Blackstone's

Handbook for Policing Students

Blackstone's

Handbook for Policing Students

Twelfth Edition

Edited by
Professor Robin Bryant
and
Sarah Bryant

Contributors:

Barry Blackburn, Dr Paul Gilbert, Dr Sofia Graça,
Kevin Lawton-Barrett, Graham Hooper, Nigel
Jones, Dr Vincent Leonard, Trish McCormack,
Susanna Mitchell, James Nunn, Dr Martin O'Neill,
Jane Owens, Mark Robinson, Vince Straine-Francis,
Robert Underwood, and Dr Dominic Wood

OXFORD
UNIVERSITY PRESS

Great Clarendon Street, Oxford, OX2 6DP,
United Kingdom

Oxford University Press is a department of the University of Oxford.
It furthers the University's objective of excellence in research, scholarship,
and education by publishing worldwide. Oxford is a registered trade mark of
Oxford University Press in the UK and in certain other countries

First Edition published in 2006
Twelfth Edition published in 2017

Impression: 1

Published in the United States of America by Oxford University Press
198 Madison Avenue, New York, NY 10016, United States of America

British Library Cataloguing in Publication Data

Data available

ISBN 978-0-19-880614-1

Printed in Italy by
L.E.G.O. S.p.A.

Contents

Part I   Overview

Part II   Policing in Context

Part III   Qualifications and Training

Part IV   General Procedures

Part V   Specific Incidents

About the Authors

Barry Blackburn

Barry is a lecturer in Criminal Justice at Canterbury Christ Church University following a career within various sectors of the criminal justice system. He specializes in the interpretation of forensic evidence and the use of research methods within the criminal justice system. Barry has recently completed research on predictive policing and firearms licensing in the UK for the Metropolitan Police.

Dr Paul Gilbert

Paul is a civil servant in the Police Service of Northern Ireland and has more than 30 years' experience of policing in Northern Ireland as a frontline officer, police trainer, and civil servant. He is also a sessional lecturer at Canterbury Christ Church University. Paul's PhD research was on the reform of policing in Northern Ireland.

Dr Sofia Graça

Sofia is a Senior Lecturer and Director of postgraduate taught provision at the School of Law, Criminal Justice and Computing at Canterbury Christ Church University. Her research interests include domestic violence and individuals' relationship with the justice system. Sofia is also interested in law enforcement and transnational cooperation, having been invited to develop research for and present at conferences organized by Europol.

Graham Hooper

Graham is a Senior Lecturer and Director of Policing at Canterbury Christ Church University. His professional background is in policing, having served for over 30 years as a police officer rising to the rank of Assistant Chief Constable. During his police career he worked in two forces—Thames Valley Police and (on secondment) to the Metropolitan Police, where he led an initiative to tackle knife crime. Graham also has extensive experience of national policing having performed a variety of senior appointments in organizations such as Her Majesty's Inspectorate of Constabulary, the Home Office and the National Policing Improvement Agency.

Nigel Jones

Nigel has been involved in cybercrime and digital forensics investigations since 1986. He created the National High Tech Crime Training Centre for the UK Police Service and has been involved in numerous cybercrime capacity building and training programmes for international organizations on a regional and global basis. Nigel is currently a Principal Lecturer in Cybercrime at Canterbury Christ Church University.

Kevin Lawton-Barrett

Kevin is a Senior Lecturer and former Programme Director for the BSc (Hons) in Forensic Investigation at Canterbury Christ Church University. Prior to this he was an operational Senior CSI at Kent Police and a trainer attached to Kent Police College, involved in the training and development of CSIs, police recruits and detectives.

Dr Vincent Leonard

Vince is the Chief Firearms Instructor for Kent Police, a position he has held as a Police Officer since 2004 and as a member of Police Staff since 2009. He has over 40 years' professional experience in the field of firearms, the majority of which has been in the area of armed policing, as a practitioner, commander, trainer and manager. Vince's research interests are in the area of judgement and decision-making.

Trish McCormack

Trish is an Instructor at Canterbury Christ Church University and has responsibility for delivery and assessment of the modules relating to the Certificate in Knowledge of Policing within the BSc (Hons) Policing Suite. Trish retired from Kent Police in 2012, leaving as an Inspector and her last role was in the training department with responsibility for Foundation Training.

Susanna Mitchell

Susanna joined Canterbury Christ Church University in 2015 and currently lectures in evidence in relation to criminal investigation. Prior to this she was a Senior Crown Prosecutor for the CPS specializing in the prosecution of rape and serious sexual offences. Susanna is still a practising lawyer and is regularly instructed by the CPS.

James Nunn

James was formerly a Roads Policing Inspector with the Metropolitan Police serving nearly 29 years, more than half of this within his specialism. He was lead for the implementation of drug drive over the prescribed limit enforcement in London and has advised the Canadian Ministry of Justice on this subject. James has an MA in Policing and Criminal Justice from Canterbury Christ Church University and is currently a PhD candidate researching traffic injury prevention at Loughborough University.

Dr Martin O'Neill

Martin is a Senior Lecturer in Criminal Investigation at Canterbury Christ Church University. He specializes in all aspects of criminal investigation and aspires to research areas such as sexual offences, domestic abuse investigations, investigative decision making and death investigation.

Jane Owens

Jane is a Senior Lecturer in Policing at Canterbury Christ Church University. She has served as a Police Officer in both Surrey and Bedfordshire Police Forces, ending her career seconded to the National Policing Improvement Agency, where she was an Implementation Officer for the development and delivery of national leadership and management training for Sergeants and Inspectors. Jane's research interests include neighbourhood policing, police governance and 'private' policing.

Mark Robinson

Mark is a serving police officer with over 24 years of experience. He is a specialist in forensic interviewing and has trained and advised officers from a number of UK and international police services. He has also trained marine, rail and air accident investigators from civil and military organizations, in basic and enhanced interview techniques. Mark has presented on the subject of forensic interviewing in the UK and abroad and holds a first class honours degree in Psychology.

Vincent Straine-Francis

Vince is a Module Leader for the BSc (Hons) Policing Cyber Security and an Instructor on the Certificate in Knowledge of Policing for Canterbury Christ Church University. He is a retired Metropolitan and Kent Police Detective. Vince spent the last seven years of his career devising Kent Police Detective training programs, and training new recruits and Specials.

Robert Underwood

Bob is a Senior Lecturer and Programme Director for the BSc in Policing Studies/Policing at Canterbury Christ Church University. He was formerly a Kent Police Officer and helped to devise the Kent Student Officer Programme. Together with colleagues, Bob was jointly responsible for the design of the Foundation Degree in Policing, which formed the basis of initial police learning in Kent.

Dr Dominic Wood

Dominic is Head of the School of Law, Criminal Justice and Computing at Canterbury Christ Church University. After organizing and chairing an international policing conference at CCCU on Knowledge Led Policing, Dominic helped to establish the Higher Education Forum for Learning and Development in Policing.

Dr Dominic Wood

Dominic is Head of the School of Law, Criminal Justice and Computing at Canterbury Christ Church University. After organizing and chairing an international policing conference at CCCU on Knowledge Led Policing, Dominic helped to establish the Higher Education Forum for Learning and Development in Policing.

Table of Cases

United Kingdom

European Court of Human Rights

European Court of Justice

Table of Legislation

EU Legislation

Table of Secondary Legislation

Table of Codes of Practice

Table of Circulars

Introduction

This twelfth edition of *Blackstone's Handbook for Policing Students* is designed and written to support trainee police officers and students on policing pre-join programmes at colleges, universities, or private sector training providers. The Handbook has six main parts (Overview, Policing in Context, Qualifications and Training, General Procedures, Specific Incidents, and Investigation and Prosecution). Each part is divided into a number of chapters and addresses a different aspect of policing and initial police training. The chapters focus in more detail on specific topics—such as Chapter 5 on the Criminal Justice System in England and Wales (in 'Policing in Context'), Chapter 15 on Unlawful Violence (in 'Specific Incidents'), and Chapter 25 on Investigative Interviewing (in 'Investigation and Prosecution').

The content has been revised and updated to reflect the needs of students undertaking pre-join programmes prior to joining the police. We have also included the content needed to meet most of the requirements of the Initial Police Learning and Development Programme (IPLDP) which underpins the training for all trainee police officers.

The authors of the Handbook have taken care to ensure the accuracy of the information contained within. However, neither the authors nor the publisher can accept any responsibility for any actions taken, or not taken, as a consequence of the information it contains. We would be grateful for feedback on the new Handbook, and for the identification of the occasional error. Reader feedback on the twelfth edition is welcome. Please email police.uk@OUP.com with your comments or queries.

Please note that references throughout the Handbook to IPLDP materials have not been reviewed or endorsed by the IPLDP Central Authority Executive Services.

1 | Introducing the Handbook

1.1 Introduction

In this chapter we provide you with guidance about how to use the Handbook, and some background information and advice on studying policing. We are familiar with the wide range of experiences that learners (either on pre-join programmes at a college, university, or private training provider, or as trainee police officers) bring to their education and training, and the Handbook has been written and set out to be both accessible and of value to all our readers.

1.2 The Handbook as a Survival Guide

The Handbook is designed to support both trainee police officers and those learners who are preparing to join the police on an approved 'pre-join' programme such as the Certificate in Knowledge of Policing (CKP). For example, to help you learn more effectively, we have omitted some of the more detailed aspects of the law and police procedure and instead provide a simplified version that shows the key points. Of course, this does not mean that the detail is not important; it is just that learning is usually easier when moving from the simple to the complex, so we start you off with the simple. In the case of the law, the full complexity will normally be introduced and explained to you by your tutors and trainers using a variety of teaching and learning methods. However, you may be expected to learn new material for yourself, and if this is so then you are likely to find Chapter 8 of the Handbook particularly useful.

The style of the Handbook represents a judgement concerning the best ways of introducing and describing a subject area. For many aspects of the law (eg as covered in Chapters 12 to 22 inclusive) we have adopted a bite-size approach for legislation and police practice. We have simplified and condensed the topics into relatively short sections of text and diagrams, each dealing with a particular topic. This would seem to suit the subject matter and the need for you, on many occasions, to assimilate and be able to reproduce the facts. In other parts of the book we have adopted a more holistic approach—for example to investigation and interviewing, covered in Chapters 24 and 25. This reflects the reality that learning the skills of investigation and interviewing involves much more than simply following the Codes and legislation. You will also need, for example, to appreciate the structure an interview can take, the forms of communication used (particularly for questioning), and the role of the interview within a wider criminal investigation.

1.3 Using the Handbook

You will sometimes look up a particular topic, but at other times you might read several sections to gain an overview. If you are an activist learner (see 8.6.5.2) you might find completing some of the tasks provides a welcome relief from simple reading! This Handbook, although large enough, does not contain the full level of detail you will need either to complete your pre-join programme or to qualify as a police officer, so we frequently refer you to further sources of information after hopefully providing you with a good general understanding of the topic in question.

1.3.1 Tasks, references, and further reading

Many of the chapters include tasks to check your understanding, or for trainee officers to use as stimulus material for the SOLAP or Learning Diary (see 8.5.4). Answers are provided at the end of each chapter. In many cases the tasks provide further ideas for you to explore, or point you in the direction of additional reading and study. For this reason it is helpful to read the answers to the tasks even though you may already be confident that you know the answer to a question.

Referencing is a standard academic system for producing evidence for your arguments, or for directing the reader towards further information. We have deliberately kept the volume of referencing in this Handbook to a minimum, generally restricting it to where the source of the ideas and information might be useful. Referencing sources is a common courtesy to those authors whose work we have utilized, and respects the intellectual property rights of others, but we have minimized it to make the Handbook more accessible to a wider range of readers: the flow is not disturbed by frequent references to other material.

We also indicate where further reading might be useful as the Handbook is very much a survival guide (see 1.2). You will find more detail and further explanation in your college or university library (including electronic resources), in your College of Policing notes (if you are on a pre-join programme) or force notes (if you are also a special constable or undertaking initial training), and from organizations such as NCALT and the PNLD, through their websites in particular. We frequently state that further information, or the source of the underpinning material we have utilized is available 'online'. The usual search techniques (using web-based search engines such as 'Google') will soon provide the relevant hypertext links.

1.3.2 Extracts from legislation, circulars, and Codes

Throughout the Handbook there are numerous extracts from primary legislation or Codes—often from Acts of Parliament. These are quoted in their original form, but sometimes with minor changes to make the meaning clearer. Often an explanation in everyday language is also given, normally in a text box to the right of the original legislation. Quotations are signified by the use of a different font (or quotation marks), while explanations and comments are in ordinary text, like this:

if when not at [his/her] place of abode.

The term 'place of abode' means the place or site where someone lives. It normally includes the garage and garden of a house and should be given its normal meaning, but it will be a question of fact for the court to decide. If a homeless person sleeps in his/her car, the car counts as an abode while he/she is asleep. However, when the same car is being driven by the same person, it is not considered as a place of abode for the purposes of the offence of going equipped (see *R v Bundy* 1977).

When changes have been made to the original, this is usually because legislation tends to use the word 'he' to cover 'he or she'. (However, in some legislation (eg for some sexual offences), 'he' really does mean just 'he'.) We have changed 'he' to 'he/she' and 'him' to 'him/her', and so on, where appropriate. We have also occasionally changed a particular word if it helps the sentence make more sense when quoted alone. Minor changes to the wording of legislation or Codes in the Handbook are shown in square brackets, as in the following example.

The original, from s 74 of the Sexual Offences Act 2003, states:

> For the purposes of this Part, a person consents if he agrees by choice, and has the freedom and capacity to make that choice.

Our revised version reads:

> For the purposes of this [offence], a person consents if [he/she] agrees by choice, and has the freedom and capacity to make that choice.

As you can see we have changed 'Part' to '[offence]' and 'he' to '[he/she]'. You will also find the detail of legislation covered in other publications. Most recent legislation is available from the government website <http://www.legislation.gov.uk>. Legislation can be confusing as it may have been subject to amendment and changed by subsequent legislation, for example the definition of a religiously aggravated offence in the Crime and Disorder Act 1998 (see 14.10) was subsequently added to by the Anti-terrorism, Crime and Security Act 2001. This added a new subsection 28(5) to the four subsections of the 1998 legislation. The government website at <http://www.legislation.gov.uk> provides 'updated' versions of much (but not all) original legislation.

It is also often the case that the words and phrases used in legislation have specific meanings that do not always correspond exactly to the same words or phrases used in everyday life, for example, you might think that 'assault' always means physically hurting somebody but see 15.2.

Further explanation of legislation can be found (for example) in sources including:

- publications such as Butterworth's Police Law and the Blackstone's publications (notably the Police Operational Handbook and the annual Police Manuals);
- via the PNLD website at <https://www.pnld.co.uk/> (note that this is a subscription service unless you have a police.uk email address);
- legal guidance from the CPS at <http://www.cps.gov.uk/legal/index.html>;
- the 'official' home of UK legislation at <http://www.legislation.gov.uk> (turning on the 'explanatory notes' can be helpful);
- the College of Policing digests (you can subscribe to these by sending an email to digest@college.pnn.police.uk); and
- the online legal databases Westlaw (<http://www.westlaw.co.uk>) and Lawtel (<http://www.lawtel.com/UK/Home>) if you are studying at university or college.

Trainee police officers and special constables can also use force resources (eg the force intranet). The NCALT learning portal for the police service at <http://www.ncalt.com> the Police OnLine Knowledge Area (POLKA) at <https://polka.pnn.police.uk> are also available to trainee officers.

> **TASK 1** Use the internet to find the definition of 'controlled area' in the law governing demonstrations in the vicinity of Parliament. It is defined within the Police Reform and Social Responsibility Act 2011.

1.3.3 Structure of the Handbook

As you might have already discovered through reading the Contents, the Handbook is divided into six parts and 27 chapters.

- **Overview**—this is mostly devoted to reference material that will be of value to students on pre-entry courses and trainee police officers. You are likely to use this part of the Handbook to check on the meaning of an acronym, remind yourself of a key date in policing, or practise the phonetic alphabet.
- **Policing in Context**—this provides the background and context to policing and law enforcement in England and Wales, including an overview of policing professional issues, the nature of crime and disorder, and the Criminal Justice System. If you are on a pre-join programme then this part of the Handbook provides you with a starting point for the required reading and research.
- **Qualifications and Training**—this is a description and discussion of what it means to work within the profession of policing, from standards of behaviour, to qualifications, to the detail of training itself.
- **General Procedures**—this examines general policing powers and procedures in detail, to the level required for initial training as a police officer.
- **Specific Incidents**—this covers the knowledge of criminal law required to undertake policing of a wide variety of incidents up to the stage of initial qualification, and hence is a particularly long and demanding part of the Handbook.
- **Investigation and Prosecution**—this looks at the processes and procedures for police investigations (including interviewing and forensic investigation), and concludes with a chapter on prosecution.

1.4 Key Aspects of Police Education and Training

In Chapters 6 to 8 inclusive we provide more detail on education and training for pre-join programmes at a college or university and for trainee officers after joining the police. Here we offer a brief introduction to some key components: pre-join programmes, the IPLDP, the NOS, the Certificate in Knowledge of Policing, the Diploma in Policing, and the PAC. The IPLDP modules set out what you need to know and the skills you require to become a police officer. The National Occupational Standards (NOS) underpin both the Certificate in Knowledge of Policing and the Diploma in Policing (the latter forming the basis for qualification as a police constable). In many forces the Police Action Checklist (the PAC) is also a key requirement in the assessment of a trainee police officer for Independent Patrol. Note that many aspects of police education and training are subject to review and change, and particularly so in the next few years with the introduction of a new Policing Education Qualifications Framework by the College of Policing.

The Handbook is linked throughout to the Certificate in Knowledge of Policing, the Diploma in Policing, and the associated NOS.

1.4.1 Pre-join programmes

Pre-join courses are provided by further education colleges, universities, and private training companies. There are currently over 60 approved pre-join programmes (some available through distance learning) available in the UK. The courses are either 'stand alone' (eg the Certificate in Knowledge of Policing) or embedded within longer programmes. If you are on a pre-join programme, you are probably aiming to join the police or other law enforcement agency as a full-time professional (eg as a PCSO or police constable). You might also be a special constable; for some embedded pre-join programmes this is compulsory. Pre-join programmes are expected to articulate with the pre-join curriculum and deliver the learning requirement of the Certificate in Knowledge of Policing (see 1.4.4 and 7.4.1).

1.4.2 IPLDP

The Initial Police Learning and Development Programme (IPLDP) forms the basis of initial policing training (that is, up to the point of confirmation as a police constable). The IPLDP consists of three sets of learning modules:

* the Induction modules (prefixed with 'IND');
* the Operational modules ('OP'); and
* the Legislation, Policy, and Guidelines modules ('LPG').

Taken together there are over 7,000 separate learning outcomes (about 5,000 of which are 'mandatory') described with the three sets of modules and it is not possible (or indeed appropriate) to cover them all in detail in a Handbook.

This Handbook covers most of the IND modules. However, some aspects of initial police training, such as First Aid, are more suited to specialist publications, and others (such as IND 8: 'Operation of information technology systems') are very dependent on individual force policy and equipment. In these instances we provide an overview of the training rather than describe the full detail. Similarly, a subject such as the multicultural nature of modern Britain and the diverse communities that you will police is better studied (we would wish to argue) using textbooks or other learning material specifically devoted to this task, rather than using this Handbook.

IPLDP Induction Modules

IND 1   Underpinning ethics/values of the police service
IND 2   Foster people's equality, diversity, and rights
IND 3   Develop one's own knowledge and practice
IND 4   Develop effective relationships with colleagues
IND 5   Ensure your own actions reduce the risks to health and safety
IND 6   Assess the needs of individuals and provide advice and support
IND 7   Develop effective partnerships with members of the community and other agencies
IND 8   Operation of information technology systems
IND 9   Administer First Aid
IND 10   Use police powers in a fair and justified way
IND 11   Social and community issues, and Neighbourhood Policing

---

The operational modules for the training of police officers are also numerous. This Handbook covers the underpinning knowledge required for most of the OP modules.

IPLDP Operational Modules

OP 1   Deal with aggressive and abusive behaviour
OP 2   Obtain, evaluate, and submit information and intelligence to support local
            priorities
OP 3   Respond to incidents, conduct and evaluate investigations
OP 4   Participate in planned operations
OP 5(a)   Search premises
OP 5(b)   Search individuals
OP 5(c)   Search vehicles
OP 5(d)   Search open areas
OP 5(e)   Search missing person
OP 6(a)   Prepare, conduct, and evaluate interviews (witness/victim)
OP 6(b)   Prepare, conduct, and evaluate interviews (suspects)
OP 7   Arrest and report suspects
OP 8   Escort suspects and present to custody
OP 9   Prepare and present case information, present evidence, and finalize
            investigations

The Legislation, Policy, and Guidelines modules covered in this Handbook are as follows:

IPLDP Legislation, Policy, and Guidelines Modules

LPG 0   Underpinning legislation policy and guidelines (Phases 3 and 4)
LPG 1   Underpinning legislation policy and guidelines (Phase 3)
LPG 2   Underpinning legislation policy and guidelines (Phase 4)

This Handbook provides you with much of the basic knowledge required for LPG 1 and LPG 2, apart from aspects that would vary depending on local force policy. We cover the areas of LPG 0 we regard as essential for the trainee police officer or pre-join student (even though some of this is designated as optional under the IPLDP).

1.4.3   NOS Units for Policing

There are 21 National Occupational Standards (NOS) that relate to initial police training. It is unlikely you will be assessed directly against the NOS units particularly if you are on a pre-join programme. Instead, the NOS units are used as a basis for two qualifications, the Certificate in Knowledge of Policing and the Diploma in Policing (see 1.4.4 for a summary and 7.4 for further detail).

The 21 NOS Units for Initial Policing

AA1   Promote equality and value diversity
AB1   Communicate effectively with people
AE1   Maintain and develop your own knowledge, skills, and competence
AF1   Ensure your own actions reduce risks to health and safety
BE2   Provide initial support to victims, survivors, and witnesses and assess their
            needs for further support
CA1   Use law enforcement actions in a fair and justified way
CB1   Gather and submit information that has the potential to support law
            enforcement objectives
CD1   Provide an initial response to incidents
CD3   Prepare for, and participate in, planned law enforcement operations
CD5   Arrest, detain, or report individuals
CI101   Conduct priority and volume investigations
CJ101   Interview victims and witnesses in relation to priority and volume
            investigations
CJ201   Interview suspects in relation to priority and volume investigations

Overview

CK1	Search individuals
CK2	Search vehicles, premises, and open spaces
DA5	Present evidence in court and at other hearings
DA6	Prepare and submit case files
GC10	Manage conflict
2K1	Escort detained persons
2K2	Present detained persons to custody
4G4	Administer First Aid

Each of the NOS units is subdivided into learning outcomes, see 8.5.1 for details.

1.4.4 The Certificate in Knowledge of Policing and the Diploma in Policing

The Certificate in Knowledge of Policing (CKP) and the Diploma in Policing are QCF Level 3 qualifications. The Certificate is likely to be delivered as either an independent and stand-alone award or as part of a longer pre-join programme offered by a college, a university, a police force, or another education provider. The Diploma is more likely to be delivered by a police force as part of the initial training for trainee police officers, and is the national minimum qualification for initial police training. A full list of the units for each qualification is shown in 7.4.1 and 7.4.2.

The units for the Certificate and the Diploma are drawn from the National Occupational Standards (NOS) for initial police training (see 1.4.3), for example BE2 which is concerned with 'providing initial support to victims and witnesses within a policing context'. In effect the Certificate represents the knowledge and understanding for each topic (hence it may be referred to as BE2K), while the Diploma covers the skills needed as well as the knowledge requirements. Each Certificate and Diploma unit is also indirectly linked with a number of other, more thematic NOS units such as NOS Unit AA1.

1.4.5 Local force policies

If you are a special constable or undertaking initial police training with a police force then this Handbook should always be read in conjunction with local force policies. This applies particularly for procedures such as writing a statement or making a pocket notebook entry, and where new technology is being introduced. You are likely to find your local policies referred to as 'Force Orders', 'Standard Operating Procedures (SOP)', or 'Policies' on your organization's intranet.

Trainee police officers may also be required to learn verbatim definitions. These are often concerned with the law, for example the definition of what constitutes theft. In this case we advise you to use the definitions given to you by your force rather than those reproduced in this Handbook or, indeed, in other textbooks. This is because there is sometimes a slight variation between forces—for example, whether the wording uses 'he' as in the original Act, or 'he/she'.

1.5 Answer to Task

TASK 1 The Police Reform and Social Responsibility Act 2011 can be located at <http://www.legislation.gov.uk/ukpga/2011/13/contents/enacted>. Demonstrations in the vicinity of Parliament are dealt with in Part 3 of the Act, 'Parliament Square Garden and surrounding area' and in ss 142–147 inclusive. You should find a hypertext link to s 142 which explains that 'controlled area' of Parliament Square is its central garden and the immediately adjoining footways. However, s 142(2) explains that the definition of 'central garden of Parliament Square' is the site in Parliament Square on which the Minister of Works was authorized to lay out the 'new central garden' by the Parliament Square (Improvements) Act 1949. This Act will be difficult to locate unless you have access to a printed resource such as the All England Law Reports (eg through a university). However, the government produces explanatory notes for most new legislation, and in this case (by careful searching) you should be able to find Annex A to the document 'Police Reform and Social Responsibility Act 2011 Guidance on the Provisions Relating to Parliament Square and Surrounding Area' (see <http://www.publications.parliament.uk/pa/cm201011/cmbills/116/en/2011116en.htm>) which provides a map of the controlled area.

2 Reference Material

2.1 Introduction

In this chapter of the Handbook we provide you with some background information as reference material to policing in England and Wales. This is likely to be of value to you whilst undertaking a pre-join programme and subsequently during your initial training as a student police officer. For example, you might encounter more experienced police colleagues, or fellow students, using an acronym or a form of jargon that you have not encountered, and the glossary in 2.3 might well provide an answer. We also include in this chapter a list of dates and key events in the history of law enforcement and policing, and these might help you set present practices (and some reactions to proposed changes) in perspective.

We also provide you with an understanding of the basic configuration of the rank structure in policing and an overview of a typical police force organizational structure. Finally, we describe and explain the conventions used by law enforcement agencies for conveying information, such as the phonetic alphabet and the codes for conveying or recording ethnicity.

This Chapter covers the arrangements in England and Wales, but many of the provisions shown here are similar in Scotland and Northern Ireland. However, it should be noted that both these nations have their own governance, laws and regulations of relevance to the police and policing.

2.2 Chronology of Law Enforcement and Policing

An understanding of the past is an important precursor to understanding the present. There are no CKP or IPLDP learning outcomes explicitly concerned with the history of policing, but IPLDP modules such as 'Understanding and being in the community' and 'Understanding social change' (both part of IND 11) are likely to be more meaningful if current practice is considered within a historical policing context. We do not provide a comprehensive history of law enforcement and the police in the UK, nor do we offer much in the way of analysis, but we do provide you with some of the background and a number of key dates in the history of policing. It is surprising to note that the police (in the UK and elsewhere) are a relatively modern phenomenon and there have been a number of notable occasions when their very existence has been challenged. If there is one key date in modern-day policing it is probably 1829 when Sir Robert Peel, then Home Secretary, introduced a Bill in Parliament for the establishment of a 'Metropolitan Police Force' for London. Perhaps this is the key observation here: the police service as we would recognize it today is barely 190 years old, and continues to be subject to fundamental changes regarding its purpose and structure. The formation of the Met is often referred to by police historians as the beginning of the 'new police', delineating the previous ad hoc local policing bodies and watch systems that existed before this point.

Here we present a brief chronology (timeline) of the significant developments in the history of the police service of England and Wales, dominated (at least in the nineteenth century) by the Metropolitan Police in London.

1829   Sir Robert Peel established the first civilian police force in London, with two Justices of the Peace in charge of the force—Richard Mayne and Charles Rowan.

1831   Period of considerable unrest and mob violence, especially in the north of England and in London.

1835   The Municipal Corporations Act 1835 established 'watch committees' to oversee policing of areas outside London.

1839–40 Provincial constabularies were established across the country for the first time.

1842   Establishment of a detective force at the London Metropolitan Police HQ, Scotland Yard (still only ten staff in 1856).

1840s–50s There was considerable hostility towards the new police, with widespread resentment about the cost and the perceived lack of police officers when needed. Some believed that any police force was illiberal.

1856   It became mandatory for local government bodies to set up police forces. Financial support was awarded by central government to forces which proved to be efficient and reliable, paving the way for the modern inspection regime by the HMIC.

1860   Over 200 borough and county police forces in England and Wales in existence. Unrest in Ireland led to the formation of the Royal Irish Constabulary, which was paramilitary from the outset.

1872   Police officers went on strike for the first time.

1878   The Criminal Investigation Department (CID) was formed, with Scotland Yard detectives being called in by county forces to lead criminal investigations well into the 1930s.

1883   The Special Irish Branch was set up as part of the Metropolitan Police to deal with attacks by Irish republicans in London, and later became known simply as Special Branch.

1901   Scotland Yard's Fingerprint Bureau was formed.

1911   Police officers were armed for the first time, after assisting the military to end a siege of armed anarchists in a London house.

1912   Establishment of special constables on a permanent basis.

1914   NUPPO, the first Police Union (unofficial) was formed. The 'Women Police' were founded.

1914–18 The First World War put enormous pressure on the police due to enlistment in the armed forces, suspension of police recruitment, and new tasks such as the pursuit of deserters.

1916   The Commissioner of the Metropolitan Police ruled that any officer joining a union was liable to dismissal.

The regularizing of women police officers as equal members of the force is generally dated from 1916, though many would argue that women were not fully accepted in the police service until the Second World War, and even then, attitudes to female police officers were often negative. Moreover, those women officers who were appointed were largely confined to duties connected with children or women offenders. The Police Federation, did not admit female officers as members until 1948.

1918–19 The police, particularly in Liverpool and London, embarked on a series of strikes for better pay and conditions, and for recognition of police trades unions. New legislation then banned police trades unions and denied the police the right to strike, but allowed the formation of the Police Federation for negotiations over pay, etc.

1921   Police motorcycle patrols were established.

1922   After the creation of Eire in 1922, the RIC became the Royal Ulster Constabulary (RUC).

1931   A two-tier entry system to the police operated briefly, based on the officer/non-commissioned ranks recruitment in the armed forces. Police officers were trained at Hendon, but this experiment with 'officer entry' was short-lived.

1935   The first police forensic laboratory was opened by the Metropolitan Police.

1937   The emergency telephone number 999 was introduced.

1946   The number of forces was reduced to 125.

1948   The Police Federation started to admit female officers as members.

1950s   The so-called 'Golden Age' of policing, characterized by apparent widespread acceptance of the legitimacy of the police, and relatively low levels of crime and disorder

Popular belief in its existence probably derives at least in part from a television series of the time, *Dixon of Dock Green*.

1964   The number of separate and distinct forces was reduced to 49.

1965   Police officer personal radios were introduced.

1973   Women police officers were fully integrated directly into the police service, performing the same duties as male colleagues.

1981   The Scarman Report into the Brixton riots in April 1981 (involving mostly young black men) gave rise to a concerted effort to improve relations between the police and minority ethnic groups.

1984   The Police and Criminal Evidence Act 1984 (PACE Act) created the Police Complaints Authority (PCA). This was in response to criticism of the police 'acting as judge and jury' in investigations into complaints from the public about the police.

1990   The Association of Chief Police Officers (ACPO) published its 'Statement of Common Purpose and Values', which emphasized that the police should be seen more as a service than as a force.

1990s (onwards) The employment of civilian staff increased in forces, as it was recognized that some traditional police officer roles could be performed just as effectively by non-warranted police staff (eg crime scene investigators).

1994   Creation of a centralized computer database for criminal records.

1997   NAFIS, the National Automated Fingerprint Identification System was created.

1999   The Macpherson Inquiry into the death of Stephen Lawrence (a black teenager murdered in London in 1993) criticized the whole police service as institutionally racist.

The RUC became the Police Service of Northern Ireland (PSNI), following the Patten Inquiry and Report.

2002   Introduction of Police Community Support Officers (PCSOs).

2003   TV airing by the BBC of The Secret Policeman video uncovering racism at a regional police training centre. The Independent Police Complaints Commission (IPCC) was established to replace the Police Complaints Authority.

2005   Formation of the Serious Organised Crime Agency (SOCA), combining several existing agencies to counter level 3 crime and criminality.

2006   Following a 2005 HMIC report, an amalgamation of police forces was proposed but then rescinded in 2006. The National Police Improvement Agency (NPIA) was formed, incorporating Centrex (police training) and other agencies such as Information Services.

2007   The Home Office was split into two parts: the 'justice' element was incorporated into a Ministry of Justice, whilst the 'security' element (including the police) became part of a new Interior Ministry. Such a division did not take into account that the police play a large role in justice as well as security (as stated in 1830 by Sir Richard Mayne at the founding of the 'new police' in London).

2008   Publication of the Flanagan Review of Policing, with recommendations on reducing unnecessary police bureaucracy and the implementation of Neighbourhood Policing.

2008–9 The 'Policing Pledge' was launched, setting out the public's right to a range of services from their local police force (eg that an emergency 999 call will be answered within ten seconds). It was subsequently withdrawn in 2010–11.

2010   A new government promises cuts in police bureaucracy, the return to the police of responsibility for charging suspects with 'low level' offences, and locally elected police and crime commissioners.

2011   The 2010 comprehensive spending review imposes budget reductions for police forces in England and Wales. By 2012 these cuts had led to a reduction in police staffing levels in many police forces in England and Wales.

2011   The first Winsor Review into police officer and staff remuneration and conditions is published with detailed recommendations on police pay.

2011   The Neyroud Review into police training and leadership recommends the establishment of a chartered professional body for policing.

Overview

2012   The first Police and Crime Commissioners (PCCs) were elected to replace Police Authorities (which had been the main instrument of local police accountability since the 1960s). They are responsible for 'hiring and firing' the chief constable and setting out a five-year Police and Crime Plan. In London, the PCC role was adopted by the Mayor's Office.

2012   The publication of the second Winsor Review into entry routes into policing, promotion, health and fitness requirements, and contribution-related pay.

2012   The College of Policing was established as a professional body for policing—at the same time the NPIA was abolished.

2013   The Home Office consults on measures intended to maintain and enhance the integrity of the police, including: a new code of ethics (covering all ranks); a single set of professional standards; a national register of chief officers' pay packages, gifts, hospitality, and second jobs; and a national register of officers who have been 'struck off'.

2013   The Lord Stevens Independent Review of Policing makes 37 recommendations including reducing the number of police forces, scrapping PCCs, a new chartered status for police officers, and changes to the qualification structure of training.

2013   Allegations that the Government chief whip Andrew Mitchell made particular derogatory remarks to police officers on duty in Downing Street lead to claims of collusion between some of the police officers involved (the repercussions were dubbed 'Plebgate' by some media).

2013   The Serious Crime Agency is formed, with a national remit to tackle serious and organized crime.

2014   An MPS police officer is jailed for a year for misconduct in public office after falsely claiming that he witnessed an altercation between the chief whip and police officers in Downing Street in 2013.

2014   The Home Secretary sets out a package of reforms of the Police Federation, including plans to withdraw some public funding of the Federation and introducing an 'opt in' to the Federation rather than the existing 'opt out'.

2014   A new Police Code of Ethics is published by the College of Policing.

2014   In the High Court Mr Justice Mitting rules that Mr Mitchell had called a police officer a 'pleb' during an incident in Downing Street in 2012.

2014   First 19 'direct entrants' to the police service (at superintendent level) are recruited (from a pool of almost 1,000 applicants).

2015   Further cuts to the budgets (c. £300 million) of police forces begin to be implemented.

2015   The Independent Inquiry into Child Sexual Abuse begins. Its terms of reference include the role of the police (in England and Wales) in investigating child sexual abuse.

2015   The hearings begin for the judicial-led inquiry into undercover policing.

2015   The College of Policing commences consultation on the requirement for police officer applicants to have a degree.

2015   ACPO (Association of Chief Police Officers) is abolished and a new organization representing police chiefs is created—the National Police Chiefs' Council (NPCC).

2016   The new inquest into the 96 deaths at Hillsborough in 1989 hears from its final witnesses.

2016   The second election for police and crime commissioners in England and Wales takes place.

2017   The Metropolitan Police appoint first ever female Commissioner—Cressida Dick. The three most senior positions in policing in England and Wales are all now headed by women—the 'Met' (MPS) (Cressida Dick), the National Crime Agency (Lynne Owens), and the chair of the National Police Chiefs' Council (Sara Thornton).

TASK 1 What is the history of your local force? See if you can establish the dates of a few key events in the last 200 years or so.

2.3   Glossary of Terms Used in Policing

You will encounter many acronyms and forms of jargon during your training. The following glossary of terms covers a wide range of the often bewildering words and phrases used within policing. Note also that many police forces also publish their own glossary of terms.

3 × 5 × 2 A 'three by five by two' intelligence form. The numbers refer to 'qualities' of the intelligence, measured in three categories, using the scales 1 to 5 and A to E, and the letters P or C.

5 × 5 × 5 A 'five by five by five' intelligence report. The numbers refer to a scale that is used to attempt to measure the reliability of, access to, and other factors about the source providing the intelligence.

16 + 1 Reference to the system used to record self-defined (as distinct from officer-defined (see IC1)) ethnicity: for example A1 is used for Indian.

ABC (1) Acceptable Behaviour Contract; (2) Activity-Based Costing, a finance/budgeting methodology that enables costs of an activity to be calculated (as opposed to a value which can only be assessed).

ABE ('A-B-E') *Achieving Best Evidence*, Guidance on Interviewing Victims and Witnesses, and Using Special Measures.

ABH Assault resulting in actual bodily harm.

ACC Assistant chief constable; a senior police officer command rank (see 2.4).

ACPO ('Ack-poh') Association of Chief Police Officers. ACPO was replaced in April 2015 by the newly formed National Police Chiefs' Council (NPCC, qv).

Active Defence A proactive approach to defence which involves a rigorous examination of police investigation procedures and the prosecution case; the title of an influential book by Roger Ede and Eric Shepherd.

ad hoc A Latin phrase meaning 'for this special purpose', which has come to mean 'off the cuff' or 'unrehearsed'.

ADVOKATE ('advokate') Mnemonic used in police training to assist the recollection of the so-called 'Turnbull' rules for witness recall (see 10.5).

AFO ('A-F-O') Authorized Firearms Officer.

Airwave The digital national police radio communication system.

AirwaveSpeak A standardized form of communication when using Airwave (qv).

Alpha/Bravo, etc The phonetic alphabet used in police communication (see 2.6.1).

AMHP Approved mental health professional.

Analyst A professional police staff member whose role (usually) is to analyse and assess crime data and intelligence, and present research findings.

ANPR Automatic Number Plate Recognition system: see 'Nexus'.

APA ('A-P-A') Association of Police Authorities (now replaced in part by APACE qv).

APACE Association of Policing & Crime Chief Executives.

APACS ('aippax') Association of Payments and Clearing Services.

APEL ('A-P-L' or sometimes 'aipull') Accreditation of Prior Experiential Learning.

APL ('A-P-L' or sometimes 'aipull') Accreditation of Prior Learning.

APP Authorised Professional Practice.

ARU ('A-R-U') Armed Response Unit.

ARV ('A-R-V') Armed Response Vehicle.

ASB Anti-social Behaviour.

ASBO ('azboh') Anti-social Behaviour Order, discontinued in 2015. The Injunction to Prevent Nuisance and Annoyance (IPNA) is seen by some as a replacement.

ASP ('asp') An informal term for an extendable metal baton (a reference to the US company Armament Systems and Procedures Inc).

Assistant commissioner Senior police rank in the Metropolitan Police, generally considered to be equivalent to a chief constable.

ASU ('A-S-U') Air Support Unit, usually in the form of police helicopters.

Attestation The formal point at which the powers and responsibilities of the office of constable are assumed, accompanied by the swearing of an oath.

AVLS Automatic (or Automated) Vehicle Location System.

Awarding Bodies Organizations permitted to issue awards and qualifications such as NVQs (qv) and the Diploma in Policing (qv).

Baton A side-handled self-protection weapon carried by uniformed police officers.

Baton round The formal term for a rubber or plastic bullet.

BAWP ('B-A-W-P') British Association for Women in Policing.

BCE Bad-character evidence.

BCS British Crime Survey (now replaced by the Crime Survey for England and Wales).

BCU Basic Command Unit (Area, Division) or sometimes Borough Command Unit (particularly amongst MPS officers (qv)).

Biometrics The use of unique human physical characteristics (such as the iris of the eye) as identifiers.

BLS Basic Life Support (part of First Aid training).

BME Black and Minority Ethnic (groups).

Bolt-on ASBO An informal term for an ASBO (qv) added after a conviction.

Border Force The UK's law enforcement body responsible for immigration and customs control.

BPA Black Police Association.

Bramshill Former centre for police leadership training in England and Wales, closed in 2015.

BTP British Transport Police.

BWC Body-Worn Camera qv BWV.

BWV Body-Worn Video.

Byford Report A review by Sir Lawrence Byford on the police investigation into the 'Yorkshire Ripper' (Peter Sutcliffe) murders between 1975 and 1981; the report was instrumental in the establishment of HOLMES (qv).

CAP ('C-A-P' or 'cap') Common Approach Path.

CAR (often 'car') Cumulative Assessment Record, used as part of assembling the SOLAP (qv).

Cat A/B/C murders ('cat A', etc) Categories of homicide (see 11.3.4).

CBO Criminal Behaviour Order.

CBRN Chemical, Biological, Radiological, or Nuclear (hazard, etc).

CCR Contact and Control Room.

CCTV Closed-Circuit Television.

CCU Computer Crime Unit.

CDRP(s) Crime and Disorder Reduction Partnership(s).

Centrex Central Police Training and Development Authority, previously responsible for national police training, subsequently subsumed within NPIA (qv).

CEOP ('see-op') Child Exploitation and Online Protection Centre, a command of the National Crime Agency (qv).

CEPOL European Police College.

Certificate in Knowledge of Policing The knowledge requirement for the assessed units of the Diploma in Policing (qv), usually undertaken as part of a pre-join programme (qv).

cf Latin for 'compare'.

Chief Officer A police officer with the rank of assistant chief constable and above: command rank.

CHIS ('chiss') Covert Human Intelligence Source (informant).

Child Sexual Abuse The collective term used to describe any form of sexual abuse of children and young persons both historically and in the present day. CSA is now a major priority for police forces (see fully Strategic Policing Requirement).

CI ('C-I') (1) Cognitive Interview; (2) Cell Intervention.

CIAPOAR Mnemonic for factors to remember when making decisions within the NDM (qv); Code of ethics, Information, Assessment, Powers and policy, Options, Actions, and Review.

CID ('C-I-D') Criminal Investigation(s) Department, now replaced in many police forces by Specialist Crime Investigations, SCI, or similar.

CIRA ('seera') Continuity Irish Republican Army, a proscribed terrorist group.

Civil Nuclear Constabulary A non-Home Office police force that provides security and protection to civil (non-military) nuclear sites in the UK.

CJPOA Criminal Justice and Public Order Act 1994.

CJ(S) A process or unit concerned with Criminal Justice (Systems).

CKP Certificate in Knowledge of Policing (qv).

CLDP Core Leadership Development Programme.

CLO ('C-L-O') Community Liaison Officer.

CLUE2 ('klue-too') A case-tracking data system.

CNC Civil Nuclear Constabulary.

CnC Command and Control system used by a number of police forces and other agencies.

Collar To make an arrest (vernacular).

College of Policing The professional body for policing.

Commander Metropolitan and City of London chief police officer rank equivalent to assistant chief constable in all other forces.

Commissioner Police rank used only in the MPS and the City of London police, signifying head of their respective forces. The commissioner of the Metropolitan Police is considered to be one of the three most senior police officer posts in the UK.

Compromise When a criminal target (a suspect) detects covert surveillance.

Confirmation The final stage of successful initial training, normally after a period of two years, when a student police officer is confirmed as a police constable.

Continuity Continuity (of evidence): an audited and continuous trail from crime scene or suspect to court, such that evidential items can be accounted for at all times, to prevent interference or contamination.

CoP see College of Policing.

CPA (1) Crime Pattern Analysis; (2) Child Protection Agency.

CPIA Criminal Procedure and Investigations Act 1996.

CPN Community Protection Notice.

CPO Crime Prevention Officer.

CPOSA Chief Police Officers' Staff Association.

CPP Crime Prevention Panels.

CPR Cardio-pulmonary resuscitation.

CPS Crown Prosecution Service, the governmental body of qualified lawyers who prosecute criminal cases before the courts.

CRaSH or CRASH Collision Recording and Sharing.

CRE Commission for Racial Equality; now the EHRC (qv).

Crimelink Crime analysis software used by some force analysts, developed by the company 'Precision' Computing Intelligence.

Crimewatch Long-running BBC TV programme that highlights unsolved crimes, usually of a serious nature.

CRO ('C-R-O') (1) Criminal Records Office; (2) Criminal (vernacular).

CROPS ('crops') Covert Rural Observation Posts (or Points).

CSAI Child Sex Abuse Images

CSI Crime Scene Investigator.

CSM Crime Scene Manager.

CSO Community Support Officer.

CSODS Child Sex Offender Disclosure Scheme.

CSP (1) Communications Service Provider; (2) Community Safety Partnership.

CSU Community Safety Unit.

CT Counter Terrorism.

CT Units Regional counter terrorism units (not in London) where forces collaborate to create additional capability and capacity to tackle terrorism and extremism.

CTM Contact Trace Material.

Cuff (1) Police vernacular for not doing something which one is supposed to do as a matter of duty or obligation; (2) To handcuff (vernacular).

Custody or custody suite A designated area in a police station (usually where the cells are located), where arrested persons are logged and processed.

CW Cannabis Warning.

Cybercrime An all-embracing term and somewhat ambiguous term to describe an ever-increasing set of crimes committed using computers and/or digital networks, or against computer systems.

Dabs Colloquial term for fingerprints.

DC Detective Constable.

DCC Deputy Chief Constable.

DCI Detective Chief Inspector.

DCS Detective Chief Superintendent; command rank.

DDA Normally a reference to the Disability Discrimination Act 1995.

Deputy assistant commissioner Senior police officer rank in the Metropolitan and City of London police forces. Equivalent to deputy chief constable in other police forces.

DFU Digital Forensics Unit.

DHRs Domestic Homicide Reviews.

DI ('D-I') Detective Inspector.

DIC ('D-I-C') Drunk in charge (of a person or object).

Diploma in Policing The minimum national qualification for trainee police officers.

Disclosure A reference to the requirement on the police and the prosecution to provide the defence with certain information and documents which might be pertinent evidence in a criminal case.

DNA Deoxyribonucleic Acid (genetic material used to obtain a 'genetic fingerprint').

Doctrine A body of knowledge and procedure concerned with police practice, notably criminal investigation—for example, as expressed in the MIM (qv) and the NCPE Volume Crime Investigation Manuals.

DPP Director of Public Prosecutions (also head of the Crown Prosecution Service).

DS Detective Sergeant.

DVCVA Domestic Violence, Crime and Victims Act 2004.

DVLA Driver and Vehicle Licensing Agency.

DVPN Domestic Violence Protection Notice.

DVPO Domestic Violence Protection Order.

EAW European Arrest Warrant.

EBP Evidence based policing.

ECHR European Convention on Human Rights.

EEK Early Evidence Kit for use after sexual assaults.

EHRC Equality and Human Rights Commission: formerly the CRE (qv).

Element (of a unit of an NOS) The units of a NOS (qv) are usually divided into two or more elements which describe more precisely the skill or competence to be attained and measured.

EPO Emergency Protection Order, used for protecting children from imminent harm.

ERO ('E-R-O') Evidence Review Officer.

ESDA ('ezzder') Electrostatic Detection Apparatus.

ETA ('E-T-A') Estimated time of arrival.

et al Latin for 'and others'.

Europol The European Union Law Enforcement Organisation.

Extended police family A reference to the wider group of law enforcement and pubic order staff, beyond the traditional full-time police—for example, special constables and PCSOs (qv).

FA ('F-A') Forensic Alliance (an independent forensic science laboratory and service).

Family of forces Term previously used by the HMIC (qv) police forces that are similar in terms of their structure, size, budget, etc. Now largely replaced by the Home Office's designation of 'Most Similar Forces' (MSF (qv)).

FAO or FOAS ('F-A-O' or 'F-O-A-S') First Attending Officer/First Officer Attending the Scene/ first responder.

FASP ('farsp' or 'fasp') First Aid Skills for Policing. An NPIA (qv) programme of five modules. Module 2 (First Aid Skills) is often undertaken as part of IPLDP (qv).

FBO Football Banning Order.

FCA Forensic Computer Analyst.

FCC Force Communications (or Control) Centre.

FCP Forward Control Point.

FDR Firearm Discharge Residue

'Federation' The Police Federation of England and Wales (qv).

Fence Vernacular for a person who buys or exchanges stolen goods.

FERRT ('fert') Fingerprint Evidence Recovery and Recording Techniques.

FGM Female Genital Mutilation.

FIO ('F-I-O') Field Intelligence Officer or Financial Intelligence Officer.

Fishing Police vernacular for any speculative attempt, particularly where the intention is to try to recover evidence of potential value in a criminal case but the grounds for doing so (and the form of evidence to be seized) are uncertain.

FLA ('F-L-A') Family Law Act 1996.

FLINTS Forensic Linked Intelligence System: a database and comparative analysis system developed by West Midlands Police.

FLO ('F-L-O') (1) Family Liaison Officer; (2) Forensic Laboratory Officer.

FMPO Forced Marriage Protection Order.

FOD ('fod') Fact Of Death, a statement from a medical professional confirming a person is dead.

FOI ('F-O-I') Freedom of Information, as in a request under the Freedom of Information Act 2000.

Forensics21 A discontinued initiative to improve police forensic services (ended in 2012).

Foundation degree/FD A qualification at higher education level. There are a number of foundation degrees in policing, many incorporating the NOS (qv) and the Diploma in Policing (qv) units for initial policing.

FPN Fixed Penalty Notice.

FSS (1) Forensic Science Society (2) Forensic Science Service (closed in 2012).

FSU (1) Family Support Unit; (2) Firearms Support Unit.

FTS Forensic Telecommunications Services.

Garda Síochána The police force of the Republic of Ireland.

GBH Category of assault: Grievous Bodily Harm.

GMP Greater Manchester Police.

GPA Gay Police Association.

H2H House-to-house (as in conducting enquiries).

Handler Vernacular term for police officer responsible for liaising with and tasking a CHIS (qv).

Overview

Handling Taking illegal ownership of stolen or otherwise illegally obtained goods.

Hate crime ACPO (qv) defines a hate crime as any hate incident (qv), which constitutes a criminal offence and is perceived by the victim, or any other person, as being motivated by prejudice or hate.

Hate incident ACPO (qv) defines a hate incident as any incident, which may or may not constitute a criminal offence, that is perceived by the victim, or any other person, as being motivated by prejudice or hate.

Hearsay A reference to information that is not given directly (orally) to the court, but is somehow second-hand. It is generally not usable in a court as evidence, although there are many notable common law and other exceptions to this general rule.

Hermes A database of missing persons maintained by the MPB (qv).

Hillsborough The grounds of Sheffield Wednesday football club, where 96 Liverpool fans were unlawfully killed in 1989. The events have come to symbolize failures in police leadership.

Hit A DNA sample which can be matched with an identified person (not always criminal).

HMIC Her Majesty's Inspectorate of Constabulary. HMIC inspects at BCU (qv) and force levels and also carries out thematic inspections (eg into police training).

HMPS Her Majesty's Prison Service.

HMRC Her Majesty's Revenue and Customs (previously 'Customs and Excise' and the 'Inland Revenue').

HOLMES, HOLMES2 Home Office Large Major Enquiry System: an information system designed to support large-scale police investigations (eg homicide).

Home Office A government department responsible for policy relating to policing and crime.

Home Secretary The senior government minister responsible for policing and security in England and Wales and for developing police reform (note: the Welsh Assembly has some devolved powers for policing in Wales).

HORTies ('hortiz') Police vernacular for the HORT/1 and HORT/2 forms relating to the production of driving documents.

HOSDB Home Office Scientific Development Branch, was part of NPIA (qv).

Hot spot A geographical location with a high incidence of crime and criminality.

HPDS High Potential Development Scheme.

HQ Headquarters.

HRA Human Rights Act 1998.

HSE Health and Safety Executive.

Ibid Latin for 'in the same place'.

IC1, IC2 to IC9 (eg 'I-C-2') A reference to Identity Codes used by police officers to record ethnicity. IC1 is White European.

ICF Integrated Competency Framework. This combined descriptions of behavioural requirements with the NOS (qv) and profiles for certain policing roles. Replaced by the Policing Professional Framework (qv) in 2011.

ICIDP Initial Crime Investigators' Development Programme.

ICO Information Commissioners Office, the regulatory office for data protection and electronic privacy.

ICV Incident Command Vehicle used in situations where public order might be a problem.

IDENT1 ('ident-wun') The national database of fingerprints.

Idents Identifications (vernacular).

IDIOM Information Database for IOM; a database for tracking and monitoring PPOs (qv).

IED ('I-E-D') Improvised Explosive Device (a 'bomb').

IIMARCH ('eye-eye-march') Mnemonic for content of briefings: Information, Intention, Method, Administration, Risk assessment, Communications, Human rights compliance

IL4SP Initial Learning for the Special Constabulary.

ILP/ILPM ('I-L-P') Intelligence-Led Policing and hence Intelligence-Led Policing Model; sometimes referred to as Intelligence Based Policing, and also referred to as Information Based Policing or Information-Led Policing.

IMPACT A College of Policing (qv) programme to improve police access to, and sharing of, information.

IMSC Initial Management of Serious Crime course.

IND Immigration and Nationality Directorate.

Independent Inquiry into Child Sexual Abuse A public inquiry (likely to take years) to examine the extent to which institutions and organizations in England and Wales have made a serious attempt to fulfil their responsibility to protect children.

Independent Patrol The ability of a trainee police officer to conduct police patrol without the constant supervision of a qualified police officer. Usually achieved after successful completion of the PAC (qv).

Informant A person who passes intelligence to a source handler: a CHIS (qv). Often a criminal, an informant is known by other criminals as a snout, grass, or nark.

INI The IMPACT (qv) Nominal Index—a 'mega' database for searching of a number of smaller databases for information concerning named individuals.

Insp. or Ins. Abbreviation for 'Inspector', a policing rank.

Institutional racism The idea that institutions can unintentionally behave in a manner prejudicial to ethnic minorities, through their written and unwritten policies and procedures.

Inter-agency Approaches that involve partnership between several agencies: for example, collaboration with the Probation Service and Social Services. See also CDRP (qv).

inter alia Latin for 'among other things'.

Interpol International criminal police organization.

Intranet Often refers in police circles to a police internal electronic information system, with restricted access rights.

IO Investigating (police) Officer, usually a detective officer (for a crime), but can be a uniformed officer (eg for traffic collisions).

IP ('I-P') Injured Person or Party (often literally the person injured in a crime involving personal violence).

IPCC Independent Police Complaints Commission: deals with serious complaints against the police, and investigates instances where police officers have used firearms. Soon to be replaced by the 'Office for Police Conduct'.

IPLDP (I-P-L-D-P or 'ipple-dip') (1) Initial Police Learning and Development Programme: the programme for initial police training managed by the Home Office since 2006; (2) Central Authority Responsible for the implementation and policy direction of IPLDP (which includes representation from the Home Office, Police Federation, and the Superintendents' Association (qv)).

ISA Information Sharing Agreement (between the police and other agencies).

ISO ('I-S-O') Individual Support Order, for a young person aged 10–17 years.

ISVAs Independent Sexual Violence Advisors.

JAPAN: *J*ustification, *A*uthorization, *P*roportionality, *A*uditable, and *N*ecessary; a checklist for policing actions.

JBB Joint Branch Board of the Police Federation of England and Wales (qv).

JRFT Job-Related Fitness Test.

Justice Ministry Responsible for the courts, prisons, probation, criminal law, and sentencing.

KUSAB ('queue-sab') *K*nowledge, *U*nderstanding, *S*kills, *A*ttitudes, and *B*ehaviours, for trainee police officers.

Latent prints Prints (such as fingerprints) which are invisible until revealed by dusting or other techniques.

Lawrence, Stephen/the Lawrence Inquiry/the Macpherson Inquiry References to the death of the black teenager Stephen Lawrence in 1993, the subsequent investigation conducted by the MPS (qv), and the reports that followed (eg as conducted by Lord Macpherson, 1999).

LCN Low Copy Number; a tiny amount of DNA recovered through advanced scientific processes.

Overview

LDR Learning Development Review. These are regular reviews during training (typically three) as part of the IPLDP (qv) approach to monitoring achievement of a student police officer's skills and behaviour.

LEA Law Enforcement Agency.

Learning Diary Kept by trainee police officers as part of the process of reflective learning. It may form part of the SOLAP (qv).

Learning Requirement A set of learning requirements that underpin the IPLDP (qv) curriculum designed by Professors John Elliott, Saville Kushner, and others (Elliott *et al*, 2003).

Level 1 Local crime signifier (used within NIM (qv)). Illegal possession of a controlled drug is a level 1 crime.

Level 2 Cross-BCU or cross-force crime signifier (used within NIM (qv)). Dealing in illegal drugs is a level 2 crime.

Level 3 National or international crime signifier (used within NIM (qv)). Organizing the importing or distribution of illegal drugs is a level 3 crime.

LGC Laboratory of Government Chemists (service provider for scientific analysis).

LIVESCAN Commercial computerized database for taking fingerprints digitally.

LOCARD Forensic database system.

loc cit Latin for 'at the place quoted'.

LPG Legislation, Policy, and Guidelines modules, part of the IPLDP curriculum (qv).

MAPPA ('mapper') Multi-Agency Public Protection Arrangements (part of the joint agency approach to managing violent and sex offenders).

MARAC Multi-agency Risk Assessment Conference.

MASH Multi-agency sharing hub.

Match An identified DNA (qv) sample.

MG 3 A form used to report to the CPS (qv) for an initial charging decision.

MG 11 Witness statement form.

MIM ('mim') Murder Investigation Manual (sometimes called the 'Murder Manual'). It was the first example of a comprehensive doctrine (qv) to assist in the investigation of serious crime, and sets out possible investigative strategies (eg forensic and the interview strategy). It was written partly as a result of the enquiry into the death of Stephen Lawrence (qv).

minutiae Latin for 'of small parts'; the individuality of a fingerprint through examination of its ridge (qv) characteristics (up to 150 characteristics in a single finger print).

Misper Missing person, or the forms used during an investigation about a missing person.

MO ('M-O') *Modus operandi* is Latin for a characteristic way of doing something. Often used to refer to a particular way of committing a crime.

MoDP Ministry of Defence Police.

MOPAC Mayor's Office for Policing and Crime (London's equivalent of a police and crime commissioner).

MoPI ('moppy') Management of Police Information.

Morris Inquiry An inquiry in 2004 into professional standards and employment issues in the MPS (qv).

MOU ('M-O-U') Memorandum of Understanding.

MPS Metropolitan Police Service: London's police force.

MSF Most Similar Force (for comparison).

Multi-agency A term employed in policing to describe approaches to crime investigation and reduction that involve partnership with non-police agencies.

NABIS ('nay-biss') National Ballistics Intelligence Service.

NACRO ('nak-roh') National Association for the Care and Resettlement of Offenders.

NAFIS ('naffiss') National Automated Fingerprint Identification System, now replaced by IDENT1 (qv).

National Crime Agency The National Crime Agency, the national law enforcement agency which has now assumed responsibility for some of the work previously undertaken by the NPIA (qv), SOCA (qv), and the CEOP (qv).

National Injuries Database A searchable national database of (mainly) victim's wounds enabling comparisons.

National Occupational Standards The National Occupational Standards (NOS) for policing were developed by Skills for Justice (qv). For initial police officer training there are currently 21 NOS.

NB Latin for 'take especial note of'.

NBPA National Black Police Association.

NCA National Crime Agency (qv).

NCALT ('enn-kalt') National Centre for Applied Learning Technology. NCALT is a password-protected, internet-based learning portal for the police service.

NCDV National Centre for Domestic Violence.

NCSP National Community Safety Plan.

NDM National Decision Model.

NDNAD National DNA (qv) Database.

NDORS National Driver Offender Re-training Scheme.

NEFPN Non-endorsable Fixed Penalty Notice.

Nexus A combined computer database system.

NFA (1) No Further (police or CPS) Action; (2) No Fixed Abode; (3) National Fraud Authority (disbanded in 2014).

NFD National Footwear Database (replaced the NFRC).

NFFID National Firearms Forensic Intelligence Database.

NFIB National Fraud Intelligence Bureau, a central access point for individuals and organizations who suspect cybercrime, overseen by the City of London police.

NFIU National Football Intelligence Unit.

NFLMS National Firearms Licensing Management System: a database containing details of all firearm or shotgun certificate holders (and those in the process of applying for certificates).

NFRC National Footwear Reference Collection (previous name for the National Footwear Database).

Nick Vernacular for: (1) a police station; (2) to arrest a person.

NID ('N-I-D' or 'nid') National Injuries Database (qv).

NIE ('N-I-E') National Investigators' Examination.

NIM ('nim' or 'N-I-M') National Intelligence Model. All police forces are required to follow the NIM, which is sometimes described as a business model for policing.

NMAT ('en-mat') National Mutual Aid Telephony, a national call-handling system for use in emergencies.

NMPR National Mobile Phone Register or the National Mobile Property Register.

Nominals Vernacular police term for those perceived to be active and often recidivist, high-volume criminals.

NOMS National Offenders Management Service.

Non-Home Office forces Police forces that are not one of the 43 county or city-based forces, for example BTP (qv).

NOS ('N-O-S' or rarely 'noz') National Occupational Standards (qv).

NPAS National Police Air Service.

NPB National Policing Board.

NPC National Policing Curriculum.

NPCC National Police Chiefs' Council, established in 2015 with the objective of coordinating operational policing at national levels, replacing ACPO (qv).

NPIA National Police Improvement Agency, phased out in 2013. Much of its previous work is now managed by the College of Policing (qv), the National Crime Agency (qv) and the Home Office (qv).

NPPF The National Police Promotion Framework, a new system for promotion to Sergeant and Inspector ranks.

Overview

NPT Neighbourhood Policing Team.

NSPIS National Strategy for Police Information Systems: a suite of databases and software to support case preparation, command and control, and custody processes.

NSY New Scotland Yard.

NTSU National Technical Services Unit.

NVQ National Vocational Qualification. There are NVQs at Levels 3 and 4 in Policing and other law enforcement roles, incorporating the relevant NOS (qv).

OCC Operations and Communications Centre.

OCD Out of court disposal (OOCD is also used).

OIC ('O-I-C') Officer in Charge.

OOCD Out of court disposal (OCD is also used).

OP ('O-P') Observation point for carrying out surveillance.

Op Operation, usually refers to a targeted police operation against a criminal problem, for example 'Op Damocles'. The name of each operation is simply taken from a list and does not reflect the nature of the operation.

op cit Latin for 'see the work cited'.

ORC ('O-R-C' or 'ork') Operational Response Commander.

OSPRE® ('osspray') Objective Structured Performance-Related Examination, these were written tests for potential police sergeants or inspectors, now subsumed within the NPPF (qv).

OST Officer Safety Training.

PAC ('P-A-C' or 'pack') Police Action Checklist. In many forces the satisfactory completion of the PAC is one of the criteria for the right to undertake Independent Patrol (qv).

PACE ('pace') Police and Criminal Evidence Act 1984.

PAS ('P-A-S') Police Advisers' (or Advisory) Service.

passim Latin for 'everywhere', but used in the sense of throughout.

PBE Pocket book entry.

PC or Pc Police constable.

PCC Police and Crime Commissioner.

PCeU Police Central e-Crime Unit, created in September 2008 and a national resource (partly funded by the Home Office (qv)), based at the MPS (qv).

PCP (1) Police and Crime Panel; (2) Police and Crime Plan.

PCSO Police Community Support Officer.

PDP The Professional Development Portfolio is a tool for recording an individual police officer's professional development. The PDP for trainee officers is the SOLAP (qv).

PDU Professional Development Unit, for trainee police officers, police officers, and other police employees.

PEACE ('peace') Mnemonic for an interviewing model, adopted by police forces in the UK. The letters represent the stages of an interview: *P*lanning and preparation; *E*ngage and explain; *A*ccount, clarification and challenge; *C*losure; and *E*valuation.

PEEL The acronym used by Her Majesty's Inspectorate of Constabulary (HMIC) to describe the three areas ('pillars') of inspection they use when assessing forces: P (police) E (effectiveness) E (efficiency) and L (legitimacy).

PentiP The Penalty Notice Processing system.

Phonetic Alphabet The system commonly used by the police to communicate letters of the alphabet.

PI ('P-I') Performance Indicator; a type of quantitative measure, used by the Home Office to assess the police service.

PIMS ('pimz') Performance Indicator Management System.

PIP ('pip') 'Professionalising Investigation Programme' at levels 1–4. Level 1 is embedded in the initial police officer training (mapped to the NOS (qv) 2G2, 2H1, and 2H2).

PIRA ('peer-rah') Provisional Irish Republican Army, a proscribed terrorist group.

PKC Policing Knowledge Certificate, more properly known as the Certificate in Knowledge of Policing, a pre-join qualification.

PLO ('P-L-O') Prison Liaison Officer (a police officer).

PM Post mortem examination.

PNAC (sometimes 'p-nack') Police National Assessment Centre (sometimes 'Senior PNAC') for superintendents and chief superintendents who aspire to chief officer (qv) ranks.

PNB (1) Pocket notebook; (2) Police Negotiation Board.

PNC Police National Computer.

PND (1) Penalty Notice for Disorder; (2) Police National Database.

PNLD Police National Legal Database.

POCA ('pocker') Proceeds of Crime Act 2002.

Police and Crime Panels Set up by the Police Reform & Social Responsibility Act 2011 to act as a 'check and a balance' on a PCC's performance.

Police Degree Apprenticeships A College of Policing led initiative creating a new entry route into policing via an apprenticeship programme (from 2020). Officers will have to undergo police training and complete a degree in policing to be confirmed in the rank.

Police Federation of England and Wales The national staff association for the federated ranks of constable, sergeant, inspector, and chief inspector, resembling a trade union.

Police Memorial Trust Charitable organization (with a national memorial in London) for police officers killed in the line of duty.

Police Now A new initiative where graduates are employed as police officers for a two-year period with a specific remit to address a particular community problem.

Police Scotland The name of the single police force in Scotland, created in 2013 when the eight regional forces merged.

Police Staff Official designation of support (civilian) staff, some of whom are operational but do not have the police officer warranted powers. Includes PCSOs (qv).

Police Superintendents' Association of England and Wales (PSAEW) The national staff association for the ranks of superintendent and chief superintendent.

Policing Protocol Order 2011 A statute-based description of the legal responsibilities of chief constables, police and crime commissioners, the home secretary, and police and crime panels.

POLKA ('polka') Police OnLine Knowledge Area, a restricted online collaborative site for sharing policing knowledge and information.

PolSA/POLSA ('polsah') Police Search Adviser.

POP/BritPOP ('pop') Problem-Oriented Policing and its UK derivative.

PPF Policing Professional Framework—replaces the ICF (qv).

PPU Prisoner Process Unit.

Predictive Policing A method for deciding how to deploy police resources based upon predicted crime patterns, using software based on mathematical algorithms.

Pre-entry course/programme See pre-join programme.

Pre-join programme A course of study leading to entry to the police service as a trainee officer. Normally offered by a commercial provider, a further or higher education college or university, often in conjunction with a police force or forces. May lead to a foreshortened period of subsequent training.

Probationer An informal term for a police officer in initial training and a reference to the probationary period. Now usually replaced by trainee police officer or trainee officer, but you may still hear the term used.

Profiling/Profilers An informal term often used in policing (as in 'offender profiling' and 'geographical profiling') but of uncertain meaning. Most often used to describe predicting the psychological traits of an unknown offender (eg when used to support the investigation into a linked serial rape case). However, the official term is behavioural analyst or behavioural adviser.

PRRB Police Remuneration Review Body.

PS or Ps Police sergeant.

PSB or PSBM The basic personal safety course often included by forces as part of IPLDP (qv).

PSD Professional Standards Department.

PSNI Police Service of Northern Ireland (previously called the RUC, Royal Ulster Constabulary).

PSO Prohibited Steps Order (for protecting children).

PSPO Public Spaces Protection Order.

PWITS ('pee-wits') Possession (of drugs) with intent to supply.

QCF Qualifications and Credit Framework—the organization responsible for accrediting qualifications in England, Wales, and Northern Ireland.

QPM Queen's Police Medal.

qv Latin for 'for which, see ....'—reference to another item or word.

R&D Research and Development Unit (usually for intelligence analysis and tasking at BCU (qv) level).

RCT Randomised Control Trial, often employed to support Evidence Based Policing (qv).

Re-coursing/Back-coursing An informal term for trainee police officers having to repeat elements of initial training, normally as a result of failure or for personal reasons.

Redcap Vernacular term for an officer of the RMP (qv).

Reflex Nationally funded project to deal with organized immigration crime.

Refs A vernacular reference to a refreshment break during a tour of duty.

Ridge and furrow Identifying features in fingerprints.

RIPA ('ripper') Regulation of Investigatory Powers Act 2000—regulates undercover police work and the use of informants, now partly subsumed by the Investigatory Powers Act 2016.

RIRA ('real I-R-A') Real Irish Republican Army, a proscribed terrorist organization.

RMP Royal Military Police.

ROLE ('role') Recognition of Life Extinct, this is a statement from a medical professional confirming a person is dead.

ROTI ('roh-tee') A written record of a taped interview (audio-taped); a summarized account.

ROVI ('roh-vee') A written record of a video-taped interview; a summarized account.

RSHO Risk of Sexual Harm Order, superseded by SROs in 2015.

RTA (1) Road Traffic Act; (2) Road Traffic Accident—now largely replaced by RTI (qv) or RTC (qv).

RTC Road Traffic Collision. The term 'collision' is preferred to 'accident' as it is more suggestive of the fact that most collisions on roads are due to human error, negligence, or a criminal act, rather than a chance event. However, the term 'accident' is still present in legislation.

RTI Road Traffic Incident.

RUC Royal Ulster Constabulary—the former police force for Northern Ireland, replaced by the Police Service of Northern Ireland (PSNI) in 2001.

RV(P) Rendezvous (point) at a crime scene or major incident.

SAB Safeguarding Adult Board.

Safeguarding A term used increasingly in policing to describe policies to address vulnerable adults and children/young persons, who may be at risk of harm through exploitation by criminals.

Sanitized The term for describing intelligence from which the identifying features and origins have been omitted.

SARA ('sarr-rer' or 'S-A-R-A') *S*can, *A*nalyse, *R*espond, and *A*ssess.

SARC ('sark') Sexual Assault Referral Centre.

SB Special Branch: a part of every police force that specializes in matters of national security and consists of non-uniformed police officers.

SCAIDP Specialist Child Abuse Investigation Development Programme.

Scarman Inquiry (Scarman Report) An official inquiry into the circumstances surrounding rioting in the Brixton area of London in 1981. It recommended reforming the law, changing police training and practice, and improving community relations.

SCAS ('Scaz') Serious Crime Analysis Section. A database of homicides and stranger rapes maintained by the NCA (qv).

SDE Self-defined Ethnicity.

SDN Short Descriptive Note (part of a case file, such as a reference to a transcription of an interview with a suspect).

Secret Policeman Reference to the video documentary made in 2003 by an undercover reporter and subsequently aired by BBC television. The documentary produced evidence of racist behaviour by police recruits at a police regional training centre.

SFO Serious Fraud Office.

SGM Second Generation Multiplex: a DNA-profiling system using seven areas for discrimination between people (1 in 50 million).

SGM+ A similar DNA-profiling system to SGM, using 11 areas for discrimination (1 in 1,000 million).

Sgt Abbreviation for 'sergeant', a policing rank sometimes also referred to as 'skipper'.

Shoe marks Informal term for footwear prints which can match a suspect to a crime scene, in the same way as DNA and fingerprints can.

SHPO Sexual Harm Prevention Order, supersedes SOPOs.

Show out A vernacular reference to a security problem on a surveillance operation when the suspect realizes that he/she is being observed.

SIA ('S-I-A') Security Industry Association.

sic Latin for 'just as it is written'.

SIO ('S-I-O') Senior Investigating Officer (usually a detective officer) investigating a serious or major crime, such as a Category A or B murder (qv), or a rape or series of rapes.

SIODP Senior Investigating Officers' Development Programme.

SIU ('S-I-U') Special Investigation Unit (for child abuse and child protection investigations).

Skills for Justice/SfJ/S4J The Sector Skills Council (SSC) for Criminal Justice, including Policing. Skills for Justice is also responsible for the National Occupational Standards (qv) for Policing and other justice-related bodies and organizations (such as the Probation Service).

Skillsmark Quality assurance scheme introduced by Skills for Justice (qv).

SLA Service Level Agreement.

SLDP Senior Leadership Development Programmes (SLDP1 and SLDP2) for chief inspector roles or above.

SLP Senior Leadership Programme.

SMART(ER) Used in reference to objectives: *S*pecific, *M*easurable, *A*chievable, *R*ealistic, *T*imely (and *E*valuated and *R*eviewed).

SMT Senior Management Team (on a BCU (qv), it usually consists of the commander, a superintendent (or a chief superintendent on large BCUs), together with one or more chief inspectors (Crime and Operations) and a business manager).

SNT Safer Neighbourhood Teams (an alternative name for Neighbourhood Policing Teams).

SO 19 Firearms unit in the MPS (qv).

SOCA ('socker') Serious Organised Crime Agency: phased out in 2013, its work is now carried out by the NCA (qv).

SOCO ('sockoh') Scenes of Crime Officer; outmoded term replaced in many police forces by CSI (qv).

SOCPA ('sockper') The Serious Organised Crime and Police Act 2005.

SOIT Sexual Offences Investigative Techniques (officer), an MPS role.

SOLAP ('soh-lap') Student Officer Learning Assessment Portfolio (see 8.5.4). In many forces this replaced the PDP (qv) for trainee police officers.

SOLO ('solo') Sex Offender Liaison Officer.

SOP ('S-O-P') Standard Operating Procedure.

SOPO ('sop-oh') Sexual Offences Protection Order, superseded by SHPOs in 2015.

Spit hood A shroud used by police to cover a detained person's face and head to protect police officers and others from spitting or biting.

SPoC/SPOC/spoc ('spock') Single Point of Contact.

SPP Strategic Policing Priorities.

SPR Strategic Policing Requirement (qv).

SRO Sexual Risk Order, supersedes RSHOs.

Stinger Pronged device for stopping cars by puncturing the tyres.

STO ('S-T-O') Specially trained officer.

STR Short Tandem Repeat: a DNA profiling methodology which replaces the SGM and SGM+ terms (qv).

Strategic Policing Requirement A statement by the Home Secretary outlining national risks and threats to England and Wales. It also states the government's expectations of police forces in terms of capacity and capability to collectively address such threats. The SPR is regularly updated.

Superintendents' Association The Police Superintendents' Association of England and Wales.

Supervised Patrol Undertaken by trainee police officers under the supervision of a qualified police officer or officers.

T&CG Tasking and Coordinating Group.

Tac/TAC team (1) Tactical Support Team—for example, used to serve a warrant; (2) Terrorism and Crime Team (MPS (qv)).

TDA or TADA Taking and Driving Away: a reference to a form of vehicle crime. Also known as TWOC (qv).

Tenprint A fingerprinting process whereby prints of all ten fingers are recorded.

Test Purchase The authorized purchase of drugs, alcohol, or other items (by an undercover police officer or another person) to provide evidence of illegal activity.

TFU Tactical Firearms Unit.

TIC ('T-I-C') Acronym for offences 'taken into consideration' by a court.

TIE (sometimes 'ty') *T*race, *I*mplicate, and/or *E*liminate (in investigations).

TNA Training Needs Analysis.

TWOC ('twok') Taken Without (or Without Owner's) Consent—normally used in reference to a motor vehicle: TDA or TADA (qv).

UC (or UC officer) Abbreviation for an undercover officer.

Undercover Policing Inquiry Judge-led public inquiry into all undercover policing since 1968.

UKBA UK Border Agency, now dissolved, its work is now carried out by Border Force (qv) and Immigration Enforcement.

UVP Ultra-Violet (Light) Photography.

VCSE Volume Crime Scene Examiner (forensic).

VDRS Vehicle Defect Rectification Scheme.

VEM ('V-E-M') Visible Ethnic Minority: refers to both individuals and communities.

VIAPOAR ('via-por') Mnemonic for the factors to take into account when making decisions, recently replaced by CIAPOAR (qv).

ViCLAS ('vy-class') Violent Crime Linkage Analysis System—a database used by SCAS (qv) in the UK, originally devised by the Royal Canadian Mounted Police (RCMP).

VIPER ('viper') Video Identification Parade Electronic Recording.

ViSOR ('vy-zor') Violent and Sex Offender Register: a database of individuals considered a potential danger to the public because of their history of violence and/or sex offending.

Vol Volume.

VOO Violent Offender Order.

VPS Victim Personal Statement.

WBA Work-based Assessment.

'Whorl' Characteristic pattern seen in fingerprints.

Winsor Review(s) Two reports (2011 and 2012) by Tom Winsor on pay, conditions, entry routes, and career pathways for police staff.

WPLDP Wider Police Learning and Development Programme.

YOT Youth Offending Team.

YPVA Young People's Violence Advisor.

> **TASK 2** There could well be terms, acronyms, and jargon particular to your local police organizations and hence not included here. Your local force might have a list on its intranet, or on a publicly available website, or (more rarely) in a published form. Use the internet to try to track down a list.

2.4 Police Ranks

You may sometimes hear the police referred to as a 'disciplined organization'. This refers not only to the need for self-discipline and restraint but also to the fact that at least parts of the organization (those parts concerned with police officers) are organized into ranks in a hierarchical fashion, involving the issuing and receiving of orders. Apart from the MPS and one or two other forces (such as the City of London), the rank structure (and the associated badges on the epaulettes of uniforms) are as follows:

Rank Structure

In order of decreasing superiority:

- chief constable (commissioner*);
- deputy chief constable (deputy commissioner*);
- assistant chief constable (commander*);
- chief superintendent;
- superintendent;
- chief inspector;
- inspector;
- sergeant; and
- constable.
    * Metropolitan and City of London equivalent ranks—see below.

In the non-uniformed equivalents 'detective' often precedes the rank, for example detective chief inspector. It is important to note that being a detective does not signify a higher or more senior police rank—it simply defines the *role* of the officer.

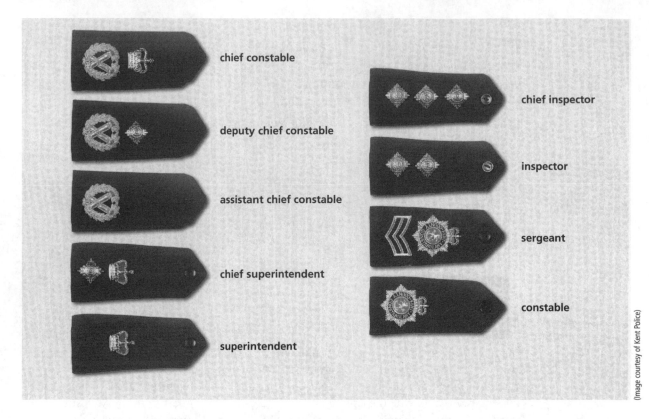

(Image courtesy of Kent Police)

In the MPS the rank structure is different for the higher ranks; the three highest ranks are commissioners rather than chief constables, and there are also two additional ranks (marked with asterisks on the MPS rank list). Note that the MPS has announced its intention to phase out two of the 11 current ranks by 2018, including the consolidation of inspector and chief inspector ranks.

MPS Ranks in 2016

- commissioner;
- deputy commissioner;
- assistant commissioner;
- deputy assistant commissioner;*
- commander;*
- chief superintendent;
- superintendent;
- chief inspector;
- inspector;
- sergeant; and
- constable.

The City of London Police is a little different again. The Border Force also has a rank structure, and its officers also wear a uniform with epaulettes, but the names of the ranks differ slightly (ranging from 'administrative assistant' to 'director general').

The insignia of the ranks may vary from force to force. You should also take the time to familiarize yourself with the insignia of uniformed members of the extended police family (see 3.4), such as special constables and PCSOs.

TASK 3 Construct a set of memory cards to help you learn the police ranks and their associated insignia. Memory cards are best made from thick paper or cardboard. (You may have used them as a child!) On one side of the card put the rank, on the other side a photograph (or a simple diagram) of the associated insignia, like so:

superintendent

(Image courtesy of Kent Police)

Now take cards at random from your collection. If the name of the rank is given then describe the insignia. Reverse the card and check your answer. If the insignia is given, then you need to name the rank. As before, turn over to check your answer.

Keep playing (alone or in a group) until you have memorized all the ranks and insignia.

2.5 Police Organization and Governance

The diagram shows a typical structure for a police force with 6,000-plus staff. There are likely to be small variations between forces.

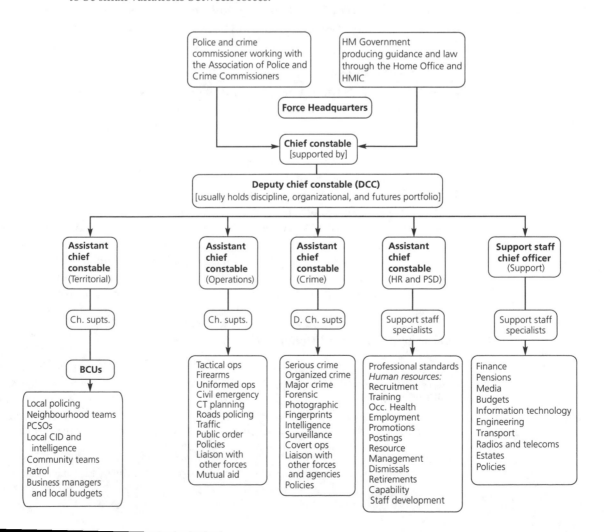

TASK 4 Find out the names and ranks of the individuals who lead your local police force. For example, who is the ACC responsible for training?

2.5.1 Police and Crime Commissioners and Police and Crime Panels

Each police force now has a democratically elected police and crime commissioner (PCC). They are responsible for holding chief officers to account, and partly funding the force from a precept (a type of local tax). Over 90 per cent of PCCs are linked to a political party, the remainder being independent.

Each PCC is answerable to a police and crime panel (PCP), the members of which are appointed. A minimum of ten of the panel members are local authority councillors (elected) and the other members are individuals with specific skills or knowledge within their police locality. The panel has only limited powers, and functions mainly as, a 'check and a balance' on the PCC and his/her actions. For example, the panel can 'review' a PCC's draft crime and police plan and make recommendations about it, but the PCC need only 'have regard to' the panel's views. The panel could not reject a PCC's plan outright. Similarly, the panel can 'veto' the PCC's recommended precept the first time it is submitted, but cannot block a re-submitted precept.

There are three important differences between a PCC and the previous local police authority:

- the PCC is a single person (as opposed to typically 17 individuals from different backgrounds, as was the case with the police authorities);
- the PCC is directly elected (rather than appointed, as was the case with local police authority members). Some have said this makes policing democratically accountable; and
- the PCC has a broader remit, as it includes holding other local crime-related agencies to account (compared with the much narrower scope of the local police authorities).

The introduction of PCCs has arguably made the political dimensions of police work more explicit and transparent, although there are still concerns that the new system could undermine police independence and lead to political interference.

The Policing and Crime Act 2017 places a duty on police, fire, and ambulance services to work together. PCCs will be able to take on responsibility for fire and rescue services where a local case is made out.

2.5.1.1 Police and crime plans

Every PCC in England and Wales is required (by the Police Reform and Social Responsibility Act 2011) to produce a police and crime plan setting out a strategy for policing and crime reduction. This must be done in consultation with the PCC's chief constable. These plans will also involve other community safety partners (eg health, local authorities, fire and rescue services) and other criminal justice agencies in setting priorities. Each plan covers a five-year period but can be revised annually. The plans are likely to contain specific objectives to be achieved. For example, one objective set by the PCC for Cumbria in 2013 was to 'Reduce the impact antisocial behaviour has on [Cumbrian] communities' with an associated priority to 'Promote restorative justice, encouraging a broader and more joined-up approach to the use of community resolutions to address offenders' behaviour, focussing on: antisocial behaviour, veterans, youth justice, rural crime' (Cumbria Police, 2014). Undoubtedly these police and crime plans have at least an indirect effect on the work of police service staff, and in many cases the effects will be relatively easy to see, in terms of changing priorities in operational policing.

2.5.2 The Policing Protocol Order 2011

The legislation that ushered in police and crime commissioners (Police Reform & Social Responsibility Act 2011) also sought to redefine and clarify the constitutional/governance positions of the key actors in policing in England and Wales— the Home Secretary, the chief constables, and the police authorities (the police authority is now replaced by a PCC in each force). This was achieved in a document called the Policing Protocol Order 2011.

Perhaps the most sensitive area the Protocol touches upon is police operational independence. Prior to the introduction of PCCs considerable concern had been expressed that some PCCs might seek to assume operational control of their local police force. The Order sought to reaffirm that operational control would remain solely in the hands of chief constables and this has largely been achieved.

2.5.3   The Strategic Policing Requirement

The major police reforms around 2011 also saw the creation of the Strategic Policing Requirement (SPR). This was a bold attempt by the Home Office to outline the commitments and priorities that would require a coordinated and joint response from the police service—to see a number of police forces acting in unison to tackle a serious national threat or risk.

The first SPR was issued by the Home Secretary in 2012, and required both PCCs and chief constables to be ready to respond with trained, equipped, and deployable resources anywhere to address incidents of terrorism, serious public disorder, or civil disaster. The SPR was reviewed, revised, and republished in 2015, and child sexual abuse was added to the list of national threats to which forces may have to respond in a collective and coordinated manner.

Along with the many regional collaborations that have sprung up between and amongst forces to deal with crime and policing issues that some found difficult to address alone, the SPR remains one of the most important statements about how constabularies are expected to work together—in effect as a national police force.

2.6   Conventions for Conveying Information

If you have ever attempted to spell out a word on the phone to another person you have probably experienced the difficulty of clarifying the difference between 'm' and 'n', 's' and 'f', and so on. Mistakes made in the context of ordinary phone calls are seldom life-threatening, but if these same mistakes were made during a police communication it could prove costly, both in time and in terms of safety. This is the reason the 'phonetic alphabet' (sometimes referred to as the 'radio alphabet') and conventions for communicating numbers, time of day, and dates were developed and subsequently adopted by police forces throughout the UK.

2.6.1   The phonetic alphabet

With the phonetic alphabet each letter is given a phonetic equivalent. This is to avoid confusion over letters which sound the same, such as 'p', 'b', and 'd'; Instead of saying 'd' the police officer will say 'delta'. The following is a list of the phonetic alphabet as normally employed by police forces in the UK (and beyond). You may well be asked to memorize and use it after you join the police.

The Phonetic Alphabet

a	Alpha	j	Juliet	s	Sierra
b	Bravo	k	Kilo	t	Tango
c	Charlie	l	Lima	u	Uniform
d	Delta	m	Mike	v	Victor
e	Echo	n	November	w	Whisky
f	Foxtrot	o	Oscar	x	X-ray
g	Golf	p	Papa	y	Yankee
h	Hotel	q	Quebec	z	Zulu
i	India	r	Romeo		

(For a time 'Indigo' was used instead of 'India' but this practice is now very uncommon in police circles.)

TASK 5 Learn the phonetic alphabet. There are various ways of doing this, including using memory cards as in Task 3. One way of testing yourself is to spell out the names of family and friends.

Overview

2.6.2 Numbers

When communicating a number (eg the age of a person), then each digit of the number is said individually. There is a further convention that the number 0 is referred to as 'zero' and not 'naught' (nor as the letter 'O'). Hence the number 2,306 (two thousand, three hundred, and six) is communicated as 'two-three-zero-six'. A less common rule is to give large numbers in pairs such as 245,671 being conveyed as 'two-four, five-six, seven-one'. However, practice does vary in this respect (particularly with phone numbers).

2.6.3 Time and date

As you might guess, police forces tend to use the 24-hour clock for conveying the time of day. So 7.26 pm is written as 19.26 and hence said as 'one-nine, two-six hours' (see 2.6.2). Dates are given as the day-month-year, in the UK style.

2.7 IC and SDE Codes

There are a number of different situations in which a police officer might need to communicate or record a person's ethnicity, based upon an individual's appearance. The system used by some police forces to communicate the perceived ethnicity of a person is known variously as 'IC codes' 'IC 1 to 6 codes', 'PNC Codes', and 'ID codes'. An officer could use this to describe a suspect's ethnicity when searching for a record on the Police National Computer (or the Police National Database). The acronym IC probably stands for 'Identity Code' (it has been around for over 30 years). There are normally six or seven categories (IC 0/IC 7 not always being used) as shown in the following table. Note that a different system might be used by some forces.

'IC' Code	Ethnicity	Example of a Nationality*
IC 0 (sometimes IC 7)	Unknown	N/A
IC 1	White North European	Swedish
IC 2	White South European (sometimes 'Dark European' or 'Mediterranean')	Greek
IC 3	Black (sometimes 'African-Caribbean')	Nigerian
IC 4	Asian (sometimes 'South Asian')	Pakistani
IC 5	Chinese/Japanese/SE Asian (sometimes 'Oriental' or 'East Asian')	Chinese
IC 6	Middle Eastern (sometimes 'Arab')	Egyptian

* Ethnicity and nationality are not the same. The examples shown here are for illustration only.

The Self-defined Ethnicity (SDE) codes (also known as '16 + 1') are codes used to record the ethnicity of a person as defined by that person him or herself. A trainee police officer will normally encounter these codes when completing forms. There are 16 ethnicity codes, plus one for 'not stated'. These are summarized in the following table.

General ethnic group	Self-declared ethnicity	SDE Code
White	British	W1
	Irish	W2
	Any other white background	W9
Mixed	White and black Caribbean	M1
	White and black African	M2
	White and Asian	M3
	Any other mixed background	M9
Asian or Asian British	Indian	A1
	Pakistani	A2
	Bangladeshi	A3
	Any other Asian background	A9
Black or black British	Caribbean	B1
	African	B2
	Any other black background	B9

Chinese	Chinese	01
Other ethnic group	Other ethnic group	09
Not stated	Not stated	NS
Total		16 + 1 (not stated)

There is less variation between police forces in the use of SDE codes (when compared with the IC Codes—see previous table) as they are determined by the Home Office (adapted from the national UK census in 2001).

> **TASK 6** Use the internet to discover some of the previous IC codes employed by the police. (What 'unofficial' IC codes can you find?) What are the inherent problems when using police officer-defined codes for radio communication?

2.8 Answers to Tasks

TASK 1 Police websites sometimes include their force history (eg the extensive MPS site at <http://www.met.police.uk/history/>). Many forces also have museums (eg the Essex Police museum at Police HQ in Chelmsford) and some may also have a comprehensive and published written history (eg Ingleton, 2002).

TASK 2 Police forces often publish a glossary of terms used in their documentation, available under the Freedom of Information Act 2000. An example of a glossary may be found at <http://www.devon-cornwall.police.uk/AboutUs/LinksAbbreviations/Pages/Abbreviations.aspx>.

TASK 3 Using memory cards (sometimes also called 'flashcards') in the era of modern information technology may seem somewhat old-fashioned but they are a tried-and-tested method that works.

TASK 4 Many police websites have a 'Who's Who' section (although not always up to date), particularly for their Senior Management Team. Kent Police SMT for example is described on this page at their site: <http://www.kent.police.uk/about_us/our_organisation/our_org.html>.

TASK 5 You might like to test yourself by trying the NASA online phonetic alphabet tester available at <http://virtualskies.arc.nasa.gov/communication/2.html>.

TASK 6 In 1975 the police in London replaced their 'RC code' ('Race Code') with a new 'Identi-Coding' ('IC') system. This assigned 'white-skinned European types—English, Scottish, Welsh, Scandinavian and Russian' to IC1; 'dark-skinned European types—Sardinian, Spanish, Italian' to IC2; 'Negroid types—Caribbean, West Indian, African, Nigerian' to IC3; 'Indians and Pakistanis' to IC4; 'Chinese, Japanese, Mongolians, Siamese' to IC5; and 'Arabians, Egyptians, Algerians, Moroccans and North Africans' to IC6. Even at the time this caused some controversy (Mackie, 1978).

An example of an unofficial IC code is 'IC 9' for people from the gypsy, Roma, or traveller community.

For operational reasons the police obviously require a quick, efficient, and timely means of communicating the ethnic appearance of a missing person, victim, or suspect. In terms of skin colour and other physical features a white South African does not resemble a black Nigerian and in some circumstances this is important. However, there are obvious definitional, empirical, and social problems in classifying individuals according to a perceived nominal categorization based on general physical appearance, skin colour, facial features, and so on. Put another way ethnicity is not defined by appearance, but the way someone looks might be part of their ethnicity. It is difficult because there is no reliable shared meaning of the descriptions 'black', 'white', 'Chinese', and so on when applied to people.

3 Policing

3.1 Introduction

The title of this chapter is 'Policing' rather than 'The Police'. This reflects Reiner's distinction that the term '"Police" refers to a particular kind of social institution, while "policing" implies a set of processes with specific social functions' (Reiner, 2000, p 1). Policing is undertaken by a range of organizations and it is for this reason that Chapter 3 examines the 'extended policing family' and 'the multi-agency approach'. This chapter also engages with the aspects of learning and development (either as a student on a pre-join programme or as a trainee police officer) supporting the claim that policing is a profession. The demonstration of certain professional qualities is likely to be required of you, whether you are a trainee police officer or on a pre-join programme. These qualities are sometimes less easy to pinpoint and identify than other aspects of learning and development (such as the acquisition of knowledge and demonstration of competencies and skills as outlined in Part III of this book), but they are just as important. If you can demonstrate these qualities you are very likely to have the potential to meet the requirements expected of a professional police officer in the twenty-first century.

Policing is always changing and evolving, but this is particularly true at the current time. A professional body for policing continues its development following the establishment of the College of Policing in December 2012. Alongside the introduction of the College of Policing, perhaps the most significant change for policing in recent years was the introduction of directly elected Police and Crime Commissioners (see 2.5.1) to replace local police authorities as the body with the main responsibility for holding chief officers to account. Without doubt, the current changes are profound, perhaps more dramatic and significant than any other changes in policing over the past 50 years or so.

3.2 Policing and Law Enforcement Agencies

The chronology of policing and law enforcement presented in 2.2 shows clearly that law enforcement in England and Wales has rarely been simply the province of the police alone. Many responsibilities for law enforcement and public order continue to be shared amongst a large number of agencies as shown in the table.

Type	Description	Examples	Comments
The 'territorial' or 'Home Office' police forces	The 43 county or metropolitan police forces in England and Wales, the single Police Services of Scotland and of Northern Ireland	Essex Police MPS Derbyshire Constabulary PSNI	What most people mean when they refer to the 'Police'
Sector-specific police forces	Police forces for specific sectors or industries (eg transport, nuclear power)	BTP CNC	Powers are at least equal to those of the territorial police forces

'Heritage' constabularies and police forces	Individual constabularies established previously under Acts of Parliament, restricted to small geographical areas	Port of Dover Police Royal Parks Constabulary Cambridge University Constabulary	Powers are the same as those for territorial police but the forces are small in size
Armed services police	Organizations responsible for policing the armed forces (eg the navy)	MoD Police Royal Military Police	Some armed services police are civilians and not members of the armed forces
Agencies	Home Office or non-statutory bodies with extensive powers of search, detention, arrest, and investigation	NCA (National Crime Agency) (for England and Wales)	The NCA has now subsumed many former agencies such as SOCA
National police 'units' or 'sections'	Normally NPCC or College of Policing supported units offering specialist support to police forces	National Wildlife Crime Unit (NWCU) Serious Crime Analysis Section (SCAS)	Normally made up of seconded police officers, but not exclusively so
Other organizations with investigatory powers	Non-police organizations with limited powers of investigation (but which might include surveillance powers)	Local Authorities HM Revenue and Customs IPCC	Some powers are governed by RIPA 2000
Other organizations with enforcement and/or regulatory powers	Regulatory bodies with responsibility for enforcing regulations	Trading Standards HSE	Powers normally fall short of arrest although they can usually prosecute
Other 'emergency services'	Services, other than the police, usually involved in the case of fire, vehicle collisions, apparent accidents, and so on	Fire and Rescue Services	Some emergency services have powers for stopping people and vehicles, entry, investigation, and prosecution
'Private' security or investigatory services	Companies and individuals from the private security industry	Security guards 'Private detectives' Debt collectors	In some cases licensing is required or forms of self-regulation
Informal policing	Social control and enforcement as a secondary occupational responsibility	Teachers Park rangers Bus drivers	Normally no powers beyond that of the civilian

Informal policing activities are also undertaken at the so-called 'secondary' and 'tertiary' levels of social control, for example by teachers and bus conductors, and through institutions such as the church and trade union organizations. These informal policing mechanisms are not underpinned by powers beyond those of every citizen and are better understood as secondary occupational responsibilities or even less tangible societal responsibilities.

Despite the increased sharing of policing powers the 'public police' still retain unique and profound powers, including those surrounding discretion (see 3.6). We still often refer to our police organizations as 'forces' although you will also hear reference to the 'police service'. In 3.4 we examine some of the 'extended policing family' roles in more detail.

3.3   The Multi-agency Approach

We noted in 3.2 that policing responsibilities are shared among a number of agencies. The police in particular are encouraged (and sometimes required) to collaborate with a number of agencies in investigating crime, and on issues concerning public protection. A 'multi-agency' (sometimes 'inter-agency') approach to reducing crime and disorder and investigating crime is officially endorsed by the Home Office and others. The Diploma in Policing units to 'Provide initial support to victims and witnesses', 'Provide an initial response to incidents', 'Conduct priority and volume investigations', and to 'Interview victims and witnesses in relation to priority and volume investigations' make explicit reference to the police officer working and consulting with other agencies, organizations, and 'relevant others'. The Policing Professional Framework (PPF, see 8.5.2) states that one of the key personal qualities required for a police constable, is

'Work[ing] in partnership with other agencies to deliver the best possible overall service to the public'. Police forces have written force policy and protocols relating to multi- and inter-agency cooperation. Multi-agency collaboration is particularly evident in the following areas:

- **Child welfare and protection:** this is likely to involve cooperation between the police, health and social services, education and children's services. For example, if you are a trainee police officer on Independent Patrol you might attend an incident concerning alleged drink-driving but also notice at the scene a child who appears malnourished, bruised, and psychologically withdrawn. The trainee police officer will report this to his/her BCU's public protection desk. Children's services will then become involved and the circumstances further investigated.

- **Domestic abuse:** similarly, a police response to domestic abuse is likely to include working with specialist domestic abuse services (such as the local Women's Aid), social and health services, housing, education, and voluntary organizations (such as Relate). A multi-agency approach is recommended to provide protection and support to the victim and his or her dependants (see 13.6.1.7). A police force is also likely to have its own specialist domestic abuse investigation units. Note, however, that none of this detracts from the presumption that the police will arrest and take action against the alleged offender if possible.

- **Reducing crime and disorder:** the Crime and Disorder Act 1998 established on a statutory basis an obligation for the police and other agencies to work together to counter and reduce crime and disorder in their localities, in particular anti-social behaviour. This takes place formally within a Community Safety Partnership (see 3.3.2).

- **Partnerships with local councils or authorities over fixed-penalty notices:** fixed-penalty notices are often issued for parking infringements or driving offences (such as those recorded by speed cameras). The partnership is likely to include close cooperation with local authority CCTV monitoring teams, especially for city centres and popular club or pub venues.

3.3.1 Multi-Agency Public Protection Arrangements

Multi-Agency Public Protection Arrangements (MAPPA) are considered by many organizations as key to the successful management of violent and sexual offenders, especially their reintegration into society after a prison sentence. The Police, Probation, and the Prison Service in each area form a 'Responsible Authority' for MAPPA, and work together with other agencies such as social services, electronic monitoring providers, registered social landlords, youth offending teams, children's services, local health services, local housing authorities, and Jobcentre plus. MAPPA guidance identifies a framework with four core functions: identifying MAPPA offenders; ensuring relevant information is shared with appropriate agencies; assessing the risk of serious harm; and managing risk.

The guidance identifies three broad categories of offenders (with some overlap):

- Category 1—registered sexual offenders as defined in Part 2 of the Sexual Offences Act 2003;
- Category 2—violent offenders sentenced to 12 months or more imprisonment, sexual offenders not included in Category 1, and offenders disqualified from working with children; and
- Category 3—other dangerous offenders who are not included in the first two categories but are nonetheless still regarded by the Responsible Authority as presenting a serious risk to the public (eg they have a previous conviction or caution that indicates that they have the potential to cause serious harm to others).

There are three identified levels of risk management. Level 1 is for offenders who can be managed by one primary agency without necessarily involving other agencies. Level 2 management involves more than one agency but is not considered to be overly challenging or complex. Level 3 is used where managing the risk requires active conferencing and senior representation from the Responsible Authority and other agencies with a duty to cooperate.

The number of 'MAPPA-eligible offenders' in the UK has been steadily increasing. In 2016 the Ministry of Justice reported there were almost 72,000 offenders in the UK (73 per cent Category 1; 26 per cent Category 2; and less than 1 per cent Category 3) and 98 per cent of cases were managed at Level 1 (Ministry of Justice, 2016).

Information about offenders is stored in a central database called ViSOR. The data in ViSOR can be accessed by the three Responsible Authority agencies, and the cases are called 'nominals'. When a case ceases to be an active MAPPA case, the information is archived and can be retrieved at a later stage if necessary. The police have a responsibility to create and maintain a

ViSOR record for offenders in Categories 1 and 3 when this is not the responsibility of the Probation Trust. Nominal records will normally be removed at the 100th birthday of an individual, after a review is conducted.

In deciding on what course of action to take it is important that 'defensible decisions' are made. This is to ensure that the Responsible Authority has taken all reasonable steps, and that the assessment methods utilized are reliable. A thorough evaluation of the collected information needs to be demonstrated, and decisions need to have been recorded and acted upon. Throughout it is important to demonstrate that the appropriate policies and procedures have been followed, and that a proactive approach has been adopted by the practitioners and managers. An important function of MAPPA is to ensure that public protection work is communicated to the public and all interested parties in a consistent manner.

3.3.2 Community Safety Partnerships

The Crime and Disorder Act 1998 made partnership-working a statutory requirement for organizations such as police authorities, local authorities, fire and rescue authorities, primary care trusts, the Probation Service, and the Drug and Alcohol Action Team. These 'Community Safety Partnerships' (CSPs) work together with Police and Crime Commissioners (PCCs) to identify and respond to crime problems within a specific area. There are about 320 CSPs in England and Wales. Trainee police officers are most likely to encounter CSPs in terms of the local force priorities.

CSPs meet regularly and discuss how to develop strategies to combat crime in the local area. Their key objectives are to:

- establish the level and extent of crime and disorder within the area;
- consult widely with the local population;
- develop a strategy aimed at tackling problems with a clear action plan with organizational responsibilities;
- review the current strategy periodically; and
- work closely with the local PCC.

The aim is to share information and working with other local public, voluntary, and private organizations to achieve agreed objectives, by means of an agreed strategy to reduce crime and improve community safety and quality of life.

3.3.3 Community Safety Units

Each police force contributes resources to a local Community Safety Unit (CSU) to coordinate the work of the police locally, in collaboration with the other local agencies such as district and county councils and primary health care trusts. (In some forces this coordinated multi-agency work might have a different name.) CSUs implement CSP strategic decisions and respond to local need through a full-time Community Safety Team. Given the local focus of CSUs there will be different priorities in different areas, but there are a number of common roles and functions. For example, they have an obligation under the Crime and Disorder Act 1998 to audit the crime and disorder problems in their respective areas and to devise suitable strategies (every three years) to prevent and reduce crime. This includes addressing quality of life issues and the fear of crime.

3.3.4 Youth Offending Teams

Youth Offending Teams (YOTs) are run by local authorities and bring together and help coordinate the work of a number of different agencies, including the police. They work with young people who are at risk of offending or reoffending, and offer support through education, employment, work placements, psychological support, and mentoring. YOTs also provide support for young people who have been arrested or have to attend court.

3.4 The Extended Policing Family

Policing involves an array of providers to form an extended policing family. This includes special constables, police support staff and police community support officers, and private security firms. This is not an exhaustive list, but it does provide an indication of the various different kinds of policing arrangements, including voluntary, regulatory, and private policing providers.

In broad terms, in March 2016 there were approximately 201,000 staff working for the police forces of England and Wales of which about 61 per cent were police officers, 31 per cent police support staff, 6 per cent PCSOs, and the remaining 2 per cent had other roles such as detention officers (author's calculations, based on data available at Home Office, 2016g). In addition, there were around 16,000 special constables serving with police forces in the UK in 2016—these figures are similar to the previous year's.

3.4.1 Special constables

Special constables ('Specials') are volunteers, and are sworn officers with full powers who undertake police duties on a part-time basis (a minimum of 96 hours per year). Most Specials are not paid employees of a police force but they are reimbursed expenses. However, a number of measures have been introduced by some forces or local authorities to 'reward' Specials for their service such as an 'allowance' or a council tax discount. They must be over the age of 18 and be a national of a country within the European Economic Area, or a national of a country outside the EEA, with the right to reside in this country without restrictions. Traditionally, most special constables undertake paid employment elsewhere; the system functions very much in the same way as the Territorial Army, or RAF, or Naval volunteer reserve forces. In most forces, they work alongside regular officers, go out on patrol, and deal with the range of activities which a patrol constable would encounter during an ordinary shift. Specials are subject to the same Code of Ethics as other police officers which means, for example, that they must not take any active part in politics. Increasingly, individuals appear to be joining the specials as a route into the regular police force, particularly as part of a pre-join scheme. Recent developments in some police services have even required future applicants to the police service to serve as special constables before applying for full-time employment. Consequently, there are a growing number of specials who are in full- or part-time education. Whilst such initiatives are currently welcomed, primarily on economic grounds, there might be issues further down the line for the status of specials as more focus is placed on what a police officer needs to know before being issued with a warrant card. For example, consider the implications if a special constable applies to his/her force to become a paid full-time police officer through the national SEARCH© assessment process (see 8.2), but is rejected (perhaps on the grounds of respect for diversity). This could raise concerns over whether he/she should retain the status of a warranted officer.

The training for specials is the IL4SC (Initial Learning for the Special Constabulary) programme, and utilizes both workplace assessments (against the NOS) and the assessment of knowledge and understanding (often deploying the Diploma in Policing learning descriptors as a basis).

3.4.2 Police support staff

In many forces, support staff can make up to a third of total numbers, and they undertake a wide range of tasks. There were approximately 62,000 police support staff in England and Wales in 2016. They were previously termed 'civilian' and this was often associated with administration or other 'non-police' work, but those days are long gone in most police forces. However, despite the extent to which police support staff have become increasingly integral to the wider policing family, such roles are undoubtedly most at risk when police budgets are cut.

> **TASK 1** Suggest some examples of the types of work police support staff might carry out.

You may be able to think of other police support staff roles (such as training) in a police force, but other important support staff roles include crime scene investigators, statement takers, detention officers, and lawyers. For some areas in policing it may be more appropriate to employ specialist support staff (cybercrime and fraud being two obvious examples) than to rely on 'omnicompetent' officers. This is part of a wider debate about the purpose of sworn officers, and the responsibilities and tasks assigned to this role.

3.4.3   **Other police forces**

As noted in 3.2, in addition to the Home Office 'territorial' forces of England and Wales there are other police forces such as:

- British Transport Police, who are responsible primarily for policing the railway network in the UK (over- and underground). With its headquarters in London, BTP has uniformed and plain clothes officers travelling on the railways and performing police functions. BTP figured very prominently in cooperation with the MPS in the wake of the tube train bombings in London on 7 July 2005.
- The Ministry of Defence Police, who guard MoD establishments (naval dockyards, airfields, and army regimental depots) across the UK (ie including Scotland). Other police forces within the armed forces are the Royal Military Police (RMP) and the RAF's Provost and Security Services (P&SS). These have jurisdiction only within their force establishments and then only for crimes which are not classified as major crimes. Murders and serious assaults are usually investigated by the local police force.
- The Civil Nuclear Constabulary (CNC), who protect civil nuclear installations and fuels in shipment and storage. All its officers are firearms-trained.

3.4.4   **Police Community Support Officers (PCSOs)**

PCSOs work alongside police constables in policing local neighbourhoods. Their role is to help reduce crime and anti-social behaviour and provide reassurance to the public. They engage with the public and identifying their concerns, and support people who are affected by anti-social behaviour, crime, or the fear of crime. They walk or travel on a limited beat where they can be seen and spoken to, and there is an emphasis on their meeting and talking to young people. PCSO uniforms are similar to those of warranted police officers but they have blue ties and their epaulettes clearly identify them as PCSOs.

PCSOs do not have a power of arrest but do have many other powers (see CoP, 2015h). All PCSOs must carry documentation detailing the powers they have been granted. There are 20 'standard' powers potentially available to the PCSO, which include the power to:

- enter and search any premises for the purposes of saving life and limb or preventing serious damage to property;
- require the name and address of a person (under some circumstances only, eg for anti-social behaviour, for road traffic offences or if the suspect is believed to have committed certain offences such as causing injury, alarm, or distress to another;
- control traffic (under certain circumstances);
- issue certain fixed penalty notices (eg for cycling on a footpath, for littering);
- require surrender of certain items (eg alcohol from persons under 18, or persons drinking in designated places);
- seize certain items (eg tobacco from a person aged under 16) and vehicles used to cause alarm; and
- remove abandoned vehicles.

Another 43 additional powers can be granted at the discretion of chief officers, such as:

- issue fixed penalty notices (for disorder; truancy; excluded school pupils found in a public place; dog fouling; graffiti and fly posting; certain other byelaw offences; driving the wrong way along a one-way street; unlicensed street vendors);
- 'deal with' begging;
- detain a person for up to 30 minutes, using reasonable force to prevent him/her from escaping;
- search detained persons for dangerous items and use reasonable force to prevent escape;
- require a person claiming to be a charity collector to provide his/her certificate, name, address, and signature.

PCSO training involves being assessed against six of the ten Diploma in Policing units, but with one unit at level 2 rather than level 3. This is similar to the training and assessment of special constables. Some PCSOs are using the scheme as a route into regular policing. Many of the PPF personal qualities (see 8.5.2) for PCSOs are identical to those for police officers.

Policing in Context

> **TASK 2**
> 1. What discretionary powers are given to PCSOs by your local police force?
> 2. Think about what you know about PCSOs and the work they do. What form do you imagine PCSO training takes, and how long might it last?

3.4.5   Other policing and law enforcement agencies

Many aspects of our lives are predominantly policed by individuals other than sworn police officers, for example the policing within most football grounds is conducted by stewards. Likewise, the policing of the night-time economy in our town and city centres (to reduce the likelihood of serious disorder) involves many more privately employed individuals than sworn police officers. There are also non-police agencies which investigate and then turn their findings over to the police to take to court, while others have investigative powers and can also prosecute their own cases. HM Revenue and Customs, for example, has powers to investigate other crimes such as evasion of VAT or other taxes, improper importing, and other matters. Likewise, the UK's Border Force employees have specific powers in relation to immigration and customs matters. There have been moves to centralize and coordinate investigative capacities across different agencies, most recently through the establishment of the National Crime Agency (NCA) in 2013. The NCA 'command' units, include Border Policing Command, Economic Crime Command, Organised Crime Command, and Child Exploitation and Online Protection Command.

3.4.6   Regulatory bodies

These are bodies which have a particular interest in specialized matters such as public health or environmental crime, and can prosecute offenders. This category includes:

- the Health and Safety Executive (HSE);
- Trading Standards Authorities;
- the National Society for the Prevention of Cruelty to Children (NSPCC);
- the Royal Society for the Prevention of Cruelty to Animals (RSPCA); and
- the Royal Society for the Protection of Birds (RSPB).

In a sense, most of these bodies focus on niche crime, such as maltreatment of animals and stealing birds' eggs. Only the work of the HSE and the NSPCC impact substantially on police work, although it seems likely that environmental crime will have a higher profile in the future.

3.4.7   The private sector

Despite the difficulties experienced by the company Group4 (now G4S) in providing the agreed policing services for the 2012 London Olympics, the government believes that private companies have an important role to play within the extended policing family. The private security industry is expanding rapidly and includes staff such as door stewards at clubs, shopping centre security personnel, train guards and security guards who patrol areas frequented by the public. The last few years have seen an increase in the number of 'gated communities' (following a US model), where access to a group of private and exclusive dwellings is controlled by uniformed guards 24 hours a day. This reassures the householders that privacy is guaranteed, and increases physical security, making burglaries, robberies, and assaults more difficult to commit or attempt. Compulsory licensing for staff is in place for many staffed security occupations such as security guarding, door stewarding and for vehicle immobilizer personnel (clampers). There is a voluntary (non-statutory) scheme in place for 'Approved Contractors'— the companies supplying private security services. More information is available on the Security Industry Authority (SIA) website.

Security extends across the community, for example through bailiffs and the use of CCTV. Bailiffs recover property that has not been fully paid for, or seize goods in lieu of debt, and may work with the police, particularly with evictions or where there is concern about public order. The extension of the policing family also includes the large surveillance system (eg monitored CCTV) across the UK, and automated number plate readers (ANPR) linked to cameras mounted on bridges and gantries to monitor vehicle movements. The use of CCTV in police surveillance work is discussed in 23.4.1.

When considering the steady growth of private security, we should not ignore the large established security companies, such as G4S and the Securitas Group. They are involved in all aspects of private security, such as cash collection from businesses, the provision of physical security, and the transportation of prisoners. There can be a blurring of roles between public policing and private policing when private companies provide security for organizations, for example at some animal research facilities external security seems to be run by the police whilst internal security seems to be managed by a private company. The degree of cooperation that exists between the two, and the distinctions between 'accountable police activity' and 'unaccountable police activity' are not always clear.

An important question raised in relation to private policing concerns the very purpose of the police. They carry out a variety of activities with a common purpose; to serve the public interest, and it is in this sense (perhaps more so than the question of how the police are funded), that the police are deemed to be public, as opposed to private. However, many police organizations receive private funding; for example, BTP are partially funded by the rail companies. Indeed, all public police services are increasingly generating income beyond that provided by government through the Home Office, and it seems likely that an increased reliance on private funding will be required to sustain an effective and efficient police service.

Finally (though we have by no means exhausted the examples of the private security industry), we may look at private investigators. These are small-scale enquiry companies (seldom exceeding half a dozen employees) which are usually staffed by ex-police officers. They are principally engaged in matters such as gathering evidence for presentation in divorce cases or tracking down missing persons. They present little in the way of conflict with the regular police, except when attempts are made to access official records or data such as vehicle number plates.

3.5 Personal Authority and Legitimacy

Authority is a key concept for the police and of particular interest to the trainee police officer and students undertaking pre-join programmes. The exercise of authority is often viewed as a mark of a professional although 'authority' is often expressed or described instead as autonomy or credibility and related concepts. If you are a trainee police officer your authority will certainly be challenged on occasions, and you will no doubt find yourself thinking deeply about your authority, and maybe about how to manage the use of it. There are a number of personal qualities that you need to exhibit before completing your training (see the PPF in 8.5.2) and some of these are clearly related to personal authority.

In the 1960s and 1970s, the educational philosopher Richard Peters (often referred to as RS Peters, who usually wrote and worked in collaboration with Paul Hirst) argued that there are different forms of personal authority which nonetheless interrelate (Peters, 1973). Although his focus was on authority in education we have adapted his work here to apply to policing.

3.5.1 The main forms of personal authority

The main forms of personal authority are considered to be:

- **epistemic**: authority from knowledge (knowing more than the next person);
- **natural** (sometimes called 'charismatic authority'): derived from personality, demeanour (non-verbal communication);
- *de facto* (from fact): authority that exists through convention rather than as a matter of right;
- *de jure* (from right): authority as a matter of right; and
- **moral**: authority that arises from a moral high ground.

Note that these categories are not intended to be mutually exclusive. As we shall see later, *de facto* and moral authorities, for example, are often linked. It is also important to note that authority here can relate to two distinct concepts. There is the general authority of the police service, often thought about in terms of legitimacy (see 3.5.3). The second is the authority of the individual police officer, which will vary from individual to individual, and it is that which concerns us here.

3.5.1.1 What do these mean for a police officer?

A police officer's *epistemic* authority stems from knowledge of the law and procedure. The public expect a police officer to know the rudiments of the law. Although members of the public may know that an offence has occurred (by applying their common sense), they will expect an officer to know which particular law or laws have been broken. In part, this expectation is fed by media portrayals of the police which often feature a police officer using the words 'I arrest you for [specifics of the offence]'. Therefore, if in a particular situation it is seen that a police officer's grasp of the law or proper procedure seems uncertain, then his or her epistemic authority will decrease. The law, policy, and guidelines studied during training (eg the IPLDP LPG modules: see 1.4.2) provide the basis for establishing epistemic authority.

Some people appear to have more *natural authority* than others through sheer presence (charisma), and are more able to take control when required. This form of authority can be developed, and trainee police officers will receive training on demeanour, use of language, non-verbal communication (body language), and other more subtle ways in which natural authority can be enhanced. Other factors are important too; being smartly dressed (polished shoes, clean and tidy uniform, etc) may seem a strangely old-fashioned topic for a Handbook of this kind but they are important aspects of a trainee officer's personal authority when, for example, giving evidence in court.

Police officers are seen to have *de facto* authority in certain circumstances, for example in the aftermath of a road traffic collision, or the expectation that road users will move out of the way of police patrol cars using their sirens and lights. This authority comes not just from the law, but through custom. In terms of the extent to which citizens trust the police and see the police as a legitimate authority, Tom Tyler in the USA and a number of academics in the UK have shown empirically that citizens appear to be more concerned with how police officers conduct themselves and carry out their duties, rather than what they achieve (see Tyler, 2003; Bradford *et al*, 2009; Myhill and Bradford, 2011; and Jackson *et al*, 2013). The focus of this research is on how perceptions of procedural justice inform the legitimacy of police authority. The *de facto* form of authority is easily lost if abused (or perceived as such), and members of the public will no doubt carry on making wry comments about the police using their sirens and lights to get back to the station more quickly for a cup of coffee and a biscuit!

It is a simple fact that police officers have powers that are not granted to other members of society. These powers are the main source of an officer's *de jure* authority, and many are covered in this Handbook. The wearing of a uniform symbolizes this form of authority, to separate a police officer from the rest of society, as does the possession of a warrant card.

Police officers are expected to subscribe to a code of ethics and behaviour which is of a higher standard than the rest of society, and this gives them not only *moral authority but also moral responsibilities*. There are certainly greater moral obligations on the police when compared to many other occupational groups, for example in terms of honesty, integrity, fairness, impartiality, politeness, and general conduct. Gross examples of inappropriate police behaviour (such as the ill-treatment of prisoners) undermine the moral authority of the police service as a whole, but there are other less dramatic examples at the level of the individual. Put simply, members of the public do not expect to witness police officers swearing in public, smoking on duty, or acting other than professionally in the role. These restrictions on the personal behaviour of police officers and the effect on their moral authority also extend to life off-duty. Where is the moral authority of a police officer who arrests an acquaintance for possession of cocaine during a raid on Saturday, having smoked cannabis with him the previous evening? How is a police officer's moral authority affected if she uses her warrant card to gain free entry to a nightclub? Retaining moral authority also requires police officers to maintain a moral perspective when dealing with the public. It is not appropriate, for example, to judge a member of the public by the same high standards that a police officer must follow, and it is partly for this reason that the 'attitude test' (see 3.6.5) is an unacceptable means of deciding whether to arrest a person.

3.5.2   Development of personal authority

If you are a trainee police officer, then it is likely that there will be opportunities for you to develop your personal authority during your initial training. These may include:

- preparing and delivering presentations to others, including groups of students and training staff;
- increasing your knowledge and recall of the law and procedure;
- observing your own behaviour, including your demeanour and use of language, for example by analysing video of your performance whilst undertaking a particular task; or
- feedback from others, including your trainers, assessors, fellow trainees, and representatives of community groups (eg whilst undertaking your community attachment).

> **TASK 3** Imagine you are a police officer and you have arrested a woman on suspicion of assault and theft in a shopping centre. The victim has identified the suspect, who cannot explain her possession of the victim's mobile phone. Give examples of how the five forms of personal authority would feature in this particular scenario.

3.5.3 Legitimacy

The issue of legitimacy is central to debates about the police role in liberal democratic societies. The existence of police authority requires individuals to willingly sacrifice a degree of personal freedom and liberty in order to secure a greater degree of collective freedom and liberty. The logic behind this way of thinking is made explicit in the writings of the seventeenth-century English philosopher Thomas Hobbes: without authority in society there would exist 'a war of all against all'. For Hobbes, therefore, the existence of any authority is preferable to none at all. This is an important point to note because, as Nozick (1974) and Simmons (2001) argued, the necessity for authority must be considered before questioning the legitimacy of authority. The difficulty in justifying police authority is illustrated by the fact that it took six attempts (from 1785 onwards) to pass a Police Bill through the Houses of Parliament, to create the 'new' police in 1829. Clearly there was opposition at the time to the very existence of a professional standing body of police in England and Wales. Today, we largely take the existence of the police for granted, and very few people seriously question whether we would be better off without any police.

Nonetheless, in terms of civil liberties, it is important to be able to justify a police presence, especially given the extent to which we could argue that such a presence may be expensive (eg at football matches) or disproportionate (such as in shopping malls). We may even go beyond justifying the mere existence of the police to consider the more pressing and ongoing debate concerning the legitimacy of the police. Here it is worth noting two distinct means through which it can be established: consensual and moral legitimacy.

3.5.3.1 Consensual legitimacy of the police

The police are quite rightly governed by the law, but the issue of legitimacy is central to debates about the police role in liberal democratic societies in other ways too. Consensual legitimacy is gained through the support of the people and communities who are being policed. It reflects the democratic aspect of policing within a liberal democracy, the notion of 'policing by consent' (Reiner, 2000). In the early years of the police the discussion about legitimacy was almost exclusively concerned with consent, and today the Home Office's focus on neighbourhood policing (see 3.9.1) places great emphasis on the importance of this issue.

From the perspective of those advocating consensual legitimacy, the police are legitimate to the extent that the public consent to policing. Of course there are differing degrees to which we might say the public consents to the police. One view is to say that the public consents passively by not opposing what the police do. On the other hand we might insist on the public having an ongoing engagement with the police in order for consent to be given actively. In practice, the kind of consent gained will be dependent upon the type of police response and the particular problem addressed. For example, if the police are required to deal with a serious threat of terrorism, then the consent will have to be passive in order to allow the police to be effective. (The more the public knew about how the police intended to counter the terrorists, the more the terrorists would also know and the police intervention might fail as a consequence.) Conversely, when the police are required to resolve low-level but persistent offending, there is a greater need for the police to communicate with the local community, to establish and agree the best way to address the problem. In this latter case, the consent must be active and ongoing. The police need to negotiate their response to the problem and ensure that the community supports, as much as is possible, any police interventions. In this respect, to ensure consensual legitimacy of the police there must be appropriate public involvement in negotiating police responses, and the response must deal effectively with the particular problem. An appeal for witnesses to an event is a common form of this nexus between police and public.

There are limits to consensual legitimacy, for example the police could theoretically be too responsive to the views of the communities being policed. As Waddington (1999) has noted, the police are required to deal with conflicts in society and in the exercise of this function they may have to police 'against' some sections of the community. A real concern exists that the police might be overly responsive to one section of the community against another. This could lead to the exclusion and/or targeting of groups of individuals who are seen to be on the periphery of a community. Put another way, the popularity of the police, which is effectively what consent measures, is no guarantee that the police are acting in a legitimate way. Equally, people's fears or concerns may not necessarily match the prevailing crime patterns, and may not help the police to focus effort appropriately.

There are various ways of establishing the legitimacy of police authority, and approval from citizens is just one. As Simmons (2001) observes, this particular way of establishing legitimacy focuses on how an authority is perceived, rather than what it does. It measures the attitudes of the recipients of the authority, rather than measuring the authority itself. In a similar vein, Bottoms and Tankebe (2012) draw attention to the limits of the procedural justice approach to ascertaining police legitimacy, on the grounds that it captures the perspective of the 'audience', but not the power-brokers themselves.

We might say that consent is a necessary, but not sufficient, aspect of police legitimacy. In liberal democratic terms, consent reflects democratic, but not liberal concerns. The liberal concerns within liberal democratic contexts are expressed more through the moral legitimacy of the police, rather than consensual legitimacy.

3.5.3.2 The moral legitimacy of the police

It is also becoming increasingly important for the police to 'do the right thing' from a moral perspective. The course of action that would be supported by a local community is not always the moral one, and the community might not support all morally correct policing actions. For example, the police will not always be able to gain consensual support for protecting a known paedophile living within a residential area, or allowing a racist organization to march through the town centre. However, the reason why the police do what they do is often a matter of moral legitimacy rather than consensual legitimacy.

As far as possible, the police will try to achieve both moral and consensual legitimacy, but this is not always possible. The former Chief Constable of Devon and Cornwall, John Alderson, has been an advocate of what he refers to as 'principled policing' for a number of years (see Alderson, 1998). He has argued that policing should be more firmly founded upon moral principles, rather than pragmatic concerns. The Human Rights Act 1998 has given legislative support to this point of view. Increasingly, police officers must take into account a number of (often different or contradictory) moral considerations in order to make professional judgements. Policing by consent remains an important part of police legitimacy, but the police must operate primarily within both legal and moral boundaries if they are to be truly legitimate.

TASK 4 What would you need to take into account if (as a police officer) you had to control a march by the British National Party through your town, knowing that the Anti-Nazi League was planning to turn up in large numbers to oppose the march? (Note that our interest here is in judgements based on police legitimacy, rather than the detail of operational orders.)

3.6 Police Discretion

According to Jones, police discretion is the 'freedom of the individual officer to act according to his or her own judgement in particular situations' (as cited in Newburn and Neyroud, 2008, p 82). We could perhaps replace the word 'freedom' with 'duty' or 'obligation' and refer to 'professional judgement', to emphasize that the concept of police discretion is founded within the notion of the 'office of constable'. This establishes the legal status of a police officer as a holder of original authority. A police officer cannot be ordered to arrest a person. He/she must take responsibility for deciding whether arrest is appropriate or not, given the circumstances (see 10.6). In this sense, discretion should be seen more as a professional burden than a freedom, as freedom implies too much subjectivity. Police officers are not robots, programmed to respond to every crime they encounter by arrest and charge, and policing is about more than law enforcement; it is carried out in the public interest with a view to securing primarily a more peaceful society. In terms of good policing, law enforcement is just one means to an end, and would be inappropriate in some contexts. For example it would not be practical or legitimate to arrest and charge for every offence because it could undermine the relationship between police and public (see 3.6.4). Nor would it be likely to have any significant impact on levels of crime (although see zero-tolerance policing models (3.9.4) and also the association between offences and criminality discussed in Chapter 4).

Thus the exercise of discretion is an important, even fundamental policing skill. Indeed, Lord Scarman stated:

> the exercise of discretion lies at the heart of the policing function. It is undeniable that there is only one law for all: and it is right that this should be so. But it is equally well recognised that successful policing depends on the exercise of discretion on how the law is enforced.... Discretion is the art of suiting action to particular circumstances. (Scarman, 1981, para 4.58)

Chan (2003) has noted that, in the early stages of initial police training, officers are hungry for basic technical knowledge; you might agree! This is understandable because police officers require the basic know-how skills in order to feel confident enough to perform duties (under the supervision of a tutor) in operational settings such as Supervised Patrol (see 3.5.1.1 on epistemic authority). Police discretion is a subject that does not fit easily under the umbrella of basic technical knowledge, unlike most of the other learning for trainee officers. Nonetheless, it is important to understand what police discretion is (and what it is not), because it is relevant to most of a police officer's everyday work. It is the vital ingredient which justifies police work as a profession, or in Neyroud and Beckley's words (2001, p 86), discretion is 'the essence of informed professionalism in policing'.

3.6.1   Defining and using discretion

Police discretion does not only apply to front-line officers. It also applies to the kinds of decisions that police managers and chief officers must make, described by Neyroud and Beckley (2001) as 'prioritizing decisions' and 'tactical decisions'. The former relates primarily to the allocation of limited resources and the latter relates to the balancing of liberty and order in a liberal democratic society. In a similar vein, Delattre (2002) discusses the need for senior investigative officers to make anticipatory and planning decisions about, for example, when to identify and release information about a serial killer. These are all good examples of police discretionary decisions and it is important for new police officers to be aware of why and how these kinds of decisions are made. However, here we will focus on discretion for front-line officers: in other words, the kind of decisions that patrol constables (and therefore trainee officers) are expected to make on a daily basis.

Discretion often involves choosing between different law enforcement options. For example, officers are regularly confronted with minor offences that present a choice of issuing fixed penalty tickets or making an arrest and taking the suspect to the police station. It has been argued that:

> Under-enforcement as opposed to choosing how to enforce the law, has led to concerns because it is seen by some to occur as a consequence of either an officer's 'misappropriation of judicial power' or an officer's 'discrimination'. (Neyroud and Beckley, 2001, pp 85–6)

Clearly anyone who is given a verbal warning or reprimand instead of being charged or arrested is unlikely to complain about it. But it could be argued that any person who has committed an offence has no defence, and merits the law's full weight of sanction, and that everyone (who has committed an identical offence) deserves to be punished in the same way. Some people think it is unfair that all offenders do not have the law enforced against them, and critics of under-enforcement point to the inconsistency in applying the law. This calls into question the fundamental right of the police to employ discretionary powers.

One simple answer (proposed by the critics of police discretion) is to remove police discretion altogether, or at least reduce the extent to which officers can draw upon it. There would be practical problems with this. For instance, the criminal justice system already struggles to cope with the existing caseload; how would it cope if the police enforced the law without discretion? Another problem is that police work is extremely difficult to manage (Reiner, 2000, Ch 2). Most officers operate alone or with a partner and as Crawshaw et al (1998, p 24) note, police supervision tends to occur after the event. These problems illustrate the extent and relevance of police discretion, but they are not arguments for keeping it.

Governments have periodically introduced legislation and guidelines to restrict the amount of discretion a police officer can use. This may be reflected in force policies as well, for example in relation to the policing of domestic violence, although 'Positive action' policies (including arrest at a domestic incident, see 13.6.1) have been applied across the UK, effectively reducing the use of discretion. If police discretion is to be maintained, however, it is important that we make a positive case for it. We need to identify a number of ways in which police discretion is often misrepresented, for example the idea that police discretion is nothing more than applying common sense.

3.6.2 Discretion and common sense

The view that police discretion is a matter of applying common sense to policing situations would appear to have some merit. It helps police officers understand how real operational experiences complement the necessarily theoretical and abstract learning which takes place during the initial period of police training. Officers learn to use the law as a means to an end rather than as an end in itself. However, it is too simplistic to view police discretion as the mere application of common sense, as this suggests that discretionary decisions are straightforward and could be applied by anyone. It also fails to distinguish between the decisions that are just simple, common sense decisions and the decisions that genuinely require the use of discretion. As Davis (1996) notes, not all choices are discretionary. Police discretion cannot be simply reduced to being a matter of making choices or decisions.

3.6.3 Police discretion and subjectivity

Another way of understanding discretion is to consider the view that every police officer has a unique subjectivity that produces different approaches to how the law is interpreted and enforced. However, although the individual subjectivities of officers clearly play an important role in day-to-day policing, this should not be confused with police discretion. Indeed, police discretion is necessary precisely because it provides a way of curbing the influence of individual subjectivity.

Should we expect all police officers to make the same decision in identical circumstances? We should note that the question is not entirely fair because in reality no two sets of circumstances are ever identical. Nonetheless, the existence of police discretion implies the answer cannot be a clear cut 'yes' or 'no'. But if every officer makes a different decision, in what sense are these decisions connected, and how do they relate to policing principles and practice? The answer is that we should expect officers' decisions to differ, but that there will be a finite number of decision categories, normally two or three. Ideally, each of these categories would represent good police decisions that could be justified and explained. (More realistically, we might expect a few officers to make decisions that fall into another separate category, one that represents bad police decisions.) There are only a limited number of valid options open for consideration because each option must adhere to professional standards, integrity, the law, and force policy. The legal philosopher Ronald Dworkin has explained this point by referring to discretion as the 'hole in the doughnut' (see Neyroud and Beckley, 2001, p 83). This analogy suggests that discretion is given meaning by the professionalism (the dough) surrounding it—the hole in a ring doughnut only exists because of the dough. If we eat the ring, the hole disappears too. Likewise, without professional standards, discretion becomes meaningless; police discretion cannot exist if there is no professional policing context.

Just as professional standards limit the number of options available to officers, the same standards also allow for different responses. Subjectivity is not an adequate answer because it would mean that law enforcement is too arbitrary. It is not acceptable that a man is arrested only because he encountered officer A, rather than officer B or C. All police responses are only valid to the extent that they can be explained and justified in terms of professional standards, and not just as a product of a subjective perspective. To reiterate and emphasize the point, discretion reduces the influence of subjectivity by providing an objective, professional guide to decision-making.

3.6.4 Discretion and judicial misappropriation

We have noted that some critics see police discretion as nothing more than an individual officer's misappropriation of judicial power. The reasoning behind this is that if an individual has clearly committed an offence an officer who decides not to enforce the law is effectively acting as judge and jury. This view is based upon a long-standing misconception of the police officer's role; that the police are merely law enforcers. Waddington (1999) observes (with reference to the surprise expressed by researchers into policing in the 1960s):

the prevailing assumption had been that policing was little more than the application of the law... Criminals committed crimes and the police captured the criminals who were tried and convicted by the courts. (Waddington, 1999, p 31)

Indeed, Waddington refers to the discretionary powers of the police as being 'discovered' in the 1960s. Of course police officers had been exercising discretion since the creation of the modern police in 1829 but it was not an aspect of police work that had received much attention. As more research has been conducted, it has been found that the police have consistently enforced the law more against certain sections of society and less against others, and to some extent the evidence suggests that this is still the case (see 3.6.5).

There can be no defence for the police discriminating against certain sections of society, but that does not mean that the police should have their power of discretion removed. Instead, maybe police officers should be seen more as 'peace officers' than law enforcers (Banton, 1964). Waddington (1999) has argued that the police use the law as and when appropriate in order to bring about a greater sense of peace and order in society. He refers also to Lord Scarman's warning following the Brixton riots in 1981 'that the maintenance of "public tranquillity" was a higher priority than "law enforcement"' (Waddington, 1999, p 42).

The police should make law-enforcement decisions based upon their interpretation of what is best for the public interest. It is this balancing act between law enforcement and the needs of society that gives rise to police discretion. The police are expected to use the law to maintain order, and therefore they need discretionary powers in order to use the law as effectively as possible, within legal boundaries. But they should not be required to enforce the law mechanically in every circumstance. In this respect the police are accountable not only to the law but also to the people they police.

3.6.5 Discretion and discrimination

The view that discretion is the means by which certain sections of society are discriminated against has arisen from research conducted since the 1960s. Why are some sections of society more likely than others to have the law enforced against them? In their defence, police officers have argued that they do not discriminate against any sections of society but respond to each individual they encounter depending on how that individual responds to them. This is referred to in police circles as the attitude test. (You will no doubt hear more experienced police officers using this phrase, or more colloquial versions.) Quite simply, an individual who is polite and repentant is less likely to have the law enforced against him/her. The supposed rationale is that he/she appears to have learnt a lesson and seems unlikely to reoffend. An intervention by a police officer is in itself an effective form of remonstration and can help to prevent repeat offending. It may not be in the public interest to pursue certain cases further, as this would contribute nothing towards achieving a more ordered society (and apart from the wasted expense, it could have a negative effect on the individual stopped). On the other hand, it is argued that if the individual stopped by the police officer is rude, abusive, and unrepentant, then it is assumed that further action needs to be taken to make sure he/she feels sufficiently reprimanded.

But such practice may just perpetuate problems in society. People who regularly come into contact with the police are more likely to be immune to police warnings and will feel more confident in challenging an officer's authority. They are more likely to be abusive and to have an existing antagonistic relationship with the police. Historically, individuals from certain ethnic minority groupings have had a disproportionately high interaction with the police, and the attitude test helps to perpetuate this. Police officers must therefore take great care in such situations.

We discussed epistemic authority in 3.5.1.1, and noted the need for police officers to have a sound knowledge of the law. Increasingly, however, in relation to police discretion, police officers also need to know what actually works in policing; what is effective and what is not effective, and why different individuals are likely to respond in different ways to similar police interventions. Clearly, a police officer with a better knowledge and understanding of the contexts in which he/she is operating will be able to apply discretionary reasoning more effectively.

Efforts have been made to promote this kind of information in police culture, and to rectify any resulting adverse or confrontational attitudes. There have undoubtedly been some low points; for example, see Macpherson (1999) and *The Secret Policeman* programme (2003). This

Policing in Context

programme was about an undercover journalist, Mark Daly, who joined Greater Manchester Police as a trainee officer and spent 15 weeks at the Bruche Centrex regional Police Training Centre, near Warrington. He secretly filmed some of his fellow trainees and the trainers delivering the programme, and recorded racist language and attitudes amongst some of his fellow trainees and inappropriate behaviour by some trainers. However, as Daly himself noted in 2003:

> The majority of the officers I met will undoubtedly turn out to be good, non-prejudiced ones intent on doing the job properly. But the next generation of officers from one of Britain's top police colleges contains a significant minority of people who are holding the progress of the police service back. (Daly, 2003)

Today's police officers are in a much better position to understand the negative way in which some people from ethnic minorities respond to the attitude test, and officers understand how to speak and act in a manner that can help break the cycle. This is due mostly to the in-service programmes for equality and diversity training and development, which are compulsory for all officers.

The important difference between discriminatory and discretionary decisions is that discrimination is based upon prejudice, whereas discretion is premised upon professional judgement (which incorporates many different factors, including the prevalence of discrimination in previous times). This requires officers to go beyond simply providing a common standard by which every individual encounter is measured. Officers are required to respond to each encounter individually, taking into account the specifics of each situation. As Rowe (2002) has noted, since the Macpherson Report (1999) policing no longer treats everyone equally but rather pursues specific policies aimed at reducing discrimination, for example by actively promoting an anti-racist agenda. It is now part of the police officer's role to break the cycle of discrimination.

TASK 5 In the following task you are given two scenarios to consider. The first is taken from the 1995 National Police Training notes and the second is our own invention.

1. You see a woman, who appears to be slightly drunk, pick up a street sign that has fallen from a wall, conceal it under her raincoat, and walk off. When stopped, she readily admits that she intends to keep it as a trophy. She is a medical student who is celebrating passing her final exam (NPT, 1995, p 4).
2. You are on duty outside a football ground when you observe a young man, clutching a can of super-strength lager, pick up an 'Away Supporters' sign that has fallen from a wall, conceal it under his hoodie and walk off. When stopped, he readily admits that he intends to keep it to start a collection. He is a football fan who is celebrating his club's victory in an important match.

In each case consider what discretion, if any, you would exercise.

3.7   Policing as a Profession

Trainee officers will often hear references during training to 'adopting a professional attitude' or 'behaving in a professional manner'. But what does this actually mean? Here we consider what it means to professionalize policing and what this means for the trainee officer.

Before we examine what 'professionalize policing' might mean, we need to consider what we might generally mean by a 'profession'.

TASK 6 Make a list of professions. What features do you look for in an occupation that makes it a profession? Are there any common features that are found in all the professions you have listed?

3.7.1   What is a profession?

We encounter the word profession in many different contexts and applied to numerous occupational groups. There is no universally accepted definition of profession, though there is a general agreement that only some occupations qualify as professions. It is also potentially confusing that the word 'professional' is often appended to an activity simply to acknowledge that its practitioners receive some form of payment for it, or that it is undertaken more seriously. (For example, we know that a reference to a 'professional gambler' means that he/she probably earns a living from gambling.) However, there is likely to be more to a profession than this.

Traditionally, there were just four professions: law, medicine, the church, and the military. Later, accountancy became a profession, and now there are many more occupations commonly regarded as professions.

There is a broad consensus in the academic world that at least some of the following are required for an occupation to also be a profession:

- an accepted *corpus* of knowledge and theory underpinning the practice of the profession;
- controls on entry to the profession, normally through qualification, coupled with a need to maintain the currency of qualification;
- autonomy, discretion, and a degree of self-regulation;
- its practitioners have a form of vocational calling; and
- a code of ethics.

For most professions, many of the control and regulatory functions are carried out by a professional body.

To illustrate these ideas and to explore them further, we now consider medical practice as an example of a profession and measure it against our list of features for a profession.

Requirements of a profession	The medical profession
Corpus of knowledge and theory	The scientific basis to medical practice (eg physiology and biochemistry), knowledge of clinical practice (eg conducting physical examinations), aspects of the behavioural and social sciences
Controls on entry to the profession and continuing professional development	Completing a recognized medical degree, followed by a period of supervised practice (eg foundation training followed by postgraduate training). There is a need to demonstrate regular Continuous Professional Development under seven headings in order to maintain a place on the professional register
Autonomy, discretion, and self-regulation	Medical doctors have significant autonomy and discretion. Their conduct is regulated by the General Medical Council (GMC). Their representative body is the British Medical Association (BMA). Their authority is largely epistemic in nature (see 3.5.1)
Vocational calling	Difficult to prove, as no clear definitions of a vocation exist. However, interviews for entry to medical degrees often attempt to test applicants for this
Code of ethics	A code is published by the GMC. It includes the need for doctors to 'make the care of your patient their first concern', to 'respect patients' dignity and privacy', and 'to give patients information in a way they can understand'

We can see that medicine matches our working definition of a profession very closely.

3.7.2   Is policing a profession?

First attempt the following task.

TASK 7 Complete the following table for the occupation of policing:

Requirements of a profession	The policing profession
Corpus of knowledge and theory	?
Controls on entry to the profession and maintenance of position	?
Autonomy, discretion, and self-regulation	?
Vocational calling	?
Code of ethics	?

You probably established that policing in the UK meets many, but not all, of our criteria for being a profession. Some of the 'missing' elements (such as the need to maintain skills and knowledge) were originally developed by the NPIA and others, and more recently the College of Policing has taken on this responsibility. There is now a 'National SIO Register' for senior investigating officers (SIOs). It is envisaged that eventually it will contain the details of all investigators accredited through the Senior Investigating Officer Development Programme (SIODP), or through other means of demonstrating competence, although progress on this appears slow. In order to remain 'live' on the register an SIO will be required to provide details of his/her relevant CPD activity (NPIA, 2008c). A similar system applies for doctors—to retain their place on a professional register they have to provide evidence to show they have kept up to date and are fit to practise (GMC, 2008).

The College of Policing (CoP) is the official professional body for policing. Since its inception the CoP has assumed many of the standards and training responsibilities of its predecessor, the NPIA. It has also extended into other areas such as accreditation (for example, of CKP providers), professional practice, evidenced-based policing, and ethics. In the long term, the CoP aspires to achieve charter status ('The Royal College of Policing') and be independent of government, for example in terms of its funding. Membership of the CoP is open to all police staff, but awareness of the CoP amongst police staff appears to be low, a problem exacerbated by the inability of the CoP to communicate directly with members and potential members (Home Affairs Select Committee, 2015).

In late 2013 the College of Policing created a 'Disapproved Register', a list of police officers who were either dismissed because of gross misconduct or who had resigned whilst facing allegations of misconduct. In July 2016 it was reported that a total of 833 names were on the register, with ranks ranging from constable to chief superintendent (CoP, 2015e). Worryingly, almost one-half of the 833 had been allowed to resign instead of facing a gross misconduct investigation (ibid). The Home Office changed the Police Regulations in 2015 to prevent this occurring in the future.

A key requirement for professionalization appears to be specialist knowledge and expertise. Sir Ian Blair commented on the role of the police service and the need for public engagement and the development of specific police knowledge (Blair, 2005). The 2011 Neyroud Review into police leadership and training proposed further steps to align policing more fully with other professions, including the establishment of a new professional body. This is an ongoing remit of the College of Policing as indicated, for example, by the development of the new Code of Ethics for policing, the extensive ongoing development of Authorised Professional Practice and the current (2017) development of a new qualifications framework for policing (pitched at HE (higher education) level).

3.7.3 Why is it important for policing to be a profession?

Some would argue that establishing and maintaining policing as a full profession is important for the following reasons:

- to develop the body of knowledge (eg doctrine) and skills required for modern-day policing (as professions usually take the lead in determining what research and development best suit their clients' needs);
- to protect the right of the police, in certain key respects, to regulate themselves;
- to improve public confidence in the work of the police: for example, a full professional register (as distinct from just a list of those 'struck off') would almost certainly imply the need for its members to regularly demonstrate that they have met the requirement to maintain their skills and knowledge; and
- to distinguish the work and the professional standing of the police officer from other members of the extended policing family (see 3.4) and other law enforcers (you might not agree that this is a good reason, but it is certainly behind some thinking).

There are alternative arguments. For example, many of the traditional professions such as law are not noted for their inclusivity, and striving for a professional status may reduce the representative nature of the policing family.

3.8 Diversity and the Police

Society is becoming increasingly more diverse, for example in terms of differences between people's ethnicity, religious beliefs, and sexual orientation. But more importantly we have become more conscious of such differences, and much more determined and willing to afford equal status to individuals from diverse backgrounds. Difference, expressed through the concept of diversity, has come to be represented as something to be celebrated, and it is now less common for difference to be seen as a barrier to the achievement of a harmonious society. Consider for example the changing ways in which anti-racist sentiments are expressed. A common slogan from previous times challenged racist views by stating that there is only one 'race' and that is the human race. Such a slogan seeks to diminish differences between people by saying that such differences are less important than the factors that unite humanity. Today though, anti-racism is expressed more commonly through the celebration of differences between individuals and groups in society, and is supported by the argument that the coming together of different values, beliefs, cultures, and perspectives makes life more interesting, more dynamic, and ultimately richer in a variety of ways.

It is important to note that diversity is about how we perceive differences between people as much as it is about the differences themselves. A simple illustration of this point is given with regards to the significance given to religious differences between communities in different contexts. For example, in most of the UK today the divisions within the Christian faith are of little significance for the majority of people. However, we know that historically this has not always been the case and more recently the divisions between Catholics and Protestants have been important factors in Northern Ireland. However, the existence of differences does not necessarily lead to tensions or problems as some may suggest, nor are differences necessarily the source of a dynamic society as others may claim. Either way, if you are (or plan to be) a professional police officer then you will be required to think carefully about issues of diversity within society, and about the various ways in which the concept of diversity informs policing. Moreover, it is the responsibility of police forces to end discrimination within their own organizations, so there is a heightened sensitivity concerning the conduct of police officers when dealing with issues that involve diversity.

> **TASK 8** We have already referred to race and ethnicity as part of diversity. Suggest some other differences between people that contribute to diversity.

3.8.1 Diversity and vulnerability

One important way in which diversity informs policing is in relation to the responsibility that the police have towards vulnerable people (see Chapter 13). People who are clearly identifiable as minorities in society will often find themselves victimized by members of majority groups, for example when individuals from minority ethnic groups are targeted by racists. Sometimes the victimization can be more subtle, and trainee police officers or CKP students need to think carefully about how their own actions are perceived. Some actions could be deemed offensive by others, even though this was not the intention. As a professional, a police officer has the responsibility to do everything possible to resolve problems, and should certainly not be adding to them. This includes ensuring that police actions are not misunderstood or misinterpreted. But vulnerability does not only arise for individuals from minority groups. For example, women are not a minority group but could be considered to be more vulnerable than men in some circumstances, for example where physical strength or financial independence are significant factors. However, a police officer needs to ensure that any judgement that a particular person may be vulnerable is based as far as possible on the likely facts about the person and the situation, rather than on the officer's own social conditioning and expectations. After all, some women are physically strong and/or financially independent, and some men are physically and financially dependent on others.

It would also be a mistake to assume that every individual from a minority group or a group that has traditionally been discriminated against will feel vulnerable. Indeed in relation to all aspects of diversity, police officers need to tread a fine line that recognizes diversity without imposing any preconceptions.

The issue of mental health is particularly useful in illustrating the complicated nature of diversity. Mental health issues exist to varying degrees in the general population and can have serious effects in terms of individual and collective well-being. But many people have preconceived ideas of what is healthy and is unhealthy, which makes recognizing diversity and difference in relation to mental health particularly difficult. Police actions in relation to mentally ill people are covered in 13.2.

3.8.2 Diversity and discrimination

Police forces have been under scrutiny for discrimination on the grounds of race for a number of decades. Both the Scarman Report, published in 1981 after the Brixton riots in London, and the Macpherson Report, published in 1999 following the death of Stephen Lawrence, refer to racial discrimination by the police and a failure to address it. In 2009 the Home Affairs Committee published an evaluation of the impact of the Macpherson Report on tackling 'institutional racism' in the police. It concluded that there were clear positive changes in the way that the police dealt with ethnic minorities and in the investigation of homicides where the victims were from ethnic minorities. There are, however, still concerns regarding the apparently disproportionate number of stop and searches being conducted on individuals from ethnic minorities, as well as a disproportionate number of individuals from African-Caribbean backgrounds featuring on the National DNA Database.

Legislation outlaws discrimination on the grounds of belief, but the subject is fraught with difficulty and it may be some time before a law is comprehensively framed which can allow criticism of belief but which prohibits actions that discriminate against belief systems. Age discrimination is unlawful, but this is a complex area since it can apply to people of any age and is closely related to the laws of employment. Older people past the conventional retirement age are more likely to be affected by this type of discrimination than young people. The Mental Health Act 2007 and the Disability and Equality Act 2010 reinforce the need to address ways in which people with mental health problems suffer discrimination, especially since the majority of such individuals report having experienced it. This is of particular relevance for police officers, given that people with mental health problems often come into contact with the police (see 13.2), and feature disproportionately within the criminal justice statistics (see Bradley, 2009). Gender discrimination is also subject to legislation. One area of particular interest for police forces is the legislation associated with forced marriages, which requires that special consideration is given when dealing with women who may be experiencing this form of victimization (see 13.6.3).

3.8.3 Promoting equality

It is important that police officers, given the powerful positions they hold in society, ensure that their own prejudices do not lead to discrimination. Our culture, gender, life experiences, family, cultural, and social backgrounds can all influence our understanding and views of the world. They can be portrayed in a variety of verbal and non-verbal ways and need to be managed by each officer during encounters with members of the public, in order to reduce their potentially harmful impact.

A number of important principles that support equality have been integrated into the standards of professional behaviour for the police (see 6.3.2). These standards are reflected in specific requirements that apply for police responses to issues such as hate crime (see 14.10), harassment (14.5), confidentiality (6.8.1), human rights (5.4), and recording information in investigations (24.3). The intention is to avoid damage to minority groups (that may otherwise feel angry, isolated, distrusting of the police, fearful, and distressed) as a result of police failure to adequately address discrimination, harassment, and/or victimization. Equality and professionalism are crucial to maintaining police legitimacy across society and to building confidence in criminal investigations.

As a public service it is important that police personnel reflect a representative cross-section of society. This will benefit policing in terms of gaining confidence and cooperation across the full range of groups within the community. Recruiting from the full range of society allows the police service to attract a wider range of skills and knowledge as well as recruiting the best people to fill vacancies.

3.8.3.1 Protected characteristics and the Equality Act 2010

The foundations of equality and diversity in the UK are enshrined in legislation. Under Equality Act 2010 it is unlawful to discriminate on the grounds of certain 'protected characteristics'. These are: age, disability, race, religion or belief, sex, gender reassignment, sexual orientation, marriage and civil partnership, pregnancy or maternity.

The 2010 Equality Act brought together all of the previous anti-discrimination laws into one Act; before the Act came into place there were several different pieces of legislation including the Sex Discrimination Act 1975 and the Race Relations Act 1976. This reform made it easier to understand and strengthen protection in some situations. The Act has certain key aims including those that concern:

- personal characteristics—restating the relevant enactments relating to discrimination and harassment;
- pay differences—certain employers will be required to publish information about the differences in pay between male and female employees;
- victimization—prohibition in certain circumstances;
- discrimination—action to be taken to eliminate discrimination and other prohibited conduct;
- equality of opportunity—to be increased; and
- family relationships—to amend the law relating to rights and responsibilities in family relationships.

Public authorities are now required to eliminate discrimination, harassment, victimization, and any other conduct prohibited by the Act in relation to the protected characteristics. They must also advance equality of opportunity and foster good relations between all people who share a protected characteristic and people who do not share it.

3.9 Approaches to Policing in England and Wales

It is perhaps misleading to suggest that the policing models and approaches described here are somehow in competition or are mutually exclusive, although there are significant points of departure between them. Rather, they focus on different things. For example, the intelligence-led policing model tends to be seen as a response to the inevitable and unavoidable existence of criminals in society and the existence of high-volume repeat criminals. On the other hand, problem-oriented policing, as the label suggests, attempts to model crime or disorder in terms of problems that we can then analyse and attempt to solve. Community-based and neighbourhood policing favour the view that crime and disorder should be seen in the wider context of the community or communities from which it originates. Zero-tolerance policing is based on the idea that an absence of effective police responses is likely to lead to an escalation of problems, from low-level anti-social behaviour and incivility towards more serious criminal activities. It therefore focuses on dealing robustly with all minor offending in order to make this outcome less likely. These different approaches to policing are premised upon conflicting views regarding what are the most pressing policing problems in society and what are the most appropriate and effective means of addressing them.

> **TASK 9** What do you think characterizes the British approach to policing? What can you point to that is essentially British about it?

3.9.1 Community-based and neighbourhood policing

Government policies and media sound bites regularly focus on the policing of communities and neighbourhoods. Looking back at the history of policing, even before the creation of what we now know as the public police, there is clear evidence of participation of the community in policing (Rawlings, 2002). Consider for example the 'Hue and Cry', the pursuit of an offender in the King's name, as portrayed in historical accounts such as Dickens' *Oliver Twist* with the baying crowd pursuing Bill Sikes. Contrast this historical (and fictional) scenario with the present day; there is an increasingly distant relationship between the public and the police, particularly in relation to the contribution of communities to policing their own localities.

Despite attempts over the last 30 years to improve police presence and community activism in protecting their own neighbourhoods, it is only in the past ten years that there have been fundamental changes in the structure and the development of legislation relating to these issues. Often perceived as the 'softer' side of policing and lower status than other policing roles (such as criminal investigation), community-orientated approaches to policing provide a cru-ial opportunity to engage with the public, proactively combat crime (through crime preven-on strategies), and address community safety and quality of life issues. This engagement is important to community problem solving, developing public confidence in the police, and providing a visual presence.

The lack of partnership approaches has received substantial criticism since the 1980s with reforms in policing attempting to build partnerships and community engagement, for example the 1991 Morgan Report. The Crime and Disorder Act 1998 provided substantial powers in addition to a statutory requirement for partnership-working. The introduction of PCSOs (see 3.4.4) increased the visible uniformed presence, and the introduction of Neighbourhood Policing initiatives and the recent promotion of the 'big society' (Newburn, 2007; Herbert, 2011) was a further step forward. These changes represent attempts to develop local approaches to policing and improve police engagement with communities with the aim of increasing public contributions to policing objectives. The Home Office consultation document *Policing in the 21st Century: Reconnecting police and the people* (Home Office, 2010d) sets out the Coalition government's vision of 'cutting crime and protecting the public' and a more 'directly account-able' police service, offering 'value for money'. This vision also proposes to 'empower commu-nities' and provide 'greater visibility and availability'. Although policing reforms are subject to consultation and implementation, the following subsections will provide a selective overview of key areas of recent initiatives to improve police community engagement.

3.9.1.1   Community policing approaches

In community policing the police seek to involve the various communities in their locality in terms of achieving local policing objectives. A key feature of this approach is the emphasis on communication and problem-solving activities between the police and community. It can also involve the community setting some priorities or engaging in policing activities. The commu-nity policing model has been widely recognized since the 1960s in the UK and strongly sup-ported by John Alderson (former Chief Constable of Devon and Cornwall Constabulary) in the late 1970s (Mawby, 2008). The serious consequences of failing to work with communities or respond to their needs were demonstrated through the Notting Hill disorders in 1958, the Brixton riots in 1981, and disturbances in Burnley, Bradford, and Oldham in 2001 (Fielding, 2005; Bowling, Parmar, and Philips, 2008). These outbreaks of community discontent resulted in civilian and police casualties and millions of pounds of damage, and sent local community relations with the police into decline. After such disturbances the inevitable examination of the causes usually results in recommendations to improve dialogue between the community and the police. Within the community policing umbrella there have been a number of approaches and activities that emphasize particular aspects of the community policing ethos, and we examine some of these in the following paragraphs.

3.9.1.2   Problem-orientated Policing (POP)

Herman Goldstein developed the concept of problem-orientated policing (POP) as a means of achieving the purposes of policing through tackling problems in communities (Tilley, 2008a). He defined POP as follows:

> In its broadest context, problem-orientated policing is a comprehensive plan for improving policing in which the high priority attached to addressing substantive problems shapes the police agency, influencing all changes in personnel, organisation, and procedures. Thus problem-orientated policing not only pushes policing beyond current improvement efforts, it calls for a major change in the direction of those efforts. (Goldstein, 1990, p 32)

This view was particularly important in the context of the police repeatedly dealing with par-ticular crimes or calls for assistance (these could be non-crime anti-social behaviour) from the public in a reactive manner. This responsive approach or 'fire brigade policing' (Rowe, 2008, p 165) would not necessarily address underlying problems in the community; rather, it could stretch the police beyond their capacity without improving public safety. By reorganizing and reconfiguring police responses in the manner described by Goldstein the police would analyse the calls from the public and examine the underlying factors causing the need for police assistance.

Particularly attention would be given to cases where repeat call-outs and minor cases could escalate to more serious problems (Rowe, 2008). The emphasis of POP in this context encourages a shift from reactive to proactive approaches to policing. Durham Constabulary have been notable employers of the POP approach in the UK, encouraged by the enthusiasm of the current Chief Constable Mike Barton. In 2016 Durham Constabulary were the only police force in England and Wales to be rated by HMIC as 'outstanding' in their effectiveness in tackling crime.

POP's systematic way of dealing with community problems was not without challenges in terms of organizational and cultural resistance, including 'crude performance management regimes, staff turnover, lack of trained analysts and interagency hostilities' (Tilley, 2008b, p 226). In addressing underlying community problems Goldstein argues that the police frequently need to engage with other private, public, and voluntary organizations. Such partnership approaches (often referred to as 'inter-agency' or 'multi-agency' approaches) are not without tension, as there may be challenges due to different organizational culture, levels of authority, and objectives (Tong, 2008). So although POP might appear a sound proposal in principle (and with some notable successes) we also need to consider the barriers to implementing such an approach. As with any concept or idea, the original intentions to improve practice can face substantial barriers. Only through the support and willingness of practitioners to engage with new approaches will the intended objectives be met.

3.9.1.3 Neighbourhood policing

The Neighbourhood Policing initiative introduced by the then Labour government was rolled out to all police services during 2008. This initiative has been seen by some as a 're-morphed' version of community policing (Joyce, 2011, p 78). Since the late 1990s there had been a shift of emphasis in policing from a focus on crime-fighting to a broader recognition of behaviours that impact on the quality of life and the fear of crime. It is these underpinning influences and the public demand for a more accessible and visible police service that have provided the motivation for reform in policing.

Among the reforms that encouraged police engagement with communities was the Police Reform Act (2002) that paved the way for the introduction of Police Community Support Officers (see 3.4.4). Their role was specifically designed to provide presence and to be accessible so the community could contribute to Neighbourhood Policing Teams (NPT). These involve PCSOs and police constables being assigned to patrol and police particular geographical areas, and to use proactive, intelligence-led, and problem-solving approaches to tackle crime and anti-social incidents within their neighbourhood. In addition to engaging with the public and hearing their concerns, NPTs are also tasked with providing solutions and engaging the community in creating safer neighbourhoods.

Neighbourhood Policing conforms to the AIIA model (NPIA, 2011b) in that it provides:

- **Access**—to local policing services through a named point of contact;
- **Influence**—over policing priorities in their neighbourhood;
- **Interventions**—as joint actions with partners and the public;
- **Answers**—sustainable solutions and feedback on what is being done.

Neighbourhood policing aims to promote 'community interaction' and to control crime and reduce fear, 'with community members helping to identify suspects, detain vandals and bring problems to the attention of the police' (NPIA, 2011b). Although these aims would predominantly appear to target low-level crime, it should be noted that the fear of crime and nuisance behaviour, the role of intelligence collection, and effective communication with the police has wider implications. Sir Ian Blair (the former Commissioner of the Metropolitan Police) argued in his Jonathan Dimbleby lecture in 2005 that:

> national security depends on neighbourhood security. It will not be a Special Branch officer at Scotland Yard who first confronts a terrorist but a local cop or a local community support officer (Blair, 2005).

3.9.1.4 Neighbourhood Watch

The Neighbourhood Watch (NhW) scheme involves bringing groups of residents together to 'create...communities where crime and anti-social behaviour are less likely to happen' (Neighbourhood Watch, 2014). It was established in 1982 and there are now approximately 150,000 schemes in the UK covering 5 million households. NhW is usually organized by volunteers and led by a coordinator who is supported by a liaison officer linked to the local police station. These local networks are part of a larger national structure supported by the National Police Chiefs' Council and the Home Office, and need to be registered with the police. NhW groups collect information about local concerns (eg criminal damage, anti-social behaviour, bogus callers, etc), and provide the police with any information regarding crimes or suspects. The police can also share information about crimes committed in their community, and offer advice on how community members can protect themselves. Police officers can encourage them to start new schemes or join established schemes by directing people to liaison officers or established coordinators. There are also other watch schemes such as Hospital Watch, Boat Watch, Business Watch, Pub Watch, Shed Watch, Church Watch, Forecourt Watch, Bicycle Watch, Country Eye, Horse Watch, Farm Watch, School Watch, and Shop Watch (Kent Police, 2010).

3.9.1.5   Volunteer roles in police work

There are two key volunteering roles in the police namely 'special constables' (see 3.4.1) and 'police support volunteers' (or simply 'police volunteers'). Police volunteers are individuals who work for the police in a variety of non-enforcement roles—these include helping with front desk responsibilities, neighbourhood watch support (see 3.9.1.4), and assisting neighbourhood policing teams with community initiatives. Typically a non-metropolitan police force will have between 100 and 200 volunteers. Police volunteers are security checked but do not hold any police powers.

3.9.2   Problem solving in the community

Attempting to solve problems within communities requires innovative responses, discretion, and imagination. It is difficult to provide an instruction manual for solving community problems, as bespoke responses are often required to address specific problems in a unique context. With this in mind it is important to remember that problem solving is based upon personal judgement informed by individual values and the information available to the decision maker at the time. However, rather than provide no direction at all, there are models of problem solving that can be useful for individuals working in the community, for example the PAT (Problem Analysis Triangle) and the SARA (Scanning, Analysis, Response, and Assessment) process. These provide practitioners with a framework for tackling problems.

The PAT (see the following illustration) provides an officer with a basis to begin to analyse a particular problem.

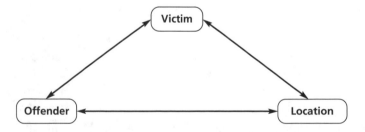

This approach has been associated with problem-orientated approaches and routine activities theory (Tilley, 2008a), and considers three main points of analysis (victim, location, and offender). Solutions are then found through identifying practical measures to address one or more of these points, for example:

• protection of the victim through crime prevention or target-hardening measures;
• providing surveillance or additional patrols in the location concerned; and
• targeting or persuading offenders to cease their disruptive activities.

While some might consider this to be a simplistic model, it does provide a rationale to responding to problems and collecting the information needed to find solutions. It demands critical and objective thinking, that can in turn provide inspiration for decision-making. Although this concept is predominantly aimed at uniformed work, there is clearly scope for it to be used more widely, including for non-crime problems.

The SARA process takes the process a step further through to assessment and review. It involves continual re-evaluation of decisions with the intention of improving practice. The key stages are

- **Scanning:** identifying a problem or a crime;
- **Analysis:** assessment of available information surrounding circumstances;
- **Response:** strategy chosen to deal with event;
- **Assessment:** review and evaluation of impact or effectiveness.

Although this model may be seen as rather mechanical, it does provide a practitioner with a framework in which to confront problems and make decisions (Bullock and Tilley, 2003, p 3).

There are other problem-solving models (with acronyms) which focus on different aspects of decision-making or problem-solving processes. Each practitioner needs to identify a method of working that suits his/her needs, and the problem being addressed.

3.9.3 Intelligence-led policing

Intelligence-led policing (ILP) was introduced in the UK in the 1990s as a new model of policing (and is also known as intelligence-based policing). Within this policing model, intelligence from a number of agencies is pooled with the explicit intention to 'disrupt, disable or undermine criminal behaviour' (Stelfox, 2008, in Newburn and Neyroud, 2008, p 146). Ratcliffe (2008) defined intelligence-led policing as 'a business model and managerial philosophy where data analysis and crime intelligence are pivotal to an objective, decision-making framework that facilitates crime and problem reduction, disruption and prevention through both strategic management and effective enforcement strategies that target prolific and serious offenders'.

ILP was progressively adopted (with varying degrees of enthusiasm) by police forces in England and Wales during the late 1990s, and retains a significant influence on strategic and tactical policing methods in the UK. Thornton claims for example, that 'the concept of intelligence-led policing underpins all aspects of policing, from neighbourhood policing and partnership work to the investigation of serious and organised crime and terrorism' (Thornton, 2007, p 3).

ILP, at its outset at least, was a crime-focused model of policing which emphasizes the countering of crime through detection, disruption, or dissuasion. In practical terms, ILP derives its philosophy and principles from the recognition that crime and criminality can be understood at some level in terms of its perpetrators, its temporal and spatial patterns, and the linkages between crimes (eg common case analysis). In terms of the perpetrators of crime, the 1993 Audit Commission report (Audit Commission, 1993) and the unpublished research of Kent Police and others appeared to demonstrate clearly that a minority of criminals are responsible for the majority of most types of volume crime. The logic ran that this minority could be identified (eg through the use of paid informants) and then targeted and 'removed' through successful detection and prosecution. This, it was hoped, could be a more effective use of police resources, compared with more reactive models. Indeed, as Heaton (2008) and others have observed, this 'targeting' of high-volume and often recidivist offenders became a cornerstone of ILP. Thus the mantra of ILP became to 'target the criminal and not just the crime' (adapted from an observation made by the Audit Commission, 1993), and this led to a much greater emphasis on intelligence gathering and analysis (the employment of increasing numbers of analysts), and a reduction in apparently ineffective reactive policing.

Opinion and research continue to differ concerning just how small a minority of criminals are responsible for just how large a majority of crime. For example, the 1993 Audit Commission report (Audit Commission, 1993) cited Home Office research, which claimed that '7% of males who had been convicted of 6 or more offences accounted for 65% of all convictions' (Home Office, 1989, p 2). Heaton argued that a more 'realistic' ratio would be 3 per cent of offenders being responsible for 24 per cent of offences (Heaton, 2000). Given that there was probably some exaggeration in early claims (particular as the oft-repeated '7% responsible for 65%' was derived in a particular context), there is nonetheless clear evidence for a skew in offending. For example, in a 2004 study in Brighton and Hove, the 'top' 40 of the 400 identified high-volume offenders were responsible for 691 convictions out of the 3,453 total (Center for Problem Oriented Policing, 2009). Further, research on repeat victimization (eg Everson and Pease, 2001) suggests that prolific offenders may be responsible for the bulk of these repeated crimes against the same person or target.

The identification of 'patterns of crime' and linking crimes together is also an important (although not a unique) feature of ILP, giving rise to the ability to deploy policing resources more effectively. This is often combined with an increased multi-agency approach to the sharing of intelligence. The analysis of crime data and intelligence (see 23.5) by both the police and partner agencies (often through CSPs) is a key factor in identifying temporal and spatial aspects of crime. This can help ensure that resources are deployed appropriately, and proactively where possible.

3.9.4 Zero-tolerance policing

Zero-tolerance policing came to prominence in the 1990s under the mayoral leadership of Rudi Giuliani in New York City and the approach adopted by his Commissioner of Police, Bill Bratton. New York City had suffered high levels of crime throughout the 1970s and 1980s, and Bratton adopted a more aggressive and robust approach to policing. It came to be known as zero-tolerance policing because it responded vigorously to all acts of low-level criminality and incivility and behaviours that detracted from the quality of life for ordinary citizens. The approach was loosely premised upon the 'Broken Windows' thesis presented by Wilson and Kelling (1982). They argued that neglect and the consequent physical problems in a community foster social disorder and eventually crime, and outlined the need to 'nip bad behaviour in the bud'. The approach was accompanied by a systematic process of managerial accountability known as Compstat, which made the achievement of crime reduction outcomes more open and transparent.

Reductions in crime followed the introduction of zero-tolerance policing in New York, and Bill Bratton became an international star of policing. However, critics later pointed to the fact that similar reductions in crime had also occurred in parts of the USA that had not adopted zero- tolerance policing methods. The overzealous and aggressive approach adopted by officers enforcing a zero-tolerance policing strategy also began to attract criticisms from the citizens of New York City once crime rates had fallen. In England and Wales, zero-tolerance policing was adopted in the late 1990s in Cleveland under the direction of Detective Superintendent Ray Mallon. However, controversy led to the suspension of Mallon and his eventual retirement from the force, and the image of zero-tolerance policing was somewhat tarnished by this experience.

Nonetheless, the notion of zero-tolerance policing regularly comes to the fore, for example following the outbreak of rioting across London and other English towns and cities in August 2011. Likewise, variations on the zero-tolerance policing approach have been developed and implemented by a number of police forces in England and Wales. The current Commissioner of the Metropolitan Police Service (MPS), Bernard Hogan-Howe, came to prominence during his time as Chief Constable of Merseyside Police through the successes of his strategy of 'Total Policing', which is seen by some as a form of zero-tolerance policing.

> **TASK 10** Consider the phenomenon of anti-social behaviour. How would intelligence-led policing, problem-orientated policing, and community-based or neighbourhood policing, adopted in their purest form (that is, to the exclusion of all other approaches), address this problem?

> **TASK 11** We have considered models of policing in England and Wales, but elsewhere in Europe other models are used. If you have travelled abroad, what differences have you noticed in policing?

3.10   Answers to Tasks

TASK 1 You might have included the following (which vary from force to force, of course, but which most forces have most support staff engaged in):

- **Crime Scene Investigators:** an operational role which in the past was undertaken exclusively by police officers, modern CSIs are often now police staff with training and qualifications in forensic investigation (see 26.3).
- **Statement takers:** many of the statements taken from witnesses and victims of crime, particularly volume crime, are taken, not by police officers but by support staff. The reason is that such statements do not have to be taken under caution (unlike statements by suspects) and therefore do not have to be taken by sworn officers. This can free up a great deal of time for police officers to pursue the investigation, and there can be a marked increase in the professionalism with which victims and witnesses are interviewed because the support staff involved are undertaking these tasks all the time.
- **Volume Crime Scene Examiners (VCSEs):** this role may not exist in all forces, but VCSEs are employed to undertake specialist forensic examination of extended areas of crime scenes on a large scale. They are particularly used in vehicle crimes.

- **Detention officers ('jailers'):** these are support staff trained in custody and holding prisoners.
- **Human resources (HR):** HR can include the whole range of specialists covering recruitment, promotions and postings, training, assessment and appraisal, retirement, secondment, dismissal, or capability issues. HR also deal with all matters relating to police support staff, including negotiations with staff associations.
- **Information technology:** these specialists are almost exclusively support staff, though some forces retain police officers where there is direct interface with police officers on patrol, for example in force communication centres or control rooms. IT often includes telephony and wireless communications (including personal radios) within its remit.
- **Lawyers:** force legal advice (civil and/or criminal) is now seen as an important resource, particularly for the chief officer team and the Police Authority, and in dealing with complaints from the public, or litigation by employees (eg employment tribunals).
- **Estates:** police forces occupy considerable numbers of buildings and possess vast stocks of property which need specialist handling, particularly in negotiations with planning authorities.
- **Finance:** with police budgets in the hundreds of millions of pounds annually, there is a need for specialist financial and budget management. In most forces, 80 per cent or more of the budget is spent on salaries or pensions, leaving a relatively small operational revenue budget to which is added the capital budget for aspects such as buildings and vehicles.
- **Administration:** from paper files to computerized records, from sickness certificates to awards ceremonies, from shotgun certificates to booking training courses, the administrative tasks in a police force are complex and numerous. The bureaucratic nature of policing inevitably creates a large administrative tail.

Force websites often provide descriptions of the roles undertaken by police staff. A good example is Essex Police and its website <http://www.essex.police.uk/recruitment/police_staff_vacancies.aspx>.

TASK 2

1. In most cases you should be able to find this information through an internet search. Some forces publish this information as a matter of routine, others as the result of a FoI request. For example, the MPS provides a list of designated powers within its publicly available 'MPS Disclosure Log'.
2. The volume and exact nature of the training is very much determined by the chief constable in each force, or the local BCU commander in terms of any specific training. There is still debate about the outline of a training package which all PCSOs should receive. Training lasts for at least five weeks, but there have been calls for much longer and more specific PCSO training systems to be set up as a form of continuous development. In most forces it would look something like this:
   - **Week 1:** an induction course, which contains health and safety instruction, learning about diversity, and some introduction to the general nature of being a community support officer.
   - **Weeks 2–4:** include attitude and behaviour development, combined with knowledge of outside agencies and other tools for successful community problem solving.
   - **Week 5:** is the 'Powers' week, where PCSOs are provided with knowledge of their existing powers and their practical effectiveness. This would also include some rudimentary safety training and training to defuse potentially dangerous situations and how to calm and manage angry people.

Finally, there will be BCU or beat training and familiarization until independent patrol.

TASK 3 The following are examples of how the five forms of authority might feature in the scenario:

Form of authority	Examples
Epistemic	You have a clear understanding of the definition of the possible offences involved in this incident. You have knowledge of the appropriate procedures to be followed and this is conveyed in speech to those present, including the victim and the offender
Natural	You use your demeanour and language to take control of the situation, including indicating when you wish a person to answer a question and in which order
De facto	Your right to question those involved is probably accepted without challenge (but not necessarily with cooperation!)
De jure	You have the authority to arrest if the circumstances require this
Moral	You demonstrate, through your behaviour and attitudes, that you do not immediately jump to conclusions concerning the sequence of events, nor attribute guilt or innocence

TASK 4 You would have had to arbitrate between the right to freedom of expression (however extreme such views may be) and the need to sustain law and order. The legitimacy of your presence might not be consensual, but it may be both legitimized in law and necessary for preservation of the peace. The police would endeavour to control the marchers by determining the safest route for the parade to follow whilst also ensuring that direct clashes with the protesters were avoided. However you managed the event, someone, somewhere would have individual freedoms circumscribed (even if only the rights of Saturday shoppers to go about their lawful business), and thus the police are using moral as well as legal legitimacy in the policing of the march.

TASK 5 You have probably spotted our intentions with this task; the two situations are very similar. The first scenario is the more serious in policing terms as you are told that the woman appears to be slightly drunk, whereas the young man is simply clutching a can of lager. In the first case the fact that she is a medical student who will soon (presumably) join the medical profession may well have influenced your thinking towards exercising discretion. However, you were not appointed to be a moral guardian of society: the place that a person holds in society should not feature in your decision whether or not to exercise discretion.

In terms of your answer you might well have considered other aspects such as the intentions of each person concerned, the precise nature of the apparent offence, and so on. The problem with presenting these scenarios in a written form (or as simulations in training) is the lack of this context; this is so important when making decisions.

When exercising discretion it is important that you are able to justify your actions to an outsider looking in—that is, to show how discretion is the result of rational decision-making rather than instinct or some other gut reaction. Doing so will also help you meet the assessment requirements of the Diploma in Policing units. During your training and assessment you must evidence your decision-making; your assessor cannot read your mind!

Taylor (1999) has produced a useful checklist for the exercise of discretion. You are asked to consider issues such as fairness, justice, accountability, consistency, and wider community interests and expectations.

TASK 6 It is highly likely that you included at least some of the following professions: medicine (eg a doctor); law (eg a barrister); Church (eg a vicar); and teaching (eg a school teacher). You may also have thought of the military (eg a General); nursing; accountancy. Did you include policing?

Professions are occupations that normally have the following qualities:

- They provide an income which is normally referred to as a salary. Interestingly, in many respects police officers are paid a wage rather than a salary—for example, below certain ranks they qualify for overtime payments calculated at an hourly rate.
- Entry to the profession is regulated and controlled. The title may be legally controlled, as in the case of the medical profession. Quite often a higher education degree in an approved area of study, or a licence is required. Members of the profession are then licensed to practise, but there are procedures for removal of the licence (which in some professions is referred to as being struck off).
- There is a code of ethics and behaviour that members of the profession subscribe to.

TASK 7 Some possible answers are:

Requirements of a profession	The policing profession
Corpus of knowledge and theory	There is a growing body of underpinning knowledge and theory for many aspects of policing, for example in operational matters and application of the law. There was also doctrinal development, undertaken by the College of Policing (eg underpinning Authorised Professional Practice). However, there is yet no universally accepted complete *corpus* of knowledge which is unique to policing
Controls on entry to the profession and maintenance of position	Entry is controlled through the national selection process. However, there are no formal academic requirements to enter the profession, beyond relatively simple tests of English and numeracy, although this might well change in the near future (see Chapter 8)
Autonomy, discretion, and self-regulation	Police officers enjoy relatively high levels of autonomy and discretion. The title of police constable is controlled so that only those that qualify are entitled to use it. Self-regulation of policing exists in a restricted form but is increasingly under challenge. The College of Policing is not yet independent of government. ACPO has been replaced by the National Police Chiefs' Council
Vocational calling	Policing is more than just a job and affects many aspects of an individual's life
Code of ethics	There is a new code of ethics

TASK 8 You would probably have picked up on race and gender, but did you get sexual orientation, age, or belief? And disability?

TASK 9 You might have included.

- it is decentralized: public policing is still largely local, autonomous, and non-political (with shades of grey, viz the Miners' Strike in 1984–5);
- policing is consensual: it cannot operate without the active support of the public;
- approaches to policing are characterized by provisions in the Human Rights Act 1998 and the PACE Act 1984, which respect human dignity and ensure fairness of process;
- police officers, for the most part and on most occasions, are unarmed;
- police officers have independence in conducting investigations; they may still exercise initiative in whether to investigate or not;
- we have an adversarial criminal justice system, which requires the prosecution to disclose evidence;
- there is a presumption of innocence until proven guilty; the burden of proof lies with the prosecution.

TASK 10 In terms of anti-social behaviour you might have suggested the following:

- **Intelligence-led policing**—target the most active and serious contributors to the anti-social behaviour. This might require the use of informants and surveillance. When these individuals have been identified, then examine all appropriate means, within the law, of removing them from exercising leadership and direction over the rest. For example, consider what offences they might have committed, whether ASBOs might be suitable, what other agencies may be engaged to bring pressure to bear (eg do we have information that they are illegally claiming benefits?), what evidence we will need, and so on. If we cannot detect the crime, it could be disrupted instead.
- **Problem-orientated policing**—the fundamental problem needs to be identified. The anti-social behaviour may simply be the visible manifestation of a less obvious problem or change. For example, the removal of fences between the gardens of local-authority-owned houses could have created open areas which are vulnerable to anti-social behaviour. If so, other agencies might need to be involved in an agreed and concerted strategy to address the underlying problem.
- **Community-based or neighbourhood policing**—first we need to talk to those that can really help us: members and representatives of the local community and the patrol officers who work with them. If young people are involved then how can we mobilize their parents and others in the community to address both the anti-social behaviour and its underlying causes? What support can be offered? In summary, do not simply view this as a question of law enforcement but more as a wider question concerning the stability and cohesion of the local community.

TASK 11 You might have noticed that:

- uniformed police officers routinely and openly carry arms (so do detectives, but concealed);
- stop and search can be more widespread than in the UK; European citizens routinely carry an identification card or identifying papers;
- there are often several types of police officer (*gendarmes, carabinieri, guardia civil, police municipale*, city police as well as national police) in the same country;
- most European police forces are nationally organized, even when they have variations in police types (such as the paramilitary *gendarmes*, as against the *agents de police* in France); and
- particularly in Eastern Europe and Russia, as well as further afield, there may be a hostility to the police or even a fear of them, especially at border controls. This is a legacy and, in some cases, a continuation of the role of the police as an arm of the state, and is associated with repression and denial of freedom. Citizens in countries which have suffered under occupation or tight state control may show contempt and loathing of the police, to a degree seldom seen in the UK.

There are other differences which you will find only by close comparative study or by investigation into the individual country's criminal justice system. Did you know, for example, that the Dutch abolished the jury system in 1804 and never reinstated it? Or that Italy has provision for a jury trial system but has never used it?

4 | Crime and Criminality

4.1 Introduction

In this chapter we take a brief look at the nature of disorder, crime, and criminality in England and Wales. Every day, social media (particularly Twitter), TV and radio, and the pages of newspapers contain reports of disorder and crime. Many articles and research papers are devoted to trying to understand criminal motivations, why people commit crimes, and why certain crimes are more prevalent than others. You will read some of these criminological texts and papers during your studies on a pre-join programme or as a trainee police officer.

In this chapter we have deliberately simplified these issues because this is not a handbook of crime or criminology, and some of the topics are very complex, drawing on psychological, philosophical, sociological, and political perspectives. In a very real sense, you will be grappling with these ideas and questions throughout your police career, and most certainly during your time as a student or police trainee.

> **TASK 1**
> * What makes a crime sensational?
> * What makes a crime of little apparent interest?
> * What makes a crime impact on a community?

Increasingly over the past 40 years, criminologists have become interested in studying the police. This has produced numerous publications concerning the organization, administration, governance and general understanding of police work (eg Newburn, 2011; Reiner, 2010; Rowe, 2014; and Caless and Owens, 2016 to name but a few). However, beyond this, criminology has also provided the police with a number of important theories about the nature of crime and criminal behaviour, which can help the police in a number of different ways. For example, the proactive policing model has been supported by developments in criminological theories concerning crime prevention, the study of victims, evidence-based policing and the spatial movements of criminals. The scope of criminological studies is too vast to cover here, but by providing a selection of important ways in which criminology informs contemporary policing, it is hoped that you will be encouraged to consult the growing body of criminological research concerning many different policing matters. But first we will consider some more basic questions, some possible definitions of crime, and some possible causes of crime.

4.2 Definitions of Crime

What is crime? We tend to think we know the answer until we begin to think through the details and test out our general ideas on some specific examples. We might say that crime is what is forbidden, that crime is activity which society would like to eradicate or prevent, or that crime is a measure of society's health: the more unbalanced the society, the more the crimes on the statute book. Technically, a particular activity is a crime because the law defines it as such. However, remember that laws are made by people so, in the end, we are back to where we started: people (albeit only certain categories of people such as judges and MPs) decide which activities are crimes. Without reference to existing concepts of crime and laws there is nothing about an activity in itself that marks it out as a crime. Consider, for example, how some forms of sexual activity between consenting adult men were treated as crimes in the recent past but are no longer treated as such. There are a very few acts that have been consistently considered crimes throughout modern history (try Task 2). Other types and definitions of crime are mutable (they change as society changes). Think about our attitudes to the environment in which we live, for example collecting birds' eggs or hunting foxes with dogs are now seen by many as unacceptable. The laws have followed suit. Currently there is debate around so-called 'legal highs'; should they be 'criminalized'? Also should drugs that are currently categorized as 'illegal' be legalized? Policy makers, practitioners, and academics will discuss these issues at length, but if they are not covered by legislation they cannot be a crime.

We will start with considering a narrow definition of crime—that is in terms of actions referred to in legislation. This provides us with a definitive statement but does not really explain why particular acts and behaviours are treated as criminal whilst others are not. However, if we look beyond the law as part of the definition of crime, we then find that the task becomes no easier. Finally, we consider the thoughts of JS Mill, a nineteenth-century philosopher who proposed that deviant behaviour might have a role in promoting beneficial changes in society (although he recognized that some deviant behaviours would be classed as crime if they caused harm to other people).

4.2.1 Crimes are defined by law

Originally, the word 'crime' actually meant judgement or accusation (from Latin *crimen*, a judgement), and it was only later that it came to be associated with the act of offence or wrong-doing. By the Middle Ages, crime was something 'against the law', and thus a crime was an action punishable by law. On one level, we now simply define crime as action which is against the law, and clearly the act needs to be against a specific criminal law. Critics of this definition of crime point to an obvious tautology—we are essentially saying the same thing twice but in a different form. Using such a circular argument, that crime is defined by law, takes us no further forward in our understanding.

4.2.2 Crimes are defined by society

Others have argued conversely that crime, is a social construction. By this they mean that no act or behaviour is in itself wrong but rather that different societies will identify different activities as crimes, according to the specific needs of a given society at a particular point in history.

TASK 2

- List three crimes that would appear to be universal.
- List three offences that are considered criminal in the UK today but were not 100 years ago.
- List three offences that are considered criminal in other parts of the world but not in the UK.

Crime can also be defined more broadly as all social wrongdoings and anti-social behaviour. This sociological approach addresses the question from the perspective of why certain acts are criminalized, but can compromise the clarity of legal definitions of particular offences.

4.2.3 Mill's principle of 'harm to others'

John Stuart Mill (1806–73) was an English philosopher. He believed it was important for the development of a healthy society that individuals should have as much freedom as possible, primarily (he suggested) because individuals who deviate from the norm can help society to advance. However, the problem for any authority is how to work out when a deviation from the norm might be beneficial and when it is not. In other words, it is not always possible to know for certain whether an individual who is acting differently is being innovative or merely criminal.

There are numerous examples throughout history of individuals (some of whom we now celebrate as heroes) who were considered a threat to society at an earlier time. Think, for example, about the suppression of scientific thinkers, such as Galileo, who were considered to be heretics, or (more recently) civil rights protesters such as Martin Luther King in the USA. In the UK today there are many examples of people and campaign groups willing to break the law, for example animal rights activists, Fathers 4 Justice, anti-abortionists, and environmentalists. These groups each believe they represent values that are not normal today but will become so in the future, in the same way that those fighting at previous times in history for equal rights for women or the abolition of the slave trade eventually came to be recognized as heroic figures.

For Mill, the way to permit individuals or groups to deviate from existing norms, and indeed to challenge them, is to allow people to make mistakes and act immorally, providing these acts do not harm others. This is Mill's famous 'harm to others' principle. It is largely from this perspective that we have established a separation between the law and morality; it is argued that the law pertains to public matters and morality to private individual concerns. This view was supported in 1957 in the Wolfenden Report into homosexuality and prostitution, in which it was argued that private acts between consenting adults should not be the concern of law enforcement (Wolfenden Report, 1957). Campaigners for gay rights have criticized this finding for putting too much emphasis on the word private, as they feel this suggests that public expressions of homosexuality should be regulated and controlled.

However, other critics have challenged the view that law and morality can be so neatly separated. They argue that there is a significant grey area which we might characterize as social morality, that it is simply not possible to insulate our private activities completely, that there will always be leakage, and our actions will always have consequences in ways that we could not have predicted. This challenges Mill's 'harm to others' principle because it suggests that others are harmed by our actions even if this was not our intention. Perhaps a good example of this, to illustrate the point, is passive smoking. For many years campaigns have encouraged smokers to stop for their own sake, but little was done to prohibit smoking in a public place. It is now increasingly regulated on grounds of the health and safety of people in the vicinity (see 14.2.1.7).

This also illustrates that harm is more widely defined today than when Mill was writing. We have become more sophisticated in identifying different forms of harm. For example, consider the extent to which we have broadened our understanding of domestic violence to include psychological, emotional, and financial harm, in addition to physical injury resulting from an assault.

4.3 The Causes of Crime

When examining the causes of crime, an important starting point is to acknowledge some fundamental differences in how we might understand crime and how these differences in turn can inform police work. Blackburn (1995) makes a distinction between crimes and criminality. He discusses crimes as a rational response to the environment in which people find themselves, and criminality as a characteristic of an individual that emphasizes their propensity to commit crimes.

4.3.1 Crime—a rational response?

Some crimes are apparently easily explained as a product of the social situation in which they occur. For example, an unemployed single mother shoplifting nappies for her baby is certainly committing a crime, but it could be said that a more serious problem is that she should be in such a difficult position in the first place. Others will point out that not all mothers in the same situation would resort to shoplifting but would find a legal solution to the problem. Irrespective of which moral position is adopted, from a policing perspective this particular crime can be understood more readily as a social response rather than as an individual failing. This view is associated with what is referred to as classical criminology, which emerged in the late eighteenth century and informed the thinking of law reformers at this time (eg Bentham, Howard, Beccaria). This view of crime suggests that anyone could become a criminal given the right circumstances, and that punishment is required to act as a deterrent to crime.

4.3.2   Criminals—a breed apart?

Conversely, it is difficult to understand the actions of a violent serial murderer as the consequence of injustices in society. No matter how bad society is, it is hard to view such brutality as a reasonable response in any sense. A contrasting explanation for the causes of crime is the concept of criminality. This view developed from what is referred to as the positivist school of criminology associated with Cesare Lombroso's *L'Uomo Delinquente* (The Criminal Man) published in 1876. Positivists differed from the classical approach to criminology by arguing that:

• criminality is determined by factors beyond the immediate control of an individual and is not a product of his or her free will;
• criminals are a certain type of individual distinct from non-criminal individuals; or
• criminals are pathological (see Jones and Newburn, 1998, pp 101–2).

4.3.3   Nature and nurture

These kinds of questions have been debated for centuries. It is often referred to as the nature/nurture debate. Nature refers to what we are born with or, in recent terms, our genetic make-up, and nurture relates to the environmental contexts in which we develop. This includes everything from our schooling, how our parents raised us, whom we chose to associate with, and every arbitrary experience that has good, bad, or indifferent outcomes. However, the nature/nurture dichotomy can often be misleading. The debates have frequently been polemical and exclusionary; that is, those favouring nature explanations would dismiss nurture as an influence and those supporting nurture explanations would exclude completely the view that nature has any part to play. Increasingly today we recognize that both nature and nurture form part of the explanation and, indeed, that it is not always easy to distinguish one from the other. Modern biology continues to uncover examples of genetic predispositions being either masked or revealed by environmental factors.

4.3.4   Hate crime

The Crown Prosecution Service define hate crime as:

> Any criminal offence which is perceived by the victim or any other person, to be motivated by hostility or prejudice based on a person's race or perceived race; religion or perceived religion; sexual orientation or perceived sexual orientation; disability or perceived disability and any crime motivated by hostility or prejudice against a person who is transgender or perceived to be transgender. (from *Hate Crime What is it?* (online))

The Criminal Justice Act 2003 dictates that if a crime is based on hostility influenced by actual or perceived religion, ethnicity, disability, or sexual orientation, then the court must state this as an aggravating factor when sentencing the offender(s). Note that there is no particular offence entitled 'hate crime'.

Interestingly, hate crime (including homophobic or racist crimes) as can be seen above, can be defined as such by the victim(s) or any other person, irrespective of the views of the police officer dealing with it. This amendment arose from the enquiry into the death of the black London teenager, Stephen Lawrence, and a subsequent report into the police investigation chaired by Sir William Macpherson. (This report famously branded the MPS as 'institutionally racist'.) The following question then arises: 'If any person present can define a crime as a "hate crime", why cannot *any* individual define *any* incident in which they feel disadvantaged, wronged, or frightened, as a "crime"?' The law provides the answer. There must have been an identifiable criminal offence (such as assault) before the qualification of whether or not it is homophobic or racist can be considered. It is the hate which is defined by the individual and not the crime. Once again, the close interrelationship between the law, society, and individuals is a key factor in understanding crime. The law surrounding harassment and hate crime is covered in 14.5 and 14.10.

4.4   Measuring Crime

There are various means of measuring crime, for example police and criminal justice statistical records, large-scale surveys (mostly government-sponsored), and small-scale academic studies. The government and criminal justice agencies use police recorded figures and the Crime Survey in England & Wales (CSEW) and Northern Ireland Crime Survey (NICS) as their key sources of information. In these surveys thousands of households are randomly selected and interviews are conducted with the aim of measuring both recorded and unrecorded crime (see 4.4.1). The Scottish Crime and Justice Survey is available from the Scottish Government Justice Analytical Services.

The under-reporting of crime by the public, the under-recording of crime by the police, political interest, and intellectual bias all contribute to distortions in the measured levels of crime at any given time. This can also lead to difficulties in making meaningful comparisons with crime levels in the past. Under-reporting and under-recording are particularly problematic for the police, and have received considerable attention in recent years. Research practices can also contribute to a distorted picture of the true extent of crime; there will always be weaknesses in any research design that involves collecting data, for example due to sample size, access to research participants, ethical barriers, organizational limitations, funding restrictions, or the methods employed. The British Crime Survey (the predecessor to the CSEW) was considered one of the most comprehensive crime surveys in the world, but no research is beyond reproach. For example, it was only in January 2009 that the BCS began including 10- to 15-year-olds in the survey and recording their experiences of crime, and it wasn't until 2016 that the CSEW began to include questions that measured the extent of fraud and computer misuse offences. Researchers constantly review their methods to ensure the crime surveys are robust and as useful as possible.

Establishing a more accurate picture of the extent of crime and ensuring that it is recorded properly are important aspects of modern policing. However, what information needs to be recorded?

4.4.1 Reported incidents and recorded crime

An important distinction needs to be made between reported crime-related incidents (eg phoned reports made by a member of the public to the police) and recorded crime. Let us consider a particular incident where the police are contacted—it may or may not involve a crime. Imagine that I have witnessed a heated argument in the street, perhaps with some pushing, shoving, and screaming. I phone the police and report it; the police will take note of the contents of my call (it will be registered or 'logged' in police jargon). This registration of the incident is what most commentators mean when they refer to reported crime. The police then have to decide whether the incident should be then recorded as an actual crime (a so-called 'notifiable offence'). They are required to use the Home Office criterion which states that if (on the balance of probability) the circumstances as reported by the caller amount to an offence, and there is no credible evidence to the contrary, then it should be recorded as a crime (Home Office, 2014c). The 'the balance of probability' element is satisfied (Home Office, 2016d) when:

- the circumstances of the victim's report amount to a crime as defined by the law (the police will determine this, based on their knowledge and the counting rules); and
- there is no credible evidence to the contrary immediately available.

The police response to incoming calls is discussed in more detail in 24.4.1.

As our incident illustrates, the decision is far from simple. In response to my call the police are required to make all reasonable enquiries to identify specific victims and secure any supporting evidence. Although pushing and shoving could technically be an offence of assault or battery (see 15.2) or a public order offence (see 14.4), this would depend on the circumstances, and these would probably not be clear from my account over the phone. More importantly, a victim is unlikely to be identified and the basic recording rule of 'no victim, no crime' would be applied. (Note, however, that there are exceptions to this rule.) Hence in my example, it is highly unlikely that the pushing and shoving that I witnessed, although registered as an incident would actually result in the police recording a crime.

Crime recording and counting methods were changed by the Home Office in 2013, and further modified in 2014, replacing the old system under which crimes were classed as either 'detected', 'undetected' or 'no crime'. There are now a total of 19 possible outcomes (McKee, 2014). The processes of reporting and recording crime are complex and full details are provided by the Home Office (2015a).

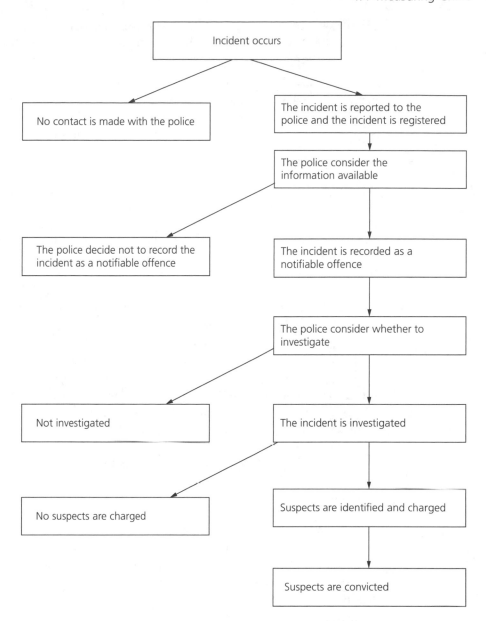

In terms of statistics, the police service as a whole claimed to have cleared up 29 per cent of all recorded crime in 2013–14 (McKee, 2014), which appeared to be an impressive record. However, it has been estimated that recorded crime represents only a small proportion of all crime committed. Data from 2002 (see the pie chart) suggests that for all crimes occurring, 47 per cent are reported, 27 per cent are recorded, 5 per cent are cleared up (these are reported, recorded, and investigated), and 2 per cent result in conviction (Wright, 2002).

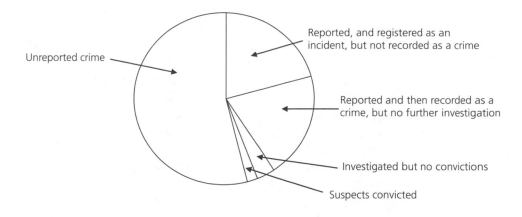

It is interesting to note that in 1771, the clear-up rate for crime was estimated as 24.6 per cent (Emsley, 1996). Of course many other factors would need to be taken into account for any meaningful comparison to be made with today's figures.

HMIC acknowledges that there is a 'degree of subjective interpretation in making decisions about how to record crimes' (HIMC, 2013a, p 3). This is a subject of some concern. Indeed, the same HMIC report concluded that in at least one police force there was serious under-recording of crime which led to victims not receiving the service they required.

4.4.2 The perception of crime

There is a general acceptance that the fear of crime and disorder has increased in recent years. For example the CSEW 2013/14 found that around 6 in 10 adults believed that crime (in the country as a whole) had risen over the past few years (ONS, 2015), despite the fact that most forms of recorded crime have actually shown a decrease in the same period (although see Farrall and Gadd (2004) for a critique). It would also appear that particular communities are more likely to believe that crime has risen significantly when compared to others, and also to worry more about crime. For example, the CSEW for 2013/14 (ONS, 2015) suggests the following demographic factors are significant in terms of perceptions and beliefs about crime:

- gender: women are more likely than men to believe that crime had risen in recent years, this was true for both national and local crime;
- age: there were also differences by age group in perceptions of crime levels but the patterns were different for the local and national measures. With regard to the national picture, the general pattern was that the perception that crime was rising increased with age (people aged 75 and over were most likely to view it as having risen in recent years). Conversely, a perception that crime was increasing locally was highest in the 35–44 and the 45–54 age groups, and then reduced with rising age. While those aged 75 and over were the most likely to think crime was increasing across the country as a whole, they were the least likely to believe that local crime levels were rising;
- location: individuals living in the most deprived areas were most likely to perceive a rise in local and national crime in recent years, whereas people living in urban areas were more likely than rural inhabitants to think that crime had risen in their local area; and
- newspapers: readers of the 'red top' (tabloid) newspapers are more likely to believe that crime has increased in recent years than those who read the 'broadsheets' or 'quality press'.

However, it is important to note that according to official statistics, those who feel most worried about crime or who perceive crime to be increasing are not necessarily those who are actually the most likely to become victims. Although having said this, it could be argued that suffering from fear of crime is itself a form of harm to an individual. For people who are very anxious and fearful about crime, the lifestyle implications can be profound, and an elderly person's statistically 'irrational' fears about crime still need to be taken into account. Think of this as some kind of calculation: the risk of an incident (such as a physical attack) may be low but the negative consequences of such an incident (were it to occur) could be very high in terms of recovery from an injury. So despite the low probability, this can be a significant issue for the individual concerned.

There are a number of reasons why many people overestimate the extent of crime and disorder. A key reason is that people tend to base their judgements not only on those 'invisible' but often very serious crimes (such as burglary or sexual crimes), but also on the more obvious local crimes. These are usually less serious but Innes (2014) refers to them as 'signal crimes' or 'signal disorders', and believes they are perceived by residents as warning signals about the level of insecurity in their neighbourhoods. Possible examples of signal crimes and disorder, particularly when a number of these examples coincide in a local community, include:

- public drinking, swearing, rowdy and uncivil behaviour by groups of individuals;
- graffiti and other forms of damage and vandalism, litter;
- evidence of drug taking and dealing, prostitution;
- speeding;
- rubbish dumped in the street or outside houses; and
- abandoned or burnt-out vehicles.

As Innes (2005, p 102) notes, 'major crimes such as homicides can and do function as signals, but (for most people, most of the time) the signals that they attend to and that assume particular salience for them are what have tended to be treated by the criminal justice agencies as less serious'. Once spotted, these signals can give rise to a heightened sense of awareness amongst individuals of other similar examples—a self-reinforcing and potentially harmful feedback loop.

4.5   Modelling Crime and Criminality

In 4.3 we provided an overview of some of the theories that attempt to explain the existence of crime and criminality. We now move on from these general theories (often concerned with human nature and society) to more detailed explanatory models and also suggest some possible responses for the police and others.

4.5.1   Opportunities for crime

Pease (2002) notes three different ways in which crime has been understood, and he defines these in terms of structure, human psyche, and circumstance. 'Structure' covers major social issues that are seen to be linked to crime, for example poverty and inequality. Human psyche concerns the attributes of the criminal as a person, in other words the reasons why he/she has a propensity to commit offences. However, the circumstance is seen by Pease as the key factor for causing crime.

Rational-choice theory assumes that when criminals decide to commit offences they go through the same kind of thought process as non-criminals making everyday, non-criminal decisions:

> It is not the case (except for a tiny handful of pathological personalities) that criminals are so unlike the rest of us as to be indifferent to the costs and benefits of the opportunities open to them. (Wilson, 1996, p 312)

This suggests that crimes occur if and when they are easy to commit, and the results are sufficiently rewarding.

Routine-activity theory is also predicated upon an understanding of the relationship between an individual's everyday experiences and his/her criminal behaviour. Importantly, it defines criminal opportunities in terms of three interrelated and necessary components: a motivated offender; a suitable target; and the absence of a guardian. The idea is that criminal opportunities arise when these three components coincide. We may observe that the number of offences might increase even if there is no increase in the number of motivated offenders. This occurs if a small number of motivated offenders are in situations where there are few guardians and plenty of suitable targets. Schools are a prime example of this kind of scenario: there are significant numbers of largely unsupervised vulnerable children with mobile phones, and there are other children who are keen to acquire these.

4.5.2   The 'hot' model

One way to consider the phenomenon of crime in society is to think about some of its constituent elements as being hot: that is, both frequently occurring and worthy of attention. The following owes much to Clarke (1999), although some terms such as 'hot offender' are of our own devising. It should be noted that with a growing proportion of crime occurring online (see 21.2) the 'hot' model of crime might need to be adapted (or even abandoned) in the future.

Hot spots are places that are particularly prone to crime, such as railway stations, shopping malls, town centres, particular shops and houses, post offices, or flats. This may be related to the easy pickings for the criminal intent on theft, shoplifting, mugging, or similar. In addition, it may also be related to opportunity, because these are places where people are more likely to be carrying large quantities of cash (railway stations close to race courses for example, or streets leading away from ATMs or cash machines) or other items of potential value (such as credit and debit cards). This leads to an unevenness of crime distribution: in a city there will be some particular and relatively small geographical areas that always or nearly always have a high crime rate (all types), but other areas will be virtually crime free. Until some preventative action is taken, these 'hot spots' will persist, and even if action is taken they may recur (see 4.6.2.2).

Hot offenders are defined as the relatively small number of people who are responsible for the majority of crime. However, opinion and research continue to differ over just how small a minority of criminals is responsible for just how large a majority of crimes (see 3.9.3). Furthermore, research for example by Everson and Pease (2001) on repeat victimization (see 'hot victims' discussed later) suggests that prolific offenders may be responsible for the bulk of these repeated crimes against the same person or target.

Hot products are the items we know are more attractive to burglars or street robbers, and there is a logic to what is stolen. Whilst flat-screen TVs are still objects of desire for burglars, the average, small-time, drug-abusing, volume criminal will go for small items of value which are easily transportable and not easily traced. This is why cash (pre-eminently) and jewellery are popular targets for thieves. Cash, of course, is easily disposed of and generally untraceable, and the bulk of rings and watches are easily converted into money. Smartphones and laptops are also popular targets. Interestingly, according to insurance claim information the most commonly stolen home possession in 2015 were bicycles.

As you might suppose, there is a mnemonic (Clarke, 1999) for rating hot products: CRAVED.

C	Concealable
R	Removable
A	Available
V	Valuable
E	Enjoyable
D	Disposable

The CRAVED model may be used as a means of judging just how attractive an object will be for a thief. A score can be assigned for each factor, and a high total CRAVED score would indicate that the object is more likely to be stolen. (Granted, it is not as simple as this, but the scoring system gives a relatively easy way of using the checklist.)

In the original work by Clarke (1999), disposability was considered to be one of the most important factors. Thieves prefer items which they can get rid of quickly and without fuss to a trusted 'fence', and will probably receive only a tenth or a fifth of the retail value of the item. Handling stolen goods is covered in 16.5.

TASK 3 Estimate how CRAVED the following articles might be:

- an iPad;
- an iPhone 7 or equivalent smartphone;
- a laptop;
- £642.89 in coins;
- a desktop computer with separate screen and keyboard;
- a CRT (non-flat-screen) television;
- a 2005 mobile phone;
- £350 in £50 notes;
- a manuscript copy of *The Lindisfarne Gospels*;
- 12 Japanese ivory *netsuke* dating from the late sixteenth century;
- a Rolex watch, engraved and dated; and
- an unframed oil painting by Rubens, measuring 23 × 19 cm.

Hot victims are perhaps the least studied and least understood part of the equation. Intuitively, it could be expected that old age, frailty, and naïvety would make a person more vulnerable than the average person, but there is little empirical evidence to support this, other than for distraction burglary (see the start of 16.4). However, studies have shown that once someone has been a victim of a certain type of crime on one occasion (particularly burglary), he/she is more likely than other people to be a victim again, even if all other variables are taken into account. Repeat victimization (if it occurs) generally takes place quite soon after the original incident. Often high crime rates and hot spots exist precisely because of repeat victimization (if not the same address, it could be the same street). Less well understood is the victimology surrounding e-enabled crime (see 21.2).

Why some people, or some premises, or some organizations should be repeat victims of crime is not always clear. There is some evidence (although not conclusive) that the original offender returns to the same places and reoffends. From a thief's perspective it may be that 'it worked once so it will work again'. Alternatively, it could be that a thief intentionally gives a house-owner time to claim on insurance for a valuable item, and then returns to steal the replacement (see eg Bowers *et al*, 1998). Whatever the explanation, we should emphasize that people who do not take elementary precautions after having been victims of crime on one occasion should not be surprised if they are targeted again.

Finally, we know that those who repeatedly victimize the same target tend to be more established lifestyle or career criminals. This all suggests that intelligence about the nature of a crime and why it is repeated in the same spot with the same victim, should help police forces predict where, when, and by whom the next attempt will be made (see eg Bowers *et al*, 2004 and more recently the claims made for 'PredPol', 2014).

> **TASK 4** Following what we have said about hot victims, what operational strategies do you think that the police should employ to help reduce repeat victimization?

Clearly, there are many possible interactions between hot spots, hot offenders, hot products, and hot victims. Hot offenders are more likely to want hot products. Hot victims are more likely to be in hot spots, and this is certainly the case for domestic burglary. Hot offenders are likely to target hot spots because, as we noted earlier, there are relatively easy opportunities for crime and relatively little chance of being caught. And of course the same offenders may return to burgle the same house again. It is hard to disentangle cause and effect, but the uneven distribution of crime cannot be ignored.

> **TASK 5** What practical policing implications can be derived from the following quotation, assuming that the argument being made is valid?
> Becoming criminal can be explained in much the same way we explain becoming a midwife or buying a car. (Wilson, 1996, p 307)

4.6   Crime Reduction

We often hear the terms 'crime prevention', 'crime reduction', and 'community safety' used both within policing and more widely. Ekblom (2001) draws subtle distinctions between these concepts, whereas Pease (2002) suggests they are different expressions of the same thing. We will use the terms interchangeably.

Crime prevention is a long-standing but often neglected policing priority. Today we recognize that all police officers have a crime prevention responsibility, and that this is not simply the role of a designated 'Crime Prevention Officer' (as was the case in the recent past). The police now have a better understanding of how preventative measures can be utilized to reduce crime, and this can be seen as an integral aspect of a police officer's duties alongside crime detection. Crime prevention can be used in a targeted and directed manner to reduce crime and to thereby free more police resources for dedicated proactive police work. Given the apparent huge growth in online crime (see Chapter 21), and the current very low rates of detection for this form of criminal activity, crime prevention measures also increasingly need to include cyber-security awareness.

Crime can be reduced to some extent through detecting crimes and imprisoning the offenders, with the result that fewer prospective offenders have the opportunity to commit crime. However, preventing crimes from happening in the first place represents a far more rational approach, and provides clear benefits to society. The targeted use of crime prevention is discussed in 3.9.2. It forms part of a problem-oriented approach to reducing crime, and is informed by routine-activity theory and the idea that there are three components of crime: the offender, the victim, and the location of a crime. Police officers should consider why a crime has occurred, and in this way preventative measures become more obvious. The police response becomes proactive as opposed to reactive.

The crime reduction agenda has also been bolstered by the move towards partnership approaches in policing (see 3.3), and the increasing emphasis on crime prevention has altered

Policing in Context

the role of the police. Crime prevention requires good intelligence and it is therefore important that police officers make the most of information from local intelligence officers. Police officers also need to share information with the local intelligence officers.

It is important that any intervention is properly evaluated (see 4.6.1 on evidence-based policing). To this end, policing in general (and crime reduction in particular) is increasingly subjected to research and evaluation, and the results of this research will help ensure that any claims used to justify preventative strategies are based on firm evidence (see eg Smith and Tilley, 2005).

4.6.1 Crime prevention and evidence-based policing

A number of professional bodies and academic authorities have promoted the idea of 'evidence-based policing' (EBP) as an approach to countering crime in the UK. The research is often carried out by police force personnel in collaboration with academic institutions (such as University College London or Cambridge University). Possibly in part as a response to funding cuts, EBP has received significant attention from the College of Policing and others in recent years, as a potential means of improving the efficiency of the police whilst reducing costs (see Sherman, 2013).

EBP has its origins in the more well-established evidence-based approaches adopted in other professions such as medicine, and adopts many of the characteristics of these approaches. It is concerned with basic research on what works best (when implemented properly under controlled conditions), and ongoing outcomes research where the issue being examined is evaluated over time. Put simply this means making changes to existing practices, and measuring the difference the changes have made to see whether or not they were effective.

EBP emphasizes the importance of utilizing a scientific approach to evaluating police practice. This would include conducting systematic reviews of existing evidence (as with the 'Cochrane Reviews' in the context of health care), and the use of 'randomized trials' and 'randomized control trials' (RCTs) and other statistical techniques to establish new knowledge. For example, RCTs were used recently as part of an EBP approach in the College of Policing evaluation of the impact of body-worn video on criminal justice outcomes of domestic abuse incidents (Owens *et al*, 2014). The authors found a 9 per cent increase in the use of criminal charges for domestic abuse incidents if the cameras were worn (a small but statistically significant difference). The use of RCTs in policing is increasing but is still relatively rare, despite its widespread application in other fields such as medical research.

4.6.1.1 Randomized control trials

An RCT is essentially an experiment that is conducted in a rigorous and scientific manner, and is considered the 'gold standard' in some forms of empirical research, depending on the type of study. Usually an RCT is used to attempt to gain knowledge about a 'population'. Here, a population is a scientific term that refers to the complete set of objects that share a common quality or characteristic (often called a 'variable') that we wish to discover more about. These 'objects' could be people, but this is by no means always the case. The quality or characteristic is normally something that can be measured. For example, we might be interested in the population of all victims of domestic abuse in the Greater London area in 2015. However, in practice we need to be as precise as possible about the population, so, for example, the exact meaning of 'victim', 'domestic abuse', and 'Greater London area' for this study would all need to be carefully defined. One characteristic all of the subjects (the victims) will probably have in common is that they will have suffered repeat victimization. We might want to find out if the police action (eg the attending officers providing a leaflet to the victim) seems to have an effect. To put it simply, does providing a leaflet seem to be mathematically correlated with a decreased, increased, or unchanged likelihood of further victimization? (This is often referred to as 'testing the hypothesis'.)

A sample of victims from the population will usually be studied, because normally the population itself is too large to form the basis of the experiment. This is the first scientific compromise in the experiment because the sample might not be representative; any effects seen for the sample might not hold true for the whole population. Indeed, the methods for selecting a sample, and just how confident we can be in generalizing from the sample to the population are themselves subjects of academic study. One particular problem in sampling (and often a

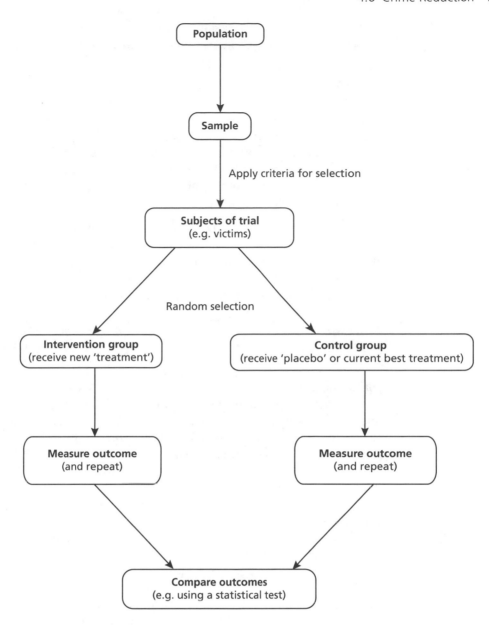

major problem in EBP) is that sample might be in part 'self-selecting'. For example, in our case the sample is likely to contain people who have had a more positive experience of interactions with the police, because they are more likely to agree to be part of the trial. They are probably not entirely representative of the population of victims of domestic abuse. For this reason, EBP researchers need to be particularly careful in extending sample-based conclusions to the underlying population from which the sample has been drawn.

After the sample from the population has been determined, the next thing is to decide who will take part in the RCT. It could be that we would like every member of the sample to be a subject of the experiment. However, there may be good reasons why we need to apply particular criteria for inclusion/exclusion—for example, some victims might be 'vulnerable adults' (see 13.7.3) who are not able to give informed consent. This is the second likely scientific compromise in the trial, because the application of the inclusion criteria might unwittingly introduce some form of bias to the outcome.

After the criteria have been applied we now have a new smaller experimental sample. The members of the sample (in our example, victims of domestic abuse) are then allocated to one of two groups: the 'intervention group', and the 'control group'. (Note that in some RCTs there could be more than two groups, for example there could be more than one type of leaflet, and we would be comparing three groups; 'no leaflet', 'leaflet A', and 'leaflet B'.) Selection for the groups is by random allocation using a 'double blind' method. It is random in that every member of the sample group (the 'subject') has an equal chance of being selected, and 'double blind' because neither the subject nor the researchers involved (the 'experimenters') know who has been allocated to which group. A double blind random allocation can even be automated (to avoid human intervention and therefore possible bias). In our example the allocation could occur automatically when the police force concerned responds to the report of domestic violence.

The 'intervention group' then receives the new treatment and the 'control group' does not. In medical trials the control group would receive an inert placebo or current best treatment, so, in our example, the subjects in the control group would receive the usual approach. For a proper double blind trial, it is important that both the subjects and the experimenters (which in our case will include the police officers implementing the new approach with the treatment group) are 'blind' to whether the 'treatment' or the placebo is being administered. But obviously, it is often almost impossible for police experimenters to be unaware of whether they are employing the treatment or the 'placebo'. This undermines the validity of any conclusions drawn, and presents major difficulties for RCTs in EBP.

For both the intervention group and the control group the outcome(s) of the trial are measured. This is often in terms of measuring a numerical quantity, such as the number of times a particular event has occurred or the average rate at which it has occurred. In our example we would be measuring rates of re-victimization for the intervention group and the control group. (As with other aspects of the RCT, we would need to carefully define from the outset what exactly is meant by 'rates of re-victimization' and how to measure them.) Note that in many trials in medicine the outcomes for each group are then measured again after a period of time, maybe several times, to check that any effect of the new treatment does not simply fade away over time. However, this approach is rarely adopted in RCTs within EBP.

The culmination of the RCT is the comparison between the outcome for the intervention group and the outcome for the control group for the particular variable. Often this means comparing two numerical values (such as 16 per cent and 22 per cent). The two values are very likely to be different, but we need to know whether the difference is big enough for us to conclude that the outcomes are significantly different, or whether the difference could be simply due to chance. Deciding whether a difference is significant (or not) is not a matter of judgement (even if the researcher is very experienced and qualified). Instead, the decision is made using a predetermined statistical test for significance. There are hundreds of statistical tests available but only a small number will be appropriate for the particular RCT. Researchers are trained in choosing the appropriate test (it will be part of the design of the RCT from the outset), and then interpreting the results. The so-called 't-test' and 'chi-squared test' are often used, but the correct choice depends on the nature of the data collected, the design of the RCT and so on. The result of a statistical test used to assess the difference in outcomes of an RCT is often stated as a level of significance (usually cited as 'p', and values of 0.05 and 0.01 are common). The p value is essentially a judgement on how likely it is that a difference can be put down to chance. If $p = 0.01$ (which is the same as 1 per cent), this would mean that the observed difference between the groups would be seen by chance in only one in a hundred cases, that is the difference is unlikely to occur simply as a chance effect, so it is likely the difference is 'real'. A rule of thumb is that the smaller the value of p the more certain we can be that a genuine effect has been measured.

4.6.1.2   Implementing EBP practice and research

Systematic evidence reviews and RCTs are normally expensive and time-consuming to carry out, and, as yet (apart from local examples such as reducing crime in a number of supermarkets in South Wales), there have been few reliable outcomes from EBP initiatives in the UK that have directly affected operational police practice. The RCTs employed sometimes fall short of the 'gold standard' adopted in other professions—for example, by employing quasi random techniques for selection rather than true random methods, and failing to implement a 'double blind' approach. There is a particular problem with premature over-generalization of results from samples to populations.

Research into EBP can result in best practice guidelines, new authorized professional practice or Codes of Practice being laid down in law. The College of Policing are actively working with police forces, Police and Crime Commissioners, academic partners, and national policing leads to produce research on the priority areas for policing (College of Policing, 2016b). The College of Policing have made EBP a part of their *National Policing Vision 2016* declaring: 'A greater emphasis on evidence-based practice will equip the workforce with the advanced skills needed to prevent crime.' They are working with identified partners in a number of different ways,

- through the 'What Works Centre for Crime Reduction' (part of the College of Policing) where they review, collate, and share the best available evidence for crime reduction;
- by embedding the best available evidence into standards and practice;
- by building capacity for research across policing by including evidence-based approaches in training, and by supporting forces to help build partnerships with higher and further education. This includes training officers about the principles of how to undertake evidence reviews (at 'evidence-based camps' events) and adding a new unit on EBP to the Certificate of Knowledge in Policing;
- through the Crime Reduction Toolkit, which can help raise awareness of evidence derived from research, and the importance of using appropriate and robust research methods.

As the Rt Hon Theresa May MP said (when she was Home Secretary): 'It is in the public interest to show that what the police are doing is really working' (Home Secretary, 2012).

4.6.2 Approaches to crime reduction

The new emphasis on integrating crime prevention into everyday police work means that police officers must continually anticipate, recognize, and assess the risk of criminal activity. Measures can then be taken to reduce the risk. These measures could be straightforward, for example simply providing the public with crime prevention advice. At other times, a more concerted effort is required to reduce the crime risk.

4.6.2.1 Reducing the opportunities for crime

An unlit pathway provides criminals with an appropriate crime location. A police officer needs to be able to evaluate what short-term measures can be taken to reduce the criminal opportunity (for example increase the guardianship of the unlit pathway by increasing police patrols), but the police must also ensure that a longer term solution is provided, for example by contacting the local council to ensure the lighting problem is addressed.

Routine-activity theory (RAT) and rational-choice theory are often used to explain the causes of crime (see 4.3). Using these different factors, we can suggest that preventative techniques could be organized under three headings: increasing the effort (eg target hardening); increasing the risks (eg CCTV); and reducing the rewards (eg marking property). Pease (2002) adds a fourth heading: 'reducing the excuses'. The relative significance of each of these strategies depends upon the particular crime in question: which strategy is most likely to have the greatest deterrent impact on the potential criminal? These ideas are illustrated in Task 6.

TASK 6 Consider the following scenarios and identify whether increasing the effort, increasing the risk, or reducing the reward would be the most effective preventative measure. (We acknowledge that, to some extent, all three would be appropriate but try to identify the one that you think addresses the problem most directly.)

1. There have been a number of thefts from vehicles in a supermarket car park. The cars targeted have had valuable items stolen from them.
2. A shop is being repeatedly targeted at night by a group of known drug addicts.
3. Small amounts of money are being stolen by a member of staff from within a bank.

Routine-activity theory suggests some other approaches that may be used in crime reduction: for example, ensuring that motivated offenders are not left unobserved where there are easy criminal targets, eg goods that could be stolen. The number of motivated offenders does not have to be reduced in order to reduce crime; they simply need to be monitored more closely. Goods could also be redesigned so they are more difficult to sell on. To some extent routine-activity theory can also be applied to help reduce the opportunities for online crime as well as the more 'well-established' crimes that involve physical locations, although some aspects of RAT are more applicable than others (Leukfeldt and Var, 2016).

4.6.2.2 The prevention of hot spots

The persistent presence of police officers, PCSOs, or local authority wardens would undoubtedly have a deterrent effect, but this cannot be sustained for long due to the cost. CCTV cameras are a possible short-term solution, especially if coordinated with police action on the ground such as 'blitzes' on pickpockets, for example.

A longer-term and better solution is to 'design out' crime, for example by installing carefully designed walkways and better street lighting. Intelligence (see Chapter 23) is also likely to be an important part of any approach to dealing with hot spots. Analysts will consider the types of crime, the times when they occur, the sorts of people who commit those crimes and the seasonal impact (if any) upon the nature of the crime. A detailed understanding and taking appropriate measures may lead to the cooling of a hot spot. Dealing with crime hotspots which occur in cyberspace normally requires the involvement of a number of national agencies and private companies (such as ISPs).

4.6.2.3 Crime prevention advice

Crime prevention is the responsibility of all police officers, but a specialist Crime Prevention Officer (CPO) can provide further advice. The crime should be considered from the perspective of the victim, the offender, and the location. Pertinent questions can then be asked about why a crime has occurred, and this can help provide the basis for practical solutions. The advice can be tailored to specific contexts, for example, regarding the most suitable locks, lighting, and other basic security measures in a home where a burglary has recently taken place. There is also specific need to tailor crime prevention messages aimed at young people, children and those at particular risk within online environments. The lessons learnt during the investigation of one particular crime incident should also be used to help prevent future criminal activities.

Police officers can encourage communities as a whole to become involved in implementing effective crime prevention strategies, for example Neighbourhood Watch schemes (see 3.9.1.4), and Street Watch. Neighbourhood Policing Teams (sometimes known as Safer Neighbourhood Teams (SNTs)), Crime Prevention Panels (CPPs), and Community Safety Partnerships (CSPs), all provide a local focus for crime prevention measures alongside the national Crimestoppers Trust, which works in collaboration with the police.

4.6.2.4 Displacement

Crime prevention can lead to crime displacement: crimes are not prevented, but merely displaced to other places or to a later time. New types of crime may also occur through criminal innovation (see the following list). Displacement is often explained as a consequence of criminality: those with a disposition to commit crimes will adapt and find different ways in which to realize their criminal disposition. The following types of displacement have been identified.

- **Temporal displacement:** the crime takes place at a later time. As an example, consider the depot that introduces a security guard overnight to counter a string of night-time burglaries. However, there is a one-hour gap between the security guard finishing and the day staff arriving, so the criminals choose this time to commit the offence.
- **Spatial displacement:** the crime happens somewhere else. In this case imagine that a high police presence is introduced in Area 1 to curb incidents of anti-social behaviour from a group of teenagers. The teenagers simply move to Area 2 and behave in the same way.
- **Displacement by type of crime:** the criminals turn to different crimes. Suppose that the local council introduces better street lighting on an estate prone to street robberies. The number of robberies falls but the number of burglaries increases in the area.
- **Displacement by innovation:** the criminals become better at what they do. An example is the increasing use of credit cards; people no longer carry large amounts of cash. This reduces the cash reward for muggers but some turn to using stolen credit cards, thereby gaining access to even larger sums of money.

Pease (1997) has suggested that the extent of displacement is often exaggerated, and that the issue is raised on ideological rather than empirical grounds, as an excuse for taking no action. He also argues that displacement is never likely to be 100 per cent, and illustrates ways in which displacement can be an advantage. For example, it might be beneficial to move a crime from one area to another to reduce its overall impact on society, or to change the type of crime committed. For example, if prostitutes are operating on the street in a residential area where many children live, it seems likely that a high police presence would move the prostitutes on to another area. Would this be beneficial or not? If the prostitutes move to a non-residential area it would clearly reduce the concern that children would be affected, although this might need to be balanced against a separate concern for the safety of the prostitutes. Some of the prostitutes might innovate and use more discreet means of operating, while others might turn to other potentially lucrative activities, for example shoplifting. The effects of displacement can be predicted and then compared with the effect in practice. As Pease puts it, displacement is positive as long as 'the deflected crime causes less harm and misery than the original crime' (Pease, 1997, p 978).

4.7 **Answers to Tasks**

TASK 1 There are many different explanations for what registers as a sensational crime in public imagination and the media. A sensational crime is often one which has something out of the ordinary, something different, even a little outrageous, to make it stand out.

Some violent crimes involving children may feature highly in the media and thus public consciousness (possibly because many of us are expected to identify with the parents of the victim, or because the vulnerability of a child evokes sympathy and pity in us), as may crimes in which single young women are involved. (There is some suggestion of an ethnic bias in reporting crimes of this type, with victims of ethnic minorities less likely to receive extensive media coverage than their white counterparts. However, this discussion is beyond the scope of this Handbook.)

Crimes which tend not to make the headlines, unless really bizarre or huge, are the so-called victimless crimes such as defrauding a large company or embezzling insurance money. There are victims of course for any crime (because that helps to define the nature of a crime), but what frightens a community or spreads anxiety is the thought that some sort of terror or dread is stalking the streets. A series of rapes can do this, especially in a small community like a town or at a college, and the abduction of a child also causes widespread concern.

TASK 2 There are a large number of possible answers, and we provide some suggestions here. The answer for 'universal crimes' is somewhat speculative.

Crimes	Examples
Universal	Theft, murder, and rape
In the UK now, but not 100 years ago	Stalking, computer crimes (eg hacking), and some types of outdoor night-time music and dancing events
In other parts of the world, but not in the UK	Adultery (Nigeria), consuming alcohol (Saudi Arabia), keeping African pygmy hedgehogs (some states of the USA)

TASK 3 There is a difference between intrinsic value and 'CRAVED'. The thieves would probably leave the coins behind because they are bulky and very heavy, but they would pocket the £350 in notes immediately. The PC would probably be left; again it is bulky and heavy. The iPad, iPhone7, and the Rolex would be easily pocketed for selling on. However, traffic in particular electronic goods is often short-lived as it is often the next-generation goods that the fences demand; the laptop may be old and heavy, and a 2005 mobile phone would yield no return. Apple Inc have introduced additional security measures in recent years to increase the difficulty of 'fencing' stolen iPads and iPhones. The Rolex might present problems because any engraving can help trace an item, but in a snatching or mugging the thieves would not stop to check. The engraving and date would reduce the price, so the fence might decide to file out the engraving.

The other items are small but would be very difficult to sell on. *The Gospels* and the Rubens' painting would be worth several million pounds, but they would be very difficult to fence on any art market. (However, organized drugs importers and traffickers have used valuable art such as paintings or sculptures as 'cash' for their transactions—the more so since the Proceeds of Crime Act 2002 made depositing large amounts of cash in a bank account subject to scrutiny and investigation.)

The *netsuke* (small carved figures) would be worth several thousand pounds each, but only through an expert dealer, and the average fence is unlikely to know what they are. That said, some thieves steal to order and might target such items specifically, but these are not likely to be volume criminals working on hot spots.

TASK 4 In this task you were asked to consider police strategies to combat repeat victimization. Some useful suggestions are included in the Police research paper, 'Biting Back: Tackling Repeat Burglary and Car Crime' available online. The popular phrase, 'once bitten, twice shy' suggests that we become more vigilant after an unpleasant incident such as being the victim of a crime, but this will not necessarily help! As we suggested in terms of burglary, by far the best predictor of future victimization is whether we have been a victim in the recent past. The police should ensure the householder receives advice on reducing the vulnerability of their property.

TASK 5 The quotation assumes that criminal behaviour will follow a rational pattern, thus hot products will be targeted by certain people in hot spots, and markets will exist for the products of crime. The predictability of this should allow the police to anticipate appropriate points at which to intervene.

TASK 6

1. Reducing the reward. The fact that the cars targeted have valuables on show suggests that the offenders are looking for easy rewards. Increasing the risk by introducing better lighting, CCTV cameras, or security guards would also be beneficial, but the most cost-effective measure is likely to be encouraging people not to leave valuables in the car.
2. Increasing the effort. We can assume that these particular offenders are desperate and therefore unlikely to be overly concerned at being caught (increasing the risk) and will be prepared to take risks for small rewards (reducing the reward). Therefore, making it physically difficult to break in by installing metal bars and stronger locks is likely to be the most effective measure.
3. Increasing the risk. The rewards are already limited and making it more difficult to take the money is impractical because of the need for employees to handle money. Therefore, increasing the risk, for example by installing CCTV, is likely to have a deterrent effect because the employees have a lot to lose if they are caught. List three crimes that would appear to be universal.

5 The Criminal Justice System in England and Wales

5.1 Introduction

In the UK the concept of the criminal justice system refers to the law, law enforcement, and dealing with transgressions of the law. The criminal justice system (the CJS) in England and Wales includes the police, the courts of law, the National Offender Management Service (NOMS), the Youth Justice Board, and the Crown Prosecution Service (CPS).

Both students on pre-join programmes and trainee police officers will need to understand a variety of different types of law and court procedures. A number of situations that involve specific types of legislation will be addressed in more detail in subsequent chapters (such as criminal and family law regarding domestic violence in 13.6), but here we will concentrate on the general aspects; how laws are made, some of the different branches of law, the principles behind criminal law, and the courts system. The system used by the courts in England and Wales is adversarial, whereas elsewhere in Europe (eg in France) the system is inquisitorial.

The adversarial model requires that a person, the defendant, is accused of an offence and is tried by a court (usually in open session), and that the defendant's guilt must be proved beyond reasonable doubt. The prosecution is conducted on behalf of the Crown, often referred to in written case law as 'R' ('Regina' or 'Rex', the Queen or King respectively, depending whether a King or a Queen is on the throne when the case is heard). The Crown Prosecutors and Senior Crown Prosecutors (SCP) are lawyers employed by the CPS to review, and when appropriate, prosecute cases investigated by the police. Associate Prosecutors (who are not lawyers) may also perform some of these functions at the level of the magistrates' courts. Crown Advocates deal almost exclusively with cases at Crown Court and Court of Appeal, and provide the CPS with advice on complex legal matters. The defendant is normally represented by a solicitor and in some circumstances by a barrister. They are known as the 'defence counsel' or 'the defence' (see Chapter 27 for more details on these roles). In an inquisitorial system (not used in England and Wales) the defendant is questioned by a judge during trial; correspondingly, the role taken by the lawyers in court is of a much lower profile.

Litigation in court is not always the best way to solve disputes between parties. Disadvantages include the costs involved with the judicial system, the length of the process, and the fact that the outcome may be perceived as unduly simplistic (there being a clear designated 'winner' and 'loser' within an adversarial system). Restorative justice can be used instead (see 10.13.2), and at its simplest is when minor crimes and incidents are dealt with on the spot by police officers. It can also involve a more formal procedure at a restorative meeting.

5.2 The Law in England and Wales

An understanding of the law in England and Wales is an important aspect of the police officer's epistemic authority (see 3.5.1), and is essential in relation to many of the NOS elements underpinning the Certificate in Knowledge of Policing and the Diploma in Policing. Law also features extensively during most Operational Modules and in LPG 1 and LPG 2.

You may have heard law referred to as: common law, statute law, case law, Acts of Parliament, Statutory Instruments, and by-laws. These all interrelate in a number of ways.

Common law (also known as judge-made law) can be traced back to the Norman invasion of Britain in the eleventh century. Local courts made decisions that were then passed by word of mouth to other courts, which with time became accepted by other courts throughout the country, creating a 'binding precedent'. Examples of common law offences include murder, manslaughter, perverting the course of justice, and escape from lawful custody. In the UK no new common law offences are created now, apart from the setting of precedents by the courts when interpreting existing law.

Statute law is the foundation of the current legal system in England and Wales. These are primary sources of law, and can be accessed electronically via the UK Statute Law Database at www.legislation.gov.uk. Bills or 'draft law' are needed to create new legislation; ministry officials write a proposal and submit it to the Houses of Parliament for a decision. If accepted it is given Royal Assent before becoming an Act of Parliament. For example, the Criminal Justice and Courts Bill was introduced in House of Commons in February 2014 for discussion and received Royal Assent just over one year later, becoming the Criminal Justice and Courts Act 2015. A regularly revised list of bills currently before parliament for consideration is available at <http://services.parliament.uk/bills/>.

Case law helps to establish the precise meaning of legislation. Decisions made by higher courts about legislation are then accepted by lower courts throughout the country. This 'doctrine of precedent' sets out how the legislation should be used by a court in similar circumstances. Although the specific circumstances of the case might change (referred to as *obiter dicta*), the court should use the same reasoning (or *ratio decidendi*) that was used by previous courts to reach a decision. An example of this would be the decisions made about identification evidence in the case *R v Turnbull* [1976] 3 All ER 549. (Note the system for referencing cases: 'R' stands for Regina (the Crown as prosecutor), 'v' for versus, and 'Turnbull' is the name of the defendant. This case can be found in Volume 3 of the 1976 All England Law Reports on p 549.) When case law has been used this is indicated as 'by way of case stated'.

Acts of Parliament are divided into sections containing, for example, definitions, offences, powers of arrest, exemptions, and interpretations of words and expressions used. An Act often includes technical details such as fines and penalties which may need frequent revision and updating. These will be provided in the form of Statutory Instruments such as Orders, Regulations, and Rules, and are often left to government ministers to reduce the pressure on parliamentary time.

Statutory Instruments (SIs) allow the details of an Act to be revised without using parliamentary procedures. They are as much part of the law of England and Wales as is the main body of the Act of Parliament. As with Acts of Parliament, SIs are given a number as well as a title, 'Criminal Justice (Electronic Monitoring) (Responsible Person) Order 2014' (SI 2014 No 163). The Home Secretary used this SI to enable private companies such as Capita and G4S to take responsibility for the electronic monitoring of people released on condition of bail or as part of a youth rehabilitation order, curfew, or community order.

By-laws are usually local laws which have been made by a local authority and approved by a Secretary of State of the government. They normally deal with local matters, for example dogs on leads in recreational areas. They can also refer to charters, which are documents created under a generic form of legislation to regulate certain activities within an organization. Examples of charters include Trades Union charters and the Department of Health Information Charter.

TASK 1 The Road Vehicle Lighting Regulations 1989 (SI 1989 No 1796) were introduced under s 41 of the Road Traffic Act 1988. Find out what regs 11–22 cover in relation to motor vehicles. (Use *Blackstone's Police Manual: Volume 3 Road Policing*, the internet, or other publications to look this up.)

5.3 **Principles of Criminal Liability**

Trainee police officers will of course be involved in non-crime incidents—for example, policing a picket line established during a strike—and will need to consider the relevant legislation. However, most of the law relevant to the first few years of service undoubtedly is of the criminal, rather than the civil form. Indeed, the list of subjects in the IPLDP LPG modules is dominated by criminal law.

We begin with the notion of 'criminal liability'—how do we *know* and then prove that a person has broken the law? There are two elements of criminal liability:

1. The *actus reus*—the action the defendant carried out, which must be proved beyond reasonable doubt (see 5.3.1).
2. The *mens rea*—guilty mindset that the defendant had at the time the action was taken, which also must be proved; that is, that the defendant intended to commit the crime. However, there are some exceptions to this (see 5.3.2).

Although the use of Latin can seem off-putting and exclusionary, these terms are commonly used in policing and so are worth remembering. We will now look at these two building blocks of criminal liability in more detail.

5.3.1 *Actus reus*

This is about a person's actions (including an omission or a lack of action). If a person is to be found guilty of a criminal offence, then it must be proved that he/she either:

- acted criminally in some way: for example committed murder;
- omitted to do an act which brought about a criminal outcome: for example knowing that someone was going to commit a crime but doing nothing to stop it or report it;
- caused a state of affairs to happen: for example, knowingly drinking a lot of alcohol and being found drunk and incapable at the wheel of a car; or
- failed to do an act which was required, and which brought about a criminal outcome: for example, by failing to ensure that a vehicle was roadworthy when offering it for hire, this leads to the criminal outcome of someone driving a car that is not in a safe condition to be driven.

5.3.2 *Mens rea*

This is about a person's thoughts or state of mind. Although the Latin term appears to be very narrow in its meaning, in reality there are a number of thought processes and levels of intent that satisfy the requirements of many offences, other than just having guilty knowledge. You will find these states of mind listed under different terms in a number of offences. The most common words are:

- 'dishonestly' such as for theft;
- 'wilfully' such as for neglect of children;
- 'recklessly' as in for causing criminal damage; and
- 'with intent' as in burglary with intent to steal.

The degree of *mens rea* in criminal offences varies between more serious situations where a person deliberately committed an offence, and less serious situations where a person failed to take appropriate care to avoid the criminal outcome of their action or inaction (usually called negligence). The level of intention is assessed by comparing the actions of the defendant with those of a hypothetical 'reasonable' or average person under the circumstances of the alleged offence. For more serious situations (eg murder and 'wounding or inflicting grievous bodily harm with intent') the law requires that the suspect has a certain intent or *mens rea*. This would also include offences for which there is an ulterior purpose other than the main criminal act, for example when a defendant is charged with burglary with intent (see 16.4.1). Here, it would have to be proved that the defendant not only intended to enter a building as a trespasser, but also intended to inflict grievous bodily harm, cause damage, or steal.

'Strict liability' offences are those for which a *mens rea* is not required (or a diminished *mens rea* is sufficient) to convict someone for breaking the law. In such cases only the guilty act (*actus reus*) needs to have occurred. Examples of strict liability offences include:

- paying for sexual services of a prostitute who is being subjected to force (s 14 of the Policing and Crime Act 2009, see 17.5.2)—it is irrelevant whether the suspect knows about the force; and
- the sale of faulty goods (s 14 of the Sale of Goods Act 1979)—it is irrelevant whether the suspect knows the goods are faulty.

Strict liability offences are usually less serious and often correspond to statutory violations, but they can also include offences where the action itself is considered so dangerous or socially unacceptable that there is no need to prove the offender's intention. It is not always clear whether a *mens rea* is required. Decisions concerning strict liability may be ultimately left to the courts.

5.3.3 Burden of proof

How do we prove that a person is guilty of a criminal offence? The law tells us that:

> throughout the web of the English criminal law one golden thread is always to be seen: that it is the duty of the prosecution to prove the prisoner's guilt. (*Woolmington v DPP* [1935] AC 462)

Therefore, in criminal proceedings the onus is on the prosecution to prove the guilt of the defendant, not on the defendant to prove his or her innocence. And furthermore, the degree of proof required for criminal cases is 'beyond reasonable doubt'. This was famously expressed by Geoffrey Lawrence (cited in Johnston and Hutton, 2005, p 133) in the following way:

> The possibility of guilt is not enough, suspicion is not enough, probability is not enough, likelihood is not enough. A criminal matter is not a question of balancing probabilities and deciding in favour of probability, a conviction must be formed beyond reasonable doubt that the accused is guilty, and this is done on the basis of the evidence provided in court.

5.4 Human Rights

The concept of human rights and the responsibilities of police officers in the preservation and maintenance of those rights runs throughout this Handbook. Human rights legislation stresses an individual's entitlement to expect certain fundamental rights as part of their social contract with the state and other forms of authority.

The protection of human rights in the UK has been significantly affected by the Human Rights Act 1998 (HRA) which came into force in the year 2000. The HRA took s 1 of the European Convention on the Protection of Human Rights and Fundamental Freedoms (which came into force in 1953, referred to as the ECHR) and, to a large extent, copied it into domestic law. There are several important features of human rights legislation under the HRA:

- all new statute law must be compatible with the rights, but there is no retrospective effect on existing law (*R v Lambert*, 2001);
- an individual may take a public authority to a UK court (rather than directly to the European Court of Human Rights) if the authority has not acted in a manner compatible with the rights;
- UK courts are required to interpret all legislation in a way which is compatible with the Convention's rights, so far as is possible (s 3); and
- public authorities (eg government and the police) cannot act in a way which is incompatible with the Convention.

Note, however, that although the HRA has no automatic retrospective effect, all new Bills from the government are examined by the Parliament's Joint Committee on Human Rights to check compatibility with human rights legislation. For example, at the time of writing the Extremism Bill, the Investigatory Powers Draft Bill, and the Policing and Criminal Justice Bill are being assessed by this Committee, as there are concerns that they may pose significant issues with respect to human rights.

All ten of the Diploma in Policing assessed units include the requirement to address the need to 'Promote equality and value diversity' in the relevant context. For example, the assessed unit concerned with providing an initial response to incidents has an assessment criterion stating that the learner must be able to identify the legislation, policies, procedures, codes of practice, and/or guidelines that relate to race, diversity, and human rights when responding to an incident. The corresponding Certificate in Knowledge of Policing unit 'Knowledge of providing an initial response to policing incidents' also requires knowledge of such matters.

5.4.1 What are the rights?

The rights are listed within the articles of the Human Rights Act 1998. Each right is considered as absolute (underlined), limited (L), or qualified (Q).

Article number	Article title
2	<u>Right to life</u>
3	<u>Prohibition of torture</u>
4	<u>Prohibition of slavery and forced labour</u>
5	Right to liberty and security (L)
6	Right to a fair trial (L)
7	<u>No punishment without law</u>
8	Right to respect for private and family life (Q)
9	Freedom of thought, conscience, and religion (Q)
10	Freedom of expression (Q)
11	Freedom of assembly and association (Q)
12	Right to marry (L)
14	Prohibition of discrimination (L)

The **Absolute rights** of an individual cannot be restricted by the interests of the community as a whole.

Limited rights do not apply in all circumstances and are limited in the articles which contain them—for example the right to liberty (part of Article 5) does not apply if the detention is lawful, such as after arrest. However, although the right to liberty may be limited, a lawfully arrested person would still have the right to security under Article 5. A further example occurs within Article 6, where there is a right for both the public and the press to have access to any court hearing. This right is subject to certain restrictions in the interests of morality, public order, national security, or where the interests of those under 18, or the privacy of the parties require the exclusion of the press and public.

Qualified rights relate to matters where interference by the public authority is permissible if it is in the public interest and can be qualified, for example to prevent disorder or crime, for public safety, or for national security. However, a public authority (such as the police) may only interfere with a qualified right if the interference is:

- lawful and is part of existing common or statute law (see 5.2), such as the power to stop and search;
- made for one of the specifically listed permissible acts in the interests of the public, such as in order to prevent disorder for public safety; or
- necessary in a democratic society because the wider interests of the community as a whole often have to be balanced against the rights of an individual (but it must still be proportionate).

There are certain aspects of the HRA 1998 which may seem strange when compared to other Acts of Parliament (eg Article 1 does not contain any rights and Article 13 does not even exist). This is partly because the HRA is a transposition of s 1 of the ECHR into domestic law.

5.4.2 Applying the Human Rights Act to everyday policing

A police officer should consider the following questions in relation to an individual or group before 'interfering' with another person's qualified rights:

1. Are my actions lawful? Is there common or statute law to support my interference with their rights?
2. Are my actions permissible? Am I permitted to interfere with their rights because it is in support of a duty, such as preventing crime?
3. Are my actions necessary? Do the needs of the many outweigh the needs of the few; in other words, must I take into account the interests of the community and balance one individual's rights against another's?
4. Are my actions proportionate? Having considered everything, will my actions be excessive or could I do something less intrusive and more in proportion to the outcome I need to achieve?

During initial police training mnemonics may be used with regard to these questions, for example:

- **JAPAN** (Justifiable, Accountable, Proportionate, And Necessary) and
- **PLAN** (Proportionality, Legality, Accountability, and Necessity).

The ability to consider these matters is assessed in the Certificate in Knowledge of Policing, which includes the assessment criteria to be able to 'Understand the legislation, national guidelines and personal responsibilities that relate to the use of police powers when dealing with suspects' (part of the unit 'Knowledge of using policing powers to deal with suspects').

> **TASK 2** How would a trainee police officer seek to follow the principles of equality, diversity, and anti-discrimination practice?

5.5 The Criminal Justice System in Practice

Once an alleged crime has been reported, there will be an investigation at some level, mostly conducted by the police. The extent and nature of an investigation will inevitably vary with the circumstances (covered in more detail in Chapters 10 and 24). A subsequent prosecution is usually conducted by the CPS on behalf of the Crown (the state). Depending on the seriousness, the cases are dealt with at different courts (see 5.5.2). The defendant may choose to represent him/herself but it is more usual to use a solicitor or barrister. The courts may be assisted by Social Services and the Probation Service. Investigation, prosecution, and court procedures are covered in more detail in Chapters 23–27.

Certificate in Knowledge of Policing students will need to demonstrate underpinning knowledge and understanding about the UK criminal justice system in many of the units. Trainee police officers will obviously come into contact with the criminal justice system. Indeed, in many forces a criminal justice placement forms part of IPLDP Phase 2 of training, and this provides an opportunity for meeting other professionals working within the system. Many of them will also be on education and training programmes linked to NOS elements determined by Skills for Justice, as is the Diploma in Policing. A number of the Diploma assessed units such as 'Conduct priority and volume investigations' relate to carrying out investigations, preparing cases, and appearing in court. The Police Action Checklist (PAC) heading 'Finalize investigations' also requires a trainee officer to demonstrate the ability to 'adhere to court procedures' and 'give evidence at court' before being declared fit to undertake Independent Patrol.

5.5.1 The classification of criminal offences

Offences are classified according to their seriousness and the level of court at which they can be tried. The three main categories of offence are summary-only offences, indictment-only offences, and either-way offences.

Summary-only offences are normally dealt with in the magistrates' court where they are governed by Part 37 of the Criminal Procedure Rules 2010. Examples of summary-only offences are common assault and being drunk and disorderly. The Crown Court may however deal with a summary offence in certain circumstances. For example, there are a small number of summary-only offences that can be added to the indictment (the formal document that sets out the offences to be heard in the Crown Court) along with connected indictable or either-way offences. These are listed under s 40 of the Criminal Justice Act 1988, and include common assault, taking a vehicle without consent, and driving while disqualified. Summary-only offences must be charged within 6 months of the offence having taken place.

Indictment-only offences are the most serious cases and can only be dealt with in a Crown Court. Examples include: murder, manslaughter, causing death by dangerous driving, rape, robbery, aggravated burglary, and wounding with intent.

Either-way offences can be tried in a magistrates' court or a Crown Court. Examples of either-way offences include theft, obtaining property by deception and assault occasioning actual bodily harm. Certain either-way offences can only be tried at a magistrates' court, for example criminal damage or aggravated vehicle taking with a cost below £5,000 and low-level shoplifting of goods worth less than £200 (ss 22–22A of the Magistrates' Court Act 1980). At the first hearing in the magistrates' court the defendant will be asked whether he/she wishes to enter a plea. In the event of a 'not guilty plea', or if the defendant chooses to 'withhold' his/her plea, a 'mode of trial' hearing will take place to decide where the trial will be held. During the hearing the crown prosecutor will make representations about where the case should be heard. The defence may object to an either-way offence going to the Crown Court, but the magistrates make the final decision. However, the defendant can 'elect' to be tried by judge and jury, and the magistrates cannot decide to the contrary. If the defendant enters a guilty plea at the first hearing in the magistrates' court then the magistrates will consider whether their sentencing powers are sufficient to deal with the matter. If not, they will commit the case to the Crown Court for sentence.

The classification for each criminal offence and its mode of trial and penalty can be found either by reference to primary sources—that is, the legal texts themselves (eg through the Home Office website) or secondary sources, such as Blackstone's Police Manuals. For example, the relevant legislation for handling stolen goods is in s 22 of the Theft Act 1968. This, in conjunction with Sch 1 and s 32 of the Magistrates' Court Act 1980, states that handling stolen goods is triable either way, with a maximum penalty of 14 years' imprisonment on indictment, or if tried summarily six months' imprisonment and/or a fine.

TASK 3 Use an appropriate textbook or the internet to determine for the offence of robbery:

- the relevant Act, including section;
- the mode of trial; and
- the maximum penalty for a person found guilty.

5.5.2   The courts

The structure of the courts system in England and Wales relates to the nature of the matters in hand and the seriousness of the cases handled by each category of court.

The diagram shows some key elements in the relationships between the various types of court in England and Wales. The courts on the left side of the diagram deal with criminal cases while those on the right deal with civil cases. Police officers are only occasionally required to give evidence at a court dealing with civil cases, for example an officer who attended a road traffic collision in which a pedestrian was seriously injured might be called as a witness in a civil court case in which claims for damages were in dispute.

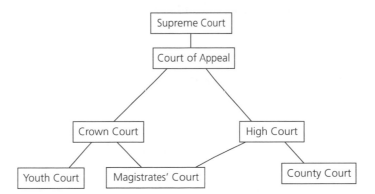

The role of the courts that deal with criminal cases is our primary concern here.

The magistrates' courts are where all criminal cases start, regardless of classification. Around 95 per cent of all criminal cases are concluded in the magistrates' court. Most summary matters stay in the magistrates' courts along with appropriate either-way offences. The more serious either-way offences and indictable-only offences tend to be sent straight to the Crown Court following the first hearing. Magistrates deal with a variety of hearings, for example, applications for bail, guilty pleas, and sentencing, not guilty pleas, trial management hearings, and trials. There are about 330 magistrates' courts across the UK.

Hearings in the magistrates' courts are presided over by a District Judge (a qualified lawyer) or a bench of three magistrates (sometime referred to as the Justices of the Peace). Magistrates are lay people drawn from the local community, and not professional judges or lawyers. Magistrates' courts also hear non-criminal cases, such as family law disputes. The Specialist Domestic Violence Courts are held in magistrates' courts.

There are limits to the sentences that can be used at a magistrates' court. The maximum custodial sentence is 6 months per individual offence, with an absolute maximum of two consecutive

6-month sentences totalling 12 months (s 154 of the Criminal Justice Act 2003). Fines at magistrates' courts cannot exceed £5,000. For either-way offences (see 5.5.1), the offender can be sent to the Crown Court for sentence if the magistrates believe that a more severe sentence is appropriate. If a defendant is dissatisfied with a verdict from the magistrates' courts, he/she may appeal to the Crown Court for matters of fact and law, and to the High Court for matters of law only.

A **youth court** is normally used for defendants aged between 10 and 17 years (unless being charged jointly with an adult or for murder or manslaughter). The procedures are very similar to those in a magistrates' court but are adapted to take account of the age of the defendant, and are not open to the public. A particular courtroom within a magistrates' court is often formally designated as a youth court. Appeals from a youth court generally go to the Crown Court.

The **Crown Court** is a first instance court (ie not an appeal court) for more serious criminal cases, including indictable offences such as murder, rape, or robbery. There are about 90 Crown Courts across the UK. They also try appeals from magistrates' courts, and 'either-way' cases (see 5.5.1) referred by magistrates' courts. The trial takes place before a judge and a jury, and members of the public (see Chapter 27). Police officers and other relevant experts may have to attend court as witnesses. On matters of fact and law, it is possible to appeal from the Crown Court to the Criminal Division of the Court of Appeal.

The **High Court** is, alongside the Crown Court and the Appeal Courts, part of the higher courts of justice in England and Wales. It hears cases at first instance and on appeal. The High Court consists of three divisions, the Queen's Bench Division, the Chancery Division, and the Family Division, and each hears different types of cases. Judges from the Queen's Bench Division hear the most important criminal cases at Crown Court.

The **Court of Appeal** normally sits in up to 12 courts in the Royal Courts of Justice in London. It considers appeals from the Crown Court (criminal cases) and the High Court (civil cases) but it also takes a few appeals from magistrates' and youth courts. Some hearings may now be recorded and broadcast (Crime and Courts Act 2013), overturning a ban dating from 1925.

The **Supreme Court** is the highest court and the final instance of appeal on points of law and important legal disputes for criminal and civil cases in England and Wales. It is presided over by 12 appointed senior judges.

Summary of the courts

Courts	Type of cases	Features	Appeals go to
Youth	Defendants aged 10 to 17 years	Not usually open to the public	Crown Court
Magistrates'	Offences triable summarily only Offences triable either way	Usually open to the public	Crown Court or High Court
Crown	Offences triable only on indictment Offences triable either way referred from magistrates' courts Appeals from magistrates' and youth courts	Judge and jury	Court of Appeal (Criminal Division)
Appeal	Appeals from Crown Court	Criminal and Civil Divisions	Supreme Court
Supreme	Appeals from Court of Appeal	Replaced the House of Lords in 2009	Final point of appeal

TASK 4 Find out the location of your nearest magistrates' court or Crown Court, and plan when to visit. You will be able to sit in the public gallery to observe proceedings.

5.5.3 Sentencing

Once a court has found a defendant guilty, it has three primary options at its disposal in terms of sentencing: community orders, fines, and custodial sentences. These options may be used together or separately, depending on the offence and the offender's circumstances. Community orders (such as removing graffiti from buildings) combine rehabilitation with punishment within the community, and are supervised by the National Probation Service. For the most serious offences, courts may opt for custodial sentences. The length of time served depends on the maximum penalty foreseen by law for the crime, the circumstances in which it was committed and on the offender (for example, whether he/she was a repeat offender).

The court may also make a conditional or an absolute discharge. For the former, the offender is discharged with the condition of not committing any other offence for a maximum of three years. If an offence is committed within the time period the offender will be convicted for breaching the conditional discharge and re-sentenced. For an absolute discharge, a person who either admitted to an offence or has been found guilty is not penalized as the process of investigation and prosecution is deemed a sufficient response to the offence committed.

Sentences must be appropriate and proportionate, taking into consideration all of the circumstances. The sentencing council sets out sentencing guidelines to help magistrates and judges decide on the appropriate sentence. For more information see <http://www.sentencingcouncil.org.uk/>.

5.6 The Police and Criminal Evidence Act 1984 (PACE)

The powers which police officers have to arrest individuals, to search people and property, to enter buildings, and to seize objects are considered in more detail later in this Handbook (Chapters 9 and 10). Many of these powers and the restrictions on their use are to be found in the Police and Criminal Evidence Act 1984 (known as the PACE Act 1984, or simply as PACE). A good understanding of a number of sections of the PACE Act 1984 (and particularly the associated Codes of Practice) is an essential prerequisite of meeting the Certificate in Knowledge of Policing unit 'Knowledge of using policing powers to deal with suspects' and the Diploma in Policing assessed unit to 'Use police powers to deal with suspects'. However, many other Certificate and Diploma assessed units also expect the candidate to meet assessment criteria concerned with legislation, policies, procedures, codes of practice and/or guidelines in many practical policing contexts.

The demonstration of knowledge of the PACE Act 1984 in practical policing contexts is also an important milestone of the PAC—for example in relation to conducting searches. Trainee officers are likely to encounter this subject matter during Phase 3 of the IPLDP and within LPG 1 'Police Policies and Procedures', particularly parts of LPG 1.4(1) and LPG 1.4(8).

The PACE Act 1984 contains key legislation in relation to:

- criminal investigation procedures in England and Wales;
- applying the principles of justice, honesty, and workability in the investigative process;
- protection of the rights of all individuals; and
- police powers for search and arrest.

5.6.1 PACE Codes of Practice

The PACE Codes of Practice provide guidelines for the conduct of investigative processes. They are divided into eight main sections, and refer to contacts between the police and the public in the exercise of certain police powers.

Code	General areas covered
A	Stop and search
B	Search of premises
C	Detention, treatment, and questioning of suspects
D	Identification of suspects
E	Audio-only recording of interviews
F	Audio-visual recording of interviews
G	Power of arrest
H	Detention, treatment, and questioning of terrorist suspects

A brief summary of each code is provided here. The Codes are available as a smartphone app, and can also be downloaded in full from the Home Office website.

Code A deals with the exercise by police officers of statutory powers of stop and search, and the requirements for police officers and police staff to record public encounters. It provides guidelines on searching people who are not under arrest, and the guiding principles for the justification needed for using a power of search, the circumstances in which the search can take place, and the responsibility of those making the search towards the individual. The considerations and recommendations for the protection of an individual's rights are also covered, leaving very little doubt about the proper extent of a search and where it can take place. In addition, the Code outlines what documentation must be completed at the end of such a search or encounter. Recent changes to Code A seek to clarify the meaning of 'reasonable grounds for suspicion' and the performance and disciplinary procedures associated with a misuse of the powers. The introduction of the Terrorism Prevention and Investigation Measures Act 2011 (TPIMS) and of the Protection of Freedoms Act 2012 and an associated statutory code of practice has already resulted in changes to Code A. As such, references in Code A to stop and search under the Terrorism Act 2000 have been removed, and other powers not related to terrorism have been added. Annex F on gender and searching has also been replaced by Annex L of Code C (Establishing Gender of Persons for the Purpose of Searching).

Code B deals with searches of premises by police officers, and the seizure of any property found (including property found on people present on the premises). It provides guidelines on how to protect a person's rights in relation to the conduct of the search and recording it afterwards. It includes pre-planned searches (with warrants issued by magistrates), as well as searches for the purposes of making an arrest, or a search for stolen or unlawfully possessed property in premises and on persons. Code B includes the powers in Sch 5 to TPIMS to enter and search premises, and clarifies that a search warrant under PACE must be executed within three months of being issued.

Codes A and B require that there is 'reasonable suspicion' for any search of individuals in school premises for weapons (as a result of the Violent Crime Reduction Act 2006, s 48).

Code C deals with the detention, treatment, and questioning of suspects by police officers, and applies primarily to suspects under arrest. However, any person who is not under arrest but who is assisting with an investigation should be treated with 'no less' consideration (Note 1A). The Code outlines the procedure for protecting an arrested person's rights whilst in detention, and the care he/she must be given while in custody at a police station. It emphasizes that discrimination against a detained person with 'protected characteristics' (listed under the Equality Act 2012) is unlawful, and sets out how custody staff can give, and obtain, specified information from the detainee, using interpreters and written translations where necessary (see 10.8 for further details). Code C underlines the rights for detainees to communicate with other people, including legal representation, and describes how to protect those rights during questioning (a written notice of the rights is required, see 10.8). Detainees aged 10 to 17 years must have an appropriate adult (see 25.5.1.1) and a person responsible for his/her welfare (usually a parent or guardian) must be informed. Code C also covers terrorism-related post-charge questioning and detention.

Code D deals with the identification of persons by police officers. It protects the rights of a suspect regarding identification before and after arrest. Identification parade procedures and identification by body samples and fingerprints, and showing witnesses photographs of suspects are all covered.

Code E deals with audio recording of interviews with suspects (arrested or not), and safeguards the rights of an individual. It sets out that the recordings must be handled securely and in confidence, and allows for breaks during interviews. Recordings are often made by secure digital network or removable media rather than on tape. The Code requires that the person is informed of the various aspects of the recording process at every stage (see 25.5.7). Recent amendments to Code E mean that voluntary interviews of suspects who have not been arrested for certain indictable offences do not have to be audio-recorded. The offences are: possession of cannabis, possession of khat, shoplifting with a value up to £100, and criminal damage of up to a value of £300.

Code F deals with audio-visually recorded interviews with suspects (arrested or not), and outlines the procedures to be followed. Such recordings can be made on tape or on a secure digital network or on removable media. At the time of writing there is no statutory requirement on the police to visually record interviews.

Code G deals with the statutory power of arrest by police officers. It outlines the correct procedures for arresting a person in order that his/her right to liberty is considered at all times (see 5.4). Code G defines a lawful arrest and explains that the justification for arrest is made up of two parts: involvement in the commission of the offence and that the arrest is necessary (s 24 of PACE, see 10.6.2). Police officers must consider all the information when deciding whether to make an arrest, particularly in situations where the suspect alleges self-defence (see 15.5.1), or when school staff allege using reasonable force to prevent pupils from committing an offence (s 93 of the Education and Inspections Act 2006). Information that may indicate a person's guilt as well as innocence should be taken into account (Code G, Notes for Guidance, 2A). Suspects should be warned that if they do not stop a certain behaviour, they may be arrested (2D). An arrest should not be made for the sole purpose of either conducting an interview (*Richardson v The Chief Constable of West Midlands Police* [2011] 2 Cr App R 1; [2011] EWHC 773 (QB)), or obtaining biometric data (2F and 2H respectively).

Code H deals with suspects arrested on suspicion of being a terrorist under s 41 of the Terrorism Act 2000. It applies in no other circumstances, and ceases to apply once the suspect has been charged with an offence (Code C then applies), released without charge, or transferred to a prison. Interpreters and written translations must be used where necessary and a written notice of rights and entitlements must be provided to each detainee (as for Code C).

If any of the Codes are breached there is a possibility of:

- disciplinary action for the police officer, depending on the circumstances (see 6.6.5);
- evidence being deemed inadmissible or unfair by a court (s 78(1) PACE Act 1984); and/or
- liability for civil or criminal proceedings.

TASK 5 For each Code, write a brief description of a situation when it might be applied. If you are a trainee officer you might have witnessed such incidents while on Supervised Patrol, and descriptions of these may provide you with material for completion of your SOLAP.

5.7 Answers to Tasks

TASK 1 You should have found that these Regulations cover the fitting of lights, reflectors, and rear markings on vehicles.

TASK 2 You may have considered a number of possible scenarios that might take place on Supervised Patrol. Remember that these rights extend to suspects as well as victims and witnesses. For example, if you are a trainee officer then you may be involved in the arrest of an individual whose grasp of spoken English is poor or non-existent, and subsequently involved in the procedures used when suspects have difficulty communicating in English. The QCF indicate that, for this element, evidence **must** come from real-life situations. Your assessor may well be able to observe your actions directly in this case but you would also need to provide evidence of your knowledge and understanding—for example, through evidence in your SOLAP cross-referred to your Learning Diary or pocket notebook.

TASK 3 For the offence of robbery, you should have found:

- the Theft Act 1968, s 8(1);
- *mode of trial*: triable on indictment only;
- *maximum penalty for a person found guilty*: life imprisonment.

TASK 4 The website <https://courttribunalfinder.service.gov.uk> can be used to find your local courts.

TASK 5 Your answers might include the following:

Policing in Context

Code A: You may have seen people being searched, for example under s 23 Misuse of Drugs Act, s 47 Firearms Act, and s 1 PACE Act 1984. Annex A of the PACE Act 1984 Code A lists the various powers of search (see 9.4.3).

Code B: you may have seen premises searches under s 17 of the PACE Act 1984, in order to arrest a person. You may also have seen searches of premises at the time of an arrest, under s 32 of the PACE Act 1984, and after arrest under s 18 of the PACE Act 1984. You may also have seen a warrant executed. All these searches would have been carried out with regard to Code B.

Code C: you may have observed people suspected of committing road traffic offences interviewed at the roadside, and the officer recording the interview contemporaneously in his/her pocket notebook.

Code D: you may have seen a witness or victim identify a suspect in the vicinity of an offence soon after the event. You may also have seen an identification parade, where a witness is asked to identify a suspect.

Codes E and F: you may have seen suspect interviews at your local police station which were recorded, and the steps taken to respect the suspect's rights—for example, explaining how he/she can obtain a copy of the recording. Many forces routinely make AV recordings of interviews.

Code G: you are very likely to have seen suspects arrested (see 10.6), and cautioned at the time of arrest.

6 | Roles, Responsibilities, and Support

6.1 Introduction

This chapter of the Handbook covers applying to join the police service and induction into a police organization. Induction is the process of 'bringing in' or initiation. In some senses it also refers to a kind of transformation—in this case from being a member of the public to becoming both a member of the public and a police constable. This is likely to take a few months.

You will discover that there are certain symbolic aspects to induction, such as the ceremony that surrounds attestation. Induction is also the assimilation into an organizational culture or cultures. In policing, the process of 'buying into' the existing organizational culture has not been without controversy. For some observers, the prevailing cultures within the police have often been characterized as male-dominated and exclusionary. Allied to this view is the suggestion that initial police training moves you from being an individual to being part of a group, and into a group where it is 'dangerous to be different'. (This is the so-called police 'canteen culture' that you may hear or read about.) The police service is aware of these criticisms and one of the driving forces behind recent changes to initial police training is to create a learning environment which is more inclusive.

We will examine the Code of Ethics produced by the College of Policing which sets out the necessary attitudes and behaviours, and the Police Regulations which also address these matters. We also explain conduct, misconduct, discipline, and complaints, and introduce the staff association for police constables, the Police Federation, and mention some of the specialist support groups such as the British Association of Women Police Officers. This is followed by a description of police IT systems (an increasingly important part of information management) and how information is stored, processed, and communicated, including confidentiality and the implications of the Freedom of Information Act 2000. The importance of effective communication is also considered as this is an essential part of discharging the responsibilities of the police officer.

Understanding the role of health and safety is an important part of a police officer's ability to make risk assessments, and this is often covered in conjunction with First Aid, a vital skill for patrol constables. A police officer's own safety and that of others will be covered in Personal Safety Training (the title varies between forces). This will involve learning self-defence and about how to manage angry and tense situations, and the appropriate use of certain police equipment such as rigid-pattern handcuffs, the ASP baton, and incapacitant spray.

6.2 Attestation and the Role of the Police Constable

After attestation a trainee police officer holds the office of probationary constable, with the position being confirmed after about two calendar years. The origins of the office of constable within law enforcement in the UK can be traced back hundreds of years, although many commentators consider the most significant starting point for the modern-day police service as the year 1829 (see 2.2).

In recent years, constables have become just one of many members of the extended police family; they no longer have a monopoly on certain traditional policing powers. They nonetheless continue to hold a special position within a police organization, as you will discover when working through this chapter and those that follow. There are also additional responsibilities for the role of constable, particularly in terms of attitudes, values, and professional knowledge. Many of the CKP and Diploma in Policing units are concerned with the need for a police trainee to demonstrate the appropriate attitudes and values, and, by extension, to have gained the necessary underpinning skills and knowledge. Similarly, one of the Induction Modules of the IPLDP is concerned with the 'Underpinning Ethics/Values of the Police Service' (IND 1). The CKP unit 'Knowledge of managing conflict within a policing context' also contains the assessment criterion that learners should be able to 'explain how to communicate with people in a way that...is free from discrimination and oppressive behaviour'.

There has been much discussion about the possible effects of an individual's personal beliefs and values, and the manner in which these are expressed in their day-to-day actions and decisions. Trainees may feel (somewhat defensively) that they are 'entitled to their opinions' with the implication that their attitudes would have no bearing on their actions. This is obviously an important issue for those engaged in police training and education, and is addressed in other parts of this Handbook. Here, however, we are concerned with how the professional development of a trainee (and the progression to confirmation as constable) links up with the wider common purpose and values of the police service.

We noted in 3.7 that the existence of a code of professional conduct is a common feature of the professions. The Police Service Statement of Common Purpose and Values was first issued by ACPO in 1990 and is reflected today, almost word for word, in most police forces' own statements. It is a relatively consistent declaration of the guiding principles of the police service, and all police officers, including trainees, are required to work towards the achievement of this statement.

According to the statement, the purpose of the police service is to:

... uphold the law firmly and fairly ...	be neither too weak nor too aggressive, and with no bias,
... prevent crime ...	not let it happen if it can be stopped first,
... pursue and bring to justice those who break the law ...	and hence we need to understand the requirements of the criminal justice system,
... keep the Queen's peace ...	not allow public disorder and criminality to occur unchallenged,
... protect, help and reassure the community ...	that is, all our communities and not just those that appear to support the police or those that we *belong to*.

In 2003 a BBC undercover reporter secretly filmed trainee officer training at the Centrex Bruche training centre (the BBC called the documentary *The Secret Policeman*). Examples of inappropriate behaviour by some trainee officers at Bruche uncovered by the documentary included:

- use of offensive racist terms to describe members of ethnic minorities, including unsubstantiated slurs on the character of the family of murdered black teenager Stephen Lawrence;
- donning an imitation Ku Klux Klan hood and threatening to knock on the door of a fellow trainee of British Asian heritage; and
- claims that they used police powers in a discriminating way against ethnic minorities.

One Centrex police trainer was also secretly filmed expressing his happiness to his group of trainees that the single police recruit of British Asian heritage had been re-coursed (required to retake certain aspects of his training), although there was no suggestion that this was as a result of racism.

> **TASK 1** If you are a trainee police officer, what does the Police Service Statement of Common Purpose and Values mean for you? Your reflections could be written up and used as evidence for your SOLAP—for example, as evidence cross referring to the assessment criteria of one of your Diploma in Policing learning outcomes. Your reflections could also feature in your Learning Diary, under the heading 'Police Policies & Procedures'.

6.2.1 Attestation of police constables

Attestation is the stage at which a trainee police officer is formally given the powers of a police constable—for example, he/she is then able to arrest someone according to the law and Codes of Practice. The legal detail is set out in s 29 of and Sch 4 to the Police Act 1996, as amended by s 83 of the Police Reform Act 2002. (Parallel legislation covers the 'non-Home Office' forces, eg in s 24 of the Railways and Transport Safety Act 2003, for BTP.) In many police organizations, attestation happens early on in a trainee officer's career—sometimes on initial appointment and certainly within the first few weeks. The warrant card can also be issued at attestation (although some forces instead issue a 'trainee police officer identity card').

There is often a formal attestation ceremony to which family and friends may be invited. The declaration is usually taken by a Justice of the Peace (magistrate). The trainee will make a formal declaration (sometimes referred to as an 'Oath') as follows:

> I...of...do solemnly and sincerely declare and affirm that I will well and truly serve the Queen in the office of constable, with fairness, integrity, diligence, and impartiality, upholding fundamental human rights and according equal respect to all people; and that I will, to the best of my power, cause the peace to be kept and preserved and prevent all offences against people and property; and that while I continue to hold the said office I will, to the best of my skill and knowledge, discharge all the duties thereof faithfully according to law.

An alternative Welsh-language version can be used in Wales and there are alternative versions for police officers in Scotland and Northern Ireland, and in the BTP.

The making of a declaration may seem somewhat old-fashioned. However, it is worth bearing in mind that the declaration police officers make has a statutory basis in law and its symbolic importance remains strong, both within police culture and in the wider political and social world.

> **TASK 2** Trainee police officers should learn the declaration for the attestation word for word! Note that you will probably be given a card to read from at actual attestation, or be asked to follow another's lead. However, you are likely to be required to memorize information on a number of occasions during training (eg definitions) and this task is good practice.

6.3 The Code of Ethics

The Code of Ethics was introduced by the College of Policing in July 2014 and issued as a code of practice under s 39A(5) of the Police Act 1996 (College of Policing, 2014a). The Code of Ethics (available from the College of Policing website) is central to the professionalization of the police service and police practices. All police officers and staff must observe the Code and ensure it is applied for all police officers, staff, and volunteers engaged in policing within the service.

The Code of Ethics comprises the policing principles (see 6.3.1) and the standards of professional behaviour (see 6.3.2) and is incorporated as a central feature of the National Decision Model (see 6.5.2). The Code complements the Police Service Statement of Common Purpose and Values (see 6.2). Initial police training will frequently involve direct contact with both the public and fellow members of the extended policing family (eg PCSOs). It is therefore important that trainees read and understand the Code as it applies to all areas of police work (details of the full Code can be found on the College of Policing website). Many of the Diploma in Policing learning outcomes are concerned with the nature and quality of the interactions with the public and between colleagues.

Qualifications and Training

Attested police officers are not employees in the conventional meaning of the term; they are instead holders of public office. One consequence of this is that all police officers' activities on and off duty are covered by the Code of Ethics and regulated by law through Statutory Instruments. Any breach of the Code of Ethics can be dealt with in a variety of ways from peer or group challenge through to using the police regulations. Professional judgement, proportionality and the severity and impact of the breach will all need to be taken into account.

The material covered here relates directly to a number of assessment criteria within the assessed Diploma in Policing units and is likely to be relevant to Phase 3 of the IPLDP and the Induction Module IND 1: 'Underpinning Ethics/Values of the Police Service'.

6.3.1   The Policing Principles

The general attitudes and approaches to police work are underpinned by the Policing Principles. This broad guidance can be applied in a variety of contexts. The Policing Principles are as follows:

1. Accountability—you are answerable for your decisions, actions, and omissions.
2. Fairness—you treat people fairly.
3. Honesty—you are truthful and trustworthy.
4. Integrity—you always do the right thing.
5. Leadership—you lead by good example.
6. Objectivity—you make choices on evidence and your best professional judgement.
7. Openness—you are open and transparent in your actions and decisions.
8. Respect—you treat everyone with respect.
9. Selflessness—you act in the public interest.

For further details see the College of Policing website.

6.3.2   The ten standards of professional behaviour

The ten standards of professional behaviour are the minimum standards that both trainee and confirmed police officers must maintain, and are listed in the Police (Conduct) Regulations 2012. They are:

1. Honesty and Integrity
Police officers are honest, act with integrity, and do not compromise or abuse their position.

2. Authority, Respect, and Courtesy
Police officers act with self-control and tolerance, treating members of the public and colleagues with respect and courtesy. Police officers do not abuse their powers or authority and respect the rights of all individuals.

3. Equality and Diversity
Police officers act with fairness and impartiality. They do not discriminate unlawfully or unfairly.

4. Use of Force
Police officers only use force to the extent that it is necessary, proportionate, and reasonable in all the circumstances.

5. Orders and Instructions
Police officers only give and carry out lawful orders and instructions. Police officers abide by police regulations, force policies, and lawful orders.

6. Duties and Responsibilities
Police officers are diligent in the exercise of their duties and responsibilities.

7. Confidentiality
Police officers treat information with respect and access or disclose it only in the proper course of police duties.

8. Fitness for Work
Police officers when on duty or at work are fit to carry out their responsibilities.

9. Conduct

Police officers behave in a manner whether on or off duty which does not bring discredit on the police service or undermine public confidence in policing.

10. Challenging and Reporting Improper Conduct

Police officers report, challenge, or take action against the conduct of colleagues which has fallen below the standards of professional behaviour.

Note that the Police Service of Northern Ireland (PSNI) has its own standards of professional behaviour, available on their website.

> **TASK 3** In March 2010 a senior police officer from Thames Valley Police was arrested and suspended from duty after allegedly setting fire to a hire car he had used while on duty, in order to destroy evidence that he was having an affair. Leaving aside the suspected criminal offences of arson, insurance fraud, and perverting the course of justice, which of the standards of professional behaviour may have been breached during the alleged incident? What are the consequences of this for both the individual concerned and the police service as a whole?

If you are a trainee officer, then your written reflections may be relevant to the knowledge requirements of the 'Underpinning Ethics/Values of the Police Service' sections of your SOLAP.

> **TASK 4** Consider standards 3, 4, and 7 of the standards of professional behaviour, and list the assessed units of the Diploma in Policing that are most relevant. What sort of evidence could a trainee officer use to meet the learning criteria for these units? Bear in mind that evidence usually takes the form of tangible objects such as written documents and by direct observation and questioning by an assessor (see Chapter 8).

6.4 The Police Regulations and Conditions of Service

Conditions of service for police constables are also regulated by law under various Police Regulations contained in Statutory Instruments. Because of their length and complexity these will not be dealt with in their entirety here, but they are presented here in a summarized and simplified form, with extra explanations in places. Full details may be found in other textbooks such as *Blackstone's Police Manual: Volume 4 General Police Duties 2017* and online. At the moment of attestation a trainee police officer becomes subject to police regulations such as the 2003 Regulations as described in the following paragraphs. Note that the Police (Performance) Regulations 2012 do not apply for trainee officers during the probationary period.

6.4.1 Restrictions on private life and business interests

These are set out in Sch 1 to the Police Regulations 2003 which states that 'The restrictions on private life…shall apply to all members of a police force' (reg 6(1)) and that:

> A member of a police force shall at all times abstain from any activity which is likely to interfere with the impartial discharge of [his/her] duties or which is likely to give rise to the impression amongst members of the public that it may so interfere; and in particular a member of a police force shall not take any active part in politics. (Sch 1, para 1)

In other words, a police officer must not pursue a course of conduct which members of the public will perceive as favouritism and especially must not be active in politics. In addition, a police officer 'shall not wilfully refuse or neglect to discharge any lawful debt' (Sch 1, para 4). This does not mean a police officer cannot have a mortgage or a car loan (as these are lawful), but any debt which could place the officer in danger of being coerced is unacceptable.

The Police (Amendment No. 3) Regulations 2012 state in reg 8 that:

> [i]f a member of a police force has or proposes to have a business interest which has not previously been disclosed, or, is or becomes aware that a relative has or proposes to have a business interest which, in the opinion of the member, interferes or could be seen as interfering with the impartial discharge of the

member's duties and has not previously been disclosed the member shall immediately give written notice of that business interest to the chief officer.

For the purposes of their integrity and credibility, police officers must disclose business interests in order that they may be checked for compatibility with the role of a constable.

> **TASK 5** Find out about the procedure for police officers to declare any business interests in your police area.

6.4.2 Personal records, fingerprints, and samples

In relation to personal records, reg 15 of the Police Regulations 2003 states that the chief officer of a police force 'shall cause a personal record of each member of the police force to be kept' throughout a police officer's service. It will contain details of the officer and his/her relatives, a history of courses attended, expertise gained, promotions achieved, and the outcomes of any disciplinary investigations.

Regulation 18 of the Police Regulations 2003 concerns taking and recording a police officer's fingerprints, for the purposes of eliminating him/her from any forensic investigation. Quite often this takes place early on in training and sometimes as part of initial training on forensic awareness. Regulation 19 of the Police Regulations 2003 obliges an officer to supply a sample such as a mouth swab for DNA analysis, again for the purposes of elimination. From April 2012, the 2003 Police Regulations have been amended so that any officer can be selected for random drug testing according to protocols described within the Police (Amendment No. 2) Regulations 2012.

6.4.3 Duty to carry out lawful orders

Regulation 20 of the Police Regulations 2003 states that every member of a police force:

> shall carry out all lawful orders and shall at all times punctually and promptly perform all appointed duties and attend to all matters within the scope of [his/her] office as a constable.

The police service has a rank structure in which supervisors and managers may require certain actions to be carried out. It is an expectation that a police officer will carry out these orders, but only if they are lawful.

> **TASK 6** If you are a trainee officer, take the opportunity to reflect upon these regulations and the police Code of Ethics. The College of Policing Code of Ethics (2014a), section 5.2 states that a police officer should:
>
> > follow lawful orders, recognizing that any decision not to follow and order needs to be objectively and fully justified.
>
> Which areas do you think are going to be easy for you to satisfy, and which areas do you need to consider at greater length? How for example would you know that an order was unlawful?

6.4.4 Discharge of a trainee police officer

Under reg 13 of the Police Regulations 2003 a trainee officer can be dismissed. This is covered more fully in 8.4.4.3 along with extending the probationary period under reg 12. However, before being discharged, a trainee can give notice of retirement (in other words, resign). Under the Police (Conduct) (Amendment) Regulations 2014 which came into force in January 2015, an officer intending to resign must obtain the appropriate authority from the Chief Officer (or his/her delegated authority).

6.5 Ethical Decision-making in Policing

The legitimacy, authority, and even effectiveness of the police depend on the exercise of ethical decision-making. In essence this means that there is an expectation on the police, from the public and others, that they make decisions based on a set of ethical principles, and not in an arbitrary manner, or according to emotional response or prejudice. However, this presents a number of questions including the fundamental question of 'Whose ethics?'. We will examine the ethical basis to policing, how ethics are reflected in decision-making, and finally the ways in which police officers might fall short of the ethical requirements expected of the police service.

6.5.1   Ethics and policing

Ethics are important for all police officers because if police methods and procedures do not meet high ethical standards then the authority of the police will be undermined, and the public may have less trust in the police and the law. The expected standards of behaviour are clearly defined in existing documents but ethics is also about personal ideas, and if a police officer's actions are to ring true, his/her own rules of moral behaviour (or personal ethics) need to correspond with the force's formal requirements. Diversity training (see 8.6.6) provides trainees with further opportunities for considering personal views and feelings about a range of possible attitudes and behaviours.

A number of official documents set out guidance (in varying degrees of detail and levels of official standing) concerning police ethics and behaviour. These documents include the Professional Policing Framework (PPF) 'personal qualities' of the police constable (see 8.5.2); the Police (Conduct) Regulations 2012; the Police (Performance) Regulations 2012; the Police Regulations 2003; and the College of Policing Code of Ethics. The Police (Conduct) Regulations 2012 contain the 'standards of professional behaviour' (see 6.3.2), guidance on police officer behaviour when off duty (see also 6.4), and misconduct procedures (see 6.6).

The police have always been affected by changes in customs, beliefs, and social morality. Policing norms are shaped by social norms, and so ethical questions concerning what police officers ought to do in particular circumstances are interpreted according to the moral values of the day. For example, there has been a shift in police practice from being responsive to being proactive, and more emphasis is placed on preventing crime.

> **TASK 7** What is policing by consent, and how might this differ from when police were introduced in 1829?

In recent years policing has been informed increasingly by the need to demonstrate value for money (sometimes through reductions in police staffing levels) and to meet targets set by government. This form of 'managerialism' has been criticized by some chief officers because it leads to police officers becoming over-concerned with meeting targets. This is problematic because it is not always easy to measure the things that police need to do.

The role of police in international peacekeeping (alongside a military presence and other supporting agencies from different parts of the world) demands an ethical consistency across different organizations with very different values and traditions. This might sometimes include British police officers working alongside officers from other countries where there is: widespread corruption; routine bribery of public officials; governments using their police as a political arm; very low rates of pay for police officers; very low status for police officers; and/or paramilitary-style force employed by the police.

> **TASK 8** Consider corruption, bribery, political use of the police, low pay, low status, and paramilitary policing. Draw a flow diagram showing how these factors might interact. Use arrows to show how one factor causes another. (An example of this particular use of arrows is shown in the diagram below: the arrow shows that poor pay leads to low status.)
>
>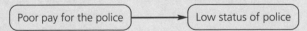
>
> Note that there are no certain answers to this exercise; you might argue that it is the low status that is causing the low pay.

One of the key skills trainee police officers have to develop during training is the ability to apply discretion (see 3.6), and this is linked with ethics. For example, imagine two trainees on Supervised Patrol are called to deal with a theft at a supermarket, with instructions to investigate the matter and decide upon a course of action. The offender is a confused 94-year-old man who has apparently picked up a bag of sweets and wandered out of the store, pursued by store detectives. The old man had technically committed a crime, but there were mitigating circumstances: his age and frailty must be taken into account, and proving 'intention permanently to deprive' (the basis of the Theft Act 1968 (see 16.2)) would be somewhat difficult. Enforcing the law might not be the most appropriate response, but a police officer has to be prepared to justify the reasons for his/her decision (see 6.5.2 on the NDM).

6.5.2 The National Decision Model

The police routinely make difficult decisions in fast moving situations, where the information may be incomplete and there may also be efforts to mislead or undermine police responses. Ethical decision-making in policing is informed by the National Decision Model (NDM). The NDM, introduced in 2012, consists of a number of elements, with the Code of Ethics being central. It related to ACPO's Statement of Mission and Values published in July 2011. The NDM is intended for use by anyone making decisions in the police service (both operational and non-operational), which in effect means virtually every employee, although the wording used within the NDM is to a large extent drawn from operational police culture.

When making decisions using the NDM the mnemonic CIAPOAR can be used as an aide-memoire:

- Code of Ethics—the policing principles and standards of professional behaviour;
- Information—gather information and intelligence;
- Assessment—assess threat and risk and develop a working strategy;
- Powers and policy—consider powers and policy;
- Options—identify the options and contingencies;
- Action—take action;
- Review.

In essence, the NDM is a risk-based model which seeks to provide the policy basis for taking ethical action, or deciding not to act. Police officers might sometimes need to work outside of policy if the circumstances require, but justification and documentation is still required. The APP outlines a number of principles that are fundamental to the NDM, to encourage and support professional judgement. As professionals, the police have to be able to make decisions in uncertain conditions, and the first consideration should be the public safety and security. When judging possible risks from decisions the possible benefits and harm must be taken into account, and it must be accepted that harm can never be totally prevented. Therefore a decision involving risk should be judged by how good the decision-making was, and not by the actual outcome, so any police officer who has followed these principles when making a decision should be supported. The principles clearly state that making decisions concerning risk is inherently difficult, and that the extent to which an officer's decisions present risks should be judged in comparison with others in a similar professional position, and that deciding whether to record decisions about risk is a matter of professional judgement. It is emphasized that examples of good risk taking should be identified and shared, and that communication and cooperation with other agencies will help improve decision-making (CoP, 2013g).

6.5.3 Police corruption

In a culture where ethical decision-making in policing is not valued, corruption may flourish. Research has shown that corruption can occur in any part of the police service, and therefore we need to understand how widespread corruption is likely to be, and how we might prevent it. In 2016, a former Merseyside police officer was sentenced to four years' imprisonment for targeting female domestic abuse victims for his own sexual gratification (CPS, 2016). In fact 'corruption for the purposes of sexual gratification' amongst police officers seems to be on the increase (HMIC, 2015b, p 110). There have been 436 reported allegations of abuse of authority by police officers for sexual gain in a period of two years (BBC, 2016).

> **TASK 9** What sort of opportunities do you think there might be for corruption in relation to drugs policing?

Corruption can take a number of forms, for example, misfeasance—doing something you should not do; non-feasance—not doing something you should do; and malfeasance—the commission of indictable crimes.

What thought processes or experiences could lead officers to act in this often illegal way? We suggest the following could all be potentially corrupting factors:

- lack of personal integrity;
- corrupt police officers providing a role model;
- the pressure for results;
- abuse or assault from members of the public;
- the difficulties in securing convictions;
- belief that sentencing was not adequate for the crime committed;
- the first arrival at the scene of a crime, when cash or goods may be lying about;
- personal financial pressures;
- handling and storing drugs from police investigations;
- the 'long hours, low reward' culture, leading to envy of others more fortunately placed;
- lack of effective supervision;
- the excessive exercise of discretion without challenge;
- feelings of bitterness or resentment at not receiving expected promotion; and
- managing informants without adequate supervision or scrutiny.

> **TASK 10** Consider the list of factors that might contribute to an officer's decision to act corruptly. Most of them are about predisposition—motivations for an officer to act corruptly. But an opportunity is also required; list the five factors from the list which provide opportunities to act corruptly.

There are a number of theories about the causes of corruption. One such theory is that the metaphorical (in some cases, actual) free cup of coffee is enough to start a police officer on the slippery slope to corruption. The idea is that from a free cup of coffee it is but a short step to a free meal, then free entry to a club, then preferential treatment, then provision of goods and inducements, and finally the offer to engage in joint criminal exploits. By accepting the free cup of coffee, the officer could be signalling a willingness to be corrupted.

> **TASK 11** How convinced are you by the 'free cup of coffee' theory? Can you see any flaws in it? Can you think of examples that might challenge the theory?

The 'bad apple' theory argues that a corrupt police officer or staff member is an isolated instance, and that the solution is to simply remove the individual officer. The 'bent for the job' theory (also known as 'noble cause' corruption) is a third explanation for corruption. It was argued that the law was so inadequately structured that substantial numbers of the guilty went unpunished, and that officers felt obliged to be devious and underhand because it seemed the only way to achieve results (see Newburn, 2015, for a literature review of police integrity and corruption).

> **TASK 12** What sort of events or feelings would make a 'bad apple' officer more likely to act corruptly, and why might other officers not succumb to the same pressures or temptations?
>
> How convinced are you by the 'bent for the job' theory? Do you accept that the end is more important than the means, and, if so, does that mean that inexperienced officers have to be taught trickery or stealth?

6.6 Misconduct and Complaints Procedures

Police misconduct and complaint procedures are governed by three pieces of legislation namely; Police (Complaints and Misconduct) Regulations 2012, Police (Conduct) Regulations 2012, and Police (Performance) Regulations 2012. These regulations are outlined in the 2015 Home Office guidance document *Police Office Misconduct, Unsatisfactory Performance and Attendance Management Procedures*, available online.

'Misconduct' includes any police officer action which does not meet the standards of professional behaviour. 'Gross misconduct' is a more serious failure to meet the standards (so serious that it could lead to dismissal). Allegations concerning the conduct of a police officer fall into one of two categories:

• 'conduct matters', which concern allegations made against a police officer by a colleague; and

• 'complaints' which are allegations made by a member of the public about the conduct of a police officer.

The process of making such allegations, the investigation and subsequent methods of disposal, are together known as the Police Complaints System.

Complaints and conduct matters can be handled by a line manager or supervisor, or if more serious by the 'appropriate authority' or the IPCC. The appropriate authority would be a chief officer (chief constable or commissioner), but he/she can delegate this function to a police officer of at least the rank of chief inspector, or another police staff member of at least a similar level of seniority. This will frequently be an officer within a Professional Standards Department.

6.6.1 Conduct matters

Police officers are required to abide by the standards of professional behaviour (see 6.3.2). This includes the tenth standard that requires a police officer to report, challenge, or take action against the conduct of any colleague whose behaviour has fallen below any of the other nine Standards. Failure to report such instances would render the officer liable for claims of misconduct. Normally, an officer should report any concerns to his/her supervisor or the Professional Standards Department, but concerns can also be raised confidentially with the IPCC (see 6.6.3) as it is designated as an official body for the purposes of public interest disclosure.

The flowchart summarizes the procedures for handling an allegation relating to 'conduct matters'. These decisions would be taken by the appropriate authority—usually local senior officers.

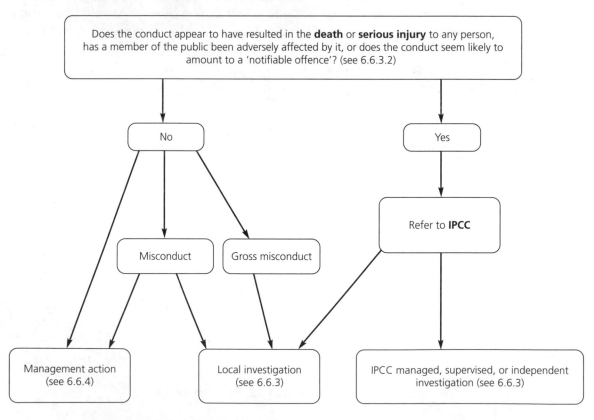

Management action includes setting expectations for future conduct and an improvement plan (see 6.6.4).

For a local investigation, the investigator is appointed by the appropriate authority, and the officer under investigation must be notified (under reg 15 of the Police (Conduct) Regulations 2012, or reg 16 of the Police (Complaints and Misconduct) Regulations 2012). Further information is provided in 6.6.3.2. A misconduct meeting or hearing might be required, and the

IPCC may be involved. The IPCC can decide to discontinue the proceedings if it becomes apparent that there is no case to answer. The possible sanctions are described in 6.6.4.

6.6.2 Complaints

Allegations made by members of the public concerning the conduct or behaviour of a police officer (trainee or confirmed) are called complaints. Examples might include complaints of rudeness, the use of excessive force, or unjustified arrest. Allegations can only be made by a member of the public who:

- claims to be the victim of the conduct;
- claims to have been adversely affected by the conduct (but is not the victim);
- claims to have witnessed the conduct; or
- is a person who is representing any of the above.

The appropriate course of action will be decided by the 'appropriate authority' (defined earlier). IPCC statutory guidance on the handling of complaints is available via its website (IPCC, 2015). The flowchart summarizes the process for managing complaints:

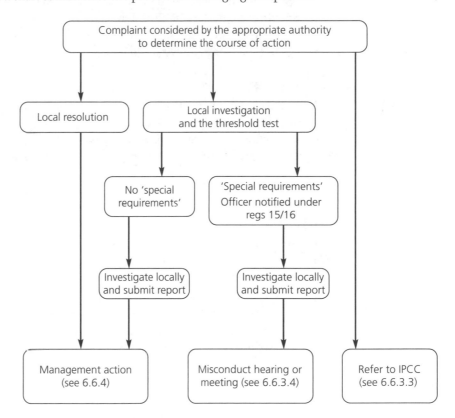

The threshold test establishes whether it appears likely that the officer who is the subject of the complaint has committed a criminal offence or behaved in such a way that disciplinary proceedings are likely to be required. If this applies, the investigation will be subject to 'special requirements', and the officer must be formally notified about the investigation (see 6.6.3.2).

6.6.3 Investigations and the Independent Police Complaints Commission

The diagram shows the different ways in which complaints and matters of misconduct are handled and the extent of the involvement of the IPCC. The diagram tapers towards the top as there are fewer high-level investigations. As you might expect, the more serious the matter, the higher the level of the investigation, and the greater the level of direct IPCC involvement. Note that the then Home Secretary Theresa May announced in March 2016 that the IPCC is to be overhauled and renamed as the Office for Police Conduct (Home Office, 2016e).

IPCC stands for **Independent Police Complaints Commission**

Beginning with the lowest level, to 'dispense or withdraw' means that the investigation is discontinued. A police force may ask the IPCC for permission to discontinue an investigation if:

- the complainant is uncooperative;
- the complaint or allegation of misconduct is harsh, is brought about with the intention of annoying, or an abuse of procedure;
- the complaint or allegation of misconduct is repetitious; or
- a local resolution is agreed (see 6.6.4).

6.6.3.1 Local investigations

A local investigation is carried out for less serious matters that do not warrant IPCC involvement. It would usually be carried out by personnel from the Professional Standards Department within a police force, and is structured in a similar way to any other police enquiry, including collecting evidence through interviews from witnesses and suspects.

6.6.3.2 Notification

The officer in question must be notified for all investigations that are:

- referred to the IPCC;
- into a complaint where special requirements apply, or
- into conduct matters where it seems likely there has been misconduct or gross misconduct, a notifiable offence, a death or serious injury.

The notice must be served in writing and as soon as practicable. It will be served under reg 15 of the Police (Conduct) Regulations 2012 or reg 16 of the Police (Complaints and Misconduct) Regulations 2012. (The same form is used for both conduct matters and complaints.) The notice may be referred to in police circles as a 'reg 15' (with a hard 'g'). It will include a description of the conduct, the outcome of the severity or threshold test, and a reminder that the officer has the opportunity to seek advice from the Police Federation. The Police Federation advises any officer receiving a reg 15/16 notice not to say anything at that stage and to seek the advice of a Federation representative. If the officer is to be interviewed, once again the advice is to contact a Federation representative who will arrange to attend the interview or, in some circumstances, help to arrange for legal representation. A notice may also be given for less serious investigations.

6.6.3.3 Investigations involving the IPCC

An IPCC-*supervised* investigation is used for complaints or allegations of misconduct which are of considerable significance and probable public concern. It will be supervised by an IPCC commissioner but conducted, directed, and controlled by the police. The complainant has the right of appeal to the IPCC.

An IPCC-*managed* investigation takes place when the alleged incident is more serious and likely to cause higher levels of public concern, and therefore the subsequent investigation must have an independent element. The IPCC direct and control the process, whilst the police conduct the investigation.

An *independent* IPCC investigation is used for incidents that cause the greatest level of public concern, have the greatest potential to impact on communities, or have serious implications for the reputation of the police service (for deaths in custody). These require a wholly independent investigation conducted in its entirety by IPCC staff.

There is no right of appeal against an IPCC-managed or independent investigation except through judicial review, a form of court proceedings which checks that the correct procedures have been used.

6.6.3.4 Misconduct meetings and hearings

After the evidence has been collected in an investigation the appropriate authority decides if the officer's behaviour amounted to misconduct or gross misconduct, and there may be various outcomes, as shown in the flowchart. A misconduct meeting may be held for an officer falling slightly short of the standards of professional behaviour, and a misconduct hearing will be held for more serious failures or when the officer already has a final written warning. The evidence collected during the investigation will be considered and the outcomes and sanctions will be determined. The possible outcomes and sanctions are explained in 6.6.4.

6.6.4 Outcomes and sanctions

There are a number of methods of disposal available on the conclusion of an enquiry into conduct matters or complaints.

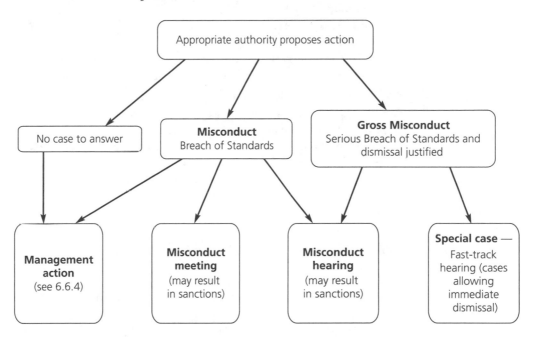

Local (or informal) resolution may be possible, in which case regulation 15/16 notices (see 6.6.3.2) are not required, no blame is attached, nor is there any need to involve disciplinary procedures. The process will not affect a trainee officer's personal development plan (usually the SOLAP, then the PDR), staff appraisal, or any subsequent misconduct hearing. Note that a police force cannot make an apology to the complainant unless the officer concerned (the officer against whom the complaint was made) authorizes it.

Management action would involve pointing out how the behaviour fell short of the standards of professional behaviour, and identifying expectations for future conduct. It could also include establishing an improvement plan and addressing any underlying causes of misconduct. It can therefore be seen as supportive.

After a **misconduct meeting** the outcome could either be no further action, management action, a written warning, or a final written warning. After a **misconduct hearing** the sanctions could be as for a misconduct meeting and also dismissal (with or without notice). The 'services' of a trainee officer can be dispensed with at any time under reg 13 of the Police Regulations 2003 (see 6.4.4).

6.6.5 Unsatisfactory performance or attendance

Unsatisfactory performance or attendance is an 'inability or failure of a police officer to perform the duties of the role or rank [he/she] is currently undertaking to a satisfactory standard or level' (Police (Performance) Regulations 2012). The 2015 Home Office document *Guidance on Unsatisfactory Performance and Attendance Procedures* suggests that informal and early interventions by a manager ('management action') should be sufficient to improve and maintain a police officer's performance or attendance (see also 6.6.4). It also states that formal action should not be taken unless the police officer has earlier been offered supportive action but had declined or failed to cooperate, resulting in no improvement.

The Unsatisfactory Performance Procedures (UPP) can also be invoked for officers on long-term sick-leave and supported by management action, but for whom returning to work during a reasonable time is unrealistic. Note that the UPP do not apply to trainee officers during their probationary period; reg 13 of the Police Regulations 2003 would be used instead (see 6.4.4).

There are three stages in the UPP with 3–12 months between each. During this time there must be improvement, and the satisfactory performance must be maintained for a year in order to avoid moving on to the next stage. However, recent changes to the regulations do allow the IPCC to recommend or direct police services to the Police (Performance) Regulation procedures if the conduct is under Sch 3 of the Police Reform Act 2002. The three stages of the UPP are:

- Stage 1: the officer is requested to attend a meeting by his/her first-line manager, and given the option of being accompanied by a Police Federation representative. An improvement notice will be issued and an action plan agreed by the officer and his/her line manager. The officer maintains the right to appeal.
- Stage 2: this is identical to Stage 1, except that the meeting is with his/her second-line manager.
- Stage 3: the officer attends a meeting with his/her senior manager. A decision will be made by three panel members consisting of at least one police officer and an HR professional.

Stages 1 and 2 can also be omitted for 'gross incompetence' relating to performance. This would be 'a serious inability or serious failure of a police officer to perform the duties of the role or rank he is currently undertaking to a satisfactory standard or level, to the extent that dismissal would be justified' but it does not include poor attendance (reg 4(1)). If the panel at Stage 3 decides that the officer's performance is unsatisfactory the following options are available: redeployment, reduction in rank (performance only), dismissal with a minimum of 28 days' notice, or an extension of a final improvement notice.

6.7 Police Representative Organizations

Until April 2015, the Police Federation had a unique status as a police representative organization in that all trainees automatically joined. However, in 2014 the Home Secretary announced the law would be changed so police officers would not simply become members by default (Home Office, 2014d). To that effect, in 2015 the Police Federation (Amendment) Regulations 2015 (a Statutory Instrument, see 5.2) was introduced, with a clause added to the 1969 Regulations. These changes mean that when a trainee joins the police service he/she can now decide whether to opt in to join the Police Federation (and currently, most choose to join). Note that in 2016 the Home Office decided that Special Constables should not be represented by the Police Federation. Other staff organizations are described in 6.7.2.

6.7.1 The Police Federation of England and Wales

England and Wales have a single Police Federation (s 64(1) of the Police Act 1996, Membership of Trade Unions), as do each of Northern Ireland and Scotland. Here we describe the Police Federation of England and Wales (the PFEW), but many of the observations also apply to Scotland and Northern Ireland. (Note that what follows is subject to change, due to the Police Federation's ongoing implementation of the recommendations from the 2014 Normington Independent Review.)

The PFEW has eight regions, with each region electing representatives to form the national Joint Central Committee. For example, Region No 2 of the Federation consists of the police forces of Cleveland, Durham, Humberside, Northumbria, North Yorkshire, South Yorkshire, and West Yorkshire. The Joint Central Committee is responsible for the national policy of the Federation.

The Federation is not a trade union in the usual sense of the term, and indeed, police officers are forbidden from joining a trade union:

> Subject to the following provisions of this section, a member of a police force shall not be a member of any trade union, or of any association having for its objects, or one of its objects, to control or influence the pay, pensions or conditions of service of any police force. (s 64(1) of the Police Act 1996 Membership of Trade Unions)

The Federation therefore does not have the right to call for any kind of industrial action such as a strike and cannot affiliate itself to the Labour Party or any other political organization. However, in many other respects the Federation was established to represent the views of its members (police officers below the rank of superintendent) on local, regional, and national levels in much the same way as any other staff association.

Each of the police forces in England and Wales has a Joint Branch Board (JBB). Within the JBB there are separate boards, representing the interests of constables, sergeants, and inspectors, as shown in the diagram. These boards each have separate agendas and meetings but also combine to form the force JBB. The JBB represents the views of police officers to the chief constable or commissioner, and to others in positions of responsibility.

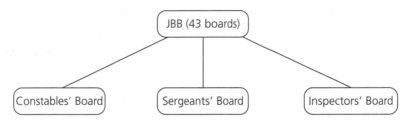

6.7.1.1 The role of the PFEW

On behalf of its members, the PFEW negotiates aspects of pay, pensions, and allowances through the Police Remuneration Review Body (PRRB). This body consists of representatives from the Police Federations (England and Wales, and Northern Ireland), the Superintendents' Association, and the National Police Chiefs' Council (NPCC) and was established through the Anti-Social Behaviour, Crime and Policing Act 2014. The members of the body meet with representatives of the government ministers responsible for the police (the Home Secretary, the Northern Ireland Secretary) and representatives of the local authorities and magistrates. The PRRB has an independent chair and deputy chair (appointed by the Prime Minister). Scotland was not included in the remit of the PRRB, and continues to use its own Police Negotiating Board.

The Federation is also represented at Police Advisory Board meetings (chaired by the Home Secretary), which consider professional subjects such as training, promotion, and discipline. After taking these discussions into account, the Home Secretary may then make proposals to amend the Police Regulations.

One of the primary functions of the Federation is to give advice and assistance to its members who are the subject of a formal complaint or internal investigation. In such circumstances the Federation's advice to an officer is to remain calm and contact his/her local Federation representative if unsure of what to do next. The IPCC have produced a leaflet concerning complaints, available from the IPCC website (IPCC, 2016a). The Federation also offers advice and assistance to police officers (including trainee officers) who sustain injuries while on duty and who wish to claim compensation from the Criminal Injuries Compensation Authority (CICA). It also offers advice and assistance to police officers (including trainees) on matters arising from the conditions of service set out in the various Acts and regulations governing the police service.

6.7.2 Other police representative organizations

There are other organizations that represent particular groups and interests, and some have links with the Police Federation. For example, the British Association for Women in Policing (BAWP) is represented on the Equality Subcommittee of the Police Federation. The BAWP seeks to address women's issues in policing and not simply to represent women; membership is open to both men and women. Further information is available on their website.

The National Black Police Association UK (NBPA) is an independent charitable organization which seeks to further the position of all police officers of 'African, African-Caribbean, Middle-Eastern, Asian or Asian sub-continent origin'. A trainee officer may join the NBPA through membership of his or her local Black Police Association (BPA), of which there are about 40 in the UK, split into nine regions. Further information is available on their website.

The National LGBT Police Network UK was established in March 2015 and aims to promote inclusiveness and equality for LGBT people who work in the police service and other crime agencies. This body replaced the Gay Police Association (GPA) which was founded in 1990 and had members in all of the UK's police forces. However, in 2014 after government funding to the GPA was cut, its membership voted to close the association from April that year. The GPA in Scotland continues as it receives separate funding from the Scottish Government.

The National Disabled Police Association (NDPA) is a registered charity and staff association which seeks to support disabled people in both the police service and the wider community. It was launched in 2004 and aims to promote better access to policing for disabled people (see their website for further information).

The Police Superintendents' Association of England and Wales (PSAEW) represents the ranks of Superintendents and Chief Superintendents (there are similar organizations for Scotland and Northern Ireland). As with the Police Federation (see 6.7.1), the PSAEW represents its members at the national Police Negotiating Board.

The National Police Chiefs' Council (NPCC) represents the interests of chief officers in England, Wales, and Northern Ireland. Chief officers are defined as police officers of the rank of ACC or above (commander in the MPS) and senior police staff equivalents. The NPCC states that its remit is to enable independent chief constables and their forces to work together to improve policing for the public. The NPCC go on to say that every police force is represented in the work of the NPCC through attendance at Chief Constables' Council. The NPCC draws on the efforts and expertise of chief officers around the country—those at the rank of assistant chief constable or above, commander in the Metropolitan Police Service and City of London Police, and senior police staff equivalents. While all chief officers have the opportunity to be involved in and shape the work of the NPCC, it is not a membership body in the traditional sense (NPCC, 2015b).

The College of Policing (CoP) is the professional body for policing whose remit is to find the best ways of delivering policing and to ensure that all officers and staff working for the police have the right knowledge and skills to do their jobs. The role of the CoP is to set the standards of professional practice within the police; to accredit training providers for qualifications such as the CKP; and set appropriate learning and development outcomes (College of Policing, 2013g). In addition, they also:

- identify, develop, and promote good practice in policing based on evidence;
- support police forces and other organizations and encourage cooperation to protect the public and prevent crime; and
- identify, develop and promote ethics, values, and standards of integrity within the police service as a whole.

Further information on the CoP is provided in 3.7.2 and other parts of Chapter 3.

TASK 13 If you are a trainee police officer, does your local force have a BPA? If it doesn't, try and find out why there is no BPA or equivalent.

6.8 Managing Police Information

Here we examine the need of police officers both to protect the confidentiality of information or data, and to share some information under the requirements of the Freedom of Information Act 2000 and the Data Protection Act 1998 (DPA). The recording of information and the confidentiality policies of the police service concerned should be explained to victims, survivors, and witnesses (IND 6.3).

Police data-gathering includes four principles, that the information gathered must be (1) Accurate, (2) Adequate, (3) Relevant, and (4) Timely. Once information is collected it is important the police adhere to legal requirements. Eight principles underpin the Data Protection Act 1998:

- Personal data must be processed fairly and lawfully and, in particular, must not be processed unless one or more of the 'conditions for processing' are met (covered in Schs 2 and 3 to the Act—for example, the individual concerned has consented or there is an urgent need because of the 'vital interests' of an individual, such as where medical history data is given to an A & E department in a hospital)

- Personal data can be obtained only for one or more specified and lawful purpose, and must not be further processed in any manner that is incompatible with that purpose or those purposes.
- Personal data must be adequate, relevant, and not excessive in relation to the purpose or purposes for which they are processed.
- Personal data must be accurate and, where necessary, kept up to date.
- Personal data processed for any purpose or purposes must not be kept for longer than is necessary for that purpose or those purposes.
- Personal data must be processed in accordance with the rights of data subjects under the DPA.
- Appropriate technical and organizational measures shall be taken against unauthorized or unlawful processing of personal data and against accidental loss or destruction of, or damage to, personal data.
- Personal data shall not be transferred to a country or territory outside the European Economic Area unless that country or territory ensures an adequate level of protection for the rights and freedoms of data subjects in relation to processing the personal data.

6.8.1 Confidentiality

Police officers (including trainee officers and special constables) will frequently encounter information of a sensitive and confidential nature. It is probably obvious, but confidentiality must be maintained, particularly in relation to witnesses, victims, and intelligence. Both the Data Protection Act 1998 (DPA) and the Human Rights Act 1998 (HRA) were enacted partly as a response to European legislation for protecting individual rights. Individual force policies may also make reference to the DPA and perhaps to the HRA (particularly those sections relevant to the right to privacy).

Police forces will collect and request information from a range of sources. The collection, storage, and disclosure of this information is subject to controls under the DPA and the Management of Police Information (MoPI). Each force has a 'data controller' who receives and considers applications for information, and decides whether the information requested can be disclosed. The DPA also provides certain rights to individuals (including witnesses and victims) for information. It is an offence under the DPA to disclose personal information without the consent of the data controller, except for the purposes of crime prevention or detection.

Confidentiality is one of the standards of professional behaviour (see 6.3.2). Police officers are expected to 'treat information with respect and access or disclose it only in the proper course of police duties'. The Policing Professional Framework (PPF) and the Code of Ethics expects the police constable to 'uphold' these professional standards. Respect for confidentiality as a theme runs through many of the Diploma in Policing assessed units. The unit that requires a trainee to 'Gather and submit information to support law enforcement objectives' contains the assessment criterion that the trainee is able to 'explain the importance of maintaining the security . . . of information'. The evidence for meeting this assessment criterion is likely to be derived from activities on Supervised Patrol, and could take the form of artefacts such as records, or direct observation by an assessor (normally a tutor constable), or witness statements. It is very unlikely that simulations in a classroom environment would meet the requirements for this criterion. The Certificate in Knowledge of Policing contains a similar assessment criterion for the knowledge aspects of this topic.

6.8.2 Management of Police Information (MoPI)

The means by which the police collect, record, share, and retain information has been the subject of some controversy in recent years, most notably as a result of the inquiry into the circumstances preceding the Soham murders (where a school caretaker killed two pupils) and the subsequent police investigations (see Bichard, 2004). The College of Policing document, *Management of Police Information* is available online. This sets out the basic principles that police organizations should adopt for the collection, recording, sharing, and retaining of information relevant to their usual work. At the level of the individual police officer, the information may take the form of intelligence and evidence gathering, details concerning domestic crime, search form completion, and pocket notebook entries.

Further, the HRA (see 5.4) requires all UK legislation to correspond with the European Convention on Human Rights. This means that any act by a public authority (such as the police) that contravenes the rights under the Convention will be unlawful. An individual's rights to privacy and family life (Article 8) can be 'interfered' with by the collection of personal information, and this interference is only permitted under certain circumstances.

The DPA places additional constraints on those holding personal data (defined in the Act as any information which can identify a living person). However, when data is used for the prevention or detection of crime, or the apprehension or prosecution of offenders, exemptions are permitted. (The College of Policing provides guidance on data protection in their *Management of Police Information* document, available on their website.)

The Code, the HRA, the DPA, and CoP information all set out an obligation to manage police information in ways that are both effective and meet certain ethical and professional standards. Much of this is at the level of the organization (rather than the individual) and are made manifest through standing orders, policies, strategies (the force 'Information Management Strategy'), and similar instruments. However, the same principles also apply for all levels of police staff, regardless of rank or role, and are likely to feature in police training after joining the police, and even on some pre-entry courses. For example, there is the need to ensure that the information that a police officer records is: necessary (for policing purposes); accurate (check the facts); adequate (do not omit important information); relevant (address the facts; record opinions only if necessary, and clearly mark as such); and timely (make the entry as soon as possible).

6.8.3 Freedom of information

The Freedom of Information Act 2000 (FoI) gives a general right of access to all types of recorded information held by public authorities, such as police forces. Each force will publish (normally online) details concerning the public's right under the FoI to access information kept by the force, and the procedures for accessing it. They will also have a publication scheme listing what information is available as a matter of routine, thereby reducing the number of requests for the same information. Not all requests for information will be successful—some of these are obvious, for example, requests relating to the identity of a Covert Human Intelligence Source (see 23.3 on the use of a CHIS), but the right to information is the norm rather than the exception. Requests can be made, and are made, on all kinds of topics.

There are two main ways that the FoI might directly affect a trainee police officer. First, he/she may personally receive a request for information under the FoI, perhaps in the form of a letter or by email. (Many people will know, for example, that a police work email is likely to be of the form x.y@force.pnn.police.uk where x is the first name, y is the surname, and 'force' is a shortened version of the name of a police force, for example BTP.) The officer should not normally respond in person but should promptly pass the request to the person responsible for handling FoI requests. Secondly, and put simply, all trainees and officers should always be aware when recording information as a police officer, that someone, someday, may apply under the FoI to view that record. Normally, and unless there are very good reasons to refuse, this will be permitted, so it is very important to choose your words accurately and carefully.

6.9 Operating IT and Communication Systems

Trainee police officers are expected to operate IT systems on both a general level (such as basic word-processing tasks and sending emails), and will also learn how to use specific police-related systems such as the Police National Computer (PNC) and the Airwave radio communication system. They might also be expected to use a particular police force information system. The ability to use 'force information management systems' is one of the requirements of the PAC under the 'Information Management' heading.

Many trainees and students on pre-join programmes are likely to already have many generic IT skills. Some police forces encourage their staff to take advantage of schemes such as the European Computer Driving Licence (ECDL). The basic skills include: searching the internet (vital for finding sites to help with all other IT skills!); creating folders; managing files (eg naming, saving, and retrieving files); word-processing documents; printing documents; using presentational software (such as MS PowerPoint); and sending and receiving emails.

6.9.1 Police information systems and databases

There are two large national databases of information for police use in the United Kingdom, the Police National Computer (PNC) and the more recently established Police National Database (PND). The PNC tends to be used by officers for 'street level' checks on a suspect, while the PND is more often employed within the context of an investigation, and is likely to contain much more detailed intelligence on individuals (both convicted and suspected). The Schengen Information System II (SIS II) operates across Europe and provides alerts concerning people and property. It is available to all police officers and police staff. In addition, a local police force is also likely to have its own databases, and you will learn about these when you enter training.

6.9.1.1 The PNC

The PNC is a large database containing information on, amongst other things, people (eg those with criminal records), vehicles (including registered keepers), driving licences, and property. It is also used by other agencies such as the Crown Court (for checking potential jurors), the Environment Agency, the Gangmasters Licensing Authority, and the United Kingdom Border Agency. A police officer could use the PNC to establish, for example, whether a driver is disqualified, or to assess the potential for a particular suspect to respond with violence. However, the PNC can do more than perform these relatively simple checks. For example, the Driver and Vehicle Standards Agency (DVSA) database is linked to the PNC, so a police officer is able to check the expiry date of an MoT and other details (such as 'advisory notices'). The linked DVLA database will reveal information relating to tests, endorsements, and so on. The PNC can also be used to search for more 'fuzzy' information such as nicknames used by offenders, tattoos, scars, hair colour, and similar distinguishing features.

The PNC is normally accessed by radio and speaking to an operator based at the Force Control Room. There is a routine to be mastered; a particular sequence of requests is made to the operator, first specifying the nature of the request (eg a vehicle check). The officer then provides his/her name and force number before stating the reason for the check. The phonetic alphabet is used to spell out words to ensure there is no mistake in transmitting the information (see 2.6.1). Officers must make a PNB record (see 10.2) of the details of the checks carried out so that his/her work is auditable.

It will certainly be emphasized during police training that there is a requirement to access the PNC in a responsible and professional manner. Inappropriate use of the PNC is viewed by police forces as a serious matter, and could lead to dismissal of a trainee police officer. (Not only is it a contravention of the PNC Code of Practice, but it is also against the law.) Unfortunately, examples of inappropriate use are only too easy to find. These have included checking on a daughter's new boyfriend and selling information to private investigators (Wadham, 2004) and in 2013, a Kent Police officer was given a prison sentence after persuading a colleague to conduct a PNC check on a man living in the officer's house (Kent Online, 2013). Alleged misuse of the PNC can lead to an IPCC inquiry (see 6.6.3) and a subsequent prosecution.

TASK 14

1. What are VODS and QUEST? You may need to use the internet or (if you are a trainee officer) ask more experienced colleagues.
2. The HMIC has carried out PNC-compliance inspections of police forces. These may be viewed via the HMIC website. Check whether your local force has yet been inspected. If so, read the report. If not, read one from your Most Similar Force (MSF) comparator.

Trainee officers are likely to be instructed on using the PNC. Effective use of the PNC is part of LPG 1 of the IPLDP, and the ability to utilize the PNC is also listed under the 'Information Management' heading of the PAC (so this will need to be demonstrated before a trainee can undertake Independent Patrol).

6.9.1.2 The PND

The PND enables information and intelligence to be shared between police forces. It was set up in 2011, partly as a consequence of the inadequacies uncovered during the Bichard inquiry into the Soham murders in 2002, and replaced the IMPACT Nominal Index. The PND contains 'POLE' data, which is information about:

- *People* (eg offenders and suspects);
- *Objects* (eg stolen vehicles);
- *Locations* (eg addresses of offenders); and
- *Events* (eg crime reports).

The data is located within five discrete but interconnected sets of records: custody, intelligence, crime, domestic abuse, and child abuse. A police force is able to check what information or intelligence is held on an individual (a 'nominal') by any other police force. Much of the information to be found on the PNC will also be present in the PND and vice versa.

6.9.1.3 Schengen Information System II (SIS II)

The Schengen Information System acts as a 'central hub' within Europe for member countries to distribute alerts across member states. UK police and border agency staff can set up and respond to alerts with international significance through the PNC. For example, alerts can be raised for persons wanted for arrest for extradition, missing persons who need police protection (including minors and adults not at risk), witnesses, absconders, people or vehicles requiring checks, and lost/stolen objects that need to be seized. Once an alert is raised it is distributed to all member states.

6.9.2 TETRA and Airwave communication

The communication protocol used by police forces in England and Wales (as with most of the other countries in Europe) is known as 'TETRA'—Terrestrial Trunked Radio. 'Airwave' (the product of a commercial company, Airwave Solutions Ltd) employs the TETRA protocols, and is the radio communications network used by the police for voice communication (eg between a police patrol and the force control room) and for communication of data. The system has replaced what many people still think of as police 'radio'. Airwave can also be used to communicate with other rescue and emergency services, and the terminals have an emergency button for use in the case of imminent personal danger. The system can be used for conventional point-to-point communication between two individuals, or it can be used by a number of people to communicate as a group (see 6.9.2.1). It is currently considered secure as it employs relatively sophisticated forms of encryption.

Trainee officers will be provided with full details about how to communicate over Airwave, including codes and protocols which are restricted to the police service (and hence not reproduced here). The phonetic alphabet is used where appropriate (see 2.6.1). Trainee officers will also be required to learn 'AirwaveSpeak', which reduces the amount of time needed to communicate information, and reduces the incidence of error or ambiguity. The table describes some of the basic rules (but be aware that there are many more).

	Description	Example
Starting the call ('calling up')	A police officer repeats the call-sign of the person (or control room) that he or she is calling and then adds his or her own call-sign	'Charlie romeo, charlie romeo...this is tango two three....'
Exchange	A police officer finishes his or her part of the exchange with the word 'Over'	'Charlie romeo, charlie romeo...this is tango two three...over'
Conveying information, asking questions, etc		'Charlie romeo, charlie romeo this is tango two three, disturbance in Tontine Street, over'
Confirming	A confirmation is often given that the message has been received and understood	'Tango two three, received, over'
Finishing the call	A police officer (or the control room) finishes the sequence of communication with 'Out'	'Charlie romeo, tango two three, suspects under arrest, out'

Airwave has limited capacity so careful management of operational use is important for police effectiveness. (There is however a 'surge' facility that allows additional capacity in times of emergency.) Capacity is particularly limited in rural areas and in underground train stations (where strict protocols are therefore particularly important). Coverage is good throughout the road systems of England, Wales, and Scotland, but there are limitations in remote areas, with no coverage at all in some places. It appears to function effectively in most circumstances, although claims were made after the riots in England during the summer of 2011 that Airwave had become 'overloaded' and police officers were forced to use their own personal mobile phones to communicate (Police Federation, 2011, p 6). This was subsequently denied by the company concerned.

The government are currently planning to replace the Airwave system with the new Emergency Services Network (ESN) which according to the Home Office (in their 2015 document *Emergency Services Network*) will provide the next generation integrated critical voice and broadband data services for the three emergency services (police, fire and rescue, and ambulance) together with other agencies such as the NCA. ESN will be a 4G mobile communications network with extensive coverage, high resilience, appropriate security and public safety functionality which will allow users to communicate even under the most challenging circumstances. At the time of writing the predicted timeline for transition to ESN is between 2017 and 2020.

6.9.2.1 ICCS

Radio communication in policing operates within a system referred to as the Integrated Command and Control System (ICCS). This allows police services to communicate internally, with one another and with other emergency services. ICCS links telephony, radio and other digital technologies, and allows a number of people to communicate directly, efficiently, and effectively as a group. In 'trunked mode operation' (TMO) a number of airwave users can communicate as a 'talk group'. (A talk group could be, for example, all the police officers involved with a particular enquiry, or staff from a variety of agencies when responding to a major incident.) Direct Mode Operation (DMO) provides voice communication between two or more handheld or mobile terminals without using Airwave. It can be used in areas with little or no coverage, but has a more limited range (usually limited to line of sight) than TETRA and uses battery power more quickly than TMO.

Capacity, congestion, and coverage are important factors for ICCS, for example, 'telephony' and 'point-to-point' occupy a lot of capacity and their use should be limited. The most efficient use of Airwave is through an open talk group (this uses the same capacity as a single point-to-point airwave communication). Mobile terminals should be set to the correct talk groups and unnecessary monitoring or usage avoided.

All users must also consider data security when using ICCS. Information that may be sensitive or operationally significant can be sanitized (see 23.5.1), or an alternative means of communication could be used. In the event of an Airwave system failure, emergency services control staff will revert to using mobile phones or the Airwave mobile phone facility, while others use status and text message with certain limitations.

For further information on ICCS and the various functions and capabilities the following sources are available online: *Standard Operating Procedure Guide on Multi-Agency Airwave interoperability* and *Standard Operating Procedure Guide on Police to Police and Inter-Agency Airwave interoperability* (both published by the NPIA in 2010), and *Airwave TeTRa (Terrestrial Trunked Radio) Technology Procedure*, from Surrey Police.

6.9.3 Mobile data devices

A number of police forces allocate mobile data devices such as smartphones, tablets, and laptops to their officers, with the intention of reducing the amount of 'paperwork'. A mobile data device provides an electronic means of:

1. entering and sharing data (eg a witness statement collected in electronic format at the scene of an incident);
2. recording and sharing location data (eg using GPS); and
3. printing some types of completed forms on a 'mini-printer' connected by Bluetooth or similar methods.

In recent years there has been considerable investment in other mobile data devices for the police service, typically in the form of BlackBerry smartphones and vehicle-mounted mobile data devices (eg in a patrol car). The intention is to free up police officer time and to improve efficiency. Deployment of these devices appears to be patchy; but the Home Office and the CoP have recently (2013) introduced a 'Digital Pathfinder' initiative, one aspect of which is to share good practice in the use of mobile data devices by police forces. Concerns have been expressed over both the cost of the devices and of ongoing data usage. However, the police use of mobile data devices is likely to grow and further expand into areas such as electronic completion of forms, particularly if the devices are linked with mini-printers. In addition, mobile data devices normally incorporate a digital camera, which (in some forces) a police officer can use to record potential evidence.

In broad terms the devices allow a police officer to access the PNC, local force tasking and briefing bulletins, missing person reports, police intelligence systems, other information systems (eg the PNLD), and information relating to an individual's name and address (eg the electoral roll, the Quick Address System), and to send emails. The exact functions and applications used on the mobile data devices are specific to each force and normally kept confidential. It is assumed that secure forms of data encryption are used, but the details are confidential.

Trainee police officers issued with a mobile data device will be informed of the relevant protocols and rules. For example, when a force-issued mobile data device is switched on it is likely to become 'visible' to the control room, therefore many police forces forbid their use whilst off duty.

6.10 Police Equipment and Technology

Police officers and Special Constables carry a range of equipment and technology when on patrol. The various items are used for personal protection (see 6.12.5), for controlling violent or potentially violent people, and for communication with other police staff. Training will be given in both the function and appropriate use of the issued equipment and technology. (Note that officers are usually prohibited from carrying unauthorized equipment or technology, but policy details vary between forces.) Here we provide a brief overview of police equipment and other items.

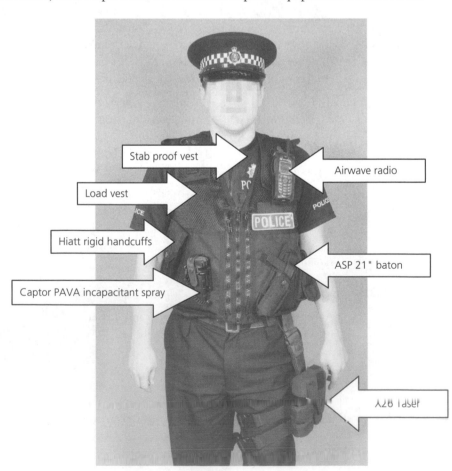

Police uniforms vary from force to force, and according to the role a police officer may be performing at a particular time. The photo shows the typical clothing and equipment worn and carried by an operational police officer. A trainee officer will become familiar with the 'Standard' (or 'Default'), 'Ceremonial', 'Public Order', and 'Specialist' (eg Dog section) uniforms for his/her force. The Standard uniform is worn on operational activities. It includes the custodian helmet for male officers and the bowler for female officers if on foot patrol, the cap if in a patrol car, and a black wicking shirt. The Public Order uniform includes a helmet, overalls, a face cover, and protective gloves. Every officer is also required to display a badge showing his/her name and/or number.

Protective equipment such as body armour and/or a stab vest is also worn for operational duties. Police officers carry equipment whilst on operational duties, such as a first aid kit, handcuffs, PAVA ('pepper') incapacitant spray (or CS spray), a baton (eg an ASP), an Airwave terminal (see 6.9.2), and a torch. In some forces officers might also carry a mobile phone and a 'taser'. Recently, an increasing number of police forces have been issuing officers with Body Worn Video (BWV). This can capture evidence of criminal behaviour and also reduce the time needed to complete statements (MPS, 2014).

Each force makes its own arrangements for purchasing equipment and technology, and some items (such as body armour) must meet Home Office quality assurance guidelines. There are opportunity costs in this approach for as the Home Office noted in 2012 'The police service currently procures equipment and services...in up to 43 different ways at a total cost of £3.3bn across 43 forces' (Home Office, 2012d, p 5). The government intends to legislate to encourage more bulk purchasing of equipment by consortia of police forces in the future.

6.11 Effective Interpersonal Communication

To 'communicate effectively' is an underpinning requirement of all the Diploma in Policing assessed units. For example, the unit 'Provide initial support to victims and witnesses' includes the assessment criterion requiring that an officer can 'communicate with individuals appropriately, taking account of pace, the victim or witnesses' level of understanding and their preferred forms of communication' (our interpretation). The Certificate in Knowledge of Policing requires that learners should 'understand the factors that affect victims and witnesses and impact on their need for support'. The PPF expects the police constable to 'Explain things well, focusing on the key points and talking to people using language they understand' and to 'listen carefully and to ask questions to clarify understanding'.

Survivors, victims, or witness can understandably be upset and disturbed by their experiences of crime, anti-social behaviour, or other incidents. It is important that officers are aware of these reactions and that sufficient time and 'space' are allowed for people to communicate what they have experienced in the course of the incident under investigation. It may be that practical and emotional support in the form of listening and reassurance is sufficient, but careful assessment might be required to determine whether additional support is required (eg medical assistance, counselling, victim support services). It is important to communicate effectively, building a rapport and gaining trust, being supportive, and keeping those affected up to date.

The ideas presented here should help you become more aware of the way you speak, and the effect it has on other people. In turn, this will help you develop strategies to help you communicate more clearly in the future, and to choose the most appropriate way to speak to another person. In 6.11.3 we will also examine the other side of the communication equation—listening skills. Non-verbal communication (NVC) is also covered (in 6.11.2) as this is an important means of communication that can easily affect exchanges between all individuals, including police officers.

Transactional analysis (TA) is explained in 6.11.1, as an example of a theory about human communication. Other theories are equally valid; for example, Shannon and Weaver's Information Theory. We are not asking you to buy into transactional analysis to the exclusion of other theories; instead we use it here as an example of the benefits that may flow from a careful and structured analysis of patterns of communication.

Qualifications and Training

6.11.1   Transactional analysis

Transactional analysis was originally developed by Eric Berne (for an introduction see Berne, 1968), and is based upon the assumption that at any one time people tend to adopt the characteristics or 'ego states' of a parent (critical or nurturing), adult, or child (adapted or free). The ego state affects their attitudes and the way they speak to each other. The ego states and the type of language used and the associated typical behaviours and attitudes are shown in the table.

Ego state	Typical words/phrases	Typical behaviour	Typical attitudes
Critical parent	'That's disgraceful!' 'You ought to…!' 'Always do it!'	Furrowed brow, pointed finger.	Condescending, judgemental.
Nurturing parent	'Well done, that's clever!'	Benevolent smile, pat on back.	Caring, permissive.
Adult	'How…'? 'When…'? 'Where…'? 'What…'?	Relaxed, logical, attentive.	Open-minded, clear-thinking, interested.
Adapted child	'Please can I?' 'I'll try harder.'	Vigorous, nodding head, downcast eyes, whiny voice.	Compliant, defiant, complaining.
Free child	'I want…' 'I feel great.'	Laughing with someone, uninhibited.	Curious, fun-loving, spontaneous.

Note that no one operates in any of these states on a permanent basis, but switches between states, even within the course of a single conversation.

> **TASK 15** If this Handbook were a person, which of the ego states would fit best and most often?

According to the theory of TA, the way a person responds will vary, partly due to the way the other person behaves or speaks (influenced by their own ego state). A trainee officer needs to be able to analyse (to some extent) the way he/she speaks and responds, and the ways that others speak and respond, and then to be able to identify the most appropriate way to manage the conversation. Having identified the ego states in play, the next task is to recognize the category of conversation or transaction, ie whether it is complementary, crossed, or ulterior.

Complementary transactions occur when the ego state of each side of the conversation correspond. Here is an example of a complementary transaction between a trainee police officer 'P' and a member of the public 'M'.

> P stops a car to give advice to the driver.
>
> **M**   I don't know why you've stopped me. Haven't you got anything better to do?
> **P**   Is this your car? I've stopped you because I've got the right, and what's your problem anyway?
> **M**   Get lost.
> **P**   You can't say that; any more lip and I'll have you.

The opening transaction is from M who appears to be in the child ego state. P's response is in the 'critical parent' ego state. The ego states correspond; it is a complementary transaction sequence:

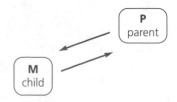

The exchange will continue in this way as long as the transactions are complementary. However, P can change the flow of the conversation by deliberately changing his/her tone and behaviour, and communicating a different ego state to create a 'crossed transaction'.

A **crossed transaction** breaks a complementary transaction. To change the style of the transaction, either P or M could employ a different ego state; let us begin the conversation again with P reacting differently.

M	I don't know why you've stopped me. Haven't you got anything better to do?
P	Hello, just a quick word, I'm PC Williams from Lewes police station. I've stopped you because one of your brake lights isn't working did you know? This could affect your safety as well as the safety of others.
M	Oh right, I didn't realize—thanks for telling me—I'll get it fixed . . . soon.
P	Thanks for your cooperation. Good afternoon.

In this case P deliberately ignores M's child ego state and adopts an adult ego state. It is a reply that has reasoning in its content, and this has an effect on M, who may not have expected this type of response. M responds accordingly in the adult ego state, which brings about a satisfactory conclusion. This is referred to as a crossed transaction, as P's response has broken the parent–child–parent pattern, and the transaction has crossed over into a different style.

In an **ulterior transaction** there are actually two different messages, an open message and a hidden message. Frequently with ulterior transactions, the open message is adult–adult, but the hidden message is parent–child or child–parent.

For example, M begins the transaction sarcastically, and emphasizes the word 'such'.	
M	It's nice to see the local police making such good use of their time.
P	Yeah, it's all part of the service to you.

This transaction is not just about words: it is also about body language and the tone of voice. The opening transaction has a hidden meaning: M dislikes the police (or at least P) and feels that the police (or P in particular) waste time, rather than catching real criminals; hence the sarcastic emphasis on the word 'such'. P's response also has a hidden meaning: hence the smirky tone and the emphasis on the word 'you'. Each component is complementary. So, unless one of the participants crosses a transaction, the dialogue will continue in this manner. The skill, therefore, is to be aware of what is happening, and to be able to cross an unproductive transaction, and thereby change the ego state of the other person.

Try using these ideas to help you understand your own and other people's styles of communication, and then choose the most appropriate way of saying what it is that you want to say.

> **TASK 16** Over the next two days, listen carefully to conversations around you. What ego states are operating and what type of transactions are taking place? Write down three brief extracts and explain what is happening in terms of transactional analysis.

6.11.2 Non-verbal communication

People may communicate anxiety, confidence, despair, or any other emotion through body language, also known as non-verbal communication (NVC). You may be able to use NVC to help build up trust with other people. It has been observed that adopting similar body postures and mannerisms communicates a positive attitude. A trainee police officer or special constable could use such techniques (in a discreet manner) when communicating with witnesses, suspects, victims, or other members of the public.

However, be wary of popular accounts concerning NVC; particular actions never have definite meanings and hand gestures (for example) are not 'windows on the soul'. (Unfortunately these kinds of scientifically unjustified 'tips and tricks' have featured in police training in the past.) In particular, the use of 'body language' in an attempt to identify deception or lying is problematic (see Vrij, 2008, for a comprehensive consideration of this). You should also be alert to 'ethnocentrism' in your interpretations of NVC, such as a refusal to make eye contact—for some ethnic groups this is related to cultural attitudes to authority, and does not necessarily indicate guilt or remorse.

6.11.3   Listening skills

Of all the skills that we develop during our lives, the ability to listen is probably the most difficult of all. We hear, but we do not always listen; this ability has to be learned and practised, and a trainee police officer will benefit from developing the ability more fully. Even the little things people say may be of critical importance when dealing with a public order situation or when investigating a crime.

Here we shall simply offer some basic advice on listening. Police training will include more detailed advice on listening skills. It is best to:

* pay full attention to the other person as he/she is speaking and to avoid looking away (think what it feels like for you when you are speaking to a person who keeps glancing away!). Use verbal and non-verbal feedback (eg nodding) to show you are listening'
* let the speaker finish before asking another question or make a comment, and don't interrupt. Most of us think we already do this but research shows that this is rarely the case! (However, there may be occasions when a police officer **must** interrupt for operational reasons.) A good way of training yourself to let someone finish is to mentally count a few seconds after he/she has stopped before you respond. You may also notice that he/she then fills this silence, and carries on speaking, almost as an afterthought. Sometimes, this extra information is of critical importance. Family doctors have long known this: often the most important part of the consultation is when the patient stands to leave and remarks, 'Oh yes doctor, there is one more thing ...'
* try echoing back to the speaker if you need to clarify something, for example by using a phrase he/she has already used—'You said, "He asked me for a cigarette,"...'. The speaker is likely to pick up the thread and continue to explain further.

6.11.4   Communication with colleagues

There are many reasons why good working relationships are important including: maintaining trust, contributing to professional performance, effective cooperation, and encouraging commitment. There is a need to communicate effectively, but also to manage conflict, challenge some attitudes and behaviour, build relationships, and work in teams. It is important to be aware of the needs of work colleagues.

The ability to prioritize accordingly can be crucial in providing an effective response. Failure to do this can result in additional pressures placed on the supervisor and the team, put the public and police colleagues at greater risk, and undermine public confidence in the police. Often these situations can be highly pressured and having an appreciation of the available support and advice from colleagues and appropriate organizations (see 11.2) can improve the speed and quality of the service to the public.

Inappropriate behaviour in policing has been a source of criticism and one that the police service continually attempts to address. There are a variety of different ways in which inappropriate behaviour can occur such as unwittingly using potentially offensive language, ignorance, and intended insults and discrimination. All police officers are expected to understand cultural sensitivities, inappropriate sexist or racist behaviour, and language. If police officers disregard these important issues it undermines the police service, supports discrimination within the service, and can put police officers and the public at risk. It could also result in disciplinary action for the officers concerned. For this reason all police officers including trainees have a responsibility to address (and where appropriate challenge) inappropriate behaviour of colleagues. When taking such actions, however, it is important to recognize the limitations of your own abilities—it may sometimes be better to seek advice or guidance from a supervisor.

6.11.4.1   Teamwork

The need to work effectively as a member of a team is reflected in a number of the Integrated Competency Framework (ICF) competencies. There are seven competencies: respect for equality and diversity, effective communication, personal responsibility, problem solving, team working, community and customer focus, and resilience.

The College of Policing lists several behaviours to build and maintain relations between team members, and also suggests a number of behaviours to avoid (see the table).

Effective team-working strategies	Poor team-working strategies
understand own role in a team	fail to volunteer to help other team members
actively take part in team tasks in the workplace	only offer to take part in high-profile and interesting activities
be open and approachable	take credit for successes without recognizing the contribution of others
make time to get to know people	work to a single agenda rather than contributing to team performance
cooperate with and support others	allow small exclusive groups of people to develop
offer to help other people	fail to offer advice or get advice from others, or play one person off against another
ask for and accept help when needed	restrict and control the sharing of information
develop mutual trust and confidence in others	prevent others from saying what they think
willingly take on unpopular or routine tasks	show little interest in working jointly with other groups to meet the goals of everyone involved
acknowledge that there is often a need to be a member of more than one team	fail to discourage conflict within the organization

Officers can demonstrate commitment by taking a full share of the workload and responding promptly to requests for help from other colleagues. It is also beneficial to clearly communicate about any difficulties encountered; this is far better than just trying to transfer the responsibility to someone else as the problems are unlikely to go away! A positive team spirit is beneficial to everyone, and all team members must take responsibility for maintaining productive working practices. The same principles apply for situations where an officer is working more as an individual rather than as part of a team; face up to responsibilities, take appropriate actions, and ensure all communications are clear.

6.11.4.2 Resolving conflicts

Occasionally, there can be disagreement between team members or with a supervisor. It is important to resolve disagreement diplomatically in order to avoid undermining police responses, as this might otherwise result in poor performance. Unless conflicts are resolved, a sense of distrust is likely to develop between team members and supervisors, and they will no longer be able to work together effectively. Individual interpersonal skills are important in trying to avoid conflict by trying to understand the views and opinions of others, and respond in an appropriate manner. You will need to understand the problem from the opposing perspective, identify the various solutions, and agree on the most appropriate way forward. One model of conflict resolution is 'CUDSA' (Confront, Understand, Define, Search, and Agree). This provides a step-by-step approach begins with confronting and understanding the problem before moving on to search for and agree to solutions.

TASK 17 The QCF Diploma in Policing assessed unit 'Support victims, witnesses and vulnerable people' contains the following assessment criterion:

The trainee police officer can, when communicating with victims and witnesses, ensure that he or she 'applies principles of equality, diversity and anti-discrimination practice' (our interpretation).

List some examples of questions that a trainee police officer might ask people, to help demonstrate meeting this assessment criterion. (In practice, Skills for Justice expect this competency to be demonstrated in a practical context on at least two occasions.)

6.12 Health and Safety

By its very nature, policing has always been and will continue to be a potentially hazardous occupation. Whilst risks are present in all work activities, operational staff are more frequently exposed to risks, for example when dealing with environmental incidents or disorderly behaviour. All employers have a duty to ensure (as far as is reasonably practicable) the health, safety, and welfare of their employees. In turn, each employee has a duty to take reasonable care for his/her own health and safety and that of other persons who might be affected by his/her acts or omissions. It is important for front-line police officers to be fit and to be provided (and use) with suitable personal safety equipment.

Health and safety may seem at times to be just another bureaucratic burden, but it is an issue police officers must consider and have in mind at all times during their day-to-day work. Health and safety duties are covered by ss 2–7 of the Health and Safety at Work etc Act 1974, and became applicable to police officers, special constabulary officers, and cadets by virtue of the Police (Health and Safety) Act 1997. Home Office publications from 1996 onwards provide guidance for police managers. A police force will also have its own published health and safety policy (eg see the 2012 Metropolitan Police document *Mayor's Office for Policing and Crime and Metropolitan Police Service Health and Safety Policy*, available online).

Health and safety-related assessment criteria feature in many of the Diploma in Policing assessment units—indeed, health and safety assessment is embedded throughout the Diploma through articulation with the NOS Unit AF1 (see 7.4). For example, the Diploma assessed unit 'Conduct police searches' has an assessment criterion to 'manage the health and safety of self and others prior to the search'. The Certificate in Knowledge of Policing unit 'Knowledge of conducting police searches' also requires learners to be able to 'explain how to maintain the health and safety of self and others during the search' when conducting vehicle searches.

Health and safety is also addressed during the IPLDP Induction Module IND 5, 'Ensure your own actions reduce the risks to health and safety'. The topics covered here are also linked with PAC heading 'Safety First' and in particular the subheadings 'Health and Safety—Legislation' and 'Health and Safety—Dynamic assessment'.

(Adapted from the Home Office publication *A Guide for Police Managers*, 1997)
All decisions must be taken with the National Decision Model in mind (see 6.5.2).

6.12.1 The employer's role in health and safety

Section 2(2) of the Health and Safety at Work etc Act (HSWA) 1974 sets out the employer's role for health and safety, stating that employers are responsible for:

- providing and maintaining plant and systems of work that are, so far as is reasonably practicable, safe, and without risks to health;
- making safe arrangements for the use, handling, storage, and transport of articles and substances;
- providing necessary information, instruction, training, and supervision for ensuring, so far as is reasonably practicable, the health and safety at work of employees;
- maintaining places of work under the employer's control in a condition which is safe and free from health risks, with safe means of entry and exit; and
- providing and maintaining a working environment for employees that is, so far as is reasonably practicable, safe, without risks to health, and has adequate facilities for their welfare at work.

(Adapted from the Home Office publication *A Guide for Police Managers*, 1997)

6.12.2 The employee's role in health and safety

Health and safety legislation places general duties on employees for example to:

- take reasonable care for their own health and safety and that of other persons who might be affected by his or her acts or omissions (s 7(a) HSWA);
- cooperate with the employer to enable the employer to comply with statutory duties for health and safety (s 7(b) HSWA);
- use correctly all work items provided by the employer, in accordance with training and instructions received (reg 14(1) of the Management of Health and Safety etc Work Regulations 1999); and
- inform their employer, or the person responsible for health and safety, of any work situation which might present a serious and imminent danger and any shortcoming in the health and safety arrangements (reg 14(2) of the Management of Health and Safety etc Work Regulations 1999).

(Adapted from the Home Office publication *A Guide for Police Managers*, 1997)
All decisions must be taken with the National Decision Model in mind (see 6.5.2).

6.12.3 Hazards, risks, and threat level

Consider the potential threats to the health and safety of a trainee police officer on foot patrol. You have probably thought of several scenarios in which the trainee police officer could be harmed. But how much harm, and how likely is it to happen? This is a matter of judgement for each different situation, but it makes it easier to judge if you think of each type of harm in terms of the hazard, the risk, and the threat level.

A hazard is something with a potential to cause harm, for example, slipping over on a wet surface, being hit by moving traffic, seizing drugs and used needles, or being hit by a meteorite. The hazard criteria are about how serious the consequences would be if the event occurs. The formal levels of classification for the hazard level are:

- high—death, major injury, or serious illness may result;
- medium—serious injuries or ill health; off work for more than three days; and
- low—less serious illness or injury; off work for less than three days.

The risk is the likelihood of such an event actually happening (see also 6.5.2 on the National Decision Model). You might have already thought that some hazards are more likely to happen than others and that the likelihood of such events also needs to be taken into account. The risk criteria are about how likely an event is: a high risk means it is very likely or near certain to occur, and medium is when it is likely to occur, and low risk is when it is very unlikely to occur.

The threat level (sometimes referred to as overall risk) is a combination of the hazard and the risk. (Note the possibility of confusing risk and overall risk; the word 'risk' may be used in these two different ways, and you will need to seek clarification if the context does not make the meaning clear.) The grid shows different combinations of hazard and risk, and the resulting threat levels.

THREAT LEVEL ↘		HAZARD		
		High	Medium	Low
RISK	High	INTOLERABLE **high** threat level	SUBSTANTIAL **high** threat level	MODERATE **medium** threat level
	Medium	SUBSTANTIAL **high** threat level	MODERATE **medium** threat level	ACCEPTABLE **low** threat level
	Low	MODERATE **medium** threat level	ACCEPTABLE **low** threat level	TRIVIAL **low** threat level

(Adapted from Home Office, 1997)

Another way of looking at assessing the threat level is to multiply the hazard and risk in an equation: hazard × risk = threat level.

For those of you who are more mathematically minded, this is not the conventional kind of formula—after all there are no numbers to put into the formula—it is just a way of summarizing the relationship to emphasize how the threat level is determined by the combination of the hazard and risk levels.

The following examples illustrate the interaction between hazard, risk, and threat level:

1. Death by meteorite—the hazard is very high as meteorites can be heavy and fall from the sky at high speeds. But the risk is low as this event is very unlikely to occur. So the threat level is low.
2. Bruising from arresting a drunken suspect—the hazard is minor. However, the risk is high as this is quite likely to occur. But the threat level is low as the consequences are unlikely to be serious.
3. Gunshot wounds when pursuing armed suspects—the hazard is serious, and there is quite a high risk of shots being fired. In this situation the threat level is high (and special precautions should be taken).

Consider another example. Imagine you are a trainee police officer on duty at the scene of a road traffic collision. Your colleague is dealing with an injured person in one of the vehicles and you are directing the traffic.

Qualifications and Training

Hazards	You could be struck by a motor vehicle and your colleague could also be hit whilst attending to the injured person, therefore the hazard level is high, as death or major injury is likely to occur if another vehicle collides with you or your colleague.
Risk	Take into account day- or night-time, volume of traffic, weather conditions, and location: the risk level is medium as it is likely or possible that you might be struck by a vehicle.
Threat level	The threat level is therefore assessed as substantial.

There has been criticism of apparent 'risk aversion' amongst some police officers, and particularly when officers are confronted with situations that pose dangers to themselves and for members of the public. The CoP state (2013f) that 'Police decision makers can, therefore, be more accurately described as professional risk takers, with risk taking being at the core of police professionalism'. Further information is available online in *Striking the balance between operational and health and safety duties in the Police Service* produced by the Health and Safety Executive.

6.12.4 Control measures

Control measures are steps that can be taken to lower the risk and therefore reduce the threat level. A five-step approach can be used, as illustrated in the following example; imagine you are a trainee police officer on foot patrol.

* **Step 1: Identify the hazards.** As a pedestrian you are exposed to danger from moving vehicles, and you could also face unpredictable confrontation with members of the public.
* **Step 2: Who may be harmed, and how?** You, a colleague, or a member of the public could be harmed by a moving vehicle, or a weapon used by a member of the public, resulting in death or major injury. Therefore, the hazard level would be high.
* **Step 3: Evaluate the risks.** Your up-to-the minute location is not always known and you are sometimes alone, as a result of which harm is possible/likely to occur. You are always at risk of walking into an unexpected situation in which harm is possible/likely to occur. You may face difficulties with radio communication, reception, and transmission, or other faulty systems, which could lead to harm. Therefore, the risk potential is medium.
* **Step 4: Record your findings.** The threat level grid shows the threat level would be substantial, so you should use control measures to lower it.
* **Step 5: Review your assessment from time to time, and revise it if necessary** .

The following control measures could be used to lower the threat level:
* in relation to the road network, adopting the correct procedures learnt during training, wearing the correct personal protective equipment (fluorescent), and using First Aid if required;
* applying techniques from training sessions for control and restraint, firearms and knife awareness, and using personal protection equipment;
* keeping the Control Room updated with your location;
* using your local knowledge and requesting all available information to assess situations; and
* being aware of the limitations of communications equipment.

TASK 18 We are not always good at judging overall risk. As an exercise, arrange the following risks in order of likelihood, putting the most likely first. They are given to you in a random order.

The likelihood of death in the next year for the average person in the UK:

* by falling down stairs;
* through being struck by lightning;
* in an aircraft crash;
* in a train crash;
* in a cycling accident;
* as the victim of homicide;
* by drowning in a bath; and
* as a consequence of lung cancer.

(Adapted from Haigh, 2006)

> **TASK 19** Imagine you are a trainee police officer carrying out a search of an aggressive young man (under s 1 of the PACE Act 1984: see 9.4.2). What would be your considerations in relation to your own and your colleagues' safety while searching him? What is your estimation of the threat level and what could be done to lower it?

If you are a trainee officer or a student studying the CKP, completion of Task 19 might assist you in preparing to meet NOS standard AF1.1 'Identify the hazards and evaluate the risks in the workplace'. In turn, this links with PAC heading 'Safety First' and the checklist subheadings 'Health and Safety—Legislation' and 'Health and Safety—Dynamic assessment'.

6.12.5 Personal safety training

Police officers are permitted to use reasonable force if necessary to prevent crime or to arrest a person (see 15.5.1). This right exists under common law and s 3 of the Criminal Law Act 1967. In addition, s 117 of the PACE Act 1984 allows a police officer to use reasonable force to exercise powers granted by other parts of PACE. A police officer may also use reasonable force in self-defence (see *R v McInnes* [1971] 1 WLR 1600 (CA)). In all cases the force used must be proportionate and exercised with due regard to the human rights of the individuals concerned.

A trainee police officer will receive practical training in protecting both him/herself and others from attack, and also about how to use reasonable force against others. (Pre-join programmes are not likely to include practical training unless it is also for special constables, but the CKP does require learners to 'understand the legislation, national guidelines and personal responsibilities that relate to responding to incidents' and to 'understand the process for providing an initial response to incidents in line with national service requirements'.) The precise title of the training may vary but in all cases, the relevant Diploma in Policing assessed unit is 'Manage conflict situations in policing'. For example, this unit has an assessment criterion that the trainee is able to 'apply personal safety techniques with issued equipment'. The training normally takes place in specialist facilities over a period of five to ten days. (In most forces it is referred to as Personal Safety Training (PST) or the Personal Safety Programme, although you might also hear reference to Officer Safety Training (OST). The title PST is now preferred, partly because some or all of the training is also used for some members of the extended police family. Alternatively, a force may have contracted with the CoP to deliver the 'Personal Safety—Basic Course'.)

Further information is available in the ACPO Centrex *Personal Safety Manual* (available on the College of Policing website), and the NPCC *Guidance on the use of Handcuffs* and *Guidance on the use of Incapacitant Spray*, available online.

These are the typical components of PST:

- **conflict management:** for example, recognizing typical signs of potential conflict;
- **searching people and places:** for example, health and safety when searching people who may have hidden weapons;
- **protective equipment:** for example, body armour, baton, and 'less lethal weaponry' such as the taser;
- **use of handcuffs and limb restraints:** for example, the use of the 'Speedcuff' rigid handcuffs and leg restraints;
- **'unarmed' self-protection skills:** for example, 'distraction strikes';
- **particular considerations when attending scenes:** for example, possible actions to be taken in the event of trying to help someone experiencing problems in water;
- **edged weapon skills:** for example, the appropriate responses to a person with a knife;
- **incapacitant sprays:** for example, the use of PAVA (Captor spray); and
- **use of batons and ASPs:** for example, the use of the 21-inch expandable baton (the ASP) and the Arnold baton.

Successful completion of PST is a target within the PAC (under the 'Safety First' heading), so trainee officers have to achieve it before Independent Patrol. However, many trainee officers will be expected to successfully complete PST before their first Supervised Patrol and, in many cases, before a community engagement. Police officers may also be expected to undertake and pass 'refresher' PST training courses later in their career.

> **TASK 20** Each force will have police officers trained in the use of equipment used for protection in Chemical, Biological, Radiological, or Nuclear incidents (CBRN incidents, see 11.6.3). What is the standard personal-protective equipment used by the UK police for such incidents?

6.12.6 First aid training

It is the duty of every police officer to 'protect life'. Inevitably police officers find themselves at incidents where there are seriously injured people, and they may also be called upon by members of the public to assist in helping with conditions ranging from a sprained ankle or scalding by hot water through to heart attacks or epileptic seizures. The public will expect a police officer to know what to do. Although specialized medical personnel will also be present (or on their way) on most occasions, a police officer will sometimes be the first person on the scene who has received any training for dealing with such emergencies.

It is for this reason that, pre-join programmes and the induction phase of training include instruction on how to administer basic First Aid. The training is likely to be based around the College of Policing programme 'First Aid Skills for Policing (FASP) Module 2—First Aid Skills'. There might also be assessment against the four elements of NOS Unit 4G4 'Administer First Aid'. Skills for Justice inform us that that the unit has been 'imported' from the Royal Marines Public Services NOS (Unit 4) and was developed by the British Red Cross in consultation with the St John Ambulance Service.

Elements of Unit 4G4—Administer First Aid

4G4.1   Respond to the needs of casualties with minor injuries
4G4.2   Respond to the needs of casualties with major injuries
4G4.3   Respond to the needs of unconscious casualties
4G4.4   Perform cardio-pulmonary resuscitation (CPR)

First Aid is also one of the headings in the Police Action Checklist and hence the successful completion of First Aid training is likely to be a necessary condition for Independent Patrol (see 8.4.2.1). First Aid training is likely to cover some or all of the following:

- **managing scenes and casualties:** for example, assessing the extent of casualties, communicating with others;
- **Basic Life Support (BLS) for Adults:** an algorithm of actions to administer immediate life support, including the need first to ensure the safety of yourself and others. It involves checking the injured person for a response, checking airways and breathing, and what to do next (recovery position, chest compression, rescue breaths, depending on the situation), and performing cardio-pulmonary resuscitation (CPR);
- **Basic Life Support (BLS) for Infants and Children:** variations on the system used for adults;
- **specific critical medical conditions:** eg shock, bleeding, spinal injuries, heart attacks, and epilepsy;
- **choking:** techniques employed to counter choking;
- **sprains, strains, and fractures:** dealing with broken bones and similar injuries;
- **scalds and burns:** what to do before more specialist medical treatment can be obtained; and
- **hypothermia, frostbite, heatstroke, and heat exhaustion:** how to treat potentially difficult medical conditions, especially for vulnerable individuals.

Most police forces expect police officers to maintain their level of First Aid training after the initial probationary period. Typically, this involves a 'refresher course' every three years or so. For more specialist roles, officers may be required to undertake specialist First Aid training, such as Kent Police's Tactical Emergency Aid Medical Support (TEAMS) First Aid Skills.

> **TASK 21** Read and reflect on the contents of Chapter 10 ('First Aid') of the 1999 Macpherson Inquiry into the death of Stephen Lawrence, at <https://www.gov.uk/government/publications/the-stephen-lawrence-inquiry>. Trainee officers may find this task provides stimulus material for completing a Learning Diary entry for Phase 1 under the 'Health & Safety' heading.

6.12.7   **Coping with stressful situations**

All professional work has the potential to create stress, but policing presents its own unique challenges in that it involves not only the usual sources of stress when working for a large organization (bureaucracy, differences with colleagues, etc) but also coping with crises, emergencies, and crime. These particular sources of stress also affect the other people involved, for example suspects, victims, and witnesses, and hence police officers often have to manage the reactions of others who are also experiencing stress. There has been a significant increase in the last few years in the number of sick days taken by police officers on the grounds of 'stress-related illness'.

It is difficult to scientifically define exactly what is meant when we say that somebody is suffering from 'stress' (as distinct from the perfectly normal short-term reactions most of us have to a challenging situation). However, most everyday definitions of stress emphasize that it is more continuous than a transient state and instead refers to a persistent collection of 'symptoms' such as psychological disturbances of anxiety, feelings of insecurity, and physiological changes such as palpitations or diarrhoea.

It is important to recognize the symptoms of long-term stress both within yourself, and others. These are many and varied and include feeling generally 'tensed up', irritable, having a short temper, sleep disturbance (particularly insomnia), problems in relationships, poor appetite, and physical symptoms such as headaches. However, professional medical advice is required to properly identify stress as a cause of these problems. Stressful situations do not necessarily give rise to long-term stress and, likewise, a person may be 'stressed' for no apparent reason.

The sources of stress in policing can be thought of as originating from three interrelated contexts: from within the person, from being a member of a police force, and from the external demands placed on police officers. It could well be that susceptibility to stress has a personality dimension. It could be that the very types of people who are attracted to policing are also more vulnerable to suffering from stress (although there is only limited research to support this idea). Being a member of a large, complex, and demanding organization such as a police force can easily lead to exposure to sources of stress. The demands placed on police officers, in terms of dealing with the results of crime and disorder (including death and injury), interacting with members of the public, offenders, and the legal profession are also obvious sources of stress. The mistakes that police officers inevitably make are sometimes very visible ones. A particularly stressful event for police officers can be responding to a critical incident, when they may witness disturbing events. No doubt many readers would have heard of the phenomenon of 'Post-Traumatic Stress Disorder', or PTSD.

There are numerous articles, books, and websites with advice on coping with stress. Police forces also have counselling facilities as well as occupational health support (eg through the 'Occupational Support Unit'). The usual advice typically centres on dealing with both the symptoms (which may require specialist medical help), and the causes of stress.

6.13   **Answers to Tasks**

TASK 1 Your response to the task may have centred on one or more of the following:

- **Ethical or moral reasons**: as a trainee police officer, you subscribe to the values of the Statement as they coincide (more or less) with your own values. Indeed, the reason you joined (or seek to join) the police was perhaps in order to 'protect, help and reassure the community'.
- **Professional reasons**: you have chosen to join a profession of your own free will and so should abide by the rules of that profession.
- **Instrumental reasons**: for example, in order to do my job as a police officer properly (or indeed, to keep my job) I need to subscribe to, and implement, the requirements of the Statement.

The circumstances surrounding the documentary and the political fallout are well documented on the internet and elsewhere. Many commentators have argued that the documentary gave added impetus to the reforms contained within the IPLDP, and particularly those aspects concerned with the values and attitudes of police officers.

TASK 2 There are many techniques for memorizing information (the author Tony Buzan, for example, has written extensively on the subject). We describe one straightforward technique here for memorizing the declaration:

1. Gather ample supplies of blank paper!
2. Now write out (or word-process) the declaration on a blank piece of paper by copying the original. Check and double-check that you have the words exactly as they should be.
3. Read the first sentence several times (not the whole paragraph) and try to commit this to memory.
4. Now turn the page and write down (or word-process), from memory, the first sentence on another piece of paper.
5. Check your recollected version against the original, correct, version word for word.
6. Repeat stages 3–5 until you have the sentence completely correct.
7. Now attempt to memorize the first two sentences together in order.
8. Repeat the process until you have the first two sentences completely correct.
9. Now add the third sentence and so on.
10. Continue until you have committed the complete declaration to memory.

This may take you some hours to achieve. The same technique can be used for memorizing other information—for example, your force might expect you to learn 'definitions'.

TASK 3 Although the police officer concerned was off duty when the alleged incidents took place you have probably noted that the standards for general conduct apply for officers both on and off duty. The standards apparently breached here include Honesty and Integrity, Duties and Responsibilities, and Discreditable Conduct.

TASK 4 The most appropriate Diploma in Policing assessed units would appear to be:

Standard	Relevant Diploma in Policing assessed unit
3. Equality and Diversity	All units
4. Use of Force	Manage conflict situations in policing
7. Confidentiality	Handle information and intelligence that can support law enforcement

(However, some alternative answers are entirely possible.)

TASK 5 In many police forces, such as Kent Police, you would need permission from at least the BCU commander, and the written notice must be given to the chief constable using the form *Notification of Secondary Business Interests*. This should be forwarded through the individual's line manager to the divisional commander or head of department for endorsement.

In many forces, the responsibility for monitoring the 'secondary business interests' of police officers and police staff is delegated to the head of HR.

TASK 6 You will have your own response to the first part of the task. In relation to receiving an unlawful order, this is most unlikely to occur, but you should still be clear about your own position. The College of Policing Code of Ethics (2014a) goes on to state:

5.3 There may be instances when failure to follow an order or instruction does not amount to misconduct. For example, where a police officer reasonably believes that an order is unlawful or has good and sufficient reason not to comply.

5.4 Any decision to not obey orders or follow instructions, or that transgresses policing policies and other guidance, must be able to withstand scrutiny.

TASK 7 The assumption is that consent should be achieved in a positive sense, through gaining the support of the public and involving them in policing decisions and strategies. There is also an emphasis on the need for police to be ever more responsive to community needs, see for example *Policing in the 21st Century: Reconnecting Police and the People* (Home Office, 2010c). In 1829, we would argue, the notion of consent was slightly different—it was measured negatively in the sense that people were consenting only to the extent that they were not proactively objecting to or protesting against policing initiatives.

TASK 8 As we suggested, there are no certain answers to this task. There are interesting examples of attempts by a number of countries to tackle, for example, corruption amongst their police officers through using the kind of analysis that you have just undertaken. For example, in Kenya, police numbers in 2004 were almost doubled and corruption subsequently fell. (However, proving that this was cause and effect is somewhat more difficult.)

TASK 9 Drugs policing, in particular, gives rise to a number of opportunities for corruption both in type and frequency (Lee and South, 2003). These include theft from arrested drug dealers, planting drugs to imply guilt, illegally protecting drug dealers (eg by classifying them as a CHIS), and participation in dealing.

TASK 10 The five opportunities from the list are:
- first arrival at the scene of a crime where cash or goods are present;
- handling and storing drugs from police investigations;
- the excessive exercise of discretion without challenge;
- managing informants without adequate supervision or scrutiny; and
- lack of effective supervision.

TASK 11 The free cup of coffee theory may seem to you to be an unlikely explanation, but imagine if a police officer uses his warrant card to secure financial advantage—for example, to gain free entry to a club. Even if he justifies this to himself on the grounds that his (non-uniformed) presence would somehow be to the benefit of the club concerned, would this not lead to at least a small sense of obligation on his part and a potential compromise of his position? As they say in the USA, 'nobody ever gave a cop something for nothing'. The situation is even more complex when a police officer has a second job.

This is not to say that accepting gratuities is always wrong. The circumstances will be a guide, as will force policy. For example, you may be offered cups of tea (or coffee!) by well-meaning members of the public if you are engaged in long and tiring public order duties, and it seems there would be little to lose and much to be gained by accepting the offer on those occasions.

TASK 12 Remember that this theory assumes that the officer has a predisposition towards corruption or deviant behaviour. If this is the case, then he/she is likely to find many reasons that will justify undertaking corrupt acts.

For a comprehensive discussion of this and other aspects of police corruption you might want to read Caless (2008a and 2008b), as well as Newburn (1999) and Miller (2003).

TASK 13 You can establish whether your local force has a branch of the BPA by searching the database on their website.

TASK 14

1. They are both features of the PNC. VODS is a Vehicle Online Descriptive Search application for helping identify vehicles. It can search for combinations of details such as make and model, colour, and VIN (see 16.8.1.1). QUEST is a Query Using Extended Search Techniques facility within PNC, and is the fuzzy capability we referred to earlier. The operator can input partial descriptions of people and produce a list of names that match the characteristics. HMIC have reported the following example of a successful outcome when using QUEST:

   In the West Midlands, counterfeit currency was used in a public house. A search was carried out on the description of a white male, 6' tall, thin build with a skinhead haircut, brown hair, aged 20–22 years. The offender had a tattoo of a swallow on his left hand. Enquiries at the scene suggested he lived in Solihull and may have been called 'Barry'. A QUEST search produced one suspect who was subsequently dealt with for the offence. (HMIC, 2005b, p 36)

You might like to conduct further research on the use of Boolean search techniques that use AND, OR, and NOT. These are also useful for conducting internet searches. Further information is available at <http://www.inbrief.co.uk/police/police-national-computer.htm>.

TASK 15 Agreed, this task requires a gross oversimplification of the theory. However, on most occasions the Handbook would appear to be in adult mode—but there are certainly also aspects of the critical and nurturing parent.

TASK 16 We obviously provide a simplified version of transactional analysis (TA). You might want to read further. A good starting point is Berne's very readable and popular 1968 book *Games People Play* (reissued in the late 1990s), which you are likely to be able pick up second-hand on eBay or at boot sales for very little. The games that Berne refers to are transactions that lead inevitably to predictable outcomes.

Note that TA is not without its critics and some of its academic standing has been damaged by popularized and oversimplified accounts. Another frequent approach (in police training) to analysing the interactions between individuals (or groups) is the use of the so-called 'Johari' window. The unusual name Johari originates from its two inventors, Joseph Luft and Harry Ingham (Luft, 1970). It proposes that one way of analysing aspects of human interaction is to identify areas of personal awareness and ignorance:

	Known to self	Not known to self
Known to others	Open area	Blind area
Not known to others	Hidden area	Unknown area

For example, the blind area includes aspects which the person does not know about him/herself but which others know. This can range from straightforward information (such as a medical complaint like halitosis) to more developed personality features, such as feelings of inadequacy, which are barely discerned by the individuals concerned and yet can be easily seen by others.

TASK 17 The kind of questions you might ask are with reference to your actions, such as entering a person's home, touching a person when conducting a search, and religious requirements for the treatment of the dead.

TASK 18 The correct order starting with the most likely, based upon statistics for 2004, is: as a consequence of lung cancer; as the victim of homicide; by falling down stairs; in a cycling accident; by drowning in a bath; in a train crash; in an aircraft crash; and finally through being struck by lightning.

TASK 19 What hazards would you identify? The man could cause you injury by using physical force, or a weapon or an object he is carrying or picks up or takes from you (eg your own personal safety equipment). He might also have an infection or infestation and could infect you with it (such as hepatitis C, tuberculosis (TB), influenza (flu), or scabies). Care will be needed as there may be needles concealed in his clothing. Therefore the hazard level is medium, as you could be absent from work for more than three days if he does attack or harm you.

In terms of the risks, you should take into account his level of agitation and aggression, how long the search will take, and what opportunity you give (or avoid giving) for him to use force against you. You should also take into consideration: the locality of the search in terms of its proximity to other members of the public; the level of illumination; and whether any colleagues are present or nearby. The risk level is medium as it is likely or possible that you might be injured, and so the threat level is calculated to be moderate.

There are many control measures you could take, for example: requesting a cover officer (if you are alone); carrying out personal safety techniques such as standing at his side when conducting the search; being aware of his movements at all times during the search; engaging him in conversation (because he will find it difficult to think of answers to questions and do other things at the same time); wearing gloves to reduce the risk of injury, and washing your hands (and other exposed body parts) afterwards. You could also carry out the search in the sight line of a CCTV camera.

TASK 20 The standard CBRN personal protection equipment issued to trained police officers in the event of an incident is the CR1 (CR stands for Civil Responder; the military are issued with their own version). The CR1 is identical to that used by the fire service in similar circumstances. CBRN incidents are covered in 11.6.3.

TASK 21 Naturally, much media attention at the time of the Macpherson Inquiry report centred on the charge of institutional racism. Unfortunately, this inadvertently diverted national attention from the very serious issue of the training of police officers in First Aid and the need to maintain their skills, throughout their careers and at all ranks. Although the Report is clear that Stephen Lawrence's death from his injuries was probably unavoidable, Chapter 10 remains a shocking catalogue of incompetence and ineptitude. It concludes with the observation that:

> [t]his evidence reinforced the Inquiry's views as to the lack of satisfactory and proper training in First Aid for officers of all ranks. Not only should officers be properly trained and be given proper refresher training at regular intervals, but it must be made plain that more senior officers need instruction just as much as junior officers. An officer in the position of [name] must be able to ensure that what is being done by his juniors is proper and satisfactory and in accordance with well-coordinated and directed training. The notion that it may be good enough simply to wait for the ambulance and the paramedics must be exploded. (Macpherson, 1999, s 10.6)

7 | Qualification and Professional Development

7.1 Introduction

In this chapter we examine the National Policing Curriculum, the qualification process for training as a police officer (including pre-join programmes), and the formal assessment systems for the professional development of confirmed officers. By 'qualification' we mean the requirements on pre-join students and trainee police officers in terms of gaining access to a policing career, gaining advanced standing, and qualifying as a police officer. At the end of the chapter we examine the new Police Education Qualifications Framework (PEQF) and the implications of the proposed changes for initial training and professional development.

7.2 The National Policing Curriculum

The National Policing Curriculum (NPC) was developed by the College of Policing to form the basis of training for a range of policing roles, responsibilities and levels. It is aligned with both Authorised Professional Practice (APP) and the NOS (see 7.4.3). The pre-join curriculum is derived from the NPC, and provides the basis for qualification through the Certificate in Knowledge of Policing (see 7.2).

A 'curriculum' normally refers to all the learning that is considered necessary for a student to achieve specified learning outcomes. Hence a curriculum normally includes or makes reference to an accepted body of knowledge, but might also include consideration of the teaching and learning methods to be employed and the skills to be gained. It will generally relate to and fit with formal qualifications.

The NPC is structured around seven themes (CoP, 2016j). The 'Core Learning' theme underpins all parts of the curriculum (and hence the other six headings), and covers four headings:

- 'ethics and integrity';
- 'communication';
- 'evidence based policing'; and
- 'leadership and management'.

The other six NPC headings are:

- 'Ensuring Public Safety' (eg first aid, personal safety, public order, roads policing);
- 'Protecting Vulnerable People' (eg countering domestic abuse, child abuse (including child sexual exploitation) and serious sexual offences);
- 'Preventing and Reducing Crime' (eg crime prevention, counter terrorism);
- 'Maximising Information and Intelligence' (eg gathering intelligence, use of police databases);
- 'Conducting Investigations' (eg investigating crime and non-crime incidents, forensic investigation, interviewing suspects and witnesses, detention, custody, case file management); and
- 'Supporting Victims'.

7.3   Overview of Qualifications

Until relatively recently the usual qualification route for police officers was through joining a police force and undertaking a two-year full-time probationary period of training. There was little, if any, accreditation of prior learning, and the same model of entry applied to all applicants. There are now some alternative routes into policing and a significant development in recent years has been the introduction of pre-join (or 'pre-entry') schemes and courses by some colleges, universities, and other providers, sometimes in conjunction with police forces. The Home Office has also introduced a fast-track inspector scheme, and changed its recruitment policy to allow direct recruitment to the rank of superintendent, and the appointment of chief constables from overseas (Home Office, 2013g).

Note that from April 2018 the new Policing Education Qualifications Framework is expected to be introduced. This will mean major changes to the current 'landscape' of policing qualifications, including prior and initial learning for police officers (see 7.7 for further information on the proposals).

The table summarizes the various routes to qualification currently available at the time of writing. APL is accredited prior learning (which will shorten the length of training and the probationary period for some trainee police officers).

Course	Qualification	APL arrangements	Comments
Traditional police training (two years)	Diploma in Policing*	N/A	In the past this was the only form of training but it is offered less often now
Certificate in Knowledge of Policing**	FE Level 3	Towards the knowledge requirements only	Sometimes called the 'CKP' or the Policing Knowledge Certificate, (PKC). A pre-employment qualification to be obtained before application. Students complete Diploma in Policing after joining the police
Foundation Degree in Policing, Police Studies, or related discipline	FdA or FdSc. Often linked with joining Special Constabulary. HE Level 5	Towards knowledge requirements. Towards competence requirements if linked with Special Constabulary	Students complete Diploma in Policing before or after joining
Honours Degree in Policing, Police Studies or related discipline	BA (Hons) or BSc (Hons) HE Level 6	Towards knowledge requirements, and also competence requirements if linked with Special Constabulary	Typically three years in duration (full-time), compared to two years for a FdA or FdSc. Students complete Diploma in Policing before or after joining

*   Changes are expected with the possible introduction of a Level 6 qualification in 2018.
** Likely to be replaced in 2018.

7.3.1   Pre-join programmes

Students on such programmes complete some of the learning and training required to become a full-time police constable before they join a police force. The College of Policing (CoP) expects the content of all pre-join programmes to articulate with the pre-join curriculum (see 7.2), and some pre-join programmes also incorporate the Certificate in Knowledge of Policing (CKP). The CoP also operates an 'Approved Provider Scheme' for pre-join programmes (particularly providers of the CKP) as part of its 'Pre-join Strategy'. At the time of writing (2017) some 62 organizations have been approved, including six that offer distance-learning options, 19 universities, 25 colleges, and one police force (CoP, 2015c). Pre-join programmes are either stand-alone (eg a course leading only to the CKP) or may be embedded within longer programmes of study, such as a Foundation degree in Policing or Police Studies.

In 2015 the College of Policing conducted a review of pre-join programmes (CoP, 2015k) and reported some concerns about the CKP amongst students, training providers, awarding bodies, colleges, and police forces. In particular, doubts were expressed concerning the level of knowledge gained by students undertaking the CKP, and about variations and inconsistencies in assessment practices and problems with the transferability of the award (ibid).

To join some forces, a current CKP certificate is a necessary (but not sufficient) requirement to join as a recruit. For example, South Wales Police require 'CKP Plus' as a preliminary to being even eligible to apply to join the police as a constable (South Wales Police, 2015). CKP Plus is achieving the CKP and also (in the case of the CKP being achieved with a provider other than South Wales Police) scoring more than 70 per cent in two multiple-choice examinations set by the force.

The successful completion of very few (if any) of the existing pre-join programmes guarantees entry to the full-time police, or even an interview with a police force. The nationally determined recruitment assessment process will still apply (see 8.2). The APL value of a pre-join programme is likely to vary between 'receiving' police forces, although the CoP has established a set of 'principles' to guide force policy. The currency of a completed pre-join programme is normally three years, or four years for a PCSO or special constable continually engaged with operational duties (CoP, 2014g, p 5). So entry to the police will need to be achieved within this time limit to gain the maximum APL for subsequent IPLDP training.

7.4 The Certificate and the Diploma

The Certificate in Knowledge of Policing and the Diploma in Policing are based around the 21 NOS units for initial policing (listed in 1.4.3). Detailed content for both the Certificate and Diploma is derived from the National Policing Curriculum (see 7.2). The CKP essentially covers the knowledge aspects of the Diploma, and equates to roughly 50 per cent of the Diploma in Policing. The evidence collected as part of the assessment for the CKP can be used as a form of APL against the requirements of the Diploma when undertaking initial training with a police force. The CKP does not include any operational work-based policing assessments, and so successful completion of this qualification does not indicate operational competency.

Each of the Certificate and Diploma units are divided into learning outcomes with associated content and assessment criteria. For example, the content for the Certificate learning outcome to 'Understand how to arrest and detain suspects in line with legal and national service requirements' is likely to cover aspects of the HRA and the PACE Codes of Practice (see 5.4 and 5.6). The assessment criteria for each learning outcome give an indication of what the learner has to do to demonstrate achievement of a learning outcome (see 8.5.1 for further details).

Both the Certificate and the Diploma are at QCF Level 3 which is roughly 'A' level standard, but it is invidious to draw simple comparisons between academic awards and hybrid occupational qualifications such as the Diploma in Policing. This is because the Diploma signifies occupational competence, which normally requires a combination of both theoretical understanding and practical application. It is reasonable that a FE Level 3 Diploma representing competence can be embedded in an HE Level 4 or 5 award (such as a Foundation degree): after all, a person's practical ability to undertake a role within a profession often falls short of his/her theoretical understanding of the same set of tasks.

7.4.1 The Certificate in Knowledge of Policing

The Certificate of Knowledge of Policing is currently offered by training providers, universities, and FE colleges, subject to approval by the College of Policing. Some training and education providers will offer Certification through awarding bodies such as City & Guilds, CMI, Pearsons, ProQual, and SfJ Awards.

The ten Certificate units cover the knowledge required for a range of policing activities. The Certificate carries a total of 29 credits (with the number of credits for each unit shown in brackets), and although it is a QCF Level 3 qualification overall, a few of the units are at Level 4.

Qualifications and Training

Certificate in Knowledge of Policing Units	Learning outcome(s)
Knowledge of handling information and intelligence (3)	Understand the legislation, national guidelines, and personal responsibilities that relate to handling information and intelligence Know how to handle information and intelligence that can support law enforcement objectives in line with national service requirements, authorisations, and protocols
Knowledge of evidence-based preventative policing (2)	Understand the features of evidence-based preventative policing Understand how to develop an evidence-based preventative policing approach in given situations Understand how to implement evidence-based preventative policing plans Understand how to review evidence-based preventative policing approaches
Knowledge of providing an initial response to policing incidents (3)	Understand the legislation, national guidelines and personal responsibilities that relate to responding to incidents Understand the process for providing an initial response to incidents in line with national service requirements
Knowledge of supporting victims, witnesses, and vulnerable people (3)	Understand the factors that affect victims, witnesses, and vulnerable people and the impact on their need for support Understand the legislation, national service requirements, and codes of practice that apply when dealing with victims, witnesses, and vulnerable people Understand the importance of effective communication with victims, witnesses, and vulnerable people Understand how to provide initial support to victims, witnesses, and vulnerable people
Knowledge of using policing powers to deal with suspects (3)	Understand the legislation, national guidelines, and personal responsibilities that relate to the use of police powers when dealing with suspects Understand how to arrest and detain suspects in line with legal and national service requirements Understand the options with regard to the disposal of suspects
Knowledge of conducting priority and volume investigations (4)	Understand the legislation, national guidelines, and personal responsibilities that relate to conducting priority and volume investigations Understand the nature of crime and its impact upon the community Understand the process for conducting priority and volume investigations Understand how to conduct priority and volume investigations in line with legal and national service requirements Understand how to prepare and document information relating to priority and volume investigations in line with legal and national service requirements
Knowledge of interviewing victims and witnesses in relation to priority and volume investigations (2)	Understand the legislation, national service requirements and professional codes of practice in relation to conducting interviews with victims and witnesses Understand how to plan and prepare for interviews with victims and witnesses Understand how to conduct interviews with victims and witnesses Understand post-interview procedures and the evaluation process for interviews with victims and witnesses
Knowledge of interviewing suspects in relation to priority and volume investigations within a policing context (3)	Understand relevant legal and organisational requirements in relation to interviewing suspects Understand the principles of interviewing suspects
Knowledge of conducting police searches (3)	Understand the legislation, national guidelines, and personal responsibilities in relation to conducting police searches Understand how to conduct police searches in line with legal and national service requirements

Certificate in Knowledge of Policing Units	Learning outcome(s)
Knowledge of managing conflict in policing (3)	Understand the legislation, national service requirements, and personal responsibilities that relate to managing conflict
	Understand conflict management techniques
	Understand requirements for recording and reporting conflict management incidents

(Table contents based on Ofqual, 2016; Crown Copyright)

The CKP qualification is intended to assess knowledge and understanding of the content of the pre-join curriculum. The College of Policing divides the pre-join curriculum into nine modules based upon nine of the ten National Policing Curriculum headings (see 7.2). If you are a CKP student you might well find that your, college, university, or training provider has mapped your course to these NPC learning outcomes.

7.4.2 The Diploma in Policing

The ten Diploma units cover the knowledge required for a range of policing activities (as in the Certificate in Knowledge of Policing) but also cover the associated skills. Each Diploma unit carries between two and five credits, making a total of 84 credits (the credit value for each unit is shown in brackets in the table).

As with other policing qualifications, the content of a course leading to the Diploma will be based upon the ten areas of the National Policing Curriculum (7.2). Students who have taken an approved pre-entry programme, or who were previously a special constable or a PCSO might be able to claim 'advanced standing' against the assessment requirements of the Diploma through APL (see 7.2).

Note that with the probable introduction of a new Policing Education Qualifications Framework in 2018 there are likely to be significant changes to the Diploma (it may even be replaced). This is discussed further in 7.7.

Diploma in Policing Units	Learning outcomes
Plan, implement, and review an evidence-based preventative policing approach (8)	Understand an evidence-based preventative policing approach
	Be able to develop a preventative policing approach in a given situation
	Be able to develop plans to support preventative policing approaches
	Be able to implement preventative policing plans
	Be able to review preventative policing approaches adopted
Support victims, witnesses and vulnerable people (8)	Understand the factors that affect victims, witnesses, and vulnerable people and how this may impact on their need for support
	Be able to communicate effectively with victims, witnesses, and vulnerable people
	Be able to provide initial support to victims, witnesses, and vulnerable people
	Be able to assess the needs and wishes of victims, witnesses and the vulnerable for further support
Manage conflict situations in policing (10)	Understand the legal and organisational requirements related to managing conflict
	Be able to apply conflict management techniques
	Be able to apply personal safety techniques with issued equipment
Use police powers to deal with suspects (10)	Understand the requirements for using police powers when dealing with suspects
	Be able to arrest and detain suspects in line with legal and organisational requirements and timescales
	Be able to report suspects in line with legal and organisational requirements and timescales
	Be able to apply alternative options with regard to disposal of suspects, in line with legal and organisational requirements

Qualifications and Training

Conduct police searches (10)	Understand legal and organisational requirements in relation to police searches
	Be able to prepare to conduct police searches in line with legal and organisational requirements
	Be able to conduct police searches of premises, vehicles, and outside spaces in line with legal and organisational requirements
	Be able to conduct police searches of individuals in line with legal and organisational requirements
Handle information and intelligence that can support law enforcement (8)	Understand legal and organisational requirements related to handling information and intelligence that can support law enforcement
	Be able to handle information and intelligence that can support law enforcement
Provide an initial response to policing incidents (8)	Understand legal and organisational requirements related to responding to incidents
	Be able to analyse information to plan responses to incidents
	Be able to provide an initial response to incidents in line with legal and organisational requirements
Conduct priority and volume investigations (10)	Understand the legal and organisational requirements in relation to conducting priority and volume investigations
	Understand the process for conducting priority and volume investigations
	Understand the nature of crime and its impact upon the community
	Be able to conduct priority and volume investigations
	Be able to document information relating to priority and volume investigations, in line with legal and organisational requirements
Interview victims and witnesses in relation to priority and volume investigations (6)	Understand the principles of interviewing victims and witnesses
	Be able to plan and prepare interviews with victims and witnesses
	Be able to conduct interviews with victims and witnesses
	Be able to evaluate interviews with victims and witnesses and carry out post-interview procedures
Interview suspects in relation to priority and volume investigations (6)	Understand the principles of interviewing suspects
	Be able to prepare for interviews with suspects
	Be able to conduct an interview with a suspect
	Be able to evaluate interviews with suspects and carry out post-interview procedures

(Adapted from Ofqual, 2016; Crown Copyright)

7.4.3   The National Occupational Standards and the NOS Units

The initial training for trainee police officers is underpinned by 21 National Occupational Standard (NOS) units (see 1.4.3 for a list of the unit titles). The National Occupational Standards are a set of statements that describe the competence required to undertake a certain occupation or to use a set of particular skills. They form the basis of qualifications for certain occupations, for example the Diploma in Policing.

Each of the ten units of the Diploma in Policing is based on one of the 21 NOS units. These ten NOS units are fully assessed within the Diploma. A further five NOS units are embedded within the ten Diploma units, and the NOS unit on searching is partly assessed. Of the remaining five NOS units, four are not assessed within the Diploma and the final NOS unit (on First Aid) is assessed separately. You should be aware that the requirements for assessments relating to the NOS can change, both in terms of the number of units and their content.

7.5   PIP Level 1

The 'Professionalising Investigation Programme' (PIP) forms the basis for training officers in criminal investigation, and is maintained by the CoP. It also underpins the system through which a police force decides what level of police response is appropriate for different types of crime. The four levels for PIP are shown in the table.

Level	Associated staff/police rank	Type of investigation or crime
1	Patrol Constable/Police Staff/Supervisors	Investigation of volume and priority crime
2	Dedicated Investigator, eg CID officer	Substantive investigation into more serious and problem offences, including road traffic deaths
3	Senior Investigating Officer	Lead investigator in cases of murder, stranger rape, kidnap, or complex crimes
4	Principal Investigating Officer/Officer in Overall Command (OIOC)/Heads of Crime	Critical, complex, protracted, and/or linked serious crime(s)

(Derived from Centrex, 2005)

PIP Level 1 is included in initial pre-qualification police training and covers interviewing techniques, investigation methods and models, law, case files, major and serious crime procedures, ranging from petty theft to 'stranger' murders. It is integrated into the IPLDP curriculum (embedded within the National Policing Curriculum) and has also been mapped against three of the NOS units used for the Diploma in Policing:

- CI101 Conduct priority and volume investigations;
- CJ101 Interview victims and witnesses in relation to priority and volume investigations; and
- CJ201 Interview suspects in relation to priority and volume investigations.

These units also feature within the operational modules of the IPLDP—for example, CJ101 and CJ201 have been mapped against OP6 'Prepare, conduct, and evaluate interviews'. It is therefore unlikely that a trainee officer will achieve PIP Level 1 until the end of his/her first year of training (at the earliest), and it is more likely to be during the second year.

After successfully completing PIP Level 1 a trainee officer will be 'signed off' as a Level 1 investigator, and be registered with his/her force as having reached this standard. However, in order to remain registered all police officers have to demonstrate on a regular basis that their skills and knowledge have been maintained.

7.6 Professional Development

In this part of Chapter 7 we examine the professional development opportunities that might present themselves to a newly qualified police officer, including applying for promotion. Towards the end of your training (or in some forces, in the second year of training) you may be asked to consider the possibility of undertaking a specialist role within your force.

One of the first decisions will be whether to specialize or generalize. You should refer to the Policing Professional Framework (see 8.5.2) personal qualities for the constable role at this point, and remind yourself what is involved in reaching the required standard for the generic role.

You will already have the behavioural competencies; the ability to complete the administration procedures associated with the role, maintain the standards of professional practice, work as part of a team, provide First Aid when required, and comply with health and safety legislation. You will also make the best use of technology and you promote equality, diversity, and human rights in all your working practices, as well as being part of an organizational response which recognizes the needs of all communities. You employ an effective problem-solving approach to all community issues in which you become involved and you make good use of intelligence to support the policing objectives of your force.

Thus equipped, you should be ready to take on any general task as a constable, and to serve anywhere in the force that you are needed. For some people that is enough and they are perfectly happy refining these competencies and behaviours, building experience, and interacting with the public on a daily basis; some officers will never want to move away from this generic role during their entire careers.

7.6.1 Specialist roles

As a trainee police officer you will have been exposed to the work of three major divisions of policing during your initial training: investigation, patrol policing, and community policing. We now examine each of the three areas in turn.

7.6.1.1 Investigative policing

A decision to follow the investigative route does not mean that you are closing off the other avenues forever. It is quite common to move in and out of roles and across the streams of central police work, but as a rule you will stay within the detective branch or department if you specialize in investigation. In many forces, the route to becoming a skilled investigator is through service on an investigation team based locally in a BCU. In some forces, this is called a 'tactical criminal investigation department' or TAC CID.

Level 1 PIP is linked with the IPLDP and the NOS units/Diploma in Policing assessment units for initial policing, so Level 1 is automatically achieved on successful completion of initial training (see 7.5).

The Initial Crime Investigators' Development Programme (ICIDP) is a police force programme for trainee detective constables (TDCs) and provides the basis for the investigation of more serious and complex criminal cases. (It is also sometimes referred to as the National ICIDP (NICIDP).) The ICIDP is linked with PIP Level 2, which is in turn linked with three NOS units relevant to serious and complex investigations; CI102, CJ102, and CJ202 ('Conduct serious and complex investigations', 'Interview victims and witnesses in relation to serious and complex investigations', and 'Interview suspects in relation to serious and complex investigations', respectively). These are more demanding than the parallel NOS units for initial police training listed in 7.4.1.

The ICIDP consists of three phases, summarized as follows. Details are available from local police forces.

- **Phase 1** (for the trainee investigator) is a period of self-study using printed materials, and typically takes a minimum of 14 weeks to complete. The content is law-based and covers property offences, assaults, drugs, firearms, sexual offences, offences against children and other vulnerable persons, cyber and digital crime, and evidence.
- **Phase 2** is typically a six-week taught course, and concludes with sitting the National Investigators' Examination (NIE), a multiple-choice examination consisting of 80 questions (10 of which do not count towards the final mark). It assesses knowledge of the four sub-areas: property offences; assaults, drugs, firearms, and gun crime; sexual offences; and evidence. At the time of writing (2017) the passmark has not been finalized but in 2016 it was set at 55.7 per cent (CoP, 2016h). There is some flexibility on how forces structure the course (eg some base it on a case study and might also incorporate a 'Hydra' simulation). However, all courses are likely to be linked to the NOS units and elements, and to articulate with the CoP specified aims and objectives and the content derived from Authorised Professional Practice (APP). In many forces, before commencing Phase 2 there is also a requirement to complete a 'tier 2' investigating interview course after initial training. The methods used for assessment of the knowledge and understanding gained during Phase 2 vary between forces (eg whether a formal written examination is set or not).
- **Phase 3** will always involve demonstration and assessment of competence in the work place against the three NOS units (CI102, CJ102, and CJ202). A tutor (normally an accredited detective constable (Level 2) or an investigative adviser) will provide supervision, and evidence must be collected in a Professional Development Portfolio (PDP). Experienced investigators (who will have been in position before the advent of the ICIDP) are able to access Phase 3 through APL procedures. On successful completion of Phase 3, investigators are 'registered' at the BCU level as qualified at PIP Level 2.

Officers may then move to internal force departments such as a central unit investigating Level 2 serious crime, or join a specialist homicide team, investigating 'Cat A' and 'Cat B' murders, manslaughter, or GBH. This will probably involve taking the **Initial Management of Serious Crime** (IMSC) course, which is designed primarily for detective sergeants and is, in effect, a bridging course between the ICIDP and the more advanced programmes for SIOs. After completing the IMSC course and attaining the rank of detective inspector, an investigator might choose to undertake the College of Policing three-week **Management of Serious Crime Investigations Development Programme** as a further career step.

The Senior Investigating Officer Development Programme (SIODP) is designed for investigators who are already qualified to at least PIP Level 2 (eg through the ICIDP) or its equivalent, and who are likely to become responsible for investigating serious crime such as homicide and rape by a stranger. Students of the SIODP are typically of detective inspector rank or above. As with IPLDP and ICIDP, the SIODP is linked with the NOS, in this case the single unit CI103, 'Manage major investigations' (with a total of five elements). The course typically lasts 15 days. A one-week 'Hydra' simulation course (based on the investigation of a serious crime) is also often recommended as a follow-up, and is in some cases a compulsory element. The SIODP is usually delivered on a regional rather than local-force basis in order to provide good access to specialist inputs, and also for economy of scale (the numbers involved are significantly lower than for the ICIDP). The course usually covers the APP investigative model (particularly in terms of initial response, gathering information, and the use of forensic investigation), multi-agency working, family liaison, resource management, the use of intelligence, record keeping (particularly in terms of policy logging and disclosure), self-evaluation and the evaluation of others, and handling the media. Evidence for claiming competence is presented in a PDP, and successful completion results in achievement of PIP Level 3.

7.6.1.2 Patrol policing

If you decide that Patrol is your preferred interest, there are plenty of roles to take, such as Traffic, Tactical Operations, Firearms, and Public Order. In this type of work you will be at the forefront of visible uniformed policing. As for investigation, specializing within Patrol will involve a fair amount of training and will follow a systematic development route. One of the things you should consider, before opting to go into the Patrol stream, is what opportunities there are for you to obtain further qualifications, and to find out whether there is a partnership programme with academic institutions. If Patrol is a 'default option' in your force, and there is little evident development or systematic learning, you might want to think twice before committing yourself. If, on the other hand, your force is pursuing partnerships, links, and development opportunities, you will find that Patrol is far from a backwater and may be the most vibrant and innovative part of your force. It very much depends on your local circumstances.

There is no doubt that Patrol can be an immensely satisfying part of policing: you will often be the first officer attending a crime scene (with all the responsibilities we outline in Chapter 11, in terms of the 'golden hour' and your vital role in the preservation of life and of evidence), and you will have a major part to play in policing demonstrations, large gatherings, public events, and disorder. Your contact with the public will be an integral part of the reassurance agenda and you will be mainly involved with the policing of volume crime and public disorder. It is the most physically demanding of all police roles, and you will also be in the forefront of dealing with violence, collisions, tragedies, and human disaster. The dynamic risk assessments for many of the roles in Patrol will be crucial for police and public safety; you should not underestimate the strains and stresses of front-line police work.

7.6.1.3 Community (neighbourhood) policing

Community and neighbourhood policing is different again. Here, you will work with smaller teams, and the work will often help form an important bridge between Patrol and Investigation. You will learn new skills and your development will probably be geared to specializing in one of a number of roles. For example, you may opt to work as a Community Liaison Officer (CLO), in which case you will get to know the leaders and members of groups within your local community and help to develop sophisticated partnership-working arrangements to meet community needs. Diversity skills will be vital, as will the accumulation of intelligence on crime in the community. You will often be the first port of call from your detective colleagues when investigating crime within your area, and your advice will be needed, and usually respected and acted upon, especially when there are local sensitivities, such as minority ethnic communities or the investigation of a homophobic crime.

You may become part of a Neighbourhood Policing Team (NPT) alongside members of the wider policing family such as PCSOs and special constables. This will involve both responding to local issues and needs surrounding crime and disorder (often in collaboration with other agencies, such as local authorities), and taking proactive action in reassuring the public. You will be a named contact for members of the local community, and will help them access their local policing services. Community policing also involves providing feedback on actions taken and the consequences.

A Family Liaison Officer (FLO) has a specialist role within community policing. They are trained in negotiation, mediation, and some group-management techniques so that their work with families (usually the victims or witnesses of crime) is as productive, reassuring, and positive as possible. A FLO can provide a focus for the family in the wake of a crime, especially a crime of violence, and will help them through the difficulties of the search for the offender, arrest, charge, and the subsequent court proceedings. In a very real sense, a FLO is the 'face of policing' to that family, and will often help them provide vital evidence. For example a FLO played a leading part in obtaining evidence in the Russell murders case in Kent in 1996. This was a particularly disturbing crime, in which a mother and her two daughters on a rural foot-path were attacked by a man with a hammer or similar instrument. The mother and one of the daughters died but the older daughter survived. In the investigation which followed, the FLO's skills were vital in gaining her trust, and this was integral to the successful prosecution of Michael Stone for the murders.

Working closely with neighbourhoods and their varied communities is, for many officers, what policing is really about, and offers its greatest rewards. This is not to say that the work is easy; to gain the community's trust and respect means working long hours, having highly developed personal skills, and understanding how community dynamics and partnerships work. The development of NPTs based on BCUs, in which there may be a mix of police officers, PCSOs, special constables, and members of other agencies, is a pointer to the importance of local and citizen-focused engagement. Should you opt for a community-policing role, you may well find yourself in time supervising the work of others, and/or managing a neighbourhood-policing team. Many officers find this a deeply satisfying activity and are reluctant to leave it. Other work, such as crime reduction, schools' liaison, and working with crime-reduction partnerships also provide considerable rewards in return for persistence, professionalism, and receptivity, but the results in terms of crime reduction are often long-term, rather than immediate. Communities appear to dislike frequent changes of police personnel and it takes time to build relationships. If you opt for community policing, you need to be aware that it is often for the long haul.

7.6.2 Personal development

Whether you seek promotion early or not, you have an obligation to sustain your continuous professional development (CPD). The nature of CPD varies from force to force; in some it means gaining the necessary experience and qualification through training (such as in Firearms, or the ICIDP programme—see 7.6.1.1). In other forces it can mean pursuing further study which links your professional development with an academic partner, resulting in a further academic award such as a two-year occupation-based Foundation degree, vocational qualifications such as an NVQ or SNVQ, or a higher education award such as a BSc (Hons) in Policing or a Master's degree. Some forces allow all these forms of CPD, which seek to develop the skills and capabilities you will need as you progress in policing (laterally or vertically). Your force is likely to have a number of academic partners through whom further professional study may be pursued, but, if not, plenty of institutions advertise their courses or programmes in publications and websites such as *Police Professional*.

Note that you will probably need permission to engage in further study, since the force has to balance your CPD with the demands of your current job. After all, studying could add up to 25 hours to the working week, although this could be justified in both organizational terms (increased professionalism) and individual aspiration. If the agreed further study is directly related to your policing function, your force might pay the fees and allow you some duty time to study, but always check first.

7.6.3 Achieving promotion

If you are a trainee police officer then your first priority will obviously be to achieve full confirmation at the end of two years' training. However, if not now, then probably at some time in the future, you may begin to think about promotion to a higher rank. Whenever possible you should talk to those already holding the substantive rank and find out what they do and why. You will also need to look at the competencies and role requirements of the generic sergeant role and any specialist functions which a supervisor performs. If you can, you should seek opportunities to 'act up' in the rank, perhaps by supervising a patrol of constables for a limited time, or by seeking temporary promotion whenever it is offered. It is helpful here to understand a difference in terminology: acting rank means that you do it for a short time, probably on a casual basis; temporary rank means that you perform the role of that rank for a period of at least three months, and you receive the pay of that rank.

It is not a requirement in the police service, as it is in the armed forces, to spend some time in the acting rank before being eligible for consideration for promotion. However, the opportunity for an officer to act in the rank above is often a good opportunity for showing that he/she can do the next job; it accrues experience in the role and gives the opportunity for assessors to make judgements on a person's actual performance, rather than simply on potential. The PEQF may introduce new qualifications for achieving promotion.

7.6.3.1   The National Police Promotion Framework

Promotion to sergeant and inspector ranks is organized through the National Police Promotion Framework (NPPF). This system was introduced in April 2015. As with much of the content of this chapter, arrangements for promotion are likely to change once the new Police Education Qualifications Framework is introduced (planned for 2018). This is explained more fully in 7.7.

For promotion from constable to sergeant, the NPPF involves four steps:

1. assessment of candidate's competence in his/her current rank through the PDR;
2. passing a formal assessment of knowledge of law and police procedure (known as the 'NPPF Step 2 Legal Examination');
3. assessment against role-specific competencies and matching these to the existing vacancies (eg by structured interviews or psychometric testing);
4. temporary promotion and work-based assessment (WBA) for a period of least 12 months, during which the individual will be required to demonstrate competence in the role (against the National Occupational Standards).

The NPPF Step 2 Legal Examination is a three-hour multiple-choice examination paper with 150 questions (140 of which count towards the final mark). The syllabus may vary from year to year. In 2017 the syllabus was divided into four categories: crime, evidence and procedure, road policing, and general police duties (CoP, 2016i). Each of the four subject categories is then further divided into greater detail (eg 'handling stolen goods'), and related to legislation where applicable. At the time of writing the pass mark for the NPPF Step 2 Legal Examination had not been finalized, but the pass-mark for the equivalent examination in 2015 was 55 per cent (CoP, 2015i).

7.7   The Policing Education Qualifications Framework (PEQF)

In early 2016 the College of Policing put forward potentially far reaching proposals to reform the professional development of police officers, as a 'key step towards establishing policing as a profession' (CoP, 2016a, p 4). As we noted in 3.7, qualifications are one of the hallmarks of a profession and the CoP's new 'Policing Education Qualifications Framework' (PEQF) represents one of the most serious attempts in recent years to reform and regularize qualifications in policing. The summary provided here is based on information available in early 2017 and represents the authors' interpretation of the proposals as they currently stand. Readers are encouraged to consult the College of Policing website for the most up-to-date and reliable information.

The CoP proposals concern:

- the qualification requirements for entry to training in policing;
- a new qualifications framework for policing involving universities;
- accreditation of prior experiential learning for police constables already in post.

Joining the police is likely to remain largely unchanged in the near future (see 8.2) and hence careful consideration will need to be given to the number of students recruited by universities (in consultation with their partner police forces) to pre-join and post-join programmes, given the limits on recruitment and the uncertain outcome of an independent selection process.

7.7.1   PEQF Proposals for Entry into Police Training

It is proposed that entrants into training should have Level 3 qualification(s), and Level 2 in English and mathematics (or equivalents). Level 2 represents attainment of 'functional skills' (eg GCSE grades C to A*), and Level 3 awards provide access to higher education (eg 'A' level grades A to E, an IB diploma, etc). The academic requirements for entry to training are likely to be in addition to some of the current requirements such as age and minimum fitness requirements. However, there might still be variations in entry requirements between forces.

It is envisaged that from 2020 three possible pathways to confirmation as a police constable will be available:

- a 'degree apprenticeship' where recruits gain an undergraduate degree whilst training (and receiving a salary, but at the level of an 'apprentice police officer');
- successful completion of a 'CoP-approved' pre-join practical policing degree (such as a BSc (Hons) Policing, where students fund themselves);
- a 'post-join' postgraduate 'conversion' programme into policing (paid for by a police force), for graduates from other disciplines such as the social sciences.

Many details have still yet to be decided. For example, the proportions of the content of the degree apprenticeship route that should be determined nationally (through the CoP) and locally (between police forces and universities) has not been settled.

7.7.2 PEQF Proposals for Professional Development and Promotion

The proposed new qualifications framework for policing will cover different ranks as shown in the table. In some cases the qualification will be achieved whilst in position rather than as a pre-requisite for appointment. Requirements for 'specialization' (eg as an investigator) are still being discussed.

Rank to be attained	Qualification required (proposed)	HE qualification level	Explanation
Police constable	'degree apprenticeship' (in general policing)	Level 6	Level 6 is equivalent to an undergraduate honours degree (eg a BA (Hons)).
Police sergeant	'higher level apprenticeship' (in leadership and management)	Level 6	
Police inspector	'postgraduate certificate' (in leadership and management)	Level 7	Level 7 is postgraduate master's level (eg an MSc).
Police superintendent	'master's apprenticeship'	Level 7	
Senior police commander	'professional doctorate'	Level 8	Level 8 is PhD level.

Table based on College of Policing and Home Office information but authors' interpretation

Accreditation of prior experiential learning for police officers currently in post (eg police constables) is also under consideration. It is proposed that they should be able to gain academic credit for their existing skills and experience. The level and scale of academic credit (APL/APEL) is yet to be determined, but the intention is to develop national standards. It is unlikely that current police officers will be obliged to gain a qualification.

Determining the balance and nature of work-based and university assessment will be important, because policing (in common with professions such as nursing) combines a number of skills and forms of knowledge. Ensuring national consistency between police forces and their university partners (allowing the transferability of qualified individuals between forces) will be important and possibly difficult to achieve.

8 | Education, Training, and Assessment

8.1 Introduction

In this chapter we examine the current programmes of education and training that feature within police training, including entry through pre-join courses. The College of Policing announced in early 2017 that entry to the police is to be significantly reformed in the coming years; the routes into joining the police service are set to change. Beyond 2020 there will be three entry routes available to potential police officers:

1. a police constable degree apprenticeship paid for and managed by a force in partnership with a university allowing individuals to obtain a policing degree and earn while they learn;
2. a specific professional policing degree;
3. for graduate entrants a graduate programme which will also be paid for by the force.

The most significant of these changes will be the introduction of a police constable apprenticeship degree programme, which will see some applicants to the police, who do not have a degree, secure employment as an apprentice police officer. Their probationary training will include not only that deemed necessary by their force, but also a requirement to complete a policing degree with a University selected by the force. The police constable apprenticeship degree will be an employer led scheme, and as such recruitment into a police service will be required. More information can be obtained about the future changes to police recruitment at the College of Policing official website <http://www.college.police.uk/What-we-do/Learning/Policing-Education-Qualifications-Framework/Pages/Policing-Education-Qualifications-Framework.aspx>.

In our examination of the current training arrangements, we will look in most detail at the training after joining the police (initial police training), and the forms of assessment that will be used to confirm fitness to practise as a police officer.

Direct vocational training, which takes place for example in police forces, is often concerned with the 'mastery' of a skill or practical knowledge acquisition. The emphasis is on being able to do something, and to do it correctly. For this reason police forces often employ classroom-based techniques which involve problem-based learning punctuated with role-plays to provide more realism. Computer-based learning might also be used: for example, via the Managed Learning Environment (MLE) of the National Centre for Applied Learning Technologies (NCALT). The learning will assessed by sitting multiple-choice examination papers. Work-based learning will take place within the Basic Command Unit (BCU) and comprise of coaching by a tutor constable leading to competency-based assessment. This is discussed in more detail in 8.6. More recently the College of Policing has launched a pre-join curriculum and an associated qualification, the Certificate in Knowledge of Policing (see 7.4), that can be delivered by a range of 'non-police' providers from private companies, further education colleges and universities.

In higher education, where undergraduate degrees in policing are taught, a student is likely to be given more responsibility for his or her own learning with teaching directed more towards further reading and independent research. However, in some cases practical application of the learning might also take place, although the realism of work-based learning may be limited unless the student is also a special constable. Emphasis in higher education will be placed on reflection, analysis, and criticality using libraries, e-libraries, and virtual learning environments

Qualifications and Training

such as Blackboard to locate resources. As a consequence, assessment will include writing academic assignments (eg essays) in addition to written formal examinations.

8.2 Applying to Join the Police

Some readers of the Handbook might already be full-time trainee officers, in which case this section might only have limited value to you. However, if you are a student on a pre-join programme at a college or university, or you are currently a special constable or a PCSO seeking to become a full-time police officer, then the following will provide a useful overview of gaining entry to the full-time police service. Note, however, that there are other options and positions within the wider police family other than becoming a regular officer (see 3.4).

Many of the 43 police services in England and Wales are currently recruiting a significant number of new staff following a temporary freeze in recent years. There are three main sources of information on becoming a 'regular' police officer:

- the recruitment departments of the police forces in England and Wales (accessible via the websites of the parent organizations)—consider not only the territorial police forces (such as the MPS) but also other police forces such as BTP;
- the 'official' College of Policing website (at <http://recruit.college.police.uk/Pages/home.aspx>); and
- a website run by Chamberlain Place Ltd (at <http://www.allpolicejobs.co.uk>), which claims to be 'the only website that lists all current vacancies in all UK police forces'. However, at the time of writing this was a paid subscription-only service.

For joining the police service as a full-time police constable all of the following are requirements (in 2017, at the time of writing):

- You need to be **eligible** to join, for example in terms of age and nationality (see 8.2.1).
- You need to submit and pass an **application process** at the level required by the force you have applied to (see 8.2.2).
- A **background** and security check and a medical check (including testing for use of illegal drugs) should indicate that there is no good reason to exclude you (see 8.2.4).
- You need to undertake and pass a **fitness** and **eyesight test** (see 8.2.4.1).

Each police service can set its own additional entry requirements so you will need to check with the organization you wish to join. Following Peter Neyroud's recommendations on police training and leadership and the second Winsor Review (2012), some forces now also require certain qualifications or experience (see 8.2.1). For others you might also need to complete a pre-application questionnaire or pass an in-force interview, and for some forces, applicants must live in the area. Meeting all of the requirements does not guarantee a job with the police force concerned. There have been occasions in the past where recruitment has been cancelled at short notice and otherwise successful applicants have been disappointed.

8.2.1 Eligibility

Eligibility in this context refers to both your general suitability for the police service and the technical requirements on you in terms of your age, fitness, and so on. There are many books and websites providing advice on the former. Many of the chapters of this Handbook will also provide insight into the skills, attitudes, and behaviour expected as part of the role of police constable. In terms of the technical requirements, in order to apply to become a full-time police constable you must be 18 years of age or over, and be in good health and reasonably fit. Officially there is no upper age limit, but the normal retirement age for police constables and sergeants is at 60 years of age and hence you are not likely to be selected if you are aged 57 or over.

The College of Policing website provides more detail on eligibility requirements. Some key points are that:

- there is no height prerequisite;
- general educational or specific pre-join qualifications are needed for some (but not all) police services, eg a GCSE qualification in English at grade C or above; the Certificate in Knowledge of Policing (and a certain level of attainment might be specified);
- experience in a police-related role may be required, eg as a 'special' or a PCSO;

- a conviction or even a caution can lead to an application being rejected (this includes anyone having received a formal caution in the last five years, or committed a violent crime or public order offence);
- you must be a citizen in the UK, European Union, European Economic Area, or Commonwealth, or a foreign national with indefinite leave to remain in the UK;
- you need appropriate physical and mental fitness to perform police duties; and
- there may be additional local force requirements, such as the ability to drive or swim, and in many cases residence in the UK for a period of no less than three years (with no nationality exemptions). For the MPS you must have lived in London for at least three of the six years prior to applying, and the ability to speak one of 25 listed languages is desirable but not essential.

It might be worth at this stage asking yourself 'Is there any reason that I know of now that will mean that I cannot join the police in the future?' For example, are your eyesight and level of health at the required levels? Do you have any convictions that might prohibit you from joining? The College of Policing provides a useful pre-application questionnaire which will help you with some of these questions.

8.2.2 The application process

After careful consideration and research the next step after checking eligibility is to apply to a police force with vacancies. None of the stages of the application and recruitment process should be taken for granted! None are straightforward and there is always a possibility of failure, and this applies particularly for completing the application form. This will often need to be completed by hand (in writing) although some forces provide the opportunity to register and submit forms online. Many applicants fall at this first hurdle because they do not assign sufficient importance to the process. The guidance that accompanies the form should be read carefully. Common sense suggests that answers should be drafted before completing a handwritten form, thereby avoiding making spelling and grammatical mistakes.

The application form is likely to involve the following:

Section(s)	Notes
Biographical details—name, DoB, place of birth, nationality, address(es), family details, employment details, etc	Straightforward information is required, but double-check that you have these right
Convictions, financial background, membership of BNP/National Front/Combat 18 or similar organizations	Criminal convictions are likely to mean your application is rejected. Your family will also be subject to checks Financial problems include County Court Judgments (CCJs) Membership of the BNP/National Front/Combat 18 or similar organizations will exclude you
Tattoos	Be honest about tattoos, even if they are not on parts of the body normally exposed to the public. The MPS policy is that no tattoos on the face, visible above the collar line, or on hands are acceptable Offensive or racist tattoos are likely to be problematic
Education and qualifications	List of your qualifications (exams passed) with dates, etc. Remember that you might be asked to show your certificates at some stage so check that you have the details correct. Some forces will require you to complete the CKP before recruitment
Personal referees	Choose your referees with care. Ensure that they can respond authoritatively on your employment or educational record
Competency questions	Usually four questions testing your understanding of the skills and qualities required of a police constable. In many respects the most important part of the form (see below)
Motivation questions	Usually five questions exploring the reasons why you wish to become a police officer

Your application form will join hundreds of others as part of an application 'sift'. The police staff responsible for assessing and grading your application (the 'assessors') deliberately do not see certain biographical details such as your ethnicity and so on, but instead judge how effectively you have answered the competency and motivation questions. Assessors will look for evidence of specific behaviours from the Policing Professional Framework (PPF) in your answers and grade them accordingly. At the time of writing these are decision-making, leadership, professionalism,

Qualifications and Training

public service and working with others. Read and think carefully about these competency behaviours (the details are to be found in the document *Police SEARCH Recruit Assessment Centre: Information for Candidates* on the CoP website).

If you pass the paper sift then you will be invited to attend an 'Assessment Centre'. This is usually a reference to the assessment process itself rather than a physical location. The assessment will probably take place at a venue within the relevant police force area, and will be conducted according to national guidelines as described in 8.2.3.

8.2.3 The Assessment Centre

Prior to attending the Assessment Centre all applicants are sent a 'welcome pack' containing a number of documents as preparation materials. It is also available via the CoP website (referred to as the 'Westshire Welcome Pack'). The Assessment Centre process follows a nationally agreed format, often referred to as SEARCH©. The pack will include information about this although you can also download this information in advance from the CoP website.

The welcome pack will also provide information about a fictitious shopping centre which underpins the storyline for the interactive and written exercises at the Assessment Centre. The applicant will play the role of a customer services officer during these exercises. This might appear strange for applying for a position in policing (and not in commerce or business), but the intention behind this appears to be to ensure that all candidates have a fair chance regardless of background (after all, a policing scenario might give a special constable an advantage). It assumes that the generic competences required by a constable can nonetheless be assessed. Preparation for the Assessment Centre could also include learning more about the force applied to (eg the name of the chief constable), practising for the interview (discussed later), and attempting numerical and reasoning tests.

The Assessment Centre takes about five hours and has five main stages as listed in the table. The candidates are allocated to syndicates (groups) so the exercises can be carried out in turn. All candidates will be under observation even during breaks—surreptitiously texting during a briefing (for example) will be noticed and not be viewed favourably. More formal assessment will also take place as shown in the table (although note that details may be subject to change by the CoP).

Stage of Assessment Centre	Number of assessments	Time allowed	Form of assessment
Interview	1	Up to 20 minutes (4 questions of 5 minutes each)	Using a subset of the NCF, graded A–D
Numerical test	1	23 minutes for 21 questions	The score is converted to an A–D scale
Verbal ability test	1	30 minutes for 28 questions	The score is converted to an A–D scale
Written exercises	2	20 minutes each	Using a subset of the NCF graded A–D
Role-play exercises	4	10 minutes each (includes 5 minutes' preparation)	Using a subset of the NCF graded A–D

The **interview** consists of four questions and will focus on exploring how each candidate has handled situations in the past. Six different competencies will be assessed during the 20-minute interview. Some competencies will be assessed more than once and oral communication will be assessed throughout the interview. The competencies being assessed are:

- Decision Making;
- Service Delivery;
- Serving the Public;
- Professionalism;
- Openness to Change;
- Working with Others.

Typically the questions begin with 'Can you give me an example of...?' and then refer to a generic situation such as overcoming a particular challenge. Examples of 'mock' Assessment Centre interviews can be found on YouTube and these might be useful in terms of appreciating the format of the interview. But a candidate should avoid being too polished and calculating and must genuinely understand and mean what he/she says.

The **numerical test** consists of a 23-minute multiple-choice examination with 21 questions and four choices for each answer. Each of the number-based simple mental arithmetic problems requires a calculation (without a calculator) involving addition, subtraction, multiplication, division, and simple percentages.

In the **verbal ability test** 28 multiple-choice questions are used. Information is provided about a situation, and the questions measure your ability to make sense of the situation. For each question in Section A there is a choice of three possible answers, and in Section B there are four options. (There is only one correct answer to each question.) A full briefing will be given before the test. Many people find the verbal ability test more demanding than the numerical test.

The two **written exercises** are more demanding still, and last 20 minutes each. The exercises are based on the contents of the Welcome Pack (discussed earlier). For each exercise written information is provided about a problem at the shopping centre, for example a memo from a colleague, a map of the centre, and letters from those involved in the complaint. The candidate, as the customer services officer, has to write a 'proposal document' using the template provided. The following abilities will be assessed: the ability to comprehend and summarize information accurately; logical structure of the responses; and spelling and grammar. An example of the written exercises is available on the CoP website.

The four **role-play exercises** each consist of a ten-minute exercise; five minutes for preparation (with written information provided about the situation) and five minutes for a role-play between the candidate as the customer services officer and an actor playing a certain role, for example a customer with a complaint. This is an opportunity for using some of the information from the Welcome Pack such as the policies of the fictitious shopping centre. Making notes in advance is a good idea as these can be used during the role-play. The positive indicators described in the NCF (shown here in italics) should be used when acting out the role. For example, the candidate could say something like:

- 'I am going to take personal responsibility for this problem by doing the following...' (*professionalism*);
- 'I've looked at the centre's policy on...and I've decided to...' (*decision making*);
- 'It may make me unpopular with...but I am still going to...' (*professionalism*);
- 'I am going to challenge the attitude of...because it may have been discriminatory' (*professionalism*);
- 'I am going to offer support to...in order that she can...' (*working with others*); and
- 'I am going to keep you updated on my progress by...' (*serving the public*).

Each of the Assessment Centre stages is marked by the assessors, and an overall mark is then calculated. The marking schemes are confidential.

After a successful Assessment Centre (expect to hear after a couple of weeks or so) you may be asked to attend an interview with your chosen police force (this does not apply in all forces). Although your performance may meet the minimum national standard at the assessment centre, this does not necessarily guarantee you a post within the force you are applying to. For example, forces may have more candidates who have met the national standard than they have vacancies, therefore may choose to prioritize candidates by those who have achieved the highest scores above the minimum standard, or by adding an additional assessment or an interview. If you are going to be interviewed, then you should find out carefully what is involved, and why an interview is being conducted at this stage.

8.2.4   Background, security, and medical checks

After a successful Assessment Centre the police force concerned will conduct a background and security check on you and your family and associates. They are likely to take up the references you supplied in the application form and check the PNC and other intelligence databases for your right to work in the UK, your address and other biographical details, any criminal convictions or cautions, your financial background, and whether you 'associate' with known criminals. If you are refused entry to the police on grounds of security there is little you can do.

You will also be asked to complete and submit a detailed medical questionnaire, countersigned by your GP. Home Office circular 59/2004 (available on the www.gov.uk website) outlines the recommended medical standards for recruitment into the police. The police force might request further information from you and/or your GP, and there might also be a 'medical' involving a hearing test, blood pressure measurements, a lung function test, and tests for alcohol, drug or substance abuse. Your BMI (Body Mass Index) might also be calculated which involves measuring your height and weight to assess if you are overweight.

8.2.4.1 Fitness and eyesight test

If you are selected for the next phase of recruitment, then you will be invited to attend a fitness assessment. At the same time you will be asked to have you eyesight examined by an optician and get the form completed and countersigned, or the force will carry out an eye-test. (This might also happen at an earlier stage—see 8.2.4.) Your unaided eyesight will need to meet certain minimum standards, you should check this with the force you are applying to.

All applicants also undertake a 'multi-stage fitness test' (the MSFT), an endurance test which involves running to and fro on a 15-metre track in time with a series of bleeps, with the time interval becoming increasingly short (the 'bleep test'). Some forces replace this with a 'circuit' of a 15m track. Most reasonably fit applicants have no great problem in meeting this requirement. To test your level of fitness mark out a 15m distance (or use your local sports centre) and then download the mp3 file with the 'bleeps' from the CoP website (<http://www.college. police.uk/What-we-do/Standards/Fitness/Pages/MSFT-pratice-recruits.aspx>) and attempt the running exercise.

8.3 IPLDP

The Initial Police Learning and Development Programme (IPLDP) is the form of police initial training used by all forces since April 2006. It also forms the basis, at least in part, of special constable training, PCSO training, and the growing number of pre-entry programmes available through colleges and universities.

The National Policing Curriculum (NPC) is made up of learning standards, which have been designed by the College of Policing to meet current police training needs for a wide variety of roles (see 7.2). Both the IPLDP and the CKP curriculum work towards a subset of the NPC learning standards, which are also mapped to the relevant National Occupational Standards, contained within the Policing Professional Framework. The NPC derived learning standards are typically spread over four phases of training and learning and are not normally delivered in a simple, linear, serial manner. A typical pattern of delivery is shown in 8.4.1. Colleges, universities, or forces may use different terminology from that used here. For example, there may be modules rather than courses, and phases might have a different meaning. Police forces are expected to ensure that the entire mandatory IPLDP curriculum is taught (NPIA, 2010b, p 3), but can choose how to structure the training as long as they remain IPLDP-compliant (Home Office, 2005c).

8.3.1 IPLDP and pre-join programmes

Educational and training providers have to demonstrate that the content and assessment of their pre-join programmes relates to the IPLDP (NPC) pre-join curriculum (NPIA, 2011a, p 12 and CoP, 2013e). This enables successful students to gain APL against parts of the full IPLDP on entry to the police. In practice it is often more straightforward for colleges and universities to deliver the underpinning knowledge requirement (for examples through the Certificate in Knowledge of Policing) rather than the embedded professional skills requirement of IPLDP. Typically, a pre-join course will include subjects that link with the IPLDP curriculum categories such as the context to law enforcement, the CJS, police powers, basic law and legislation relevant to policing (eg theft, traffic offences, etc), and more advanced criminal law (eg sexual offences). There is currently significant variation between pre-join course providers.

8.4 The Probationary Period and Confirmation

After joining the police all trainees undertake the Initial Police Learning and Development Programme through the Diploma in Policing (see 8.3). Trainees who have passed the CKP may only need to cover part of the Diploma as most of the knowledge aspects for each topic will have already been covered. In this part of Chapter 8 we examine the likely pattern of training over the two-year 'probationary period', how trainees are assessed as competent, the probationary period, and confirmation. We also consider what might happen to trainees who experience problems during training.

8.4.1 The pattern of training

The IPLDP approach to the initial training of police officers consists of four phases as shown here:

Phase	Typical activities
Phase 1: Induction	Introduction to the force • Practical and organizational needs, eg dress code, uniform, Federation, etc • Learning about IPLDP, ethics, and diversity • Undertaking First Aid and Officer Safety Training (eg self-protection) • Introduction to the use of technology, eg Airwave, PNC, etc • Job-Related Fitness Test
Phase 2: Community safety and partnerships	• Receiving a crime and disorder 'package' • Community safety
Phase 3: Core police learning and Supervised Patrol	• Classroom learning of the bulk of LPG modules (including case studies, eg in public order) • Operating a 'Crime Investigation Model' • Undertaking Supervised Patrol
Phase 4: Additional learning and Independent Patrol	• Classroom learning (a minimum of 30 days/6 weeks) of the more complex LPG modules (including case studies), eg child abuse and sexual offences • Developing police practice (particularly local practice) • Undertaking Independent Patrol

A community placement or engagement of at least 80 hours is likely to be included (Home Office, 2004 and NPIA, 2010a). The phases might not be delivered in this order, and could be interwoven throughout the two-year probationary period as shown in the timeline table. Details concerning the Learning Diary, SOLAP, and PAC are given later in this chapter.

Timeline in weeks	Stage	IPLDP phases	Activities	Milestones
1–2	Induction	1	Learning about the organization, Health & Safety, Personal Safety Training (PST), First Aid, etc	Undertaking the Job-Related Fitness Test Completion of first Learning Diary entries, and attestation
3	Community engagement	2	Placement with a community group (this might occur instead at a later stage)	Completion of first SOLAP entry
4	Area familiarization	1	The work of a BCU	Completion of more Learning Diary and SOLAP entries
5–10	Taught courses	1 and 3	Legislation, procedures, and other subjects	Successful completion of assessments
11–12	Supervised Patrol	3	Coaching and assessment	Beginning Supervised Patrol and completion of some QCF Diploma unit learning outcomes
13–18	Taught courses	1 and 3	Legislation, procedures, and other subjects	Successful completion of knowledge element assessments
19–21	Supervised Patrol	3	Coaching and assessment	Completion of some QCF Diploma unit learning outcomes
22–27	Taught courses	4	Legislation, procedures, and other subjects	Successful completion of assessments
28	Supervised Investigation	3	Coaching and assessment	Completion of some QCF Diploma unit learning outcomes

Timeline in weeks	Stage	IPLDP phases	Activities	Milestones
29–32	Taught courses	4	Legislation, procedures, and other subjects	Successful completion of assessments, six of the QCF units and the PAC Satisfactory Learning Development Review and Independent Patrol status
33–35	Supervised Patrol and Supervised Investigation	3	Coaching and assessment	Beginning Independent Patrol and completion of some remaining QCF Diploma assessment units
36–69	Independent Patrol	4	Patrol and/or investigation, assessment against QCF Diploma assessment units, taught courses	Completion of some remaining QCF Diploma assessment units
70	Independent Patrol	4	Meeting with supervisor	Second Learning Development Review
71–104	Independent Patrol	4	Patrol and/or investigation, assessment against QCF Diploma units	Completion of remaining QCF Diploma assessment units and the SOLAP Final Learning Development Review, and Confirmation

For Supervised Patrol, Independent Patrol, and confirmation in particular, there are significant variations in the timings between forces. Some forces choose to concentrate most of the taught elements of training in the first 52 weeks. Forces often elect to organize their training in terms of a series of courses or modules designed to deliver the requirements of the IPLDP. For example, West Yorkshire Police structures its training in the following way:

A typical structure for training (West Yorkshire Police)

Phase 1 (3 Weeks)

The first two weeks are an induction into the organisation at Bishopgarth, Wakefield. During this time recruits will be given more information about what the two years as a student officer will be like. They'll don the uniform for the first time and begin to see the responsibilities & obligations that come with it.

On week 3 the uniform is set aside for a while and they change location to the University of Huddersfield where they begin to develop the knowledge and understanding required by the modern Police Officer by looking at wider social issues affecting policing.

Phase 2 (4 Weeks)

Students continue at the University for a further three weeks covering such areas as: Equality, Diversity & Rights; Professional Development and delving further into Social & Community Issues. The final week of this phase consists of a five-day community placement, based in the Division (area) to which they'll be posted. They are there to observe and learn about a section of the community that they're likely to encounter and be expected to engage with, when on patrol. This allows them the opportunity to interact with the communities outside of the policing context. They don't wear uniform at all during Phase 2.

Phase 3 (24 Weeks)

This phase begins with 13 weeks of Legislation, Procedures and Guidelines training back at Bishopgarth. This is achieved through a combination of classroom-based training and practical exercises. It includes two weeks of detailed IT training in the key computer systems in general use within West Yorkshire Police. During this fortnight, one day is set aside for Public Order training at our dedicated training site. By the end of this part students look forward to a week of annual leave. On their return from leave they begin gaining practical experience with a tutor constable in a Professional Development Unit (PDU) at an Operational Division for at least ten weeks. This may be extended if necessary, to accommodate individual development needs.

Phase 4 (Up to the end of Year 2)

Once a student is judged as fit for independent patrol, which is measured against set criteria, they commence Phase 4 and head out on their own for the first time. This doesn't mean they are alone; they are part of a team. Students will be monitored and assisted by colleagues and supervisors throughout the rest of the two years and beyond. During the second year they also receive a further five weeks of formal training which is split between Bishopgarth and the University; with a further community placement week. These will be grouped into three fortnights, spaced through the second year. Students actually spend 75 per cent of the first two years working at division, gaining practical experience.

Study

There will inevitably be some private study to do as you would expect with any training course or vocational qualification, but much of it is based upon students' experiences and how they have used those to develop. As the programme progresses they build a portfolio (Student Officer Learning & Assessment Portfolio—SOLAP) which catalogues learning and development, both in the training establishments and the work place. This substantially contributes towards two of the modules, which together with a handful of assignments for the University draw[s] on experiences of the programme.

As with many other vocational qualifications there will be a need to study outside work time, indeed some people will have family members who are currently doing that. Time invested now will result in successful completion of the programme and a rewarding career in the Police Service. Officers who fail to submit work when required will be failing to meet our standards.

Support

Don't worry—it is our aim to guide students through the programme and see them succeed but we do accept that some people will find it more taxing than others. Above all we want to see 100% effort and an officer who is prepared to respond positively to feedback. The first thing to realise is that this is a packed course, the majority of which is work place-based. It is important that recruits find time to complete the necessary study and work, as leaving things to the last minute will lead to huge problems. Any student who is unsure of anything must ASK. We can't help if no one speaks to us. Standards are set throughout the course, though 'pass' marks may vary from one aspect to another. Extra support is available at every stage and we aim to focus development based upon individual needs.

Beyond the first two years

When you have successfully completed the programme you are awarded a Foundation Degree in Police Studies. In terms of further study, you could, at your own expense, seek to turn this into a full degree in a suitably linked subject. There may also be the possibility in the future of being awarded further credits for work-related study which could also lead to a full degree.

Also, you will now be eligible to apply for one of the many diverse job opportunities that exist within the Organisation so you can begin to shape your own career.

(West Yorkshire Police, 2010, reproduced by kind permission of West Yorkshire Police.)

TASK 1 Find out about the pattern of training for the police force in your area, and how it relates to IPLDP Phases 1 to 4.

8.4.2 The probationary period

The probationary period is the time that a trainee officer is technically under or in 'probation'. A trainee is not a confirmed constable and is subject to the regulations that apply to trainee police officers (see 6.4). The probationary period is normally two years for full-time trainees. Part-time training (now increasingly available) has an extended probationary period calculated according to Annex C of the Police Regulations 2003: training at half the full-time rate will take twice as long.

As with other aspects of initial training, the length of the probationary period may change in the future. In some forces APL (accredited prior learning) shortens the length of training and the probationary period. This may be particularly important for PCSOs and special constables who subsequently join up as police officers. Foreshortened training through APL might also be open to trainees joining from other professions, or through approved pre-join routes in higher and further education.

8.4.2.1 Independent Patrol

Attaining the right to undertake Independent Patrol is a key milestone in the professional development of a trainee police officer. Training is far from over, but he/she can now undertake many police functions associated with fully qualified (confirmed) officers without the need for constant supervision.

Independent Patrol normally occurs after about week 30 in training, although this does vary significantly from force to force. As with many aspects of initial police training, the timing of Independent Patrol remains under discussion. (The traditional approach was simply to say that, all other criteria being satisfied, it would happen on a certain week, but this makes less sense in an era of competence-based occupational standards.) A number of written reports have also highlighted problems that some forces faced in organizing and assessing the Independent Patrol phase of initial training.

A trainee's suitability for Independent Patrol is assessed against various criteria, including a subset of the QCF units, the Police Action Checklist (the PAC, see 8.5.3), and normally takes place after a Learning Development Review (see 8.5.4.3). As you would expect, the main aim is to ensure that the trainee is competent and safe to undertake Independent Patrol, including holding the appropriate values and behaviour (eg against the five PPF qualities of decision-making, leadership, professionalism, public service, and working with others: see 8.5.2). Note that completing the PAC is only one trigger for Independent Patrol, and does not automatically lead to it.

A trainee police officer normally receives confirmation of competence against the PAC from a Professional Development Unit (PDU) supervisor/assessor during IPLDP phases 1, 2, or 3. Some forces may also expect trainees to have acquired advanced driving skills before granting Independent Patrol status.

8.4.3 Confirmation

All being well, after two years (104 weeks) a trainee police officer should be deemed 'fit for confirmation of appointment'. However, in our view, the criteria for confirmation under the IPLDP remain less than clear and we suggest you seek a definitive statement of what is required. However, *some* or *all* of the following are likely to be involved:

* successful completion of the Level 3 Diploma in Policing (see 8.5.1);
* attainment of the five personal qualities of the PPF role profile for police constable (see 8.5.2);
* satisfactory completion of the SOLAP (see 8.5.4);
* satisfactory completion of the PAC (see 8.5.3);
* a 'successful' final Learning Development Review (see 8.5.4.3);
* a minimum academic attainment; and/or
* other requirements such as a level of fitness (the Job-Related Fitness Test), ability to administer First Aid, and being able to drive a car to a certain standard.

Note that these requirements are not mutually exclusive because they interrelate and overlap. For example, the SOLAP is likely to cross-reference with the PAC, and the Learning Development Review will involve the five personal quality areas. The list could also be summarized in IPLDP language as the successful completion of Phases 1 to 4.

8.4.4 What can go wrong?

We have no wish to be negative, but things can sometimes go wrong.

8.4.4.1 Could I get sacked?

At the outset it is important to note that, as for qualified police officers, most trainee police officers are not employees in the usual sense of the term. Technically they are 'holders of public office' (and for BTP the situation is especially complicated). This means that the conditions of employment for trainee police officers are particularly complex. In terms of dismissal (officially called 'dispensing with your services') and resignation ('retirement'), the main source of definitive information are the Police Regulations 2003, Statutory Instrument No 527. The Regulations can be found on the www.legislation.gov.uk website, but the important detail is set out in separate annexes.

For the trainee officer, probably the most important paragraphs in the Police Regulations 2003 are regs 12 and 13 (often known colloquially as Reg (pronounced with a hard 'g') 12 and Reg 13). Some of the other police regulations are covered in Chapter 6. As with many aspects of police training, the position regarding probation, the Regulations, and complaints may be reviewed. The Morris Inquiry in particular highlighted the complexity of current arrangements (Morris *et al*, 2004).

8.4.4.2   Extension of the probationary period

Regulation 12 provides for the usual probationary period (two years for full-time student police officers) to be extended. Details are given in Annex C to the Regulations. The usual reasons for extending the probationary period are interrupted training due to illness or personal problems, or when an officer is 'back-coursed' and required to retake a stage of training, perhaps because of failure. Forces are unlikely to allow an indefinite extension to the probationary period and will usually provide a trainee officer with detailed information concerning the implementation of 'Reg 12' on the local level.

8.4.4.3   Dispensing with a trainee officer's 'services'

Regulation 13 allows for your dismissal. It is worth quoting in full:

(1) Subject to the provisions of this regulation, during [his/her] period of probation in the force the services of a constable may be dispensed with at any time if the chief officer considers that [he/she] is not fitted, physically or mentally, to perform the duties of [his/her] office, or that [he/she] is not likely to become an efficient or well conducted constable.
(2) A constable whose services are dispensed with under this regulation shall be entitled to receive a month's notice or a month's pay in lieu thereof.
(3) A constable's services shall not be dispensed with in accordance with this regulation and any notice given for the purposes thereof shall cease to have effect if [he/she] gives written notice to the police authority of [his/her] intention to retire and retires in pursuance of the said notice on or before the date on which [his/her] services would otherwise be dispensed with; and such a notice taking effect on that date shall be accepted by the police authority notwithstanding that less than a month's notice is given.
(4) Where a constable has received a notice under this regulation that [his/her] services are to be dispensed with and [he/she] gives written notice of [his/her] intention to retire and retires under paragraph (3), [he/she] shall nevertheless be entitled to receive pay up to and until the date on which the month's notice [he/she] has received would have expired or where [he/she] has received or is due to receive a month's pay in lieu of notice [he/she] shall remain entitled to that pay notwithstanding the notice [he/she] has given under paragraph (3).

Regulation 13 dismissals are rare and would normally come at the end of a long process during which support and guidance will be offered. If you are issued with a Reg 13 notice, we suggest you contact your representative at the JBB (the Police Federation, see 6.7.2) or take other advice.

Note that the grounds for dismissal ('not fitted, physically or mentally, to perform the duties of [his/her] office, or that [he/she] is not likely to become an efficient or well conducted constable') are quite broad. For example, persistent failure in assessments or examinations could be considered grounds to consider that a trainee is not mentally fit to continue training. However, more common reasons for being dismissed or resigning are inappropriate behaviour or failing to maintain a certain level of fitness. The 'balance of probability' is used as the standard of proof for deciding whether the grounds for dismissal have been met.

There are obvious reasons for resigning before being dismissed, particularly in terms of future employment prospects. However, this would not mean the trainee would escape prosecution if the grounds for dismissal arose from a criminal act.

8.5   Assessment

Assessment can be formative or summative. Formative assessment takes place throughout the learning period to help determine learning needs while summative assessment takes place at the end of a period of learning to judge what has been learnt.

Students on pre-join programmes leading to the Certificate in Knowledge of Policing will be assessed through written work. Tutors will compare trainees' written explanations and descriptions against the assessment criteria. For example, one assessment requirement is to demonstrate 'knowledge of gathering and submitting information to support law enforcement objectives within a policing context', so trainees might be asked to submit a description of a number of pieces of legislation and national policy or guidelines in relation to gathering, submitting, retaining, recording, and disseminating information. Other forms of assessment are also likely to be employed, consistent with the need for valid, reliable assessment of your knowledge and understanding (rather than the practical skills of policing). These forms of assessment could include multiple-choice type examinations, timed essays, assignments, verbal questioning, formal written examinations, and assessed scenarios. There is no commonly agreed pass-mark for the CKP and practice appears to vary with the course provider. For example, to achieve the CKP with Coventry University a minimum pass-mark of 75 percent is required for each 'closed book' assessment (Coventry University, 2015). The Home Office Select Committee expressed some concern in 2015 on the standards set by some providers of the CKP, noting that 'it cannot be right that one provider has a 100 per cent success rate for the qualification (Home Office Select Committee, 2015, para. 72).

8.5.1 The assessed Diploma in Policing units

Successful completion of the entire QCF Diploma in Policing award is just one of the requirements for becoming a qualified police constable (see 8.4.3 for the others). As described in more detail in 7.4.1, each of the ten QCF units within the Diploma is linked with the National Occupational Standards (NOS) for initial policing. In effect, each Diploma unit consists of:

- one main NOS unit; and
- selected aspects of the five embedded NOS units (AA1, AB1, AE1, AF1, and CA1).

(The two 'Search' Diploma units also include part of NOS Unit CD3.)

All of the units can be assessed incrementally during the two-year training period, and a number of the assessment units can be completely signed off in the work place during the taught phase of training. However, as shown in the table, before undertaking Independent Patrol a trainee officer must be assessed as competent on at least one occasion in six of the Diploma units (NPIA, 2010a, p 35), and three of the Diploma units can only be finally assessed during Independent Patrol and hence in the work place.

Name of Diploma in Policing assessed unit	Required *before* going on Independent Patrol	Final assessment *during* Independent Patrol
Plan, implement and review an evidence-based preventative policing approach	✓	
Support victims, witnesses and vulnerable people	✓	
Handle information and intelligence		
Provide an initial response to policing incidents	✓	
Use police powers to deal with suspects	✓	
Conduct investigations		✓
Interview victims and witnesses in relation to priority and volume investigations		✓
Interview suspects in relation to priority and volume investigations		✓
Conduct police searches	✓	
Manage conflict situations in policing	✓	

8.5.1.1 Components of a QCF Diploma unit

Each QCF Diploma unit is a self-contained and free-standing expression of a particular part of the role of police constable, with a description of how competence for this part of the role can be assessed. Each unit contains learning outcomes (usually between two and five) and assessment criteria. An example of a learning outcome is to 'be able to communicate effectively with victims and witnesses' (see 7.4 for a full list). The learning outcomes have been mapped with the IPLDP learning descriptors. There will be one or more assessment criteria for each learning outcome. Each assessment criterion is a 'can do' statement that can be adapted for assessment, for example the learner can 'communicate with individuals appropriately taking account of pace, their level of understanding and their preferred form of communication'. Each unit also includes additional information such as a description of the aims of the QCF unit, the linked NOS units, and specific assessment requirements, for example the number of times competence must be practically demonstrated.

You achieve a QCF unit when it has been confirmed that you have provided reliable, valid, and sufficient evidence (in the correct format) to demonstrate your competence. The quality of evidence is more important, than the volume. Competence will be achieved at different times for different people but there will probably be a system in place to encourage (and even require) you to follow a given schedule. In theory, you could be given credit if you can already meet a standard (perhaps having worked as a special constable before joining as a full-time trainee) through the accreditation of prior learning (APL), or prior experiential learning (APEL), but to date this has been difficult to implement.

8.5.1.2 A detailed examination of one Diploma unit

We will work through an example to show how a unit is likely to be assessed. We have chosen the unit **'Provide an initial response to policing incidents'** to look at its component parts in more detail. It is an average size QCF unit with a credit value of four, three learning outcomes (see 7.4 for a full list), and 13 assessment criteria. The underpinning training for this unit is likely to begin relatively early and it also demonstrates the links between the Diploma, the NOS, and other aspects of training, for example the PAC. It links with one of the embedded NOS units, AA1.

First, an overview of the unit itself. (We reproduce extracts from the QCF units, taken from the Register of Regulated Qualifications to be found at <http://register.ofqual.gov.uk/>, which are Crown copyright.) The QCF provides the following summary:

> This unit covers providing an initial response to incidents, including: crime, non-crime and traffic incidents. The learner will need to be able to gather information on the incident, establish the nature of the incident, and plan their actions accordingly. In the case of a major or critical incident, when first on the scene, they will need to take control of the incident until relieved by the appropriate person.

It is clear that plenty of learning is required, including practising skills and acquiring knowledge and understanding. The final assessment for it will probably be during Supervised or Independent Patrol. The first requirement will be to gain adequate **knowledge** of legislation and police procedure concerning a whole range of incidents—'crime, non-crime and traffic incidents'. This will include at least a working knowledge of the legislation surrounding public order offences (eg s 4 of the Public Order Act 1986), violent incidents (eg s 47 of the Offences Against the Person Act 1861—Actual Bodily Harm), and so on. You will also need to be familiar with:

- police procedure, such as the correct use of the pocket notebook and making police statements (to be able to 'gather information on the incident');
- critical incident management ('take control of the incident'); and
- health and safety, human rights, and respect for diversity (as always).

This knowledge and understanding is likely to be achieved incrementally during the first year or so of training (and is covered in other parts of this Handbook).

In terms of the **skills**, for this unit knowing how to communicate with the control room and fellow officers is essential, and personal safety training might also be required. You may also need to know how to support witnesses and victims, how to protect the scene (for forensic purposes), and possibly how to administer First Aid.

The unit has three **learning outcomes**, which effectively subdivide the unit into logical stages. It states that the learner will:

1. Understand legal and organizational requirements related to responding to incidents.
2. Be able to analyse information to plan responses to incidents.
3. Be able to provide an initial response to incidents in line with legal and organisational requirements.

The first two learning outcomes are concerned with all the actions required (mental as well as physical) before actually arriving at an incident. The third learning outcome relates to the events and police actions after arrival. It makes sense to group these learning outcomes

Qualifications and Training

together, since the quality of the police response is likely to depend (at least in part) on the quality of the planning.

Each learning outcome has a number of linked **assessment criteria**. For example, the third learning outcome about the actual responses to incidents, requires the trainee police officer to be able to:

3.1. analyse all available information to establish the nature of incidents
3.2. prioritise actions in accordance with the nature of incidents
3.3. take control of incidents
3.4. communicate with those already at the scene
3.5. apply proportionate personal safety techniques where necessary
3.6. preserve the scene and any potential evidence
3.7. prioritise casualties in line with their needs
3.8. provide support to victims, survivors, witnesses and others in line with their needs
3.9. adapt own actions according to any contingencies and changes in the nature of incidents
3.10. include others who need to be involved at the earliest opportunity
3.11. make records of actions taken to respond to incidents

8.5.1.3 Demonstrating attainment of a QCF unit

The evidence for attainment of a QCF unit features at the level of the assessment criteria. One aspect is demonstrating that you have the required knowledge, and this applies for nine out of the ten units. Formal demonstration of the appropriate knowledge (eg of legislation or police procedure) will be required before a trainee is given the opportunity to demonstrate how to apply the knowledge in a real policing context.

The assessment of knowledge is most likely to occur in a classroom environment, and can be assessed by:

- responding to verbal questioning;
- multiple-choice or short-answer tests (sometimes called 'Knowledge Evaluation Exercises');
- written answers to questions;
- written assignments with deadlines;
- assessed practical exercises, role-plays, or discussions; and
- other means (eg online assessments).

The assessment of knowledge can be one of the most confusing aspects of initial training, so all trainee officers are strongly advised to carefully read the information provided about assessment of the knowledge element of the QCF assessment units, and to ask about the assessment strategies and criteria if you are unclear. A key question might be 'How do I pass the knowledge element for my QCF assessment units?'

You might also need to ask:

- Is there a pass-mark, and if so what is the pass-mark? (In some forces it is 60 per cent for each subject area.)
- If there is no pass-mark, then how are pass/fail decisions made for the knowledge element?
- What happens if I don't pass? (In some forces failure on one component of an assessment can be balanced by a particularly good mark for another ('condonement')).
- Who moderates the examinations or assessments and what is the process for external quality control?

For example, in other Level 3 Diploma units (such as those for the construction industry) the minimum pass-mark in written examinations is 70 per cent and moderation is carried out by the awarding bodies concerned. Whatever the forms of assessment, it is important that you are clear on what is being formally assessed. For example, there are over 250 learning outcomes in the IPLDP Induction Modules alone.

8.5.1.4 Work place assessment

The QCF Diploma in Policing unit 'Provide an initial response to policing incidents' (see 8.5.1.2) explains that competence must be demonstrated practically on three occasions, covering two different types of incident. Competence is assessed using the Diploma unit assessment criteria, and is likely to involve one or more of the following:

- **Direct observation** is a very common form of evidence for competence. Put simply, a suitably qualified person (normally a tutor, an assessor constable, or PDU assessor—the terms vary from force to force) observes a trainee carrying out a particular work-related task and confirms that the actions meet the standards. Before and after the event the assessor will explain the process. He/she will use the criteria to help decide whether the evidence is appropriate and sufficient.
- **Questioning** by the assessor might also be used, although during an observation the assessor should be as unobtrusive as possible.
- **Testimony from witnesses** can provide evidence to show that a trainee has met a particular assessment criterion. The witnesses are most likely to be the trainee's tutors and more experienced and qualified police colleagues. Other people can also provide testimony, but they need to be credible, and occupationally competent for the relevant unit.
- **Written evidence** or 'work products' come in a wide variety of forms. Common sources of written evidence include police statements written by the trainee, PNB entries, *pro forma* documents he or she has completed (eg FPNs), and reports. The assessor will obviously be interested in how far these products demonstrate that the trainee has achieved the assessment criteria for an assessment unit, but will also be checking on aspects such as authenticity (ie checking that it is the trainee's own work).
- **Artefacts** are tangible objects such as photographs (eg of a cordon the trainee helped establish) or tape recordings (eg of an interaction with a member of the public). This evidence is indexed and cross-referenced in the trainee's SOLAP (see 8.5.4). A written description of the background and context for the artefact will also be required.

In some circumstances a force may consider it more appropriate to test competence by using a **simulation** or role-play rather than by observing a real-life situation. All ten QCF Diploma in Policing assessment units permit simulation to some extent. This is an advantage in terms of safety and convenience; after all it might be difficult to arrange the necessary circumstances for a trainee on Supervised Patrol, and some situations are so complex it makes sense to use simulation for each separate element. Certain first-aid skills are more appropriately evidenced through simulation (using realistic mannequins) than for real. For assessment through simulations you may need to think carefully: unless particularly carefully designed and organized, simulations often lack the rich detail of real-life contexts, and this ambiguity can make it more difficult to devise an appropriate response.

> **TASK 2** Which learning outcomes of the QCF Diploma unit 'Use police powers to deal with suspects' must be practically demonstrated through competence in the work place, and on how many occasions?

8.5.1.5   Claiming achievement of a QCF unit

You should be proactive in claiming competence towards learning outcomes of a QCF unit: familiarize yourself with the assessment criteria—it is in your own interest. The whole process provides a series of opportunities to demonstrate your skills. A single incident or one simple task that you have completed could potentially be used as the basis of evidence for a whole range of QCF units. These opportunities should be exploited as it will help you complete the assessment more quickly. You should certainly avoid leaving it to the last minute: if you leave it too long, you will discover that, as with stamp collecting, you will have many 'doubles' for 'Conduct police searches' but you are still looking for the elusive 'Manage conflict situations in policing'! Remember too that the assessment criteria for certain units may be demonstrated outside the context of traditional policing—for example, during a community placement in your second year of training. A suitably qualified person from outside your force may be able to confirm competence, but check with your force.

If you feel that you do not have sufficient opportunity (particularly on Supervised Patrol) to demonstrate attainment of a learning outcome of a QCF unit, or if you feel that your assessor has it wrong, you should speak to one of your tutors. Forces are required to follow certain quality assurance procedures and these will almost certainly include the right to appeal against an assessment decision. All forces will have a published policy which sets out the grounds for an appeal and the processes involved. Normally an appeal is made to the person responsible for the PDU where the decision was made, rather than to the assessor who made the decision.

TASK 3 Use the internet to locate and download the specifications for the NOS Unit 4G4 'Administer First Aid' (see the Skills for Justice website at <www.sfjuk.com>). This NOS unit is often assessed as part of police training but does not form part of the Diploma itself. What are the knowledge and understanding requirements?

8.5.2 ### 8.5.2   The Policing Professional Framework (PPF)

The PPF describes the personal qualities that are required for each rank (eg Superintendent) and role (eg call controller) in the police service. It consists of a set of **role profiles** and the associated **personal qualities** required.

The role profile and personal qualities for trainee police officers are the same as for police constables. Skills for Justice (the sector skills council for the CJS and responsible for the PPF) gives the role profile for a police constable as:

> The frontline of the criminal justice system and community engagement. Under general supervision, but often operating independently. Responsible for the protection of life and property, the prevention and detection of crime and the maintenance of public order through a range of sworn powers in line with organisational standards. (Skills for Justice, 2011)

The police constable role profile is essentially the NOS embedded within the ten QCF Diploma in Policing units (see 7.4.1), so any trainee officer achieving the Diploma will automatically attain the role profile of constable. However, the personal qualities (shown in the table) will also need to be demonstrated. Police forces are expected to contextualize the role profiles and personal qualities within their own training and HR processes.

Personal quality	Component	Description
Decision-making		Gathers, verifies, and assesses all appropriate and available information to gain an accurate understanding of situations. Considers a range of options before making clear, timely, justifiable decisions.
Leadership	Openness to change	Positive about change, adapting rapidly to different ways of working and putting effort into making them work. Flexible and open to alternative approaches to solving problems.
	Service delivery	Understands the organisation's objectives and priorities, and how own work fits into these. Plans and organises tasks effectively, taking a structured and methodical approach to achieving outcomes.
Professionalism		Acts with integrity, in line with values and ethical standards of the Police Service. Takes ownership for resolving problems, demonstrating courage and resilience in dealing with difficult and potentially volatile situations. Upholds professional standards, acting honestly and ethically, and challenges unprofessional conduct or discriminatory behavioural standards.
Serving the public		Demonstrates a real belief in public service, focusing on what matters to the public and will best serve their interest. Understands the expectations, changing needs and concerns of different communities and strives to address them. Builds public confidence by talking to people in local communities.
Working with others		Works cooperatively with others to get things done, willingly giving help to others, is approachable, developing positive working relationships. Explains things well, listens carefully, and expresses own views positively and constructively.

(Based on Skills for Justice, 2011)

Qualifications and Training

8.5.3   **The PAC**

The Police Action Checklist (the PAC) is part of the system for checking whether a trainee police officer is ready to begin Independent Patrol (see 8.4.2.1). It is cross-referenced to a subset of the NOS units and hence links with at least some of the QCF assessment units which form the Diploma in Policing. Therefore completing the PAC complements the achievement of the Diploma units and does not compete with or stand apart from this process.

The PAC has ten main headings and each heading is broken into a number of specific requirements.

Action Checklist

Safety first

- First Aid
- Health & Safety—Dynamic assessment
- Health & Safety—Reporting
- Personal Safety Training (PST/OST, etc)
- Fitness test—according to force policy

Information management

- Utilize the PNC
- Utilize force information management systems (eg intelligence/crime reporting/command and despatch)

Patrol

- Demonstrate patrol priorities in accordance with NIM
- Demonstrate communication with control rooms

Search

- Conduct stops
- Demonstrate lawful search—persons
- Demonstrate lawful search—premises
- Demonstrate lawful search—vehicles

Investigation

- Use CCTV during an investigation
- Demonstrate initial crime scene management
- Conduct the initial investigation and report of missing persons
- Conduct the initial investigation and report of volume crime
- Conduct the initial investigation and report of a domestic incident
- Conduct the initial investigation and report of racist and/or hate crime
- Conduct the initial investigation and report in relation to a child protection and/or vulnerable person incident
- Conduct the initial investigation and report of a sudden death
- Demonstrate initial RTC scene management
- Interview—conduct a witness interview using the PEACE model
- Interview—conduct a suspect interview using the PEACE model
- Demonstrate correct handling of exhibits
- Provide support and advice to victims and witnesses
- Respond to developments during an investigation

Disposal

- Report for summons
- Make lawful arrests
- Convey a suspect into custody

Custody office procedures

- Present suspect to custody in accordance with force procedures
- Obtain fingerprints
- Obtain photographs
- Obtain DNA sample
- Complete pre-charge procedures

Finalize investigations

- Complete case files (eg summons and post-charge files)
- Prepare for court or other hearings
- Present evidence to court or other hearings

Road policing

- Check driving documents
- Demonstrate vehicle stops
- Complete traffic documents—including HO/RT1/FPN(E)/CLE2/VDRS
- Demonstrate correct administration of the appropriate tests for drink-/drugs-driving offences

Property

- Complete property register

The PAC is largely concerned with performance and is not generally used as a tool for trainee officer development. It is also usually contextualized—that is, performance is also judged in the light of a trainee's developing personal qualities (part of the PPF role profile for police constables (see 8.5.2)).

Before a trainee officer can be considered for Independent Patrol an assessor will confirm his/her competence against all the PAC subheadings. Note that successful completion of the PAC does not necessarily guarantee eligibility for Independent Patrol. Some police forces will expect more—for example, a certain level of driving skills.

In many forces there will still be formal training alongside Independent Patrol, and in all forces collecting evidence towards completion of the remaining QCF assessment units will certainly continue. Under the IPLDP, there should be at least 30 days of 'protected learning time' after being granted Independent Patrol, and before Confirmation.

8.5.4 The SOLAP

The SOLAP is the Student Officer Learning and Assessment Portfolio. It is a record of achievement constructed during initial training, and is a key document as it charts a trainee's progress towards becoming professional and competent, and ready for confirmation as a constable. Some forces emphasize that the portfolio firmly belongs to the trainee officer, but this does not mean that it is confidential to him/her, nor does this ownership necessarily provide any kind of protection in the case of legal action.

The SOLAP is a physical or an electronic document (stored in a folder on the force intranet or housed on a Virtual Learning Environment such as Blackboard). It has to follow certain national requirements, but forces are permitted to customize it: from the relatively trivial act of adding a force logo to the more significant step of deciding to release the SOLAP requirements to trainees in stages, rather than as a whole at the outset.

Much of the advice we have provided concerning the assessment of the QCF Diploma units applies to the completion of the SOLAP. So, for example, it should be started as soon as possible and any incidents attended should be fully exploited for evidence gathering. Records of crime and incident numbers should be kept so that the material for the SOLAP can be found when needed. Some forces provide SOLAPs from previous trainee officers (anonymized), to help show what is required.

8.5.4.1   Components of the SOLAP

A typical SOLAP will be made up of the following (the format may vary from force to force and is also subject to periodic revision):

The SOLAP

Chapter	Contents	Comments
1	Student Officer Personal Profile	You provide brief biographical details (name, DoB, etc), together with a list of your previous educational and other achievements. You are expected to keep this up to date
2	Student Officer Role Profile	Information concerning the Student Officer Role Profile, including PPF, QCF units, the NOS, the PAC, assessments, and appeals
3	Introduction to the Phases of Learning	A description of the four IPLDP phases
4	The Learning Modules	A description of the three sets of IPLDP Learning Modules (the IND, OP, and LPG modules listed in 1.4.2) and how the curriculum is structured
5	Learner Development Framework	A description of Learning Diaries and Learning Development Reviews. You will be expected to keep a Learning Diary and take part in the Learning Development Reviews (or equivalent)
6	Police Action Checklist	Information concerning the PAC. You need to achieve the PAC before Independent Patrol
7	Diploma in Policing/QCF units/ National Occupational Standards	Detailed information concerning the Diploma in Policing, the compulsory QCF units, and the links with the NOS
8	Assessment Process	Information concerning assessment of the knowledge element, competence, collecting evidence, the assessment process (Induction, planning, etc), and a useful detailed example of an assessment activity
9	Overview of Assessment Methods	Note that this chapter is concerned with the assessment of your competence
10	Overview of Assessment	A description of the main forms of documentation involved in the assessment process, for example induction records, witness testimony forms, and an evidence index
11	Glossary of terms	A 'jargon-buster' of acronyms used in the IPLDP assessment process

In addition, there are a number of appendices which contain either additional information or templates to use in order to complete a SOLAP. We examine some of the key components of the SOLAP in more detail in 8.5.4.2 and 8.5.4.3.

8.5.4.2   The Learning Diary

The Learning Diary is included in Chapter 5 of the SOLAP, and provides a structured account of learning during the probationary period. Most forces will expect reflective and evidenced entries, using the subheadings provided so that judgements can be made on progress, competency can be evidenced for assessment purposes, and future development can be planned. Some forces emphasize the need for critical reflection by renaming the Learning Diary a Reflective Diary or similar.

Under the IPLDP, the Learning Diary subheadings normally reflect the stage of training. For example, in the first few weeks during the initial induction phase they might relate to the introduction to the organization, and during a community placement the subheadings are likely to encourage reflection on what has been learnt during the placement, and so on. During the first two phases of training entries should be made every week, and later on a monthly basis. Diary entries can be structured to address the following:

- What happened?
- How did you, and the others around you, respond?
- What was the outcome of the events?
- What could you do differently, or better, in the future?

In most cases the Learning Diaries also have a 'golden thread' running through all components, about ethics, respect for diversity, relationships with colleagues, and health and safety. There is also normally a section for tutors and trainers to complete, and this helps monitor its completion as well as ensuring the tutor provides useful feedback. It is not formally assessed in the way that a written examination would be, but the entries can be used as partial evidence towards completion of some of the QCF Diploma in Policing units' assessment criteria.

The following (fictitious) Learning Diary entries provide an idea of what is generally expected.

Trainee Police Officer: PC Phillips

Crime

When we were on night duty mobile patrol, my tutor and I were sent along with other patrols to an alarm activation at a newsagents on a housing estate where suspects had been seen to make off on foot with cigarettes and alcohol.

Key learning points:

Choosing the right search parameters when called to incidents.

What surprised me?

My tutor did not drive us straight to the shop but began an area search for the suspects some way away. He said he had judged how long it took for the alarm to be notified to control, how long it took for us to be sent to the call, and how far the suspects could have travelled on foot in that time.

How will I put this learning into practice?

In the future, if that happens or similar I will also notify control that I will not go straight to the scene. I will judge how long it has been since the incident took place, judge the suspects direction of travel, and then begin my search away from the scene. I will also consider sitting in the car with the engine switched off, waiting and listening, and also requesting a dog patrol (if there is one) to attend to track the suspect.

Intelligence

Today in our briefing we were given intelligence about a known criminal suspected of burglaries in our area during the daytime. The MO is to gain entry via insecure windows at the back of terraced houses, make an untidy search and take high-value electronic equipment in pillow cases from the house, and leave via the front door.

Key learning points:

The importance of intelligence to police operations.

What surprised me?

Whilst on foot patrol today, my tutor and I saw the suspect from the briefing on a housing estate, trying to hide from us in a back garden. We checked with the homeowner that the suspect did not have permission to be in the garden. His behaviour, the information we had, the time of day, and location were our grounds to look for stolen property and we carried out a s 1 PACE search. In a pillow case quite close to the suspect there was an iPod and another mp3 player. I arrested the suspect as this was necessary for one of the reasons we learnt about during training.

How will I put this learning into practice?

This incident really showed me the importance of intelligence. I will pay more attention to briefings from now on as the information in them helps my patrol skills and gives me the idea to pay attention to specific areas and to specific people. I can see that intelligence-led policing can really work and help me to add to my reasons for needing to do a s 1 PACE search. I will also go to the Intel unit when I've got time to get up to date information on disqual drivers and their cars.

Investigation and interview

When I saw what my tutor constable said when he interviewed a shoplifter I had arrested in the shopping centre, I saw how to prove the offence by interview.

Key learning points:

Questioning techniques for interviewing.

What surprised me?

I was expecting him to use the proper words like 'Did you dishonestly appropriate the property from the shop with the intention of keeping it?' But he just used open questions and everyday language and kind of managed the conversation and asked questions like 'Why did you go into the shop?', 'What were you thinking about when you picked up the bottle of scotch?', 'How much money did you take to go shopping today?', 'What did you want to do with the scotch?'.

How will I put this learning into practice?

In my interviews I will try to get to the truth, but not by using the words from legislation but instead I will speak like in a general conversation, which should get a better response from the suspect for the points we may need to prove. I will try to use open questions to get as much information from the suspect and begin my questions with 'Tell me about . . . ' This seems to be a better way of interviewing.

Non-crime incidents

Today my tutor and I were requested to attend a misper call about a 10-year-old boy who had gone missing from his home.

Key learning points:

An appropriate initial response to child mispers.

What surprised me?

Before we started to fill in the misper form my tutor asked the parents if they had looked for him. They said they had searched the whole house but he said that he still had to do another search. I watched him searching the house and garden looking for where a child that age could be. We looked for gaps or spaces which would be big enough. Then in an old shed at the bottom of the garden we found him. My tutor asked the parents some questions and the child about why he had hid himself like that. I didn't realise that there are two types of misper: absent or missing.

How will I put this learning into practice?

When I get the report of a misper (not just absent), esp a child, I will start by making a full search of the home, even if the family have said they have done it already. This might save a lot of time in the long run and might prevent a large-scale search involving lots of time and people. I will look for any spaces which would fit a child and try hard to find these spaces in the first place.

Police policies and procedures

Today we attended the scene of a road traffic collision with two cars. None of the drivers had passengers or were injured. The vehicles had very slight damage and the collision took place at a T-junction at very slow speed.

Key learning points:

The importance of following force policy.

What surprised me?

I did not have any suspicion that the drivers had been drinking, but my tutor reminded me it is force policy to give a breath test to every driver in a road traffic collision (Road Traffic

Act powers). I was surprised that even though it was only 8.30 am, one of the drivers proved positive and I arrested him.

How will I put this learning into practice?

In the future I will take care to follow force policy and test every driver in a crash, whether I suspect them of drinking or not. I will do this whatever the situation for the crash and whether any other driving offences are suspected.

Protecting people

When we were on foot patrol in the shopping centre today, my tutor asked me to imagine I was a thief, to look around at the shoppers, and to consider who was the most likely to be a victim of a crime when out shopping.

Key learning points:

Crime prevention is just as important as crime detection.

What surprised me?

When I looked around I saw people paying no attention to their valuable property. I saw people (all ages) carrying mobiles in their hands, just giving a thief the chance to just snatch them. There were also some people holding money in notes in their hands and a lot of older and more weaker looking women carrying their purses very high up in their handbags which could also easily be snatched. We began giving advice to some of these people about the risks of what could happen.

How will I put this learning into practice?

Whenever it is the situation to offer crime-prevention advice I will do it. For example, if I see an old person keeping their purse near the top of their bag I will go and tell them that it could be snatched and that they could think about fixing a chain onto the purse at one end and attaching the other end to their bag.

Stops and searches

While out with my tutor today I saw a number of searches being carried out by other officers. Some of the searches did not go that well and the suspects in some were clearly not that compliant.

Key learning points:

The importance of following a professional 'stop, account, and search' routine.

What surprised me?

Most of the searches where the suspects were more compliant were the ones where the searching officers said the PACE Codes of Practice requirements for searching. What I saw was the searching officers going through them using GO WISELY. This seemed to have the effect that the suspects thought they really knew they had the right so they did not try to obstruct or resist so much.

How will I put this learning into practice?

When I carry out my searches I will do exactly the same thing and use GO WISELY to remind me of what to say. Before today, I thought I was only taught it to help me remember it for my exam, but now I see how important it is and the good effect it has on people being searched.

Traffic

Today on mobile patrol, we must of stopped about 15 vehicles. Every time it was to give the driver some advice.

Key learning points:

The police can help with driver and passenger safety.

What surprised me?

The reasons why we stopped the vehicles did not seem to be major issues eg for no seat belts, children that were too small for the front seat, parking near crossings, and minor speeding. Then, after speaking to my tutor, I realized that we have a role for road safety and that it is part of our job to prevent injury to drivers, passengers, or pedestrians, not just 'catch criminals'. Because if we can prevent someone's head hitting the windscreen or another passenger if in a crash by reminding them to wear a seat belt or wearing it properly, then we might have saved a lot of pain and misery. Also parking near crossings needs to be stopped as it risks the lives of people crossing. Also we learnt recently in class that 30 mph areas are there for a purpose and going over the speed limit even a bit could be the difference between life and death for a pedestrian.

How will I put this learning into practice?

Even when I am v busy with calls to attend, I will try to take the time to give advice to road-users. I will say to them that the problem is in the unexpected situations that can happen very fast so cannot be avoided. It will be difficult for me sometimes to give advice to a road user like when I am tired and hungry, but I must remember that one day I might not take the chance to say something and just after he is involved in a crash and is injured or even dies. I would find that very hard to cope with.

8.5.4.3 Learning Development Reviews

A Learning Development Review (LDR) gives rise to documents that are more formal than the Learning Diary. LDRs are based on structured meetings with tutors and assessors involving reviews and critical self-assessment. The trainee officer then writes this up as a formal document, based on the personal qualities and role profile of the police constable. The LDRs (usually around ten) are documented in Chapter 5 of the SOLAP. There are three key reviews during training:

- the review for Independent Patrol, involving completion of the PAC;
- an interim review, for example after the first year of training (week 52); and
- the final review for confirmation (at week 92, see 8.4.3), probably involving completion of the QCF Diploma assessed units plus other professional requirements.

These LDRs are essentially a progress report and an agreement of what actions might be needed within a specified timescale. The SMART model of objective setting may be used when agreeing targets (Specific, Measurable, Relevant, Achievable, and Timed). Any disciplinary matters might be included in this part of the SOLAP. Note that forces are permitted to replace the National IPLDP Learning Development Reviews with their own local approach if they can meet the criteria laid down by NPIA (2009d, p 4). This would include linking the LDR to the PFF role profile for police constables (see 8.5.2).

8.5.5 Fitness assessment for police officers

All trainee officers take the 'job related fitness test' (the JRFT). This involves a bleep test and a dynamic strength test, and is very similar to the MSFT used during the selection for recruitment (see 8.2.4.1). All police officers and staff requiring personal safety training are required to take a fitness test (College of Policing, 2014e).

A retake is allowed for any trainee who fails the JRFT, probably at about week nine. Obviously, he/she would be well advised to do some fitness training in the intervening weeks. Forces are normally supportive and may suggest a programme of activities. There may be a third and final chance to pass. Failure at this stage may lead to a 'Reg 13' and dismissal from the force (see 8.4.4), but policy can vary, so the local force and perhaps also the local Police Federation representative should be consulted (see 6.7.1) in such circumstances.

8.6 Learning as a Trainee Police Officer

In this part of the chapter we look at the various ways in which trainee officers learn, but the ideas and information provided here are also useful for learners on pre-join programmes. The learning is structured so that it starts off with relatively simple tasks, and will involve acquiring

Qualifications and Training

largely factual knowledge. It then moves on to how to apply the ideas in practice. This is all deliberate as this seems to be the best way to learn according to learning theories (see 8.6.5). All learners can apply these (and other) theories themselves, to help develop more effective ways of learning independently.

The IPLDP philosophy is to encourage police forces to adopt educational principles and practices that suit adults from all personal and educational backgrounds and with all learning styles. It is worth noting that police training has existed in the UK for over 150 years, and that hundreds of thousands of trainee officers have been successfully trained. This does not mean, of course, that police training was perfect in the past nor, indeed, that it is now (HMIC, 2002), and we tend not to hear much from those who have been unsuccessful! However, it is clear that many people from all sorts of backgrounds have successfully trained to become police officers and moved on to rewarding careers in policing.

It will sometimes be appropriate to perform tasks in simulated situations, so that you can easily rectify mistakes and clarify any misunderstandings. Eventually, though, it will be appropriate for you to go onto the streets and begin the process of policing the community, first on Supervised Patrol and later on Independent Patrol. As this is initially a daunting prospect, trainees are allocated a tutor, coach, or mentor for support, and will probably also be attached to a Professional Development Unit (PDU).

8.6.1 Learning and PDUs

Professional Development Units (PDUs) provide important aspects of initial police training. They also assist police officers who have transferred from other forces and support police officers back into policing duties eg after a period of illness, although practice does vary significantly from force to force. They are usually physically based within the BCU, and may be known as Probationer Development. In some forces there may be a PDU in every BCU, whilst in others a single PDU serves the whole force. Staffing also varies, as does the management structure and the types of resource available, so it is difficult to describe a typical PDU. A police officer of inspector rank or above is likely to be responsible for a PDU, and will line-manage sergeants and PCs (sometimes referred to as training officers) based there.

The PDU is likely to work alongside the other departments, and might be part of the training department (in fact you might receive all your training at the PDU, including classroom-based teaching). You can expect a PDU tutor (sometimes called a tutor constable or assessor constable) to be an experienced officer with skills in coaching and assessment. Whatever the particular arrangements, the PDU is likely to be of crucial importance for trainees, an observation supported by the Home Office (2005b, p 22): 'The importance of the role of the Professional Development Unit in providing and supporting...learning experiences throughout the whole of the probationary period cannot be overstated.' Some BCUs seem to struggle to support a large number of trainees (HMIC, 2005a, p 17), and there has also been some criticism concerning the lack of police management support for some force PDUs.

8.6.1.1 The advantages of a PDU

PDUs provide trainee police officers with the opportunity to apply learning in a controlled environment. So, instead of being immediately plunged into a world of reactive policing, a trainee can reinforce selected aspects of his/her learning through simulations of genuine policing tasks. These may be based around particular needs for the force, especially towards the end of training.

Another advantage is that the tutor and student to carry out activities on a one-to-one basis (Home Office, 2005c). A trainee will be able to discuss what he/she intends to do and say at an incident (a pre-brief) and will then be able to deal with the incident itself in an effective, safe, and professional manner, albeit in a monitored or co-pilot fashion with the tutor/coach. The incident can then be discussed afterwards (debrief). This helps trainees use the different stages of the learning cycle (see 8.6.5.3). Learning Diary entries (see 8.5.4.2) can provide further opportunities for self-assessment and reflection.

Within the PDU, staff members assess trainees' competence against the QCF Diploma in Policing units and the PAC. In turn, the Home Office expects the assessors to be competent to perform this task, demonstrated through undertaking an assessor's award perhaps (Home Office, 2005b; NPIA, 2010a).

8.6.2   Teachers, trainers, and learning

In a class of up to 16 people, there is every chance that each learner will prefer to learn in a different way (see 8.6.5.2 on 'preferred learning styles'). Therefore, it is obviously a challenge for the training staff to accommodate each learner with an appropriate activity. A popular approach in police training is 'facilitation', where trainers adopt styles and techniques to bring out (or 'tease out') ideas and views from the group whilst at the same time reducing their own role as conventional didactic 'stand at the front and talk' teachers.

We will describe a number of activities commonly employed by trainers. The intention is that all members of a group will be engaged at least once during a session. Some trainers will use evaluation sheets to find out more about the effectiveness of different methods.

The **'boardblast'** is a very popular teaching method used by police trainers. The tutor will invite responses which will be written down on a board or flipchart and then discussed. This will be assessed by the tutor and revisited at different stages of the lesson, and is often a very effective method (but is sometimes used to excess). Another occasional disadvantage to the boardblast approach is that most of the class will have very limited knowledge and hence the suggestions might not cover all the required aspects for the topic.

Written case studies are also used. These involve working on a practical example of a police-related problem. Details will be given to an individual or a group, who will then read the material and form conclusions about its content to demonstrate understanding of the subject.

Demonstration can be used for practical topics involving the use of the body in the psychomotor domain (see 8.6.5.1). The tutor will demonstrate the movements so the student can repeat the activity afterwards.

Group-work is a very common method in police training. For small-groups, students share ideas among the group and for this to work well, each member should be actively involved in the task. When the group reports back its findings, the trainer or trainers will probably act as a facilitator and will tease out the learning.

Large-group work usually involves allocating responsibility to small groups for researching part of a larger topic. They work away from the training room, and use books, reference material, and computer-based learning. After an agreed time the large group reassembles and the small groups each present their findings to everyone. Alternatively, a large group of students may be presented with information, perhaps from a specialist or a guest speaker, or by watching a video clip.

Individual work provides an opportunity for the student to work alone. This could take a variety of forms, ranging from conducting interviews for research to writing an assignment under exam conditions.

Electronic learning often uses computer-based learning (CBL) packages, which are now available both nationally and locally. CBL activity can be carried out individually or in small groups, both inside and outside the classroom environment. Trainee officers and/or special constables are likely to have access to the resources on the NCALT website (a username and password are needed). There are an increasing number of electronic resources available through NCALT, particularly case studies that link with the IPLDP learning outcomes and phases. For example, Phase 3 case studies include Public Order, Civil Dispute, Sudden Death, and Stop and Search, and for Phase 4 they include Counter Terrorism, Missing Persons, Burglary, and Child Protection.

Facilitated discussions are particularly useful for exploring attitudes and behaviour. The discussion might be initiated by watching a DVD, or by reflecting on the presentation of a guest speaker. Trainers encourage students to share their thoughts with others. If this is the case, then trainee officers should be prepared to maintain confidentiality as private and sensitive matters may be disclosed (but remember that confidentiality does not protect a trainee from disciplinary action concerning inappropriate language, attitudes, or behaviour).

Presentations are used for some topics. If the subject matter is appropriate for this form of delivery (eg an introduction to the Theft Act 1968), or time is short, then trainers may well deliver a presentation, often using Microsoft PowerPoint software. Throughout the presentation, trainees are given the opportunity to ask questions and make notes. Different trainers will have different approaches to delivering presentations, which may or may not coincide with a student's learning style. For example, some may use the technique of progressively revealing bullet points which, although it will keep the attention of many in the class, can be

Qualifications and Training

irritating to some (most trainers welcome feedback on matters such as this). Finally, a Virtual Learning Environment (such as Blackboard) is likely to contain copies of the presentations.

Role-plays involve trainees 'playing' given roles in an imaginary situation, for example in a simulated 'stop and account' scenario, one trainee will act as a police officer and the other a member of the public. Role-plays are normally used when a trainee has gained sufficient knowledge and skills (particularly in terms of police procedure) to make them meaningful. Some police forces use semi-professional actors or volunteers from the local community to play roles, and this can contribute to diversity training. The debrief also provides useful learning opportunities (a trainee could even be videoed to assist with this). Note that role-plays and simulations cannot normally be used as evidence against achievement of the assessment criteria of the Diploma in Policing units. However, a trainee officer can reflect on what has been learnt from a role-play in his/her Learning Diary Phase 3.

The **community engagement** is seen as an important way in which trainee officers learn about the diverse communities they will police and their own attitudes towards the various community members (see 8.6.4). The IPLDP places great emphasis on trainees adopting a self-critical approach (Home Office, 2004) involving active self-questioning of his/her existing beliefs and attitudes. Evidence of this self-critical approach can be included in Learning Diary Phase 2 entries under headings such as 'What challenged you during the engagement, in what ways, and how did you respond?'

Syndicate exercises involve students working in small groups as a syndicate. A syndicate is a group of people where each assumes a certain role. For example, one student might be a member of the public complaining about anti-social behaviour in her street. Other members of the syndicate will play the role of the local PC, the police BCU commander, and so on. The various issues are explored from the different perspectives. Syndicate exercises can be useful learning devices but need to be carefully organized and managed by trainers, with detailed instructions and briefing on the roles played by students. For example, if the syndicate group is quite large (six or more) certain members of the group might not participate, or the issues might be only be examined in token and ineffective ways because of time restraints.

Finally, trainers will ensure that trainee officers have access to the NPIA 'blended' learning resources that support IPLDP. These include extensive student notes, audio notes (mp3 versions of the student notes), and the Authorised Professional Practice (APP) consolidated professional guidance.

8.6.3   Coaching

In police training, coaching is normally carried out one-to-one, and will be one of the responsibilities of a tutor or mentor, particularly when a trainee is based with a PDU (see 8.6.1). The stage at which a PDU allocates tutors to trainees will vary between forces, but as soon as you have been given details of your tutor(s) you should arrange to meet up. At the meeting you may find yourself talking about your background, how you came to join the police, and what you are aiming for. You should also mention the name you would like your tutor to use for you. However, bear in mind that your relationship with your tutor will develop over time—so do not say too much at first if it makes you feel uncomfortable. If you have a paper-based SOLAP that contains any feedback from your training staff at university or training centre then take it with you, so your tutor can start to get to know you. You could share entries from your Learning Diary (see 8.5.4.2) to help illustrate your strengths and weaknesses. Together you can use these to create a development plan for the future. Making a list of subjects that you have already learned in theory can help with planning on how to create opportunities for applying the learning in the work place.

Your tutor will use a variety of techniques to help you learn. For example questioning can involve closed questions (with a yes or no answer), open questions which need fuller answers, and reflective questions to check your understanding; all of these are useful. If your tutor uses multiple questions you need to answer one question at a time to avoid confusion. And 'leading' questions might lead you to agree when you don't! (Remember, this could equally well apply to your own use of questions, so you should always be aware of what style of questions you are using.)

Coaching often takes place before and after attending an incident as part of Supervised Patrol. The incidents may have been carefully selected by the PDU: that is, they wait for a particular type of incident to be reported (such as a suspected shoplifting incident) and then accompany you to that incident. Or you might attend any incident that day, regardless of its nature. Your response (but not necessarily on the first occasion) will be important in terms of your subsequent assessment against the Diploma in Policing units (see 8.5.1).

Pre-briefs are a good way of preparing. Your tutor will question you about the theory you have learned in the training room, and about how you intend to deal with the incident. After the incident, at the de-brief he/she will probably ask you to reflect and make notes about what went well, and what did not go quite so well (the notes can also be used for Learning Diary entries). The ELC (see 8.6.5.3) can help structure reflection on important questions such as 'What happened at the incident?' and 'What are you going to do differently (or better) next time?'.

The tutor feedback serves two main purposes: to reassure you that your contribution has been recognized and noted, and to help you develop the skills and abilities required. Feedback is often structured as a kind of sandwich; first an observation on something you did well, then discussing a developmental point, and then returning to something else you did well.

8.6.4   Learning from the community

Under the IPLDP, all trainee police officers are expected to undertake at least 80 hours of community engagement, normally as part of Phase 2 or Phase 3 (if a police force uses this terminology). These hours could be a continuous week of block placement or perhaps one or two days per week for a number of months. For at least 24 of the 80 hours, a trainee will be based with a community group or a public, private, or voluntary organization such as a care home, a refugee support centre, or a youth-offending team. A particular emphasis is placed on the opportunities the placement provides in relation to ethnicity and diversity (by 'issues around diversity' the police service normally means gender, disability, gay and lesbian groups, and age). However, the community engagement can also be used to give the trainee an insight into the community's expectations of the police. Examples of this kind of placement include being based in local supermarkets, hospitals, schools, and housing authority units. Other examples of community placements (the other 56 hours) include attachments to 'low-profile' policing units and one-day visits to local community groups.

Trainee police officers on community engagement are not likely to be in uniform (or carrying personal safety equipment), and it may be decided that it is best not to reveal to the 'clients' at the placement that the fresh face is a trainee police officer. This is normally to allow trainees to interact as naturally as possible with the clients of the organization, particularly if some of them could be hostile to the police. If this is the case for you, bear the following in mind:

- Your force will have conducted a risk assessment concerning the placement but, if you feel uncomfortable in terms of your own personal safety, then you should make this known to your force. If the problem persists, then you may wish to contact your Police Federation representative (see 6.7.1).
- There will be standard operating procedures (SOPs) in place to govern the relationships between your force and the organizations involved and also what you should do under certain circumstances—for example, in the case of questions concerning health and safety. Familiarize yourself with these.

To make the most of a community engagement you should find out about the organization in advance. It may have a website setting out its aims and objectives. You should try and find out how it is funded and if it is inspected in some way (inspection reports may be available online). When on placement, you should engage with the people there—for example, staff and clients of the organization. They will be as interested in you as you are in them, so you will probably find this quite easy. You should keep in mind the objectives of the community placement; the aim is for you to learn about community issues. Think also about how you could evidence the skills and knowledge you gained from the placement. For example, how could you demonstrate that your understanding of the ethics and values of the police service has been enhanced?

Trainees are sometimes required to present findings from a community engagement to fellow trainee officers and perhaps even members of your Supervised Patrol BCU. Your experiences will also form the basis for Learning Diary entries in the SOLAP (see 8.5.4), or could be used in a professional assignment. It is also likely to be relevant to some of the Diploma in Policing assessment unit learning outcomes and the relevant NOS units, in particular the embedded NOS Unit AA1 'Promote equality and value diversity'.

You will probably learn from the community in other ways too, for example from guest speakers and community representatives. You should make a real effort as a learner to engage with the guest speakers and achieve as much as possible from the session.

> **TASK 4** You are on community engagement at a centre that provides support for young people who have been excluded from full-time secondary education. The young people at the day centre have been told t hat you are a student and that you are there to learn about their experiences and the work of the support group. However, they have not been told that you are a student police officer. During a break you observe one young person offering to sell what appears to be Ecstasy, a class B drug (see 12.5.1.1) to his friend. What do you do?

8.6.5   Improving your learning

To help you learn more easily you need some understanding about the different ways adults learn. This varies between individuals, and educational background is usually an important factor. You may be a student on a pre-join programme, or have entered the police family earlier in another police-related role (eg as a PCSO), or have recently left full-time further or higher education (up to 30 per cent in recent years), whilst a number of you might not have undertaken training or study for a long time.

8.6.5.1   Domains of learning

Many of our day-to-day actions centre on three main areas of activity and these are also important for learning. Understanding these areas will help you to assess your own competencies and evaluate your own educational and training needs. It will then be easier for you to learn and revise for exams, and will provide you with a route map through any learning experience. The three areas are referred to as the 'learning domains' (eg Bloom *et al*, 1956 and subsequent publications in this series). They are:

- The cognitive domain which is associated with the ability to reason, and will include learning subject matter such as law, legislation, policy, and procedure, about which we have to think.
- The affective domain which is associated with feelings and emotions, for example, the way people react to situations (such as provocation), and their values and prejudices. A cliché in police training is that 'attitudes can be caught or taught', and therefore a great deal of your training will involve learning to adopt appropriate attitudes and behaviours towards the public and your colleagues, in areas such as respect, race and diversity, team working, community and customer focus, effective communication, problem solving, personal responsibility, and resilience.
- The psychomotor domain is associated with physical dexterity, for example, personal safety training, First Aid training, using a breath test machine, and traffic control.

Within each domain there are levels of complexity, beginning with the easiest (on the left) and progressively becoming more difficult towards the right, as shown in the table.

For the cognitive domain ('the head'):

Knowledge →	Comprehension →	Application
The ability to recall facts, words, or phrases, eg a definition of an Act or a section of law	To understand and be able to explain component parts of policy, procedure, or legislation, eg the meanings of words within definitions, the variations and exceptions	To use this knowledge and understanding to apply previous learning to a set task which is either simulated, paper-based, or in the work place

For the affective domain ('the heart'):

Receives →	Responds →	Values
Listens to or sees demonstrated an attitude which is to be learned eg 'We want you to be a non-discriminator, regardless of the prejudices you may actually have'	Outwardly shows the learned attitude or behaviour, but does not necessarily believe in it, eg 'I have prejudices, but I will not discriminate because I've been told I must not'	Adopts the learned attitude or behaviour and, without request or prompting, owns the feeling personally, eg 'Even though I have prejudices, I believe it is wrong to discriminate and therefore I will not do so'

For the psychomotor domain ('the hands'):

Imitation →	Manipulation →	Precision
Performs the skill as a result of copying or repeating what has been observed, eg resuscitation techniques in First Aid	Executes the skill with some instruction or coaching	Carries out the skill alone without copying, instruction, or the necessity for coaching

For a session involving mainly the cognitive domain, you will probably be asked to assimilate at least some of the knowledge about the subject in advance; for example, learning an offence in the form of a definition. This is sometimes referred to as a 'pre-read' but you are of course required to learn material, and not just read it! There may be a check to assess whether you have gained the appropriate level of knowledge. A trainer or tutor will then probably move you on to the next level in the cognitive domain (from knowledge to comprehension) and check your understanding and clarify any misunderstandings. Finally, you will be given an opportunity to develop your learning further, using one or more of the methods listed in 8.6.5. This will involve the third level of the domain—applying your learning.

Similar activities will be used in the other two domains for attitudinal and skills-based subjects, probably starting at the simplest level and moving incrementally to the more complex. Trainee officers will be coached and mentored in preparation for assessment against the Diploma in Policing units and the embedded National Occupational Standards (see 7.4).

8.6.5.2 Preferred learning styles

People seem to prefer to learn in different ways (Kolb, 1984) and researchers have discerned the existence of four main learning styles; activist, theorist, pragmatist, and reflective. Most people fit into one or two of these styles. The **activist** learning style involves being actively involved with a task, for example taking part in simulations or role-plays; setting tasks or writing questions or case studies; taking part in computer-based learning, for example through the NCALT website; and/or using pre-formed questions before sessions so that learning can be continually checked. The **theorist** learning style involves having a logical outlook and developing underlying theories; reading about a subject and drawing independent conclusions; challenging the underlying assumptions; and/or designing logical diagrams to summarize the subject matter as a sequence of points to be learned. The **pragmatist** learning style involves thinking or dealing with the problem in a practical way, rather than using theory or abstract principles; finding the use of theory and discussion frustrating; and/or looking for the practical applications for learning. The **reflective** learning style involves learning in a slow, deliberate way; taking a step back and looking at a subject from all angles before drawing a conclusion; discussing issues. Participation in simulations or role-plays may not seem that useful.

TASK 5 You can find out more about your own learning style(s) by taking part in an online questionnaire: go to the Learning Styles interactive website at Canterbury Christ Church University: <http://www.canterbury.ac.uk/graduate-skills/preview/audits/learning-styles/index.html>.

8.6.5.3 **The Experiential Learning Cycle (ELC)**

We all know the sayings that 'if you don't succeed the first time, then try, try again' or 'we all learn by our mistakes'. Much of your learning will take place through your own experiences, and as adults we can actually teach ourselves, at least in part. This process can be represented as a diagram showing the experiential learning cycle (ELC), adapted from the work of David Kolb (Kolb, 1984).

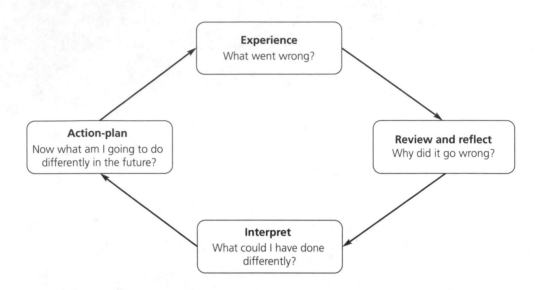

TASK 6 Think of a situation you found yourself in recently where afterwards you decided to do something differently next time. Now relate those circumstances to the ELC diagram, starting with Experience and moving clockwise through the diagram.

The four stages to the cycle are as follows:

- *Experience* (called 'Concrete Experience' in the Kolb original): this is direct experience, often through practical application. A trainee police officer will often want to know what the practical applications of the session will be and get 'hands on' as soon as possible. A police trainer may provide prompts, for example 'think of times in your own life when you have been subject to bullying or harassment'.
- *Review and reflect* ('Reflection'): what does the experience mean to me? This stage is the beginning of understanding. A task such as 'describe your feelings when you were bullied or harassed' may be given.
- *Interpret* ('Abstract Conceptualization'): this involves placing the experiences in some form of theoretical and more abstract framework such as 'How do victims feel about this?'
- *Action-plan* ('Active Experimentation'): the stage of action-planning is how we take this learning forward and test it against reality, such as 'What can a police service do to support victims of harassment?'

TASK 7 A trainee police officer, as part of Personal Safety Training, starts learning how to handcuff a suspect by taking part in supervised practice using a manikin (dummy). The trainer, observing the student practise and testing the results, then asked: 'Were there any risks to you during the cuffing? How tight did that feel for the suspect? What might you have done differently?'

That night the trainee reads up on how to handcuff suspects; the reasons for doing it in particular ways, force procedure, and the human rights of the suspect. The next day, presented with a fellow trainee to handcuff, she thinks: 'Now what did I do wrong yesterday and what did it say in those notes I read? I'll try it like this today.'

Identify in the above, each of the four stages of Kolb's ELC.

8.6.5.4 **Studying and study skills**

We acknowledge that learning 'policing' is sometimes a confusing and disorientating experience. In some cases we even have to unlearn before we can learn. For example, if you do not know that there are major legal differences between the offences of robbery and burglary, you will have to unlearn what you thought you knew already, which can be disconcerting and discouraging! Taylor (1986) suggests that the discomfort we experience is actually a necessary part of adult learning. In particular, she discerned four distinct phases of the learning experience, as shown in the diagram.

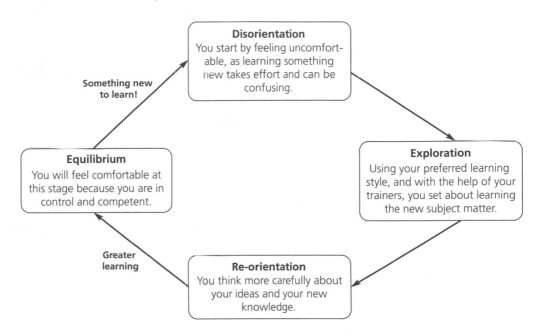

In summary, learning something new is often initially characterized by feelings of discomfort and anxiety. Bear this in mind when studying and it will help you cope; it is quite normal to have some ups and downs as you learn.

There are numerous guides, books, and websites which can be used to help develop your study skills. For example, if you are also undertaking a higher education award as part of your education and training, then you may find it useful to work through Dr Stella Cottrell's *Study Skills Handbook* (Cottrell, 2013). Students based at a college or university will almost certainly find that support for study skills is available. The following skills are all required:

- reading skills;
- note taking and writing skills;
- memorizing and revising for assessments;
- using libraries, learning centres, and e-learning resources;
- researching and using internet search engines; and
- time management.

Finally, note that you may have undiagnosed difficulties in learning which could affect your ability to study. Colleges and universities often offer screening for such problems when students first join.

> **TASK 8** Find out about the reading technique SQ3R, perhaps by using Google or another internet search engine. This will also prove useful to you if you decide to train as an investigator over the next few years.

8.6.6 **Diversity training in the police**

One of the reasons for undertaking a community engagement (see 8.6.4) is that it provides real and complex opportunities for a trainee police officer to witness and learn from the views and experiences of members of the diverse communities that make up the UK.

In general terms, diversity is about the range of features found in human life and culture including ethnicity, religion, gender, physical ability, age, sexual orientation, customs, and language. We ought perhaps to celebrate diversity as part of the richness of human cultures, but diversity is sometimes thought of as a form of 'otherness'—that is, qualities that make 'them' different from 'us'. We also examine diversity as a key theme in policing in 3.8.

Trainee officers need to think carefully about their own experiences and attitudes, and how these might affect the way they relate to the diverse range of people encountered in policing work. What skills are needed to work effectively in the community, and how can diversity training help with developing these skills? Diversity training is usually placed within IPLDP module IND 2, but it will be assessed in a variety of contexts. One of the assessment units embedded in the Diploma in Policing (NOS Unit AA1.1) includes the element to 'Promote equality and value diversity', and this is likely to be assessed through direct observation of a trainee's actions, the records he/she kept, and testimony from witnesses.

There is a tendency in some police environments to view diversity training as a form of inoculation. In fact, you sometimes hear police officers saying that they have 'had' their diversity training as if it were some form of one-off injection that would protect them for the rest of their careers. Perhaps it would be more appropriate to see diversity training as just the start of a process that will continue throughout your career.

8.6.6.1 Questions you might need to consider

You might need to consider the following questions during diversity training:

- What are my existing beliefs and attitudes about the diversity I encounter in people?
- How will my beliefs and attitudes affect the way that I behave during my everyday and professional life?
- How will my behaviour affect other people around me?

But at the outset, why is it important to consider these questions? It is important because our beliefs, attitudes, and values can spill over into our work, and for a police officer this includes whilst on duty. Hence if you hold prejudices and bias towards certain groups of people (as most of us do, to some extent at least), you are more likely to act upon your prejudices if you are not aware of them, and your conduct may fall short of the standards expected of trainee police officers.

Finally, respect for diversity makes good policing sense. You are more likely to gain the cooperation of others, to secure information and intelligence, and hence to progress an investigation, if you are aware of the pluralistic nature of the communities within the UK and have some understanding of how best to work in such contexts.

8.6.6.2 Looking inwards

As an individual, you will view the world in your own way, but you also need to remember that other individuals each have their own world-view that deserves respect. To consider these issues fully, you will need to genuinely engage with your lecturers, trainers, your colleagues, and most of all, yourself. In particular, you will need to examine what you know about yourself in relation to diversity and the following issues:

What I know about myself as an individual:

- how I currently behave;
- my current values, beliefs, and attitudes; and
- how my background has influenced me.

What I know about myself as a trainee police officer:

- my responsibilities and the duties I have to perform;
- my career history; and
- how the law affects me and the policies I have to follow.

> **TASK 9** Take the time to think, then jot down your thoughts about the points above—you might find it quite hard to see yourself in these ways. Reflect upon your ideas—which parts have you found easy, and which parts have been more puzzling? Do you know why? Through asking yourself these questions, you will be preparing yourself for genuine engagement with police service diversity training.

TASK 10 Consider:

- your experiences in life so far and those you are likely to have in the near future;
- your prejudices, assumptions, and stereotypical views, and their consequences;
- your view of the world you live in and the people within it; and
- your ability to mix well in a social environment with people from other backgrounds and cultures.

Again, take time to think about each point in turn. You may find it useful to think what your friends and family would say about any prejudices you might have. Make brief notes and reflect upon your answers.

8.7   Answers to Tasks

TASK 1 Well, how does it compare? Do not be surprised (or concerned) to find significant variation from the national template.

The internet will give you access to brief descriptions of a number of force approaches to structuring initial training, and it is surprising how varied these can be.

TASK 2 Outcomes 2 and 3 must each be demonstrated on two occasions.

TASK 3 You should have found that the knowledge and understanding requirements of Unit 4G4 are:

1. Limitations and risks of applying First Aid to others.
2. How to detect an obstructed airway and methods of clearing obstruction.
3. How to check for signs of life and for life-threatening conditions.
4. Methods of CPR and how to use this appropriately.
5. How to manage an unconscious casualty and the main causes of unconsciousness.
6. Precautions to be taken when performing CPR.
7. Different types of wound and their treatment.
8. Methods for controlling bleeding.
9. Signs and symptoms of shock.
10. Recognition and treatment of sprains, strains, and fractures.
11. Main safety considerations when dealing with burns or scalds.
12. How to recognize and assess the severity and extent of injuries.
13. Appropriate treatments for hypothermia, frostbite, heat-stroke, and heat exhaustion.
14. How to recognize and respond to local danger and risks when dealing with casualties.

TASK 4 This would be a difficult issue for any trainee police officer. You have probably been attested, and hence have assumed the full responsibilities and powers of a constable and yet you are barely trained and even less experienced. You are with the organization to learn, not to disrupt their usual ways of working. However, dealing in drugs is a serious offence.

Your force will have standing operating procedures to help you decide what to do, and these often involve you taking advice from your supervisor and referring to the policies of the organization concerned. The important point is not to keep this to yourself.

TASK 5 You will find that the site will describe each of the categories as 'activist', 'theorist', 'pragmatist', and 'reflector' and undertaking the online questionnaire would have placed your preferred learning style into a grid.

Where the two lines intersect gives you some measure of your preferred learning style. It shows that I am a predominantly activist learner. According to the site this means that I seek hidden possibilities; I learn by talking with others; I get totally involved; I take risks; I am enthusiastic, working quickly and involving others, and my favourite question is 'What if?'.

The site is not the only way of exploring your preferred learning styles. A popular method in police training is to use Honey and Mumford's Learning Styles Questionnaire. Further details may be found at <http://www.peterhoney.org>.

Qualifications and Training

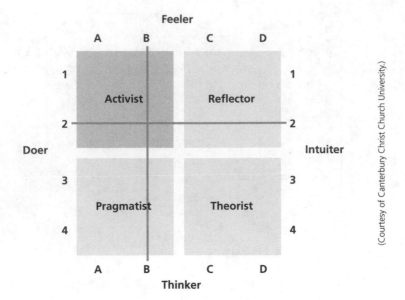

(Courtesy of Canterbury Christ Church University.)

TASK 6 Not everyone finds that the Kolb process works for them. Indeed, there are a number of more general critiques of the theory underlying ELC. Rogers, for example, has argued that 'learning includes goals, purposes, intentions, choice and decision-making, and it is not at all clear where these elements fit into the learning cycle' (Rogers, 1996, p 108).

TASK 7 The supervised practice with a dummy is the experience stage.

The trainer asked, 'Were there any risks to you during the cuffing? How tight might that feel for the suspect? What might you have done differently?'—this is the review and reflect stage.

The trainee reads up on how to handcuff suspects and reads about the reasons for doing it in particular ways, including force procedure and the human rights of the suspect—this is the interpret stage.

The next day she has the chance to practise handcuffing again and thinks, 'After what happened yesterday, and because of what I read last night I'll try it a bit looser'—this is the action-planning stage.

TASK 8 SQ3R stands for:

- Survey/Skim the material you need to read;
- formulate Questions that you expect the material to answer;
- do the Reading;
- Recall what you have read; and
- Review.

TASKS 9 and 10 Your answers will reflect your own particular experiences and thoughts.

As background reading you might wish to consider looking at the 2003 HMIC thematic inspection *Diversity Matters*, which examined training on matters of race and diversity in the police service. This report should be available from your police force. The Equality and Human Rights Commission document '*Police and racism: What has been achieved 10 years after the Stephen Lawrence Inquiry report?*' is available online.

9 | Stop, Search, and Entry

9.1 Introduction

This chapter describes police procedures and duties in relation to stop and search for people and vehicles, searching premises, and powers of entry into premises. These procedures will be used by trainee police officers on Supervised and Independent Patrol.

'Stop and search' is an umbrella term given to the 19 or more powers to detain people for the purposes of search, with s 1 of the PACE Act 1984 being used most frequently. According to PACE Act 1984 Codes of Practice, the main purpose of stop and search powers is to 'enable officers to allay or confirm suspicions about individuals without exercising their power of arrest' (Code A, para 1.4).

There is some controversy surrounding the use of police stop and search powers in relation to people from visible ethnic minorities. Stop and search has been particularly associated with racial harassment; it is claimed that visible ethnic minority people have been subject to stop and search to a disproportionate extent compared with their proportion in the general population. For further information see the latest Home Office Statistical Bulletin *Police Powers and Procedures England and Wales* on the gov.uk website. There are, however, arguments concerning the statistical basis for this claim, which highlight the difference between the 'resident' and 'available' populations in particular policing areas (eg see Waddington *et al*, 2004) because some sectors of the resident population are more likely to be out on the streets. However, as Newburn noted, 'irrespective of whether or not police stop and search powers are used . . . in a discriminatory fashion, it seems undeniable that this is how they are experienced by minority ethnic communities' (Newburn, 2007, p 787). If the police misuse their powers this is likely to create public mistrust (see Code A, para 1.4). Police officer bias can have discriminatory effects, so officers are encouraged to recognize and challenge the way in which bias and stereotypes can influence their own decision making. You can use exercises such as the Harvard Implicit Association Test (available online) to help identify some of your own personal biases.

This chapter also covers the recording of all stops and searches. This is a conventional quantitative measurement of police performance, and each force has policy guidelines on when and how these powers may be used. The main thing to remember is that whatever search power is used, it must conform to the guidelines set out in the PACE Act 1984 Codes of Practice.

Powers of entry are also covered for searching, for example searching a property directly after an arrest for dangerous articles or property relating to a criminal offence (s 32 of the PACE Act 1984). Other powers of search after arrest are also covered, including some which require authorization from a senior police officer (s 18 of the PACE Act 1984) and those which are provided under warrant issued by a Justice of the Peace (s 8 of the PACE Act 1984). A separate Code of Practice on Powers of Entry applies for regulatory bodies such as the Health and Safety Executive and the Environment Agency, available on the Home Office website. Finally, the practicalities of searching premises, vehicles, and open land are also considered.

General Procedures

9.2 Definitions of Places and Other Locations

Various categories of locations that apply to stop and account and searches are referred to in the legislation. The definitions of locations and places given here are also relevant to other aspects of law-enforcement work.

A **public place** is anywhere 'the public or any section of the public has access, on payment or otherwise, as of right or by virtue of express or implied permission' (s 1(1)(a) of the PACE Act 1984). The public have a right to use roads and footpaths, and other public areas during opening hours. They have express permission to enter cinemas, theatres, or football grounds having paid an entrance fee and they can remain there until that particular entertainment is over, when permission to be there ends. There is an implied permission for persons to enter privately owned buildings to carry out business transactions with the owners, and to use a footpath to the front door of a house to pay a lawful call on the householder. That implied permission remains until withdrawn by the householder or the owner of the business premises. Places to which the public has ready access include a private field (if that field is regularly used, even by trespassers), or a garden (if it is accessible by jumping over a low wall). Ultimately, it would be a question of fact for the court to consider whether all members of the general public can gain ready access to the place and whether a landowner has given permission for the public to use a privately owned place.

A **private place** is land or premises which are privately owned to which the general public does NOT have ready access, for example a private residence or a private office block. Privately owned land or premises that is used by the general public during opening hours (and is therefore a public place at that time) reverts to being a private place during closing times.

Premises is a very general term and under s 23 of the PACE Act 1984 includes vehicles, vessels, aircraft, hovercraft, offshore installations, renewable energy installations, and tents and other moveable structures.

A **dwelling** is any place where a person or people live and is defined in two pieces of legislation. A dwelling is:

- '[a]ny structure or part of a structure occupied as a person's home or as other living accommodation (whether the occupation is separate or shared with others) but does not include any part not so occupied, and for this purpose "structure" includes a tent, caravan, vehicle, vessel or other temporary or moveable structure' (s 8 of the Public Order Act 1986);
- '[a]n inhabited building, or a vehicle or vessel which is, at the time of the offence, inhabited (irrespective of whether or not the person who occupies the vehicle/vessel is present at the time of the burglary)' (s 9(4) of the Theft Act 1968).

A **place of residence** is not defined in law so would be a question of fact for the court to decide, but is likely to be similar to a dwelling.

9.3 Stop and Account

Polices officers can speak to anyone in the ordinary course of their duties, and members of the public have a civic duty to help the police prevent crime and locate suspects (PACE Code of Practice A, Note 1). When an officer requests a person in a public place to account for him/herself, there is no national requirement for the officer to make any record of the encounter or provide a receipt (para 4.12 of PACE Code A). However, police forces have discretion if there are concerns over local disproportionality in the use of stop and account; they can request officers to record the self-defined ethnicity of persons stopped in this way, or who are detained with a view to searching but are not searched (Code A, Note 22A). The person should be given information about how to report any dissatisfaction with respect to the way he/she has been treated, if he/she requests it (Code A, Note 22B).

9.4 Stop and Search Powers

In the year ending 31 March 2016, there were 386,474 stops and searches conducted by police in England and Wales under s 1 of PACE, s 60 of the Criminal Justice and Public Order Act

1994, and s 44/47A of the Terrorism Act 2000, a fall of 28 per cent compared with the previous year (Home Office, 2016f, p 4). However, during the same period those individuals from Black (or Black British) groups were six times more likely to be stopped by police than those from White groups, an increase over previous years (ibid, p 6).

There are over 19 different powers to stop and search, such as for drugs (see 9.4.3.1) and firearms (s 47 of the Firearms Act 1968). Section 1 of the PACE Act 1984 introduced a further power to stop and search for stolen items or 'prohibited articles' and is perhaps the most commonly used. Many stop and search powers (such as under s 1 of PACE) require the officer to have 'reasonable grounds for suspicion', whereas others do not (such as under s 60 of the Criminal Justice and Public Order Act 1994 (see 9.4.3.3)). Any decision to stop and search, however, must always be based on objective criteria. The full list of stop and search powers is given in Annex A to the PACE Code of Practice A and we discuss some of these in more detail in 9.4.3. Finally, although not a power to stop and search *per se*, in 9.5 we cover road checks for locating particular people, under s 4 of the PACE Act 1984.

According to PACE Code A, para 3.1 and the Terrorism Act 2000 Codes of Practice, para 5.1.1, 'all stops and searches should be carried out with courtesy, consideration and respect for the person concerned. This has a significant impact on public confidence in the police'. Typically then, the powers remain under constant scrutiny from oversight bodies, for example in 2013, HMIC published the report *Stop and Search Powers: Are the police using them effectively and fairly?* (HMIC, 2013b). It indicated that the police had very little understanding about how the powers should be used most effectively and fairly to cut crime, and that they were rarely targeted at priority crimes in particular areas.

In April 2014, the Home Secretary announced the Best Use of Stop and Search Scheme (BUSSS) to support a more intelligence-led approach, to achieve greater transparency and community involvement in the use of the powers (Home Office, 2014b). Forces are not required by law to use BUSSS, although most have chosen to opt in. HMIC inspections check for compliance, and any force not complying with all the features of the Scheme can be suspended (Home Office, 2017, p7). The Home Secretary suspended 13 police forces from the BUSSS in February 2016 (HMIC, 2016a).

HMIC reported on the progress made in *Stop and Search Powers 2* (HMIC, 2015c), and in response to the report's first recommendation, the College of Policing (2015m) produced a definition of a fair and effective stop and search. This states that a search is fair and effective when:

- the search is justified and the lawful use of the power stands up to public scrutiny;
- the officer has a genuine and objective reasonable suspicion that stolen or prohibited articles will be found in the person's possession;
- the person understands why he/she has been searched and feels that the search has been conducted with respect; and
- the search is necessary and is the least intrusive method a police officer could use to establish whether a member of the public has a prohibited article or an item for use in crime with him/her.

In summary, any decision to carry out a stop and/or search must be fair, and the reasons must of course be lawful and be able to withstand legal scrutiny. The method of the search must follow the proper procedures, and records must be made to that effect. In addition, the interactions with the public during the whole encounter must be professional. It is vital that stop and search powers are used in a manner that is transparent and accountable. Further guidance on the use of stop and search is provided as the Authorised Police Practice on the College of Policing website.

Stop and search information from each force is available to anyone as data downloads from data.police.uk. Police supervisors have the responsibility to monitor the use of the powers by individual officers (Code A, para 5.5), and if standards of professional behaviour (see 6.3.2) are not maintained, performance or misconduct procedures may be instigated (Code A, para 5.6).

The Certificate in Knowledge of Policing requires learners to 'understand legal and organizational requirements in relation to searching individuals' and to 'understand legal and organizational requirements in relation to searching vehicles, premises, and open spaces'. The ability to 'demonstrate lawful search of persons, premises, and vehicles' is a requirement within the

General Procedures

PAC heading 'Search' and can also contribute evidence for the attainment of the Diploma in Policing assessed unit 'Conduct Police Searches'. Note that the unit requires that an officer can conduct searches on the appropriate 'grounds and legal authority', and identify and deal with any potential risks such as offensive weapons, assault, sharps (eg hypodermic needles), or hazardous substances. As with most Diploma assessment criteria, the evidence is likely to be through an assessor's direct observation of a real search. Competence will need to be demonstrated against the learning outcomes on at least two occasions in the work place.

9.4.1 Stop and search procedures

For any stop and search the rights of the individual must be safeguarded. Therefore, s 2 of the PACE Act 1984 and the PACE Codes of Practice always apply. Code A, para 1.1 of the Codes of Practice states that police officers must use their powers to stop and search 'fairly, responsibly, with respect for people being searched, and without unlawful discrimination' (see 3.8.3.1 on 'protected characteristics' which are particularly relevant to avoiding discrimination). In addition, 'any misuse of the powers is likely to be harmful to policing and lead to mistrust of the police' (Code A, para 1.4). The police also have a responsibility to safeguard and promote the welfare of all persons under the age of 18 (s 11 of the Children Act 2004). The procedures to be followed are described in detail in 9.4.1.1 to 9.4.1.5.

9.4.1.1 Reasonable Grounds for Suspicion

Many stop and search powers require 'reasonable grounds for suspicion', for example s 1 of the PACE Act 1984 and s 23 of the Misuse Drugs Act 1971. A search is more likely to be 'effective, legitimate and secure public confidence' if the grounds for suspicion are based on a range of 'objective factors' (Code A, para 2.8A).

The test for 'reasonable grounds for suspicion' (Code A, para 2.2) has two parts:

1. a genuine suspicion in the mind of the officer that he/she will find the object for which the power of search is being used; and
2. the suspicion must be reasonable, formed on an objective basis from facts, information and/or intelligence which contribute to the high probability that the object will be found and that a reasonable person would also draw the same conclusions.

The police officer must be able to explain the basis of the suspicion by reference to a specific aspect of the person's behaviour, or to intelligence or information about the person. This must be relayed to the person being searched (see 9.4.1.2), and also recorded (see 9.4.1.5). The power to stop and search should not be related to a suspicion that the person has committed an offence. Rather, the suspicion would be that he/she is likely to be in possession of an object related to a suspected offence (for which a person may be legally searched (see 9.4.2.3)). This would include a suspected offence committed by another person. An example of this would be searching a child under the age of criminal responsibility who was being used as a 'mule' by an adult to carry unlawful items such as drugs, stolen property or even firearms (Code A, para 2.2A, Note 1B and 1BA). The two scenarios at the end of 9.4.2.3 illustrate how the grounds for a s 1 PACE search stop and search may be established.

The grounds can be based on the general behaviour of the person, the time, and the location. The officer must be able to explain his/her suspicion in terms of specific aspects of the person's conduct or behaviour (Code A, para 2.6B). For example, imagine an officer on mobile patrol is passing through an area where intelligence indicates burglaries are a current problem, and she sees a man jump down from a high garden wall. She can see the outline of a large square, flat object inside his zipped jacket, and that he is struggling to hold it in place. She asks him why he did not use the front door of the house, and about the object he has inside his coat. He fails to explain. She also notices that he is short of breath, is impatient, sweating, and is constantly backing away. All these observations can contribute to reasonable grounds for stop and search. Previous convictions can also play a part in an officer's decision to stop a person and ask for an explanation concerning his/her presence and behaviour. For example, imagine that intelligence indicates a spate of car thefts during the hours of darkness in a certain area, and a man with previous convictions for car thefts is seen looking in car windows at night. If he is unable to provide a satisfactory explanation, and taking the behaviour into account, an officer could form reasonable grounds for suspicion.

The reason for stopping and searching a suspect cannot be based upon physical appearance alone, (unless the police have information or intelligence giving a specific description of a suspect) particularly with regard to 'the protected characteristics', such as age, sex, race, religion, or belief (see 3.8.3.1 for a full list). Generalizing (ie stereotyping) groups of people as being more likely to take part in criminal activity must be avoided (Code A, para 2.2B(a) and (b)). Reasonable grounds can include descriptions from witnesses that refer to personal factors about a suspect (for example age, clothing, hair colour, and height), as these would help pinpoint a particular person (Code A, para 2.4). But this information alone would not be sufficient grounds for carrying out a stop and/or search—more specific information would be required, for example that the person was carrying a gun. To illustrate this further, imagine that a police officer receives information from a member of the public that a bearded dark-skinned young man wearing a white tunic has tucked a knife into his ankle boot at the ticket office of a train station. This could provide reasonable grounds to stop and search a bearded dark-skinned young man wearing a white tunic on the station platform, but only because he matches the description of the person who was seen to tuck a knife into his boot.

Refusing to answer any questions can never be used to provide reasonable grounds for suspicion (Code A, para 2.9), nor can grounds be established retrospectively through questioning (Code A, para 2.11). However, if reasonable grounds materialize during an encounter, the person can then be detained for a search. It would be essential at that point to provide the person with the relevant information (see 9.4.1.2).

For certain categories of people and in certain situations, the requirements for reasonable grounds are different. For a person who is believed to be a member of a 'gang' or group (see 15.8), a police officer may have reasonable grounds to stop and search such a person if reliable information or intelligence exists (Code A, para 2.6 and Note 9A). The same applies for protest groups, where unlawful objects could be brought to meetings or marches (Code A, para 2.6A). Here it is not always necessary for the searching officer to have reasonable suspicion that each and every member of the suspected group is in possession of a prohibited article before carrying out a search of an individual within that group (*Howarth v Commissioner of Police of the Metropolis* [2011] EWHC 2818 (QB)).

9.4.1.2 Information a police officer must provide before the search

Reasonable steps must be taken to provide certain information to the person to be searched (or to the person in charge of a vehicle which is to be searched). These requirements are explained in s 2 of the PACE Act 1984 and Code A, para 3.8 of the Codes of Practice. If these are not followed in full, any of the evidence thus obtained could be challenged in court (PACE Code A, para 1.6).

The information that must be provided to the person who is going to be searched can be summarized by the mnemonic GO WISELY.

G	Grounds of the suspicion for the search
O	Object/purpose of search
W	Warrant card (if the officer is in plain clothes or if requested by the person)
I	Identity of the officer performing the search
S	Station to which the officer is attached
E	Entitlement to a copy of the search record
L	Legal power used
Y	You are detained for the purposes of a search

It is important that police officers comply with all aspects of GO WISELY. In the case of *O (a juvenile) v DPP* (1999) 163 JP 725, it was decided that a breach of s 2 of the PACE Act 1984 would render a search (and probably any later arrest and detention) unlawful. In *R v Bristol* [2007] EWCA Crim 3214, it was reported that a search had been carried out under s 23 of the Misuse of Drugs Act 1971. The defendant was convicted of obstructing a police officer, but the conviction was later overturned on appeal because s 2 of the PACE Act 1984 had not been followed. A search was also deemed unlawful in another case (*Browne v Commissioner of Police for the Metropolis* [2014] EWHC 3999 (QB)), as the searching officer failed to abide by s 2 of the PACE Act 1984 and used excessive force; damages were awarded for assault.

9.4.1.3 Conducting the search

During the search the police officer must comply with PACE Code A (see 5.6. and other parts of this chapter). The officer must also act in accordance with the Code of Ethics (see 6.3), adhere to the nine Policing Principles (see 6.3.1), and comply with the Standards of Professional Behaviour (see 6.3.2).

The search must be kept **relevant**: the extent of the search must relate to the object the officer is looking for. For example, if a witness has seen someone putting an object into a certain jacket pocket or the glove compartment of a vehicle, then only that location can be searched (para 3.3). The person or vehicle can be detained for the purpose of such a search, but the length of time must be reasonable and kept to a minimum (para 3.3). Vehicle search procedures are covered in more detail in in 9.8.2.2.

The following points also apply for searching a person under stop and search powers; the officer:

- must seek the **cooperation** of the person. Under s 117 of the PACE Act 1984 reasonable force may be used as a last resort (see 15.5.1), but only after attempts to search have been met with resistance (para 3.2);
- cannot search a member of the **opposite** sex if it involves removal of more than outer coat, jacket, gloves, headgear, or footwear, or be present at such a search unless the person being searched specifically requests it (para 3.6);
- cannot require any person to **remove any clothing in public** other than an outer coat, jacket, and gloves (however, the person can be asked to remove more clothing voluntarily (Note 7));
- can **place his/her hands** inside the pockets of outer clothing and feel round the inside of collars, socks, and shoes (para 3.5);
- can search a person's **hair**, but only if this does not require the removal of headgear (para 3.5);
- can carry out a **more thorough search**, for example requiring the removal of a T-shirt (but without exposing intimate body parts) - this must take place out of public view, for example in a police van or at a nearby police station (see para 3.6);
- can carry out a search which **exposes intimate parts** of the body (see 9.4.1.4), but not as a routine extension of a previous less intrusive search where nothing had been found.

If the person to be searched is vulnerable on grounds of age, gender, mental ill-health or physical or learning disabilities, then the vulnerability should be identified and consideration given to seeking the assistance of an appropriate person (eg carer). A check should be made that the person understands what is going to happen, and that the search is necessary and proportional (College of Policing (APP), 2016).

If the person to be searched is a child, then the child's safety and welfare should be considered, and the manner adopted and the information provided about making a complaint must be appropriate to the child's age. The searching officer must also defuse any challenging behaviour by the child, and identify an appropriate adult (eg parent) who can assist. When it is necessary to search a child under ten (this is only likely to happen in exceptional circumstances), the search should be carried out in a safe and controlled area, and if at all possible, in the presence of an appropriate adult (College of Policing (APP), 2016).

9.4.1.4 Intimate Searches

It is very rare, but it is sometimes necessary to carry out an intimate search involving exposure of intimate body parts (for example, if there are reasonable grounds for suspecting that a man has a knife concealed in his underpants). In the year ending 31 March 2016 only 77 intimate searches were carried out by police in the whole of England and Wales (Home Office, 2016f, p 6). In such a situation, the officer must first consult with a supervisor, to discuss why this is necessary and proportionate. Unless the supervisor refuses permission for the search, the final decision on whether to proceed rests with the officer at the scene. If a supervisor cannot be contacted within a reasonable time, the officer must take into account the need to carry out the search without further delay, the reasons why the intimate search is necessary and whether reasonable steps have been taken to consult a supervisor.

The intimate search must be carried out at a nearby police station or other nearby location out of public view, but not in a police vehicle. In terms of the people present, the search must be carried out:

- by an officer of the same sex as the person being searched;
- with at least two people present (except in urgent cases where there is a risk of harm to the person or others);

- with an appropriate adult present if the person is a child or vulnerable adult (Code C, Annex A, para 11); and
- out of sight of anyone not required to be present, and of anyone of the opposite sex (apart from an appropriate adult requested by the person being searched).

Cooperation should be encouraged, and to minimize embarrassment the person should at all times be wearing some of his/her clothes (his/her clothes are removed and put back on depending on which part of the body is being searched). The search should be conducted as quickly as possible, and he/she should be allowed to get dressed as soon as the search is over. For the genital area, only a visual examination is permitted, and only if it is necessary for the search. If an item is suspected to be inside a body cavity, the person will have to be arrested before a more thorough search can take place (Code C, Annex A, para 11).

9.4.1.5 Recording the search

If the person is not subsequently arrested, a record of a search must be made, either electronically or on paper (s 3, PACE and Code A, para 4.1). The record should be made as soon as possible after the search (s 3(2)(b), PACE and Code A, para 4.1). The following information must be recorded:

- the date, time, place, object, and grounds/authorization of the search(Code A, para 4.3);
- the person's ethnicity (as given, or if different, the officer's perception (see Code A, Annex B);
- the officer's identity (Code A, para 4.3).

Where a search exposes intimate parts of the body, the record must include the reasons why such a search was necessary, the name of the supervisor contacted for permission, and the timing of the contact and permission. If a supervisor was not contacted, the reasons for this must be recorded, including the steps taken to contact a supervisor.

Note there is no requirement for an officer to record the name, address, and date of birth of the person searched, or a person in charge of a vehicle which has been searched (Code A, para 4.3A), so this information should not be requested unless there are other reasons. Officers should consider carefully how to ask the person about his/her ethnicity. The BUSSS recommendations state that the results of the search should also be recorded, and whether the items were linked to the reason for the stop and search.

The person must be asked if he/she wants a copy of the record, and if he/she does, it should be provided immediately if possible. Alternatively, a receipt can be provided, and this must explain how a copy of the full record can be obtained, including access to an electronic copy of the record (Code A, para 4.2). However, it may be completely out of the question to provide a record or a receipt at the time, for example during serious public disorder or if an officer is called to an incident of higher priority (Code A, para 4.2A). The person is entitled to a copy of the record at a later time if the request is made within three months (Code A, para 3.8(e)).

If the person is arrested and taken to a police station, the record of the search will be made on the custody record (s 3(2)(a) and Code A, para 4.2B). The custody officer must ask the person if he/she wants a copy of the search record and if so, it should be provided as soon as practicable (Code A, para 4.2B).

After searching an unattended vehicle (or anything in or on it) a record of the search must be left, preferably inside the vehicle. For a vehicle that is locked, the record should be attached to the outside (see Code A, para 4.8 and s 2(7) of the PACE Act 1984).

9.4.2 Stop and search (s 1 of the PACE Act 1984)

This is often referred to simply as 'stop and search' although the Act refers to it as 'stop, search and detain'. We will refer to it here as 's 1 PACE stop and search' to distinguish it from the other 18 stop and search powers. If during a search an article is found for which there are reasonable grounds to suspect it to be stolen or prohibited, it can be seized (s 1(6), PACE Act 1984). An officer does not have to be in uniform to carry out a s 1 PACE stop and search.

9.4.2.1 Appropriate locations for an s 1 PACE stop and search

This type of search can be carried out in any public place (see 9.2.). This can include a garden or yard, or other land attached to a dwelling, but a person cannot be searched under s 1 PACE if he/she lives in the dwelling or has the resident's permission to be there (s 1(4)). A s 1 search cannot be carried out inside a dwelling under any circumstances (s 1(1)(b)). The same principles apply to searching a vehicle on land attached to a dwelling: a vehicle in such a location cannot be searched under s 1 PACE if the person who lives there is in charge of the vehicle or has permitted it to be there (s 1(5)(a) and (b)).

The search must be carried out at the place where the person or vehicle was first detained, or 'nearby' (Code A, para 3.4). 'Nearby' is defined in Code A, Note 6 simply as 'within a reasonable travelling distance', and as there is no guidance from case law, the term should be interpreted relatively cautiously. If a vehicle is stopped for a search in a busy street, the officers could take it into the nearest side street. This would ease any possible traffic congestion, maintain the health and safety of all concerned, and is very likely to count as 'nearby'.

9.4.2.2 Who or what can be searched under s 1 PACE?

Having made sure that all of the requirements covered in 9.4.2.1 are satisfied concerning the location, under s 1(2)(a) of the PACE Act 1984 an officer can search:

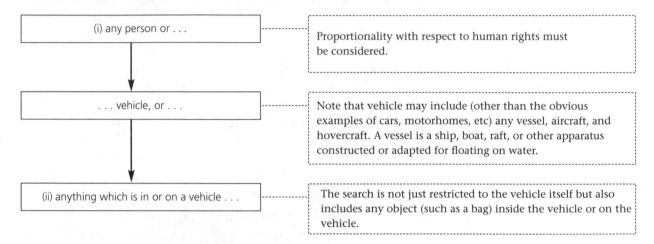

9.4.2.3 What items are included under s 1 PACE?

The search can only be for stolen or 'prohibited' articles. Stolen articles include any article for which there are reasonable grounds for suspecting it to be stolen. The following table provides further details about prohibited articles.

Prohibited article	Description
Offensive weapons (including firearms, (see 18.3.1)	Includes any article 'made, intended, or adapted' for causing injury to a person (see 18.2.1), for use by anyone. See also s 1(9) PACE and Code A, Note 23
Bladed or sharply pointed articles	Includes *any* bladed or sharply pointed article apart from a small folding pocket-knife (see 18.2.3)
Any articles used in the course of or in connection with certain criminal offences	Includes any article made, intended, or adapted for use (by anyone) in the course of or in connection with burglary (see 16.4), taking a conveyance (see 16.8.2), fraud (see 16.9), or criminal damage (see 20.2)
Fireworks	Only if possessed in contravention of any firework regulations (see 14.9)

Note that some items (such as drugs and items for use in terrorist activities) do not fall within this definition of prohibited articles, and therefore other statutory powers of search must be used to search for such items (see Code A, Annex A).

Scenario 1: Searching a Suspected Burglar

One evening, at the start of a night duty, you are provided with an electronic briefing containing information that a number of burglaries have taken place on the local housing estate. The suspect's *modus operandi* (MO) is to enter the rear of dwellings through insecure doors or windows during the early hours of the morning, and take small electrical items.

Later on, at 02.00 hours, you are on mobile patrol when you are called to several reports from members of the public regarding a prowler in the rear gardens of a number of houses within the housing estate. You make a search of the area on foot and locate a suspect hiding in the back garden of a house carrying a small rucksack which obviously contains several items. You carry out a PNC check of the suspect on the details he provides, and there is a record of an individual with the same details who has previous convictions for burglary. A colleague speaks to the occupant of the house and asks if the suspect lives there and whether the suspect has permission to be in the garden. The occupant unambiguously replies 'no' to both questions.

Under these circumstances you can justify your 'reasonable grounds' to carry out a s 1 PACE search: you have the intelligence you gained from the earlier briefing regarding the burglaries in the area, the behaviour of the suspect and the fact that he is a trespasser, and your suspicion that the rucksack carried by the individual might contain stolen articles. Having established your reasonable grounds for suspecting that you will find stolen or prohibited articles on the person, and after you have complied with the Codes of Practice (see 5.5.5) you go ahead and detain the suspect for the purposes of a s 1 PACE search.

Scenario 2: Searching a Vehicle in Relation to a Suspected Street Robbery

A street robbery takes place within your area in which a suspect jumps out of a car and allegedly steals a mobile phone from a pedestrian at knifepoint. Part of the registration number of the car is reported by a witness. Some minutes later you see a car fitting the description of the one used in the robbery in the driveway of a nearby house, and note that the registration matches the part-registration given by the witness. You locate the resident, who says that nobody in the house has any connection to the car, or has given permission for it to be there. These observations and information justify your 'reasonable grounds' for suspecting that you will find stolen or prohibited articles in the vehicle as a result of the robbery, and therefore you go ahead and search the vehicle. Throughout the search you remember to comply with the Codes of Practice (see 9.4.1).

TASK 1 There are a number of requirements that must be met when making a search under any of the 19 statutory powers. Some of these relate to providing certain information to the person being searched. Write down what a police officer would have to say before and during a search. Work out a system to help you remember the different points that must be covered (eg make a mind-map or your own mnemonic).

If you are a trainee police officer then completion of this task will help towards meeting the CK1 knowledge requirements in the SOLAP under the headings 'Legal and organizational requirements' and 'Searching individuals'.

9.4.3   Other stop and search powers

There are many other important and useful stop and search powers apart from under s 1 PACE. These include search powers under s 47 of the Firearms Act 1968 (for firearms, see 18.3.5), s 7 of the Sporting Events (Control of Alcohol etc) Act 1985 (for alcohol and fireworks at sporting events, see 14.7.1) and s 289(3) of the Proceeds of Crime Act 2002 (for cash obtained through unlawful conduct, see 16.5.2).

Here we will cover in more detail:

- s 23 of the Misuse of Drugs Act 1971 stop and search for controlled drugs;
- s 60 of the Criminal Justice and Public Order Act 1994 stop and search powers for offensive weapons and bladed or sharply pointed articles;
- s 54(1) of the Animal Welfare Act 2006 stop and search powers to prevent cruelty to non-wild animals; and
- ss 43 and 47A of the Terrorism Act 2000 stop and search powers to prevent acts of terrorism.

Other stop and search powers such as s 6 of the Public Stores Act 1875 and s 4 of the Crossbows Act 1987 are used less frequently. The full list is in Annex A to PACE Code of Practice A.

9.4.3.1   Stop and search for drugs

Section 23 of the Misuse of Drugs Act 1971 contains powers for searching persons and vehicles in relation to drugs offences, as shown in the flowchart. (The list of prohibited articles under s 1(7) of the PACE Act 1984 does not include drugs.) The offences relating to the unlawful possession, supply, and manufacture of controlled drugs are covered in Chapter 12.

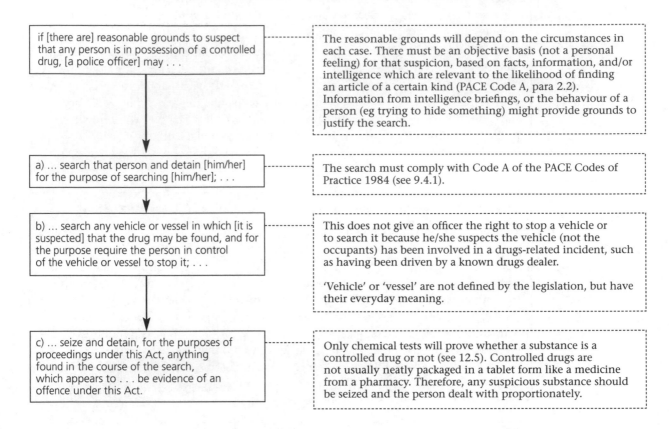

if [there are] reasonable grounds to suspect that any person is in possession of a controlled drug, [a police officer] may . . .

The reasonable grounds will depend on the circumstances in each case. There must be an objective basis (not a personal feeling) for that suspicion, based on facts, information, and/or intelligence which are relevant to the likelihood of finding an article of a certain kind (PACE Code A, para 2.2). Information from intelligence briefings, or the behaviour of a person (eg trying to hide something) might provide grounds to justify the search.

a) . . . search that person and detain [him/her] for the purpose of searching [him/her]; . . .

The search must comply with Code A of the PACE Codes of Practice 1984 (see 9.4.1).

b) . . . search any vehicle or vessel in which [it is suspected] that the drug may be found, and for the purpose require the person in control of the vehicle or vessel to stop it; . . .

This does not give an officer the right to stop a vehicle or to search it because he/she suspects the vehicle (not the occupants) has been involved in a drugs-related incident, such as having been driven by a known drugs dealer.

'Vehicle' or 'vessel' are not defined by the legislation, but have their everyday meaning.

c) . . . seize and detain, for the purposes of proceedings under this Act, anything found in the course of the search, which appears to . . . be evidence of an offence under this Act.

Only chemical tests will prove whether a substance is a controlled drug or not (see 12.5). Controlled drugs are not usually neatly packaged in a tablet form like a medicine from a pharmacy. Therefore, any suspicious substance should be seized and the person dealt with proportionately.

A person's demeanour or behaviour, specific intelligence about the person or vehicle, or the presence of objects associated with drugs could help form reasonable grounds for a search for possession (College of Policing (APP), 2016). However, merely suspecting a person to have used a controlled drug in the past, or to have been in the presence of drug users, is probably not enough to justify a reasonable suspicion. This could include situations where the officer notices the smell of cannabis, or a 'passive scanning' police dog senses the presence of illegal drugs. (Such situations might however provide good cause to investigate the person or vehicle further, for example, through a PNC or intelligence check, and this could lead to new findings that could justify a suspicion that drugs are present, thereby providing sufficient reasonable grounds.)

Where a premises might need to be searched, there must of course be reasonable grounds to suspect that controlled drugs or documents associated with illegal drug transactions are in the possession of a person on any premises. In such circumstances a warrant may be issued to search the premises. Any person on the premises may be searched as long as this is specified in the warrant (s 23(3)). Grounds to suspect possession of an item are not required prior to the individual being searched, but the decision should still be based on objective factors connected with the reason for searching the premises, not upon personal prejudice (Code A, para 2.29). Further information on searching premises is provided in 9.8.

It is an offence to intentionally obstruct an officer during the course of a s 23 search, whether or not any drugs are found (s 23(4), Misuse of Drugs Act 1971). However, in *R v Pasaihou Garjo* [2011] EWCA Crim 1169 it was reiterated that for an offence of obstruction to be prosecuted, the detention of the suspect must first of all be lawful and have satisfied the requirements under s 2(2) of the PACE Act 1984 (see also *R v Bristol* [2007] EWCA Crim 3214 in 9.4.1.2). This offence is triable either way and the penalty is a fine or imprisonment (summarily six months, and two years if on indictment).

9.4.3.2   Stop and search for psychoactive substances

Section 36 of the Psychoactive Substances Act 2016 (PSA) creates a power to stop and search a person, where a police officer has reasonable grounds to suspect that the person has committed, or is likely to commit an offence under the PSA. (There is no power to search for simple possession as it is not an offence to possess a psychoactive substance, apart from inside a custodial institution, see 12.5.1.2 for details on PSA offences.) Similar search powers in respect of vehicles, and vessels and aircraft are also available (ss 37 and 38), and if it is impracticable to search a vehicle where it was initially stopped, the vehicle can be taken elsewhere (s 37(3)).

Any item found in the course of a search under ss 36–38 PSA can be seized and retained (s 43) if the officer reasonably believes the item is evidence relating to a PSA offence, or that the item is a psychoactive substance. Consequently, even though simple possession of a psychoactive substance is not an offence, a small amount of a suspected psychoactive substance can still be seized after a ss 36–38 search. Items seized under s 43 can only be retained for as long as necessary for forensic examination, investigation, or as evidence in a trial (s 49). For small amounts of a psychoactive substance (that seem to be for personal use only), the item must be returned to the owner, and not retained and disposed of (s 50), as no offence has been committed. The offences relating to the production, supply, and manufacture of psychoactive substances are covered in Chapter 12.

9.4.3.3 Stop and search for incidents with serious violence

Section 60 of the Criminal Justice and Public Order Act 1994 applies in situations where it seems likely that a serious breakdown in public order has occurred or might occur. It empowers a senior police officer to authorize stop and search for offensive weapons or other dangerous instruments. Once this power has been granted, a police officer can carry out a stop and search without having prior reasonable grounds to suspect that the person or vehicle is carrying weapons or dangerous articles (s 60(5)). The public are often informed (using leaflets, Twitter and other means) that a s 60 authorization has been made for a specific geographical area.

The decision to authorize the use of s 60 powers is based on a senior officer's objective and reasonable belief that one or more of the permitted grounds apply ((aa), (a) or (b), see the flowchart), and that it is necessary to use the powers to achieve a legitimate aim (College of Policing (APP), 2016). The table explains the meaning of key terms used in the wording of the legislation shown in the flowchart.

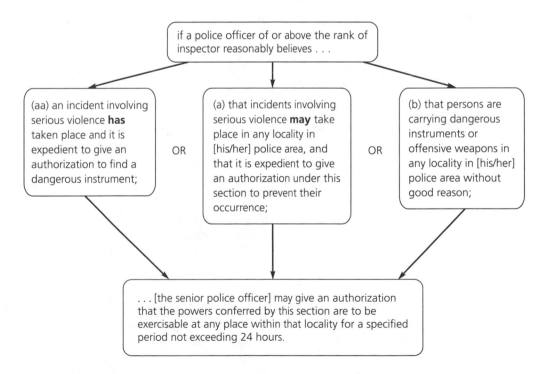

The Best Use of Stop and Search Scheme (BUSSS) sets a higher standard than Code A, for example the authorizing officer must be at least an assistant chief constable or commander. It also states that forces should communicate with the public in the search area, if practicable in advance and afterwards, to explain the reasons and outcomes of the authorization. A full description of the BUSSS can be found on the gov.uk website.

Term	Explanation
Dangerous instruments	Any bladed or sharply pointed article whatever its intended purpose (see 18.2.3)
Offensive weapon	This means the same as in s 1(9) of the PACE Act 1984 (see 9.4.2.3 or 18.2.1)
	For the purposes of s 60(1)(aa), an offensive weapon also includes 'any article used in the incident to cause or threaten injury to any person, or otherwise to cause intimidation', which could include a firearm as defined in s 57 of the Firearms Act 1968 (Code A, Note 23)
Carrying	Carrying a dangerous instrument or an offensive weapon means having it in his/her actual possession
Vehicle	Includes a caravan

Any pedestrian can be stopped for the purposes of being searched (including anything he/she is carrying), as can any vehicle, including its driver and any passengers. However, para 2.14A of the Codes of Practice provides guidelines; officers should select whom or what to search after objectively assessing the nature of the incident or the weapon involved and comparing this with those persons or vehicles he/she thinks are most likely to be associated with that incident or those weapons. When making the selection, officers must take care not to unlawfully discriminate (see 9.4.1). The power should not be used for any unconnected purpose, and it must only be used for the reasons for which the authorization was provided. The search must comply with s 2 of the PACE Act 1984 (see 9.4.1 onwards), and the person is entitled to a 'written statement' about the search within 12 months (para 2.14B). In *Roberts, R (on the application of) v The Commissioner of the Metropolitan Police* [2012] EWHC 1977 (Admin), it was agreed that although there was potential for racial discrimination in the exercise of a random search power such as s 60, it remains compatible with the Articles in the European Convention on Human Rights.

A driver or pedestrian who fails to stop when required commits a summary offence (s 60(8)) with a penalty of one month's imprisonment and/or a fine. A police officer can seize a dangerous instrument or an article which he/she reasonably suspects to be an offensive weapon (s 60(6)). The authorization also permits an officer in uniform to require a person to remove clothing or anything else if the officer reasonably believes that he/she is wearing it to try and conceal his/her identity. Such an item can also be seized (s 60AA(2)(b)). A person who fails to remove an item of clothing when required to do so by a constable (under this legislation) commits a summary offence (s 60AA(7)), with a penalty of six months' imprisonment and/or a fine.

TASK 2 A town has recently experienced several outbreaks of serious public disorder between two rival gangs. The disorder has mainly occurred in the local park. Subsequently, an order is in force under s 60 of the Criminal Justice and Public Order Act 1984.

An officer on patrol in the local park sees a young man wearing a full-face ski mask which is concealing the man's face. Under what circumstances can the officer ask the young man to remove the mask? Choose one of the following:

1. The officer reasonably believes that the person is carrying a dangerous instrument or an offensive weapon.
2. The officer reasonably believes that the person is attempting to conceal his/her identity.
3. No further circumstances are required as a s 60 order is in force.
4. The officer reasonably believes that the person is likely to be involved in violence.

9.4.3.4 Stop and search in relation to prevention of cruelty to animals

The Animal Welfare Act 2006 provides powers of stop and search to help prevent cruelty to non-wild animals. A vehicle may be stopped and detained under s 54(1) of the Animal Welfare Act 2006 to search it to prevent animal suffering (s 19(1)), or to seize an animal that is suspected of being involved in animal fighting (s 22(1)).

The officer must be in uniform to exercise this power. The vehicle may be detained for as long as is reasonably required (s 54(4)) for a search or inspection to be carried out (including the exercise of any related power under this Act). The search must take place where the vehicle was first detained or nearby

Two other Acts provide powers of stop, search, and seize in relation to animal protection:

- the Wildlife and Countryside Act 1981 (s 19(1)) to help prevent taking and killing of wild birds and other animals; and
- the Wild Mammals (Protection) Act 1996 (s 4), which relates to vehicles as well as to persons.

9.4.3.5 Stop and search in relation to terrorism

The Terrorism Act 2000 (TACT) provides two types of stop and search powers to help prevent acts of terrorism; one for which reasonable suspicion is required to search persons and vehicles (ss 43 and 43A respectively), and the other for which suspicion is not required (s 47A) for searching persons and/or vehicles in specified locations (requires prior authorization by a senior police officer). In the year ending 31 March 2015, the Metropolitan Police Service stopped and searched 411 persons under s 43 of TACT, but none under s 47A (Home Office, 2015c). The TACT Codes of Practice set out the basic principles for the use of powers by police officers under these sections. Before any search under TACT the officer conducting the search must provide the GO WISELY information, as for any other stop and search (see 9.4.1.2).

For a s 43 TACT search a police officer must reasonably suspect that a person is a terrorist (s 43(1)). The person can be searched to discover whether or not he/she has in possession (including carrying) anything which may constitute evidence that he/she is involved in terrorism. This power may be used at any time or in any place if the criteria of reasonable suspicion has been met; no authorization is required (para 3.2.1). As for searches under s 1 of PACE, the searching officer does not have to be of the same sex as the person being searched, nor be in uniform (paras 3.2.5 and 3.2.6). If a police officer stops a vehicle to search such a person (s 43(4A)), the vehicle and anything in or on it can be searched (s 43(4B)(a)) for anything which may constitute evidence that the person is a terrorist (para 3.2.2). However, any other person in the vehicle cannot be searched unless there are sufficient grounds for suspecting that he/she is also a terrorist. It is not sufficient that he/she is in the company of a person who is suspected of being a terrorist (para 3.2.3).

Under s 43A of TACT a vehicle can be stopped and searched if a police officer reasonably suspects that it is being used for the purposes of terrorism. An unattended vehicle can also be searched (para 3.3.1). When a vehicle is searched, it must be for evidence that it is being used for terrorist purposes (para 3.3.1). The driver, any passengers, and anything on or in the vehicle can also be searched, as can anything carried by the driver or passengers. Items that are reasonably suspected to be related to terrorism can be seized and retained (s 43(4) and s 43A(3)).

Under s 47 of TACT an **authorization** from a senior police officer permits any person or vehicle to be searched in a specified area or place (s 47A(1)), without the need for reasonable suspicion in relation to the person or the vehicle (s 47A(5)). However, the authorizing officer must reasonably suspect a terrorist act will be forthcoming and that the authorization is necessary to prevent such an act (ss 47A(1)(a) and 47A(1)(b)(i)). The area or place must be no larger than necessary, and the time period only as necessary to prevent such an act (s 47A(1)(b)(ii) and (iii)). When an authorization is in place, a police officer in uniform can stop any vehicle or pedestrian in the specified area or place in order to search:

- a pedestrian and anything he/she is carrying (s 47A(3));
- a vehicle and anything in or on the vehicle, its driver and any passengers, and anything carried by the driver or passenger(s) (s 47A(2)).

The search can only be for evidence that the vehicle is being used for terrorist purposes or that the person is a terrorist (s 47A(4)) (TACT Codes, para 4.9.2). Items that are reasonably suspected to be related to terrorism can be seized and retained (s 47A(6)).

9.5 Road Checks (s 4 of the PACE Act 1984)

A senior officer can authorize a road check to determine whether a vehicle is carrying people connected with an indictable offence (a witness or suspect), or people who are unlawfully at large (s 4 of the PACE Act 1984). There must be reasonable grounds for suspecting that the person is, or is about to be, in the locality. Road checks cannot be used for road traffic or vehicle excise offences.

The road check must be authorized by a senior officer in writing because the rights of all the individuals stopped must be considered—every vehicle will be stopped in a certain area. The authorization must specify the time, place, and reason for the check.

The authorizing officer must be a superintendent or above but if unavailable, an officer of a lower rank can authorize a road check (see s 4(5) of the PACE Act 1984). Any use of the power to impose a road check has to comply with PACE Code of Practice A. When actually stopping the vehicles s 163 of the Road Traffic Act 1988 must be followed (see 19.4.1).

> **TASK 3** Consider the health and safety implications of holding a road check. What are the considerations applicable to police officers and to the general public?

9.6 Search of Premises on Arrest

Section 32 of the PACE Act 1984 provides the police with powers to search premises in which a person was arrested for an indictable offence, or where he/she was immediately prior to the arrest (see 10.8.5). Section 18 of the PACE Act 1984 goes further and provides for searches of *any* premises associated with a suspect arrested for an indictable offence. There must be reasonable grounds for believing that there is evidence relating to that offence on the premises. The searches must be relevant, for example, there is no justification for searching for a petrol generator in a toilet cistern (s 18(3)) and (s 32(3)). Note that items related to legal privilege, for example letters from the suspect's legal representative cannot be seized (s 32(8) and (9) PACE). Details on procedures for searching premises are given in 9.8.2.1.

Any seized items can be referred to as exhibits in any subsequent statement the officer makes (see 10.12. on duty statements and 11.2.6 on exhibits). The use of photographic evidence should be considered to capture the property in the exact location it was found. If the evidence is stored electronically, for example on a computer, the computer can be seized (s 20 PACE Act 1984) in order that the evidence can be suitably reproduced (see 21.5. on seizing computers).

The information here provides some of the underpinning knowledge required to achieve the PAC checklist heading 'Search'. The relevant Diploma in Policing unit is 'Conduct Police Searches'. Competence must be demonstrated practically during three real searches (once for each type of search; vehicles, premises, land), ensuring that all assessment criteria are covered. The relevant Certificate in Knowledge of Policing unit is 'Knowledge of Conducting Police Searches'.

9.6.1 Section 32 PACE searches

When a person is arrested for an indictable offence, the premises he/she was in immediately prior to the arrest can be searched (s 32(2)(b) of the PACE Act 1984), as shown in the flowchart.

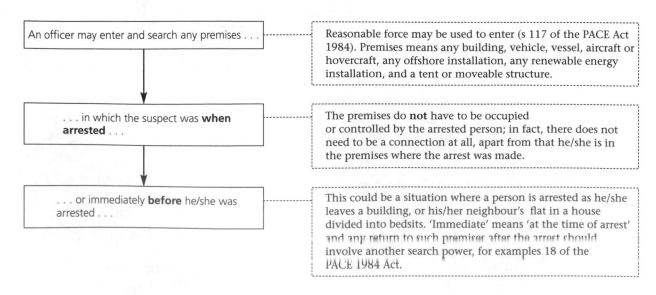

An officer may enter and search any premises . . .

Reasonable force may be used to enter (s 117 of the PACE Act 1984). Premises means any building, vehicle, vessel, aircraft or hovercraft, any offshore installation, any renewable energy installation, and a tent or moveable structure.

. . . in which the suspect was **when arrested** . . .

The premises do **not** have to be occupied or controlled by the arrested person; in fact, there does not need to be a connection at all, apart from that he/she is in the premises where the arrest was made.

. . . or immediately **before** he/she was arrested . . .

This could be a situation where a person is arrested as he/she leaves a building, or his/her neighbour's flat in a house divided into bedsits. 'Immediate' means 'at the time of arrest' and any return to such premises after the arrest should involve another search power, for examples 18 of the PACE 1984 Act.

When using these powers to search a block of flats or a bedsit the search must be limited to the dwelling where the arrest took place (or where the arrested person was immediately before), but any communal areas, for example stairs or a hallway, can also be searched. Any item found on the person or premises can be seized (s 19 PACE).

Note that if the arrest is unlawful (eg if it was not necessary (see 10.6.4)) then a subsequent s 32 search would also be unlawful (see *Lord Hanningfield of Chelmsford v Chief Constable of Essex Police* [2013] EWHC 243 (QB)).

9.6.2 Section 18 PACE searches

Any premises associated with a suspect arrested for an indictable offence (see 5.5.1) can be searched (s 18 PACE), but the search must be authorized. This power of search is useful because a person who has committed a suspected crime is unlikely to keep items related to the crime in his/her personal possession for long; the items are more likely to be in his/her home or workplace, for example. In addition, it is reasonable to suppose that a suspect has committed other undetected crimes, so the premises might contain evidence of previous and related criminal activity. There must be reasonable grounds to suspect that there is evidence on the premises that relates to either the offence in question, a similar offence, or to some other related indictable offence (s 18(1) of the PACE Act 1984). For example, a man who has been arrested for stealing a smartphone could have his car searched for other stolen items, but remember that the search must be relevant. Anything found during a s 18(1) search can be seized, and retained (s 18(2)) for long as necessary (s 22 of the PACE Act 1984).

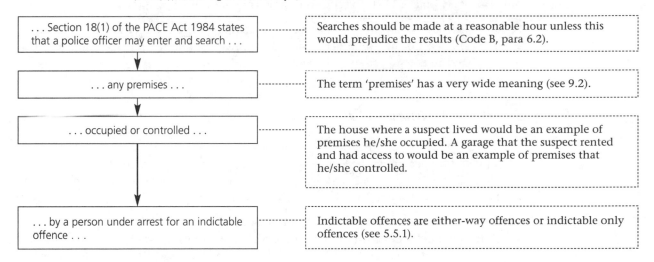

If appropriate, the search can take place before the arrested person is taken to the police station (s 18(5)). For example, imagine a suspect arrested for theft of lip-sticks at a store says she has some other stolen make-up at home, mixed up with her lawfully-obtained items. There would then be justification to search her home while she is present and before taking her to the police station, so she can identify the stolen items.

Authorization for s 18 PACE searches is given in writing by an officer of the rank of inspector or above, and is normally obtained in advance of the search (s 18(4)). The authorizing officer must be satisfied that the necessary grounds exist, and that the premises are occupied or controlled by the arrested person; mere suspicion of occupancy or control is not sufficient (Code B, para 4.3). If possible, the authority should be recorded on the Notice of Powers and Rights, and signed. Details of the grounds and the evidence sought should be recorded on the notice, the custody record, the search record, and in the officer's PNB. When the premises are searched before the arrested person is taken to the police station (under s 18(5)), prior authorization is not required, but an inspector (or a higher ranking officer) must be informed as soon as practicable afterwards (Code B, para 4.3).

9.7 Search Warrants for Evidence of Indictable Offences

Section 8 of the PACE Act 1984 sets out the grounds and procedure to be followed when applying for a warrant to search premises as part of an investigation into an indictable offence, and also provides a power to seize certain evidence. A s 8 warrant would be used for a suspect who has not been arrested; after arrest s 18 or 32 of the PACE Act 1984 could be used (see 9.6. and 10.8.5). Other statutes provide particular powers for the police to enter and search premises in certain circumstances, such as the Theft Act 1968 (stolen property) or the Misuse of Drugs Act 1971 (controlled drugs). In such cases the police will be able to obtain a search warrant under that enactment. Any search warrant application (as well as the subsequent search) must comply with ss 15 and 16 of the PACE Act 1984.

The warrant is issued by a Justice of the Peace. There must be reasonable grounds for believing that an indictable offence has been committed, and that the object of the search is likely to be of substantial value to the investigation (but it must not be subject to legal privilege, excluded material, or special procedure material).

In addition, at least **one** of the following conditions must apply:

- It is not practicable to communicate with a person who is entitled to grant entry to the premises or to the evidence.
- Entry to the premises will not be granted without a warrant.
- The purpose of a search may be frustrated or seriously prejudiced unless a constable arriving at the premises can secure immediate entry.

A 'specific premises warrant' applies for just one premises and an 'all premises warrant' applies to any premises occupied or controlled by the person specified in the application (and can include specified premises). For an all premises warrant the Justice of the Peace must be satisfied that it is really necessary, for example due to the particulars of the offence or because it is not reasonably practicable to specify every single premises which might need to be searched.

Premises may be entered and searched on more than one occasion under the same application, although the second and any other subsequent entries must be separately authorized by an officer of the rank of inspector or above.

9.8 Searching Premises, Vehicles, and Open Land

Here we cover the practicalities of conducting searches of vehicles, premises, and open spaces. In major and serious crimes the Senior Investigating Officer may require that a forensic examination is carried out first, followed by a search for intelligence materials. Then the building will be searched as described here.

It should be remembered that volume crime activities such as frauds (particularly card fraud) and drug sales can be used to fund terrorist activities. If premises and vehicles searches uncover evidence that leads to grounds for suspicion, the information should be passed to the appropriate authority.

9.8.1 Planning a search

Proper planning is essential for the success of a search, and for large or complex searches a Police Search Advisor (PolSA) should be consulted. ACPO (2006c) recommended using the IIMARCH mnemonic when planning a search, as a reminder to consider all of the following (see also 11.7.1):

- Information—why the search is needed, intelligence, local issues.
- Intention—the aim or reason for the search, the target material.
- Method—how the search and management of it will be conducted.
- Administration—maps, plans, transport, equipment.
- Risk assessment (see 6.12. to 6.12.4).
- Communications—such as which channel to use, mobile and landline numbers, code words.
- Human rights compliance.

A risk assessment of the venue will consider the physical risks, such as the safety of buildings and the contents, as well as the likelihood of resistance from occupants. Force intelligence systems and local knowledge could provide information on any contingency plans already in place for the premises, and any warnings regarding occupants. This will inform decisions regarding the number of officers and whether a PolSA and/or a specialist search team are required. For vehicle searches it is essential that roadside safety is considered: appropriate traffic control and safety systems must be in place. Searches should certainly not be carried out on blind bends or adjacent to fast-moving traffic.

The size of the search area and the relative size of the target objects are very important factors to consider when planning the size of the search team: searching for a small article in a large and cluttered house will be difficult. For outdoor searches, the terrain or surface vegetation is a further consideration—the search officers can obviously be more widely spaced when searching for a larger object on short grass. The officer in charge of a premises search may use a floor-plan or labels to identify the rooms to avoid confusion between, say, a large number of bedrooms. The search must be conducted systematically.

Personal safety equipment (helmets, gloves, knee protectors) and tools to access hides, dismantle equipment, or even dig in gardens may be required. Search dogs are an invaluable tool for specialist targets such drugs, cash, blood, and firearms (although dogs can damage fragile forensic evidence). A CSI may be useful for photographic recording and specialist packaging advice. In searches related to computer crime (or involving digital materials) a member of the Digital Forensics Unit may be required.

If it seems likely that more than a few items will be seized, it is good practice to appoint an exhibits officer. He/she will also be able to reduce problems associated with documentation and continuity, and will help ensure that force protocols regarding the handling, exhibiting, and storage of exhibits are closely followed. It is important that sufficient packaging material, transport, and storage facilities are available for the anticipated quantity of evidence. Officers should complete a PNB entry for finds in addition to completing any log entries.

> **TASK 4** Imagine you are a police officer, and you and a colleague are required to arrest a person on suspicion of theft. You follow the suspect to the vicinity of her house, but lose sight of her at the last moment. The house has a front and a rear entrance, so how are you going to carry out the arrest, and what are your considerations at this time?

9.8.2   Conducting the search

The correct authority, search records, and other paperwork must be in place prior to embarking on the search. The warrant or other authority should be served even if the occupier has agreed to the search. The officer in charge should manage the search closely and control the movements of personnel and effectively manage their deployment, depending on the complexity of each room or zone.

It is good practice for searchers to work in pairs inside buildings and vehicles and to maintain contact with each other. After the search each could check the other's work as a form of 'peer review'—this is useful because no one has ever 'seen it all before'. All the objects that have been moved and searched should be returned to their original positions (as found), and any damage should be meticulously recorded, and also authorized by the person in charge of the search.

9.8.2.1   Searching buildings

The search must be focused and detailed. It should start at a logical point, following the plan drawn up by the officer in charge of the search. Randomly poking about in a room is not a systematic procedure. Note that some work environments such as factories and commercial garages are exceptionally hazardous environments.

If there is anybody on the premises the officer in charge should identify him/herself and state the purpose and grounds of the search, and also identify and introduce any other officers involved (Code B, para 6.5). This does not apply if there are reasonable grounds for believing that alerting the occupier would frustrate the object of the search, or put officers in danger (Code B, para 6.4). No consent is required for unoccupied premises, or if no one who is entitled to grant access (an owner or tenant for example) is available. In a lodging house, a search should not be made solely on the basis of the landlord's consent; every reasonable effort should be made to obtain the consent of the tenant, lodger, or occupier (Code B, para 5.2). If practicable, the consent must be given in writing on the Notice of Powers and Rights before the search (Code B, para 5.1).

Section 117 of the PACE Act 1984 allows the use of reasonable force if, for example, the occupier is absent, or has refused entry or does not reply (see also Code B, para 6.6). A copy of the Notice of Powers and Rights should be given to the occupier, or left on the premises if they are empty (Code B, para 6.7). Specimen copies may be available during police training.

The precise choice of search pattern (spiral, zone, grid, or strip) is often a matter of personal choice but, above all, the search must encompass all possible parts of the building under scrutiny. In the case of a house the space is already divided into zones by the walls and floors, but larger structures can be more complex. It is essential that every effort is made to ensure all areas are searched effectively—there are likely to be voids behind drawers and under cupboards, and any access panels must be removed. Remember that many enterprising criminals attempt to hide evidence, for example beneath floorboards or in a water tank.

A police officer who is lawfully on any premises has a general power under s 19 of the PACE Act 1984 to seize anything he/she has reasonable grounds for believing that:

- it has been obtained in consequence of the commission of an offence;
- it is evidence that relates to an offence which he/she is investigating, or to any other offence; and
- it is necessary to seize it to prevent it being concealed, lost, damaged, altered or destroyed.

The seized items can be retained for as long as necessary (s 22 of the PACE Act 1984) but see also 10.9.1.

9.8.2.2 Searching vehicles

Vehicles can be regarded as having five main areas: the engine bay, the passenger cabin, the boot, the exterior, and the underside. These should be searched systematically in turn. Vehicles contain a significant number of possible voids for the concealment of contraband, and indeed commercial vehicles intended for illegal drugs importations may have specially constructed voids built into their structure. For example, in 2016, Nottinghamshire police, during investigation into an organized crime group involved in smuggling large amounts of cocaine and heroin into the UK, discovered a number of vehicles that had been rebuilt to include secret compartments.

In terms of safety, apart from the danger of working alongside traffic, the specific dangers associated with all vehicles are moving parts and electricity, so always remove the ignition key and apply the handbrake. In addition, some vehicle owners have been known to place needles in seats and razor blades beneath access panels to prevent theft, so proceed cautiously.

9.8.2.3 Searching open spaces

External searches, whether for evidence or a missing person, can become very complicated, especially if the area to be covered is large, or there are outbuildings, vehicles, and/or drains. The weather, local dangers (such as capped wells and barbed wire), and the large distances that may be involved also make it more difficult. The assembled team must be motivated and effectively directed. Maps and plans of the area are essential, but so is local knowledge—all intelligence and information sources should be examined for useful information (this is likely to have also been done at the planning stage). A further complication is that the offender, any accomplices, the public, and the media may have access to the search area, especially when cordoning is impractical.

On open and featureless ground, police tape is normally used to divide the area into strips, grids, or zones. If a line search is used, on any return 'sweep' the boundary of the previous sweep is always covered again. The whole line stops when something (a ditch or hedge, for instance), bars the way, and the object is normally searched immediately.

A search of remote areas and woodland, in particular, can reveal caches of weapons or explosives, or hides containing stolen materials. Effective searches can be expected to turn up a wide variety of material that is unrelated to the offence under investigation, but any item such as a timer, electrical equipment, or a mobile phone found in a surprising, suspicious, or unexpected place should be treated with caution. These are rare events, but see 11.6. for more details on the actions that should be taken, in particular at the scenes of suspicious devices.

9.8.3 After a search

When finishing a search, officers should take away all their equipment and leave any paperwork required for the owner or occupant. The appropriate records must be made including details such as the people present, the area searched, and the evidence found. The records would be in the officer's PNB for a small search and in separate documents for a larger search. A large amount of evidence would be recorded in an exhibits register, and this would be referred to as an exhibit in individual officers' PNB entries.

At the end of the search the officer in charge will almost certainly debrief the team (if used) and conduct a final 'walk through' to assess the completeness of the search, particularly if the target material has not been found or if damage has been caused. If the occupier is present, then he/she should be shown the condition of the property. Photographs of damage (and the absence of damage) are very useful in this respect. The property must be left secure if force was used to secure entry.

TASK 5 Imagine you are a police officer. You are called to your custody area where your inspector is waiting to give you a signed 's 18' authority to search the premises of a person in custody for burglary of a shop which sells mobile phones. The burglary took place yesterday and the person in custody was not in possession of any stolen property at the time of arrest.

- What are your considerations before leaving the custody area?
- What are you going to do on arrival at the premises to be searched?
- How will you conduct the search?
- What will you do before leaving the premises?

9.9 Answers to Tasks

TASK 1 You are likely to find that making a mind-map and working on your own mnemonic or other way of remembering will really help fix the key points in your mind. Of course, you have GO WISELY to use, too.

TASK 2 The power is not absolute and cannot be exercised unless the officer reasonably believes that he is wearing the item to conceal his identity, so response 3 is incorrect. There is no reason to believe he was carrying a dangerous instrument or an offensive weapon, or that he was likely to be involved in violence, so responses 1 and 4 are incorrect.

Therefore, the answer is 2. The officer must reasonably believe that the young man was attempting to conceal his identity.

TASK 3 Considerations at road checks:

1. Wear personal safety equipment, including high-visibility clothing.
2. Carry out the road check in an area which is well lit by street lamps.
3. Use signs to reduce the speed of vehicles entering the checking area.
4. Remain alert to the presence of vehicles at all times.
5. Reduce the risk to the general public by asking them to stay in or near their vehicles.
6. Bear in mind the possibility that a vehicle might fail to stop at the road check.
7. Only use the correct techniques (from training) to bring to a halt a vehicle which has failed to stop.
8. Give clear indications to drivers of what the driver should do.
9. Communicate with colleagues and remain with the main group involved in the check.
10. Select a location with clear views of oncoming traffic.
11. Select a location which is suitable to stop vehicles (particularly large vehicles), such as a lay-by.
12. Provide the opportunity for vehicles to return to the traffic flow safely.
13. Consider the classification of the road and the speed of oncoming traffic if it is part of the 'fast road network' such as a dual carriageway.
14. Make allowances for the safe stopping distances of moving traffic during periods of adverse weather conditions.
15. Avoid certain locations if practicable, such as road junctions, bends, the brow of a hill, and crossings.

TASK 4 You probably considered the following:

1. How can you secure all entrances so she cannot escape (eg through the back door)?
2. Should and can you obtain further support from your colleagues to achieve this?
3. With the back door secured, knock on the door or ring the bell to locate the suspect.
4. If there is no response, consider what reasonable grounds you have for believing that she is on the premises—for example, can you see her through the window, or have you had the entrances and exits under continuous observation since she entered the premises?
5. Is this now developing into a pre-planned event for which you should consider calling for further assistance?

General Procedures

TASK 5 You probably considered the following:

1. Is there a door key in the prisoner's property that you can take in case there is no one at the premises to allow you entry?

2. Is the 's 18' authorization signed and in your possession?

3. At the premises you must follow the PACE Act 1984 Codes of Practice for searching premises: identify yourself; state the purpose and grounds of the search; and identify and introduce anybody with you (Code B, para 6.5).

4. Limit your search to the extent that is reasonably required for the purpose of discovering evidence relating to burglary and mobile phones.

5. A copy of the 'Notice of Powers and Rights' should be given to the occupier or left on the premises if no one is present.

10 Initial Investigation, Arrest, Detention, and Disposal

10.1 Introduction

In this chapter, we look in detail at the law surrounding detention and arrest, and collecting evidence—both from a crime scene and from people; victims, witnesses, or perpetrators of a crime. Some form of initial investigation will be needed to help decide the appropriate course of action. It is of course vital that police officers know the law and how to apply it in relation to detaining a person, carrying out an arrest, and taking a suspect into custody. Further details on investigation, interviewing, and forensic procedures are covered in detail in Chapters 23 to 26.

The use of police powers to detain, arrest, and gather evidence must be shown to be justified and proportionate to events in question. The exercise of powers should be consistent with the Human Rights Act 1998 and the provisions of the Police and Criminal Evidence (PACE) Act 1984, and the associated Codes of Practice (see 5.6.1). A professional approach is of prime importance when processing the arrest and detention of a suspect. A fundamental liberty is being taken away from the detained person, and officers must be clear about the police powers to take such an action. Risk assessments must also be made when a person is detained, especially when there is a risk of self-harm. 'Death in custody' is a devastating occurrence to all concerned (for example the death of Darren Lyons in 2015 following his arrest by Staffordshire Police), and is treated very seriously by the IPCC investigators (IPCC, 2016b). In addition, any failure to follow proper procedure could lead to a criticism of police actions, and can help the defence counsel; a case could be lost as a result. A guilty person might walk free and possibly offend again, all because of a procedural or technical lapse.

Many people are not likely to be familiar with the criminal justice process. Over the years, police officers become very familiar with the layout of a police station, the location of the cells, the role of the custody officer, interview procedures, cautions, statements, and legal jargon. They become so used to it in fact that much of it becomes automatic—part of the nature of professionalism. However, witnesses, suspects, and victims might be anxious or confused, so they will need to have things explained, and their uneasiness or discomfort anticipated. Reassurance can be offered from day one in law enforcement. In addition, an individual is also much more likely to respond positively if he/she is treated with respect. A suspect may start to talk, a victim may feel able to describe what happened, a witness may explain what he/she saw, felt, smelt, touched, or tasted. All this could provide vital evidence in a case.

General Procedures

10.2 The Pocket Notebook

The pocket notebook (the PNB) is used to make a written record of the details of incidents and other pertinent information, particularly whilst on patrol. This would include a statement made by a suspect or a description given by a witness. A PNB entry is also necessary to meet some requirements under PACE (see 5.6). Typically a PNB is issued to trainees soon after joining a police force, and local force policy will be explained on how to complete a PNB, where it should be stored, its surrender, the issuing of new PNBs, and so on (in accordance with the Management of Police Information procedures: see 6.8.2). The rules of disclosure apply to PNB entries (see 24.3.3).

The main functions of the PNB are to:

- note the start and finish time of each period of duty;
- keep a record of significant information collected during an incident in order to comply with the Criminal Procedure and Investigations Act 1996 (see 24.3);
- make a contemporaneous account (as the events unfold) or if this is impossible, as soon as reasonably practicable afterwards;
- state clearly where another police officer (eg your assessor whilst on Supervised Patrol) has been consulted when writing an entry (see 10.2.3); and
- increase the extent and accuracy of recall in court (see 10.2.3 and 27.5.3).

The language used in PNB entries must be clear, factually based, and avoid the use of exclusionary terms. Where other official police documents exist (such as 'stop and search' forms) it is not normally necessary to complete a PNB entry as well (but see local policy). Police officers must keep their PNB in a safe place whilst on and off duty and inform their supervisor straight away if it is lost.

Some forces (eg Dyfed-Powys) now equip at least some officers with mobile data devices which can be used for some tasks instead of the handwritten PNB. The software is designed to provide secure access to databases such as the PNC and electoral roll. These devices have a facility to complete standard *pro forma* documents that can then be uploaded to a force network, but they are not often used (at the time of writing) to record other information, for example statements made by suspects. Other forces are moving towards replacing the traditional written PNB completely with an electronic alternative. The Metropolitan Police, for example, equips officers with an Apple iPad mini with ultrafast Vodafone 4G (Vodafone, 2015). In the longer term, it is suggested that the introduction of the Emergency Services Network (ESN) will bring a more standardized approach and avoid the need for officers to carry two hand-held devices. The programme has been described as 'one of the most technologically advanced systems worldwide', but also as 'inherently high risk' (National Audit Office, 2016). Consequently, for the time being, most trainee officers will probably follow the time-honoured tradition of carrying a police pocket notebook.

10.2.1 How to use the pocket notebook

The importance of the PNB and its proper use cannot be overemphasized. All police forces place obligations upon officers to record certain matters within it, and the courts can examine it if it is used by an officer while giving evidence (see 27.5.3). Therefore, certain rules apply, and if these are not followed then the accuracy or even the authenticity of the entries could be questioned. A number of Diploma in Policing assessed units refer to the need to keep accurate, legible, and complete records, and the PNB is in effect a set of records.

The following depicts some pages from a PNB outlining the general rules that police officers should apply for making PNB entries:

01

Write the day, date, and year at the beginning of entries for each day and underline them

DO NOT LEAVE SPACES

If spaces are left then ——— draw ——— a ——— line, to ———

indicate nothing further can be added. ———

Always make the pocket book entries in, black, ink. ———

Make all entries legible. ———

WRITE	Entries should be made in the pocket book as the event happens. If the ———
THE	circumstances make it impossible to do so at the time, then the entry should be
TIME	made as soon as practicable after the event, and the reason for the delay should
IN THIS	also be noted eg: 'Whilst using officer safety techniques, I was unable to make any
COLUMN	entries'. ———
USING	Each entry should include the time and name the location where the notes ———
THE	were made.———
24 HR	Entries must only be written in single lines of writing on the lines of the pages of
CLOCK	the book (except when drawings are made, in which case, draw across the page). —

Use every line and page of the pocket notebook and do not write anywhere else in the book such as inside the cover. ———

Do NOT overwrite errors. ———

Do NOT erase or obliterate errors. ———

Any mistake should be crossed out with a single line (~~so it can be read~~) and ———

initialled beside the deletion. Any correction should then be written straight after the initials.———

If two pages are turned over by mistake a diagonal line should be ———

drawn across the blank pages and 'omitted in error' written across the page. ———

Do NOT tear out or remove any of the pages or parts of the pages. Write all ———

SURNAMES in BLOCK CAPITALS. ———

Write down the names and addresses of victims, suspects, and witnesses. ———

Write down all identifying features such as serial numbers of property, including vehicles or documents, e.g. the registration numbers of vehicles. ———

What a person says should be 'written down in direct speech!' and the conversation recorded verbatim or word for word. ———

General Procedures

TASK 1 Why should we avoid the term 'Christian name' when referring to a witness?

10.2.2   Example of a PNB entry

The following shows how the rules are applied in a PNB entry.

		01
	Wednesday 16ᵗʰ January (0000)	

	Duty 0600–1600 ———— Patrol ZZ 10 ————
	Refreshment time 0900 and 1400——————
0545	Briefing at ZZ————
0550	Collected keys for ZZ 10 patrol vehicle index number ZZ 00 ZZZ ————
0600	Checked vehicle seats and feet areas for property—no trace of any property ————
0605	Commenced patrol ————
0610	At the time stated on the date above, I was alone on mobile patrol in uniform ————
	travelling in an easterly direction along Sheerbury Road, Ramstone, ————
	approximately 50 metres east of the junction with Applebreaux Road, when I saw —
	a Fordover motor vehicle, index number YY 00 ZZZ being driven in the same ————
	direction approximately 20 metres in front of me. There was a clear unobstructed —
	view of this vehicle. I caused the vehicle to stop in Sheerbury Road, 20 metres ————
	West of the junction with Applebreaux Road and spoke to the driver who was the —
	sole occupant of the car. The driver identified him/herself to me as First Middle —
	LASTNAME, born 00/00/00 address 101 Hernegate Road,Ramstone, Kentshire. ————
Q	'May I see your driving licence and insurance for this vehicle please?' ————
R	'Haven't got my insurance with me because I have only just bought the car ————
	yesterday, but here's my driving licence'. Driving licence details ————
	LASTN000022FM9ZZ ————
Q	'As you are unable to produce your insurance to me right now and as I need to ————
	ask you some more questions relating to your insurance, I would like to take the —
	opportunity to inform you of your rights at this point'. I cautioned Mr LASTNAME
	and told him was not under arrest. ————
Q	Where is your insurance certificate right now?' ————
R	'I guess it's on its way in the post, I rang them yesterday' ————
Q	'What is the name of your insurance company?' ————
R	'I'm not sure—can't remember.' ————
Q	'How much did you pay for the insurance?' ————
R	'Again, sorry, I can't remember.' ————
Q	'How long have you owned this vehicle?' ————
R	'One day, I bought it yesterday.' ————
	PNC check no trace LASTNAME. PNC vehicle check LASTNAME RO at address ————
	given. Voter's register check confirmed LASTNAME living at address I completed ————
	an HO/RT/1 form. ————

General Procedures

Q	'As you haven't been able to produce your insurance to me now, please produce your certificate of insurance and this form at a police station within 7 days. Have you got any questions, and do you understand what you have to do?' LASTNAME gave no reply.
Q	'I have been making a record of our conversation, would you please read these notes I have made, and if you agree they are a true record of what we have said, and then sign my notes to that effect?' This is a true record. FM Lastname
Q	'As you have been unable to produce your certificate of insurance to me here, I am going to report you for the offence of failing to produce or not having a certificate of insurance for this vehicle.' I cautioned LASTNAME and there was no reply. These notes were made at the time between 0610 and 0630. CL Underwood PC 118118:
0630	Resumed patrol.
0900	Refs ZZ
0945	Resumed patrol.
C	No insurance—unacceptable because of possible consequences for passengers in the vehicle, pedestrians and property owners if vehicle was involved in a collision.
I	PNC check showed vehicle had no insurance.
A	Vehicle was stopped safely , driver spoken to on the footpath beside car.
P	S 136 RTA 1988 to stop vehicle, no insurance covered by s143 RTA 1988.
O	Could have used verbal warning, but due to the serious offence and possible outcome, prosecution is in public interest.
A	20 minutes for questioning and reporting the driver was proportionate here.
R	Driver remained calm. Safe environment throughout.

The reasons for making a particular decision need to be clear. The National Decision Model (see 6.5.2) provides a suitable framework for making decisions, and the mnemonic CIAPOAR can be used to ensure that a PNB entry includes all the aspects that need to be taken into account. The College of Policing Authorised Professional Practice suggests that brief notes should be made against each letter of the mnemonic:

C	Code of Ethics—have all the principles been considered during the decision-making process?
I	Information—where did it come from and what did it consist of?
A	Assessment—was there a risk, how was it assessed, and what was the outcome?
P	Powers and policy—which ones were used and were they legally justified?
O	Options—which ones were available and why were they selected?
A	Action—was it proportionate, legal, accountable, and necessary?
R	Review—what went well, did not go so well, or could be done differently in the future?

More information is provided on the College of Policing's Authorised Professional Practice website at <http://www.app.college.police.uk/>.

General Procedures

Top Ten Hints for Using a PNB

1. It should be carried at all times on duty.
2. It should be used to record evidence (not opinion, except in cases of drunkenness).
3. It is a supervisor's responsibility to issue a new one when needed.
4. The general rules (see ELBOWS(S)) should always be applied.
5. Make use of the useful information it contains (such as an aide memoire for the caution).
6. It may be referred to while giving evidence.
7. It remains police property.
8. Diagrams should be included (where appropriate) as part of the written notes.
9. On duty, additional pieces of paper should not be used to supplement the PNB, or as an alternative.
10. Don't lose it!

The rules concerning PNB entries can be summarized by the mnemonic 'no ELBOWS(S)', commonly used in police training.

E	no Erasures
L	no Leaves torn out/Lines missed
B	no Blank spaces
O	no Overwriting
W	no Writing between lines
S	no Spare pages
(S)	but Statements should be recorded in 'direct speech'

10.2.3 PNB entries and conferring with others

The College of Policing APP is clear that as a general principle, a police officer should not confer with others prior to recording his/ her personal account of an incident (CoP, 2013d). However, if other police officers have been involved in the same incident, then there may be occasions when it is necessary for them to consult with each other so that the notes can be as full and comprehensive as possible, but a record to the effect that consultation has taken place (including names, dates, times, locations, and the reasons for consultation) must be made. Police officers who are involved in an incident are legally permitted to confer with each other about their involvement together, before they give their first account in a PNB or statement (*R (on the application of Saunders & Anor) v The Association of Chief Police Officers & Ors* [2008] EWHC (Admin) 2372).)

Firearms officers have come under particular scrutiny in recent years with regard to conferring. In 2005, Jean-Charles de Menezes was shot and killed by MPS firearms officers in 2005 in mistaken belief that he was a 'suicide bomber'. In the subsequent inquest the coroner criticized the practice of MPS firearms officers having 'conferred' when writing their notes some 36 hours after the fatal shooting. The same practice was criticized after Mark Saunders was shot dead by MPS firearms officers in 2008 (*R (on the application of Saunders & Anor) v The Association of Chief Police Officers & Ors* [2008] EWHC (Admin) 2372). MPS firearms officers were also challenged over conferring after they shot Mark Duggan in 2011 (*R (Delezuch) v Chief Constable and R (Duggan) v ACPO* [2014] EWCA Civ 1635). As a result, the College of Policing issued the following guidance for firearms officers: officers should not as general practice confer with others before writing their accounts, although there may of course be a need to converse in order to resolve an ongoing safety or operational matter. Most importantly, each officer's honestly held recollection of the incident should be recorded individually, as there should be no reason why an officer should need to confer about what was in his/her mind at the time force was used. However, if discussion must take place on other issues, then a record must be made of the time, the date and place of the conferring, the content of the discussion, who was involved and the reasons why it took place.

TASK 2 Formulate your own system for remembering the general rules concerning PNB entries—for example, a mind-map or mnemonic.

10.3 Cautions

From the moment a police officer suspects a person of committing an offence, the suspect has the right to certain information. This 'caution' or 'warning' is to protect the suspect's rights and keep him/her informed of the possible consequences of what he/she says (or doesn't say) during an investigation. Code C, para 10 of the PACE Codes of Practice outlines when a warning or caution must be used during the investigative process. Case law states that a caution is required 'when, on an objective test, there are grounds for suspicion, falling short of evidence which would support a *prima facie* case of guilt, not simply that an offence has been committed, but committed by the person who is being questioned'(*R v Nelson and Rose* [1998] 2 Cr App R 399). The type of caution described here should not be confused with the cautions used in out of court disposals (see 10.13.2).

There are three different cautions for use during investigations, and each is used at a different stage. The 'when questioned' caution is used at arrest and interview, the 'now' caution is used just before a person is charged with an offence, and the 'restricted' caution is used only for interviews after charge. In all cases the suspect is being warned about how his/her words can be used as evidence, and that whatever he/she says (or doesn't say) can be used in evidence.

There is no need to provide a caution:

- when asking for a person's identity or the identity of the owner of a vehicle;
- when asking for a driver's name and date of birth under the Road Traffic Act 1988 (see Code C, para 10.9, and 19.4.2);
- when asking a suspect to read and sign records of interviews and other comments (see Code C, para 11 and Note 11E, and 'unsolicited comments' in 10.4.1); or
- before conducting a search (see Chapter 9).

A police officer using a caution must have a thorough understanding of the 'when questioned', 'now', and 'restricted' variations of the caution, so that the meaning can be passed on to the suspect. Minor deviations in the wording of cautions are acceptable. However, if the Codes are clearly breached then any evidence obtained will probably be rendered inadmissible. Police officers must always record when a caution has been given (a PNB entry or on a record of the interview), including the type of caution used (see Code C, para 10.13).

10.3.1 The importance of the proper use of a caution

The correct version of the caution must be used or the evidence obtained might be rejected by the court. For example, in *Charles v Crown Prosecution Service* [2009] EWHC 3521 (Admin) the defendant was arrested for being drunk in charge of a motor vehicle (s 5(1)(b) of the Road Traffic Act 1988: see 19.9.3). At the police station the suspect provided a positive specimen of breath for a breath test and was informed that he would be charged with a s 5(1)(b) offence. He was later interviewed about the incident and given the wrong type of caution. During the interview, the suspect admitted to actually driving the vehicle and the charge was therefore changed to the more serious offence of driving a vehicle on a road above the prescribed limit, but the conviction was quashed due to the incorrect procedures.

Some people, particularly those who do not have English as their first language, may not understand the formal wording of a caution. There is an obligation under PACE to ensure that the detained person understands the caution (Code C, para 10.7 and Note 10D) but this may not be possible at the time of arrest: a full explanation of the caution might only be possible at interview, once an interpreter is present. When in doubt, an interpreter who is fluent in the suspect's own first language should attend the custody area (and may be needed during the interview process as well, see 25.4). The caution can be given in the Welsh language where appropriate. The wording of the Scottish caution is slightly different, but officers in England and Wales are unlikely to use it (because a suspect who has committed an offence in Scotland but who is arrested in England or Wales would either be escorted back to Scotland for interview, or a member of the Scottish police force would travel to interview the suspect).

10.3.2 The three parts to a caution

There are three parts to a caution (Code C, para 10.5), as shown in the diagram:

General Procedures

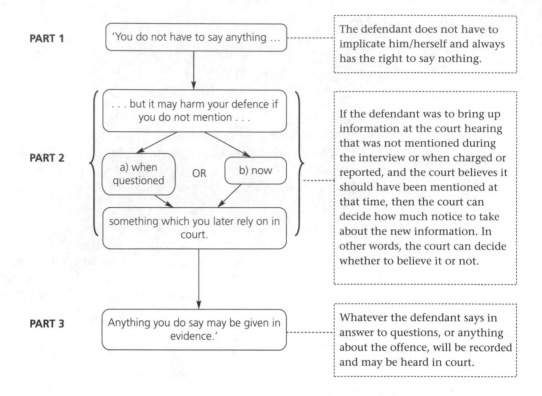

10.3.3   Use of the 'when questioned' caution

The 'when questioned' caution is given to a suspect at the time of arrest, unless:

- it is impossible to give the caution, for example if the person is very intoxicated (Code C, para 10.4 and Code G, para 3.4); or
- the caution has been given earlier (eg when a person who is suspected of committing an offence has attended a police station voluntarily to be interviewed (see 10.6 and Code C, para 3.21)).

The 'when questioned' caution is also used at the start of an interview, and when continuing with an interview after a break (see also Chapter 25 on interviewing).

At the same time as being cautioned, certain additional information must be provided depending on the circumstances and location of the interview. For example, a suspect who has been arrested must also be reminded of the entitlement to free legal advice, and a suspect who has not been arrested must be clearly told that he/she is not under arrest. Further details are provided in 25.5.5.

10.3.4   The use of the 'now' caution

The 'now' caution is the suspect's last chance to have anything recorded about the offence (see Code C, para 16.2). It is used at the end of an investigation, for instance when charging a detained person with an offence, or at the end of reporting a person for an offence (see 10.13.1.1).

Some suspects who are to be prosecuted may not need to be arrested (see 10.6). When inform-ing such a suspect of the impending prosecution there is no requirement under the Codes of Practice to use the 'now' caution, but it can still be used. If it is not used this may help the defendant's case if he/she provides 'new information' at the hearing; he/she could simply claim that there had been no earlier opportunity. This could be seen as a 'fair point' and the court might be more likely to believe the new information (see Code C, Note 10 G and see 25.5.9.2). Therefore it is advisable to always use the 'now' caution after informing a person that he/she may be prosecuted.

10.3.5   The use of the 'restricted' caution

If a suspect is interviewed after being charged (this is unusual, see Code C, para 16.5) then the 'restricted' caution is used. It is referred to as such because it is shorter than the other cautions. The following words could be used: 'You do not have to say anything unless you wish to do so, but anything you do say may be given in evidence.' The interviewer should also remind the detainee about his/her right to legal advice.

> **TASK 3** Imagine an officer arrests a young woman. First, decide which caution he should use. Secondly, imagine that he uses the standard words but it seems the woman does not understand what he means. Write down a simplified wording he could use to explain the caution to her.

10.4 Unsolicited Comments by Suspects

An arrested suspect must be taken to a police station before being interviewed about the relevant offences (Code C, para 11.1). Note that any questioning the person regarding his/her involvement in a criminal offence is regarded as 'an interview'. However, an arrested suspect may suddenly say something relevant to the offence, that could be used in evidence. Such utterances are referred to as 'unsolicited' or voluntary comments, and are of two types: relevant comments and significant statements.

A **relevant comment** includes anything which might be relevant to the offence (Code C, para 11.13 and Note 11E), for example 'That other person you've arrested, it was them that did it, you'll see, just ask them you've been talking to, they'll back me up, you'll see!'

A **significant statement** includes anything which could be used in evidence against the suspect (Code C, para 11.4A). The term derives from Part III of the Criminal Justice and Public Order Act 1994 and must have been made in the presence and hearing of a police officer (or other police staff member). It could be a direct admission of guilt, for example 'I wish I never done it now, but I lost it, the knife was on the table and I just kept stabbing, stabbing and stabbing!'.

All unsolicited comments made by suspects should be recorded in a PNB entry, noting when the comment was made and signed by the police officer. When practicable, the suspect should be asked to read it, and if he/she agrees that it is a true record, he/she should endorse the record with the words 'I agree that this is a correct record of what was said' and then sign (Code C, Note 11E). If the suspect does not agree with the record, the officer should add the details of any disagreement to the PNB recording, for the suspect to read and sign as an accurate account of the disagreement. Any refusal to sign should also be recorded (Code C, Note 11E).

10.5 Identification of Suspects by Witnesses

Some criminal offences are witnessed by members of the public who may feel able to recognize and identify the perpetrator(s). Obviously this could provide useful evidence. (Here, 'identify' does not mean that the witness can provide the suspect's name, just that the witness can point out who it was.) The Codes of Practice must be followed, in order to safeguard the rights of a possible suspect (see 10.5.1). If the witness is successful in pointing out a person, the circumstances under which the identification was made must be recorded (see 10.5.2).

Such an identification process by a witness is only permitted when there is not already enough information to justify the arrest of any particular person. In such circumstances the identity of the suspect is 'not known'(Code D, para 3.2). (The identity of a suspect who has been arrested is regarded as 'known' (Code D, para 3.4) even if the police are not certain of his/her name. When investigating a suspect who has been arrested, different identification procedures are used, such as VIPER video identification parades, see <http://www.viper.police.uk/>.)

10.5.1 The identification process

Before asking a witness to pick out a particular person a record should be made of the witness's 'first description' of the suspect (Code D, para 3.2a). Ideally, it should be recorded as a PNB entry. Then the witness should be asked to identify the suspect. Care must be taken to avoid directing the witness's attention to any individual (Code D, para 3.2b). The identification may be compromised if the witness's attention is drawn to any individual (see Note 3F). However, a witness can be asked to look carefully at the people around, or in a particular direction. This might be necessary to ensure that the witness does not overlook a possible suspect, or to encourage him/her to make comparisons between several people. If there is more than one witness, they must be taken separately to attempt an identification (Code D, para 3.2c);

additional officers are likely to be required. The police officer accompanying the witness must make a full PNB record of the action taken as soon as possible (Code D, para 3.2e).

The witness will have had two opportunities to see the suspect: first, around the time the offence was committed, and second, when taken to make an identification. The visual evidence from the first sighting may be disputed in court, but this is less likely if the 'Turnbull' guidelines have been followed (see 10.5.2).

10.5.2 ADVOKATE

The guidelines for identifications were set by case law in *R v Turnbull* (1976) 63 Cr App R 132. The mnemonic ADVOKATE is a useful way to remember the main points:

A	Amount of time the suspect was under observation
D	Distance between the witness and the suspect
V	Visibility (eg what was the lighting like, what were the weather conditions?)
O	Obstructions to his/her view of the suspect
K	Known or seen before (does he/she know the suspect and, if so, how?)
A	Any reason for remembering the suspect
T	Time lapse between the first and any subsequent identification to the police
E	Errors between the first recorded description and the suspect's actual appearance

In terms of the **Amount** of time the suspect was under observation, for how long was witness looking at the suspect, and from what positions (it is very unlikely that the suspect was in exactly the same position for the whole period) and from what distances? It should also be noted if were there any breaks (however brief) in the observation, and whether it was a frontal, rear, or profile view.

In terms of the **Distance** between the witness and the suspect, how far away was the witness from the suspect when the incident took place? The distance is likely to vary during the course of the observation and will rarely be one measurement, so the longest and the shortest distance, and the timings should all be recorded. In a street, the kerbstones can serve as a guide as they are usually one metre long.

In terms of the **Visibility**, consider the light levels; was it day or night, and if at night were the street lamps on? The weather conditions must be included in detail—it is not sufficient to say 'It was raining'; terms such as heavy rain or drizzle should be used. The effect of sunlight should be considered; where was the sun in relation to the suspect and the witness, and were any shadows cast? If possible, state the distance of available visibility. It is important to record whether the witness was wearing glasses or contact lenses, or if he/she needs corrective lenses.

In terms of **Obstructions** to his/her view of the suspect, any obstruction between the witness and the suspect should be described in detail. It is insufficient to say, for example, that the view was obstructed by a hedge—how tall, how wide, how dense was it? A glass obstruction should be described as clean/dirty, frosted/clear/double-glazed, and whether there was any glare or reflections from the sun or other sources. The extent of the obstruction as perceived by the witness must be ascertained. Record the distance between the witness and any obstructions.

In terms of whether the suspect is **Known** to the witness is he/she a friend, relation or a work colleague? If already known, how long has the witness known the suspect, and how well? When did he/she last see the suspect? Has his/her description changed in the interim period (eg a change of hair style)?

In terms of the existence of **Any** reason why the witness should remember the suspect, consider any distinguishing feature or peculiarity of the person, or the very nature of the incident itself that made the person memorable. (This can also relate to previous sightings.) What, if anything, first attracted the witness's attention? What has stuck in his/her mind?

In terms of **Time**, how much time elapsed between the witness seeing the suspect at the incident and obtaining a first description? And how much time elapsed between the first description and the subsequent identification?

In terms of **Errors** between the first recorded description of the suspect and his/her actual appearance, how similar is the first description to the actual appearance of the suspect? Any errors or differences between the first description, and the actual appearance of the suspect when he/she was identified must be noted to show integrity of the evidence (eg a suspect is identified while wearing a black sweatshirt without a hood when the original description recorded a hooded top).

One of the most important issues to consider when using this process of identification is whether it is actually required. If there is sufficient evidence to justify an arrest, the suspect should be arrested instead.

TASK 4 A police officer attends an incident involving criminal damage to a garden wall. The householder tells her that it all happened about 20 minutes ago and that he can definitely identify the person who did it, and knows where he is likely to be. What should the officer do, and what should she say?

10.6 Arrest Without Warrant

A police officer may need to arrest a person whom he/she suspects of committing a criminal offence. This would usually be 'arrest without warrant', a general power, derived from s 24 of the PACE Act 1984 and governed by Code G of the Codes of Practice. The police also have other powers of arrest without warrant, for when a person has breached bail conditions, for example (see 10.6.5). In the year ending 31 March 2015, 950,000 arrests were made by police in England and Wales, a fall of 7 per cent on the previous year (Home Office, 2015h). Warrants for arrest are covered in 10.7.

The right to liberty is an important principle under Article 5 of the European Convention on Human Rights (see 5.4) and the power to arrest and detain a person liberty clearly challenges that right (Code G, para 1.2). It is therefore obvious that this power should only be used for the right reason and at the right time. The information provided here will contribute towards the Certificate in Knowledge of Policing unit 'Knowledge of Using Police Powers to Deal with Suspects' and the knowledge evidence to meet assessment criteria requirements of the Diploma in Policing assessed unit 'Use Police Powers to deal with Suspects'. It is also relevant to the PAC heading 'Disposal' and in particular 'make lawful arrests', and also contains material likely to be relevant to Phase 3 of the IPLDP LPG 1 under the 'Police Policies and Procedures' heading, particularly LPG 1.4(1).

A suspect who has committed an offence does not have to be arrested. He/she could be reported for the offence, granted street bail, or issued with a fixed penalty notice; these are covered later in this chapter. A suspect can also attend a police station voluntarily to assist the police with the investigation of an offence, and may leave at any time unless he/she is subsequently arrested (Code C, para 3.21). Note that if the rights of an individual are not observed, the investigation will be discredited at best, and at worst discontinued. There could also be claims for damages for an unlawful arrest and false imprisonment (Code G, para 1.3).

Police officers must use their powers to arrest fairly, responsibly, with respect for the suspect, and without unlawful discrimination (Code G, para 1.1). Indeed, the Equality Act 2010 makes it unlawful for police officers to discriminate against, harass, or victimize, any person on the grounds of the 'protected characteristics' of age, disability, gender reassignment, race, religion or belief, sex and sexual orientation, marriage and civil partnership, pregnancy and maternity.

10.6.1 The two elements for a s 24 PACE arrest to be lawful

Under PACE Code G, para 2.1 two elements must both be satisfied for a s 24 arrest to be lawful:

1. the person has been involved, has attempted to be involved or is suspected of involvement in the commission of a criminal offence; and
2. there are reasonable grounds for believing that the person's arrest is 'necessary' (see *Shields v Merseyside Police* [2010] EWCA Civ 1281).

10.6.2   Reasonable grounds for suspicion

It is important to bear in mind that although words such as 'suspicion', 'grounds', and 'belief' are in common usage, they have particular meanings within the context of policing and the law. In a law enforcement context the following meanings apply:

- A **reasonable** conclusion is one that one or more people would agree on as a result of the same personal experience or understanding. It is a practical, level-headed, and logical result.

- **Grounds** for something include a reason or argument for a thought to exist.
- To **suspect** something is to think that it is probably true, although you are not certain.
- To **believe** something is a stronger and more concrete conclusion.

Therefore, in order to decide whether there are reasonable grounds to suspect, the component parts of that offence must be considered, and whether or not a like-minded person party to the same facts would draw the same conclusions about the suspect and the offence. The opportunity, motive, presence of mind, means, and incentive for committing the offence should all be considered. Alternatively, certain facts might be known about the suspect, so a person who fits the same profile in terms of employment, description, name, or clothes, or has previous convictions for similar offences and lives near the crime scene, could be identified; any of these could contribute to grounds for suspecting (see *Chief Constable of West Yorkshire v Armstrong* [2008] EWCA Civ 1582).

The suspicion required to make an arrest under s 24 PACE must contain reasonable and objective grounds based on known facts and information. If information that appears to be reliable is given to a police officer, then he/she can use that information as reasonable grounds for making an arrest (*R (Rawlinson & Hunter Trustees) v Central Criminal Court; R (Tchenguiz and R20 Limited) v Director of the Serious Fraud Office* [2012] EWHC 2254 (Admin) ('Tchenguiz')).

The suspicion must be related to both the likelihood that the offence has been committed, and that the suspect is the person who committed that offence (Code G, para 2.3A). Accordingly, a police officer must not only take account of facts which might indicate a person's involvement but also information that might dispel suspicion, such as claims of innocence (Code G, Note 2). For example, common and statute law provide defences to assault for school staff in relation to the use of 'reasonable force' (see 10.8.3 and 15.5) against their pupils (under s 93 of the Education and Inspections Act 2006), so these defences should be taken into account (Code G, Note 2A). PACE Code G, Note 2B emphasizes that an arresting officer must pursue all lines of enquiry in order to fulfil his/her obligations as an investigator under para 3.5 of the Criminal Procedure and Investigations Act 1996 Code of Practice (see 24.3).

Note, however, that an arrest can never be justified simply on the basis of obeying the orders of a supervisor or manager (*O'Hara (AP) v CC of the RUC* [1997] 1 Cr App R 447). The supervisor or manager must provide sufficient information so that the arresting officer can generate his/her own reasonable grounds for suspicion (see *Commissioner of Police of the Metropolis v Mohamed Raissi* [2008] EWCA Civ 1237) and *(1) Sonia Raissi (2) Mohamed Raissi v Commissioner of Police of the Metropolis* [2007] EWHC 2842 (QB)). If the information is too sensitive to be passed to a more junior officer, then the supervisor or manager would have to make the arrest.

10.6.3   Involvement in the commission of a criminal offence

The first element of a lawful arrest under s 24 of the PACE Act is a person's involvement, suspected involvement, or attempted involvement in the commission of a criminal offence (Code G, para 2.1). The guidance in para 2.3 provides more detail on the circumstances in which this might apply. The table provides summaries and illustrative scenarios set in an electrical goods shop, with a police officer who is on duty but not in uniform. (Remember, however, before arresting the person the officer must be certain that element 2 is also satisfied: that it is necessary to arrest the suspect. The officer must have clear reasons in mind for the necessity (see 10.6.4).)

Level of involvement	Example
A person is about to commit an offence (s 24(1)(a))	The officer sees a woman, who is obviously not a member of the shop staff, walk up to a display of batteries, select a multi-pack, and put it under her coat. She then walks towards the entry/exit of the shop, making no attempt to pay for it. The officer stops her as she is about to leave the shop.
A person is in the act of committing an offence (s 24(1)(b))	The officer sees a man walk up to a display of DAB radios, cut a security link, pick up a radio, and walk towards the door of the shop past the check-outs, without paying for the radio. The store alarm is activated and the man continues to walk out of the shop. The officer concludes that the man is stealing the radio and stops him just outside the shop.
There are reasonable grounds for suspecting a person to be about to commit an offence (s 24(1)(c))	The officer sees a man walk up to a display of mobile phones. He appears to be extremely nervous. The officer sees him take a metal cutter out of his pocket and reach out with the tool towards the security chain of the mobile and appears to be about to cut the chain. But then he is disturbed. He puts the tool back in his pocket and walks away. A few seconds later the same man returns to the display of mobiles, takes out the same tool, places the tool around the security chain, and sets off the alarm. At this moment the officer decides he has reasonable grounds for suspecting that the man is about to commit an offence.
There are reasonable grounds for suspecting a person to be committing an offence (s 24(1)(d))	The officer is just outside the shop and notices a woman standing just inside, near the doorway. She is holding an unpacked, brand-new set of hair straighteners under her arm with the lead hanging down. She has a large handbag and appears nervous. The officer sees her put the straighteners into her bag. She then walks towards the door as if to leave the shop. The officer notes the obvious facts: the straighteners should be in their packaging; the woman should not be so anxious to leave the shop quickly; and she should not have put the straighteners in her bag. This all forms reasonable grounds for the officer to suspect that the woman is in the process of committing an offence of theft.
There are reasonable grounds for suspecting an offence has been committed and that a particular person is guilty of the offence (s 24(2))	The officer is just outside the shop and notices a woman run out of the shop clutching an apparently unpackaged white and chrome-coloured object. The store alarm is activated. He runs after her but loses sight of her in the crowd. A short while later he spots a woman who looks the same as the suspected shoplifter; he believes it is her. He decides he has reasonable grounds for suspecting she had stolen something from the shop.

Section 24 of the PACE Act also caters for situations in which it will be clear that an offence has definitely been committed. For example, a camera shop owner who deals with *every* sale in his shop sees a woman walk up to a display of cameras, pick one up, and walk towards the door of the shop without paying for it. The store alarm is activated. The shop owner decides that she has stolen the camera and runs out and stops her, and then calls the police. In such circumstances, the officer (if it is also **necessary**) could arrest any person:

- **who is guilty of the offence** (s 24(3)(a)). For example, the shop owner describes the suspect's actions to the officer in the presence and hearing of the suspect and the suspect does not refute the allegations;
- **for whom there are reasonable grounds for suspecting to be guilty** (s 24(1)(b)). Imagine that the camera shop owner in the example had run after the suspect, but could not catch up with her. He calls the police and supplies a first description of the woman. The description is passed to an officer who the next day sees a woman fitting the description. He decides therefore that he has reasonable grounds for suspecting her of the theft.

10.6.4 Reasons that make an arrest 'necessary'

In 10.6.1 we explained that there are two elements for a lawful arrest under s 24 PACE: involvement in the commission of an offence, as discussed earlier; and that the arrest is 'necessary' (Code G, para 2.4). An arrest is deemed to be necessary if one or more of the following reasons (s 24(5)) apply:

1. to ascertain a person's name;
2. to ascertain a person's address;
3. to prevent injury, damage, indecency, or obstruction;
4. to protect a vulnerable person;
5. to ensure prompt investigation; or
6. to prevent a suspect disappearing.

General Procedures

There must be reasonable grounds for believing that the arrest is necessary (*Richardson v The Chief Constable of West Midlands Police* [2011] 2 Cr App R 1; [2011] EWHC 773 (QB)). The officer's belief must also be objectively reasonable (*Hayes v Chief Constable of Merseyside Police* [2012] 1 WLR 517), the implication being that any other officer in the same position would be likely to have the same belief. The necessity to arrest an individual using these reasons should be proportionately justified, carefully balanced, and accompanied by substantive grounds. Note that a suspect who has arranged to attend a police station voluntarily could be arrested on arrival if new information had come to light after the arrangement was made and it was not practicable to make the arrest any earlier (PACE Code G, note 2G).

These six reasons are set out in full in s 24(5) of the PACE Act 1984 and Code G, para 2.9, available online. The table lists the six reasons and the mnemonic ID COP PLAN.

I	Investigation	To allow the prompt and effective investigation of the offence or of the conduct of the person in question.
D	Disappearance	To prevent any prosecution for the offence from being hindered by the disappearance of the person in question.
C	Child	To protect a child or other vulnerable person from the relevant person.
O	Obstruction	To prevent the relevant person causing an unlawful obstruction of the highway.
P	Physical injury	To prevent the relevant person causing physical injury to him/herself or any other person.
P	Public decency	To prevent the relevant person committing an offence against public decency.
L	Loss or damage	To prevent the relevant person causing loss of, or damage to, property.
A	Address	To enable the address of the relevant person to be ascertained.
N	Name	To enable the name of the relevant person to be ascertained.

10.6.4.1 To ascertain a person's name or address

It should be made clear to the suspect that his/her name and address is required in relation to an offence, so the investigation can proceed. If the suspect refuses, the officer must always explain that it may lead to arrest. The officer should ask the person in an assertive manner, and it may be necessary to ask more than just once. (Remember, this is not a power to arrest any person who simply refuses to give his/her name or address.)

An officer may also arrest a suspect where there are reasonable grounds for doubting the name or address provided is correct (Code G, para 2.9(b)). There must be a logical reason for believing the information is not correct, for example:

- the person cannot provide any identifying documents (eg a driving licence with a photograph);
- there is no record of the name or address in the voters' register or telephone directory;
- the officer suspects the person is using the name or address of a close relative with the same details; or
- the officer suspects the name or address is fictitious because it is the name or address of a famous person or character.

Code D of the Codes of Practice provides guidance on the definition of a unsatisfactory address. It would include an address where the location does not exist. Other examples of unsatisfactory addresses include where the person's name does not appear at the address on the voters' register, or if the person is leaving the UK very soon never to return, or is of 'no fixed abode' and cannot supply a permanent address. However, an address can be regarded as satisfactory if someone else at the address (eg an employer or relative) will accept service of the written charge and requisition on the person's behalf. This procedure could be used for a person whose home address is not in the UK.

10.6.4.2 **To prevent injury, damage, indecency, or obstruction**

A reason for arresting someone could be to prevent the person:

- **causing physical injury to any other person (Code G, para 2.9 (c)(i))**: for example, if investigating an offence of throwing fireworks in a street or public place (s 80 of the Explosives Act 1875), the officer might conclude that the suspect may harm somebody else;
- **suffering physical injury (Code G, para 2.9 (c)(ii))**: for example, if investigating the offence of being a pedestrian on the carriageway of a motorway (s 17(4) of the Road Traffic Regulation Act 1984), the officer might conclude that the suspect may suffer physical injury from a passing vehicle veering off the main carriageway;
- **causing loss of or damage to property (Code G, para 2.9 (c)(iii))**: for example, if the offence of interference with a motor vehicle or trailer (s 9 of the Criminal Attempts Act 1981), the officer might conclude that the suspect's actions could cause damage to the vehicle;
- **committing an offence against public decency (Code G, para 2.9 (c)(iv))**: for example, if investigating for the offence of using profane or obscene language (Town Police Clauses Act 1847), an officer might conclude that the suspect was committing an offence against public decency; or
- **causing unlawful obstruction of the highway (Code G, para 2.9 (c)(v))**: for example, if investigating for an offence of wilful obstruction of the highway (s 137 of the Highways Act 1980) and the suspect was stopping or slowing vehicles on a road, the officer might conclude that the person needed to be removed.

10.6.4.3 **To protect a child or other vulnerable person**

It might be necessary to arrest a suspect if he/she is risking the health and safety of a vulnerable person or child (Code G, para 2.9 (d)). For example a parent is suspected of abusing their children at home and so the arrest is necessary to protect the children.

10.6.4.4 **To allow the prompt and effective investigation**

An investigation might be hindered or delayed if the suspect is not arrested. PACE Code of Practice G para 2.9 (e) sets out the circumstances for the reason for arrest being 'to allow prompt and effective investigation of the offence or conduct'. For example, it might be necessary to arrest a suspect who is unlikely to attend the police station voluntarily to be questioned (para 2.9 (e)(i), Note 2F). There might also be a need to take fingerprints, footwear impressions, samples, or photographs of the suspect (Code G Note 2H). All these actions would not be possible unless he/she had either consented or been arrested. Code G para 2.9 (e) suggests other circumstances where this reason would apply. These include where there are reasonable grounds to believe that the person:

- has made false statements (eg date of birth) or presented false evidence (eg a forged driving licence);
- may steal or destroy evidence (eg disposing of stolen property from a burglary);
- may alert co-suspects or conspirators (who could then arrange to go into hiding); or
- may intimidate or threaten witnesses.

10.6.4.5 **To prevent the disappearance of the person in question**

Arrest can be necessary if there are reasonable grounds for believing that the suspect will otherwise fail to attend court. This because after arrest, street bail can be used (see 10.13.3.1), and this can help deter the suspect from trying to evade prosecution. Arrest may also be the best solution if a person is homeless and cannot provide a suitable contact address for issuing a written charge and postal requisition. This is explained in more detail in PACE Code G, para 2.9(f).

10.6.5 **Arrest without warrant by other persons**

Any person may arrest another person if the offence concerned is an indictable offence and a constable is not present to carry out the arrest (s 24A(3)(b) of the PACE Act 1984). The arrest must also be necessary in order to prevent the suspect escaping before a constable can arrest him/her, or to prevent injury (to the suspect or to another person) or to prevent damage to property. The person carrying out the arrest must either have seen the suspect committing an indictable offence or have reasonable grounds for suspecting the suspect to be committing an indictable offence (for example the person has seen a man he does not recognize climbing into his neighbour's house through a window and suspects burglary is being committed). The arrest could also be carried out later (s 24A(2)). For example a store detective sees a woman commit a theft and is unable to apprehend her at the time, but sees her soon afterwards and arrests her then.

10.6.6 Arrest in other circumstances

A police officer also has powers to arrest in circumstances that are unrelated to a suspected offence (see PACE Code G, Note 1A). These include arresting a person who:

- fails to answer police bail to attend police station (s 46A PACE, see 10.13.3);
- has been bailed to attend court and who is suspected of breaching, or is believed likely to breach, any condition of bail (s 7(3) of the Bail Act 1976, see 10.13.3);
- is unlawfully at large, to return him/her to prison (s 49 of the Prison Act 1952);
- is a young person who has absconded from the place where they are required to reside, and to return him/her there (s 32(1A) of the Children & Young Persons Act 1969);
- might not have the right to remain in the UK, so examination is required (Schedule 2, Immigration Act 1971);
- is suffering from mental disorder, to remove him/her to place of safety for assessment (s 136 of the Mental Health Act 1983, see 13.2.2);
- has tested positive in a preliminary roadside test (s 6D of the Road Traffic Act 1988, see 19.9.4.4); or
- is causing or may cause a breach of the peace (a common law power, see 14.3).

> **TASK 5** Think of a practical example for each of the offences of unlawful possession of drugs (see 12.5.2), criminal damage (see 20.2), robbery (see 16.3), and a s 5 Public Order Act offence (see 14.4.3.1). Consider the circumstances under which you (as a member of the public and not a police officer) could arrest for these offences and what possible reasons you could have for believing the arrest to be necessary.

10.7 Warrants of Arrest

A warrant is a formal written document issued by a magistrate or judge that authorizes the arrest of a named individual or a group of people. It is normally addressed to the police and directs them to carry out an action on behalf of the court. A police officer can execute a warrant without having physical possession of the warrant at the time (s 125 of the Magistrates' Courts Act 1980). A warrant of arrest is often used in relation to a failure to:

- pay fines (s 76(1) or (2) of the Magistrates' Courts Act 1980);
- appear at court (s 55(2) of the Magistrates' Courts Act 1980);
- answer bail (s 7(1) of the Bail Act 1976).

A warrant may also be issued for the arrest of a witness required in a court if he/she has not attended despite having been summoned. For non-appearance at court the warrant will be issued under s 97 of the Magistrates' Courts Act 1980 (for a magistrates' court), and under s 4 of the Criminal Procedure (Attendance of Witnesses) Act 1965 for a Crown Court.

There is a power of entry under s 17(1)(a) PACE to search a premises to execute an arrest warrant issued 'in connection with or arising out of criminal proceedings' (subsection (i)). The wording 'is deliberately widely drawn' (Home Office Circular 88/1985, para 8), so for example a constable can enter and search premises to arrest a person for non-appearance in court or failing to pay fines in relation to a criminal offence.

> **TASK 6** Find out how a police officer should execute a warrant.

> **TASK 7** What is the 'European Arrest Warrant'? How does it work?

10.8 **Making an Arrest**

Here, we deal with the process of making an arrest and a police officer's responsibility to protect the suspect's rights. Making an arrest is an important milestone to achieve within the Police Action Checklist. The 'Disposal' heading of the PAC is particularly relevant here, especially the confirmation that an officer can make lawful arrests. The relevant Diploma in Policing assessed unit is 'Use police powers to deal with suspects'. The evidence for the achievement of these assessment criteria will come from successfully conducting arrests whilst under supervision on at least two different occasions. The information provided here is also relevant to the Certificate in Knowledge of Policing unit 'Knowledge of Using Police Powers to Deal with Suspects'.

10.8.1 **Preparing to make an arrest**

When an arrest is planned or imminent, a police officer must plan in advance where possible. The circumstances might be difficult, for example the precise location and circumstances of the suspect are unlikely to be known. (Note that unless it is unavoidable, a young person should not be arrested at his/her place of education, but if this is necessary the principal or his/her nominee must be informed of the arrest (Code G, Note 1B).)

10.8.1.1 **Risk assessment and arrest**

A police officer should make a risk assessment about a planned arrest, guided by the National Decision Model (see 6.5.2). Inevitably there are risks when force is used to enter and search in unplanned situations: it is impossible to predict who or what might be encountered. Consideration should be given to whether it is really necessary to immediately enter the premises. It might be better to stay outside, watch the front and back, and secure the area until colleagues with appropriate equipment and resources arrive (see 6.12 on health and safety).

The risk assessment could be made in advance on the way to an incident or it may need to be done at the incident itself. The risk assessment is ongoing and may need to be modified when approaching a suspect to make the arrest. An officer should consider how his/her demeanour, presence and attitude might influence the other person's reaction. If the suspect becomes agitated or aggressive, the officer could issue a verbal warning outlining the behaviour of the individual and the consequences of his/her actions. (There is no legal obligation to do this.)

10.8.1.2 **Power of Entry to Arrest**

There is a power of entry under s 17(1) PACE to enter and search premises in order to arrest a person on warrant (see 10.7), or a person suspected of committing an offence (arrest without warrant, see 10.6). It applies for any indictable offence and for certain summary offences, as listed in the table.

Summary offence with a power of entry in order to arrest	Legislation
Prohibition of uniforms in connection with political objectives	s 1 of the Public Order Act 1936
Causing fear or provocation of violence s 4 public order offences	s 4 of the Public Order Act (see 14.4.3.3)
Failing to stop when driving a vehicle or cycle when requested	s 163 of the Road Traffic Act 1988 (see 19.4.1)
Driving or being in charge of a vehicle when unfit through drink or drugs	s 4 of the Road Traffic Act 1988 (see 19.9.2)
Being under the influence of drink or drugs when operating railways and trams, etc	s 27 of the Transport and Works Act 1992
Using violence to secure entry	s 6 of the Criminal Law Act 1977 (see 15.7)
Trespassing on premises whilst an interim possession order is in place	s 76 of the Criminal Justice and Public Order Act 1994
Trespassing with a weapon of offence	s 8 of the Criminal Law Act 1977 (see 16.4.3)
'Squatting' on premises	s 7 of the Criminal Law Act 1977
Squatting in a residential building	s 144 of the Legal Aid, Sentencing and Punishment of Offenders Act 2012 (see 14.8.4)
Causing harm or distress to animals	ss 4, 5, 6(1) and (2), 7, 8(1) and (2) of the Animal Welfare Act 2006 (see 13.8.1)
Bringing animals into the UK (risk of rabies)	s 61 of the Animal Health Act 1981

General Procedures

Section 17(2) of the PACE Act 1984 explains the factors that must be taken into account before entering, for example whether there are reasonable grounds for believing that the person is on the premises—can he/she be heard, or seen through a window? This power of search is limited to the extent that is reasonably required to achieve the objective (s 17(4)). For example, if the entry and search was to find and arrest a certain person, there is no justification for opening and looking inside a tobacco tin. If a police officer has made an unlawful entry, any evidence of criminality (such as the seizure of controlled drugs) may be excluded by the court under s 78 of the PACE Act 1984 (see *R v Veneroso* [2002] Crim LR 306 (Crown Ct)). When searching a flat or bedsit, the communal areas such as hallways, stairs, and shared kitchens and bathrooms can also be searched. A neighbouring flat cannot be searched 'just in case', but of course any of the flats could be searched if there was reason to believe that the person was in that particular dwelling.

Other s 17(1) PACE powers of entry apply for arrests in other circumstances, unrelated to the investigation of an offence (see 10.6.5). This could include the arrest of:

- a person who has escaped (after being arrested, or from involuntary custody at a psychiatric unit) , but only under circumstances of hot pursuit, not after a period of days or weeks;
- a person who has escaped from a prison, remand centre, young offenders' institution, or secure training centre;
- a young person or child who has escaped after being detained having committed 'grave crimes'; or
- a child who is absent from local authority care.

10.8.2   Information to be given on arrest

Under s 28(1) of the PACE Act 1984 and Code G para 2.2, when a person is arrested the officer must tell the person at the time of the arrest:

- that he/she is under arrest (even if it seems obvious): and
- the reasons and the necessity for the arrest (see 10.6.1).

The actual words 'I arrest you' are recommended (although this is not essential). It is definitely not sufficient for the officer to simply place a hand on the suspect's shoulder; he/she must be clearly informed in words (s 28(2)), and provided with sufficient information to understand what has happened, and why (Code C Note 10B). An arrest is not lawful unless the suspect is fully informed of the arrest and reasons at the time or as soon as practicable (Code C, para 10.3), unless this is not possible because, for example, the suspect runs off. In addition, for an arrest to be lawful, the reason given must be correct.

To fulfil the requirements of both s 28 and Code G, para 2.2 an officer might say:

> I have just seen you run out of the shop with a joint of meat under your arm. I heard the store alarm sound at the same time and I therefore suspect that you have stolen the meat. I am arresting you on suspicion of theft of that meat as the arrest is necessary to allow the prompt and effective investigation of the offence by interviewing you at the police station and by searching premises occupied or controlled by you for evidence relating to similar offences.

10.8.3   Using force during an arrest

During an arrest the use of force may be required, but this must be 'reasonable' (for example see s 117 of the PACE Act 1984). The arresting officer must have an honest belief that the force used was reasonable and appropriate in the circumstances (similar to the requirements under s 3 of the Criminal Law Act 1967). The force would be 'reasonable' if the arresting officer met with force, and had to use equal force to negate it, and then use more force to take control (see also 15.5.1). Such procedures are covered in staff safety training.

Section 3 of the Criminal Law Act 1967 (see the flowchart) provides a defence for the use of force for law enforcement activities.

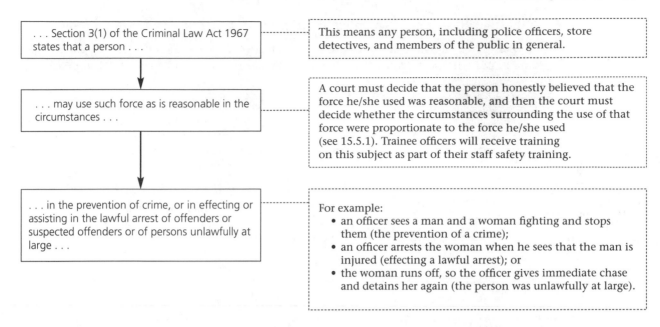

Note that if a police officer restrains a person, but does not at that time intend or seem to intend to arrest him/her, then the officer is committing an assault, even if an arrest would have been justified (see *Fraser Wood v DPP* [2008] EWHC 1056 (Admin)). In *Chief Constable of Merseyside Police v McCarthy* [2016] EWCA Civ 1257, the court decided that use of a Taser for the second time, lasting 10 to 11 seconds (guidelines indicate an initial five second burst is recommended), was not a use of unreasonable force, due to the officer's genuinely held belief that he and others close by were under the threat of immediate attack.

10.8.4 What to do after an arrest

First, the suspect must be cautioned (see 10.3). Second, unless it is impracticable to do so, the officer must record in his/her PNB:

- the nature and circumstances of the offence leading to the arrest;
- the reason or reasons why the arrest was necessary;
- that a 'when questioned' caution was given; and
- anything said by the person at the time of arrest.

If the arrest took place in a location other than in a police station, the suspect can be searched by a police officer (s 32 of the PACE Act 1984) if there are reasonable grounds for believing that he/she may present a danger to any person (s 32(1)), or is in possession of anything which could be used to escape from custody (s 32(2)(i)) or which could be evidence relating to an offence (s 32(2)(ii)). The search must only be to the extent required to find the particular item—for example, if the search is for a car battery, there is no reason for looking in a trouser pocket (s 32(3)). In public, a person cannot be required to remove any clothing other than an outer coat, jacket, or gloves, but his/her mouth may be searched (s 32(4)).

A person who has been arrested can be photographed on the street (s 64A(1A) of the PACE Act 1984). This can be without consent (either withheld, or it is not practicable to obtain it). Before the photo is taken the person can be required to remove anything worn on or over part of the head or face, and an officer can remove it if the person refuses (s 64A(2)). However, if a religious garment is to be removed the person should first be taken out of public view so the photograph can be taken in private.

10.8.5 Searching premises after an arrest

After a person has been arrested for an indictable offence, the premises he/she was in immediately prior to the arrest can be searched (s 32(2)(b) of the PACE Act 1984). In addition, any other premises associated with that person can also be searched under s18 of the PACE Act 1984, with authorization. Further details on these types of searches is given in 9.6, and the practical procedures for searching premises are covered in 9.8.2.1.

10.8.6 Taking the suspect to a police station

A person who has been arrested must be taken to a police station (s 30(1) of the PACE Act 1984 and Code C, para 11.1A) without delay. The only exception (s 30(10)) is if a delay could:

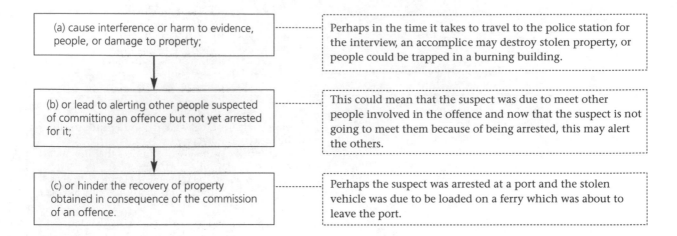

Before placing the detainee in the police vehicle it is advisable to:

- search the suspect (see 10.8.4) for possible weapons;
- use restraints such as handcuffs, whilst considering human rights (see 5.4) and the limitations of reasonable force (see 10.8.3);
- search the area in the vehicle where the suspect will sit to locate any unexpected items, and remove police equipment such as items of clothing, stationery and bags;
- check that rear-door 'child' locks are activated and that electric windows are deactivated;
- position another officer (rather than the suspect) behind the driver if the vehicle has no barrier between the front and rear seats;
- accompany the suspect in the rear of a van, or in its cage, and be able to communicate with the driver at all times; and
- search the vehicle on arrival at the police station (in the presence of the suspect).

Any discussion of the alleged offence on the way to the police station should be avoided. This is because any questioning of a person regarding his/her involvement or suspected involvement in a criminal offence is considered to be an interview, and interviews must be carried out under caution in a suitable place (Code C, para 11.1A). However, if a suspect freely provides information, then follow the guidelines in relation to significant statements and relevant comments (see 10.4 and 25.5.5) on how this is used during interviewing).

10.8.7 'De-arresting' a suspect

Any person arrested in a place other than at a police station must be released if there are no longer any grounds for keeping him/her under arrest (s 30(7) of the PACE Act 1984). For example a suspect might initially refuse to provide his/her name but then provides it on the way to the police station. A record must be made of such a release in the officer's PNB explaining the circumstances, and why the reasons for the arrest no longer exist.

10.8.8 The suspect has committed further offences

After the arrest and taking the suspect to the police station it might become apparent that he/she has committed further offences. The police officer has to decide whether to arrest the suspect again, for the further offences(s). The officer will need to reflect as follows: if the suspect had committed only the further offences and was not at a police station, would there be a need to arrest him? If the answer is 'yes' then he should be arrested for the further offences (s 31 of the PACE Act 1984). All the procedures that apply for any arrest must be carried out in full for this second arrest (such as stating why the arrest is necessary (see 10.6.4) and cautioning the suspect appropriately (see 10.3)).

TASK 8 Consider the following scenario:

An officer is on patrol just outside a tool shop. He sees a man run out of the shop carrying an unpacked, brand-new drill with the label still attached. The shop alarm is activated. During the earlier briefing at the police station the officer had been told that this shop had suffered a number of walk-in thefts over the last few days. He therefore decides to arrest him.

He says (on a bad day):

> Hey...you're not going anywhere, you've got to come with me, I'll tell you why later...for now just do as I say...have you got a problem with that? Got anything to say, well it doesn't matter. Come on, give me that drill.

Take a moment to write down what is wrong as far as the PACE Act 1984 and the Codes of Practice are concerned.

Next write down what he should have said to the person.

This task will help develop the knowledge and understanding requirement of the Certificate in Knowledge of Policing unit 'Knowledge of using police powers to deal with suspects' and the Diploma in Policing assessed unit competence 'Use police powers to deal with suspects'. It could also form the basis of an entry in the SOLAP and in particular the 'legal and organizational requirements' evidence sections.

10.9 Retaining Items in Relation to an Offence

Certain items found on a suspect or at a crime scene may be required as evidence during a subsequent investigation and prosecution. These items are often referred to as 'seized property'. (The use of the word 'property' in a policing context means any article, object, or item which comes into the possession of the police (whether ownership details are known or not), and includes 'found property' (eg lost items handed to the police, see 13.7.1.1).)

Property can be seized directly from the suspect after his/her arrest. The item(s) may either be directly linked to the crime (eg objects suspected to have been stolen), or be other items which need to be sent for forensic examination, such as a suspected illegal substance. Other items can also be seized which may have been abandoned at or near the scene of the crime but cannot immediately be linked to the suspect, such as a crowbar found in a front garden. Such items are likely to require forensic examination to establish if there is a link between the suspect and the offence.

10.9.1 Retention and storage of seized property

The main guidance regarding retention of seized property is found in s 22 of the PACE Act 1984, although detailed guidance will also be given during training with a police force. Note that s 22(4) states that 'nothing may be retained if a photograph or copy would be sufficient'.

The legislation describes two main reasons for retaining items:

(a) for the purposes of a criminal investigation, for use as evidence at a trial for an offence, or for forensic examination or for investigation in connection with an offence;

(b) in order to establish its lawful owner...where there are reasonable grounds for believing that it has been obtained in consequence of the commission of an offence.

Contamination must be minimized when seizing and retaining items, and a record of continuity must be kept (see 11.2 and 26.2). Seized items 'may be retained so long as is necessary in all the circumstances' (s 22), but common respect for the property rights of others (as described, for example, in the Human Rights Act 1998) would suggest that any item that is no longer relevant to an investigation should be returned to its owner as soon as possible. Each police force is likely to have a 'Property Management Policy' that sets out the protocols for return (see eg that of Merseyside Police, available online). For mobile phones, each phone has a unique serial number which will be listed on the National Mobile Property Register (NMPR), available online. This can be used to identify the registered owner and establish whether the phone has been stolen. Further details are available online.

General Procedures

> **TASK 9** If you are a trainee police officer you should familiarize yourself with the forms and procedures relating to seized property. Once seized, where are such items initially stored and, if required, where are they stored for longer periods of time?

10.10 Presentation of Suspects to Custody Officers

For most suspects, being arrested is a highly charged emotional event, and police officers must maintain a professional approach throughout. An arrest is the start of a long process, and all staff involved have a responsibility to preserve the suspect's rights throughout the detention.

The information provided here is relevant to the PAC custody office procedures checklist, (particularly 'provide grounds of arrest to custody officer' and 'search suspect and place in cell where appropriate') and the PAC 'disposal' checklist in relation to 'convey a suspect into custody'. The Diploma in Policing does not include a specific assessed unit addressing custody procedures, but the unit 'Use police powers to deal with suspects' requires the ability to 'Keep the custody officer informed of progress to enable them to make a decision on disposal'. Practical competence must be evidenced on at least two occasions in the work place.

10.10.1 Arrival at the police station with an arrested person

Once at the police station, the person should be taken before a custody officer as soon as practicable (Code C, para 2.1A). The police officer who brings in the suspect should note the arrival time (the 'relevant time' (s 41(2) of the PACE Act 1984)) in his/her PNB. This is to provide continuity of evidence between time of arrest and of arrival at the police station, and subsequent authorization and detention by the custody officer. A suspect cannot normally be detained for more than 24 hours from the relevant time without being charged or released.

10.10.2 The custody officer

The custody officer is usually a police officer of at least the rank of sergeant, but in some forces a police support employee is designated as a 'staff custody officer'. The custody officer's main duty is to ensure that any person in police detention is treated according to the PACE Act 1984 and the Codes of Practice, and that certain events are recorded on a custody record, usually through the NSPIS Custody and Case Preparation Programme. The entered information will automatically update the Police National Computer (see 6.9.1.1), and will also be available for the preparation of case files (see 27.4).

When an arrested suspect is taken to the custody suite, the custody officer must be informed of the relevant circumstances of the arrest; ie the suspect's involvement in the commission of a criminal offence, and the reason(s) why the arrest was necessary. This is obligatory under s 24 of the PACE Act 1984 and Code G, para 2.2. The arresting officer would say for example:

> At 11.00 hours today I was on duty outside an electrical shop in the High Street when I saw this person run out of the shop with a brand-new digital radio under his arm. I heard the store alarm sound at the same time and I therefore suspected that he had stolen the radio. I arrested him on suspicion of theft of the radio to allow the prompt and effective investigation of the offence by interviewing him here at the police station, and also to obtain authority from an inspector to search any premises occupied or controlled by him for evidence relating to similar offences of theft.

The officer should stay with the suspect during the initial stages of the custody process.

If there is insufficient evidence to charge a detainee and the investigating officer does not believe it is necessary to see him/her again, the custody officer will release the person without charge as the need for detention no longer applies (Code C, para 1.1). This process is called 'refused charge', and it will be the end of the matter unless fresh evidence is found.

10.10.3 Charging and detaining a suspect

The custody officer must decide if there is enough evidence to charge the arrested person at this point (s 37(2) of the PACE Act 1984). If there is not sufficient evidence the suspect can still be detained if the custody officer has reasonable grounds for believing that the detention is necessary to secure or preserve evidence relating to the offence (eg to carry out searches for evidence), or to obtain such evidence by questioning the suspect.

The precise time that the custody officer authorizes the detention is called the 'authorized time' (s 41(2) of the PACE Act 1984). (This is different from the 'relevant time' referred to in 10.10.1.) The need for continued detention will be reviewed not more than six hours from the 'authorized time', and further reviews will be conducted at nine-hourly intervals after that. The reviews are carried out by an inspector, and the timings are sometimes referred to as the 'custody clock'. Section 40A(2) of PACE permits review of a detention by telephone, but only when it is not reasonably practicable to use video-conferencing (s 45A).

10.10.4   The detainee's rights after arrest

If the custody officer decides to detain the person he/she must inform the detainee of the grounds, and record the grounds for detention in the detainee's presence (Code C, para 3.4). If he/she is incapable of understanding, is violent, or is in need of medical attention, the grounds must be given as soon as practicable (para 1.8). The custody officer must also make sure the detainee is clearly informed about certain rights that apply throughout the whole period of detention (PACE Act 1984, Code C, para 3.1). The rights are:

1. to have someone informed of his/her arrest;
2. to consult privately with a solicitor and receive free legal advice; and
3. to consult the PACE Act 1984 Codes of Practice.

The detainee must be given two written notices explaining the rights and other arrangements (Code C, para 3.2). Detainees who need an interpreter must be given appropriately translated notices (Code C, para 13.1). The first notice sets out the three rights noted above and also the arrangements for obtaining legal advice, the right to a copy of the custody record, and an explanation of the caution. The second notice sets out the detainee's entitlements while in custody, for example the provision of food and drink, access to toilets, and so on (see Code C, Notes 3A and 3B).

The custody officer (or other custody staff as directed) must ask the detainee whether he/she would like legal advice and for someone to be informed of his/her arrest. The detainee will be asked to sign the custody record to confirm his/her decisions (Code C, para 3.5). The custody officer must also note on the custody record whether the detainee requires:

*   medical attention, for example as a result of an injury or lack of medication;
*   an appropriate adult, for example the parent or guardian for a juvenile, or a relative or guardian for a mentally vulnerable person (see 25.5.1.1);
*   help with checking documentation, for example providing clarification of any of the rights; or
*   an interpreter, for example for detainees who cannot speak English, or who have speech or hearing impairments.

The custody officer will also assess whether the detainee will be a risk to him/herself or to others. This will include checking the PNC and consulting with the arresting officer and appropriate healthcare professionals, for example a custody nurse (Code C, para 3.6).

10.10.4.1   The detainee's right to have someone informed of the arrest

The detainee may have one friend, relative, or interested person informed of his/her whereabouts as soon as practicable (s 56 of the PACE Act 1984 and Code C, para 5.1). If the first attempt fails, the detainee can suggest two other people to be contacted. At the discretion of the custody officer or the officer in charge of the investigation, further attempts can be made to contact other people until the information has been conveyed to one person. For a young person in detention (under 18 years) the person responsible for his/her welfare must be informed. The detainee should be given writing materials if he/she requests, and be allowed to telephone one person (in addition to the person informed above) for a reasonable time.

10.10.4.2   Delaying the detainee's right to contact

The right to contact people and to legal advice can be delayed if the offence involved is indictable or it seems that the communication is likely to lead to:

- interference with or harm to evidence or other people;
- alerting other people who are suspected of committing an indictable offence, but not yet arrested; or
- hindrance to the recovery of property.

Delaying a detainee's right to legal advice (s 58 of the PACE Act 1984 and Code C, Annex B) is very rare, and must be authorized by an officer of the rank of superintendent or above. Any decision to delay trying to inform someone of the suspects whereabouts (under s 56, see 10 10.4.1) must be authorized by an officer of at least the rank of inspector, and the delay must not be longer than 36 hours (s 56 of the PACE Act 1984 and Code C, Annex B).

10.10.4.3   Receiving visits

At the custody officer's discretion the detainee can receive visits from friends, family or others who are likely to take an interest in his/her welfare, or from a person in whose welfare the detainee has an interest (Code C, para 5.4). Such visits are subject to the availability of supervising staff, and any possible hindrance to the investigation will also need to be considered (Code C, Note 5B).

10.10.5   Searching the detainee

The custody officer has the power to search the detainee, or can ask another officer to carry out a search. The searching officer must be of the same sex as the detainee (s 54(9) of the PACE Act 1984). The custody officer will decide the extent of the search, but it must not be intimate (ss 54(6) and (7), and see also 26.6.1). The forensic examination of suspects is covered in 26.6.

A strip search can be authorized, but only if it is reasonably considered that the detainee has concealed an article which he/she would not be allowed to keep and a strip search is necessary to find the article (Code C, Annex A, para 10). A strip search involves removal of clothing, and must be in accordance with Code C Annex A para 11. For example it must be carried out by an officer of the same sex with at least two other people present, but away from other people in general, and in a safe place. The search should be conducted with regard to sensitivity, and as quickly as reasonably possible. The detainee can be required to lift his/her arms and stand with his/her legs apart. In relation to establishing the gender of persons for the purposes of searching, see Code A, Annex F. An intimate search examining the whole of a person's body (including orifices) must be authorized by an officer of at least the rank of inspector, and he/she must have reasonable grounds for believing that the detainee may have concealed on his/her person:

- anything which could be used to cause physical injury to him/herself or others; or
- a class A drug (see 12.5.1.1), and possessed it with the appropriate criminal intent before being arrested (s 55(1)).

A record of all or any of the items found during a search must be made. This could be on the custody record, or elsewhere (in which case the location must be noted on the custody record (Code C, para 4.4)). Clothes and effects can only be seized if there are reasonable grounds for believing they may provide evidence relating to an offence, or if the custody officer believes the detainee would use the items to harm him/herself, to damage property, to interfere with evidence, or to try to escape (s 54 (3) and (4)). It was held that taking away clothing under s 54 to avoid its use as a ligature is not a breach of Article 8 of the ECHR (see 5.4), as long as the requirements of the Codes of Practice are followed (*Davies (by her mother and litigation friend) v Chief Constable of Merseyside Police* [2015] EWCA Civ 114).

The custody officer is responsible for any of the detainee's possessions that are unrelated to the offence and are not going to be used as evidence (Code C, para 4.1), and must arrange their safekeeping.

General Procedures

> **TASK 10** In Task 8 of this chapter a police officer saw a man run out of the shop carrying an unpacked, brand-new drill and heard the shop alarm go off. The officer knew from recent briefings that this shop had suffered a number of walk-in thefts over the last few days. He had therefore arrested the man and taken him to the police station. What should the police officer say to the custody officer?
>
> Completion of this task would help towards achieving the knowledge requirements of the SOLAP.

10.11 Statements from Witnesses and Victims

An important part of any investigation is supporting witnesses (who may also be victims) through the process of making a witness statement. This is recorded on an MG 11 form, which will be included in the case file (see 27.4.2). Victim personal statements (see 10.11.2) are also recorded on an MG11 form, either following on from the first part of a witness statement or on a separate form.

The MG 11 form is available as a paper or an electronic version. The paper version has a front sheet and continuation sheets if required. The back of the form (once completed) is for police and prosecution use only, in order to protect witnesses. Abbreviations and jargon should not be used. On handwritten copies black ink should be used, and any written mistakes should be crossed out with a single line and initialled in the margin (no overwriting or correction fluid). Use a paperclip rather than a staple if there is more than one page.

Some of the following guidance is adapted from the unpublished document 'A Guide to Form MG11, General Completion' by Kent Police.

10.11.1 Witness statements

Witness statements are generally compiled by the interviewing officer after he/she has interviewed the witness (see 25.6), and they have together agreed the facts that are to be recorded. The officer should outline to the witness the consequences of stating anything which is false or that he/she does not believe to be true, and draw his/her attention to the need to sign a declaration to that effect at the end of the process.

The witness's name should be written out in full at the top of the form, using capitals for the family name only. (If capitals are used throughout, then underline the family name.) Where a witness statement refers to a person, the name the witness gives that person should be used. For all descriptions of a person, object, or incident, ADVOKATE must be adhered to in full (see 10.5.2). Descriptions should be recorded in detail, and any uncertainties fully recorded.

Witness statements must record only what the witness has experienced directly through his/her senses. Opinion should not be included, apart from a relevant expert providing an expert opinion, or a competent witness stating whether another person was drunk (see 12.2.1).

Exhibits (items that could be used as evidence in court) must be given a reference number that includes the initials of the person from whom the police officer takes the exhibit. So, for example, the bag of shopping Alice Stoner gave to PC Hoddim will have the reference number AMS/1. The other bag (the orange bag held by the man on the pavement) will have the reference number CU/1 because it was the first item of evidence collected by PC Underwood in this incident (see 11.2.6 for more on numbering of exhibits).

General Procedures

General Procedures

MG 11 (T)

RESTRICTED (when complete)

WITNESS STATEMENT

(CJ Act 1967, s.9; MC Act 1980, ss.5A(3) (a) and SB; MC Rules 1981, r.70)

URN ☐☐☐☐

Statement of: *Alice Marion STONER*

Age if under 18: *over 18* (if over 18 insert 'over 18')   Occupation: *Customer service assistant*

The unique reference number will be generated by the unit or department that deals with case file.

This statement (consisting of *one* page(s) each signed by me) is true to the best of my knowledge and belief and I make it knowing that, if it is tendered in evidence, I shall be liable to prosecution if I have wilfully stated anything in it, which I know to be false, or do not believe to be true.

Complete the number of pages **after** the statement is finished.

Signature: *AMStoner*   Date: *01.03.00*

Tick if witness evidence is visually recorded ☐ *(supply witness details on rear)*

Always begin with the time, day, date, and location. Use the words used by the witnesses (for example 4 p.m. rather than the 24 hour clock).

At 4.00 p.m. on Wednesday 1st March 0000, I was in Kerrie's corner shop which is situated on the north pavement of the High Street at its junction with Hythewell Road, Maidbury. I was standing by the fruit which is located inside the shop approximately 10 metres from the front door but my view of the front door was obscured by upright shelving. The shop sells groceries and is approximately 15 metres by 15 metres with one door for customers in and out. There is shelving fixed to the walls and three lines of upright shelving along the entire length of the shop which is approximately 2 metres high. I could not see any other customers inside the shop at the time, but I could see the shop assistant but only when she leant over to the shelf. She was unpacking ~~some bacon out of a box~~. I would describe the assistant as … [ADVOKATE]. I will refer to her as Assistant one.

All descriptions must follow ADVOKATE

Any uncertainties must be included.

For starting a new paragraph, do not leave any whole blank lines. There is no need to rule off the space at the end of a line.

I then heard some sort of a struggle approximately 10 metres away from me towards the back of the shop. I didn't see anything because there was shelving in between me and the scuffle. I heard a man's voice say in a cross way 'what's it to you if some of us ain't got nothing to eat' or something like that and then I heard a long bang like a box falling over or a door slamming. Then I heard a thump and a shout outside. I picked up my bag and went over to the door and Assistant one was standing there rubbing her head like it was hurting. I could see a man in a dark blue or black jacket half lying on the ground outside, holding onto something orange, but I didn't have my glasses on so I couldn't see what it was quite. I would describe the man as… [ADVOKATE]. He was rubbing his leg like it was hurting him a lot.

Utterances must be recorded in direct speech. Hearsay evidence (she said that he said) should be recorded in direct speech.

The officer who wrote the statement on behalf of the witness must write this declaration at the end of the statement.

From the back of the shop, another assistant and a customer came walking towards me. I would describe the assistant as … [ADVOKATE] and will refer to her as Assistant two. Assistant two had a telephone in her hand. I would describe the customer as … [ADVOKATE]. This customer and Assistant two went out of the front door and held on to the man, but he didn't look like he was struggling much. At 4.10 p.m. the same day two police officers arrived at the shop, one male and one femle. One of them (PC Hoddim) came into the shop and spoke with Assistant one. I found a bag with some shopping in it by the cold cabinet, which I gave to PC Hoddim (exhibit labelled and marked AMS/1). Then I went out and spoke to the lady officer. AMStoner

The witness should sign at the foot of every page, and after the last word of the statement.

This statement was taken by me at 13.26 hours on Saturday 28th March 0000 at Maidbury Police Station. At the end I read it over to Alice Stoner and she read and signed it in my presence. C.Underwood PC 118118, 01.03.00

The officer must sign and date (including his/her rank and number) immediately after the last word of the declaration and at the end of each page.

Signature: *AMStoner*   Signature witnessed by: *C Underwood PC 118118*

PTO

MG 11 (T)

RESTRICTED—FOR POLICE AND PROSECUTION ONLY
(when complete)

Witness contact details

Home address: *31 JENNER ROAD, MAIDBURY, KENT*

.... Postcode: *MA99 1XX*

Use capital letters for all this part.

Home telephone No: *1234567* .... Work telephone No: *123456789* ....

Mobile/Pager No: *1234567* .... E-mail address: *N/A* ....

Preferred means of contact: *HOME PHONE*

Male/~~Female~~ (delete as applicable) Date and place of birth: *12.00.65 BIG CITY*

For example, if previously married.

Former Name: *N/A* .... Height: *163cm* Ethnicity Code: *W1*

Dates of witness non-availability: *see MG 10*

If no MG 10 form is available, then record the relevant information here.

....

Witness care

(a) Is the witness willing and likely to attend court? ~~Yes~~/No. If 'No', include reason(s) on form MG6. What can be done to ensure attendance?

....

(b) Does the witness require 'special measures' as a vulnerable or intimidated witness? ~~Yes~~/No. If 'Yes' submit MG2 with file.

(c) Does the witness have any specific care needs? ~~Yes~~/No. If 'Yes' what are they? (Healthcare, childcare, transport, disability, language difficulties, visually impaired, restricted mobility or other concerns?)

....

....

....

Witness Consent (for witness completion)

a) The criminal justice process and Victim Personal Statement scheme (victims only) has been explained to me: Yes/~~No~~

b) I have been given the leaflet 'Giving a witness statement to the police—what happens next?'   Yes/~~No~~

c) I consent to police having access to my medical record(s) in relation to this matter: Yes☐ No☐ N/A☑

d) I consent to my medical record in relation to this matter being disclosed to the defence: Yes☐ No☐ N/A☑

e) I consent to the statement being disclosed for the purposes of civil proceedings e.g. child care proceedings (if applicable):   Yes☐ No☐ N/A☑

f) The information recorded above will be disclosed to the Witness Service so that they can offer help and support, unless you ask them not to. Tick this box to decline their services: ☑

Remember to get the witness to sign here.

Signature of witness: *AMStoner*

Statement taken by (print name): *PC 118118 UNDERWOOD* Station: *Maidbury Police Station*

The time and date the statement was made should be recorded in your PNB.

Time and place statement taken: *17.50 01.03.00 MAIDBURY POLICE STATION*

General Procedures

10.11.2 Victim personal statements

The victim will provide a statement as a witness, but can also make a further statement as a victim. A victim personal statement (VPS) provides extra information on how the crime has affected the victim and what support he/she may need. A VPS can also be made by the relatives or partners of homicide victims, or the parents (or carers) of children or of adults with learning difficulties. It will form part of the case file and is used during the court process, particularly in sentencing and applications for bail.

A VPS is normally made immediately after a witness statement on the same MG11 form. This is known as a Stage 1 VPS. A caption should be inserted between the evidential part of the statement and the VPS, to emphasize this separation, for example:

> I have been given the Victim Personal Statement leaflet and the VPS scheme has been explained to me. What follows is what I wish to say in connection with this matter. I understand that what I say may be used in various ways and that it may be disclosed to the defence.

A separate or an additional VPS can be made at a later stage. This is called a Stage 2 VPS, and the same caption should be used to emphasize that it is a VPS and not an evidential witness statement. If a previous VPS has been made, the caption should include the phrase 'This statement adds to what I said in my previous victim personal statement'.

The officer should explain that the victim can express anything he/she chooses, including:

- whether he/she wants to be told about the progress of the case;
- whether he/she would like extra support (particularly if appearing as a witness at a trial);
- whether he/she feels vulnerable or intimidated;
- whether he/she is worried about the suspect being given bail (eg if the suspect and victim know each other);
- if racial hostility is felt to be part of the crime, or if he/she feels victimized because of his/her faith, cultural background, or disability;
- whether he/she is considering trying to claim compensation from the offender for any injury, loss, or damage suffered; and
- whether the crime has caused, or made worse, any medical or social problems (such as marital problems).

Victims can choose whether the VPS will be heard in court (either read out by the victim or the CPS, or from a recording). There may be consequences for a victim's privacy if the statement is heard in open sessions, particularly if it is reported by the media. If it is not heard and the defendant is found guilty, the contents of the VPS will still be considered as part of the evidence prior to sentencing. All this must be clearly explained to the victim.

The completed statement should be sent to the CPS with information on any arrangements made, and the victim's preferences. Further guidance on victim personal statements is available on the Ministry of Justice website.

10.12 Duty Statements

A duty statement is a witness statement made by a police officer as a witness to events. The general guidance for completing MG11 forms still applies (see 10.11.1) but there are additional considerations. On the back of the MG11, for the 'home' contact details (at the top) a police officer should use his/her work address, email, and telephone number. The Witness Care and Witness Consent sections do not need to be filled in for a duty statement: simply put 'N/A' where appropriate.

When referring to other police officers, the first time an officer is mentioned the family name should be in capitals, with his/her rank and number. If the same officer is mentioned again, only the rank and name need be used. Witnesses should be referred to using either both names, or Mr/Mrs (etc) and the family name in capitals. The first time a suspect is named in a duty statement, his/her full name should be used with the family name in capitals, but after that only his/her family name.

MG 11 (T)

RESTRICTED (when complete)

WITNESS STATEMENT

(CJ Act 1967, s.9; MC Act 1980, ss.5A(3) (a) and SB; MC Rules 1981, r.70)

URN

Enter your rank and force number.

Statement of: *Charlotte UNDERWOOD*

Age if under 18: *over 18* (if over 18 insert 'over 18')   Occupation: *Police Constable 118118*

Sign with your rank and number.

This statement (consisting of *one* page(s) each signed by me) is true to the best of my knowledge and belief and I make it knowing that, if it is tendered in evidence, I shall be liable to prosecution if I have wilfully stated anything in it, which I know to be false, or do not believe to be true.

Signature: *C. Underwood PC 118118*   Date: *01.03.00*

Use the 24 hour clock and use 'at' not 'at approximately'.

Always begin with the time, day, date, location, and other persons present. Do not include your name, title, number, or station in the main body of the text.

Tick if witness evidence is visually recorded ☐ *(supply witness details on rear)*

At 1600 hours on Wednesday 1st March 0000 I was on uniformed patrol in a marked police vehicle with PC 69900 HODDIM. At this time we attended Kerrie's Corner shop, 98 High Street, Maidbury, Kentshire. As we arrived I saw a man who I now know to be Nathan JONAH born 09.09.1973 sitting on the pavement holding a plastic carrier bag approximately 1 metre from the front door of the shop on the pavement outside. I got out of the car and walked towards JONAH. I would describe JONAH as... The plastic carrier bag JONAH was holding looked as if it contained something lumpy. I heard JONAH shout 'That's it, you're all for it now!' and he tried to stand up, but stumbled and fell. As I approached him I could smell intoxicating liquor on his breath, his speech was slurred, and his eyes were glazed. He tried to stand up again but could not. He was drunk or otherwise intoxicated. He was groaning and looking downwards with his eyes shut sometimes.

This is hearsay evidence (she said that he said), and should be recorded in direct speech; see 10.9.

A woman came up to me and introduced herself as Mrs STONER. She said in the presence and hearing of the suspect 'I heard him say "what's it to you if some of us 'ain't got nothing to eat" and then I heard a long bang—I think he pushed the shop assistant against the wall behind the door and ran out'. PC HODDIM came over with a shop assistant from the store, a person I now know to be Janis DEE. In the presence and hearing of the suspect I said to Mrs DEE 'Can you please tell me what happened?' Mrs DEE replied 'I was filling the refrigerator with packets of bacon when this bloke here took a pack from out of the box on the floor. He walked around the store for a little while, well staggered really. I tried to stop him and then he just walked out without paying for it.' At 1635 hours the same day I said to the suspect JONAH 'As a result of what this person has told me I am arresting you on suspicion of theft of a pack of meat from the shop. Your arrest is necessary for the prompt and effective investigation of the offence and because you are drunk you may suffer physical injury to yourself'. I then cautioned him to which he replied 'It wasn't me, you've got the wrong person ... why me?' ... As JONAH was drunk I believed that he may present a danger to himself or others if he had possession of a weapon. I also believed he may have other articles from the store which he had not paid for. Therefore I searched him before placing him into the police vehicle. I looked inside the bag he was carrying and it contained a large packet of meat which I seized (exhibit labelled and marked CW/1). JONAH was placed in a police vehicle and conveyed to Maidbury Police Station arriving at 1645 hours the same day where he was introduced to the custody officer PS BENN.

Arrests must be recorded in direct speech, but the caution does not have to be. Any response from the suspect must be accurately recorded.

Sign and date after the last word of the statement, and include your rank and number.

For a duty statement, the signature does not need to be witnessed.

C. Underwood PC 118118, 01.03.00

Sign at the foot of every page, and include your rank and number.

Signature: *C. Underwood PC 118118*   Signature witnessed by: *n/a*

PTO

General Procedures

10.13 Methods of Disposal of Criminal Suspects

Here we describe the various methods of 'disposing' of a criminal suspect. We have split these into three main categories: directing to court, out-of-court disposals, and bail.

10.13.1 Directing to Court

Once an investigation has been concluded and a decision to prosecute has been made by the police or the Crown Prosecution Service (see 27.2), the defendant will be formally accused of committing a criminal offence. In less serious cases, the defendant will receive a formal accusation by way of a written charge and postal requisition by a public prosecutor. In more serious cases the charge will be read out to the suspect in a police station.

10.13.1.1 Written charge and postal requisition by a public prosecutor

Criminal proceedings can be instituted by a written charge and a postal requisition (s 29(1) and (2) of the Criminal Justice Act 2003), after a police officer reports a suspect at the roadside for a road traffic offence, or a suspect attends a police station voluntarily at an officer's request (reporting for an offence). This has largely replaced the former practice of issuing a summons to attend court.

To report a person for the purposes of issuing a written charge, the officer must:

1. state the offence(s) involved;
2. gather evidence in the usual way, ie using the senses, for example what was seen or heard;
3. point out the offence(s) to the suspect;
4. caution the suspect using the 'when questioned' caution (follow PACE Code C, para 10.2) and also inform him/her that he/she is not under arrest, but that any failure to cooperate or to answer particular questions may affect his/her immediate treatment;
5. make a written record of the questions and answers about the offence(s) in his/her PNB, including points to prove and negations to available defences;
6. offer the PNB to the suspect to read and sign that the notes are a true record of the interview (see Code C, para 11.11);
7. tell the suspect 'I am reporting you for the offence(s) of ...'; and
8. caution the suspect (using the 'now' caution: see 10.3).

The evidence is used to form a case file (see 27.4) which is then submitted by the officer in the case for review. If the decision is to prosecute, the public prosecutor will issue a written charge to the suspect. This will describe the relevant offence and state the Act under which the offence was created. The public prosecutor will also issue a requisition which requires the suspect to appear before a magistrates' court. The documents will be served by post, with copies sent to the court named in the requisition.

10.13.1.2 Charging at a police station

The custody officer (for minor offences) or the CPS (for more serious offences) will decide whether a suspect should be charged, or released without charge (see also 27.3). For a juvenile or a vulnerable adult, any action taken should be taken in the presence of an appropriate adult (Code C, para 16.1 and Note 16C).

A person who is going to be charged (or the appropriate adult) is given a written notice (an MG4 form, see 27.4.2) which includes the following details:

- reference number of the case and custody record number;
- time and date the charge is made;
- the suspect's details, including name, address, and date of birth;
- the name of the police officer who charged the suspect (not necessarily the 'officer in the case') and the name of the custody officer who 'accepted the charge'; and
- any reply from the suspect in response to charge.

The charge will always include the 'now' caution (see 10.3.4) and for an assault is likely to be worded as follows:

'You are charged with the offence(s) shown below. You do not have to say anything. But it may harm your defence if you do not mention now something which you later rely on in court. Anything you say may be given in evidence. On (date) at (town) in the county of (name of county) you assaulted (name of victim) contrary to section 39 of the Criminal Justice Act 1988.'

After a suspect has been charged or informed that he/she may be prosecuted for an offence, the suspect must not be interviewed any further unless it is necessary for the following reasons (listed in Code C, para 16.5):

- to prevent or minimize harm or loss to some other person, or the public;
- to clear up an ambiguity in a previous answer or statement; or
- in the interests of justice for the detainee, to have new information relevant to the offence put to him/her to comment on (new information having come to light since he/she was charged or informed about the possibility of being prosecuted).

If an interview is needed a 'restricted' caution must be given at the start (see 10.3.5).

After being charged, the suspect will usually be released, with or without bail (see 10.13.3.2). The custody officer may however decide that he/she should be kept in custody, if for example the person has no current abode, his/her name is not known, or for a more serious offence (see s 38(1) PACE and s 25 of the Criminal Justice and Public Order Act for a full list). A suspect who has been charged and kept in custody will be brought before a magistrates' court at the next sitting.

10.13.2 Out-of-Court Disposals

Custody officers and other decision-makers have a duty to consider whether an out-of-court disposal (OOCD) would be more appropriate for the offender than prosecution. This type of disposal is also known as neighbourhood justice. The National Decision Model (see 6.5.2) can help ensure consistent and effective decision-making when considering an OOCD. The views of the victim(s) must always be taken into account. The College of Policing Authorised Professional Practice provides further information on the neighbourhood justice outcomes framework (College of Policing, 2015j).

Restorative justice has been successfully used over a number of years for some offences and some offenders. At its simplest minor crimes and incidents are dealt with on the spot by police officers. Community resolutions can include elements of restorative justice and are also aimed at adults or youths for lower-level crime (see 14.2.1.3 in particular). A more formal procedure may also be used if the victim and offender agree, in which they are brought together in a restorative meeting facilitated by an appointed police officer or volunteer. For more serious or persistent matters which cannot be dealt with immediately, a series of meetings with additional participants may be needed to seek longer-term reparative solutions.

Here we cover PNDs and adult, youth, and foreign national cautions. Cannabis and khat warnings are covered in 12.5.3.2, and OOCDs for young people who cause ASB are covered in 14.2.1.3. Note that the cautions covered here are a method of disposal and must not be confused with the other forms of cautions used in investigations (see 10.3).

10.13.2.1 Penalty notices

The Penalty Notice for Disorder (PND) scheme was introduced in 2001 under ss 1–11 of the Criminal Justice and Police Act 2001. PNDs allow perpetrators aged 18 or over to pay a fine without going to court. The key aims and objectives of the penalty notice schemes are:

- to reduce the amount of time that law enforcement officers spend completing paperwork and attending court;
- to increase the amount of time law enforcement officers spend on the street;
- to reduce the burden on the courts; and
- to deliver swift, simple, and effective justice that carries a deterrent effect.

The term 'Fixed Penalty Notice' is used in a number of different circumstances, but the common factor is that the recipient has to pay a fixed penalty or charge. The first penalty notices were introduced over 50 years ago for motoring and road traffic offences (see 19.12.4). The Anti-Social Behaviour Act 2003 also provided for local authority personnel and PCSOs to issue penalty notices (also sometimes referred to as fixed penalty notices) for graffiti, and other minor offences such as littering, or dog control offences. The Anti-Social Behaviour, Crime and Policing Act 2014 enabled PCSOs, police and council officers to issue Fixed Penalty Notices for failing to comply with a Community Protection Notice, and for Public Spaces Protection Offences (see 14.2.2). Civil Enforcement Officers issue Penalty Charge Notices (PCN) for de-criminalized parking/waiting offences in most parts of the UK. PCNs are also used in

London for some moving traffic offences related to bus lanes, no-entry signs, restricted turns and yellow box junctions.

A police officer who has reason to believe that a person aged 18 or over has committed a relevant offence can issue a penalty notice (s 2(1) of the Criminal Justice and Police Act 2001). It can be issued on the spot by an officer in uniform ('street issue'), or at a police station by an authorized officer, usually the custody officer. In some forces PNDs can be issued using mini computerized printers instead of hand-written PND tickets, so officers will need to be familiar with the type of PND forms used locally. The national data-sharing system for recording PNDs (PentiP (Penalty Notice Processing)) can be used to check for unpaid penalties from previous incidents.

A person who accepts a PND is not admitting to a crime; he/she is simply supporting a suspicion by a police officer that an offence has been committed, and recognizing there will be no further proceedings. It would not affect a defendant's 'good character' (see 24.2.5.2, 27.4.5 and *Regina v Hamer* [2010] WLR (D) 235).

The offences for which a PND can be used are shown in the tables.

PND Offence with a fine of £90	Legislation
Wasting police time/giving false report	Criminal Law Act 1967, s 5(2)
Using public electronic communications network in order to cause annoyance, inconvenience, or needless anxiety	Communications Act 2003, s 127(2)
Knowingly giving a false alarm to a person acting on behalf of a fire and rescue authority	Fire and Rescue Services Act 2004, s 49 (England only) Fire Services Act 1947, s 31 (Wales only)
Causing harassment, alarm, or distress	Public Order Act 1986, s 5
Throwing fireworks	Explosives Act 1875, s 80
Drunk and disorderly	Criminal Justice Act 1967, s 91
Selling alcohol to person under 18 (anywhere)	Licensing Act 2003, s 146(1)
Supply of alcohol by or on behalf of a club to a person aged under 18	Licensing Act 2003, s 146(3)
Selling alcohol to a drunken person	Licensing Act 2003, s 141
Purchasing or attempting to purchase alcohol on behalf of a person under 18 (includes licensed premises and off-licences)	Licensing Act 2003, s 149(3)
Purchase of alcohol for consumption in licensed premises by person under 18	Licensing Act 2003, s 149(4)
Delivery of alcohol to person under 18 or allowing such delivery	Licensing Act 2003, s 151
Destroying or damaging property worth £300 or under	Criminal Damage Act 1971, s 1(1)
Unlawful possession of cannabis and its derivatives	Misuse of Drugs Act 1971, s 5(2)
Theft (retail) of property worth £100 or under (but see* at the end of this table)	Theft Act 1968, s 1
Breach of fireworks curfew (2300–0700hrs)	Firework Regulations 2004, reg 7 (Fireworks Act 2003, s 11)
Possession of a category 4 firework	Firework Regulations 2004, reg 5 (Fireworks Act 2003, s 11)

* For 'theft from a shop' (other than by an employee) only one such PND should ever be issued to an individual, and only for incidents where the value of the goods does not exceed £100 and the property has been recovered (consuming the stolen property may be an exception).

PND Offence with a fine of £60	Legislation
Dropping or leaving litter or refuse except in a receptacle provided for the purpose in a Royal Park or other open space	Royal Parks and Other Open Spaces Regulations 1997, reg 3(3–5), and the Parks Regulation (Amendment) Act 1926, s 2(1)
Using a pedal cycle, a roller blade, etc except on a Park road or in a designated area	
Failing to remove immediately any faeces deposited by an animal for which that person is in charge	
Depositing and leaving litter	Environmental Protection Act 1990, ss 87(1) and 87(5)
Throwing stones at a train	British Transport Commission Act 1949, s 56
Trespassing on a Railway	British Transport Commission Act 1949, s 55
Drunk in the highway	Licensing Act 1872, s 12
Consumption of alcohol by a person under 18 in a bar	Licensing Act 2003, s 150(1)
Allowing consumption of alcohol by a young person (aged under 18) in a bar	Licensing Act 2003, s 150(2)
Unlawful possession of khat and its derivatives	Misuse of Drugs Act 1971, s 5(2)

The recipient of a PND has 21 days to decide whether to pay the penalty or request a court hearing. In some areas an education option is available as an alternative; he/she must complete the course and pay for it. Failure to take any of these options may result in a fine (one and a half times the penalty amount) or court proceedings.

If after receiving a PND it comes to light that the person may have committed a more serious and non-penalty offence during the same incident, the further offence can be investigated and prosecuted separately (see *R v Gore: R v Maker* [2009] EWCA Crim 1424; WLR (D) 240). The flowchart shows the process model for issuing a PND (adapted from the current Home Office operational guidance (Home Office, 2013b)).

A person who has been given a PND may be photographed on the street (s 64A(1A) of the PACE Act 1984). This can be without consent (either withheld, or it is not practicable to obtain it). Before the photo is taken the person can be required to remove anything worn on or over any part of the head or face, and if he/she refuses an officer can remove it (s 64A(2)). However, for a religious garment the person should be taken out of public view before removing the garment and photographing the person.

The flow chart summarizes the system for using penalty notices.

General Procedures

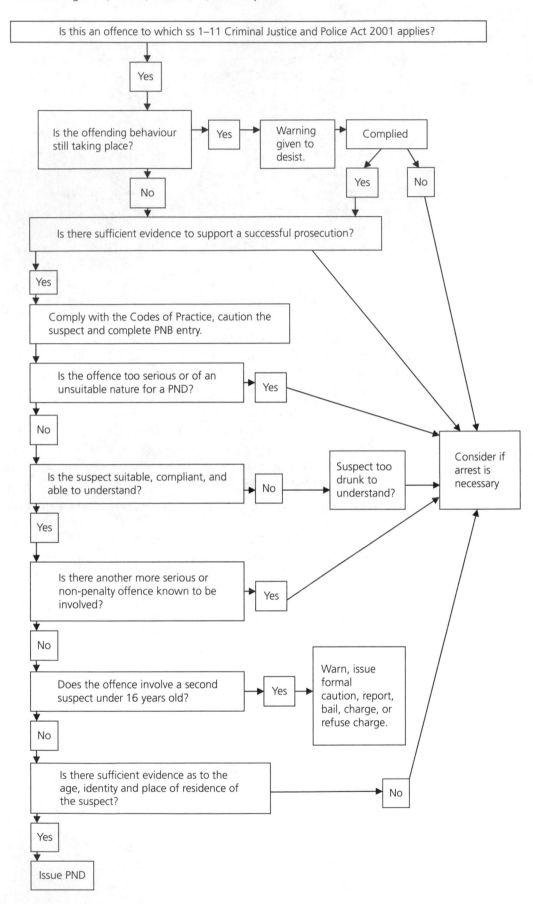

10.13.2.2 Adult cautions

Sections 22–27 of the Criminal Justice Act 2003 introduced two new types of caution for adults (aged 18 years and over); the simple caution and the conditional caution. They involve a formal warning given by a senior police officer, or by another police officer on the instructions of a senior police officer.

Simple cautions can be given to a person who has admitted guilt for certain summary or either-way offences (see 5.5.1). They cannot be used for the offences listed in SI 2015/790 (s 17(3) of the Criminal Justice and Courts Act 2015). To use a simple caution, all of the elements of the offence must be proved (*R (on the application of W) v Chief Constable of Hampshire Constabulary* [2006] EWHC 1904 (Admin)). The caution is recorded on the PNC, and can be taken into consideration by the court if the recipient is later convicted and sentenced for a further offence. Further details are provided in the Home Office Circular 016/2008 and in the Ministry of Justice guide *Simple Cautions for Adult Offender*, available online.

A conditional caution is similar to a simple caution but has rehabilitative or reparative conditions attached. It can be used to address the offender's behaviour, or to make reparation for the effects of the offence on the victim and others. For example, for person who has been involved with low-level alcohol-related crime and/or disorder, the condition could be to remain sober. Failing to comply with the conditions will result in criminal proceedings, and the caution will be cancelled. If there are reasonable grounds for believing that an offender has failed (without reasonable excuse) to comply with any of the conditions, he/she can be arrested without warrant (s 24A of the Criminal Justice Act 2003). Conditional cautions can be given by a police constable, an investigating officer, or a person authorized by the prosecutor. Five requirements must be met for a conditional caution:

1. The officer has sufficient evidence that the person has committed an offence.
2. The police officer or relevant prosecutor (or other authorized person) decides that there is sufficient evidence to charge the person with the offence and that a conditional caution should be given.
3. The offender admits the offence to a police officer (or other authorized person).
4. The effect of a caution and the consequences of failing to observe a condition must be explained to the offender.
5. The offender signs a document that sets out details of the offence, and that he/she admits guilt and consents to the caution and the attached conditions.

Further details are provided in the CPS Conditional Cautioning Code of Practice, available on the CPS website.

10.13.2.3 Youth cautions

The Crime and Disorder Act 1998 provides for the youth caution (s 66Z(1)) and the youth conditional caution (s 66A) for young people aged between 10 and 17 years. They can be used even if the recipient has previous convictions (for any offence). The suspect must admit the current offence, and must also be referred to the Youth Offending Team (YOT, see 3.3.4) as soon as practicable (ss 66ZB(1) and 66A(6A) respectively). Further information can be obtained from the *Youth Out-of-Court Disposals Guide* (Ministry of Justice and the Youth Justice Board, 2015).

For a youth caution the officer must have sufficient evidence to charge for the offence, and must also believe it is not in the public interest to give a youth conditional caution or to prosecute. An appropriate adult must be present when the caution is given (s 66ZA(2)). For a young person receiving a second youth caution, the YOT will be expected to make an assessment, and if appropriate arrange a voluntary rehabilitation programme (s 66ZB(2)).

Youth conditional cautions are the next level up from a youth caution, and conditions are placed on the perpetrator. The five requirements listed in 10.13.2.2 must all be met (ss 66A(1) and 66B(1)–(6)), and both the views of the victim and the behavioural needs of the young person should be taken into consideration.

General Procedures

10.13.2.4 Foreign national offender conditional cautions

A person who offends in the UK may be a foreign national with no right to enter or remain the UK. It may be in the public interest if he/she is not prosecuted in the courts but instead receives a caution and leaves the UK. The primary conditions for these cautions are that the offender must cooperate with the authorities and then leave the UK and not return for five years. Secondary rehabilitative conditions can be imposed, including attending a treatment course (for drug addiction for example) prior to departure. Reparative conditions can also be imposed such as paying compensation, repairing damage, and apologizing to the victim.

10.13.3 Bail

Bail is a process of attempting to ensure that a person appears at a specified time at a specified place such as a police station or court. Bail can be used during an investigation to allow more time for police officers to conduct further enquires, as there is a time limit on how long a suspect can be held without being charged (see 10.10.3). The 'custody clock' can be stopped and the suspect released on bail to return to the police station at a later date, when the clock would be restarted, and would carry on from the time it had been stopped. At the time of writing, legislative changes to pre-charge bail were being considered in Parliament with a view to being incorporated into the Policing and Criminal Justice Bill. Bail can also be used to bind a defendant to appear in court having been charged.

10.13.3.1 'Street bail'

Street bail is a discretionary power which allows police officers to release an offender on bail without taking him/her to a police station. The offender must attend a specified police station at a later specified date (ss 30A–30D of the PACE Act 1984). This saves time as the offender does not need to be taken to or processed at the police station, and more time is also available for investigation. For legal representatives, parents, and appropriate adults, there are improved opportunities to plan and prepare.

A decision to grant street bail should follow the normal arrest procedures in s 24 of the PACE Act 1984 (see 10.6). Statements concerning guilt are not relevant to the decision to grant bail—interview and examination of evidence will take place later. The following questions must be considered when deciding whether to grant street bail.

1. What type of offence has been committed and how serious is it? There is no definitive list of offences for which street bail can be granted; it is a matter for a police officer's discretion. However, it is unlikely that street bail would be granted for a serious offence.
2. What has been the impact of the offence? The impact on the victim, the offender, and other persons should all be considered.
3. Would a delay in dealing with the offender result in loss of vital evidence? It might be necessary to take him/her to a police station to preserve and examine forensic evidence which could otherwise be lost.
4. Is the person fit to be released back onto the streets? For example, a drunk driver or a person with mental health problems may not be in a fit state to be released, and for a juvenile, consideration must be given to his/her welfare.
5. Does the person understand what is happening? This particularly applies to vulnerable people who would normally require the assistance of an appropriate adult during an investigation (see 25.5.1.1).
6. If released on bail, is the person likely to commit a further offence? Street bail should not be used if there are reasonable grounds to believe that he/she might continue the offending behavior or commit another offence, for example, where people have been fighting.
7. Has the person provided a correct name and address? The identification and address details provided must be believed to be correct.

If street bail is appropriate the decision should be explained to the offender, and a street bail notice issued. It is important that the person understands the requirement to attend a police station on a specified date, and that he/she is not being legally discharged and may also be subject to court proceedings or other disposal actions. A verbal explanation covering the points 1–7 should be given, even though these are also clearly stated on the notice provided. The length of time for street bail is partly determined by how long it is likely to take to carry out the investigation, but force policy might also apply (maximum periods may be specified).

Conditions may be imposed on the bail (s 30A(3A) of the PACE Act 1984) to ensure the person surrenders to custody when required, does not commit an offence while on bail, and does not interfere with witnesses or otherwise obstruct the course of justice (whether in relation to him/herself or any other person). Some types of conditions are not permitted, for example requiring residence at a bail hostel, or a surety (a commitment to pay if the person does not return). The street bail notice given to the suspect will list the conditions, and name the police station at which the conditions can be varied.

There is a power to arrest without warrant if there are reasonable grounds for suspecting any of the bail conditions have been broken, or for failing to answer bail at the specified time (ss 30D and 30A of the PACE Act 1984).

10.13.3.2   Bail from a police station

The overarching power for the police to grant bail and to require individuals to report back to the police station is contained in s 47(3) of PACE. There are five main reasons for bail being given:

Circumstances for granting bail	PACE subsection	Return location	Conditions can apply?
Further investigation and evidence gathering is planned as there is insufficient evidence to support a charge at present	s 34(5)	police station	no
Insufficient evidence to support a charge and no further investigation planned, but review is required	s 37(2)	police station	yes
Sufficient evidence to support a charge but consultation with the CPS is required to agree charges	s 37(7)(a)	police station	yes
Sufficient evidence to support a charge but consultation with the CPS is required to agree on an alternative form of disposal, such as a caution (see 10.13.2.2)	s 37(7)(b)	police station	yes
After a person has been charged with an offence	s 37(7)(d)	court	yes

A person who has been released on bail who then fails to attend the police station or court at the appointed time, or is suspected of breaking attached conditions can be arrested without warrant under s 46A(1) of the PACE Act 1984 (see 10.6.5).

10.13.4   Wanted persons

If the identity of a suspect is known and all local lines of enquiry to trace and arrest him/her have failed, or if he/she has not answered bail to a police station or court, a police officer can circulate the person's details on the PNC (see 6.9.1.1). This will need authorization from a supervisor or manager, who will assess the seriousness of the situation. Most volume, priority, and major crime offences (see 24.2.3 for definitions) will be judged as sufficiently serious for a person to be placed as 'wanted' on the PNC, as will the situation when a person has absconded from prison. Further examples are provided by Humberside Police (2015).

> **TASK 11** What offence, if any, is committed by a person who fails to return on bail to a police station, or fails to surrender to custody at a court after having been bailed?

10.14   Handover Procedures

After initial enquiries into a suspected crime (eg taking statements, collecting potential evidence, the arrest of a suspect) the arresting officer may 'hand over' responsibility for the subsequent investigation to another colleague, for example a volume-crime investigator (see Chapter 24). In some forces the case files are handed over to a Criminal Justice Unit or Department where 'case-builders' obtain further statements and evidence, and (if appropriate) prepare files for submission to the CPS (see 27.4.2). Practice varies; in some forces the arresting officer may be expected to see the process through to a more advanced stage.

The key principle for handovers is that the information provided will enable the receiving colleague to become as familiar with the circumstances of the alleged offence as the arresting officer. The 'handover package' will include documents and references to artefacts (eg forensic evidence and special property). It will also include a general checklist (the 'single source document'), which will be likely to list the following:

Checklist entry	Examples/notes
Names of the alleged offender(s)	Provide names, DoB, and custody numbers
The arresting officer's account of the circumstances leading up to arrest	Remember to avoid offering opinion in this section
Investigation checklist	• A series of tickbox lists addressing the arrest (including a copy of PNB entries); • searches; • exhibits; • scene and forensic evidence; • detainee and custody considerations; and • PNC/force intelligence database checks
Witness details and statements	• names, addresses, and contact numbers of witnesses; and • a summary of witness statements
Other officers involved	• details of those who also attended; and • copies of their PNB entries and statements

Note that the single source document could be 'relevant material' (see 24.3.1), so it must be included on the MG 6C form.

10.15 Answers to Tasks

TASK 1 The 'first' or 'given' name is the term to use, rather than 'Christian' name. The latter is a reflection of a time when the assumption was made that all UK residents subscribed (at least notionally) to Christianity as a religion.

TASK 2 The use of mind-maps as tools for learning and analysis was pioneered by Tony Buzan and others. The website <http://www.mindtools.com/pages/article/newISS_01.htm> has some useful advice on the application of Buzan's ideas. Of course, we have provided you with the no ELBOWS(S) mnemonic already, but developing your own mnemonic is good practice and will help fix the ideas in your long-term memory.

TASK 3 There are many examples, but you might have considered the following:

> The caution means that you have the right to silence and you do not have to say anything or reply to any question you are asked. Anything that you say now or during the rest of the investigation can be given to the court for consideration. However, if you choose not to say anything now or during the investigation and then you decide to say something during the court proceedings instead, the court can deal with this fresh evidence as they choose, including ignoring it.

TASK 4 She should:

1. obtain and record a first description from the householder;
2. ask the householder if he would consider accompanying her to the locations mentioned to attempt an identification;
3. explain to him that she will not direct his attention to any individual but that he should look carefully at each person present.

TASK 5 Whatever examples you chose, each should have clearly addressed:

- a person's involvement, or suspected involvement, or attempted involvement in the commission of a criminal offence; and
- the reasonable grounds for believing that the person's arrest is necessary.

TASK 6 She should:

- locate the person who is subject of the warrant through the use of intelligence, a stop check, the PNC, or her local force database;
- identify herself, then confirm the identity of the person, and then arrest and caution him/her;

- endorse the back of the warrant (also known as 'backing up');
- record the event in her PNB;
- send the 'backed-up' warrant to the appropriate court, following local procedures.

If she is not in possession of the warrant at the time of the arrest and the person asks to see it, she must show it to him/her as soon as is practicable.

TASK 7 The European Arrest Warrant (EAW) is an EU-wide arrest warrant which allows for the extradition of a person suspected of a serious crime from a participating EU country. The application is made by a judge in one country to a judge in the country where the suspect is known to be present. The process is therefore within and part of the criminal justice systems of both countries. Previously, 'extradition' was highly politicized, and people or cases were subject to long delay, political processes, appeals, and so on. The aim of the EAW is to speed things up. Further details may be found at <http://www.asser.nl/Default.aspx?site_id=8&level1=10783>, but the process may change in the future due to Brexit.

TASK 8 You probably considered the following:

1. An arrested person must be informed by the arresting officer that he/she is under arrest (s 28(2) and Code G, para 2.2).
2. The arrest is not lawful unless the arresting officer at the time, or as soon as is practicable, informs the person of the grounds for the suspicion (s 28(3)).
3. The arrested person must be informed about his/her involvement (or suspected or attempted involvement) in the commission of a criminal offence, and the reasonable grounds for believing that arrest is 'necessary' (Code G, para 2.2).
4. The officer must caution the arrested person (Code G, para 3.4).

For the second half of the task, your answer was probably along the following lines:

> I have just seen you run out of the shop with a brand-new drill under your arm. I heard the store alarm go off at the same time and I suspect that you have stolen the drill. I am therefore arresting you on suspicion of theft of the drill. Your arrest is necessary to allow the prompt and effective investigation of the offence, and also, because you were running away, to prevent any prosecution for the offence being hindered by you leaving the area. You do not have to say anything, but it may harm your defence if you do not mention when questioned something which you later rely on in court. Anything you do say may be given in evidence.

TASK 9 The different categories of seized property might have separate forms for recording the details, but similar information is likely to be required such as:

- sequential number (to be attached to the item(s) for the purposes of recognition);
- name and address of the person from whom it was taken;
- location where it was taken into police possession;
- details of the police officer who took possession;
- exhibit reference (if known);
- description of article(s);
- reasons for taking into police possession;
- proposed disposal method for the property (eg returned to owner or destroyed); and
- current location of the property.

The appropriate form should be completed and a copy attached to the property before it is stored. Each force will have its own procedures but if the main property store cannot be accessed because it is closed (eg at night), the property will have to be kept in a 'transit store' (a secure cupboard). It will later be transferred to the main store by the property officer.

TASK 10 You probably considered the following:

> I have just seen this person run out of a shop with a brand-new drill under his arm. I heard the store alarm sound at the same time, and I suspected he had stolen the drill. I arrested him on suspicion of theft of the drill. This was necessary to allow the prompt and effective investigation of the offence by interviewing him, and also to prevent him leaving the area as this could prevent a prosecution for the offence.

TASK 11 Section 6(1) of the Bail Act 1976 states that it is an offence for person who has been released on bail in criminal proceedings to fail without reasonable cause to surrender to custody. This is a summary offence and the penalty is three months' imprisonment and/or a fine.

General Procedures

11.1 Introduction

This chapter is primarily concerned with the general procedures to be followed when attending incidents, including crime scenes. Throughout we link the subject matter to police officer initial training, but the content will also be useful to those undertaking a pre-join programme at a college or university. We also examine attending and dealing with incidents involving loss of life, often sudden deaths, although not necessarily of a suspicious nature.

The police have a responsibility to respond and deal with many types of incident, but the majority of police everyday activities can be described as 'Steady State' policing. There are also 'Rising Tide' incidents, which are unexpected and cannot be planned for. Examples include large-scale rail, road, air, and sporting disasters or acts of terrorism. They may be classed as emergency, major, or critical incidents (see 11.5). 'Planned Operations' are where the police have had advanced warning of a situation (eg a large demonstration) and will have contingency plans in place (see 11.7).

The police will attend volume crime scenes and minor incidents more often than major crime scenes. In a number of key respects, the principles of attending a volume crime scene are no different to those employed when attending the scene of a major crime: the differences might simply be those of scale. However, as we note in 11.5, emergencies, major, and critical incidents may give rise to crime scenes of significant geographical size and complexity (such as the bombings in London in July 2005) and the events might require multi-agency emergency responses, adding to the demands of crime-scene management.

The material covered here is particularly relevant to three of the Diploma in Policing assessed units: 'Conducting priority and volume investigations' and 'Provide an initial response to policing incidents' and 'Conduct Police Searches'. In particular, the following learning outcomes and assessment criteria are relevant:

Name of Diploma unit	Learning outcome	Assessment criteria
Conduct priority and volume investigations	Understand the process for conducting priority and volume crime investigations	• Summarise the methods used to protect scenes • Summarise the methods used to protect evidence
	Be able to conduct priority and volume investigations	• Gather information, intelligence and evidence to support the investigation in line with organisational procedures and lines of enquiry • Identify the need for any additional support for investigations • Take the necessary steps to protect and preserve the scene

Name of Diploma unit	Learning outcome	Assessment criteria
Provide an initial response to policing incidents	Understand legal and organisational requirements related to responding to incidents	• Explain the duty of care that Police Officers have to the public when responding to incidents • Explain why different incidents require different initial responses
	Be able to analyse information to plan responses to incidents	• Gather information and intelligence regarding incidents
	Be able to provide an initial response to incidents in line with legal and organisational requirements	• Analyse all available information to establish the nature of incidents • Prioritise actions in accordance with the nature of incidents • Take control of incidents • Preserve the scene and any potential evidence • Include others who need to be involved at the earliest opportunity
Conduct police searches	Understand legal and organisational requirements in relation to searches	• Explain how to secure potential evidence from search scenes
	Be able to conduct police searches of premises, vehicles and outside spaces in line with legal and organisational requirements	• Maintain the integrity of seized items, including through the use of appropriate packaging and storage

It covers parts of PIP Level 1 'Responding to Incidents' and is also relevant to parts of the Certificate in Knowledge of Policing units, 'Knowledge of conducting priority and volume investigations' and 'Knowledge of providing an initial response to policing incidents'.

11.2 General Procedures at Crime Scenes

Deployment to any incident has the potential to generate numerous challenges, for example unlawful violence against persons and premises, and public disorder. Victims and witnesses may also need support, including first aid, and in the case of more serious injuries, an ambulance or paramedics may be required.

The scene of an incident (such as a road accident) normally requires a police officer to make a judgement about the scale and type of response required so that the appropriate help and support is made available through the police and other agencies. We discuss this issue later but initially concentrate on crime. A crime scene is frequently the most important component of any criminal investigation, because it is very likely to contain physical and electronic evidence which could identify suspects, corroborates or refutes statements made by witnesses, and demonstrates guilt or innocence. Early and effective protection of the crime scene ensures that the greatest amount of potential evidence is available for recovery and, therefore, maximizes its value to the investigation.

Crime scenes are not purely geographical locations to which we can apply an address, postcode, or map reference; a victim or suspect in a crime such as a sexual assault is also a crime scene. Treating a person (especially a victim) as a crime scene may be distressing and potentially offensive to the person and to his/her family or friends, but it is vital that we consider people as sources of evidence and intelligence. This is to ensure that we effectively 'protect and preserve' them, and recover the evidence or intelligence we need. Anything that could be a source of evidence or intelligence is also part of a crime scene, including articles related to the offence, such as weapons and vehicles, computer hard drives, digital storage media, as well as the intangible such as networked environments.

Some of the biggest 'offenders' in relation to poor scene preservation are victims of crime, so any opportunity to encourage good scene management is vital, and will pay dividends. Call centre staff should be trained to explain what the victims or informants could do to help preserve evidence, and the FAO (First Attending Officer) can instruct victims and the public on simple issues such as staying clear of the crime scene and not handling evidence. Victims are often vital sources of physical evidence (especially in offences against the person and sexual assault) and preventing their contamination by others (such as supportive family members) is important. Sexual assault victims should be forensically examined before they smoke, eat, drink, wash, or go to the toilet (unless absolutely necessary) because such activity can destroy evidence. This is sometimes very difficult to explain and may be a source of considerable conflict, yet the problem can be solved with a diplomatic and respectful approach.

Nearly all officers carry a personal mobile phone with a camera, and it might be tempting to use it to photograph a crime scene. This may occasionally assist an investigation in the early stages (eg when a wet shoe mark is evaporating). However, generally, it is better not to use the camera on a personal mobile phone at a possible crime scene because the phone would then become a source of evidence and would normally be retained for analysis of the image in its original state.

11.2.1 Early priorities at crime scenes—the FAO

The overriding principle at any incident is that all attending officers rigorously ensure the safety of the public, their colleagues, and themselves. Some of the people present at a scene of a criminal offence may be emotional, aggressive, or confused and might represent a danger. In addition, damage to premises, such as by fire, may weaken the structure of a building, resulting in further hazards.

Prior to responding to an incident, officers should ensure that they know the basic information required to ensure they are prepared and safe. This includes a meaningful address or location, an idea of the incident type and the location of any rendezvous points (RVPs). While travelling to the scene of an incident, a 'dynamic' risk assessment should be made based on the information gathered from the initial report (see the introduction to 24.4.1). The assessment should be based upon:

- what is known (objective fact/information) or believed (subjective fact/information) to have happened;
- the number of people likely to be present;
- any information on the PNC and local intelligence databases about the individuals involved (eg that a suspect has been violent in the past);
- if any weapons are present at the scene;
- any risks associated with the location and local community sensitivities.

11.2.1.1 Arriving at a crime scene

The first police officer who attends the scene (possibly as the result of an emergency call) is known variously as the FAO, the First Officer at the Scene (FOAS), or sometimes the Initial Responder; different forces use different terms. We use FAO in the remainder of this chapter. The FAO may be of any rank and position within the organization—indeed, it could be a trainee police officer—this will entirely depend on who happens to arrive first. For example, it was a special constable in Community Safety at Thetford (Norfolk) who was first on the scene of a serious assault, and he had to manage the scene and deal with first aid as well as keeping his control room informed.

The first few minutes after a **major crime** may be confusing and the FAO should control any person in the vicinity, including colleagues, and direct them to carry out urgent tasks where appropriate. Many of the members of the public near the incident may be potentially valuable witnesses and must be identified swiftly. The FAO may also have to arrest a suspect. It should be remembered that all physical evidence is expendable when balanced against human life. Hence the FAO should not preserve a crime scene to the extent that it causes delays which aggravate a victim's injuries or increase any risks to life and limb. This is not to say that physical evidence can be disregarded during the life-saving process; the FAO can advise the ambulance crew where not to tread and can carefully move furniture away from the victim to facilitate medical aid when *necessary*. However, if such actions are carried out, it is essential that moved items are left in their new position and not moved again in an attempt to recreate the original crime scene. This is because moving furniture, switching on lights, and even opening doors represents contamination (in its loosest sense, but see 11.2.5.1) and may remove items from their original context. All these actions must be reported to the crime scene investigator (CSI) early on in the investigation and should also be recorded as PNB entries (see 10.2). Further details on forensics are covered in Chapter 26, and Chapter 24 covers investigative actions at crime scenes more generally.

As soon as the initial response and emergency treatment of any casualties has been completed all police officers, including the FAO, and other personnel attending crime scenes should withdraw. They should only re-enter if approved, and protective clothing must be worn for their own safety, and to avoid adding more misleading material to the scene.

11.2.1.2 The golden hour

The first period of any incident, particularly in major crime and critical incidents, is often described as the 'golden hour'. This is a shorthand reference to the need to identify witnesses and preserve a scene quickly so that evidence can be protected or gathered while it is still fresh and undisturbed. For example, bloodstains should be sampled or protected before they are diluted by rain, shoe impressions (shoe marks) may need to be covered in poor weather, and the body of a deceased person could be initially examined before rigor mortis sets in.

It is also advantageous to identify and interview witnesses whilst their recollections are still clear. A police officer should always listen carefully to witnesses and evaluate what they say in the light of what is already known. He/she will of course record what is said as a PNB entry, and may also make a note of further questions to ask or other lines of enquiry (see 24.4.1.2 and 24.4.3).

11.2.1.3 Cordons

Cordons are erected as a visible barrier to identify the parameters of crime scenes or other incidents, such as fires. A flimsy cordon tape is clearly not a physical barrier: it is more of a 'statement' to help limit and control access for relevant personnel. In criminal investigations, they are generally only used for more serious offences such as major crimes and fatalities.

Cordons are set up using police tape, and this should be done promptly to completely prevent public access. The golden rule is to cordon a larger area than seems immediately necessary. The tape should be securely attached to carefully chosen fixed objects, but any objects that might be a source of evidence should not be used, for instance a parked car, as the action of the wind or people moving the tape could erase evidence such as bloodstains and fingerprints. The size of the cordon should not be determined by the location of convenient fixed objects: if necessary, the tape can be affixed further out until poles are available. Whilst installing the tape the officer must also control witnesses and keep them out of the freshly cordoned area, and this is sometimes difficult. Further information about cordoning bomb scenes is provided in 11.6.2. A single cordon (or the inner or first cordon) must encompass specific areas:

- the venue of any incident or suspected offence;
- all possible routes into or out of the venue;
- any location where physical evidence could possibly be found: for example, communal bins, under cars in the street, nearby gardens; and
- any location identified as significant by witnesses.

A secondary cordon (the outer cordon) can also be installed to manage the public's access and view, and is strictly a matter of control. If the public can see significant evidence then the cordon is almost certainly too small. It also makes sense to position the outer cordon so that vehicles can turn around, minimizing local congestion. Once the inner cordon is in place, nothing—not even a patrol car—may leave or enter it until sanctioned by a CSI, unless it is required to save life—for example, an ambulance or fire appliance. Vehicles moving through the cordoned area may damage vital evidence, for example at bomb scenes components of the device may be picked up by the tyres of emergency vehicles and driven out of the scene. Additionally, the offender might have leant against a vehicle outside the venue of the offence when he made off, so CSIs may need to examine every vehicle within the cordon or, on occasions, every vehicle in the street.

The powers available to the police to secure crime scenes were considered in the case of *DPP v Morrison* [2003] EWHC 683 (Admin). In a serious incident in a shopping centre involving groups of young people, the police had sought to cordon off four areas in the shopping centre to secure and preserve evidence. Morrison was arrested for obstruction of a police officer in the lawful execution of his duty (and a Public Order Act offence) after he had walked into one of the cordoned areas, despite being told not to do so by police. He was initially convicted but appealed, and the Crown Court allowed the appeal, stating that there was no lawful authority to erect the cordon, and therefore the police were not acting in the lawful execution of their duty. The prosecution in turn appealed to the High Court. The High Court considered case law and existing legislation and decided that where a public area is to be cordoned, it was unlikely that anyone would have a right to stop police from doing so, but that on private property the police were entitled to assume that the owner would consent to cordoning. The shopping area in the *Morrison* case was privately owned but had a public right of way, so the cordoned areas were a public place (see 9.2), and the police were therefore entitled to install a cordon there. The appeal was successful. On a practical level, this decision makes it clear that in certain circumstances police officers might need to obtain search warrants (under perhaps s 8 of the PACE Act 1984) in order to remain on private premises for the purposes of a crime scene search.

11.2.2   The rendezvous point and the Common Approach Path

The rendezvous point (RV point or RVP) is vital to the smooth running of the investigations at the scene, and should have been carefully chosen early on in the investigation. It may have to accommodate a number of vehicles, rest stations, major incident vehicles, and even a command tent. RVPs should never be placed in a narrow street with restricted access. They should always be in a roadway or on land with good access, which is unconnected to the investigation. When attending the scene of a suspicious explosion, care must be taken to search the RVP for secondary devices which have been deliberately placed to cause maximum casualties to the emergency services. In incidents involving firearms officers, forensic personnel and other emergency services will normally attend the RVP rather than the crime scene as a matter of safety.

The Common Approach Path (CAP) is a designated route from the edge of the cordon into the crime scene proper. If the scene is 'empty' (there are no living victims) there will be more time to choose the most suitable route, but in any case it should not be the route likely to have been taken by victim or offender. Nor should it necessarily be the route taken by the FAO, as he/she was acting early on without full knowledge of the facts. The selected route should minimize damage to potential evidence, particularly material which is small or almost two-dimensional—such as shoe marks and blood. Wherever possible, the CAP should be laid on solid ground, as this will help prevent evidence being accidentally concealed; this could mistakenly happen if personnel walked on a CAP over soft materials such as soil. Ideally the CAP should be marked with tape but, in the early stages, this may not be possible. If tape is used it should not be anchored with rocks and other debris in the vicinity, since one of these may have been a weapon. Once selected the CAP should be guarded by a scene control officer.

Some of the problems associated with CAPs are:

- over-eagerness to establish a CAP through the rear of the premises: entering the premises via a back door and searching for a key may destroy vital evidence;
- selecting the route for a CAP in a flat, featureless field;
- a lack of choice due to a building having only one entrance; and
- no immediate available means to mark the CAP.

One of the early tasks of the CSI is to search the CAP for evidence, and if this is found the CSI may want to re-route it, or else record and remove potentially valuable material.

11.2.3   The crime scene log and attending personnel

Perhaps the most important document at the crime scene is the log, a booklet or sheet upon which the details of all attending personnel are recorded. In essence, it records any event that could have led to contamination of evidence. The log should contain details of:

- every person already at the scene when the FAO arrived;
- every person who subsequently attended the scene and the time of attendance;
- every person who entered the crime scene or inner cordon, with the time of attendance and the reason; and
- preferably, a description of the CAP so that every person attending the scene can familiarize themselves with it prior to entry.

Whilst the scene control officer should be visible it is the responsibility of all attending personnel (including trainee police officers on Supervised or Independent Patrol) to seek him/her out. Logging or resourcing databases which manage deployments and information at incidents (such as STORM and the older systems like CAD and OIS) do not record officer deployments in sufficient detail and should not be relied upon.

It is the responsibility of the scene control officer and every individual to ensure the log is completed correctly. The log must be copied and will probably be disclosed to the defence (see 24.3.3), who will study it and compare it to statements, PNBs, and other scene logs. Failure to properly maintain the log may mean that some or all of the evidence removed from the scene could be deemed as inadmissible by the CJS.

11.2.3.1   Non-police personnel at crime scenes

Ambulance crews should be allowed controlled access in order to save life. They are generally aware of how to behave in a crime scene but may have to be reminded not to touch anything needlessly and to show caution where they walk. The FAO could accompany the crew and point out apparently significant evidence to be avoided, and should take their names for later elimination (particularly of shoes, clothing, and fingerprints). Clearly, ambulance personnel should wear gloves, as should the FAO. Efforts to resuscitate by ambulance staff can generate very considerable quantities of debris, such as wrappers and used medical equipment. This material should be left at the scene for the attending CSI.

A doctor is not always required to establish that a death has occurred since ambulance crews will make a 'recognition of life extinct' (ROLE), sometimes referred to as 'Fact of Death' (FOD). In this case the attending officer should take any forms they produce and ensure these are returned to the police station. If a doctor attends, he/she should wear protective clothing, and disturb the body as little as possible. The use of oral, rectal, or deep-tissue thermometers is not generally permitted because this can interfere with biological evidence in particular, such as DNA. If there is any concern that the death may be suspicious (see 11.3) the doctor or ambulance crew should be requested not to turn the body nor search through clothing to view hypostasis or injuries until a CSI is in attendance. Certification of death is carried out by a doctor afterwards, but he/she could also be asked for an opinion as to the cause of death, particularly if the deceased has apparently suffered a sudden death and is known to the doctor.

Other police colleagues (including senior officers) should not enter the inner cordon unless:

- the offender is likely to be within and must be apprehended;
- they are saving life;
- they can assist in urgent and immediate acts to prevent loss of the scene (eg putting out a small and manageable fire); and/or
- a dog is required to pick up a track from within the cordon.

In the case of deaths, there is no requirement for a senior officer to enter the scene once death has been confirmed, or to confirm that a death is suspicious, because every additional person in the crime scene can potentially destroy or contaminate evidence.

The CSI will attend at the RVP (see 11.2.2) and will liaise with the FAO and other personnel, to decide how to proceed. In general terms, the CSI's initial role is to gather information, start with photography where appropriate, and advise detectives and uniformed police on the arrangements for any arrested persons. Once this has been achieved he/she will examine the CAP, record and recover vulnerable evidence from it, and occasionally move the CAP to another location. It is common for the CSI to enter the scene with the doctor to certify deaths or examine a deceased person.

The **Crime Scene Manager** (CSM) is appointed in a major crime enquiry to manage the scene and deal with scientific resources. In some cases a single CSM may be appointed, who will deal with all parts of the investigation. In a more serious or complex case there may be a number of CSMs and a **Crime Scene Coordinator** (CSC). Typically, the CSM will be hands-on, but will also be flexible enough to attend strategy meetings and deal with other issues.

A variety of emergency personnel may attend a scene and will be recorded in the log if they enter the crime scene, unless it is a serious incident and is impractical. The following groups will also keep their own records of attendance:

- the fire service;
- Explosives Ordnance Disposal (EOD) (in the case of explosions or suspected explosive devices);
- HM Coastguard and RNLI;
- mountain rescue and lowland search organizations (with dogs).

Other personnel who may attend as required include forensic scientists, borough or district surveyors and structural engineers (to assess the safety of damaged buildings), National Grid (for gas leaks), and scaffolding contractors (to support damaged structures in order to prevent collapse). However, once cordons are in place, no one should enter the crime scene until sanctioned and briefed by a CSI unless the safety of the public or attending personnel is at risk. At a non-crime incident there will be an incident commander who should be consulted.

General Procedures

11.2.3.2   Powers of entry for CSIs and experts

There is often confusion over powers of entry for CSIs, scientists, and computer experts at crime scenes as prior to the Police Reform Act 2002 very little thought was given to this. However, the following now applies:

- Section 18 of the PACE Act 1984 permits entry to a premises for police officers in relation to a person who is under arrest for an indictable offence, and s 38 of the Police Reform Act 2002 modified this to permit entry for a civilian designated as an 'investigating officer';
- Section 16 of the PACE Act 1984 (concerned with the execution of warrants by police officers) authorizes civilians and specialists to attend with the police. Code B, para 2.11 refers to a 'designated person' accompanying police officers as having powers to search and seize evidence.

In many cases, however, formal permissions are not required because the occupier will invite the police to attend and enter the property.

11.2.4   Fast-track actions

In every major crime the senior investigating officer (SIO) will consider fast-track actions which might resolve the investigation rapidly. These decisions are taken after careful consideration, and are noted in the decision log or policy file (which records the decision-making process of the senior officer). However, in the very early minutes of an investigation, some actions may be necessary to prevent the loss of evidence or facilitate the apprehension of a suspect. These can include the following:

- the use of a dog to track the offender, particularly if the scent is not contaminated—the dog may have to enter the inner cordon;
- the immediate collection of evidence which is in danger of being lost, such as wadding and cartridge cases being blown down a street by the wind, photographing the image on a computer screen, powering off a smartphone (which might otherwise be remotely 'wiped');
- switching off a cooker if it might start a fire;
- covering shoe marks and tyre marks in poor weather, using boxes or bin lids taken from an area well away from the crime scene;
- an urgent search of the street (sometimes called a flash search) for evidence which has been discarded, especially when the area is busy; and
- controlling large groups of people in confined situations (eg a pub) which might cause the loss (or gain) of fibre evidence.

In these circumstances care must be taken to make the right decision. Protective clothing (at the least, clean medical-style gloves) might be needed to prevent contamination of the evidence. Police officers (including supervised trainees) should be prepared to justify their actions (or lack of them) to the senior investigating officer.

11.2.5   Forensic considerations at volume crime scenes

The attending police officer may be required to take a crime report, assess the likely *modus operandi* of the offender, record losses, identify potential witnesses, and assess the scene for the potential attendance of a CSI. Overall, fewer actions will be taken by CSIs and police officers at a volume crime scene (compared with a major crime scene). The police will also try to minimize disruption to normal life in the immediate vicinity of the crime. If the CSI is delayed, a police officer may need to:

- close doors to control children and pets (instead of using cordon tape);
- close windows and consider boarding up in inclement weather;
- if boarding-up is to be arranged, ensure the original window is left, rather than being immediately removed by the contractor;
- cover shoe marks inside with a chair (not a piece of paper which is more likely to be moved or trodden on);
- bring broken glass and property inside, handling it by the edges and wearing gloves (as moisture makes fingerprinting difficult);
- cover shoe and tyre marks outside with bin lids, trays, or boxes, even in sunny weather;
- on a bed use the blanket or quilt to funnel any material to a corner of the room; and
- allow the victims to make drinks and food and facilitate this, unless doing so would damage good evidence or cause a health risk.

Whilst these actions may help a victim's state of mind, there are other considerations which must be borne in mind, such as the preservation of evidence. In the presence of DNA rich material a mask should be worn (if available) to prevent contamination from the officer. Another important consideration is to protect any articles that have to be moved by wearing gloves and handling material carefully: **gloves do not protect fingerprints from being destroyed**. Third, continuity must be considered, as the police officer who moves articles of interest should—technically—exhibit them. Local protocols should be followed on this issue. Details of investigative forensic procedures are covered in Chapter 26.

11.2.5.1   Preventing Contamination

Contamination is the transfer of trace evidence by any means other than direct or indirect involvement with the crime, be it accidental or deliberate. The term is also broadly used to describe damage to evidence or altering its state in some way that is not required for its preservation. Consider the contamination issues regarding vehicles, prisoners, and colleagues. For example, if a police officer is tasked to deal with a suspect and has previously been to the crime scene, then he/she could potentially contaminate the suspect with material from the scene. This may reduce the value of evidence that links the suspect with the crime scene.

Certain forms of forensic evidence are, in all practical senses, incontrovertible (eg DNA evidence, see 26.5.3). Nonetheless, such evidence will be scrutinized by the defence in a criminal case, with the intention of casting doubt on the integrity of an exhibit (see 11.2.6) and to have it disallowed by the judge. An effective defence team will look for errors in continuity, packaging, and handling, and for any possible source of contamination. The following general advice applies to reduce the risk of contamination:

- wear new surgical-type gloves and a face mask, as a minimum, when dealing with exhibits or whilst inside a crime scene. (In the absence of a face mask, at the very least, all persons present should avoid coughing or talking over exhibits.);
- store exhibits properly to prevent decay and damage. Property stores should be cool and dry. Electronic exhibits should not be stored on plastic shelving or sources of magnetic fields (motors and speakers for example);
- never deal with exhibits from two facets of the same offence, such as from the victim and the suspect;
- do not deal with clothing from one person in an offence (eg take it out of packaging) in a room that has previously been used for sampling another person;
- do not place a prisoner in a cell until it has been cleaned.

In relation to vehicles, two people from the same offence (such as victim and suspect) should never be conveyed in the same vehicle, even at separate times, until all parties have been forensically examined. Police vehicles which could contain blood in any form should be cleaned or washed down once any forensic examination has been completed, and all patrol cars should be regularly and fastidiously valeted.

11.2.6   Exhibits and exhibiting

According to common law 'it is within the power of, and is the duty of, constables to retain for use in court things which may be evidence of crime' (*R v Lushington, ex p Otto* [1894] 1 QB 420). The 'things' can include physical objects, such as a knife, and are often referred to as exhibits (as they may be exhibited to a court or 'shown to a witness [at interview] and referred to by him in his evidence' (ibid)). The ruling in *Lushington* from 1894 later formed the basis of important sections of the PACE Act 1984 (s 19 on the seizure of material, s 20 in relation to computers and digital evidence, and s 22 which describes police powers to retain seized material). Under a Code of Practice within the Criminal Procedure and Investigations Act 1996, any police officer investigating alleged crimes 'has a duty to record and retain material which may be relevant to the investigation' (see 24.3.2 on recording and retaining).

A police officer or a member of the public who finds an article which may be used as evidence should 'exhibit' it, which involves formally recording certain details about the object. If the item was originally found by a member of the public, then this process will be completed by a police officer, but the finder's initials and name will be recorded on the exhibit label and used as part of the exhibit number. The police officer will also be responsible for taking a statement from the person about how and where it was found. The items will be packaged and labelled by the police officer who found or received the item from a member of the public. Police officers and CSIs are advised not to accept an unpackaged exhibit from anyone other than a member of the public, as this is a potential cause of contamination.

The item must be properly packaged to preserve the evidence (see 26.7 for details) and labelled. Packaging materials normally have labels printed on the outer surface which can be used for noting facts; otherwise a simple label can be affixed. For labelling, the basic information required is:

- **name** of the person exhibiting (ie the person who first found the item);
- an **exhibit number**: normally the initials of the person exhibiting the item and a sequential number (see 10.11.1 for an example);
- a **description**, which should be brief and to the point—to prevent other people shortening the description for convenience (index numbers or serial numbers should be included for clarity); and
- the **date, time, and place** the exhibit was found;

It is the mark of a professional to make detailed notes about the exhibit to assist other investigators. If detailed and accurate records are not kept about the contents of a package, another person might open it to check the contents, and this could cause contamination. Detailed notes should be made about any identifying marks, the size of clothing, any damage or stains, any logos or identifying features, serial numbers, and the precise location of the exhibit and its orientation. The procedures for storing items as they come into police possession are described in 10.9.

11.2.6.1   Signing exhibit labels

The exhibit label records the **continuity** (or chain of custody) of the exhibit. Ideally, the chain should be unbroken from its seizure until it arrives at court, so every person who takes control of the exhibit should sign the label (and later write a statement) unless local protocols dictate otherwise. The movement of bulk quantities of exhibits is often recorded on a *pro forma* by the driver, and major crime exhibits officers do not normally write a statement for every receipt of every exhibit. If, however, police officer X temporarily passes a packaged exhibit to officer Y for comment but it remains in X's custody, then Y need not sign the label. An example might be where X asks for a casual opinion, for example 'Is this a ball-peen hammer?' However, if another person Z gives a professional opinion or transports the exhibit to another place, then Z should sign the label and write a statement describing his/her actions.

11.2.6.2   Firearms as exhibits

Safety must always be considered when dealing with firearms as exhibits. That said, firearms are excellent sources of evidence. They provide ballistics evidence, and their smooth surfaces are good sources of fingerprints, and DNA can be collected from their rough control surfaces such as the grip, slide, and trigger (and from the muzzle if it has been in contact with skin or saliva). We will look at the different types of firearm and the associated law in Chapter 18.

All police forces will have strict protocols in place for entering firing ranges, accepting weapons from members of the public, and seizing them during searches. For health and safety reasons, all personnel at a crime scene should treat every weapon as if it is loaded and call for a firearms officer to make it safe. For weapons suspected of being involved in crimes it is normal practice for a photographer or CSI to be present during the making-safe process. Whilst making it safe a firearm should not be pointed at the floor or wall if people could be below or on the other side of the wall. None of the controls should be tampered with apart from those necessary to make it safe, nor should it be 'dry-fired'.

In addition no-one should:

- handle or move a firearm unnecessarily or move, or drop another article onto a firearm;
- move a firearm by poking a pen, or any other object, into the barrel or trigger guard;
- stand in front of a firearm or point a firearm at any person, even when 'made safe'.

Every person who handles a firearm should clearly demonstrate that it is safe, for example when passing it to or receiving it from another person. In terms of labeling, there may be force policies for firearms at scenes or in storage (often a red label means it has not been made safe, and a green label that it has). Loaded firearms should not be conveyed to the police station or laboratory unless this is necessary and suitable safety measures are in place.

Above all: presume every firearm is loaded and ready to fire. In reality, very few guns can fire by being dropped or knocked, since the majority of them have in-built safety features, but the consequence of a weapon firing by accident can obviously be extremely serious.

11.2.7 Attending major crime scenes

At the scene of a major crime many of the actions that should be taken by the first attending officer (the FAO: see 11.2.1) are common to the procedures to be followed at any crime scene. The FAO should attempt to:

* provide First Aid and get assistance from an ambulance crew, when necessary;
* cordon off the scene (as wide as practicable) and refrain from entering the scene and prevent unauthorized entry, except to preserve life or prevent further damage; and
* create a CAP for all who come to the crime scene (see 11.2.2) and begin a 'scene attendance log' (see 11.2.3).

If deaths have occurred the bodies should not be covered, but if they are in public view the public should be removed or screening should be installed until the first attending CSI arrives with a small tent.

Evidence collection can also commence, such as recording witness details and any comments they make, and recording if anything is disturbed or moved. Assistance may be needed to preserve the scene. It is vital to maintain communication with the force control centre and keep them informed. The FAO should also of course remain calm, be positive, and manage the situation until help arrives.

> **TASK 1** In what ways might the subsequent investigation into a major crime differ from other investigations?

Most police forces have specialist (often centrally based) departments or units which deal with major crime investigations. The investigation is headed usually by a specially trained senior investigating officer, usually at least a detective inspector or detective chief inspector. Many of the elements involved in investigating major crime have been covered elsewhere in the Handbook and we do not repeat them here.

11.3 Incidents Involving Deaths

Police officers will almost certainly encounter death and injury as the result of major and critical incidents. However, for other incidents a person may have died through natural causes such as illness and old age; for example, the local police station might be called by the neighbour of an elderly person to report that they have not seen them for some time or that there are other circumstances which give cause for concern. Of course, these situations are not restricted to the elderly: it is a particularly distressing task to attend a scene of the death of a child or young person.

Any death which occurs outside the hospital environment and is in some way unexpected is referred to in police circles as a 'sudden death'. All sudden deaths will be subject to some form of investigation, but of course this does not mean that the death is associated with criminal activity. A police officer in early attendance at a scene of a fatality could reflect on the following:

* Is the event which probably caused death at this scene likely or possible? (For example: could this banister support this body?)
* For a suicide, were the means available to the victim?
* Are any of the injuries puzzling? (For instance there may be unexplained bruises to limbs or the head and neck.)
* Would the victim have been physically capable of the act? (Was he/she strong or tall enough? Could a woman of this stature have pulled the trigger on a rifle and shot herself?)
* Is there any sign of a struggle? (The location may appear particularly disordered, but it could have been like that anyway.)
* Is anything apparently missing? (eg an ornament, jewellery box, firearm, or car—and what is the evidence for this?)
* Is there evidence of a possible forced entry? (Damaged door locks, scratched or dented paintwork around windows, footwear marks on doors, and splintered frames are all suspicious, but there may be an entirely innocent explanation.)
* Does the position or state of the body fit logically with the information received?

If there is any uncertainty, the scene can be treated as 'suspicious' until proven otherwise.

11.3.1 Police actions for incidents with deaths

The general procedure to follow for sudden deaths will vary from force to force, although all subscribe to certain basic principles (and relate to the procedures for attendance at a crime scene: see 11.2). A police officer should:

1. ensure his/her own safety before approaching, as the scene of a death can be dangerous (particularly if there have been multiple deaths);
2. decide whether there is a chance the person is still alive: could First Aid be administered—is an ambulance required?
3. establish and use a CAP (see 11.2.2) to preserve the scene;
4. touch nothing until a visual inspection has been made and beware of bodies in contact with live electrical systems, as well as toxic fumes, poisons, firearms, needles, and body fluids;
5. consider that any death might be the result of crime if it is in any way suspicious.

The officer should make a PNB entry (see 10.2) which records the location, position, and general description of the body, including any visible injuries. Any evidence should also be noted, such as physical evidence in the immediate area, or from witnesses. Obviously, if the identity of the deceased is known this should be included—any relatives or friends who are present can be asked.

There are also administrative considerations. The attending officer should arrange for the death to be certified by a doctor, nurse, or paramedic, and take any paperwork they produce. If they have disturbed the scene in any way the time and nature of the disturbance should be noted. A supervisory CID officer and CSI should be contacted as appropriate for any unexpected death (such as unexplained, apparent suicide, accident, fire, decomposed remains, etc). If the victim is under the age of 18 then this must be reported clearly to the control room because an investigative policy regarding the deaths of children will be activated. If the deceased is a visiting serviceman/woman (on or off duty), the Visiting Forces Act 1952 may be relevant (regardless of whether the death is suspicious). The investigation could then be taken over by a foreign authority, such as the US Air Force, but the police should meanwhile maintain control of the investigation.

The officer should take control of the scene and anything within it or near it which may be associated with the death (a weapon, drugs, alcohol bottles, suicide note). If the death is not suspicious then force policy may require the officer to search the deceased for signs of injury and to take from him/her any valuables—these should be packaged and stored securely according to local protocols. Any sudden death could be the result of a crime, so an investigative mindset should be employed throughout the process even if the circumstances appear to be innocent, because there is a possibility that the scene has been staged in order to delay or prevent a murder investigation.

After the examination at the scene the body will be removed. If relatives need to be informed this must be done as soon as possible by a police officer (in person unless the conditions are exceptional). Police forces across the UK carry out this task for each other when distance makes it difficult. A family liaison officer can be used in cases of murders, roads fatalities and other incidents.

You should also be aware that police officers are likely to suffer psychologically as a result of dealing with a sudden death. Whilst many appear to shrug off what they have seen they may still be affected, perhaps by depression or post-traumatic stress disorder (PTSD). Any person who is accustomed to taking control in difficult situations may feel powerless and overwhelmed when confronted by the distress of relatives, and the very fact that they are unaccustomed to such feeling can cause additional difficulties. You should be aware of a variety of possible effects of this on police officers, ranging from being generally upset to severe changes in behaviour. Some officers are not apparently affected by a large-scale incident, yet may become upset at a single death when they identify (in some way) with the deceased, or their family and friends. Every police force has structures in place to provide support and assistance: getting help is not a sign of weakness.

11.3.2 **Certifying death**

Where there might be the slightest chance a victim is alive, medical assistance should be obtained. A medical professional (a doctor, nurse, or ambulance crew) is required to attend the scene to certify that death has occurred or to make a ROLE (see 11.2.3.1). There are some exceptions to this rule based upon the notion that a person is 'obviously dead' but, for the trainee officer it is better to err on the side of caution and seek advice. This author, on one occasion, reluctantly called a police surgeon to a skeleton.

> **TASK 2** Suggest a type of injury which would definitely cause death (and therefore not require a medical professional to certify death).

The procedure for certifying death depends on whether the death was expected or unexpected, as shown in the diagram.

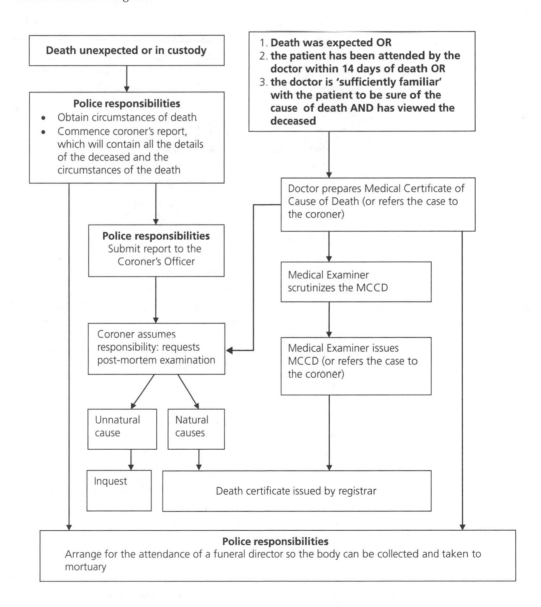

In April 2012 the system permitting doctors to certify death became more complex owing to the offences committed by Dr Harold Shipman. Doctors should now prepare a Medical Certificate of Cause of Death (MCCD), to be scrutinized by 'Medical Examiners' (a doctor not associated with the MCCD) before being fully issued. This process is expected to be implemented throughout England and Wales in April 2018, but in the meantime, follow local force protocols.

11.3.3   Investigations and changes to the body after death

The body changes quite quickly after death, and this can assist investigations. The most immediate change is the colour of the skin: having lost its blood flow it can appear lifeless and wax-like within a few seconds.

Hypostasis occurs when the blood settles to the lowest parts and enters the skin creating a port-wine-coloured stain. This is also known as post-mortem lividity or *livor mortis*. It occurs because the blood drains downwards, so where a body is upright, blood drains to the lower parts of the limbs, cheeks, and ears. After three to four hours, the blood clots (solidifies) and can no longer flow, so if the body is subsequently moved, the dark areas will no longer be on the lower or underside parts of the body. Pressure can cause distortion to the pattern of hypostasis; any areas of skin that have been under pressure will be pale because they are uncoloured by blood. These effects can be produced by the texture of fabrics and clothing seams, and even by floor tiles.

Rigor mortis occurs when chemical changes in the muscles gradually cause them to stiffen. The process normally begins in the head and works down the body. In very general terms it might start after four hours and disappear after 24 hours (when the body begins to break down biologically). However, the process is dependent upon a number of factors, particularly the ambient temperature (the process is quicker at higher temperatures). Crucially, immediately after death the body becomes limp and will flop to rest on adjacent structures, and if left for a number of hours, rigor mortis will stiffen it in that position. If subsequently moved, the body will be rigid and fixed in that initial posture—it will not flop against the surrounding structures.

The core temperature of the deceased will equalize with the ambient temperature after death, so it will usually fall in the UK climate. The relationship between the lowering of the core temperature and the ambient temperature is well documented but not so reliable (as is commonly depicted on television) that the pathologist can give an estimate of the time of death to within a few minutes. The ambient temperature, amount of clothing, and general health of the victim may all affect the temperature drop. Then, due to decay and insect activity, the body temperature may increase.

Other changes to the body will depend on the conditions. If the weather is not too cold it will begin to break down quite rapidly, which may attract a variety of animals which will feed upon it. Blowflies are the most mobile carrion feeders and will appear first, followed by successive waves of insects and other animals. The results include putrefaction and even dispersal of bones over time. In hot or dry environments the body may become mummified. The process of change in a body after death is covered by a specialist field: forensic taphonomy.

In relation to suicides there are some commonly held expectations, but many of these are untrue (or at least only partly true). These expectations (with the reality in brackets) include that:

- There should be a suicide note (but not every suicide victim writes a note);
- Women never shoot themselves in the face (some do);
- Farmers always use a shotgun (many do not);
- Vets always use animal tranquilizers or other drugs (many do);
- Those who cut their wrists or throats always make tentative cuts first (many do).

Suspicion and an enquiring mind can be beneficial at any sudden death but investigators should rely on observation and experience rather than generalization. The chief issues with suicide are that the person must have had access to the object which caused their death and must have been physically capable of committing the act.

11.3.4   Murder investigations

Murder investigations involve a huge investment of police time and resources. Most murders are committed by close family members, or others known to the victim, and although the circumstances leading to such events are often shocking on a domestic scale, it is the abduction and murder by strangers (particularly of children) which attracts most media attention and police resources.

> **TASK 3** What is the CATCHEM database and what does it tell us about a particular category of victims and their murderers?

The level of resources put into a murder investigation depends on the classification of the murder. Murders are classified as Category (Cat) A, B, or C within a more general system of categorizing major crime. Cat A and Cat B murder investigations will be led by an SIO who will probably be centrally based, while a Cat C murder could be investigated by detectives in a local BCU. However, there are variations on these basic categories, and a Cat C murder can often turn out to be more complicated than first thought, requiring more than just a local response.

The 'Murder Investigation Manual' (the 'MIM') and the 'Practice Advice on Core Investigative Doctrine' (ACPO, 2006a and ACPO Centrex, 2005, respectively) offer an investigative model which will be used as the template for major violent crime enquiries by most police forces. The model consists of five stages (fast track, theoretical process, planned method of investigation, suspect enquiries, and disposal).

> **TASK 4** Imagine you are a trainee police officer. You are called to a crime scene in a part of town with many multiple-occupancy dwellings. The body of a young woman is slumped on the floor of a blood-splattered bed-sitting room. Curious and worried onlookers are present, and the landlord of the property (who discovered the body) is nervously waiting for you just inside the bedsit door. He says that he heard a disturbance and a lot of screaming. He used his master key to open the door and has not touched anything. What do you do to ensure proper incident management, remembering Stage One of the MIM includes 'crime-scene and evidence preservation'? What are your tasks in priority order?

11.4 Railway Incidents and Fires

Railway property and any scene where there is (or has been) a fire present particular risks. The policing of most railways and the London Underground is the responsibility of British Transport Police (BTP) but there are occasions where other forces will be engaged in activities relating to railway property. This could include the pursuit of suspects, searching railway property for missing persons or property related to crime, assisting at incidents and accidents, or providing cover when BTP are not immediately available. BTP officers' training is augmented by Personal Track Safety (PTS) courses: most other police forces do not offer this certification.

11.4.1 Incidents and offences on railway property

Railways and their associated infrastructure are exceptionally dangerous places. The risks include:

- being struck by a train whilst crossing a track (even at a level crossing or pedestrian gate);
- being struck by a train whilst walking onto a track to retrieve property, rescue a pet, or another person;
- electrocution by the 'third rail' or overhead power lines, or by signaling equipment;
- bumps, trips, and falls.

The electrical conductors which carry the power for trains are either a third rail or overhead, suspended between gantries. It should always be assumed that such conductors are 'live' because the power runs continuously and is not switched off when no train is present. Given that they carry so much power, death is almost certain if a person or anything they are touching comes into contact with railway power conductors. Overhead power lines can also arc, transmitting electricity through the air to nearby objects. If a person has fallen onto the third rail there is nothing which can realistically be done until the power is turned off, and police officers should be absolutely certain that this has been done before acting in such circumstances; there is no room for ambiguity. Further dangers are posed by 'rolling stock' (engines and carriages), particularly as in modern trains these are fast and relatively silent in operation. Railway apparatus (ie railway equipment other than rolling stock) is also dangerous: electrical components, moving parts, and trip hazards are universal. Therefore, police officers engaged on foot pursuits or assisting on railway property, for example at a station, should continuously consider their safety and those of colleagues and the public. **Essentially: there is no reward worth the risk of stepping onto a railway line.** Most force policies will require the abandonment of foot pursuits if the suspect enters railway property, unless there is an immediate risk to life and the officer feels that the situation warrants entry to the track area (after a dynamic risk assessment).

For searches, special measures called 'Safe Systems of Work' (eg stopping trains and cutting the power) should be arranged before carrying out *any* search on operating railway lines or associated property, and it is wise to post a lookout for any carriages or engines that are still moving, however slowly. When searches of railway property are required, close negotiation with Network Rail and train operating companies is essential to reduce the risk of accidents and—where practicable—minimize disturbance to the network. BTP would be pleased to accommodate other forces in this respect. Under the Railway Safety Accreditation Scheme, BTP can accredit organizations and selected personnel with powers to deal with anti-social behaviour by issuing Fixed Penalty Notices and enforcing by-laws. Their presence is intended to act as a visible deterrent and reassurance as well as to free up BTP officers for more frontline duties.

Apart from the common offences which might be committed on railways, such as thefts (especially of cables), attacks on ticket machines, assaults, and criminal damage, specific legislation applies for crime and trespass on the railway network. Some of it is quite old, and 'translation' of the Victorian English can be difficult.

11.4.1.1 Trespass and authorized crossing point offences

Under s 16 of the Railway Regulation Act 1840 it is an offence to wilfully trespass on any railway or railway premises and to refuse to leave when asked to do so by any officer or agent of the railway company. The wilful behaviour is evidenced by a **refusal to leave**. The Regulation of Railways Act 1868 prohibits a person from crossing a railway line other than in an authorized place (eg level crossings or and pedestrian crossings). Under s 23 a person commits an offence if he/she crosses at an unauthorized place after being warned to desist by a servant or agent of the railway company.

Nearly a century later the British Transport Commission Act 1949 added legislation on trespass to cover trespass along 'railway lines, embankments, tunnels and sidings or any "works" (equipment) and electrical installations' (s 55). The section raises the issue of being in 'dangerous proximity' of lines and electrical installations. It is important to note that the investigating officer must produce evidence of a notice exhibited at the station nearest the place of the offence providing a clear public warning not to trespass on a railway. These signs are most obviously seen at the ends of platforms and at pedestrian and level crossings. The trespass is a summary offence and can be dealt with by a £60 PND (see 10.13.2.1).

11.4.1.2 Throwing objects and causing damage to railway property

Section 56 of the British Transport Commission Act 1949 makes it an offence to throw, or cause to fall, any object (stone, or thing likely to cause damage) into or upon any rolling stock or static equipment on any railway or siding or any 'works' or which is likely to cause injury. It is immaterial whether the train or equipment is in motion or is static. This is a summary offence and can be dealt with by a £60 PND (see 10.13.2.1).

The Offences Against the Person Act 1861 is a more complex but overarching piece of legislation which discusses 'unlawfully and maliciously' throwing or causing objects to fall. If an intent to injure or endanger any person on a train can be proved, then an offence has been committed (ss 32 and 33). Drunkenness and failing to follow by-laws is covered in s 34. Section 17 of the Railway Regulation Act 1842 applies for misconduct by railway employees.

The Malicious Damage Act 1861 (s 35) covers placing items (eg a railway sleeper), on a railway, and also covers the removal of rails, turning (or switching) points, and showing or hiding signals. There must be intent to obstruct, overthrow, damage, or destroy an engine, carriage, or truck. This offence is triable on indictment only and the maximum penalty is life imprisonment. Section 36 deals specifically with obstructing engines, or carriages, or railways. The offence is triable either way and it is not necessary to prove intent.

11.4.2 Attending a fire

Fires are caused by the oxidation of fuel which creates heat. In order for a fire to occur three elements are required: a fuel source (such as furniture, hay, or petrol), oxygen, and an external heat source to cause ignition. Once a fire has started the heat generated can speed up the rate of burning so yet more heat energy is liberated, causing a chain reaction effect. A fire can be extinguished by removing one of the three elements; removing the fuel, starving the fire of oxygen, or reducing the temperature with water. Fires in buildings will often self-extinguish or just smoulder once most of the available fuel or oxygen has been consumed. In such a situation opening a door or window will introduce fresh air (containing oxygen) to any remaining hot fuel, and the fire can suddenly explode into an inferno within seconds. The heat from fires spreads by convection (hot air rises), conduction (heat travels through solid objects), and radiation (glowing heat that crosses empty space). Fires can grow very fast, and the chain reaction effect means that small fires, which appear to be insignificant, can spread quite rapidly. During a drought the fuel load in outdoor environments such as grasslands, forests, and gardens, is so dry that the fire spreads far faster than would normally be expected.

Fires are emotional scenes: occupants of buildings and those whose homes have been damaged or destroyed will be suffering from a combination of fear, relief at surviving, anger, grief, and utter despair at perhaps losing everything they own. There may be irrational or angry outbursts levelled at anyone, and this might include physical assault. A number of agencies are available to assist such victims, for example the local authority can provide temporary accommodation, and practical assistance may be sought from the Salvation Army or Citizens' Advice. If a family member or colleague has died or been injured as a result, then more specialist support can be arranged through Victim Support, the NHS, a Family Liaison Officer (FLO), and charities such as Cruse Bereavement Care.

11.4.2.1   The role of the police at fires

The overriding principle at fire scenes is to prevent the loss of life (including police officers' lives) and to take action to save lives. The critical issue of your own safety as a police officer is covered in 6.12, and this principle extends to fighting fires: police officers should not attempt to take action against anything but the smallest of fires. Police officers have powers under s 17 of the PACE Act 1984 to enter a premises to save life or prevent damage, and PCSOs have powers under the Police Reform Act 2002, Sch 4, Part 1, but no unnecessary risks should be taken to save lives, protect property, or rescue animals.

Police officers at a fire scene where the Fire and Rescue Service (FRS) is not in attendance should employ the METHANE mnemonic (see 11.5.2). During the early phase of an incident response officers may decide that a fire is small enough to tackle with available fire-fighting equipment (or imaginative use of a hose or towel). But it may seem that the fire could spread and grow. Whatever the verdict, the control room must be kept informed. They will contact the FRS who will decide whether or not to attend. The control room will also contact relevant security companies, homeowners, and key holders of houses or businesses so that they can take appropriate action. If there is any conceivable risk to people in nearby properties, the street, or in passing vehicles then decisive action must be taken: evacuate all nearby properties and keep everybody clear. Follow the old adage: GET OUT and STAY OUT. If the FRS is already in attendance the FAO should make contact with the senior fire officer present and act as a conduit for information at the scene. Police officers are likely to have relevant local knowledge about occupants, business activity on the premises, and/or information about any perceived risks or relevant force contingency plans in place in the area.

People in or near the fire may already have burning clothes or hair, but these can also 'spontaneously combust' at a distance due to the radiant heat. Such victims may well panic and be unable to follow advice. They should be pushed into a lying position on the ground, and the flames smothered with a coat or blanket. The horizontal position is particularly important to prevent convected heat rising from burning clothes and damaging the eyes and mouth. Victims may need urgent first aid and hospitalization, but early decisive actions can save lives and reduce further injury.

Putting out the fire and saving lives is the role of the FRS, but police officers can assist by controlling the public (s 37 of the Road Traffic Act 1988), assisting with evacuations, and closing roads (ss 35 and 163) as appropriate. If the cause of the fire is unknown or suspicious then force policy will almost certainly require the attendance of a patrol supervisor or inspector, CID, and a CSI. An incident may be deemed to be 'serious' if injury or significant loss occurs, and an appropriate police response and investigation will take place.

Any large fire will inevitably attract onlookers, many of whom will merely wish to watch, but some may be intent on stealing rescued property or may even try to enter the property to steal. Scene security, management of the public, and a continuing eye on traffic problems need to be maintained. Some arsonists will return to observe the activity at the scene and a few may even obstruct attempts to extinguish the fire. At one fire in Kent, the offender repeatedly attempted to disable the fire hydrant in the street outside a fire until police arrived and arrested him. We cover offences that may be committed by persons obstructing firefighters in 11.4.2.2.

11.4.2.2 Fire and Rescue Service powers and obstruction offences

The Fire and Rescue Services Act 2004 confers a number of powers on the FRS and its members in relation to emergencies, particularly for incidents which are likely to cause death or serious illness or injury, or where there may be serious harm to the environment and any plants or animals in it. This applies for fires or situations where there is a major risk of a fire, road traffic incidents, other types of emergency, and also covers actions required to prevent consequent damage to property (s 44(1)). Authorized FRS staff can enter premises by force, move or break into vehicles, close roads, control the traffic, and restrict access in order to achieve these aims (s 44(2)).

If a person interferes with or obstructs firefighters in the course of their work, he/she could be charged with an offence under the Emergency Workers (Obstruction) Act 2006 (EWOA) or the Fire and Rescue Services Act 2004, for example:

- obstructing or hindering personnel engaged in emergency operations when extinguishing a fire or protecting life and property in relation to a fire (or going anywhere to deal with it or prepare for it) (s 1 EWOA);
- obstructing a person who is assisting a firefighter (s 2 EWOA);
- obstructing or interfering with an employee of a fire authority who is entering a property or vehicle by force, or carrying out other emergency work under s 44 of the Fire and Rescue Services Act.

The full Acts are available on the www.legislation.gov.uk website.

11.5 Attending Emergency, Major, and Critical Incidents

Initial police training is likely to cover the police role in handling emergencies, major incidents, and critical incidents, and emergencies. These are all similar in terms of their scale and significance, and it is for this reason that we have grouped them together in this part of Chapter 11. Trainee officers are most likely to attend genuine emergency scenes out of all of these types of incident. Further information is available from the College of Policing website.

An **emergency** is defined by s 1 of the Civil Contingencies Act 2004 as 'an event or situation which threatens serious damage to human welfare in a place in the United Kingdom' including one or more of the following:

- human illness or injury or loss of life;
- homelessness or damage to property;
- disruption of a supply of money, food, water, energy, or fuel;
- disruption of transport, communication, or health systems and services;
- serious environmental damage (eg radioactive contamination);
- war or terrorism which threatens serious damage to the security of the UK.

A **major incident** is an emergency that requires the implementation of special arrangements by one or all of the emergency services, or that involves a significant number of people, and could require:

- the initial treatment, rescue, and transportation of a large number of casualties;
- the handling of a large number of enquiries likely to be generated both from the public and the news media, usually made to the police;
- the need for large-scale combined resources of the police and other agencies such as the Fire and Rescue Service and Ambulance Service or Trust;
- the mobilization and organization of the emergency services and partner organizations, for example a local authority, to cater for the threat of death, serious injury, or homelessness to a large number of people.

(Adapted from material provided by Wiltshire Police, no date.)

A **critical incident** is 'any incident where the effectiveness of the police response is likely to have a significant impact on the confidence of the victim, their family and/or the community' (College of Policing, 2013). Any incident—such as harassment—can escalate to being critical, while other incidents are often clearly significant in the early phases (such as an apparent murder, train crash, or a large fire).

Police officers in training will practise and rehearse effective ways to intervene to resolve a problem such as a domestic dispute, dealing with a shoplifter, or calming people down who have been involved in a minor road collision. They will learn to defuse, control, restrain, or manage any of a great variety of incidents. But what about an incident which has the potential to 'go major' and get really out of hand? There are fewer opportunities for practising for such events.

TASK 5 Try and imagine what your first response would be if you were the first police officer to arrive at:

- a serious road collision;
- the scene of a brawl in which someone had been knifed;
- an accident on a railway line;
- a burning house where people are trapped on upper floors; or
- a situation where a child is being held hostage.

What would your responsibilities be, as opposed to your instincts? What would you be expected to do? Is there an order in which you should do things? What seem to be the priorities at the scene? What should be your priorities at the scene? What communication is needed and with whom?

Every force and every emergency service will have contingency plans to deal with a wide range of emergencies and incidents, and for some types of incident this will be a legal requirement under the Civil Contingencies Act 2004. There will be generic plans for certain types of emergency such as an aircraft crash, an influenza pandemic, or a siege incident with a hostage.

Large-scale incidents of any type are not simply 'dealt with' and then closed: there are serious issues to consider surrounding the impact upon the community at large, such as a fear of further crime and disorder, or where the public's expectations of the police have not been met. Thus the perception of a high level of vulnerability, the scale of the incident and the feelings held by victims and families must be appropriately addressed through effective communication which must be managed closely. Liaison with victims, their families and the community at large is important for a number of reasons, not least of which is to restore public confidence.

11.5.1 Early priorities at a major incident

The actions of first police officer on the scene are crucial to the proper and managed outcome of the incident, and relying on instinct is not sufficient in such situations. For example, at a large brawl in a club, bringing the scene under control is not best effected by an officer wading into the middle of the fracas and grabbing someone at random—this is likely to provoke more violence. House-fire incidents may also tempt a trainee officer to act heroically, but without the proper apparatus or an understanding of how fires develop (see 11.4.2) and the risk of structural collapse of the building, he/she may become a victim rather than a rescuer. A police officer needs to follow proper procedures, and to think and act calmly and rationally in order to:

- assess the situation and work out what is going on;
- communicate as quickly as possible; and
- prioritize actions.

TASK 6 Imagine you are a police officer attending an incident in which a man with a hostage appears to have barricaded himself into a semi-detached house in a cul-de-sac. About a dozen people are milling about, and the event has been described to you by two very excited and incoherent witnesses. You have one other police officer to assist you. Assuming that police back-up will arrive within ten minutes and other emergency services (fire and rescue service, ambulance) are also on their way (with an estimated time of arrival of 15 minutes), what would be your list of things to do in priority order at such an incident?

The FAO is in control of the incident (as 'Silver', the forward Commander: see 11.5.3) until he/she is relieved by someone of superior rank. The incident may include a crime scene, so preservation of evidence and keeping the scene clear and untouched is very important. In an emergency involving firearms or the risk of violence, the FAO would not let other emergency services go forward into the 'line of fire' either. Most ambulance trusts will not permit their personnel to enter firearms-related crime scenes as a matter of safety: consider that North West Ambulance Service forbade its staff from approaching the multiple scenes involved in the 'rampage' of Derrick Bird in 2010.

It is actually unlikely that a FAO would be alone for that long, unless the incident is in a really remote and inaccessible place, or there are corollary problems (such as a natural disaster of some kind) and access roads are blocked. A senior officer may arrive quite quickly but, if not, the golden hour is the responsibility of the officers present. All this sounds complicated and difficult to remember; however, training and experience enable police officers to maintain clear priorities and to follow procedures properly, acting calmly, positively, purposefully, and promptly.

11.5.2 METHANE

The **METHANE** mnemonic sets out the standard College of Policing APP procedure for emergencies (and replaces the previously used CHALETS mnemonic). The table outlines the key aspects of the procedure, and further information is available under *Civil Contingencies* on the College of Policing website.

M	Major?	Should a major incident be declared?
E	Exact?	What is the exact location of the incident?
T	Type?	What type of incident is it? Is there a threat to life? Is there a fire or the risk of a building collapse? Some other serious incident such as a sudden death?
H	Hazards?	Are any hazards present or suspected? There may be immediate dangers such as a fire or flood or potential dangers such as flood water or the presence of hazardous substances.
A	Access?	How is the incident accessed? What are the safest routes into and out of the venue? Where should the RVP be situated?
N	Number?	What is the number, type and severity of casualties? Identify the number of casualties and what seems to be wrong with them. How severe are their injuries?
E	Emergency services?	What emergency services are present and are others needed? Fire and rescue service/ambulance/coastguard?

Out of all the services that may attend such an incident, only the police will be constantly alert to the possibility that a crime has been committed, and that the emergency, major, or critical incident could also be a crime scene (see 11.2). For example, after a road traffic collision, consideration must be given as to whether the driver was under the influence of drink or drugs; and after a fall from a height, did the woman fall or was she pushed; is this a natural or a suspicious death? Police officers should be suspicious and be alert to any signatures or characteristic signs that there is something wrong. For example, a witness may remark 'funny thing—that man hanging round all morning', or an officer may spot an article at the scene (or nearby), such as an empty wallet or purse. This might suggest that all is not what it seems, and problem-solving skills can help clarify ideas.

> **TASK 7** Describe a problem-solving and decision-making model you have encountered.

11.5.3 Control and responsibility

There is a standard command sequence in use in all police forces across the UK. The levels refer to the function of the command level and not necessarily to the rank of the officers concerned (see the College of Policing Authorised Professional Practice website on *Operations and Command Structures* for further information).

Levels of Command

Gold	Strategic command of the incident, usually at police headquarters or at a designated strategic police command centre
Silver	Tactical police command at a forward point closer to the scene of immediate crisis
Bronze	Operational local response at the crisis point itself (eg cordons or firearms), often carried out by a number of people (Operational Response Commanders or ORC), rather than one designated commander

When a more senior officer becomes available the command level will transfer to the officer with the higher rank. Therefore whilst on Independent or Supervised Patrol a trainee officer may be 'Silver' for a short period of time before a more senior or more experienced officer arrives on the scene. This tiered structure is considered by many in the police service to work effectively (and has been exhaustively tested) at local or force level and also at national level.

A risk assessment must be carried out to facilitate a proportionate response in the right sequence. The senior officer carrying out the assessment will ask the person who is 'Silver' at the time for information about the situation.

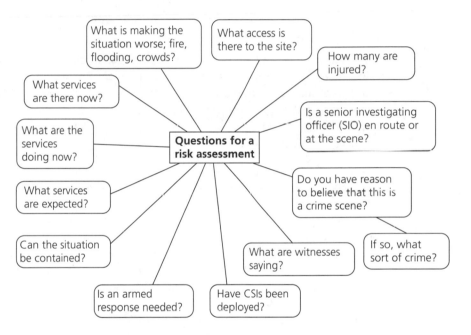

Resources should not be committed too early, unless there is a clear picture of what is happening on the ground, because over-resourcing is wasteful and inefficient. Police officers attending an incident are clearly not available for deployment elsewhere, and swamping a site with armed officers, dog teams, and underwater search teams is not necessary if the incident turns out to be trivial.

In the case of missing persons (especially when there may be other factors, possibly criminal) there are many components to the response: search teams are called out, assessments of transport needs are made, command and control, strategic, and tactical responses are all set up, and the control room will alert other emergency services. For larger incidents the invoking of 'military aid to the civil power' (MACP) might be required. Specialists such as explosives ordnance (bomb disposal), helicopters, search and rescue, engineers, nuclear, chemical, and radiological detection and containment units, and a host of others may be called upon. Note that deployment of armed officers is usually a top-level command decision ('Gold'), made by a chief superintendent or chief officer.

TASK 8 What problems might potentially arise within command structures? Make a list of what could go wrong and what would avoid problems.

At some incidents there may be bystanders, and they may be a help or a hindrance. Control of people's movements is essential, even at a relatively limited incident. Well-intentioned people may offer to help and any volunteers can be used effectively to direct and contain people, to direct traffic, and conduct evacuation until more help arrives. However, bystanders may not always be so helpful; police and other emergency service support can be delayed because of 'rubber-neckers'—passers-by who want to see what is going on. This is often an impediment to effective scene management, and police officers should always be prepared to move such onlookers away from the incident. There is another and very important reason why the area itself must be controlled: it could be a crime scene, and controlling access and the preservation of evidence is of absolutely vital importance (see 11.2).

Newspapers, internet sites, Twitter, social network sites, radio, and television have apparently inexhaustible appetites for crime stories. This quest for the news story has produced an edgy, sometimes fraught, relationship between the media and the police. The media can definitely help with appeals for information to help solve complex crimes, raise awareness of danger, alert the public to emergencies or major disruption, or appeal for help with searches for missing people. The media offer the potential to engage with large numbers of people very quickly and locate suspects or witnesses who have left the local area. However, the media can also be rather superficial and sensationalist in an endless quest for headlines (see Leishman and Mason (2003) for more detail).

The management of information from the police must be carefully monitored. Too much information could put informants at risk, limit the range of questions that could be asked to a potential suspect, or result in the disposal of crucial evidence. Withholding information from the media can provide the police with a broader range of investigative tactics; unfair presentation of witnesses, victims, or suspects by the media can undermine their credibility before due process has taken place.

> **TASK 9** The media have an understandable appetite for dramatic stories. How long do you think it might take for the media to respond to a major incident such as a train crash?

A police officer should never be tempted to give media interviews; each force will have a specialist unit for these functions (and some BCUs have their own media relations staff too). An officer's comments might inadvertently be misleading—he/she might not have the full picture and is unlikely to have much experience in communicating through the media. In major cases the police will hold a press conference to brief the press and provide up-to-date and appropriate information.

11.6 Attending Scenes with Suspect Devices

Suspect devices include bombs, incendiary devices (designed to start or sustain a fire), and CBRN (chemical, biological, radiological, and nuclear) devices, with or without explosive triggers. Any incident involving a suspect device is most certainly an extreme case of a major or critical incident. Incidents involving CBRN devices are still rare, but they have been known. In 1995, a small and secretive Japanese sect called Aum Shinrikyo released small quantities of diluted Sarin (a nerve gas) inside a crowded Tokyo subway in the morning rush hour. Twelve people died and around 5,000 people required hospital treatment for their injuries. Had the gas been in concentrated form, the Japanese authorities believe that thousands could have died.

Terrorist incidents can be regarded as those incidents that involve the use or threat of violence (often extreme violence) to further or to publicize a political or extremist belief. The definitions of terrorism and extreme violence are considered further by Matassa *et al* (2003). The Terrorism Act 2000 provides particular powers for situations which might involve terrorism. Similar powers are available under other primary legislation or procedure, but the Terrorism Act 2000 provides wider powers than under other legislation to stop and search and to arrest (see 9.4.3.5).

General Procedures

If any suspect device is encountered, its precise nature cannot be determined by visual means alone. The cardinal rule is: do not touch it. The role of the FAO in managing such an ultra-critical incident is to create a very wide space around the suspect device (as wide as is practicable), and to get people out of the area. Whilst the requirement to preserve evidence is high, this is secondary to public safety at all times.

11.6.1 Cordons and the Terrorism Act 2000

An area can be 'designated' as a cordoned area under s 34 of the Terrorism Act 2000 by a police officer holding the rank of superintendent or above (or under s 34(2), by any other constable if he/she considers it urgent). Police officers have certain additional powers in a designated cordoned area (s 34(1)). Under s 36(1) a police officer can:

- order a person to immediately leave a cordoned area or any premises adjacent to a cordoned area, and to move a vehicle from a cordoned area (if he/she is the driver or in charge of the vehicle);
- arrange for the removal of a vehicle from a cordoned area or for it to be moved within a cordoned area; or
- prohibit or restrict pedestrian or vehicular access to a cordoned area.

(Note that legislation regarding BTP and MOD police officers is slightly different.)

If a person fails to comply with any of these requests he/she commits an offence (s 36(2) of the Terrorism Act 2000). However, a defence is available if the accused can prove a reasonable excuse for the non-compliance (s 36(3)). This offence is triable summarily only and the penalty is three months' imprisonment and/or a fine.

11.6.2 Suspected explosive devices

Alerts for suspected explosive devices present major demands on police and other emergency service resources, and hoaxes can be just as disruptive as the real thing (in the initial stages at least). Nonetheless, it must be assumed that every suspect device has the potential to kill and injure. The mnemonic **BOMB ALERT** provides a useful summary of the procedures to be followed.

B	Buildings: evacuate
O	Occupants: get them out and away
M	Move people right away from the scene
B	Back off: there could be secondary devices or other targets
A	Accurate information relayed back to control
L	Locate witnesses
E	Evacuate the neighbourhood of the device
R	Rendezvous (RV) points for arriving support
T	Tape off a cordon at the most practicable distance

As a general rule, cordons for small objects (up to briefcase size), should be placed at least 100 metres away from the device. For larger items (eg cars), the cordon should be a minimum of 200 metres, and for very large objects (eg large vans), the cordon should be a minimum of 400 metres away. The initial cordons may be installed by the fire or ambulance services during the rescue phase, using red and white tape. The outer cordon will generally be installed by the police using blue and white tape, and will be managed by scene control officers who permit authorized entry as required, and record activity in their crime scene log (see 11.2).

Streets lined with buildings provide a blast corridor for an explosion so personnel are safer behind 'hard cover' (eg concrete buildings) with no line of sight of the suspected device. No person should be located behind or beneath windows or other glass panels, however far away from the device.

The CAP to the object should be marked out if practicable (see 11.2.2), consistent with the overriding priority of personal and public safety. The force control room should be informed of the precise location of the device (see 11.5.2), especially if a wider evacuation is taking place outside the immediate cordon, but note that hand-held radios or mobile phones must not be used within 10 metres of the suspect object, and vehicle-based radios must not be used to transmit within 50 metres.

General Procedures

11.6.3   CBRN incidents

A chemical, biological, radiological, or nuclear (CBRN) incident has the potential to cause extreme devastation and very widespread loss of life. Fortunately this type of incident is rare and all forces will have detailed contingency plans—the considerations and procedures are the same as for any other type of suspect device. A CBRN attack can be hard to recognize, but any reports of groups of people suddenly collapsing or feeling unwell, or of a strong or noxious smell could indicate the presence of chemicals. Other types of CBRN attack (eg involving nuclear radiation) will not be perceptible, in the early stages at least.

In a suspected CBRN incident the **Steps** procedure must be followed. The step number corresponds with the observed number of casualties.

For a Step 3 incident, a METHANE assessment should be made if at all possible, but police safety must not be compromised.

Step	Number of casualties	Procedure
Step 1	One	Approach the site using the usual procedures.
Step 2	Two	Approach with caution and do not discount any possibility. Report arrival and do not touch any object. Report updates continually.
Step 3	Three or more	Do not enter the scene. Create an RV point outside the area and await instructions.

11.6.4   Attending the scene of a bomb explosion

After a bomb explosion there is likely to be devastation, wreckage, smoke, flames, badly injured people, dead bodies (and parts of bodies), noise, and confusion. The role of the FAO is the same in principle as for a train crash or major road traffic accident: take charge, clear those who can walk out of the area, close off the area with a cordon, attend to the injured if possible, and treat the area as a crime scene. In addition to the METHANE principles (see 11.5.2), the mnemonic ICICLE provides guidance on the procedures to be followed:

I	Identify the source of threat or suspicion
C	Communicate all available details to force control
I	Investigate the circumstances
C	Contain the threat to people where possible
L	Lead and reassure people at the scene
E	Ensure that major incident procedures are put in hand

Nothing can prepare a trainee police officer (or anyone) for the emotional impact of witnessing such scenes; indeed, many police officers present at the immediate aftermath of a major disaster report experiencing an initial sense of helplessness. However, it has been said (and in our view rightly) that what distinguishes a police officer from the general public is not his/her exercise of powers, or uniform, or knowledge of the law, but knowing what to do in an emergency. That knowledge can only come from training and experience.

TASK 10 Note the priority actions now in response to (1) a suspect CBRN device; and (2) a subsequent detonation. What should be done first and thereafter?

11.7   Planned Operations

'Planned Operations' are where the police have had advanced warning of a situation or event and as a consequence will have been able to develop suitable contingency plans, tactics, and strategies. Examples include disruption at sea and airports due to strikes, pre-planned demonstrations, and large music festivals. As soon as the necessity for such an operation has been identified, it is given an operational name to distinguish it from other incidents. The 'operation' covers the period from instigation, through planning, execution, and debrief. We provide a summary here, but more details are available on the College of Policing website.

11.7.1 Planning an operation

All police organizations have contingency plans for identified risks in their own areas, with a degree of flexibility to cover all eventualities. A range of tactical options are available for use for planned operations. Some of these tactics are used as part of 'steady state' policing (see 11.1) such as police dogs, batons and building entry, while others are more specialized, for example the use of armed response personnel who can fire attenuating energy projectiles and CS smoke. Other tactical options include shield tactics, air support, vehicle tactics, barricade/obstacle removal, cordons and intercepts, water cannon, containment, and evidence-gathering teams.

The hierarchy of command, known as Gold, Silver, and Bronze (GSB) (see 11.5.3), is nationally recognized by the police, partner agencies, and other emergency services. At each level of GSB, tactical advisers from the police and external organizations provide knowledge, understanding, and skills for the planning phase and for responding to changing circumstances throughout the duration of the operation. For example, Gold Command could elect to convene a 'strategic coordinating group', or Silver Command could assemble a 'tactical planning group' to develop a strategy.

Commanders and coordinating groups require specific, accurate, and relevant information at each stage of the operation, so a dedicated intelligence function will be required (see Chapter 23). This will be located centrally within the GSB incident room, or elsewhere, for example at the Force Intelligence Bureau. A Community Impact Assessment (CIA) is made to judge the extent to which businesses, community groups, families, and individuals may be affected by the proposed police response, providing vital information for planning a successful operation. Personnel from within the police family (eg neighbourhood teams), and external representatives from the third sector (charitable and non-profit-making organizations, community bodies), can all provide input for the CIA.

Gold Command (or 'Gold') determines the strategy and plans the police response accordingly. All the relevant information is recorded in a single document, the 'operational order'. The personnel participating in the operation are briefed as required, following the categories set out in the IIMARCH model (see the table).

IIMARCH heading	Key features
Information	Such as evaluated intelligence, results of the community impact assessment, length, duration, and location of the operation
Intention	Objectives of GSB strategies, tactics, policies, powers, and procedures
Method	Process by which the tactics, policies, powers, and procedures will be used
Administration	Logistics pertaining to start times, location, and lengths of duty and periods of refreshment
Risk assessment	Based on gathered information from intelligence sources
Communications	Including media broadcasts and inter-operability between personnel
Human rights and other legalities	Preserving the rights of individuals and groups and adhering to codes of practice in the use of legislation

The police information (see 6.8.2) generated by an operation must be collected, recorded, shared, and retained in accordance with ACPO guidelines. These specify the use of the Government Security Classifications Policy (GSCP), under which information is classified as either: Official, Secret, or Top Secret.

11.7.2 Participating in a planned operation

In the course of a planned operation police officers will of course follow the tactics outlined in the operational order, but within these limits individual officers will probably need to decide what specific actions to take. They should use the National Decision Model (see 6.5.2) as a framework for taking a decision. Records of any decisions made and actions carried out should be made in accordance with the PACE Codes of Practice (see 5.6) and the rules of disclosure (see 24.3.3). Police officers will usually make a record as a PNB entry (see 10.2), although this might not be possible at the time, depending on the circumstances.

The operational order may specify the use of personal protective and operational equipment (see 6.10), particularly if the use of force is likely to be required. The use of force to challenge unacceptable behaviour will be covered under personal safety training (see 6.12.5) and limited by legislation such as the Human Rights Act 1998 (see 5.4) and common law. Each individual officer must remember that his/her own health and safety is just as important as maintaining the health and safety of others (see 6.12).

11.7.3   Effective communication for planned operations

Effective communication with partners, communities, and other stakeholders helps to build trust and confidence and ensure that the appropriate strategy is adopted. Openness and transparency can help identify the potential for further escalation of problems, and make it less likely that unplanned (and less suitable) police response tactics will be used. All officers participating in an operation have an individual responsibility to maintain effective interpersonal communication (see 6.11). Various communication channels are available to GSB during planning and during the operation itself, such as:

* open data, for example police.uk, Data.gov.uk, and Ordnance Survey OpenData;
* face-to-face, for example public meetings, under-represented groups, independent advisory groups, partnership working, and information sharing;
* digital and social media, for example platforms such as Facebook, Twitter, YouTube, and Blog, social media monitoring, and digitally enabled meetings;
* corporate communication (traditional media), for example press releases and statements, television, radio, and newspaper interviews.

After a planned operation there will be a debriefing process to identify examples of good practice and opportunities for improvement. This could help streamline procedures and reduce demands for frontline staff in the future. The information from the debrief should be recorded and retained for revelation and disclosure (see 24.3.3). Further information on debriefing can be found on the Authorised Professional Practice website at <http://www.app.college.police.uk>.

11.8   Answers to Tasks

TASK 1 You may have noted that major-crime investigations are often long term and complex, especially when dealing with 'stranger murders' or 'stranger rapes'.

You could note, too, that crimes of violence attract considerable media interest and widespread publicity which, whilst helpful in publicizing the crime, have the potential to adversely affect an investigation if not handled properly.

TASK 2 When a person is decapitated.

TASK 3 Although it is beyond the scope of this Handbook (and not something that you are likely to encounter unless you become an SIO) you might like to research the CATCHEM (Central Analytical Homicide and Expertise Management) database. Research conducted on child murder with a sexual motive revealed complex mathematical relationships between places of abduction, and aspects of the offender. This is described in Aitken *et al* (1995). One inferential model the authors describe suggests that, in the case of a boy victim aged 0–10 who has been abducted, there are high probabilities that the offender lives within five miles of the contact point (75 per cent chance) and is aged 21+ (77 per cent).

The pioneering work of Aitken *et al* continues to be developed and extended by, amongst others, the Serious Crime Analysis Section (SCAS, now part of the NCA).

The research used has now been applied to the more general crime of homicide (Francis *et al*, 2004). For example, if the victim is aged 18–24, male, ethnically of Asian background, unemployed, and 'stabbed in a rage', then the model predicts that the offender is over 21 (68 per cent likelihood), also Asian (55 per cent), and an acquaintance of the victim (60 per cent).

TASK 4 The priority at the scene of a major violent crime is the preservation of life followed by the preservation of evidence.

You would probably note that the first priority would be not to let anyone else over the threshold of the crime scene, and that might well extend to the area outside the bedsit, to include stairs, stairwell, communal areas, and adjoining corridors or passages. You would clear people away (including the landlord), and close off the scene as swiftly as possible. You would enter the room, principally to ascertain whether the presumed victim is still alive. If she is you would follow the Airways, Breathing, Circulation (ABC) procedures, or possibly the 'Hands-only CPR' method as recommended by the British Heart Foundation and publicized by Vinnie Jones in early 2012 (see <http://www.bhf.org.uk>). Your duty is to support her until the paramedics arrive, and you would also ensure that nothing else was touched.

You would be in urgent communication with your force control centre, describing what you can see, the location, and any other relevant requirements, such as the attendance of paramedics, an ambulance, and a doctor. You would request the attendance of CSIs and probably the duty SIO or duty detective officer, since it is evident that a violent crime has been committed, possibly murder.

Then what? If you had a colleague with you, you could share the note taking, including the names and addresses of all those present, whether they have volunteered as witnesses or not. (Bear in mind the need to 'record, retain, reveal, and disclose' that we discuss in 24.3.) You would ask the landlord (whose details you have also recorded) for information about the victim and possible visitors she had had that day, including of course any information about the other person or persons present at the apparent altercation. You would log your actions, begin arranging the CAP, and note anything which you observed (such as a murder weapon, scattered possessions, blood splashes, and so on).

TASK 5 Your answers could well have been 'I do not know', which would have been entirely understandable even if you are a trainee police officer. (In fact your trainers might be more worried if you claimed already to know the answers to these questions.) We aim to go on to provide you with some general principles and some possible answers.

TASK 6 Your list could read something like this:

- Clear the immediate scene and note any injuries to anyone.
- Ensure that the area around the house (the 'stronghold') is evacuated and move people as far from the scene as possible.
- Continue to ask for information on what has happened, but calm any hysterical or over-excited people.
- Create a CAP in and out of the incident (see 11.2.2).
- Clear a wide area to receive the support once it arrives, and identify a suitable RVP (ensure that arriving vehicles are kept away from the scene itself).
- Keep in constant communication with your control centre, making sure that they know what is happening and what you are doing.
- Use your colleague proactively to control the immediate area, to talk to witnesses, to communicate with the incoming support.
- Find out all you can about the alleged hostage-taker, including name and any relationship with anyone likely to be inside the house with him.
- Make notes: keep a careful log (see 11.2.3) of what has taken place to the best of your knowledge, recording names and addresses of witnesses (see 24.4).
- If it is safe to do so, try to open a dialogue with the hostage-taker, making sure that he understands that you are a police officer and emphasizing that your aim is to end this incident peacefully, without anyone getting hurt.

Trainee officers could compare this list to the one provided during training. No doubt there will be many points in common.

TASK 7 There are many. The usual model taught during police training adopts a six-stage process, starting with defining the problem:

General Procedures

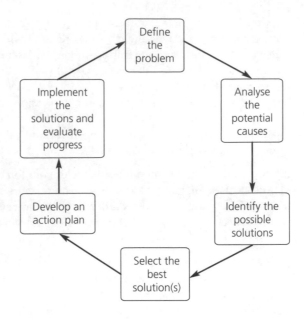

TASK 8 The 'Gold, Silver, Bronze' system has come under critical scrutiny in recent years. In his report into the investigation of the Soham murders, Sir Ronnie Flanagan made the following observation:

> Ironically, the overlaying of the Gold, Silver and Bronze command structure on this operation contributed to a lack of clarity of command of the incident, particularly in relation to the role of the SIO and was subject to comment in the internal review. (Flanagan, 2004, p 13)

The report also contained a recommendation that when applied to homicide the system should be clarified. A number of the Flanagan recommendations were subsequently adopted in NPIA guidance and subsequently feature in the CoP Authorised Professional Practice.

TASK 9 We were not exaggerating when we discussed the extent of media interest earlier. In the case of the Watford train crash in 1996, Hertfordshire police reported that media interest in the incident commenced within five minutes of the crash happening (Moses, 1997). And more recently, in January 2013, when a gunman began shooting at Lone Star College, near Houston, Texas, one student was tweeting during the incident. Justin Lear of CNN responded, and even asked if she had any photos. For an edited version of the tweets see <http://storify.com/mashable/student-tweets-during-school-shooting>.

TASK 10

1. The role of the police officer does not include identifying the type of device. His/her role would be to contain the scene, evacuate anyone within the cordon, and manage the site until help arrives. He/she should be communicating to the force control centre to tell them everything he/she can see and otherwise perceive, including the location of the device and its description, following the METHANE mnemonic. Note that it is unwise to allow the walking injured to simply leave: even if they appear well they may be contaminated and require decontamination and treatment.
2. Secondary devices would be a major concern. The ICICLE principles should be applied.
3. Further information is available from the *Civil Contingencies* section of the College of Policing website.

12 Alcohol, Drugs, and Substance Abuse

12.1 Introduction

Many of the incidents encountered by a trainee police officer on Supervised and Independent Patrol will be alcohol or drug-related, particularly on late shifts. The health and safety of all persons present must be considered: the potential for injury can be very high. Intoxicated people are sometimes subject to rapid mood swings, happy one minute and then violent the next, and others who are normally quite reserved may lose some of their normal social inhibitions and behave unpredictably. Although this chapter is mainly concerned with the application of the law surrounding alcohol- and drugs-related incidents, initial police training and pre-join programmes also provide an introduction to the wider issues surrounding alcohol and other forms of drug and substance abuse. Drink- and drug-driving is covered separately in 19.9.

A common perception is that 'binge drinking' of alcohol has increased amongst the young, but the reality appears somewhat more complex. The number of young people drinking to excess appears to have dropped in recent years, but those that do abuse alcohol do so more often and to a greater extent (Fuller, 2008). In another survey it is suggested that between 2003 and 2014 the number of 11–15-year-olds trying alcohol has actually dropped by 23 per cent (Institute of Alcohol Studies, 2016). This could, however, be linked to an increased use of other substances.

According to the 2015/16 Crime Survey for England and Wales (CSEW), around 8 per cent of adults (aged 16–59) had taken a drug controlled by the Misuse of Drugs Act 1971 in the last year, which equates to around 2.7 million people. This level of drug use was similar to the 2014/15 survey, but slightly lower than a decade ago (10.5 per cent in the 2005/06 survey). The same survey, estimated that 0.7 per cent of adults aged 16–59 (around 244,000 people) had used a psychoactive substance during 2015/16, with the 16–24 age-group accounting for around two-thirds of these.

12.2 Alcohol-related Offences and Powers

There is no doubt that alcohol causes problematic behaviour for a minority of users. In a recent report, 76 per cent of police respondents stated they had received an injury whilst dealing with drunken members of the public and 65 per cent indicated that they had been injured on more than one occasion (Institute of Alcohol Studies, 2015). In the same report police practitioners were surveyed on the perceived effectiveness of the available disposal methods, in terms of reducing alcohol-related crime and disorder. Just over half of the respondents agreed that charging offenders was the most effective method. Out-of-court disposals (see 10.13.2) were seen as less effective, with 44 per cent of respondents stating that fixed penalty notices did not work, and 41 per cent claiming that dispersal notices (see 14.2.2.1) had poor results. A further 56 per cent of respondents agreed that cautions and conditional cautions were also ineffectual (Institute of Alcohol Studies, 2015).

According to the Home Office's *Modern Crime Prevention Strategy*, the percentage of all violent incidents, in which the victim believes the offender(s) to be under the influence of alcohol, has fluctuated between 48 and 59 per cent since 2004. Latest figures estimate that the cost to society of alcohol-related crime is £11 billion and that 36 per cent of penalty notices for disorder (see 10.13.2.1) were issued for the offence of being drunk and disorderly. The *Local Alcohol Profiles for England* indicate that in the period 2014/15 there were 1.1 million estimated hospital admissions where an alcohol-related disease, injury, or condition was the primary reason for admission, or a secondary diagnosis. Of these admissions, there were about 5,000 road or pedestrian traffic accidents and 8,000 intentional injuries including assaults (Public Health England, 2016).

Here we explore the legislation and powers available to a police officer to deal with people who have drunk alcohol to excess and those which help to prevent the consumption of alcohol by young people. The word 'alcohol' is used in some legislation. It is defined in s 191(1) of the Licensing Act 2003 as spirits, wine, beer, cider or any other fermented, distilled, or spirituous liquor.

12.2.1 Drunkenness as an offence

The terms 'drunk' and 'drunkenness' are not defined in law. As a precedent, the case of *R v Tagg* [2002] 1 Cr App R 2 determined that the everyday meaning of 'drunk' should be used. The *Oxford English Dictionary* defines drunk as 'having drunk intoxicating liquor to an extent which affects steady self-control' (*Shorter Oxford English Dictionary*, 2002, although the 1933 edition was cited in that case). The Court of Appeal also accepted that the *Collins Dictionary* definition (used by the judge in the original case under appeal) and the *Shorter Oxford English Dictionary* definitions were essentially the same, and were helpful in determining the existence of a state of drunkenness.

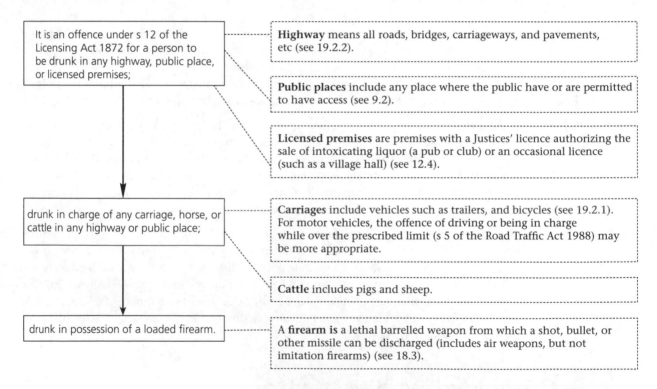

The court itself must decide whether or not a suspect was drunk. Generally, the opinion of a witness is inadmissible as evidence, but for drunkenness a 'competent witness' may give evidence that, in his/her opinion, a person was drunk (*R v Davies* [1962] 1 WLR 1111). A competent witness is defined as a person who understands questions, and can respond coherently, and would of course include a police officer. The witness should also provide facts to support the opinion, for example, that the person was unsteady on her feet, had glazed eyes and slurred speech, or that her breath smelt of intoxicating liquor.

This offence is triable summarily and the penalty is one month's imprisonment or a fine. A fixed penalty notice can also be used (see 10.13.2.1).

12.2.2 Drunk and disorderly behaviour

The precise meaning of the term 'disorderly behaviour' is not defined by statute but its everyday meaning is 'unruly or offensive behaviour'. Under s 91(1) of the Criminal Justice Act 1967, it is an offence for any drunken person to display such behaviour in any highway, public place, or licensed premises,

This offence is triable summarily only, and the penalty is a fixed penalty notice (see 10.13.2.1), a fine, or one month's imprisonment.

12.2.3   Drunk in charge of children

Under s 2 of the Licensing Act 1902, it is an offence for a person to be drunk while 'having charge' of a child under the age of seven years in any highway, public place, or licensed premises. The precise meaning of 'having charge' is not defined by statute, but probably means some sort of care or control over the child(ren); the suspect must be the only person with the child, or alternatively everyone in a group with the child must be drunk. The offence is triable summarily and the penalty is one month's imprisonment or a fine.

> **TASK 1** Imagine you are a trainee police officer. In your area you often see a habitual drunk who often drinks large quantities of strong lager and then becomes very abusive to passing members of the public. You are requested to deal with this. How would you approach her and what long-term solution could improve the situation? Look at s 34(1) of the Criminal Justice Act 1972 to help determine a suitable course of action.

12.2.4   Controlled Drinking Zones

A local authority can designate an area as a 'controlled drinking zone' (s 235 of the Local Government Act 1972) to help control ASB. It is not an offence to drink alcohol in a controlled drinking zone, but it is an offence to fail to comply with a request to surrender alcohol or to cease drinking. However, note that Home Office advice is that 'it is not appropriate to challenge an individual consuming alcohol where that individual is not causing a problem' (Home Office, 2009b). Local policies will determine how to dispose of any confiscated alcohol. The offence of failing to comply is triable summarily and the penalty is a fine. A fixed penalty notice can also be used (see 10.13.2.1).

12.3   Alcohol and Young People

Concern about young people drinking alcohol has increased considerably over the past few years. Certain legislation addresses this in relation to young people on licensed premises. Other legislation is available to help limit their alcohol consumption in other places to which the public has access.

On a more general note, if an officer encounters a 'child' carrying unopened cans of alcohol, then he/she should at least consider whether the child had bought the cans (and his/her welfare), and take action accordingly. This applies even if there are no grounds to reasonably believe that the child has been consuming alcohol (or is about to consume it) at a relevant place.

12.3.1   Confiscation of alcohol from young people

A police officer (in or out of uniform) or a suitably designated PCSO may confiscate alcohol (or anything reasonably believed to be alcohol) from a young person in a 'relevant place' (s 1(1) of the Confiscation of Alcohol (Young Persons) Act 1997). A relevant place includes:

- any public place, for example streets, parks, and shopping centres (but not licensed premises such as pubs or clubs); and
- any other place to which the person has unlawfully gained access, such as gate-crashing a party at a private house where the trespasser did not have the consent of the homeowner to gain entry.

The officer must inform the person of his/her suspicion under s 1(1) (s 1(4) of the Confiscation of Alcohol (Young Persons) Act 1997), and as shown in the diagram an officer can require alcohol to be surrendered.

Specific Incidents

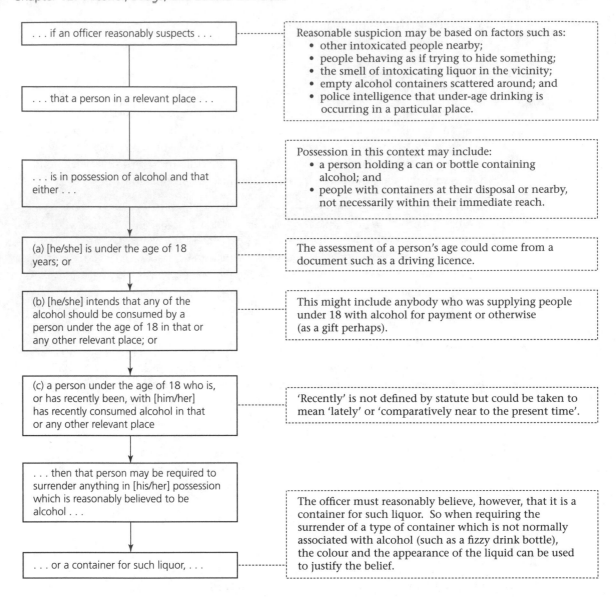

. . . if an officer reasonably suspects . . .

Reasonable suspicion may be based on factors such as:
- other intoxicated people nearby;
- people behaving as if trying to hide something;
- the smell of intoxicating liquor in the vicinity;
- empty alcohol containers scattered around; and
- police intelligence that under-age drinking is occurring in a particular place.

. . . that a person in a relevant place . . .

. . . is in possession of alcohol and that either . . .

Possession in this context may include:
- a person holding a can or bottle containing alcohol; and
- people with containers at their disposal or nearby, not necessarily within their immediate reach.

(a) [he/she] is under the age of 18 years; or

The assessment of a person's age could come from a document such as a driving licence.

(b) [he/she] intends that any of the alcohol should be consumed by a person under the age of 18 in that or any other relevant place; or

This might include anybody who was supplying people under 18 with alcohol for payment or otherwise (as a gift perhaps).

(c) a person under the age of 18 who is, or has recently been, with [him/her] has recently consumed alcohol in that or any other relevant place

'Recently' is not defined by statute but could be taken to mean 'lately' or 'comparatively near to the present time'.

. . . then that person may be required to surrender anything in [his/her] possession which is reasonably believed to be alcohol . . .

The officer must reasonably believe, however, that it is a container for such liquor. So when requiring the surrender of a type of container which is not normally associated with alcohol (such as a fizzy drink bottle), the colour and the appearance of the liquid can be used to justify the belief.

. . . or a container for such liquor, . . .

The person must be required to state his/her name and address (s 1AA) and be told that it is an offence to fail to comply (without reasonable excuse) with a requirement under s 1(1) or (1AA). A young person suspected to be under 16 can be removed to his/her place of residence or a place of safety (s 1AB) (see 13.3.3 and 14.2.2.1). This offence is triable summarily and the penalty is a fine. Local policy on the disposal of surrendered alcohol varies between forces.

12.3.2 Persistently possessing alcohol in a public place

It is an offence for a person under 18 to be in possession of alcohol without reasonable excuse in any relevant place on three or more occasions within a year (s 30 of the Police and Crime Act 2009). The offence is triable summarily and the penalty is a fine.

> **TASK 2** Imagine you are a police officer and you see a young teenager at a bus station drinking alcohol. What requirements will you make of him? Write down a list of things you would have to say for the requirements to be lawful.

12.4 Premises Licensing Legislation

The Licensing Act 2003 includes legislation to address drunkenness in 'relevant premises'. Relevant premises in this context are premises where alcohol can be sold by retail (for example a pub or a shop), club premises with a certificate (eg a working men's club where alcohol is supplied by or on behalf of a club to members), but also any premises with 'permitted temporary activity' (such as a village hall hired out for a wedding reception).

Staff managing or working in places where alcohol is served have a legal responsibility to try to prevent drunkenness and disorder. People with these responsibilities are listed in s 140(1) of the Licensing Act 2003, and are referred to here as responsible staff (a term of our own invention, not a legal term). They include:

- the holder of a premises licence;
- the designated supervisor of a licensed premises;
- any person who works at the premises in a capacity which authorizes him/her to prevent disorderly conduct;
- any member or officer of a club (with a club premises certificate) who has the capacity to prevent disorderly behaviour; and
- the user of a premises with permitted temporary activity, at the permitted time.

12.4.1 Disorderly conduct

An offence is committed by responsible staff who knowingly allow disorderly conduct on licensed premises (s 140(1) of the Licensing Act 2003). This offence is triable summarily and the penalty is a fine.

A drunk or disorderly person commits a summary offence under s 143(1) of the Licensing Act 2003 if without reasonable excuse he/she:

- fails to leave relevant premises (when requested to do so by a police officer or a responsible staff member); or
- enters (or attempts to enter) relevant premises having been requested not to enter.

A police officer must respond to requests from responsible staff to help expel or refuse entry to a drunken person (s 143(4) of the Licensing Act 2003). Reasonable force may be used to encourage the person to comply (see *Semple v Luton and South Bedfordshire Magistrates' Court* [2009] EWHC 3241 (Admin) and 15.5.1).

12.4.2 Providing a drunk person with intoxicating liquor

Responsible staff who knowingly sell (or attempt to sell) alcohol to a person who is drunk on relevant premises commit an offence under s 141(1) of the Licensing Act 2003. It is also an offence for anyone to obtain or attempt to obtain alcohol for a drunken person on relevant premises (s 142(1)). These offences are triable summarily and the penalty is a fine. They are also penalty offences for the purposes of s 1 of the Criminal Justice and Police Act 2001.

12.4.3 Powers of entry

There is a power of entry to any place if there is reason to believe that an offence under the Licensing Act 2003 is being committed or is about to be committed (s 180(1) of the Licensing Act 2003). Reasonable force can be used (s 180(2)). The term 'any place' is defined in s 193; it includes vehicles, vessels, or moveable structures, licensed or not.

There is also a power of entry under the Licensing Act 2003 to any place with a club premises certificate if there is reasonable cause to believe that an offence relating to supplying a controlled drug has been committed (see 12.6.2), or is about to be, or is being committed at that moment (s 97(1)(a)), or that a breach of the peace may occur (s 97(1)(b)). Whilst exercising this power reasonable force may be used (s 97(2)).

For premises with permitted temporary activities, under s 108(1) of the Licensing Act 2003 a police officer may enter the premises at any reasonable time to assess the effect of the event in relation to prevention of crime and disorder, public safety, the prevention of public nuisance, and the protection of children from harm. There is no specific offence of obstructing a police officer under s 108, but an offence under the Police Act 1996 could be considered (obstruction in the lawful execution of police duties (see 15.4)).

12.4.4 Selling alcohol to children and young people

Alcohol cannot legally be sold to a person under the age of 18 years. It is an offence to:

- sell alcohol to a person under 18 in any place (s 146(1) of the Licensing Act 2003)—this is also a penalty offence (see 10.13.2.1); or
- knowingly allow the sale of alcohol on relevant premises to an individual aged under 18 (s 147(1) of the Licensing Act 2003).

Specific Incidents

A further more serious offence is committed if on two or more different occasions (within a period of three consecutive months) alcohol is unlawfully sold on the same licensed premises to a young person under 18 (s 147A of the Licensing Act 2003). These offences are triable summarily and the penalty is a fine.

TASK 3 In the course of an investigation into offences concerning public indecency and criminal damage it is found that many of these offences are committed by people who have consumed large amounts of intoxicating liquor on relevant premises. This intake of alcohol may have contributed towards these offences being committed.

How could the licensing authority of the premises be informed about such activities?

12.5 Controlled Drugs and Psychoactive Substances

Police officers will frequently encounter people who have been using controlled drugs or psychoactive substances. Risk and hazard levels should be carefully assessed when dealing with people 'under the influence'. Personal safety equipment may be required as the consequences of contamination from bodily fluids or equipment used by a drug addict can be very serious. The merest micro-cut from a virus-contaminated sharp article could cause a life-threatening infection. Demonstration of appropriate health and safety measures form part of the PAC Safety First requirements and the assessment criteria for many Diploma in Policing assessed units.

12.5.1 Definitions of Controlled Drugs and Psychoactive Substances

A controlled drug is a drug that is subject to legal control. They are classified as such because of their harmful effects on the human body, in particular the brain, and the fact that many people find the psychoactive effects of these substances enjoyable and therefore hard to resist. New substances are added to the Home Office list as they come to the attention of the authorities. Any alteration to the chemical composition of a controlled drug makes it a different substance, and it will therefore not be subject to the existing controlled drugs legislation. Such an altered substance might however be a 'psychoactive substance', and would therefore be covered by the Psychoactive Substances Act 2016 (see 12.5.1.2).

12.5.1.1 The Definition of a Controlled Drug

Controlled drugs contain one or more defined chemical compounds with recognized effects, and are classed as Class A, B, or C (Misuse of Drugs Act 1971) according to the potential for harm they are thought to present.

Class A	eg Ecstasy, heroin, cocaine, crack cocaine, 'magic mushrooms' (containing psilocin), and LSD
Class B	eg cannabis leaves, cannabis resin, amphetamines, and barbiturates
Class C	eg khat, tranquillizers (such as Temazepam), and some painkillers

---

A full list of controlled drugs can be found on the Home Office website.

In the financial year ending 2016, there were 29,949 seizures of Class A drugs, which is about the same as the previous year. Cocaine was the most commonly seized Class A drug. Seizures of Class B drugs were down 13 per cent on the previous year (115,126 seizures), with herbal cannabis accounting for the vast majority (97,218 seizures, a total of 30,493 kilograms). There were 5,128 seizures of Class C drugs in 2015/16, a decrease of 18 per cent compared with 2014/15 (Home Office, 2016h).

The illegal use controlled drugs often involves particular equipment, to smoke or inject a substance for example. Some examples of this equipment are shown in the photographs.

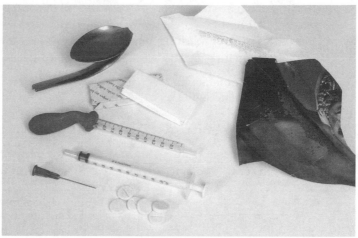

Heroin 'gear'

Crack Smoking equipment
(Photographs from Drugscope 2013, copyright free)

Recognizing controlled drugs is very difficult as there are so many different forms, shapes, colours, and sizes including pills, tablets, liquids, powders, and resins. Therefore, a police officer who finds such substances without pharmaceutical company packaging should not try and identify it, but should act on the suspicion that it is a controlled drug. You are advised to make yourself familiar with the 'street drugs' now in circulation, including their appearance and slang names (see the excellent 'encyclopedia' resource available on the DrugWise website).

12.5.1.2   The Definition of a Psychoactive Substance

In the legislation a 'psychoactive substance' is any substance (other than controlled drugs, alcohol, or tobacco) which is capable of producing a psychoactive effect in a person who consumes it (s 2(1)(a) of the Psychoactive Substances Act 2016). In recent years, perhaps with a view to circumnavigating the controlled drugs legislation, many new psychoactive substances (sometimes referred to as NPS) have been manufactured, and these so-called 'legal highs' are often sold online and in 'head shops'. New legislation such as the Psychoactive Substances Act 2016 (PSA 2016) has been drafted to counter these activities.

Psychoactive substances include mephedrone, 'spice' (an example of a synthetic cannabinoid), 'GBL' (gamma butyrolactone), 'GHB' (gamma hydroxybutyrate), and 'Salvia' (derived from the plant Salvia divinrum; a 'herbal ecstasy').

Psychoactive substances also include everyday retail items such as:

- solvent-based glues;
- correction fluids/thinners;
- marker pens;
- any kind of aerosols;
- anti-freeze;
- nail varnish/nail varnish remover;
- nitrous oxide (an aerosol spray propellant found in whipped cream canisters).

Where substances are sold by a retailer for their intended use, eg cleaning, gardening, industrial use, their sale will not be an offence unless there is evidence that the cashier is aware of a likelihood that the product in question may be consumed for its psychoactive effect.

Specific Incidents

It is not an offence to possess a psychoactive substance (except in a custodial institution (s 9 of the PSA 2016)). However, there are dedicated police powers to stop and search for psychoactive substances (s 36 for searching individuals, s 37 for searching vehicles, and s 38 for boarding and searching vessels or aircraft), see 9.4.3.2 for further details.

The 2015/16 Crime Survey for England and Wales refers to psychoactive substances, and a new Psychoactive Substances (NPS) resource pack can be found on the gov.uk website.

12.5.2   Unlawful possession of a Controlled Drug

As a police officer in training, the most frequently encountered drugs offence is unlawful possession. In order to commit this offence (s 5(2) of the Misuse of Drugs Act) a person must:

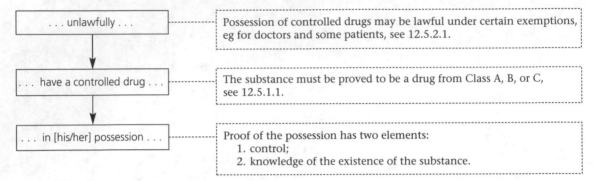

Through case law it has been established that two elements are required in order to establish possession of a substance; control of the substance and knowledge of its existence. Possession can be actual (on his/her person), or constructive (eg under his/her control in a vehicle or house some distance away).

Elements required to prove possession	Explanation
1. Control of the substance itself or a container in which it is held	Control of a substance is indicated by the rights the person has over the substance, and generally amounts to ownership. It would certainly include items found on a person or in his/her property, but would also include items that a person has ordered and paid for by post but has not yet received. Having control would also include having custody when a person knows he/she has temporary or partial responsibility for an item, with the owner's consent or knowledge.
2. Knowledge of the existence of a substance	The suspect must know of, or suspect the existence of a substance. If it was inside a container, it must be proved that the suspect knew about the container and that it contained a substance.

Both of these elements must be satisfied to prove that the person was in possession of the substance. It is not sufficient for a person to have something in his/her pocket (ie control) if he/she is not aware it is there. Nor can a person be said to be in possession if he/she knows that a substance is in a particular bag, but the bag is not in his/her custody or control. The situation is less straightforward if the substance was found on shared premises.

As an example, imagine that a man is searched using the powers under s 23 of the Misuse of Drugs Act 1971 (see 9.4.3.1), and in the man's pocket the officer finds kitchen foil with traces of brown powder on it. After examination, the brown powder is identified as heroin. To prove the offence of possession it must therefore be shown that:

- the foil with the powder was in his pocket, and he knew the powder was there (it does not matter whether or not he knew the substance was a controlled drug);
- the powder was heroin; and
- he was not lawfully entitled to possess the drug.

In relation to stop and search, controlled drugs are not prohibited articles under s 1 of the PACE Act 1984, but s 23(2) of the Misuse of Drugs Act 1971 has its own power of search (see 9.4.3.1).

12.5.2.1   **Exemptions permitting lawful possession of a controlled drug**

Most people found to be in possession of a controlled drug, will not be in lawful possession of the substance. Possession is lawful for some workers as part of their work, for example as suppliers to the pharmaceutical trade, and as doctors (if proper prescribing records are kept). Such exemptions are provided under the Misuse of Drugs Regulations 2001 and made by the Home Secretary under s 7 of the Misuse of Drugs Act 1971. Patients who have been prescribed controlled drugs are also provided for under the exemptions. Regulation 6 allows police officers, police support employees, customs officers, and postal workers to possess drugs whilst acting in the course of their duties.

12.5.3   **Unlawful possession of cannabis and khat**

Cannabis is a Class B drug, and khat (a herbal stimulant which is usually chewed) is a Class C drug. With the aim of providing a consistent nationwide approach to personal possession by adults, an intervention framework for unlawful possession of both drugs is used.

12.5.3.1   **Intervention model for the unlawful possession of cannabis and khat**

The model helps provide a justifiable and proportionate response, and the intention is to send out the message that cannabis and khat are harmful and illegal. There are three levels of intervention but the guidance emphasizes that arrest remains the first presumption, although discretion can be used at all times. Cannabis and khat warnings are covered in more detail in 12.5.3.2.

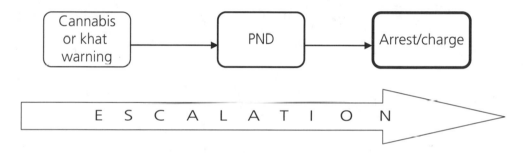

Under this model, PNDs and warnings can only be used if the person:

- is aged 18 years or over and has verifiable personal details; name, date of birth, and address;
- is not vulnerable (see 13.2);
- is competent enough to grasp the meaning of the officer's questions and his/her own replies;
- is not under the influence of alcohol or drugs at the time the warning or PND is issued;
- possesses an amount of cannabis or khat only suitable for personal use (in the officer's judgement);
- is not in possession of any other drug; and
- admits the possession of cannabis or khat (this only applies for warnings, and not for PNDs, see 12.5.3.2).

Aggravating factors must be taken into consideration when deciding which option to take in the intervention model. If there are no aggravating factors then a warning is the likely outcome. If there are one or more aggravating factors, then discretion should be used to decide whether to issue a PND or make an arrest. The location where the person is found to be in possession can be an aggravating factor. This could be a previously identified 'hot spot' for anti-social behaviour due to cannabis/khat use (eg a corner of a park) or any place young people are more likely to be such as a playground or youth club. Aggravating factors also include smoking cannabis or chewing khat in a public place or in the view of the public, or being a repeat offender (including other criminal offences) or someone who continually engages in anti-social behaviour. A further factor would be appearing to fail to recognize the seriousness of the possession.

The PNC can be used to find out whether the suspect has received a relevant warning or a PND, as they cannot be used more than once. There is no need to employ each stage of the model in sequence: arrest can be used even if the suspect has never received a relevant warning or a PND, depending on the officer's discretion. If the suspect does not admit the unlawful possession, a PND can only be used if there is sufficient evidence (see 12.5.2) to prove the offence. For suspects aged under 18, a youth caution can be used as an alternative (see 10.13.2.3).

The large flowchart with the shaded boxes shows the main factors to take into account when dealing with suspects in possession of cannabis or khat. Individual circumstances and the use of discretion mean that the diagram can only provide an indication of the more usual outcomes, and does not cover every eventuality. The shaded boxes relate to the intervention model.

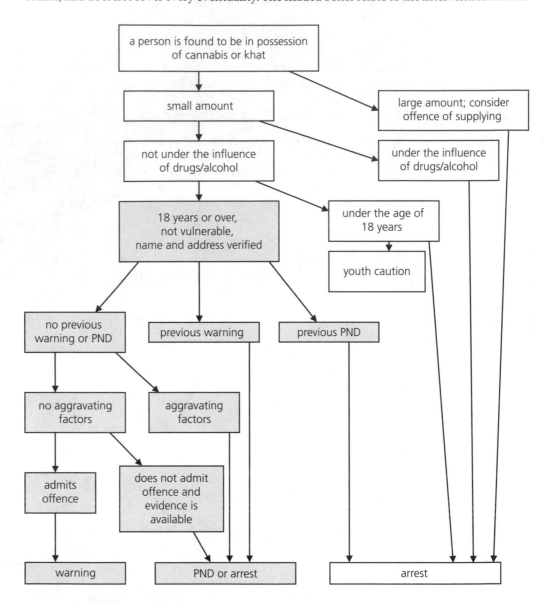

12.5.3.2 Cannabis and khat warnings

These warnings can only be issued when there are no aggravating factors (see 12.5.3.1), and when the person is compliant with the procedure, admits to the offence, and has no previous records of relevant warnings, PNDs, or convictions. The current guidance is that no more than one warning should be issued to an individual. However, under the previous guidance two warnings were allowed, so warnings issued after 26 January 2009 must be taken into account when deciding a level of intervention, whereas those issued before this date should not (although they do of course form part of the general previous offending history).

There is no formal group of words for a cannabis or khat warning, but ACPO recommends that the terms 'cannabis warning' or 'khat warning' are used (rather than 'street warning'). The officer should tell the suspect that the warning will:

- be recorded and added to local police databases for future reference;
- produce a record of a detected crime for the purposes of statistics as a recordable crime;
- not amount to a criminal record or conviction; and
- lead to the issuing of a PND or arrest if he/she is found in unlawful possession of cannabis or khat in the future.

Two useful ACPO documents are available online; National Policing Guidelines on KHAT Possession for Personal Use Intervention Framework (England & Wales Only) and Guidance on Cannabis Possession for Personal Use Revised Intervention Framework.

12.5.3.3   Possession of small amounts of cannabis or khat: practical aspects

For suspects in possession of small amounts of cannabis or khat a police officer should investigate the suspected unlawful possession, remembering to follow the PACE Codes of Practice to protect the rights of the individual (see 10.3 on cautions). The officer should try to establish whether there is any lawful excuse for possession (see 12.5.2.1 and 12.5.4), or if there is any evidence of a more serious offence such as intent to supply (see 12.6.2 and 12.6.3). The drugs should be seized and secured according to local policy (see 10.9 and 11.2.6). The incident should be recorded at the time as a PNB entry. The recording requirements must also be satisfied, and stop and search forms will need to be completed (see 9.4.1). Intelligence reports and crime reports can be completed later.

Any arrest must be 'necessary' (see 10.6.4). For details on issuing a PND for possessing cannabis or khat, see para 3.2 of the Home Office operational guidance available at <http://www.justice.gov.uk/downloads/oocd/pnd-guidance-oocd.pdf>.

> **TASK 4** If you are a trainee police officer, find out the common street names, prices, and the appearance for the most common Class A, B, and C drugs in your policing area.

12.5.4   Defences and penalties for unlawful possession of a controlled drug

In addition to the possession being lawful (see 12.5.2.1), a number of other circumstances can provide a defence (s 5(4), the Misuse of Drugs Act 1971). For example a woman who finds drugs in her son's pocket and removes the item, will temporarily possess the drugs, as would a member of the public who finds a package containing drugs and takes it to a police station. The flowchart provides more details about these particular circumstances and the conditions that must be satisfied.

Preventing unlawful possession under s 5 of the Misuse of Drugs Act 1971 is defined as:

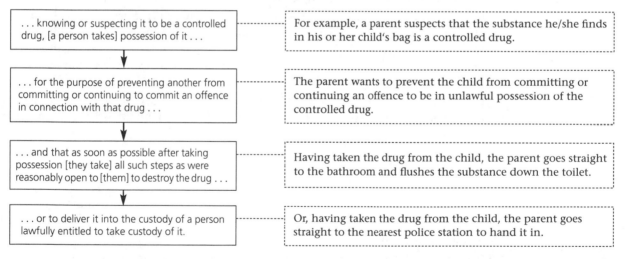

Other defences are available under s 28 of the Misuse of Drugs Act 1971. These relate to two main issues: whether the suspect knew or believed the substance was a controlled drug (s 28(3)(b)(i)) and whether the suspect was entitled to possess that particular drug (s 28(3)(b)(ii)). The onus is on the suspect to prove that he/she did not know or suspect some relevant point of fact alleged by the prosecution. Trainee police officers are unlikely to be involved in this process.

Offences involving Class A, B, or C drugs are triable either way and the penalty is imprisonment and/or a fine. The lengths of prison sentences are shown in the table. Unlawful possession of cannabis can also be dealt with by way of a PND for £90 (see 10.13.2.1 and 12.5.3).

Class	As a summary offence	As an indictable offence
A	Six months	Seven years
B	Three months	Five years
C	Three months	Two years

Specific Incidents

> **TASK 5** Establishing whether someone is in unlawful possession of controlled drugs is not always straightforward. Identifying a substance as a controlled drug is relatively straightforward but proving possession is more complicated. Consider the following three scenarios and try and decide whether possession has been established in each case.
>
> 1. Before going out to a party one night person E puts some cannabis into a wallet. He goes out and gets very drunk and can't remember the night's events. He returns home the next day and puts his coat containing the wallet back into his wardrobe. Some days later he puts the coat on again forgetting it contains the wallet with the cannabis. He is subsequently stopped and searched by the police and the cannabis is found. Is he guilty of unlawful possession?
> 2. During a s 23 search, controlled drugs in the form of tablets are found in the jeans pocket of person F. He claimed that the tablets had been prescribed to him by a doctor some months ago but that he had lost them, so obtained another prescription from his doctor for some more tablets. He says he later found the missing tablets at the back of a drawer and put them in his jeans pocket, where they are found by the police. Was he in unlawful possession of the tablets at the time?
> 3. Person G was entertaining visitors when a search warrant under s 23(3) of the Misuse of Drugs Act 1971 was executed. A small quantity of heroin was found on the sofa in between two guests and G admitted to the police officers present that she was the owner. But when she was formally interviewed she withdrew the admission but provided information about the identity of a person she claimed was of the true owner of the heroin. She also stated that one of her visitors had probably had drugs in his possession in her flat and that another had been preparing to take heroin before the search took place. Are the circumstances sufficient for G to have been in control of the drugs?

12.6 Production and Supply Offences

Drugs legislation has been carefully worded so that it is not only the illegal end user who is subject to prosecution, but also (and perhaps more importantly) the people involved in supply chain. The legislation relating to the illegal production and supply of controlled drugs is in ss 4–6 of Misuse of Drugs Act 1971. Defences to production and supply offences relate to proving possession, and whether the substance in question actually is a controlled drug, but see also 12.5.6 on s 28 and other defences for possession. For psychoactive substances, productive and supply offences are covered in ss 4–7 of the PSA 2016. As for controlled drugs, certain activities such as work carried out by health care professionals or as approved scientific research are exempted for the purposes of this Act (s 11).

12.6.1 Production of controlled drugs or psychoactive substances

It is an offence to produce a controlled drug or be concerned in its production (s 4(2) of the Misuse of Drugs Act 1971). The only person who can lawfully produce controlled drugs are manufacturers under licence from the Secretary of State. Growing plants and carrying out chemical processes are included under the umbrella term 'producing', while 'being concerned in the production' would include delivering chemicals, providing premises, or providing finance.

For production of cannabis plants, the Home Office recommends charging under s 4(2), as the charge of 'cultivation of cannabis' (s 6(2)) does not allow for confiscation proceedings (Circular 82/1980). The defences outlined in s 28 of the Misuse of Drugs Act 1971 (see 12.5.4) apply to both these offences.

Offences involving production of drugs are triable either way and the penalty is imprisonment and/or a fine. The maximum lengths of prison sentences are shown in the table.

Class	As a summary offence	As an indictable offence
A	Six months	Life
B	Six months	14 years
C	Three months	Five years

Section 4(2) offences for a Class A drug are 'trigger' offences under s 63B of the PACE Act 1984: a sample can be demanded from a person in police custody (see 26.6 on taking samples from people).

The intentional production of a psychoactive substance is an offence under s 4(1) of the PSA 2016. The person must know or suspect that the substance is a psychoactive substance and also:

- intend to consume it for its psychoactive effects; or
- know (or be reckless as to whether) it will be consumed by another person for its psychoactive effects.

These offences are triable either way. The penalty is a fine and/or imprisonment (12 months if tried summarily, and up to seven years' imprisonment on indictment).

12.6.2   Supply offences

These offences (including offering to supply) are covered under s 4 of the Misuse of Drugs Act 1971 (for controlled drugs), and under s 4 of the PSA 2016 for psychoactive substances. A court must treat the offence more seriously if it was committed in or near to a school, or if the suspect used a courier under the age of 18.

For controlled drugs, supply offences are covered under s 4(3) of the Misuse of Drugs Act 1971 as shown in the diagram.

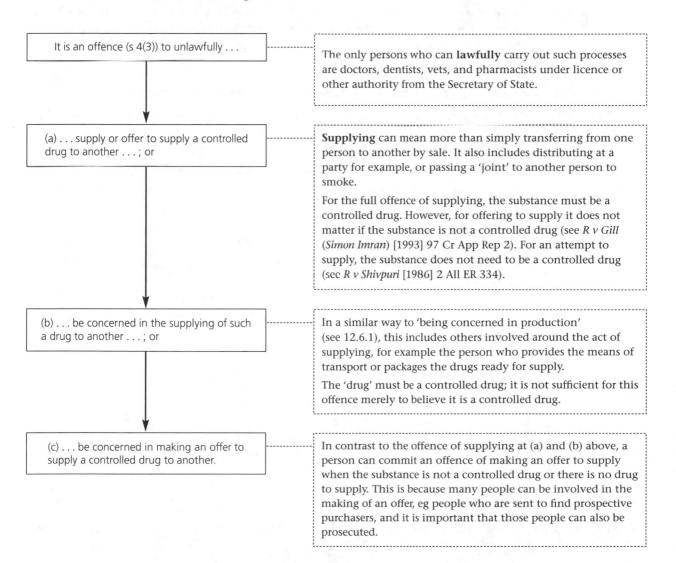

The defences outlined in 12.5.4 also apply here. The penalties are the same as for the production of a controlled drug (see 12.6.1). The offence is a trigger offence: a police officer can demand a sample from a suspect in custody.

For psychoactive substances, it is an offence to intentionally supply such a substance to another person (s 5(1) of the PSA 2016). This only applies if the supplier knows or suspects (or ought to) that the substance is psychoactive, and if he/she knows (or ought to know or suspect) or is reckless as to whether another person is likely to consume it for its psychoactive effects. The parallel offences concerning an offer to supply are covered under s 5(2). These offences are all triable either way, and the penalty is a fine and/or imprisonment (12 months if tried summarily, and up to seven years' imprisonment on indictment).

12.6.3 Possession with intent to supply

Possession of a controlled drug with intent to supply is an offence under s 5(3) of the Misuse of Drugs Act 1971. The substance in question must be a controlled drug (unlike the s 4(3) supplying offence), but need not be the drug the suspect believes it to be, so a suspect who believed the drug was heroin can still be guilty even if it is found to be cocaine. It is not relevant whether the possession is lawful, so a chemist or police officer in lawful possession could commit this offence if he/she intended to unlawfully supply the drug. The defences outlined in s 28 of the Misuse of Drugs Act 1971 also apply to s 5(3) (see 12.5.4). The penalties are the same as for the production of a controlled drug, and the s 4(3) offence is a trigger offence: a police officer can demand a sample from a suspect held in custody (see 12.6.1).

For psychoactive substances, possession with intent to supply is covered under s 7(1)(a) of the Psychoactive Substances Act 2016. The suspect must know (or suspect) that the substance is psychoactive (s 7(1)(b)), and intend to supply it to another person for consumption (by any person) for its psychoactive effects. Offences under s 7 are triable either way. The penalty is a fine and/or imprisonment (12 months if tried summarily, and up to seven years' imprisonment on indictment).

12.6.4 Occupier or manager of premises used for controlled drug offences

This offence (s 8 of the Misuse of Drugs Act 1971) concerns persons who occupy or are concerned in the management of a premises, and who 'knowingly permit or suffer' any of the following activities to take place there:

(a) producing or attempting to produce a controlled drug;
(b) supplying, attempting to supply, or offering to supply a controlled drug to another;
(c) preparing opium for smoking;
(d) smoking cannabis, cannabis resin, or prepared opium.

There must be evidence that one of these activities has actually occurred (see *R v Auguste* [2003] EWCA Crim 3329). For example, in relation to (b) above, there must be evidence of a controlled drug actually being supplied on the premises: the simple existence of sufficient quantities and equipment for supplying controlled drugs is insufficient to prove the offence (see *Regina v McGee* [2012] EWCA Crim 613). The suspect does not need to know what type of controlled drug is involved.

To be an 'occupier' the person does not have to be a tenant or owner, but needs to have sufficient control over the premises such that he/she could prevent drug-related activities. A student who pays for a room on campus would be regarded as an occupier. A person 'concerned in the management' does not have to have a legal interest in the premises, and would include a trespassing squatter (see *R v Tao* [1976] 3 All ER 65). A cleaner would be neither an occupier nor concerned in the management. To 'knowingly permit or suffer' the activity would include having suspicions but choosing to take no action, and also trying to stop the activity but without success. Powers are available to close premises (licensed, enclosed, open, residential business) that are being used for controlled drug offences (see 14.2.2.4).

Offences under s 8 are triable either way. If tried summarily the penalty is a fine and/or imprisonment (six months for Classes A and B, and three months for Class C). On indictment the penalty is a fine and/or up to 14 years' imprisonment.

12.6.5 Import and export of controlled drugs or psychoactive substances

The legal import and export of controlled drugs requires a licence, and is covered under s 3(1) of the Misuse of Drugs Act 1971. Without a relevant licence it is an offence under s 170 of the Customs and Excise Management Act 1979 to knowingly acquire possession or be concerned in transporting, storing or concealing such drugs, or be concerned in any fraudulent evasion or attempted evasion of such a restriction. These offences are triable either way. The penalty for a Class A or B drug is imprisonment (life and 14 years, respectively), and for Class C on summary conviction three months' imprisonment and/or a fine, and on indictment, five years' imprisonment.

For psychoactive substances, it is an offence to intentionally import or export such a substance (s 8(1) and (2) PSA 2016, respectively). The person must know or suspect (or ought to know or suspect in the circumstances) that the substance is psychoactive. He/she must also intend to consume it for its effects, or know or be reckless as to whether some other person is likely to consume it for its effects. Offences under s 7 are triable either way, and the penalty is a fine and/or imprisonment (12 months if tried summarily, and up to seven years' imprisonment on indictment).

TASK 6

1. Make a list of factors and circumstances that would provide reasonable grounds for suspecting a person is in unlawful possession of drugs with intent to supply.
2. What would a police officer have to say to a person before carrying out a search under s 23 of the Misuse of Drugs Act 1971?
3. Having found an unidentifiable substance, what are some of the reasons that would make it necessary to arrest the person?

12.7 Answers to Tasks

TASK 1 Look at s 34(1) of the Criminal Justice Act 1972 to help with the answer.

- The health and safety of the individual is paramount—is she injured in any way, and how drunk is she?
- What offence has she committed? Is she just drunk, or drunk and disorderly?
- Is arrest necessary to prevent her from causing physical injury (to herself or others) or could the matter be dealt with in another way?
- What other agencies could you involve?

Some forces have a local agreement whereby a person can be taken to an approved treatment centre for alcoholism. If this was the case the police officer could treat her as being in lawful custody for the purposes of the journey (s 34(1) of the Criminal Justice Act 1972).

TASK 2

- Introduce yourself, giving your name and your station.
- Explain that you suspect he is under 18 years of age.
- Tell him that he is in a public place.
- Make clear to him that you wish him to surrender any intoxicating liquor in his possession, and to give his name and address, and that failure without reasonable excuse to comply is an offence.

TASK 3 Some forces have a member of staff who is responsible for representing the police at applications for premises licences or renewals. He/she should be notified of incidents where suspects have been drinking excessively, and the information can then be taken into account when deciding on granting or renewing licences.

TASK 4 Some common unlawfully used controlled drugs are:

- **amphetamines** (speed, whizz, w, billy, uppers, phet, amph, wizz, white, sulphate, snow, sprint, bomb, base, paste, dexies). The average UK street price is £12 per gram;
- **cocaine** (coke, crack, charlie, sniff, white, ching, powder, snow white, snuff, rock, nose candy, okey cokey, fairy dust, Bolivian marching powder, toot, wrap). The average UK street price is £52 per gram, and £10–20 for a 'rock' of crack cocaine weighing 0.25 grams;
- **heroin** (smack, crack, brown, gear, shit, jack, skag, henry, horse, needles). The average UK street price is £10–20 per 2g bag; and

- **cannabis** (weed, skunk, pot, dope, bud, green, blow, hash, ganja, grass, draw, puff, gange, shit, spliff, wacky backy, pukka, rocky, joint, hashish, resin, doobie, gear, bush, smoke, leaf, stash, buddha, rasta pasta, chill, mary jane, to blaze, marijuana, squidgy black, rock, purple haze, sensimilia, hemp, herb, blow, soap, blunt). The average UK street price for cannabis resin is £30 per quarter ounce.

More information is available at <http://www.drugwise.org.uk/>.

TASK 5

1. Yes. In *R v Martindale* (1986) 84 Cr App R 31 (CA), Lord Laine stated that:

   > Possession does not depend upon the alleged possessor's powers of memory. Nor does possession come and go as memory revives or fails. If it were to do so, a man with a poor memory would be acquitted, he with a good memory would be convicted.

2. Yes, his possession was lawful. The original possession of the tablets was lawful and the lawfulness continues with time (see *R v Buswell* [1972] 1 WLR 64).

3. No, she cannot be said to be in control of the drug. There is insufficient actual or physical control of the heroin in this situation (see *Adams v DPP* [2002] All ER (D) 125 (Mar)).

TASK 6

1. Factors and circumstances that would provide reasonable grounds for suspecting a person is in unlawful possession of drugs with intent to supply might include:

   - intelligence that drugs are being supplied or used in that particular area;
   - information on the descriptions of people supplying or using drugs in that area;
   - behaviour of the person (eg is he/she trying to hide something, or is getting ready to throw away something small, seemingly with the intention that you will not notice?); and
   - behaviour of people who approach the person (eg do a series of individuals separately approach the person, exchange small items, and then walk away? Note that these may be very open acts, to try and avoid attracting attention).

2. Before the search, the police officer must explain the purpose of the search, explain the grounds, tell the person about his/her entitlement to a copy of the record of search, show a warrant card (if out of uniform), explain to the person that he/she is being detained for a search, state the legal search power title to be used (s 23 of the Misuse of Drugs Act), and provide the name of his/her police station and his/her (the officer's) name. This can be summarized by the mnemonic GO WISELY (see 9.4.1 for full details).

3. See 10.6.4 for the reasons that can apply for making an arrest, for example:

   - preventing injury through the use of the drug(s);
   - ensuring a prompt investigation through the questioning of the suspect and the analysis of the drug(s).

13 Protection from Violence, Abuse, and Neglect

13.1 Introduction

Some people at certain times in their lives may need protection from violence, abuse and neglect, and require support and guidance, for example from social services or the health service. The police will often be tasked with the initial protection of vulnerable people, young people, and people who may lack the mental capacity to make decisions. In this chapter we explore how the police can respond to these situations, and describe the procedures and available powers. Coordination between different agencies may not be straightforward, and an initial assessment will often be needed to help establish the most appropriate course of action. For example, the police inevitably come into contact with people with mental health difficulties, but they are not obliged to assume direct or indirect responsibility. Other partner agencies are often better equipped to deal with such issues and may have statutory responsibility for providing support and services (although the police will often assist (see the Mental Health Act 1983 Code of Practice and the College of Policing Authorised Professional Practice, particularly the sections *Engagement and communication, Major investigation and public protection, Public order, and Detention and custody*)). It is also important to ensure that individuals are treated fairly and do not suffer discrimination (s 149 of the Equality Act 2010). Vulnerable people need help with accessing services and justice, and protection from crimes committed against them (including hate crimes).

The chapter concludes with an examination of how the law seeks to prevent harm to animals.

13.2 Mentally Vulnerable People

Police officers and others working in law enforcement will often encounter people who behave in ways that may seem strange, or who seem to be unable to think clearly. This could be due to a mental illness that causes distorted thoughts and feelings, or they may find it hard to take in basic facts and make decisions, or be under the influence of drugs (illegal or otherwise). A person with a mental disorder may often find it hard to make rational decisions. This incapacity may be transient during severe episodes of illness, or more persistent, during periods of enduring mental illness. The College of Policing APP provides comprehensive guidance on responding to people with mental health problems or learning disabilities (CoP, 2016g), and the mental health charity MIND has published a good practice guide for the police (2013), and a guide for prosecutors and advocates (2010).

The police may be involved with individuals with mental ill health in two rather different ways; as part of accessing healthcare or in a law enforcement capacity (CoP, 2016g). A common misconception is that people who suffer from mental disorder (mental illness) are likely to be violent, but this is not the case. Most pose no physical threat to others, but are simply confused or unable to cope. Police training will include guidance on how to recognize the symptoms of

Specific Incidents

mental illness, and further advice is provided through NCALT. Here we will examine the relevant legislation and parts of the MHA Code of Practice (Department of Health, 2015). The Mental Health Act 1983 (MHA) is used in relation to people with mental illness. The Mental Capacity Act 2005 (MCA) is used if a person is incapable of making a decision and requires care for any other reason, such as a medical condition. The scenario in 13.2.4 illustrates this further. Note that under the MHA, dependence on alcohol or drugs is not considered a disability or a disorder (s 1(3)).

13.2.1 Interacting with mentally vulnerable people

Mental ill health includes a variety of disorders, including psychotic disorders (such as schizophrenia), mood disorders (such as depression or bipolar disorder), and a variety of personality and anxiety disorders (such as panic attacks and phobias). Learning disabilities cover a wide range of conditions with 'significant impairment of intelligence and social functioning' (s 1(4) MHA). With such a wide definition, officers need to assess each situation on an individual basis. Individuals with learning disabilities can be especially vulnerable, and are likely to have a limited understanding of police work and the justice system. Some may also have difficulty recalling events, understanding questions, and communicating effectively. Others may acquiesce to suggestions of events and actions in order to appease the interviewer. It is therefore very important that individuals with learning disabilities are identified as such when giving witness statements (see 10.11 and 25.6), and that this information is passed to the CPS. A doctor or a mental health practitioner can help identify whether an individual has a learning disability. Support agencies such as Victim Support can provide assistance to people with mental disabilities, for example if they are asked to testify in court.

Trainee police officers have to learn how to deal with these situations effectively and maintain their own and others' safety. People experiencing fear, paranoia, confusion, anger, hearing voices, and frustration may become aggressive, and police officers need to know how to minimize the effects. For example, when dealing with individuals displaying signs of mental ill health, you should look out for possible signs of aggression such as sweating, clenched fists, rapidly moving eyes, frowning, increased reaction to sound, raised voices, and threats. You should also avoid any physical contact with them unless you are sure that it will not be perceived as threatening. Consider taking a step backwards to show you are giving the person space, move slowly, and as little as possible, but keep your hands visible. Make a visual check for weapons and remove anything dangerous, particularly sharp objects, from the individual's reach. You should maintain an adequate distance and may remove your headwear, as this may be seen as threatening. However, you should be cautious, and keep in a safe position.

Establishing good communication may be difficult, but is essential when dealing with a person with mental ill health. You should explain what you are doing and repeat it, to ensure that you are being understood. Use a calm low-pitched tone and reassure the individual of what you are trying to achieve. A Medic Alert bracelet could provide useful information and the individual should be asked about it. Ask the person why he/she is upset, but avoid challenging or reasoning against delusions.

When you call for further assistance ask for lights and sirens to be turned off. Ensure that only one officer talks at a time, do not whisper to your colleagues, and avoid using your radio where possible. Any onlookers should be removed from the scene.

A person with mental ill health may be unpredictable, so you may need to prevent him/her from engaging in harmful behaviour. You may need to use force to do this, but make sure that it is only used as a last resort and that it is absolutely necessary and proportional in the circumstances. You may also need to use force to protect the public and yourself, and again, the degree and type of force must be necessary and reasonable. Before using any force, consideration should be given to the various strategies that can be employed to help minimize aggression, as discussed previously.

There will probably be local policies in place between law enforcement agencies and practitioners to ensure a fair and adequate treatment of individuals experiencing mental ill health. You should familiarize yourself with the local policy to ensure that you can provide best service in such situations.

13.2.2   Disturbed behaviour in public places

It is not an offence to be mentally disordered in a public place. Many people who live in the community suffer from mental ill-health and cope well with their everyday lives. However, if a person in a public place (see 9.2 for definitions of public and private places) seems to be in need of immediate care and control, a police officer has the power to remove him/her to a place of safety (s 136 MHA).

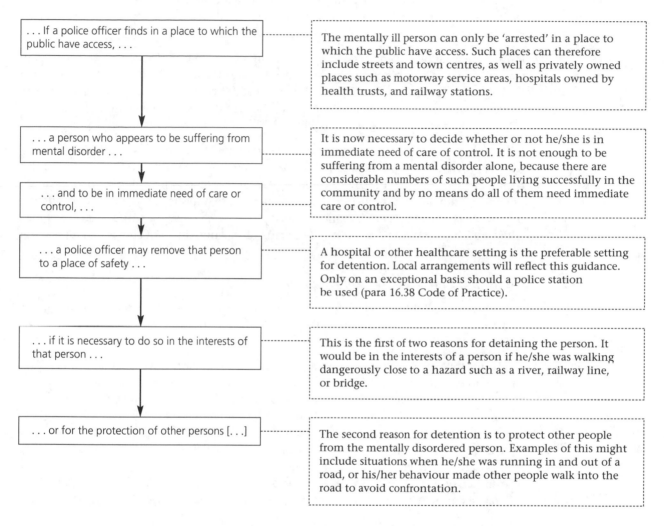

. . . If a police officer finds in a place to which the public have access, . . .	The mentally ill person can only be 'arrested' in a place to which the public have access. Such places can therefore include streets and town centres, as well as privately owned places such as motorway service areas, hospitals owned by health trusts, and railway stations.
. . . a person who appears to be suffering from mental disorder . . .	It is now necessary to decide whether or not he/she is in immediate need of care of control. It is not enough to be suffering from a mental disorder alone, because there are considerable numbers of such people living successfully in the community and by no means do all of them need immediate care or control.
. . . and to be in immediate need of care or control, . . .	
. . . a police officer may remove that person to a place of safety . . .	A hospital or other healthcare setting is the preferable setting for detention. Local arrangements will reflect this guidance. Only on an exceptional basis should a police station be used (para 16.38 Code of Practice).
. . . if it is necessary to do so in the interests of that person . . .	This is the first of two reasons for detaining the person. It would be in the interests of a person if he/she was walking dangerously close to a hazard such as a river, railway line, or bridge.
. . . or for the protection of other persons [. . .]	The second reason for detention is to protect other people from the mentally disordered person. Examples of this might include situations when he/she was running in and out of a road, or his/her behaviour made other people walk into the road to avoid confrontation.

Hospital or ambulance transport should be used if a person needs to be transported to a place of safety (as set out in agreed local policies). Police transport should only be used in cases of extreme urgency or where there is a risk of violence (Code of Practice, para 16.32).

13.2.2.1   Detention in a place of safety

A place of safety would include social services residential accommodation, a hospital, a police station, an independent hospital or care home for mentally disordered persons, or any other suitable place (if the occupier is willing temporarily to receive the patient). The definition of a place of safety is provided in s 135 of the MHA. A person removed from a public place to a place of safety may be detained there, but only:

- to be examined and assessed by a registered medical practitioner;
- to be interviewed by an approved social worker; or
- while necessary arrangements are made for his/her treatment or care.

The detention period must not exceed 72 hours, beginning at the time of arrival in the first place of safety (s 136(2) of the MHA and Code of Practice, para 16.26).

At the time of writing (2017), Parliament is discussing the Policing and Crime Bill, which is likely to introduce changes to the MHA. This could include banning the use of police cells as a place of safety for children suffering from mental ill health, and only allowing their use as such for adults in exceptional circumstances.

A person in a health service place of safety (such as a hospital) may develop signs of apparent mental ill health, and therefore need care and control. This should be provided by the doctors

Specific Incidents

and nurses (using their powers under s 5 of the MHA and Code of Practice, para 16.20) and the police should not be called to intervene under s 163 of the MHA.

13.2.2.2 Detention of a mentally disordered person at a police station

If a detained person is excluded from a hospital as a place of safety and taken to a police station, the name of the person who made the exclusion decision (and the reasons for it) must be recorded (Code of Practice, para 16.62). A person detained in a police cell as a place of safety for lack of a suitable alternative, should not be detained there for more than 24 hours (Code of Practice, para 16.40).

If no offence has been committed the person cannot be arrested under s 24 of PACE. However, if a person has to be taken to a police station as a place of safety under s 136 of the MHA, then Code C of PACE applies (Code of Practice (para 16.66)). He/she would therefore have the same rights as a person who has been arrested, and a police officer would have the power to search him/her under s 32 PACE (see para 16.68).

In investigations, an appropriate adult must be present when a 'mentally vulnerable' or 'mentally disordered' person is interviewed (see 25.4.2 and 25.5.1.1). There are exceptions to this requirement, namely if it seems it could lead to: interference with evidence (related to an offence, an individual, or property); alerting someone else suspected of committing an offence; or preventing the recovery of illegally obtained property. An interview without an appropriate adult must be approved by an officer of the rank of superintendent or above, and it must not represent harm to the individual (PACE Code C).

13.2.3 Disturbed behaviour in private places

A police officer might need to help or restrain a mentally disordered person in a private place, such as the person's home. For a private place, the powers of removal and detention are different from those that apply for a public place.

If it seems that the person might be a danger to him/herself or to others, then a police officer can try to explain the need for treatment. If the person does not agree to this, then police control should be contacted to request the attendance of an Approved Mental Health Professional (AMHP). A police officer should remain at the scene until the AMHP arrives. Once an AMHP begins to assess a person for possible detention he/she assumes overall responsibility for coordinating the process of assessment (Code of Practice, para 14.41), and for arranging transport to hospital if required. Police officers have no obligation to stay until the end of the assessment, unless it is unsafe to leave (Code of Practice, para 16.34). The AMHP might ask for assistance during the transportation of the patient to hospital, but see 13.2.3.2.

It may seem that an AMHP is not required, but a breach of the peace is likely. The police can detain a person in order to prevent this (but see 14.3. on 'breach of the peace' and the use of force). If the person is suspected of committing an offence, there may be reasons to arrest him/her, but this is not necessarily the most appropriate way of dealing with a mentally disordered person.

13.2.3.1 Using force to enter

If the person refuses to let anyone in and there is no one else present to grant entry, then force can be used, but only if:

- the police officer has a magistrate's warrant (under s 135 of the MHA) authorizing a search to remove persons believed to be suffering from mental disorder;
- there is a breach of the peace (see 14.3); or
- the entry is necessary to save life or limb, or to prevent serious damage to property (s 17(1)(e) PACE, see 13.7.2 and 20.1, respectively).

13.2.3.2 Removing a person in a private place to a place of safety

If a person is in a private place and there has been no breach of the peace and no offences have been committed, he/she cannot be detained or removed (under the MHA) to a hospital or other place of safety unless he/she consents, is 'sectioned' for admission to hospital (see 13.2.3.3), or there is a magistrate's warrant in place (see 13.2.3.1).

If an AMHP arranges for the detention of a person and his/her removal to hospital, the police may be involved in transportation, but only for more challenging patients. The extent of such police involvement will be set out in locally agreed policies (Code of Practice, para 14.48).

13.2.3.3 'Sectioning'

This is an unofficial term that refers to the procedures that can be used when a person in a private place seems to need urgent psychiatric hospital treatment, but will not seek it voluntarily and presents a danger to him/herself or to others. The person can be 'sectioned' (the term is used with reference to a section of the MHA). The application is made by an AMHP or the nearest relative, and is considered by two medical health practitioners (or just one in an emergency). If the application is agreed, a police officer may be asked to help remove the person to hospital (but see 13.2.3.2), by force if necessary (s 6 MHA). A 'section application form' must be completed and signed prior to any such police involvement.

13.2.4 The Mental Capacity Act 2005

The Mental Capacity Act 2005 (MCA) provides a broad legal framework which aims to protect vulnerable people aged 16 years or over (s 2(5)) who do not have the capacity (ability) to make their own decisions. (This could be through illness, unconsciousness, alcohol, drugs, or a severe learning disability that has been present since birth.) The Act also empowers and offers protection to carers and others (such as police officers) who find themselves involved in the protection of vulnerable people. Of particular interest is s 5, which provides the power to carry out acts related to the care or treatment (including restraint) of a person who lacks capacity. The MCA Code of Practice (Department for Constitutional Affairs, 2007) provides guidance on how the Act should be interpreted, and is not just for police officers and health care professionals. The National Mental Capacity Forum was set up in 2015 to work with a variety of stakeholders (including health services, police, and social care) to improve local implementation of the MCA.

The following scenario is presented here from the perspective of a police officer. As you read on about the meaning of the term 'capacity' and making decisions, you might find it useful to consider how the Act might apply in practice.

> Two police officers have been asked by a paramedic team to attend a bedsit in town. An extremely thin and naked man is lying in bed with several open wounds on his body which look as if they could have been caused by hypodermic needles. He appears heavily intoxicated, and is suspected of using controlled drugs. Blood-filled syringes are strewn all around the bed and the floor of the room and the man appears to be bleeding from body orifices. The police officers consider the health and safety of the people around them as a priority so they and the paramedics don protective clothing and remove dangerous and contagious items to a toxic chemical receptacle and a 'sharps box'. The paramedics have tried to persuade the man to go to hospital but every time they have got close to him he has mumbled and moved away violently. The police officers also try to communicate with him, but without success. They must now decide how to help him, and under which legislation.
>
> In these circumstances the use of the Mental Health Act 1983 is inappropriate, partly because the person is not in a public place (and so s 136 would not apply), but also because the man is in need of immediate medical and not psychiatric care. Although he might be suffering from a temporary mental disorder, it is his inability to make a decision and gain medical attention that is the immediate concern. The Mental Capacity Act 2005 can be used in these circumstances, to facilitate making arrangements for transporting him to hospital for medical treatment.

13.2.4.1 General principles underlying the Mental Capacity Act 2005

Section 1(1) of the MCA provides some key principles, for example that a person:

- must be treated as if he/she has capacity (see 13.2.4.2) unless it can be established otherwise (s 1(2));
- must not be treated as incapable of making a decision unless all practicable steps have been taken to help him/her to do so, without success (s 1(3)); and
- must not be treated as if he/she is unable to make a decision just because he/she is known to have made an unwise decision previously (s 1(4)).

The Act also specifies that any decision or action that is taken must be in the person's best interests (s 1(5)) and must avoid (as far as possible) interfering with his/her rights and freedom (s 1(6)).

13.2.4.2 Judging a person's mental capacity

Capacity is the ability to take in information and use that information to make decisions. A lack of capacity could be caused by an impairment or disturbance in the functioning of the mind or brain (s 2(1)), for example through a learning disability, dementia, brain damage, or toxic confusion caused by drugs or another noxious substance. The lack of capacity could be permanent or temporary (s 2(2)). Of course, any evaluation can only be made on the balance of probabilities.

The process of judging of a person's capacity will focus on the person's ability to make decisions. Section 3 of the Act provides specific guidance on how to judge a person's ability to make a decision. No reference can be made to the person's age or appearance, nor should any unjustified assumptions be made based solely on the person's condition or behaviour (s 2(3)). A functional test may be used to check, for example, if he/she is able to: understand and retain any information relevant to a decision; use information to help make a decision; or inform another person of a decision. The means of communication used by either party is not important; it could be talking, writing or typed text, a sign language, or other gestures.

13.2.4.3 Acting on behalf of a person who lacks capacity

Under s 4 of the MCA the decision made and any subsequent action must be in the person's best interests. He/she must be encouraged to participate as fully as possible in any act or decision, and all reasonably practicable steps should be taken to achieve this. The likelihood of the person having the capacity at some point in the future must be considered, and if there is no immediate need to make a particular decision, and he/she is likely to regain the capacity to make the decision, then it should be delayed until he/she has recovered sufficiently.

If the person cannot make decisions and therefore lacks capacity, a decision might need to be made on his/her behalf. As far as possible, the person's wishes and feelings should be considered, especially his/her usual beliefs and values (if known). The views of the following people should also be taken into account:

- his/her carer;
- anyone else he/she would like to be consulted; and/or
- anyone with power of attorney or a deputy appointed by a court.

Actions carried out in connection with the care or treatment of a person do not incur any liability (s 5) if prior to those acts, reasonable steps were taken to establish that the person lacks capacity, and it was reasonably believed that the actions were in the person's best interests. If a decision relates to life-sustaining treatment, any consideration that it would be better if the person was allowed to die should be avoided.

If the actions are resisted (despite efforts to communicate and to encourage participation) then restraint may be needed. But there must be a reasonable belief that restraint has to be used to prevent harm to the person, and the restraint must be proportional (s 6). Actions defined as restraint under s 6 include using force (or threatening to use it) in order to apply care or treatment, and restricting a person's liberty of movement, whether or not he/she resists. It does not include depriving a person of his/her liberty (within the meaning of Article 5 of the ECHR), or contravening a decision made by a court or a person with a relevant power of attorney.

13.2.4.4 Applying the Mental Capacity Act 2005

In the scenario at the start of 13.2.4, all practicable steps to help the man have been unsuccessful. The attending police officers and paramedics believe he needs urgent treatment in hospital. On the balance of probabilities he is suffering from toxic confusion which has caused an impairment or disturbance of his mind or brain. He is therefore unlikely to have the capacity to make the decision to go to hospital and appears to be incapable of understanding the information relevant to the decision—that is that he is seriously ill and needs treatment. The police officers and paramedics have tried to communicate with him and to encourage him to participate in making the decision to go to hospital but their efforts have failed. There is no information pertaining to family, friends, or carers, and there is no indication of how he might have wished to be treated when he had capacity.

Specific Incidents

The police officers and paramedics have taken all reasonable steps required to establish that he lacks capacity, and that he cannot make the relevant decision. Therefore they need to make a decision on his behalf. The least restrictive action or decision to avoid interfering with his rights and freedom is to ensure he receives hospital treatment. They judge that the least restraint required under the circumstances is to help him onto a stretcher for transportation to hospital.

13.2.4.5 Ill-treatment or neglect of a person who lacks capacity

Some people have particular caring or legal responsibilities for an individual who lacks capacity, and may also have a power of attorney. It is an offence under s 44 of the MCA for any such carer or responsible person to ill-treat or wilfully neglect the person.

The offence is triable either way and the penalty is a fine or imprisonment (summarily 12 months, and five years on indictment).

TASK 1

1. What is your local force's policy in terms of the use of s 136 MHA powers?
2. A police officer is called to the home of the parents of a young man (over 18) who seems to be suffering from a mental disorder. On arrival, the parents inform her that he is in his bedroom, and holding the door handle to stop anyone opening the door. Using the minimum force necessary (and limiting your answers to the Mental Health Act 1983):
   (a) how could she gain entrance for the parents, and
   (b) what options are available should she decide that the young man is in need of medical attention in relation to his apparent mental disorder?

13.3 Safeguarding Children

The Children Act 1989 was seen as an important development in safeguarding the welfare of children in the UK. It placed great emphasis on encouraging multi-agency working and supporting children and families, and heralded an approach to child welfare that made children the primary concern. This also led to the 'Working together to safeguard children' national guidance. However, cases such as the tragic death of Victoria Climbié in the year 2000 demonstrated that more needed to be done to protect children from harm. The inquiry into the death of Victoria Climbié, headed by Lord Laming (2003), provided a number of key recommendations designed to ensure thorough investigation of potential crimes, proper training for investigators, and appropriate and effective inter-agency working. In response to the Laming recommendations, the government produced 'Every Child Matters', and eventually the Children Act 2004. These promote child welfare, and inter-agency working, placing statutory obligations upon local authorities to cooperate with other agencies. Indeed, the police should support other agencies in their work when there are concerns for a child's well-being (whether or not a crime has been committed), such as under ss 17 and 47 of the Children Act 1989 (Home Office, 2015e, p 34). The role of child commissioner was created, and Local Safeguarding Children Boards (LSCBs) were set up in regions throughout the country. LSCBs ensure that clear guidance and procedures are in place, and provide multi-agency training.

Note that the age definition of a child in the Children Act 1989 is any person under the age of 18 (s 105). Legislation often refers to children or young people of a particular age, for example 'a child under the age of 12'.

13.3.1 Investigating child abuse

Each police force will have a specialist Child Abuse Investigation Unit. Whilst there may be regional differences in the exact nature and scope of their work, these teams will usually be staffed by nationally trained investigators (trained in ICIDP or equivalent), who will have also been expected to have undertaken the National Specialist Child Abuse Investigator Development Programme (SCAIDP). There is an expectation that all officers interviewing children in relation to abuse will be trained to a very high standard in witness interviewing.

Once a referral is made to such a team, either from an internal notification or from an external agency (eg social services), the investigators will decide what type of investigation is required. These may often begin as joint agency investigations, although where criminal offences are suspected the police will take a lead role. According to s 47 of the Children Act 1989, the local authority has a duty to investigate where it believes that a child might be suffering from significant harm. The police have certain powers under s 46 of the same Act in relation to police protection (see 13.3.3), and the first consideration will be to secure the welfare of a child or children. Once this has been achieved a thorough criminal investigation can take place, and other agencies will work to assure the current and future welfare of the child.

In incidents involving children, it is not uncommon for child abuse to be an underlying factor. Specialist units are available to assist trainee officers with decision-making where a child's welfare is a concern. A wide range of incidents may be associated with child abuse, such as:

- domestic abuse;
- missing children, including those truanting from school;
- children engaged in criminality, including bullying and abusing others;
- children abusing animals;
- children involved in sexual exploitation or prostitution;
- parental drug or alcohol abuse.

Further information is available from the College of Policing in *Risk and associated investigations*, available online. Sexual offences involving children are covered in 17.7.

13.3.2   Protecting children from harm

Children are sometimes exposed to significant harm by their parents, relatives, and other people involved in their care and supervision. The Children Act 1989 (s 31(9)) states that harm can include:

- ill-treatment or the impairment of health or development;
- impairment suffered from seeing or hearing the ill-treatment of another;
- sexual abuse; and
- forms of ill-treatment which are not physical.

An alternative definition categorizes child abuse into four distinct types: physical, emotional, sexual, and neglect (ACPO *Guidance on Investigating Child Abuse and Safeguarding Children* (2nd edn) (2009)). Unsurprisingly, one of the risk factors associated with suspicious child deaths include a previous history of violence to children (see ACPO, 2014a). More recently, the Counter-Terrorism and Security Act 2015 (s 36) introduced the obligation for Local Authorities to establish 'Channel' panels to try and prevent children being harmed through being drawn into terrorism. The panels (which include the local chief officer of the police) assess the likelihood of this, and arrange for support to be provided (Home Office, 2015e, p 19).

Some of the legislation in the Children and Young Persons Act 1933 (CYPA) is considered here (see also 13.1.1.2). The Offences Against the Person Act 1861 and the Sexual Offences Act 2003 are also relevant (see Chapters 15 and 17 respectively).

13.3.2.1   The offence of child cruelty

This offence can be committed by a person aged 16 or over who is responsible for caring for a child under 16. The offence is committed when such a carer willfully 'assaults, ill-treats, neglects, abandons or exposes' the child or causes him/her to be treated in a way which is likely to cause unnecessary suffering or 'injury to health' (s 1(1) of the CYPA). The 'injury to health' includes:

- physical injury, or loss of 'sight, hearing, limb or organ of the body'; and
- psychological problems such as 'mental derangement'.

The offence is triable either way and the penalty is a fine or imprisonment (summarily six months, and ten years on indictment).

13.3.2.2   Cigarettes and young people

A constable in uniform has a duty to seize any cigarettes, tobacco, or cigarette papers in the possession of a young person who is smoking in a street or public place (s 7(3) of the CYPA). This applies for a young person who either is, or appears to be, younger than 16. Any seized items should be disposed of according to local force policies and procedures.

Selling cigarettes, cigarette papers, or tobacco to young people under the age of 18 years is an offence under s 7(1) of the CYPA (under s 7(2) if automatic machines are used). However, shopkeepers may be relieved to know that under s 7(1A) it is a defence if it can be proved that he/she 'took all reasonable precautions and exercised all due diligence to avoid the commission of the offence'. The offence is triable summarily and the penalty is a fine. If a person is convicted of a s 7(1) or 7(2) offence on two or more occasions within two years, a magistrates' court can apply a restriction order under s 12. This bans the offender from selling or managing premises for selling tobacco-related products. It is a summary offence for a person to knowingly contravene such an order, and the penalty is a fine.

13.3.2.3 Injuries to children from heating appliances

Carers have a responsibility to ensure that children are kept safe when heating appliances are in use. Under s 11 of the CYPA a person over 16 commits an offence if a child under 12 is killed or suffers serious injury because the carer allowed 'the child to be in a room containing an open fire grate or any heating appliance'. The appliance must have been 'liable to cause injury to a person by contact with it' and 'not sufficiently protected to guard against the risk of being burnt or scalded without taking reasonable precautions against that risk'. The penalty for this summary offence is a fine.

13.3.3 Police protection

The police have a statutory duty to safeguard the well-being of children (s 11 of the Children Act 2004). Police officers have a power to take children under 18 into police protection, if the child's safety seems to be at immediate risk were no action taken (s 46 of the Children Act 1989). Note however, that police protection is an emergency power and should only be used when absolutely necessary, the principle being that wherever possible the decision to remove a child/children from a parent or carer should be made by a court (Home Office, 2015e, pp 31, 58). In such circumstances the local authority will apply to a court for an Emergency Protection Order (EPO).

Apart from in exceptional circumstances, no child should be taken into police protection until the initiating officer (see 13.3.3.2) has seen the child and assessed the circumstances. A child can be in police protection for up to 72 hours (s 46(6) of the Children Act 1989).

Where possible, officers should speak with the child, but take care to avoid 'contaminating' any future interviews. The child's responses should be recorded word for word. If a criminal investigation is initiated, the guidance set out in *Achieving Best Evidence in Criminal Proceedings: Guidance on interviewing victims and witnesses, and guidance on using special measures* should be followed. Once officers have secured the safety and well-being of the child, the case should be referred to the Specialist Child Abuse Investigation Unit or its equivalent (see 13.3.1).

13.3.3.1 Procedure for police protection

Police protection can involve moving the child to a safe place, or preventing his/her removal from a safe place. Section 46(1) of the Children Act 1989 states that where a police officer 'has reasonable cause to believe that a child would otherwise be likely to suffer significant harm' he/she may:

1. remove the child to suitable accommodation and keep him/her there; or
2. take all reasonable steps to ensure that his/her removal from a hospital (or other place in which he/she is accommodated) is prevented.

There are two separate and distinct roles for the police in relation to police protection: the initiating officer and the designated officer (Home Office Circular 17/2008). The designated officer will be at least the rank of inspector and cannot be the initiating officer for the same case. He/she must independently overview the circumstances in which the child was taken into protection.

13.3.3.2 The role of the initiating officer

The initiating officer takes the child into police protection, undertakes the initial enquiries, and completes a Police Protection Form as soon as possible. Under s 46(3) of the Children Act 1989, the initiating officer must as soon as is reasonably practicable also:

- inform the local authority where the child was found, of the police protection steps that have been taken (and are proposed) concerning the child, and the reasons;
- tell the authority in which the child usually lives ('the appropriate authority') where he/she is now being accommodated;
- inform the child (if he/she appears capable of understanding) about the steps taken and the reasons, and about any further police protection steps that may be taken;
- try and establish the wishes and feelings of the child;
- ensure that a designated officer has been assigned for the case; and
- arrange for the child to be moved to local authority-provided accommodation ('suitable accommodation' (see 13.3.3.4), if the child is not already in care.

In addition, as soon as is reasonably practicable, the initiating officer must contact the adults who have been caring for the child (s 46(4)). As well as the child's parents, this would include every person who has parental responsibility for the child (see 13.3.3.3) and any other person with whom the child was living immediately before being taken into police protection. The adults who have most recently been caring for the child must be told about the police protection steps taken (or planned) concerning the child, and the reasons.

13.3.3.3 The meaning of 'parental responsibility'

Parental responsibility in terms of the Children Act 1989 means 'all the rights, duties, powers, responsibilities and authority which by law a parent of a child has in relation to that child and [his/her] property'. It can be held by parents, the step-parents, and in certain circumstances, by other people or administrative bodies such as a local authority. The question of who has parental responsibility is covered in ss 2 and 3 of the Children Act 1989. The key points are:

(a) If the father and mother were married to each other when the child was born, they will each have parental responsibility (s 2(1)). (The father is no longer the 'natural guardian' of his legitimate child (s 2(4)).)
(b) If the biological parents were not married to each other when the child was born, the mother will have parental responsibility, and so will the father if the child was jointly registered after 1 December 2003 (s 2(2)).
(c) More than one person can have parental responsibility for the same child at the same time (s 2(5)), and each may act alone to meet that responsibility (s 2(7)).
(d) A person who has parental responsibility for a child does not cease to have the responsibility simply because another person acquires such responsibility for the child (s 2(6)).

The spirit of the legislation is that all the parties including the parents, the child, and the local authority must be kept informed and given reasons for any actions. The child's wishes must be listened to, but not necessarily followed.

13.3.3.4 Suitable accommodation

Suitable accommodation will be local authority accommodation, a registered children's home, or foster care (see Home Office Circular 44/2003), or relatives or other appropriate carers, if the designated officer and social services consider it appropriate. The child may also be taken to hospital if medical attention is required.

The circular also emphasizes that a child under police protection should not be taken to a police station unless there is absolutely no alternative, and under no circumstances should he/she be taken into the custody suite or cell area.

TASK 2 Jo is a single parent struggling to care for 4-year-old Sam. The child has been ill, and Jo does not want to take any more time off work. Her parents often care for Sam while Jo is at work.

However, on one occasion the parents are unavailable to help. Jo realizes that there is no food in the house and, when Sam is asleep, she goes out shopping. During the journey, her car breaks down.

Sam wakes up and becomes distraught. Having heard the child screaming hysterically, the neighbours call the police. Although the officer can clearly hear Sam inside, all the doors and windows are shut and Sam cannot open the door.

(a) What power of entry, if any, is available?
(b) What offence might Jo have committed?

13.4 Missing Persons

There are a number of reasons for a person to 'go absent or missing'. These include:

- children or young people (predominantly teenage girls) who run away from home, normally for one or two days, often because of some recent or chronic issues at home. This is the single biggest demographic group of absent or missing persons (NPIA, 2010b, p 11);
- children who are missing through abduction (either by a non-custodial parent, direct physical abduction by a stranger, or through other means such as internet grooming (see 17.7.6));
- adults (predominantly men) who go absent probably in an attempt to escape from problems in their home lives. These cases are much less likely to be resolved quickly;
- vulnerable adults such as the aged and the mentally ill who become lost;
- adults who have been abducted, for example for purposes of sexual assault or people trafficking.

The vast majority of absent or missing persons are found very quickly and have suffered no harm (or the report turns out to be unfounded). A few are found dead after many weeks, and some are never found. 'Absent' and 'missing' have different meanings, and are associated with different levels of risk. A person is absent when not at a place where he/she is expected or required to be, and a person is missing if his/her whereabouts cannot be established, and the circumstances are out of character, or the context suggests he/she might be subject of crime, or at risk of harm to him or herself or another (CoP, 2016c). The level of risk is clearly higher for a person who is missing.

A person will be categorized as 'absent' if there seems to be no apparent risk, or he/she is simply not where expected. In these circumstances the police are not likely to launch an investigation. However, 'absent' cases must be carefully monitored, and the actions to locate the individual should be agreed early on, as should a review to reassess level of risk . If the level of risk increases, an escalation to the category of 'missing' should be considered. The onus is to view 'going absent' as a possible indicator of potentially something else, and not just as an event in its own right. For example, a child might go absent because he/she is being abused at home, and in such circumstances the safe recovery of the child might be just the start of further investigations.

Missing person incidents sometimes become critical incidents (see 11.5), requiring the support of services other than the local force. A search for a missing person can entail a considerable expenditure of resources and time, including rural and urban searches, dragging waterways, and exhaustive enquiries, particularly if the missing person is in some way vulnerable, such as a child or a mentally ill adult. If there is a criminal aspect to the disappearance, a major crime unit (or equivalent) could be involved, especially if there has been a suspicious death.

The national policy on the police response to 'misper' incidents was extensively redrafted in the light of the Soham murders in 2002. That case highlighted the reliance of smaller police forces on 'mutual aid' for large-scale searches. This is part of the argument for merging forces into larger organizations, which are then capable of mounting such searches independently.

13.4.1 Missing person enquiries

For all missing person reports the initial response should consist of, at least, recording the incident, conducting a risk assessment, agree on the first steps to trace the missing person, a timeline set for reviewing decisions taken (CoP, 2016e). Each case varies but there are standard considerations that always apply when the initial report is received by the call taker, not least of which is to identify whether the person is 'missing' or 'absent' (see 13.4). The majority of missing person enquiries relate to children, so a thorough knowledge of the procedures related to the disappearance of a child is vital.

It is also important to keep an open mind and consider different reasons and scenarios that may explain why that person is missing. Officers should avoid making assumptions, and should communicate with those who have more experience in cases of missing persons. The safety of the missing person should be the prime consideration of everyone involved in the investigation. If relevant, forensic evidence should be collected as soon as possible before it is compromised or lost (within 24 hours for high-risk cases and within seven days for medium-risk cases). This will help speed up the investigation by ruling out suspects, and will also avoid the need for later requests to the person's family (as this could cause them further distress)

(CoP, 2016c). Police forces should consider how to provide the best support for the missing person's family, as they are likely be under considerable stress due to the circumstances, and may also be required to provide detailed information on the disappearance.

The main guidance is available online in the following documents:

- *Major investigation and public protection: Missing persons* (CoP, 2016c)
- *Missing Children and Adults—A Cross Government Strategy* (Home Office, 2011);
- *Guidance on the Management, Recording and Investigation of Missing Persons* (ACPO, 2010c); and
- *Interim Guidance on the Management, Recording and Investigation of Missing Persons 2013* (ACPO, 2013).

The first task in a 'misper' (missing person) enquiry is to conduct a risk assessment, even if it is not yet clear whether the person is missing or just absent. Information is required about the person and his/her circumstances prior to the disappearance, particularly any factors which indicate vulnerability and their lifestyle. The disappearance of a child (taken here to mean a person under the age of 18) is always medium or high risk, and concern would be even higher for a child on the Child Protection Register. The College of Policing have produced a set of quick reference guides that you may find useful in supporting your work when dealing with a missing person (CoP, 2016d). Police officers can use the following checklist to collect the information required for the risk assessment.

Factor	Yes/No/Unknown
1. Is the person likely to self-harm or attempt suicide?	
2. Is the person likely to be the subject of a crime in progress, eg abduction?	
3. Is the person vulnerable due to age, infirmity, or any other factor?	
4. Are the weather conditions inclement to the extent that this would seriously increase the risk to health, especially where the missing person is a child or an elderly person?	
5. Does the missing person need essential medication or treatment not readily available to them?	
6. Does the missing person have any physical illness, disability, or mental health problems?	
7. Does the person have the ability to interact safely with others in an unknown environment?	
8. Has the person been involved in a violent, homophobic, and/or racist incident or confrontation immediately prior to his/her disappearance?	
9. Has the person been subject to recent bullying?	
10. Has the person previously disappeared and suffered or been exposed to harm?	

If a person had left intentionally then certain items (for example credit cards and money) are likely to be missing. He/she might be involved with crime or have employment or financial problems—there may be evidence of this. If there seems to have been a violent struggle the person may have been abducted, and the scene must be preserved for evidential and investigative purposes.

The levels of risk suggested by ACPO (2010c) and the College of Policing (2016c) are shown in the table (our summary):

Level of risk	Criteria
High	The risk posed to the missing person is immediate and there are substantial grounds for believing that he/she is in danger through vulnerability; or he/she may have been the victim of a serious crime; or there are substantial grounds for believing that the public is in danger
Medium	The risk posed is likely to place the person in danger or the person is a threat to others
Low	There is no apparent threat of danger to the missing person or the public

The particular actions needed for each level of risk form part of police training. However, searching for the missing person is an obvious early step to take. This would probably initially involve a thorough search of the person's house, garden, and any adjoining premises (children can hide in very small spaces) and could be extended to include the surrounding area concentrating first on the person's 'habitual haunts', and then hazardous places such as pools, streams, caves, empty buildings, and so on.

Preparation should be made to widen the search systematically, including making house-to-house enquiries. Work place or school absence records can help establish a person's recent movements and activities. Personal papers belonging to the missing person could be viewed (depending on the circumstances), and retained as possible evidence. Local and national police databases should also be interrogated. A list should be made of all relatives, friends, contacts, and work colleagues/fellow trainees in case these are needed, and recent photographs that are a good likeness should be obtained. It may seem an obvious idea to examine any digital devices known to belong to the missing person(smartphones, tablets etc) and their online activities (such any social network sites they might use), but there is no automatic legal right for the police to do so (the missing persons has the right to privacy) – so be guided by local force policy.

The reliability of any person giving information should be considered. Ian Huntley, a caretaker at a school in Soham murdered two young girls, and provided false information to the police early in the investigation about where he had last seen them. All police forces now have to collate information on all absent and missing persons in each police force. This work is carried out by Missing Person Coordinators.

13.4.1.1   Special considerations for missing children

Missing children are particularly at risk of abuse. The Human Rights Act 1998 places a duty on public authorities to protect any person who may be at risk, so the police have a duty of positive action on the investigation of missing persons. All reports of missing children must be properly investigated, and are never considered as low risk.

Children in care ('looked after children') make up a large proportion of cases of missing children, and they often have other needs that compound their vulnerability. Carers may use the term 'unauthorized absence' in relation to some missing children, but the police should avoid using it when recording a missing child (ACPO, 2010a, p 17) as this might cause confusion. If a looked after child is not where the carers expect but his/her whereabouts are known or thought to be known (eg staying with a friend), it is the responsibility of the care staff to search and make enquiries. If the child is then reported to the police as missing, the police might want to consider searching the same area again. If there is suspicion that the child may be at risk of serious harm, it may be appropriate to use the Child Rescue Alert (CRA). This involves seeking help from the public, for example through TV, radio, text messages and other social and digital media (CoP, 2016f).

> **TASK 3** Consider the following scenario:
>
> A 16-year-old boy has been reported as missing by his mother. Checks with his school showed that he did not arrive at school that morning, despite having left his house (an isolated farm) at the normal time and in school uniform. His whereabouts are unknown and he may have been missing for as long as ten hours. There are indications that he has recently become moody and depressed, and may have been subject to some bullying at school. He is asthmatic and needs regular medication. He is a keen shot and has his own shotgun for using on the farm. He had a quarrel with his father the night before; his father had refused to allow him to go out with friends that evening. The father says the boy acts rebelliously.
>
> 1. You might note that there are a number of vulnerabilities, or potential areas for concern, in this case. What further information is required?
> 2. If the missing person enquiry becomes prolonged, what national guidance is available to help plan the ongoing police investigation?

13.5   Modern Slavery and Human Trafficking

Modern Slavery is an umbrella term that includes human trafficking and slavery, servitude and forced or compulsory labour. These crimes all involve exploitation. A system that involves slavery is one where one or more persons seem to have ownership over another person(s).

Slavery is prohibited under the European Convention on Human Rights (Article 4, ECHR). Slavery, servitude, and forced labour were first criminalized in 2010 under s 71 of the Coroners and Justice Act 2009. The Modern Slavery Act 2015 (MSA) consolidated these offences and explicitly addressed human trafficking. Slavery, servitude and forced or compulsory labour are all offences under s 1 of the MSA. The Act also introduced an Independent Anti-Slavery Commissioner, with a UK-wide remit to improve the prevention, detection, investigation, and prosecution of modern slavery offences and identification of victims (MSA, Part 4).

The UK's strategy to address modern slavery is organized around four 'Ps' (HM Government, 2014a). These are:

- pursue (by prosecuting and disrupting offenders);
- prevent (individuals from offending);
- protect (vulnerable people from exploitation and raising awareness and resilience for modern slavery); and
- prepare (by improving victim identification and support).

13.5.1 Human Trafficking

Human trafficking is often a complex phenomenon of significant national and international importance. It consists of arranging or facilitating the travel of a person, with the view to that person being exploited (by the trafficker or someone else). The victim can be of any age, and whether he/she consents to travelling is irrelevant, and the travelling can be to or from the UK, or within the UK (s 2 of the MSA). Human trafficking impacts different areas of policing and incorporates a variety of offences, offenders, and forms of victimization. Police officers may come across trafficking victims whilst on patrol or when responding to incidents. Human trafficking does not always entail a sophisticated and complex operation; the exploitation of any one individual by another, for example with the promise of work in another part of the country, may also fall into this category.

Human trafficking should not be confused with human smuggling; smuggling involves bringing a person into a country illegally, after which the relationship between the parties ceases (Article 3 of the Protocol against the Smuggling of Migrants by Land, Sea and Air supplementing the UN Convention against Transnational Organized Crime).

13.5.1.1 Exploitation of trafficked persons

Sexual exploitation was the most common form of exploitation for which potential adult victims were referred in 2014 (IDMG, 2015, p 9). It is more likely to affect women and girls. Some victims are forcibly taken from their homes and used in the sex trade, while others voluntarily travel to another destination, unaware of the exploitation that will ensue. This is further complicated by the fact that some victims initially agree to travel to work in the sex industry, but are unaware of the working conditions that will be imposed (eg number of clients, type of sexual activity, and pay). For the purposes of human trafficking, all the forms of sexual exploitation that are covered by Part 1 of the Sexual Offences Act 2003 and s 1(1)(a) of the Protection of Children Act 1978 (indecent photographs of children) are considered as forms of exploitation. Section 33A of the Sexual Offences Act 1956, related to the offence of keeping a brothel, can also be important in relation to sexual exploitation.

Labour exploitation is when the victim is forced to work under unacceptable conditions. It often involves threats or physical harm, restrictions of movement, debt-bondage, withholding wages, retention of identity documents, and threats of denunciation to the authorities of the illegal status of the worker. It can be found in a variety of industries, such as factory work, construction, and catering and hotels. Commercial organizations operating in the UK with an annual turnover of more than £36m are required to disclose the steps they have taken to ensure their business does not involve modern slavery (including their supply chain), or to make a statement that they have taken no such action (s 54 of the MSA). The majority of potential child victims referred through the National Referral Mechanism (see 13.5.3) concern labour exploitation (IDMG, 2015, p 9).

Servitude involves providing services, but through threat or coercion. For example, domestic servitude is when victims are forced to clean or cook in other people's homes. Unlike slavery, servitude does not involve 'ownership', but the victim will often have little chance of improving or changing his/her conditions, and may also be the target of sexual abuse. Offenders may have attracted victims through the promise of employment or patronage (eg promising the parents of a child that they will provide her with an education). Victims of servitude are often from abroad, but some originate in the UK.

The circumstances under which a person is found can be used to help to determine whether he/she is being held for the purposes of slavery, servitude, and forced or compulsory labour. Factors such as vulnerability due to age, familial relationship to the offender, or mental or physical illness should be considered (s 1(4)(a) of the MSA). The type of activity and the context are also relevant, for example the work or provision of services may involve sexual exploitation, removal of organs, threats or deception (MSA s 1(4)(b)).

13.5.2 The context of modern slavery and human trafficking

Victims often come from the poorer communities in their country of origin. Poverty places individuals at a greater risk of victimization, especially where there is pressing need for money (such as a relative being ill). Any country with a relatively low socio-economic status is likely to be targeted for victims by human traffickers, and women are more likely to be victimized for two reasons: they usually have lower wages and greater difficulty in accessing education in their home country, and secondly, they may be more in demand in the country of destination (eg as female sex workers). The victims are recruited in a variety of ways, from advertisements for work, to abduction and kidnapping. Their travel documents may or may not be legitimate, for example, a trafficker may arrange a new identity for a child and appoint him/herself as a guardian, thus controlling almost every aspect of the child's life. Corruption in the country of origin (including by government officials) can impede the investigation and prevention of human trafficking.

In 2015, 3,266 potential victims were referred (to the National Referral Mechanism, see 13.5.3) but previous estimates suggest the true number of victims is far higher, probably between 10,000 and 13,000 (NCA, 2015, p 3; IDMG, 2015, p 7). Victims are often reluctant to come forward and report their exploitation, so its true prevalence is difficult to assess. Public authorities (including police authorities) have a statutory duty to notify the Secretary of State when there are reasonable grounds that a person may be a victim of slavery or human trafficking (s 52 of the MSA), and this should at least help improve the accuracy of the data. The details required for such a notification are specified in Schedules 1 and 2 of the MSA (Duty to Notify) Regulations 2015, but should never include data that could lead to potential victims being identified (by anyone).

13.5.3 Responding to trafficking

The National Referral Mechanism (NRM) is a system for triggering formal identification and support for victims of slavery and human trafficking. Under the NRM, 'first responders', which include certain public bodies and NGOs, must refer potential victims to the appropriate 'competent body'. The competent body for individuals from the European Economic Area (the EU countries together with Iceland, Liechtenstein, and Norway) is the UK Human Trafficking Centre (UKHTC), and for non-EEA individuals the competent body is UK Visas and Immigration. Trained 'case owners' will then decide whether the individual in question is a victim of modern slavery. If there are reasonable grounds to consider that this is the case, the victim is entitled to state-funded support while further evidence is gathered to decide whether he/she is (more likely than not) a victim of modern slavery (IDMG, 2015, p 7).

Victims are brought into the country through various points of entry. Initial indicators that a person may have been trafficked include: human rights breaches; threats or actual harm to family members; deprivation of food, water, and sleep; the withholding of medical care; being forced to perform sexual acts; having wages partly or totally withheld; debt-bondage; working excessive hours; not having access to identity documents such as a passport, or having restricted freedom of movement.

Cooperation from victims is often essential for the successful investigation and prosecution of human trafficking offenders, so every effort must be made to form a supportive and trusting relationship. It is important not to judge or stereotype victims of human trafficking, as their circumstances are often unique and difficult to understand for the outsider.

When the victims are children, other indicators of trafficking might be present, such as the unexpected possession of goods and money, exhibiting self-confidence and maturity beyond their years, appearing to have no money but having a mobile phone, or having to pay debts. Such a child may be unable to give details of a contact person or an address, go missing from local authority care, be cared for by adults who are not their parents, have a difficult relationship with their 'parents', or be one of several unrelated children living at an address. In addition, he/she is unlikely to be registered with a GP or be enrolled at a school. For children trafficked within the UK, additional factors that may be particularly relevant include signs of physical abuse, being sexually active and having sexually transmitted diseases or unwanted pregnancies, reports of sexual exploitation, evidence of substance abuse, contact or relationships with significantly older adults or adults outside their normal circle, accounts of social activities with no plausible explanation for funding, street homelessness, self-harming behaviour, and forming online relationships with adults.

Children are not deemed capable of consent and are therefore seen as victims of trafficking if they are being transported to do work, even if they were not forced or deceived. Some children may not be aware that they are being trafficked and others may deliberately conceal the fact. An officer who suspects that a child may be a trafficking victim has the power to remove the child to a safe place (or prevent the child's removal from a safe place) for a maximum of 72 hours (s 46 of the Children Act 1989 (see 13.3.3)). If there is a risk to life or likelihood of serious harm, the police can apply to a court for an Emergency Protection Order (see 13.3.3).

It is sometimes very difficult to respond effectively to victims of human trafficking. For example, the victim may not understand English, might have learning and communication disabilities, or may have suffered trauma leading to mental ill health. Other difficulties include the victim needing medical assistance or having financial dependants. They might also fear reprisals, or fear any authority due to an insecure or illegal immigration status. Their cultural or religious beliefs, shame and fear of dishonour or of forensic medical examination (especially in victims of sexual abuse) can present additional difficulties. Each of these aspects should be taken into account when interviewing suspected victims. Efforts must be made to communicate with them effectively and to reassure them of the role of the police and to explain any required procedures. Police officers should be mindful of their own conduct, gender, and appearance, and the possible effects on victims. Some victims may have experienced long periods of isolation, and may as a consequence feel dependent on their captor, and therefore may not want to cooperate in bringing him/her to justice. Adequate physical, psychological and medical support should be provided from the early stages of the investigation.

Police officers who come into contact with suspected victims should ensure they are safe and receive medical assistance as required, and inform a supervisor and a senior detective officer of the situation. An intelligence report should be submitted and the UKHTC notified as soon as possible using the National Referral Forms. When dealing with children, the local authority children's social care service and police Child Abuse Investigation Unit should also be notified.

To prevent a person from engaging in modern slavery the police can apply to a magistrates' court for a Slavery and Trafficking Prevention Order (STPO) or a Slavery and Trafficking Risk Orders (STRO) (s 2 of the MSA) to restrict certain individuals' behaviour. An STPO lasts for at least five years and can be imposed following a conviction for a modern slavery offence, or be issued as a stand-alone order. For an STRO, the risk of harm posed by an individual must be assessed, and the order can only be issued if there is evidence 'beyond reasonable doubt' of the activities or a risk of harm. The minimum duration of an STRO is two years. Breaching a STPO or a STRO is a criminal offence, punishable with up to five years imprisonment. The maximum custodial sentence for slavery (including human trafficking) is 12 months if tried as a summary offence, and life imprisonment if tried under indictment (s 5 of the MSA).

13.6 Family Violence and Oppression

Here we cover a variety of offences that can occur when some members of a family or social group seek to maintain control over other members of the group. This includes domestic abuse, 'honour'- based violence, female genital mutilation, and forced marriages; these issues have recently been addressed by governmental policy, particularly in terms of violence against women and girls (Home Office, 2016a). Other forms of familial abuse include abuse of older people, child to parent abuse, and sibling abuse.

Managing incidents of violence in family settings presents particular difficulties, because investigations into domestic or 'honour'-based violence may be hampered by the non-cooperation of the extended family or the community. In addition, officers should be aware that when a victim has an insecure immigration status, the records of any police investigation may become part of his/her application to stay in the UK.

Certain victims will have specific needs or characteristics that make them particularly vulnerable, such as age, gender, sexual orientation, disability, cultural background, immigration status, or profession. In relation to vulnerable adults, consideration should be given to the Local Government Association's *Guidance on adult safeguarding and domestic abuse: a guide to support practitioners and managers*.

13.6.1 Domestic violence and abuse

There is currently no legal definition of domestic violence and abuse. The Home Office (2013a) proposes the following definition:

> any incident or pattern of incidents of controlling, coercive, threatening behaviour, violence or abuse between those aged 16 or over who are, or have been, intimate partners or family members regardless of gender or sexuality. The abuse can encompass, but is not limited to psychological, physical, sexual, financial and emotional [abuse].

A new offence of controlling and coercive behaviour in an intimate or family relationship was introduced by the Serious Crime Act 2015. The offence is designed to address patterns of non-violent abuse in ongoing relationships, because this had proved difficult to prosecute under other legislation. The repetitive nature of the behaviour and its cumulative effect on the victim did not always meet the criteria for for common assault or stalking and harassment offences.

Violence in the domestic context should be prosecuted as any other violent crime (see Chapter 15). In terms of police action, the approach should be pro-arrest, and to gather as much evidence as possible. Detailed guidance on the investigation of domestic violence is available in *Authorised Professional Practice on domestic abuse* published by the College of Policing in 2015. The APP guidance updates and in many ways reinforces the information previously published on behalf of ACPO (NPIA, 2008a), and underpins much of what is written here. It emphasizes a multi-agency approach and the need for officers to take 'positive action' whenever reasonable and within their powers.

A Domestic Violence Disclosure Scheme ('Clare's Law') was introduced in the UK in 2014 (UK Parliament, 2013). It allows an individual to find out whether his/her partner has a history of violence. Members of the public have a 'right to ask' (similar to the Child Sex Offender Disclosure Scheme) and a 'right to know'. If the police receive relevant information, they can disclose it to the person at risk after making the appropriate checks (Home Office, 2012b).

13.6.1.1 Civil responses to domestic violence

The Family Law Act 1996 (FLA) provides opportunities under civil law to counter domestic violence and abuse. The FLA was modified by the Domestic Violence, Crime and Victims Act 2004 and provides the basis for most of the provisions covered here.

A non-molestation order requires a person to refrain from molesting another named person. The applicant (an 'associated person' (s 62(3) of the FLA)) could be a spouse, ex-spouse, civil partner, or a current or former cohabitant. Under s 42A of the FLA it is a criminal offence to breach a non-molestation order without reasonable excuse (the person must know of the existence of the order). If the CPS fails to act, the victim may be able to use contempt of court proceedings. The offence of breaching a non-molestation order is triable either way and the penalty is a fine or a maximum of five years' imprisonment.

An occupation order allows an owner, tenant, spouse, or a civil partner to seek the removal of one occupant (the abuser) from his/her home (s 33, FLA). The abuser will be forbidden from entering the property (s 33(3)). A power of arrest may be included under s 47(1)) for a breach of the order (although this is only a civil offence). These orders can be difficult to obtain, often because of the abuser's property rights (Herring, 2007, p 270). The lengthy procedures involved are an obvious disadvantage for victims.

Domestic Violence Protection Orders (DVPOs) and Domestic Violence Protection Notices (DVPNs) have been rolled out in police forces in the UK from 2014. A DVPN is imposed by the police in the immediate aftermath of a domestic violence incident, and prevents the abuser from having contact with the victim or returning to the victim's home for a maximum of

48 hours. (The authorizing officer for this notice needs to be at least at superintendent rank.) Within 48 hours of a DVPN being issued, an application needs to be made to a magistrates' court for a DVPO, a civil order under which there will be a further no-contact period (14–28 days' duration) for the victim and the offender. The aim of DVPNs and DVPOs is to give victims more time to decide whether to leave the abuser or to apply for a non-molestation or occupation order.

Prohibited Steps Orders (PSO) are used to prevent a suspect removing a child from the applicant (s 8 of the Children Act 1989). They do not necessarily prohibit contact with a child, but may impose restrictions on certain activities without prior permission from the court (for example taking the child abroad or out of the local area). The orders can be applied for by anyone with parental responsibility for the child (as described by Part 1 of the Children Act 1989, see 13.3.3.3). A breach of a PSO is a civil contempt of court; there is no power of arrest attached to this order.

The National Centre for Domestic Violence (NCDV) assists victims with the application for emergency injunctions, and can be a very important point of call to ensure that a victim is safe and able to escape violence. The NCDV offers an electronic third party injunction referral system and provides a secure on-line ASSIST programme that enables police officers access to court papers related to non-molestation and occupation orders (NCDV, 2015a; NCDV, 2015b).

13.6.1.2 Responding to domestic violence incidents

The Crime Survey for England and Wales estimates that approximately 1.2 million women and 650,000 men (aged between 16 and 59 years of age) experienced domestic abuse between April 2015 and March 2016 (ONS, 2016b). When a domestic violence incident is reported to the police there are likely to be numerous previously unreported incidents—47 per cent of the victims interviewed for the BCS 2009/10 had been victimized more than once and 30 per cent three or more times (Flatley *et al*, 2010). (The Crime Survey for England and Wales (which replaced the BCS) provides more recent data but it is only indicative, as no more than five repeat offences are recorded (Walby, Towers, and Francis, 2014).) It is also common for victims of domestic violence to experience other forms of inter-personal violence such as sexual assault and stalking (Walby and Allen, 2004). Despite the commitments made by many forces, the HMIC's 2014 review of police responses to domestic violence was damning (HMIC, 2014). Hence it is essential that greater efforts are made to take positive action from the start.

The first part of the response is usually the call taker, or the front desk staff. He/she must ensure the safety of victim, as well as gathering and recording information. The 2015 CoP document *Call handler and front counter staff response to a domestic abuse incident* (CoP, 2105b) provides full guidance on the appropriate response. The following information will be required:

- the location and identity of the people involved;
- whether anyone at the scene is disabled, intoxicated, has special needs or is injured;
- whether there any weapons at the scene, and if so, have they been used;
- whether any children are present at the scene, and if so, are they safe;
- whether there are any communication difficulties (will an interpreter be needed?);
- whether anyone present has a history of domestic abuse or violent behaviour;
- whether anyone present has a relevant court order.

The victim's demeanour (and that of others present) and any background noise should also be noted (but should not necessarily be taken as an accurate indicator of the situation). The caller should be told when the police are likely to arrive, and that he/she should avoid disturbing any possible evidence. Information should be sought to enable the best possible response; some victims may be calling from unfamiliar locations, or the situation may be changing continuously.

All the information should be recorded and disseminated, although an abridged version can be used when a rapid deployment is required. The call-taker should inform the attending officer whether his/her supervisors have been briefed of the incident. Officer safety must be considered and back-up may be necessary.

It is important to understand that domestic violence often involves repeat victimization, an aspect that is sometimes overlooked by first response officers (HMIC, 2011, p 10). If there has been no previous contact with the police, this does not mean there has been no prior abuse.

The police should address the incident in its wider context, and take into account for example whether the perpetrator has previously committed similar abuse, or if the victim has already been subject to a risk assessment. The victim might also have been through a MARAC (see below), and have a safety codeword for contacting the police when seeking assistance (CoP, 2015b). Any electronic or paper-based records should be checked for relevant information.

If the suspect is at the scene, the call-taker should keep the caller on the line in order to ensure the best possible response to the incident, and also to gather evidence (which could be used in a subsequent prosecution). If the suspect is no longer present, the caller should be advised to keep safe, for example by locking all doors and windows, and taking a mobile phone with him/her or keeping phone lines open if using a fixed line. (Note that if the caller says that the suspect has left, this might not be the case as the suspect could be forcing the caller to say as much.) A departed suspect may return at any time, so a key word should be agreed for the caller to use if the suspect returns. A description of the suspect should be obtained and circulated by the police officers in the area, and checks on the suspect should be conducted, including using ViSOR and the PND. If the caller is a child, as much information as possible should be gathered, particularly to ensure the child's safety (CoP, 2015b).

An incident or crime report should be completed using the appropriate force system. This will ensure that domestic violence incidents are not ignored without the proper support being provided to victims, and that any follow-ups are also fully completed. The computer-aided dispatch (CAD) must remain open for domestic violence incidents until a risk assessment has been carried out and the victim contacted (CoP, 2015b).

13.6.1.3   Attending a domestic violence crime scene

The first priority is the safety of everyone at the scene. Consideration should be given to taking the victim to a place of safety, if this cannot be assured in his/her own home. The responding officer should try to build a rapport with the victim to provide reassurance, but also to help with the initial investigation, and ensure a successful handover (CoP, 2015g). The risk for the victim, children, and officers present (particularly in relation to the use of weapons) must be re-assessed, and risk management safety planning must be initiated. Officers should also ensure the preservation of the relevant evidence if any prosecutions seem likely. Everything said by the suspect, victim, or children must be accurately recorded. The information given to the call-taker should be confirmed and any discrepancies investigated, (for example, the arrival of the police might change the dynamic of the situation, and cause the victim to mistakenly believe that he/she is no longer in danger).

The victim and/or the suspect may deny officers access to the premises. The officer will have to judge whether for example the victim is being controlled or coerced (to prevent entry or to say that the suspect has left). Should the suspect deny entry, officers should ask to speak to other members of the household. If entry is refused, officers may have grounds to use the power of entry under s 17 of the PACE Act 1984 (to arrest for an indictable offence or to save life and limb, see 10.8.1.2). If this power is used, a full PNB record must be made, including the reason for using it. Arrest for a breach of the peace (see 14.3.2) may also be considered. If children are deemed to be in danger, s 48 of the Children Act 1989 could also be used (see also 13.3.3 on using police protection powers).

If a suspect has left the scene, then his/her description should be confirmed and circulated. Officers should then speak in more detail with the persons present, and consider whether photographic and video evidence is required. For any children are at the scene, a record should be made about each child's welfare, communication ability, demeanour, name, date of birth, sex, address, doctor, primary carer, and school. If no children are immediately apparent, officers should still be alert for signs of children, as they may have been kept away from the immediate scene.

It is very important that officers gather as much evidence as possible to ensure a successful prosecution. Research suggests that the use of body worn video might help increase the number of criminal charges in situations of domestic abuse, and may be particularly useful in helping officers gather evidence at the scene and the context of the offences (Owens, Mann, and Mckenna, 2014).

First accounts should be obtained from each individual as soon as possible after the events, especially any description of an absent suspect. Each person should be seen separately and in a safe environment, and video recording can be used. When the versions of the events differ considerably there may be a need to establish which person is the victim. An injured person could be the victim, but the aggressor can also be harmed when a victim acts in self-defence. The arrest of both parties should be avoided if at all possible. The apparent victim(s) should be offered support at this stage (see 13.6.1.6).

Forensic evidence should be gathered (an early evidence kit (EEK) could be used, see 17.6.1.1) to avoid over-reliance on the victim's statement in a future prosecution. Officers should be proactive in gathering and using photographic evidence in domestic violence investigations. A victim's non-intimate injuries should be photographed as soon as possible after the event, and later when injuries may become more apparent. Photographs of injuries should be used to assist interviewing and help decide bail. Copies should be attached to the evidence file to be sent to the CPS and judiciary. Chapter 11 provides more details on general procedures to be followed when attending crime scenes.

Risk assessments must be carried out for all incidents involving domestic violence. Many forces use an *aide mémoire* (such as the DASH risk assessment checklist) to assist with this. The primary risk assessment must be carried out as soon as possible by the attending officer or first responder. (In some forces the risk assessment is the responsibility of specially trained staff such as the domestic abuse specialist officer or coordinator, but the first officer at the scene might still conduct the risk assessment under supervision.) Relevant information includes the frequency of repeat victimization, the seriousness of the injuries, any escalation of violence, and details of the victim and the suspect. Domestic violence is often part of a pattern of coercive and controlling behaviour, so the context of the situation must be taken into account when assessing risk, and not just the current incident. All staff involved with the ongoing investigation, including the custody officer, should be encouraged to contribute information. If several risk factors are identified it may be necessary to inform the victim and notify the relevant support services. Victims should not be asked to sign risk assessments as it is the responsibility of the officers to determine the level of risk to be assigned to each case. The degree of risk should be continuously reviewed, usually by the first responding officer, to ensure the correct level of protection for victims. The primary risk assessment underpins the immediate safety planning. Secondary risk assessments are conducted in some cases, and by specially trained staff, but this does not happen in all forces. It is therefore imperative that the first risk assessment is thorough, and consistently reviewed.

13.6.1.4 Investigating and follow-up for domestic violence incidents

The management of the investigation is dependent on local practices and on general guidance. The 'right first time' principle applies; the investigation should be thorough. It does not need to be conducted by domestic abuse specialist officers, but, they can provide useful information and guidance. High-risk cases should be investigated by officers trained at PIP level 2 or above.

The investigation should consider the following points:

1. any history of domestic abuse;
2. any relevant police intelligence (local, national, and international), sources of intelligence include the Police National Database (see 6.9.1.2), the Violent Offenders and Sex Offenders Register, house-to-house enquiries, other information from witnesses, and CCTV images and covert surveillance (see 23.4);
3. any relevant medical information (with consent);
4. information held by housing, social care, and probation services;
5. any civil orders and child contact agreements (including disputes);
6. evidence from professionals and staff from the emergency services who witnessed the abuse;
7. hearsay evidence may be acceptable, for example a witness's report of something said by a suspect or a child's account of events (see 24.2.5);
8. technology and social media may also provide useful information, for example, the victim may have threats of violence.

Other lines of enquiry include house-to-house enquiries, automatic number plate recognition (for example, to ascertain the victim and suspects' whereabouts), bank accounts and other financial information (the victim's earnings might be under the suspect's control), covert surveillance (for example, in situations of harassment), and prison intelligence. Bad character evidence (see 24.2.5) may also be useful to secure a conviction if used with other evidence (CoP, 2015e).

Interviews should explore details of the incident and possible existing evidence, for example details of witnesses; the victim's physical and emotional injuries; details of family members; the history of the relationship and any previous incidents or threats (including with other partners); whether children were present; whether the parties are separated; whether any civil action has been taken; whether any sexual offences have been disclosed; the points to prove; and the victim's perception of the future relationship in terms of the likelihood of further abuse. When interviewing the suspect, it is important to consider the victim's safety if disclosing information provided by the victim. The first officer at the scene should also be interviewed when relevant, and the interview recorded.

If a witness decides to withdraw from the investigation a domestic abuse officer should take a comprehensive withdrawal statement including the witness's reasons, confirmation of the truthfulness of his/her original statement, whether he/she was put under pressure to withdraw, with whom he/she has discussed the matters, whether he/she is considering civil proceedings, and were the prosecution to continue, the perceived impact on the witness and any children. This statement and a report from the officer for the case should then be sent to the CPS. The statement may be used as evidence in the prosecution of the current or other incidents. The risk assessment and safety plan for the victim should also be reviewed.

All reports of domestic violence must be recorded following the National Crime Recording Standards, particularly as domestic violence may be associated with other crimes such as child abuse and harassment. All relevant information should be passed to police domestic abuse coordinators, who will liaise with the Tasking and Co-ordination Group (see 23.6). The accuracy of the existing data can then be monitored and further statistical information can be produced for sharing with partner agencies and other police personnel.

TASK 4 One of the partners in a long-term domestic relationship complains that she has been punched by the other. What offence has potentially been committed?

13.6.1.5 Methods of disposal of suspects

Police officers have a duty of positive action when responding to incidents of domestic abuse (CoP, 2015a). This often means arresting the suspect, but this is not always possible or the best solution. The decision to arrest a suspect should not be influenced by the victim's opinion or whether previous complaints have been withdrawn. If the decision is not to arrest, the reasons need to be recorded. Alternatives to arrest include reporting the suspect for an offence and proceeding by way of a written charge, or informing the suspect (verbally and/or in writing—a 'police information notice') that further similar actions may amount to harassment (see 14.5.1).

General codes of practice and CPS guidance on domestic violence should be used when deciding whether to charge a suspect (CPS, 2013b, and the CPS, *Domestic Abuse Guidelines* available online). The CPS Domestic Abuse Charging Advice Sheet should also be consulted (CPS, 2015). The victim should be informed if the decision is against prosecution. The use of cautions in cases of domestic violence is discouraged, although they are sometimes used for a first incident where there is no intelligence of related incidents.

When considering releasing the suspect on bail (see 10.13.3), risk factors should be taken into account and the victim consulted. Any attached conditions should ensure that the victim, children, and witnesses are protected. The conditions must be such that they can be policed effectively, and not conflict with existing court orders. If the suspect is forbidden from contacting the victim then it should be made clear that 'contact' means directly or indirectly, in person or through social media. It is important to be clear that the conditions of bail apply to the suspect's behaviour (not the victim's), and that breaches of bail will be treated seriously, even if the suspect and the victim become reconciled. Before a suspect is released from a police station, the victim should be informed where possible, and the notification recorded. The police should help arrange (as required) for the suspect and the victim to remove their belongings from their joint residence (as required), especially if this could otherwise lead to a breach of bail conditions. All control rooms and databases should be updated regarding the suspect's bail conditions.

13.6.1.6 Safety and Support for the victim

In providing support for victims and ensuring their safety, it is paramount that communication is clear, that the risk assessment is accurate and consistently reviewed, and that appropriate safety planning is devised. Domestic abuse victims are entitled to an enhanced level of service under the *Code of Practice for Victims of Crime* published by the Ministry of Justice (2015).

The following points should be explained to the victim:

* the reasons for the method of disposal;
* how to access support services provided;
* that the incident will be recorded on police IT systems; and
* that the information and evidence from the current incident could be used to support future prosecutions. Other support could involve helping arrange for the victim to move into a refuge, or installing a panic alarm (particularly if the suspect does not live with the victim).

Victims should be informed as soon as possible, and no later than within one working day, of any developments regarding the suspect (such as his/her arrest, interview under caution, a decision to prosecute or use an out-of-court disposal, a decision not to prosecute (and the reasons), or the date, time, and location of a first court hearing). Victims must also be informed if the suspect is released, whether without charge or on police bail. If the suspect is released on bail, any conditions imposed (and any change to or cancellation of the conditions) must be communicated to the victim. Reports of a breach of bail should of course be followed up promptly.

The victim must be offered the opportunity to make a Victim Personal Statement (see 10.12). This is a good way of capturing the context of the offending and of conveying the impact of the events to the court. A restraining order on the suspect could be used (see 14.5.7.1), and the implications of this should be fully explained. Victims should be told about the possibility of seeking help from Victim Support (VS), and about community support services, and places of safety. They should also be given referral details for an IDVA (Independent Domestic Violence Advisor). Note that the police should only refer victims to support services when they have the victim's explicit consent (CoP, 2015f). The location of temporary emergency accommodation (if used) should never be revealed to the suspect.

The police should assist the victim and the IDVA in developing and implementing a safety plan. Advice on home security (from Crime Prevention Officers), personal alarms, mobile phones, and CCTV can all be included. Other safety schemes include cocoon watch schemes (neighbours, family, and relevant agencies contact the police in case of further incidents); police watch schemes (regular patrolling of a certain area); and sanctuary schemes (provision of extra support so the victim does not have to go out, and the creation of a safe room from where he/she can call the police). Neighbourhood policing teams should be kept informed about domestic violence and associated levels of risk in their geographic area.

Victims of domestic violence with an unstable immigration status can have additional financial difficulties because their access to benefits may be restricted. If the violence occurred within the first two years of the relationship, the victim can however appeal for indefinite stay in the UK.

When a person is killed by a partner or former partner, the Secretary of State can arrange for a 'domestic homicide review' with the aim of preventing further deaths (s 9 of the Domestic Violence, Crime and Victims Act 2004). The reviews can involve chief officers of police, local authorities, probation officers, and health and social services.

13.6.1.7 Multi-agency work and wider initiatives to counter domestic violence

Multi-agency approaches are very important in preventing and addressing domestic violence incidents. Provision varies across the country, but good practice often involves a Local Strategic Partnership (LSP) which brings together representatives from local authorities, public and private sectors, community and voluntary organizations. Clear information-sharing agreements (ISAs) can facilitate multi-agency cooperation. Multi-agency work is also facilitated through:

* MAPPA (Multi-Agency Public Protection Arrangements), where the police, the Prison Service, and the Probation Service help to manage risk from violent and sexual offenders in the area (see 3.3.1).

- MARACs (Multi-Agency Risk Assessment Conferences), often coordinated by local police forces. They provide a forum for the sharing of information developing a multi-agency risk management plan for each case. The police have a significant role in the work of a MARAC, particularly in detaining perpetrators and referring cases. High risk victims of domestic abuse should be referred to MARACs.
- SABs (Safeguarding Adult Boards), which decides whether and how to intervene when there is suspicion that an adult in the area has needs for care and support and is experiencing or at the risk of abuse or neglect, and is unable to protect him/herself as a result of the needs experienced.
- MASHs (Multi-Agency Safeguarding Hubs), where services are co-located to facilitate communication in a given area. They are usually dedicated to protect children but may also have information-sharing protocols for adults.
- IDVAs, who work with police officers to provide independent support, risk assessment, and safety planning for victims. They are important in helping the police fast-track the investigation of domestic abuse incidents and can testify as an expert witness. IDVAs should be kept informed of any changes in police practice and updated regularly on the cases.
- SDVCs (Specialist Domestic Violence Courts), set up to improve victim protection, increase offender accountability, and to promote multi-agency cooperation.
- DHRs (Domestic Homicide Reviews), a multi-agency review where a person aged 16 or above has died due to possible abuse, neglect, or violence in a domestic context.
- YPVAs (Young People's Violence Advisors) who support domestic abuse victims aged 16 to 18 in a similar way IDVAs support adult victims.
- ISVAs (Independent Sexual Violence Advisors) who provide targeted support to victims of sexual violence.

Other strategies to reduce domestic violence include the DASH risk assessment checklist (Home Office, 2009d, p 32), and a College of Policing course on domestic violence for police officers and CPS professionals.

13.6.2   'Honour'-based crime

'Honour' based crime can include domestic or sexual abuse, forced marriage, or female genital mutilation. It involves attempts to maintain control in a family or social group to protect certain conceptions of honour and will often involve violence, hence the term 'honour'-based violence (HBV). The perpetrators believe that an individual has brought shame to the family or community through his/her behaviour. Inverted commas are often used for the word 'honour' in this context, because although the perpetrators may believe they are defending a certain notion of honour with their actions, honour is not accepted in the UK as an excuse for violence or oppression.

It is very difficult to establish accurate numbers of 'honour'-based crimes, due to high levels of unreported cases and inconsistencies in police recordings of such crimes (Iranian and Kurdish Women's Rights Organisation, 2014). There have been some extremely violent and high profile cases such as the murder of Banaz Mahmod in 2006 by her relatives. These draw attention to the need to clearly identify cases as HBV so proper support can be provided for the victims. Although most victims of HBV are women (cases tend to occur in very male-dominated cultures), men can also be the targets of HBV, for example if they are gay or if they support victims of HBV.

In 2015, HMIC published a report on the police response to HBV, forced marriage and female genital mutilation. It reported that few forces correctly understood the isuues or had adequate procedures in place to handle such cases (HMIC, 2015d, p 8).

It is important that cases of HBV are identified early on so they are managed properly. Cases are prosecuted under the specific offence committed (eg, assault, kidnap, rape, threats to kill, or murder) but should be flagged up as HBV in the case file. The victim may be at risk from his/her own family and community, so great care is needed when discussing the case with anyone else, particularly family members or others, for example translators from within the same community. In some cases, contract killers may be hired by the family, or distant relatives living in other areas of the country can pose a threat. Thus a victim can be at risk even after leaving his/her community. Ensuring the victim's safety is a priority, and the level of risk should not be underestimated. Information should be gathered not only about the victim but also about the alleged offender—he/she may be using younger members of the family to commit the criminal acts or to deflect attention from him/herself.

13.6.3 Forced marriage

Forcing a person to marry is a criminal offence under s 121 of the Anti-social Behaviour, Crime and Policing Act 2014. The victim can be physically, emotionally, or psychologically pressured to marry by means of threats, physical or sexual violence, or other forms of coercion directed at the victim or a third person. If the victim lacks the capacity to consent under the Mental Capacity Act 2005 (see 13.2.4), any type of conduct can amount to the offence. Some victims are not coerced or threatened but are deceived into going abroad, and are unaware that the purpose of the trip is a forced marriage (for a prosecution it is not relevant whether the marriage took place). A forced marriage should be distinguished from an arranged marriage; the latter is a legal practice in which a third party arranges for two consenting people to marry.

Possible cases of forced marriage must be identified and flagged up in the early stages so that appropriate management can be put in place. The Forced Marriage Unit (the FMU, a joint Foreign and Commonwealth Office and Home Office unit) provided assistance for 1,220 possible cases of forced marriage in 2015, of which 80% of the victims were female and 20% male (Home Office 2016b, p. 3). Whilst most cases involve individuals from South Asian communities, forced marriage also occurs in communities from the Middle East, Europe, Africa, and North America (HM Government, 2014b, p 10). For appropriate management of the case to be put in place, information must be gathered about the alleged offender, as well as the victim and the community.

Extensive guidance on best practice in responding to situations of forced marriage can be found in HM Government's 'Multi-agency practice guidelines: Handling cases of Forced Marriage'. One of the most important recommendations is to recognize that there may be only one chance to speak to a victim of forced marriage (for example because travelling is imminent)—the 'one chance rule' (HM Government, 2014, p 21). The attending police officer should contact the designated person in their organization with expertise in forced marriages (often the same person leading the response in cases that involve the safeguard of children, protection of vulnerable adults or victims of domestic abuse). If access is not immediately possible, then information should be gathered to establish the facts and help with the referral. The individual must be seen in person, alone and in a place where the conversation cannot be overheard (victims may otherwise suffer retaliation from spouses and other family members when coming forward in situations of forced marriage). The victim should be reassured of the confidentiality of the conversation. The options available should be fully explained to the individual but his/her decision must be accepted. A risk assessment exercise should be performed (for example, using DASH mentioned above). Any evidence of abuse or threats of abuse should be sought and documented. Any criminal offence committed in the context of a forced marriage (either before or after the marriage) will also be prosecuted (CPS, 2014).

The case should be discussed with the Forced Marriage Unit, and the victim referred to appropriate local and national support groups if he/she agrees. Police and social service records should be checked for past referrals of family members including siblings, for example for situations of domestic abuse or missing persons within the family. If relevant, a restricted entry in the force intelligence system should be created, and a crime report submitted. Officers should reassure the victim about confidentiality, assess the need for immediate protection and agree an effective method of contacting the victim discreetly in the future.

For individuals with certain disabilities, a communication specialist could be used. If the person is under 18, a police protection referral should be made (see 13.3.3). Similarly for adults with support needs, a referral should be made to the designated person responsible for safeguarding vulnerable adults, and activate local safeguarding procedures (see 13.7.3).

A Forced Marriage Protection Order (FMPO) can be issued by a civil court to a person who seems to be planning to implement a forced marriage. The recipient of the order is obliged to hand over the passport of the person at risk, or to reveal his/her whereabouts if missing. Breaking an FMPO is a criminal offence, with a penalty of up to five years' imprisonment (s 120 of the Anti-social Behaviour, Crime and Policing Act 2014). The maximum custodial penalty for arranging a forced marriage is 12 months' if tried summarily, and seven years if tried on indictment.

13.6.4   Female genital mutilation

Female genital mutilation (FGM) occurs when part or all the external female genitalia (see WHO, 2008) are removed or injured for no medical reason. It is also referred to as female circumcision and female genital cutting, and is usually performed by a female 'cutter', before puberty starts. Perpetrators of FGM often believe that they are protecting an important part of their cultural identity, and FGM may be presented as an occasion for celebration and a rite of passage. Whilst it is important to try to engage with the communities where FGM is performed, FGM is a violation of human rights (particularly the rights to health, security, and physical integrity, and the right to be free from torture and cruel, inhuman, or degrading treatment), and can cause serious health problems and even death. The offence is punishable with a maximum of 14 years' imprisonment (Female Genital Mutilation Act 2003 (FGMA) and ss 70-75 of the Serious Crime Act 2015).

Although FGM has been a crime under English law since the 1980s, no prosecutions were made until 2014. The College of Policing published APP guidance on addressing FGM in 2015, which pivots on prevention, protection, and prosecution (CoP, 2015d). Further information is also available in *A Protocol between the Police and the Crown Prosecution Service in the investigation and prosecution of allegations of FGM* (available online). This stresses the importance of early consultation between the police and the CPS.

13.6.4.1   FGM offences

FGM offences include carrying out FGM, assisting a girl with carrying out FGM on herself, or assisting a non-UK person outside the UK to perform FGM on a UK person (ss 1(1) and (4), 2, and 3 of the FGMA). For a victim under 16 years of age, the persons responsible for her (such as a parent, or someone assuming similar responsibility even if only temporarily) are committing an offence of failing to protect her, with a maximum penalty of seven years' imprisonment (s 3A of the FGMA). Carrying out FGM and failure to protect a girl from FGM may be prosecuted in the UK, even if the acts were committed in another country.

13.6.4.2   Prevention of FGM

Police officers who suspect that FGM is likely to occur should consider the need to take immediate action to protect anyone at risk, and inform a supervisor or specially trained officer. There may be indicators that suggest that FGM is being planned for a particular girl, for example preparing for a trip, absence from school, and/or a special ceremony. The safety of the girl is paramount, and an assessment of risk of significant harm should be conducted. It could be classed as a critical incident and the 'Golden Hour' principle applied (see 11.2.1). The girl could be taken into police protection for up to 72 hours (see 13.3.3).

A strategy meeting will be arranged (within a day at most) between the local authority children's social care and health professionals. The parents will be informed of the law and the dangers of FGM, but if it seems that the girl is still at risk of FGM the emergency protection powers and orders under ss 46 and 44 of the Children Act 1989 can be used. A risk assessment should also be conducted for other female family members. If it is known that a particular woman has undergone FGM, a multi-agency meeting must be convened and a risk assessment carried out for any girls in her family.

13.6.4.3   Investigating FGM

FGM is a crime and amounts to child abuse when carried out on girls, so a robust investigation must be conducted. Victims may not know that the events they experienced amounted to FGM and/or that it is illegal in the UK. They are often unwilling to report FGM and support a prosecution, so officers may be reluctant to address cases of FGM for fear of being branded racist or culturally insensitive, but this should not deter them from exercising their duty of protection. Officers rely heavily on information and support from other agencies to identify and address FGM. Covert tactics should also be considered and any opportunities for gathering intelligence should be maximized.

Indicators that FGM has occurred include absences from school and noticeable changes in behaviour when the girl returns (such as difficulty sitting straight, complaining of pain, and being secretive). For suspected cases of FGM, local safeguarding procedures should be followed. For known cases of FGM where the victim is under the age of 18 years, all registered health and social care professionals and teachers have a duty to report it to the police (s 5B of the FGMA).

A case would be 'known' if the FGM has been verbally disclosed by the victim or visually identified by the professional involved. Failing to report a known case to the police is not a criminal offence, but is treated as a serious disciplinary matter (CoP, 2015d). Medical evidence will be required for known cases of FGM.

The anonymity of the victim must be preserved for life, so the publication of information that may lead members of the public to identify her is forbidden. Any breach of this is punishable with a fine (s 4A and Sch 1 to the FGMA).

13.6.4.4 FGM Protection Orders

FGM Protection Orders (FGMPO) can be issued by the High Court or a family law court, to protect girls at risk of FGM (s 5A and Sch 2 to the FGMA and the Serious Crime Act 2015). They can also be used for girls who have already undergone FGM as they are at further risk if they are threatened by other witnesses in an investigation. Applications for an FGMPO can be made by the victim, local authorities, or a third party authorized by the court (such as the police, a healthcare professional, a teacher, a friend, or a family member). Breaching an FGMPO is an either-way offence (the penalty is up to 12 months' imprisonment if tried summarily, and 5 years on indictment). A breach can also be treated as a civil matter, as contempt of court (see s 5A and Sch 2, 4 (3) and (4) to the FGMA).

13.7 Support for Victims, Witnesses, and the General Public

Law enforcement is often seen as the main police priority, but this is not the only role of the police. In terms of police legitimacy (see 3.5.3 and 3.5.4) there is a clear need to engage with the community, and to act as a 'police service' in addition to being a 'police force'. The general public expects the police to keep everyone safe, so police powers include being able to use force to enter property to save life and limb in emergency situations. It has also long been recognized that children should be afforded particular protection, but more recently the needs of vulnerable adults have also received attention. In terms of criminal justice, it is also important that all victims and witnesses are adequately supported so they can provide good evidence during prosecutions.

13.7.1 Providing support for members of the general public

In the following sections, we cover some of the services provided by the police that are unrelated to law enforcement, such as dealing with lost property, and helping people who become ill in the street. A few might argue that the role of the police in the twenty-first century should not include these time-honoured and traditional activities. Others might suggest that they serve to enhance and secure police legitimacy in an ever more demanding society.

13.7.1.1 Lost property

Traditionally, although not a statutory obligation, the police have provided the repository for property found in public spaces. The police also maintain records of property reported as lost so that any article that has been found can be returned to its owner at the earliest opportunity. Other organizations provide a similar service, such as road and rail transport companies, but only for property lost or found in their own vehicles or premises.

A person finding property is not obliged to hand it over to the police, but should take all reasonable steps to find the owner to avoid being suspected of committing theft (see 16.2). This might include reporting it to the police, and indeed, items such as passports and driving licences are more likely to be quickly and safely returned to the owner if the police take responsibility for making the contact. Generally, police policy is that a police officer (and others such as a PCSO) who finds lost property should record and deposit it at the police station.

Police staff on patrol or at the front counter of police stations will inevitably be handed lost property from members of the public. It is vital that the officer makes an accurate record, and a full entry should be written if a PNB is used (see 10.2). The description of the item(s) should refer to simple facts such as measurements, and unique identifying features such as serial numbers. Assumptions should be avoided; a gold coloured watch incorporating the name of a leading manufacturer may not be the genuine thing! The description of such an article should state that it is a watch made of yellow metal, together with the wording on the face.

13.7.1.2 Illness in the street

Police officers on patrol will often encounter individuals who are ill, or seem ill. The conditions may be minor or more serious, such as heart attacks, and will also include people suffering from severe mental health problems. A person who appears to be drunk or under the influence of drugs might instead be unwell, or have been assaulted or otherwise injured.

A first task for a police officer in this situation is to decide whether the person is likely to be ill, and if so to determine the nature of the illness. It is worth checking to see if the person is carrying documentation or wearing MedicAlert jewellery relating to an illness or medical treatment.

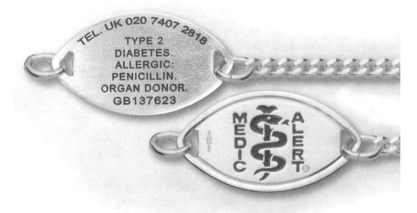

Image reproduced with permission of the MedicAlert foundation.

Police officers should call for an ambulance if it seems necessary, without assuming that a bystander or witness has already done so. A person cannot be forced to go to hospital, but the ambulance staff will be able to provide support. Where appropriate the police officer should provide First Aid as the preservation of life is always paramount.

The identity of the person should be established where possible, but this will not always be straightforward. If asking the person and checking his/her personal documentation (and any MedicAlert jewellery) does not provide the identity, another person at the scene may know the person and be able to help. The PNC can also be checked for descriptions to see if there are any matches on the wanted or missing persons indexes. If necessary, CCTV can be checked to establish the person's prior movements. A supervisor could arrange for the description of the person to be circulated if all else fails.

Officers on patrol may also encounter people who are suffering from memory loss. It is important to try and find out whether this is due to an injury or some pre-existing condition,such as dementia, as this will influence the steps to take next. Determining the cause of memory loss can obviously be difficult, but witnesses might be able to help. We cover dealing with mentally vulnerable people in 13.2.

An officer also has a responsibility to safeguard any property the person might have, for example, a bag or money in a pocket. If possible, this should be kept with the person, for example if he/she is taken to hospital. However, if this is not practical, the property should be taken to a known relative if possible, or as a last resort to the police station for safekeeping. The police officer should, where possible, also ensure that the appropriate relatives are notified. The ill person may not wish a relative to be informed, but this will be a matter of judgement. The police officer must ensure that decisions are justifiable and clearly documented, and a supervisor should be consulted if in any doubt.

The officer should accompany the person to hospital if the illness seems to be serious and/or life-threatening as the information he/she can provide could be important for a medical diagnosis.

13.7.2 Entering property to save life or limb

The police have the legal power to enter and search premises to save life or limb (s 17(1)(e) of the PACE Act 1984). The power of search is limited to the extent that is reasonably required to achieve the particular objective (s 17(4)). For example, if a property is entered and searched to find a person who needs medical treatment, there is no justification for searching a bathroom cabinet. Nor can the power be used to search a home to identify relatives of a person who is unconscious in hospital. If the conditions do not satisfy s 17 then the entry is unlawful, and any evidence of criminality (such as the presence of controlled drugs) may be excluded by the court in a subsequent prosecution (under s 78 of the PACE Act 1984 (see *R v Veneroso* [2002] Crim LR 306 (Crown Ct)). The officer does not need to have reasonable grounds for believing that anyone is on the premises. For a building with flats, all the flats can be searched.

In the case of *Baker v Crown Prosecution Service* [2009] EWHC 299 (Admin), it was further decided that entry and search under subsection (e) can be carried out:

- without seeking the permission of the occupant (this might be self-defeating);
- without giving the occupant a reason if it is impossible, impracticable, or undesirable to do so;
- to save someone from him/herself as well as from a third party; but
- only to the extent that is reasonably required to satisfy the objective for using the power of entry (s 17(4) PACE Act 1984).

These powers should only be used if 'something serious' seemed to have occurred (or was likely to occur) within the property, and not 'simply on the basis of concern for the welfare' of someone in the premises, as shown in *Syed v DPP* [2010] EWHC 81 (Admin). In this incident the officers attended after a neighbour reported a disturbance. On arrival, there was no sign of a disturbance but the officers attempted to enter the premises, stating to the occupant that they were 'concerned about the welfare of person(s) within'. The occupant refused entry, assaulting one officer and spitting at the other, and was subsequently charged with an offence under s 89 of the Police Act 1996 (see 15.4). On appeal the conviction was quashed; it was held that the officers had not been acting in the lawful execution of their duty because the criteria for using s 17(1)(e) had not been met.

Reasonable force may be used to secure entry (s 117 of the PACE Act 1984) where any part of the PACE Act 1984 grants a power of entry. If met with force, an officer might have to use equal force to negate it, and then use even more force to take control. This is covered as part of personal safety training. In a prosecution, the court has to determine whether an officer honestly believed that the force he/she used was reasonable and proportionate in the circumstances (see 15.5.1). The principles are similar to the use of force during an arrest (s 3 of the Criminal Law Act 1967, see 10.8.3).

13.7.3 Public protection

In the police environment, the term 'Public protection' has a broad meaning. It is associated with the management of violent and sexual offenders (see MAPPA 3.3.1), but the term is also applied to protecting victims through investigating incidents involving sexual offences, violence, child abuse, vulnerable adult abuse, domestic abuse, hate crime, and missing persons.

13.7.3.1 Abuse of Vulnerable Adults

Any person can be a victim of abuse and in need of protection, but particularly those who are vulnerable because of their condition or their situation, for example very elderly and infirm people or adults who self-harm, or abuse alcohol or drugs.

Any adult (aged 18 years or over) is deemed to be vulnerable (Department of Health, 2000) if he/she:

- needs (or may need) community care services due to mental, physical, or learning disability, age or illness:
- is unable (or may be unable) to take care of him/herself; or
- cannot protect him/herself against significant harm or exploitation.

ACPO (2012b) identified two main types of incidents where adults may suffer abuse: those involving serious abuse including GBH or serious sexual assault, and those which involve a serious incident in a care or health-care environment. Potential forms of abuse can include a physical, sexual, psychological, discriminatory, institutional, or financial nature, but can also include acts of omission and neglect. Abusers can perpetrate multiple offences against one person a number of times, or abuse groups of people at the same time. Offenders can be from any section of society, and can include relatives, care workers, professional staff, volunteers, and strangers. The abuse can take place in a range of contexts including day care, residential or nursing situations, as well as hospitals or indeed the person's own home. Motivation for the abuse can include punishment, fraud, and sexual pleasure. A victim may be reluctant to report the abuse if the suspect is his/her primary carer, and the victim might then be obliged to move into institutional residential care.

The key responsibility of the first officer at the scene is to protect the victim from further harm, to preserve evidence, and identify any criminal offences. When communicating with a vulnerable victim, an officer should do so in a way that considers their preference, age, and understanding (see 13.2.4 and 25.6). In the context of safeguarding vulnerable adults, judging the risk of harm is difficult, due in part to an adult's right to make his/her own decisions and choices, and the fact that a victim may not see him/herself as vulnerable. For a vulnerable adult in custody, the PACE Codes of Practice provide a number of safeguards to protect his/her rights, including the appointment of a responsible adult. There is currently no single statutory framework for safeguarding adults equivalent to the Children Act 1989 (which legislates for child protection (see 13.3)).

Further information is available online in ACPO's *Guidance on Safeguarding and Investigating the Abuse of Vulnerable Adults*, and the Department of Health's *No Secrets: Guidance on Developing and Implementing Multi-Agency Policies and Procedures to Protect Vulnerable Adults from Abuse*. The Home Office *Code of Practice for Victims of Crime 2015* (available online), can also be helpful in making decisions about how to best meet victims' rights and entitlements. Indeed, a multi-agency approach to communication and decision-making may safeguard the victim and prevent further abuse by addressing the immediate protection needs of the victim at the earliest opportunity.

13.7.4 Providing support for victims and witnesses

Officers at the scene of an incident need to consider the needs for support of victims, witnesses, or suspects (and others affected by the incident) in an ethical and appropriate manner (see 6.3). Victims and witnesses may have suffered a physical injury and stress, and may also be emotional, confused, aggressive, angry, and/or scared. The type of support required will vary depending on the incident and those involved, and could involve providing reassurance, first aid, and information on issues on procedures relating to the incident (legislation, courts, and available services). Specialist medical help might also be required. It is important that the appropriate procedures and legislation are followed and that anxiety or vulnerability is not increased. Officers should therefore keep victims and witness informed. Where vulnerability has been identified the person's wishes should be discussed with them and met where appropriate (this could include further support such as 'Special Measures' (see 27.5.2.5)). The support needs of witnesses, survivors, and victims can change over time.

One important reason for offering suitable support is that it will facilitate the collection of evidence. For further guidance in relation to intimidated witnesses see 14.6. and 25.4.

13.7.4.1 Information and support for victims

Working with victims of crime is an important part of police work, but victims and their families often find it hard to understand the complexities of criminal investigations and legal proceedings. Establishing a good relationship with victims increases the chances that they will cooperate effectively with the investigation and prosecution. Victims must be treated with dignity and respect, regardless of the specific circumstances of the crime. They may have experienced very traumatic events and require particular support. Some victims are considered as vulnerable (eg due to their age or the type of crime suffered) and require additional forms of support. Police officers should consider the well-being of individuals from a broad perspective and be aware of the full range of support services. Specialist support for victims of domestic abuse is covered in 13.6.1.6, and for sexually motivated offences in 17.6.1.

Victims have certain entitlements as described in *The Code of Practice for Victims of Crime 2015* (available online). A victim is defined in the Code as 'a natural person who has suffered harm, including physical, mental or emotional harm or economic loss which was directly caused by a criminal offence' or is a close relative of a person 'whose death was directly caused by a criminal offence'. The Code requires enhanced levels of support for victims 'of the most serious crime, persistently targeted victims and vulnerable or intimidated victims'. It extends to businesses, and to the families of the deceased as appropriate. There are separate entitlements for adult victims (Chapter 2, Part A) and child victims (Chapter 3, Part A). The entitlement remains

Specific Incidents

if a suspect is charged or convicted of the crime, and regardless of whether the entitled person collaborates with the investigation.

The Code also sets up duties for service providers, including the police. All victims making an allegation of criminal conduct should within five days be provided with the *Information for Victims of Crime* leaflet (or be referred to a relevant website with the same information). 'Priority victims' (identified by the police as such) are entitled to an 'enhanced service', and must be given this information within one day. This would include victims of the most serious crimes, persistently targeted victims, and vulnerable or intimidated victims. Victims must also be told about the Code and how to access its provisions. Those entitled to special measures should have these clearly explained, and any specific measures identified as necessary to help victims give evidence should be recorded and shared with Witness Care Units and the CPS.

Victims must be given information and contact details about relevant services (see 13.7.4.2). The police must explain that victim details are usually passed on to victims' services unless the victim requests otherwise. However, explicit consent must be obtained from a victim of sexual offences or domestic violence, or bereaved close relatives, before forwarding the details to victims' services. Victims can choose to self-refer to the services at a later date. The police referral should be done within two working days of an allegation being reported by a victim. Victims of the 'most serious crime' should also be informed of the availability of pre-trial therapy, if needed.

A Victim Personal Statement (VPS) can also be made (see 10.11.2), and this must be raised at an early stage for the most serious crimes, for persistently targeted, and vulnerable or intimidated victims, and for parents or guardians of vulnerable or child victims. (Other categories of victim must be informed of this opportunity only when completing a witness statement.) A police officer can however use his/her discretion, and offer the opportunity to make a VPS to any victim at this stage, when appropriate.

The police must keep victims informed about the suspect. Victims must be informed within five days (one day for enhanced service) of a suspect being arrested, interviewed under caution, released without charge, released on police bail, or if there are changes in the conditions to their bail or it is cancelled. Any decisions to prosecute or to give the suspect an out-of-court disposal must be communicated to the victim within the relevant time limits (one or five days), including all police cautions and decisions and reasons not to prosecute. The police must also inform victims of the date, time, and location of the first court hearing and bail conditions (including any decisions regarding breaches of these conditions). When considering out-of-court disposals, a victim should also be asked for his/her views when practicable, and these should be taken into account.

Once a trial has started the CPS, Witness Care Units, and other agencies take over responsibility for providing information to victims. The exception is when the police are nominated as the single point of contact with victims, in which case it may be necessary to keep victims updated of any developments.

13.7.4.2 Support services for victims

Victim Support (VS) is a non-governmental agency that offers support primarily to victims and witnesses of crime, and to anyone else who may have been affected, such as the family members of a victim. It also provides assistance to witnesses, and runs the Witness Services in courts across the country. The full range of VS services are listed and described on their website. The service is staffed by specially trained volunteers who offer free and confidential service to victims of crime. (All VS volunteers carry photographic identity cards.) They offer support such as advice on how to improve personal safety or how the criminal justice system works, crisis management, and long-term help. A crisis is often due to a serious form of crime but could also result from non-crime incidents such as a road traffic collision or a sudden death. Specially trained support staff can provide assistance to bereaved family members of victims of violent deaths. Finally, VS also offers information on compensation and insurance schemes.

Other support services include Citizens Advice, social services, mental health, bereavement and relationship counsellors, and medical practitioners. Particular care needs to be taken with vulnerable people (eg due to age, disability, mental health issues, children, and those who feel intimidated). Note that police officers are in a good position to inform victims of violent crime about the Criminal Injuries Compensation Scheme.

13.7.4.3   Crime prevention advice for victims

The security of a building should be considered after a fire (see 11.4.2) or a burglary (see 4.5.2) as other criminals can exploit perceived weaknesses and commit further crimes. Simple crime prevention and reduction advice, access to good information (perhaps from a Crime Reduction Officer), ideas on alarm installation, and other 'target hardening' techniques can all be useful. Some victims are repeatedly targeted by offenders (see 4.5.2 on 'hot victims') and, in many cases, the scale of the offences can become quite alarming, particularly in relation to property-repair scams, or in households where domestic violence is an issue.

A basic level of support can be offered by patrols occasionally visiting vulnerable victims to check on their welfare and give advice. Neighbourhood Watch schemes should be encouraged (see 3.9.1.4), and victims and their neighbours can be told how to contact Neighbourhood Policing Teams to promote engagement with the local police and build a rapport.

13.8   The Prevention of Harm to Animals

The first legislation to protect animals in the UK was 'An Act to Prevent the Cruel and Improper Treatment of Cattle' in 1822. Indeed, this was the first animal welfare legislation passed by a parliament anywhere in the world. Research indicates that there may be links between animal abuse and human abuse (see NSPCC, 2005; Flynn, 2011), so this issue has a wider significance.

The legislation covered here is from:

* the Animal Welfare Act 2006 (for non-wild animals; 'gardens, farms and zoos');
* the Wildlife and Countryside Act 1981 (for all types of wild animals, including invertebrates);
* the Wild Mammals (Protection) Act 1996 (for wild mammals only); and
* the Hunting Act 2004.

Note that the definition of 'animal' and 'wild animal' varies slightly between the Acts.

13.8.1   The Animal Welfare Act 2006

This Act applies only to animals that are vertebrates; that is, mammals, birds, reptiles (eg snakes), and amphibians (eg frogs). It does not cover invertebrates (animals without a backbone) such as insects, snails, or worms. It also refers to 'protected animals', which are defined as a type of animal that is either:

* normally domesticated in the UK (such as a cat);
* under the control of a person (such as a cow kept in a farmer's field); or
* not living wild (such as a lion; note that a lion that has escaped from a zoo is not truly living wild).

The Animal Welfare Act 2006 places a 'duty of care' on animal owners (eg farmers and pet owners) in an attempt to ensure the basic needs of animals are met, as well as outlawing certain forms of suffering. Offences which can be committed under the Animal Welfare Act 2006 include causing or permitting unnecessary suffering (s 4), mutilation (s 5), docking of dogs' tails (s 6), administration of poisons (s 7), arranging animal fighting (s 8), failure of person responsible for animal to ensure welfare (s 9), and transfer of animals by way of sale or prize to persons under 16 (s 11). All the offences listed in the following paragraphs under the Animal Welfare Act 2006 are triable summarily and the penalty is imprisonment not exceeding 51 weeks and/or a fine.

Other parties involved in investigating possible animal welfare offences include local authorities and the state veterinary service. The RSPCA in association with ACPO and Centrex published guidance notes for the Animal Welfare Act 2006, and these are available online. Guidance for dealing with dangerous dogs is available from Defra (Defra, 2009).

13.8.1.1   Causing unnecessary suffering to an animal

Section 4(1) of the Animal Welfare Act 2006 concerns causing unnecessary suffering to a protected animal (defined at the start of 13.8.1).

Specific Incidents

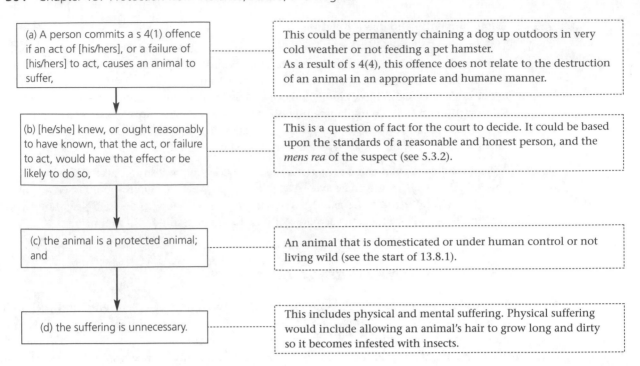

The meaning of 'unnecessary' includes when the suffering could reasonably have been avoided or reduced (s 4(3)). Note that some acts that cause suffering can be considered as justified and proportionate if there is a legitimate purpose (for example, for the animal's benefit, or to protect a person, property, or another animal, or is compliant with the Animals (Scientific Procedures) Act 1986).

There is a separate offence (s 4(2)) where the perpetrator does not directly cause the unnecessary suffering but instead permits it to be caused by another person (or fails to prevent this). Person A can commit an offence through the actions of B if:

- A is responsible for, owns, or is in charge of the animal (permanently or on a temporary basis); or
- A has the care of or control over B, and B is under the age of 16 and has responsibility for the animal.

A court will decide what person A could reasonably have done in the circumstances to prevent the unnecessary suffering.

13.8.1.2 The duty to ensure welfare

A person who is responsible for an animal has a duty to ensure its welfare. Section 9(1) of the Animal Welfare Act 2006 states that a person commits an offence if he/she does not meet an animal's needs, which under s 9(2) include its need for a suitable environment and diet; to be able to exhibit normal behaviour patterns, including any need it has to be housed with, or apart from, other animals; and to be protected from pain, suffering, injury, and disease.

13.8.1.3 Mutilation of a protected animal and docking dogs' tails

Under s 5(1) of the Animal Welfare Act 2006 a person commits an offence if he/she mutilates a protected animal. The definition of mutilate is interference with the sensitive tissues or bone structure of an animal (excluding permitted procedures carried out by a veterinary surgeon). It is also an offence for a person who is responsible for an animal to permit another person to mutilate, or to fail to prevent another person from mutilating a protected animal (s 5(2)). This legislation does not apply to the removal of a dog's tail, or in certain circumstances specified by the regulations of an appropriate national authority (eg the armed services).

The docking of a dog's tail is covered in s 6 of the Animal Welfare Act 2006. It is an offence to remove a dog's tail (or part of it), other than for medical treatment (or cause to be removed). The legislation is mainly intended to prevent the removal of dogs' tails for purely cosmetic reasons, and does not apply if the dog is a 'certified working dog' less than six days old. (A dog is a certified working dog if: evidence has been given to a vet; a national authority has proved the dog will be used for work (eg pest control or emergency rescue); or the dog is of a specified working type.)

13.8.1.4   Administration of poisons

Section 7(1) of the Animal Welfare Act 2006 states that a person commits an offence if without lawful authority or reasonable excuse he/she administers (or causes to be administered) any substance to a protected animal, knowing it to be poisonous or injurious. This includes any substance which, due to the quantity or manner in which it is administered or taken, has a harmful effect (such as large amounts of salt).

A person responsible for any animal also commits an offence by permitting or failing to stop someone else allowing the animal to take poisonous substances (s 7(2)). This only applies if the person responsible for the animal knew that the substance was poisonous and did not intervene.

13.8.1.5   Transfer of animals by way of sale or prize to persons under 16

Section 11(1) of the Animal Welfare Act 2006 states that it is an offence to sell an animal to a person whom the seller has reasonable cause to believe is under the age of 16 years. Here, selling an animal includes 'transferring, or agreeing to transfer, ownership of the animal' (s 11(2)).

Section 11(3) explains what this means for a person offering an animal as a prize to a person aged under 16 years. The person offering the prize does not commit the offence if the arrangement takes place:

- face to face and the young person is accompanied by a person aged 16 years or over;
- not face to face (eg by telephone) but with the consent of the relevant carer; or
- in a family context.

13.8.1.6   Animal fighting

An animal fight involves placing a 'protected animal' with any animal (including a human) for 'fighting, wrestling, or baiting'. Section 8(1) of the Animal Welfare Act 2006 states that a person commits an offence if in relation to an animal fight he/she arranges it, receives money, provides publicity, bets on the outcome, participates, possesses items for use in a fight, trains animals, or keeps relevant premises. It is also an offence to be present at an animal fight, without lawful authority or reasonable excuse (s 8 (2)), or to knowingly supply, publish, show, or possess with intent to supply a video-recording of an animal fight (s 8(3)).

It is also an offence to be present at an animal fight, without lawful authority or reasonable excuse (s 8 (2)), or to knowingly supply, publish, show, or possess with intent to supply a video-recording of an animal fight (s 8(3)).

Section 22(1) of the Animal Welfare Act 2006 states that a police officer may seize an animal if it appears that it has been involved in a s 8(1) or (2) offence. There is also a power to enter and search non-dwelling premises (s 22(2)) for the purpose of exercising a power under s 8(1), if the officer believes a relevant animal is there.

13.8.1.7   Protected animals in distress

Animals in distress may need to be taken into police possession, and some might need to be destroyed. The powers are provided under ss 18 and 19 of the Animal Welfare Act 2006, and local force policy should also be considered. Animal inspectors also have the same powers. It is an offence to intentionally obstruct a person acting under s 18 of the Animal Welfare Act 2006 (s 18(12)).

Section 18(1) of the Animal Welfare Act 2006 states that, if there is a reasonable belief that a protected animal is suffering, an officer may 'take, or arrange for the taking of, such steps as appear to be immediately necessary to alleviate the animal's suffering'. This in itself would not authorize destruction of an animal (s 18(2)). An animal inspector or police officer may destroy a protected animal (or arrange for another person to do so), either at the site or at another location, but only if the animal's condition is so poor that this would be in its own interest. This must be certified as such by an attending vet (s 18(3)) or there must be no reasonable alternative and the need is so urgent that it is not reasonably practicable to wait for a vet (s 18(4)).

A protected animal may be taken into possession by an animal inspector or police officer if a veterinary surgeon certifies that it is suffering, or is likely to suffer if its circumstances do not change (s 18(5)). If the officer believes that action is needed urgently (and it is not reasonably practicable to wait for a vet) then he/she may act alone (s 18(6)). Any dependent offspring may also be taken into possession (s 18(7)). An animal taken into possession can be removed to a place of safety, cared for (either on the premises where it was being kept or at another suitable place), and marked for identification purposes (s 18(8)).

There is a power of entry (s 19(1)) to non-residential premises to search for a protected animal, and to exercise any power under s 18. A warrant under s 19(4) would be required for a similar entry and search of a private dwelling. A police officer or animal inspector must reasonably believe that there is a protected animal on the premises, and that it is suffering (or if the circumstances of the animal do not change, it is likely to suffer). Reasonable force may be used for an entry under s 19(1) if necessary, but only if it appears that entry is required before a s 19(4) warrant can be obtained and executed.

13.8.1.8 Other powers under the Animal Welfare Act 2006

A police officer may enter and search any premises to arrest any person he/she reasonably suspects of committing an offence under ss 4, 5, 6(1), 6(2), 7, 8(1), and 8(2) of the Animal Welfare Act. This power is provided under s 17 of the PACE Act 1984.

A vehicle may be stopped and detained under s 54(1) of the Animal Welfare Act 2006 in order to search it to prevent animal suffering (s 19(1)) or to seize an animal that is suspected to have been involved in animal fighting (s 22(2)). A police officer must be in uniform to exercise this power. The vehicle may be detained for as long as is reasonably required (s 54(4)) for a search or inspection to be carried out (including the exercise of any related power under this Act). It may be searched either at the place where it was first detained or nearby (see 9.4.1 on procedures for searches).

13.8.2 Cruelty to wild animals

The law concerning cruelty to wild animals is to be found largely in:

- the Wildlife and Countryside Act 1981 (for most types of wild animal—mammals, birds, frogs, toads, fish, insects, and snakes, but there are notable exclusions, see 13.8.2.1); and
- the Wild Mammals (Protection) Act 1996 (a mammal is an animal whose female produces milk for the nourishment of its young, such as rabbits, foxes, squirrels, hedgehogs, bats, and dolphins).
- the Hunting Act 2004 (which forbids hunting wild mammals with dogs).

The offences of cruelty to wild animals described here are all summary offences, and the penalty is six months' imprisonment and/or a fine.

13.8.2.1 The Wildlife and Countryside Act 1981

Section 1 of the Wildlife and Countryside Act 1981 covers wild birds. A 'wild bird' is any bird of a species that lives wild as a resident or visitor to the European territory of any member state. Game birds (such as pheasants) are not considered wild birds for the purposes of this Act, and there are also other current exceptions (as determined by the Secretary of State for the Environment), such as wood pigeons and herring gulls.

Under s 1 of the Wildlife and Countryside Act 1981 it is an offence to intentionally:

- kill, injure, or take any wild bird;
- take, damage, or destroy the nest of any wild bird while that nest is in use or being built; or
- take or destroy an egg of any wild bird.

Other types of wild animal are protected under s 9 of the Wildlife and Countryside Act 1981, under which it is an offence to intentionally kill, injure, or take 'any' wild animal. However, there are some exclusions (for example rats and rabbits), and it will be for a court to decide whether a particular animal is covered under s 9.

Section 19 of the Wildlife and Countryside Act states that if a police officer suspects with reasonable cause that any person has committed an offence under this Act he/she may search that person and anything in his/her possession and seize and detain evidence (see 9.4.1 on searching). He/she may also enter premises other than a dwelling to arrest a person in relation to these offences (see 10.8.1.2).

13.8.2.2 The Wild Mammals (Protection) Act 1996

Under this Act a mammal is wild if it is not of a kind that is commonly domesticated in the British Islands, and is not the kind of animal that would normally be under the control of a person. It is an offence to mutilate, kick, beat, nail, or otherwise impale, stab, burn, stone, crush, drown, drag, or asphyxiate any wild mammal with intent to inflict unnecessary suffering (s 1 of the Wild Mammals (Protection) Act 1996).

The following are not offences under the Wild Mammals (Protection) Act 1996:

- mercy-killing (and attempts) such as putting an injured badger 'out of its misery';
- actions under authorization, for example by a vet; and
- lawful killing by traps, dogs, birds, or poisons.

If a police officer has reasonable grounds for suspecting that a person has committed an offence under the Wild Mammals (Protection) Act 1996 he/she may stop and search the person (including a vehicle) and seize any relevant items. Code A of the PACE Act 1984 Codes of Practice would apply (see 9.4.1).

13.8.2.3 The Hunting Act 2004

This Act covers hunting wild mammals with dogs. This is only allowed for certain types of wild animal and in certain circumstances as stated in Sch 1. In any case, no more than two dogs may be used, and the animal should be shot dead by a competent person as soon as it is found or flushed out.

Hunting with dogs is allowed for situations where the wild animal:

(a) could otherwise cause serious damage to livestock or its food, game or wild birds, crops, growing timber, fisheries, other property or the biological diversity of the area;

(b) is hunted for human or animal consumption;

(c) is to be used as food for a bird of prey;

(d) is a rabbit or rat;

(e) is impeding the rescue or recapture of another escaped animal; or

(f) is part of a field trial or competition;

(g) is being hunted as part of a research or study programme.

A number of amendments to the Hunting Act 2004 were proposed in July 2015, including allowing the use of more than two dogs to stalk or flush out wild mammals. The discussion of these amendments was however postponed and the law remains unchanged.

TASK 5

- In the Animal Welfare Act 2006 an animal can only 'suffer' physically. True or false?
- What are the three different ways a 'protected animal' may be defined under the Animal Welfare Act 2006?
- There have been anonymous reports about a flat where a dog has been left alone while the residents have gone on holiday. Could a police officer enter the premises under s 19 of the Animal Welfare Act?
- A police officer attends an incident where a cat has been found with a discharged firework taped to its body which had been recently ignited. The cat is still alive but badly injured. The suspects were seen running into a nearby house. Restricting your answer to the Animal Welfare Act 2006, what power of entry, if any, could she use if required to enter and arrest the suspects?

13.9 Answers to Tasks

TASK 1

1. There are likely to be policy agreements with local Social Services and the Healthcare Trusts.

   (a) A dynamic risk assessment of the situation should be made first. Can she safely enter the room or should she seek the assistance of other officers with appropriate personal safety equipment? Entrance can be gained by seeking the permission of the parents/owners of the property to unscrew the door handle and withdrawing the bar a little, so the handle on the other side no longer works. Then she could turn the handle herself to open the door.

(b) She should find out if the young man will voluntarily go to hospital. If not, an AMHP should be called to see if he can be taken into hospital under one of the sections within the MHA.

TASK 2

1. Under s 17(1)(e) PACE an officer 'may enter and search any premises for the purposes of saving life or limb or preventing serious damage to property'. The witness evidence of hearing hysterical screaming and the suspicion that the child is alone and cannot open the door together justify the use of s 17 to save the life and limb of the child.
2. It would appear that Jo has committed an offence under s 1 of the Children and Young Persons Act 1933. This is committed by any person who is 16 years old or over who has responsibility for a child under the age of 16 years and who 'willfully assaults, ill-treats, neglects, abandons or exposes the child in a manner likely to cause unnecessary suffering or injury to health'. In these circumstances Jo has 'abandoned' Sam in a manner likely to cause unnecessary suffering or injury to health. It appears that, although an offence has been committed, the child is no longer in immediate danger and arrangements could be made (perhaps with relatives) for the child's safety while Jo is absent. If there was any reason to believe the child was in immediate danger the officer could consider taking Sam into police protection and arresting the mother. However, prosecution guidelines must be followed and the guidance of a CPS representative would be required. Whatever action is taken, it must be proportionate.

TASK 3

1. The boy needs regular medication: has he taken it with him? Are there factors which will make his medical condition worse (such as stress-induced asthma)? Can the condition be life-threatening in any way? Is his shotgun (and any other weapons on the farm) accounted for? Has any ammunition gone missing? Has he mentioned any particular individuals in connection with the apparent bullying at school, or about revenge? Was the quarrel with his father more serious than usual? What could have caused his depression and anxiety? Has he ever talked (or hinted) about suicide? Does he have a religious belief or strong ethical principles? Has he taken drugs? Has he ever been in trouble with the police?
2. The College of Policing provides guidance in *Major investigation and public protection: Missing persons* (CoP, 2016c). The ACPO guide *Interim Guidance on the Management, Recording and Investigation of Missing Persons 2013* supports the ACPO 2010 guidance. Both are available online.

TASK 4

You probably considered the following:

1. Through questioning, a police officer would be able to determine whether the injury affects the health or comfort of the victim in more than a trivial way.
2. Through questioning and observation, a police officer would be able to collect and collate evidence concerning the injury and whether it can be seen or felt by the victim or witnesses. Remember that the police officer him/herself is a witness too.
3. If there is no evidence of the offence of actual bodily harm, then common assault could be considered as an alternative.

TASK 5

1. False. In the Act, 'suffering' means physical or mental suffering and related expressions shall be construed accordingly.
2. Section 2 states an animal is 'protected' if it is: of a kind which is commonly domesticated in the British Islands; under human control (permanently or temporarily); or otherwise not living in a wild state.
3. Section 19 does not authorize entry to part of a premises which is used as a private dwelling. Under these circumstances a warrant will need to be obtained, under s 19(4).
4. She may enter and search any premises to arrest any person she reasonably suspects of committing an offence under s 4 of the Animal Welfare Act 2006, using s 17 of the PACE Act 1984 (see 10.8). Local force policy must be followed in relation to using force to gain entry in such circumstances.

14 Policing Public Order, Anti-social Behaviour, and Harassment

14.1 Introduction

The Crime Survey for England and Wales (ONS, 2017) estimates the effects of crime and disorder on the quality of people's lives. In the year ending June 2016 survey, 10.2 per cent of people perceived the levels of anti-social behaviour (ASB) in their local area as 'high'. In the same period the police recorded 1.8 million incidents of ASB which compares with the 4.5 million notifiable crimes (see 4.4.1) recorded by the police. An estimated 29% of respondents reported experiencing or witnessing ASB in their local area, a small increase from 28% in the previous year, but overall, the number of ASB incidents decreased by 6 per cent compared with the previous year.

Anti-social behaviour is not a 'crime' as such, but the term covers a number of disruptive activities, some of which are criminal offences. Consequently, this chapter looks not only at these offences but also considers some of the powers designed for the policing of social disorder generally, in both private and public places.

Dealing with civil disputes (eg trespass or debt) and court orders (concerning, eg, access to children or repossession of property) is not normally the responsibility of the police service in England and Wales. However, the police are often first at the scene when such a situation escalates, and even if it begins as a civil dispute it may erupt into an incident where criminal offences are committed. For some cases of civil dispute, and where no offences have been committed, the police can suggest an alternative remedy in the civil courts could be pursued. If, for example, a person is harassed by a neighbour, an injunction can be brought about under s 3(1) of the Protection from Harassment Act 1997 (see 14.5.1.4). In other circumstances, the police can apply for a civil order such as a Domestic Violence Protection Order (see 13.6.1.1).

The methods for policing demonstrations have drawn attention in recent years, particularly the controversial use of 'kettling' to contain and control crowds. The police have a 'negative duty' to not restrict, hinder or prevent peaceful protest as well as a positive duty to protect citizens who want to exercise their right to demonstrate; 'the right to peaceful assembly' in the European Convention on Human Rights (ECHR). This right is now enshrined in the Human Rights Act 1998, as the freedom of thought, conscience and religion (Article 9), the freedom of expression (Article 10) and the freedom of assembly (Article 11)—see 5.4. There have been a number of HMIC reports on the policing of protest, including a major review in 2009 after the protests at the G20 summit (HMIC, 2009, revised 2011). An HMIC report in 2011 recommended that the police retain an adaptable response to the changing nature of protest (HMIC, 2011), and so police training is likely to be designed to reflect these ongoing changes. In this chapter we examine the common law employed by the police to contain protesters to reduce the threat of large-scale disorder.

Specific Incidents

14.2 Countering Anti-social Behaviour

There has been increasing interest in the role of the community and victims in working with the police to address ASB. The Anti-Social Behaviour, Crime and Policing Act 2014 (ASBCPA) provides some relatively new approaches which aim to change the way in which ASB incidents are managed, by focusing on the impact on the victim and less on the behaviour itself. In addition, local authorities, the police, and courts now have new powers to tackle ASB, replacing earlier interventions such as Anti-social Behaviour Orders (ASBOs) because the process of application was slow, bureaucratic, and expensive. In addition, the ASBO failed to change the behaviour of perpetrators, who then went on to commit breaches. The orders consequently did not provide long-term protection to victims and communities.

The ASBCPA provided new powers and injunctions to help the police and local authorities address ASB and disorder. In terms of these powers, ASB is broadly categorized as either housing related or non-housing related. The latter occurs in a public place such as a shopping precinct or city centre. Housing related ASB on the other hand will include disputes between neighbours over lifestyle clashes, high hedges, litter, noise, boundary disputes, and the behaviour of children. It also includes more serious incidents of ASB, where the behaviour of one household causes serious problems within a whole neighbourhood and may involve harassment, violence, and criminality. The Home Office guidance *Anti-social Behaviour, Crime and Policing Act 2014: Reform of anti-social behaviour powers: Statutory guidance for frontline professionals* July 2014 is available online.

14.2.1 Tackling ASB at the level of the individual

If a police officer has reason to believe that a person has been acting (or is acting) in an 'anti-social manner' a police officer can require that person to give his/her name and address (s 50(1) of the Police Reform Act 2002). An anti-social manner is one that 'caused or is likely to cause harassment, alarm or distress to any person' (s 2(1)(a) of the ASBCPA). It is an offence for such a person to fail to give his/her name and address when required (including giving a false or inaccurate name or address (s 50(2) of the Police Reform Act 2002)). This offence is triable summarily and the penalty is a fine.

14.2.1.1 Civil injunctions

Injunctions to Prevent Nuisance and Annoyance (IPNAs) were introduced under the ASBCPA (along with Criminal Behaviour Orders) to replace ASBOs, and can be used at an early stage to stop or prevent individuals engaging in ASB. They are intended for use in non-housing related ASB where the behaviour either caused or was likely to cause harassment, alarm, or distress, and for housing related ASB where the conduct is capable of causing nuisance or annoyance.

A wide range of organizations can apply for such an injunction, such as local councils, social landlords, the police, and Transport for London. They are issued by the county court and High Court for over 18 year olds, and the Youth Court for under 18 year olds (the relevant YOT must also be consulted (see 3.3.4)). Unlike their predecessor (the ASBO), there is no need to prove an injunction is 'necessary', and they are obtainable on a civil standard of proof (balance of probability). IPNAs can require the perpetrator to address the causes of their ASB, and can also include prohibitions. Breaching an injunction is not a criminal offence but must be proved to criminal standard (beyond reasonable doubt). The penalty for a breach for under 18 year olds is a supervision order or, as a very last resort, a civil detention order of up to three months for 14–17 year olds. For over 18s the penalty is civil contempt of court with an unlimited fine or up to two years in prison.

14.2.1.2 Criminal Behaviour Orders

Criminal Behaviour Orders (CBOs) were introduced under the ASBCPA (along with Civil Injunctions), to replace ASBOs, and are designed to deal with the most persistently anti-social individuals who engage in criminal activity. CBOs are issued by a criminal court on conviction for any criminal offence, but the ASB does not need to be part of the offence. The court must be satisfied beyond reasonable doubt that the offender had already engaged in behaviour that caused or was likely to cause harassment, alarm, or distress to any person, and that making the order would help prevent the offender from engaging in further similar behaviour. For example, a defendant could be brought before a court and found guilty of criminal damage, and if there was additional evidence that he had engaged in ASB, the court could be asked to make a CBO. The CBO can require the perpetrator to address the causes of his/her ASB (eg attend an anger-management course), and can also include prohibitions. For under 18-year-olds, Youth Offending Teams must be consulted (see 3.3.4).

Breaching a CBO is a criminal offence, so the breach must be proved beyond reasonable doubt. On summary conviction the penalty is up to six months' imprisonment or a fine or both and, on indictment, up to five years' imprisonment or a fine or both.

14.2.1.3 Out-of-court disposals for young people

Out-of-court disposals are favoured by the Government for dealing with young people in the first instance who cause ASB (Home Office, 2014a). Examples include:

- Acceptable Behaviour Contracts (ABC): a written agreement between a local agency and the perpetrator of ASB to desist from the unacceptable behaviour. To encourage compliance, the terms contained in the contract should be discussed with the perpetrator before they are drafted.
- Community Resolutions: these can be used with both adults and juveniles to help draw up an informal agreement between parties. They are aimed at first-time perpetrators who show genuine remorse for their victim(s).
- Mediation: this is a facilitated conversation between the perpetrator and victim (all parties attend voluntarily). Any solution should be agreed by all parties, and the meditator can draw up a document to formalize the decisions.
- Parenting Contract: this can be considered if it seems that the parent or guardian is a bad influence on the child under 18, or if supervision is lacking. They are similar to an ABC, but are signed by the parent or guardian. They could be considered if the perpetrator is under the age of criminal responsibility and there are no other more appropriate interventions for the child.
- Support and counselling: drug and alcohol dependency can contribute to causing ASB, so early supportive interventions can be instigated.
- Verbal warnings: these are issued by the police, the council, or a housing officer if ASB has occurred (or is likely) and the individual's behaviour is considered as unreasonable.
- Written warnings: as with a verbal warning, these should include details of the behaviour, why it is unacceptable and its impact on any victims.

14.2.1.4 Victim engagement

Two new measures in the ASBCPA 2014, community triggers and community remedies, enable victims and others to contribute to decisions about managing ASB in their area.

The new community trigger system allows victims of ASB or another person acting on their behalf to formally request that ASB incidents be reviewed by the police and local councils (or other relevant bodies). They will then determine whether a certain threshold has been reached, usually three complaints over a six-month period (although this can be locally defined). The persistence and harm (or potential harm) caused by the ASB will also be taken into consideration. Agencies must inform the victim if the threshold has been met, and if it has, a case review will take place with a problem-solving approach. Where an action plan is required, it will be discussed with the victim and a timescale for action agreed.

A community remedy allows victims of ASB to be able to choose the most appropriate out-of-court punitive, reparative, or rehabilitative actions to be taken against perpetrators of low-level crime and the ASB. This will be recorded in a community remedy document which can be used by a police officer, PCSO (if designated), or a relevant prosecutor when a conditional or youth conditional caution is proposed (see 10.13.2.2 and 10.13.2.3). To invoke a Community Remedy there will need to be:

- evidence indicating that the person has committed an offence or ASB that would warrant the use of a caution or court proceedings for a civil injunction;

- an admission from the perpetrator of the behaviour or the offence and an agreement to participate in the community remedy.

If the perpetrator fails to comply with a conditional or youth conditional caution, court proceedings can be used.

14.2.1.5 Evicting tenants and Absolute Ground for Possession

Absolute Ground for Possession (AGP) can be used by landlords to evict tenants where ASB or criminality has already been proven by another court. The police should not be directly involved in any AGP-related action (it is a civil matter), but they should be aware of it existence in providing advice to landlords etc. It can be used for secure and assured tenancies in both the social and private sector.

The landlord does not need to prove that it is reasonable for him/her to be granted possession if the property has been closed for more than 48 hours under a closure order for ASB, or the tenant, a member of the tenant's household, or a person visiting the property has breached a civil injunction or been convicted of certain offences. These offences include the breaching of a criminal behaviour order (CBO) or a noise abatement notice, and serious offences such as violent and sexual offences, criminal damage, possession of offensive weapons and drugs. The behaviours amounting to the breach or the convicted offence need to have occurred in the locality of the property, or to have affected a person with a right to live in the locality, or the landlord or his or her staff/contractors.

A landlord first needs to serve a notice of the proceedings on the tenant. This must be within three months where a closure order has been used, or within 12 months of the relevant conviction or finding of the court in relation to a breach. The notice is valid for 12 months.

14.2.1.6 Nuisance or disturbance on hospital premises

It is an offence (s 119(1) of the Criminal Justice and Immigration Act 2008) for a person on NHS premises to cause a nuisance or disturbance (without reasonable excuse) to an NHS staff member who is working there or is otherwise there in connection with work, and to refuse (without reasonable excuse) to leave when asked to do so by a police officer or an NHS staff member.

Here, NHS premises includes:

- NHS hospitals in England, and any building or other structure on hospital grounds (land in the vicinity of the hospital and associated with it); and
- any vehicles associated with the hospital and situated on hospital grounds (includes an air ambulance).

This offence cannot be committed by a person who is there to obtain medical advice, treatment, or care for him/herself, but can be committed by someone who has already received it or has been refused it during the previous eight hours. An NHS staff member includes agency and contract workers, students, and volunteers. A police officer who reasonably suspects that a person is committing or has committed a s 119(1) offence can remove him/her from the premises using reasonable force if necessary (s 120(1)). The offence of causing a nuisance (s 119(1)) is triable summarily, and the penalty is a fine.

14.2.1.7 Smoking in a smoke-free place

Under s 7 of the Health Act 2006, a person commits an offence if he/she smokes in a 'smoke-free' place. Smoking includes the smoking of cigarettes (hand-rolled and manufactured), pipes, cigars, herbal cigarettes, and the use of water-pipes (eg 'hubble-bubble' pipes).

Smoke-free places include 'enclosed or substantially enclosed premises which are open to the public, and shared workplaces', and are defined in the Smoke-free (Premises and Enforcement) Regulations 2006. Briefly, 'enclosed premises' have a ceiling or roof and are wholly enclosed except for doors, windows, or passageways, while 'substantially enclosed premises' have a ceiling or roof but the permanent openings in the walls are less than half of the total areas of walls, known as the '50% rule'. (Here, 'walls' include structures which 'serve the purpose of walls and constitute the perimeter of premises', and a 'roof' includes any fixed or moveable structure or device which is capable of covering all or part of the premises as a roof, including, for example, a canvas awning.) Therefore premises with a ceiling or roof that have large permanent openings in the wall (more than half of the total wall area) are not subject to this legislation.

This offence is triable summarily and the penalty is a fine.

14.2.1.8 Dangerous dogs and anti-social behaviour

Dogs must be kept under control, and prevented from injuring people or other dogs. The owner of a dog or the person in charge of it at the time (A) commits an offence under s 3(1) of the Dangerous Dogs Act 1991 if the dog is dangerously out of control in any place. The offence is aggravated if the dog causes injury to a person (B) or an assistance dog. However, these offences do not apply if the dog is in a dwelling or forces accommodation (in the building, or partly in it, or in part of it) and B was in (or entering) as a trespasser, or if A was present and believed B to be trespassing.

The basic offence is triable summarily and the penalty is six months' imprisonment and/or a fine. The aggravated offence is triable either way. If tried summarily the penalty is six months' imprisonment and/or a fine. On indictment the penalty is 14 years if a person dies as a result of being injured, 5 years in any other case where a person is injured, and 3 years if an assistance dog is injured or dies.

Guidance for dealing with owners or breeders of dangerous dogs (defined in s 1 of the Dangerous Dogs Act 1991) can be found in *Dangerous Dogs Law Guidance for Enforcers*. Legislation in relation to protecting the dogs from cruelty can also be considered (see 13.8.1).

14.2.1.9 Injunctions for gang-related violence

An injunction can be taken out against an individual, to prevent him/her from engaging in, or encouraging or assisting, gang-related violence (s 34(3) of the Policing and Crime Act 2009). The police or a local authority apply to a county court (or the High Court) for the injunction. Further details on the definition of a gang, and other legislation to help reduce the harm associated with gangs are provided in 15.8.

A power of arrest (s 43(2)) may be attached to an injunction in case of it being breached. The Home Office has issued Statutory Guidance on s 34(3) injunctions (Home Office, 2010d).

> **TASK 1** The case of *Rice v Connolly* [1966] 2 QB 414 clearly decided that a person need not give his/her name and address unless there is power to make an arrest for a crime. In the case of a woman who has not been arrested but is nonetheless acting in an anti-social manner, can a police officer require her to provide her name and address?

14.2.2 Community-based measures for tackling ASB

The police often work with the local council to find long-term sustainable solutions in areas where ASB is a regular problem. However, police officers can often deal with an individual's behaviour straightaway and provide immediate short-term respite to a local community.

14.2.2.1 Dispersal Orders

A dispersal order allows a police officer in uniform or a designated PCSO to direct any person committing or likely to commit ASB, crime, or disorder to leave an area for up to 48 hours. The orders can be used for a person over the age of 10 (or who appears to be over 10). The ASB must be contributing (or be likely to contribute) to causing harassment, alarm, or distress to members of the public in the local area or to the occurrence of crime and disorder.

The direction to leave must be necessary to remove or reduce the likelihood of the behaviour. The order must be authorized by an officer of at least the rank of inspector. The direction to disperse must be given in writing unless it is impracticable, and should specify the area to and the time period for which it applies, and can also determine the route and the time recipient(s) should leave by. The police officer or PCSO can require the person to hand over any items that could be used to commit ASB, crime, or disorder, but this is not a power of seizure so no force can be used. A young person under 16 receiving such a direction can be taken home (unless there are reasonable grounds for believing that he/she would be likely to suffer significant harm there) or to a place of safety. If he/she is unwilling to go voluntarily, the word 'remove' has been held to mean 'take away using reasonable force if necessary' (*R (W) v Commissioner of Police for the Metropolis and another, Secretary of State for the Home Department, interested party* [2004] EWCA Civ 458).

Failing to hand over the requested item, or breaching a dispersal order is a summary offence. The penalty for failing to hand over items is a fine, and for breaching an order up to three months in prison (for over 18 year olds only) and/or a fine.

14.2.2.2   Community Protection Notices

A Community Protection Notice (CPN) is designed to address ASB caused by an individual aged over 16, or by businesses and other organizations. The ASB needs to be having a detrimental effect on the quality of life for people in the locality, and to be unreasonable and persistent/continuing. Council and police officers, PCSOs (if designated), and social landlords can issue CPNs. A written warning must first be given to the perpetrator, stating the problem behaviour, requesting that it should stop, and stating the consequences of continuing. The CPN can include requirements to desist from or stop specified activities, and to take reasonable steps to avoid further ASB.

Breaching a CPN is a criminal offence and the penalties can include a fixed penalty notice (see 10.13.2.1) up to £100, or on summary conviction a fine for contempt of court. In the case of a conviction, the prosecuting authority can ask the court to impose a remedial and/or a forfeiture order. As examples, remedial action could be for the perpetrator to clear up rubbish, and under a forfeiture order, items that were used to commit the ASB could be seized (such as spray painting equipment).

14.2.2.3   Public Spaces Protection Orders

A Public Spaces Protection Order (PSPO) is issued by a council and is designed to manage a specific problem which is caused by individuals or groups in a particular public place, and is injurious to the local community. The ASB must be having (or is likely to have) a detrimental effect on the quality of life for local people, and is (or is likely to be) persistent or continuing in nature and unreasonable. The restrictions imposed by the order must be proportionate and justified, and could include making requirements such as keeping dogs on a lead, and prohibiting the consumption of alcohol in a particular area. A PSPO takes precedence over any by-law which already prohibits an activity in the restricted area, for example a 'controlled drinking zone' (see 12.2.4). Access to public spaces can also be restricted (including certain types of highway) if ASB is occurring there, for example an alleyway could be closed to everyone except the inhabitants of the adjacent houses.

It is an offence for a person, without reasonable excuse, to fail to comply with a PSPO requirement, or to do anything prohibited by a PSPO, apart from in relation to alcohol. A PSPO prohibiting alcohol consumption is only breached when a person is challenged and fails to stop drinking or surrender the alcohol. (This effectively allows peaceful consumption of alcohol in an area with a PSPO relating to alcohol.) Breaching a PSPO is a summary offence and the penalty is a fine. A fixed penalty notice can also be used (see 10.13.2.1).

14.2.2.4   Closure Notices and Orders

These can be used to close premises (licensed, enclosed or open, residential, and business) that are causing nuisance or disorder. A closure notice applies for 24 hours, but can be extended. A closure order is a longer-term solution and can be issued subsequent to a closure notice if it seems necessary. The court must be satisfied that the notice or order is necessary to prevent the nuisance or disorder from occurring, continuing, or recurring. Residents cannot be prohibited from accessing their home by a closure notice, but will have to leave if a closure order is issued.

A closure notice is initially issued for 24 hours. The council or a police officer (of at least the rank of inspector) must be satisfied on reasonable grounds that the use of the premises has resulted (or is likely to result if the notice is not issued) in nuisance to members of the public, or disorder near the premises. The notice can be extended by up to 24 hours by a council's chief executive officer or a police superintendent. When a closure notice is issued, an application for a closure order must also be made to the magistrates' court. The court can extend the closure notice if necessary for a further 48 hours, so that a closure order can be issued. It is a criminal offence to enter or remain on premises in contravention of a closure notice or extension, and the penalty is an unlimited fine or imprisonment of up to three months, or both. It is also an offence to obstruct a police officer or local council employee who is serving a notice, or entering or securing the premises. The penalty is imprisonment of up to three months, an unlimited fine, or both.

A closure order can be used if it seems necessary. The court must be satisfied that without it there will be serious nuisance to members of the public, or disorderly, offensive, or criminal behaviour on the premises. It is a criminal offence to remain on or enter premises in contravention of a closure order without reasonable excuse, and the penalty is imprisonment of up to six months, an unlimited fine, or both.

> **TASK 2** Imagine you are a trainee police officer on Supervised Patrol in a part of a city which has a significant and persistent problem with anti-social behaviour, and is therefore subject to an authorization under s 34 of the Anti-Social Behaviour, Crime and Policing Act 2014. This allows you to disperse people from the locality if you believe this is required. During your patrol, you see a group of children, some seeming as young as six, running in and out of nearby houses and intimidating passers-by. What precise powers would you have to deal with the children involved?

14.3   Breach of the Peace

You have no doubt heard of the phrase 'breach of the peace'. There is some considerable debate concerning both its meaning and whether the police should still have powers in this respect. This is partly because the law surrounding a breach of the peace is somewhat unusual: it is not a criminal offence, nor is it part of statute law, but is instead part of common law (see 5.2). Case law has set a precedent in defining its meaning (see 14.3.1). Some police forces discourage their officers from the use of police powers in relation to a breach of the peace, whereas others continue to view it as an important means of reducing the likelihood of harm taking place. In all cases the police use of breach of the peace should be consistent with Article 5 (the right to liberty and security), Article 10 (the right to freedom of expression), and Article 11 (the right to freedom of assembly and association) of the Human Rights Act 1998 (see 5.4). During recent protests the police have used likelihood of an imminent breach of the peace as the reason for the containing ('kettling') of large numbers of protesters at the same location for extended periods of time. The use of 'containment' as a public order measure remains controversial, as does the use of breach of the peace legislation.

Any person committing a breach of the peace can in law be arrested by any other person (although in most cases this will be a police officer, rather than a member of the public). Having been arrested, individuals can be detained until there is no likelihood of a breach of the peace recurring. They may then be released without further action or be 'bound over' (see 14.3.3).

14.3.1   Definition of breach of the peace

The case of *R v Howell* [1981] 3 All ER 383 provides a definition of the meaning of breach of the peace:

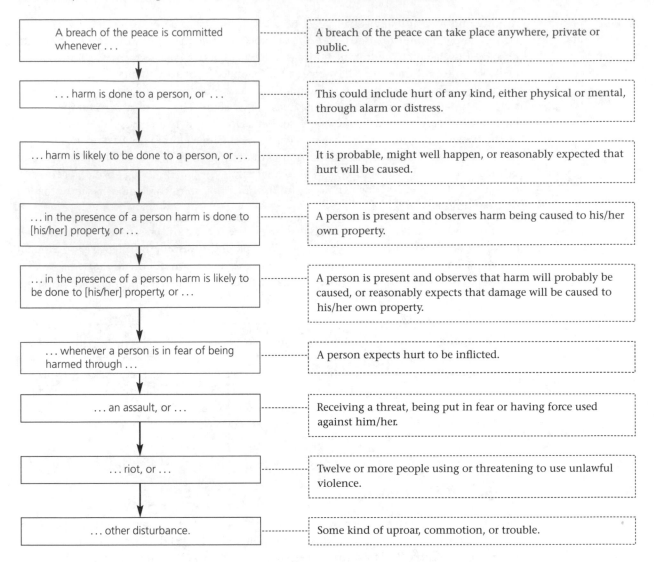

A breach of the peace is committed whenever . . .	A breach of the peace can take place anywhere, private or public.
. . . harm is done to a person, or . . .	This could include hurt of any kind, either physical or mental, through alarm or distress.
. . . harm is likely to be done to a person, or . . .	It is probable, might well happen, or reasonably expected that hurt will be caused.
. . . in the presence of a person harm is done to [his/her] property, or . . .	A person is present and observes harm being caused to his/her own property.
. . . in the presence of a person harm is likely to be done to [his/her] property, or . . .	A person is present and observes that harm will probably be caused, or reasonably expects that damage will be caused to his/her own property.
. . . whenever a person is in fear of being harmed through . . .	A person expects hurt to be inflicted.
. . . an assault, or . . .	Receiving a threat, being put in fear or having force used against him/her.
. . . riot, or . . .	Twelve or more people using or threatening to use unlawful violence.
. . . other disturbance.	Some kind of uproar, commotion, or trouble.

14.3.2 Powers of arrest and entry for breach of the peace

Breach of the peace is unique. It can take place in many different ways, but whatever the situation, it must satisfy the elements set out in the case *R v Howell*.

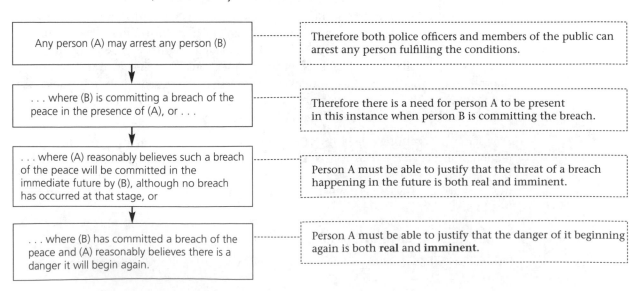

Any person (A) may arrest any person (B)	Therefore both police officers and members of the public can arrest any person fulfilling the conditions.
. . . where (B) is committing a breach of the peace in the presence of (A), or . . .	Therefore there is a need for person A to be present in this instance when person B is committing the breach.
. . . where (A) reasonably believes such a breach of the peace will be committed in the immediate future by (B), although no breach has occurred at that stage, or	Person A must be able to justify that the threat of a breach happening in the future is both real and imminent.
. . . where (B) has committed a breach of the peace and (A) reasonably believes there is a danger it will begin again.	Person A must be able to justify that the danger of it beginning again is both **real** and **imminent**.

For the arrest to be lawful, the person making the arrest must identify the all-important ingredients of harm and compare the actual circumstances with the definition. The breach must have taken place in his/her presence, or the threat of a breach or its renewal must be both real and imminent.

Under common law (see 5.2) an officer is entitled to enter either private or public premises in order to make an arrest for a breach of the peace, or to prevent such a breach. Once the breach has come to an end the officer should not remain on private premises (unless there is another reason to do so) and should leave within a 'reasonable time'. If he/she is assaulted (eg by a resident of the property) during that reasonable time, this could be regarded as an assault on a police officer in the lawful execution of his/her duty. However, if the officer has not left within a reasonable time, his/her presence may be unlawful and therefore he/she might not be protected under criminal law (*Robson v Hallett* [1967] 2 QB 939).

14.3.3 Binding-over after an arrest for breach of the peace

After arrest for breach of the peace, the police can release the person without further action when it is deemed that a risk of a breach no longer exists. However, in other circumstances the CPS may decide (s 3(2)(c) of the Prosecution of Offences Act 1985) that further action is needed to reduce the risk of another breach. The person will appear before a magistrates' court, which can issue a binding-over order which can refer to general terms of protection, or it can be more specific by naming people. The order can also require the recipient to keep the peace for a specified time, and/or enter into a recognizance for a specified sum (an agreement to pay a financial penalty to the court if brought back after any subsequent breaches).

TASK 3 In August 2012 at King's Cross underground station in London a group of around 30 to 40 individuals were stopped from making their way to the Notting Hill Carnival in order to 'prevent a breach of the peace'. Some of the men were reported by the press to be wearing 'body armour'. The men were believed to have travelled from north London in order to 'cause trouble' at the carnival. They were held until the police judged there was no risk of disorder and then released without charge. An MPS Commander was reported as saying 'On the arrests at King's Cross we received intelligence that members of a north London gang were heading towards the carnival. They were spotted on the Underground and they were detained until the carnival was over. There was no doubt they were planning on causing trouble' (London Evening Standard, 2012).

In November 2003, a woman climbed the gates of Buckingham Palace to protest at the visit of US President George W. Bush. She then unfurled the Stars and Stripes flag on top of the gates with the words 'ELIZABETH WINDSOR AND CO...HE'S NOT WELCOME' written on the flag. After about two hours she voluntarily climbed down from the gates and was reportedly arrested by the police on suspicion of criminal damage and breach of the peace.

Compare the use of breach of peace powers in the two examples.

14.3.4 Containment

Containment (also known as 'kettling') is used by the police to maintain public order and safety. It involves putting a cordon around a large number of people and confining them to a relatively small, easily managed public area, and police officers decide who remains inside the cordon and for how long. The police argue that the likelihood of an imminent breach of the peace provides them with common law powers to confine people in this way, but this has been challenged in the courts.

For containment to be lawful, the following should be considered:

- at common law, an apprehended breach of the peace must be imminent;
- circumstances dictate what is imminent, but it is not an inflexible concept;
- actions can be justified only if they are proportionate, reasonable, and necessary;
- when steps are required to keep two or more different groups apart, a combination of their actions can be considered when deciding if there is an imminent breach of the peace; and
- depending on the circumstances, action may be taken which affects people who are not actively involved in the breach of the peace.

These five points are derived from *R (on the application of Hannah McClure and Joshua Moos) v Commissioner of Police for the Metropolis* [2012] EWCA Civ 12 and *Laporte v Chief Constable of*

Gloucestershire Constabulary [2007] 2 AC 105. In the former case the containment was justified by the reasonable apprehension of imminent and serious breaches of the peace likely to be caused by the arrival of another substantial crowd of protesters at an airbase. The justification was not the violent and unruly behaviour of the main crowd. (See also *Moss v McLachlan* [1985] 1 RLR 76 in relation to the policing of the 1984 miners' strike.)

The police must not use containment until they have taken all other possible steps to prevent the breach or imminent breach of the peace and to protect the rights of third parties (*Austin v Commissioner of Police of the Metropolis* [2009] 1 AC 564). The containment of children is lawful if s 11 of the Children Act 2004 is followed, regarding the welfare of the children (*R (on the application of Castle and others) v Commissioner of Police for the Metropolis* [2011] EWHC 2317). It should be noted that people released from containment have no obligation to provide personal information, nor is it acceptable for them to be photographed (*Susannah Mengesha v Commissioner of Police of the Metropolis* [2013] EWHC 1695 (Admin)). Further information on the use of containment can be found in the *Manual of Guidance on Keeping the Peace* (ACPO, 2010e).

14.4 The Public Order Act 1986

The Public Order Act 1986 deals with a wide range of behaviours and offences, in descending order of seriousness: riot (s 1), violent disorder (s 2), affray (s 3), fear or provocation of violence (s 4), intentional harassment, alarm, or distress (s 4A) and non-intentional harassment, alarm, or distress (s 5). As you might expect, the least serious offences are the most commonly committed.

14.4.1 Intoxication is not a defence

Some people accused of Public Order Act 1986 offences may claim in their defence that they were intoxicated at the time of the offence. However, s 6(5) of the Public Order Act 1986 specifically states that in these circumstances a person will be taken by the court to have the same level of awareness as if he/she had not been intoxicated, unless it can be proved that either the intoxication:

- was not self-induced (eg 'spiked' drinks); or
- was caused solely by the taking or administration of a substance in the course of medical treatment (eg prescribed medicine).

Note that s 6(5) does not apply to s 4A of the Act, as s 4A was introduced at a later date.

14.4.2 Locations for public order offences

Offences under ss 4, 4A, and 5 of the Public Order Act 1986 are for the most part only committed in a public place, but in certain circumstances they can also be committed within the confines of a private place, for example a communal area such as a shared laundry in a block of flats (see *Le Vine v DPP* (2010) DC (Elias LJ, Keith J) 6/5/2010). These offences can also apply when the conduct occurs in the confines of a private place, but it causes a person who is in a public place to be harassed, alarmed, or distressed. For example, if a householder attaches a poster to the inside of his front-room window, and it offends a person in the street outside (a public street), the offence has been committed. (However, if the poster was in a side window and was seen by a neighbour from inside his own house (perhaps through a side window), then the offence has not been committed. Other legislation is available for circumstances which are completely private, for example the Protection from Harassment Act 1997 (see 14.5.1).)

The more serious public order offences (riot, violent disorder, and affray) can take place in private, as well as in public places (see 9.2 for definitions of public places).

14.4.3 Offences under ss 5, 4A, and 4

Sections 5 and 4A of the Public Order Act 1986 are used for relatively minor forms of public disorder such as persistent swearing and shouting. Section 4 is used for more serious public disorder, involving fear or provocation of violence.

The distinctions between offences under ss 5, 4A, and 4 require careful consideration and still cause some debate in legal and police circles. The offences are compared in the table to highlight important differences between them.

	s 4	s 4A	s 5
Intentions of the suspect	Intends to cause fear of violence or to provoke violence	Intends to be threatening, abusive, or insulting	No intention, but is aware that the conduct is threatening or abusive
Recipient of the conduct	Conduct aimed towards a specific person	Conduct does not have to be aimed towards a specific person	Conduct does not have to be aimed towards a specific person (but has to be carried out in the hearing or sight of a person likely to be caused harassment, alarm, or distress)
Includes disorderly behaviour?	Does not include disorderly behaviour		Includes disorderly behaviour
Distribution of material?	Includes distribution of material		Does not include distribution of material
Outcome of the behaviour	No specific outcome is required to prove this offence	An identifiable person must be harassed, alarmed, or distressed	No specific outcome is required to prove this offence

Before looking at the sections in detail, you might find it useful to consider the definitions of key terms used in the legislation:

- Abusive: using insulting or degrading language
- Alarm: a state of surprise, fright, fear, terror, and panic
- Behaviour: a display of conduct involving the treatment of others
- Disorderly behaviour: rowdy, unruly, boisterous, loud, raucous, or unrestrained conduct
- Display: to show or exhibit for all to see, such as placing a sign or poster in a window
- Distress: a feeling of suffering, anguish, and misery
- Distribute: to hand out, share out, give out, or issue to a particular person or people, not just simply leave 'lying about'
- Harassment: a feeling of annoyance, persecution, irritation, and aggravation
- Insulting: disrespectful, especially if done in a way that is offensive or suggesting that a person is beneath consideration (but in a way that is more than causing annoyance or bitterness)
- Sign, leaflet, pamphlet, or poster or other visual representation: containing pictures, text, or images
- Threatening: a physical or verbal act which indicates that harm will be inflicted. It can also include violent conduct
- Words: can be spoken, shouted, or written
- Writing: a notice containing lettering or other visible form of text.

14.4.3.1   Section 5 of the Public Order Act 1986

The offence is also referred to as causing non-intentional harassment, alarm, or distress. Section 5 of the Public Order Act 1986 states that a person is guilty of this offence if he/she uses threatening or abusive words or behaviour, or disorderly behaviour, or if he/she displays any writing, sign, or other visible representation which is threatening or abusive, and this is done within the hearing or sight of a person likely to be caused harassment, alarm, or distress thereby.

The key features of s 5 offences are that:

- the conduct does not have to be aimed towards a specific person;
- the conduct must take place within the presence of a person who can see or hear the conduct, but that person does not need to be identifiable;
- the type of conduct must be likely to cause harassment, alarm, or distress;
- any material used (such as a poster) does not have to be distributed;
- the suspect must intend or be aware that his/her conduct is threatening or abusive in general terms; however,
- there is no need to prove he/she actually intended to cause any person to be harassed, alarmed, or distressed.

You may feel that the last two bullet points appear contradictory, but consider the example shown here. A police officer (PO) is interviewing a suspect (S), and the precise nature of a s 5 offence becomes more clear; the suspect might intend his/her conduct to be threatening or abusive but still have no intention to make any person harassed, alarmed, or distressed.

PO	Why did you behave like that, back there in the street?
S	I was trying to be…hard in front of my mates.
PO	Didn't you think about the effect it might have on other people?
S	Not really, no—I was only messing about.
PO	What was the point of it all then?
S	Not a lot—I was only showing off, I'd had a bit, but I wasn't off my head. I knew what I was doing, yeah, and I wanted to be loud and proud, just to show my mates I could do it. They just laughed, made out I was acting stupid.
PO	Yes, and you might have upset a few older people passing by; how do you think they felt hearing that lot?
S	I just didn't think—yeah, I knew they were there…But if I did, I didn't mean to upset them…

There are three defences to this offence (listed in s 5(3)):

- he/she was in a public place but had no reason to believe that anybody could hear or see the conduct;
- he/she was inside a dwelling (place of residence) and had no reason to believe that the words, behaviour, or conduct could be seen or heard by a person in a public place, for example, a poster was on a wall inside the front room, and could not be clearly seen from outside; or
- that the conduct was reasonable and did not cause anybody to be harassed, alarmed, or distressed, for example he/she shouted at a group of people who were carrying out an unlawful act outside his/her home.

This offence is triable summarily and the penalty is a fine. It can also be racially or religiously aggravated (see 14.10.4).

TASK 4 Take a moment now to consider what evidence a police officer would need before making a decision whether to consider a woman for a s 5 Public Order Act 1986 offence.

1. Who would provide evidence?
2. What evidence would they be able to provide?
3. What evidence would a police officer present at the scene be able to provide?

14.4.3.2 Section 4A of the Public Order Act 1986

A s 4A offence is often referred to as causing intentional harassment, alarm, or distress. A person is guilty of this offence if he/she uses threatening, abusive, or insulting words or behaviour, or disorderly behaviour, or displays any writing, sign, or other visible representation which is threatening, abusive, or insulting, with intent to cause a person harassment, alarm, or distress thereby causing that or another person harassment, alarm, or distress.

The key features of s 4A offences are that:

- the suspect intends the conduct to be threatening, abusive, or insulting and to cause a person harassment, alarm, or distress;
- the conduct does not have to be aimed towards a specific person;
- at least one identifiable person must be harassed, alarmed, or distressed; and
- if material is used it need only be displayed (and not distributed).

This piece of legislation is aimed at supporting the most vulnerable members of the community, who may be specifically targeted because of their inability to respond appropriately to intentionally directed acts which cause them harassment, alarm, or distress. These victims may feel particularly uncomfortable as witnesses, so every opportunity should be taken to support them throughout any police or legal process.

As a possible defence, a suspect could demonstrate that:

- he/she had no reason to believe his/her words, behaviour, or conduct inside a dwelling (a place of residence) could be seen or heard by a person anywhere outside, for example a man was reading out loud from a book but the windows were shut (s 4A(3)(a)); or
- his/her conduct was reasonable, for example if a woman in her front room opened the window and shouted at two people tampering with her car outside (s 4A(3)(b)).

This offence is triable summarily and the penalty is six months' imprisonment and/or a fine. This offence can be racially or religiously aggravated (see 14.10.4).

14.4.3.3 Section 4 of the Public Order Act 1986

A s 4 offence is also referred to as fear or provocation of violence. A person is guilty of this offence if he/she uses towards another person threatening, abusive, or insulting words or behaviour, or if he/she distributes or displays to another person any writing, sign, or other visible representation which is threatening, abusive, or insulting. The intent must be to:

- cause that person to believe that immediate unlawful violence will be used (against him/her or another) by any person; or
- provoke the immediate use of unlawful violence (by that person or another);
- cause that person to believe it is likely either that such violence will be used or be provoked.

For this offence, the intentions of the suspect are the key issue; the actual effect of the behaviour on other people is not relevant. The intention must be to make the recipient (the person (or persons) to whom the conduct is addressed) feel fear, or to provoke other people or another person to be violent. Despite the fact that the actual effect of the conduct is not relevant for this offence, for the intentions of the suspect to be held to be genuine, his/her conduct must be directed towards a recipient who must be present at the time when the words or behaviour are used. The recipient must be able to see or hear the conduct (or the suspect must at least believe that the recipient is able to see or hear the conduct (see *Atkin v DPP* [1989] Crim LR 581)).

The suspect's intentions may be to cause fear of violence. If so, the suspect must intend the recipient to fear that violence will be used (or is likely to be used). The threatened violent acts do not need to involve the suspect or the recipient directly. The violent acts could be threatened against another person, or threatened to be carried out by another person, and not by the suspect.

Alternatively, the suspect could have the intention (a determined state of mind) to provoke any person to use violence. For example, an extremist at a demonstration shouts at an animal research worker, 'A dog is for life, not just for you to torture and experiment on, you sadist! You'll get the same, I promise you that!'. If the intention is to provoke the other demonstrators to be violent, the offence is committed.

The key features of s 4 offences are that:

- the conduct must be directed towards a person or persons present at the scene;
- any material used is distributed and not just displayed;
- the suspect must intend or be aware that his/her conduct is potentially threatening, abusive, or insulting (but it does not matter whether the recipient actually feels threatened, abused, or insulted);
- the suspect may intend to cause fear or provoke a reaction of violence (but it does not matter whether the conduct actually has either of these effects);
- if the suspect intends to cause fear (that violence will be or is likely to be used), the intention need only be to cause the recipient to feel fear; and
- if the suspect intends to provoke violence, the intention can be to provoke any person present.

A police officer may enter any premises to arrest any person reasonably suspected of committing an offence under s 4 of the Public Order Act 1986 (s 17 of the PACE Act 1984: see 10.8.1.2). The offence is triable summarily and the penalty is six months' imprisonment and/or a fine. This offence can be racially aggravated (see 14.10.4).

Specific Incidents

> **TASK 5** Imagine you are a trainee police officer on Independent Patrol. You encounter a man who is shouting in an incoherent and aggressive manner, and it seems to you that the behaviour is likely to be capable of causing harassment, alarm, or distress. Consider how you will deal with this situation if there is no one else in the area at the time to whom this conduct is aimed and hence it appears to be directed solely at you.
>
> While drawing your conclusions, refer to *DPP v Orum* [1988] Crim LR 848 and *Harvey v DPP* [2011] EWCA Crim B1.

> **TASK 6** Imagine you are a trainee police officer on Independent Patrol. You see a man walk up to the door of a club and adopt an aggressive posture towards the door supervisor. You are about two metres away. The aggressor has clenched fists, bulging eyes, and has taken up a 'boxing' position. The suspect then pushes his shoulder into the door supervisor's chest causing the door supervisor to move back. You hear the suspect say 'You're a dead man'. You believe that the door supervisor is about to be attacked and so you arrest the suspect under s 4 of the Public Order Act 1986.
>
> When you return to the club to obtain a statement from the door supervisor, he is not willing to make a statement. Does it seem likely that a successful prosecution could be brought against the suspect under these circumstances?
>
> When drawing a conclusion, consider *Swanston v DPP* (1997) 161 JP 203.

14.4.4 Serious public order offences

These offences under the Public Order Act 1986, in increasing order of seriousness, are affray (s 3), violent disorder (s 2), and riot (s 1). These offences all involve unlawful violence and can be committed in private as well as in public. Violence is essentially aggressive or hostile conduct towards property or persons, and includes acts capable of causing injury even if no injury or damage is caused, for example throwing a full can of beer towards a person, even if it falls short (see s 8 of the Public Order Act).

The legislation describing offences under ss 1–3 also uses the term a 'person of reasonable firmness' (sometimes referred to as the 'hypothetical bystander'). This is not defined under law but can be taken to mean an average person in terms of their reaction to violent incidents around them (ie not someone who is unduly frightened by the most minor of incidents, nor someone who is completely hardened to violent behaviour).

14.4.4.1 Affray

For an affray (s 3 of the Public Order Act 1986) the threat of violence needs to be capable of upsetting others. The primary objective of the law is to protect the general public around the affray and therefore the court will consider how a hypothetical person of reasonable firmness (see 14.4.4) who witnessed the incident would feel (*R v Sanchez*, The Times, 6 March 1996).

Therefore, there are in effect three parties involved in an affray:

1. the individual making the threats;
2. the person subject to the threats who must be present; and
3. at least one bystander.

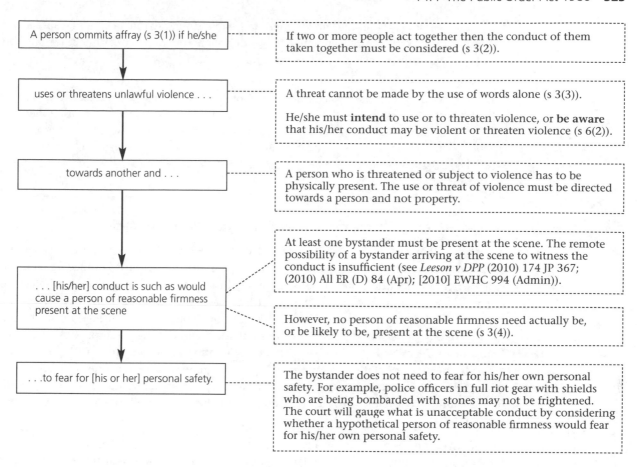

| A person commits affray (s 3(1)) if he/she | ┄┄ | If two or more people act together then the conduct of them taken together must be considered (s 3(2)). |

| uses or threatens unlawful violence . . . | ┄┄ | A threat cannot be made by the use of words alone (s 3(3)).

 He/she must **intend** to use or to threaten violence, or **be aware** that his/her conduct may be violent or threaten violence (s 6(2)). |

| towards another and . . . | ┄┄ | A person who is threatened or subject to violence has to be physically present. The use or threat of violence must be directed towards a person and not property. |

| . . . [his/her] conduct is such as would cause a person of reasonable firmness present at the scene | ┄┄ | At least one bystander must be present at the scene. The remote possibility of a bystander arriving at the scene to witness the conduct is insufficient (see *Leeson v DPP* (2010) 174 JP 367; (2010) All ER (D) 84 (Apr); [2010] EWHC 994 (Admin)). |
| | ┄┄ | However, no person of reasonable firmness need actually be, or be likely to be, present at the scene (s 3(4)). |

| . . .to fear for [his or her] personal safety. | ┄┄ | The bystander does not need to fear for his/her own personal safety. For example, police officers in full riot gear with shields who are being bombarded with stones may not be frightened. The court will gauge what is unacceptable conduct by considering whether a hypothetical person of reasonable firmness would fear for his/her own personal safety. |

In drawing a conclusion about the conduct of the suspects and the person of reasonable firmness, the court can consider evidence from witnesses at the incident (including police officers), the extent of any injuries, and recordings such as from CCTV or the media.

This offence is triable either way. The penalty if tried summarily is six months' imprisonment, and/or a fine, and on indictment three years' imprisonment.

14.4.4.2 Violent disorder and riot

For the offence of violent disorder (s 2 of the Public Order Act 1986), three or more persons must be present together and use (or threaten to use) unlawful violence. There must be an intention to use or threaten violence, or an awareness that the conduct may be violent or may threaten violence.

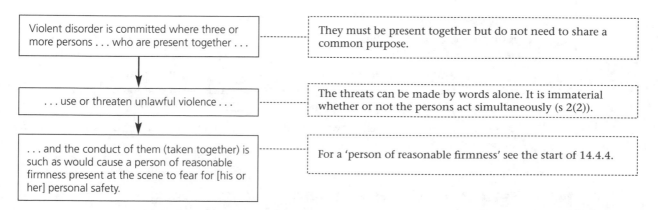

| Violent disorder is committed where three or more persons . . . who are present together . . . | ┄┄ | They must be present together but do not need to share a common purpose. |

| . . . use or threaten unlawful violence . . . | ┄┄ | The threats can be made by words alone. It is immaterial whether or not the persons act simultaneously (s 2(2)). |

| . . . and the conduct of them (taken together) is such as would cause a person of reasonable firmness present at the scene to fear for [his or her] personal safety. | ┄┄ | For a 'person of reasonable firmness' see the start of 14.4.4. |

If it is only possible to arrest and investigate one person out of such a group, then he/she can still be charged with this offence, but it must still be proved that at least two other people using or threatening violence were present, and they must be mentioned in the charge. However, there is no requirement for a common purpose to be held by those using or threatening behaviour (see *R v NW* [2010] EWCA Crim 404).

This offence is triable either way. The penalty if tried summarily is six months' imprisonment and/or a fine, on indictment five years' imprisonment.

Specific Incidents

The offence of riot (s 1(1) of the Public Order Act 1986) is similar to that of violent disorder, but twelve or more people must be present. Charges of riot are very rare. A riot offence is triable on indictment only and the penalty is ten years' imprisonment.

> **TASK 7** Imagine you are a trainee police officer on Independent Patrol. You respond to a call from a customer of a local nightclub alleging that a member of the door staff has pushed a female customer out of the door and that she fell over as a result of the push. There are no other witnesses to the incident and no CCTV footage. Disregarding the investigation of the assault, could an investigation into an affray be sustained? Refer to *R v Plavecz* [2002] Crim LR 837 for your answer.

14.4.5 Hatred on the grounds of race, religion, and sexual orientation

The original Public Order Act 1986 was amended to address 'stirring up' (the phrase used in the legislation) or inciting hatred against a group of people on the grounds of race, religion, or sexual orientation. Racial hatred means 'hatred against a group of persons defined by reference to colour, race, nationality (including citizenship) or ethnic or national origins' (s 17 of the Public Order Act 1986). Religious hatred (s 29A of the Public Order Act 1986) means hatred against a group of persons defined by reference to religious belief (for example Christianity or Islam) or to a lack of religious belief (for example atheists and humanists). Hatred on the grounds of sexual orientation means 'hatred against a group of persons defined by reference to sexual orientation whether towards persons of the same sex, the opposite sex or both' (s 29AB of the Public Order Act 1986). Further guidance on this is provided in a Ministry of Justice Circular (2010).

The offences can be committed in a public or a private place, although the effects of the actions must be felt in a public place. The different ways 'stirring up' can be caused are listed in various sections of the Act, as shown in the table. A separate offence (such as criminal damage) can also be aggravated on these grounds, see 14.10 for details.

Activity	Racial	Religious or sexual orientation
Using threatening words or behaviour, or displaying written material	s 18	s 29B
Publishing or distributing written material	s 19	s 29C
Public performance of a play	s 20	s 29D
Distributing, showing, or playing a recording	s 21	s 29E
Broadcasting threatening images or sounds	s 22	s 29F
Possessing racially inflammatory material	s 23	s 29G

In practice, the offences a police officer is most likely to encounter are those involving the use of threatening words or behaviour or the display of written material. Some possible defences are that:

- the acts were part of a programme service (eg on a television programme);
- the acts took place in a private place and were not noticeable to a person in a public place; or
- the suspect was not fully aware of the possible effects of his/her actions.

These offences are triable either way and the penalty is a fine or imprisonment (six months summarily and seven years on indictment).

14.5 Protection from Harassment

Harassment exists in a variety of forms, for example during episodes of stalking, pestering, persecution, and causing annoyance. A number of offences are available to help to deal with the often traumatic experience of being harassed. If complaints are not investigated and addressed in the first instance, relatively minor incidents may develop into much more serious offences such as kidnap, assault, and even murder.

When responding to complaints of harassment, the police priorities are to:

- investigate every report of harassment;
- preserve the safety and protect the lives of all victims;
- approach the harassment proactively;
- use a multi-agency approach when necessary;
- deal with offenders effectively, using any means within the criminal justice system.

Further information can be found in Practice Advice on Investigating Stalking and Harassment, available online.

14.5.1 The Protection from Harassment Act 1997

Sections 1 to 5 of the Protection from Harassment Act 1997 can be applied in a wide range of situations, including disputes between partners in a relationship, disputes between neighbours, stalking and campaigning. The offences described in the Protection from Harassment Act 1997 are harassment without violence (s 2), stalking (s 2A), breaching an injunction (s 3(6)), putting people in fear of violence (s 4), stalking involving fear of violence or serious alarm or distress (s 4A), and breaching a restraining order (s 5(5)).

The behaviour must be oppressive, unreasonable, and unacceptable, such as that displayed during an act of stalking (for which the offence was originally designed), and be of the sort that a reasonable person would find harassing (s 1(2) of the Protection from Harassment Act 1997). Harassing a person includes alarming the person or causing the person distress (s 7(2)). In legal terms, only a person can be harassed, so an employee can be harassed but not a company or a corporate body (s 7(5) of the Protection from Harassment Act 1997).

For these offences (ss 1–5) the perpetrator must know or ought to know that his/her actions are likely to cause the relevant effect on the victim. The judgement on whether a suspect 'ought to know' is made by considering whether a reasonable person in possession of the same information would know that the actions would have these effects. The final decision whether or not particular behaviour led to a person being alarmed, distressed, or fearful is taken by the court.

Clearly, the Protection from Harassment Act 1997 is a potentially valuable piece of legislation that offers a number of options for providing support to victims of harassment. However, a considerable amount of evidence is required to secure a successful prosecution under this Act, and proving a course of conduct in particular can be difficult. Advice from the CPS should be sought at an early stage.

14.5.1.1 A 'course of conduct'

Under s 1(1) of the Protection from Harassment Act 1997 a person must not pursue a 'course of conduct' which amounts to harassment of another or of two or more persons, which the perpetrator knows or ought to know amounts to harassment. The conduct cannot be just a one-off event; it must be a course of conduct; this means it must occur on more than one occasion. A course of conduct exists when conduct is directed towards:

- an individual on at least two occasions (s 7(3)(a)); or
- two or more people, and on at least one occasion in relation to each of those persons (s 7(3)(b)).

By precedent it has been decided that it is not just the number of incidents that is important, but whether those incidents are connected (*Lau v DPP* [2000] All ER (D) 224). However, it is less likely that the court will accept that behaviour constitutes a course of conduct if there is a long period of time between the events under consideration. The course of conduct does not have to comprise similar types of conduct: indeed, often it is not obvious that separate incidents are connected, so be aware of this during any investigation. However, a number of irregular and unconnected incidents in a turbulent and unpredictable relationship in which all parties concerned play a part, does not amount to a course of conduct (see *R v Curtis* [2010] EWCA Crim 123 and *R v David Roger Widdows* [2011] EWCA Crim 1500). A court may decide that there was a sequence of separate incidents instead (see *(1) Buckley (2) Smith v DPP* [2008] EWHC 136 (Admin)).

Conduct includes speech, letters, and emails, so evidence will need to be gathered from a wide range of sources such as diary entries, emails, letters, photographs, and interviews with witnesses. A person might make an initial bona fide enquiry for example, but this could become harassing if it is followed up in a manner that is persistent (see *DPP v Hardy* [2008] All ER (D) 315 (Oct)).

The conduct can also involve more than one person. An example of where a group of people could be guilty of harassment would involve three people, X, Y, and Z, who stand along the route which H takes to work in order to give her a threatening letter. They give her the letter, and later Z makes a threatening phone call to her. Provided that H feels alarmed or distressed, and X, Y, and Z knew (or ought to have known) that their actions were likely to be alarming or distressing, then X, Y, and Z would all be committing an offence (s 7(3A) of the Protection from Harassment Act 1997).

That a suspect did not make contact himself on a particular occasion was held to be irrelevant: in *James v CPS* [2009] EWHC 2925 (Admin), a client who was receiving local authority care made repeated calls to the office but received no reply. The eventual victim returned the calls on a number of occasions and was verbally abused. Also the offence of harassment does not have to include actually carrying out the conduct; mere planning or otherwise assisting with the course of conduct can amount to the offence.

14.5.1.2 Harassment without violence

It is an offence under s 2(1) of the Protection from Harassment Act 1997 for a person to pursue a course of conduct which involves harassment of one or more persons (s 1(1)(a) and 1(1A)(a)). Once initiated a person continues to pursue a course of conduct even when he/she does not personally harass the victim but aids, abets, counsels, or procures another who carries it out instead (s 7(3A)). The suspect(s) must know (or ought to know) that the behaviour amounts to harassment (s 1(1A)(b)).

The course of conduct can be to persuade a person to carry out a particular act or to omit to carry out a particular act. The offender might try to persuade a person to do something that he/she is **not** under any obligation to do (s 1(1A)(c)(ii)). For example, an animal rights extremist might pressurize a person working with animals in research to supply information on work practices. This offence can also be committed when there is an intention to persuade a person to omit to do something that he/she is entitled or required to do (s 1(1A)(c)(i)). For example, an animal rights extremist might pressurize a person to stop working for a company that uses animals for research.

The offence can also be committed when the course of conduct is intended to persuade *any person* to change his/her current routine (s 1(1A)(c)(i) and (ii)). This may form part of a wider campaign about political or social issues. It must be directed towards two or more person(s) in the first instance and occur on at least one occasion in relation to each of those persons.

As a possible defence to a s 2 offence, the suspect could try to show on the balance of probabilities that he/she acted either 'in reasonable circumstances' (this will be for the court to decide, probably using the 'reasonable person' test as in s 1(2)), or in the course of his/her work, for example as a police officer or court official. Full details of the defences are given in s 1(3) of the Protection from Harassment Act 1997.

This offence is triable summarily and the penalty is six months' imprisonment and/or a fine. It can also be racially or religiously aggravated (see 14.10.4).

14.5.1.3 Stalking

The offence of stalking is covered under s 2A of the Protection from Harassment Act 1997. The suspect's acts (or omissions, although no examples are provided) must be associated with stalking. The acts include: following the person, watching or spying on him/her, loitering in any place (whether public or private), contacting (or attempting to contact) him/her by any means, monitoring his/her use of electronic communications (eg the internet or email), interfering with his/her property, and publishing any statement or other material relating to or originating from him/her (or purporting to). For stalking that causes fear of violence or serious alarm or distress, see 14.5.1.6.

The suspect must pursue a course of conduct (as for s 2(1) offences) that involves harassment (s 2A (2)(a)), and it can be targeted at one or more persons (subsections (1)(a) and (1A)(a), respectively). The behaviour must be such that the suspect(s) must know (or ought to know) that it amounts to harassment (s 2A (2)(c)). A person who starts a course of conduct is regarded as continuing it even when the latter acts are carried out by someone else arranged by the suspect (s 7(3A)). This offence is triable summarily and the penalty is six months' imprisonment and/or a fine. It can be racially or religiously aggravated (see 14.10.4).

14.5.1.4 Isolated events causing distress

If distress is caused only on one occasion this does not constitute a course of conduct, and may instead be the subject of a claim in civil proceedings under s 3(1) of the Protection from Harassment Act 1997. The legislation has recently been amended so that a company (as well as a person) can apply for an injunction against individuals. The result of a civil claim can be damages (a court order to pay money) and/or an injunction (a court order to impose sanctions on the offender). If an injunction is breached, an offence is committed triable either way. The penalty is a fine or imprisonment (six months summarily and five years on indictment). There are no racially or religiously aggravated versions of the civil proceedings under s 3 of the Protection from Harassment Act 1997.

14.5.1.5 Putting people in fear of violence

This offence is described in s 4 of the Protection of Harassment Act 1997 and involves more than sending insulting or abusive letters or emails. The conduct must be targeted at an individual and be calculated to alarm or cause distress. It must also be oppressive and unreasonable (as identified in *Thomas v News Group Newspapers Ltd* [2001] EWCA Civ 1233, [2002] EMLR 78).

There are several key differences from the harassment (s 2) offence we described earlier. For s 4 offences:

- the victim must believe the violence will happen (as opposed to believing it might happen);
- the victim must fear the violence personally (and not on behalf of somebody else, such as a family member) (*Caurti v DPP* [2002] Crim LR 131); and
- the fear of violence cannot be conveyed through a third party.

In most other ways, the conditions for this offence are similar to those for the offence of harassment (s 2) described in 14.5.1.2; the court decides what is reasonable or unreasonable, it is an offence to pursue or assist the conduct, and there must be a course of conduct amounting to harassment within the meaning of s 1 (see 14.5.1, and *Haque v R* [2011] EWCA Crim 1871). Other relevant case law includes *R v Curtis (James Daniel)* [2010] EWCA Crim 123, [2010] 1 WLR 2770 and *R v Widdows (David Roger)* [2011] EWCA Crim 1500, (2011) 175 JP 345.

The defences to this offence are similar to those for s 2 but with one major addition: that the suspect's course of conduct was pursued reasonably for his/her own protection or for protection of another or of property (belonging to him/her or another). This offence can be racially or religiously aggravated (see 14.10.4) and is triable either way. The penalty is a fine or imprisonment (six months summarily, and a maximum of ten years on indictment).

14.5.1.6 Stalking involving fear of violence or serious alarm or distress

These offences are covered under s 4A(1) of the Protection from Harassment Act 1997. Under s 4A(1)(a) the suspect's course of conduct must amount to stalking (see 14.5.1.3) and also cause the victim:

- to fear on at least two occasions that violence will be used against him/her (s 4A(1)(b)(i)); or
- serious alarm or distress which has a substantial adverse effect on his/her usual day-to-day activities (s 4A(1)(b)(ii)).

For these offences the behaviour must be such that the suspect must know (or ought to know) that his/her acts will have these effects on the victim (ss 4A(2) and 4A(3)). In *R v Qosja (Robert)* [2016] EWCA Crim 1543, it was held that to prove fear of violence, there must be evidence from the victim that he/she feared there would be violence directed at him/her (not just a possibility of violence).

The defences to this offence are given in s 4A(4), and are similar to the defences for s 4. The offence is triable either way and the penalty is a fine or imprisonment (12 months summarily, and ten years maximum on indictment). A suspect found not guilty of this offence could instead be found guilty of an offence under ss 2 or 2A (s 4A(7)). The s 4A offence can be racially or religiously aggravated (see 14.10.4).

14.5.1.7 Restraining orders

A court can make a restraining order under s 5 of the Protection from Harassment Act 1997 against a person who has been convicted (s 5(1)) or acquitted (s 5A) of any offence, to protect a person from harassment. A restraining order will place restrictions on a person's future behaviour. It may last indefinitely or for a period stated by the court, and it can be varied or discharged on application. The order will be recorded on the PNC, the police local intelligence database, and the PND. Breaching a restraining order is an offence (s 5(5)) and the penalty is a fine or imprisonment (six months summarily, and five years on indictment).

TASK 8 Imagine you are a police officer. You are requested to attend an address in your area where a complaint of harassment has been made. Write brief answers to the following questions:

1. What evidence would you need to collect to prove an offence under either s 2 or s 4 of the Protection from Harassment Act 1997?
2. What other methods could be used to stop the conduct?
3. How could future evidence be recorded?
4. What reason(s) would make an arrest necessary in these circumstances?

14.5.2 Preventing harassment and the Criminal Justice and Police Act 2001

Harassing or intimidating behaviour by individuals towards a person in his/her home is an offence under the Criminal Justice and Police Act 2001 This legislation should not be seen as a way of stopping people from carrying out their lawful rights to protest peacefully or express strong opinions. Nor is it intended to prevent a fan from standing outside the home of his/her favourite television celebrity or to stop media commentators from trying to record first-hand comments from people in the news. Rather, this legislation aims to provide a balance between the right to carry out such activities and the right of other individuals in their own homes to be protected from harassment, alarm, or distress.

The legislation referred to here provides more than one tool to deal with this type of situation (see 3.6 on discretion). The direction to leave is useful, but of course it does not prevent the same protesters from returning and continuing with the same type of behaviour. Charging a person with an offence (causing harassment, distress, or alarm), however, is a more serious matter. Therefore you will need to consider carefully which of the powers to use and this will depend on factors such as the number of people in the vicinity of the person's home, their behaviour and purpose, and the impact of their presence on the resident(s) and people in the surrounding area.

14.5.2.1 Causing harassment of a resident

Behaviour that may cause harassment, alarm, or distress (ss 42 and 42A of the Criminal Justice and Police Act 2001) and would include persistent, sustained, and aggressive hammering on a door; climbing onto the roof of a dwelling, and aggressive use of banners or placards to block or impede access.

As well as causing distress to a resident inside his/her dwelling, other categories of people can also be affected such as other people present with the resident or people living nearby. Courts will use the 'reasonable person' test to decide whether a person would find the relevant activities significantly disturbing. A police officer does not have to be present when the behaviour occurs; for example, recordings from a resident's CCTV could be used as evidence of the protestors' activities and the distress caused. This offence is triable summarily and the penalty is six months' imprisonment and/or a fine.

14.5.2.2 Giving directions to prevent harassment, alarm, or distress

Under s 42(1) of the Criminal Justice and Police 2001 Act a police officer has the power to give 'directions' to a person (or a group) in order to prevent him/her/them from causing harassment, alarm, or distress to residents (or other people in the vicinity). The wording of a direction (s 42(2)) might be 'You have caused harassment and distress to people living in this area. I therefore require you to leave immediately'.

The direction can be given orally or in writing, and will instruct the person(s) to leave the vicinity and for a specified period (not exceeding three months) and conditions may be attached. An officer of any rank can give the direction (s 42(6)) but it will usually be given by the most senior officer present. An offence is committed under s 7A if a person who has received a direction to leave then fails to leave, or leaves but then returns within the specified time period to try to persuade a resident to follow a particular course of action. This offence is triable summarily and the penalty is six months' imprisonment and/or a fine.

14.5.3 Sending nuisance communications

If the nuisance behaviour involves a form of communication such as telephone calls or letters, then alternative offences can be considered. This is particularly useful if a course of conduct is not evident.

14.5.3.1 Sending items to cause distress or anxiety

Under s 1 of the Malicious Communications Act 1988 it is an offence for a person to send, for the purpose of causing distress or anxiety, any item (including electronic communications) which contains:

- indecent or grossly offensive content (s 1(1)(a)(i));
- a threat (s 1(1)(a)(ii)) (unless it was made reasonably to reinforce a demand (s 2));
- information which is false and known or believed to be false (s 1(1)(a)(iii)); or
- any article which is entirely or partly, indecent or grossly offensive (s 1(1)(b)).

This offence includes letters, parcels, and other articles sent by post. It also includes electronic communication such as emails, text messages, and oral or other communication transmitted by means of a telecommunication system, for example landline or mobile telephone (s 2A(a) and (b)). Sending includes delivering by hand, transmitting, and causing to be sent (s 3) by the sender, but does not include the actions of the service provider. The offence is triable summarily and the penalty is six months' imprisonment and/or a fine.

14.5.3.2 Improper use of public electronic communications network

It is an offence under s 127 of the Communications Act 2003 to send (or cause to be sent) a message by means of a public electronic communications network (eg mobile and landline telephones) which is grossly offensive, indecent, obscene, or menacing (s 127(1)), or false, or to persistently use the network for the purpose of causing annoyance, inconvenience, or needless anxiety to another (s 127(2)). These offences are triable summarily and the penalty is six months' imprisonment and/or a fine. A PND can be used for a s 127(2) offence (see 10.13.2.1).

> **TASK 9** Imagine you are a trainee police officer on Supervised Patrol and you have been asked to attend the address of a person who reports being harassed by people in the street outside his house. Suggest some factors you would need to consider in order to decide whether to direct anybody away from the house and whether to investigate for an offence.

14.6 Intimidation of Witnesses, Jurors, and Others

Witnesses often feel vulnerable and concerned about the consequences of their actions, and some become victims of intimidation by the suspect(s) in the case. For example, suspects or their associates might attempt to intimidate witnesses and victims to dissuade them from giving evidence in court. The 'No witness, No justice' project is a joint initiative between the CPS, NPCC, the Home Office, and the Cabinet Office's Office of Public Service Reform. It highlights the importance of providing support to people who are crucial in the successful prosecution of offenders, and that the police have a duty of care towards them. The Home Office report (1998) 'Speaking Up for Justice' argues that in this context intimidation is not simply a matter of explicit threats of physical harm to a witness or victim but also includes other less tangible forms: for example, threats made to third parties such as a wife, son, or daughter; financial threats (such as withdrawing support for a dependant). It is important therefore that police officers involved assess the needs of intimidated witnesses and be aware of the various supporting agencies including: Victim Support, the Witness Service, Anti-Social Behaviour Units, Housing Associations, Witness Care Units, Crown Prosecution Service, Prison Service, and other voluntary organizations (eg specific support such as sexual violence or domestic violence).

In *Osman v United Kingdom* (1998) 29 EHRR 245, it was decided that national authorities (such as the police) have an obligation to take preventative measures to protect an individual whose life is at risk through the criminal acts of others. In cases involving death threats, there must be a real and immediate risk to the life of the identified individual(s). Reasonable steps must be taken to assess those threats (known as the Osman threshold) and protect the individuals concerned. However, if the assessment does not suggest that there is a real and immediate risk, the police and other authorities cannot be held negligent if subsequent harm falls upon the victim (*Chief Constable of Hertfordshire v Van Colle (Administrator of the estate of GC, deceased) & Anor: Smith v Chief Constable of Sussex* [2008] UKHL 50).

The offences of intimidation are triable either way and the penalty is a fine or imprisonment (six months summarily, and five years on indictment).

14.6.1 Intimidation relating to civil proceedings

Intimidation relating to civil proceedings is covered under the Criminal Justice and Police Act 2001. For current civil proceedings (s 39(1)) the victim of the intimidation can be a witness in any civil proceedings in the Court of Appeal, the High Court, the Crown Court, a county court, or a magistrates' court. The suspect must have carried out an act which causes intimidation and is intended to either obstruct, pervert, or otherwise interfere with the course of justice.

For civil proceedings in the past (s 40(1)) the person suspected of intimidation must know (or believe) that his/her victim had been a witness in the relevant proceedings, and the intimidation must take place within the period from the start of the proceedings until 12 months after the end of the proceedings.

14.6.2 Intimidation relating to criminal proceedings

This is covered under the Criminal Justice and Police Act 2001. The person suspected of intimidation must have carried out an act (or acts) which either intentionally caused harm to (or threatened to harm) another person. The threatened harm or intimidatory act can be financial or physical, and can be directed against either the person or his/her property (s 51(4)). The person making the threat commits an offence even if a third party is used to convey that threat (s 51(3)). During the relevant periods there is a presumption of an intention to intimidate unless the suspect can prove otherwise (s 51(7) and (8)).

For current criminal proceedings (s 51(1)) the victim of the intimidation must be either assisting in the investigation, a witness or potential witness, or a juror (or potential juror) in proceedings for the offence. The suspect must have carried out an act which causes intimidation and is intended to either obstruct, pervert, or otherwise interfere with the course of justice. The act must occur between the start of the investigation and the end of the proceedings, for example at the conclusion of a court hearing.

For criminal proceedings in the past (s 51(2)), the suspected intimidator must know (or believe) whilst carrying out the acts that his/her victim has assisted in an investigation into an offence (eg as a witness), acted as a juror, or concurred in the relevant verdict. In addition, the intimidatory acts must take place within a certain time frame. Note that a person can of course both assist with an investigation and be a witness in court, in which case the longer time frame applies.

Role of the intimidated victim in criminal proceedings	Time period in which the intimidation occurs	
	Starts	Ends
A person who assisted with an investigation	The start of any assistance in the investigation (or the start date as believed by the suspect)	Twelve months after any assistance was given
A witness or juror during the court hearing	The start of the court proceedings	Twelve months after the end of the trial or appeal

14.7 Sporting Events Offences

Sports-related offences do not feature within the compulsory LPG modules of the IPLDP, but we cover them here since the policing of football matches often features as part of the training of trainee police officers whilst on Supervised or Independent Patrol. Hence, although the policing of football matches is not a common occurrence for every police officer in England and Wales, trainee officers might be involved in it, particularly in forces covering large towns and cities. Many football clubs will take steps to inform their supporters of the main points of the law and the regulations governing behaviour, for example see Stoke City's 'Customer Charter' online.

The offences described in this section are covered under the Sporting Events (Control of Alcohol etc) Act 1985 and the Football (Offences) Act 1991. Currently, football is the only sport which it is considered necessary to control. Statistics on football-related arrests and banning orders can be found on the gov.uk website. The CPS website provides useful guidance on the policy for prosecutions.

14.7.1 The Sporting Events (Control of Alcohol etc) Act 1985

The Sporting Events (Control of Alcohol etc) Act 1985 only applies to sports grounds, certain sporting events, and designated periods relating to those sporting events. It applies to football matches only if both the particular sports ground and match have been 'designated' by the Secretary of State (see Sch 1, Art 2(1) of Statutory Instrument 2005 No 3204, available online). Note that the list of designations may vary from year to year to reflect changes in the organization of football leagues.

The following events are examples of matches which would be likely to be designated for the purposes of the Sporting Events (Control of Alcohol etc) Act 1985, as they meet both the ground and the match (teams) criteria:

- A football match played between Bristol City and Scunthorpe United at Bristol City's ground, Ashton Gate. This is because Ashton Gate is a designated sports ground and both teams are currently members of the Football League.
- A match played between Dover Athletic and Manchester United at Dover, because Crabble football ground is a designated sports ground and Manchester United is currently a member of the Football Association Premier League.

The legislation does not apply to any sporting event in which players are not paid, nor if spectators are admitted free of charge, such as amateur weekend matches on school sports fields or recreation grounds.

Offences under the Sporting Events (Control of Alcohol etc) Act 1985 can only be considered if they occur during the period commencing two hours before the start of a football match and ending one hour after the end of the match. For example, if a football match is scheduled to start at 7.45 pm and the match ends at approximately 9.30 pm, the period of this match would be from 5.45 pm to 10.30 pm. (We ignore here the added complexity of 'added time' for stoppages, or extra time to decide a match, or the match starting late.)

14.7.1.1 Transport of passengers to sports events

Supporters will often travel to sports event by train, coach, or minibus. Drivers, owners, and passengers of some types of vehicle which are used for the principal purpose of carrying passengers for the whole or part of a journey to or from a designated sporting event are subject to legislation under s 1 of the Sporting Events (Control of Alcohol etc) Act 1985.

Public service vehicles covered by this legislation include buses and coaches, passenger trains, and minibuses. It is an offence under s 1(2) to knowingly cause or permit intoxicating liquor to be carried on such a vehicle. This applies to the operator of the public service vehicle and to the person who has hired it. (It also applies to a 'servant or agent' of the operator or hirer.) It is also an offence for such a person to have intoxicating liquor in his/her possession (s 1(3)) or to be drunk (s 1(4)) while on a vehicle to which this section applies. This offence is triable summarily only and the penalty is a fine for s 1(2) or (4) offences, and three months' imprisonment and/or a fine for an offence under s 1(3).

Minibuses and larger motor vehicles (that are not public service) vehicles are covered by s 1A of the Sporting Events (Control of Alcohol etc) Act 1985. They must be adapted to carry more

Specific Incidents

than eight passengers and be in use for the principal purpose of carrying two or more passengers. It is an offence to knowingly cause or permit intoxicating liquor to be carried (s 1A(2)) on such a vehicle. This offence can be committed by the driver, the vehicle's keeper (or his/her servant or agent), and by anyone who has hired or borrowed the vehicle from its keeper (or his/her servant or agent), or the servant or agent of the person to whom the vehicle is made available.

It is also an offence for such a person to have intoxicating liquor in his/her possession (s 1A(3)) or to be drunk (s 1A(4)) on a vehicle to which s 1A applies. This offence is triable summarily only and the penalty is a fine for s 1A(2) or (4) offences, and three months' imprisonment and/or a fine for a s 1A(3) offence.

14.7.1.2 Alcohol and drinks containers at a designated sporting event

Section 2(1) of the Sporting Events (Control of Alcohol etc) Act 1985 is often imposed for football matches where there is a potential for disorder. Under this legislation it is an offence to possess alcohol or drinks containers likely to contain alcohol. The containers covered by this legislation are defined in s 2(3) as 'any article or other portable container for holding any drink, which when empty is normally discarded or returned to (or left to be recovered by) the supplier and which is capable of causing injury to a person struck by it'. This obviously includes bottles and cans, including when crushed or broken, and parts of such containers. (Containers for holding any medicinal product (within the meaning of the Medicines Act 1968) are not included.)

Section 2(1) applies at any time during the period of a designated sporting event when the person is either in any area of the sports ground from which the event may be directly viewed, or entering (or trying to enter) the sports ground. The offence is triable summarily and the penalty is three months' imprisonment and/or a fine.

It is also an offence for a person to be drunk inside the ground, or to be drunk while entering or trying to enter a ground at any time during the period of a designated sporting event at that ground (s 2(2)). This offence is triable summarily and the penalty is a fine.

14.7.1.3 Fireworks, flares, and similar articles during a designated sporting event

Section 2A of the Sporting Events (Control of Alcohol etc) Act 1985 covers the possession of fireworks and similar objects at designated sporting events. The prohibited objects (s 2A(3) and (4)) include fireworks, rockets, distress flares, fog signals, pellets and fumigator capsules (for testing pipes), and any other item which is for 'the emission of a flare for purposes of illuminating or signalling, or the emission of smoke or a visible gas'. It does not include matches, cigarette lighters, or heaters.

The times and places to which this legislation applies are the same as for the possession of alcohol at a sports ground, as is the penalty (see 14.7.1.2).

14.7.1.4 Powers of entry and search for sports grounds

Section 7 of the Sporting Events (Control of Alcohol etc) Act 1985 allows a police officer to enter and search any part of the ground if he/she has reasonable grounds to suspect that an offence under the same Act is being committed (or is about to be committed), or to enforce the provisions of the Act. This relates to the possession of alcohol, fireworks, and similar articles and applies during the period of a designated sporting event at any designated sports ground (see 14.7.1). There is a power to search a person (s 7(2)) or a vehicle (s 7(3)) if there are reasonable grounds to suspect that an offence under this Act has been committed (or is about to be committed). See 9.4.1 for details on search procedures.

14.7.2 The Football (Offences) Act 1991

The Football (Offences) Act 1991 deals with problem behaviour at football matches. It covers throwing objects, racist chanting, and pitch invasions. The definition of a designated match is very similar to the definition for the Sporting Events (Control of Alcohol etc) Act 1985, as is the time period. The Football (Offences) Act 1991 also applies if the match does not take place, using the advertised starting time as a point of reference.

Throwing objects at a designated football match is an offence under s 2 of the Football (Offences) Act 1991. The objects must be thrown without lawful authority or excuse (for the suspect to prove) at or towards the playing area, or any adjacent area to which spectators are not generally admitted, or any area in which spectators or other persons are or may be present. This offence is triable summarily and the penalty is a fine.

Indecent or racist chanting at a designated football match is an offence under s 3(1) of the Football (Offences) Act 1991 if the chanting is of an 'indecent or racialist nature'. Chanting means the repeated uttering of any words or sounds, by one or more people (s 3(2)) and 'racialist nature' means it is 'threatening, abusive or insulting to a person by reason of [his/her] colour, race, nationality (including citizenship) or ethnic or national origins'. The offence is triable summarily and the penalty is a fine.

Spectators going onto the playing area (a 'pitch invasion') at a designated football match commit an offence under s 4 of the Football (Offences) Act 1991. This includes 'any area adjacent to the playing area to which spectators are not generally admitted, without lawful authority or lawful excuse (which shall be for [the suspect] to prove)'. This offence is triable summarily and the penalty is a fine.

TASK 10 As a trainee officer on Supervised Patrol, you are deployed to a football match. The club concerned plays within the Football Conference National Division (currently the Blue Square Premier), so you can therefore assume that both the ground and the matches played in the ground are designated under both the Sporting Events (Control of Alcohol etc) Act 1985 and the Football (Offences) Act 1991. Consider each of the following offences and match them against the situations given in the table by putting the appropriate letter(s) in the right-hand column. The first answer has been given to you. You may need to consult the original legislation for the detail.

(a) s 2(1) of the Sporting Events (Control of Alcohol etc) Act 1985;
(b) s 2(2) of the Sporting Events (Control of Alcohol etc) Act 1985;
(c) s 2 of the Football (Offences) Act 1991;
(d) s 3 of the Football (Offences) Act 1991;
(e) s 4 of the Football (Offences) Act 1991;
(f) s 1(2) of the Sporting Events (Control of Alcohol etc) Act 1985;
(g) s 1(3) of the Sporting Events (Control of Alcohol etc) Act 1985;
(h) s 1(4) of the Sporting Events (Control of Alcohol etc) Act 1985; and
(i) s 2A of the Sporting Events (Control of Alcohol etc) Act 1985.

1.	You see a fan fumbling for money to pay for a cup of tea from the refreshment stand. When you approach, he is hardly able to stand and his breath smells of intoxicating liquor, his eyes are glazed, and his speech is slurred.	b
2.	You are on duty at the edge of the pitch near the entrance to the players' tunnel as the teams enter after half-time. You see a dark metal object hit the ground near your feet and notice one of the players stop and grab his head in pain. You look up and see a youth in the crowd with his right hand raised as if he has just thrown an object.	
3.	One of the mid-field players is black. Every time he receives the ball you hear opposition supporters make 'monkey' sounds and shout racist abuse.	
4.	You are on duty outside the ground and you see a fan waiting to get a ticket. He has a four-pack of lager cans under his arm.	
5.	Before the start of a match you see a supporter near the front of ticket queue. He finishes drinking from a can, drops it and crushes it with his foot. He then looks around before picking up the crushed tin, and putting it in his coat pocket.	
6.	One of your responsibilities is to monitor the away supporters as they arrive by coaches and minibuses hired for the occasion. You notice a person drinking from a bottle of cider on one of the minibuses. As the vehicle stops, the driver opens the door and you see one of the other passengers stand up and offer the driver a can of lager. Another passenger then falls down the steps of the minibus, apparently drunk.	
7.	At the end of a match when the final whistle is blown the two teams start to leave the pitch. A group of fans go onto the pitch to follow the players and congratulate them.	
8.	At the end of a match in early November, you see a youth reach into his pocket as the crowd is leaving the ground. As he rummages in his pocket, a firework falls out.	

14.8 Criminal Trespass and Outdoor Gatherings

Travelling people with no fixed abode sometimes find a temporary place to live on privately owned land. This may cause anxiety and distress for the owners of the land or for local residents. However, if the intention of the trespassers is not to reside, gather, or disrupt lawful activity or if only one trespasser is involved, then the situation might be a civil matter (see 14.8.5). If it is clear that a trespasser clearly intends to disrupt lawful activity this is likely to amount to a criminal offence (see 14.8.2). Separate legislation is available to deal with difficulties arising from large outdoor music and dancing events (see 14.8.3).

14.8.1 Criminal trespass or nuisance on land

This offence is described under s 61(1) of the Criminal Justice and Public Order Act 1994. At least two suspects must be planning to live on the land for a period of time, and they must have been asked to leave by the owner or legal occupier. In addition, the suspects must have either:

- caused damage to the land or to property on the land, or used threatening, abusive, or insulting words or behaviour towards the occupier, a member of his/her family, or an employee or agent of his/hers; or
- have six or more vehicles with them on the land (a vehicle includes caravans and unroadworthy vehicles).

A senior police officer present at the scene must reasonably believe that these conditions have been fulfilled. He/she may then direct those persons to leave the land, and to remove any of their vehicles and other property from the land. If the trespassers will not leave, s 62 of the Criminal Justice and Public Order Act 1994 provides a power to seize and remove their vehicles. This also applies if a person fails to remove any vehicle on the land, or leaves and returns within three months (s 62(1)). It is an offence (s 61(4)) for a person to fail to leave as soon as is reasonably practicable, or to leave and then re-enter within three months. These offences are triable summarily and the penalty is three months' imprisonment and/or a fine.

14.8.2 Aggravated trespass on land

Sections 68 and 69 of the Criminal Justice and Public Order Act 1994 cover trespassers who disrupt or obstruct any lawful activity taking place on land or adjoining land (hence the 'aggravated' nature of the trespass). This would include protesters at a military base. Land would include agricultural buildings, footpaths, bridleways, and cycle tracks that cross the land. The summary offence of aggravated trespass is provided under s 68(1). The penalty is three months' imprisonment and/or a fine.

A senior police officer at the scene of an aggravated trespass has the power to direct a person to leave the land (s 69 of the Criminal Justice and Public Order Act 1994). He/she must reasonably believe that:

- the person is committing (or has committed or intends to commit) aggravated trespass; or
- more than one person is trespassing, and they intend to intimidate other people there who have a right to be there, and deter or obstruct them from lawful activity.

Under s 69(3), it is an offence for a person who has been directed to leave if he/she fails to leave the land as soon as practicable, or having left, re-enters as a trespasser within three months (beginning with the day on which the direction was given). It is a defence if the accused can show that he/she was not trespassing, or that he/she had a reasonable excuse for failing to leave as soon as practicable or for re-entering as a trespasser. The offence is triable summarily and the penalty is three months' imprisonment (maximum) and/or a fine.

14.8.3 Open-air gatherings with music at night

Although complaints about excessive noise from gatherings in residential properties are often dealt with by local authority personnel, complaints about larger gatherings in the open air may sometimes require police action. Sections 63, 64, and 65 of the Criminal Justice and Public Order Act 1994 can be used to deal with such situations. The type of gathering (also referred to as an 'open-air rave') is defined in s 63; more than 20 people must be present out of doors at night with amplified music with repetitive beats. The music must be loud or go on for a long time, and be 'likely to cause serious distress to local residents'.

The Act includes the power for police officers to give directions to people present at such gatherings (and to people travelling to the locality). There are some predictable exemptions; the following categories of people cannot be given directions under ss 63–65:

- the occupier of the land ('the person entitled to possession of the land by virtue of an estate or interest held by him [or her]' (s 61(9)) or any member of the occupier's family;
- any employee or agent of the occupier; and
- any person whose home is situated on the land.

14.8.3.1 Dispersal powers for open-air gatherings with music at night

A power is available to disperse people (ten or more) who are at a gathering with music at night, or waiting together at the location for such an event to start (s 63(2)). It also applies for two or more people who are making preparations for such an event.

The direction must be made by an officer of at least superintendent rank, and if not communicated by him/her may be communicated by any constable at the scene (s 63(3)). A person will be regarded as having received the direction if reasonable steps have been taken to bring it to his/her attention (s 63(4)). It is an offence (s 63(6)) if a person (knowing that a relevant direction has been given) then fails to leave the land as soon as reasonably practicable, or leaves and re-enters within seven days. If the suspect can provide a reasonable excuse, this may be a defence (s 63(7)). A person who has been directed to leave a gathering who then moves on to (or prepares for) another similar gathering within 24 hours commits an offence under s 63(7A). The offences are triable summarily and the penalty is three months' imprisonment and/or a fine.

Section 65 of the Criminal Justice and Public Order Act 1994 provides powers to direct persons to desist from proceeding towards a gathering to which s 63 applies. The police officer must be in uniform and within five miles of the gathering. It is a summary offence (s 65(1)) for a person not to comply with such a direction and the penalty is a fine.

14.8.3.2 Powers of entry and seizure for open-air gatherings with music at night

A power of entry to the police when dealing with night-time open-air musical events is provided under s 64 of the Criminal Justice and Public Order Act 1994; police officers may need to be deployed to determine whether the gathering is covered under s 63 (ie is a 'rave', see the start of 14.8.3). If a police officer of at least the rank of superintendent reasonably believes that the relevant circumstances exist then he/she may authorize any constable to enter the land (s 64(1)). A warrant is not required (s 64(3)). If the s 63 conditions are met, then s 63 directions can be given.

Vehicles and sound equipment belonging to a person (or appearing to) may be seized if he/she has received a s 63 direction and has (without reasonable excuse) failed to remove them, or removed them but then returned within seven days and entered with them as a trespasser.

14.8.4 Squatting in a residential building

It is an offence for a trespasser in a 'residential building' to live or intend to live there for any period of time (s 144(1)(c) of the Legal Aid, Sentencing and Punishment of Offenders Act 2012). The person must have entered as a trespasser, and the means of entry be such that he/she must (or should) know that it was trespass (s 144(1)). The offence does not apply if the person stays on after the end of a lease or licence (s 144(2)). A building includes any temporary or moveable structure or part of a structure, and is 'residential' if it was designed or adapted as a place to live before the time of entry (s 144(3)). A police officer in uniform has the power (s 17 PACE) to enter and search premises to arrest a person for this offence (see 10.8.1.2). It is triable summarily and the penalty is six months' imprisonment and/or a fine.

14.8.5 Police involvement in civil trespass

Police officers will frequently be called to incidents where a person unlawfully enters land or premises owned by another. This is civil trespass, and is not a criminal offence. The trespasser may become criminally liable if, for example, the acts and/or the intent amount to criminal trespass (see 14.8.1), burglary (see 16.4), or living or intending to live in a residential building for any period of time (see 14.8.4).

Specific Incidents

Accordingly, in civil trespass incidents the actions of police officers are limited to identifying whether any criminal offences have been committed, remaining to prevent any taking place, and offering advice about civil remedies to both owners and trespassers. The owner should request the trespassers to leave, but if they do not and the owner decides to try and remove the trespassers by force (likely to be difficult), the police should remain in order to prevent a breach of the peace (see 14.3) or to identify any criminal offences, for example unlawful personal violence (see 15.1).

Consequently, at an incident where civil trespass is alleged, a police officer should:

1. Locate the owner of the land/premises and speak with him/her to try and establish the circumstances surrounding the complaint, the identity of the trespassers and their location, and if any criminal acts have taken place. If no criminal offences have been committed the limitation of police involvement should be emphasized.
2. Locate the alleged trespassers and seek to establish their identity (should they wish) and any claim to lawful entry they might have (in order to help the owner and the trespassers come to a common understanding). The officer should also explain that if they commit a criminal offence or a breach of the peace, they may be liable to arrest and prosecution, and that the owner can obtain an order from a civil court to eject them.
3. Attempt to bring about an amicable agreement between the two parties through dialogue, if no criminal offences have been committed.
4. Remain at the incident if it seems that criminal offences may be committed.
5. Make a full PNB entry (see 10.2) of the events and what was said.

14.9 Fireworks Offences

Under the law, a firework is any device which burns and/or explodes to produce a visual and/or audible effect, and is intended for use as a form of entertainment. Some fireworks offences relate to misuse that could cause danger or annoyance, some relate to the time of year, and some relate to the age of the person buying fireworks. Of particular concern in recent years has been the use of powerful fireworks such as 'aerial shells, aerial maroons, shells-in-mortar and maroons-in-mortar', which can register sound levels above 120 dB—about the noise level of a jet aircraft 100 metres away, and could also be used to damage or even destroy large objects such as cars. The sale of these products to the public in the UK is banned, but people can purchase them abroad and bring them back to the UK.

Relevant legislation includes the Explosives Act 1875, the Fireworks Act 2003, the Fireworks Regulations 2004, and the Fireworks (Safety) Regulations 1997. It is an offence for any person:

- to throw, cast, or fire any firework in or into any highway, street, thoroughfare, or public place (s 80 of the Explosives Act 1875);
- to wantonly (deliberately) throw or set fire to a firework in the street to the obstruction, annoyance, or danger of residents or passengers (s 28 of the Town Police Clauses Act 1847).

It is also an offence for anyone under the age of 18 years to possess fireworks in a public place, except for indoor fireworks (reg 4 of the Fireworks Regulations 2004). Indoor fireworks include caps, sparklers, and 'throwdowns'. (A throwdown is a paper or foil package that contains substances which explode when thrown onto the ground.)

These offences are triable summarily. Alternatively a PND can be used (see 10.13.2), apart from an offence under s 28 of the Town Police Clauses Act 1847.

14.9.1 Selling fireworks

A special licence is required for a trader to sell fireworks to the public throughout the year. Traders without a special licence can only sell fireworks to members of the public during the following periods:

- first day of Chinese New Year and three days prior to this;
- Diwali and three days prior to this;
- between 15 October and 10 November; and
- between 26 and 31 December.

Under s 12(1) of the Consumer Protection Act 1987 it is an offence to supply fireworks (including sparklers but excluding all other indoor fireworks) to persons under the age of 18 years. This offence is triable summarily, and the penalty is a fine.

14.9.2 Firework curfews

A 'firework curfew' is a period of time where the general use of fireworks is not permitted. Under reg 7(1) of the Fireworks Regulations 2004 it is an offence for a person to use an 'adult firework' (essentially all fireworks other than indoor fireworks) between 2300 and 0700 hrs the next day except for during the periods shown in the table. Other exemptions apply for local authority employees using a firework during a local authority display or national commemorative event.

Curfew exemption event or date	Exemption period ends
First day of the Chinese New Year	0100 hrs the following day
5 November	Midnight
Diwali	0100 hrs the following day
31 December	0100 hrs the following day

This offence is triable summarily and the penalty is six months' imprisonment and/or a fine, or a PND can be used (see 10.13.2 on PNDs).

14.9.3 Restrictions on large fireworks for public displays

Public displays frequently use large fireworks, known as category 4 fireworks. They may only be used by an appropriately qualified person (reg 5 of the Fireworks Regulations 2004). Members of the general public are prohibited from possessing such fireworks, except for any person who is employed by a local authority, or who is involved in public or commercial firework displays. A breach of reg 4 or 5 is a criminal offence under s 11 of the Fireworks Act 2003. The offence is triable summarily, and the penalty is a fine.

14.10 Hate Crime

Hate crime is defined on the CPS website as:

> [a]ny criminal offence which is perceived by the victim or any other person, to be motivated by hostility or prejudice based on a person's race or perceived race; religion or perceived religion; sexual orientation or perceived sexual orientation; disability or perceived disability and any crime motivated by hostility or prejudice against a person who is transgender or perceived to be transgender.

In 2015/16, 62,518 hate crimes were recorded by the police, an increase of 19 per cent compared with 2014/15. The hate crimes were categorized as follows, with some falling into more than one category (Home Office, 2016c):

- race hate crime (79%);
- sexual orientation hate crime (12%);
- religion-based hate crime (7%);
- disability hate crime (6%);
- transgender hate crime (1%)

The Home Office has published *Action Against Hate: The UK government's plan for tackling hate crime* (available online). This sets out the UK government's programme of actions to tackle hate crime in England and Wales. A key consideration for the police when identifying a potential hate crime is the victim's perception. In most forces the policy is to record a crime as a 'hate crime' if the victim perceives it as such. Often, victims expect the attacks to continue or are terrified of future victimization. An incident involving hate crimes can spread trepidation through a community, and may also develop into a critical incident (see 11.5).

There are several specific Acts that refer to crime offences, including the Public Order Act 1986 (see 14.4.5), the Football Offences Act 1991 (see 14.7.2), and the Crime and Disorder Act 1998 (see 14.10.1).

Specific Incidents

In all cases of hate crime, the police are expected to identify and record crimes as such, to thoroughly investigate hate crimes, and to offer an appropriate level of support to victims. Trainee officers are unlikely to be involved beyond the early stages of an investigation (see 24.5). In addition to the usual considerations (eg forensic awareness) extra sensitivity around the needs of victims from minority communities is often needed. Further guidance can be found in *Hate Crime Operational Guidance*, available online. Probationer constables are likely to cover these matters in the initial learning and development phase of their training, and this often involves a contribution from local minority communities or groups.

Racially or religiously motivated assaults, criminal damage, public order offences and harassment can be charged under the Crime and Disorder Act 1998 as the 'aggravated' version of the basic offence (see 14.10.1). These carry a heavier sentence on conviction. For a basic offence triable on indictment, a person who is found 'not guilty' of the aggravated version of that offence can still be found guilty of the basic offence. This is known as the 'alternative verdict' (s 6(3) of the Criminal Law Act 1967). For summary-only basic offences, there is no power for the court to return an alternative verdict; therefore the defendant is more likely to be charged with both the basic and the racially or religiously aggravated offence. At the time of writing (2016) there are no 'aggravated' versions of charging for hate crimes motivated by a person's disability, sexual orientation, or transgender identity. However, if such a motivation is shown to be present, then this would be taken into account in the sentencing of an offender. For further information on the number of prosecutions for certain types of hate crime, see the CPS report *Hate Crime Report 2014/15 and 2015/16*, available online.

14.10.1 The definition of racially or religiously aggravated

This is explained in s 28(1) of the Crime and Disorder Act 1998. An offence becomes racially or religiously aggravated for the purposes of ss 29–32 if the offender demonstrates hostility (s 28(1)(a)) or is motivated by hostility (s 28(1)(b)) on racial or religious grounds. Providing evidence for the suspect's behaviour is likely to be easier than providing evidence for his/her motivation.

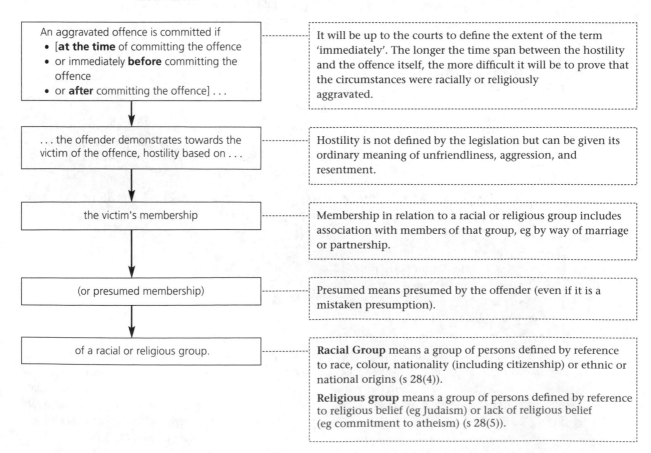

A person is held to have demonstrated hostility even if his/her behaviour might be partly motivated by other factors with no racial or religious basis (s 28(3)), but this is a question of fact for the court to decide. For example, in the case of *Johnson v DPP* [2008] EWHC 509 (Admin), two car park attendants were the victims of hostility, partly based upon their job status and partly upon their membership of a racial group. It was subsequently held that a racially aggravated s 5 Public Order Act 1986 offence had been committed against them. The accused (who was black) had made reference to the skin colour of the attendants, and told them to leave the black community in which they were working and to go to a predominantly 'white' area.

Note that of course people working in law enforcement are themselves fully entitled to protection from any racial or religious aggravation.

14.10.2   Racially or religiously aggravated assaults

Under s 29(1) of the Crime and Disorder Act 1998, the following types of assault as a basic offence can be racially or religiously aggravated:

* common assault (see 15.2.1);
* any offence under s 47 of the Offences Against the Person Act 1861 (see 15.2.2); and
* any offence under s 20 of the Offences Against the Person Act 1861 except for s 18 'with intent' offences (see 15.3).

The motivation for the basic offence must be taken into account—it must be racially or religiously motivated. For example, in the case of *DPP v Roshan Kumar Pal* (unreported, 3 February 2000) the charge of racially aggravated common assault was not proved. Even though the assault on an Asian-heritage caretaker was accompanied by abuse, the assault was held to be motivated by the perceived low status of the victim's job, and not by racism. If the racial or religious aggravation aspect of the offence charged is not proved, the court can substitute the basic offence in most cases.

Aggravated s 20 and s 47 offences from the Offences Against the Person Act 1861 are triable either way and the penalty is a fine or imprisonment (summarily, six months and seven years on indictment). Aggravated common assault offences are triable either way and the penalty is a fine or imprisonment (summarily, six months and two years on indictment).

14.10.3   Racially or religiously aggravated criminal damage

These offences are covered in s 30 of the Crime and Disorder Act 1998. A person is guilty of this offence if he/she destroys or damages property belonging to another (see 20.2), and the acts are racially or religiously motivated. Case law extends the meaning of the term 'belonging' to include having control or custody for property (as used in the Criminal Damage Act 1971 and the Theft Act 1968). There is no need to identify a specific victim and therefore spray-painting racist graffiti on a wall would probably be an example of this offence. The offence is triable either way, regardless of the value of the property damaged. The penalty is a fine or imprisonment (summarily, six months and up to 14 years on indictment).

14.10.4   Racially or religiously aggravated public order offences

Section 31 of the Crime and Disorder Act 1998 covers the aggravated forms of basic public order offences. The table shows the basic public order offences (see 14.4), and the corresponding racially or religiously aggravated offences.

Basic offence (Public Order Act 1986)	Racially or religiously aggravated offence (Crime and Disorder Act 1998)
Fear or provocation of violence (s 4)	s 31(1)(a)
Intentional harassment, alarm, or distress (s 4A)	s 31(1)(b)
Causing harassment, alarm, or distress (s 5)	s 31(1)(c)

In *Norwood v DPP* [2003] EWHC 1564 the regional organizer of the British National Party for Shropshire was found guilty of a racially aggravated s 5 Public Order Act 1986 offence. A few weeks after the 9/11 terrorist attack in New York he displayed a poster which included the words 'Islam out of Britain' and 'Protect the British People' and an image showing one of the 'twin towers' in flames, along with a crescent and star surrounded by a prohibition sign. It was displayed in his flat window and could clearly be seen from the street. However, where the offence is motivated towards the individual victim (and not towards members of his/her racial group) it is not held to be racially aggravated. For example, in the case *DPP v Howard* [2008]

EWHC 608 (Admin), an off-duty police officer heard his neighbour shouting 'I'd rather be a paki than a cop.' It was held that the only motivation for the neighbour's shouting was his intense dislike and hostility towards the police (and as a consequence an offence under s 5 of the Public Order Act 1986), and therefore the comments had not been racially aggravated.

The penalty for a s 31(1)(a) or (b) offence (triable either way) is a fine or imprisonment (summarily, six months, and two years on indictment). An offence under s 31(1)(c) is triable only summarily as it relates to a summary-only basic offence (s 5 of the Public Order Act), and therefore has no alternative verdict. The penalty is a fine.

14.10.5 Racially or religiously aggravated harassment

This is covered in s 32 of the Crime and Disorder Act 1998. The offences are racially and religiously aggravated forms of basic offences from the Protection from Harassment Act 1997, s 2 (harassment) and s 4 (putting people in fear of violence).

The offences of aggravated harassment (s 32(1)(a)) and aggravated putting people in fear of violence (s 32(1)(b)) are triable either way and the penalty is a fine or imprisonment (six months for a summary offence, and on indictment two years (s 32(1)(a)) and seven years (s 32(1)(b)). For trials on indictment, a person who is found not guilty can still be found guilty of the relevant basic harassment offence (s 32(5) and (6) of the Crime and Disorder Act 1998).

TASK 11 Consider the following groups of people. In relation to racially or religiously aggravated offences, decide whether they constitute a racial or a religious group, or neither or both:

1. Jews (see *Seide v Gillette Industries* [1980] IRLR 427);
2. Rastafarians (see *Dawkins v Crown Suppliers (Property Services Agency)*, The Times, 4 February 1993, [1993] ICR 517);
3. Muslims (see *J H Walker v Hussain* [1996] ICR 291); and
4. Gypsies (see *Commissioner for Racial Equality v Dutton* [1989] QB 783).

14.11 Answers to Tasks

TASK 1 A constable in uniform may require a person to give his or her name and address if the constable has reason to believe that a person has been acting (or is acting) in an anti-social manner within the meaning of s 2(1)(a) of the Anti-Social Behaviour, Crime and Policing Act 2014. This power is provided by s 50(1) of the Police Reform Act 2002.

Further, s 50(2) states that an offence is committed by any person who:

    (a) fails to give [his or her] name and address when required to do so under subsection (1), or
    (b) gives a false or inaccurate name or address in response to a requirement under that subsection.

TASK 2 Since the young people in the group appear to be local residents, you would not be able to prohibit them from returning to the area within 48 hours, but if you reasonably believe they are between 10–15 years old you could take them back to their homes or to a place of safety, having provided them with a written direction first. However, for children who are clearly less than 10 years old such a direction cannot be used, nor is there a legal power to take them home or remove to a place of safety. You could visit the parents and try to offer advice.

TASK 3 In the first example the available intelligence and the use of body armour would appear to provide reasonable grounds for believing that harm was likely to be caused by a person or persons at the carnival.

For the Buckingham Palace example there was no evidence in the description given:

- of harm being done or being likely to be done to a person;
- that, in the presence of a person, harm was done to his/her property;
- of a person fearing being harmed through assault, riot, or other disturbance.

It would therefore be very difficult from the information in the description alone to prove a breach of the peace in this case.

TASK 4 You probably considered the following:

1. The officer would collect evidence from the woman and other people in the area.
2. Their statements could provide evidence that the suspect was aware that:
   * while she was in a public place, anyone could hear or see her conduct; and
   * her conduct was unreasonable and was likely to cause harassment, alarm, or distress.
   Evidence could be gathered from people in the public area at the time confirming that they felt alarmed or distressed.
3. The officer could provide evidence about the suspect's conduct (what the officer actually saw and heard), and that there were other people in the public area at the time.

TASK 5 A police officer can also be harassed, alarmed, or distressed, but remember that this is a question of fact to be decided in each case by the magistrates. The magistrates may take into account that police officers often see incidents of disorderly conduct, and may therefore have developed a tolerance of such words and conduct. The evidence of other people in the area is an important factor.

TASK 6 In the case of *Swanston v DPP* (1997) 161 JP 203, the incident had occurred in a very small area and the officer was within about 1.5 m of the suspect. Unless the door supervisor had impaired hearing or sight, he could not have failed to understand what was said or failed to see the actions committed by the suspect. In the *Swanston* case, the prosecution proved that the suspect had the intention of causing the door supervisor to fear that violence was going to be used against him. Those facts were proved by the admissible evidence, including evidence from the police officer who witnessed the incident.

TASK 7 In *R v Plavecz* [2002] Crim LR 837, having been found guilty of affray, the defendant appealed. The court decided that affray is a public order offence and is inappropriate where the incident is essentially 'one on one', and the conviction was therefore quashed. It is doubtful therefore, given the circumstances outside the nightclub, that an investigation for affray could be sustained, but always seek guidance from the CPS in such matters.

TASK 8

1. For either of these two offences to be proven, you would need evidence to prove a course of conduct: for example letters, photographs, or eyewitness accounts. If the harassment involved phone calls, you would seek police force assistance to liaise with the service provider in order to obtain evidence of the calls. You would clarify with the victim whether there had been any previous instances of harassment or being put in fear of violence, and whether the police were informed or any civil remedy taken under s 3 of the Act. You would collect statements from colleagues who had seen the victim on previous occasions, and collect evidence from any other witnesses and paperwork, letters, and photographs from the victim, and exhibit them in a statement (see 10.12). The case could be discussed with a CPS Evidence Review representative or anyone involved in the investigation in an advisory capacity.
2. If the suspect was known and a course of conduct could not be proved but the victim had been harassed or put in fear of violence, you could warn the suspect. The warning would be recorded as a PNB entry, and you would also make sure it is recorded on the force database for future reference. This could be evidence towards proving a course of conduct in the future.
3. The victim should be advised to:
   * seek legal advice, as pursuing a civil remedy under s 3 of the Act could be appropriate;
   * contact Victim Support;
   * contact his/her phone service provider if the phone was being used to harass or put him/her in fear of violence, to arrange for a block to be placed on 'number withheld' incoming calls.
   * keep a diary of events, retain physical evidence (such as letters), and take photographs of any visible evidence.
4. If a course of conduct could be proved or suspected, the suspect could be arrested, but only if there was a reason for the arrest being necessary. This could be to protect a child, or to allow the prompt and effective investigation of the conduct of the person in question, or to prevent any prosecution for the offence being hindered by the disappearance of the person in question.

Specific Incidents

TASK 9 The following are factors for consideration:

- How many times has the victim been harassed by people congregating outside his own home?
- Has he asked the people to leave the area?
- How many people are in the vicinity and what are they doing?
- What is the purpose of their gathering?
- What is the impact on the person in his home?
- Is there sufficient evidence to investigate the offence, or can the situation be better resolved in its early stages by directing the people to leave the area?

TASK 10 The answers are as follows:

1b, 2c, 3d, 4a, 5a, 6fgh, 7e, 8i.

TASK 11 The answers are:

1. Racial group and religious group.
2. Not a racial group but a religious one.
3. Not a racial group but a religious one.
4. Racial group but not a religious one.

15 Unlawful Violence Against Persons and Premises

15.1 Introduction

Unlawful personal violence is a very common occurrence, and police officers are called to investigate such incidents with alarming frequency. It is also estimated that in the year ending June 2016, one in three violent incidents were not recorded at all, the highest under-recording rate for all crime categories. Likewise, in 2016, violence against the person offences recorded by the police increased by 24 percent, representing 1,035,162 reported crimes, the highest number recorded in a 12-month period since the introduction of the National Crime Recording Standard (ONS, 2017) in April 2002.

A number of different offences are covered in this chapter, both against individuals and premises. These offences include:

- common assault under s 39 of the Criminal Justice Act 1988;
- common assault by beating under s 39 of the Criminal Justice Act 1988;
- assault occasioning actual bodily harm under s 47 of the Offences Against the Person Act 1861;
- unlawful and malicious wounding, or inflicting grievous bodily harm (GBH) under s 20 of the Offences Against the Person Act 1861;
- wounding or causing grievous bodily harm with intent to do grievous bodily harm, or to resist or prevent arrest (referred to as 'GBH with Intent') under s 18 of the Offences Against the Person Act 1861;
- assaults on the police and obstructing a police officer under s 89(1) of the Police Act 1996; and
- assault with intent to resist arrest under s 38 of the Offences Against the Person Act 1861.

The general provisions of criminal law of course apply to violence and abuse in domestic settings; there are no offences that relate specifically to domestic violence.

Before going into the details of the offences, the various meanings of the word 'assault' must be considered. There is no legal definition of assault. In *R v Brown* [1993] 2 All ER 75, Lord Templeman referred to the definition of assault as that adopted by the Law Commission in their Consultation Paper No 122, *Legislating the Criminal Code: Offences against the Person and General Principles* (1992), para 9.1. This stated:

> in common law an assault is an act by which a person intentionally or recklessly causes another to apprehend immediate and unlawful personal violence and a battery is an act by which a person intentionally or recklessly inflicts personal violence upon another.

Clearly there is a distinction between a victim experiencing the application of force by battery and apprehending the threat of an application of force, although both can amount to an assault (*R v Rolfe* (1952) 36 Cr App Rep 4). So whenever the word assault is used, the intended meaning must be considered.

In November 2015 the Law Commission submitted a proposal for reforms on offences of violence against a person (Law Commission, 2015). The proposals included recommendations for changes in sentencing for offences, as the hierarchy of offences should range from the least to the most the harm caused. This hierarchy should be better reflected in sentencing (particularly for offences under s 20 (malicious wounding or grievous bodily harm) and s 47 (assault occasioning actual bodily harm)). The Law Commission also argues that some of the language in the current legislation is archaic (for example 'grievous' and 'malicious') and therefore requires updating. However, the most fundamental changes under consideration for these offences concern the requirements for intention and recklessness with respect to serious injury. Currently there must be either an intention to cause injury or recklessness as to the risk of injury. The proposed changes would instead create a liability where there is no foresight about the degree of harm that could be caused.

During incidents involving unlawful violence the health and safety of the public and police officer(s) is paramount, so police officers should always consider whether personal protective equipment is required. Incidents involving violence can be difficult to control. Often there is little time to assess a situation and plan a response because the events can be spontaneous. On receipt of a call requesting police assistance at a violent incident, call handlers will obtain as much detail as possible and relay it to the attending officers (see 24.4.1.1). If the identity of the suspect is known he/she can be checked on the PNC. Risk factors for physical violence include a history of violent or disturbed behaviour, substance or alcohol abuse, and previously expressing an intention to harm others. While travelling to the scene, the deployed officers will carry out a risk assessment based on the information from the initial report (see 11.2.1). The National Decision Model (see 6.5.2) should be applied to meet priorities such as safety of victims and the preservation of evidence (see 11.2). Once at the scene a reassessment of the victim and officer safety should be made, including the immediate risk posed by access to, or use of, weapons. The need for First Aid or other medical assistance (such as an ambulance) for anyone present will need to be assessed. In a domestic setting, the parties involved might need to be separated, especially if children are present (see 13.6). If the suspect(s) are present the FAO should watch for warning signs of incipient further violence—as well as verbal threats be aware of other signs of threatening behaviour such as the stance of the person, facial signs (eg snarling, jaw clenching), their use of their arms and hands (eg giving an aggressive 'come on' gesture with the hands or having clenched fists) plus increased breathing rate and pupil dilation (although these are more difficult to identify, particularly at a distance). If you are a trainee police officer or a special constable you will be given further information on this during Officer Safety Training (OST), and particularly the problems of interpreting so-called 'body language'. If the alleged offender has left the scene, then his/her identity and description should be obtained from the people still present, and broadcast to other police patrols in the area (see 10.5).

Early investigative actions will be crucial for there to be any chance of a successful prosecution; accurate records must be kept of anything said by the suspect (see 10.2), and evidence might need to be recorded, for example by taking photographs. If the suspect is to be arrested, a further risk assessment is needed, and reasonable force can be used if required (see 10.8.1.1 and 15.5.1). Local force policy varies on how the suspect will be transported to a police station (see 10.8.6).

The information given here is likely to be relevant to trainee police officers during Phase 3 of the IPLDP and for LPG 1 under the 'Crime' heading.

15.2 Common Assault and Occasioning Actual Bodily Harm

Historically, the Offences Against the Person Act 1861 provided magistrates with the opportunity to imprison or fine anyone committing the common law offences of assault or battery (see 15.2.1). The same statute provided the offences of assault occasioning actual harm, GBH, and GBH with intent. Assault and battery remained as common law offences until they became summary offences by virtue of s 39 of the Criminal Justice Act 1988.

The CPS advises prosecutors and the police to consider both the level of injuries and the likely sentence that a court would apply when deciding how to charge a case of assault. They should take into account the *Sentencing Council's Definitive Guideline on Assault* (published in March 2011). In general, if there are no serious injuries, then the offence should be charged as common assault. The police can make the charging decision on common assault, as it is a summary offence (Director's Guidance 2013). If the injury is serious the charge should be ABH. For an injury which is considered to be 'really serious', the charge should be GBH. There may be instances where it is necessary to deviate from this general principle (Sentencing Council, 2012).

15.2.1   Common assault

Under s 39 of the Criminal Justice Act 1988 there are two possible offences:

* common assault as a threat; and
* common assault by battery.

The naming of common assault offences is widely acknowledged to be confusing; attempts (as yet unsuccessful) have been made to revise the legislation concerned. The two forms of common assault are alternatives and should never be charged together (see *DPP v Little* [1992] 1 All ER 299). They are triable summarily only, and the penalty is six months' imprisonment. Note that these offences can be racially or religiously aggravated (see 14.10.2).

15.2.1.1   Common assault (threat)

Common assault as a threat can take a number of forms:

* common assault (threat)—any act which makes a victim understand he/she is going to be immediately subjected to some personal violence. An example of this would be: 'I'm going to bitch-slap you bruv!'. This could be done by social media, or letter, if there was some immediacy to the threat being carried out and the victim believes violence is going to occur (*R v Constanza* [1997] Crim LR 576). This includes when there is no means to carry out the threat such as holding a replica gun against a person and threatening to shoot him/her, if the victim believes there is a threat of violence (see *Logdon v DPP* [1976] Crim L R 121, DC);
* conditional threat (or conditional assault) conveys a threat on condition of another event, for example 'get out the car or I will cut you'. Bodily harm would be expected to follow any refusal made by the victim. If the victim gets out of the car, the suspect would still be guilty of assault.

Non-conditional threat (or unconditional assault) is not considered an assault, for example, John says to Sue, 'Get me a glass of water', Sue refuses and John says, 'If your brothers weren't here I'd thump you.' The words of the threat already tell you that John is not going to assault Sue and therefore there is no immediate threat.

In the context of common assault as a threat is:

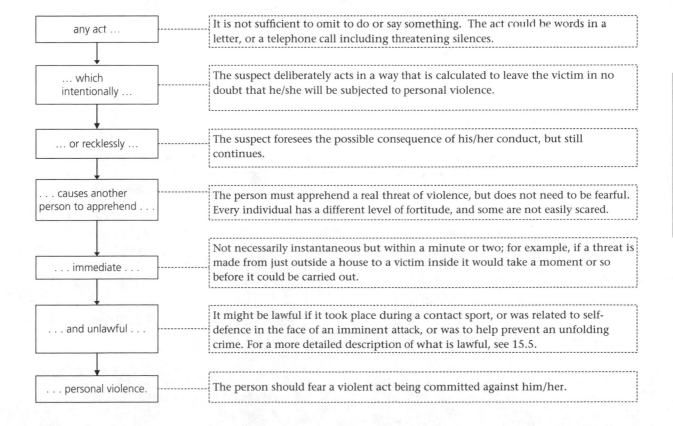

any act ...	It is not sufficient to omit to do or say something. The act could be words in a letter, or a telephone call including threatening silences.
... which intentionally ...	The suspect deliberately acts in a way that is calculated to leave the victim in no doubt that he/she will be subjected to personal violence.
... or recklessly ...	The suspect foresees the possible consequence of his/her conduct, but still continues.
... causes another person to apprehend ...	The person must apprehend a real threat of violence, but does not need to be fearful. Every individual has a different level of fortitude, and some are not easily scared.
... immediate ...	Not necessarily instantaneous but within a minute or two; for example, if a threat is made from just outside a house to a victim inside it would take a moment or so before it could be carried out.
... and unlawful ...	It might be lawful if it took place during a contact sport, or was related to self-defence in the face of an imminent attack, or was to help prevent an unfolding crime. For a more detailed description of what is lawful, see 15.5.
... personal violence.	The person should fear a violent act being committed against him/her.

Specific Incidents

15.2.1.2 Common assault (battery)

Common assault by battery (beating) involves the actual use of force by an assailant on a victim but only results in very minor or no perceivable injury. It is the intentional or reckless application of force on another, and can range from a push to a punch, and depends on how much harm is done, and the injury received.

A 'battery' (as in common assault by battery) is any act by which a person:

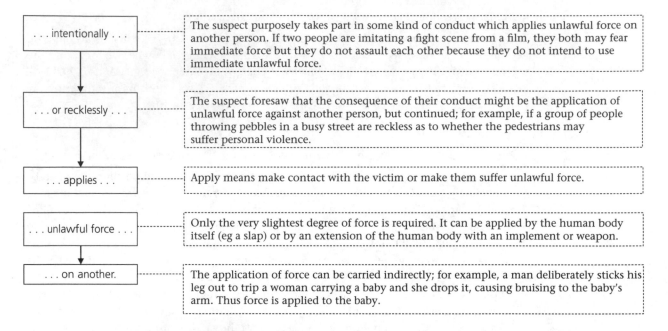

. . . intentionally . . .	The suspect purposely takes part in some kind of conduct which applies unlawful force on another person. If two people are imitating a fight scene from a film, they both may fear immediate force but they do not assault each other because they do not intend to use immediate unlawful force.
. . . or recklessly . . .	The suspect foresaw that the consequence of their conduct might be the application of unlawful force against another person, but continued; for example, if a group of people throwing pebbles in a busy street are reckless as to whether the pedestrians may suffer personal violence.
. . . applies . . .	Apply means make contact with the victim or make them suffer unlawful force.
. . . unlawful force . . .	Only the very slightest degree of force is required. It can be applied by the human body itself (eg a slap) or by an extension of the human body with an implement or weapon.
. . . on another.	The application of force can be carried indirectly; for example, a man deliberately sticks his leg out to trip a woman carrying a baby and she drops it, causing bruising to the baby's arm. Thus force is applied to the baby.

TASK 1 Consider the following incidents in relation to s 39 of the Criminal Justice Act 1988, and state for each which offence has been committed:

1. Two men have been arguing in the street and one man has pushed and shoved the other, but very little force has been used upon the victim, who is therefore uninjured. What offence has been committed, common assault or common assault by beating?
2. During a dispute between two women in a car park no force was used, but one of them was left in no doubt that she was about to face unlawful personal violence. What offence has been committed?

15.2.2 Actual Bodily Harm (ABH)

This offence is usually referred to as Assault Occasioning Actual Bodily Harm (AOABH) and is covered under s 47 of the Offences Against the Person Act 1861. Note that here the word assault is being used to mean some sort of physical attack. The main factor which distinguishes common assault by beating from AOABH is the degree of injury. *R v Donovan* [1934] 2 KB 498 at 509, [1934] All ER Rep 207 suggested that 'bodily harm has its ordinary meaning' and includes 'any hurt or injury calculated to interfere with the health or comfort of the prosecutor. Such hurt or injury need not be permanent, but must, no doubt, be more than merely transient and trifling'.

The injury must therefore be real and it should be capable of being seen or felt by the victim (or by witnesses such as a police officer). It also includes psychiatric injury/illness or psychological damage (*R v Ireland* [1998] AC 147 (HL)), and a hysterical and nervous state of mind brought about by the threat of violence. All of these latter 'injuries to the mind' must be supported by medical evidence (see *R v Chan Fook* [1994] 2 All ER 552, [1994] 1 WLR 689, 99 Cr App Rep 147, [1994] Crim LR 432).

The term 'harm' can have a broad meaning, for example in one case the victim visited her ex-partner who cut off her ponytail. Although hair grows outside the body and might therefore be considered as dead, and the victim did not feel physical pain in the normal sense, such an act was held to amount to Actual Bodily Harm (see *DPP v Smith (Michael Ross)* [2006] EWHC 94 (Admin), [2006] 2 All ER 16).

The aspects of intention or recklessness are the same for actual bodily harm as they are for common assault by beating; it only needs to be proved that the assault was intended or that it was carried out recklessly. There is no need to prove that the accused intended to cause injuries amounting to actual bodily harm (or was reckless as to whether injuries amounting to actual bodily harm would be caused).

This offence is triable either way. The penalty if tried summarily is six months' imprisonment and/or a fine, and five years' imprisonment on indictment. This offence can be racially or religiously aggravated (see 14.10.2).

15.3 Unlawful and Malicious Wounding or Inflicting Grievous Bodily Harm

Section 20 of the Offences Against the Person Act 1861 states that it is an offence to 'unlawfully and maliciously…wound another person' or to 'inflict grievous bodily harm [upon another person]'. The suspect must know that the actions would result in some kind of injury, but does not necessarily have to foresee the degree of injury. The injuries can be caused either with or without a weapon.

To understand this offence, careful consideration needs to be given first to the meaning of certain words. 'Grievous' should be taken to mean 'really serious' (*Director of Public Prosecutions Appellant; and Smith Respondent* [1961] A.C. 290); see 15.3.1 for details. 'Unlawfully' means 'without lawful justification' (as opposed to cases of lawfully inflicted injury, eg some instances of self-defence, see 15.5). 'Maliciously' means:

- an actual intention to do that particular kind of harm; or
- recklessness (unreasonably persisting in taking that risk) as to whether such harmful consequences would occur as a result of the actions taken. For example, in the possible transmission of a sexually transmitted infection by sexual activity, it would be reckless for the suspect to take that risk (*R v Dica* [2004] 3 All ER 593 Court of Appeal).

Note that, although malice (ill-will or a malevolent motive) must be present, it does not have to be towards the victim personally.

15.3.1 The extent of the injury

The injury must amount to either wounding or grievous ('really serious') bodily harm. Wounding is defined as breaking of all the layers of the skin. A wound can be a minor injury requiring just stitches, but it can equally be a lot more serious, for example 'a wound' is likely to require surgery if any organs are damaged or if there is a risk of infection. A wound does not have to be caused with a weapon (though of course this is often the case, eg using a deliberately smashed glass for the attack).

Grievous bodily harm is not defined in the Act but case law has established that it should be given its ordinary meaning, which is 'really serious bodily harm' (*DPP v Smith* [1960] 3 All ER 161). The bodily harm must be serious, but not necessarily dangerous or permanent.

The CPS list (CPS, 2009b) suggest the following as examples of GBH:

- injury resulting in some permanent disability, that is loss of function;
- visible disfigurement;
- broken or displaced limbs or bones;
- injuries with substantial blood loss, usually requiring blood transfusion;
- injuries resulting in lengthy treatment or incapacity;
- psychiatric injury (expert evidence is required).

GBH does not have to include an assault or a battery (see 15.2.1). For example, a person infecting his/her partner knowingly with the HIV virus while concealing the infection from the partner is committing the offence of grievous bodily harm. There have been at least ten convictions for GBH based on the reckless transmission of HIV in England and Wales. Telephone calls that would result in serious psychiatric injury to the victim can also amount to grievous bodily harm.

This offence is triable either way, and the penalty if tried summarily is six months' imprisonment and/or a fine, and up to seven years' imprisonment on indictment. This offence can be racially or religiously aggravated (see 14.10.2).

Specific Incidents

15.3.2   GBH with intent

The full name for this offence is 'wounding or causing grievous bodily harm with intent to do grievous bodily harm or to resist or prevent arrest'.

Section 18 of the Offences Against the Person Act 1861 states it is an offence to:

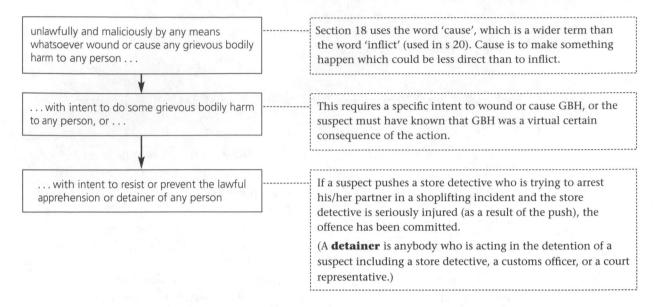

| unlawfully and maliciously by any means whatsoever wound or cause any grievous bodily harm to any person . . . | Section 18 uses the word 'cause', which is a wider term than the word 'inflict' (used in s 20). Cause is to make something happen which could be less direct than to inflict. |

| . . . with intent to do some grievous bodily harm to any person, or . . . | This requires a specific intent to wound or cause GBH, or the suspect must have known that GBH was a virtual certain consequence of the action. |

| . . . with intent to resist or prevent the lawful apprehension or detainer of any person | If a suspect pushes a store detective who is trying to arrest his/her partner in a shoplifting incident and the store detective is seriously injured (as a result of the push), the offence has been committed.

(A **detainer** is anybody who is acting in the detention of a suspect including a store detective, a customs officer, or a court representative.) |

The main difference between simple grievous bodily harm (GBH) and this offence is the element of intent. Of course intent is sometimes difficult to prove, although there will be some obvious examples, for instance if a weapon is used.

This offence is triable on indictment only and the penalty is life imprisonment. There was no perceived need to create a racially or religiously aggravated offence for this offence as the maximum sentence is already life imprisonment.

15.4   Assaulting, Resisting, or Obstructing Police Officers

This applies to police officers acting in the lawful execution of their duties, and to anyone assisting a police officer in the lawful execution of his/her duties. Assault to resist arrest is a separate offence. Note that here the word 'assault' is being used to mean some sort of physical attack.

Section 89 of the Police Act 1996 (due to be amended) currently states it is an offence for any person:

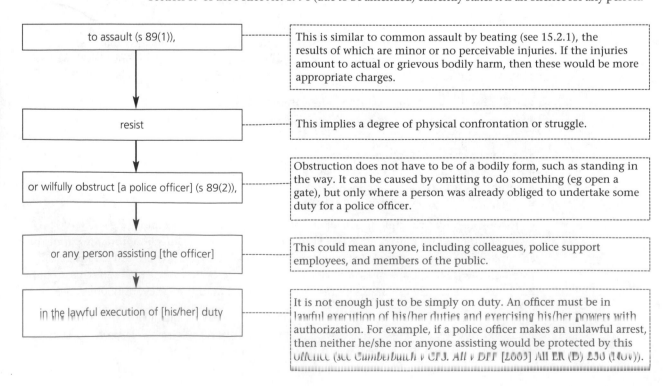

| to assault (s 89(1)), | This is similar to common assault by beating (see 15.2.1), the results of which are minor or no perceivable injuries. If the injuries amount to actual or grievous bodily harm, then these would be more appropriate charges. |

| resist | This implies a degree of physical confrontation or struggle. |

| or wilfully obstruct [a police officer] (s 89(2)), | Obstruction does not have to be of a bodily form, such as standing in the way. It can be caused by omitting to do something (eg open a gate), but only where a person was already obliged to undertake some duty for a police officer. |

| or any person assisting [the officer] | This could mean anyone, including colleagues, police support employees, and members of the public. |

| in the lawful execution of [his/her] duty | It is not enough just to be simply on duty. An officer must be in lawful execution of his/her duties and exercising his/her powers with authorization. For example, if a police officer makes an unlawful arrest, then neither he/she nor anyone assisting would be protected by this offence (see *Cumberbatch v CPS, Ali v DPP* [2009] All ER (D) 230 (Nov)). |

These offences are triable summarily and the penalties are a fine or imprisonment (six months for a s 89(1) offence and one month for a s 89(2) offence).

For the offence of resisting arrest, s 38 of the Offences Against the Person Act 1861 states it is an offence to:

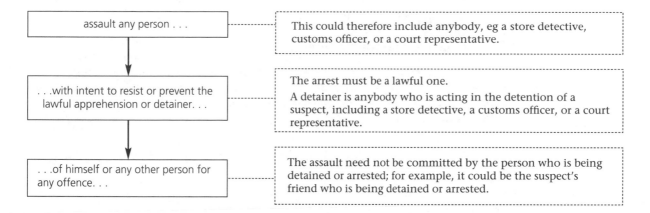

It is important that the police officer is acting in the line of duty, for example if on premises conducting a search. If the officer's presence is not lawful then he/she cannot make a lawful arrest, and any attempt to make an arrest could even amount to an assault. A person who resists in these circumstances could claim self-defence to an assault (and thereby avoid prosecution for the offence of resisting arrest). The offence of resisting arrest is triable summarily and the penalty is two years' imprisonment.

15.5 General Defences to the Use of Violence

There are a great many defences to the application of force, for example self-defence (also known as common law self-defence). Self defence is not however defined by statute, and therefore it is a question of fact for the courts to decide whether a particular act amounts to self-defence. In *Dewar v DPP* [2010] EWHC 1050 (Admin) it was reaffirmed that there is a two-part test to self-defence:

- that the individual believes that he/she was acting in self-defence; and
- that the force used was reasonable in the circumstances (see 15.5.1).

There is no need to consider which person was the initial aggressor (see *Marsh v DPP* [2015] EWHC 1022 (Admin)). The timing of the use of force can also vary, for example in the case of *R v Bird* ([1985] 1 WLR 816) she believed she was about to be hit and so she hit her partner first. The definition of reasonable force is examined in more detail in 15.5.1.

Reasonable chastisement can be a defence, but this does not apply for chastisement that involves assault occasioning actual bodily harm, unlawfully inflicting grievous bodily harm, causing grievous bodily harm with intent, or cruelty to a child, when the assailant is the child's parent (s 58 of the Children Act 2004). The Education Act 1996 removed the right of schools to use corporal punishment. (This was appealed by a Christian School in 2005 and was unsuccessful (UKHL 15; [2005] 2 AC 246).)

That consent was given for the use of force can be a defence. In sports, the level of force used must be appropriate and in keeping with the rules of the game (see *R v Barnes* [2004] EWCA Crim 3246) and *R v Coney* (1882) 8 QBD 534). Consent can also be used as a defence in a medical context (for example that the act was a necessary part of medical treatment), and for piercings or tattoos. It might also be used where there has been 'horseplay' or rough and undisciplined play where there is no intention to cause injury (*R v Jones (Terence)* (1986) Crim LR 123). The defence of consent cannot however be relied on in offences under s 47 and s 20 OAPA 1861 where the injuries resulted from sadomasochist activities (*R v Brown* [1993] 2 All ER 75 House of Lords).

Intoxication can only be used as a defence for crimes of specific intent, such as offences under s 18 (maliciously inflicting grievous bodily harm with intent). The other more common types of assault (common, causing actual bodily harm, assault of a police officer) require no specific intent and therefore this defence cannot apply. For this defence to succeed the court must take into account the degree of intoxication, to determine whether the defendant would have been capable of forming the intent to bring about a specific result.

Other defences include that the force was applied in order to defend property, by accident or in the course of preventing a crime.

15.5.1 The meaning of 'reasonable force'

The use of reasonable force for self-defence, defence of property, and law enforcement is defined in law, for example its use for certain powers of arrest and entry provided under s 117 PACE (see 10.8.2 and 13.7.2). The general meaning of 'reasonable force' is expanded upon in s 76 of the Criminal Justice and Immigration Act 2008. This also provides a number of defences, for example:

- self-defence (a common law defence, see s 76(2)(a) of the Criminal Justice and Immigration Act 2008);
- defence of property (a common law defence, see s 76(2)(aa) of the Criminal Justice and Immigration Act 2008); and
- the use of force in the course of prevention of crime, or in making an arrest (s 3(1) of the Criminal Law Act (s 76(2)(b)), see 10.8.2).

For these defences, the person must have had an honest belief that it was necessary to use force and the degree of force used was not disproportionate (see *Palmer v R* [1971] AC 814). Both these conditions must be fulfilled. The person's perceptions of the circumstances at the time will be taken into account, as well as the reality of the situation. For example, the defendant might have had a mistaken belief as to the circumstances but if this misunderstanding is considered to have been reasonable in that context, then a jury could find the defendant not guilty (*R v Williams (Gladstone)* [1987] 3 All ER 411, 78 Cr App Rep 276). Also, it is not reasonable to expect all defendants in the heat of the moment to be able to judge the precise degree of force required. Therefore, a person who uses the force honestly and instinctively thinking that it was necessary will be provided with some leeway.

However, note that a police officer commits an assault (as in common assault by beating, ABH, or GBH) if he/she restrains a person without intending or purporting to arrest him/her. This applies even if an arrest could have been justified (see *Fraser Wood v DPP* [2008] EWHC 1056 (Admin)).

15.5.1.1 Defending against intruders in a dwelling

Where a person is defending him/herself or others from intruders in their home, it might still be reasonable in the circumstances to use a degree of force that might otherwise be considered disproportionate. The resident may have been under intense pressure, with little time to think rationally about the minimum level of force required to stop an intruder. Amendments were made to s 76(5)(a) of the Criminal Justice and Immigration Act 2008 in 2013. This states that the force used by an individual must always be reasonable in the circumstances as he/she believes them to be, and introduces the idea of disproportionate force. For example, a burglar breaks into a home, and the resident awoken from a deep sleep goes downstairs where a struggle ensues. The resident punches the burglar, knocking him out. This might be considered disproportionate, but is reasonable taking the circumstances into account. However, if the resident then started beating the unconscious burglar, this would be considered grossly disproportionate, and therefore unreasonable and unlawful. A resident who shot indiscriminately at burglars with a gun (*R v Martin* [2002] 2 WLR 1) was held to have used grossly disproportionate force.

This only applies for a resident acting in self-defence or to protect others in his/her home and the force used was disproportionate and not grossly disproportionate. The use of disproportionate force to protect property however is still unlawful. Further information regarding the defence of property is available in the Parliament briefing paper 'Householders and the criminal law of self-defence' available online.

15.5.2   **Positional asphyxia**

In some very rare circumstances the use of restraint by police officers has the potential to result in serious injury or death to the person being restrained. Leaving aside the possibility of a cardiac arrest, one of the more serious risks is positional asphyxia (PA), also referred to as postural asphyxia. This is when a person's body position or posture affects the ability to breathe, and can be exacerbated by pressure applied to the person's back. It may occur through poorly executed or ill-thought-out restraint techniques, or be consequent to some form of accident, such as fainting onto a chair or other raised surface. Asphyxiation can also be caused by obliging a person (particularly if overweight) to remain seated with his/her chest close to his/her knees.

To reduce the risk of PA, police forces, prisons, and medical organizations generally recommend that restrained persons are held face down for only the shortest possible period of time. In addition, pressure on the back or chest (such as controlling the person with a knee or the restrainer's body weight) must be limited as much as possible. The risk of PA is increased for people who are under the influence of alcohol or drugs, or unconscious, who are overweight, who have engaged in a violent struggle or heavy exercise, or who are under extreme stress. Prevention is relatively simple: pressure should not be applied to the chest area or the back; a seated person should not be forced or left to lean forward; and detained persons should be made to stand or sit upright as soon as possible, for example after handcuffs have been applied.

The warning signs of impending PA are relatively clear and include:

- suddenly becoming quiet, limp, or agitated—any change in consciousness should be considered;
- complaining of not being able to breathe—even if the detainee has an aggressive demeanour, any such complaint should be taken seriously;
- noisy breathing, gurgling or choking, foaming saliva, convulsions;
- signs of cyanosis (blue lips, eyelids or gums—often difficult to spot);
- signs of force or stress in the face and neck, such as raised blood vessels or bleeding.

The potential for in-custody deaths from positional asphyxia will be lessened by exercising caution and common sense. Officers should pay close attention if there is a risk, and in the event of asphyxiation, any hold or position potentially affecting the subject should be removed and his/her clothing loosened. If this does not improve the person's condition then CPR should be performed. However, it should be noted that resuscitation in such circumstances often fails. More details can be found in Belviso *et al* (2003).

15.6   **Threats to Kill**

Section 16 of the Offences Against the Person Act 1861 (as amended by Sch 12 to the Criminal Law Act 1977) is about making threats to kill. One way this offence can be committed is straightforward: A threatens to kill B and intends that B will believe the threat.

- Annie says to Bob 'You've 'ad it, you're dead, I'll do it..., you're dead': Annie wants Bob to believe that her threat to kill him is real.

The other way this offence can be committed is slightly more complicated: person A communicates a threat to kill, and intends that B should believe the threat. But the threat is not about killing B, it is about killing another person C. (It is irrelevant whether C knows about the threats.)

- Adam says to Babs 'That Colin—he's finished now, I'll sort it—final like, stone cold, dead': Adam intends that Babs should believe that his threat to kill Colin is real.

To prove this offence, it is not necessary for A to actually intend to kill anyone, but it must be proved that A intends that B should believe and fear that this would be carried out. The threats made by A can be premeditated or spontaneous, and can be communicated by any means including through email or a social networking site. There does not have to be the sense that the killing would be carried out immediately. The offence could be useful where there has been no assault (eg if an assault has been prevented), yet the victim B was in fear that it would be carried out.

Threats to kill are relatively common and it is often difficult to prove an offence has occurred because it is often one person's word against another. There are also defences such as A only made the threat against B in self-defence. For this offence, the threat to kill should be plain for the jury to see (*R v Solanke* [1970] 1 WLR 1). If it is not obvious, then perhaps a charge under s 4 of the Public Order Act 1986 or a charge of affray would be more appropriate (see 14.4).

This offence is triable either way, and the penalty if tried summarily is six months' imprisonment and/or a fine, and on indictment ten years' imprisonment.

TASK 2 A police officer attends each of the following incidents. Using the information given here decide what offence or offences may have been committed in relation to the injuries sustained by the victims. In some cases you may wish to give more than a single answer.

1. Two people are arguing in the street. The dispute reaches a point where one of the couple head-butts the other, who then has a severe nosebleed.
2. An apparently drunken man throws a glass bottle from a moving car in the direction of a woman waiting at a bus stop. The bottle hits the shelter and breaks. A large fragment of flying glass hits the woman on her head, causing a deep wound which bleeds profusely. The woman's skull can easily be seen through the wound. Subsequently, the victim attended accident and emergency at a local hospital and had several stitches inserted.
3. CCTV images show a woman taking goods from a clothes shop and hiding them under her jacket. A store detective follows her out and into the street and stops her. He explains who he is and why he is detaining her. She makes a sudden move, pushing the store detective backwards. He falls over and grazes his hand.
4. After months of alleged harassment by local youths in the street outside her house, the occupant comes out and slaps one of the youths, leaving a large red mark on his cheek.

15.7 The Use of Violence to Enter Premises

It is an offence to use violence to gain entry to premises occupied by any person opposing the entry (s 6 of the Criminal Law Act 1977). Convictions for this offence are usually in the context of domestic disputes, for example, a man trying to force his way into his own flat is committing an offence if his live-in partner is inside and does not want him to come in. A police officer suspecting that such an offence may have been committed should run through a mental checklist before acting, to ensure that the circumstances match all the requirements of the relevant legislation.

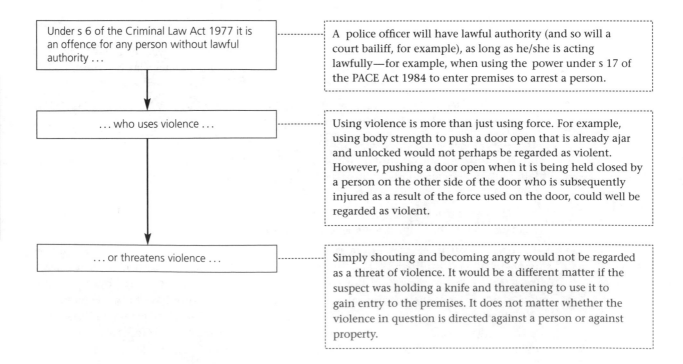

Under s 6 of the Criminal Law Act 1977 it is an offence for any person without lawful authority . . .

A police officer will have lawful authority (and so will a court bailiff, for example), as long as he/she is acting lawfully—for example, when using the power under s 17 of the PACE Act 1984 to enter premises to arrest a person.

. . . who uses violence . . .

Using violence is more than just using force. For example, using body strength to push a door open that is already ajar and unlocked would not perhaps be regarded as violent. However, pushing a door open when it is being held closed by a person on the other side of the door who is subsequently injured as a result of the force used on the door, could well be regarded as violent.

. . . or threatens violence . . .

Simply shouting and becoming angry would not be regarded as a threat of violence. It would be a different matter if the suspect was holding a knife and threatening to use it to gain entry to the premises. It does not matter whether the violence in question is directed against a person or against property.

Specific Incidents

So for this offence, the suspect must not have lawful authority to enter, and must either use violence or threaten to use violence:

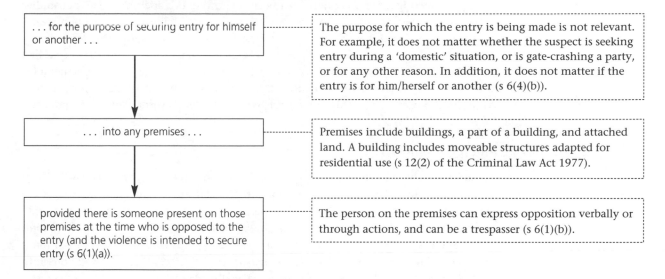

... for the purpose of securing entry for himself or another ...

The purpose for which the entry is being made is not relevant. For example, it does not matter whether the suspect is seeking entry during a 'domestic' situation, or is gate-crashing a party, or for any other reason. In addition, it does not matter if the entry is for him/herself or another (s 6(4)(b)).

... into any premises ...

Premises include buildings, a part of a building, and attached land. A building includes moveable structures adapted for residential use (s 12(2) of the Criminal Law Act 1977).

provided there is someone present on those premises at the time who is opposed to the entry (and the violence is intended to secure entry (s 6(1)(a)).

The person on the premises can express opposition verbally or through actions, and can be a trespasser (s 6(1)(b)).

This offence does not apply for a home owner, tenant or legally intended occupier who comes home and finds squatters have entered. The exemption does not include however using or threatening violence towards the trespasser. The trespasser can be asked to leave, and it is an offence under s 7 of the Criminal Law Act 1977 if he/she refuses to do so. Section 144 of the Legal Aid, Sentencing and Punishment of Offenders Act 2012 also created an offence of squatting in a residential building (see 14.8.4).

The offence of using violence to gain entry is triable summarily, and the penalty is six months' imprisonment and/or a fine. There is a power of entry to arrest under s 17 of the PACE Act 1984 for this offence (see 10.6).

TASK 3 Charlie and partner Sam have been facing up to the fact that their three-year relationship is drawing to an end. Recently there have been several episodes where they shouted angrily at each other, and both of them have taken to going out separately and getting very drunk. They share a house which is owned jointly.

One evening Charlie stays at home while Sam goes out to a club. Sam arrives home in the early hours of the following morning, very drunk, to find the front door will not open with the key. Sam begins to bang on the door with his fists, and the awakened neighbours hear Charlie shouting from inside the house to stop the banging and to go away. One of the neighbours calls the police who attend the scene to find Sam still banging the door. In relation to s 6(1) of the Criminal Law Act 1977, has Sam committed an offence?

15.8 Gang-related Violence

The issue of 'gang'-related violence has received considerable attention in recent years. In 2011, HM Government claimed in *Ending Gang and Youth Violence: A Cross-Government Report* that 'gang members carry out half of all shootings in the capital and 22% of all serious violence.'

UK legislation (s 34(5) of the Policing and Crime Act 2009) defines a gang as a group that consists of at least three people; uses a name, emblem, or colour or any other identifiable characteristic; and is associated with a particular area: (this may seem a little vague). ACPO used a working definition of gang that includes the notion of a relatively durable, predominantly street-based group of young people who see themselves (and are seen by others) as a discernible group and engage in a range of criminal activity and violence. The members of the group may also identify with or lay claim over territory, have some form of 'identifying structural feature', and/or be in conflict with other similar gangs (Home Office, 2012c). Some research (eg Harris *et al*, 2011) suggests that we need to be cautious about labelling offenders as gang members. This is because such labelling may have the unwanted effect of a 'self-fulfilling' prophecy, and make it more difficult for supposed gang members to break away.

Studies commissioned by Westminster Joint Health and Well Being Board have shown there is a higher level of mental health issues within the gang population compared with the general population and the offender population of the same age group (Madden, 2015). Other studies have shown that 86 per cent of gang members were identified as having antisocial personality disorder, over half suffered from alcohol dependence, anxiety disorder, or drug dependence, and 34 per cent had attempted suicide, 25 per cent had suffered psychosis, and 20 per cent had depression. It is becoming more common to see mental health problems in UK gang members (and in the US it has been shown that gang-affiliation is associated with conditions such as anxiety, mood disorder, conduct disorder, post-traumatic stress disorder, and attempted suicide (Hughes *et al*, 2015)).

15.8.1 Tackling gang violence

New measures have been introduced to tackle problems associated with gangs. The Anti-Social Behaviour, Crime and Policing Act 2014 created new offences such as threatening with a knife in a public place or school (see 18.2.4) and possessing illegal firearms with intent to supply (s 2(A) of the Firearms Act 1968), the latter carrying a maximum penalty of life imprisonment. The Act also increases the maximum penalty for importation of firearms to life imprisonment (s 50 and 5(A) of the Customs and Excise Management Act 1979). For investigations into gang-related crime the police can apply for an 'Investigation Anonymity Order' for any person who gives information to the police (see 25.7) and this can help persuade witnesses to cooperate. Gang activity can also be inhibited through the use of injunctions under s 34 of the Policing and Crime Act 2009 (see 15.8.1.1 and 14.2.1.9).

15.8.1.1 Gang Injunctions

'Gang injunctions' can be used to deter individuals from engaging in, or encouraging or assisting with gang-related activities including violence. Councils and Police Chief Officers are able to apply for an injunction under s 34(3) of the Policing and Crime Act 2009 to forbid a person from being involved in gang-related violence or gang-related drug dealing activity.

The application is made to a high or county court (for over 18s), and it must be shown that the person has engaged in, encouraged or assisted, or needs to be protected from being drawn into more serious activity involving violence or drugs. The 2015 Home Office document *Injunctions to Prevent Gang-Related Violence and Gang-Related Drug Dealing* provides more detailed guidance. For 14–17-year-olds the application for an injunction is made to a youth court. Local partners can also apply (such as registered social landlords, housing associations, transport agencies, probation, and youth offending teams). Local authority and other key partner agencies may also be involved as they have a responsibility to protect and improve the well-being of a child (s 10 of the Children Act 2004).

A gang injunction can last for up to two years and can prohibit a respondent from:

- associating in public with named gang members;
- visiting or travelling through a particular area or areas;
- being in charge of a particular species of animal (if it has been used to intimidate others);
- posting videos that promote their gang or threaten rival gangs on video-sharing websites; or
- uploading details of gang 'meet-ups' on social networking websites.

If the injunction is for more than a year then the court will hold a review four weeks before the end of the first year to decide whether it should be extended or varied. For a young person, the review must take place at least four weeks before his/her 18th birthday.

Although a breach of a gang injunction is a civil matter, and would therefore be dealt with as a contempt of court, the prohibition is likely to include an arrest power for a breach. Adults breaching the injunction could be remanded in custody, or on bail with conditions. For 14–17-year-olds, supervision orders (attending regular appointments with a mentor or supervisor), activities orders (attending rehabilitative programs), or curfews can be used (Home Office, 2015d).

15.9 Managing Violent Offenders

Violent Offender Orders (VOO) were introduced in 2009 under the Criminal Justice and Immigration Act 2008, with the aim of reducing reoffending (Home Office, 2009a). They are civil orders and set restrictions or conditions that limit an individual's behaviour, for example preventing him/her from going to certain locations, attending certain events, or having contact with specified individuals (s 102 of the Criminal Justice and Immigration Act 2008). VOOs cover a period of between two and five years.

The order is requested by a chief police officer and issued by a magistrates' court. The court must be satisfied that a VOO is necessary to protect the public or any particular member of the public from serious physical or psychological harm. The recipient of a VOO must be aged 18 or over and have been previously sentenced to at least 12 months' imprisonment for a serious violent offence (or be subject to a hospital or supervision order (or an equivalent) after being found not guilty due to insanity (s 99)). The offender can have committed the relevant crimes outside the UK (s 99(4)).

Multi-Agency Public Protection Arrangements (MAPPA) are used to help the police, the Prison Service, and the Probation Service to manage risk from violent and sexual offenders (see 3.3.1). A national database (VISOR, the Violent and Sex Offenders Register) lists all individuals who pose a risk of serious harm to the public. It is accessible to the police, probation and prison services and supports the development of MAPPA.

15.10   Answers to Tasks

TASK 1

1. Common assault by beating (battery): only the very slightest degree of force is required to constitute a battery and little or no visible injury is necessary to prove the offence.
2. Common assault: if a person is threatened with immediate unlawful personal violence of a minor nature, he/she is the victim of common assault (remember that assault is the threat of violence or harm, not the harm itself).

The suspect can only be charged or reported for the offence of common assault, or common assault by beating (battery), not both.

TASK 2 The problem with this type of scenario is that you lack all the other information that would be available in a real incident. However, based entirely on the limited information available to you in the questions, the following are the possible offences that could be considered:

1. Here, in order to have sustained a nosebleed the health and/or comfort of the victim is most likely to have been 'interfered with', so AOABH under s 47 of the Offences Against the Person Act 1861 is most likely to be the appropriate offence.
2. All layers of the victim's skin have been broken and therefore the injury is a wound. More evidence is required to ascertain the suspect's intentions (this will come from witnesses and by interviewing the suspect). The offence could be GBH or GBH with intent.
3. Two options here perhaps; as far as the injury is concerned, a graze may have interfered with the health and comfort of the store detective, therefore AOABH under s 47 of the Offences Against the Person Act 1861 could be considered. When the aspect of detention/arrest is also taken into consideration, then assault with intent to resist lawful arrest under s 38 of the Offences Against the Person Act 1861 may also be appropriate.
4. Once again, a large red mark may have interfered with the health and comfort of the young man, therefore AOABH under s 47 of the Offences Against the Person Act 1861 could be considered. Alternatively, the red mark could be considered as a minor or hardly perceivable injury, so this might be a common assault by beating (s 39 of the Criminal Justice Act 1988).

Prosecution guidelines or charging standards are available on the CPS website.

TASK 3 Section 6(1) of the Criminal Law Act 1977 states that any person who, without lawful authority, uses or threatens violence for the purpose of securing entry into any premises for [him/her]self or for any other person is guilty of an offence provided that:

• 'a person is present on those premises, and he/she is opposed to the entry which the violence is intended to secure'; and
• 'the person using violence or threatening the violence knows that that is the case'.

In the circumstances it appears that Sam is only hammering on the door with his fists and therefore the actions of Sam fall short of the 'violence' that is required for this offence. If Sam's actions escalate to the likelihood of damage being caused, or threats or use of violence, then the offence would be committed provided that Sam knew Charlie was on the premises and opposed the entry.

16 | Theft, Fraud, and Related Offences

16.1 Introduction

This chapter examines the law and procedure concerned with a number of criminal offences associated with theft and fraud. We present the basic knowledge of the criminal law required for many pre-join programmes and for initial police training. This Handbook will provide you with the essence of the most relevant law and some interpretations (both academic and from case law or precedent), but there is no substitute for reading and understanding the law itself.

Of all the dishonest criminal offences police officers will deal with early in their careers, theft will probably be the most common. Theft includes shoplifting and stealing from an employer, as well as a number of other similar crimes. The primary source of legislation relating to theft is to be found in ss 1–6 of the Theft Act 1968. There are many legal complexities surrounding theft and we will simply examine the basic principles involved. Trainee officers are likely to be involved in most stages of the investigation of theft and 'simple' types of fraud, from reporting to investigation and possibly prosecution. They are less likely to become involved in complex fraud investigations, beyond the initial stages. This is particularly the case for large-scale credit card fraud, where difficult decisions need to be made concerning the 'screening' of reported offences to decide which should be the subject of a secondary investigation (see 24.4.3) and in reference to the NIM (see 23.6). The investigation is likely to be handled by a specialist unit (which might also deal with cybercrime (see Chapter 21)).

The information is this chapter is relevant to the PAC requirement that trainee police officers conduct initial investigations and report volume crime. It will also provide the opportunity to develop the underpinning knowledge required for a number of Certificate in Knowledge of Policing and Diploma in Policing assessed units, and for trainees' Phase 3 Learning Diary entries (particularly the 'Crime' heading) and SOLAP. Note, however, that the IPLDP curriculum is subject to periodic 'maintenance' and hence a check should be made with each force to find out precisely what aspects of the criminal law and police procedure around theft, fraud, and related offences are required.

16.2 The Definition of Theft

A person is guilty of theft (s 1 of the Theft Act 1968) if he/she 'dishonestly appropriates property belonging to another with the intention of permanently depriving the other of it'. A thief is a person who commits a theft or in everyday language, steals something. We examine each of the five key concepts for theft in turn.

Dishonesty is not defined by the Act, but s 2(1) of the Theft Act 1968 defines where a person will **not** be treated as dishonest. The person is **not** acting dishonestly if he/she believes that:

- he/she had the lawful right to take the item (eg a man sees a woman leaving with his bag and decides to take it back from her);
- he/she would have had the owner's consent if the owner had known the circumstances (eg your neighbour is on holiday and you are looking after his garden, but your lawnmower breaks down so you take his from his shed to cut your grass); and
- the owner cannot be discovered by taking reasonable steps (eg a person finds cash in the street).

But s 2(2) of the Theft Act 1968 states that a person may be treated as dishonest if property is taken, even if the person would have been willing to pay for it. A court must decide if a person acted dishonestly. To prove dishonesty, it would need to be shown that a reasonable person would consider the action(s) dishonest and that the defendant knew that his/her actions would be viewed as dishonest by those standards (see *R v Ghosh* [1982] QB 1053).

Appropriation is given the following meaning in s 3(1) of the Theft Act 1968. It is:

- assuming the rights of an owner of property by keeping it or controlling its movements (eg a girl takes a pen from a shop display and puts it in her pocket); or
- obtaining property innocently and later keeping it and using it as his or her own (eg hiring a ladder and not returning it).

However, when an innocent purchaser pays the right price for property which later turns out to be stolen, he/she will not have committed theft. For example, if a man buys a second-hand bicycle in good faith and then discovers it is stolen, he will not have committed theft (s 3(2) of the Theft Act 1968). It will then be a matter for a civil court to decide who is now the rightful owner—the prior owner or the innocent purchaser. However, if the man finds out the bicycle had been stolen, and decides to keep quiet (or sell it on), then he might have committed theft.

Consent to appropriation may be in doubt if the person has been deceived about the nature of the circumstances. Nor can a person consent to appropriation if he/she is not of sound mind (including having serious learning difficulties, see *R v Hinks* [2000] 4 All ER 833).

Property within the Theft Act 1968 (s 4) includes money and physical items, but also other things such as ideas, see 16.2.1 for details.

Belonging to a person (s 5) means that the person is either the owner or he/she has:

- a proprietary right or interest, for example the owner of a car takes her car to garage for repairs. The mechanic spends time and money on parts repairing and servicing the car. He would now have a proprietary right of interest in the car as he has put an investment into it, and now has part ownership until the debt is settled or agreed. If the owner takes the car without settling or agreeing the debt this might be theft. (see *R v Turner* (No 2) [1971] 1 WLR 901);
- possession, for example whoever has the vehicle in his/her possession. Whether that possession is lawful depends on the circumstances and the timing. If the owner of the car took it without having paid then his/her possession might not be lawful; or
- control, for example the mechanic who carries out the repairs on the car.

The intention to permanently deprive (s 6(1)) is shown by a person treating another person's property as if it were his or her own. This could include:

- lending and borrowing over an extended time scale (eg borrowing a sewing machine from somebody and then lending it to someone else); or
- pawning an item (eg going to a pawnbroker's shop with another person's laptop and receiving a loan of money in exchange).

The offence of theft is triable either way. If the value of the property stolen is less than £5,000, the offence is tried summarily (s 22A of the Magistrates' Courts Act 1980). The penalty if tried summarily is six months' imprisonment and/or a fine, or for retail property worth £100 or less a PND can be used (see 10.13.2). The penalty on indictment is up to seven years' imprisonment. The police powers for entry and search provided under PACE 1984 for indictable offences (see 10.8.5) apply for all suspected thefts (s 176 of the Anti-Social Behaviour, Crime and Policing Act 2014).

16.2.1 The definition of property within the Theft Act 1968

Property in the context of the Theft Act 1968 has its usual common meaning of a moveable object (such as items for sale in a shop) or an individual's personal property (which includes a wide variety of things such as wallets, smartphones, illegal drugs, pets), and money (notes and coins). However it also includes intangible items, for example air in an oxygen tank, space in a skip, and trademark logos (but not electricity (see 16.7)). 'Things in action' are also taken to be property under the Act. By 'things in action' the law is referring not to tangible objects, but instead to rights eg to sue (to take civil legal action against another). For the trainee police officer, considering property as a 'thing in action' is most likely to occur in connection with alleged crime involving bank or building society accounts, for example which a person entrusted by an organization makes out a cheque to him/herself. When we deposit funds in a bank account the ownership of the money passes to the bank but in turn we gain under the law the right to 'sue' the bank for this amount back (this right to sue is the 'thing in action'). If somebody else tries to dishonestly debit our bank balance by transferring money to their own account, they are unwittingly attempting to steal our right to sue for the money, not the money itself.

16.2.1.1 Land as property

Land itself generally cannot be stolen (although rights to land can), so if, for example, a home-owner goes on holiday and her neighbour moves the fence over a little to increase the size of his garden (and hence decrease the size of hers), this would not be regarded as theft. (The victim would have to pursue such a matter in a civil court.) However, if a trustee in charge of an estate or a person with a power of attorney chose to sell another's land for profit, this could amount to theft. Turf, top soil, and cultivated trees and shrubs, and parts of buildings (roof tiles, fireplaces, and fixtures and fittings) are sometimes removed without permission. These items are all regarded as 'real property' so taking such items could therefore amount to theft. Whole buildings however cannot be stolen as such.

16.2.1.2 Wild plants and animals on land

The taking of wild plants, fruit, flowers, and fungi only amounts to theft if they are taken:

* for sale, reward, or a commercial purpose; or
* in such a manner that the plant or fungus cannot grow back (eg they have been uprooted).

The taking of wild animals from land can be regarded as theft but only if:

* the animal has been tamed and was kept in captivity such as in a zoo or a home; or
* the animal had been killed there without the landowner's permission, and taken (ie poaching).

Note however that other legislation such as the Wildlife and Countryside Act 1981 might prohibit the taking of certain wild animals and plants in a wider range of circumstances.

> **TASK 1** Now that you know what constitutes a theft, think of three incidents of theft that you are aware of, either through the media or other means, and try and identify the five elements of theft within each of those incidents.

16.3 Robbery and Blackmail

Robbery and blackmail are two separate offences under the Theft Act 1968, but there are some similarities. Robbery is theft involving the use of physical force (or the threat of force) to appropriate property belonging to another person. For blackmail, pressure is also put on the victim with the aim of causing him/her a loss. However, for blackmail no property needs to have been taken and no physical force needs to be involved for the offence to be proved.

16.3.1 Robbery

Robbery is the act of stealing from a person whilst using (or threatening the use of) force or violence (s 8 of the Theft Act 1968). It is an aggravated form of the primary offence of theft and therefore, for robbery to be proved, theft has to be proved first. Force or a threat of force must be used immediately before, at the time of the theft, and in order to carry out the theft.

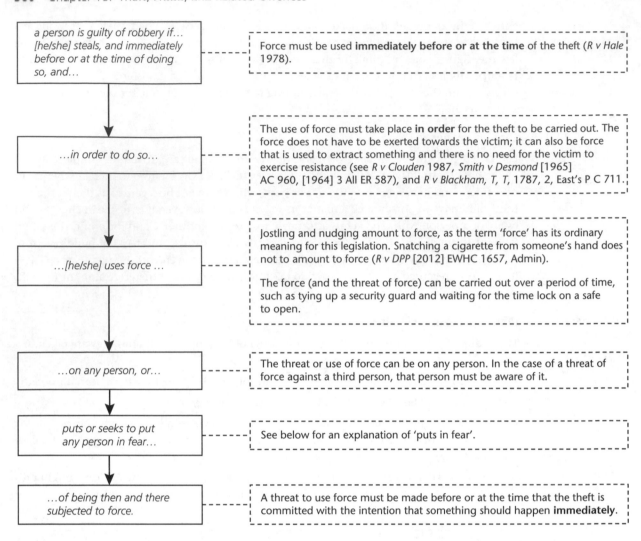

There are two main ways the 'puts in fear' element of the offence could be established:

- The victim's statement could show that he/she was put in fear; note however that the measure of fear is not important, because the fortitude shown by different people will inevitably vary (see *R v DPP*; *B v DPP* [2007] EWHC 739 (Admin), 171 JP 404); or
- the state of mind of the suspect (as seeking to put a person in fear of force) could be evidenced from the suspect's statement. It could also be proved by evidence from other witnesses or circumstantial evidence, such as the suspect wielding an offensive weapon.

When force is threatened, but the force is to be used against a third person, he/she must know about it; he/she must 'apprehend' the force. For example, imagine a man goes into the bank and passes a note to the bank teller to hand over cash or he will stab the woman behind him in the queue. The woman does not know the threat has been made, so even if the teller hands over the money this would not be robbery (although it might be blackmail, see 16.3.2).

In terms of the timing of the force or threat of force, if a suspect says 'Give me your mobile now, or I'll stab you', and the mobile is handed over it would be robbery. If however a suspect says to a victim, 'If you don't give your mobile to me before the end of school this afternoon, I'm going to stab you'; it is not robbery as the threat of force is for the future, but it might be blackmail. If force is used after the theft, it would not be robbery but the two separate offences of theft and assault could be considered. An example of this could be a man snatching a woman's mobile phone from her hand without force and then pushing her over. Similarly, if at the end of a fight, as an afterthought, a man sees the opportunity to dishonestly take an item of property from somebody he has injured in the fight, then that is not robbery; it is assault and theft.

Note that all five elements of theft must be proven (see 16.2) to have applied at the time of the robbery. For example, in *R v Vinall and another* [2011] EWCA Crim 6252, it was held that although violence had been used at the time a pedal bike was initially taken, there was no intention to permanently deprive until later when the suspects decided to abandon the cycle, and so the original conviction of robbery was unsafe.

The offence of robbery is triable on indictment only and the maximum penalty is life imprisonment.

16.3.2 Blackmail

A person commits the offence of blackmail if he/she makes any unwarranted demand with menaces, with a view to making a gain for him/herself or any other person, or with intent to cause a loss to any other person (s 21(1) of the Theft Act 1968). The demand must be unwarranted and unreasonable. Some demands may be considered reasonable, for example in relation to the repayment of a debt.

The evidential requirements are shown in the table.

Evidential requirement	Explanation
Demand	The demand can be made orally or in writing
With a view to gain or loss	The loss or gain must be financial in nature
Menaces	This should be given its ordinary dictionary meaning, for example has a threatening quality or action
The demand must be unwarranted	The court must decide whether the demand was unreasonable, and whether the suspect believes it was reasonable and proper

The offence of blackmail is triable on indictment only and the maximum penalty is 14 years' imprisonment.

TASK 2

a) Chris is carrying a bag full of shopping in the town centre when the handle breaks and the bag falls to the ground. Jo grabs the bag and makes off, but it breaks open, spilling the contents onto the ground. Jo picks up one of the items and then runs into Chris, causing her to fall over heavily and break her arm. Has Jo committed the offence of robbery?

b) Mike is a bailiff and he arrives at Stav's home to collect £500 on order of a court. Mike tells Stav if he does not hand over the money he will come in and seize £500 worth of property. Has Mike committed the offence of blackmail?

16.4 Burglary and Trespassing

Burglary is a so-called 'volume' and 'acquisitive' crime. Students on pre-join programmes could be set an 'investigation' activity based on a burglary when knowledge concerning the needs of victims, the legislation involved, human rights and similar will be assessed. Trainee police officers will undoubtedly encounter crimes of burglary whilst on Supervised and Independent Patrol. Indeed, burglary may feature as a case study during Phase 3 of the IPLDP.

Burglary is a serious offence; aggravated burglary (see 16.4.2), for example, carries a maximum sentence of life imprisonment. Not all burglaries are reported, sometimes because the victim is unaware that the burglary has occurred or is reluctant to be involved with the police. Research also suggests that an increasing number of burglaries are committed with the main aim of obtaining vehicle keys to steal vehicles (Allcock *et al*, 2011 and Chapman *et al*, 2012).

There is also the phenomenon of distraction burglary (in some forces called 'artifice' burglary), where entry is gained to the home of a person (very often an elderly person) by an offender pretending to be an official. An important case in establishing this type of offence was *R v Boyle* [1954] 2 QB 292, [1954] 2 All ER 721. Boyle was charged with burglary (or 'house breaking' as it was then known) as he had falsely represented himself as employed by the BBC to locate radio disturbances. He thereby gained admittance to the person's home and stole a handbag. On appeal against conviction it was held that the use of deception to gain entry meant he was a trespasser. Artifice burglars usually commit 'spree offences' (a series of similar crimes within a short period of time), probably because the net haul from each residence is relatively small.

The legislation concerning burglary is to be found in ss 9–10 of the Theft Act 1968. We look separately at the basic offence of burglary, then at aggravated burglary, and finally at various aspects of trespass associated with this type of crime.

16.4.1 The basic offence of burglary

The basic offence of burglary is set out in s 9 of the Theft Act 1968. There are two subsections which describe the main ways the offence can be committed, as shown in the diagram.

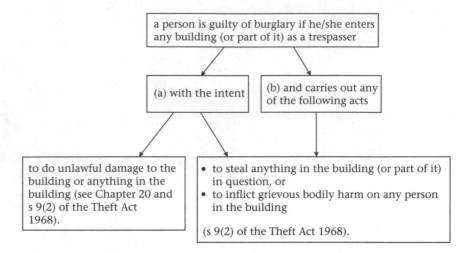

Certain terms, such as 'entry', 'trespasser', and 'building' need to be carefully defined in order to fully appreciate the range of activities that might count as burglary under s 9(1) of the Theft Act 1968.

Entry can be gained in a number of clearly defined ways:

- In person, by walking or climbing into a building, either completely or by inserting a body part (eg an arm or a leg) through a window or letter box. However, there must be more than minimal insertion; sliding a hand between a window and frame from the outside of a building in order to release the catch would be insufficient.
- Using a tool or article as an extension of the human body to carry out one of the relevant offences. In these circumstances no part of the body needs to be inserted, only the article that is being used to gain entry. The article must be used for more than just gaining entry; using a crowbar just to prise open a door would not qualify as the full offence, but a length of garden cane pushed through the letter box of a shop to hook a scarf from a display would qualify as the full offence.
- Using a blameless accomplice in a similar way to using an article as an extension of the suspect's body. Here, for example, a child under 10 years of age (below the age of criminal responsibility) could be lifted through a small window to obtain property from inside. Note that if the child only prepared an entry point the offence has only been attempted.

Trespass involves a person entering a building or part of a building (for the purpose of committing one of the relevant offences) in one of the following ways:

- entering a building for a purpose other than the intended purpose of that building, for example going into a shop with the intention to steal (rather than an intent to browse or buy);
- entering by some kind of deception, for example pretending to represent a utility company for the purpose of reading a meter and being invited into the building ('distraction burglary', referred to earlier);
- crossing over a demarcation line of some kind, unlawfully and without invitation or permission, whether or not the owner knows he/she is trespassing;
- exceeding a general consent to enter premises, such as entering your father's address at night to steal something (see *R v Jones; R v Smith* [1976] 3 All ER 54, [1976] 1 WLR 672).

The person must have guilty knowledge (*mens rea*: see 5.3.2) that what he/she is doing amounts to trespass, or alternatively, not care about whether he/she is trespassing. The trespass must also be voluntary.

(Image © Zoe Lawton-Barrett)

Burglary involves entering a building as a trespasser

The word **'building'** is used within the Theft Act 1968, but is not defined there. However, the meaning of 'a building' is reasonably well established through case law:

- 'building is an ordinary word, which is a matter of fact' (*Brutus v Cozens* [1973] AC 854, 861);
- a building is 'a structure of considerable size and intended to be permanent or at least to endure for a considerable time' (*Stevens v Gourley* (1859) 7 CBNS 99); and
- 'a building need not necessarily be a completed structure; it is sufficient that it should be a connected and entire structure' (Judge Lush in *R v Manning & Rogers* (1871) CA). A house under construction becomes a building when it has all its walls and a roof.

Examples of buildings other than houses include garages and garden sheds, but force policy and procedures may vary with regard to burglary from different types of building.

A dwelling is defined within the Theft Act 1968 as an inhabited building or a vehicle or vessel which is inhabited at the time of the offence (the occupier need not be present at the time of the burglary). An inhabited houseboat moored at a river bank is regarded as a building for the purposes of the Theft Act 1968. Similarly, a motor home or caravan inhabited during a holiday is a building (but not when it is parked and empty during the winter). However, a tent would not be included since it is not a semi-permanent structure. We provide further information on the definitions of premises and locations in 9.2.

This legislation also covers part of a building, and when a person is lawfully within a building but enters a part of it that he/she is not meant to enter (for example if a customer in a shop goes behind the counter to take money out of the till). It will be a matter for the jury to decide whether the area in question amounts to 'part of a building' from which the general public are excluded (see *R v Walkington* [1979] 2 All ER 716, [1979] 1 WLR 1169).

16.4.1.1 Sections 9(1)(a) and 9(1)(b)

Subsection 9(1)(a) relates to intent only, while s 9(1)(b) relates to actually carrying out the acts (as shown in the diagram at the start of 16.4.1).

For an offence under s 9(1)(a) of the Theft Act 1968 the suspect must enter a building (or part of a building) as a trespasser and intend to:

- steal anything in the building;
- inflict grievous bodily harm on anyone in the building; or
- unlawfully damage the building or anything inside it.

However, the acts do not have to be committed, only intended. The intent can be proved in a number of ways (or in combination), such as the suspect admitting to having guilty knowledge or criminal intent to commit the offence. Alternatively, other suspects (who admit to involvement in committing the offence) might name the suspect as an accomplice.

Circumstantial evidence can also help prove intent, such as finding the suspect in the building in possession of property that is known to originate from the premises. Witness statements, and the arresting officer's observations on the suspect's proximity to the crime scene when he/she was arrested could also be used. Fingerprint evidence could also indicate the suspect had been at the location (see 26.6).

If the offence relates to an intent to inflict GBH then the entry must have been made with that in mind. Consequently, in relation to proving the offence, the same degree of evidence of intent will be required as would be needed to prove intent under s 18 of the Offences Against the Person Act 1861 (see 15.3.2).

Under s 9(1)(b) of the Theft Act 1968, burglary involves trespassing and committing acts which amount to:

- theft (or attempted theft); or
- inflicting GBH (or attempting to inflict GBH).

(Note that subsection (b) does not include inflicting unlawful damage.) In relation to inflicting GBH, the meaning of 'inflict' includes situations where force is applied indirectly (*R v Wilson* (1983)). For example, it would include a situation where a woman in her home is frightened by a burglar and as a result falls down the stairs and breaks her leg; harm has been inflicted by the suspect, even though there has been no application of force. For further information on judging whether the acts amount to an attempt, see 22.2.

An offence under either subsection is triable either way, and the penalty if tried summarily is six months' imprisonment and/or a fine. If tried on indictment the maximum penalty is ten years' imprisonment (14 years if the building or part of the building was a dwelling), and at least three years for a third domestic burglary.

16.4.2 Aggravated burglary

Aggravated burglary (s 10 of the Theft Act 1968) involves the use of weapons or explosives to commit burglary. The types of weapon or explosive (articles) covered by this legislation are shown in the table, and can be recalled by the mnemonic WIFE.

Article	Details	Theft Act 1968
Weapon of offence	Any article made or adapted for use for causing injury or incapacitation to a person, or intended for such use (see 18.2.1 on offensive weapons)	s 10(1)(b)
Imitation firearm	Anything which has the appearance of being a firearm, whether capable of being discharged or not (see 18.8)	s 10(1)(a)
Firearm	Includes an airgun or air pistol (see 18.3) and 'component parts' of a firearm (ie parts essential to discharging the weapon such as the gun barrel, chamber, cylinder), but not 'additions'*	s 10(1)(b)
Explosive	Any article manufactured for the purpose of producing a practical effect by explosion (not fireworks or matches), or intended by the person having it for that purpose	s 10(1)(c)

* see 18.3.1.1 for details.

The phrase 'has with him' has the same meaning as 'constructive possession' which means he/she is carrying the item, including an item in a bag the person is carrying. (The meaning is therefore not the same as under the Firearms Act 1968 where the item can be at a short distance, for example in the boot of a car 50 metres away.) Anyone else who is present and knows about the constructive possession is also regarded as having constructive possession.

The point in time when the offence is committed depends upon the subsection and the type of burglary:

- for a s 9(1)(a) burglary, the offence is committed the moment a person enters a building with intent (and has in his/her possession one of the WIFE articles);
- for a s 9(1)(b) burglary, the offence is committed when the person commits the theft or grievous bodily harm (and has in his/her possession one of the WIFE articles).

This offence is triable by indictment only and the penalty is life imprisonment.

16.4.3 Trespass offences related to burglary

A trespass or vagrancy offence may be committed if an offender enters a premises but his/her actions do not amount to burglary.

Trespassing with a weapon of offence is committed when a person is on any premises as a trespasser (after having entered as such) and has a weapon of offence in his/her possession without lawful authority or reasonable excuse (s 8 of the Criminal law Act 1977). It is different from burglary under s 9(1)(a), because there is no intent to commit theft, GBH or damage. The offence is triable summarily and the penalty is three months' imprisonment and/or a fine.

Trespassing with an intent to commit a sexual offence is covered under s 63 of the Sexual Offences Act 2003. The offender must be on premises or land without the owner's or the occupier's consent and know that he/she is trespassing (or be reckless as to whether he/she is trespassing). There must also be an intent to commit a sexual offence while there, and this could be proved from statements from the offender or intended victim, or items seized from the offender at the scene (such as a knife). The intent can be formed at any time, for example before entering the premises, or only later while on the premises. It is immaterial whether any sexual offence is actually committed. The offence is triable either way. The penalty if tried summarily is six months' imprisonment and/or a fine not exceeding the statutory maximum, and on indictment ten years' imprisonment.

The Vagrancy Act 1824, particularly s 4, could be used when a suspect is found on enclosed premises in the open air or land for any unlawful purpose, such as preparing to commit a burglary or theft. 'Enclosed premises in the open air' would include a house, a shed, or a warehouse, and can mean inside a room or a building. But it does not include the situation where a person is on premises where he/she is entitled to be, but has been found in a particular room. For example, a man could not be found guilty of this offence if he wandered from a communal hallway into a private room which was part of the same premises, because the room itself would not be an enclosed area in the open air (*Talbot v Oxford City Justices*, The Times, 15 February 2000). Enclosed premises can also include an outdoor area such as an enclosed garden or yard that has a defined boundary, and it does not matter if there are gaps in the fence or boundary enclosure. It would not include a university campus truncated by roads and footpaths (see *Akhurst v DPP* [2009] WLR (D) 96).

The person must be on the enclosed premises for an unlawful purpose, so it would not include a person who is hiding from the police following a burglary because the unlawful purpose must be current (*JL v CPS* [2007] WLR (D) 202). Nor would it include a homeless person who sleeps in a shed for just a night or two (but see 14.8.4 if residency is suspected). The offence under s 4 of the Vagrancy Act 1824 is triable summarily and the penalty is three months' imprisonment and/or a fine.

TASK 3 Georgia enters a house as a trespasser with intent to steal jewellery for which there is a demand at local car boot sales. While she is on the premises, and as a precaution against capture, she takes a screwdriver from a cupboard under the stairs. She continues the search, still with the screwdriver. Twenty minutes later, the occupier returns and Georgia stabs her, causing serious injury. Has burglary been committed? Give reasons for your answers. (Consider only the offences relating to burglary here.)

16.5 Stolen Goods and the Proceeds of Crime

Stolen goods includes 'money and every other description of property, except land, and includes things severed from the land by stealing' (s 34(2)(b) of the Theft Act 1968). For this offence goods are considered to be 'stolen goods' if they have been obtained through theft, blackmail, or fraud (ss 1 and 21 of the Theft Act 1968, and s 1 of the Fraud Act 2006, respectively).

Stolen goods also include any gain or return from the disposal of the original stolen items such as money or other items which have been received in exchange (s 24(2) of the Theft Act 1968). These are known as 'notionally stolen goods'. After the original theft there is often a whole chain of events, and each of the handlers in this process commits the offence of handling stolen goods, if each has guilty knowledge (*mens rea*) that the goods were originally acquired by a theft. The chain will only be broken when a person receiving the goods is unaware of their origins.

We also cover the Proceeds of Crime Act 2002. It is not always possible for a criminal to benefit from a crime if the items remain in their original state. In the majority of cases, the profits have to be realized, exchanged, or hidden to be of any worth, for example through money laundering.

16.5.1 Handling stolen goods

This offence is described in s 22 of the Theft Act 1968 and is committed when a person handles goods that they know or believe to have been stolen. The person can receive the items, or agree to or assist with their retention, removal, disposal or realization by another person. This could be for the benefit of, another person. It is also an offence to make arrangements for any of these acts.

The meaning of receiving has been established through case law as 'gaining possession or control', and would obviously include carrying or holding the goods. But it also includes having control over goods, which is when a person has remote possession; the goods could be kept in storage in a garage or lock-up, for example. The receiver does not need to gain in any way from handling the goods, but he/she must know that the goods are stolen at the time of their receipt, and there must be proof that the goods were actually received. If the receiver is still negotiating the receipt of the goods, then such an act might be construed as 'arranging' one of the acts which constitute handling. When a person has been charged with receiving stolen goods the onus is always on the prosecution to prove the case. The suspect would have been given an opportunity at interview to explain how he/she had innocently acquired the stolen property. If the jury sees the explanation as reasonable then the defendant might be acquitted. If no explanation is given then the judge might direct the jury to the fact the defendant had been found with stolen property and did not account for this (see *R v Schama, R v Abramovitch* (1914) 11 Cr App Rep 45, 79 JP 184).

The offence of handling stolen goods can also be committed by a person who is involved in the retention, removal, disposal, or realization of the goods, where:

- retention means continuing to possess something (especially when someone else wants it);
- removal means taking something away from the place where it was;
- disposal means passing on, getting rid of, giving away;
- realization means obtaining money or profit by selling something.

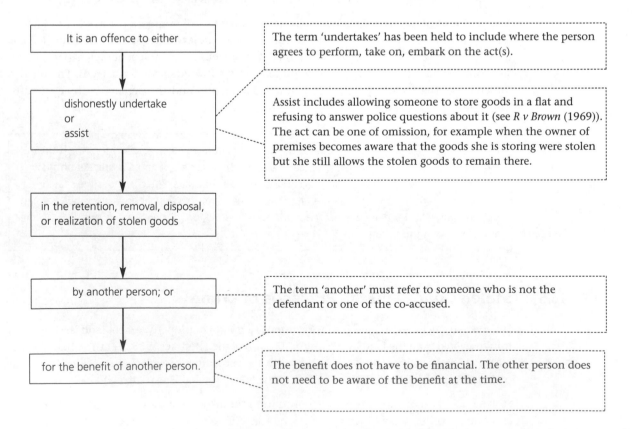

It is an offence to either

⬇

dishonestly undertake
or
assist

⬇

in the retention, removal, disposal, or realization of stolen goods

⬇

by another person; or

⬇

for the benefit of another person.

The term 'undertakes' has been held to include where the person agrees to perform, take on, embark on the act(s).

Assist includes allowing someone to store goods in a flat and refusing to answer police questions about it (see *R v Brown* (1969)). The act can be one of omission, for example when the owner of premises becomes aware that the goods she is storing were stolen but she still allows the stolen goods to remain there.

The term 'another' must refer to someone who is not the defendant or one of the co-accused.

The benefit does not have to be financial. The other person does not need to be aware of the benefit at the time.

The offence of handling stolen goods is triable either way. The penalty if tried summarily is six months' imprisonment and/or a fine, and up to 14 years' imprisonment on indictment. Note that all five elements of theft must be proven (see 16.2) to have applied at the time of the robbery.

Specific Incidents

16.5.1.1 Knowing or believing that items are 'stolen goods'

The handler must know or believe that items have been stolen for his/her actions to be dishonest; suspicion would not be enough. The knowledge or belief could be proved by direct evidence from the thief, admission by the handler, or circumstantial evidence, such as non-standard packaging, or where the goods were offered for sale. A suspect would know the goods were stolen if he/she had been told by the thief or burglar or someone with first-hand knowledge, or might believe that they were if there was no other likely explanation in the circumstances (see *R v Hall* [1985] 1 QB 496).

The court has to decide what is dishonest by everyday standards, and whether the suspect was aware he/she was dishonest by those standards. The suspect may claim to have had a right to the property in law, or would have the owner's consent or that the owner cannot be traced, but none of these is relevant. It would also be perfectly correct to direct a jury to use common sense, such as when a person chooses to become deliberately blind to the circumstances of goods being stolen (see *R v Griffiths* (1974) 60 Cr App Rep 14). In the case of *Hall*, two men carried out a burglary, and took the stolen property, mainly silver and ornaments, away in three suitcases. The following morning the police observed the two men meeting Hall at his flat, and raided it 10 minutes later. The property was recovered along with the cases, and all three men were arrested. When interviewed, Hall initially admitted that he knew it was stolen property, but later denied he knew. He was convicted of receiving stolen goods. On appeal he argued that he did not know or believe the goods to be stolen. The appeal was dismissed, concluding there could be no other reasonable explanation (see *R v Hall* [1985] 81 Cr App R 260 on the distinction between knowledge, belief, and suspicion).

16.5.1.2 The distinction between 'handling' and 'theft'

It is important to distinguish clearly between 'handling' and 'theft'. The following factors will be taken into account: whether the theft was complete, whether there was a break in the proceedings, and whether the suspected handler became involved only after the theft had occurred.

For example, Ellis goes to a large out-of-town electrical store. She steals two radios from the store, and hides them in a bin outside the store. Sal then takes the radios. The table presents a number of different scenarios to illustrate some differences between handling and theft.

Offences committed by Sal the accomplice

Sal's actions ...	Offence committed by Sal
Sal is waiting by pre-arrangement and takes the radios away	Theft
Sal arrives half an hour later by pre-arrangement, and takes the radios away	Theft, particularly if the proceeds are to be shared out between Ellis and Sal. However, handling may be considered if Sal subsequently pays Ellis for the goods
Sal is told where the radios are, but only *after* they have been stolen. Sal then collects the radios	Handling

A thief can become a handler of the property that he/she originally stole, but only if he/she loses control of the property and later decides (whilst the goods can still be referred to as stolen goods) to have dealings with the property once again.

When a thief steals property he/she will often attempt to move it on swiftly. Therefore, when a short time goes by after the theft and an individual is caught with items reported as stolen, he/she owes an explanation as to how he/she came by the property. In the case of *Cash* (*R v Cash* [1985] QB 801, [1985] 2 All ER 128) nine days was considered a reasonable period of time for the possession to be 'recent', and so the 'doctrine of recent possession' could apply.

16.5.1.3 Wrongful credits

In this context a credit is 'wrongful' if the funds concerned were derived from theft, blackmail, fraud, or stolen goods. A person is guilty of an offence under s 24A of the Theft Act 1968 if he/she fails to take reasonable steps for a wrongful credit to be cancelled. The wrongful credit must have been made to an account kept by him/her, (including a joint account or any account in which the person has any other right or interest). He/she must know or believe the credit is wrongful. The maximum sentence for this offence is 10 years' imprisonment.

16.5.2   Proceeds of crime offences

It is an offence under the Proceeds of Crime Act 2002 (POCA) to benefit from any kind of proceeds of crime. For example, the proceeds of crime can be converted into assets in order to make their origin appear legitimate—this would include money laundering. POCA 2002 makes reference to the proceeds of crime as 'criminal property', defining it as any property which the suspect knows or suspects to be or represent, the benefit from any criminal conduct (s 340(3)) in the UK (s 340(2)). Criminal property includes money; property (real, personal, inherited, and moveable); things in action such as patents, copyrights, and trademarks; and other intangible or incorporeal property such as property rights, leases, or mortgages (s 340(9)). Real property is land and things forming part of the land, such as plants and buildings, and moveable property is not attached to the land (eg furniture, art, books, or household goods).

There are three main offences under POCA which cover most eventualities in benefiting from the proceeds of crime:

* **Concealing, converting, or transferring criminal property** (s 327(1)). A person commits an offence if he/she conceals, disguises, converts, transfers, or removes any criminal property from the UK. For example, a man knows that his wife brings back large quantities of alcohol from cross-Channel ferry trips to sell on to local young people. He hides the money behind the panel of the bath in their house. He is guilty of concealing criminal property. Lodging, receiving, retaining, or withdrawing can amount to converting (*R v Fazal 2009* [2009] EWCA Crim 1697).
* **Involvement in arrangements for criminal property** (s 328(1)). A person commits an offence if he/she enters into (or becomes concerned in) an arrangement which he/she knows (or suspects) will help with the acquisition, retention, use, or control of criminal property, by (or on behalf of) another person. The suspect must know or believe it was criminal property when the arrangement was made (see *R v Geary* [2010] WLR (D) 228). For example, a man derives a considerable income from targeting vulnerable householders. He carries out a roof inspection and deceives the victim about its condition, and carries out unnecessary 'repairs' for cash. His live-in partner knows how the money is obtained, and has opened several bank accounts for depositing the profits. Therefore she has been concerned in an arrangement that will help in the retention or control of criminal property.
* **Acquisition, use, and possession of criminal property** (s 329(1)). For example a small-time drug supplier gives some of her profits from selling drugs to a friend. He knows where the money comes from and uses it to buy food; he has 'used' criminal property.

There is a power of search for premises (s 289(1) POCA) if a police officer has reasonable grounds for suspecting the presence of cash obtained through unlawful conduct (s 304(1)), or intended to be used by any person for an unlawful purpose. The officer may also search a suspect and any article he/she possesses at that time (s 289(2) and (3)). The officer's presence must be lawful, and he/she must comply with s 2 of the PACE Act 1984 and the PACE Codes of Practice (see 9.4.1).

16.5.2.1   Defences and penalties

Three defences are available for offences under ss 327(1), 328(1), and 329(1) of the POCA 2002:

* the suspect makes or intends to make (with reasonable excuse) an 'authorized disclosure' to a police, customs, or nominated officer, concerning his/her actions;
* the suspect knows (or reasonably believes) that the criminal conduct took place outside the UK and that it was not unlawful in that other country (s 327(2) and (2)A); and
* law enforcement authorities (such as the police) have a defence if they convert or transfer seized criminal property, for example they place seized money in an interest-earning account.

An additional defence is available for s 329(1) where a person acquires, uses, or has possession of the criminal property for 'adequate consideration'. A shopkeeper could claim this defence if she sells goods to a customer and the customer pays with money that comes from crime. Solicitors or accountants who receive money for costs also have this defence.

The s 327, 328, and 329 offences are all triable either way and the penalty is a fine or imprisonment (six months summarily or up to 14 years on indictment).

> **TASK 4**
>
> 1. In the context of 'handling stolen goods', which, if either, of the following statements is true?
>   a) For the purposes of committing an offence of handling, 'stolen goods' includes money but not land.
>   b) Property obtained as a result of a fraud under s 1 of the Fraud Act 2006 is considered to be 'stolen goods' for the purposes of the offence of handling.
> 2. A police officer carries out a lawful s 1 PACE Act 1984 stop and search on Terri and complies with the PACE Codes of Practice throughout the process. Terri is an 18-year-old persistent offender and prolific shoplifter. His current favoured MO is to steal items such as chocolate and clothes from shops, to sell on quickly and cheaply. Local intelligence has indicated that Terri has also become a courier for local drug suppliers. Intelligence also indicates that he has an extremely modest lifestyle; he does not own any vehicles, lives alone in a one-room bedsit, doesn't drink, but occasionally smokes cannabis. He is registered unemployed, receives state benefits, and has no close family. During the search, £100,000 in used £50 notes is found concealed in various locations in his clothing. Terri cannot account for this money and there is no evidence of its origin. What would be the likelihood of a successful prosecution for acquiring, retaining, using, or controlling the criminal property under s 328(1) of the POCA 2002? Refer to the cases of *R v NW, SW, RC & CC* [2008] EWCA Crim 2 and the conjoined cases of *R v Allpress; R v Symeou; R v Casal; R v Morris; R v Martin* [2009] EWCA Crim 8 for your answer.

16.6   Going Equipped

This offence is described in s 25 of the Theft Act 1968. A wide range of articles are used to carry out (or help carry out) burglary or theft, such as equipment for removing security tags from clothes, or for gaining entry to vehicles or buildings (including keys). The offence is not committed by simple possession of the articles alone. The suspect must be away from his/her place of abode and be on his/her way to carry out a theft or burglary (see *R v Ellames* [1974] 3 All ER 130). A direct connection to a specific burglary or theft does not need to be established, but it must be possible to prove that the article is intended to be used to commit crime (by the suspect or another person). The offence cannot be committed when coming away from the crime.

In terms of possession of the article, the phrase used in the legislation is 'has with him' which includes having it ready to hand, such as in a nearby bush a few feet away, or in a car parked outside the address he intends to break into. Note that the meaning of 'has with him' here is not the same as it is for aggravated burglary (which is more constructive possession, such as in his/her pocket, see 16.4.2).

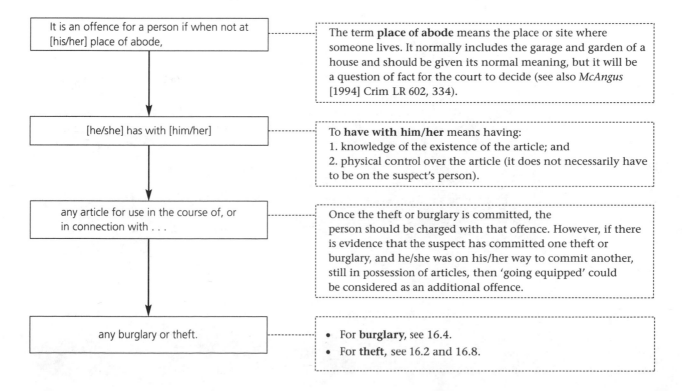

| It is an offence for a person if when not at [his/her] place of abode, | The term **place of abode** means the place or site where someone lives. It normally includes the garage and garden of a house and should be given its normal meaning, but it will be a question of fact for the court to decide (see also *McAngus* [1994] Crim LR 602, 334). |

| [he/she] has with [him/her] | To **have with him/her** means having:
1. knowledge of the existence of the article; and
2. physical control over the article (it does not necessarily have to be on the suspect's person). |

| any article for use in the course of, or in connection with . . . | Once the theft or burglary is committed, the person should be charged with that offence. However, if there is evidence that the suspect has committed one theft or burglary, and he/she was on his/her way to commit another, still in possession of articles, then 'going equipped' could be considered as an additional offence. |

| any burglary or theft. | • For **burglary**, see 16.4.
• For **theft**, see 16.2 and 16.8. |

This offence is triable either way, and the penalty is six months' imprisonment and/or a fine if tried summarily, and up to three years' imprisonment on indictment.

16.7 Abstracting Electricity

Electricity does not fall within the definition of property in the Theft Act 1968, and therefore it cannot be stolen, in legal terms. Here, the term 'abstracting' means illegally taking and using something. The abstracted electricity could be from the mains or from a battery, in a caravan for example. As electricity is not property within the Theft Act 1968, an entry into premises with the sole intention of abstracting electricity will not amount to burglary.

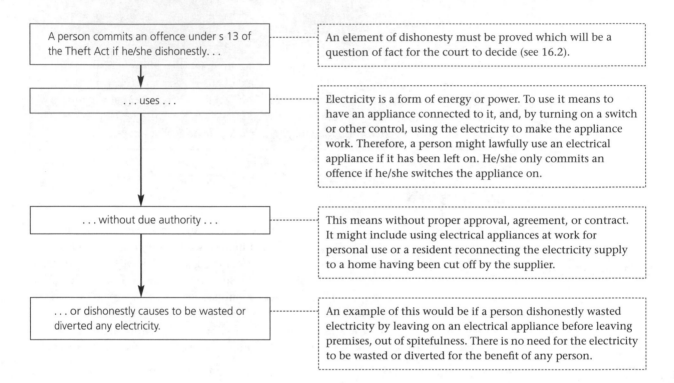

A person commits an offence under s 13 of the Theft Act if he/she dishonestly. . .	An element of dishonesty must be proved which will be a question of fact for the court to decide (see 16.2).
. . . uses . . .	Electricity is a form of energy or power. To use it means to have an appliance connected to it, and, by turning on a switch or other control, using the electricity to make the appliance work. Therefore, a person might lawfully use an electrical appliance if it has been left on. He/she only commits an offence if he/she switches the appliance on.
. . . without due authority . . .	This means without proper approval, agreement, or contract. It might include using electrical appliances at work for personal use or a resident reconnecting the electricity supply to a home having been cut off by the supplier.
. . . or dishonestly causes to be wasted or diverted any electricity.	An example of this would be if a person dishonestly wasted electricity by leaving on an electrical appliance before leaving premises, out of spitefulness. There is no need for the electricity to be wasted or diverted for the benefit of any person.

This offence is triable either way and the penalty is six months' imprisonment and/or a fine if tried summarily, and up to five years' imprisonment on indictment.

TASK 5

1. At each of her BCU briefings throughout the past week, a police constable has been informed about a series of car thefts in her area. One night, she is on patrol in a narrow street of terraced houses with no front gardens or driveways. She knows that a prolific car thief lives there. She notices a car being parked in the street outside his house and goes over. She speaks to the driver and notices gloves, a large bunch of approximately 40 car keys, and a short length of scaffolding pole in the foot-well of the passenger's seat. What could she say to him? Could the offence of 'going equipped' have been committed? What questions does she need to ask in order to establish if this offence has actually been committed?

2. Which of the following offence(s) are neither a 'theft' nor a 'burglary'?:
   a) robbery;
   b) entering a building as a trespasser with the intent to cause damage; and
   c) abstracting electricity.

> **TASK 6** On the way home from a nightclub in the early hours of the morning, Daisy walks through an industrial estate where there are a number of storage warehouses. She decides to go into one of the warehouses without permission, through an open door, with the intention of finding somewhere to sleep for the night. Having entered the warehouse, she forces open a door to another room and in so doing damages the lock. Once inside the room, she switches on an electric fire to keep warm and falls asleep until awoken by a security guard patrolling the industrial estate. Has she committed burglary? Give reasons for your answers.

16.8   Theft of Vehicles and Related Offences

Every year thousands of cars are stolen in England and Wales. Where do they go and why are they stolen? How do we identify stolen vehicles? Here we examine some of the legal aspects and police procedures surrounding a number of vehicle crimes.

The police will receive reports of vehicles being stolen by telephone, through online crime reporting systems, and occasionally personally whilst on patrol. The Police National Computer (see 6.9.1.1) will be updated and if the registration number of the stolen vehicle is spotted by a police officer or an automatic number plate reader system (ANPR), action will be taken. If a stolen vehicle is found by the police, then they can arrange for an approved recovery operator to take it to a secure location (reg 4 of the Removal and Disposal of Vehicles Regulations 1986). It may be examined by a CSI, depending on local policy. (The owner of the vehicle or their insurance company has to pay the recovery and storage fees (Removal, Storage and Disposal of Vehicles (Prescribed Sums and Charges) Regulations 2008).)

Some vehicles are stolen for resale, and their origin will often be disguised when sold on (see 16.8.1.2). Other vehicles may be broken down for parts, particularly older vehicles, as they may have a higher overall value as parts. The cost of vehicle repairs motivates some owners to arrange (or merely claim) that the vehicle has been stolen, so he/she can claim on the insurance.

Other vehicles are taken for 'joyriding'; the vehicle is driven for excitement or as a means of transport, usually for only a brief period of time. This is not theft because there is no intention of permanently depriving the owner of the vehicle. The offence of TWOC (taking a conveyance without consent, see 16.8.2) was created as a separate offence in the Theft Act 1968 to cover these circumstances. TWOC may also result in damage and injury, so we also describe 'aggravated vehicle taking'. We also cover 'interference' and 'tampering' with motor vehicles, along with the theft of pedal cycles.

16.8.1   Detection of stolen vehicles

There are a number of ways of establishing that a particular vehicle is a stolen vehicle and some everyday clues can trigger an alert police officer to investigate a little further. For example:

- Is it a type of vehicle that is more likely to be stolen? (see Task 8)
- Is the vehicle displaying the correct registration plates? Do the plates look as though they have been replaced or have new plates been stuck over the old plates? Do the plates seem different from the rest of the car—for example, is the car clean and the plates old and dirty, or the other way round; or are the plates plain, with no reference to a vehicle dealership?

To investigate further, a police officer will need to establish the specific identifying features of a vehicle such as the VIN number (see 16.8.1.1).

16.8.1.1   The identifying features of a vehicle

Vehicles normally have a number of identifying features unique to each vehicle, and these can be easily recalled by using the police mnemonic VICE as shown in the table. The identifying features are recorded on DVLA databases along with the colour, make, and model of the vehicle. Police control-room personnel have access to databases listing the positions of the stamped-in VIN, the VIN plate, and the engine number for all vehicle makes and models.

V	Vehicle Identification Number (VIN)	The 17-character VIN unique to that vehicle. The VIN is displayed on the dashboard (visible through the windscreen) on most vehicles. All vehicles used on or after 1 April 1980 have the VIN on a metal plate attached to a part of the vehicle not normally subject to replacement, and in a conspicuous and accessible position.
I	Index number or registration plate	All mechanically propelled vehicles used on public roads require a registration mark (number).
C	Chassis number (same as VIN)	All vehicles used on or after 1 April 1980 will have their 17-character VIN stamped into the chassis or frame of the car. The location is often described in the vehicle handbook.
E	Engine number	Engine numbers are often tucked away in locations most easily seen when (or if) the engine is taken out of the vehicle. Engines are also sometimes replaced, so the fact that an engine number cannot be found should not in itself be a cause for suspicion.

(Image © Kevin Lawton-Barrett)

Example of a VIN on the chassis of a VW camper van

16.8.1.2 Disguising stolen vehicles

When a vehicle is reported as stolen it is recorded on police and other databases using the VICE identifying features. So if it is to be sold on or used long term it needs to have a new 'identity'. The new VIN and other VICE features have to be taken from a similar vehicle so that the colour and make, etc will match that of the stolen vehicle. Often, the new identifying features will be taken from a vehicle that has been severely damaged, and has been reported as such to the DVLA on a V23 form. (A V23 is sent to the DVLA either by an insurance company whenever a total loss payment is made on a vehicle, or by a police officer when reporting a vehicle that has been 'written off' in an accident. It is legal to repair these vehicles and use them on the roads, but there will be evidence of extensive repairs.)

The perpetrator first obtains the identifying features of a damaged vehicle (see 16.8.1.1) with a V23 form, and then steals a similar vehicle. The identifying features from the damaged vehicle are transferred to the stolen vehicle (and the damaged vehicle is usually scrapped). The stolen vehicle with its new identity will then be sold to an innocent purchaser.

Thus police officers must be alert to vehicles with identifying features that do not exactly match the database records. Some vehicles are exported as their resale value may be higher in other countries.

16.8.1.3 Procedure for checking vehicle VICE details

The recommended procedure is outlined in the diagram. If the vehicle needs further examination, a force vehicle examiner can carry this out.

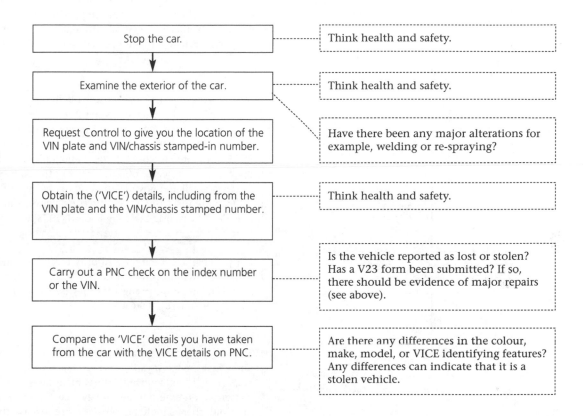

TASK 7 In 16.8.1.3, references are made to stopping the car, examining the car, and locating the VIN and VIN/chassis number. What powers or regulations (1) allows a police officer to stop and examine a car; and (2) require the car to be equipped with a VIN or chassis number?

16.8.2 Taking a Conveyance without the Owner's Consent or Authority (TWOC)

This offence (TWOC) is described in s 12 of the Theft Act 1968. 'Taking a conveyance' is a very common offence in England and Wales and, unfortunately, modern technology has so far failed to deter criminals from this activity. Note that a conveyance is any equipment constructed or adapted for the carriage of a person or persons whether by land, water, or air. (It does not include a conveyance constructed or adapted for carrying items other than people, such as the pedestrian-controlled vehicle used by postal workers to transport mail. Pedal cycles are not included under this legislation either; taking a cycle is covered by another subsection described in 16.8.3.)

The legislation allows those who have lawful authority to move a conveyance, for example:

- bailiffs can remove a vehicle where loan repayments are overdue;
- the police or the DVLA can remove a vehicle that appears to have been abandoned; and
- the Fire and Rescue Services or the local council can remove an inappropriately parked vehicle.

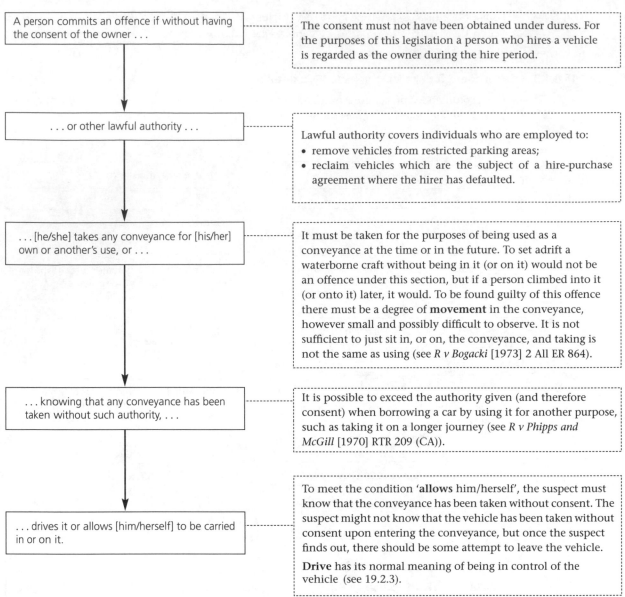

A person commits an offence if without having the consent of the owner . . .

The consent must not have been obtained under duress. For the purposes of this legislation a person who hires a vehicle is regarded as the owner during the hire period.

. . . or other lawful authority . . .

Lawful authority covers individuals who are employed to:
• remove vehicles from restricted parking areas;
• reclaim vehicles which are the subject of a hire-purchase agreement where the hirer has defaulted.

. . . [he/she] takes any conveyance for [his/her] own or another's use, or . . .

It must be taken for the purposes of being used as a conveyance at the time or in the future. To set adrift a waterborne craft without being in it (or on it) would not be an offence under this section, but if a person climbed into it (or onto it) later, it would. To be found guilty of this offence there must be a degree of **movement** in the conveyance, however small and possibly difficult to observe. It is not sufficient to just sit in, or on, the conveyance, and taking is not the same as using (see *R v Bogacki* [1973] 2 All ER 864).

. . . knowing that any conveyance has been taken without such authority, . . .

It is possible to exceed the authority given (and therefore consent) when borrowing a car by using it for another purpose, such as taking it on a longer journey (see *R v Phipps and McGill* [1970] RTR 209 (CA)).

. . . drives it or allows [him/herself] to be carried in or on it.

To meet the condition '**allows** him/herself', the suspect must know that the conveyance has been taken without consent. The suspect might not know that the vehicle has been taken without consent upon entering the conveyance, but once the suspect finds out, there should be some attempt to leave the vehicle.

Drive has its normal meaning of being in control of the vehicle (see 19.2.3).

Case law provides a number of clarifications in relation to this offence. For a floating conveyance the movement can be caused by a sail, but cannot 'be natural movement' created by waves or water currents (see *R v Miller* [1976] Crim LR 147). A conveyance must be taken for the purpose of being used as such (including future use), and not just for 'mischief' (see *R v Stokes* [1982] Crim LR 695). A vehicle ceases to be 'taken' once it has been recovered by the victim, police, or insurance company, but this would probably not include simply receiving a report from a member of the public reporting its whereabouts.

A possible defence (s 12(6) of the Theft Act 1968) is that the person believes that he/she has the consent of the owner or had other lawful authority. This offence is triable summarily and the penalty is six months' imprisonment and/or a fine.

The basic offence of taking a conveyance cannot be attempted (see 22.2 on criminal attempts), as the offence is not indictable. The offence of vehicle interference or tampering with a motor vehicle can be used instead (see 16.8.2.2). Note that as theft is an indictable offence, the offence of theft could also be considered if some form of attempt has taken place.

> **TASK 8** Approximately 1,000 vehicles are taken without the owner's consent in the UK every day. What type of vehicle seems most likely to be taken in your area? If you are a trainee police officer, your area should be able to provide you with factual information on this, including where the vehicles are stolen from, and what happens to them.

16.8.2.1 Aggravated vehicle-taking

A further offence may have been committed under s 12A(1) of the Theft Act 1968 if damage or injury is caused when a vehicle is taken without consent. Injuries may also include shock, and damage includes any damage caused during the whole incident and does not have to be deliberately inflicted.

Section 12(A)(1) of the Theft Act 1968 states that a person commits the offence of aggravated vehicle-taking if he/she first of all commits:

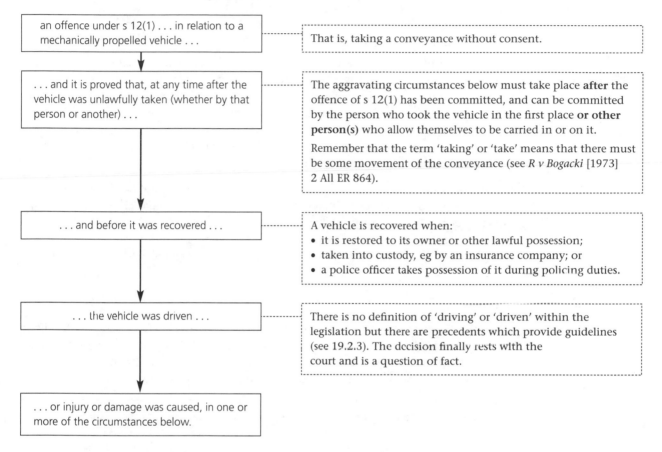

an offence under s 12(1) . . . in relation to a mechanically propelled vehicle . . .	That is, taking a conveyance without consent.
. . . and it is proved that, at any time after the vehicle was unlawfully taken (whether by that person or another) . . .	The aggravating circumstances below must take place **after** the offence of s 12(1) has been committed, and can be committed by the person who took the vehicle in the first place **or other person(s)** who allow themselves to be carried in or on it. Remember that the term 'taking' or 'take' means that there must be some movement of the conveyance (see *R v Bogacki* [1973] 2 All ER 864).
. . . and before it was recovered . . .	A vehicle is recovered when: • it is restored to its owner or other lawful possession; • taken into custody, eg by an insurance company; or • a police officer takes possession of it during policing duties.
. . . the vehicle was driven . . .	There is no definition of 'driving' or 'driven' within the legislation but there are precedents which provide guidelines (see 19.2.3). The decision finally rests with the court and is a question of fact.
. . . or injury or damage was caused, in one or more of the circumstances below.	

The aggravating circumstances (s 12A(2)) for this offence are that:

- the vehicle was driven dangerously on a road or other public place. The courts would consider whether the vehicle was driven 'dangerously' (see 19.8.1). For definitions of 'road' see 19.2.2, and for 'public place' see 9.2;
- an accident occurred (due to the driving of the vehicle) which caused injury to a person or damage to property other than the vehicle. Here an 'accident' is an unintended occurrence which has an adverse physical result, and the court can also take into account what an 'ordinary' person would consider to be an accident (see *R v Morris* [1972] RTR 201); or
- the vehicle suffered damage after being taken, for example by colliding with something. It can be caused by a person other than the person who first took the vehicle.

Possible defences include that the dangerous driving, damage, or accident had occurred before the suspect took the vehicle or that he/she was not in or on the vehicle, or in its 'immediate vicinity' when the dangerous driving, accident, or damage occurred (s 12A(3)). Immediate vicinity is a question of fact for the court to decide. Even if the suspect can disprove aggravating factors, he/she can still be found guilty of the basic offence (s 12A(5)).This offence is triable either way. If the value of the property damaged or destroyed is less than £5,000, the offence is tried summarily (s 22 of the Magistrates' Courts Act 1980). The penalty is a fine (no upper limit) or imprisonment (six months summarily, or two years on indictment). If the accident caused death, the penalty is up to 14 years' imprisonment.

16.8.2.2 Interference and tampering with motor vehicles

When a suspect takes a conveyance without the consent of the owner, in many cases he/she will go through a process of selecting a vehicle, gaining entry either forcibly or by trying door handles, overcoming anti-theft devices such as alarms and steering locks, and then applying a technique such as 'hot wiring' to start the engine. This process inevitably takes time, and sometimes the suspect can be apprehended before the vehicle is taken. However, TWOC is a summary offence (and therefore cannot be attempted under s 1(1) of the Criminal Attempts Act 1981: see 22.2). So the offences of interfering with and tampering with motor vehicles were created to cover situations where TWOC seems to have been attempted.

Section 9(1) of the Criminal Attempts Act 1981 states that it is an offence for a person to interfere with a motor vehicle or trailer, or with anything carried in or on a motor vehicle or trailer with the intention of committing:

- 'theft of the motor vehicle or part of it';
- 'theft of anything carried in or on the motor vehicle or trailer'; or
- the offence of taking a conveyance.

However, actually proving intent is tricky. In 5.3, we discussed the two main building blocks to a criminal act: *actus reus* (the act itself), and *mens rea* (an intention to commit an act). In this case, the act cannot simply be preparation but needs to go further than this. Unfortunately, case law provides us with little guidance on what interference actually means in practice. Nonetheless, it must be proved that the suspect had at least one of the three intentions, but it is not necessary to prove which particular one. This is a summary offence and the penalty is three months' imprisonment and/or a fine.

Tampering as an activity is more readily understood than interference, and the legislation (s 25(1) of the Road Traffic Act 1988) refers specifically to vehicle brakes. It is an offence for a person without lawful authority or reasonable cause to tamper with the brake or any other part of its mechanism, or to get on or into the vehicle. This applies to motor vehicles on a road or in a local authority parking place. It is a summary offence and the penalty is a fine or imprisonment for up to three months.

16.8.3 Taking a pedal cycle

A pedal cycle is not a conveyance for the purposes of s 12(1) of the Theft Act 1968, so the taking of a cycle is not a TWOC offence, but is covered as a separate offence under s 12(5). It includes riding a pedal cycle knowing it to have been taken by another person without consent or lawful authority. The penalty for this offence is six months' imprisonment and/or a fine.

TASK 9 Which of the following would constitute an offence of interfering with a motor vehicle?

1. Trying to removing a horse box from the tow bar of a vehicle in order to steal the horse box.
2. Attempting to remove a go-kart from the garden of a house in order to steal it.
3. Opening the unlocked front driver's door of a car to steal a satnav fixed to the dashboard.
4. Putting super glue in a car door lock to prevent the owner from opening the door.

16.9 Fraud and Bribery Offences

The various Theft Acts (1968, 1978, and 1996) also contained sections addressing aspects of what we tend to call fraud and deception. This proved confusing and much of the law surrounding the crime of fraud is now encapsulated instead in the Fraud Act 2006. In the last report before it closed, the National Fraud Authority (NFA) estimated that annual losses due to fraud in the UK amount to £52 billion (NFA, 2014). More recently, Experian (based on research by the University of Portsmouth) claim that annual losses are closer to £193 billion (Experian, 2016). Younger people are most likely to be victims of consumer fraud (Button, 2009), but all age groups are vulnerable. See the NFA's *Fraud typologies and victims of fraud* (still available online) for interesting further details on the profiles of fraud victims. The responsibilities previously covered by the NFA have now passed to a number of bodies including the City of London Police, the National Crime Agency, the Home Office, and the Cabinet Office.

Generally speaking, the police will only take reports of fraud if the events are imminent or in progress, or if the suspect is known locally or easily identified, or if the victim is vulnerable and perhaps unable to use the telephone or internet. In all other cases, reports will be made to Action Fraud, the national reporting centre for fraud and internet crime in the UK. If a report is taken by the police, a crime reference number is generated and the case referred to the National Fraud Intelligence Bureau (NFIB), run by the City of London Police. A number of support services are available to victims of crime (see 13.7.4). For more information visit the Action Fraud website.

Section 1 of the Fraud Act 2006 states that the offence of fraud can be committed in one or more of three distinctive ways:

1. by false representation, for example returning stolen goods to a shop to try to obtain a refund (s 2);
2. by failing to disclose information, for example omitting important information when applying for a job or health insurance (s 3); and
3. through abuse of position, for example whilst driving a local authority minibus, demanding fares from local residents when the service is actually free (s 4).

For all of these offences there is the same intent; to make a gain for him/herself or another or to cause a loss to another or to expose another to a risk of loss. The gain or loss can be temporary or permanent and could involve 'personal' property, 'real' property, things in action, and other intangible property, such as the name of a company or the copyright to a product. This is similar to the definitions of property under the Theft Act 1968.

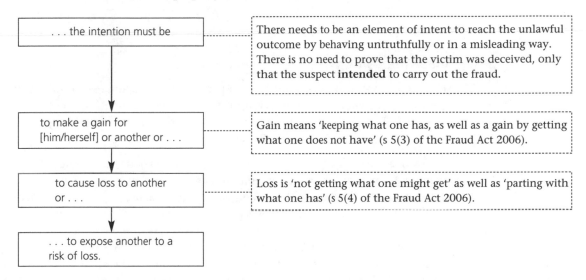

The offences are all triable either way and the penalty is a fine or imprisonment (12 months summarily or up to ten years on indictment).

16.9.1 False representation

Section 2 of the Fraud Act 2006 states that a person commits an offence if he/she 'dishonestly makes a false representation and intends…to make a gain for [him/herself] or another, or to cause loss to another or to expose another to a risk of loss'. This would include a person who advertises an item for sale (including online), purporting it to be genuine when he/she knows it is a fake. Even if nobody sees the ad or responds, the person has still risked causing somebody a loss. The offence is committed the moment the item is listed.

The term 'dishonesty' is not defined in the Act, but in case law it has been held to relate to the test of whether the dishonesty would challenge the standards of a reasonable and honest person, and whether the conduct was considered dishonest by the suspect him- or herself (see *R v Ghosh* [1982] QB 1053).

A representation can be made to a device or machine which is designed to receive, convey, or respond to communication; for example, bank ATMs or coin-operated cigarette dispensers (s 2(5)). A representation is **false** (s 2(2)) if it is;

• 'untrue'; for example, using foreign coins or objects to obtain cigarettes from a machine; or
• 'misleading'; for example, assuming the identity of a charity worker and shaking a stolen charity collection tin in a busy street.

Recent case law makes it clear that the suspect must intend that the false representation will cause a gain or loss (*R v Gilbert* [2012] EWCA Crim 2392).

16.9.2 Failure to disclose information

Section 3 of the Fraud Act 2006 states that a person commits an offence if he/she 'dishonestly fails to disclose to another person information which [he/she] is under a legal duty to disclose, and intends, by failing to disclose the information to make a gain for [him/herself] or another, or to cause loss to another or to expose another to a risk of loss'.

The failure to disclose can be made by an oral or written omission. The legal duty to disclose (and some examples of a failure to disclose) derives from:

- statute, for example where a company must publish yearly accounts under company law, but fails to do so;
- assumed good faith, such as failing to disclose a serious illness in order to reduce health insurance premiums;
- the express or implied terms of a contract, from the custom of a particular trade or market; such as an estate agent failing to reveal to a client all the bids she received for a property, so her friend can buy it at a lower price;
- the existence of a fiduciary relationship (where a person is entrusted with another person's financial arrangements), for example where a solicitor does not tell his client there is another beneficiary to a contract.

To provide evidence for this offence, it is often easiest to show that there was a failure to pass on information to the victim. He/she will then have a legitimate claim for seeking damages for non-disclosure, and will also be able to clarify his/her position regarding future consent.

16.9.3 Abuse of position

This offence (s 4) can be committed by a person who occupies a position in which he/she is expected to safeguard (or not to act against) the financial interests of another. The offence is committed if he/she dishonestly abuses that position intending to make a gain for him/herself or another, or to cause loss to another or to expose another to a risk of loss.

The offence could apply for anyone who has relied upon or has knowledge of another person's financial affairs, such as between an employer and an employee, between a trustee and a beneficiary or between cohabitees. The meaning of the term 'abuse' in this context is not defined in law but is held to have its normal everyday meaning, and it can be an act or a failure to act (s 4(2)). Examples might include a person who has access to the bank account of a vulnerable relative and takes money for their own use, or where housemates pool money to pay bills and one of them is entrusted to pay the bills, but instead misuses the money dishonestly. The abuse must take place at the time the suspect occupies the position of trust, and not later. For example, a woman leaves a company but still has the contact details of clients stored on a disc, and then sells the information to another company. As she does not occupy the position at the time she formed the dishonest intent, the s 4 offence is not committed (although she might have committed an offence of possessing an article for committing fraud, see 16.9.4).

16.9.4 Possession, making, or supplying of articles for committing fraud

A person can commit an offence by 'going equipped' (see 16.6) to carry out a fraud, rather than actually having committed the fraud itself. In this context, going equipped means being in possession or control of articles for use in frauds (s 6 of the Fraud Act 2006) or making or supplying such articles (s 7).

The articles can include clothing to imitate company representatives, mechanisms to slow down electricity meters, and bogus satellite TV cards, as well as false identity cards (see 16.9.7), credit cards, cheque books, shopping bags, till receipts, passports, and driving licences. It also includes a computer program or data held in electronic form (see 21.2).

Section 6 of the Fraud Act 2006 covers possession or having the article under his/her control. For possession, the person must have immediate physical control over the article and know that it is there. Having control would include having physical control at a distance (eg possessing the key to a cupboard where the item is kept) and also knowing that the article was there. If one person is shown to be in possession of an article, then any other person present who is also aware of the possession is also guilty of possession.

Unlike most other statutory preventative measures, this offence can be committed anywhere, including when the articles are located in the suspect's home. (Statutory preventative measures are pieces of legislation designed to prevent criminal offences from taking place, for example 'going equipped' to steal and 'carrying offensive weapons'.)

Section 7 of the Fraud Act 2006 states that a person commits an offence if he/she makes, adapts, supplies (or offers to supply) any article, knowing that it is designed or adapted for use in the course of or in connection with fraud (or intending it to be used to commit or assist with the commission of fraud). An example of this could be a man offering to make a false ID card for a woman, when he knows she is going to use it to pose as a charity collector and collect donations from the public. Under s 1 of the PACE Act 1984, a police officer has the power to search (see 9.4.2) for articles made or adapted for use in fraud.

The offences are triable either way and the penalty is a fine or imprisonment (12 months summarily, five years on indictment for a s 6 offence, and ten years on indictment for a s 7 offence).

16.9.5   Dishonest obtaining of services

Section 11 of the Fraud Act 2006 covers obtaining a service by dishonest means. The services must be of a type for which payment is generally required and would include bus or train rides, haircuts, a stay in a hotel room, downloading music, dry-cleaning, admission to a sports event, table attention at a restaurant, and tuition. The service must be obtained through a dishonest act (not an omission), such as using a false credit card, giving false personal details, and making false promises or agreements. The proof of the dishonesty should follow the guidelines in *R v Ghosh* [1982] QB 1053 (see 16.2 on dishonesty). The offence is triable either way and the penalty is a fine or imprisonment (12 months summarily or five years on indictment).

16.9.6   Making off without payment ('bilking')

If no dishonest representation takes place and a person had every intention to pay for goods before the property was obtained, but then makes off without paying, an offence is committed under s 3 of the Theft Act 1978 (rather than fraud under s 1 of the Fraud Act 2006). This particular offence is often referred to as 'bilking'. For example, a person might fill up with petrol on the forecourt of a filling station with every intention of paying for the petrol, but on seeing the staff otherwise engaged and no other customers around, decide to drive off without paying. Note that this offence only applies if 'payment on the spot' is the norm in that particular situation, such as collecting goods on which work has been done (eg shoe repairs) or paying for a service which has been provided (eg a haircut). It does not apply if a customer has a credit arrangement or a 'tab' with the service provider. The offence is triable either way and the penalty is a fine or imprisonment (six months summarily or two years on indictment).

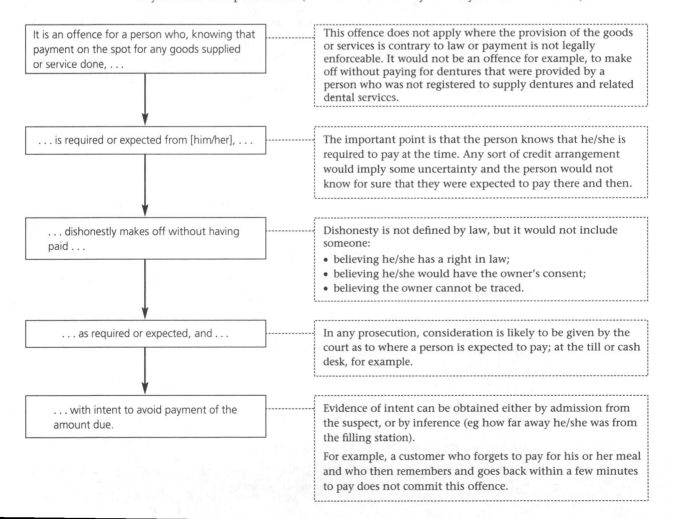

It is an offence for a person who, knowing that payment on the spot for any goods supplied or service done, ...	This offence does not apply where the provision of the goods or services is contrary to law or payment is not legally enforceable. It would not be an offence for example, to make off without paying for dentures that were provided by a person who was not registered to supply dentures and related dental services.
... is required or expected from [him/her], ...	The important point is that the person knows that he/she is required to pay at the time. Any sort of credit arrangement would imply some uncertainty and the person would not know for sure that they were expected to pay there and then.
... dishonestly makes off without having paid ...	Dishonesty is not defined by law, but it would not include someone: • believing he/she has a right in law; • believing he/she would have the owner's consent; • believing the owner cannot be traced.
... as required or expected, and ...	In any prosecution, consideration is likely to be given by the court as to where a person is expected to pay; at the till or cash desk, for example.
... with intent to avoid payment of the amount due.	Evidence of intent can be obtained either by admission from the suspect, or by inference (eg how far away he/she was from the filling station). For example, a customer who forgets to pay for his or her meal and who then remembers and goes back within a few minutes to pay does not commit this offence.

TASK 10 At what stage of a visit to a restaurant are the following offences potentially committed by people who fail to pay for a meal:

- s 1 of the Fraud Act 2006;
- s 3 of the Theft Act 1978; and
- s 11 of the Fraud Act 2006?

To answer the question, complete the table by describing in the right-hand column the likely actions and thought processes of the customers at each stage of the visit to the restaurant, linking these to ss 1 and 11 of the Fraud Act 2006 and s 3 of the Theft Act 1978. The case of *DPP v Ray* [1974] AC 370 may assist.

People enter the restaurant and order a meal	
Having ordered the meal, they wait at the table for it to be served	
The meal is served to the table	
Having consumed the meal, they are expected to pay	
They leave the restaurant	

16.9.7 False and fake identification documents

The Licensing Act 2003 (Mandatory Licensing Conditions) requires all licensed premises to have age verification checks, and this will usually rely on documentation provided by customers. Some young people use a false identification document, which could be:

- a genuine and unadulterated document being used by a different person;
- a genuine document that has been altered; or
- a fake document (a copy of a genuine document, or a form of ID that does not exist).

Possession without reasonable excuse of a false identity document or an identity document which relates to another person is an offence under s 6(1) of the Identity Documents Act 2010, is triable either way. The penalty is a fine or imprisonment (six months summarily or two years on indictment).

Possession of an identity document which is false, which the person knows or believes to be false, and intends to use it to establish personal information about him/herself or to induce another to ascertain personal information about him/her is an offence under s 4(1) of the Identity Documents Act 2010. This offence is triable on indictment only and the maximum penalty is 10 years' imprisonment, a fine or both.

The Home Office document *False ID Guidance: July 2012* available online provides details on how to recognize genuine acceptable forms of ID, the most common forms of false ID, and the procedures for dealing with found ID documents.

16.9.8 Bribery

The Bribery Act 2010 provides an effective legal framework to combat bribery in the public and private sectors. It also includes offences relating to bribery of foreign officials, and commercial organizations that allow their agents to commit bribery. An organization will have a defence if it provides evidence of having policies and practices in place that prohibit bribery.

The offences relate to bribing another person and to accepting a bribe. Two particular terms used within the legislation have particular meanings:

- 'improper performance' means failing to perform a function or activity with good faith, or impartially (s 4); and
- 'relevant function or activity' includes all functions of a public nature, for example those carried out by public authorities (such as the police), and all activities connected with a business, trade, or profession (s 3).

The offences are triable either way and the penalties are a fine or imprisonment (one year if tried summarily, and 12 years on indictment).

16.9.8.1 Bribing or attempting to bribe another person

Under s 1(1) of the Bribery Act 2010, it is an offence for person P to offer, promise or give a financial or other advantage to another person in order to:

Specific Incidents

- bring about an improper performance by any person of a relevant function or activity; or
- reward any person for such improper performance (s 1(2)).

It is sufficient for P to intend to induce or reward the misconduct; the actual outcome of P's actions are irrelevant. It is also sufficient for P to know or believe that the acceptance of the advantage in itself constitutes the improper performance of a function or activity (s 1(3)). The advantage can be offered, promised, or given by P directly or through a third party (s 1(5)).

16.9.8.2   Requesting, accepting, or benefiting from a bribe

Under s 2(1) of the Bribery Act 2010, person R commits an offence if he/she requests, agrees to receive, or accepts an advantage if:

- R intends improper performance (by anyone) to follow as a consequence (s 2(2));
- R's request (in itself), agreement, or acceptance amounts to improper performance (s 2(3));
- R accepts the reward for anyone's subsequent improper performance(s 2(4)).

It is irrelevant whether R actually receives any advantage. The meaning of 'advantage' is a question of fact for the court to decide.

16.10   Answers to Tasks

TASK 1 You probably considered the following:

1. Was the person dishonest?
2. Did he/she take the property?
3. To whom did the property belong?
4. Did the person show an intention never to give the property back to its owner?

TASK 2 (a) The circumstances do not amount to an offence of robbery because violence was not used in order to steal. This is because Jo picked up the bag and attempted to run off with it; she did not use force to steal it. Jo then picked up an item from the ground and ran into Chris, causing her to fall over and break her arm, and it was only then that force was used. It was used only after the theft had taken place. Force was not used immediately before, at the time, nor in order to steal the bag and the goods, and therefore robbery has not been committed.

(b) The circumstances do not amount to blackmail. Although the threat is unpleasant and detrimental to Stav, it is perfectly lawful as Mike is acting on behalf of a court, and the request is reasonable.

TASK 3 The following offences are likely to have been committed:
- burglary with intent to steal (s 9(1)(a) of the Theft Act 1968), since Georgia entered as a trespasser with the necessary intent;
- burglary (s 9(1)(b) of the Theft Act 1968) has been committed since Georgia, having entered as a trespasser, inflicts grievous bodily harm on the occupier; and
- aggravated burglary (s 10 of the Theft Act 1968) has taken place because, whilst committing the s 9(1)(b) burglary, Georgia was armed with a weapon of offence at the time of the search for something to steal.

TASK 4

1. Both statements are true.
2. Without identifying the specific criminal conduct (or at least recognizing the type of criminal conduct which produced the money in the first place), there is unlikely to be a successful prosecution. The case of *R v NW, SW, RC & CC* [2008] EWCA Crim 2 was important with respect to the interpretation of the POCA 2002. The Court of Appeal ruled that the CPS could not just focus on inexplicable affluence, make the assumption that there was no lawful reason for its presence, and then presuppose that the affluence must result from the proceeds of crime. Unless there is evidence that Terri had the necessary knowledge or suspicion that the property represented a benefit from criminal conduct, there could not be a successful prosecution under s 328(1) of the POCA 2002. Even if it could have been proved that the money was from the unlawful supply of controlled drugs, it was decided in *R v Allpress; R v Symeou; R v Casal; R v Morris; R v Martin* [2009] EWCA Crim 8 that, if a suspect's only role in relation to the drug money was to act as a courier on behalf of another, such property did not amount to property for which the court could have ordered confiscation from him under the POCA 2002. Therefore, only if it could have been

Specific Incidents

proved that Terri had benefited (eg by receiving payments for passing on the money), could he have been successfully prosecuted under s 328(1) of the POCA 2002.

TASK 5

1. In response to this task you may have considered:

- **Has he 'control' over a pair of gloves, a large bunch of approximately 40 car keys, and a short length of scaffold pole?** Yes, they are in his car and in his sight.
- **Can the gloves, a large bunch of approximately 40 car keys, and a short length of scaffold pole be considered as 'any article'?** Yes.
- **Could the articles be used in the course of or in connection with any 'burglary' or 'theft'?** Yes, these are articles which are often used for breaking into cars. (Eg the short length of scaffold pole can be used to break a steering lock.) However, it is not clear at this point whether or not the person has used the articles for any burglary or theft, or whether he was going to use them for such in the future. In order to be found guilty of going equipped the suspect must have some future intention to carry out a burglary or theft and therefore this would need further investigation.

A further consideration is whether the suspect is 'at his place of abode'. There are two issues here. Is the man parked outside his own house? The police officer will need to verify whether it is his house; confirmation could be acquired by making a personal visit to ask inhabitants of the house, checking the voters register, or perhaps asking to see utility bills. And if it is his house, is sitting in a parked car outside a house (with no driveway) equivalent to being 'at his place of abode'? This would be a question of fact for a court to decide.

2. (c) only; abstracting electricity. Interestingly, even though it was mentioned in 16.8 that TWOC is not theft, the Theft Act 1968 (s 25(5)) specifically states that for purpose of going equipped, TWOC will be treated as theft.

TASK 6 No burglary has been committed. Although Daisy entered the storage warehouse as a trespasser, her intention was to sleep, and not to commit any of the offences specified in s 9(1)(a) of the Theft Act 1968. Once inside the warehouse, she damaged the door (which is property), and also abstracted electricity by using the fire, but neither damage to property nor abstraction of electricity are included in the acts listed under s 9(1)(b) of the Theft Act 1968 (which is confined to theft and grievous bodily harm).

TASK 7

1. Section 163 of the Road Traffic Act 1988 states that 'a person driving a mechanically propelled vehicle on a road must stop on being required to do so by a constable in uniform' (see 19.4.1). A police officer will be authorized as an examiner by his/her chief officer (see 19.5) and will therefore have the authority to test a vehicle on a road, for the purposes of ascertaining compliance with:
   - the construction and use requirements including lighting; and
   - the requirement that the condition of the vehicle is not such that its use on the road would involve a danger of injury to any person.
2. All wheeled vehicles first used on or after 1 April 1980 should be equipped with a plate which clearly shows the vehicle identification number, the name of manufacturer, and the type approval number (possibly on a separate plate). The plate should be in a conspicuous and readily accessible location on a part not normally subject to replacement. This is described under reg 67 of the Road Vehicles (Construction and Use) Regulations 1986. The VIN should also be stamped on the chassis or frame and together these identifying features can be matched against details on PNC to enable identification of stolen vehicles.

TASK 8 Note that reliable statistics for the cars most likely to be stolen are not available, as the Home Office no longer collect these figures. The Honest John website provided the following information on the most frequently stolen cars in 2013 (in descending order): Vauxhall Astra, Ford Fiesta, Volkswagen Golf, Vauxhall Corsa, BMW 3 Series, Ford Focus, Ford Mondeo, Honda Civic, BMW X5, and Land Rover Defender.

TASK 9

1. This would be interference (a horse box is a trailer).
2. No, because a go-kart is not a motor vehicle adapted or intended for use on the road.
3. Yes, there is an intention to commit theft of an item which is 'carried in or on the motor vehicle' so this counts as interference.
4. No, there is no intention to steal the vehicle, anything in or on it, or take it without the owner's consent so this would not count as interference.

TASK 10 People enter the restaurant and order a meal. There is an expectation that people who enter a restaurant will pay for food which is prepared for them and served accordingly. By entering a restaurant, therefore, people imply that they have the means by which to pay for goods which are ordered and the intention to do so unless there is a special credit agreement whereby payment can be delayed until a later date. If people enter the restaurant with the appearance of being paying customers (the false representation), but with an express intention not to pay for the meal they are about to order and consume (the property), or knowing they do not have the means to pay for it, they will commit a s 1 Fraud Act 2006 offence of 'fraud by false representation'. This is because the 'dishonest representation' took place before the property was obtained.

Having ordered the meal, they wait at the table for it to be served. When people enter a restaurant and order the meal, initially intending to pay but then change their mind about paying before it is obtained, then the offence is again one of s 1 'dishonest representation', as once more they assume the role of paying customers (the false representation) before the meal is obtained (the property).

The meal is served to the table. When obtaining a meal at a restaurant, some of the charge is for the service that the customer receives. If the customer implies that he/she is an ordinary customer but intends not to pay for the service of the meal, then an offence of 'obtaining services dishonestly' may be committed (s 11 of the Fraud Act).

Having consumed the meal, they are expected to pay. If people who enter a restaurant intend at the start to pay for their meal, but then change their minds after their meal is served, then the dishonesty has occurred after obtaining the property, so this cannot be a s 1 offence. However, because the meal was served to the table, a s 11 offence of 'obtaining services dishonestly' may be committed.

They leave the restaurant. If the people continue to make out that they are ordinary customers, intending to pay (eg waiting for the bill), and then slip out of the restaurant at a convenient moment without paying, there is dishonesty, but it takes place after obtaining the property and the offence is more likely to be s 3 Theft Act 1978; that is, 'bilking'. The CPS can provide advice on choosing the most appropriate charge (see 27.2).

17 | Sexual Offences

17.1   Introduction

The incidence of sexual offences in England and Wales is notoriously difficult to determine, beset as it is by issues of under-reporting and lack of definitional clarity. The most recent data from the Office of National Statistics (2016a) reports that the police recorded 108,762 sexual offences in 2015–16. (This combines data from the Crime Survey for England and Wales (CSEW), Home Office police recorded crime, the National Fraud Intelligence Bureau, and the Ministry of Justice Criminal Justice Statistics Quarterly Update.) The figures represent a 14 per cent increase on the previous year. According to the CSEW, this increase is mainly explained by current rather than historical offences (contrary to the explanation suggested for the increase in sexual crimes recorded for 2012–13), greater willingness to come forward from victims, and an improvement in police recording practices for sexual offences (ONS, 2014, pp 13 and 33). Between 2015 and 2016 there were 36,438 recorded rapes (an increase of 16 per cent from the previous year), and 72,324 other recorded sexual offences (a rise of 13 per cent).

A number of assumptions surrounding sexual offences have been refuted through research over the years. These include 'rape myths', such as assuming that rape only happens to certain types of women or that women in some way provoke the offence (Croall, 2011, p 267), these are spurious arguments that used to arise for example for rape prosecutions where the victim was a prostitute. Another myth is that a rape is usually committed by a stranger in a dark alley attacking a woman. For female victims of the most serious sexual offences, around 90 per cent knew their attackers, and only 15 per cent had reported the case to the police (Ministry of Justice *et al*, 2013, p 6). However, so pervasive are some of these myths, particularly in relation to the expected behaviour or victims, that the CPS and the Metropolitan Police Service developed a joint action plan on rape that aims to address some of these misconceptions (CPS and MPS, 2015a).

Establishing that the victim did not consent to a sexual act is another problematic aspect of this type of offence. The Sexual Offences Act 2003 defines consent and presumptions about consent (ss 74 to 76). It is also presumed that there is no consent if the victim is under 16. In 1991, a landmark case made it clear that it has never been the fact that by marriage, a woman irrevocably consents to sexual intercourse with her husband, irrespective of her state of health or any objections to the act (*R v R* [1992] 1 AC 599, HL). In a more recent case a husband was convicted of raping his wife on a number of occasions from 1970 onwards. This case cited the *R v R* decision as exploding the myth that it was ever acceptable (*R v C* [2004] EWCA Crim 292). The situation is not always clear in relation to consent, for example when a victim had consumed large amounts of alcohol, or changed his/her mind about engaging in sexual activity. The issue of consent will be discussed in more detail in 17.6.2.

More recently, there has been increasing concern about the sexual abuse of children, and particularly the use of technology to facilitate grooming of victims and to share images of child abuse. The possession and sharing of illicit images of children will be covered in more detail in 17.4.2. Individuals concerned with the safety of children can raise concerns with the police, who in certain circumstances will be able to disclose information in order to protect children, under the Child Sex Offender (CSO) Disclosure Scheme (see 17.8).

The police tend to define policy in terms of 'serious' sexual offences and 'other' sexual offences. There is no collective official definition of 'serious' and in a sense every sexual offence is a serious one. For example, 'flashing' (see 17.2) is not normally included within the category of serious sexual offences, but its impact on victims might well be serious, and it has been suggested that this type of sexual crime, alongside voyeurism and image-related offences, may be precursors to more serious offending. However, the police consider that a distinction between 'other' and 'serious' is needed for a number of reasons, including the pragmatic necessity to make decisions on the deployment of resources and the development of policy. Many police forces will make reference to the use of the word 'serious' in the context of the Sexual Offences Acts of 1956 and 2003 and derive definitions in this way. In broad terms the following are normally considered as serious sexual offences when committed against adults (including attempts to commit these offences):

* rape (vaginal, anal, and oral);
* sexual assault by penetration;
* sexual assault where the assault is particularly serious (or is aggravated such as by including a person with a mental disorder);
* causing a person to engage in sexual activity without consent; and
* any other offence of a sexual nature deemed especially serious by the investigating officer.

Where the offences relate to children, they will always be treated as serious because by their very nature they relate to issues of safeguarding, and other abuse may have occurred.

Reports to the police of sexual offences will arise from a variety of circumstances and in a number of forms. For example, the police may attend the scene of rape at a club, or a victim might phone the police or attend in person at a local police station. There may also be referrals from a Sexual Assault Referral Centre (SARC). The report might be of a very recent sexual assault or of a rape that took place some 20 or more years ago. Because the vast majority of laws are not retrospective, when a sexual offence is reported many years after the event, the law that applied at the time of the offence is still relevant (as illustrated in the convictions of high-profile celebrities such as Rolf Harris, Gary Glitter, and Stuart Hall). Even though the range of sexual offences currently on the statute books appears to cover many eventualities, it may not cover historical reports. For instance, rape law prior to the 1990s would only cover vaginal penetration, and not anal or oral. The latter form of penetration was added to the definition of rape in the Sexual Offences Act 2003. As a result, on a practical level, the date upon which the offence was committed focuses the investigation toward a particular piece of legislation and case law. For example although oral rape was not an offence in itself the 1990s, it could still have constituted an offence of indecent assault.

The investigation of sexual offences has been a problematic area for the police, although the situation has improved markedly since the documentary made by Roger Graef in 1982. This showed the unsympathetic manner in which three male police officers interviewed a woman who had reported to the police that she had been raped. Given the particular controversies surrounding the police investigation of rape in the past, it is perhaps not surprising that there is detailed guidance in this area, particularly from NPIA/College of Policing, ACPO, and the CPS (eg ACPO, 2010a for an abridged version; a fuller version is made available to police forces).

The rate of attrition (between a report being made to the police and successful prosecution) is particularly high in sexual offences cases and has been the subject of much official, professional, academic, and media interest. There is undoubtedly an increased emphasis within the police service on improving both the rate of reporting of sexual crimes and the proportion that are brought to a successful prosecution or outcome (Angiolini, 2015).

17.2   Acts of a Sexual Nature in Public Places

Exposure is covered by s 66(1) of the Sexual Offences Act 2003. It is commonly referred to as 'flashing'. A person commits an offence if he/she exposes his/her genitals and intends that someone will see this and be caused alarm or distress. It is not necessary for a person to actually have seen the exposed genitals or to have been distressed as a result; the offence is still committed. It can be committed in a private or public place (see 9.2 for definitions of places).

The important points to prove would be the double intention specified in the offence—an intent that someone will see, and an intention to cause alarm or distress. Therefore, a 'streaker' planning 'merely' to cause amusement by intending others to see his exposed genitals, does not commit this offence, because of the lack of intention to cause alarm or distress. Similarly, a nudist who, on a site specifically set aside for naturism, does not conceal his or her genitals but has no intention to cause alarm or distress, will therefore not commit the offence.

This offence is triable either way and the penalty is imprisonment (summarily, six months and two years on indictment).

Outraging public decency is covered by common law which states that it is an offence:

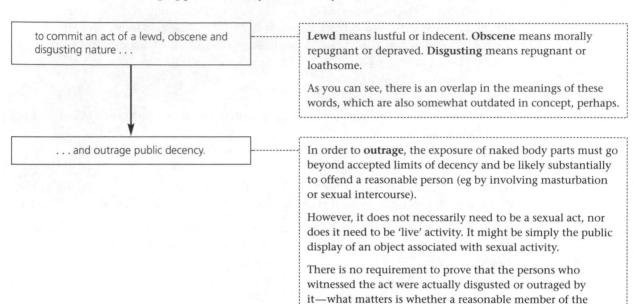

The public must have access to (whether they have a right to such access or not), or be able to see the relevant location, such as a private balcony in public view (*R v Walker* [1996] 1 Cr App R 111; *Smith v Hughes* [1960] 1 WLR 830). It must also have been possible for more than one person to witness the act.

This offence is triable either way and the penalty is imprisonment (summarily, six months and unlimited on indictment).

Sexual activity in a public lavatory is an offence under s 71 of the Sexual Offences Act 2003. There is no need for any person to witness the activity, and if there are witnesses, they do not have to be in any way outraged or distressed. The activity must be such that a reasonable person would regard it as sexual in nature. This offence is triable summarily only and the penalty is six months' imprisonment and/or a fine.

17.3 **Voyeurism**

Voyeurism is an offence under s 67(1) of the Sexual Offences Act 2003. Usually a suspect (commonly known as a 'Peeping Tom') secretly observes another person undressing or having sexual intercourse (a 'private act') for the purposes of the suspect's own sexual gratification.

Section 68(1) of the Sexual Offences Act 2003 explains that, for the purposes of s 67, a person does a private act if he/she is in a place which would reasonably be expected to provide privacy, such as in a home or hotel (but not on a beach or in an open-plan changing room) and at least one of the following conditions is met:

- his/her genitals or buttocks, or her breasts are exposed or covered only with underwear (see *R v Bassett* [2008] EWCA Crim 1174);
- he/she is using a lavatory; or
- he/she is participating in 'a sexual act that is not of a kind ordinarily done in public' such as sexual intercourse or oral sex.

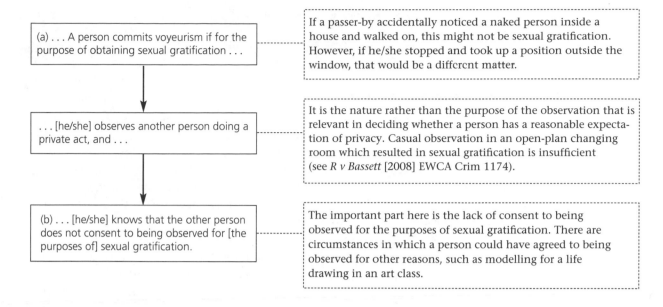

(a) . . . A person commits voyeurism if for the purpose of obtaining sexual gratification . . .

> If a passer-by accidentally noticed a naked person inside a house and walked on, this might not be sexual gratification. However, if he/she stopped and took up a position outside the window, that would be a different matter.

. . . [he/she] observes another person doing a private act, and . . .

> It is the nature rather than the purpose of the observation that is relevant in deciding whether a person has a reasonable expectation of privacy. Casual observation in an open-plan changing room which resulted in sexual gratification is insufficient (see *R v Bassett* [2008] EWCA Crim 1174).

(b) . . . [he/she] knows that the other person does not consent to being observed for [the purposes of] sexual gratification.

> The important part here is the lack of consent to being observed for the purposes of sexual gratification. There are circumstances in which a person could have agreed to being observed for other reasons, such as modelling for a life drawing in an art class.

There is a form of voyeurism linked to 'dogging' (outdoor sexual activities); however, if the 'doggers' encourage people to watch, the offence of voyeurism is not committed because consent has been given. Other offences, however, may have been committed, depending on the particular circumstances. Aggravating factors for voyeurism include threatening the victims to dissuade him/her from reporting the offence (CPS, 2012b).

17.3.1 Facilitating voyeurism and the use of equipment

Voyeurism using live link equipment is covered by s 67(2) of the Sexual Offences Act 2003. Person A commits an offence if he/she operates equipment with the intention of enabling another person B to observe, for sexual gratification, a third person C doing a private act. Person A must know that C has not consented to this. For example, a landlord commits an offence if he operates a webcam so that people on the internet can gain sexual gratification from viewing his tenant having sex. The landlord must know that the tenant did not agree to this. There is no need to prove that the landlord personally gained sexual gratification.

The recording of images in relation to voyeurism is covered by s 67(3) of the Sexual Offences Act 2003. It is similar to the legislation under s 67(2), except that the acts are recorded and not just transmitted. Circulating images or recordings are deemed aggravating factors by the Sentencing Guidelines Council, particularly when offenders are motivated by commercial gain (Sentencing Guidelines Council, 2007).

Installing equipment and adapting structures for voyeurism is covered by s 67(4) of the Sexual Offences Act 2003. The offence is committed even if the installation or adaptation is never used. A 'structure' can include a tent, vehicle, vessel, or some other temporary or moveable structure.

These offences are triable either way and the penalty is imprisonment (summarily, six months and two years on indictment).

> **TASK 1** Consider the following scenarios, and what offences might have been committed:
>
> 1. On the drive back to their home ground, four members of a rugby club team have taken to celebrating their wins by exposing their naked buttocks ('mooning') at the rear window of the team bus. A police officer is asked to deal with the most recent incident, that had occurred in the busy main high street. What offence might have been committed?
> 2. John is visiting his friend's house. He is having a meal when he decides to go to the toilet upstairs. When he reaches the landing he realizes that his friend's daughter Jane (aged 17) is using the lavatory with the door ajar. Rather than retreat until she has finished, John is aroused and stays on the landing watching her. He is disturbed by one of his friends. Could John be guilty of voyeurism? Does Jane's age matter?

17.4   Sexual Images Offences

Many aspects of adult pornography are completely legitimate, but if it involves 'extreme images' or indecent images of children, it will be illegal.

17.4.1   Possession of extreme pornographic images

This offence is covered by s 63(1) of the Criminal Justice and Immigration Act 2008. It is an offence to be in possession of an 'extreme pornographic image' (s 63(2)). An image includes moving images and electronic data that can be converted into an image, and/or stored on mobile phones or a computer drive for example (s 63(8)). An image is said to be pornographic if it appears to have been produced solely or principally for the purpose of sexual arousal (s 63(3)), and it must be explicit and realistic. An image is regarded as 'extreme' (see s 63(7)) if it depicts (or appears to depict) activities which:

- threaten a person's life;
- depicts rape or non-consensual sexual penetration (this was added by the Criminal Justice and Courts Act 2015, and therefore does not apply to material held prior to 13 April 2015);
- result in (or are likely to result in) serious injury to a person's anus, breasts, or genitals (including surgical reconstructions);
- involve sexual interference with a human corpse (necrophilia); or
- involve a person performing an act of intercourse or oral sex with an animal (bestiality), where any such act, person, or animal depicted in the image is or appears to be real (s 63(7)).

The offence of possession of an extreme pornographic image does not apply for 'excluded images' as defined in 17.4.1.1 (s 64(2)). Defences for possessing extreme images (s 65 of the Criminal Justice and Immigration Act 2008) include that the person: had a legitimate reason for possessing the image; had not seen the image and did not know (nor had any cause to suspect) it was an extreme pornographic image ; or had received the image without any previous request having been made, and did not keep it for an unreasonable time.

The offence cannot be prosecuted without the consent of the Director of Public Prosecutions. It is triable either way and the penalty is 12 months' imprisonment and/or a fine if tried summarily. For trials on indictment the penalty is imprisonment (three years for images which depict life-threatening acts or involve serious injury, and two years for images which involve necrophilia or bestiality).

The Ministry of Justice has issued guidance for dealing with the offence of possession of extreme pornographic images, available on the CPS website. The Internet Watch Foundation (IWF) now operates an internet hotline for the public and IT professionals to report potentially illegal websites.

17.4.1.1   Excluded images

These images are excluded in the sense that they would not be of concern for the offences under s 63(1) of the Criminal Justice and Immigration Act 2008 (see 17.4.1) or s 62(1) of the Coroners and Justice Act 2009 (for child sex abuse imagery, see 17.4.2). For material to be regarded as an excluded image, it must be part of a full-length mainstream or documentary film classified by the British Board of Film Classification (BBFC), and will not be considered as pornographic if shown as part of the complete film. However, if parts of the classified work have been extracted solely or principally for the purpose of sexual arousal, they will no longer count as 'excluded' (s 63(3)). Such cases will be a question of fact for the court to decide, for example, part of a film could have been unintentionally recorded, or reproduced for a purpose other than pornography.

17.4.2   Images of children and pornography

Sexualized images of children are used by paedophiles as both 'stimulus' masturbatory fantasy material and also as a possible disinhibitor for actual abuse of children. To help protect children from harm and exploitation, in addition to the general legislation relating to extreme pornography (see 17.4.1), further legislation is available in relation to images of children. Early legislation only applied to photographs and pseudo-photographs, but new legislation specific to drawings and other fantasy-style images was introduced in 2009. For the purpose of legislation relating to child sexual abuse imagery (or 'child pornography'), any person under the age of 18 is a child, except in cases where the defence of marriage apply.

Some photographs of children may appear indecent but are not indecent in terms of the legislation (s 1 of the Protection of Children Act 1978). Exception 1A is that the photograph was of a person aged 16 or over, and that at the time of the alleged offence, the person and the suspect were married or lived together as partners in an enduring family relationship. Exception 1B is that the photograph is for use in criminal investigation or proceedings, in any part of the world.

17.4.2.1 Possession of an indecent photograph of a child

Section 160(1) of the Criminal Justice Act 1988 states that it is an offence for a person to have in his/her possession any indecent photograph or pseudo-photograph of a child. A pseudo-photograph of a child could, for instance, involve a child's naked body with an adult face added to it. The law does not define 'indecent'. According to *R v Stamford* [1972] 2 QB 391, it is up to a jury to decide whether an image is indecent or not based on 'recognized standards of propriety' (not necessarily their personal views—see also *R v Neil* [2011] EWCA Crim 461).

Defences (s 160(2)) include: having a legitimate reason for possessing the image; having not seen the image, nor having cause to suspect what it was; and receiving the image without requesting it and not keeping it for an unreasonable time. The offence is triable either way, and the penalty is a fine or imprisonment (six months if tried summarily, and five years on indictment).

17.4.2.2 Producing and distributing indecent photographs of children

This offence is covered in s 1 of the Protection of Children Act 1978, and is explained in more detail in the flowchart.

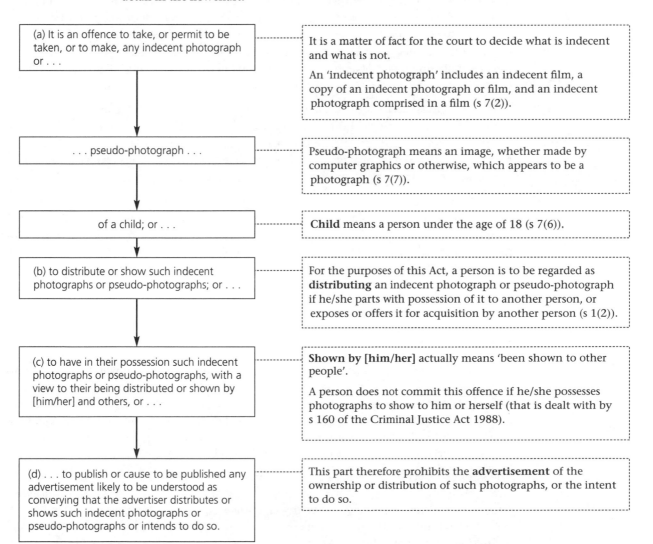

Two defences to this offence are listed in s 1(4) of the Protection of Children Act 1978:

- the defendant had a legitimate reason for distributing, showing, or having possession of the photographs or pseudo-photographs; and
- the defendant did not see the photographs or pseudo-photographs, or saw them and did not know they were, nor had any cause to suspect them to be, indecent.

The offence is triable either way. If tried summarily the penalty is six months' imprisonment and/or a fine, and on indictment the penalty is ten years' imprisonment.

17.4.2.3 Possession of a prohibited image of a child

Under s 62(1) of the Coroners and Justice Act 2009 it is an offence to be in possession of a prohibited image of a child (under 18). An image (moving, still, or in data form) is said to be prohibited if it is either pornographic (produced for the purpose of sexual arousal) or 'grossly offensive, disgusting or otherwise of an obscene character'. In addition, the image must either focus solely or principally on a child's genitals or anal region, or portray a child as a witness or participant for: sexual intercourse or oral sex with a person or an animal (the animal can be dead, alive, or imaginary); masturbation; or penetration of the anus or vagina (with a part of the body or anything else).

Defences for possession of a prohibited image of a child (s 64) are similar to those for possessing an indecent photograph of a child (see 17.4.2.1). The offence is triable either way and the penalty is a fine or imprisonment (12 months if tried summarily, and three years on indictment).

17.4.3 Disclosing private sexual images with intent to cause distress

'Revenge pornography' is when private sexual images, usually of a former partner, are made available to the public as a form of revenge against that other person. It is now an offence to disseminate to the public (or a section of the public) films or photographs of a sexual nature, without the consent of the portrayed person, and with the intent of causing him/her distress (s 33(1) of the Criminal Justice and Courts Act 2015). It is not an offence to disclose the images to the portrayed person. Images that have been altered (for example using software that enables the manipulation of photographs) are also included in the remit of this offence, but not if the unaltered images were non-sexual, and only became sexual due to the alteration(s).

Defences include that the disclosure: is necessary to prevent, detect or investigate a crime (s 33(3)); or relates to preparation or publication of journalistic material which is in the public interest (s 33(4)). A further defence is that there was reasonable belief that the images had already been released for reward, and there was no reason to doubt the portrayed person had not consented to the release, for example as commercial pornography (s 33(5)).

The offence is triable either way, with a penalty of a fine and/or 12 months' imprisonment if convicted summarily and a fine and/or a maximum of two years' imprisonment if convicted on indictment. One of the first people to be convicted was sentenced to six months' imprisonment (suspended for 18 months), ordered to undertake unpaid work, fined costs, and became subject to a restraining order. This tough approach is intended to act as a deterrent to what is assumed to be an increasingly common phenomenon.

17.5 Prostitution

A prostitute is defined as 'a person…who, on at least one occasion and whether or not compelled to do so, offers or provides sexual services to another person in return for payment or a promise of payment to [him/her] or a third person' (s 51(2) of the Sexual Offences Act 2003). Almost all public manifestations of prostitution are illegal. So for example it is an offence for a prostitute to be clearly waiting for potential customers in a public place, or for a person to be seen to actively seek the services of a prostitute in a public place.

The strong association between street prostitution and drug dependence, and between off-street prostitution and organized crime has been recognized by ACPO in its *Strategy & Supporting Operational Guidance for Policing Prostitution and Sexual Exploitation* (available online). Although prostitution is illegal in many of its manifestations and not all prostitutes are exploited, many are in a vulnerable situation, a fact that was particularly evident in the case of the Ipswich murders in 2006. Drug dependence, violence and intimidation may play a large part in explaining prostitution, but low self-esteem and having been abused as a child are also significant factors. Some victims of trafficking are also forced into prostitution. It is therefore important to determine whether an offence was committed, whether the person prostituting him/herself is in need of any kind of assistance, and which support organizations could help.

17.5.1 Soliciting in a public place

Some of the activities relating to prostitution are described in s 1(1) of the Street Offences Act 1959. This states that it is an offence for a person (male or female) to:

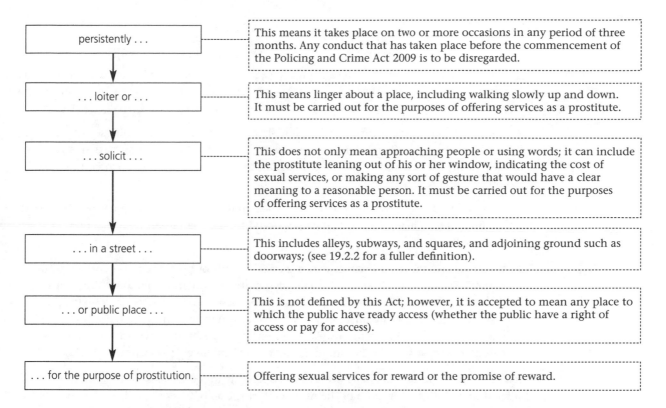

persistently . . .	This means it takes place on two or more occasions in any period of three months. Any conduct that has taken place before the commencement of the Policing and Crime Act 2009 is to be disregarded.
. . . loiter or . . .	This means linger about a place, including walking slowly up and down. It must be carried out for the purposes of offering services as a prostitute.
. . . solicit . . .	This does not only mean approaching people or using words; it can include the prostitute leaning out of his or her window, indicating the cost of sexual services, or making any sort of gesture that would have a clear meaning to a reasonable person. It must be carried out for the purposes of offering services as a prostitute.
. . . in a street . . .	This includes alleys, subways, and squares, and adjoining ground such as doorways; (see 19.2.2 for a fuller definition).
. . . or public place . . .	This is not defined by this Act; however, it is accepted to mean any place to which the public have ready access (whether the public have a right of access or pay for access).
. . . for the purpose of prostitution.	Offering sexual services for reward or the promise of reward.

This offence is triable summarily and the penalty is a fine or a court order requiring the offender to attend three meetings with a 'suitable person' (specified in the order).

17.5.2 Procuring the services of a prostitute

It is an offence for a person to solicit the services of a prostitute in a public place (s 51(A) of the Sexual Offences Act 2003). This is known as 'kerb crawling' when carried out from a vehicle. The offence is triable summarily and the penalty is a fine.

The penalties are more severe in relation to paying or offering to pay for the service of an 'exploited prostitute'. This is when a third person motivated by gain (for him/herself or another) has used exploitative conduct to induce or encourage provision of the sexual services anywhere in the world (s 53A of the Sexual Offences Act 2003). The conduct can include the use of force, threats (not necessarily violent), coercion, and deception. It is irrelevant whether the services are actually provided, or whether the 'client' is aware of the exploitative context. ACPO emphasizes that anyone exploited through prostitution needs help and support, most often in the form of access to health and welfare services (ACPO, 2011e, p.4). This offence is triable summarily and the penalty is a fine.

> **TASK 2**
>
> 1. Two police officers are on uniformed patrol near a railway station and notice a woman standing in the car park. As they approach she walks away towards the town centre, but returns a few minutes later. Later, the officers see two cars stop next to her. Each time the occupants of the cars talk to the woman and then drive off. What could the officers do?
> 2. A person offering a professional body-piercing service passes round a mobile phone amongst a group of strangers. It shows images of genitals and female breasts into which sharp metal objects of various shapes and sizes have been inserted. In relation to the possession of extreme pornographic images, have any offences been committed?

17.6 Sexual Assault, Rape, and Other Sexual Offences

This part of Chapter 17 covers the following offences within the Sexual Offences Act 2003:

- rape (s 1);
- assault by penetration (s 2);
- sexual assault (touching) (s 3); and
- causing another person to engage in sexual activity without consent (s 4).

In law, for these offences the offender must be aged 10 or over, and victim can be of any age. Remember that the question of consent is of paramount importance when considering whether a sexual act relevant to these sections amounts to an offence.

The term 'sexual' now appears in ss 2, 3, and 4, as well as many of the child sex offences. An activity will be sexual if a reasonable person would consider it is obviously sexual (s 78 of the Sexual Offences Act 2003). This would cover, for example, masturbation, which most people would consider to be sexual.

Paragraph (b) of s 78 covers more ambiguous activities which may or may not be sexual, depending on the circumstances or the intentions of the perpetrator (or both). A two-stage test may be applied:

1. Would a reasonable person consider the general nature of the act to be potentially sexual in nature? For example, if another person penetrates a woman's vagina with his/her finger, this is likely to be considered by most reasonable people to be a potentially sexual act.
2. What are the specific circumstances of the person carrying out the potential sexual act? (This might include his/her intentions.) For example, if the penetration was carried out by a GP as part of a necessary medical examination, it would be unlikely to be considered as sexual.

If a person has a hidden sexual motive to an apparently innocent activity, this will not be considered sexual for the purpose of the Act; in effect the activity would fail the first part of the test. The general opinion is that the definition under s 78 excludes obscure sexual fetishes.

Whatever the situation, the term 'sexual' is defined so as to make it clear that not every potentially sexual activity will automatically be considered as sexual under s 78. However, a number of observers have pointed to the possible tautological problems with s 78 definitions of sexual (it defines sexual in terms of itself) and you might consider researching this further.

17.6.1 Initial police response to sexual crime

All reports of serious sexual assault made by complainants should be taken seriously, although there has been considerable debate recently as to whether all complaints should automatically be assumed to be true. Certainly, an investigation should be initiated. Part of the historical context of rape complaints was the poor response from the police as Roger Graef demonstrated in the 1980s Thames Valley Police video. Victims felt that they were being subjected to investigation rather than the perpetrator, and that they were having to convince the police that they were genuine victims. To redress this balance, it became modern police practice to treat the victim as if he/she was always telling the truth. Recently this approach has been criticized because by simply believing the complainant the police effectively reverse the burden of proof against a suspect, and label the suspect as guilty at the outset of an investigation (Henriques, 2016). The Henriques Independent Review of Operation Midland (an MPS-led investigation of historical abuse), was critical of this practice, for example in the investigation of Lord Bramall for sexual offences. He was subjected to a home visit from the police in circumstances that were stressful for himself and his elderly wife (and she later died without knowing that he had been exonerated). The review suggested that even cursory investigation of the claims against Lord Bramall would have demonstrated that parts of the complaint did not withstand scrutiny, and that no further investigation could be justified.

Interestingly, Henriques (2016) also suggested that even the use of the term 'victim' was value laden. Whilst this observation was disputed by the police, Henriques suggests that people who report alleged crimes to the police should be regarded as 'complainants' as they only become 'victims' in the truest sense once a court has decided guilt. For the purpose of this text, the words 'victim' and 'complainant' will be used synonymously, with no value judgements attached to either terms. Whatever terminology is ultimately used within policing circles, there is little doubt that an objective investigation is the fairest and most appropriate approach, consistent with the values of the Criminal Justice System.

The initial investigation into an alleged serious sexual offence is conducted by the response officers and detectives allocated to investigate the crime. Some police forces have specialist units dedicated to investigating rape and serious sexual assault (eg the MPS Sapphire Teams). If the victim is a child (under 16) then other specialist police staff may also be involved. An officer of at least detective sergeant rank will be appointed to lead the investigation, and will review its progress on a regular basis. ACPO's *Guidance for the Investigation and Prosecution of Rape* (ACPO, 2010a) is also applicable to other types of 'serious' sexual offences. It promotes the use of a multi-agency approach to the investigation of rape.

Some forces (for example Kent Police) also provide extra training to uniformed response officers in order to ensure that appropriate levels of investigation and support are given within the initial investigation. A new role was also created in the mid-2000s, in many forces known as a 'specially trained officer' (STO) or SOIT (Sexual Offences Investigative Technique) officer in the MPS. The training for these roles is at PIP level 1 (see 7.5). The trained officer will become the single point of contact (SPOC) between the victim and the investigative team, and also provide early support to the victim. In theory, the same officer will support the victim through-out the investigative process through to court, and sometimes beyond. In practice this role is shared with Independent Sexual Violence Advisors and other volunteer agencies.

A number of the Diploma in Policing units are relevant to the early stages of a sexual offence enquiry, notably the units 'Provide an initial response to policing incidents' and 'Support victims, witnesses and vulnerable people'. The material covered here is also likely to be relevant to the equivalent CKP units 'Knowledge of providing an initial response to policing incidents' and 'Knowledge of supporting victims, witnesses and vulnerable people'.

17.6.1.1   Information from the complainant

A rape or serious sexual assault is often first reported to the police by the complainant but often some time after the event. It may also initially be reported as domestic violence perhaps due to mistrust in the justice system, fear of not being believed, or fear for his/her personal safety (or that of his/her children). Maintaining the complainant's anonymity is therefore an important part of investigating sexual offences.

A victim of rape or other serious sexual offences may be reluctant to disclose events of a traumatic and intimate nature. He/she could also suffer from 'post traumatic stress disorder', which can take on a variety of expressions: a very emotional or a very withdrawn initial reaction; symptoms of extreme anxiety or depression; denial; rage; hyper-vigilance; flashbacks; and other behavioural disorders. There may also be severe disorientation before he/she can begin to readapt to 'normal' life where the incident no longer takes a central role (Mason and Lodrick, 2013).

A trainee officer is unlikely to be involved much beyond the initial stages of investigation into an alleged serious sexual offence. As for other incidents, the priority of the 'first officer on the scene' will be the protection of the victim and any other individuals at risk (see 11.2.1). They will not be expected to take a detailed account from the victim (this is the STO's responsibility) but still need to be mindful that this could be the first stage of a prolonged investigation. An initial report should be taken (eg location, identity, times, description of suspect, etc) and accurate and relevant entries made in the PNB (see 10.2), followed by rapid referral to line managers and the STOs. The FAO should remain the single point of contact with the victim until an STO is appointed to the case, and should communicate the complaint to the relevant departments (usually criminal investigation and specialist investigation teams).

Report-takers should display active listening (see 6.11.3) and concern for the victim when taking the statement. It is important to establish a relationship of trust with the victim early on as this will encourage him/her to provide as much detailed information as possible at a later stage. The focus should be on assessing the immediate safety of the victim, and be sufficient for briefing of the officers investigating the events.

Certain questions must be addressed during the initial stages. These depend on the urgency of the report and include, amongst other things, asking the identity of the person making the report (and for phone calls, his/her location), the location and time of the incident, whether the person making the report is the victim or a third party (and if the latter, in what capacity), the nature of the incident, the location and identity of the suspect, and details of any known injuries (ACPO, 2010a, pp 24–5). Later, victims should be provided with information on rape

Specific Incidents

crisis centres and local victims support organizations. Any decision to arrest the offender (or involve him/her in any other way in the investigation) should consider the risk that this may present to the victim.

Forensic requirements must be considered (see 11.2), including the use of evidence-recovery methods if appropriate (see 26.6). Sexual assault victims should not smoke, eat, drink, wash, or go to the toilet (unless absolutely necessary) until they have been forensically examined as the preservation of physical evidence is essential. An Early Evidence Kit (EEK) can be used during the initial response to secure relevant forensic evidence. The kit usually includes a plastic container to collect urine samples, sheets of toilet paper, a mouth swab and a mouth rinse.

17.6.1.2 Information from others

Reports may be made by third parties, in which case the report-taker should try to establish in which capacity the third party is acting (eg as a witness or a member of a victim support organization). The third party should be provided with the contact details of an investigating officer (IO) so that any further information can be provided later if necessary. Direct police contact with the victim should usually be avoided without the knowledge of the third party. This does not mean, however, that contact with the victim should be avoided altogether; a risk assessment should be made under the supervision of an IO, who should consider using a STO to take matters forward. If the third party identifies an offender, the IO should consider further investigation and an arrest if there is reasonable suspicion of the offence having taken place. If the third party making the report is from another agency, the recording and investigation should follow the pre-agreed information-sharing protocols. The information should be auditable (eg recorded in an IT system) and can be used, for example, to analyse trends and patterns of offending.

Specialist sexual violence services should be made aware of any anonymous reports. The IO should consider ways to corroborate whether there is enough evidence to amount to reasonable suspicion and a subsequent arrest.

17.6.2 Consent

In many sexual offence cases, particularly those relating to ss 1–4 of the Sexual Offences Act, in any subsequent prosecution the court will focus on the issue of consent. A defence is available if the suspect believes that consent was given, but he/she would also have to prove that this belief was reasonable. The court will decide whether the belief was reasonable after considering the circumstances and the steps that the suspect took to obtain consent (s 1(2) of the Sexual Offences Act 2003). In general terms, the court will seek to establish whether the suspect made a conscious effort to initially establish consent and then monitor the consent—the other person might change his/her mind and withdraw consent, indicated by a change of physical expression or voice tone, for example.

Establishing that consent was given is often difficult, as in many cases the only way to do this is by assessing the statement of the complainant against that of the accused. In order to address this difficulty and to ensure that officers steer away from the myths surrounding rape (see the introduction to this chapter) the CPS and the Commissioner of the Metropolitan Police issued a joint Action Plan. This encourages the police to look more closely at the behaviour of the accused when trying to establish whether consent was granted or not, rather than focusing solely on the complainant (CPS and Police, 2015b). The action plan includes an aide-memoire with information on consent that summarizes relevant legislation and dispels some of the myths associated with rape.

Section 74 of the Sexual Offences Act 2003 states that a person consents if he/she agrees by choice, and has the freedom and capacity to make that choice. A choice has not been made freely if the person has, for instance, taken part under duress, through being blackmailed, or if put in fear of violence. Capacity to agree means the ability to decide either way, and to be able to communicate the decision. If a person is 'unable to refuse', through intoxication (see *R v Bree* [2007] EWCA Crim 256) or mental disorder, for example, then he/she does not have the capacity to make the choice. The general definition of consent under s 74 of the Act is wide enough to encompass circumstances where the victim feels compelled to have sex (eg in *R v Jheeta* [2007] EWCA Crim 1699 the victim mistakenly feared she would be fined by the police), and therefore could not be said to have consented. It covers a multitude of circumstances.

The Sexual Offences Act 2003 introduced two sets of presumptions which courts can make in relation to the guilty knowledge of the defendant: evidential and conclusive presumptions about consent.

Evidential presumptions about consent are covered in s 75 of the Sexual Offences Act 2003. The defence can provide evidence that the victim did in fact consent (to contradict the presumption that consent was not given). The defence will need to convince the judge (through the use of evidence) that there is a definite issue about consent, and then produce relevant evidence from the defendant, a witness, or the victim under cross-examination. If the judge is not convinced, the jury will be directed to find that the victim did not consent, and that the defendant could not have reasonably believed that consent was given. The jury will only be asked to assess whether the defendant's belief that consent had been granted was reasonable if his/her reasoning is not merely 'fanciful or speculative' (*R v Ciccarelli* [2011] EWCA Crim 2665). Under s 75 the court will presume that the victim did not consent if evidence presented in court proves that the circumstances involved any of the following: use of or fear of immediate violence against that or another person; unlawful detention; unconsciousness; inability to communicate due to physical disability; and/or substances that are capable of stupefying or overpowering (such as drugs) that were non-consensually administered. It also has to be proved that the defendant knew of these circumstances and that the defendant carried out the act in question.

Conclusive presumptions about consent are covered in s 76 of the Sexual Offences Act 2003. This covers circumstances in which the victim has been deceived. The presumption about consent (ie the lack of consent) is conclusive and final: if the victim has been deceived, no amount of evidence can prove that consent had been given. The court will presume that the victim did not legally consent and that the defendant had no reasonable belief that consent had been given, if it is proved in court that the defendant intentionally:

- deceived the complainant about the nature or purpose of the relevant act (eg telling the victim it was a necessary medical procedure); or
- impersonated an individual personally known to the victim, with whom the victim would have consented to such activity (eg the defendant pretends to be the victim's current sexual partner and engages in sexual activity during complete darkness).

(Of course, it also has to be proved that the defendant carried out the relevant act.)

Interestingly, recent case law has made it clear that certain deceptions that fall outside s 76 can be dealt with as lack of consent under s 74. These include deceptions concerning the gender of the perpetrator, whether a condom will be used, and blackmail. It has also been suggested that where a person lies about his/her HIV status this too could negate consent under s 74 of the Sexual Offences Act 2003. This will surprise many as a previous case (*R v B* [2006] EWCA Crim 2945) seemed to suggest that this would amount to GBH rather than rape. However, in *R v Justine McNally* [2013] EWCA Crim 1051 the Court of Appeal clarified that in *R v B* the assailant was silent about his HIV status, and that this is different from an actual deception.

17.6.3 Rape

This is covered under s 1 of the Sexual Offences Act 2003 and can only be committed by a man, but the victim can be male or female.

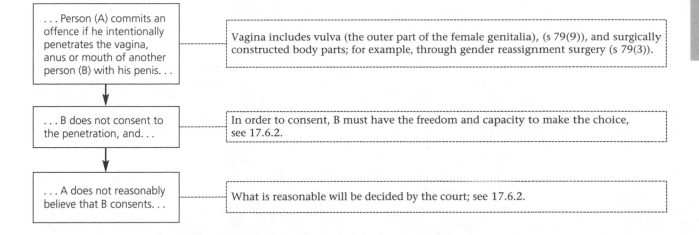

... Person (A) commits an offence if he intentionally penetrates the vagina, anus or mouth of another person (B) with his penis...	Vagina includes vulva (the outer part of the female genitalia), (s 79(9)), and surgically constructed body parts; for example, through gender reassignment surgery (s 79(3)).
... B does not consent to the penetration, and...	In order to consent, B must have the freedom and capacity to make the choice, see 17.6.2.
... A does not reasonably believe that B consents...	What is reasonable will be decided by the court; see 17.6.2.

There are some important points to consider about penetration, which also apply for other sexual assaults:

- the very slightest degree of penetration is still penetration (*R v Hughes*, 1841);
- it is a continuing act from entry to withdrawal (s 79(2)); person (A) may have penetrated person (B) with B's consent, but B then changes his/her mind (quite legitimately) and makes this clear. If A does not withdraw, this amounts to a continuing penetration; and
- references to a part of the body also include surgically constructed parts (in particular through gender reassignment surgery) (s 79(3)). This leaves open the possibility that the offence can be committed by a person with a surgically constructed penis who was not born a man.

The offence of rape is triable on indictment only and the maximum penalty is life imprisonment.

17.6.4 Assault by penetration

This is an offence under s 2 of the Sexual Offences Act 2003; person A commits an offence if he/she intentionally penetrates (with a part of his/her body or anything else) B's vagina or anus without B's consent. Person A must be sexually motivated and not have a reasonable belief that B consents. Penetration is a continuing act from entry to withdrawal, and references to body parts include surgically constructed parts (see 17.6.3). The issue of consent can be considered by looking at the general definition under s 74, or any of the evidential or conclusive presumptions in ss 75 or 76 (see 17.6.2). Rather than seeing this offence as a form of rape (because it involves the act of penetration), it is perhaps more appropriate to see it as an aggravated form of sexual assault. It is now (since the Sexual Offences Act 2003) a separate offence with higher penalties than previously. The penalty for penetrative sexual assault offence can be life imprisonment, whereas prior to 2003 the maximum sentence was only 10 years. The offence of assault by penetration is triable on indictment only.

17.6.5 Sexual assault

This is covered under s 3 of the Sexual Offences Act 2003, and the details are shown in the flowchart.

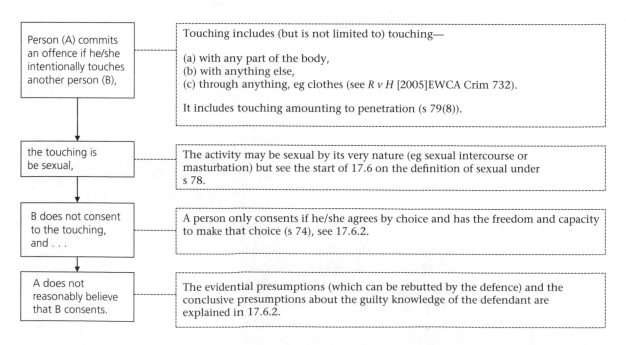

Unlike the old offence of indecent assault, the s 3 offence requires an actual touching of the person (along with the other relevant points to prove) before an offence is complete. Note the very broad definition of 'touching' provided in the flow chart. In circumstances where the suspect has only tried to touch in a sexual manner, then this could be an attempted offence (see Chapter 21).

This offence is triable either way. The penalty is six months' imprisonment and/or a fine if tried summarily, and ten years' imprisonment on indictment.

17.6.6   Causing another person to engage in sexual activity without consent

It is an offence to intentionally cause another person to engage in sexual activity if he/she does not consent, and the perpetrator does not reasonably believe that consent has been given (s 4(1) of the Sexual Offences Act 2003). An example of this type of offence is where a man threatens to stab a woman with a knife if she does not perform a sexual act in front of him. She performs the sexual act for fear of being assaulted. He has caused her to engage in sexual activity, although there was no contact between the two of them. It would also need to be proven that there was no consent and no reasonable belief in consent. The difficulty for police investigators in these types of cases is that these offences are often committed in private with no witnesses present. A thorough investigation will be needed, as other elements of proof might be uncovered, for example evidence from the suspect's phone. An extreme age difference between offender and victim, and general vulnerability of the victim are aggravating factors. The penalty is six months' imprisonment and/or a fine if tried summarily, and ten years' imprisonment on indictment.

If the sexual activity involves penetration, the offence is more serious. Under s 4(4), the perpetrator (A) can cause penetration involving person B in a number of different ways. It can be:

(a) penetration of B's anus or vagina by anything;
(b) penetration of B's mouth with a penis (any man's);
(c) penetration of any person's anus or vagina by B, using part of B's body, or any item; or
(d) penetration of any person's mouth with B's penis (if B is a male).

This would cover group situations where groups of people cause others to engage in penetrative sexual activity with other people in the group. Some of the group may facilitate the offences by restraining the victim whilst others engage in the penetrative activity. The participants could of course be prosecuted for rape or conspiracy to rape, but this has often proved difficult when groups of people have been involved. However the s 4(1) offence can be used to cover the conduct of all persons involved, and is classed as a serious sexual offence. Therefore any of the people involved who were found guilty could be put on the sexual offences register, not just those who actually penetrated the victim.

It is triable on indictment only and the penalty is life imprisonment.

> **TASK 3** Many victims of rape will be concerned about their identity becoming known during the investigation and any subsequent court case. What legislation is available to provide anonymity in relation to complaints of rape and restrictions on evidence at trials for rape?

17.6.7   Sexual activity with an animal or a human corpse

Sexual intercourse with an animal is covered under s 69 of the Sexual Offences Act 2003. It involves penile penetration of animals by humans, and of humans by animals. The animals and the human participants must be alive and the penetration can be of the vagina or the anus. This activity is also known as bestiality. The offence can also be committed by allowing or causing such an act. (Note that penetration of an animal with an object does not come under this legislation but could be pursued through legislation for prevention of cruelty to animals—see 13.8.)

Penetration of a human corpse is covered under s 70 of the Sexual Offences Act 2003 and can be committed by men or women. Any part of the body or any object can be used to perform the penetration, and any part of the corpse may be penetrated. The offender must have some kind of sexual motivation, and must know or be reckless about whether he/she is penetrating a corpse.

These offences are triable either way. The penalty if tried summarily is six months' imprisonment and/or a fine not exceeding the statutory maximum, and two years' imprisonment on indictment.

17.7   Children, Young People, and Sexual Offences

Sexual activity between an adult and a child under the age of 16 is unlawful. Here we cover some of the sexual offences legislation that applies specifically to offences involving younger victims. (The offences listed in 17.6 can also be considered where the child did not consent.) For a victim under 13 years of age the law considers that he/she cannot give consent in any sense, so the offences are of strict liability.

Sexual contact may take place between an adult (aged 18 or over) and a child under 16, or between children both of whom are aged under 16. Whilst all of these activities might be sexual offences, some of the activities will attract criminal sanction whilst others might not.

First, where a person aged 10 or over engages in sexual activity with another child, and the activities are clearly non-consensual, the prosecutor could employ any of the offences in ss 1–4 of the Sexual Offences Act 2003 (see 17.6).

Secondly, where an adult engages in sexual conduct with a child under the age of 13, there are offences of rape, assault by penetration, sexual assault, and causing or inciting sexual activity that do not rely upon proof of lack of consent (ss 5–8 of the Sexual Offences Act 2003). In essence, these offences are of strict liability due to the age of the child. In many ways the offences covered by ss 5–8 effectively mirror the offences under ss 1–4 of the Sexual Offences Act, apart from the requirement to prove age of the child, the irrelevance of consent and the addition of the term 'incitement' in s 8 to criminalize conduct aimed at encouraging children under 13 to engage in sexual activity. In all other respects the requirements of proof are the same (for example for rape, intentional penetration of the vagina/anus/mouth with a penis must be proved).

Thirdly, where an adult (aged 18 or over) engages in sexual activity with a child between the ages of 13 and under 16, where lack of consent does not feature, the Sexual Offences Act 2003 creates a series of further offences designed to criminalize such conduct (ss 9–12 of the Sexual Offences Act 2003). Again, there is no need to prove that consent was not given, although consent may be relevant to mitigation and/or sentence if a person is convicted. In these cases, the adult might be able to use a defence of reasonable belief that the child was 16 or over, but this would be dependent upon the circumstances of the case.

Finally, there may be circumstances where both parties engaging in sexual activity are under the age of 16. Section 13 of the Sexual Offences Act 2003 makes it possible for those under the age of 16 to be guilty of sexual offences under ss 9–12. However, providing there is true agreement (and, for instance no coercion by one of the parties), a prosecution is not always considered in the public interest. Further details on this are given in the Rape and Sexual Offences Guidance on the CPS website. Under s 13 of the Sexual offences Act 2003, children charged with any of these offences would be subject to a lower maximum sentence of 5 years' imprisonment.

Grooming and child sexual exploitation have received particular attention in the political and law enforcement fields in recent years, particularly due to a number of high-profile cases involving individuals, groups of individuals, and gangs that sexually exploited children. As with prostitution, such practices may form part of lucrative and international business empires. We consider some of the measures to tackle these problems in 17.7.6 and 17.8.

17.7.1 Child rape

Rape of a child under the age of 13 is an offence under s 5 of the Sexual Offences Act 2003. It can only be committed by a man, but the victim can be male or female. For this offence, the victim's anus, vagina, or mouth must be penetrated by the offender's penis. The sexual organs can have been constructed through surgery (as with s 1 rape: see 17.6.3) and penetration is a continuous act from entry to withdrawal (s 79(2)).

Whether the victim appears to consent or otherwise agree to the activity is of absolutely no relevance, nor can the defendant contend that he thought the victim was aged 16 or over. Proof that the victim was under the age of 13 must be provided for a prosecution. This offence is triable on indictment only and the maximum penalty is life imprisonment.

For a victim aged 13–15 years there is no specific offence, so the offence will need to fit the general definitions for rape under s 1 (see 17.6.3), and lack of consent would need to be proven. Where lack of consent is difficult to prove, or the circumstances reveal willing participation, then offences from ss 9–12 could be considered (see 17.3.5)

17.7.2 **Sexual assault of a child**

Sexual assault by penetration of a child under the age of 13 years is an offence under s 6 of the Sexual Offences Act 2003. The penetration can be carried out using any part of the body (such as a finger) or a separate object, and can be committed by a male or a female. The child does not need to be aware of the nature of the penetrating object. As for other offences, penetration is a continuous act from entry to withdrawal (s 79(2)). This offence is triable on indictment only and the maximum penalty is life imprisonment.

Sexual assault on a child under the age of 13 without penetration is covered by s 7(1) of the Sexual Offences Act 2003. It involves intentionally touching a child under the age of 13 in a sexual manner (see 17.6.5 for more detail on the meaning of 'touching' and 'sexual'), and can be committed by a male or a female. This offence is triable either way and the penalty is six months' imprisonment and/or a fine if tried summarily, and 14 years' imprisonment on indictment.

For these offences (s 6 and s 7) the victim must be less than 13 years old, and proof of this must be provided for a prosecution. Whether the victim appears to consent or otherwise agree to the activity is of absolutely no relevance. Nor would it be possible for a defendant to contend that he/she thought the victim was aged 16 or over.

For a victim aged 13–15 years old with non-consensual activity, offences under ss 1–4 can apply. If, however, the activities seem to have been consensual, a prosecution under s 9 or 10 could be considered.

17.7.3 **Sexual activity with a child**

It is an offence under s 9 of the Sexual Offences Act 2003 for a person (male or female) to intentionally touch a child in a sexual manner. For further explanation of the terms 'touching' and 'sexual', see 17.6.5. Where the child is less than 13 years old it is more likely that the suspect would be prosecuted under s 6 or s 7 for such activities, but the prosecutor will decide which is the most appropriate.

For a s 9 offence the child victim has to be under 16, and proof of age is required. The accused will have a defence if he/she reasonably believed the victim was aged 16 or over, so the investigation should seek evidence that could justify the suspect's belief. Prior to 2003, only young men under the age of 23 were able to use this defence, but any person charged with child sex offences can now use it. Where a child is aged under 13 years, the defence is not available.

The s 9(1) offence (assault with no penetration) is triable either way, and the penalty is six months' imprisonment and/or a fine if tried summarily, and 14 years' imprisonment on indictment. If the sexual activity involves penetration, then a more serious form of the offence is committed, under s 9(2). (Such an activity where the victim is under 13 would be prosecuted under s 6.) Section 9(2) of describes the acts carried out by the suspect (person A) that can constitute this more serious offence:

(a) he/she penetrates the child's anus or vagina (with a part of A's body or anything else);
(b) person A is a man and uses his penis to penetrate the child's mouth;
(c) he/she causes a part of the child's body (eg a finger) to penetrate A's anus or vagina; or
(d) person A forces a boy to put his penis in A's mouth.

This offence is triable by indictment only, and the penalty is up to 14 years' imprisonment.

17.7.4 **Causing or inciting a child to engage in sexual activity**

These offences (under s 8 and s 10 of the Sexual Offences Act 2003) can be committed by a man or a woman, and can involve the child acting alone or with another person. The offender might not be physically involved and no sexual activity actually has to occur; incitement alone can amount to the offence.

Causing or inciting a child under 13 years old to engage in sexual activity is covered by s 8 of the Sexual Offences Act 2003. If the sexual activity caused or incited involves no penetration the offence is committed under s 8(1), and under s 8(2) if penetration is involved. Section 8 therefore creates four separate offences: causing non-penetrative sexual activity; causing penetrative sexual activity; inciting non-penetrative sexual activity; and inciting penetrative sexual activity. Proof of age is once again required, consent is irrelevant, and the defendant will not be able to use a defence that he/she thought the child was older.

Section 8(1) offences (no penetration is caused or incited) are triable either way. The penalty is six months' imprisonment and/or a fine if tried summarily, and 14 years' imprisonment on indictment. Section 8(2) offences (penetration is caused or incited) are triable on indictment only and the maximum penalty is life imprisonment.

For a victim under 16 years of age, these activities are covered by s 10 of the Sexual Offences Act 2003. Non-penetrative sexual activity is covered under s 10(1) and penetrative sexual activity under s 10(2). Reasonable belief that the child was aged 16 or over is available as a defence for this offence. The s 10(1) offence is triable either way. Consent is again irrelevant to the offence, but might be relevant to mitigation and sentence. The penalty is six months' imprisonment and/or a fine if tried summarily, and 14 years' imprisonment on indictment. An offence under s 10(2) is triable on indictment only and the penalty is imprisonment for up to 14 years.

17.7.5 Causing a child to witness sexual acts

There are two offences under the Sexual Offences Act 2003 where the offender causes a child to witness sexual acts: where the offender commits the sexual acts him/herself (s 11) and where other people commit the acts (s 12).

For the s 11 offence the offender must know or believe that the child will be aware of the sexual acts in some way (eg seeing it live, or on a webcam, or hearing it), and gain some sexual gratification from the child's presumed awareness. However, the victim does not actually have to be aware of the activity (eg if the child does not notice). For the s 12 offence the offender must gain sexual gratification from causing a child to watch a third party involved in sexual activity (live or recorded). The child need not be coerced to watch, and may even agree to watch; this is irrelevant to whether the offence has been committed. In the case of *R v Abdullahi (Osmund) Mohammed* [2006] EWCA Crim 2060, the Court of Appeal made it clear that the showing of material and the sexual gratification did not have to occur at the same time. It was possible therefore to show a child sexualized videos with the intention to gain sexual gratification some hours later.

These offences are both triable either way. The penalty is six months' imprisonment and/or a fine if tried summarily, and 10 years' imprisonment on indictment.

TASK 4 Imagine you are a trainee officer and you are asked to attend the home of a 15-year-old girl. She alleges that a family friend has been visiting the house on a regular basis, and he has sometimes massaged her genitals. If the allegations are substantiated could he have a defence to any possible charge? Would it make a difference if the victim was 12 years old?

17.7.6 Countering grooming and organized child sexual exploitation

Grooming and child sexual exploitation has gained considerable attention in the political and law enforcement fields in recent years, particularly due to a number of high profile cases involving individuals, groups of individuals and gangs that have sexually exploited children. Grooming is now addressed under several offences, and measures are being put in place to counter child sexual exploitation.

17.7.6.1 Meeting a child following sexual grooming

Section 15 of the Sexual Offences Act 2003 provides an offence of meeting or travelling to meet a child following sexual grooming. The overall aim of this legislation is to criminalize behaviour where an adult contacts a child on one or more occasions and meets (or intends to meet) the child in order to commit any offence under Part One of the Sexual Offences Act 2003 against him/her.

Surprisingly, this offence cannot be committed by a person less than 18 years old. Bearing in mind the rapid growth in the use of the internet and social media, particularly by young people, it would seem likely that some 16- or 17-year-olds are likely commit such acts. and at present this is not addressed under this legislation.

The victim (B) must be under 16 years of age. However, if the suspect (A) reasonably believed that B was 16 or over, then A has not committed this offence.

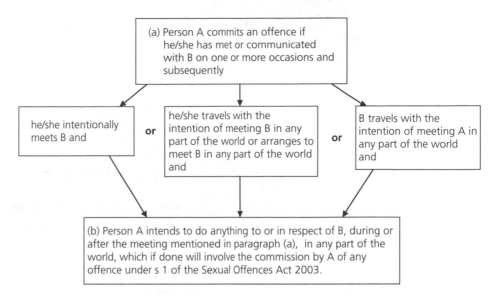

The communication between the two need not be sexualized, for example it could seem to be about attending a sporting event. The contact can be by any means, such as meeting up, a letter, an email, messages on a social networking site, or SMS texts.

A Sexual Risk Order (SRO) can be used to try and prevent online sexual approaches to children under 16, if it is feared that the person intends to meet a child and commit sexual abuse (see 17.8).

17.7.6.2 Child sexual exploitation

Child sexual exploitation occurs whenever a child under 18 years of age engages in sexual acts for a reward such as drugs, alcohol, food, accommodation, treats, money, gifts, or even simply some attention from a particular person. The reward can also be to a third person, in which case it is more likely to be money or drugs. For this offence, the sexual act can be carried out by the young person on another person, or by another person on the young person. The exploitation can involve technology (for example, asking the child to send sexual images on a mobile phone). People who sexually exploit children generally have power over them, usually as a result of being older, more 'savvy' and having more disposable income. Instances of violence, coercion and intimidation are not uncommon, and usually occur because the child has no means to escape the violence (Department for Children, Schools and Families, 2009, p 9).

Child sexual exploitation can be difficult to identify. Common indicators of abuse have been covered in 13.3, and include from the most obvious signs of physical violence (such as bruises or cigarette burns), to the child having expensive possessions that cannot be easily explained. Such children may also have health problems, including sexually transmitted diseases, and can also display a range of behavioural problems such as going missing for periods of time, skipping school or being disruptive in class, having mood swings, using drugs and alcohol, and inappropriately sexualized behaviour (NHS, 2013).

Any child can suffer sexual exploitation, including those coming from stable and loving families, but risk factors include being homeless or in care, having had a recent bereavement, experiencing low self-esteem or caring for a family member with an illness (NHS, 2013). A history of domestic violence in the family, living in a chaotic environment, a history of abuse, having parents with a history of substance abuse, and experiencing social exclusion are also added risk factors. Other factors that place children at risk of sexual abuse are: unsupervised use of social networking websites, having learning difficulties, suffering from mental ill-health, being unsure about their sexual orientation, having a history of substance abuse, having friends who are sexually abused, being excluded from mainstream education, being bullied, and being in a gang or living in an area with gang associations (College of Policing, 2014f). Girls are more likely to be sexually abused than boys (although it is likely that victimization of boys is underestimated), and there is a higher rate of victimization amongst black and ethnic minority children when compared to their proportion in the overall population (Office of the Children's Commissioner, 2012, p 14). Sexual exploitation can have a devastating impact on children, with many suffering from health problems (such as drug and alcohol abuse, self-harming and mental health problems), going missing or offending as part or as a result of their exploitation (Office of the Children's Commissioner, 2012, pp 49, 50).

Specific Incidents

'Hotel Notices' can be used to help investigate organized groups involved in child sexual exploitation. Under the Anti-Social Behaviour, Crime and Policing Act 2014 the police can require the owner, operator or manager of a hotel or B&B (or similar) to provide information about their guests (including, name, address and age). Failure to comply with the notice without a reasonable excuse, or giving information without taking reasonable steps to verify it, or knowing that it is incorrect are criminal offences under s 118 of the Anti-Social Behaviour, Crime and Policing Act 2014 punishable with a fine of up to £2,500.

17.8 Protecting the Public from Sexual Harm

Records of sexual offenders are kept by the police on what is commonly called the 'sex offenders register' (part of ViSOR, see 3.3.1). Part 2 of the Sexual Offences Act 2003 determines that offenders convicted for certain sexual offences, for example rape and certain child sex offences committed by adults, are required to notify the police of personal information such as their name and address (s 80) and this information is stored on the register. The requirements were extended in 2012 to include other offender information such as bank and credit card details, and if he/she is living in a household with a child (s 83(5A)(h)). Notification requirements are imposed for a fixed or indefinite period, depending on the sentence received, and offenders have three days to notify the police of any relevant changes. The offender can appeal against the notification requirements and these can be revised (s 82). Failure to comply with a notification order is an either-way offence under s 91, with punishment ranging from a fine to five years' imprisonment.

A **Sexual Harm Prevention Order** (SHPO) is applicable to anyone convicted or cautioned for a sexual or violent offence. It can be issued by a court upon conviction or the police or National Crime Agency (NCA) can apply to a magistrates' court. The order is issued if it is deemed necessary to protect the public or a specific member of the public in the UK or overseas from sexual harm. The offender must have committed any of the acts in Sch 3 or 5 to the Sexual Offences Act 2003, and been convicted as a result, either in the UK or abroad. SHPOs replaced Sexual Offences Protection Orders and broadly build on the same principles, but one key difference is that for SHPOs the risk is of 'sexual harm' whereas for the defunct SOPOs a risk of 'serious sexual harm' was required. SHPOs can prohibit an individual from travelling overseas and have a fixed term of not less than five years. Individuals are subject to the same notification requirements as registered sex offenders and must notify the police of their name and address within three days of the order being served. The breach of a SHPO is an offence, triable either way. The punishment is up to six months' imprisonment or fine if tried summarily, and a maximum of five years' imprisonment if tried on indictment.

A **Sexual Risk Order** (SRO) is a preventative order applicable to an individual who seems likely to present a risk of sexual harm to the public, as a result of having committed an act of a sexual nature. But unlike a SHPO, the individual does not need to have been convicted or cautioned for committing this act (s 122A of the Sexual Offences Act 2003). The order prohibits the individual from committing specified actions, which can include travelling overseas. It also requires the recipient to provide his/her name and address to the police within three days of the order being served. The police or NCA apply to a magistrates' court for an SRO and must have a reasonable belief that it is necessary to protect the public or specific members of the public in the UK or overseas from sexual harm. SROs have a fixed term of at least two years (s 122A), except for those with international travel prohibitions which must last for at least five years (s 122C). Breaching a SRO is a criminal offence, punishable with a maximum of five years' imprisonment (s 122H of the Sexual Offences Act 2003). SROs replace Risk of Sexual Harm Orders.

Under the **Child Sex Offender Disclosure Scheme** (CSODS) a member of the public can ask the police about a particular person with access to children, to find out whether that person has a record for child sexual offences. (This is sometimes referred to as 'Sarah's law' in memory of Sarah Payne who was killed by a convicted sex offender.) The police will disclose any relevant information to the people who are deemed most capable of protecting the children at risk (usually parents, guardians, and carers), but not necessarily to those who made the request for information. The disclosure is given confidentially, and only if the police believe it is in the child's interests. Information on convicted sexual offenders is not immediately and widely disclosed to the public to avoid any public backlash, and also to ensure that registered sex offenders engage with the system, rather than 'going underground'.

The CSODS information request can be made in person, by telephone or email. Individuals making the request in person (for example, by walking into a police station) should be allowed to do so privately, and will be informed about how the process will be conducted and the associated timescales. Within 24 hours there should be an initial risk assessment and minimum standard checks using PNC, ViSOR and other local intelligence systems. Immediate action must be taken if it seems there is an imminent risk to a child, following existing procedures for safeguarding children (see 13.3.3). There are five further stages for the CSODS (see the Home Office's *Child Sex Offender Disclosure Scheme Guidance*, available online).

17.9 Answers to Tasks

TASK 1

1. Section 66 of the Sexual Offences Act only applies to exposure of a person's genitals, not the buttocks (although it is possible that 'mooning' may also result in exposure of the genitals, even though this was not intended). However, in any case the suspects might claim their intention was to entertain or amuse, not to alarm or distress. In the common law offence of Outraging Public Decency, there must be a deliberate act that is lewd, obscene, or disgusting. In *R v Rowley* [1991] 4 All ER 649, Lord Simon decided that outraging public decency goes considerably beyond offending the sensibilities of 'reasonable' people. Therefore the local evidence-review representative or CPS representative should be asked whether the common law offence might be committed by members of the rugby team. The public order offences could also be considered, for example s 5 of the Public Order Act—non-intentional harassment, alarm, or distress.

2. Section 67(1) of the Sexual Offences Act 2003 appears to have been committed in these circumstances. The voyeurism offence can be committed within private premises. Jane is engaged in a private act (going to the lavatory) and John is observing her under conditions where it is reasonable for her to expect privacy. It is clear from the circumstances that John did not seek consent and it is unlikely that it would have been given in these circumstances (such evidence could be provided by Jane). Her age is irrelevant in these circumstances. The most tricky element in the case would be to prove that John's observations were for the purpose of sexual gratification, although it is likely that this would be left to a court to determine.

TASK 2

1. The woman could be investigated under s 1(1) of the Street Offences Act 1959 as 'persistently loitering or soliciting in a street or public place for the purposes of prostitution'. To prove 'persistently' there must be evidence of the behaviour on two or more occasions in any period of three months. The police officers should speak to the woman and, having found out her name, address and date of birth, check whether she has any record of soliciting in the last three months. If she is a persistent offender they may need to consider further action. Otherwise they could warn her about the possible consequences of continuing her behaviour, ensuring of course that the warning is recorded in the appropriate place according to local procedures. This will provide evidence that she has already been acting in this way to any police officer who may need to check in the future. Each police officer should record the incident in his/her PNB.

2. This offence can certainly be committed by the possession of extreme images stored on a mobile telephone. However, body piercing carried out hygienically and with consent is unlikely to result in serious injury to a person's breasts or genitals. If the owner of the mobile was a professional piercer trying to get business he/she could claim the images were for advertising and not for sexual arousal, and is likely to have a defence.

TASK 3 Section 7 of the Sexual Offences (Amendment) Act 1976 provides anonymity for victims of rape. This includes attempted rape, aiding, abetting, counselling, and procuring rape or attempted rape, incitement to rape, and conspiracy to rape. The anonymity can be waived by a victim at any time, and some victims choose this route to raise awareness for the benefit of other victims (for example the late Jill Saward, who was sexually assaulted in an Ealing Vicarage in 1986).

TASK 4 For the offence of sexual activity with a child (s 9(1) of the Sexual Offences Act 2003), there is a defence available if the girl is at least 13 years old and the perpetrator reasonably believed that the girl was over 16. There would be no defence if the girl was younger than 13 years.

18 | Weapons Offences

18.1 Introduction

In recent years, governments and the NPCC have encouraged a more 'robust' approach to charging individuals found carrying offensive weapons, with the intention of deterring potential offenders. In this chapter we outline the legislation that covers the use and ownership of weapons (including firearms), and prohibits possession of weapons in certain circumstances.

According to the Crime Survey for England and Wales, in the year ending June 2016, the police recorded 29,306 offences involving a knife or sharp instrument, a 9 per cent increase compared with the previous year (ONS, 2017). Just over half of the offences were assault with injury or assault with intent to cause serious harm, and the majority of the others were part of a robbery.

Type of offence	Number of offences
Threats to kill	2,335
Assault with injury and assault with intent to cause serious harm	15,447
Robbery	10,508
Rape	336
Sexual assault	127
Homicide	206
Attempted murder	347
Total	29,306

The expectation now is that all people aged 16 or over involved in knife crime (including possession) will be charged, and younger people will be issued with a warning (ACPO, 2010b) and referred to a Youth Offending Team (see 3.3.4).

Policies aimed at reducing the number of offensive weapons being carried in public form part of the multi-agency approach described in 3.3. For example, the Violent Crime Reduction Act 2006 makes provision for members of school staff to search pupils, including walk-through scanners for detecting weapons. Part 7 of the Education and Inspections Act 2006 describes the use of reasonable force by school staff, and the circumstances when confiscation from pupils would be lawful. In most cases school policies on searching and seizing of offensive weapons will have been agreed with the local police.

Health and safety should be of primary concern when weapons may be present—the PAC Safety First checklist is relevant as are many of the Diploma in Policing assessed units. 'Ensure your own actions reduce risks to health and safety' is one of the NOS units 'embedded' within the Diploma (see 7.4).

18.2 Weapons Offences

Firearms, knives, clubs, crossbows, batons, and swords are all clearly weapons, but so is a simple length of rope in the wrong hands (see 18.7.1). Serious wounding and possibly death can result from the use of these items, but many people possessing such items seem relatively unconcerned about this and offer some sort of excuse. In some cases, individuals found in possession of such articles may be genuinely vulnerable to attack by others, but whatever the circumstances, it is a police officer's responsibility to attempt to prevent crimes involving the use of these weapons and, if at all possible, to detect the presence and remove such items before they are used.

18.2.1 Offensive, dangerous, and specified weapons

An offensive weapon for the purposes of the Prevention of Crime Act 1953 is any article made, adapted, or intended for causing injury (s 1(4)). This clearly includes firearms, but the unlawful use or possession of firearms is more likely to be prosecuted under separate legislation (see 18.3–18.8).

A 'made article' has been made or manufactured for the purposes of causing injury to people, for example a flick knife or telescopic baton. The courts need no proof of such an item's intended use. An 'adapted article' is something which has been modified in some way for the purposes of causing injury, for example a broken bottle with sharp edges, or a potato embedded with protruding razor blades. A jury can decide whether or not articles have been specifically adapted to be offensive weapons, but proof that the defendant had no reasonable excuse for possessing such an item is still required. For example, in the case of *Prosecution right of appeal (No 23 of 2007), sub nom R v R* [2007] EWCA Crim 3312 it was decided that gloves filled with sand were offensive weapons as the prosecution had produced evidence that similar gloves had been advertised for sale on a website as 'self-defence gloves'. An 'intended article' is any item in the suspect's possession, with which he/she intends to cause injury. The precise nature of the article is not important: it is what the suspect intends to do with it. A pillow can be an offensive weapon if it can be proved that the suspect intended to use it to cause injury to a frail relative. Once again, gathering evidence through interview is important because it must first be proved that the suspect intended to cause injury with the article. Only then will any reasonable excuse be considered (see *R v Sundas* [2011] EWCA Crim 985).

Certain items that are undoubtedly offensive weapons are also classified as 'dangerous weapons' for the purposes of s 28 of the Violent Crime Reduction Act 2006, and 'specified' for the purpose of s 141 of the Criminal Justice Act 1988. The table lists some examples with descriptions (quotes are taken from the relevant Acts and Statutory Instruments).

Item	Comments
Disguised knife	'Any knife which has a concealed blade or concealed sharp point and is designed to appear to be an everyday object of a kind commonly carried on the person or in a handbag, briefcase, or other hand luggage (such as a comb, brush, writing instrument, cigarette lighter, key, lipstick or telephone)'
Stealth knife	'A knife or spike, which has a blade, or sharp point, made from a material that is not readily detectable by apparatus used for detecting metal and which is not designed for domestic use or for use in the processing, preparation or consumption of food or as a toy'
Knuckleduster	'Band of metal or other hard material worn on one or more fingers, and designed to cause injury'
Telescopic truncheon	'A truncheon which extends automatically by hand pressure applied to a button, spring or other device in or attached to its handle'
Baton	'A straight, side-handled or friction-lock truncheon'
Shuriken, Shaken or Death Star	'A hard non-flexible plate having three or more sharp radiating points and designed to be thrown'
Push dagger	'A knife the handle of which fits within a clenched fist and the blade of which protrudes from between two fingers'
Belt-buckle knife	'A buckle which incorporates or conceals a knife'
Swordstick	'A hollow walking-stick or cane containing a blade which may be used as a sword'
Handclaw	'A band of metal or other hard material from which a number of sharp spikes protrude, and worn around the hand'
Hollow *kubotan*	'A cylindrical container containing a number of sharp spikes'

Specic Incidents

Item	Comments
Footclaw	'A bar of metal or other hard material from which a number of sharp spikes protrude, and worn strapped to the foot'
Balisong or Butterfly knife	'A blade enclosed by its handle, which is designed to split down the middle, without the operation of a spring or other mechanical means, to reveal the blade'
Blowpipe or blow gun	'A hollow tube out of which hard pellets or darts are shot by the use of breath'
Kusari gama	'A length of rope, cord, wire or chain fastened at one end to a sickle'
Kyoketsu shoge	'A length of rope, cord, wire or chain fastened at one end to a hooked knife'
Manrikigusari or *kusari*	'A length of rope, cord, wire or chain fastened at each end to a hard weight or hand grip'
Samurai sword (or other similar curved blade)	'A sword with a curved blade of 50 cms or over in length which is measured in a straight line from the top of the handle to the tip of the blade'

The law regarding weapons is different in some other countries, and some are easily obtainable elsewhere and can then be brought into the UK.

18.2.2 Possessing an offensive weapon in a public place

Section 1(1) of the Prevention of Crime Act 1953 states that it is an offence for:

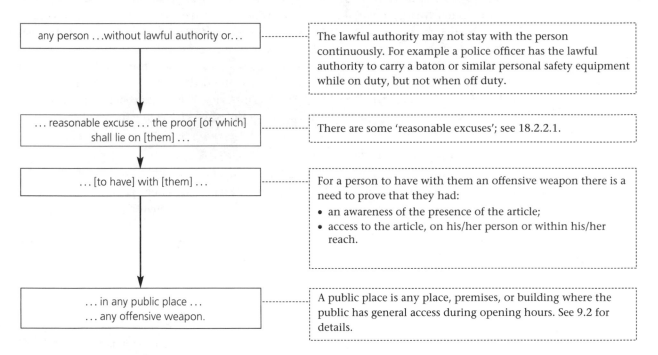

Of course, some items that might be classed as offensive weapons may have innocent uses, and the person would therefore have a reasonable excuse for carrying such an item (see 18.2.2.1).

A police officer has the power to search for offensive weapons under s 1 of the PACE Act 1984 (see 9.4.2). This offence is triable either way and the penalty is a fine or imprisonment (six months if tried summarily and four years if tried on indictment).

18.2.2.1 Reasonable excuses

A person may have a reasonable excuse for possession of an offensive weapon in a public place if he/she fears for his/her safety: for example a woman who feels she is about to be assaulted (and cannot escape) and picks up a chair to defend herself. Other reasonable excuses include having an innocent reason, such as a chef carrying kitchen knives on his way to work.

Unreasonable excuses include:

- Forgetfulness—for example forgetting that there is a machete under the seat in his/her car; see *R v McCalla* (1988) 87 Cr App R 372. However, when the forgetfulness is combined with other circumstances (eg 'relating to the original acquisition of the article') it will be for the court to decide whether there was a reasonable excuse (see *R v Vasil Tsap* [2008] EWCA Crim 2679). An example might be when a weapon is left by a passenger in a taxi and the driver moves it to the front of the vehicle intending to dispose of it. If the taxi is later stopped by the police the driver may claim to have forgotten that the weapon was there (see *R v Glidewell* LTL 19/5/99, The Times, 14 May 1999).

- Ignorance—not knowing the true identity of the item, for example, believing that a truncheon is a telescope.
- General self-defence—'just in case' he/she is attacked.

In any prosecution the burden of proving a reasonable excuse for possession of an offensive weapon lies with the defendant. Therefore, officers should gather as much evidence as possible—before, during, and after interview under caution, in relation to any likely reasonable excuse.

18.2.3 Possessing a bladed or sharply pointed article in a public place

The Criminal Justice Act 1988 (CJA) created the offence of having a bladed or sharply pointed article in a public place (s 139(1)) in an attempt to prevent serious crimes involving the use of such items. Historically, under the Prevention of Crime Act 1953, if the defendant had been in possession of an item such as a kitchen knife, pair of scissors, or large pocket knife, he/she would not be found guilty if the court could be persuaded on the balance of probabilities that he/she had had a reasonable excuse (see 18.2.2.1). We define some key terms as follows:

- 'Bladed' includes any kind of bladed article, for example a kitchen knife, scissors, a craft knife, a pocket knife, a dagger, or any other article which has been given a cutting edge or blade. Pocket knives with a blade less than 7.62 cm (3 inches) long which cannot be locked in the open position are exempt from this legislation.
- 'Sharply pointed' includes any kind of sharply pointed article, for example a needle, geometry compasses, or any other article which has been given a sharp point.

A court must decide whether an article has a blade or is sharply pointed, so the onus is on the prosecution to prove that the article fits the relevant description. For example, in *R v Davis* [1998] Crim LR 564 the suspect was carrying a screwdriver which the court was asked to consider as a 'bladed article capable of causing injury'. The court decided that it was more important to decide whether the screwdriver had a cutting edge or point than to consider whether it was capable of causing injury. Therefore, unless a screwdriver has a pointed end or has been sharpened to make a blade, it is not an article for the purposes of this Act. There is a power to search for bladed, or sharply pointed articles under s 1 of the PACE Act 1984 (see 9.4.2).

Some defences that are likely to be considered are shown in the table. General self-defence, ignorance, or forgetfulness are not defences: see the description of reasonable excuses in 18.2.2.1.

Defence	Example
Lawful authority	The lawful authority may not stay with the person continuously. For example, a police officer would have lawful authority to have a bladed or sharply pointed article after seizure and before placing it into a property store. Members of the armed services will also have lawful authority to carry articles such as bayonets whilst on duty, but may be liable for prosecution if such an article was carried off duty
For use at work	A joiner uses wood chisels with very sharp cutting edges and may need to carry them in a bag in the street while moving between jobs. The work can be casual and the bladed article does not have to be used on a regular basis (see *Chahal v DPP* [2010] EWHC 439 (Admin)). He/she, however, would not be able to use this claim if he/she had a chisel in a nightclub whilst socializing
Religious reasons	Followers of the Sikh religion may carry *kirpans* (a small rigid knife) for religious reasons
Part of any national costume	Whilst wearing national costume, some Scots carry a skean dhu (a small dagger, tucked in the top of the socks). However, this defence could not be used if the person was carrying the knife but not wearing national costume

It is very important to gather evidence to counter any defences that may be offered later. The offence is triable either way and the penalty is a fine or imprisonment (six months if tried summarily and four years on indictment).

> **TASK 1** A police officer on patrol notices scissors and several craft knives inside a vehicle on the floor by the passenger seat. What needs to be considered and what action might be needed?

18.2.4 Weapons in schools

Section 139A of the Criminal Justice Act 1988 prohibits certain weapons on school premises (ss 139A(1) for bladed or sharply pointed articles, and ss 139A(2) for other offensive weapons). Here, a 'school' is an educational institution providing primary and secondary education (s 14(5) of the Further and Higher Education Act 1992), and school premises include land used for the purposes of a 'school', including open land such as playing fields or playgrounds (s 139A(6)) of the CJA 1988).

The classification of these offences and powers of search are the same as for possessing an offensive weapon in a public place (see 18.2.1). For searching a person, it is not necessary for the officer to have grounds to suspect that he/she is in possession of a weapon, but the decision should still be based on objective factors connected with the reason for searching the premises (PACE Code A para 2.29). This is covered in more detail in 9.4 on stop and search. The officer does not have to be in uniform to enter school premises if he/she suspects a s 139A offence and reasonable force can be used to secure entry. If offensive weapons, or bladed, or sharply pointed articles are found, they can be seized (s 139B of the CJA 1988).

Defences for a s 139A offence include that the article or weapon was for use at work, educational purposes, religious reasons, or as part of a national costume, see also 18.2.3. The offence is triable either way with a penalty of a fine or imprisonment (six months if tried summarily and four years on indictment).

18.2.5 Threatening with a weapon in a public place or school

It is an offence to threaten a person in a public place or on school premises with an offensive weapon or bladed or sharply pointed article. For 'offensive weapons' the offence is covered under s 1A of the Prevention of Crime Act 1953 (POCA), and for an article with a blade or sharp point, under s 139AA of the CJA. The threat must be intentional and unlawful (see 18.2.2) and create an immediate risk of 'serious physical harm' (harm that amounts to grievous bodily harm (see 15.3.1)).

These offences are aggravated versions of the basic possession offences, so many of the definitions of terms are the same and have been described elsewhere in detail. For example for 'public place' see 9.2, for 'school premises' see 18.2.4, for 'offensive weapon' see 18.2.1, and for 'bladed or sharply pointed article' see 18.2.3.

If the suspect is found not guilty of either of the aggravated offences at court, he/she can still be found guilty of one of the relevant basic possession offences (s 10 of the Prevention of Crime Act and s 12 of the CJA 1988).

The offences are triable either way with a penalty of a fine or imprisonment (one year if tried summarily and four years on indictment).

18.2.6 Possession of a weapon in a private place

The offences we have discussed so far relate to the possession of weapons in public places or schools. For similar incidents on private property (eg inside a dwelling) s 64 of the Offences Against the Person Act 1861 could be considered. For this, it is an offence to possess, make, or manufacture any item with intent to commit, or enable any other person to commit, any other offence within the Act. The items include explosive substances (eg gunpowder), 'engines', machines, instruments, and 'any other dangerous or noxious thing'. The penalty is imprisonment for up to two years.

18.2.7 Manufacture, import, sale or hire, etc of offensive weapons

For certain types of weapon it is an offence for a person to manufacture such an item or sell or hire it to anyone. The offence also includes offering such a weapon for sale or hire, or exposing it or possessing it for the purpose of selling, hiring, lending, or giving it to another person. If the weapon in question is a 'specified weapon' (see 18.2.1), the offence is committed under s 141 of the Criminal Justice Act 1988. For a 'flick knife' or a 'gravity knife' the offence is committed under s 1 of the Restriction of Offensive Weapons Act 1959. This covers certain types of knives, such as a knife with a blade which opens automatically by hand pressure (sometimes known as a flick knife or flick gun) or where the blade is released by the force of gravity or by centrifugal force, sometimes known as a gravity knife.

This offence is triable summarily with a penalty of six months' imprisonment and/or a fine.

18.2.7.1   Selling bladed or pointed items to young people

Under s 141A(1) of the Criminal Justice Act 1988 it is an offence to sell to a young person (under 18) a knife, a knife blade, a razor blade, or an axe. This also applies for any other article which has a blade or which is sharply pointed, and which is made or adapted for use for causing injury to a person. The offence is triable summarily with a penalty of six months' imprisonment and/or a fine.

18.2.8   Arranging the minding of a dangerous weapon

Under s 28 of the Violent Crime Reduction Act 2006, a person commits an offence if he/she uses another person to look after, hide, or transport a 'dangerous weapon' for him/her. These weapons include those in the table in 18.2.1, firearms (but not air weapons, see 18.3.1 and 18.6) and the sharp and bladed articles referred to in 18.2.7.1. The arrangements must help make the weapon available for an unlawful purpose; ie that the weapon is available for the offender to use at a particular time and place, and that its possession would either constitute an offence in itself, or be likely to lead to the commission of an offence. The 'minder' would not be committing a s 28 offence, but might be committing a weapons possession offence (see other parts of this Chapter). The s 28 offence is triable either way.

> **TASK 2** Ahmed, a 17-year-old at a local FE College carries a knife 'for his own personal protection'. He is under threat from others at the college and has good grounds to fear for his safety. Putting aside any discussion of whether Ahmed has a reasonable excuse: what factors should be taken into account when deciding what action (if any) to take?
>
> Note that these considerations may be relevant to the Certificate in Knowledge of Policing assessed unit 'Knowledge of supporting victims, witnesses and vulnerable people' and the knowledge element of the Diploma in Policing assessed unit 'Support victims, witnesses and vulnerable people'.

18.3   Firearms

Each force will have specially trained and equipped personnel to deal with all firearms incidents and the deployment of firearms officers will be considered for all such incidents. However, there always remains the possibility that a trainee police officer could find him/herself unexpectedly at the scene of a firearms incident. He/she may also come across firearms during a premises search, or may be deployed to investigate people using air weapons, or required to investigate whether a firearm is legally owned. The procedures to be followed when attending an incident where a firearm has been found are covered in 11.2.6.2, and forensic aspects of firearms are covered in 26.5.6. The Home Office website contains further guidance on firearms legislation.

18.3.1   Definition of a firearm

Section 57(1) of the Firearms Act 1968 provides a definition of a firearm as shown in the flowchart. Firearms are loosely grouped into four categories under the Act:

1. Section 1 firearms (covered under s 1 of the Firearms Act 1968).
2. Shotguns.
3. Air weapons.
4. Prohibited weapons.

Specic Incidents

An item referred to as an imitation firearm may or may not be a firearm in a legal sense, but might be a replica (see 18.8).

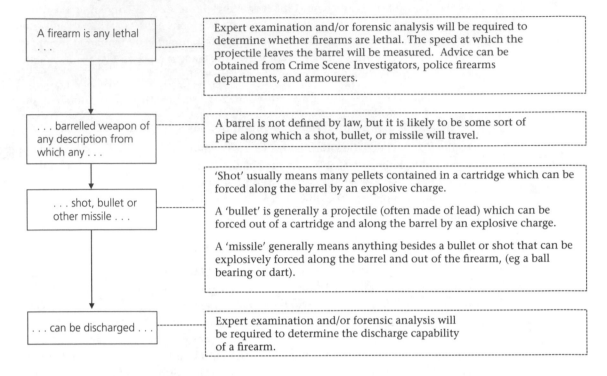

A firearm is any lethal . . . → Expert examination and/or forensic analysis will be required to determine whether firearms are lethal. The speed at which the projectile leaves the barrel will be measured. Advice can be obtained from Crime Scene Investigators, police firearms departments, and armourers.

. . . barrelled weapon of any description from which any . . . → A barrel is not defined by law, but it is likely to be some sort of pipe along which a shot, bullet, or missile will travel.

. . . shot, bullet or other missile . . . → 'Shot' usually means many pellets contained in a cartridge which can be forced along the barrel by an explosive charge.

A 'bullet' is generally a projectile (often made of lead) which can be forced out of a cartridge and along the barrel by an explosive charge.

A 'missile' generally means anything besides a bullet or shot that can be explosively forced along the barrel and out of the firearm, (eg a ball bearing or dart).

. . . can be discharged . . . → Expert examination and/or forensic analysis will be required to determine the discharge capability of a firearm.

18.3.1.1 The parts of a firearm

A firearm consists of 'component parts' which are essential for it to work (such as the trigger mechanism and the firing pin), and 'additions' (also known as accessories) such as magazines, sights, torches, trigger guards, grips, sound moderators, and flash eliminators. The component parts are all required to make a firearm fully functional. Because they are vital to this functioning, they are legally controlled so that they cannot be separately brought together to construct an uncertificated firearm (see 18.3.2).

The photograph shows a self-loading pistol (SLP), an example of a s 1 firearm. The main parts of a firearm are identified. The ammunition is stored in a 'magazine', which is then inserted into the frame within the grip. Pulling and releasing the top-slide inserts a round of ammunition into the breech end of the barrel, and also 'cocks' the action.

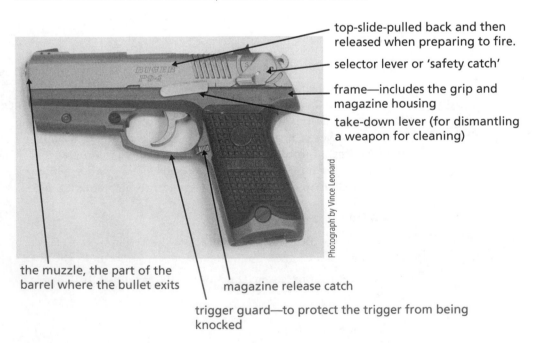

top-slide-pulled back and then released when preparing to fire.

selector lever or 'safety catch'

frame—includes the grip and magazine housing

take-down lever (for dismantling a weapon for cleaning)

the muzzle, the part of the barrel where the bullet exits

magazine release catch

trigger guard—to protect the trigger from being knocked

Photograph by Vince Leonard

The second photograph shows another SLP, partly dissembled to reveal some of the internal mechanism.

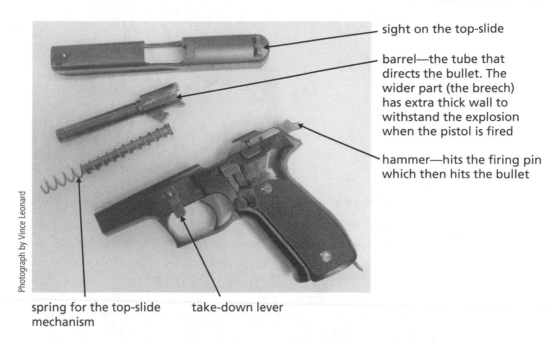

sight on the top-slide

barrel—the tube that directs the bullet. The wider part (the breech) has extra thick wall to withstand the explosion when the pistol is fired

hammer—hits the firing pin which then hits the bullet

Photograph by Vince Leonard

spring for the top-slide mechanism

take-down lever

Pulling the trigger fires the weapon—the explosion produces hot gases that force the bullet down the barrel, and push the top-slide backwards to release the empty cartridge case. The mechanism is 'self-loading' in that it also feeds the next round of ammunition from the magazine into the breech end of the barrel. The trigger can then be pulled again to fire another round, and the whole process can be repeated until the magazine is empty. (In contrast, for an automatic weapon the trigger does not need to be pulled once for every round that is fired; simply holding the pressure on the trigger will cause it to fire repeatedly until the ammunition has all been fired.)

The barrel of a firearm can be smooth or rifled. Smooth-bore weapons enable the easy passage of shot. Although normally associated with lead shot, as used in sport shooting, these weapons can also fire a single or several larger lead 'slugs'. Generally, smooth-bore weapons have a limited range, are less accurate than rifled firearms and produce a spread of shot. They are however often used to commit crimes because to the spread of shot means that accuracy is not required. For rifled-bore weapons the inside of the barrel is grooved (rifled) in a spiral pattern, with 2–16 clockwise or anti-clockwise grooves. These cause the bullet to spin, giving it stability and increasing the firing accuracy and range.

Calibre is the measurement of the diameter of the barrel. In rifled weapons this figure is normally expressed in metric or imperial figures (eg 7.62 mm, 9 mm, .38 inch, .357 inch). The units are readily convertible between the two measuring systems. In Britain and the US, calibre is measured differently for smooth-bore weapons because it was difficult for engineers in the past to be accurate to hundredths of one inch. The calibre is determined by the mass of a lead sphere that would exactly fit the barrel and the sphere's mass as a fraction of a pound. A 12-bore (UK) or 12-gauge (US) is a barrel diameter into which a lead ball with a mass of one-twelfth of a pound would just fit (approximately 1.33 ounces or about 37 g).

Sound moderators (also known as 'silencers') are designed to reduce the noise or flash of a firearm. Detachable sound moderators are generally subject to certificate control, but integral sound moderators, and those for air weapons are not. A flash eliminator reduces the flash from the round exiting the barrel and thereby aids the firer's vision (especially when firing in low light). It will be for a court to decide whether a particular sound moderator or flash eliminator could be used with the firearm in question, and whether the suspect had it for that purpose.

18.3.1.2 Ammunition

A conventional round of modern ammunition to be used in a handgun, rifle, or carbine consists of a cartridge, (normally made of brass) and a bullet (usually made from lead or lead alloy) covered wholly or partially with a copper jacket. The base of the cartridge has a 'primer' which will ignite when struck by the firing pin. This sends a flame through a 'flash-hole' to the main body of the cartridge, which ignites the propellant powder. The propellant burns and creates gases in the 'head-space' between the propellant and the bullet head. The expanding gases force the bullet from the cartridge into the barrel, from which it exits.

Specic Incidents

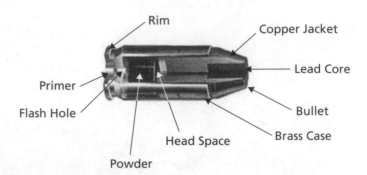

Diagram by Vince Leonard

Shotgun cartridges work on the same basic principle, but the outer covering is plastic or cardboard, and they contain shot rather than a bullet. Full details are provided in 18.5.

18.3.2   Firearms certificates

A certificate is needed for s 1 firearms, shotguns, some types of ammunition, and any component parts of a firearm (see 18.3.1.1). Other categories of firearm such as air weapons and some imitation firearms do not require certificates. It is an offence to have a s 1 firearm or a shotgun without the requisite certificate (see 18.4.2 and 18.5.1, respectively).

A police officer has the power to demand the production of a firearm certificate from any person whom he/she believes to be in possession of any firearm(s) or ammunition requiring a firearms certificate (s 48(1) of the Firearms Act 1968). The interpretation of the term 'demand' varies between forces; for some it means the certificate should be produced on the spot, while in others it could be produced at some specified time in the future. If the person does not produce the certificate and permit a police officer to read it (or otherwise show that he/she is entitled to have the items in his/her possession), then the firearm or ammunition may be seized and retained (s 48(2)). A police officer can also require the person to give his/her name and address.

18.3.3   Other offences relating to possession of firearms

Apart from not having the relevant certificate for a firearm (see 18.3.2), there are other offences related to possession of a firearm. For example, under s 19 of the Firearms Act 1968 it is an offence to have in a public place certain types of firearm and ammunition, without lawful authority or reasonable excuse (see 18.2.2.1 on excuses). This applies to:

- loaded shotguns;
- air weapons (loaded or not);
- any s 1 firearm (loaded or not);
- prohibited weapon (loaded or not);
- imitation firearms; and
- ammunition suitable for use in a s 1 firearm.

In relation to air weapons the offence is triable summarily and the penalty is six months' imprisonment and/or a fine. For other types of weapon, the offence is triable either way.

Possessing a firearm with the intention of causing fear is also an offence under s 16A of the Firearms Act 1968. It is an offence for a person to have in his/her possession any firearm or imitation firearm with intent to cause (or enable any other person to cause) any third person to believe that unlawful violence will be used. The offence is triable on indictment only and the penalty is ten years' imprisonment and/or a fine.

It is also an offence to be in possession of a firearm or an imitation firearm at the time of arrest (s 17(2)). Pretending to have a firearm by putting a hand with extended fingers inside clothing to look like a gun does not constitute an imitation in terms of a s 17(2) offence (*R v Bentham* [2005] UKHL 18).

18.3.4   Requesting a person to hand over a firearm or ammunition

Health and safety always come first. Health and safety in relation to firearms found at crime scenes is covered in 11.2.6.2.

Specic Incidents

Under s 47(1) a police officer can require any person to hand over a firearm (and/or ammunition) for examination if the officer has reasonable cause to suspect that he/she has a firearm (with or without ammunition) in a public place, or if he/she is committing or is about to commit a 'relevant offence'. Relevant offences for the purposes of this legislation include other offences from the Firearms Act 1968, such as carrying a firearm with criminal intent (s 18), trespassing in a building with a firearm (s 20(1)), or trespassing on land with a firearm (s 20(2)). It is a summary offence to fail to hand over a firearm or ammunition when required to do so (s 47(2)). The penalty is three months' imprisonment and/or a fine.

18.3.5 The power to stop and search for firearms

This is provided by s 47 of the Firearms Act 1968 (s 47(3) for a person and s 47(4) for a vehicle). It applies if a firearms offence has been committed or is about to be committed, but, as ever, health and safety comes first. In order to carry out such a search, s 2 of the PACE Act 1984 and the associated Codes of Practice must be followed (see 9.4.1). A power of entry (s 47(5)) is available to search for firearms.

18.3.6 Young people and access to firearms

For all types of firearms (including imitations and ammunition) it is a summary offence under the Firearms Act 1968 to sell or hire such an item to a person under 18 (s 24(1)), and for a young person under 18 to purchase such an item (s 22(1)). It is also an offence to give, lend or otherwise part with a s 1 firearm or ammunition to a person under 14 (s 24(2)). A defence is available for the s 24 offences if it can be shown that there were reasonable grounds to believe the young person was older than the relevant age limit (as applicable, s 24(5)).

Other legislation applies to specific types of firearms and this is covered where the various categories of firearm are described separately.

18.3.7 Trading in firearms

Section 3(1) of the Firearms Act 1968 prevents any person from trading or carrying out any business with firearms (including air weapons) without being registered as a firearms dealer. Activities will include manufacturing, selling, exposing for sale, repairing, and testing firearms. These offences are triable either way, and the penalty is six months' imprisonment and/or a fine if tried summarily, and five years' imprisonment on indictment.

18.3.8 Ball bearing ('BB') guns

A typical BB gun will not be classified as a firearm as they are not lethal, neither do they fit the definition of an imitation firearm (see 18.8) for the purposes of offences under the Firearms Act 1968. However, many 'firearms incidents' involve BB guns; a national overview can be found at <http://www.infertrust.org/issues_bb_guns.asp>.

The term 'BB gun' is derived from the small round plastic or aluminium balls they fire, which resemble ball bearings. They are powered by a spring, batteries, or gas (eg carbon dioxide) from an external aerosol canister. However, if the gun appears to be more powerful than a typical BB gun or has large projectiles, the power level may need to be assessed by a forensic laboratory, because it might be sufficiently powerful to be classified as an air weapon or a 'section 1 firearm'. If the projectiles are forced out by gas from a self-contained cartridge (resembles a bullet and casing), then the weapon will be classed as a prohibited weapon (see 18.7).

18.4 Section 1 Firearms

Section 1 firearms include a broad range of firearms. They are defined in s 1 of the Firearms Act 1968 as any firearm except for shotguns, legal air weapons, prohibited weapons, and imitation firearms. A sawn-off shotgun (see 18.5) is classed as a s 1 firearm.

18.4.1 Common types of Section 1 Firearms

There are many different types of firearm that fall under s 1 of the Firearms Act 1968, in terms of their design. We describe some of the main types here. The legal classification of firearms is covered later in the chapter.

A **revolver** is a hand-held firearm that derives its name from the cylinder that contains the ammunition, as shown in the photograph. This revolves as the weapon is fired, to align a new round of ammunition with the breech of the weapon. The usual number of rounds contained in the cylinder of a revolver is six (hence the 'six gun' of the American cowboy) but this can vary with the make and model.

Revolving Cylinder

Photograph by Vince Leonard

A **self-loading pistol** (SLP) is a hand-held firearm fed by a magazine (often removable, see 18.3.1.1). They are often (and mistakenly) referred to as an 'automatic' pistol (see 18.3.1.1). The magazine of an average modern 9 mm SLP contains about 15 rounds. Some can however contain many more rounds, depending in part on the calibre of the weapon.

A **carbine** is a rifle with a short barrel. Originally, a carbine was a short musket or rifle intended for use by mounted troops, but the accepted meaning of the term has changed.

Photograph by Vince Leonard

short barrel

magazine

A **rifle** has a long rifled barrel, and is deigned to be an intrinsically accurate and long distance weapon (many have a large sight mounted on the top). The ammunition is fed from a magazine. For a bolt action rifle the ammunition is loaded into the breech by means of a hand operated bolt, and the empty cartridge case remains in the breech until extracted by use of the bolt mechanism. This type of weapon fires one round at a time. A self-loading rifle on the other hand operates in a similar way to a self-loading pistol, and will often have a 'change lever' so they can also fire in automatic mode; when the trigger is depressed the weapon will continue to discharge until the magazine is empty.

Photograph by Vince Leonard

Change lever

18.4.2 Legislation relating to s 1 Firearms

It is an offence to have a s 1 firearm without the appropriate certificate (s 1), as shown in the flowchart.

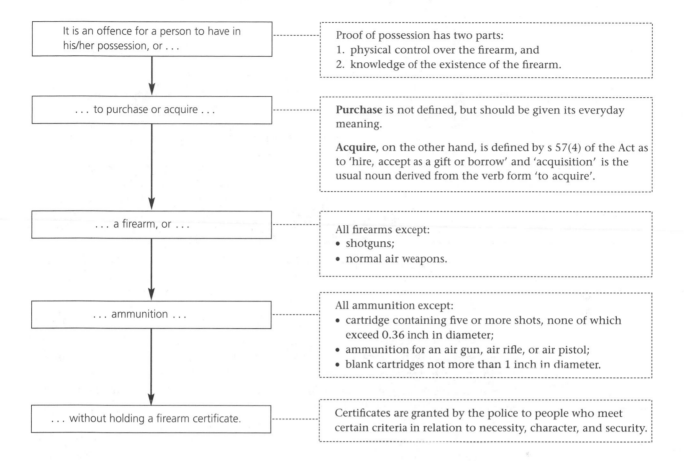

| It is an offence for a person to have in his/her possession, or . . . | Proof of possession has two parts: 1. physical control over the firearm, and 2. knowledge of the existence of the firearm. |

| . . . to purchase or acquire . . . | **Purchase** is not defined, but should be given its everyday meaning. **Acquire**, on the other hand, is defined by s 57(4) of the Act as to 'hire, accept as a gift or borrow' and 'acquisition' is the usual noun derived from the verb form 'to acquire'. |

| . . . a firearm, or . . . | All firearms except: • shotguns; • normal air weapons. |

| . . . ammunition . . . | All ammunition except: • cartridge containing five or more shots, none of which exceed 0.36 inch in diameter; • ammunition for an air gun, air rifle, or air pistol; • blank cartridges not more than 1 inch in diameter. |

| . . . without holding a firearm certificate. | Certificates are granted by the police to people who meet certain criteria in relation to necessity, character, and security. |

This offence is triable either way and the penalty is a fine or imprisonment (six months if tried summarily, but if on indictment five years, and seven for a sawn-off shotgun).

In some circumstances a s 1 firearm might not require a certificate. This is a complex area, but special arrangements are in place for certain types of firearm, including antique firearms and handguns used for killing animals. Criminals have been known to take advantage of this possible loophole by legally acquiring antique firearms and then using them to carry out street shootings and robberies. Members of rifle and pistol clubs, visiting overseas forces, and theatrical performers in a show are also excluded from the requirement to hold a firearms certificate. A blank firing revolver which had been modified to render the barrel unobstructed was judged not to require certification under s 1 because it had no cylinder or other structure for containing the bullets or rounds (*Simon Rogers v R* [2011] EWCA Crim 1549).

The age restrictions for s 1 firearms are shown in the table. An empty box means the activity is not permitted. Note that a person of any age can carry a s 1 firearm for a person over 18 during a sporting activity.

The person may	Under 14	Age 14+	Age 15+	Age 17+	Age 18+
Hold a firearm certificate	*	✓	✓	✓	✓
Carry a firearm for a person over 18 during a sporting activity	✓	✓	✓	✓	✓
Receive a s 1 firearm as a gift		✓	✓	✓	✓
Purchase or hire a s 1 firearm					✓

* A parent can be granted a certificate (or have an existing certificate varied) that includes a child under 14, if for example the child is to participate in competitive target shooting.

18.5   **Shotguns**

There are different designs of shotguns, with different loading systems. Subsection 1(3)(a) of the Firearms Act 1968 provides the definition of a shotgun as shown in the flowchart.

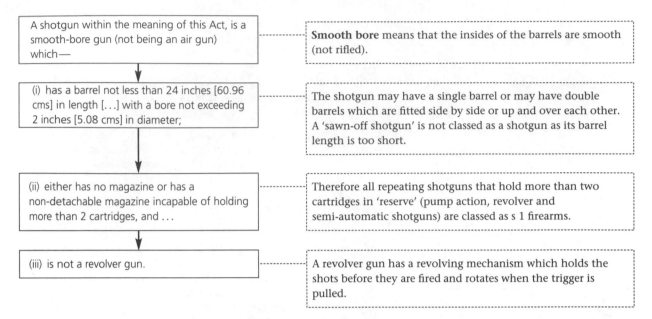

A shotgun within the meaning of this Act, is a smooth-bore gun (not being an air gun) which—

Smooth bore means that the insides of the barrels are smooth (not rifled).

(i) has a barrel not less than 24 inches [60.96 cms] in length [...] with a bore not exceeding 2 inches [5.08 cms] in diameter;

The shotgun may have a single barrel or may have double barrels which are fitted side by side or up and over each other. A 'sawn-off shotgun' is not classed as a shotgun as its barrel length is too short.

(ii) either has no magazine or has a non-detachable magazine incapable of holding more than 2 cartridges, and ...

Therefore all repeating shotguns that hold more than two cartridges in 'reserve' (pump action, revolver and semi-automatic shotguns) are classed as s 1 firearms.

(iii) is not a revolver gun.

A revolver gun has a revolving mechanism which holds the shots before they are fired and rotates when the trigger is pulled.

A typical shotgun cartridge consists of a plastic or cardboard tube containing shot and protective wadding, with a brass battery cup at the base containing the primer. The propellant is contained in the cartridge directly above the primer and separated from the shot by a 'driving wad', which is a circular piece of plastic or compressed fibrous material. In modern shotgun ammunition, this wad is usually integral to a 'chalice', which holds the shot. (The type and positioning of the wadding varies between manufacturers, and this can be useful forensically, particularly when a shotgun barrel has been shortened.) When the shotgun is fired the propellant burns, and this rapidly creates hot gases. This forces all the shot and wadding out through the barrel. The wadding prevents the spherical shot being deformed in the barrel (non-spherical shot would tend to stray from the intended path).

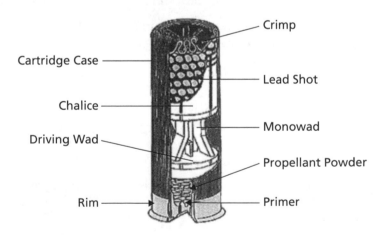

Diagram by Vince Leonard

The most commonly owned and used type of shotgun has no magazine but is double barrelled, either over-and-under or side-by-side. The cartridges are individually loaded into each barrel by 'breaking' the weapon to allow access the rear part of the barrel where the cartridges are inserted.

Pump-action shotguns have a single barrel and a magazine for cartridges. After firing, the empty cartridge is extracted by sliding the fore-end backwards, and the next one loaded by sliding it forwards.

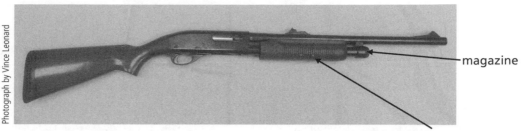

magazine

'fore-end' that 'pumps' the cartridges into the breech end of the barrel

A self-loading shotgun (often referred to as a semi-automatic) has a magazine from which the cartridges are loaded into the breech and then discharged in a similar manner to a self-loading pistol. The loading and extraction mechanism is operated by the gas created when a cartridge is discharged. This allows the weapon to be fired as fast as the trigger can be pulled.

18.5.1 Shotgun certificates and age restrictions

A shotgun certificate (also referred to as a 'licence') is granted by the chief police officer of the force in which the applicant lives. Shotguns are frequently used for sporting purposes (eg clay pigeon shooting) and for shooting game. Therefore, unless there is a specific reason to refuse the application it will normally be granted, in marked contrast to the issue of certificates for s 1 firearms. Possessing, purchasing, or acquiring a shotgun without holding a relevant certificate is an offence under s 2(1) of the Firearms Act 1968. The offence is triable either way and the penalty is a fine or imprisonment (six months if tried summarily and five years on indictment).

A number of conditions are placed upon the holder of a shotgun certificate. An important requirement is that shotguns will be kept secure when not in use, for example in a specially designed steel gun cabinet. It is an offence for a person to fail to comply with a condition relating to a shotgun certificate (s 2(2)). This offence is triable summarily and the penalty is six months' imprisonment and/or a fine.

In certain circumstances, however, a person may 'have' a shotgun without a shotgun certificate, such as when borrowing a shotgun from a person (who holds a certificate) and then using it on that person's land in his/her presence. Nor is a certificate required in order to possess the type of shotgun cartridge that has many small pellets (ie five or more shot pellets in a cartridge with pellets not more than 0.36 inches in diameter).

The age restrictions specifically for shotguns are shown in the table; an empty box means the activity is not permitted. Note that a person of any age can have an assembled shotgun in his/her possession if supervised by a person aged at least 21 years with a certificate, and there is no age limit to having a shotgun certificate.

The age restrictions that apply for firearms in general are covered in 18.3.6.

The person may	Under 14	Age 14+	Age 15+	Age 17+	Age 18+
Hold a shotgun certificate		✓	✓	✓	✓
Possess an assembled shotgun if supervised by a person aged 21 or over with a certificate	✓	✓	✓	✓	✓
Receive a shotgun as a gift			✓	✓	✓
Have an uncovered/unsecured shotgun			✓	✓	✓
Purchase or hire a shotgun					✓

It is an offence to gift a shotgun or ammunition to a young person under 15 (s 24(3)). A defence is available if it can be shown that there were reasonable grounds to believe the young person was 15 or over (s 24(5)).

> **TASK 3**
>
> 1. Describe the general characteristics of a firearm.
> 2. What are the powers to demand production of certificates?
> 3. Under what circumstances can a person be required to hand over a firearm or ammunition for examination?
> 4. What firearms are covered by s 1 and so require a s 1 certificate?
> 5. What ammunition is covered by s 1 and therefore requires a s 1 certificate?
> 6. Describe the specifications of a shotgun that would be legal in the UK.

18.6   Air Weapons

Air weapons include air pistols, air guns, and air rifles. They are usually less dangerous than other firearms because the pellets are discharged from the barrel relatively slowly and are relatively low mass. (Remember that kinetic energy is related to both the square of the speed and the mass.) The velocity is low because the pellets are propelled by air pressure alone, rather than by an explosive charge. However, air weapons are capable of causing serious injury including blindness. Fatalities are also not unknown, particularly with children—in 2013, a 24-year-old man died in Sheffield after being shot in the head with an air rifle. Air weapon offences make up more than half of all recorded firearms offences and it is clear they should be taken very seriously.

The photograph shows an air pistol that uses a sliding mechanism to generate the air pressure to 'cock' the spring so it is ready to fire.

Photograph by Vince Leonard

The pressure in an air-weapon can also by folding the barrel into the 'broken' position; this system is used for air rifles.

There are many different types of design of air weapons and unless you know how to safely handle firearms you should always ask someone who knows about firearms to assist you in their safe handling and storage.

An air weapon does not require a certificate under s 1 of the Firearms Act 1968 unless it exceeds the authorized kinetic energy. The kinetic energy can be measured by a forensic laboratory, and if it exceeds 6 ft lb (for air pistols), or 12 ft lb (for air weapons other than air pistols) the firearm would be regarded as a s 1 firearm. Any air weapon with a self-contained gas cartridge system (containing compressed gas and a pellet) is automatically classed as a prohibited weapon under s 5 of the Firearms Act (see 18.7). For further information see the Firearms (Dangerous Air Weapons) Rules 1969.

18.6.1   Age limits for possessing and firing air weapons

Age restrictions applying to all firearms (including air weapons) are covered in 18.3.6. Other legislation applies specifically to air weapons and this is covered here.

For a person under the age of 18 it is an offence to 'have' with him/her an air weapon or ammunition for an air weapon anywhere and at any time (s 22(4)) unless he/she is a member at a rifle club and firing at targets, or the weapon is being fired at a gallery and does not exceed .23 calibre (s 23(2)).

On private land with the landowner's permission, a young person aged 14–17 years can use (ie fire) an air weapon, but under 14s must be supervised by a person of 21 years or over. If the pellets go beyond the premises (eg a house, garden or other enclosed private place), an offence is committed unless the owner of the adjoining property gave permission (s 23(1 and 1A) and s 21A(1 and 2)).

A young person aged 14–17 years can use an air weapon anywhere if supervised by a person aged over 21 (s 23(1)). However, it must be remembered that without lawful authority or a reasonable excuse it is an offence to carry any firearm (including air weapons) in a public place (see 18.3.3).

These offences are triable summarily and the penalty is a fine.

18.6.2 Preventing access to air weapons for young people

The legislation described in 18.3.3 helps prevent young people having access to firearms in general, including air weapons, but other legislation applies specifically to air weapons. Subject to the exemptions for supervisors of young people outlined in 18.6.1, it is an offence:

- to make a gift or to otherwise part with any air weapon or ammunition to a young person under 18 (s 24(4));
- for a person in possession of an air weapon to fail to take reasonable precautions to prevent a young person under 18 from having an air weapon (s 24(ZA)(1)).

A defence is available if it can be shown that there were reasonable grounds to believe the young person was aged 18 or over (s 24(5)).

These offences are triable summarily and the penalty is a fine.

TASK 4

1. A 16-year-old boy has been firing an air rifle from his parents' bedroom window at baked-bean cans on top of their garden wall and some of the pellets have clearly gone into the neighbour's garden. What offence has the boy committed?
2. A young person is seen carrying an air rifle in a street. Police questioning establishes that she is 17 years old. What offence, if any, has she committed?

18.7 Prohibited Weapons

Parliament decided that the general public have no reasonable need to possess certain types of potentially highly dangerous weapon such as machine guns, PAVA (an incapacitating pepper spray), or CS spray.

(Images courtesy of Kent Police)

The two canisters on the left are examples of CS Spray and those on the right, pepper spray. All are examples of s 5 prohibited weapons.

Under s 5 of the Firearms Act 1968, no one may possess or make such items without special authority. The table shows some of the more significant prohibited features along with some examples. There are some exceptions to these prohibitions (ie such firearms would not be prohibited), as shown in the final column of the table (information derived from the CPS website).

Prohibited feature	Example of a prohibited firearm	Permitted exceptions
Short barrel (less than 30cm) or short overall (less than 60cm)	handguns, revolvers	If also an air weapon, a muzzle-loading gun or a firearm designed as signalling apparatus
Can discharge a noxious liquid, gas, or other thing.	stun guns, (including 'conducted energy devices' such as a 'Taser'), aerosol incapacitant sprays, eg CS	
Two or more missiles can be successively discharged without repeated pressure on the trigger	machine guns	
Self-loading or pump-action with a rifled barrel	short-barrelled rifles	If chambered for .22 rim-fire cartridges
Self-loading or pump-action with a short smooth-bore barrel (barrel less than 24", or overall length less than 40")	self-loading shotguns	If chambered for .22 rim-fire cartridges, or an air weapon
Smooth-bore revolver gun	'Dragon'	If also designed for 9mm rim-fire cartridges or a muzzle-loading gun
Can project a stabilized missile	rocket launcher	If also for line-throwing or pyrotechnics, or designed as signalling apparatus
Has a self-contained gas cartridge system	Brococks	
Ammunition designed to explode on or just before impact, or containing a noxious substance		
A firearm disguised as another object	pen guns, key fob guns, and phone guns	

It is an offence to possess, purchase, acquire, manufacture, sell, or transfer a prohibited weapon or ammunition (s 5(1) of the Firearms Act 1968) without written authority from the Defence Council (the Secretary of State for Defence, other MoD Ministers, the Chiefs of Staff, and senior civil servants). This offence is triable either way and the penalty is a fine or imprisonment (six months if tried summarily and ten years on indictment).

> **TASK 5** A firearms incident at Hungerford in Berkshire in 1987 shocked the public and led to calls for changes in legislation (there are numerous websites that will provide the details). Consider the subsequent White Paper, *Firearms Act 1968: Proposals for Reform* (Cm 261, 1987) and the amendment to the 1968 Act effected by s 1 of the Firearms (Amendment) Act 1988. Why was a change in the list of prohibited weapons thought to be necessary at this time?

18.8   Imitation Firearms

The Firearms Act 1982 states that an imitation firearm is any item that looks like a s 1 firearm (see 18.4) and can be readily converted (see 18.8.1) into a firearm of a type requiring a firearm certificate under s 1 of the Firearms Act 1968 (see 18.4.2).

A replica firearm on the other hand resembles a firearm but cannot be readily converted to a s 1 firearm. However, a replica may still require a certificate if one or more of its working parts constitute components of a firearm (see 18.3.1.1).

(Images courtesy of Kent Police)

On the left a real Mauser, on the right the imitation

18.8.1 Readily converted imitation firearms

An imitation firearm is 'readily convertible' if it can be converted without special skills or special tools (s 1(6) of the Firearms Act 1982). Here, a 'special tool' is a tool which would not generally be used in the home for construction and maintenance. So if an imitation firearm can be converted with a normal screwdriver, it is regarded as readily convertible.

Ultimately only a court can decide whether a particular item requires a certificate, and testing at a forensic laboratory would usually be required before commencing any prosecution. If a certificate is required but the owner does not have one, then he/she has committed an offence. There might be a defence if it can be shown that he/she did not know (and had no reason to suspect) that the imitation firearm was readily convertible (s 1(5) of the Firearms Act 1982).

18.8.2 Other offences relating to imitation firearms

It is an offence to have an imitation firearm in a public place without lawful authority or reasonable excuse (s 19 of the Firearms Act 1968) as for any other firearm (see 18.3.3). It is not an offence to have a replica of a firearm in a public place.

It is also a summary offence for a person under 18 years of age to buy an imitation firearm, and for anyone to sell an imitation firearm to a person under 18 years of age (s 24A of the Firearms Act 1968). The penalty is 12 months' imprisonment and/or a fine.

18.9 Answers to Tasks

TASK 1 You probably considered the following:

1. Do the occupants have a reasonable excuse for the presence of the items?
2. Who do the items belong to?
3. Does it seem likely that a crime could be prevented if the matter is investigated further?
4. How would a police officer progress this matter further? Are the circumstances such that an arrest is necessary?
5. Could a police officer deal with the matter by reporting the suspect?

TASK 2 You probably considered the following:

1. Is Ahmed above the age of criminal responsibility?
2. What type of knife is it?
3. Has it been made, adapted, or intended to cause injury?
4. For how long has Ahmed been carrying the knife?
5. Will he hand it over?

TASK 3

1. Any lethal barrelled weapon of any description from which any shot, bullet, or other missile can be discharged. This includes a prohibited weapon (lethal or not), any component part of a lethal or prohibited weapon, and any accessory designed or adapted to diminish the noise or flash caused by firing any such weapon.
2. A police officer may demand the production of the relevant certificate from any person whom he/she believes to be in possession of a s 1 firearm (or ammunition) or a shotgun.

3. When a police officer has reasonable cause to suspect a person of having a firearm in a public place (with or without ammunition), or to be committing (or be about to commit) an offence relevant to the Firearms Act 1968, anywhere other than in a public place.
4. All firearms except shotguns, prohibited weapons, air weapons (unless 'specially dangerous'), or imitation firearms (unless converted).
5. Any ammunition for a firearm except:
   - cartridges containing five or more shot, none of which exceeds .36 inch in diameter;
   - ammunition for an air gun, air rifle, or air pistol; and
   - blank cartridges with 1 inch maximum diameter.
6. The shotgun must have a smooth bore and the barrel must be at least 60.96cm long and no more than 5.08cm in diameter. It must not be a revolver gun, and must have either no magazine, or a non-detachable magazine that can hold only one or two cartridges.

TASK 4

1. It is generally an offence for a person under the age of 18 to have an air weapon (or ammunition for an air weapon), but there are exceptions. For example, it is not an offence for a person aged 14 years or over to possess the air weapon on private premises with the consent of the occupier, and he/she does not have to be supervised. However, it is an offence to use an air weapon to fire a missile beyond those premises (s 21A of the Firearms Act 1968).
2. A person commits an offence if, without lawful authority or reasonable excuse, he/she has with him/her in a public place any loaded or unloaded air weapon (s 19 of the Firearms Act 1968).

TASK 5 As a result of the shootings at Hungerford on 12 August 1987, it was considered that certain firearms were so dangerous that they should be classified as prohibited weapons. These include self-loading and pump-action rifles (other than those chambered for .22 rim-fire), and certain self-loading and pump-action shotguns (see the White Paper *Firearms Act 1968: Proposals for Reform* (Cm 261, 1987) and the amendment to the 1968 Act (effected by s 1 of the Firearms (Amendment) Act 1988)). The 1968 Act was also amended so that a firearm certificate was required for certain shotguns.

19.1 Introduction

Road and traffic legislation and procedure can appear confusing and complicated, but a trainee police officer will still be expected to demonstrate competence in many areas during supervised and independent patrol. This chapter covers the terms commonly used in the legislation, the offences related to circumstance and manner of driving, collisions (the preferred term for accidents), and drink- and drug-driving. It also covers non-driving highways offences such as wilful obstruction and the use of fireworks near highways.

Much of the legislation and regulation surrounds safety and the protection of individuals who use the roads. The safety of UK roads has improved significantly. However, roads incidents are the most likely cause of premature death for individuals under the age of 25, and cause a significant number of avoidable deaths across all age groups. About a quarter of all deaths in the UK each year are considered avoidable, the second most common cause being due to a road traffic incident (most avoidable deaths are due to medical conditions, such as heart disease). In 2015 there were 1,730 road traffic deaths (compare this to 518 homicides), and 22,144 people were seriously injured on the roads. Drivers failing to look properly is the most common cause of collisions (44 per cent), but the most common cause for fatalities is loss of control (31 per cent). Road death and injury are of course tragedies for the individuals concerned, but they also have a significant financial cost to society as a whole, with estimates for 2015 amounting to around £2m for each fatality (£3.2bn in total) and £230,000 for each serious injury (£4.6bn in total). Pedestrians, motorcyclists, and cyclists are particularly vulnerable (Department for Transport, 2016).

There is also a link between offending on the roads and other forms of criminality. Rose (2000) demonstrated that 79 per cent of disqualified drivers had a criminal record (four times higher than the average for the general population), approximately 50 per cent of dangerous drivers had a previous conviction, and approximately 25 per cent were convicted of an offence within a year (three times the average). Interestingly, drink-drivers were less likely to have a criminal record (40 per cent) than other groups of serious traffic offenders, and 'only' 12 per cent were convicted again within a year. However, these figures are still about twice the average for the general population. Nunn (2016) found that 82 per cent of drug-drivers had previous convictions of which 82 per cent had drugs convictions and 53 per cent had convictions for serious motoring offences. Junger *et al* (2001) also identified links between 'risky' traffic behaviour and more general violent crime, and similarly Chenery *et al* (1999) demonstrated in a famous study the links between the relatively minor offence of illegal parking in disabled bays, active criminals, and illegal vehicles. All of this leads us to the notion of 'self-selecting' road and traffic behaviour that police officers could usefully consider as indicators of perhaps more serious criminal predisposition. The enforcement of road traffic offences and the imposition of penalties will of course also deny criminals the use of the roads and hence disrupt their other criminal activities.

The National Police Chiefs' Council (NPCC) roads policing strategy 2015–2020 aims to reduce the number of collisions leading to road death and serious injury, and to combat organized crime and terrorism through flexible enforcement based upon intelligence, professional judgement, and discretion. Through working with partners, the aim is to provide a visible and technological presence on our roads, and to penalize and educate errant drivers, thereby influencing the behaviour of all road users (NPCC, 2015). There are four strands to the strategy:

- Safety—to reduce risk;
- Security—to disrupt organized crime and terrorist use of the road network;
- Effective—the use of data to improve safety and security;
- Efficiency—efficient roads will promote public confidence and efficient communication will deliver cost effective harm reduction.

These strategic objectives can only be achieved by effective partnership working. Further information is available in the *Partner agencies* section of the College of Policing Authorised Professional Practice, available online.

'Working in the carriageway' accounts for a significant number of police fatalities and is one of the most dangerous working environments for police officers. The police are governed by the Health and Safety at Work etc. Act 1974, and each police service will therefore have risk assessments (see 6.12.3) for this type of work. Trainee constables should be familiar with these assessments and the associated risk mitigation strategies. Working in the carriageway is also governed by the New Roads and Street Works Act 1991 and the Highways Act 1980. These require all individuals (including police officers) to wear suitable high visibility clothing whilst working in the carriageway (and failing to do so may constitute a criminal offence). For roads with a speed limit over 50mph the jacket must comply with the European Standard EN 471 to class 3 (service-issue high visibility jackets will comply with this).

Trainee police officers will be instructed, shown, and assessed on the detail of police procedure in terms of stopping a vehicle, actions to be taken when attending the scene of a recent collision, and so on. Where appropriate, we provide some of these details (in 19.4.1 for example, on stopping vehicles). Officers should also be guided by local policies and the College of Policing *Road Policing* Authorised Professional Practice, available online.

19.2 Definitions Relating to Vehicles and Roads

Road traffic legislation has inevitably developed as times have changed, and new terminology has been introduced to deal with advances in technology. Terms that were valid for the Highways Act 1835 may seem archaic but should be seen in context. It is essential that an officer has understanding of the terms used as they often determine the relevant powers and responsibilities.

19.2.1 Definitions of vehicles

Within road traffic legislation various terms are used to describe the different types of vehicle and other wheeled objects such as carriages, conveyances, and cycles. The following table explains some of these terms, but is by no means comprehensive.

Vehicle type	Definition	Examples
'Vehicle'	According to the Vehicle Excise and Registration Act 1994, a vehicle is: 'a mechanically propelled vehicle, or anything (whether or not it is a vehicle) that has been, but has ceased to be, a mechanically propelled vehicle' The ordinary dictionary meaning can also be used	Milk float, ride-on grass cutter
'Mechanically propelled vehicle'	'Mechanically propelled' means that the vehicle is powered by a motor (driven by electricity, petrol, diesel, or other fuels). The meaning is not defined by any Act of Parliament, so whether a particular vehicle is a mechanically propelled vehicle is therefore a question of fact for a court to decide	Car, van, lorry, go-ped, quad bike, speedway motorcycles, Formula One racing cars, self-balancing personal transporters (Segways, hoverboards, etc), invalid carriages such as powered wheelchairs and scooters

Vehicle type	Definition	Examples
'Motor vehicle'	This is a mechanically propelled vehicle that is intended or adapted for use on roads (s 185 of the Road Traffic Act 1988)	Car, van, lorry, self-balancing personal transporters (Segways, hoverboards, etc)
'Motor bicycle'*	This means a motor vehicle which has two wheels and a maximum design speed exceeding 45kph. If powered by an internal combustion engine, the cylinder capacity must exceed 50cc. It includes a combination, such as a motor vehicle and a side-car (s 108 of the Road Traffic Act 1988)	Motorcycle with two wheels, includes those fitted with a sidecar.
'Bicycle'	This includes a 'motor bicycle' (ie a motorcycle) for the purposes of vehicle excise duty	
'Moped'*	Moped means a motor vehicle which has fewer than four wheels and if first used before 1 August 1977, has an internal combustion engine with a cylinder capacity not exceeding 50cc, and pedals that can be used for propulsion. In any other case, a moped must have a maximum design speed not exceeding 50 kph (note this covers electric-powered two wheelers) and, if propelled by an engine, have a cylinder capacity not exceeding 50cc (s 108 of the Road Traffic Act 1988)	
'Pedal cycle'	This must be designed so it can be propelled by pedals, and includes electrically assisted pedal cycles (reg 3 of the Pedal Cycles (Construction and Use) Regulations 1983)	Mountain bike, racing bike, BMX bike
'Carriage'	This means a motor vehicle or trailer (s 191 of the Road Traffic Act 1988). The ordinary dictionary meaning also applies	Any motor vehicle described above, and caravans
'Conveyance'	This is a vehicle constructed or adapted for transporting person(s) by land, water, or air, but not one constructed or adapted for use 'only under the control of a person not carried in or on it' (s 12(7) of the Theft Act 1968)	Motorcycle, bus, boat, and plane

*De-restriction kits are available for mopeds (to allow speeds over 50 kph and/or increase the cylinder capacity), and for 125cc learner motorcycles, to increase power. If such alterations are made the vehicle becomes a motor bicycle and the rider must conform to the relevant licence requirements (see 19.3.1.1).

Some vehicles do not fit within obvious categories. These include mini-motos (small motorcycles designed for use on private land), go-peds (effectively a child's scooter with a petrol or electric engine) and self-balancing personal transporters such as Segways and hoverboards. All of these have been held to be motor vehicles (carriages) for the purposes of s 185 of the Road Traffic Act 1988. The Crown Prosecution Service provides advice on these on their website in the *Definitions of a motor vehicle* section. This includes the references by case stated (ie the relevant case law) regarding mini-motos, go-peds, and self-balancing personal transporters. Full details of the legal requirements are also given on the CPS website; see also *Coates v CPS* [2011] EWHC 2032 (Admin). In some circumstances, the use of such vehicles may be an offence against the Highways Act 1835 (see 19.11.3).

19.2.2 Definitions of roads, highways, and related terms

Legislation relating to road and traffic policing often includes the words 'road', 'highway', and 'public place'. Each term is used in different pieces of legislation, though the term 'road' is used far more frequently, particularly since the introduction of the Road Traffic Act 1988.

* A road is defined as any (length of) highway to which the public has access, and includes bridges over which a road passes (s 192 of the Road Traffic Act 1988). The limits of a road are the hedgerows, walls, fences, or building lines on each side, so a public footpath alongside a road is part of the road.
* A highway (s 5 of the Highways Act 1835) is defined as a road, bridge, carriageway, cart-way, horse-way, bridleway, footway, causeway, church way, or pavement.
* A public road is a road maintained at the public's expense (for the purposes of vehicle excise duty legislation), as defined in s 62 of the Vehicle Excise and Registration Act 1994. Note: care must be taken as a road to which the public have access (eg not gated or blocked) may not be a 'public road'; if in doubt consult the Highways Authority for the area.

Note the potentially confusing overlap between a road and a highway: in practice this does not matter as each relates to individual pieces of legislation.

Specific Incidents

A number of other terms are also used:

- 'other public place' is a place that any member of the general public has access to, without needing specific permission, but it will be for a court to decide (see also 9.2). It is likely to include car parks, turning areas, and parks. The term is used in a number of places in the Road Traffic Act 1988, for example in relation to insurance (s 143(1)(a)), collision reporting (s 170) , driving standards (ss 2 and 3), offences surrounding driving-related death (ss 1, 2B, 3ZB, and 3A) and drink or drug drive offences (ss 4, 5, and 5A);
- a carriageway is a 'way' that is marked or arranged in a highway, over which the public have a right of way for the passage of vehicles, but does not include cycle tracks (s 329 of the Highways Act 1980);
- a bridleway is a highway over which the public have a right of way on foot, on horseback, or leading a horse (s 329 of the Highways Act 1980);
- a footpath is a highway not adjacent to a road, over which the public have a right of way on foot only (s 329 of the Highways Act 1980);
- a footway (such as a pavement) is a highway adjacent to a road over which the public have a right of way on foot only (s 329(1) of the Highways Act 1980);
- a street includes roads, lanes, alleys, subways, squares, and any other similar places open to the public. It also includes doorways, entrances to premises, and any ground adjoining a street (*Smith v Hughes* [1960] 2 All ER 859).

The maintenance of a private road is usually the responsibility of the landowner; this one is in a good state of repair. Private roads may or may not be subject to public rights of way.

(Photo by Kevin Lawton-Barrett)

19.2.3 Definitions relating to driving

Legislation relating to road and traffic policing often refers to 'driving' and 'attempting to drive'. The term 'driving' is not defined in any Act, but there are precedents which provide guidelines. The decision finally rests with the court and is therefore a question of fact. The court will consider:

- the degree to which the person had control over the direction and movement of the vehicle;
- the length of time the person had control;
- the point at which the person stopped the driving; and
- the use of the vehicle's controls by the person in order to direct its movement.

Attempting to drive is not defined by statute, but the general principles for attempted offences should be applied; an attempt is the last action before the full offence is committed, and is more than merely preparatory to the act (see 22.2.1). For example, trying to start a vehicle which will not start because it has a fault could be considered as attempting to drive.

19.2.4 Using, causing, permitting use of, and keeping a vehicle

Many road traffic offences are committed by the people who use the vehicle (eg the driver or another, see below), but some offences relate to causing or permitting a vehicle's use. This would apply to vehicle owners and people who hold supervisory responsibilities for example. You need to have a clear understanding about the meanings of 'using', 'causing', and 'permitting'. The level of knowledge of the circumstances is the key to determining each individual's liability. We will illustrate the principles in the context of an employer, an employee, and a defective vehicle , but 'using', 'causing', and 'permitting' also occur in other circumstances, for example within families or between friends. It is also important to note that it will be for the courts to decide as a question of fact whether any of these offences has been committed in particular circumstances; the descriptions we provide here are only general guidelines.

We can briefly summarize the differences between using, causing, and permitting as follows: imagine an employer runs a company van which has a defective tyre, and his female employee drives it. Even if he is not aware of the defect then the offence would be 'using' would still be committed. If, knowing about the defect, he sent her out in the vehicle this would be 'causing', and if he allowed her to borrow the van and use it at the weekend for her own purpose, this would be 'permitting'. We provide more details in the following paragraphs.

Using a vehicle is not the same under road traffic law as driving a vehicle; for example, a vehicle can be 'in use' while parked, or while being towed. The user of a vehicle can be:

* the driver of a vehicle, including an employee driving a company vehicle for business purposes;
* the employer, if the vehicle is a company vehicle used on company business. The employer can be held responsible for committing an offence (as a user) relating to a vehicle defect even if he/she is unaware of the defect: in some circumstances, both the employer and the driver (an employee) can be held responsible;
* the owner of a vehicle, if it is being driven by another person with the owner present and for the benefit of the owner; or
* a person steering a vehicle, for example when being towed.

For causing the use of a vehicle, the 'causer' must have the authority to make a subordinate carry out a particular action, and must know about the unroadworthy state of the vehicle. In some cases, a company rather than a person can be held responsible for causing the use of an unroadworthy vehicle if the company director knows the vehicle is defective. (However, many companies allow employees to use company vehicles for private purposes, and in such circumstances it is unlikely that the employer could be held responsible for causing the vehicle to be used.) Also, note that if a person tows a vehicle, then he/she is causing it to be used on a road.

Permitting use of a vehicle has two elements that must be satisfied. The 'permitter' must:

* be in a position to either allow or forbid its use—such permission can be given verbally, in writing or merely implied; and
* have knowledge of (or 'turn a blind eye' to) the unroadworthy state of the vehicle or its lack of documentation.

Therefore a 'permitting' offence is committed by an employer who knows about a defect on a company vehicle, and allows an employee to use it for business purposes (for relevant case law see the House of Lords judgment in *Vehicle Inspectorate v Nuttall* [1999] 1WLR 629, available online). If either of these elements cannot be proved, then offences relating to the 'use' of the vehicle could be considered.

Keeping a vehicle is when a person ('the keeper') has day-to-day responsibility for a vehicle. It is a question of fact for a court to decide who is a keeper as no legislative definition exists. The 'registered keeper', on the other hand, is the person to whom a vehicle is registered, ie whose details appear on a national register of vehicles (see 19.3.3). Consequently a registered keeper may either be the keeper or he/she may not; (see *Mohindra v DPP* [2004] EWHC 490 (Admin)).

The legal owner of a vehicle could be the 'keeper' or the 'registered keeper', although this should not be assumed. It could alternatively be a financial institution which provided a loan for the purchase, or an insurance company that has paid out on a claim in relation to the vehicle.

TASK 1 Imagine you are a police officer. You see a car being towed by a van, driven by an older man, in a car park with unrestricted access used as a cut through between two roads. The car has all four wheels on the ground and is being towed with a tow rope. There is a person who looks quite young in the driving seat of the car, turning the steering and operating the brakes. You stop the vehicles and speak to both individuals. The van driver is the owner of both vehicles, and the person in the car is his 15-year-old son. You also note that one of the car tyres is defective. The car engine will not start and they say they are taking it to a local garage for repair.

What is the status of each vehicle, each individual, and the location? Who may be liable for any offences discovered?

19.3 Vehicle and Driver Documents

The act of driving and the use of vehicles are subject to licensing, statutory requirements, and testing. These regimes create various documents which a police officer needs to understand in order to deal with incidents, so this section will explain the key points. We will also cover some of the offences which may be committed if all is not in order, and some of the police powers which may be available in such circumstances.

19.3.1 UK driving licences

In the UK, a driver must have the appropriate licence entitlement for the classes of vehicle that he/she drives. The licence shows the categories of vehicle that a person is entitled to drive. UK driving licence regulation and design has changed a number of times over recent years, mainly to bring the UK into line with EU regulation, the latest amendments being in July 2015. This section will primarily deal with UK driving licences but also provides some information on licences from other countries.

Driving licences in the UK are administered by the Driver and Vehicle Licensing Authority (DVLA). The DVLA database contains a 'driver record' for each driver, which shows his/her licence and driving history, and any Driver and Vehicle Standards Agency (DVSA) test passed. Updates are indicated by a 'marker' on the record, for example 'test passed' or 'licence revoked'. The PNC contains 'driver files' which are up-to-date copies of all the DVLA driver records, and the file will have a 'DD' tab if the driver is disqualified.

Offences relating to driving licences under the Road Traffic Act 1988 include:

- driving a motor vehicle on a road otherwise than in accordance with a licence authorizing him/her to drive a motor vehicle of that class (s 87(1)); this includes drivers on provisional entitlements who fail to comply with licence requirements;
- causing or permitting another person to drive on a road if that person does not have a licence authorizing driving that class of vehicle (s 87(2)); and
- failure to update a change of address on a driving licence (s 99(5)).

19.3.1.1 Vehicle categories and codes on driving licences

There have been several changes to the licence vehicle category designations over time, and older licences will use some of the discontinued categories. The first table shows the categories that currently apply (early 2017). For a full explanation of the pre-2013, pre-1996, pre-1990, and pre-1986 arrangements, see the gov.uk website.

Licence vehicle category	Type of vehicle	Minimum driver age
Moped AM	2- or 3-wheeled vehicles with speed range of 15.5 mph–28 mph (25–45 km/h) Small 3-wheelers (up to 50 cc and below 4 kW) Light quadricycles (under 350 kg, top speed 45 km/h)	16
Moped p	2-wheeled with a design speed of over 28 mph (45 km/h) but not exceeding 31 mph (50km/h), with an engine capacity not exceeding 50 cc if powered by internal combustion. No longer issued, but if held it will be shown (as well as AM and q)	
Moped q	2- or 3-wheeled vehicle with top speed of 15.5 mph (25 km/h) and engine size less than 50 cc if internal combustion, granted with an AM licence entitlement	
A1	Small motorbikes up to 11 kW and 125 cc (power-to-weight ratio not more than 0.1 kW per kg) Motor tricycles with a power output 15 kW or less	17
A2	Medium motorbikes up to 35 kW (power-to-weight ratio not more than 0.2 kW per kg). The power of a restricted engine must be at least half its original power (or it will be category A)	19
A	Motorbikes, unlimited size/power, with or without a side-car. Motor tricycles with power output over 15 kW	24 (direct access) 21 (progressive access)

Licence vehicle category	Type of vehicle	Minimum driver age
B1	Light vehicles and quad bikes, 4 wheels up to 400kg (550kg if designed to carry goods)	17
B	Cars and light vans	17
B auto	Cars and light vans with an automatic gearbox	
B+E	Cars and light vans with a trailer up to 3,500 kg	
C1	Goods vehicles weighing between 3,500 kg and 7,500 kg, (with or without a trailer; 750 kg maximum trailer weight)	18*
C1+E	As for C1 but with a trailer over 750 kg (combined weight not exceeding 12,000 kg)	
C	Goods vehicles over 3,500 kg, with a trailer up to 750 kg	21*
C+E	Goods vehicles over 3,500kg with a trailer over 750 kg	
D1	Passenger-carrying vehicles with 9 to 16 passenger seats (minibuses), max length 8 m and trailer up to 750 kg	21*
D1+E	As for D1 but with a trailer over 750 kg (combined weight not exceeding 12,000 kg	
D	Bus with more than 8 passenger seats, and trailer up to 750 kg	24*
D+E	As for D but with a trailer over 750 kg	
F	Agricultural tractors	17
G	Road rollers	21
H	Tracked vehicles	
K	Mowing machines or pedestrian-controlled vehicles	16

* lower age limits apply for armed services personnel and when certain conditions apply. Details can be found on the 'Information on Driving Licences' leaflet available from the gov.uk website.

To start riding a motorbike legally on a road, a licence with a provisional entitlement for the relevant category is required, and also Compulsory Basic Training (CBT). This training takes place at approved training centres and includes basic handling and bike control. It includes a practical on-street assessment and a knowledge test of the Highway Code. A CBT certificate is valid for two years and is shown as a marker on the DVLA driver record. It can be retaken if it expires. Once the rider obtains a full motorcycle entitlement a valid CBT is no longer required.

Note that the motorcycle categories prior to 19 January 2013 were different (see the second table). A full explanation of the process for obtaining motorcycle licences can be found on the gov.uk website.

Pre 2013 Licence motorcycle category	Type of vehicle	Minimum driver age
A1	Light motorcycles with an engine size of up to 125 cc and a power output of up to 11 kW (14.6 bhp)	17
A	Medium-sized motorcycles up to 25 kW (33 bhp) and a power-to-weight ratio up to 0.16 kW/kg (with or without a side-car)	17
	Large motorcycles (over 25 kW (33 bhp) and a power-to-weight ratio over 0.16 kW/kg)	19

Electrically assisted pedal cycles are classified as pedal cycles (see 19.2.1) so a driving licence is not required. Similar exemptions are made for powered wheelchairs and powered scooters designed for people with disabilities.

19.3.1.2 The driver and issue number

Every UK driving licence holder has a driver number. This is the unique reference by which DVLA identifies an individual, and is assigned to a single driver record. A foreign licence holder (with no UK licence) can have a UK driver number if he/she has been dealt with for an offence in the UK and issued with penalty points. It is essential to check the details of a foreign licence holder against the 'driver file' on the PNC, because the driver may have UK penalty points or even be disqualified. It should be noted that a person may have more than one driver number if he/she has been dealt with by the DVLA using slightly different data on different occasions (eg omitting a middle name, giving names in different order, an error in the date of birth). There is a means by which a number of such driver records can be brought together (police service DVLA liaison officers can provide details).

The driver number contains three clusters of information about the driver: family name (five letters); gender and date of birth (six numbers); and a final cluster (five characters). The table shows how to interpret the driver number WILLI 611205 RS9KY for the driver Robert Stuart Williamson.

Cluster	Description	Example
1	The first five letters of the family name. If the name has less than five characters, the remaining spaces are made up using the figure 9 (ie TODD9))	WILLI
2	The first and last digits are derived from the year of birth	611205 shows the year of birth is 1965
	The second and third digits represent the month of birth and the gender. For a female, 5 is added to the second digit, so for a female born in November the cluster would be x61xxx, and for a female born in July, it would be x57xxx	611205 shows he was born in November and is male.
	The fourth and fifth digits show the day of birth:	611205 shows he was born on the 20th of the month
3	The first two characters represent the person's initials	RS9KY (if there is only one initial, 9 is used in place of a second initial, eg R9)
	The third number and the final two letters are computer-generated, and are used to avoid duplicate records. If the first 13 digits of the driver number are unique then the third digit will be a 9, otherwise it will be an 8 (or a 7 in the case of a triplicate, and so on).	RS9KY

The issue number on the driving licence is situated adjacent to the driver number on the front of the licence. A driver's first issue number is randomly generated, and is increased by one on his/her subsequent licences (ie if on first issue the number is 35, the next licence will be 36 and then 37, and so on). Only the current licence is valid as drivers are not allowed to hold more than one licence. The driver file on the PNC shows the issue number of the current valid licence, so this should be checked against any licence provided.

19.3.1.3   UK driving licences

A UK driving licence is a photocard about the size of a credit card and is valid for ten years. The licence can be a full or provisional licence, and shows the driver's current driving entitlements and personal information. Additional licence information can be accessed online using the driver number and the holder's NI number and postcode. The issue number should be checked via the Police National Computer driver file to confirm it is the person's most recently issued licence. Penalty points should also be checked on the PNC as these are no longer endorsed on the actual licence. Note that a driver may produce an old-style paper licence which is still valid, usually because he/she has not recently changed his/her name or address

Provisional licences have a green background with a clear pictogram of an L plate on the front. It will show only provisional entitlements, as they are not issued to drivers with a full entitlement in any category. Full licence photocards have a pink background with an EU flag on the front, and show all the holder's full entitlements. Full licence photocards do not show any provisional entitlements so these would need to be checked against the driver file on PNC.

The latest version of the full driving licence photocard (from 6 July 2015) is shown here. They have improved security features such as tactile (raised) surfaces, engraved text, changing colours, and complex background designs.

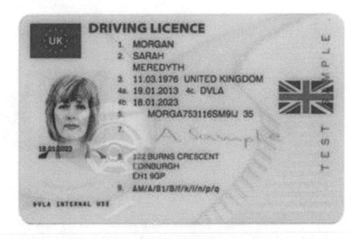

On the front of the card, the issue and expiry dates are shown ((4a) and (4b) respectively). The driver and issue number are shown at (5). The categories of valid vehicle entitlement are shown at (9), with EU directive categories in capitals and UK local categories in lower case.

On the back of the card column 9 shows all the possible entitlements (see 19.3.1.1) and columns 10 and 11 show the valid entitlements for the licence holder, with start and expiry dates. Column 12 lists the DVLA restriction codes that apply for each entitlement. (There are many restriction codes, for example code 01 is 'eyesight correction' for the driver, code 40 is for 'modified steering' on a vehicle (this may apply to a disabled driver), and code 101 is 'not for hire and reward' and may be applied to the minibus entitlement. A breach of the restrictions would amount to driving not in accordance with a licence.)

The DVLA leaflet ref INS57P provides a good explanation of most of the features shown on photocard licences. It is available on the gov.uk website, and can be printed off and kept as a reference.

19.3.1.4   Provisional entitlements and learner drivers

All provisional entitlements impose certain requirements on the driver, and these vary according to the category of vehicle. A breach of any of the requirements will amount to the offence of driving otherwise than in accordance with a driving licence (s 87(1) of the Road Traffic Act 1988). The conditions under which a provisional licence holder can drive a vehicle are set out in reg 16 of the Motor Vehicles (Driving Licences) Regulations 1999. The main requirements relate to 'L' plates and supervision.

L plates must be displayed on front and back of the vehicle while it is being driven by a provisional licence holder in England. The plates must be clearly visible to other road users within a reasonable distance (reg 16(2)(b)). The correct dimensions for an L plate are shown in the diagram, and it can have rounded corners. D plates can be displayed in Wales, but they must be replaced with L plates if driving in England.

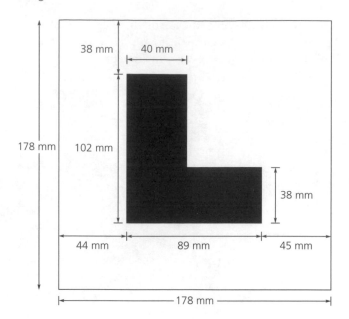

L plates are often 'cut down' for mounting on motorcycles, but this is not permitted. Any vehicle with a cut down L plate (see the photograph) is not displaying a proper L plate, so is not complying with a provisional entitlement requirement, and is therefore driving 'not in accordance with a licence'.

(Photograph courtesy of James Nunn)

Supervision is required for drivers with a provisional entitlement when driving vehicles with four or more wheels (such as those in category B, C, D, and derivatives of these). The supervision must be provided by a 'qualified driver' (reg 16(2)(a)). He/she must be at least 21 years old, have the relevant driving experience, and have had a full British (including Northern Ireland) or an EU Community licence (see 19.3.1.7) with the relevant entitlements for at least three years (reg 17(1) and (2)).

There are some situations where a driver with a provisional entitlement can drive without supervision, such as:

- driving certain categories of motor vehicle, for example, a three-wheeled vehicle;
- riding a moped, or a motorcycle (with or without a side-car);
- driving on an exempted island (except for large goods vehicles and passenger-carrying vehicles); or
- driving a motor vehicle having just passed the relevant driving test (but the driver must have a relevant certificate authorizing the driving).

Provisional licence holders should not drive a vehicle with a trailer (reg 16(2)(c)), unless he/she is learning and being supervised for a vehicle in the +E category. In such circumstances the towing vehicle should have an L plate on the front and the trailer should have a L plate on the back (reg 16(5)).

19.3.1.5   **Disqualification**

A disqualification prohibits an individual from driving any motor vehicle on a road. It can only be imposed by a court as a result of a conviction for a relevant offence, and is a punishment for the individual (as well as a move to protect the public). The DVLA driver record will be marked as such, and a Disqualified Driver (DD) tab will appear on his/her file on the PNC. The driver's licence will also be revoked (see 19.3.1.6).

Disqualification can occur in a number of different circumstances:

- endorsement and penalty points have been given;
- discretionary disqualification;
- obligatory disqualification;
- 'Disqualified Til Test Passed' (DTTP); and
- disqualified in absence.

Penalty points are recorded ('endorsed') on the person's DVLA driver record. The number of points for an offence depends on the type and seriousness of the offence. If 12 points are accumulated ('totted up') in a three-year period, the driver can be disqualified. However, this is not obligatory and a driver can put forward special reasons to the court. (It is quite possible for a driver to have more, even considerably more, than 12 current points.)

Discretionary disqualification is one of the penalty options for certain offences, including 'failing to stop after an accident' (see 19.7.2). Obligatory disqualification applies for certain offences such as driving over the prescribed limit for alcohol or drugs, or dangerous driving where the Road Traffic Act 1988 sets out minimum periods of compulsory disqualification. The length of a disqualification will be determined by the court, subject to the minimums set for obligatory disqualifications, and will relate to the nature of the offence and the drivers previous offending. In very exceptional circumstances an individual can be disqualified for life (*R v Tunde-Olarinde* [1967] 2 All ER 491), although the guidance from the Court of Appeal is that this can be counterproductive with regard to rehabilitation, and must be related to the risk posed by the individual to the general public.

A DTTP disqualification requires the individual to pass a DVSA test (normal or extended, depending on the offence) to regain his/her licence, and can be discretionary or obligatory depending on the offence. A DTTP marker will be shown on the individual's driver record. A DTTP is often imposed in addition to a conventional period of disqualification, ie disqualified for two years and DTTP. The person cannot drive any motor vehicle on a road for two years, but after this period, the disqualification reverts to DTTP-only. At this stage the 'Disqualified' marker on the DVLA driver record and the DD (disqualified driver) marker on the PNC driver file will disappear, but the DTTP marker will remain until a test is passed. He/she will be allowed a provisional licence (to be able to legally drive, to practise for, and take the test). However, if the requirements of the provisional entitlement are not fulfilled he/she is dealt with in the same way as any other disqualified driver, ie under s 103(1)(b).

A person can be disqualified even if absent from court. Courts are reluctant to take this action but it is sometimes required where an individual persistently fails to attend court knowing that he/she is likely to be disqualified. The CPS Legal Guidance for road traffic offences clearly states that 'It is no defence for a person disqualified in their absence to claim that they did not know that they had been disqualified'. Therefore individuals found to be driving in such circumstances should be dealt with in the same way as any other disqualified driver.

A person is guilty of an offence under s 103(1) of the Road Traffic Act 1988 if, while disqualified from holding or obtaining a licence, he/she obtains a licence or drives a motor vehicle on a road (s 103(1)(a) and (b) respectively). Evidence of the original disqualification must be provided to the court (see *Mills v DPP* [2008] EWHC 3304 (Admin)) This could be a certificate of conviction under s 73 of the PACE Act 1984, the defendant's admission (at interview or in court), or a statement from a person who was in court when the disqualification was imposed.

These offences are triable summarily. The penalty for obtaining a licence while disqualified is a fine. The penalty for driving a motor vehicle on a road while disqualified is imprisonment for up to six months and/or a fine, discretionary extension of the disqualification, and obligatory endorsement (six penalty points).

Specific Incidents

19.3.1.6 Revocation

When a licence is revoked the individual's licence is effectively suspended, pending resolution of the circumstances, and the person is no longer authorized to drive under any of the entitlements on the licence. Licences can be revoked by the DVLA for a number of reasons, such as:

- failing to surrender a licence when required. The DVLA is notified by a court when an endorsement is imposed, and will write to the licence holder requesting surrender of the licence within 28 days, and stating that if it is not surrendered it will be revoked. If it is not surrendered the DVLA will inform the individual by post that the licence has been revoked. The record will be updated to show the licence as expired;
- disqualification—when an individual is disqualified from driving (see 19.3.1.5), the DVLA will mark the licence as revoked on the driver record and add the disqualification. At the end of a fixed period disqualification the individual must re-apply for a licence, and until it is obtained the DVLA driver record will still show it as revoked;
- medical grounds— the licence holder (or a third party with an obligation to inform) tells the DVLA that the person has a notifiable medical condition. Full details of the notifiable conditions can be found on the gov.uk website. The revocation will only be cancelled after suitable medical reports have been received or a specified symptom-free period has passed;
- the licence has been issued in error by the DVLA.

The circumstances under which a licence can be revoked will often need to be explained to individuals, as many people do not understand the process. Depending on the reasons for the revocation, the DVLA driver record will show the licence as revoked or expired. (Sometimes the DVLA will alter the expiry date of the licence rather than revoke it in the normal way.) Note that a person with a revoked licence is not disqualified from driving; this would need to be imposed by a court. Driving with a revoked licence is 'driving not in accordance with a licence' which is a different offence from driving while disqualified.

New drivers can also have their full entitlement revoked to a provisional entitlement. The intention is to deter poor driving. The Road Traffic (New Drivers) Act 1995 introduced this for new drivers during the first two years of driving after research revealed that new drivers were more likely than other groups of road users to be involved in collisions as a result of poor driving. A new driver is effectively on a two-year probation, during which the full entitlement licence will be automatically revoked if the driver receives obligatory endorsement(s) (s 2(1)(b)) which accumulate to six or more penalty points (s 2(1)(d)). The revocation is automatically applied when the DVLA is notified (by a court or police central ticket office) that points have been given and the threshold has been reached. The individual will return to provisional status (and must of course comply with the relevant requirements for the category of vehicle being driven, such as supervision (see 19.3.1.4)). This can only apply the first time an individual has a full entitlement (ie a person can only have his/her full entitlement revoked once (s 7)).

> **TASK 2**
>
> 1. How could a disqualified driver or 'new driver' with a revoked licence conceal the fact that he/she is disqualified?
> 2. How could a police officer on patrol check whether a person is disqualified?

19.3.1.7 Foreign Licences

There are significant numbers of non-UK drivers now residing in the UK, and their status with regard to driving and licensing depends on the person's country of origin. If he/she holds a licence from one of the other 27 EU countries (a 'Community licence') then the holder is treated as if a UK licence is held, and can continue to drive on it (until the age of 70). Such a licence can be exchanged for a UK licence at any time, but this is not compulsory. For a driver with a non-EU licence, the licence will remain valid for 12 months after entering the UK as a visitor, and 12 months after becoming a resident. (An individual's status as either a visitor or resident (and any change in status) will be a matter of fact for a court to decide, but a permanent address, employment, or enrolment of children at a local school may all be indicators of residence.) Once the 12-month period has expired he/she will need to obtain an appropriate UK licence to drive legally.

If the person holds a licence from certain designated countries then it can be exchanged for a UK licence within five years of arrival, although this is not compulsory. The 'designated countries' are: Andorra, Australia, Barbados, British Virgin Islands, Canada, Falkland Islands, Faroe Islands, Hong Kong, Japan, Monaco, New Zealand, Republic of Korea, Singapore, South Africa, Switzerland, and Zimbabwe.

A driver with a non-UK licence can still be dealt with for driving matters. If endorsements are imposed, a UK driver number will be allocated and a 'non-licence holder' driver record will be created at the DVLA. A full explanation of the particular circumstances of drivers with a non-UK licence is provided at: <https://www.gov.uk/driving-nongb-licence>, but officers should also follow local policies.

19.3.2 Insurance

All motor vehicles used on the road or other public place in the UK must have a valid third party liabilities insurance policy, or a 'security' (a financial deposit by a large organization). Third party insurance means the policy will pay out if another person's property is damaged, or if someone other than the policy holder is killed or injured (s 145(3)(a)). Insurance cover is usually described as fully comprehensive, third party only, or third party fire and theft (TPF&T). Numerous terms and conditions apply, and these indicate which parties in an incident will be paid, depending on the circumstances. The cost of each policy is based on the risk as assessed from the information provided by the policy holder. Any failure to disclose correct or full information may amount to fraud under s 2 or 3 of the Fraud Act 2006. Insurers can provide insurance certificates electronically, for example by email or via a website (s 147 of the Road Traffic Act 1988).

The policy will specify the cover in terms of the use of the vehicle and the individuals concerned. It can apply to the policy holder only or to the policy holder and named drivers. 'Any driver' policies are sometimes issued (often for company vehicles) and these usually have conditions, such as all drivers must be over 25 years old or employed by the policyholder. In terms of the use of the vehicle, the cover will only apply to specific uses, such as Social Domestic and Pleasure (SDP), commuting to a fixed place of work, or business use. If any of the conditions are breached the vehicle will not be insured.

One potentially confusing condition is a clause that allows the policyholder to drive any vehicle with the owner's permission. (Previously, this was standard on all comprehensive policies but this is no longer the case, and some drivers do not realize this.) An 'any vehicle' clause never allows the policy holder to drive another vehicle that he/she also owns, nor will it apply for any named drivers on the policy. Some any-vehicle clauses require that the vehicle is also insured separately by its owner, and may also include a further clause stating that this cover does not extend to recovering vehicles seized by the police for a 'no insurance offence. It should also be noted that 'any vehicle' clauses only ever provide basic third party cover.

The details of each policy will vary, and it will only be possible to verify that cover is in place if the identity of the driver and use of the vehicle can be confirmed and the full details of the cover are known.

The policy must be issued by an insurer registered with the Motor Insurers Bureau (MIB) to be valid in the UK. The policy holder will receive a certificate of insurance (hard copy or electronic) from the company, and this will include at least the following features:

Specific Incidents

> **Insurance Company Name and Address:**
> AAA Insurance Ltd.
> The High Street
> Maidbury MB1 1AB
> Registration Number: AA 00 AAA
>
> Certificate number: 000/999/123
> Policyholder's name: Orlando SMITH Expiry date: Noon 16th December 2016
> Permitted Drivers: Verity SMITH, Noah KAY
> Limitations as to use: Use for social, domestic, and pleasure purposes, including travel between the driver's home and place of work.

Note that the existence of an insurance certificate does not prove that a vehicle is insured—the policy might have been cancelled after the certificate was issued. The MIB maintains a database of all insured vehicles, available via the vehicle file on the PNC, so officers should always refer to this. Short duration policies are often not shown on the MIB database, so further enquiries would be required to establish an accurate picture of the insurance status. The MIB run a help line for police officers who have stopped a vehicle on the street and have enquiries regarding its insurance, although this is not available 24/7 at the time of writing. The force control room can provide current telephone numbers for officers to call direct.

19.3.2.1 Driving a vehicle without adequate insurance cover

If a vehicle is not properly insured, any individual who uses, causes, or permits (see 19.2.4) its use on a road or other public place commits an offence contrary to s 143(1) and (2) of the Road Traffic Act 1988. The registered keeper (see 19.3.3) is guilty of an offence (s 144A of the Road Traffic Act 1988) if it is kept (see 19.2.4) without insurance (unless the vehicle has a Statutory Off Road Notification (SORN) where the registered keeper has declared the vehicle is off- road).

A vehicle without adequate insurance can be seized under s 165A of the Road Traffic Act 1988 (see 19.4.3 for details of the procedure).

There are a number of exceptions to the offence of driving without adequate insurance, which must be substantiated. These include vehicles:

- kept by the registered keeper at a location which is not on a road or other public place;
- not kept by the registered keeper at the relevant time, for example whilst lent to another person;
- that have been stolen and not recovered before the relevant time;
- driven by an owner who has deposited £500,000 with the Accountant General; or
- owned by authorities (such as councils, police authorities, the NHS, Army, or Air Force).

It is a defence if it can be proved that the user did not own the vehicle (nor had he/she hired it), and he/she was acting in the course of her/his employment and had no reason to believe that the vehicle was not properly insured (s 143(3) of the Road Traffic Act 1988).

19.3.2.2 Foreign Insurance

There are a significant number of individuals who have come to the UK with foreign registered vehicles. The insurance from the driver's home country will still be valid, but may be time-limited by the policy terms and conditions. However, as soon as a visitor becomes a UK resident (see 19.3.1.7) he/she must take out a policy with a UK MIB registered insurance company (see also 19.3.3 on UK-registering a foreign vehicle).

19.3.3 Vehicle registration and licensing

A new vehicle is generally first registered in the UK by the motor trade. The DVLA issues a registration document to the keeper and assigns a registration mark to the vehicle (also known as a registration number or an index number). The Vehicle Excise and Registration Act 1994 (VERA) provides much of the relevant legislation.

Some older vehicles will need to undergo registration in the UK, for example when the vehicle has only been used on a private estate or has been imported. Vehicles brought into the UK by a visitor must be registered in the UK after six months or when he/she becomes a resident, whichever is sooner. Once a vehicle is registered (or becomes subject to registration) it is also subject to the UK insurance and testing criteria.

The registration mark of a particular vehicle can be changed for a number of reasons. These include a 'cherished transfer' (also referred to as a 'private plate', although the DVLA term is 'personalized vehicle registration numbers'). Another reason for a change is that a vehicle was exported and then imported back into the UK. Records are cross-referenced on the PNC vehicle file so any previous registration numbers for a particular vehicle will be shown, as will all vehicles that have had a particular registration number.

19.3.3.1   The vehicle registration document and number plates

The vehicle registration document (the V5 or more recently the V5C) is proof that the vehicle is registered, and shows the details recorded on the register. The current version (red front cover) was introduced in 2010, and revised in 2012. People with the old style documents with a blue front cover were encouraged to change them, although this was not compulsory. The document contains a wealth of information regarding the vehicle which can be useful in the investigation of a variety of offences.

A vehicle is not properly registered if any of the particulars recorded in the register are incorrect or incomplete. It is an offence to use a vehicle that is not properly registered on a road or in a public place (s 43C(1) of VERA 1994). Other registration documents offences include failure to notify the DVLA about the disposal of a vehicle, or a change of vehicle details. Most of these offences are covered under the Road Vehicles (Display of Registration Marks) Regulations 2001 and VERA 1994. Defences for using a vehicle that is not properly registered include that no reasonable opportunity was given to supply the name and address of the registered keeper (eg if the person had only just bought the vehicle), or if there were reasonable grounds for believing that the recorded particulars were correct.

The registration mark or index number is shown on the 'number plate' of a vehicle. The plate should use a standard font, and it should not be customized in any way. These and further details on number plates may be found on the DVLA website.

(Image reproduced with the permission of the DVLA)

Local memory tag denoting where a vehicle is first registered. AB refers to Peterborough.

Age identifier which changes twice yearly in March and September. The number 51 refers to September 2001.

Random letters which will never include I or Q and which uniquely define the vehicle.

Offences relating to number plates (mostly under the Road Vehicles (Display of Registration Marks) Regulations 2001) include: no number plate or an obscured number plate; forgery of a number plate; incorrect fitting, number, or position of plates; and incorrect style, size, and spacing of characters. These are all summary offences.

19.3.4   Annual testing and 'MOT' test certificates

The majority of vehicles used on roads will be subject to testing. Any motor vehicle registered under the Vehicle Excise and Registration Act 1994 must be tested every year (after a certain period from registration) if it is to be used on a road (s 47 of the Road Traffic Act 1988). This also applies to any vehicle that is subject to registration, even if it has not actually been registered (see 19.3.3 on newly imported vehicles for example). The use of the term 'MOT' for the annual test has become common place and is also used officially, it derives from the 'Ministry of Transport' (a predecessor of the Department for Transport) which previously administered the process. The MOT system is administered by the Driver and Vehicle Standards Agency (DVSA). Vehicles are grouped into different categories for the purpose of testing and test fees (see gov.uk for details and the DVSA MOT testing manuals for each vehicle category).

For most vehicles, the first test is required when the vehicle reaches three years from the date of first registration (s 47(2)). For large goods vehicles, coaches, buses, ambulances, and private hire vehicles the first MOT is required one year from registration (s 47(3)). For older vehicles that are newly registered in the UK (see 19.3.3) the schedule for MOT testing starts from the date of manufacture which is taken to be the last day of the year during which its final assembly was completed.

It is an offence under s 47 for a person at any time to use (or cause or permit to be used) a motor vehicle on a road without a test certificate apart from the vehicle:

• being driven to a pre-arranged MOT test;
• being driven from a failed MOT test to a garage for repairs by previous arrangement (reg 6(2 (a)(i) of the Motor Vehicle (Test) Regulations 1981); or
• being towed from a failed MOT to a place it is to be broken up for scrap (reg 6(2)(a)(iii)(B)).

The results of tests are uploaded immediately and the 'MOT expiry tab' on the PNC vehicle file will be updated. Police officers should cross reference the information with the MOT data held on the vehicle file of the PNC. The MOT history of any vehicle is available to anyone on the gov.uk website.

19.3.5 Vehicle excise duty

Vehicle excise duty is payable on any vehicle used or kept on a public road, and is covered under s 1 of VERA 1994. The system is also referred to as 'vehicle licensing' and 'road tax'. The registered keeper is responsible for paying vehicle excise duty, and for arranging a Statutory Off Road Notification (SORN). A vehicle with a SORN can be kept off road without paying vehicle excise tax. The PNC vehicle files include an excise licence field, and any vehicle's excise duty status can be accessed on the gov.uk website. It has been held that a vehicle is 'kept' on a public road even if it is only there for a very short period (s 62).

The taxation classes include private/light goods vehicles (PLG, such as family cars and light vans), buses, and heavy goods vehicles. (Note that the category 'bicycle' refers to two-wheeled motorcycles rather than pedal-powered bicycles.) Some types of vehicle are exempt from duty such as vehicles for disabled people, fire engines, and ambulances. Most vehicles manufactured before 1 January 1973 are also exempt, except for large goods vehicles and buses (see s 5(2) and Sch 2 of VERA 1994). Exempted vehicles are subject to a 'nil licence' and will appear as such on the vehicle licensing register.

It is an offence for any person to use or keep a non-exempted vehicle on a public road if no vehicle excise duty has been paid (s 29(1) of VERA 1994). It is also an offence for the registered keeper to keep an untaxed vehicle off-road without making a SORN (s 31A(1)).

19.4 Stopping a Vehicle and Examining Documents

Police officers on foot or mobile patrol will sometimes need to stop vehicles in relation to driving standards, or because the vehicle is being used for some other criminal activity. Stopping vehicles and inspecting documentation are covered by particular police powers, and further powers may be available if any offences are disclosed.

19.4.1 Police powers to stop a vehicle

All police officers have the legal power to stop any mechanically propelled vehicle on a road (s 163 of the Road Traffic Act 1988) and do not need to have any form of suspicion or authorization. The police officer must be on duty and in full uniform, and give a clear direction to the driver to stop. Health and safety considerations are key in relation to where the officer makes the request, and to where the vehicle can actually stop (see 19.1). Failing to comply is a summary offence and the penalty is a fine. If the driver flees, a power of entry into premises in order to arrest for this offence is provided in s 17 of the PACE Act 1984 (see 10.8.1).

19.4.2 Driver and vehicle information checks

Police officers can now check all driver and vehicle documentation electronically by the side of the road, and there is now a clear expectation that officers will verify the status of the documentation before allowing a driver to proceed.

Here, a 'driver' is:

- any person driving a motor vehicle on a road;
- any person the officer has reasonable cause to believe had been driving a motor vehicle on a road at the time it was involved in an accident; or
- any person who the officer has reasonable cause to believe has committed an offence in relation to the use of a motor vehicle on a road, for example 'quitting' (see 19.5.2.3).

Driving licence checks are carried out on the PNC (including by the person's home post code if there seem to be discrepancies). MOT status can be checked through the PNC vehicle file or over the internet, and insurance details can be accessed on the MIB database (through the vehicle file on the PNC). The MIB help-line can also provide useful information.

19.4.2.1   Requiring documents for examination

If it is not possible to make electronic checks at the scene of an incident, a police officer can request production of the following documents:

- his/her driving licence (s 164(1));
- an appropriate insurance certificate (s 165(1)) (on paper or in electronic format on a suitable device (s 165(2A)));.
- the vehicle's MOT test certificate (s 165(1)); and/or
- CBT certificate (motorcyclists only) (s 164(4A)).

When a learner driver on a provisional entitlement is driving a motor vehicle on a road or is believed to have been involved in an accident or to have committed a road traffic offence (see 19.4.2 for details), the requirement to produce a licence also applies to the person supervising him/her (s 164(1)(d)). A police officer can also request any person driving or otherwise 'using' a registered vehicle (see 19.2.4) to produce the vehicle's registration document (s 28A(1) of VERA 1994).

Under the Road Traffic Act 1988, if the driver cannot produce the insurance or MOT certificate when required, a police officer can require the person to state his/her name and address and the vehicle owner's name and address (s 165(1)), and in some forces there may still be the option of issuing a HO/RT/1 form for production of documents within seven days (see 19.4.2.3).

19.4.2.2   Requesting information from a driver

A police officer may require a 'driver' (see 19.4.2) to state his/her date of birth (s 164(2)) if he/she fails to produce his/her licence, or produces a licence that is unsatisfactory (eg it seems to have been altered or it contains information that seems incorrect). This also applies for a person who is supervising a learner driver at the time of an accident or an offence, and there is reason to suspect that he/she (the supervisor) is under 21 years of age.

19.4.2.3   Failing to produce documents or provide information

Under the Road Traffic Act 1988 it is a summary offence for a person when required to fail to:

- produce his/her licence or state his/her date of birth (s 164(6));
- produce his/her CBT certificate (motorcyclists only) (s 164(6));
- state his/her name and address and the name and address of the owner of the vehicle (s 165(3));
- produce a certificate of insurance or an MOT certificate (s 165(3)).

Failing to produce the registration document is an offence under s 28A(3) of VERA 1994 (except when the vehicle is subject to a lease or hire agreement). However, a person will not be prosecuted for failing to produce any of these documents if the officer then issues a HO/RT/1 form and the driver then produces the documents:

- within seven days in person at a police station (specified by the driver at the time of the request);
- as soon as reasonably practicable (a question of fact for a court to decide); or
- at a later time if the driver can prove it was not reasonably practicable to do so before the day on which written charge proceedings were commenced.

For drivers of mechanically propelled vehicles and pedal cyclists suspected of dangerous, careless, or inconsiderate driving or cycling (ss 2, 3, 28, and 29; see 19.8 onwards) there is a separate offence of failing to provide his/her name and address to any person having reasonable grounds for requiring the information (s 168 of the Road Traffic Act 1988).

Specific Incidents

TASK 3

1. What checks should be undertaken to verify the identity of a driver and the validity of any documents produced?
2. What problems might there be in establishing a person's true identity?
3. What extra checks could a police officer carry out to make sure he/she has been given the person's real name and address?

19.4.3   Seizing a vehicle

Under s 165A of the Road Traffic Act 1988, a police officer has the power to seize a vehicle if he/she has reasonable grounds for believing that the driver does not have a suitable licence or that the vehicle is not adequately insured. To seize a vehicle a police officer must be in uniform and have requested to see the relevant documents. He/she must also warn the driver that the vehicle will be seized unless the documents are produced immediately. (However, if it is impractical to warn the driver then a warning is not required (s 165A(6)).) More than 1.5 m million uninsured vehicles have been seized since the power became available in 2005, with some 121,000 seized in 2015 and 72,000 during the first half of 2016 (MIB, 2016).

If the driver has failed to stop or has driven off, the vehicle may be seized at any time in the 24-hour period following the incident. A police officer has the legal power to enter premises to seize a vehicle, including from the driveway or garage associated with a private dwelling-house. The officer must have reasonable grounds for believing the vehicle to be present, and reasonable force may be used if necessary.

TASK 4 Imagine you are a police officer. You stop a high performance car using your powers under the Road Traffic Act 1988. The driver is young but has an appropriate licence and the PNC check shows that the vehicle is insured. A driving licence enquiry shows he has nine current points on his licence for three speeding offences.

- What questions would you put to him about his insurance policy?
- How would you check that the insurance company knows about the endorsements on the drivers licence and that the policy has been issued in full knowledge of the risk?

TASK 5 Imagine you are a police officer. Whilst on Independent Patrol you have stopped a vehicle using your powers under the Road Traffic Act 1988 and a vehicle check on the PNC shows the MOT has expired.

- What are the defences to not having a valid test certificate?
- What questions will you put to the driver to negate any defences?

19.5   Construction and Use of Vehicles

Construction and use legislation relates to the maintenance of a vehicle to a roadworthy standard, and the circumstances in which it may create a danger to other road users. The legislation is written in the form of regulations, notably the Road Vehicles (Construction and Use) Regulations 1986 and the Road Vehicles Lighting Regulations 1989. There are also offences under the Road Traffic Act 1988 where no specific regulations apply. Some construction and use offences can be evidenced with a superficial examination of the vehicle, while other more complex matters will require expert training.

A police officer can undergo further training and be designated as an authorized vehicle examiner (s 67 of the Road Traffic Act 1988). An examiner is authorized to test a vehicle (and drawn trailer) on a road to check compliance with construction and use requirements.

19.5.1   **Tyres**

When dealing with tyre offences it is important to record sufficient information so the specific tyre on a vehicle can be identified when presenting evidence. This will include a description of the tyre including its size and rating, the dimension and description of any defects, and its location on the vehicle. For the location the usual system is to state front (F) or rear (R), and nearside (N/S) or offside (O/S). Nearside is the side closest to the kerb when driving on the left, and offside is the side further from the kerb (and the driver's side on a right-hand drive car). So the tyre at the front of the car on the driver's side would be the F/O/S.

The terms used to describe the various parts of a tyre are shown in the diagram. It may also be necessary to specify whether a side wall was the inner (the side you cannot see from beside the vehicle) or the outer (the side to the outside of the vehicle).

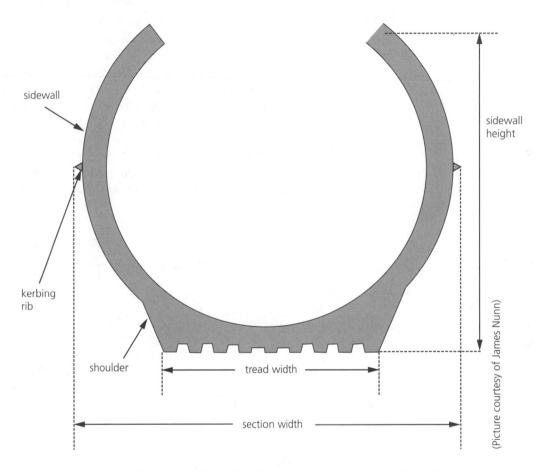

(Picture courtesy of James Nunn)

For use as evidence, all the identifying details, codes, and features on the wall of a tyre should be noted, including serial numbers and characters relating to the type of tyre. This will include the make and model of the tyre, ie Pirelli P6000.

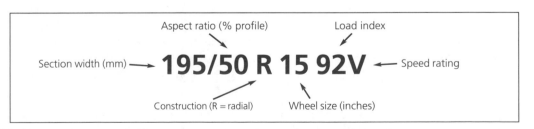

On initial examination the side wall information can appear confusing as the format has been developed over time, and uses various international standards and units of measurement. The side wall information shown in the box can be interpreted as follows:

• the section width is 195 mm, this is the distance between the outer edge of each sidewall under normal inflation, it is always greater than the tread width;

- the aspect ratio compares the height of the side wall with the section width, and is stated as a percentage (a 'low ratio' is also known as a 'low profile' in common parlance). In this case the figure is 50 per cent, so as the section width is 195 mm the side wall height must be 97.5 mm. Some older tyres may not have a stated aspect ratio; it is generally 80 per cent in such cases;
- the letter 'R' denotes that the tyre has a radial construction, and indicates the way the steel or fabric belts are arranged within the structure of the tyre. Almost all tyres on cars now are radial; other belt arrangements include bias-belted ('B') and cross-ply ('-') which are now used primarily for motorcycle tyres. There may also be another letter (H, V, or Z); this is a duplication of the speed rating information;
- the wheel rim diameter (the metal part) in inches;
- the load index (or rating); and
- the speed rating (H,V, or Z; in increasing order of maximum speed).

Other information may be present on the side wall, such as whether the tyre is 'tubeless' or 'tube type' (ie it requires an inner tube). If there is an arrow (often with the word 'direction') the tyres must be fitted so that the wheel rotates in that direction when the vehicle moves forwards. There may also be an 'inside' or 'outside' marker; again tyres should be fitted as indicated. The week and year of manufacture is indicated by a set of numbers preceded by 'DOT', and the final numbers will be the week and the year. For example 2313 would indicate the 23rd week of 2013; this information can help identify a tyre.

19.5.1.1 Offences relating to tyre condition and maintenance

Tyres on vehicles and trailers must be in good condition and suitable for the purpose for which they are being used. They must also be inflated to the correct pressure. The photograph shows an under-inflated tyre.

(Photograph courtesy of James Nunn)

Regulation 27 of the Road Vehicle (Construction and Use) Regulations 1986 applies for vehicles and trailers used on roads with pneumatic (inflatable) tyres and covers a range of problems relating to tyre condition and use. (This regulation does not apply to agricultural motor vehicles with a maximum speed of 20 mph; for vehicles that have broken down or are en route for breaking up; or vehicles being towed at not more than 20 mph.) Tyres should not in any case be in such a condition that they could cause damage to the road surface or persons (reg 27(1)(h)).

Tyres must be the correct type for the vehicle (taking into account the types of tyres fitted to the other wheels), and for the road conditions or purpose. Some wear is permitted, depending on the type of vehicle. The following types of damage are not allowed:

- cuts anywhere on the surface of the tyre, longer than 25 mm or 10 per cent of the section width of the tyre (whichever is the greater), and also deep enough to reach the ply or cord (see the photograph for an example);

(Photograph courtesy of James Nunn)

- lumps, bulges, or tears (the photograph shows a small bulge in the tyre)

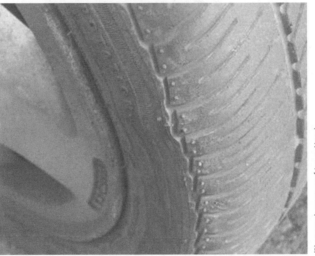

(Photograph courtesy of James Nunn)

- exposed ply or cord; the photograph shows cord exposed on the extreme right of the tread-width.

(Photograph courtesy of James Nunn)

For private cars and vans (driving licence category B and Private Light Goods vehicles (see 19.3.5)) and their trailers, the tread grooves should be at least 1.6 mm deep over the whole central three-quarters of the tread-width. A depth gauge should be used to measure accurately.

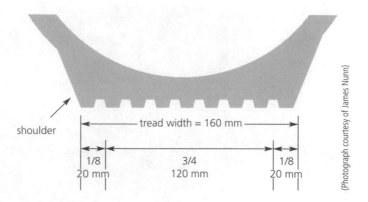

The outer eighths (on each side of the tread-width) can have patches with less than 1.6 mm of tread (as long as there are no cuts, and no cord or ply is exposed). The photograph shows a tyre with insufficient tread in at least part of the central area. So this tyre is illegal.

The width of the central three-quarters of the tread-width can be calculated as follows:

1. Measure the width of the tread, ie the surface of the tyre in contact with the road (total width = 160 mm).
2. Obtain the width of the central three-quarters of the tread-width by dividing the total tread-width by 4, then multiplying by 3 (160 mm/4 = 40 mm, and then 40 mm × 3 = 120 mm). Or alternatively use a calculator to multiply the tread-width by 0.75, (160 mm × 0.75 = 120 mm).
3. Obtain the width of each of the two outer eighths of the tread-width by dividing the total tread width by 8 (160 mm/8 = 20 mm).
4. Check that your calculations are correct by adding the value for the central three-quarters to twice the value for the outer eighth (120 mm + 20 mm + 20 mm = 160 mm, hence correct).

Measurements will need to be done accurately, but one-eighth at the edge of the tread-width is a relatively small amount so if an area with insufficient tread is clearly visible at first glance, it is likely to be more than just the outer eighth (but it will still need measuring!). The photographs show worn areas on different parts of the tread-width (the first shows wear to both outer edges, the second shows wear to just the inner edge, and the third to just the outer edge). Areas where there is no visible tread pattern remaining are described as 'devoid of tread'. All these tyres were worn beyond the legal limit, ie more than the outer eighth has insufficient tread.

For other types of vehicle (such as motorcycles, larger passenger vehicles, and larger goods vehicles) the groove depth over at least three-quarters of the tread-face must be at least 1.0 mm. The area with at least 1 mm tread depth must be continuous but can be towards one side (it does not have to occupy the central three-quarters of the tread-face). Therefore a legal tyre can have no tread over the whole of the inner or the outer quarter of the tread-face, or the inner and the outer eighth, or other combinations of areas. (Note however that certain types of tyre (usually for high performance motorcycles) are manufactured with no grooves on the outer eighths of the tread width.) The photograph shows a motorcycle tyre with tread across the whole tread-face, but which is worn to below the legal limit.

(Photograph courtesy of James Nunn)

For mopeds (see 19.3.1.1, categories AM, P, and Q) all the original tread pattern grooves must be visible. In the photograph no tread is visible in the central area, so this is illegal.

(Photograph courtesy of James Nunn)

19.5.2 Lights on vehicles

The position, style, maintenance, and colour of vehicle lights are important for road safety. Police responsibilities include identifying vehicles with faulty lights, testing and inspecting lights, and bringing the faults to the attention of the owner and/or driver. Drivers should use their vehicle lights with consideration towards other road users. Police officers can offer advice to drivers on this; for example, lights should not cause undue dazzle or discomfort to other people using the road.

The following information relates in part to the Road Vehicles Lighting Regulations 1989. There are two main categories of lights: obligatory lights (must be fitted and maintained), and optional lights.

TASK 6 A range of lights is now available for temporary attachment to the roof of a vehicle. Find out whether blue lights are permitted for use in this way.

Specific Incidents

19.5.2.1 Obligatory lights

Here we will examine the obligatory lights required for a car as this is the most common type of vehicle on the road. Other classes of vehicle have different requirements, as described in the regulations.

The obligatory lights on the front of a car are: position lights ('side lights'), dipped, and main-beam headlights and direction indicators. On the back of the car the obligatory lights are: position lights, direction indicators, stop lights (brake lights), fog lights, a registration-plate lamp, and a reflector (albeit not strictly a light). A 'hazard warning-signal device' to operate the direction indicator lights on the front and back of the car is also obligatory. These obligatory lights are often clustered together.

Position lights must be present on all four corners of a vehicle, to indicate the vehicle's presence and width to other road users. The front position lights ('side lights') are white and not particularly bright, and are often switched on by the first click of the switch near the steering wheel. The rear position lights ('tail lights') are red, and are operated by the same switch as the front position lights. They are less bright than brake lights. Position lights must be lit when the vehicle is moving at night (between sunset and sunrise) and during the day if visibility is reduced. They may also be required when a vehicle is parked on a road at night, see 19.5.2.4 for details.

Dipped-beam headlamps are powerful white lights at the front of the car. They illuminate the road ahead, but should shine downward and to the left to avoid dazzling drivers of oncoming vehicles. The dipped-beam headlights are often switched on at the second position of the light switch. They must be lit when the car is being driven during hours of darkness, but are not required by law on roads with street lighting with a 30-mph limit or less (position lights are still required) or if the vehicle's fog lights are illuminated. They should also be used during the day in seriously reduced visibility. The dipped-beam headlights do not need to be illuminated if the car is being towed. The illumination of dipped-beam headlights is usually indicated on the vehicle display by the illumination of a green lamp or pictogram.

Main-beam headlights ('full-beam') are very bright white lights at the front of the car which shine straight ahead to illuminate the road over a long distance. They are usually operated with a pull or push of a switch near the steering wheel when dipped-beam headlamps are already on. If the front fog lamps are in use (in seriously reduced visibility), the use of main-beam headlights can be counterproductive as the light will reflect back from the fog causing the driver to be dazzled, reducing the distance the driver can see.

The main-beam headlight switch must be wired so that they can be 'dipped' by the driver to avoid dazzling oncoming traffic. This involves no movement inside the headlamp unit; the dipped-beam headlights are simply switched on and the main-beam headlights are switched off. The illumination of main-beam headlights is indicated on the vehicle display as a blue lamp or illuminated pictogram.

Direction indicators are found at each corner of the car (and sometimes at the sides) and are used to indicate to other road users that the driver is intending to move the car to the right or left. They must be amber and flash between 60 and 120 times a minute. They are usually operated by pushing a switch near the steering column upwards or downwards. There must be some sort of indicator near the driver to show that the direction indicators are activated. If an indicator flashes very fast this usually indicates that one of the other bulbs in the circuit has failed.

The rear registration-plate lamp is white, and illuminates the rear plate when the position indicator lights are switched on. It should not shine directly backwards (to avoid dazzling the driver of any following vehicle).

Rear stop lamps ('brake lights') are red and very bright. They are positioned at the rear corners of the car and must operate when the main (primary) braking system (eg foot brake) of the car is applied. They warn other road users that the vehicle brakes have been activated and therefore the vehicle may be slowing down or stopping.

Rear fog lamps are red and very bright, similar to stop lamps. They are operated by an independent switch (which may be part of the main lighting switchgear), and will only work when the headlights are illuminated. They should be used only if visibility is reduced, as they might prevent following drivers from noticing any illumination of the stop lamps, and this can obviously be dangerous. They do not need to be used when the car is towing a trailer.

Hazard warning signalling uses the same lamps as the direction indicators. It is controlled by a switching device that makes all the direction indicators flash at the same time. It operates automatically in some vehicles when the driver brakes hard. It should only be used:

- when the vehicle is stationary, to alert other road users of an obstruction;
- when moving on a motorway or dual carriageway, to warn drivers behind of an obstruction ahead; or
- by the driver of a bus when children under 16 are getting on or off, or to summon help.

The switch to activate this device must be in reach of the driver. The switch button often has a small triangle which lights up when the hazard warning lights are on.

19.5.2.2   Optional lamps

Some optional lamps perform the same function as obligatory lights: for example, extra front-position lights (side lights), extra stop lamps, extra direction indicators, and extra dim/dipping and hazard warning devices. As they have the same functions as obligatory lights, they must be maintained and in full working order, just like the obligatory lights (which must still be fitted as described earlier).

Other optional lamps include lamps such as reversing lights and front fog lights. They are not obligatory so do not have to be maintained. They must not, however, be in such a condition as to cause danger or be used in such a way that they cause undue dazzle or discomfort to other road users.

19.5.2.3   Vehicle lights when driving at night

The position lights must be used as soon as the sun sets and until the sun rises. Dipped headlights should be used during the 'hours of darkness' which starts half an hour after sunset and ends half an hour before sunrise. The times for sunset and sunrise are available on police databases (via the control room), but these times can also be found in newspapers and on the internet.

> Remember:
> - hours of darkness for dipped headlights; and
> - sunset and sunrise for sidelights.

19.5.2.4   Parking without lights at night

On a road with a speed limit of 30 mph or less some types of vehicle can be parked without illuminated position lamps between sunset and sunrise. This applies to passenger vehicles (including cars and mini-buses, but not buses), light goods vehicles, motorcycles, and invalid carriages, but not to a vehicle with a trailer or a projecting load. The vehicle must be in a designated parking area or lay-by, or be parked at least 10 m from a junction, facing the right way (on either side in a one way street) and close to the kerb.

19.5.2.5   Legitimate use of a vehicle with defective lights

A vehicle with defective lights may be driven in some circumstances without an offence being committed. This is only permitted during the day (between sunrise and sunset), and the lights must have become defective during that journey, or arrangements must have already been made to repair the fault (reg 23(3) of the Road Vehicles Lighting Regulations 1989).

There are numerous other exemptions to the lighting regulations in regs 4 to 9, so unusual circumstances will need to be considered on a case-by-case basis.

Specific Incidents

TASK 7 Consider each of the following statements in turn, and decide if each statement is true or false:

1. The term 'hours of darkness' refers to a period from half an hour after sunset to half an hour before sunrise.
2. The legislation that covers the use of lights on vehicles is the Road Vehicles (Construction and Use) Regulations 1986.
3. The permitted flash rate of an indicator lamp fitted to a vehicle is between 80 and 100 pulses per minute.
4. Hazard-warning signals on a vehicle may be used lawfully when the vehicle is being towed by another vehicle.
5. A defect occurring during a journey during daylight hours is a defence to a defective light fitted to a vehicle.
6. A reversing light is an optional lamp.
7. The term 'obligatory light' means a light that is required by the legislation to be fitted to a vehicle.

19.5.3   Danger of injury from the use or poor maintenance of vehicles or trailers

There are numerous circumstances where the use of a vehicle or trailer may pose a danger or nuisance to other road users. Some of these are specifically addressed in the legislation (see 19.5.3.1 and 19.5.3.2), but many are not. Section 40 of the Road Traffic Act 1988 and reg 100 of the Road Vehicle (Construction and Use) Regulations 1986 are worded so they can be used to cover a wide range of situations related to maintenance and incorrect use of a vehicle. The offences relate using a vehicle, including causing or permitting its use (see 19.2.4). The vehicle must be on a road.

If the use involves a danger of injury to any person, this is an offence under s 40A of the Road Traffic Act 1988, if the danger is due to:

- the condition of the motor vehicle or trailer (or of its accessories or equipment);
- the purpose for which it is used;
- the number of passengers carried by it or the manner in which they are carried; or
- the weight, position, or distribution of its load or the manner in which it is secured.

If the use of the vehicle causes nuisance but not danger, then reg 100 of the Road Vehicle (Construction and Use) Regulations 1986 can be used.

Offences under these sections can be used for defects which do not fall within specific regulations. This could include suspension or bodywork defects, or extra wide wheels which stick out far beyond the bodywork (these can make contact with pedestrians or their clothing as the vehicle passes by). Jagged edges on bodywork (see the photograph of the wheel arch of a van) can cause injury to other road users. Bodywork and parts must be secure or they could cause injury or collisions (see the photograph of the loose bodywork on a motorcycle).

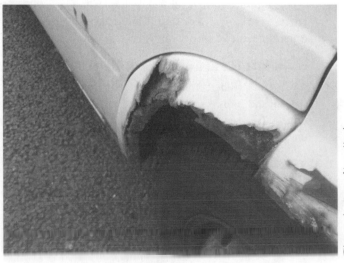

Photograph courtesy of James Nunn

(Photograph courtesy of James Nunn)

19.5.3.1 Poor maintenance and some associated offences

When considering the condition of a vehicle, a general rule is to take account of how it was first constructed, as this provides a guide to how it should be maintained. If a component part is missing or not working, an offence is likely to have been committed. Specialist equipment and training may be required to deal with some of these matters. Here we list just some of the offences under the Road Vehicles (Construction and Use) Regulations 1986 that relate to poor maintenance of a vehicle:

- The wipers and washers (those that are required to be fitted) must be maintained in efficient working order and be properly adjusted (reg 34). Split blades as shown in the photograph are not allowed.
- An audible warning instrument (horn) must be fitted to any motor vehicle with a maximum speed of more than 20 mph (reg 37).
- The braking systems (including the handbrake) must be maintained in good working order and be properly adjusted (reg 18(1)). Brake fluid should be clear and amber coloured; in the first photograph you can see it is opaque which shows it is contaminated with water and has formed an emulsion. There should be no evidence of fluid leaking from the brake system (see the photograph which shows where fluid has leaked over the inside of a wheel).
- Exhaust systems and silencers must be maintained in good working order, and must not be altered to increase the noise made by escaping exhaust gases (reg 54).
- Motorcycle exhausts must be the correct type (only for a moped or motorbike first used after 1 January 1985, reg 579A(1) or (4)). The silencer should be either the original fitted by the manufacturer or an approved British Standard replacement, and must comply with noise requirements. (A motorcycle should not be used on a road if its exhaust is marked 'not for road use' or similar.)

Vehicle emissions must not contain any smoke, visible vapour, grit, sparks, ashes, cinders, or oily substance that causes (or is likely to cause) damage to property, or injury or danger to other road users (reg 61). Some police services have instruments to test vehicle emissions, but this is usually undertaken by local authority environmental services or the DVSA.

(Photograph courtesy of James Nunn)

(Photograph courtesy of James Nunn)

(Photograph courtesy of James Nunn)

(Photograph courtesy of James Nunn)

Specific Incidents

19.5.3.2   Incorrect use of a vehicle and some associated offences

There are many ways in which a vehicle can be used incorrectly under the Road Vehicles (Construction and Use) Regulations 1986. Here we cover some of the more commonly encountered scenarios such as:

* Loads carried by a vehicle must not be a danger or nuisance to any person or property. The weight, packing, distribution, and adjustment of a load must be taken into account (reg 100(1)). The load carried by a motor vehicle or trailer must be secured if necessary, by physical restraint: for example, the luggage on the roof bars of a car must be tied down (reg 100(2)).

- Passenger numbers must not exceed the number that seats allow (reg 100(1) and (3)). For example, passengers must not be carried in the rear of a small van with no fixed seating.
- The horn (reg 99) must not be used when the vehicle is stationary (other than an emergency involving another vehicle, or when using a reversing or boarding-aid alarm). In addition, the horn must not be used by moving vehicles on restricted roads between 2330 and 0700 hours.
- Noisy engines; excessive noise from motor vehicles on roads must be avoided by the driver taking reasonable care (reg 97).

19.5.3.3 Stationary vehicle offences

The regulations on stationary vehicles are covered under the Road Vehicles (Construction and Use) Regulations 1986. The engine must be turned off when the vehicle is stationary for any length of time to prevent noise or exhaust emissions (reg 98), and it is an offence to leave the engine running whilst stationary in a confined space with other vehicles. The engine must also be turned off and parking brake applied when the driver stops and leaves the vehicle ('quitting'), unless there is another person in the vehicle who is licensed to drive it (reg 107, and s 42 of the Road Traffic Act 1988). This would apply for example to a driver who parks outside a shop and runs inside to buy something. Certain exemptions apply to emergency service vehicles and to vehicles with machinery that requires the engine to be running.

19.5.3.4 Head and eye protection for motorcyclists

Helmets or other suitable protective headgear must be worn by anyone driving or riding on a motor bicycle (defined in 19.2.1). It is an offence under s 16 of the Road Traffic Act 1988 to drive or ride on a road without such protection. The design of the headgear is regulated by the Motor Cycles (Protective Helmets) Regulations 1998. The helmet must bear a mark indicating compliance with the British Standard (BS 6658:1985) or the equivalent EU standard, or it must be of a type which seems likely to afford similar protection. A helmet must be securely fastened by straps or other fastenings, and an additional strap under the jaw must be used to secure a chin cup (reg 4). Under the regulation, a helmet that is not secured is 'not being worn'. Helmets are not required for some people in some circumstances, such as:

- a person using a ride-on motor mower;
- turban-wearing followers of the Sikh religion, whilst on a two-wheeled motorcycle;
- passengers in a side-car; and
- any person pushing a two-wheeled motorcycle on foot.

Riders or drivers of three-wheeled vehicles do not need to wear a helmet if the distance between any two wheels on the same axle (front or back) is at least 460 mm. The distance between the wheels is measured between the centre of the area of contact with the road for each wheel. Under reg 4, if the two wheels are less than 460 mm apart they are regarded as a single wheel, so the vehicle would be classed as a motor bicycle.

Eye protection is not required by law, but if used, it must meet the British Standards EN 1938:1999, or an offence is committed under s 18(3) of the Road Traffic Act 1988.

19.5.3.5 Seatbelts

The requirements for the use of seatbelts depend on the age of the person and where he/she is sitting. The requirements are provided in ss 14, 15, 15A, and 15B of the Road Traffic Act 1988, the Motor Vehicles (Wearing of Seat Belts) Regulations 1993, the Motor Vehicles (Wearing of Seat Belts by Children in Front Seats) Regulations 1993, and the Motor Vehicles (Wearing of Seat Belts) (Amendment) Regulations 2006.

A summary of the requirements is shown in the table (based on rules 99–102 of the Highway Code, available online). In addition, some older or classic cars may not have seatbelts fitted.

Seatbelt requirements

	Front seat	Rear seat	Who is responsible?
Driver	Must be worn if fitted	Not applicable	Driver
Child under 3 years of age	Correct child restraint must be used	Correct child restraint must be used. If unavailable in a taxi, the child may travel unrestrained	Driver

	Front seat	Rear seat	Who is responsible?
Child from 3rd birthday up to 1.35 m in height (or 12th birthday, whichever they reach first)	Correct child restraint must be used	Correct child restraint must be used where seat belts are fitted. Adult belt must be used if correct child restraint is not available in a licensed taxi or private hire vehicle, or for reasons of unexpected necessity over a short distance, or if two occupied restraints prevent fitment of a third	Driver
Child over 1.35 m (approx 4ft 5ins) in height, or 12 or 13 years	Seat belt must be worn if available	Seat belt must be worn if available	Driver
Passengers aged 14 and over	Seat belt must be worn if available	Seat belt must be worn if available	Passenger

If a child seat or restraint is used it should be suitable for the weight of the child concerned and fitted in accordance with the manufacturers specifications.

In some situations a seatbelt does not have to be worn, such as:

- a driver engaged in deliveries (eg delivering post or newspapers) or collections if the distance between the stops is less than 50m;
- a driver reversing a vehicle, or supervising a learner driver who is reversing a vehicle (or conducting a manoeuvre which includes reversing);
- an examiner conducting a driving test, if wearing the belt would be dangerous;
- people in vehicles being used for police purposes (see local policy; as a general rule the exemption is not used and may vary in relation to people under arrest) and vehicles being used for fire brigade purposes;
- taxi drivers while 'plying for hire', answering calls for hire, or carrying passengers, and private-hire drivers while carrying passengers;
- people taking part in processions organized by, or on behalf of, the Crown;
- people holding a medical certificate providing exemption from wearing a seatbelt (provided the certificate is produced at the time or within seven days, or includes a relevant letter issued within the EU (in relation to a Community licence holder));
- a disabled person wearing a disabled person's belt;
- the vehicle is driven under a trade excise licence (which allows untaxed vehicles to be driven by the motor trade) for the purposes of investigating or remedying mechanical fault; or
- where the seatbelt is an inertia type which is locked as a result of being, or having been, on a steep incline.

19.5.4 Vehicle identification regulations

Under reg 67 of the Road Vehicle (Construction and Use) Regulations 1986 all wheeled vehicles registered after 1 April 1980 should have a Vehicle Identification Number (VIN) plate. It will be fitted in a conspicuous and readily accessible location (on a part not normally subject to replacement). It will show the VIN and the manufacturer. It may also show the type approval number (that confirms that the vehicle meets UK standards), but this is sometimes on a separate plate. The VIN will also be stamped on the chassis or frame.

VINs on EU-market vehicles have 17 characters in a unique combination of numbers and letters. A few vehicles have non-standard VINs, usually on imported vehicles that were originally sold outside the EU (often right-hand drive vehicles from Japan).

A VIN can be matched against details on the PNC to help identify a suspected stolen vehicle (see 16.8.1). Most police services will have officers specially trained to deal with auto crimes who should be able to assist with a suspicious VIN or VIN plate.

> **TASK 8** Imagine you are a police officer. You suspect a particular vehicle has a number of serious defects so you signal to the driver to stop (using powers under the Road Traffic Act 1988).
>
> - In terms of health and safety, what factors must you consider?
> - What will you to say to the driver, and if you find a defect what will you do next?

19.6 Pedestrian Crossings and Road Signs

Over the years, the number of road signs and regulations in England and Wales has increased in an attempt to keep the road environment as safe as possible for all road users. These signs and regulations, however, are only of value if road users comply with them. Police officers can of course detect non-compliance offences, but they can also help the public develop road-safety awareness. Note that some moving traffic offences have been decriminalized in some boroughs. A comprehensive explanation of road signs is provided in the Department for Transport publication *Know your Traffic Signs* available on the gov.uk website.

19.6.1 Pedestrian crossings

The following table shows the key characteristics of the three main types of pedestrian crossing described in the Zebra, Pelican, and Puffin Pedestrian Crossings Regulations 1997.

Pelican	Pedestrians can push a button to operate traffic lights to bring vehicles to a stop. The traffic light sequence is the same as for normal lights except that, after the red light, the amber light flashes to indicate that vehicles may proceed, but only if the crossing is clear
Puffin	Sensors detect anyone waiting to cross and change the traffic lights accordingly for vehicles to stop. The sequence is the same as for regular traffic lights
Zebra	These are not supported by traffic lights. Pedestrians walk across a section of road indicated by alternate white and black stripes. Drivers and riders of vehicles are warned of the presence of a crossing by two black and white striped poles with yellow flashing beacons on top, on each pavement

19.6.1.1 Layout of crossings

The limits of crossings are marked out by two parallel lines of studs across the carriageway, as shown here.

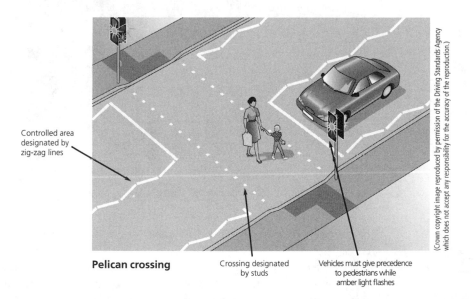

Controlled area designated by zig-zag lines

Pelican crossing

Crossing designated by studs

Vehicles must give precedence to pedestrians while amber light flashes

(Crown copyright image reproduced by permission of the Driving Standards Agency which does not accept any responsibility for the accuracy of the reproduction.)

The stop line for a Pelican or Puffin crossing is a solid white line across the road, just before the first line of studs. The line at the start of a Zebra crossing is a broken white line as the driver has to give way to pedestrians. Drivers and riders must not cross the stop or give-way line if pedestrians are on the crossing (or of course if the traffic lights are red for a Pelican or Puffin crossing).

The controlled area of a crossing is a certain length of road before (entry) and after (exit) a crossing. It is indicated by white zigzag lines painted along the edge and the middle of the road (between two and 18 zigzags, depending on the road layout in the immediate vicinity).

Where there is a refuge for pedestrians or a central reservation on a zebra crossing, each part of the crossing is treated as a separate crossing.

19.6.1.2 The correct use of crossings

The regulations for the use of crossings are given in the Zebra, Pelican, and Puffin Pedestrian Crossings Regulations 1997, and give rise to several offences which can be committed by drivers or pedestrians. Pedestrians have precedence over vehicles at (or approaching) zebra crossings (reg 25), and at pelican crossings when the amber light is flashing (reg 26). They must not delay on a crossing longer than is necessary to use the crossing in a reasonable time (reg 19).

For vehicles, the following rules apply:

- No overtaking within the controlled area when approaching any crossing (reg 24).
- All vehicles must stop at red/steady amber lights at Pelican or Puffin crossings (reg 23).
- No stopping in the controlled area of any crossings (reg 20) unless it is to allow pedestrians to cross, to prevent injury or damage, to make a right or left turn, to carry out building work or maintenance of the road or crossing, or to remove obstructions from the road (regs 21 and 22). (This does not apply to pedal cycles or public service vehicles, nor if the vehicle is beyond the driver's control.)
- No stopping on the actual crossing, unless the way is blocked or it is necessary to avoid injury to persons or damage to property (reg 18).

Contraventions of these regulations amount to an offence under s 25(5) of the Road Traffic Regulation Act 1984, and Sch 2 to the Road Traffic Offenders Act 1988.

19.6.2 White lines along the centre of the road

Solid white line systems are used to prohibit overtaking where visibility and vision is limited, or to separate lanes of traffic on roads going up a hill. The lines may be continuous on both sides or continuous on one side and broken on the other, and they can also be separated by an area in between (with hatched markings). The various layouts are set out in reg 26 of the Traffic Signs Regulations and General Directions 2002 and are covered on p 64 of the *Know Your Traffic Signs*.

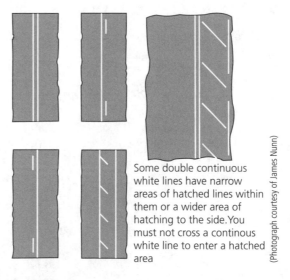

Some double continuous white lines have narrow areas of hatched lines within them or a wider area of hatching to the side. You must not cross a continous white line to enter a hatched area

(Photograph courtesy of James Nunn)

The presence of at least one continuous white line in the centre of the road means that no vehicle is permitted to stop on either side of the road. Note, that this also applies if there is a broken line on one side (reg 26(2)(a)). This regulation does not apply to dual carriageways, nor to vehicles used for fire brigade, ambulance, or police purposes. Exceptions also apply for vehicles that have stopped in order to:

- allow passengers to board/alight from a vehicle;
- allow goods to be loaded or unloaded from the vehicle;
- facilitate building or demolition work;
- enable the removal of any obstruction to traffic, road works, or public utility work; or
- avoid an accident.

Exceptions also apply for vehicles that are prevented from proceeding by circumstances outside the driver's control, or are required to stop by law or with the permission or direction of a constable in uniform or a traffic warden.

Crossing a solid white line is also covered by the regulations. If there is a continuous line closest to the driver in the direction of travel, vehicles must not to cross or straddle it (reg 26(2)(b)), irrespective of whether the other line in the system is broken or continuous. This does not apply when a vehicle is turning right or when the action is unavoidable when passing a sta tionary vehicle, a pedal cycle, a horse, a road-maintenance vehicle moving at 10 mph or less, or an accident. Nor does it apply when complying with directions from a police officer or a traffic warden in uniform. The offences relating to crossing white lines are committed under s 36(1) of the Road Traffic Act 1988, reg 10 of the Traffic Signs Regulations 2002, and Sch 2 to the Road Traffic Offenders Act 1988.

19.6.3 Disobeying a traffic sign

This is an offence only in relation to signs of the prescribed type (listed under reg 10 of the Traffic Signs Regulations and General Directions 2002) that have been lawfully placed on or near a road (s 36 of the Road Traffic Act 1988). Drivers are therefore under no obligation to heed informal signs erected by members of the public.

Regulation 10 of the Traffic Signs Regulations and General Directions 2002 creates two lists of relevance to s 36 of the Road Traffic Act 1988:

List 1: contravention of a sign on List 1 is an offence under s 36 of the Road Traffic Act 1988.
List 2: these are selected signs from List 1. Contravention of these signs creates a significant danger, and may lead to disqualification or endorsement of the driver's licence.

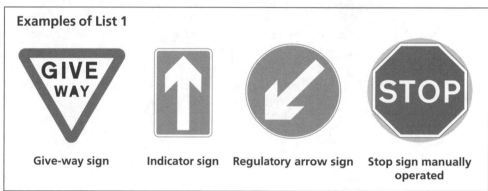

Examples of List 1

Give-way sign   Indicator sign   Regulatory arrow sign   Stop sign manually operated

(Crown copyright images reproduced by permission of the Department for Transport)

Examples of List 2

Stop sign   No-entry sign   Red light of permanent or portable traffic signal

(Crown copyright images reproduced by permission of the Department for Transport)

19.6.4 School crossing patrols

Local councils can designate locations where children cross roads on their way to and from schools (or from one part of a school to another) as a 'patrolling place'. Here, a school crossing patrol (in uniform) can hold up a prescribed sign to stop traffic to allow people to cross (s 28 of the Road Traffic Regulation Act 1984). Vehicles must stop before reaching the crossing place (so people crossing are not impeded) and remain stationary for as long as the sign continues to be exhibited (s 28(2)). Police officers may be required to undertake this function on occasions.

It is a summary offence to fail to comply with the requirements of a school crossing patrol, or cause a vehicle to move when the sign is exhibited (s 28(3)). The penalty is a fine, and the driver may also be disqualified.

TASK 9 For each of the following road traffic signs, find an image to show either the symbol for the sign or the sign as marked on the road surface itself.

1. Vehicular traffic entering the junction must give priority to vehicles from the right: for example, a mini-roundabout.
2. Priority is to be given to vehicles from the opposite direction.
3. Warning of a weak bridge.
4. Prohibition of vehicles exceeding a stated height.
5. Drivers of large or slow vehicles to stop and phone for permission to cross a level crossing.
6. Route for use by buses and pedal cycles only.
7. Route for tramcars only.
8. Stop sign, manually operated.
9. Convoy vehicle, no overtaking.
10. Stop for road works.
11. Vehicles to stay to the right of a vehicle involved with mobile road works.
12. Zigzag lines for an equestrian (horse) crossing (also called 'Pegasus') or Toucan crossing (crossing for pedestrian and cyclists to use together).
13. Line markings across a junction at which a vehicle must give way.
14. Variations of double white-line markings, including the use of hatched areas.
15. Variations of yellow bus-stop markings.
16. White lines and hatched areas dividing lanes or a main carriageway from a slip road (on motorways or dual carriageways).
17. Yellow grid markings within a box junction preventing entry without a clear exit.
18. Red-light signal of permanent/portable traffic signals and green filter arrows.
19. Tramcar not to proceed further.
20. Intermittent red-light signals at railway level crossings, swing bridges, etc.
21. Matrix prohibition.

19.7 Road Traffic Collisions

It is common to refer to collisions between vehicles as 'accidents' and the older police term of RTA (for Road Traffic Accident) has even entered popular language. However, it is more common now in police circles to refer to a Road Traffic Collisions (RTC) or a 'crash' rather than an accident. This change of terminology reflects the thinking that incidents of this nature are not random acts of chance, but have causes. There are often a number of factors which come together to create the circumstances, these can include driver error, driver distraction, poor appreciation of a hazard, and so on. However, the term 'accident' is still used frequently during police training and features in much of the relevant legislation.

Road traffic collisions are very common and result in a large number of injuries. In 2015 (the latest available report) there were 186,189 road user casualties (Department for Transport, 2016). There has been a general downward trend since 2003 (except in 2014), but it is still as if the whole population of a county the size of Carmarthenshire or the district of Bury in Greater Manchester (ONS, 2016c) were to be injured every year, year after year.

Other terms that are commonly used in relation to collisions are:
- Damage Only (where there is only vehicle damage and no injury);
- Non-Reportable Damage Only (NRDO) where there are no grounds for a police report;
- Personal Injury (often referred to as a PI); and
- Killed or Seriously Injured (the term KSI is widely used).

Officers attending collisions are legally obliged to report certain types of collisions, known as 'reportable accidents' (see 19.7.2.1). All police services are obliged to submit statistical data regarding collisions to the Department for Transport (referred to as STATS19).

19.7.1 Management of collision scenes

The police have a number of key responsibilities when responding to collisions. These include the need to preserve life, to coordinate the emergency services involved (eg the Fire and Rescue

Service), to secure, protect, and preserve the scene (see 11.2), to lead and manage the subsequent investigation into the incident, and to liaise with relatives of the injured or killed. Incidents with a serious injury or fatality should be treated as a crime scene, with specialist officers undertaking forensic reconstruction and related activities, but a basic understanding of legislation and procedure is required for all officers. In the initial response to a collision on the strategic road network (such as motorways), the police work very closely with the highways agencies. In England the agency is 'Highways England' staffed by Highway England Traffic Officers Service (TOS), (formerly known as Highways Agency Traffic Officers (HATOs) and often still referred to as such). In Wales there are two trunk road agencies staffed by Welsh Government Traffic Officers. The English and Welsh highway agency traffic officers have some powers related to the control and direction of traffic, but they are obliged to follow the direction of a police constable.

Here we provide a summary of the key police responsibilities, but for further information see also *CLEAR Keeping Traffic Moving,* available from the College of Policing online library. CLEAR is a mnemonic for Clear, Lead, Evaluate, Act, and Re-open. It is part of a Government initiative for improving incident management and traffic congestion on the strategic road network, and aims to clarify the priorities of the various organizations involved in traffic incident management, and promote partnership working. It is hoped that this will improve incident management and reduce the duration of incidents. Further detail on the management of emergency incidents on highways is available on the gov.uk website, and police service training will reflect this best practice.

19.7.1.1 Dynamic risk assessments

When attending incidents on roads, police officers should conduct a dynamic risk assessment, taking account of the location, the vehicles, and the people involved. A dynamic risk assessment involves continually evaluating the changing circumstances and adjusting the assessment accordingly.

In relation to the location, the physical layout or position on a road can increase the risk, for example bends in the road prevent approaching drivers from seeing the incident. The weather conditions or a low winter sun can also reduce the visibility. The speed, volume, and movements of passing traffic should also be considered as should any additional problems such as fallen trees or electricity cables. Some locations may suffer poor radio and/or mobile phone coverage, hindering communication between officers at the scene and their control rooms.

All the vehicles involved should be identified; as you might expect multi-vehicle incidents can compound risk factors or create new ones. The contents and the post-impact condition of some vehicles may present additional hazards; spillage of fluids, the high voltages used in modern electric vehicles, specific chemical hazards posed by vehicles that have caught fire, and body fluids from casualties should all be taken into account. If you are unsure, advice should be taken from fire and rescue units who are specialists in such hazards. Some of the vehicles might have been involved in criminal activity (always carry out PNC checks) creating additional complications. Specialist equipment such as lighting or screening is also important and should be available via force control rooms, particularly if there has been a fatality or there are special recovery requirements, for example for abnormally heavy loads or vehicles that have left the carriageway.

All the people at the scene should be accounted for; it is not uncommon for individuals to be thrown some distance from the vehicles, so this possibility should be considered. Their demeanour and any need for medical attention should be taken into account, and support provided as appropriate. The PNC could be used to help establish whether any of them have been involved in criminal activity that could present additional risks at the scene.

19.7.1.2 ACE-CARD actions for road traffic incidents

The 'ACE-CARD' mnemonic can be used to help remember the sequence of considerations and actions required when responding to a road or traffic incident. This approach is summarized in the table.

Specific Incidents

Letter:	Abbreviation for:	Meaning:
A	**A**pproach	Before approaching gather as much information as possible. Approach incidents from the rear, where possible.
C	**C**aution (signs)	Place warning signs and cones correctly (see 19.7.1.4). If on a motorway and the matrix speed restrictions need activating, contact FCC (or the local highways control room if present). Establish an appropriate 'exclusion zone' around the incident.
E	**E**xamine (the scene)	Decide whether further assistance is needed. Employ the critical incident procedures if required (see 11.5).
C	**C**asualties	After protecting the scene check that all casualties have been found and administer first aid if required. Take details of casualties before they are taken from the scene.
A	**A**mbulance (and Fire and Rescue Service and other support agencies)	Control and manage the scene. Provide a safe working area for the support agencies.
R	**R**emove (the obstructions)	Recovery services should be contacted (via FCC) asap but no vehicle should be removed until potential evidence is secured. Breakdown vehicles should be controlled by police or designated Highways Agency personnel (see 19.7.1).
D	**D**etailed (investigation)	Reporting and subsequent investigation according to local and national policy.

19.7.1.3   Special considerations for police use of the motorway hard shoulder

Motorists are not permitted to use the hard shoulder except in emergencies. The police may however drive on the hard shoulder (for guidance see the College of Policing Authorised Professional Practice and *Roadcraft: The Police Driver's Handbook*). Police exemption from Motorway regulations is covered in reg 16 of the Motorways Traffic (England and Wales) Regulations 1982.

The College of Policing Authorised Professional Practice suggest that driving on the hard shoulder ('hard shoulder running') should be kept to a minimum, and that officers should remember that the hard shoulder:

- may be in use as a live lane;
- could be obstructed by stationary vehicles or moving vehicles straying into the hard shoulder;
- may be unsafe because of dirt and debris.

Officers driving on the hard shoulder should also keep to an appropriate speed, and remember that if attending a stationary vehicle (especially in darkness), the driver or passengers may be standing or walking on the hard shoulder.

19.7.1.4   The correct locations for signs

It may be necessary to cone off part of the carriageway, in which case a cone taper will be used to guide motorists into the lanes that are still open. Signs must be placed to warn motorists, with more than one sign required for roads with higher speed traffic. On single carriageways, warning signs should be placed on both directions of approach. The minimum requirements for cone taper warning signs are shown in the table:

Speed limit	Number of signs	Clear view to the first sign	Distance for the signs (before the start of the cone taper)
70 mph (motorways)	3	100 m	300, 600, and 900 m
50–60 mph	2 or 3 (depends on safety considerations)	100 m	300 and 600 m (and 900 m if a third sign is used)
40–50 mph	2	100 m	200 and 400 m
30 mph or less	1	100 m	50 m

(Adapted from College of Policing APP for the management of incidents)

19.7.2   Driver obligations after a collision

The Road Traffic Act 1988 takes a common-sense approach to collisions (referred to as accidents in the Act) and dictates that the drivers involved must stop and be prepared to provide details to anyone who reasonably requires information, or report the incident to the police (s 170). The information might be needed for compensation claims for repairs, injuries, or deaths. Police officers in training will no doubt be carefully assessed on what information must be exchanged after a collision, and the offences committed by a person who fails to meet his/her obligations in this regard.

19.7.2.1   Reportable Accidents

If an accident meets certain criteria, then the driver has to provide particular information to other people, or failing that, report the incident to the police (s 170(1) of the Road Traffic Act 1988); this is known as a 'reportable accident'. The criteria for a reportable accident concern the location of the accident, the vehicle type, and whether there is any damage or injury apart from to the driver and his/her vehicle. (The definition of an 'accident' is not provided by statute and remains a question of fact for the courts to decide. However, in *R v Morris* [1972] RTR 201 'accident' was held to be 'an unintended occurrence which has an adverse physical result'.)

For an accident to be reportable, the location of the vehicle at the moment of the collision is important. It must have been on a road or other public place which could include hospital grounds, household garage blocks, private roads, or motorway service areas (see 9.2 and 19.2.2 for further discussion on the definition of a public place). If the vehicle leaves the road or other public place and ends up in a private dwelling, or grounds adjacent to the road or public place, this is still a reportable accident. If a collision takes place at any location other than a road maintained at public expense, evidence will be required to prove that it is a public place (for example concerning the frequency of use, by whom, and under what circumstances).

The vehicle must be mechanically propelled (see 19.2.1) and the collision must be due to its presence on a road or other public place. This includes vehicles intended or adapted for use off-road (eg dumper trucks and off-road motorcycles) and covers a wider range of vehicles than 'motor vehicles' (see 19.2.1). The phrase 'due to the presence' implies that the incident would not have occurred had the vehicle not been there, and does not mean that the vehicle was necessarily directly involved. It may be that the presence of the vehicle purely created the circumstance where other vehicles were involved in an incident. The classic example of this is a legally parked car that creates a slight narrowing of the available space which leads to a collision; had the car not been present the collision would not have occurred.

The damage must be to another vehicle such as a bicycle, or to property such as a road sign, garden wall, or certain animals. Note that lamp posts belong to the local highways authority or the local council.

(Photograph courtesy of James Nunn)

The damage can be to private property, but the vehicle must have been on a road or other public place immediately before the incident. The damage does not have to be permanent or beyond repair, but the physical appearance must have been altered in some way. Certain types of animals (horses, cattle, asses, mules, pigs, sheep, goats, and dogs) are classed as property in this context. For injuries, the injury must be to a person other than the driver of the vehicle, for example passengers, pedestrians, or people in other vehicles. The injury can be shock as well as actual bodily harm.

When attending a reportable accident, the police officer must make a report to record all the details, including making a judgement on the cause of the accident. There may be a tendency or time pressures to complete a less thorough report where it seems that no criminal offence has been committed, however, a full record of the events should still be made (see 10.2). This is because the officer might be called as a witness in a civil court case, for example if a pedestrian had been seriously injured in a collision and is claiming compensation. There is currently no national collision reporting form so each officer must be familiar with the reporting processes in his/her area.

19.7.2.2   Information required after a reportable accident

All the driver(s) at a reportable accident must stop and remain at the scene for as long as necessary to provide information to others (s 170(2) of the Road Traffic Act 1988). Failing to stop at any accident is a serious offence and is committed even if the person later reports the accident to the police.

At the scene, a driver must provide particulars to anyone who has reasonable grounds for needing the information; this could include the driver or rider of any other vehicle involved, the passengers in any of the vehicles, property owners, pedestrians, or their representatives. The driver must provide: his/her name and address; the name and address of the vehicle's owner; and the identification marks of the vehicle (eg the vehicle registration number). Failing to stop or report an accident is a summary offence under s 170(4) of the Road Traffic Act 1988. The penalty is six months' imprisonment and/or a fine, and the offender may also be disqualified.

If the driver cannot or does not provide the relevant information at the time of the accident, then he/she must 'report' the accident and provide the relevant information to the police as soon as reasonably practicable, and certainly within 24 hours (s 170(3) and (6) of the Road Traffic Act 1988). He/she must report in person to a constable or police station; it is not sufficient to telephone or email. It is a matter for a court to decide what is 'reasonably practicable' for the particular circumstances.

A relevant insurance certificate must be produced by the driver where personal injury is caused to another person (an 'injury accident'). The certificate should be shown to a police officer and any person having reasonable grounds for seeing it, for example the injured person (s 170(5)). If this is not possible at the time the driver must report the accident to the police and produce the insurance as soon as is reasonably practicable and, in any case, within 24 hours (s 170(6)). Failing to produce proof of insurance after an injury accident is a summary offence under s 170(7) of the Road Traffic Act 1988 and the penalty is a fine. When the police attend many of these arrangements no longer apply as officers are generally able to ascertain insurance status at the scene of the incident using the MIB database through the PNC.

> **TASK 10** In many police forces the policy is to conduct a preliminary breath test on every driver involved in a road traffic collision. What legislation provides this power? What computer checks could be carried out on the drivers involved?

(Photo by Kevin Lawton-Barrett)

19.8 Offences Relating to Standards of Driving

Standards of driving are assessed as sufficient when a driver passes his/her driving test, but this minimum standard should be maintained. This is defined, for the purposes of the Road Traffic Act 1988, as the standard of a 'competent and careful' driver, and it will be for a court to decide, based on the facts presented. Offences relating to the standard of driving are listed at the start of the Act. Here we cover the following offences (from the Road Traffic Act 1988 unless otherwise stated):

- causing death by dangerous driving (s 1);
- causing serious injury by dangerous driving (s 1A);
- dangerous driving (s 2);
- causing death by careless or inconsiderate driving (s 2B);
- careless and inconsiderate driving (s 3);
- causing death by driving whilst unlicensed, disqualified, or uninsured (s 3ZB);
- causing the death of another person whilst under the influence of drink or drugs (s 3A);
- careless and inconsiderate cycling (s 29);
- driving elsewhere than on a road (s 34); and
- wanton and furious driving (s 35 of the Offences Against the Person Act 1861).

For ease of explanation the offences will not be dealt in the order in which they are presented in the Act. We will examine what we mean by dangerous driving and careless and inconsiderate driving, and then consider the offences that relate to the consequences of such activity.

19.8.1 Dangerous driving

The legislation considers there are two main causes of dangerous driving: the driver's manner and actions during driving and the condition of the vehicle. These are fully defined in s 2 of the Road Traffic Act 1988.

Section 2A(1) states that a person is regarded as driving dangerously because (a) the way he/she drives falls far below what would be expected of a competent and careful driver; and (b) it would be obvious to a competent and careful driver that the driving would be dangerous (a question of fact for the court to decide).The minimum standard of driving applies during the driving test, with knowledge and application of the Highway Code also setting the standard at which a competent and careful person should drive. The Highway Code therefore provides a useful guide when interviewing and gathering evidence for this type of offence. The following are examples of driving activities which may support an allegation of an offence under s 2A(1):

- racing or competitive driving style;
- driving at a speed which is highly inappropriate for the prevailing road or traffic conditions;
- aggressive driving, such as sudden lane changes, cutting into a line of vehicles, or driving much too close to the vehicle in front;
- disregard for traffic lights and other road signs which, on careful analysis, would appear to be deliberate, or disregard for warnings from fellow passengers;
- overtaking in circumstances where it could not have been carried out safely;
- impaired driver ability, such as having an arm or leg in plaster, or impaired eyesight, or too tired to stay awake;
- using a mobile phone for talking or text messages (*R v Browning* [2001] EWCA Crim 1831; [2002] 1 Cr App R (S) 88).

The dangerous condition of a vehicle (s 2A(2)) is judged from the perspective of a 'competent and careful driver...if it would be obvious...that driving the vehicle in its current state would be dangerous'. The weight or height of the vehicle, as well as any load carried, should be considered in the context of the location and road conditions. Examples of s 2A(2) circumstances include driving with a load which presents a danger to other road users, and driving with actual knowledge of a dangerous vehicle defect.

When gathering evidence for dangerous driving, the Construction and Use Regulations 1986 and the Highway Code provide useful benchmarks. A wide range of defences are available (see 19.8.3), so where appropriate, evidence should be collected to negate these. It is for a court to decide whether it would be 'obvious' that the driving was dangerous. The penalty is a fine or imprisonment (six months if tried summarily and two years on indictment).

19.8.2 Careless or inconsiderate driving

Legislation concerning careless or inconsiderate driving is provided within s 3 of the Road Traffic Act 1988. An offence is committed by a person who drives a mechanically propelled vehicle on a road or other public place without due care or attention or without reasonable consideration for other persons using the road or public place. Whether the driving was careless or inconsiderate is a question of fact for the court to decide.

Careless driving (driving without due care and attention) is defined in law as when the standard of driving falls below what would be expected of a competent and careful driver (s 3ZA(2)). (Note the difference between this offence and dangerous driving (see 19.8.1) where the standard falls *far* below the expected standard.) Examples of careless driving would include a driver who fails to look behind whilst reversing, or crosses the white line when overtaking without checking for oncoming vehicles, or using the right-turn direction indicator and then turning left. The driver's knowledge of the circumstances can be taken into account, and any factors that he/she should have been aware of.

For inconsiderate driving, another person must be inconvenienced by the suspect's driving. This would include:

- 'cutting across' the path of another vehicle, for example when turning or changing lanes without prior warning;
- cutting in at the front after passing a long line of waiting traffic;
- causing traffic problems by failing to conform to directional arrows;
- forcing other drivers to take evasive action by failing to drive correctly;
- deliberately performing skids at high speed or making 'handbrake turns';
- driving on footpaths; or
- driving off-road across grassland, with disregard for other users of the space.

A driver can only be charged with careless or inconsiderate driving, not both. They are both summary offences, and the penalty is a fine, an endorsement and discretionary disqualification, or a £100 FPN and a driving licence endorsement of three penalty points.

19.8.3 Defences to dangerous, careless, or inconsiderate driving

There are various defences for dangerous or careless or inconsiderate driving. These are summarized in the following table.

Defence	Explanation
Automatism	Automatism is 'the involuntary movement of a person's body or limbs' (*Watmore* v *Jenkins* [1961] 2 All ER 868), and it must occur very suddenly with little or no warning. This could be due to an epileptic fit (with no prior symptoms) or a wasp sting. Case law has established that falling asleep at the wheel or a hypoglycaemic diabetic coma are not automatism
Unconsciousness or sudden illness	This would include situations where a person suddenly becomes unconscious as a result of circumstances beyond his/her control, such as being hit on the head by a stone that has smashed through the windscreen. Case law has established that falling asleep at the wheel or a hypoglycaemic diabetic coma are not beyond the driver's control
Assisting in the arrest of offenders	Here, the driver might have a defence if he/she intentionally shunted a suspect's car off the road in order to help the police arrest the suspect (*R* v *Renouf* [1986] 2 All ER 449)
Duress by threats	The suspect must be able to show that he/she drove dangerously due to a threat (that he/she could not otherwise avoid or escape)
Duress of necessity (of circumstances)	The suspect must be able to show that he/she had to drive dangerously to avoid death or serious injury (to any person), and that it was not reasonable to act otherwise in the circumstances
Sudden mechanical defect	This does not apply if the driver is already aware of the defect or it could have been easily discovered by superficial examination, for example of tyres (*R* v *Spurge* [1961] 2 All ER 688)
Authorized motoring event	A person will not be guilty under s 1, 2, or 3 of the Road Traffic Act if he/she drove in accordance with an authorization for a motoring event given by the Secretary of State (s 13(A) of the Road Traffic Act 1988)

19.8.4 Other offences involving dangerous driving

Section 35 of the Offences Against the Person Act 1861 states that it is an offence for anyone 'having the charge of any carriage or vehicle…[to cause] or cause to be done bodily harm to any person' by wanton or furious driving, racing, other wilful misconduct, or wilful neglect. This could be used on occasions when dangerous driving has taken place, but the Road Traffic Act 1988 does not cover the circumstances, so it cannot be used as the basis of a prosecution. Such circumstances would include when:

* the driving was not on a road or other public place;
* the vehicle used was not a mechanically propelled vehicle (eg it was a bicycle or horse-drawn vehicle); or
* the statutory Notice of Intended Prosecution was not given (see 19.12.5).

The offence can only be committed if the driver has a degree of subjective recklessness: he/she must appreciate that harm was possible or probable as a result of the driving (*R* v *Okosi* [1996] CLR 666). It is triable by indictment only and the penalty is two years' imprisonment. Disqualification is discretionary, although endorsement (three to nine points) is obligatory if the offence was committed in a mechanically propelled vehicle.

Riding a cycle carelessly, inconsiderately, or dangerously on a road is an offence under the Road Traffic Act 1988. This can be riding 'without due care and attention, reasonable consideration for other persons using the road' (s 29), or riding dangerously (s 28(1)). These offences are triable summarily and the penalty is a fine.

19.8.5 Causing death by driving

Road deaths have a devastating effect on families and the community, and the police have a responsibility to investigate and provide support for those affected. A family liaison officer (usually referred to as a FLO) can be appointed to provide information, build confidence and gather any information from the family which would be helpful to the investigation. Friends and relatives of the deceased may want to visit the scene and leave memorials or tributes (local authority policies might apply).

The offences are all under the Road Traffic Act 1988 and are categorized by the type of driving that caused the death. It is not relevant whether the person who died was in the suspect's vehicle at the time of the incident. The offences are as follows:

* causing death by dangerous driving (s 1);
* causing death by careless or inconsiderate driving (s 2B);

Specific Incidents

- causing death by careless or inconsiderate driving whilst under the influence of drink or drugs (s 3A);
- causing death by driving whilst unlicensed, disqualified, or uninsured (s 3ZB).

For a s 3A offence there must be evidence of careless or inconsiderate driving whilst under the influence of drink or drugs. The driver can be unfit through drink or drugs (s 4), over the prescribed limit (ss 5 or 5A), or have refused to provide a specimen (s 7) within 18 hours of the driving, or refused permission for it to be laboratory tested (s 7A(6)). These are explained in more detail in 19.9.

Note that for a s 3ZB offence, the manner of the driving must have contributed to causing the death but it does not have to be the sole reason. It is not necessary to prove careless or inconsiderate driving, but the mere presence of a vehicle on a road is insufficient (see *R v Hughes* [2013] UKSC 56). Driver licensing, vehicle insurance and disqualification are covered earlier in this chapter.

The table compares some key aspect of the various causing death by driving offences, and also shows the mode and trial and the penalties.

Section of the Road Traffic Act 1988	(s 1)	(s 2B)	(s 3A)	(s 3ZB)
Type of vehicle	mechanically propelled vehicle		mechanically propelled vehicle if unfit to drive (otherwise motor vehicle)	motor vehicle
The location	on a road or other public place			on a road
Mode of trial	indictment only	either way	indictment only	either way
Minimum mandatory disqualification	two years	one year	two years	one year
Endorsement	obligatory	obligatory 3–11 points	obligatory	obligatory 3–11 points
Retaking driving test	compulsory and extended	discretionary	depends on alcohol/drug level	discretionary
Custodial penalty	14 years	six months summarily, five years on indictment	14 years	six months summarily, two years on indictment

19.8.6 Causing serious injury by dangerous driving

Causing serious physical injury to another person by driving a mechanically propelled vehicle dangerously on a road or other public place is an offence under s 1A of the Road Traffic Act 1988. Serious injury means physical harm, which amounts to grievous bodily harm as set out in the Offences Against the Person Act 1861 (see 15.3.1). A defendant found not guilty of this offence could still be convicted of dangerous driving (see 19.8.1) or careless or inconsiderate, driving (see 19.8.2).

The offence is triable either way and the penalty is a fine or imprisonment (12 months if tried summarily and five years on indictment).

TASK 11

1. The following is a list of some of the main contributory factors to reported road accidents in 2014 (taken from *Reported Road Casualties Great Britain: 2014 Annual Report*, available on the gov.uk website). Put them in order, with the most frequently occurring first.

- Pedestrian failed to look properly
- Slippery road (due to weather)
- Sudden braking
- Driver failed to look properly
- Loss of control
- Careless, reckless or in a hurry

- Failed to judge other person's path or speed
- Following too close
- Vehicle travelling too fast for conditions
- Poor turn or manoeuvre.

2. List three national road policing priorities.

TASK 12

1. Who would be held to be 'driving' in each of the following scenarios? Use the case suggested as guidance.

   (a) Jerry sits in the driver's seat and lets the car freewheel downhill with the steering lock on. See *Burgoyne v Phillips* [1982] RTR 49.

   (b) Maz, a passenger in a car 'driven' by Mel, sees a friend walking along the roadside towards the moving car. To frighten the friend, Maz snatches the steering wheel from Mel's grasp to make the car veer in that direction. Would Maz be held to be 'driving'? See *DPP v Hastings* [1993] 158 JP 118.

   (c) Hari is in the driving seat of the car and 'driving' along the road. Pat leans over from the front passenger seat and steers the car, while Hari manipulates the other controls. Hari's view forward is partially obscured by Pat. After some distance, the car runs into a ditch, while Pat is steering. Pat had been able to reach both the handbrake and the ignition key and knew the consequences of using the various controls, but did not have access to the foot pedals. See *Tyler v Whatmore* [1975] RTR 83. Who was driving?

2. Answer questions (a) and (b) by selecting the correct option(s) from the following list.

   (a) Where can dangerous driving and causing death by dangerous driving be committed?

   (b) In what location(s) does s 35 of the Offences Against the Person Act 1861 apply?

       (i)   Anywhere?

       (ii) On a road?

       (iii) In a public place other than a road?

       (iv) In a public place only?

19.8.7   Other offences involving standards of driving

Some acts that amount to poor driving may not fall within the scope of the offences of dangerous, careless, or inconsiderate driving, but they may still amount to an offence, albeit of a less serious nature. Combined with other factors, the poor driving could contribute towards one of the more serious offences but would not, in most circumstances, constitute one of the more serious offences *per se*. Exceeding the speed limit is an important example of poor standards of driving, and is covered by s 89(1) of the Road Traffic Regulation Act 1984.

The following driving standards offences are derived from the Road Vehicles (Construction and Use) Regulations 1986:

- driving (or causing or permitting any other person to drive) a motor vehicle on a road if the driver is in such a position in the vehicle that he/she cannot have proper control of the vehicle or have a full view of the road and traffic ahead (reg 104). The penalty is an obligatory endorsement (three points) and a discretionary disqualification or a fixed penalty;

- opening a vehicle door on a road (or causing or permitting it to be opened) and injuring or endangering any person (reg 105). Note that anyone in the vehicle can commit this offence, not just the driver. If a child opens the door it is likely the driver would be deemed to have permitted the offence. The maximum penalty is £1,000 fine or a fixed penalty;

- driving a motor vehicle on a road if the driver is in such a position as to be able to see directly, or by reflection, a TV or similar apparatus (reg 109). This does not apply to satnav apparatus or other apparatus used to display information about the state of the vehicle, nor to devices that help the driver see the road adjacent to the vehicle;

- driving a motor vehicle on a road while using a hand-held phone or a similar device (reg 110). (Communication by two-way radio, such as 'CB', is excluded from this offence, although obviously the general need for safe driving still applies.) This offence can also be committed by anyone supervising a driver with a provisional licence. Where an employee commits an offence using a hand-held phone provided by his/her employer, the company can also be held liable if they have failed to prohibit the employee from using it while driving on company business. The penalty is an obligatory endorsement (three points), a discretionary disqualification, and a fine. Alternatively an FPN can be issued (see 19.12.4).

Members of the police service and other emergency services are granted some exemptions from road traffic regulations. However, police officers are expected to drive at least as well as other motorists and should aim to provide a positive role model for other drivers—consider this in relation to personal authority (see 3.5). It is very important that a police officer's driving meets the relevant standards and that he/she is fully aware of local police service policies before taking on any emergency response.

TASK 13

1. What other offences might be considered for a person using a hand-held mobile telephone while driving, apart from the offence derived from reg 110 in the Road Vehicles (Construction and Use) Regulations 1986?

2. Driving while using a phone is clearly a significant distraction; what other circumstances or activities might adversely affect standards of driving?

19.8.8 Driving in places other than a road

The law surrounding 'off-road' driving is covered in s 34 of the Road Traffic Act 1988. This states that an offence is committed by a person who:

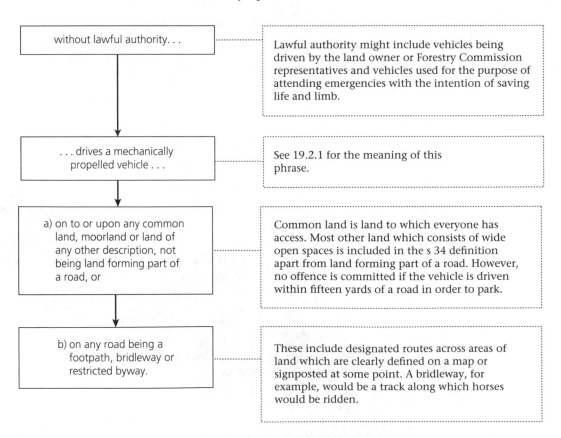

without lawful authority. . .	Lawful authority might include vehicles being driven by the land owner or Forestry Commission representatives and vehicles used for the purpose of attending emergencies with the intention of saving life and limb.
. . . drives a mechanically propelled vehicle . . .	See 19.2.1 for the meaning of this phrase.
a) on to or upon any common land, moorland or land of any other description, not being land forming part of a road, or	Common land is land to which everyone has access. Most other land which consists of wide open spaces is included in the s 34 definition apart from land forming part of a road. However, no offence is committed if the vehicle is driven within fifteen yards of a road in order to park.
b) on any road being a footpath, bridleway or restricted byway.	These include designated routes across areas of land which are clearly defined on a map or signposted at some point. A bridleway, for example, would be a track along which horses would be ridden.

This offence is triable summarily only, and the penalty is a fine.

19.9 Drink- and Drug-driving

It is an unfortunate fact that a proportion of the driving population choose to drive whilst under the influence of an intoxicant, be it alcohol or some other substance. It is inevitable that police officers will come into contact with such individuals and must know how to deal with them accordingly.

There are three driving offences relating to driving while under the influence of alcohol or other drugs, and these are all contained within the Road Traffic Act 1988:

* driving, or attempting to drive, or being in charge of a mechanically propelled vehicle whilst unfit to drive through drink or drugs (s 4);
* driving, or attempting to drive, or being in charge of a motor vehicle with alcohol (s 5) in excess of the prescribed limit; and
* driving, or attempting to drive, or being in charge of a motor vehicle with a specified drug (s 5A) in excess of the prescribed limit.

The s 4 offence is a very different offence compared with the s 5 and s 5A offences. The key difference is that, for a s 4 offence, the prosecution has to prove that the suspect's ability to drive was actually impaired, whereas for a s 5 or 5A offence the only evidence required is a certain alcohol or drug concentration in the blood, breath, or urine (depending on the offence). They also involve different categories of vehicle.

Due to the complex nature of these offences and the numerous historical challenges to the procedures, the Department for Transport now issues standard forms to be used for investigating these offences. These are MGDD/A through to MGDD/F, and are available online. You should check that any hard copies available at custody units are in fact the most up-to-date versions.

We will first consider some key terms and concepts in the legislation relating to alcohol, drugs, and driving, and then go on to look at preliminary and evidential tests in more detail.

19.9.1 Key terms from the legislation

The notion of a person being 'in charge of a vehicle' only occurs within ss 4, 5, and 5A of the Road Traffic Act 1988 and there is no legal definition for this but case law focuses on control of the vehicle and likelihood to drive. Therefore each set of circumstances is a matter of fact for a court to decide. They would take into account whether a person had some control of the vehicle, whether the person had the keys, or was in or close to the vehicle. Being 'in charge' can also include supervising a provisional licence holder (see *Leach v Evans* [1952] 2 All ER 264 and *Haines v Roberts* [1953] 1 All ER 344).

Some defendants claim a defence in relation to being 'in charge', and it may be necessary to negate this. For example, a man might attempt to prove that there was no likelihood of him driving the vehicle in the near future, but simply stating this as an intention to not drive is insufficient (see *CPS v Thompson* [2007] EWHC 1841 (Admin)). A suitable defence could be that he had booked a hotel room for the night, or that the vehicle had been wheel-clamped (see *Sheldrake v DPP* [2003] 2 All ER 497 and *Drake v DPP* [1994] RTR 411 respectively). The defence might also claim that in reality the driver was too badly injured to be able to drive or that the vehicle was severely damaged, but the court can disregard these two circumstances and still find the defendant to have been 'in charge' as these matters relate to the likelihood of driving (see *CPS v Thompson* [2008] RTR 70) rather than an actual ability to do so (s 4(4) of the Road Traffic Act 1988).

The term 'drug' has a different meaning depending on whether the offence is under s 4 or s 5A. For s 4 offences a drug is any substance which can cause an intoxicating (psychoactive) effect. This includes all 'controlled drugs' and other synthetic psychoactive substances (see 12.5.1). For an offence under s 5A, the drug must be one of the 17 drugs listed in s 5A, and no other drugs or substances can be taken into account A particular individual can be simultaneously investigated for a s 4 and s 5A offence, so the difference in the meaning of the word 'drug' is important. The Department for Transport advises that if sufficient evidence is present, then officers should proceed with both a s 4 and s 5A process.

19.9.2 Unfit through drink or drugs

These offences are covered under s 4 of the Road Traffic Act 1988. The diagram shows this in detail (s 4(1)).

Specific Incidents

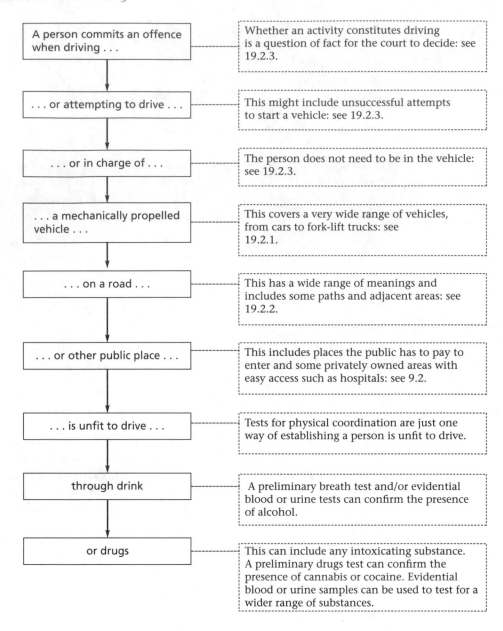

A person commits an offence when driving . . .	Whether an activity constitutes driving is a question of fact for the court to decide: see 19.2.3.
. . . or attempting to drive . . .	This might include unsuccessful attempts to start a vehicle: see 19.2.3.
. . . or in charge of . . .	The person does not need to be in the vehicle: see 19.2.3.
. . . a mechanically propelled vehicle . . .	This covers a very wide range of vehicles, from cars to fork-lift trucks: see 19.2.1.
. . . on a road . . .	This has a wide range of meanings and includes some paths and adjacent areas: see 19.2.2.
. . . or other public place . . .	This includes places the public has to pay to enter and some privately owned areas with easy access such as hospitals: see 9.2.
. . . is unfit to drive . . .	Tests for physical coordination are just one way of establishing a person is unfit to drive.
through drink	A preliminary breath test and/or evidential blood or urine tests can confirm the presence of alcohol.
or drugs	This can include any intoxicating substance. A preliminary drugs test can confirm the presence of cannabis or cocaine. Evidential blood or urine samples can be used to test for a wider range of substances.

There is no need to administer a preliminary test for alcohol or drug levels before arresting a driver for this offence, but an officer can choose to do so. By administering a preliminary test and getting a positive result the officer may avoid having to arrange for medical confirmation that the person's condition is due to the presence of alcohol or a drug. (The officer could then go straight to requesting the doctor or health care professional to take blood for an evidential test, see 19.9.5.) Remember that the result of a preliminary test for drugs will be negative if the intoxicant is not one of those covered by the test.

The suspect's level of impairment and ability to drive properly is assessed by the police officer by the observations made during a preliminary impairment test (see 19.9.4.1). However, this would clearly not be required for a man who is so intoxicated that he falls out of the vehicle and is unable to stand.

If a preliminary test for alcohol or drugs had not been carried out or was negative, the doctor or health care professional (custody nurse) at the police station will examine the person and judge if his/her condition is due to intoxication (with any substance). If the examination shows that the person's condition is due to intoxication, then an evidential test will be used (blood or urine) to prove the presence of alcohol or a drug in the body, see 19.9.5.

A suspect arrested for a s 4 offence can also be investigated for a s 5 or a s 5A offence. If there is sufficient evidence, a suspect should be charged with more than one offence, and they will be dealt with independently. Section 4 can also be used if the driver is over the limit for alcohol but the vehicle involved is not a motor vehicle (assuming there is sufficient evidence of impairment).

The evidence presented to a court for a s 4 offence is likely to include:
• the style of driving before the accused was stopped;
• his/her demeanour at time of stop (speech, unsteadiness);

- the results of any preliminary tests;
- the report by a medical examiner whilst in custody (particularly if screening specimens are not obtained to prove the presence of alcohol or drugs in the body); and
- the results of evidential drug tests (using blood or urine samples).

Remember that it might be necessary to present evidence to counter an 'in charge' defence that the driver was not likely to drive (see 19.9.1).

An arrest for a s 4 offence would be under s 24 of the PACE Act 1984. (There is no power of arrest for a s 4 offence under the Road Traffic Act 1988.) A power of entry to arrest for a s 4 offence is available under s 17(1)(c)(iiia) of the PACE Act 1984, but note that this only applies if there are reasonable grounds for believing that the suspect is on the premises (see 10.8.1.2).

Offences under s 4 of the Road Traffic Act 1988 are triable summarily and the penalties are:

- for driving and attempting to drive whilst unfit due to drink or drugs (s 4(1)): six months' imprisonment and/or a fine, and obligatory disqualification; and
- for being in charge of a vehicle whilst unfit due to drink or drugs (s 4(2)): three months' imprisonment and/or a fine, and discretionary disqualification.

19.9.3 Driving, attempting to drive or being in charge of a motor vehicle when over the prescribed limit

There are two prescribed limit offences, s 5 relates to alcohol and s 5A relates to 17 specified drugs. The offences under s 5 and 5A only require evidence that the level of the substance in the suspect was over the prescribed limit, and evidence that the person was driving, attempting to drive, or was in charge of a motor vehicle.

19.9.3.1 Alcohol in excess of the prescribed limit

This offence relates to having alcohol over the prescribed limit in blood, breath, or urine. The flowchart shows the wording for a s 5 offence; bold-edged boxes emphasize the features that distinguish a s 5 offence from a s 4 offence.

Section 5 states that it is an offence for a person to:

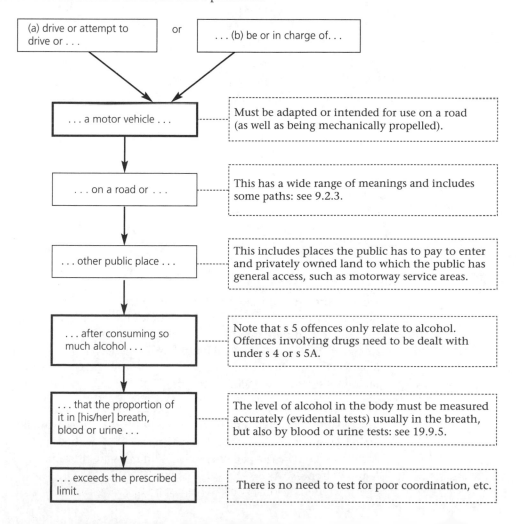

The prescribed limits are shown in the table. Note the units: microgrammes (µg), milligrammes (mg), and millilitres (ml). A good way to help memorize these figures is to remember that the digits in each measurement add up to eight.

Type of sample	Amount of alcohol per 100 ml
Breath	35 µg
Blood	80 mg
Urine	107 mg

These offences are triable summarily and the penalties are:

- for driving or attempting to drive above the prescribed limit (s 5(1)(a)): six months' imprisonment and/or a fine, and obligatory disqualification; and
- for being in charge of a vehicle above the prescribed limit (s 5(1)(b)): three months' imprisonment and/or a fine, and discretionary disqualification.

19.9.3.2 Specified controlled drug in excess of the prescribed limit

Section 5A of the Road Traffic Act 1988 relates to driving with certain specified drugs over the legal limit in the blood. The drugs covered by s 5A and their legal limits are shown in the table.

Controlled drug	Limit (microgrammes (µg) per litre of blood)
Amphetamine	250
Benzoylecgonine	50
Clonazepam	50
Cocaine	10
Delta-9-Tetrahydrocannabinol (THC*)	2
Diazepam	550
Flunitrazepam	300
Ketamine	20
Lorazepam	100
Lysergic Acid Diethylamide (LSD)	1
Methadone	500
Methylamphetamine	10
Methylenedioxymethamphetamine	10
6-Monoacetylmorphine	5
Morphine	80
Oxazepam	300
Temazepam	1,000

* the active ingredient in cannabis

Some of the drugs on the list are regularly prescribed by doctors to help patients with conditions such as anxiety. However some people obtain these drugs by other means and use them for recreational purposes, often at higher dosage levels than recommended by the manufacturer. For these drugs, the legal limits have been set very high, much higher than the levels for a person taking the drug at the medicinal dosage. This is to avoid penalizing drivers who are taking these drugs for medical reasons.

The wording and layout of s 5A is very similar to that of s 5; this was deliberate as the criminal justice system is very familiar with s 5 and how it is used. The flow chart for s 5 offence (in 19.9.3.1) can be applied for s 5A, replacing 'alcohol' with 'drugs', and 'breath, blood, or urine' with 'blood only'. The penalties for s 5A offences are the same as the penalties for the equivalent s 5 offences.

Specific Incidents

Defences are available if the suspect can show that the specified controlled drug had been prescribed or supplied for medical or dental purposes (s 5A(3)(a)), and were taken in accordance with the instructions (s 5A(3)(b)), and that immediately before taking the drug, its possession was not unlawful (see 12.5.2). These defences cannot be used if the suspect did not follow professional advice about the amount of time that should elapse between taking the drug and driving (s 5A(4)(a)and (b)). The advice could be from the person prescribing, supplying, manufacturing, or distributing the drug.

19.9.4   Preliminary tests

Preliminary tests are frequently referred to as roadside screening tests. There are two types of preliminary tests; preliminary impairment tests, and tests for the presence of alcohol or certain drugs. Preliminary tests are covered in s 6A (breath), s 6B (impairment), and s 6C (drug) of the Road Traffic Act 1988. A police officer does not need to be in uniform to require a person to take part in a preliminary test. However, the police officer actually administering a preliminary test must be in uniform (except after an accident). A Home Office statistical return form must be completed after administering a preliminary test. More recent equipment will do this automatically. Preliminary tests can also be used in police stations and hospitals.

In some situations there may be many individuals at a scene, so it might not be clear who was driving. It should first be clarified who was in each vehicle at the time of the accident; witnesses may be able to help on this matter. However, remember that a police officer only has to 'reasonably believe' that a person was driving a vehicle at the time of the accident, so if no one admits to being the driver then more than one person from the vehicle can be tested. It may also be the case that a number of individuals were 'in charge' of the same vehicle, and all be subject to testing.

A power of entry is available in order to administer preliminary tests (s 6E of the Road Traffic Act 1988), but only after an accident in which the police officer reasonably suspects a person has been injured. The power can be used for any place, using reasonable force if necessary.

The flowchart summarizes the circumstances for administering preliminary tests.

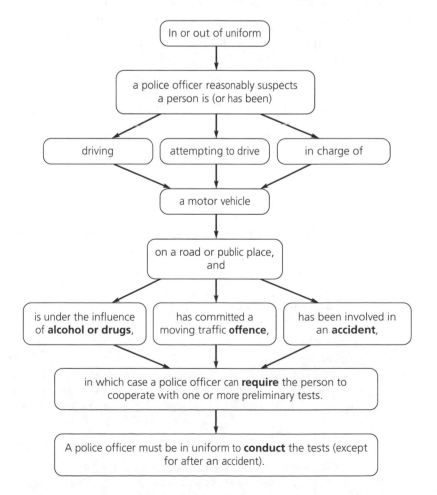

In or out of uniform

↓

a police officer reasonably suspects a person is (or has been)

↓

driving   attempting to drive   in charge of

↓

a motor vehicle

↓

on a road or public place, and

↓

is under the influence of **alcohol or drugs**,   has committed a moving traffic **offence**,   has been involved in an **accident**,

↓

in which case a police officer can **require** the person to cooperate with one or more preliminary tests.

↓

A police officer must be in uniform to **conduct** the tests (except for after an accident).

Specific Incidents

The meaning of the term 'accident' has not been defined by statute and remains a question of fact for the courts to decide (see 19.7.2.1). When any such incident seems to be due at least in part to the presence of a motor vehicle on a road it 'is a fair basis on which a police officer may request the provision of a specimen of breath' (Lord Widgery CJ in *R v Morris* [1972] RTR 201).

19.9.4.1 Preliminary impairment test

The preliminary impairment test in current use is the Field Impairment Test (FIT). It is used for s 4 offences, and is carried out by suitably trained officers. The test involves requesting the subject to undertake a number of specific tasks, such as walking in a straight line or judging time with his/her eyes closed. The tasks and subsequent recording of the observations are set out in the MGDD/F form. Failing the test provides the officer with grounds for arrest.

19.9.4.2 Preliminary breath tests for alcohol

Screening tests for alcohol are primarily used for s 5 offences, but can also be used for s 4 offences. For s 5 offences the preliminary test is used to find out if it is *likely* that there is suffi-cient alcohol in the subjects system to provide grounds for suspicion that an offence has been committed. If positive, it also allows the officer to consider arrest. For s 4 offences the tests can confirm the presence of alcohol, in which case it will not be necessary to arrange for a doctor or other health care professional to attend at the station to determine 'a condition due to …'.

There are currently two styles of preliminary breath-test device approved by the Secretary of State. Electronic devices include models such as the Lion Alcolmeter 500, the Alcosensor IV, the Draeger Alert, and the Draeger Alcotest 7410 or 6820. Non-electronic devices (such as Alcotest 80 and R80A and the Alcolyser) involve the inflation of a bag, and are used less often. All of the devices test air that has come from deep within the lungs. Officers should become familiar with the devices deployed within their area, and ensure that the manufacturer's instructions and local police service policies are followed.

For conducting the test, the police officer must make the requirement of the suspect in a form of words that complies with the legislation, including the implications of failing to comply. There is no prescribed format, but officers will be advised on any locally agreed form of words during training, and it may be specified in local police service policy.

The officer must also ask the person when he/she last drank alcohol or smoked as this can disrupt the test results if the test is taken within a certain time period. However, failing to ask these questions will not invalidate the test (*DPP v Kay* [1998] EWHC 258 (Admin)), nor will an innocent failure to follow the instructions render the arrest and subsequent evidential test unlawful (although the results may be considered as less reliable).

To carry out the test the driver should be asked to take a deep breath and to blow into the machine in one continuous breath until requested to stop. The person should be told the result of the test. A positive result from a preliminary breath test justifies arrest because it allows the officer to suspect that the proportion of alcohol in the person's breath or blood exceeds the prescribed limit. The reason for the arrest is the suspicion, not that the breath test has pro-duced a positive result. The suspect must be told the reasons for the arrest and that he/she is under arrest (s 6D(1) of the Road Traffic Act 1988) and must be cautioned. An evidential test for alcohol should then be carried out (see 19.9.5.1 and 19.9.5.2).

A patient in a hospital must never be arrested (s 6D(3)). However, should such a wrongful arrest take place, a subsequent and lawfully obtained evidential specimen will not become unlawful (*DPP v Wilson* [2009] EWHC 1988 (Admin)).

19.9.4.3 Preliminary drug tests

Screening tests for drugs are used mainly for s 5A offences but can also be used in relation to offences under s 4. For s 5A offences the preliminary test is used to find out if it is *likely* that there is sufficient drug in a person's body to provide grounds for suspecting that an offence has been committed, and therefore arrest. For s 4 offences the tests can confirm the presence of certain drugs. Once confirmed there will then be no need to arrange for a doctor or other healthcare professional to determine 'a condition due to…' at the police station.

The test is carried out on a sample of saliva and currently identifies the presence of cocaine and cannabis (or more precisely its active ingredient THC). These feature on the s 5A list of drugs, and are two of the most commonly abused drugs. According to recent research, they seem likely to account for the vast majority of drivers under the influence of a drug (Department for Transport, 2013). The next drug proposed for inclusion in the saliva test is amphetamine, but at the time of writing the timescale for this is uncertain.

There are currently two devices approved by the Home Office for roadside screening for these drugs. These are the Draeger DrugTest 5000 and the Suretec DrugWipe 3S. Both use the same technology to detect the drugs but display the results in different ways. Police services may use either or both of the devices, although their use may be restricted to specific departments or units. Any officer who is required to carry out testing will receive device-specific training.

A person may be under the influence of a drug that cannot be detected by the device. If an officers suspects this is the case and can justify an arrest, the fact that it is not possible to screen for a particular drug is not relevant, and is no bar to arrest.

19.9.4.4   What to do after a preliminary test

The actions depend on the preliminary test that has been used and whether the subject completed the test satisfactorily. The diagram summarizes the actions that should be taken in relation to the outcomes from preliminary tests. There is a power of entry in order to arrest a person who has provided a positive preliminary test and has been involved in an injury accident (s 6 of the Road Traffic Act 1988).

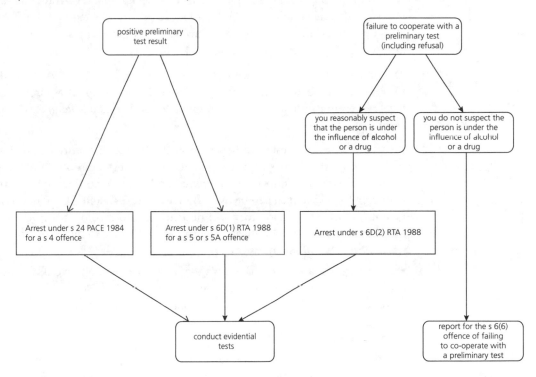

If the results of a preliminary breath test for alcohol are negative but due to the person's demeanour the police officer suspects the driver is under the influence of drugs then he/she should consider:

- administering a preliminary impairment or drugs test (if he/she is qualified and has the apparatus available) and proceed as for a s 4 or a s 5A offence; or
- arresting the driver on suspicion of the s 4 offence of driving whilst unfit, using s 24 of the PACE Act 1984 powers of arrest.

If the result of a preliminary drugs test is negative but the impairment or demeanour observed suggests intoxication, following options can be considered:

- administer a preliminary breath test for alcohol if this has not already been done;
- arrest under s 5A if it seems likely the intoxication is caused by one of the other 15 specified drugs on the s 5A list; or
- arrest under s 4 if there is sufficient evidence of impairment to consider the driver as 'unfit'.

If the result of a preliminary test is negative and there is no evidence of impairment, and no other offences have been committed, then the driver is free to leave.

Specific incidents

The number of opportunities that should be provided for completing a preliminary test will be determined locally. If the driver does not take the test correctly, refuses to participate, or is unable to complete a preliminary test, for example due to a medical condition, this is considered a 'failure to provide'. If there is reasonable suspicion that he/she is under the influence of alcohol or a drug (as appropriate), then he/she should be arrested and evidential tests will be carried out. If alcohol or drugs are not suspected, the person should instead be reported for the offence of failing to cooperate with the provision of a specimen for a preliminary test (s 6(6) of the Road Traffic Act 1988). The person's true identity will need to be ascertained (through computer checks with Control), and identification documentation obtained from the person. The address he/she gives must be checked as genuine. He/she should be interviewed under caution (all recorded in the officer's pocket notebook), and then reported for the offence of failing to cooperate with a preliminary test and cautioned again. This offence is triable summarily and the penalty is obligatory endorsement (four points) and discretionary disqualification.

19.9.5 Evidential tests

The results of evidential tests for drugs and alcohol can be used as evidence in a court for an offence under ss 3A, 4, 5, or 5A of the Road Traffic Act 1988. The specimens are usually provided at a police station (or hospital if the suspect is a hospital patient) but some may also be conducted at the roadside. The requirement for an evidential test (all types) is made at a police station or hospital, but the requirement for an evidential breath test can also be made at the roadside. It is usual to arrest a suspect before making the requirement for an evidential test, although this is not compulsory by law. A suspect who is also a hospital patient cannot be arrested (s 6D(3) of the Road Traffic Act 1988).

At a police station, a suspect cannot delay providing a specimen for an evidential test in order to obtain legal advice. There can only be a delay in exceptional circumstances and where a legal representative is available for immediate consultation (*Chalupa v CPS* [2009] EWHC 3082 (Admin)).

If there is reasonable cause to believe that the suspect has a drug in his/her body (eg from a preliminary drug-test result or the medical examiner's opinion), a blood or urine specimen should be taken for a suspected s 4 offence, and a blood specimen for a suspected s 5A offence. A single blood specimen can be used to investigate a s 4 and 5A offence as long as there is sufficient quantity (the laboratory will need to be informed of this intention). For alcohol, an evidential breath test will always be used in preference to blood or urine tests (s 7(3) of the Road Traffic Act 1988) unless:

- there is reasonable cause to believe that a medical reason prevents the use of a breath test;
- the approved device is not available; and/or
- there is cause to believe the device gave an unreliable result.

19.9.5.1 Evidential breath tests for alcohol

The test can be required and conducted at (or near) a place where a relevant preliminary breath test has been administered, at a police station, or in a hospital (s 7(2) of the Road Traffic Act 1988). There is no need to have already carried out a preliminary breath test if the suspect is being investigated for the offences of causing death by careless driving when under the influence of drink or drugs, or for being unfit to drive (ss 3A and 4 of the Road Traffic Act 1988 respectively).

Two samples of breath are required for the test, and the process and period of time in which the two samples are collected is called a 'cycle'. The two samples must be obtained from the same cycle in order for the test to be valid. Only the sample containing the lower proportion of alcohol will be used as evidence, and the other will be disregarded (s 8(1) of the Road Traffic Act 1988). The samples will be analysed by a device approved by the Secretary of State (currently the Camic Datamaster, the Lion Intoxilyzer 6000, or the Intoximeter EC/IR). The person operating the machine (often the custody officer) will have been trained to use it and will check that it is working properly. MGDD forms must be used to record the breath-test procedure and the completed forms will constitute the 'notes made at the time'.

The suspect must be warned that failing to provide a suitable specimen (two samples) may render him/her liable to prosecution (s 7(7) of the Road Traffic Act 1988, please note para A12 in the current MGDD/A). Each organization will have its own policy on how many attempts can be allowed for the suspect to provide a sufficient volume of air in a proper manner (s 11(3) of the Road Traffic Act 1988). Note that regurgitation of stomach contents does not affect the accuracy of the measurements (see *McNeil v DPP* [2008] EWHC 1254).

The prescribed limit for alcohol in the breath is 35 μg of alcohol per 100 ml of breath (see 19.9.3), but the police do not proceed unless the level is above 40 μg (see MGDD/A, section A20). After the test, the MGDD forms are completed and if the result is above the prescribed limit the driver can be charged and bailed to court.

If the driver fails to provide two samples of breath, the offence of 'failing to provide a specimen of breath for an evidential breath test' (s 7(6)) has been committed. Refusing to provide suitable samples is equivalent to failure (s 11(2) of the Road Traffic Act 1988), including when not enough breath is provided (see *Rweikiza v DPP* [2008] EWHC 386 (Admin)). The suspect must be allowed sufficient time to provide the samples in each subsequent cycle; otherwise a subsequent prosecution may fail (see *Plackett v DPP* [2008] EWHC 1335 (Admin)). The suspect is not obliged to mention any medical condition which could account for failing to provide enough breath, but the court does not have to accept the excuse if he/she later claims that this is the case (see *Piggott v DPP* [2008] WLR (D) 44). If the testing machine registers an error on the second sample in each of two cycles, then further breath samples can be required (at another police station or using another machine for example) and failing to comply is an offence (s 7(6)), even though previous samples were supplied (see *Hussain v DPP* [2008] EWHC 901). In *Bielecki v DPP* [2011] EWHC 2245 (Admin) it was decided that a court could draw an inference (ie draw their own conclusions) whether a request for a specimen of breath that was translated by an accredited interpreter will have been understood by a non-English speaking suspect.

19.9.5.2 Blood and urine specimens

These may be required under s 7(3) of the Road Traffic Act 1988 (see the start of 19.9.5). For a suspected s 4 or s 5 offence, either type of specimen can be used, but for a s 5A offence it must be a blood sample. The requirement to provide a specimen of blood or urine can only be made at a police station or hospital. If the driver refuses (or is unable) to provide blood or urine samples, then he/she will have committed the offence of failing to provide samples for an evidential test (s 7(6) of the Road Traffic Act 1988).

Before a blood or urine sample is taken the driver must be told:

- for a suspected s 5 offence, the reason(s) why breath specimens cannot be taken (from the list under s 7(3) in 19.9.5); and
- that he/she is therefore required to give a sample of blood or urine; and
- that failing to provide the specimen could result in his/her prosecution.

Specific Incidents

Where there is an option, blood is the preferred medium. Apart from medical considerations, the driver cannot choose whether the sample will be blood or urine. Before proceeding with a blood test the driver should be asked if there are any medical reasons for not taking a blood sample. The sample must of course be taken by a medical examiner or health care professional. After the sample has been obtained the driver can be bailed to return to the police station when the results arrive back from the laboratory. Blood and urine samples are usually sent to the laboratory by post, although blood samples for a s 5A analysis must remain refrigerated and arrangements vary between police services.

19.9.5.3 Allowing for the delay between the offence and taking samples

As the human body continually breaks down alcohol it is assumed that the level of alcohol in a suspect's breath, blood, or urine at the time of an alleged offence will gradually decrease over time (if no more alcohol is consumed). It is a fact in law that a court will assume the level of intoxicants in the body at the time of the alleged offence were not less than the levels measured in the evidential test (s 15(2) of the Road Traffic Offenders Act 1988).

However, the accused may claim the 'hip-flask defence', insisting that he/she consumed alcohol or drugs after the offence but before the evidential sample was taken (eg that he/she ran off after a collision and went for a drink before the police arrived), or that he/she consumed intoxicants from a container (the proverbial (and sometimes actual) hip flask) in the vehicle after the preliminary test. This is formally referred to as 'post-incident drinking'. If he/she can prove this, the assumption under s 15(2) (see previous paragraph) cannot be made.

If a driver provides an evidential specimen and alleges he/she has consumed further intoxicants since the time of the alleged offence, 'back calculations' can be used to establish that the driver was in excess of the legal limit when the incident occurred. These calculations are based on the time elapsed since the offence, the subsequent consumption of alcohol, and the estimated rate of elimination of alcohol from the human body. Evidence for back calculations should be recorded on Form MGDD/D at the police station. However, if this defence is not raised until later, the relevant laboratory should be provided with as much information as can be obtained from the case papers and the officer in charge of the case.

The following information is relevant, where available:

- the type and quantity of alcohol consumed before the incident and, if possible, the times at which individual units of alcohol were consumed;
- the type and quantity of alcohol allegedly consumed after the incident but before the test;
- the driver's characteristics: weight, height, build, age, sex, and any medical conditions;
- details of any food consumed from six hours before the offence until the provision of a breath or laboratory specimen; and
- details of any medication taken regularly or within four hours prior to drinking.

TASK 14

1. If you are a trainee police officer, find out what preliminary test equipment is available for you to use and how to use it. This information should be available at your police station or from your service policy documents.

   - Are you only authorized to use equipment to test for breath alcohol, or could you test for drugs as well?
   - Would you be allowed to carry out a preliminary impairment test?

2. The suspected commission of a moving traffic offence is one reason for requiring a driver to be tested for the presence of alcohol in his/her body. Give some examples of moving traffic offences under the Public Passenger Vehicles Act 1981, the Road Traffic Regulation Act 1984, and the Road Traffic Offenders Act 1988.

19.9.6   Drink- and drug-driving, and admission to hospital

Some drivers need to be admitted to hospital after an accident. Investigations in these circumstance are covered under s 9 of the Road Traffic Act 1988, and a MGDD/C form is used. A hospital is defined by the Act as an institution which provides medical or surgical treatment for in-patients or out-patients. The term 'patient' is not defined and will be a question of fact for the court to decide, but generally speaking a patient is a person who is currently on hospital grounds receiving medical treatment (or waiting to receive medical treatment).

19.9.6.1   Obtaining samples from a hospital patient

The regulations governing such procedures are given in s 9(1) of the Road Traffic Act 1988. A general description of preliminary and evidential tests is given in 19.9.4 and 19.9.5.

Before a requirement is made or any test carried out on the person, the medical practitioner (usually a doctor) in immediate charge of the patient's case must be notified about the proposed tests. The procedures must be explained and the doctor must be given the opportunity to object (s 9(1) of the Road Traffic Act 1988), as the welfare of a patient is paramount. A further complicating factor is that the suspect might receive drugs as part of his/her medical treatment, and these could interfere with the accuracy of the analysis of any sample taken.

If the doctor does not object, the patient can be asked to cooperate with a preliminary test. If the result of the test is negative, the patient must be told that no further action will be taken by the police in relation to investigating a drink or drug driving offence. If he/she does not cooperate and refuses to have the test, he/she should be reported for an offence under s 6(6) of the Road Traffic Act 1988. Note that a hospital patient cannot be arrested for failing to cooperate with a preliminary test (s 6D(3)).

Evidential tests will be carried out if the result of the preliminary test is positive (or the patient fails to complete the test). The outline procedure is shown in the diagram.

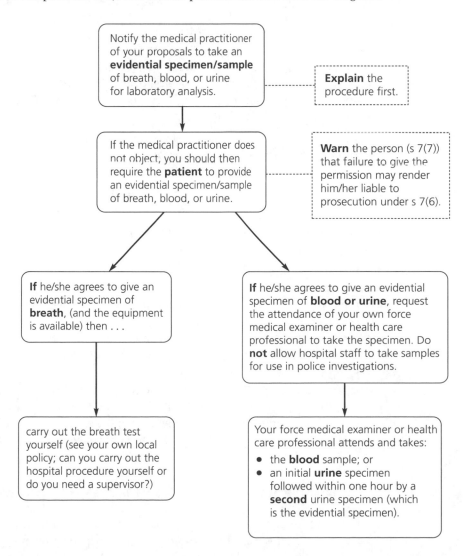

For a blood sample, a police medical practitioner or health care professional must take the specimen. If this is not possible, then another medical practitioner may be asked (this is very rare), but he/she should not have a responsibility for the clinical care of the patient.

An unconscious patient (described as 'incapable of giving valid consent' on the MGDD/C) is not able to take part in a breath test and so a blood sample will be required, and once again the relevant medical practitioner must be notified (see s 9(1A) of the Road Traffic Act 1988). In such circumstances it is lawful for a medical practitioner or health care professional to obtain a specimen of blood (s 7A(3)), but it must not be subjected to a laboratory analysis until the patient regains consciousness and gives permission (s 7A(4)). It is an offence to refuse such permission (s 7A(6)).

> **TASK 15** A trainee police officer is required to attend the accident and emergency department at the local hospital. There she makes a lawful requirement for a sample of breath, blood, or urine from a patient who was driving a vehicle at the time of a collision. Unfortunately, whilst waiting for the police medical practitioner to arrive, the patient is discharged from hospital and leaves the building.
>
> Does the obligation for the patient to provide that sample still stand? Refer to Webber v DPP [1998] RTR 111 for your answer.

19.10 Using Vehicles to Cause Alarm, Distress, and Annoyance

The police have a number of powers under s 59 of the Police Reform Act 2002 for situations when people are using motor vehicles in an anti-social manner or racing, and therefore causing concern for other people in the area. There may be reasonable grounds under the Road Traffic Act 1988 for believing that a mechanically propelled vehicle has been driven carelessly or inconsiderately (s 3 of the RTA 1988), unlawfully off-road (s 34 of the RTA 1988), or that a motor vehicle is involved (or is likely to be involved) with other motor vehicles in unlicensed on-street racing. If, as a result of the way the vehicle is being driven, members of the public are caused (or are likely to be caused) alarm, distress, or annoyance, a police officer may take the following actions, using reasonable force when required (s 59(3)(d)):

- require a moving vehicle to stop (s 59(3)(a));
- seize and remove the vehicle, after warning the driver (s 59(3)(b)); and
- enter certain types of premises (but not a dwelling-house or attached garage or garden) in order to stop or seize a vehicle (s 59(3)(c)).

Failure to stop is an offence under s 59(6) of the Police Reform Act 2002. It is triable summarily, and the penalty is a fine.

The driver must be warned that his/her vehicle will be seized if the improper use continues. However, no warning need be issued if:

- it would be impracticable to do so;
- a warning has already been given on that occasion;
- there are reasonable grounds for believing that such a warning has been given on that occasion by someone else; or
- the officer has reasonable grounds for believing that the person has been given a warning (by any police officer, in respect of any vehicle being used in the same or a similar way) on a previous occasion in the previous 12 months.

The warning applies to both the driver and that particular vehicle. Therefore it applies to future stops when anyone is driving that vehicle, and it also applies to the driver no matter what vehicle he/she is driving. The wording to be used in the warning notice is not specified in the legislation, and police services may have pre-formatted forms for use in these circumstances.

19.11 Other Offences Relating to Vehicles and Highways

There are a number of offences that relate to vehicles and highways. Here we cover the new legislation that removes the clamping of vehicles parked on private land, and some other non-driving highways offences that might cause distress or inconvenience to other road users.

19.11.1   Immobilizing vehicles parked on private land

Historically some private individuals and organizations had immobilized or moved vehicles that have been parked on private land. The owner/driver then had to pay a release fee. This caused considerable public consternation, and as a result it is now a summary offence under s 54(1) of the Protection of Freedoms Act 2012 if a person without lawful authority:

* immobilizes a motor vehicle by attaching an immobilizing device, for example a wheel clamp (s 54(1)(a)); or
* moves or restricts the movement of a vehicle, for example by towing it away or blocking its movement with another vehicle (s 54(1)(b)).

The notion of 'lawful authority' is the significant issue here. The 'law of contract' does not provide the landowner or operator of a commercially run car park with the lawful authority to immobilize or move a vehicle, even when the terms and conditions of the parking are clearly displayed and the vehicle is parked for a longer period than permitted (s 54(2)). So a car park operator who clamps a vehicle in such circumstances is likely to have committed an offence. However, for a car park where the movement of vehicles in and out is restricted by the use of a rising-arm barrier the situation is different. If a car driver does not pay the parking fee and therefore cannot leave because the barrier remains down, no offence is committed by the car park owner or operator as the car has not been immobilized or removed (s 54(3)).

Note that this offence cannot be committed by anyone who is entitled to remove a vehicle, as he/she would have lawful authority to move the vehicle. An example might be when a representative of a hire company retrieves a vehicle after the hire agreement has expired (s 54(4)). Note also that the offence requires an intention to prevent or inhibit the removal of the vehicle. So, a householder who shunts a vehicle a few metres along the road (away from the entrance to his driveway for example), does not commit the offence, because he did not intend to prevent the driver from accessing and using the vehicle.

19.11.2   Road-related Anti-Social Behaviour

Some of the more common offences are described here.

Wilful obstruction is an offence under s 137 of the Highways Act 1980. It is an offence for a person:

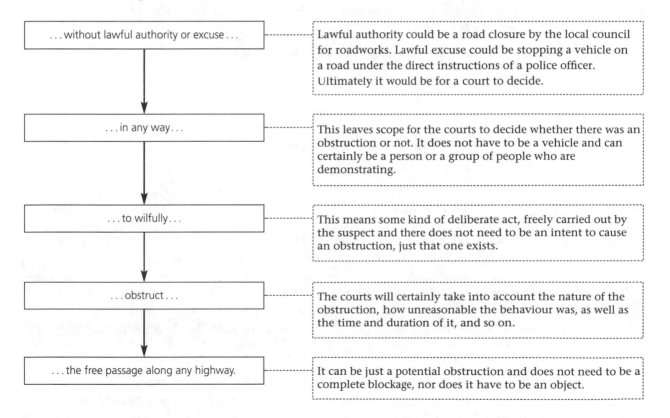

. . . without lawful authority or excuse . . .	Lawful authority could be a road closure by the local council for roadworks. Lawful excuse could be stopping a vehicle on a road under the direct instructions of a police officer. Ultimately it would be for a court to decide.
. . . in any way . . .	This leaves scope for the courts to decide whether there was an obstruction or not. It does not have to be a vehicle and can certainly be a person or a group of people who are demonstrating.
. . . to wilfully . . .	This means some kind of deliberate act, freely carried out by the suspect and there does not need to be an intent to cause an obstruction, just that one exists.
. . . obstruct . . .	The courts will certainly take into account the nature of the obstruction, how unreasonable the behaviour was, as well as the time and duration of it, and so on.
. . . the free passage along any highway.	It can be just a potential obstruction and does not need to be a complete blockage, nor does it have to be an object.

Specific Incidents

This offence is triable summarily and the penalty is a fine.

'Unauthorized campers' can be directed away from 'any land forming part of a highway, any other unoccupied property, or any occupied land without the consent of the owner' under s 77 of the Criminal Justice and Public Order Act 1994. This allows local authorities to direct people who are residing in vehicles in such locations to leave with the vehicles and any other property they have there.

Vehicles or trailers must not be left in a dangerous position on a road (s 22 of the Road Traffic Act 1988). It is an offence for a person in charge of a vehicle to cause or permit:

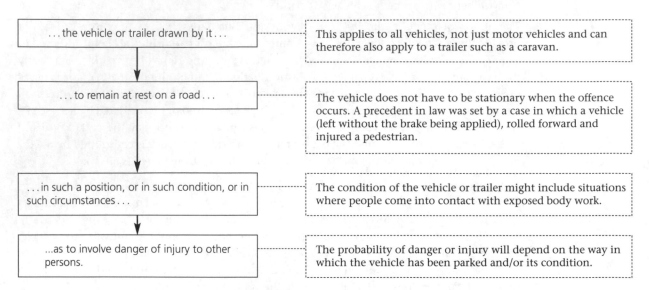

This offence is triable summarily and the penalty is a fine.

Lighting fires or letting off firearms near a highway is an offence under s 161 of the Highways Act 1980. This prohibits any person (without lawful authority or excuse) from:

- depositing anything on a highway which leads to someone getting injured;
- lighting a fire on or over a carriageway; or
- discharging a firearm (or firework) within 50 feet of the centre of a highway if it could injure a user of the highway.

This offence is triable summarily and the penalty is a fine.

Interfering with road signs, other traffic equipment, or vehicles may put other road users at risk. Section 22A of the Road Traffic Act 1988 states that it is an offence to (intentionally and without lawful authority or reasonable cause) cause anything to be on or over a road, or interfere with a motor vehicle, trailer, cycle, or with traffic equipment (directly or indirectly) if this is likely to cause injury to a person or damage to property.

Traffic equipment is defined as:

- anything lawfully placed on or near a road by a highway authority;
- a traffic sign lawfully placed on or near a road by a person other than a highway authority; and
- any fence, barrier, or light lawfully placed on or near a road (eg to protect street works), or any item placed under the instructions of a chief officer of police.

This applies only if the activities would be regarded as obviously dangerous to a reasonable person or bystander. The reasonable person or bystander does not have to be a motorist (*DPP v D* [2006] EWHC 314). It is irrelevant that the suspect was unaware of the potential danger; this will be a question of fact for the court to decide given the circumstances. The offence is triable either way and the penalty is a fine or imprisonment (six months summarily and seven years on indictment).

Repairing vehicles in the street is a relatively common practice, but it may cause nuisance to other residents, or environmental damage. Under s 4 of the Clean Neighbourhoods and Environment Act 2005, it is an offence in some circumstances to 'carry out restricted works on a motor vehicle on a road'. This includes the repair, maintenance, servicing, improvement, dismantling, installation, replacement, or renewal of a motor vehicle (or of any part of or accessory to a motor vehicle). However, a householder who repairs his/her own vehicle in the street and gives no reasonable cause for annoyance to persons in the vicinity does not commit this offence as the work is not for gain or reward or as part of a business. Nor is any offence committed if the work is required after an accident or breakdown and the repairs were necessary on the spot or carried out within 72 hours.

Skips placed on or near highways can present hazards. Permission must be given by a highways authority for placing a skip on a highway (s 139(1) of the Highways Act 1980), and conditions must be met in relation to its size, the way it is lit and its position on the road (s 139(2)). An offence is committed if the skip is placed without permission (s 139(3)), or the conditions are not met (s 139(4)). These are summary offences and the penalty is a fine.

Holding or getting onto a motor vehicle (or an attached trailer) that is moving and on a road, in order to be towed or carried is an offence (s 26(1) of the Road Traffic Act 1988). This is a summary offence and the penalty is a fine.

> **TASK 16** Several complaints have been made by residents in the neighbourhood of a club. They say that at closing time they have seen people throwing rubbish bins and other items about the streets, tampering with traffic lights, and deflating vehicle tyres.
>
> What offences might have been committed?

19.11.3 Riding vehicles on a pavement

The use of mini-motos (miniature motorbikes), go-peds (petrol-driven scooters), and self-balancing personal transporters (eg Segways and hoverboards) may pose potential risks to the health and safety of other road and pavement users. There have been a number of fatalities and serious injuries, and many members of the public consider their use as an example of anti-social behaviour. All of these types of vehicle have been held to be motor vehicles (see 19.2.1.1) and must therefore comply with the usual road traffic laws. It is an offence to 'wilfully ride a carriage' on a pavement (s 72 of the Highways Act 1835) and the meaning of carriage includes motor vehicles.

19.12 Methods of Disposal for Motoring Offences

There are several ways of dealing with a suspect who has committed a road traffic offence, and the decision will be based upon a number of factors including local policy and the police officer's discretion (see 3.6). The methods of disposal for such offences include:

* a verbal warning;
* reporting a suspect for the purposes of issuing a written charge;
* the VDRS (Vehicle Defect Rectification Scheme);
* a TOR (Traffic Offence Report);
* an FPN (fixed penalty notice);
* arrest and charge.

The first flowchart summarizes the early stages of the investigative process for dealing with motoring offences. Note there may be some local variation about the use of police note books (PNB in the flow chart), as well as matters relating to the issue of the HO/RT/1 form, FPNs, and the use of the VDRS. Officers should therefore follow local arrangements.

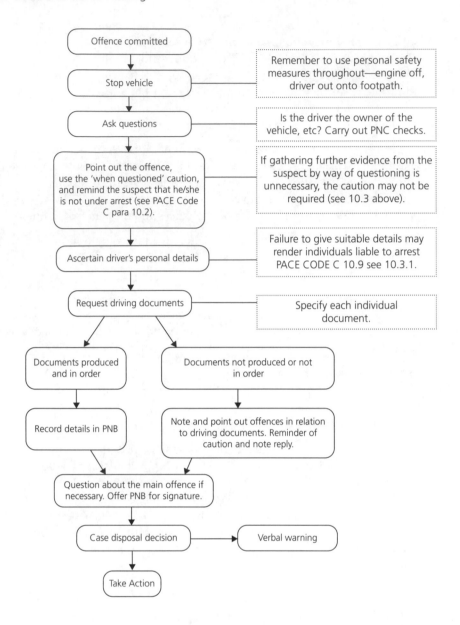

The second flow chart shows the various disposal options if a verbal warning is not appropriate. Any disposal option other than a verbal warning will require the officer to ascertain the personal details of the suspect, including a suitable address for the issuing of a written charge (often referred to as suitable for 'the service of a summons') should that be necessary. If a person refuses to provide this information he/she may be liable to arrest, and once in custody can be charged with traffic offences as for any other offence (see 10.13.1). Prior to charge, the arrested person may choose to provide the required details, and local policies vary on how to proceed. Not all the disposal methods may be available to all officers on all occasions, and processes and back-office arrangements can vary significantly between forces. Note that criminals sought in connection with serious crimes often come to the attention of the police through committing minor road traffic offences. If a suspect has been arrested for the other offences, he/she can also be charged with the road traffic offences.

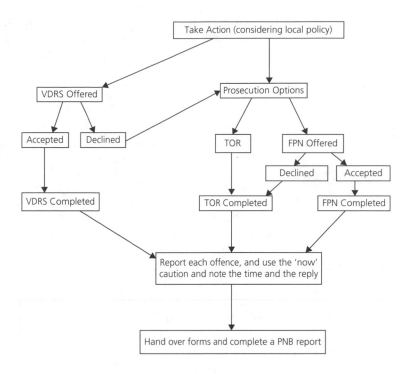

19.12.1 Reporting for the purposes of issuing a written charge

The suspect must be reported for the purposes of issuing a written charge (see 10.13.1.1) for all methods of disposal, apart from giving a verbal warning with no further action. The processes involved in each may vary, for example it is slightly different for completing a Traffic Offence Report (see 19.12.3) compared with issuing an FPN (see 19.12.4)).

19.12.2 Vehicle Defect Rectification Scheme

Drivers of vehicles that are found to be in an unsuitable condition can be given the opportunity to use the Vehicle Defect Rectification Scheme (VDRS). This is a way of dealing with certain minor vehicle defects without the need to prosecute or issue an FPN. The use of the VDRS will be subject to local police service instructions and officers should be clear about when it can be used. Deciding whether to use the VDRS will also depend on the circumstances of the offence and the officer's discretion.

The advantages of the VDRS include:

- the defects are rectified, which contributes to road safety;
- the offender does not have to go to court; and
- improved police and public relations: many people will only come into contact with the police during the investigation of road traffic matters, and the VDRS is partly supportive, rather than wholly punitive.

When considering using the VDRS the police officer must point out the offence to the person responsible for the vehicle and inform him/her that no further action will be taken if he/she agrees to participate in the scheme. However, the person should also be informed that participation in the VDRS is voluntary. If the driver declines the VDRS, he/she will be normally be issued with a TOR or an FPN, however, officers should follow local policy.

The driver must repair the defect or renew the faulty body within 14 days of the notice being issued and then submit the vehicle for examination at a Department for Transport approved testing station (an MOT testing station) where the VDRS form should be endorsed to confirm the fault is rectified. The driver must then send the completed form to the Central Ticket Office (or as guided by local policy) within the time specified. If the driver fails to return the form within the specified time, he/she can be prosecuted by way of written charge (as if the VDRS had not been used). The copy of the form will be returned after 21 days to the relevant police officer for the reporting process (this stage may depend on service operating procedure, as will the following). He/she will need to write a duty statement (see 10.12) which will include evidence relating to the offence, in the same way as for reporting a suspect for the purposes of issuing a written charge (see 19.12.1). The officer will submit a case file (see 27.4), including a report requesting the issue of a written charge. The charge will outline the offences for which the driver was reported.

19.12.3 Traffic Offence Report (TOR)

In the majority of police services most officers either offer advice for minor offences (where there has been no collision) or issue a Traffic Offence Report (TOR). Many police services are moving away from using FPNs in favour of TORs as they provide a choice of disposal options, such as driver improvement courses (only available for some offences), conditional offers with the same penalty as an FPN, or a written charge summoning the offender to court.

The format of a TOR varies between police services; some are provided in booklets of 10 with at least two self-carbonating copies for each to record details of the driver, the offence, and the vehicle involved. Generally the first copy is kept by the issuing officer (the reverse side is in effect an MG11 duty statement (see 10.12) and should be completed according to local policy). The second copy is given to the driver. As the driver could in the end be prosecuted, the reporting procedures for issuing a written charge (see 10.13.1.1) should be followed and recorded on the notice, and the driver asked to sign the entry. The completed TOR is sent to the force's central processing department for a decision on the most appropriate disposal method. The procedures for issuing TORs vary between police services so officers should be guided by local police service policy.

19.12.4 The fixed penalty system

The fixed penalty system for motoring offences (Pt III of the Road Traffic Offenders Act 1988) provides offenders with the opportunity to pay a fixed fine instead of going to court (s 54 of the Road Traffic Offenders Act 1988). The FPN system is similar to the Penalty Notice for Disorder (PND) system for anti-social behaviour offences (see 10.13.2.1). Note that the use of FPNs is subject to local policy, and that most parking offences have now been de-criminalized, for example, in London, officers can only issue FPNs for unnecessary obstruction. There are two types of FPN:

- non-endorsable fixed penalty notices (NE-FPN), for offences which do not add penalty points to an offender's driving licence (parking, seatbelts, and vehicle lighting offences);
- endorsable fixed penalty notices (EFPN), for offences which add penalty points to an offender's driving licence (eg contravening a red traffic light, failing to stop at a stop sign, and driving a vehicle with defective tyres).

An FPN can only be issued to the person actually committing the offence or driving the vehicle involved; an FPN cannot be used for people who cause or permit an offence (see 19.2.4 for 'cause' or 'permit'). In some circumstances an FPN can be issued by leaving the documents on the vehicle without the need for the driver to be present, such as a parking ticket affixed to a car's windscreen. An FPN can be issued to non-UK offenders and UK offenders, as well as those with no fixed abode, irrespective of whether the offence is endorsable. A financial penalty deposit can be requested from any offender who does not have a satisfactory address in the UK (see 19.12.4.4).

If the FPN is not accepted, the driver will have to be reported. A fine for an FPN must be paid within 28 days (to the Central Ticket Office in the area) or it will be increased by 50 per cent, and can also be recovered by the courts.

For offences involving commercial vehicles (eg breaches of drivers' hours rules, overloading of vehicles) the fixed penalty value can be increased, depending on the circumstances and the severity of the offence (see the VOSA *Guide to graduated fixed penalties and financial deposits*, available online).

19.12.4.1 Issuing a non-endorsable fixed penalty notice

When a police officer in uniform has reasonable grounds to believe that a person is committing or has committed a fixed penalty offence (and local policy indicates this is the suitable disposal option), an FPN can be issued. If the driver is present the police officer should:

1. point out the offence;
2. caution the driver using 'when questioned' and inform him/her that he/she is not under arrest (PACE Code C, para 10.2);
3. question the driver and allow him/her to ask questions (in relation to the offence(s));
4. if the driver fails to cooperate or answer any particular questions after being cautioned, he/she should be informed that failing to provide their name and address for example, may make him/her liable to detention or arrest (PACE Code C, para 10.9, see also 10.3.1);
5. check that the driver wishes to proceed with an FPN;
6. complete and issue the NEFPN;
7. report the driver or owner for the offence;
8. use the 'now' caution (see 10.3.4).

For a small number of parking offences an NEFPN can be attached to a stationary vehicle (s 62(1)). Note that it is an offence for any other person to remove or interfere with an FPN fixed to a vehicle.

The flowchart below summarizes the process.

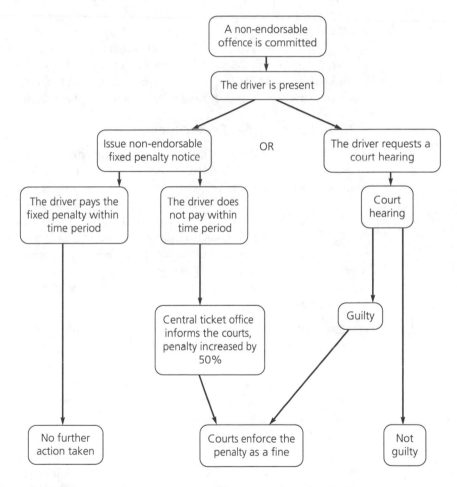

19.12.4.2 Endorsable fixed penalty notices

Where the penalty for the offence is obligatory endorsement, s 54 of the Road Traffic Offenders Act 1988 states that an EFPN may only be used if:

- the driver produces his/her licence for inspection and surrender;
- the driver's file on the PNC can be checked to view the endorsement history;
- the total points including the new proposed points must not add up to 12 or more (the driver would be liable to disqualification); and
- the driver accepts an EFPN.

The procedure for issuing an EFPN is the same as that for a standard FPN, except for checking and retaining the driving licence and providing the driver with a receipt for the licence. If the proposed new points would take the total to 12 or more an EFPN cannot be used and the driver will have to be reported for prosecution. If the driver does not have his/her driving licence available, a provisional EFPN should be issued and the driver must produce his/her licence for inspection at a police station (of his/her choice) within seven days.

19.12.4.3 Conditional offer of fixed penalty

A conditional offer for a fixed penalty can be sent to the alleged offender if the FPN cannot be handed to a driver or attached to a vehicle (s 75 of the Road Traffic Offenders Act 1988). This could apply for speeding offences detected by automatic camera devices, or when a police officer sees a driver disobeying a road sign but it is impossible or too dangerous to follow, or when a TOR has been issued and no suitable education course is available. The conditional offer will state the circumstances of the alleged offence, the relevant fixed penalty, and explain that no further proceedings will take place in relation to the offence for 28 days from the date of issue. If payment is made within that period (and for obligatory endorsement offences the licence is surrendered), there will be no court proceedings. Police officers and staff at Central Ticket Offices can arrange for conditional offers to be sent.

19.12.4.4 Roadside Deposit Scheme

If a driver has been issued with an FPN or conditional offer but is unable to provide a satisfactory UK address at the time of an offence, the police officer can request a financial penalty deposit. The officer can prohibit the use of the vehicle and physically prevent its use (eg with a wheel clamp or a wire rope lock through the steering wheel) until the deposit is paid. Once paid, the driver can then choose whether to allow the deposit to be used as payment of the penalty, or request a court hearing. If he/she is found not guilty in court the deposit will be returned. Further information is available in the *VOSA Guide to graduated fixed penalties and financial deposits*, available online. This procedure will probably only be available to specialist roads policing units; officers should check which local arrangements apply.

19.12.5 A Notice of Intended Prosecution

The rights of an individual suspected of committing certain road traffic offences are safeguarded under the Road Traffic Offenders Act 1988. He/she must be informed at the earliest opportunity of his/her suspected involvement in an offence, usually by means of a Notice of Intended Prosecution (NIP). This will specify the nature of the offence and the time and place where it is alleged to have been committed. It applies for offences listed in s 1(1) of the Road Traffic Offenders Act 1988, such as: dangerous driving; dangerous cycling; careless and inconsiderate driving; careless and inconsiderate cycling; failing to conform with the indication of a police officer when directing traffic; failing to comply with a traffic sign; and speeding offences (see Sch 1 to the Road Traffic Offenders Act 1988 and for a full list on the www.legislation.gov.uk website).

Section 1(1) states that a person cannot be prosecuted for any of these offences, unless he/she has been either:

- warned at the time of the offence of the possibility of prosecution (a verbal NIP, s 1(1)(a)), this is often described as the 'Warning Formula' and is reproduced in report books; or
- served with a written charge within 14 days of commission of the offence (s 1(1)(b)); or
- served with a NIP within 14 days of commission of the offence, setting out the possibility of prosecution (s 1(1)(c)).

It is advisable to provide the NIP as a document, because if the suspect later claims not to have fully understood a verbal NIP it would be the responsibility of the prosecution to prove the contrary (see *Gibson v Dalton* [1980] RTR 410). The NIP can also be served by post when necessary. This could be, for example, in relation to a speeding offence detected by an automatic camera device (s 89(1) of the Road Traffic Regulation Act 1984), or when a police officer observes a vehicle go through a red traffic light and it is too dangerous to follow. A PNC check (see 6.9.1) on the registration number of the vehicle will provide the name and address of the registered keeper (see 19.2.4). The registered keeper must then state who was driving the vehicle at the time of the incident (s 172(2) of the Road Traffic Act 1988); a failure to comply is an offence (s 172(3)). In *Whiteside v DPP* [2011] EWCA 3471(Admin) it was decided that:

- a NIP has been lawfully served as long as it has been posted (even if the recipient does not receive it);
- the recipient does not have a defence simply because he/she has no knowledge of the NIP being sent, unless it can be proved that under the circumstances it was not reasonably practicable to have been made aware of it;
- the offence is committed even if a recipient of the NIP does not know that he/she is obliged to state who was driving.

A NIP is not required when the vehicle concerned has been involved in an accident (s 2(1)), unless the driver failed to stop (see 19.7.2). Nor is it required if an FPN (see 19.12.4) has been issued at the time the offence was committed (s 2(2)). The final methods of disposal after the NIP has been served include a written charge or a conditional offer of a fixed penalty (see 19.12.4.3).

19.12.6 National Driver Offender Retraining Scheme (NDORS)

Another out-of-court disposal option for road traffic offences is the National Driver Offender Retraining Scheme (NDORS). Courses available include the National Driver Alertness Course and the National Speed Awareness Course (s 89(1) of the Road Traffic Regulation Act 1984). The driver must hold a current driving licence, and his/her actions and the circumstances must be such that there would be a realistic prospect of convicting him/her for the offence. If he/she has previously attended a NDORS for the same offence, it must have been more than three years ago. For more information, see the *National Driver Offender Retraining Scheme (NDORS): Guidance on Eligibility Criteria for NDORS Courses*, available online.

TASK 17

1. Imagine you are a police officer. Write down the sequence of what you would need to say and do when dealing with a driver in each of the following three situations:

   (a) driver unable to produce driving documents;
   (b) an offence for which you can use an FPN; and
   (c) an offence for which you can use the Vehicle Defect Rectification Scheme.

2. Find out about and list the road traffic offences for which a non-endorsable FPN can be used.

19.13 Answers to Tasks

TASK 1 Both of the vehicles are still 'motor vehicles' for the purposes of the legislation regardless of the fact that the car engine does not work and it cannot self-propel. Both of the individuals are 'drivers' as both have control of the movement of their particular vehicle, it is irrelevant that the youth driving the car cannot drive legally due to his age; he is still driving. The location of the incident would be a 'public place' and not a road or highway, therefore, only the offences applicable to public places can be considered. The older man would be 'using' both vehicles; he is driving the van and the car is being used for his purpose, namely being taken to a garage for repair. He will also be permitting the offences committed by his son in the car, knowing they were going to occur but continuing to allow them. The son would be using the car for the purpose of any offences relating to his use of that vehicle, so he would be driving not in accordance with a licence, driving without insurance, and driving with a defective tyre. The MOT status of the towed car would also need to be ascertained.

TASK 2

1. Knowing that he/she was likely to be disqualified from driving, a person might contact the DVLA to obtain a duplicate licence before the court hearing and then submit one and keep the other. Alternatively, the person could obtain a stolen old-style paper licence (without a photograph) and produce it to assume the identity of another person.

2. The officer should carry out PNC checks and local database checks such as the voters' register, and also ask for the person's name and date of birth to match them with the details held on the databases. The issue number on any licence produced can be checked to find out if the licence is valid. Local knowledge would be very important here as he/she would be able to ask about the description of localities and names of places to help verify the identity of the driver.

TASK 3

1. The PNC will be the primary source of information. The driver file should be checked to verify the driver's identity, driving licence status, and address; this can be cross-referenced with the person's file for marks, scars, and so on. The vehicle file will provide details regarding the vehicle's MOT and excise licence status. It will also link to the MIB insurance database which will show the details of any policy in force. Further enquiries can be made via the MIB help line if further details regarding insurance are required.

2. It is not uncommon for individuals to give slightly different details to an officer on the street to those given to other authorities such as DVLA; this may or may not be intentional. For example, a different name order, the omission or inclusion of middle names, or a slightly incorrect date of birth can all cause problems.

3. The details should be checked; a police officer should:

   - always check the driver and vehicle details with the PNC to establish if they match;
   - use the PNC to check whether the driver has a criminal record;
   - request further proof of identity, for example passports and credit cards;
   - request a voters' register check through the control room; and
   - request telephone numbers and ask the control room to call the numbers to verify the existence of the person.

By the cross-referencing of all the information currently available to officers on the street it should be possible to identify an individual and verify his/her driving status. There may be no need to use an HO/RT/1.

TASK 4 Many insurance companies are reluctant to insure high risk drivers in high performance vehicles. If they do, the premiums are likely to be very high. You might ask the driver about his insurance; the cost of the policy, how he pays for it (this could be cross-referenced with employment information, does it seem likely that can he afford it), how was the policy arranged (in person, over the internet, direct with the company, or through a broker), does he have any other driving qualifications or a black box fitted in the vehicle that could permit a discount?

The police officer should then contact the insurance company directly (using the information held on the MIB database via the PNC vehicle file), and speak to a police liaison representative, or contact the MIB help line to find out if there was full disclosure when the policy was taken out. If not, the insurance company may cancel the policy on the spot (the driver was insured when he was stopped so cannot be prosecuted for no insurance), or make a note to contact him for further payment. There may be evidence of a fraud offence (see 16.9) which can be investigated further.

TASK 5 Defences to using a motor vehicle on a road without a test certificate are that the vehicle is:

- being driven to a pre-arranged MOT test;
- being driven from a failed MOT test to a garage for repairs by previous arrangement (reg 6(2)(a)(i) of the Motor Vehicle (Test) Regulations 1981); or
- being towed to a place to be broken up for scrap, after failing an MOT (reg 6(2)(a)(iii)(B)).

Possible defences to not having a valid test certificate could be countered by asking the driver for the starting point, destination and reason of his/her journey.

TASK 6

Blue flashing lights are only allowed for certain types (and uses) of vehicle, such as police vehicles, and those owned by HM Revenue and Customs for use in pursuit of serious crime. The number of types of vehicles on the list continues to grow.

TASK 7

1. True. The term 'hours of darkness' refers to a period from half an hour after sunset to half an hour before sunrise.
2. False. It is the Road Vehicles Lighting Regulations 1989 as amended by the Road Vehicles Lighting (Amendment) Regulations 1994.
3. False. The correct rate is 60 to 120 pulses per minute.
4. False. The lawful circumstances are:

   (a) while stationary, to warn other road users of a temporary obstruction;
   (b) to summon assistance to the driver, conductor, or inspector of a bus (PSV);
   (c) on a motorway or unrestricted dual carriageway to warn following drivers of the need to slow down due to a temporary obstruction ahead; and
   (d) in the case of a school bus, while loading or unloading (or about to do so) passengers (under 16 years of age), provided the bus displays the statutory yellow reflective signs indicating the presence of schoolchildren.
5. True.
6. True.
7. True.

TASK 8 As you approach the vehicle, you would need to consider health and safety implications and consider the potential problems associated with:

- the vehicle moving through deliberate or accidental action by the driver;
- the engine still running (the driver could move off quickly);
- the handbrake not being applied (again for a quick pull away, or the vehicle may roll);
- the location of the ignition keys; and
- traffic passing by the location.

You could follow the following sequence:

1. Speak to the driver, introduce yourself, and outline the reason for stopping the vehicle.
2. Ask the driver for his/her name, address, and date of birth, and for his/her connection with the vehicle (is he/she the owner too?).
3. Ask the driver for details of his/her intended destination and the place where he/she began the journey.
4. Examine the vehicle whilst considering the potential health and safety implications associated with:

   - moving parts inside the engine compartment such as thermostatically controlled cooling fans;
   - high temperatures associated with parts such as brakes, exhaust systems, radiators, and engines;
   - harmful liquids such as hydraulic fluids, battery acid, anti-freeze, and hot engine coolant;
   - sharp objects such as exposed tyre cords or faulty bodywork;
   - movement of the vehicle and anything in, on, or under the vehicle;
   - movement of other vehicles and persons around you; and
   - the surface upon which you and the vehicle are positioned and the existence of harmful objects or substances.

5. Note any possible offence(s), detected in the usual way by gathering evidence using your senses (ie what you saw, felt, smelt, and so on).
6. Point out the possible offence(s) to the driver.
7. Caution him/her using the 'when questioned' caution, and follow PACE Code C, para 10.2 by informing the person that he/she is not under arrest.
8. If the person fails to cooperate or answer any particular questions after being cautioned, he/she should be informed that a failure to provide a name and address for example, may make him/her liable to detention or arrest (PACE Code C, para 10.9 (see 10.3.1)).
9. Note the questions and answers about the offences as PNB entries, for example when did he/she last inspect the vehicle, was he/she already aware of the defect, and how long ago did the journey begin? The PNB entry should be offered to the driver to read and sign that the notes are a true record of the interview.
10. The driver could then be reported for the offences and cautioned.

TASK 9 See the Highway Code (available online) for answers. You can also practise your understanding using the 'Practise your driving theory test' page on the gov.uk website.

TASK 10 The legislation that provides the power to implement such a policy is s 6A of the Road Traffic Act 1988; whilst in uniform or not, if a police officer reasonably believes that a person is driving, has been driving, is attempting to drive, or is in charge of a motor vehicle on a road or public place at the time of an accident, he/she may require the person to cooperate with one or more preliminary tests including a breath test. The officer must be in uniform to administer the test.

The computer checks that could be carried out on such driver include:

1. a PNC check to:

   - discover if the driver is wanted, or disqualified from driving;
   - check the driver's driving licence and insurance status;
   - check the status of any insurance to cover the driving in the circumstances. This may be a policy in the driver's name (on the current vehicle or another), or a policy applicable to the current vehicle permitting the driver's use;
   - check the MOT status of the vehicle;
   - ascertain if there are any reports regarding the vehicles being stolen; or
   - establish details of the keepers of the vehicles;

2. local checks to determine whether the driver's name and address are valid.

TASK 11 The order is as follows, with percentages for 2014. The total is over 100 per cent as some collisions/accidents have more than one contributory factor.

1. Order	Factor	Percentage of main contributory factors*
(d)	Driver failed to look properly	42%
(g)	Driver failed to judge other person's path or speed	23%
(f)	Driver careless, reckless, or in a hurry	16%
(e)	Loss of control	15%
	Poor turn or manoeuvre	14%
(j)	Slippery road (due to weather)	13%
(a)	Pedestrian failed to look properly	10%
(i)	Travelling too fast for conditions	9%
(c)	Sudden braking	8%
(h)	Following too close	7%

2. The NPCC document *Policing the Roads in Partnership—5 Year Strategy 2015–2020* (available online) lists four priority areas: 'SAFE', safe roads, free from harm by reducing road casualties; 'SECURE', secure roads, free from criminality and terrorism; 'EFFECTIVE', effective data-led patrolling and partnership working; 'EFFICIENT', efficient roads promotion policies, and improve public confidence.

TASK 12

1. (a) Jerry is driving.
   (b) Maz is not driving.
   (c) Both Hari and Pat are driving.
2. (a) (ii) and (iii): it applies on a road or in a public place.
   (b) (i) it applies anywhere.

TASK 13

1. Using a hand-held phone while driving could easily amount to failing to have proper control of the vehicle, or even dangerous driving (see 19.8.1).
2. Other 'careless driving' activities may include lighting a cigarette, turning round and looking at children, searching for a station on the radio, changing CDs, looking for sunglasses, looking in the mirror and applying make-up, or any other similar action that diverts attention from driving.

TASK 14

1. Trainee police officers are likely to receive instruction quite early on in the use of an Electronic Breath Screening Device (ESD), and to use one during Supervised Patrol. It is usually a hand-held device, with a disposable mouthpiece that is changed for each test.

In relation to preliminary drug test devices, each force has different policies relating to which staff can carry out this procedure, so trainee officers might not be trained in the use of such a device straight away.

A preliminary impairment test can only be conducted by an officer who has been approved for it by his/her chief officer.

2. Moving traffic offences include contravention of traffic regulations (for example speed limits), and failing to comply with traffic signs and directions (for example traffic lights).

TASK 15 Yes, in such circumstances the required sample may then be taken at a police station, regardless of whether an appropriate breath-analysis machine is available. See *Webber v DPP* [1998] RTR 111.

TASK 16 Section 22A of the Road Traffic Act 1988 states that a person is guilty of an offence if he/she intentionally and without lawful authority or reasonable cause:

(a) causes anything to be on or over a road;

(b) interferes with a motor vehicle, trailer, or cycle; or

(c) interferes (directly or indirectly) with traffic equipment.

TASK 17 For all of these situations the officer should first point out offence(s), then caution and inform the driver that he/she is not under arrest, but that a failure to cooperate or to answer particular questions may make him/her liable for detention or arrest (see 10.3.1). Then the officer should question the suspect and note the answers given. The next stage will vary:

1(a) Driver is unable to produce driving documents when required: the next stage is to check the PNC for all the vehicle and driver-related information. Most police services no longer allow officers to use HO/RT/1 forms requesting production of documents at a police station—check your local arrangements. Then report the suspect, and administer the caution (the 'now' version).

1(b) Fixed penalty offence: for a non-endorsable offence with driver present the officer should then: complete and issue NE-FPN, and report and caution the suspect (the 'now' caution). The driver can refuse the offer of an FPN and elect to go to court instead. If the driver is not present the completed NE-FPN should be fixed to the vehicle.

For an endorsable offence when the driver is present, the next stage is to offer an EFPN in lieu of court, report the suspect, and give the caution (the 'now' version). The driver must be in possession of his/her licence and be willing to submit it. The number of endorsement points should be checked through the PNC. If the proposed points would take the total to 12 or more an EFPN cannot be used. If the licence would have more than 12 points or the driver refuses the offer of a EFPN, then the driver should be reported for the offence, usually via a TOR or Process report. If the licence is not available but all the other conditions are met, a provisional EFPN can be issued.

1(c) VDRS offence: offer VDRS and issue form if accepted, then report and caution the suspect (the 'now' version). If the VDRS offer is refused then the driver should be reported for the offence, usually via a TOR or Process report.

2. The following offences can all be dealt with by a non-endorsable fixed penalty notice:

Road Traffic Act 1988

s 14	No seatbelt—adult, front or rear
s 15(2)	No seatbelt—child in front of vehicle
s 15(4)	No seatbelt—child in rear of vehicle
s 16	No helmet—motorcycles
s 19	Parking heavy goods vehicle on verge or footway
s 22	Leaving vehicle in dangerous position
s 23	Unlawful carrying of passengers on motorcycles
s 24	More than one person on a pedal cycle
s 34	Driving a motor vehicle off-road
s 35	Failure to comply with traffic directions
s 36	Failure to comply with traffic signs
s 40A	Using vehicle in dangerous condition, etc
s 41A	Construction and Use Regulations relating to brakes, steering, and tyres
s 41B	Construction and Use Regulations relating to weight (goods and passenger vehicles)
s 42	Other Construction and Use Regulations relating to lighting offences
s 87(1)	Driving other than in accordance with a driving licence
s 163	Failing to stop vehicle for constable in uniform
s 172	Failing to notify the police of driver's identity

Highways Act 1835

s 72	Cycling on the footway (not Scotland)

Highways Act 1980

s 137	Obstruction of highway by a vehicle

Specific Incidents

Road Traffic Regulation Act 1984

s 5(1)	Contravention of Traffic Regulation Order outside London
s 8(1)	Contravention of Traffic Regulation Order inside London
s 11	Breach of experimental traffic order
s 13	Breach of experimental traffic scheme inside London
s 16(1)	Use of vehicle contrary to temporary prohibition/restriction orders at roadworks
s 17(4)	Contravention of motorway regulations
s 18(3)	Contravention of one-way traffic on trunk road
s 20(5)	Contravention of restriction/prohibition of use of vehicle on a particular road
s 25(5)	Breach of pedestrian crossing regulations
s 29(3)	Use of vehicle in street playground
s 35A(1)	On-road parking restrictions, etc
s 47(1)	Failure to pay excess charge at parking place
s 53(5)	Breach of parking place Designation Order, etc
s 53(6)	Breach of parking place Designation Order, etc
s 88(7)	Contravention of minimum speed limit
s 89(1)	Speeding offences

Vehicle Excise and Registration Act 1994

s 33	Using or keeping vehicle without excise licence
s 42	Driving or keeping vehicle without registration mark
s 43	Driving or keeping a vehicle with obscured registration mark
s 43C	Using incorrectly registered vehicle

Road Vehicles (Display of Registration Marks) Regulations 2001

	Registration mark not in prescribed format

Greater London Council (General Powers) Act 1974

s 59	Parking on footways, verges, etc

Zebra, Pelican, and Puffin Pedestrian Crossing Regulations and General Directions 1997

reg 24	Overtaking a moving or stationary vehicle in controlled area of a crossing

20 | Damage to Buildings and Other Property

20.1 Introduction

In this chapter we examine the law surrounding damage to property, much of which stems from the Criminal Damage Act 1971. We also look at legislation to help protect ancient monuments and heritage sites in the UK. An understanding of these aspects of the law will help a trainee officer with achieving the requirement to 'Conduct the Initial Investigation and Report of Volume Crime According to (the) National Policing Plan' under the PAC heading 'Investigation'.

Criminal damage is both one of the most common crimes in England Wales and often one of the most visible (it is an example of one of the so-called 'signal crimes' described in 4.4.2). It often comes to the notice of the police through reports from the public, property owners, and others. However, intelligence might also feature, particularly in terms of identifying and taking action for 'taggers' (individuals who spray graffiti on buildings or trains or other objects as a form of stylized self- or group-identification). Likewise, the tags themselves might also provide useful information for building intelligence about the activities of a local criminal 'gang' (see 15.8 and 23.6).

The investigation of criminal damage, arson, and 'heritage crime' (eg the illegal removal of objects from archaeological sites) provides good examples of the multi- and inter-agency approach to crime reduction described in 3.3. For example, detection of criminal damage might well involve (or be led by) PCSOs and Local Authorities, suspected arson investigation is often carried out by specialist fire and emergency service investigation teams (subject to local agreements), and cultural crime detection might well involve partnership with Historic England, the English Heritage Trust, and others.

Police officers have a power of entry to search premises in order to prevent serious damage to property (s 17(1)(e) PACE Act 1984).

20.2 Criminal Damage

In terms of criminal damage, a trainee officer is most likely to encounter graffiti and minor damage to fences, cars, and bus shelters. Occasionally, the damage can be much more serious, when, for example, the damage has been caused by fire or involves culturally important buildings. Graffiti is among the most common forms of criminal damage, and to help reduce its prevalence it is a summary offence under the Anti-Social Behaviour Act 2003 to sell aerosol paint containers to a young person under the age of 16 (s 54(1)).

Section 1(1) of the Criminal Damage Act 1971 describes the offence of criminal damage. It states that an offence is committed by a person who 'without lawful excuse destroys or damages property belonging to another, intending to destroy or damage any such property or being reckless as to whether any such property would be destroyed or damaged'.

The damage must be to something 'real'; that is, something that you could touch. It can be land ('real estate') or personal items including money (eg a wad of notes). It includes wild animals in captivity (but not wild flowers). Criminal damage also includes destroying an item (ie the property is no longer any use and cannot be repaired). The cost of such 'damage' would be the cost of replacing the item.

The property must belong to another person who has custody, control, a right, an interest, or is in charge of the property. (This is in contrast with the offence of criminal damage, life endangered (see 20.2.1).) It is possible for a person to criminally damage their own property but only if it also belongs to somebody else (eg if the property is jointly owned).

The person carrying out the offence must either intend to cause the damage, or be reckless as to whether the property would be damaged. Recklessness is explained in the flowchart.

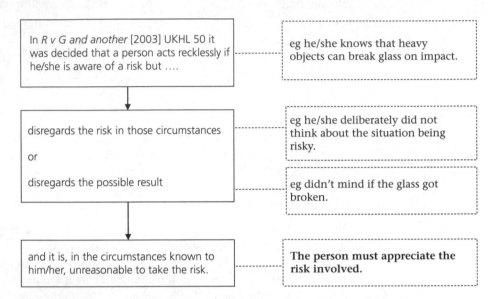

The person must also not have a lawful excuse for causing the damage. A person would have lawful excuse if they had an honestly held belief that:

- he/she had permission from the owner of the property (or an appropriate person) to cause the damage; for example, a recovery operator is authorized by a car owner to load the car onto a recovery vehicle, and damages it in the process. This would also apply if the operator believed that the owner would have given permission but is unable to do so (eg having been taken to hospital unconscious);
- that his/her own or another's property was in immediate need of protection by reasonable means, if for example a car had slipped down a steep embankment and was likely to slip still further, and a recovery operator damages it when pulling it back up onto the road.

This offence is triable either way. If the value of the property damaged or destroyed is less than £5,000, the offence is tried summarily (s 22 of the Magistrates' Courts Act 1980). The penalty is six months' imprisonment and/or a fine if tried summarily, and ten years' imprisonment on indictment.

> **TASK 1** Robyn, after her arrest for being drunk and disorderly, smears her own excrement on the walls of the police station cell. Discuss whether this constitutes criminal damage.

20.2.1   Criminal damage endangering life

The offence of 'criminal damage, life endangered' (s 1(2) of the Criminal Damage Act 1971) is committed by a person who destroys or damages property intending (or being reckless as) to endanger life. To prove the offence, there is no requirement for the offender to try to kill someone or for any actual injury or harm to occur. There is only a necessity to prove that the damage was caused intentionally or recklessly and that there was potential for another to be harmed as a result of that damage being caused.

For this offence the property can belong to the offender or to another person. For example, an angry man deliberately damages the brakes of his own car knowing that his partner will be driving it later that day, and intending her life to be endangered. The damage caused must also be the cause of the danger: for example, shooting at someone in a room through a window both endangers life and damages the window, but it is the bullet that endangers the life, not the damage from the window, so this would not be criminal damage life endangered.

This offence is triable by indictment only and the penalty is life imprisonment.

20.3 Arson

Arson is destroying or damaging property by fire. It is covered under s 1(3) of the Criminal Damage Act 1971. For a person to be found guilty of this offence at least some of the damage must have been caused by fire (excluding smoke damage). For the offence to be proved there must be an intent or an element of recklessness in relation to the use of fire.

The penalty is six months' imprisonment and/or a fine if tried summarily, and up to life imprisonment on indictment.

> **TASK 2** For what reasons might the crime of arson be committed? Can the behavioural profiling of arsonists be of potential value to the police and others?

20.4 Threats to Damage

This offence is covered in s 2 of the Criminal Damage Act 1971 and there are two points to prove in relation to such a threat:

- the conduct that is threatened must refer to damage; and
- the extent of the threatened damage must constitute an offence under s 1 of the Criminal Damage Act 1971. This can include acts of simple damage under s 1(1), as well as criminal damage where life is endangered (s 1(2)).

However, the offence of making threats to damage cannot be committed if the threat involves an element of recklessness as to whether the property would actually be destroyed or damaged (see 20.2 in relation to the meaning of 'reckless'). For example, imagine an angry woman shouts to a neighbour 'if your kid keeps throwing stones over my wall, I'll start chucking them back, and no, I don't care what it does'. She is reckless as to whether damage is caused so she would not have committed the offence of 'threats to damage'.

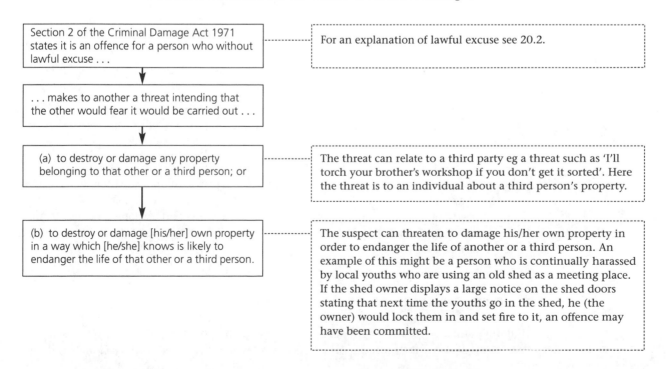

Section 2 of the Criminal Damage Act 1971 states it is an offence for a person who without lawful excuse . . .

For an explanation of lawful excuse see 20.2.

. . . makes to another a threat intending that the other would fear it would be carried out . . .

(a) to destroy or damage any property belonging to that other or a third person; or

The threat can relate to a third party eg a threat such as 'I'll torch your brother's workshop if you don't get it sorted'. Here the threat is to an individual about a third person's property.

(b) to destroy or damage [his/her] own property in a way which [he/she] knows is likely to endanger the life of that other or a third person.

The suspect can threaten to damage his/her own property in order to endanger the life of another or a third person. An example of this might be a person who is continually harassed by local youths who are using an old shed as a meeting place. If the shed owner displays a large notice on the shed doors stating that next time the youths go in the shed, he (the owner) would lock them in and set fire to it, an offence may have been committed.

A stated intention to destroy or damage the property can be communicated in any way—for example, email, text message, fax, letter, or phone call—and it could be an idle threat: there need be no intention to actually carry it out. The recipient does not have to believe the threat will be carried out immediately (if at all), nor does the recipient need to be put in fear. In any prosecution it will be for the court to decide whether what was communicated had enough substance and immediacy to constitute a threat. In some circumstances it might be more appropriate to consider an offence under s 4 of the Public Order Act 1986 (see 14.4.3.3).

This offence is triable either way and the penalty is six months' imprisonment and/or a fine if tried summarily, and ten years' imprisonment on indictment.

20.5 Possessing an Article with Intent to Cause Criminal Damage

This offence is covered in s 3 of the Criminal Damage Act 1971.

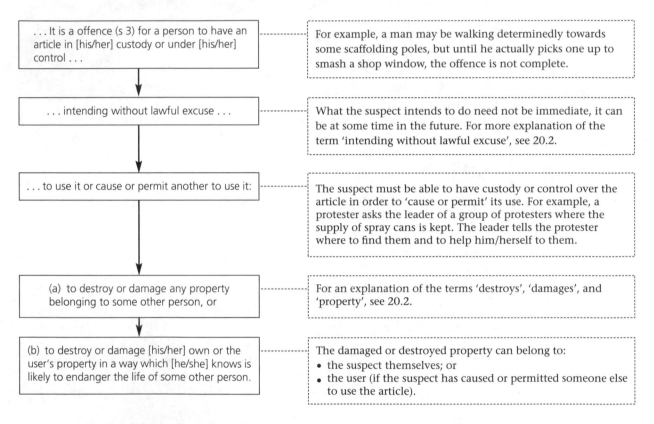

The type of article involved here can be anything tangible. The Law Commission, who advised on the Act, explained that:

> [t]he essential feature of the proposed offence is to be found, not so much in the nature of the thing, as in the intention with which it is held. (Law Commission No 29, para 59)

This offence is triable either way. The penalty is six months' imprisonment and/or a fine not exceeding the statutory maximum if tried summarily, and ten years' imprisonment on indictment.

A power to search for articles made or adapted for use in the course of or in connection with an offence under s 1 of the Criminal Damage Act 1971 is provided under s 1(2)(a) of the PACE Act 1984. Any person or vehicle (and anything in or on a vehicle) can be searched and detained for the purpose of such a search. Section 2 of the PACE Act 1984 and its Codes of Practice must be followed, including providing the person with the information listed in para 3.8 of Code A (GO WISELY, see 9.4.1 on search procedures).

20.6 Causing Damage to Heritage Sites

Buildings and sites of historic interest have had some form of legal protection in the UK since 1000. Initially, only the most important ancient sites were protected, such as Stonehenge and the great castles. Over the years, however, further specific legislation has been introduced and this provides protection to many types of historic site such as:

- scheduled monuments (an archaeological site or building that is of national importance, eg Stonehenge or Dover Castle);
- listed buildings (over 500,000 in England alone including small houses, street furniture, and lighthouses—the exact figure is not known);
- protected marine wreck sites (52 in English coastal waters);
- protected military remains of aircraft and vessels of historic interest (includes losses during peacetime);
- conservation areas (local authority designated areas of special architectural or historic interest; around 9,000 in the UK);
- Registered Parks and Gardens (gardens of stately homes, public parks, and cemeteries on a national register; over 1,600 in the UK);
- Registered Battlefields (43 in the UK, eg at Hastings); and
- World Heritage Sites (25 in the UK, eg Canterbury Cathedral, Stonehenge, and Hadrian's Wall).

20.6.1 Legislation to protect heritage sites

A number of authorities (local authorities, the police, and English Heritage) share the responsibility to enforce legislation designed to protect heritage sites. Partnership-working (see 3.3) plays a fundamental role in tackling heritage crime, both at a local operational level and nationally at a strategic level. However, this is a challenging task due to the shared responsibility, the relative rarity of incidents, and the lack of expertise and understanding of the nature of the possible 'harm'.

20.6.1.1 The Ancient Monuments and Archaeological Areas Act 1979

It is an offence under s 28 of the Act to damage or destroy (without lawful excuse) a 'protected monument' (defined in s 28, and includes a scheduled monument). The person must know that it is a protected monument and intend to destroy or damage it, or be reckless as to whether it would be destroyed or damaged. The offence is triable either way and the penalty is a fine and/or imprisonment (six months if tried summarily and two years on indictment).

Other sections of this Act may also be relevant to the trainee police officer:

- s 42 under which it is a summary offence to use a metal detector in a 'protected place' without the written consent of English Heritage, and an either-way offence to remove an object in such circumstances;
- s 9 under which it is an either-way offence to damage, demolish, or alter a listed building.

20.6.1.2 The protection of wrecks and military remains

The Protection of Wrecks Act 1973 can be used to designate an area containing a 'protected wreck'. All wreck material (eg fixtures 1and fittings, coins, cannon, and wreck timbers) must be reported to the 'Receiver' at the Maritime and Coastguard Agency.

The Protection of Military Remains Act 1986 makes it an offence to interfere (without a licence) with the wreckage of any crashed, sunken, or stranded military aircraft or designated vessel. The Act provides two levels of protection, depending on whether the site is designated as a 'protected place' or a 'controlled site'. Greater restrictions are placed upon activities at the latter. Investigations under this Act usually relate to diving and are undertaken by the Ministry of Defence supported by the police and English Heritage. Most of the offences in relation to this Act are triable either way.

20.6.2 Offences relating to cultural objects and treasure

We have already referred to the legislation around the use of metal detectors (see 20.6.1.1). Further legislation is available to help regulate the trade in 'cultural objects' and 'treasure' found at archaeological or other heritage sites. It is an offence to:

- dishonestly deal in a tainted cultural object knowing or believing that the object is tainted (s 1 of the Dealing in Cultural Objects (Offences) Act 2003). A 'cultural object' is defined as an object of historical, architectural, or archaeological interest. It is 'tainted' if a person illegally excavates an object from its original position in the ground, or removes it from a

Specific Incidents

building, structure, or monument of historical, architectural, or archaeological interest in the UK or elsewhere (after 30 December 2003). The offence is triable either way.

- fail to notify the district coroner within 14 days of finding 'treasure' (s 8(3) of the Treasure Act 1996). 'Treasure' includes old gold, silver, or bronze coins, collections of prehistoric metalwork, and objects found with such coins or metalwork (s 1 of the Treasure Act 1996). The reporting of treasure is dealt with through the Portable Antiquities Scheme. This is a summary offence.

20.7   Answers to Tasks

Task 1 The excrement will not have destroyed the walls of the police cell, but the walls will need to be cleaned and have therefore been damaged. The cost of the damage will be equal to the cost of the cleaning operation. The suspect will need to be interviewed to prove or disprove whether she intended to damage the walls or was reckless as to whether or not the damage was caused. If the drunken state was self-induced, it will not be a defence.

Task 2 Arson is regularly found to be the single biggest cause of fire. In 2007 a Home Office analysis of incidents identified particular motives for setting arson in the UK, as shown in the table.

Form of arson	Motive	Proportion of all arson (year 2000 data)	
		Property	Vehicles
Youth disorder and nuisance	Vandalism and boredom	36%	39%
Malicious	Revenge, racism, clashes of beliefs/rivalries, or personal animosities	25%	3%
Psychological	Mental illness or suicide	26%	13%
Criminal	Financial gain and fraud, or the concealment of other crimes (theft, murder, etc)	13%	45%

(Based on Home Office, 2007)

However, there are alternative but complementary ways of understanding the causes of arson. For example Canter and Fritzon (1998) identified two main categories; person-orientated (towards self or others) arson and object-orientated arson. A further distinction is possible, namely in terms of the motive being either expressive (eg to express some form of emotion or psychological need) or instrumental (eg to serve as a means of achieving another goal). This gives rise to fourfold typology, as summarized in the table:

	Person-orientated	Object-orientated
Expressive	Directed inwards (towards the offender) possibly as the result of anxiety, depression, or suicidal tendencies	Directed at an object (eg building) but for symbolic or emotional needs of the offender
Instrumental	Directed outwards (to others), possibly as revenge for perceived wrongdoing	Directed at an object (eg building), but where arson is a consequence of another motive, for example to hide evidence of a burglary

(Based on Canter and Fritzon, 1998 and Fineman, 1995)

Canter and Fritzon (1998) found that there were statistically significant associations between each of the four motive categories and the offender's social and psychological background. For example, repeat arsonists tended to fall into the expressive/object-orientated category, whereas an expressive/person-orientated arson was more likely to be committed by a person with a history of psychiatric problems. This approach thus provides a potential basis to 'profile' unknown offenders on the basis of the types of arson incidents observed. The Home Office and others see some virtue in this approach in terms of aiding arson investigation (Home Office, 2007, p 15).

21 | Cybercrime

21.1 Introduction

Cybercrime is one of many terms coined over the past 20 or more years to describe criminal activities involving some form of electronic or digital technology. The various terms have led to confusion among victims, investigators, others in the criminal justice system, and the media in particular. The term cybercrime has become more widespread since the creation of the Council of Europe Cybercrime Convention (commonly known as the Budapest Convention on Cybercrime), and is now the common term for a plethora of criminal activities. Although the terminology used in the cybercrime arena may be confusing, there are in effect five main ways that technology can impact on crime and these may be categorized as follows:

- Technology as the target of crime—in the UK, this is often referred to as, 'cyber-dependent' crime. It includes such crimes as 'hacking', where a computer is accessed illegally. The hacker may simply wish to show that he/she has the knowledge and skills to 'hack' into a security protected computer or computer system. There are other, more sinister and damaging reasons for hacking, such as stealing data stored on the computer, or restricting access by legitimate users to damage a business. This type of crime is usually investigated by highly trained staff in specialized cybercrime or computer crime units at national or local level.

- Technology as an aid to crime—where a traditional crime is committed and technology is used to support the commission of the acts. In the UK, this is now sometimes called 'cyber-enabled' crime. An example would be where a blackmail demand is made by email or other form of electronic communication, but the primary offence does not involve technology (for example food product contamination or kidnap). The blackmail offence could be committed without the use of technology, but is easier for the criminal (and often more difficult for the investigator to trace the messages). At a more contemporary level, the resources of the internet may be used to commit crimes such as harassment, racial, and other types of abuse, such as the sharing of images of child abuse amongst paedophiles. The list of crimes that may be aided by technology is almost limitless, and it is extremely difficult to imagine a crime that cannot be aided by technology in one form or another.

- Technology as a communications tool to plan or enact crime—for example, where a group of criminals use modern technology to communicate with each other about their plans or other information about a proposed crime. The criminals presume or hope that their communications are not being monitored but in any case will often use encryption (which in any event is often built-in to popular instant messaging smartphone applications such as *WhatsApp*) and anonymous services. Law enforcement agencies may find it difficult to identify that a communication even took place.

- Technology as a witness to crime—is an increasingly important tool in combating not only criminal activities, but also other types of behaviour investigated by the police, for example antisocial behaviour. The ubiquitous nature of CCTV (see 23.4.1) appears to have led to an over-reliance on such material, to the detriment of traditional investigative techniques. While digital recordings are an extremely valuable tool for law enforcement, other enquiries should still be made to support or counter the evidence available in digital form, as it may only tell part of the story.

- Technology as a storage medium—includes the deliberate or inadvertent storage of data on any device that may become evidence in an investigation. It is extremely important that the data and the devices are handled correctly from the very contact with the police, and throughout any investigation or legal process. If the first officer does not preserve it correctly, there is the potential that any evidential value may be lost forever. On some occasions any police personnel may deal with such data, but there may also be cases where specialist support is required (see 21.5).

Police officers are expected to know what to do in cases involving digital technology, and these scenarios are becoming increasingly common. He/she will need to know what actions to take (and why) as these may differ depending on the type of technology that is encountered. Younger officers will be more familiar with day-to-day use of technology, but still will be required to deal with it in a manner that will ensure the integrity of any evidence that may be derived from digital devices. The temptation to 'take a quick look' at a computer or cell phone must be resisted.

The fact that technology may be involved in the commission of a crime should not in itself make the offence in question or its investigation more difficult. The vast majority of technology related crimes fall under traditional laws, and only those at the more serious end of the scale are covered by specific legislation such as the Computer Misuse Act 1990. Some offences (such as grooming, see 17.7.6) may be committed online or offline, and are likely to be covered under other legislation such as the Protection of Children Act 1978. (This was initially used mainly in relation to analogue photographs, but it is now a key piece of legislation in combating the presence and distribution of such images on the internet.)

Today's police officer must be able to recognize new forms of crime in new environments, and take appropriate actions. It is only a few years ago that a conversation about the cloud would be about the weather, but in 2017 it is more likely to be about data storage, a topic of increasing interest and relevance to investigators. Access to data stored 'in the cloud' is problematic from the legal perspective, given that the location of storage may be in another country. So in a criminal investigation, the seizure of such data may take place under one jurisdiction while the data is stored under another jurisdiction. The potential problems this can create are being addressed by the Council of Europe with the creation of a Guidance Note on cloud evidence and a proposal to create an additional protocol to the Budapest Convention (available online). Technological change will continue to increase exponentially and this will place extra requirements on police officers to keep up to date with potential new uses of technology on criminal behaviour. New ways of abusing technology for criminal purposes will always develop, and present a challenge for policing.

21.2 Examples of Cybercrime

The extent of cyber-enabled and cyber-dependent crimes is the subject of some debate, and estimates of, the economic consequences of these crimes for the UK vary widely. Cybercrime and fraud involving the internet are becoming more prominent, and catching up with other crime types numerically. In January 2017 the Office for National Statistics reported an estimate of 3.6 million frauds (for example, fraud conducted using stolen debit or credit card details) and 2 million computer misuse offences as compared to 6.2 million 'traditional' types of crime (ONS, 2017). The National Crime Agency's Cyber Crime Assessment 2016 estimates that the annual cost of cybercrime to the UK economy amounts to billions of pounds, and is set to increase year on year (NCA, 2016, p 3).

The Home Office has been working with a number of police forces on collecting information concerning the scale and nature of cyber-enabled crime. This involves 'flagging' crimes where the reporting officer determines (on the balance of probabilities) that the offence was committed in full or in part using a digital device such as computer, a computing network or a device such as a smartphone or tablet. Examples include where a crime involved the use of a social media site (such as Facebook), or sites such as eBay to commit fraud. However, crimes where a mobile phone has been used to make phone calls or send text messages would not be flagged, nor would crimes when a PC and printer have been used to attempt to produce a counterfeit ticket for an event. Inevitably, as we have already noted, there are likely to be numerous cases where the decision to flag or not falls in a grey area.

There is no doubt at all that the volume of cyber-enabled crimes is increasing. The range and variety of such crimes (including cyber-dependent crime) also appears to be developing. We provide some examples of cyber-enabled and cyber-dependent crimes, and cyber ASB.

Many organized crime groups have moved their activities online, as the potential rewards are greater and are less likely to be detected. These types of crime can be very hard to detect and investigate as they can be carried out from any location in the world. In addition, when a computer system appears to be under attack, it is often not clear if the change in function is an attack or a non-criminal malfunction, or other activity. The initial response of information security professionals, understandably, is to mitigate the effects of the incident and bring any effected service back to normal. These incidents many not even be reported as a criminal attack. The extent of the crime can also be difficult to determine, such as whether it is a stand-alone incident or part of a wider series. Online criminals often target a huge number of victims, each for fairly small amounts. Victims will sometimes not even notice this, but even if they do, reporting it to the police is often futile, as an individual loss of less than £10 where the evidence is probably abroad, is not likely to be investigated. Criminals adopting this method can make millions of pounds, with very little chance of capture. At the very minimum, such victims should be advised to report small value online fraud through to Action Fraud (see 21.3.1).

21.2.1 Abuse of network activities

Abuse of network activities are examples of cyber-dependent crimes. Computers are often linked in huge networks within and between organizations and individuals. Their potential can also be exploited by criminals or people who want to cause disruption and commit 'cyber-ASB'. For example in a DDoS attack multiple requests or messages are sent out to the target network to intentionally overload the processing systems, and prevent it from carrying out its normal intended functions.

You have no doubt heard the term 'spam' in relation to unwanted and unsolicited emails. Spamming is when huge numbers of communications are sent out to sell a product or to distribute malware. The malware could have a variety of functions, one of which is simply to send out another wave of electronic communications to cause disruption. Spamming can also be used to help set up botnets, where a network of computers is taken over without the user's knowledge, rather like a parasite can take over and harm a living organism. The affected computers can be remotely controlled and assigned to a variety of tasks, all without the knowledge of the computer user, who might only notice that the machine seems to be working rather slowly.

Activity	Example
DDoS attacks	ICMP flood, peer-to-peer forms of attack
PBX hacking (phreaking)	Trading CBX/PBX maintenance port numbers and passwords
Spamming	SpamSoldier sending out SMS messages from Android OS phones
Botnets	Rustock botnet sending spam

21.2.2 Trespass, illegal access, or interception

Hacking is when a person intentionally accesses a computer without the knowledge or permission of the legitimate user. It is seen by some as an entertaining intellectual challenge but has inevitably been put to criminal use, for example stolen personal and business data can be sold on to organized crime groups. It also includes the interception of VoIP calls (for instance Skype services). Simple hacking is a criminal act in its own right, however it is often used to facilitate other criminal activity, and in such circumstances hacking becomes a more serious matter.

21.2.3 Malware

Malware is software that has been created to be used with a **mal**icious intent, to cause harm through disrupting digital devices and networks. It can operate in a number of different ways, and is referred to by a number of different terms, some of which are listed and explained in the table.

Name/type of malware	How it operates	Examples
Virus	Part of the coding helps it spread and replicate by inserting a copy of itself in another program	'Drive-by' websites, ransomware (eg Citadel malware) and Loozfon malware (Android operating system)
Trojan	A form of malware which is 'smuggled' into a computer or network and which then performs unauthorized actions such as deleting data or secretly providing a 'backdoor' to enable another person to take over an infected computer.	'Man-in-the Browser' (and 'Boy in the Browser') trojans secretly re-route web traffic from a victim's browser through an offender's own system, allowing the offender to capture passwords and other sensitive information (eg banking details).
Spyware	Logs a person's activities on the internet, collecting and collating information that is used to target them.	Spyware that is used for (often unwanted) 'pop up' advertising in web browsers. Also includes 'key loggers' to secretly and remotely record a user's logon and password details.
WORM	A standalone program that replicates itself over a computer network (without the need for a host program). 'WORM' is an acronym for 'Write Once Read Many'.	They sometimes are delivered by an email that then looks at a person's address book and sends a copy of itself, often along with a message that purports to come from the sender.

One of the most prominent forms of virus at the time of writing is ransomware (see also 21.2.6). It blocks user access to a computer and files, and is accompanied by a demand for a 'fee' to restore access to the affected data. The Europol Internet Organised Crime Threat Assessment (IOCTA) 2016 recognizes that ransomware has become a major problem, overshadowing the more traditional malware threats such as trojans that capture confidential banking details.

21.2.4 Offensive material and illegal services

The anonymity afforded to internet users is exploited by people who wish to share and obtain offensive images and material, whether for personal satisfaction or commercial gain. Such material would include images of sexual abuse of children (see 17.4.2) and internet hate crime (see 14.10 on hate crime). A recent phenomenon has been the use of SMS sexually explicit images by individuals wishing to humiliate or harm ex-partners (see 17.4.3). The internet is also used for offering illegal services, such as the sale of illegal drugs or weapons. The table shows some of the different ways the internet is used as a means of committing hate crime and providing illegal services.

Activity	Description	Example
Internet hate crime	Distributing material electronically intending to stir up hatred	Extremist political webpages glorifying violence against ethnic minority groups
Cybersex	Sharing sexual images without the permission of the person portrayed	Sexting via smartphones
Pharmaceuticals, controlled substances and alcohol	Selling prescription-only and other restricted drugs through the internet	Illegal online pharmacies
Weapons and firearms	Selling weapons and firearms over the internet to people with no legal right to ownership	Alleged market in weapons through 'dark web'
Revenge Porn	The publication of explicit material portraying someone who has not consented for the image or video to be shared	An ex-partner publishing intimate photographs of a former partner on social media without his/her permission

The Dark Net or Deep Web is increasingly used to commit crimes. This is the part of the World Wide Web that is not visible to the normal user and requires special software to access it. Criminal activity in this arena is typically more difficult to investigate due to the anonymity it provides. The vast majority of activity on the internet cannot be found by using the popular search sites, such as Google; alternative tools are required to access these areas. One such tool is 'The Onion Ring' ('TOR'), which is advertised as 'free software that helps you defend against traffic analysis, a form of network surveillance that threatens personal freedom and privacy, confidential business activities and relationships, and state security' (Tor, 2016). As with many ideas and developments that are created for lawful purposes, criminals exploit these new technologies for their own unlawful purposes.

21.2.5 Cyber aggression

This can be on an interpersonal level such as cyber-harassment and cyber-bullying through social media sites (see the table for examples), but would also include conflict and espionage conducted through the internet. Despite anxiety in the media, there have as yet been no clear documented cases of cyber-terrorism. The IOCTA however has established that methods that have been employed to commit cybercrime are now being applied to people smuggling and terrorism; these are becoming cyber-enabled to an increasing extent.

Activity	Description	Example
Cyber-harassment	Using digital means to harass, threaten or unreasonably embarrass a person	Repeated sending of bullying SMS texts
Cyber-stalking	Constant monitoring, contacting and spying by digital means	Stalking an ex-partner using GPS tracking systems on a smart phone
Libel	Libeling of a person online	Allegations made through a Twitter account

21.2.6 Theft, fraud, and extortion

The cyber-enabled crimes of theft and fraud are particularly common, and ransomware is a clear example of extortion. There are numerous ways of conducting theft, fraud, and extortion through the internet, as shown in the table.

Activity	Description	Example
Re-chipping, unblocking telecommunication devices	Changing a SIM card; re-programming a mobile telephone	Unblocking services via software and hardware
Advanced fee fraud	Requesting by digital means an upfront payment for non-existent goods or services	Scams such as the West African '419' fraud
Identity theft/Identity fraud	Obtaining another person's personal and/or official information online, normally to commit an offence	Creating a false profile on a social networking site using someone else's name and details
Online auction fraud	Offering items which are then not delivered, or are misrepresented in some way	Using digital images to portray a non-existent item for auction; offering an apparently expensive item but is simply a description
User account theft	Using various means to collect information about a person's computer or network account	User-accounts (eg on websites and forums, and Xbox live accounts) are hacked
Phishing	Trying to steal login, password and personal identification numbers using electronic means	Emails that seem to be from a tax office requesting details to be completed online
Spear phishing	Personalized and individualized phishing, so often more credible	An email with authentic details harvested from a social network site seeming to be from a person's employer, but which contains malware
Phone-based scams	Trying to persuade a person to provide information to later conduct theft	Phone call purporting to be from recipient's bank, or an SMS stating the person has won a prize
Cyber-squatting, domain name piracy	Registering domain names that are similar to well-known brands, intending to gain or profit	A confusingly similar company domain-name is chosen to make a profit from unwary consumers
Ransomware	A form of malware that allows a criminal to lock a computer from a remote location, and then display a pop-up window informing the owner that the computer will not be unlocked until a sum of money is paid	A ransomware demand is accompanied by an accusation of illegal activity, or a pornographic image appears on the locked screen. This makes it more difficult to seek help so the recipient is more likely to simply pay the ransom

Specific Incidents

It is now highly likely that virtual currency such as Bit Coin will be the currency of choice for criminals committing crimes of extortion such as Ransomware. Although Bit Coin transactions are in the public domain, tracing the individuals involved is more difficult than tracing traditional bank transactions, due to participants using anonymous services.

21.2.7 IPR crime

Intellectual Property Rights crime is frequently cyber-enabled. This includes intellectual property theft where images and designs are taken and used without consent, for example downloading music or text without authority from the owner or composer.

Activity	Description	Example
Intellectual property theft	Stealing intellectual property, such as images and designs	Hacking a company's computer systems to steal software for computer chip design
Copyright infringement	Making unauthorized copies of digital content	Torrents used to share music and video, 'warez' software, commercial DVD copying, android boxes used to access streaming of films and sport without payment
Trademark infringement	Unauthorized use of a registered trademark	Selling of goods online using the logo from another company
Counterfeiting	Producing an imitation version	Using digital means to make forged £20 notes
Circumventing conditional access systems	Bypassing access systems to paid products or services	Satellite TV card sharing using customized Linux firmware

21.3 Responding to Cybercrime

Cybercrime is considered to be a recent phenomenon, however it has impacted on UK policing for more than 20 years. It was only in 2001 that the first national response was created in the form of the National High Tech Crime Unit. Although somewhat of a cliché, 'prevention is better than cure' remains a sensible piece of advice with respect to cyber-enabled and cyber-dependent crime. As a policing student you will no doubt be given advice on protecting yourself by safeguarding your digital information and remaining safe online, and it is now increasingly likely that members of the public will ask you for advice on computer security. There are resources available to assist you in both roles. Measures include ensuring that antivirus software is up to date, that you have all the latest security patches for the operating systems that you use and that passwords you employ are as secure as possible. In the UK, there are a number of online resources that provide useful information and guidance. These include the 'ThinkUKnow' campaign (run by CEOP, the Child Exploitation and Online Protection) which aims to increase young people's understanding of online safety (CEOP, 2013). Another useful site is GetSafeOnline.org which provides advice for individuals and businesses. It is an unbiased resource that could provide useful information for police officers in protecting themselves as individuals, and for providing advice to the public.

At the level of organizations, security measures are normally put in place to counter activities such as network intrusion attacks. Organizations that use online purchasing will generally employ 'user authentication' methods to help counter potential fraud.

21.3.1 International measures to counter cybercrime

In 2011, the United Kingdom acceded to the Budapest Convention on Cybercrime. This is a major international treaty designed to harmonize legislation and enable the effective investigation of cybercrime. It is hoped it will improve international cooperation among nations, including the rapid transfer of electronic evidence across international borders where required.

From the perspective of the police officer, the importance of the Convention lies in its procedural provisions. It sets out procedures for processes such as:

- the rapid preservation of stored data;
- the preservation and partial disclosure of traffic data;
- the legal means available to produce evidence;
- the search and seizure of computer data;
- the real-time collection of traffic data; and
- the interception of content data.

In addition, the Convention contains a provision that facilitates some types of transborder access to stored computer data (which does not require mutual legal assistance). It also provides for the setting up of a 24/7 network to help ensure speedy assistance among the signatory parties. This makes it easier and faster for those countries to seek assistance from one another in cybercrime and electronic evidence cases. The 24/7 network point of contact for the UK is housed by the National Crime Agency and as a party to the Convention, the UK can use these provisions during an investigation. For example vital data could be preserved in another country, if it is also a party to the Convention. While police officers are unlikely to make use of such procedures on a daily basis, it is nonetheless important to know they exist—in any investigations there may be vital digital evidence, and this by its very nature is often transient. Prompt actions are often necessary to capture the relevant data and increase the prospects for a successful prosecution.

If the country to which a request is made is not a party to the Budapest Convention, there are other options to preserve data. The G7 countries' 24/7 network was created to enable data to be preserved, pending an application for legal assistance (which of course may take many months, during which the requested data may otherwise be deleted by normal business processes). The National Crime Agency is the UK contact point for this network. The network is managed internationally by the US Department of Justice (USDOJ). The number of requests to US providers has reached such a level that companies such and Facebook, Microsoft, and Google now have their own dedicated procedures for handling direct contact from international law enforcement.

21.3.2 National measures to counter cybercrime

The national law enforcement response to cyber-dependent crime is coordinated and directed through the relatively new National Cyber Crime Unit (NCCU), part of the National Crime Agency (NCA). In effect the NCA has responsibility for 'high end' cyber-dependent crime investigations as these are too complex, serious, or multinational to be investigated solely by local police cybercrime units. For example, the NCCU is likely to be actively engaged in countering the development of malware and exploit kits that are used to facilitate large-scale fraud.

The NCCU works closely with the Child Exploitation and Online Protection (CEOP) Centre (also part of the NCA), and engages with business and industry in countering cyber-dependent crime. On the international level the NCCU has close links with the European Cybercrime Centre (EC3) based with Europol in Den Haag.

A National Fraud Intelligence Bureau (NFIB) has been created by the City of London Police as a central access point for individuals and organizations who suspect cyber-dependent crime. 'Action Fraud' is a national fraud and internet crime reporting centre (run by the Home Office's National Fraud Authority). It is responsible for collating all reports of fraud, including cyber-dependent fraud, and can use the information to identify patterns of criminal activity, and thus facilitate investigations. Thus responsibility for cyber-dependent investigation is not restricted to the police service. The banking industry already supplements the police resources available to investigate plastic-card crime: for example, the industry body APACS sponsors the work of the Dedicated Cheque and Plastic Crime Unit (DCPCU).

21.3.3 Local level police responses to cybercrime

Police forces in the UK each have their own locally based resources to investigate cyber-dependent crime. This will typically involve a 'High-Tech Crime Unit' (eg Lincolnshire Police); a 'Computer Crime Unit' (eg Strathclyde Police); a 'Digital Forensics Unit' (eg Kent Police); or even be part of an 'Economic Crime Unit'. These units have often evolved from former 'Fraud Squads', and tend to be relatively small in size. Most of their work appears to be taken up with child abuse investigations. The MPS has its 'FALCON' unit (Fraud and Linked Crime On-Line) with police investigators deployed exclusively to investigate cyber-enabled fraud and other crimes. A number of forces (for example, Sussex and Surrey) have combined their resources to form joint units for the investigation of cyber-dependent crime. However, in 2014 HMIC concluded that the majority of the 18 police forces it reviewed were 'not yet able to identify or understand fully the threats, risks and harm posed by cybercrime' (HMICb, 2014, p.11).

Many cyber-enabled and some cyber-dependent crimes are effectively 'screened' to decide whether further investigation is appropriate. Level 1 or 2 plastic card crimes, if investigated, are likely to be tackled by a force-based unit, although forces do not have the resources to investigate all reported incidents (particularly credit and debit card offences such as 'card not present' fraud where items' payments are made over the internet or by phone). Any Level 3 plastic card-related crime is likely to be passed to the NCA for investigation.

Although the investigation of cyber-dependent crime will invariably involve the collection of 'traditional' forms of evidence (eg in written form) there might also be digitally based evidence such as a deleted file recovered from a PC hard drive, or the address book from a mobile phone SIM card. Police officers at crime scenes must ensure the correct actions are taken so that evidence is not destroyed or contaminated (see 21.5). The forensic techniques required from recovery to analysis (often known as digital forensics) are a specialist field within investigation. The good practice guidelines for the handling of digital evidence recommend that digital evidence strategies should form part of the wider investigative process (ACPO, 2007a and ACPO, 2012a). Police forces may choose to 'outsource' some digital forensic analysis to non-police contractors, who are also expected to meet the good practice guidelines.

21.4 Legislation and Cybercrime Offences

Where a crime has been 'cyber-enabled' then legislation will probably already exist to address the particular crime concerned. For example, many crimes that occur online, or with other digital characteristics, are prosecuted under 'non-cybercrime' legislation such as the Fraud Act 2006. It is also that case that some cyber-dependent crimes will be prosecuted as other offences. For example, hacking will be often be prosecuted as extortion (even though hacking is explicitly covered by the Computer Misuse Act 1990 (CMA)). This is often because the penalty for the 'traditional' offence (in this case extortion) will carry the heavier penalty on conviction.

Other legislation can be used to deal with the 'grey' area between cyber-enabled and cyber-dependent crime. For example, a stolen phone with a blocked IMEI will not work on a network. (A mobile phone is uniquely identified by its International Mobile Equipment Identity (IMEI) number, and network service providers can use this to blacklist stolen phones.) Therefore criminals in possession of a stolen phone will often seek to change the IMEI so it can be used again, possibly in a crime. The phone can be unblocked or otherwise re-programmed using unofficial hardware and software acquired through the internet. It is a criminal offence to unblock a phone by altering an IMEI (s 1 of the Mobile Telephones (Re-programming) Act 2002 (MTRA)).

21.4.1 The Computer Misuse Act 1990

For cyber-dependent crime the main legislation in England and Wales is the Computer Misuse Act 1990 (CMA), together with its various amendments (principally within the Police and Justice Act 2006). The four main offences under the amended CMA are shown in the table. Offences under ss 1 and 2 relate to unauthorized access whereas the more serious s 3 offence involves unauthorized acts.

Section	The offence	Explanation and examples
1	Unauthorized access to computer material	Prohibits activities such as accessing a person's iPad using his/her name and pin number. It is simply enough to prove that the suspect knows that the access was unauthorized – there is no need to prove the suspect had any intent to do something (such as steal a password to a website) after gaining access.
2	Unauthorized access with intent to commit or facilitate commission of further offences	An example of this offence would be hacking a person's PC to locate his/her bank details with the intent to access the account online and make payments from it (here, the further offence could be theft).
3	Unauthorized acts with intent to impair	This would include spreading viruses, hacking a PC and deleting files, and Distributed Denial of Services (DDoS) attacks. The scope of s 3 was broadened to include 'impair' as the original legislation required that changes be made to the files or programs on the computer, which did not cover DDoS attacks.
3A	Making, supplying or obtaining articles for use in an offence under section 1 or 3	This would include for example, supplying 'kits' to enable DDoS attacks that would enable the sowing of 'Trojans' within a company's network.

The CPS explain on their website that, for the purposes of the CMA 1990 the word 'computer' is defined under case law (*DPP v Jones* [1997] 2 Cr App R, 155, HL) as a 'device for storing, processing and retrieving information'. This is a wide-ranging definition that would certainly include tablet devices, smartphones, and perhaps even an internet-connectable fridge.

The CMA 1990 applies where the person was in the UK when he/she committed the relevant acts, and/or the relevant 'computer' was physically located in the UK. Hence, even though a non-UK offshore cloud computing service might be used to commit an offence, provided that the offender was in the UK at the time of the offence it is still covered under the CMA 1990.

They are all either way offences, and the penalty for each when tried summarily is a fine or a maximum of 12 months' imprisonment. For convictions on indictment the penalty is either a fine or imprisonment, a maximum of two years for a s1 or 3A offence, five years for a s 2 offence, and ten years for a s 3 offence.

21.5 Seizure and Packaging of Computers and Other Digital Devices

Where digital evidence is recognized and dealt with by the police, the person dealing with the seizure must follow certain procedures. The importance of this cannot be overstated! The way in which the evidence is handled at this initial stage will impact on its admissibility in any subsequent criminal justice proceedings. Your actions may mean the difference between evidence being accepted or rejected at trial. The volatile nature of this type of evidence, along with the ease in which the data held on digital devices may be altered, mean that special considerations apply for seizure and packaging of digital devices at crime scenes. Where a computer seizure is planned, the Digital Forensics Unit (or Computer Crime Unit) should be contacted in advance for advice, and where necessary they will also attend the scene. DFU personnel are specially trained to recover data and present it in a form acceptable to the criminal justice system. In doing so they will be mindful of ss 19 and 20 of the PACE Act 1984 (which provide the legal basis for the seizure of data) and the ACPO good practice guidelines for Computer-Based Electronic Evidence (ACPO, 2012a). The latter outlines (p 6) four principles of digital evidence which must be adhered to:

- Principle 1: *No action taken by law enforcement agencies, persons employed within those agencies or their agents should change data which may subsequently be relied upon in court.* For the trainee police officer this means, for example, that they should not turn on a PC that is off (see 21.5).

The remaining three principles are more relevant to specialists but are included here for completeness:

- Principle 2: *In circumstances where a person finds it necessary to access original data, that person must be competent to do so and be able to give evidence explaining the relevance and the implications of their actions.*
- Principle 3: *An audit trail or other record of all processes applied to digital evidence should be created and preserved. An independent third party should be able to examine those processes and achieve the same result.*
- Principle 4: *The person in charge of the investigation has overall responsibility for ensuring that the law and these principles are adhered to.*

Apart from data and programs that may be stored on a digital device, its plastic, metal, and glass surface may provide useful evidence. The outer skin of most computers is mildly textured and commonly will not yield fingerprints (in volume crime). However, the screen and areas which are not normally seen, such as the inside, under the support foot and at the rear, are often very smooth and may yield fingerprints. Local policy must be followed for all seizures and storage of computers and associated equipment, particularly relating to packaging. In serious or major crimes great care must be taken: the whole device may be required for DNA and fingerprint analysis. This may present a conflict between the physical and digital evidence retrieval—and must be resolved prior to any activity.

A key point is that a computer that is to be seized as part of an investigation should never be turned off ('powered off') by going through the usual domestic or workplace routine (by first closing down Windows, etc). Instead, the power supply must be interrupted, see 21.5.1 and 21.5.2. Just as important—a digital device that is turned off must not be turned on ('powered on').

Specific Incidents

Computers attached to networks present particular challenges in terms of seizure. If as an FAO, you encounter a network during an unplanned seizure, you should contact your DFU or equivalent for advice. Further information may be found in Bryant and Bryant (2014).

If you are a member of police staff you also should refer to the *PCeU First responder* guide, available through your force. An alternative source of guidance (available via law enforcement agencies) is the document *Electronic evidence guide—a basic guide for police officers, prosecutors and judges, produced by the Council of Europe (COE)*. This guide provides advice on how to handle traditional computer-based evidence, and also deals with the process of capturing evidence from devices that are already turned on, as an alternative to 'pulling the plug'. This process, known as Live Data Forensics (LDF) is becoming increasingly important and necessary, as a significant amount of data is held in temporary memory and this evidence may otherwise be lost when the computer is turned off as recommended. LDF requires very skilled and knowledgeable staff as well as specialized tools, and should not be attempted by untrained personnel. The increasing need for LDF in daily police work reinforces the advantages of contacting your digital forensics unit in advance of any search and seizure activity where digital evidence is likely to be encountered. The COE guide also gives advice on the capture of evidential materials during online investigations, which is a different process. Online investigations include circumstances where a police officer may seek to capture information of evidential value from a web page or other internet resource. In these instances, it is not simply a case of going online and downloading the data. The considerations are dealt with in the guide. The guide also has easy to use flow charts to be followed during search and seizure exercises; officers could print these off and use them as guidance when attending crime scenes where involve electronic evidence might be involved.

21.5.1 Unplanned seizures of digital equipment

Where a seizure is unplanned, contact should be made with the Digital Forensics Unit (or Computer Crime Unit) for advice. The scene should be secured and people moved away from the equipment and any power supplies. If the printer is still printing then it should be allowed to complete its run and the screen should be photographed (if it is displaying).

In the meantime:

- do not power on or off any device;
- do not touch any key or the mouse;
- do not interfere with any other device on a network;
- do not use the telephone system; and
- treat any 'advice' from the owner or user with caution.

The layout of the devices and associated cabling should be photographed or sketched where practicable. Separate photographs should be taken of the computer from the front, sides and back, and of any cables and devices such as portable drives that may be connected to the computer.

For small portable devices local policy should be followed, but in no circumstances should call lists, pictures, or any other files be viewed. If the devices are unconnected to other devices, then the DFU may suggest a simple seizure, but remember that some of these devices can still communicate with other systems on a network, through Wi-Fi, Bluetooth and infrared. It is also possible to remotely delete contents of devices such as iPhones, iPads, and similar devices. To prevent such wireless communications a Faraday bag can be used, but a good temporary solution is to completely enclose a device in kitchen foil.

The ACPO *Good Practice Guide for Digital Evidence, Version 5* (available online) also makes it clear that seized hard drives should be placed in anti-static bags, tough paper bags, tamper-evident cardboard packaging, or wrapped in paper and placed in aerated plastic bags.

21.5.2 Procedures for computers and mobile devices that are switched on

In general terms, the power supply to a computer (PC, laptop, netbook, iPad, etc) should not be interrupted by anyone who has not received the relevant training. The only exception to this rule is when the computer is executing instructions to format the logical drives or other 'destructive' activity; this will be explained during initial training. An appropriately trained person (following DFU advice) should interrupt the power supply, normally by removing the power lead from the back of the PC base unit. (Unplugging it from the mains would not necessarily cut the power supply as the computer might have an uninterruptible power supply (UPS).) Removing the power supply to a computer prevents automated routines from being activated—these might otherwise destroy vital evidence on the hard drive. Laptops can be a particular problem in unplanned seizures because removing the power lead will not close them down. DFU procedure may be to remove both the battery and the power cable, but as in all matters concerning the seizure of digital equipment, local force policy must be followed. Any removed battery must also be seized.

For mobile phones and smartphones that are powered on, similar general advice applies (but check local policy). The officer should take the following actions in this order:

- photograph the device (particularly the screen);
- make a PNB record of any on-screen text and imagery that might be visible, and in what state the device is in (for example, is it loading a web page?); and then
- power it down in the most appropriate manner. (However, there are some circumstances where local policy might determine that you leave the device powered on.)

'Live data forensics' is an important but relatively new investigative tool for devices which are found powered-on. Some of the data on such devices would be unrecoverable if the device was turned off (for example data in temporary memory of a device). Live data forensic procedures allow such data to be recovered from a device that is found powered-on. This is a specialist field and should only be undertaken by trained and equipped staff, who have the requisite knowledge and skills to recover the data, while minimizing any 'contamination' (ie changes to the data).

21.5.3 Packaging digital equipment

Force policy must be followed for 'bagging and tagging' digital equipment. This will usually be to use see-through plastic bags, and to use one bag per PC base unit if these are seized. The bag must be properly sealed and a cardboard exhibit label attached if the bag has no pre-printed label. However, polythene bags will obliterate fingerprints if they touch any smooth surfaces, so care must be taken. In serious or major crimes great care must be taken: remember that the whole device may be required for DNA and fingerprint analysis.

For small, portable digital devices the following procedures are likely to apply:

- package different media separately (eg USB pens separately from CDs);
- note the exact number of items in each bag (eg 'a large quantity of CDs' is not likely to be an adequate description);
- where applicable, keep media in their cases (remember to check inside cases);
- do not fold or bend or put any labels on discs;
- seize cradles/power packs for tablets, smartphones, PDAs and similar equipment; and
- keep packaged devices away from sources of magnetism, including during transport (eg not close to car radios).

Force-specific policies will exist in relation to seizure and packaging of smartphones and mobile phones. This may include storage in Faraday bags and boxes to prevent the device communicating with the network.

Specific Incidents

22 | Attempts, Conspiracy, and Encouraging or Assisting Crime

22.1 Introduction

In this chapter we discuss legislation designed to deal with suspects who stop just short of committing indictable offences but can nevertheless be prosecuted for attempting to commit the full offence, or for conspiracy. In addition, those accomplices who are not the actual perpetrators of an offence who encourage or assist in the commission of a crime from a distance are also considered. This relatively new legislation has a slighter wider scope than the common law offence of incitement that it replaces. These kinds of offences are referred to as inchoate—meaning anticipatory or preparatory. People who are accused of the offences described in this chapter are also sometimes loosely or informally described as 'accessories' to a crime.

22.2 Criminal Attempts

A person planning a criminal offence might not actually commit the full offence. This could be because the suspect lost his/her nerve, or was disturbed, or simply found that his/her intentions or plans were impracticable. The offence of a criminal attempt can be used to penalize a criminal for carrying out an act just short of committing a full offence. This offence (a criminal attempt) is described under s 1(1) of the Criminal Attempts Act 1981:

> If with intent to commit the offence to which this section applies, a person does an act which is more than merely *preparatory* to the commission of the offence, [he/she] is guilty of attempting to commit the offence.

The attempted offence must be an indictable offence (ie it can be tried on indictment in a Crown Court or either way at a magistrates' court or a Crown Court—see 5.5.1), however, see 22.2.3 for certain indictable offences which cannot be attempted. Summary offences cannot be attempted in terms of this legislation, but see 22.2.4.

The mode of trial is the same as for the main offence. For either-way offences the penalty is the same maximum penalty as the substantive offence when tried summarily. For an indictable only offence the maximum penalty is the same as for the substantive offence.

22.2.1 Attempts and Criminal intent

The suspect must have formed criminal intent (*mens rea*) in all three of the areas shown in the table:

The suspect must have the intent to	Example
Commit the full offence	The suspect intended to steal a car or to rob a person
Take part in a series of acts which will lead to a final outcome of committing the full offence	The suspect made a point of collecting the tools together, going to a house, and forcing a window in order to break in
Carry out all the elements of the offence	In order to attempt a theft, for example, the suspect must have acted dishonestly with the intention of appropriating the property belonging to another and of permanently depriving the other of it

For a person to be found guilty of an attempt to commit an offence, the suspect must have more than an intention to do it (*R v Campbell* [1991] Crim LR 268). The suspect must demonstrate his or her guilty intent by carrying out acts, and crucially, these must be more than just preparing to commit the full offence. Therefore, it would not be enough if the suspect had some cloth and a container of petrol in a bag, and transported them to the rival's house; his/her actions might still be considered as preparatory. If, on the other hand, the suspect went to the front door of his/her rival's house with cloth soaked in petrol, put it in the letter box, and then used a lighter to try to set light to the cloth, this would show a clear intent to carry out the offence of arson. These acts would probably be considered as 'more than merely preparatory' and could therefore constitute an attempt under the Criminal Attempts Act 1981.

The final act carried out by the accused must be in combination with all the other preparatory acts, and have no aim other than to complete the full offence. For example, a group of people might be seen getting out of a van close to a fenced enclosure containing scrap copper. They cut a hole in the fence that would be big enough for someone to climb through. On seeing a security guard, they quickly leave but are stopped some miles away. One of the group still has some wire clippers in his pocket and another throws a pair of bolt croppers out of the van. They have done more than merely prepare to steal the metal; they have committed an attempt under s 1(1) of the Criminal Attempts Act 1981 (see *Davey v Lee* (1967) 51 Cr App R 303).

It is sometimes difficult to identify the fine line between preparatory acts and attempts to commit crime. However, this is primarily a jury's decision, and is based upon 'common sense'. In *R v Geddes* the court provided a useful suggestion on how to interpret the law: does the available evidence demonstrate that the defendant has performed an action which shows that he/she has actually tried to commit the offence in question, or has he/she merely become ready to put him/herself in a position or equipped him/herself to do so (*R v Geddes* (1996) 160 JP 697)? It is not sufficient that the defendant made preparations, obtained suitable materials or equipment, got ready, and put him/herself in a position to commit the offence charged. With regard to theft, the law introduced the specific offence of Going Equipped to Steal (s 25, Theft Act 1968, see 16.6). It states that a person is guilty of an offence if, 'when not at his place of abode, he has with him any article for use in the course of or in connection with any burglary or theft'. One can see here how the law seeks to cover all eventualities of criminal endeavour—walking down the street with implements to steal a car would not amount to an attempt, but the offence deliberately designed to address this kind of conduct—Going Equipped to Steal—does.

For an attempt, if the person **believes** that he/she is committing an offence, he/she will still be regarded as having attempted it, even if it is proved later that it would not have been possible to commit the full offence (s 1(3)(b)). For example, a woman is paid money to travel from another country to the UK with a suitcase that she believes contains heroin. On arrival at the UK port her suitcase is searched and she admits to importing heroin into the UK. However, tests on the substance in the suitcase reveal it to be harmless vegetable matter, and not drugs. The offence of importing controlled drugs has not been committed, but she has still attempted to commit the crime (*R v Shivpuri* [1987] AC 1).

The more recent case of *L v CPS* (2013) QBD (Admin) demonstrates that the prosecution need to prove more than the person's mere presence at the scene of a robbery to convict him/her of involvement in attempted robbery. A group of youths were accused of acting together to attempt to rob young children of their phones. All were convicted. However, an appeal was allowed in the case of L as there was insufficient evidence to demonstrate that he encouraged the attempted robbery at any stage. His mere presence amongst the group of offenders was found to be insufficient to convict him of attempted robbery.

22.2.2 Thorough planning and practical preparation

Section 1(2) of the Criminal Attempts Act 1981 states that there must be evidence that the person actually planned to personally carry out the act, rather than just planning it (in which case someone else could have carried it out): 'the person does an act which is more than merely preparatory to the commission of the offence'. If there is something else to be done before the completion of the offence, it does not amount to an attempt.

As has been alluded to, it does not matter (for the offence of criminal attempt) whether the attempted offence would actually have been impossible to carry out (s 1(2)). Two examples demonstrate this.

1. A woman who fires a bullet at the body of a man lying on a bed intending to kill him, but she did not know he was already dead. Even though the full offence of murder is impossible, she has still in fact attempted to kill someone.
2. A man tries to steal property from a woman's pocket. He inserts his hand but finds nothing because the pocket is empty. Even though the full offence of theft is impossible he has still attempted to commit the offence of theft.

22.2.3 Offences that cannot be criminally attempted

Section 1(4) of the Criminal Attempts Act 1981 lists several categories of offence that cannot be 'attempted', such as summary offences. There are also a number of indictable offences that cannot be attempted. These include:

- conspiracy to commit an indictable offence: that is, an agreement between people to commit an offence;
- aiding, abetting, counselling, procuring, or suborning the commission of an indictable offence: for example, a person knew all the circumstances concerning a particular murder and did everything apart from deliver the fatal kick to the head; and
- assisting offenders: for example, knowingly helping offenders avoid arrest or concealing information, perhaps by paying money to a witness to stop him/her giving testimony in any trial.

The reason these particular offences cannot be attempted is because they are in of themselves preparatory (criminal) conduct. In other words, one cannot 'attempt an attempt'.

22.2.4 Summary offences and attempted criminal acts

As we have already noted, summary-only offences cannot be attempted in terms of the Criminal Attempts Act 1981. However, certain summary offences amount to attempts to commit certain acts because the law has specifically enshrined the act of attempt. Examples here include, 'attempting to drive whilst unfit through drink or drugs' (see 19.9.2), and 'interfering with vehicles' (see 16.8.2.2). The latter was created to cover situations where a person's actions effectively amount to an attempted 'Taking a conveyance without the owner's consent' offence (see 16.8.2), but could not be charged as such because TWOC is a summary offence.

TASK 1 The following case relating to an attempt subsequently went to appeal. Predict the result of the appeal and explain your reasoning.

A man was seen by a teacher in the lavatory block at a school. A cider can carrying the man's fingerprints was found in one of the cubicles and his rucksack, containing a large kitchen knife, some rope, and a roll of masking tape, was found in some nearby bushes. He was charged and convicted of attempted child abduction, the prosecution putting forward the argument that he had been hiding in the lavatories to abduct a child. He appealed on the grounds that he had not attempted to commit the offence (*R v Geddes* [1996] Crim LR 894).

22.3 Conspiracy

This brief overview will concentrate upon statutory conspiracy to commit an offence, as described in the Criminal Law Act 1977. For the sake of clarity, however, it is worth mentioning that under common law there are non-statutory conspiracies, such as conspiracy to defraud and conspiracy to corrupt public morals or outrage public decency. Further information on these is available on the CPS website. The word conspiracy is usually used to describe a secret plan by a group of people to do something unlawful or harmful—bear this in mind when seeking to understand this offence.

Conspiracy (s 1 of the Criminal Law Act 1977) is seen as an 'incomplete offence' (as are attempts to commit crime). This is because it is committed as soon as the parties agree to a course of conduct being undertaken to commit the main offence (known as the substantive offence). The conspirator does not have to commit the substantive offence to commit conspiracy. Note that a person can still be found guilty of conspiracy even if the commission of the substantive offence is impossible due to the existence of particular circumstances (subsection (b)). Thus, if two people agree a course of conduct to kill Molly it does not matter if (unknown to them), she was already dead.

For there to be a conspiracy, at least two people must make the agreement. There can be no criminal conspiracy where a person acts alone, and mere negotiation does not constitute an agreement (*DPP v Nock* [1978] AC 979). Conspiracy, then, is a group activity. However, if a person enters into an agreement and then withdraws, this does amount to a conspiracy, and the withdrawal would be regarded only as mitigation (*R v Gortat and Pirog* [1973] Crim LR 648). In addition, there are certain classes of people who by definition cannot be guilty of a conspiracy. Firstly, the intended victim of a crime cannot be guilty, and unsurprisingly a conspiracy cannot be said to exist when a child under 10 is the only other person in an agreement to commit crime (s 2 of the Criminal Law Act 1977). Finally, a husband and wife cannot be guilty of conspiracy to commit crime if they are the only people in the agreement. This particular exclusion of liability appears to relate to the traditional notion that when two people are married they become 'one', in the eyes of the law. If, however, they both entered into a conspiracy with a third party (so that there were then three people in the conspiracy) they could all be guilty of the offence.

You might ask how is it possible to prove that parties have entered into a criminal conspiracy to commit a crime. That is a good question. As you might expect, such agreements are usually made in private with no other parties present. However, the conspiracy can often be proven by the parties' pursuit of a common purpose, for example the things they do to further the cause of the conspiracy. Evidence of criminal conspiracies is usually found in material seized by the police—for example SMS messages on phones, emails, and paper-based documents showing plans to commit a crime.

As stated above, the fact that the commission of an offence is impossible, is not a bar to conviction for conspiracy. In certain circumstances convictions can take place in England and Wales where parties conspire to commit other offences abroad (s 1A Criminal Law Act 1977).

If found guilty, the sentence for conspiracy is the same as for the substantive offence planned. Because conspiracies are indictable-only offences, they can only be tried at a Crown Court, and as a Crown Court trial is a costly process, the CPS only support charges for conspiracy when it is in the public interest. If substantive offences have been committed, the CPS are more likely to charge for these rather than a conspiracy, unless many people have only been involved at the conspiracy stage.

22.4 Encouraging or Assisting Crime

The commission of a crime often involves two or more accomplices but they may not all actually perpetrate (carry out) the offence. Some accomplices are at the crime scene but 'merely' offer encouragement, while others might assist in the commission of a crime from a distance, providing information, transport, or financial support.

A person who encourages or assists in a crime (but does not perpetrate the main offence) may believe or claim that he/she was not a true accomplice. However, under the Serious Crime Act 2007 there are three criminal offences in which a person becomes criminally liable for encouraging or assisting another person to commit an offence. Together they replace the common law offence of incitement (now abolished), and also provide additional scope for prosecution in cases where the crime has not yet taken place; previously there was no criminal liability for assisting the commission of an offence unless the offence had been committed or attempted. The legislation providing for these offences came into force on 1 October 2008 and does not apply retrospectively, so would only apply for conduct since that time.

Note that a person cannot be convicted of encouraging or assisting a crime for which he/she is the intended victim. For instance, a 16-year-old schoolgirl could not be convicted of encouraging or assisting her teacher to engage in sexual activity with her. The teacher would commit the sexual offence of breach of a position of trust, but the girl could not be convicted of encouraging or assisting it as she is the person protected by that particular piece of legislation (s 51 of the Serious Crime Act 2007).

22.4.1 Intentionally encouraging or assisting an offence

This is covered by s 44 of the Serious Crime Act 2007, which states that an offence is committed by a person who:

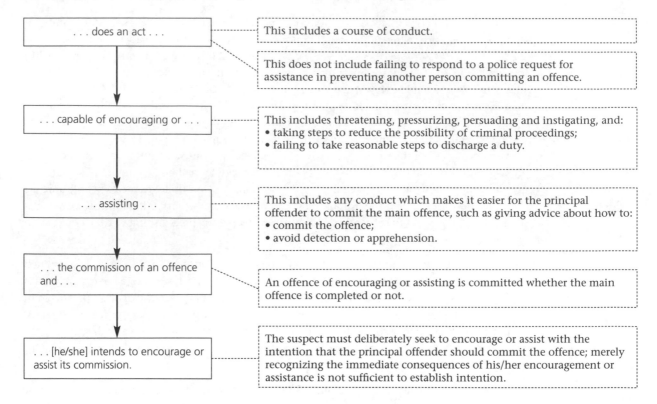

We provide a few examples to illustrate some key points:

1. At a noisy and angry street protest, a police officer speaks to Dodie (a protestor) to try and help him calm down, but Dodie becomes increasingly irate and aggressive. Due to the loud noise, the officer is unable to summon assistance from a colleague. Instead the officer requests Neil, another protestor, to help restrain Dodie, but Neil refuses. Neil's refusal would probably not be regarded as encouraging or assisting a person to commit a criminal act.
2. Frankie lends a baseball bat to a neighbour who is scared that someone might possibly break into his house to steal some antiques. Frankie knows that a baseball bat is sometimes used as a weapon to injure people, but gives it to her neighbour with the sole purpose of helping him feel more confident. Subsequently an intruder is seriously injured by the neighbour using the baseball bat. For Frankie, this would probably not amount to assistance or encouragement to cause grievous bodily harm.
3. Kristoff is married to Shazia but is having an affair with Bella, one of Shazia's workmates. Kristoff intends to murder Shazia and dispose of the body and make it seem that she has moved away. Bella knows all about Kristoff's plan and agrees to provide him with up-to-date information on Shazia's whereabouts during the day to give Kristoff a better opportunity to act without being caught. Another work colleague overhears Bella talking about the plan, and contacts the police. Bella has intentionally assisted in the commission of murder.
4. Brown works for a double-glazing firm and in return for payment gives his friend Mal a spare key from a recently installed door, knowing that Mal is likely to use the key to burgle the house. One night Mal enters the house, and steals cash and jewellery. Brown has intentionally assisted in the commission of burglary (for burglary, see 16.4).

22.4.2 Believing one or more offences will be committed

This relates to belief rather than intent. An offence is committed under s 45 of the Serious Crime Act 2007, when a person 'does an act capable of encouraging or assisting the commission of an offence' (the main offence). He/she must believe that the main offence will actually be committed and that his/her act will encourage or assist its commission.

This differs from the s 44 offence in that for a s 45 offence the person (A) offering the encouragement and assistance to B must believe that B will commit the offence, and that his act will encourage or assist its commission. It is immaterial whether the main offence is completed or not.

The following is likely to constitute a s 45 offence.

> Black is a car salesman who makes a copy of a key to the most expensive car on the forecourt where he works. During an evening out, he gives the spare key to his friend Steve, knowing that Steve will probably steal the car in the near future. Steve does not steal the car but is arrested during a burglary and is found in possession of the spare key. During his interview, Steve outlines his reasons for possessing the spare key, including Black's involvement. In this example, Black has committed the s 45 offence because, although he did not intend that Steve should commit theft, Black still believed that Steve would commit the offence. It is irrelevant that the offence was not actually committed by Steve.

The s 46 offence is very similar to the s 45 offence, but applies in circumstances where there are a number of possible main offences planned by person B (rather than just one), and person A (providing the encouragement or assistance) does not know which offence(s) B is going to commit. No main offence needs to actually be completed. As an example of a possible s 46 offence see the following:

> Tilly has been disqualified from driving and pays her friend Jas to drive her to the next town late one night. From what Tilly has said recently, Jas has a good idea that Tilly has plans to carry out three offences: a serious assault in one house and two burglaries. Scared of getting caught, Jas drops Tilly off around the corner from the first house and drives off. Tilly then decides to delay her plans until another time and texts Jas to pick her up. Here, Jas believed that at least one of the three offences was going to be committed, and therefore she can be prosecuted and convicted for encouraging or assisting the commission of offences that she believed were going to be committed.

Other examples include a gun shop owner providing guns to a criminal gang knowing they will use them in criminal enterprises such as robbery, but being unclear as to specifics, and providing cutting agents to drug dealers to mix with illegal drugs in order to supply them to others, being unaware of what class of drugs they may be supplying and to whom (*R v Omar Saddique* [2013] EWCA Crim 1150). A further example in relation to organized crime would be where a person supplies a crime gang with various number plates for vehicles upon request. He knows they commit robbery, burglary, and murder, and often do so using stolen cars on false number plates. He is unaware which crime will be committed, but he knows the false number plates will be used.

22.4.3 Possible defences to encouraging or assisting offences

If the defendant can prove that it was reasonable for him/her to act the way he/she did (in the circumstances he/she was aware of or believed existed) this may be a defence (s 50) to an offence under ss 44, 45, or 46. When determining what was reasonable, the following will be considered:

- The seriousness of the anticipated main offence: it might be reasonable to encourage or assist in the commission of a minor offence in order to prevent a more serious offence being committed. For example, Peta infiltrates a gang who are conspiring to commit an armed robbery. He tells one of the other members of the gang to steal a car for the gang to use when making off from the robbery. Peta's intention is to look credible in front of the other gang members so he can achieve his main objective of preventing the robbery from taking place. Therefore he may have a 'reasonable' defence.
- The purpose of the act of encouragement or assistance: it might be reasonable to encourage or assist in the commission of a minor offence in order to prevent more serious harm from being inflicted. For example, Manny and Sam are members of a teenage gang on a housing estate. Sam meets with other members of the gang and together they plan to attack a rival gang and stab the leader, Taz. However, Manny does not want to attack Taz and succeeds in persuading Sam and the others to smash the windows of Taz's car instead. Manny is charged with encouraging Sam to commit criminal damage, but may have a 'reasonable' defence that his actions were to prevent a more serious offence.

- The authority under which he/she was acting: it might be reasonable to encourage or assist in the commission of an offence if it was done for the benefit of collecting evidence during an investigation by law enforcement agencies. For example, Boris, a 15-year-old, is tasked by a local authority trading standards department with going into a local shop and purchasing a lottery ticket.

The defendant may be able to plead impossibility as a defence if appropriate. If the crime that he/she encourages or assists would be impossible to commit, then he/she cannot be convicted. This is because a person can only be convicted if his/her acts are genuinely capable of encouraging or assisting a crime, which cannot apply if it is impossible for the main offence to be committed. However, a person could still be convicted of a criminal attempt as an alternative (see 22.2.2). Remember also a person cannot be convicted of encouraging or assisting a crime for which he/she is the intended victim (see the introduction to 22.3).

The maximum penalties for an offence under ss 44, 45, or 46 of the Serious Crime Act 2007 will be the same as the maximum available on conviction for the relevant main offence.

The number of prosecutions for the offence of assisting or encouraging a crime are low compared with other crimes, partly because it is difficult to prove a guilty intent.

22.5 Answer to Task

TASK 1 The suspect had never had any communication nor made any other contact with any of the pupils. As a result, the Court of Appeal concluded that the acts of the suspect were merely preparatory and that the suspect had not attempted to abduct a child or children.

23 | Intelligence

23.1 Introduction

This chapter examines in detail the place of criminal intelligence and how it is used to support policing objectives. We will also consider some of the components of intelligence gathering: sources, source handling, surveillance, research and development, the intelligence 'target package', and some of the laws and rules about what can and cannot be done with intelligence. Some of the material may not appear immediately relevant to the work of a trainee police officer, but after you join you will discover its importance as you move through your training. Many of the serious and organized-crime investigations which result in a successful prosecution have their origins in good intelligence. Very few investigations into level 2 crime (and few of those at level 1) would be effective without intelligence, and certainly much police time would be ill directed and fruitless. However, intelligence is not the only tool available; this Handbook also describes other complementary approaches, such as forensic investigation.

Significant cases such as the Rhys Jones murder on Merseyside in 2007 and some arrests for suspected terrorist offences have highlighted both the importance and the difficulty of converting intelligence into evidence. In each case the police had information and intelligence from numerous sources but it proved highly problematic to convert the intelligence into admissible evidence. In the case of Rhys Jones, the police were able to use new legislation which allowed a key witness to give evidence as a 'protected' witness (see 24.2.4.1), and the police also obtained recordings of conversations (using hidden audio devices) and key forensic DNA evidence. Through these means the identity of the offenders was confirmed. However, in the case of the terrorist suspects, these evidential links could not be established in the same way and the suspects were released without charge. Even if certain intelligence is not used by the prosecution as evidence, it may still be relevant material within a particular criminal investigation and as such might need to be scheduled and revealed to the prosecutor as unused material (see 24.3). This could very well be sensitive material, but it would still need to be scheduled, if deemed relevant (see 24.3 for more information on the requirements under the CPIA).

The Certificate in Knowledge of Policing includes the assessment criterion that learners should be able to 'describe the National Intelligence Model or a model relevant to their organisation and explain how it fits within their organisation'. The Diploma in Policing assessment unit concerned with gathering and submitting information requires the trainee to be able to 'describe the National Intelligence Model . . . and explain how it fits within their organisation'. An understanding of the National Intelligence Model (the NIM) is an important requirement for trainee police officers, and it features either explicitly or implicitly within many parts of the IPLDP, including PIP Level 1, the IND modules, and particularly the OP 2 module. The NIM is covered in 23.6.

As a trainee police officer you will come into contact with the public in the majority of your working time. You may therefore be in one of the best positions to gather intelligence that could impact upon crime and criminality in your locality and the wider community. You need to be alert to the possibilities of gathering intelligence, understand how you should record it, how you can input it into the intelligence system, how it is assessed, and how it is ultimately utilized. Often through the force strategic 'Tasking and Coordinating Group' (T&CG) process, your area will have an intelligence collection plan, identifying what particular information they want to be collected at a particular time. This will be decided after a consideration of local crime trends and particular crime patterns (see 23.6.1 for more on this). However, this does not prevent you as an individual putting other information into the system, information that is unrelated to the collection plan. The information may be vital to ongoing investigations. If you think it is important, there is no harm in you submitting the material, as it can be assessed later by other more experienced colleagues (see 23.5.2 on submission procedures).

As with many aspects of operational policing, extensive Authorised Professional Practice guidance on this subject is available from the College of Policing (under the Intelligence Management heading). The CoP guidance was published in 2013 and some of the material is yet to be updated, and so should be read alongside other reference material. Note also that for obvious reasons neither the CoP guidance nor this Handbook will provide confidential details of police intelligence gathering, collation, analysis, and dissemination.

So, what is 'intelligence'? The police deal with three distinguishable forms of incoming data:

- **Information**: normally from a source that needs no confidentiality constraints or protection. It is overt information, such as a call from the public advising the police of an occurrence.
- **Intelligence**: is more difficult to define but is generally considered to be information derived from many sources (some confidential) that has been recorded, graded, and evaluated.
- **Evidence**: can be either information or intelligence, and is generally material that can be admitted in a court of law and abides by the 'rules of evidence'—that is to say, it is admissible.

It is essential that a police officer is able to recognize these three as distinct because each requires different types of action. The Diploma in Policing requires that a trainee police officer is able to 'distinguish between information and evidence' (part of the assessed unit 'Gather and submit information to support law enforcement objectives'), and the Certificate in Knowledge of Policing requires learners to be able to 'define how to distinguish between information and evidence, and the procedures to follow for each'.

For example, we might have information concerning an increase in the number of thefts of radios from cars in a particular area. If we link this information to a change in payment policy by a local drug dealer (who is now accepting goods in lieu of money in payment for drugs) we begin to derive intelligence from the information.

Criminals will usually go to some lengths to prevent knowledge about what they do leaking out. They often seek to protect key questions about a crime or a criminal; the when, where, how, and why. Finding out about criminal intentions before a crime is committed, or using covert (hidden) methods after a crime has been committed, is one aspect of intelligence-led policing (ILP). Good examples of this are covert surveillance of a person purchasing drugs from a drug dealer, or making a video recording of a person suspected of involvement in crime. In the 2015 Hatton Garden burglary, the police were able to video-record some of the people responsible for the crime while they were in a café discussing their involvement. Without such covert evidence, it would sometimes be difficult to prosecute all of those involved in similar cases. Such covert work often infringes upon the private lives of individuals, so this type of activity is carefully controlled under the Regulation of Investigatory Powers Act 2000 ('RIPA'), and the police would need to seek authority under that Act. Some of the methods for obtaining intelligence, information, and evidence (and how they are managed) are explained in the remainder of this chapter.

23.2   Sources of Intelligence

There are many sources of intelligence, ranging from information picked up during conversations with a member of the public to specialist covert surveillance operations (see 23.3 and 23.4 for details). A police officer can let colleagues know that he/she is interested in a particular individual, and would welcome any useful information gleaned in the course of interviews. The same applies of course to police patrols, who often spend some part of their duty deployment on open observation and interaction with the public. Information can also be obtained from prisons, via the force Prison Intelligence Officer (PIOs). Formal intelligence gathering in prisons is subject to strict protocols and risk assessments, but plenty of miscellaneous and open information about criminal targets is available from prison visits, interviews, preparations for release, and so on (see CoP 2013b for further details).

Police forces also share information with other forces, particularly through the Police National Database (see 6.9.1.2). Police forces should routinely communicate information which, though itself trivial or incomplete, might have a bearing on the activities of someone in another police force area (Bichard, 2004). Information can also be obtained under the provisions of the Proceeds of Crime Act 2002, which places obligations on certain occupational groups such as bank managers and solicitors; they must report the handling of sums of money for which there is little or no apparent justification as this may indicate criminal activity (see 16.5.2)..

23.2.1 Open sources of intelligence

The first and most obvious source of 'open' intelligence about crime and criminality is likely to come from the general public. People notice all kinds of things and should be encouraged to report to the police anything that is odd, suspicious, or out of character. There is much to be gleaned about the lifestyles of criminals from simple observation or from general conversations with members of the public. Criminals live within communities, they have to go shopping, wear clothes, and socialize, and of course they are very likely to have families, hobbies, or interests which have nothing to do with crime. A profile can be built up of a criminal's daily habits: where he/she shops or goes for a drink, what cars he/she drives, and so on. Neighbours, garage mechanics, newsagents, dog walkers, joggers, parking attendants, crossing attendants, fitness instructors, and the like may all have information that could be useful in an investigation.

> **TASK 1** Can you suggest some other open sources of intelligence? These would be available to any member of the public.

There may be specific practices and policies regarding open source searches in the area where you work, so as a trainee officer make sure you find out about these before you do anything on your own initiative. Some sources can be more straightforward for example gleaning information from a local newspaper. Most provincial newspapers are served by a small army of volunteers who send in reports every week, and it is sometimes possible to pick up open references to criminal targets.

23.2.2 Online sources of information

The internet is increasingly becoming a valuable source of open intelligence—for example, through social networking sites and online forums. If you decide you wish to use open online sources within your work however, it is not as simple as it sounds. First because the open web is so huge and effectively free from much control, a lot of the information lacks provenance and indeed could be inaccurate, unreliable, or even false. It might also be impossible to use it as evidence in a court of law because the authors may be untraceable. There are, however, several ways in which open source material might assist a police investigator, for instance by identifying a suspect's associates, or confirming information that is already suspected.

Remember though that an open source search leaves a 'footprint'—Locard's principle, that 'every contact leaves a trace'. Without careful planning you may inadvertently leave a police footprint. You may, for instance have searched using a police web address. Bearing in mind that many modern criminals are computer 'savvy', a criminal only needs to find out the police have searched for him to realize that he is of interest to the police. Many hours of work could have been lost by over-zealousness on the part of a well-intentioned but inexperienced officer. Open source searches can be of value in gathering further intelligence but it must be done properly. For further information, see the College of Policing APP (Managing Intelligence: Intelligence Collection).

23.3 Covert Human Intelligence Sources

The police term for an informant or source is 'CHIS', which stands for Covert Human Intelligence Source. Criminals use many more descriptions (mostly unflattering) such as 'grass', 'snout', and 'nark'. Many intelligence sources are themselves criminals as they are normally the only people with real access to criminals, their plans, and their activities.

It is interesting to note that many government agencies are permitted to use sources to gain intelligence (provided for in the Home Office Codes of Practice under the Regulation of Investigatory Powers Act 2000 (RIPA)). Such agencies and departments include HM Revenue and Customs, the Ministry of Defence, the Department of Health, the Department for Work and Pensions, the Environment Agency, the Armed Forces, and the Food Standards Agency. Any agency using a CHIS must have a responsible authorizing officer and observe the other RIPA requirements. Local authorities must obtain judicial approval for surveillance activities and the use of CHIS (ss 37 and 38 of the Protection of Freedoms Act 2012).

23.3.1 The definition of a CHIS

A member of the public who simply volunteers information about criminals or crimes is not generally defined as a 'source'. A person is regarded as a source (s 26(8) of RIPA) if he/she establishes or maintains a personal or other relationship with a person for the covert purpose of:

- obtaining information or providing access to information to another person; or
- disclosing information obtained by the use of such a relationship, or as the consequence of the existence of such a relationship.

In essence this means that a CHIS is someone who cultivates another person to obtain information, or who provides access to information, or who discloses information. Notice that the words criminal or unlawful are not used here. This is because the information need not necessarily be crime-related, at least to start with. It is the 'covert' part which is important. (Thus, solicitors or bank officials who pass details of suspicious activity to the police are not sources because they are working in an open relationship with the police and not acting covertly.)

In general terms the term 'covert' usually means hidden, but RIPA provides a precise legal definition (s 26(9)(b)–(c)):

> a purpose is covert in . . . a relationship if it is conducted in a manner which is calculated to ensure that only one of the parties to the relationship is unaware of the purpose [and] . . . [a] relationship is used covertly, and information obtained is used or disclosed in a manner that is calculated to ensure that one of the parties to the relationship is unaware of the use or disclosure in question.

What this means in straightforward terms is that the person being cultivated by the CHIS (or from whom information is obtained because of that relationship) does not know that the CHIS is informing the police. As an alternative, consider this as a working (but strictly speaking, 'non-legal') definition: a CHIS is tasked by the police with cultivating or sustaining a relationship with a third person, and that third person does not know about the police involvement.

Under RIPA, any use or conduct of a CHIS by the police will always require authorization granted by the force authorizing officer (a senior police officer, usually a detective superintendent or higher) who is answerable to a surveillance commissioner with a national remit. The authorization (or 'authority') will normally last 12 months.

23.3.2 Source handling

Most forces use a qualified and experienced detective constable as a source handler, probably paired with another (perhaps less experienced) handler. It is good practice to have two handlers so that a CHIS (who could be manipulative and might have his/her own agenda) has less chance of exerting control over the handlers. A further advantage is that two can share the responsibility of handling, welfare issues, and recording of meetings with a CHIS. Sometimes, especially when meetings or intelligence taskings are urgent, there have to be 'singleton' meets between one handler and a source, but most forces recommend that this should never be routine.

The dedicated source-management unit is staffed by a CHIS controller, CHIS handlers, and support staff. The CHIS controller is responsible for the supervision, management, and control of all the staff in the unit. The CHIS handlers are responsible for the day-to-day management and recruitment of CHISs.

> **TASK 2** What qualities do you think would make a good source handler? Discuss this with your colleagues and produce a list of attributes, skills, and competencies necessary to handle a covert source with access to criminal information.

Handlers are usually detectives who have undergone an intensive training programme during which they learn (through scenarios and role-play) how to keep control when tasking informants, arranging secure meetings, and handling devious, dishonest, manipulative, and fantasizing sources.

A handler submits a report with details of the intelligence he/she has obtained from the CHIS, and writes a separate note to his/her controller detailing the meeting itself. The intelligence is passed in its raw state to the Research and Development unit or Force Intelligence Bureau, where it is assessed against what is already known, considered in the wider context, and then sanitized (see 23.5.1).

23.3.3 Restrictions on the use of sources

We have already noted that RIPA provides the definitions of a source and what is meant by covert, but the Act also determines the legal and practical parameters for handling a CHIS. We do not go into all the detail of the Act here, but there are special safeguards for vulnerable or young people, and a regular audit of authorizations by a surveillance commissioner, appointed nationally under a chief surveillance commissioner.

Attention is also drawn throughout RIPA to proportionality and to Articles in the Human Rights Act 1998 legislation, particularly with respect to the right to a private life. RIPA provides the necessary framework for the ethical and legal use of CHISs by properly trained source handlers who are aware of the full extent of their powers (but will not abuse them), as well as ensuring that the risks are proportionate to the expected gain. To make this a little more concrete, a source with excellent access to the upper echelons of criminality would not be used to establish the identity of a local graffitist.

TASK 3 We noted earlier that a police CHIS is often a criminal, because it is usually through criminals that access can be gained to other criminals. What do you think the problems might be for a police force when recruiting and using an active criminal as a CHIS? Aside from the ethical and moral considerations, what practical difficulties might there be? How might they be met and overcome?

23.3.4 The consequences for the CHIS

When allowing a crime to go ahead, the CHIS can be designated as a participating informant (PI). This does not mean that the source will not be charged if he/she is involved in a crime (particularly if any pre-arranged limit to involvement in the crime has been exceeded). However, the sentencing judge would be made aware of the assistance the CHIS had provided.

Even when not active as a PI, an informant may be able to take advantage of the new 'assisting prosecutions' legislation contained within the Serious Organised Crime and Police Act 2005. A formal agreement can be made with an offender in order to secure evidence for the prosecution of other offenders. In most cases, the police will try to keep the identity of a CHIS confidential, the main reason being that if the information became common knowledge the person might be at risk. The police and the Crown Prosecution Service usually adopt what they see as a pragmatic approach: if there is a risk to the source, the prosecution is very likely to be withdrawn and charges dropped, and the source can be used again. No one can pretend that these are easy judgements; you may like to read further on this matter: see Harfield and Harfield (2005 and 2008).

23.3.4.1 Motivation of informants

The handler should identify a potential source's primary motive or motives (even before recruitment takes place), because this will affect how the CHIS should be handled. The primary motivation at the outset needs to be sufficient to sustain the source throughout the long period of gathering intelligence. This is a very under-researched area and hence what follows should be treated with some caution.

TASK 4 Consider for a moment why someone might decide to become a source for the police. Why would you betray your criminal colleagues? How would you keep it up, week after week, month after month? How do you keep the secret of your relationship over a period of time that may extend to many years?

Many sources will suggest that money is a key motivator, but he/she might well be able to make more money from the criminal enterprise he/she is reporting on, so we must look a little deeper; motivation is psychologically complex. For example, an experienced and 'lifestyle' criminal might inform on other criminals threatening his/her dominance. Other sources may be motivated by distaste for the crimes committed by the target criminal. In one case a young woman (with two young children) was motivated to inform on her brother, a prominent local criminal, because she had seen him downloading child sex abuse images on his computer and suspected that he was an active paedophile.

It is easy to overlook the human needs of sources: like most people, they want affection, praise, contact, reward, encouragement, and a sense of being valued. Handlers can provide all these things for a source, but he/she might become too emotionally dependent upon a handler and be unable to function adequately (in other aspects of his/her life) without the handler's help. This can lead to problems. Other ethical dilemmas may also arise: for example, imagine a CHIS drug-user overdoses on drugs purchased with the money he received from the police. To what extent would the police be ethically, morally of legally responsible? Police handlers are acutely aware of safety issues surrounding any human sources, and will make complex arrangements to protect a source's identity, and prevent it from being revealed to other criminals. The consequences of any mistakes in this regard could be catastrophic for the source, hence the need for caution. Police officers have a legal duty of care and confidentiality towards sources, so they must take every step to protect their identities (*Swinney v Chief Constable of Northumbria* [1996] EWCA Civ 1322).

As a trainee police officer you need to be aware of the risks a source may face by talking to the police. It is essential that you are cautious and try to minimize any risk by acting professionally, and keeping the information given to yourself until you are able to input it into the intelligence system. For instance, just because a person has given you information about a local crime matter does not automatically mean that all his/her family and friends know about it too. Assuming that they all know could have serious consequences for the source, especially if the friends and family find out from you in casual conversation and have different views about assisting the police. It might be useful to see yourself as a sponge, sucking up information and keeping it in, rather than giving information away! It is important to be aware that you could also be told anything—from the criminal activities of members of the public to the criminal activities of colleagues or even celebrities. It is important to faithfully record the information as given, and avoid prejudging whether it is true or not; that will be considered later, if and when the information is investigated.

23.3.5 Undercover officers and 'test purchase' operations

A highly trained police officer can work to penetrate a group of criminals, for example posing as a drugs importer or as a document supplier (eg for passports). However, the risk must be proportionate to the outcome. An undercover officer would only be used in relation to very serious crimes, such as high-profile robberies, conspiracy to murder, organized crime, or terrorism. All operations using an undercover officer require authorization, and the risk assessment for this must be very detailed. Officers cannot sustain undercover roles for long and need to be reintegrated into the police force before they are compromised or exhausted by the continuous strain ('turned or burned'). This requires fastidious timing by the handler and supervisors, in order to maximize the benefits. Recent problems with undercover police activities have led to calls for more stringent supervision of such police practices. For example, an HMIC report criticized an undercover police officer for defying management instructions when working undercover with a group of environmental campaigners (HMIC, 2012a); the trial against the activists subsequently collapsed. Recent revelations relating to the misuse of undercover operatives (for instance in the Stephen Lawrence murder investigation) have turned the spotlight on police decision making, particularly the decisions to deploy such tactics. For further information, see the *Stephen Lawrence Independent Review: Possible corruption and the role of undercover policing in the Stephen Lawrence case*, available online. A public inquiry, led by Lord Justice Pitchford will also report on undercover policing. Convened in 2015, it is expected to be some considerable time before the report is delivered.

Test purchase operations are used relatively frequently, and involve a police officer posing as a potential buyer for an illegally acquired item such as drugs. The whole transaction is monitored carefully (surveillance teams deployed and uniformed officers on hand), and when the moment is right, the dealer or seller is arrested and charged. The advantage for the police of such 'sting' operations is that an officer only needs to appear once in one location, thereby reducing the risk. The advantage in terms of criminal justice is that the criminal is caught in the act, and is therefore more likely to plead guilty. This saves time and expense, both for the police and the criminal justice system.

Officers planning and undertaking such operations must be sure that the proposed operation is proportionate and does not entrap individuals into committing offences they would not normally commit. If there is a lack of proportionality, or obvious entrapment, this could lead to either an application under s 78 of the PACE Act 1984 to have the evidence obtained rendered inadmissible, or the defence will put forward an abuse of process argument for illegality (that is a court will not allow a prosecution to continue as it is 'unfair').

> **TASK 5** What qualities and competences are required for a good undercover officer? What logistical and operational problems might arise? What needs to be considered when planning a test purchase operation?

23.4 Surveillance

The term 'surveillance' is used in an everyday sense and in a legal sense, and the meanings are slightly different. For the general public, surveillance generally means watching over something, but in a police and legal sense it generally means covert surveillance, where the subject of the surveillance is unaware that he/she is being monitored, and the monitoring is planned in advance. The use of covert surveillance is tightly controlled by the Regulation of Investigatory Powers Act 2000 (RIPA, see 23.4.2). However, other types of monitoring, such as the use of CCTV by local authorities, generally do not involve the planned observation of a particular person and so are not regulated so closely (but see 23.4.1).

Principles about liberty and freedom must be respected; the surveillance might risk infringing the 'right to privacy and family life' (see 5.4). For obvious reasons we only provide a general description of what is involved here. Details are provided during initial training, as and when appropriate.

23.4.1 CCTV

The simplest and most obvious form of open surveillance is the ubiquitous CCTV camera, overlooking public and private premises, walkways, town centres, banks, railway stations, airports, and even police stations. The benefit of CCTV is that it gives 24-hour coverage of a location and its images are retrievable within a certain period; the disadvantage is that the location of the cameras is fixed—cameras cannot follow a target round a corner. In addition, CCTV cameras are usually easy to spot, so an aware criminal will note the locations of cameras and avoid them, or wear something which disguises his/her features.

CCTV cameras are usually operated by local authorities or shop security officers. If an operator spots a person behaving suspiciously and decides to observe him/her using the CCTV for a while, this is not covert surveillance as it is not part of a planned operation; the observation is spontaneous as it is in response to immediate circumstances. The police can arrange to have access to recordings from a particular CCTV camera (as in the Jamie Bulger case, when two children enticed a toddler away and later killed him). Furthermore, some forces have live access to CCTV coverage and can therefore respond immediately to any incidents unfolding on the screens. The procedures for arranging to view CCTV footage are covered in 24.4.1.3.

Some local authorities and other organizations (see Sch 1 to RIPA for a full list) carry out directed surveillance using CCTV for their own enforcement activities, for example to monitor criminal behaviour such as fly-tipping. Sections 29 to 35 of The Protection of Freedoms Act 2012 introduce powers for the Secretary of State to issue codes of practice for surveillance camera systems, as well as a system for regulating such activities, spearheaded by a Surveillance Camera Commissioner. These provisions came into force on the 1 July 2012, and the Codes of Practice were issued in June 2013 (Home Office, 2013d). The Information Commissioners Office (ICO) recently revised the Codes that regulate the use of surveillance cameras and personal information by businesses and organizations (other than public authorities), see 23.4.2 for further information.

Recently the use of automatic number plate recognition systems (ANPR) has come under scrutiny by the surveillance commissioners, who concluded that ANPR cameras are sometimes utilized for covert purposes (see 23.4.2). In such circumstances authorization under RIPA will therefore be required (see 23.4.2.2).

23.4.2 Covert surveillance

Covert surveillance does not include discreet spontaneous observations of a crime that is unexpectedly taking place. Surveillance is planned in advance and is defined as covert:

> if, and only if, it is carried out in a manner that is calculated to ensure that the persons who are subject to surveillance are unaware that it is or may be taking place. (s 26(9), RIPA)

The Act divides covert surveillance into two types; directed and intrusive, depending on the location of the target and hence the level of intrusion. Directed surveillance is when the person is anywhere apart from residential premises or a vehicle, and intrusive surveillance is when the person is in residential premises or in a vehicle.

Directed surveillance is defined in s 26(2) of the RIPA, as shown in the diagram.

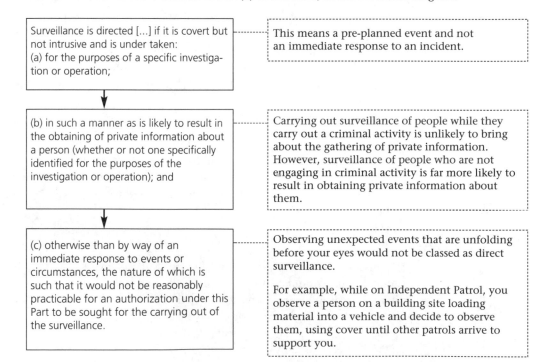

The provisions in RIPA are intended to ensure that police actions are proportionate and justified; the JAPAN principles apply here: Justification, Authorization, Proportionality, Auditable, and Necessary. More recently, police have used the mnemonic PLAN—Proportionate, Lawful, Auditable, Necessary (and some have added the letter E for Ethical), so it is possible that these terms may be used interchangeably, depending upon local policies and practices.

An example of directed surveillance might be the installation of a concealed camera in a tree opposite a suspect's residence so a surveillance team could see when the subject was about to leave. The camera would have to be positioned so that only the suspect's premises was under surveillance. If the camera captured the neighbours' house and their activities, this would be 'collateral intrusion' and authority could be withheld until the risk of intrusion is minimized or avoided. If CCTV is to be used for a covert pre-planned investigation, then authority should be sought.

Intrusive surveillance (s 26(3) of RIPA) is described in the second flow-diagram. An example of intrusive surveillance would be using a hidden listening device in a hotel room. It would also be intrusive if the listening device was installed outside the room but consistently provided information of the same quality and detail, as might be expected from a device installed inside the room (s 28(5)).

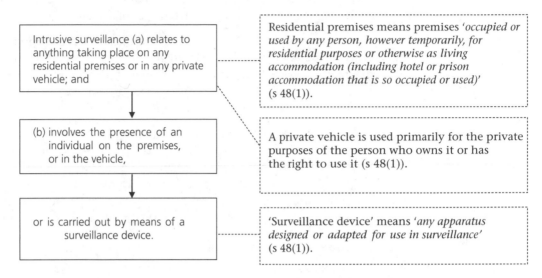

Intrusive surveillance (a) relates to anything taking place on any residential premises or in any private vehicle; and

Residential premises means premises *'occupied or used by any person, however temporarily, for residential purposes or otherwise as living accommodation (including hotel or prison accommodation that is so occupied or used)'* (s 48(1)).

(b) involves the presence of an individual on the premises, or in the vehicle,

A private vehicle is used primarily for the private purposes of the person who owns it or has the right to use it (s 48(1)).

or is carried out by means of a surveillance device.

'Surveillance device' means *'any apparatus designed or adapted for use in surveillance'* (s 48(1)).

Surveillance is not intrusive if it is carried out by a tracking device designed or adapted principally for the purpose of providing information about the location of a vehicle (s 28(4)(a)), or if it is a one-sided consensual interception (eg of a postal service or telecommunication system) with no intercept warrant (s 28(4)(b)). In a landmark case relating to the lawfulness of monitoring communications between suspects and a solicitor, the House of Lords (now the Supreme Court) concluded that RIPA Pt II allowed the covert surveillance of communications between lawyers and their clients. This was somewhat surprising as those communications might well be covered by legal professional privilege, and a person in custody has enshrined rights to consult privately with his/her legal representative (*In re McE (Appellant) (Northern Ireland) & In re M (Appellant) (Northern Ireland) & In re C (AP) and another (AP) (Appellants) (Northern Ireland)* [2009] UKHL 15).

More recently, the Court of Appeal was asked to deliberate on the case of two men who had been arrested for violent robbery and burglary. The police on three occasions had bugged the prison van used for their transport, and overheard incriminating remarks. Amongst other arguments, the defendants argued that the prison van should be regarded as akin to a prison cell, which in their view made it a private residential premises within the context of intrusive surveillance. If this was the case, then the authority for the surveillance should have been by a chief officer of police not the superintendent. They also argued that the surveillance in itself was not necessary or proportionate, and that their convictions should be quashed because the surveillance evidence should have been rendered inadmissible under s 78 PACE (see 25.5.1.2). In a clear judgment, the Court of Appeal did not agree that the prison van was private or residential, and accepted that as one offender was yet to be found, the police action had been necessary and proportionate. The appeal was dismissed (*R v Plunkett and Plunkett* [2013] EWCA Crim 261). The case is a good illustration of the importance of clear decision-making by the investigators, to demonstrate both reasonableness and good faith.

23.4.2.1   Covert surveillance methods

Surveillance work involves a variety of approaches, depending on the information required.

Static observations can be carried out from a fixed vantage point (an Observation Point or OP); for example, from a park bench or an unmarked parked police vehicle. If the OP is on private property, then special provisions apply: the identity and safety of the property's owner or user must not be compromised. The surveillance could be either directed or intrusive, depending on the location of the subject under observation.

Mobile conventional surveillance involves officers following the subject on foot or in a vehicle. If only the position and movements of the subject are recorded, then this is directed surveillance. The teams who undertake this type of work are highly trained and such operations are carefully planned. Two key factors to consider are the awareness of the subject and the location. A tightly knit rural community would be a difficult location as strangers and unknown cars will 'stand out' in a small village or a quiet residential street. Different but equally complex problems occur in busy high streets, where it is difficult to keep the target in sight. Some criminals use sophisticated counter-surveillance techniques to shake off such surveillance, though by doing so they of course demonstrate that they probably have something to hide.

Mobile technical surveillance involves attaching tracking devices to vehicles, packages, or other items. If the device is used to simply identify the position of an object, then this is directed surveillance. Tracking by GPS is commonly used by the police and private-sector organizations; you may have seen security vans for transporting money with a sign indicating that the vehicle is being tracked.

Audio and visual surveillance employs devices such as binoculars, cameras, or recording equipment. These can be used when following a subject, or observing and recording him/her from an OP. Microphones and sound-recording equipment can be used to record a subject's speech when an undercover officer engages him/her in conversation in order to obtain evidence or intelligence; 'wearing a wire'. The use of audio-visual equipment for surveillance is tightly regulated and the authorization must relate to the specific methods to be used.

23.4.2.2 Authorization for covert surveillance

Authorization for covert surveillance must be given in writing and is valid for three months. It will be scrutinized (usually monthly in the case of intrusive surveillance) by a surveillance commissioner. The authorization can be withdrawn and the operation cancelled if he/she is not satisfied that the grounds were reasonable and the justification proportionate. Any intelligence obtained is also likely to be destroyed.

For directed surveillance, the authorization should be given in writing by a police officer not below the rank of superintendent. In urgent cases, oral authorizations may be given by a superintendent, but only for 72 hours (and written authority should be provided within the 72-hour period). Intrusive surveillance is a highly specialized area of police work and will only be authorized if it involves serious crime. All such operations must be authorized by a person holding the rank of chief officer (ie assistant chief constable rank and above) and the authorization must be approved by a surveillance commissioner.

Some operations involve the use of a CHIS, OPs, and mobile surveillance, and therefore multiple applications for authority need to be considered. These complex procedures ensure that the police (and other agencies) operate in a system which is open to both scrutiny and monitoring, and in compliance with the Human Rights Act 1998.

23.4.3 Communications Data

Communications data can provide valuable intelligence to the police and other agencies, particularly when investigating organized crime and terrorism. Communications data has two main components: entity data (about a person or organization making the communication) and 'events data' about the existence and timing of the communication. It does not include the content of the communication, ie what was said or written.

One of the most controversial changes in the new Investigatory Powers Act 2016 (IPA) is the new power under s 87, which allows the Secretary of State to require a telecommunications operator to retain 'relevant communications data' for investigative reasons (see 23.4.3.2 for more details). It is hoped that the legislation includes adequate safeguards to ensure these powers are not used inappropriately. To this end, the Act was amended a number of times during its parliamentary stages. Trainee police officers are unlikely to be involved in the collection of intelligence gained from communications data but need to be broadly aware of the controls surrounding its request and collection.

23.4.3.1 Entity data and events data

Communications data consists of entity data (about a person or organization) and events data (the timing of telecommunications events) (s 261(5) IPA).

Entity data identifies the person or organization making the communication, or the location of the communication equipment being used and/or the network through which the data are transmitted. Examples include:

- the 'header' of an email which identifies the IP address of a sender;
- the postal address on a letter;
- the location of a mobile phone (eg using cell site analysis);
- 'reverse look ups' (eg whose mobile phone is this?);
- a password used by a subscriber.

Events data is concerned with data about how a communication service has been used, such as a list of numbers called by a particular mobile phone, or a list showing when letters have been delivered to a particular address.

23.4.3.2 Communications Data and Investigation

Communications data can be obtained by the authorities from telecommunications providers for the purpose of specific investigations or operations (s 61 IPA), but it must meet the necessity and proportionality criteria defined under the IPA. The public authority must consider (s 2(2)):

- whether there are other less intrusive means to obtain the information;
- the sensitivity of the material;
- the public interest in the integrity and security of the telecommunications systems; and
- protecting privacy.

Many police officers use the PLANE mnemonic to assess their approach; the gathering of the data must be Proportionate, Lawful, Auditable, Necessary, and Ethical (although other mnemonics are also used, see 23.4.2). The data gathering must be authorized by a designated senior officer who is independent of the specific investigation or operation (unless there are exceptional circumstances (s 63(2), IPA). An authorization to obtain usually lasts for one month, although extensions are available.

In some serious and complex investigations, communications data can provide vital evidence. Part 4 of IPA allows the Secretary of State to require a 'telecommunications operator' to retain 'relevant communications data' for investigative reasons (s 87). 'Relevant communications data' (s 87(11)) is any data that can be used to:

- identify the source or recipient of the communications;
- the nature (time, pattern, etc) of communication; or
- the nature and location of systems used for communications.

The retention of the data must be necessary and proportionate (s 87(1) IPA), and a retention notice from the Secretary of State, authorized by a judicial commissioner is required. The duration of the retention arrangements cannot exceed one year.

A recent case in the European courts (Judgment in Joined Cases C-203/15 *Tele2 Sverige AB v Post-och telestyrelsen* and C-698/15 *Secretary of State for the Home Department v Tom Watson and Others*) suggested that indiscriminate retention of communications data was wrong, because there were insufficient safeguards to ensure the power was only used in very serious cases.

23.4.3.3 The Investigatory Powers Act 2016

The IPA received Royal Assent in November 2016 and aims to:

- consolidate and clarify existing police and intelligence services powers in relation to obtaining communications data and data about communications (as discussed above);
- create independent oversight of certain warrants (judicial sanction will be required);
- create an office of Investigatory Powers Commissioner; and
- make provision for the retention of internet records (as discussed above).

It is envisaged that the new legislation will help combat serious crime and terrorism more effectively. Whilst extensions are available for some of the powers, the government suggest that built-in safeguards will ensure they are only used in appropriate circumstances. Many of the investigative powers in the Act were already in place (eg under statute law, case law, and EU Directives) and have merely been consolidated. The IPA consists of

- Part 1: this describes responsibilities in relation to privacy, and provides offences relating to unlawful interception of communications and the unlawful obtaining of communications data;
- Part 2: this describes the circumstances in which communications interception is lawful, and how any obtained material should be managed;

- Part 3: this sets out the manner in which communications data can be obtained, including authorization and management of the material;
- Part 4: this concerns the authorizations for retention notices served upon telecommunications operators and the resulting obligations; and
- Parts 5 and 6: these describe the powers and warrants in relation to equipment interference.

Other parts of the Act deal with bulk personal dataset warrants, and other miscellaneous provisions. Note that some Parts of the Act are not yet in force (see the legislation.gov.uk website for updates and more details).

23.5 Managing, Processing, and Using Intelligence

Intelligence should be managed, processed, and analysed so that it can be effectively and legally used by the police and other agencies. We might note, in passing, that for crime at Level 3 the national intelligence agencies link closely with the police. For example, HM Revenue and Customs includes an investigation branch (part of the National Crime Agency) and uses intelligence-led principles to track illegal imports (of any kind: drugs, people, contraband). The Security Service (MI5) also uses intelligence from police sources to counter threats to national (internal) security.

23.5.1 Collection of information

The police collect information every day. But it should only be collected if it is deemed relevant for a policing purpose, such as the preservation of life, maintaining order, and investigating and detecting crimes. This provides the legal basis for the police to deal with that information, for instance by recording it, sharing it with other agencies, or simply retaining it for future use. Information is collected (sometimes as a result of strategic direction, see 23.6), collated, evaluated, and disseminated; APP terms this 'the intelligence cycle'.

23.5.2 Intelligence reports

Intelligence is usually reported by police officers on a $3 \times 5 \times 2$ form ('three by five by two'). The numbers refer to 'qualities' of the intelligence, measured in three categories, using the scales 1 to 5 and A to E, and the letters P or C. For example, for a CHIS the scales refer to his/her reliability, the reliability of the intelligence, and the level of security to be implemented. There are a number of Diploma in Policing assessment criteria where the ability to complete parts of such forms is required.

A summary of the $3 \times 5 \times 2$ approach is given in the table (note that headings might vary from force to force).

Reliability of source (Do we trust him, her, or it?)	Reliability of intelligence (Do we believe the specific intelligence?)	Distribution (Who can see it?)
1. Reliable 2. Untested 3. Not reliable (ie intelligence has normally turned out to be incorrect in the past)	A. Known directly (eg direct observation by CCTV) B. Known indirectly but corroborated C. Known indirectly D. Not known E. Suspected to be false	P. Lawful sharing is permitted C. Lawful sharing permitted, but with conditions

All combinations of scales are possible, for example a piece of intelligence may be graded as '2 by B by P'. A police officer will complete the main body of the form with the intelligence (the who, when, where, why, and how). The grade concerned with distribution (sometimes referred to as the 'Handling Code') is then normally completed by the force Intelligence Unit.

These $3 \times 5 \times 2$ forms are a major part of the intelligence in-flow into a police force's 'Research & Development' unit (or 'Force Intelligence Bureau'—the name varies from force to force). They ensure that reports are circulated to those who need to know; this will usually be the Tasking & Coordination Group (see 23.6). Reports dealing with a common theme may be collated from a number of sources and be circulated as a single composite intelligence item (further protecting each source).

The information may be 'sanitized'—this is the removal of any features of the intelligence that could identify the source or the circumstances in which the intelligence was obtained. For example, no R&D staff would allow a report to go into circulation which began:

> At 5.30 pm, on Tuesday 15 August, 'Jimmy the shark' saw Sam 'Toucan' Belmont in the Three Feathers pub in Harpenden, and gave Jimmy ...

Aside from the inappropriate use of nicknames instead of real names, obvious indicators in the text such as 'Jimmy the shark' could quickly identify the source, which would be likely to compromise his/her access as well as putting him/her at personal risk. The 'need to know' principle applies to protecting sources, because the police want the source to continue his/her covert relationship with the target. R&D staff may return to the handler(s) with requests for directions to pursue and more targets; a productive source will be heavily tasked.

The importance of accuracy in reporting as well as objectivity cannot be understated. You may be convinced of the accuracy of the information you have gained from a source, however, this raw information still has to go through a process of collation, evaluation, and analysis in order to assess its reliability and validity (see 23.5.3 onwards). It is also essential that information is recorded and input into the system promptly. There is little use in gathering some important information if you are going to sit on it and wait until you come back from days off or leave to submit it. Trainee police officers should try to input any information you gather on the day you receive it, and before you go off duty. This professional approach will stand you in good stead in the future.

23.5.3   Analysing intelligence

At some point in the distribution chain (this varies from force to force), analysts will analyse the intelligence, for example establish and identify the MO (the *modus operandi*). This is how the criminal has carried out the offence—how did the burglar gain access to the property, what type of items were taken, where did he/she look? If the offender is known, the findings may be incorporated into a subject profile, or a problem profile if the identity of the offender has not yet been established.

The next stage will be to try and match a particular event with what is already known about other similar crimes. In some forces, this happens with the raw intelligence, in others with the sanitized version. Either way, the assessed intelligence helps analysts to fill out the picture.

The NIM (see 23.6) suggests that intelligence analysis should be undertaken within four main areas:

- Problem profiling—for example, the identification of crime hot spots (see 4.5.2).
- Subject profiling—analysing the actions of suspected criminals and their associates, and of victims. This will involve building up an understanding of the criminal networks involved, through link and association analysis.
- Tactical assessment—essentially a management-support function undertaken by the analyst and involves recommendation of the deployment of resources based on the intelligence available.
- Strategic assessment—involves likely future developments in criminal activity (eg the impact of an international event or the introduction of new technologies). Strategic assessment is normally undertaken by a senior or principal analyst.

Crime pattern analysis, network analysis, and case analysis and crime trend analysis are just four of the techniques which might be employed by the analysts. There are up to ten different analytical techniques (ACPO, 2008), although research shows that in practice often significantly fewer than ten are used (eg Cope *et al*, 2005).

As an example, APP describes how crime trend analysis helps to identify patterns in crimes or incidents in a particular locality. It could help to identify whether particular crimes are rising, or whether they are decreasing. This could be important for the allocation of scant resources to the problem. If the problem is decreasing those resources could be deployed more effectively elsewhere. Crime trend analysis would also be able to identify whether particular crimes or incidents are happening within particular time frames. Some crimes, for instance, rise in particular seasons, such as robberies at holiday resorts or burglaries at Christmas. Such analysis might also be able to identify where crime has been displaced and is now operating in another locality. For instance a successful drive to remove street crime from a particular location may only serve to move it to another location nearby. Crime trend analysis might be able to identify this pattern early so that further responses can be managed.

The theoretical and empirical methods that underpin the ten techniques include the creation and testing of hypotheses and the drawing of inferences. Analysts also use various software packages, for example the 'Analyst's Notebook' from the i2 company. The R&D unit in turn will try to gather enough intelligence to construct a 'targeting package' for the Tasking and Coordination Groups to consider (see 23.6.2).

23.5.4 Intelligence 'packages'

An intelligence package is a number of items of intelligence with related content (the term comes from the idea of bundling different items together). An ideal package would a be highly accurate picture of how particular crimes are carried out in a given locality, by whom, with what success, how the acquisitions from the crime are fenced, how money is laundered and by whom, what the likelihood is of repeat victimization, and how the crime series is likely to develop. However, many lack such detail and are much more likely to combine hard intelligence and reasoned speculation.

The intelligence package is fundamental to police operational planning at the T&CG level (and above). Intelligence packages are not just put together as a response to crime, but may also be used to support other objectives, such as planning appropriate levels of policing for a demonstration.

23.5.5 Dissemination

As discussed, intelligence may be disseminated to others within the policing family, such as other officers and staff in your force, or police forces or agencies elsewhere. Because of concerns about risk, such disseminated intelligence is likely to be sanitized to protect sources. However, police forces also have sharing agreements or arrangements with other agencies (ie social services), and various extra considerations apply. Firstly, the sharing agreement might be a legal requirement made by judge in court (for instance in family proceedings). Secondly, and more usually, the police will enter into information sharing agreements with partner agencies to ensure a professional and joined up approach. It would be difficult indeed if social services and police could not share relevant information in a child neglect investigation or a child abuse investigation. Despite any agreements, police must give due consideration to issues of proportionality, risk, data protection and freedom of information, as well as the human rights of those affected by any sharing of information. In some restricted circumstances, dissemination could involve the provision of information under statute or common law in order for a parent to protect their child from a potential abuser (the Child Sex Offender Disclosure Scheme, see 17.8). Even in these cases, however, particular care needs to be demonstrated to ensure lawful disclosure. For further information, see the information management section of APP, under the heading 'sharing'.

23.6 The National Intelligence Model

The NIM was launched by NCIS in 2000, and is concerned with using intelligence to determine priorities for policing. The Home Office describes the NIM as 'a validated model of policing... representing best practice in the use of intelligence to fight crime' (Home Office, 2001, p 45). All police forces in England and Wales are required to implement the NIM. The NIM is also utilized by the National Crime Agency and local Community Safety Partnerships (see 3.3.2).

The NIM should perhaps be clearly distinguished from ILP, although the two are often juxtaposed. (For example, the 2007 ACPO practice advice 'Introduction to Intelligence-led Policing' is almost entirely devoted to the NIM, and the Bichard Inquiry explains that the purpose of the NIM is to 'enhance intelligence-led policing' (Bichard, 2004, p 119).) The key difference between the two is that whereas ILP is essentially concerned with using intelligence to counter crime, the NIM is more concerned with using intelligence to determine priorities for policing. Further information on the NIM and its associated Codes of Practice (2005), can be found in APP under the heading 'intelligence management'.

23.6.1 **Key features of the NIM**

The key part of the NIM process is shown in the centre of the diagram: the Tasking and Coordinating Process, overseen by Tasking and Coordination Groups (T&CG). This determines the operational responses to crime and disorder, and prioritizes intelligence requirements (eg identifying car-crime hot spots, or obtaining information about a series of burglaries). The arrows on the diagram show how intelligence and other factors influence decision-making.

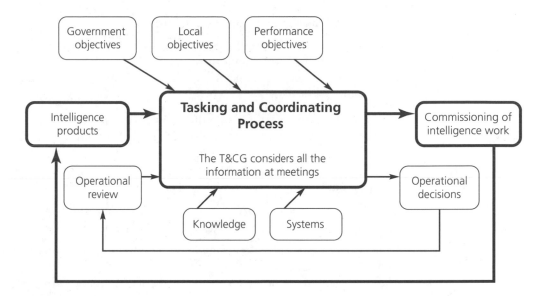

The bold lines indicate the key aspects of the process and emphasize the use of intelligence products to determine what further intelligence work needs to be commissioned. It is a continual cycle of policy development, implementation, and review, and bears some resemblance to Kolb's learning cycle, referred to in 8.6.5.3.

The Tasking and Coordinating Process is conducted at three levels to correspond with the specified levels of incident:

- Level 1 (local BCU level) in relation to local crime capable of being managed by local resources (which may include the most serious crime) and anti-social behaviour;
- Level 2 (force and regional) in relation to force, inter-force, and regional criminal activity, usually requiring additional resources; and
- Level 3 (national) in relation to the most serious and organized crime.

The classification of the crime is significant for resourcing. A single BCU does not have the resources to cope with, say, a group of criminal associates carrying out thefts from ATMs (cash machines) across the force area. A force-level response (Level 2) would be needed, and this would usually be centrally coordinated and directed. Level 3 crime is dealt with by linking with national agencies such as the NCA, in cooperation with its international counterparts.

Whether on a national, regional, or local scale, the use of assessed intelligence to inform operational decision-making follows the same principles as set out in the NIM. Care must be taken to avoid isolating the work at one level from the work at other levels. Related issues at different levels must be taken into account to ensure that opportunities are not missed, and that appropriate resources are allocated.

23.6.2 **The tasking and coordinating process**

At the heart of the business process are the **Strategic** Tasking and Coordination Group (Strategic T&CG) meetings. Most forces will have a Strategic-level T&CG dealing with serious Level 2 crime. The purpose of the meetings is to initiate a Control Strategy which will establish the intelligence requirements and set the agenda for prevention, intelligence, and enforcement priorities. The Strategic T&CG do not routinely determine the operational tactics to be deployed, but instead maintain an overview of priorities. So, for example, if the Strategic T&CG required that ATM raids were to be made a priority, then specialist operations such as surveillance and CHIS recruitment would be 'tasked' to challenge that criminal network. Strategic issues are considered every six months at force-level Strategic T&CG meetings. Members of a Strategic T&CG include the force-wide senior management team, intelligence specialists, crime analysts, and other senior staff as required.

A second category of T&CG meetings also takes place: the **Tactical** Tasking and Coordination Group meetings. At a BCU level (level 1) the Tactical T&CG meets at least every two weeks. The group comprises the senior supervisory officers and support staff from the local area, and they apply the planned response to the Control Strategy, review progress, and make changes to plans if judged appropriate. They can call on other agencies to assist in tactical decisions, but compared with Strategic T&CG meetings there is generally not such a wide range of senior staff present at Tactical T&CG meetings.

23.6.2.1 Inputs to the tasking and coordinating process

The T&CGs are informed by intelligence products which have been researched and written by analysts working with police officers (see 23.5.3). Both the strategic planning at force level and the local-tasking operational planning at BCU level are guided by these intelligence products and other forms of analysis.

Strategic Assessments are long-term strategy documents, usually produced every six months. Tactical Assessments review the progress of current operations and approaches. The T&CGs also commission, and are subsequently informed by intelligence products. These include target/subject profiles about named offenders, victims, or networks and problem profiles about issues of concern such as a hot spot or the increased availability of a particular street drug.

The decisions taken by the T&CG will be influenced by a number of other factors such as:

- Government objectives: for example, to raise the profile of thefts from cars, or deal with public order issues.
- Local objectives: including force objectives, such as dealing with problem families, problem estates, local disorder, and so on. These views will have been canvassed both by the police, through community liaison officers, and through local government councillors, local authority officials, and other parts of local government. All will be conveyed to the area or BCU commander (usually a superintendent) through routine meetings and consultations, and will be arranged into local objectives.
- Performance objectives: the long-term (yearly) objectives for the BCU will also be taken into account. These may be to develop strategies to reduce all crime locally (and might include reducing burglaries by a specific percentage, for example), or dealing with anti-social behaviour, or arrest rates, or 'brought to justice' data. These determine the BCU Commander's strategic approach.
- Knowledge: the professional knowledge required by staff in order to contribute fully to the NIM and other aspects of police work. It includes knowledge of legislation, codes of practice, and force policies.
- Systems: the IT systems and associated procedures for the storage, retrieval, analysis, and dissemination of intelligence information.

23.6.2.2 Outputs from the tasking and coordinating process

Implementation of the Control Strategy will include the commissioning of new intelligence work and making operational decisions to improve the management of crime and the local community. Teams may be assembled to tackle particular issues, and budgets are set; the overtime budget is frequently of particular significance.

As well as the weekly or fortnightly Tactical T&CG meetings at BCU level there are likely to be daily meetings to monitor and direct daily aspects of police work. The daily meetings (sometimes known as 'Intelligence Daily Briefing' meetings, or more colloquially in some forces as 'Morning Prayers') are part of the process of ensuring that the T&CG strategy is implemented and kept on track.

23.6.3 Links with the wider policing role

The NIM is intended to be the engine room that drives the policing machine. Police officers undertake much of their non-reactive work at the direction of the T&CG, to help policing in their area to be coordinated, specific, and focused. The full picture is considered at T&CG meetings, of which the intelligence on criminal matters is only a part. For example, it would not be appropriate for the T&CG to recommend an operation targeting thefts from cars when local priorities were largely focused on reducing alcohol-related violence. (However, the BCU Commander may still judge that disrupting car thefts is a temporary but urgent priority.)

23.6.4   The NIM in practice

To illustrate the way in which the NIM is used in policing we will track through a crime from start to finish.

Suppose we receive several reports of an 'artifice burglary' (see the start of 16.4). The reports will enter the process as information, and a key early requirement will be for analysts to assess the criminal's MO such as the type and location of targeted property (see 23.5.2). The findings may be incorporated into a subject profile (if the offender is known) or a problem profile (if his/her identity has not yet been established).

The T&CG may then task the police staff who are responsible for gathering intelligence to find out whether there is access to this type of criminal (perhaps through a regular 'fence'), and whether there is knowledge locally of such individuals. The T&CG will assign a priority to the investigation and will commission further work, such as checking the force's criminal databases, and trying to match other spree offences in the force area or in neighbouring forces. (Artifice burglars tend not to 'work their own patch', perhaps because they run the risk of being recognized.) Analysts might note, for example, that the offences have all taken place within half a mile of a railway station, in which case the force may approach British Transport Police for help, and look at relevant CCTV footage.

Suppose the frequency of artifice burglaries increases, and one of the victims becomes seriously ill as an indirect consequence of the theft (quite a common occurrence). At the next T&CG meeting, the priority level of the case is raised and the operational plans developed accordingly. The BCU Commander will take into account government objectives, local feelings about the nature of the crime, media pressures, and the chances of catching the culprit.

Now imagine that a CHIS (see 23.3) provides useful information to her handler and a report is submitted. It is assessed by the R&D unit and compared with other intelligence. We now have a name, a preferred location, and a clear idea of the MO. An operation is mounted, two people are arrested, and a case is prepared. The final outcome for the offender could be a prison sentence, a caution (see 10.13.2), a fine, seizure of assets, or community service. Other outcomes might include displacing the activity of artifice burglars (see 4.6.2.4), the development and implementation of a crime reduction (prevention or disruption) strategy (see 4.6), and probably some useful media coverage.

The NIM process has led to an assessment of the nature of the crime, to tasking the intelligence-gathering parts of the force, and giving the crime a higher priority level in the midst of competing claims for attention. The newly acquired intelligence was assessed and used to develop a package of operational measures through the T&CG, the resulting police action disrupted that type of crime, and probably reassured the community to some extent. This is a simple example of the business-process model of policing, and the same principles will operate whether the issue is the vandalizing of cars or a more serious crime enquiry, such as systematic violent assaults on young people near a sports centre.

TASK 6 Now it is your turn: using the NIM, describe what would happen if the BCU Commander wanted to deal with:

1. a crime hot spot involving alcohol-fuelled violence;
2. a spate of break-ins into vehicles;
3. a series of attacks on students to steal credit cards.

What factors do you think would influence the prioritizing of the crimes? What would you expect the crime analysts to provide? How would you task the collection of intelligence? What operational considerations would there be?

23.7   Answers to Tasks

TASK 1 Open sources of intelligence have grown rapidly in recent years, largely as a result developments such as social networks. Whereas in the past we might have needed to search manually through paper copies of newspapers and magazines selling used cars for evidence of possible 'ringing', now we can use the search facilities available on most websites. Indeed, the widespread availability of information is causing some concern with crimes such as identity theft and 'spear phishing' (putting aside the obvious general desire to maintain personal privacy). As an experiment, try to find out as much about yourself as you can by using freely available internet resources. For example, start with <http://www.192.com> and enter your own name. You may be surprised at what you (and others) can find out.

TASK 2 You may have come up with the following :

Integrity and honesty; patience and attention to detail; strong-minded and not easily diverted; adaptable (can think on his/her feet) and flexible; firm sense of duty but objective; understands the 'bigger picture' of force needs and intelligence requirements; reticent or discreet; knowledgeable about crime and criminals; professional in the relationship (courteous but not close); good listener, empathetic ('emotional intelligence'); ordinary/normal in appearance, so can blend into a crowd; resilient and stable as a personality and willing to work long or unsocial hours.

In practice these qualities, skills, or attributes appear not to be commonly found together. A good source handler can be trained to a high level, but there must be strong character traits already there upon which the training can build. You can see that it takes someone with considerable investigative experience and 'life skills' to succeed in this role.

TASK 3 The first consideration for the police is whether, if the identity of the informant is made known, there will be a serious risk to his/her life (or of serious harm or injury). In such circumstances the identity of the 'informant' will never be revealed. The prosecution of a case in open court would probably be abandoned if the informant was the main source of evidence.

You might also have referred to the difficulty of using an active criminal as a source. If a CHIS takes part in an organized crime, or is involved in criminal planning, he/she could be charged and brought before a court. A further difficulty is deciding whether, in order to obtain the intelligence, the crime should be allowed to go ahead with the source taking part.

The use of informants is discussed further in Dunnighan and Norris (1996 and 1999).

TASK 4 Motivation is notoriously difficult to understand and identify, and particularly so with informants. As Canter and Alison (2000) noted, the motivation that a person may put forward for their actions is not necessarily the most useful for understanding that person's actions, and will be only one of a number of possible explanations. Perhaps an obvious answer to what motivates a CHIS would be 'money' but the amounts paid out to informants are normally quite small, usually less than £100. (The total amount paid out yearly by police forces in England and Wales to all their informants is currently approximately £80,000—figure derived from BBC, 2017.)

TASK 5 For a good undercover officer the following would all be relevant; resilience, self-sufficiency, strong professionalism, the ability to work alone, the ability to pass yourself off as something you are not, the focus and concentration to know what intelligence is needed, a very good relationship and trust with your handler, and a personal inclination towards the clandestine.

Logistical and support problems include a good cover story (both for the criminal target and to explain the officer's absence back in the force), payment, nothing to identify the officer as from the police (in clothing, residence, possessions), career planning, reassuring family members, diverting curious colleagues, and so on. There are a host of problems associated with going undercover long term and a team of people are used to support the lone officer.

In planning a Test Purchase (TP) operation, you would have to think about the original intelligence and its reliability, the patterns of movement (and MO) of the target criminal, when to insert the TP officer, how to monitor what is happening, how to intervene and disrupt or arrest, and whether you have the authorization to proceed.

TASK 6

1. You should consider the location of the hot spot, for example is it in a town centre, or close to a series of pubs or clubs? When does crime happen? Would a police presence act as a deterrent? Who is likely to have brought the incidents to police attention? What would be the feelings and fears of the local community?
2. Are the vehicle owners reporting the crime? What is taken? Is there a pattern? What is the location? Are particular kinds of car targeted? What preventative action would help? (This could

include leafleting car owners, making warnings in the media not to leave valuables on view, or providing CCTV coverage.)

3. Are the credit card thefts seasonal (ie do they occur in the summer, at the start of a new term, or in the run-up to Christmas)? What is the MO? What do students do about it? Is violence involved? How is the crime reported? Are women students more at risk than men? Are there criminals on the database who specialize in this sort of crime? What preventative action might you recommend? (Hint: think about crime prevention, raising awareness, liaison with college and university authorities to put cash points on campuses, credit card theft-prevention schemes, talking to the banks, posters near ATMs, security awareness, CCTV, and so on.)

24.1 Introduction

A criminal investigation is defined in s 22 of the Criminal Procedure and Investigations Act 1996 (CPIA) as 'an investigation conducted by police officers with a view to ascertaining whether a person should be charged with an offence, or whether a person charged with an offence is guilty of it'. The CPIA Codes of Practice state that this includes investigations set up in the belief that a crime is about to be committed.

It can sometimes be confusing for student officers to understand where they 'fit' within a criminal investigation, particularly as there are a number of guidance documents that focus upon particular aspects of investigation, for example the *Practice Advice on the Management of Priority and Volume Crime (The Volume Crime Management Model)* (2009) (often referred to as VCMM), APP available on the College of Policing website and the *Murder Investigation Manual*, 2006). It may be helpful to distinguish between guidance relating to the *management* of investigations, and guidance that relates to the *process* of investigation. Both of these make a difference to the expected police response, and both provide examples of the minimum standards expected in particular situations. The VCMM sets out the minimum standards for volume crime investigations (see 24.2.3), while the MIM and APP both identify key stages within investigations, and provide investigators with the main considerations for making decisions in individual cases. Once a case is allocated to an investigator, he/she must follow APP guidance on how to progress the investigation.

The CPIA 1996 is clearly central to the correct procedures being followed for an investigation. It is vital that investigators know when any particular investigation has begun, so they can ensure compliance with the CPIA 1996 and the associated Codes of Practice. The CPIA defines the roles of investigator (wide enough to encompass both detectives and others), disclosure officer, and officer in the case. (No distinction is made between detectives and others within a police investigation.) Each role is accorded particular duties in a criminal investigation. Amongst the most important duties are the need to record, retain, and ultimately reveal (to the prosecutor) relevant material, and the necessity to pursue all reasonable lines of enquiry whether they point towards or away from the suspect. Many see the CPIA 1996 as relating only to disclosure, but it also relates to the conduct of investigation overall. The Act makes an important distinction between revelation and disclosure, the former relates to material revealed to the prosecutor by the police on the relevant forms (MG6 series), whilst disclosure relates to material disclosed to the defence by the prosecutor (see 24.3.3). Much of the recent legislation in relation to investigation was enacted to combat fears that the police had historically withheld important information, ignored exonerating facts, and simply constructed cases against individuals who were sometimes innocent. High profile miscarriages of justice often demonstrated these failings in abundance (such as the 'Guildford Four' and the 'Maguire Seven', the 'Birmingham Six', the case of the Taylor sisters, and Stefan Kiszko). For more information on these and other miscarriage of justice cases, see Eddlestone (2012).

The following legislation is also relevant to undertaking investigations and therefore underpins what we describe here:

- the Criminal Justice and Public Order Act 1994 (CJPOA);
- the Police and Criminal Evidence Act 1984 (PACE Act) and Codes of Practice 2004;
- the Human Rights Act 1998 (HRA);
- the Regulation of Investigatory Powers Act 2000 (RIPA), and
- the Serious Organised Crime and Police Act 2005 (SOCPA)

All investigators, at whatever level of accreditation, are expected to understand relevant legislation that impacts upon their investigative role, and keep abreast of changes as and when they occur. The College of Policing releases a monthly digest to assist officers to maintain their knowledge.

24.2 Key Principles for Investigations

Before we look at the detailed process of investigation, there are some key points to consider. How should investigators approach their work? And how are resources allocated for investigations where there are many competing priorities?

APP makes it clear that all investigators at all levels should adhere to some core principles when conducting investigations. These include honesty, integrity, and confidentiality. Additionally, investigators are expected to conduct effective investigations proportionately, within the law, and in a transparent fashion. These core principles echo the recently released Code of Ethics for police officers (College of Policing, 2014). Conducting investigations in this manner arguably makes for more successful investigative outcomes, thereby improving public confidence in not only the effectiveness of investigations, but also the objective and fair manner in which they are undertaken. Investigators also need to be mindful of the Code of Practice for Victims of Crime (2015v) which provides important standards for updating victims regarding the progress of investigations, the treatment they should expect from the police in given circumstances, and referral to victim support.

24.2.1 The 'investigative mindset'

There is plenty of guidance from ACPO, the College of Policing, and others about the law surrounding investigation, procedural matters, and the application of forensic investigation. However, there is comparatively little available guidance on the mental processes involved in investigation: that is, the forms of cognition and decision-making required to see an investigation to a successful conclusion. The phrase often found in the professional literature is the 'investigative mindset' (eg see ACPO Centrex, 2005, p 60) but it is far from clear what this means in practice. Most often it is a reference to what are considered the best ways for investigators both to make sense of the information (eg an eyewitness statement) and potential evidence (eg a DNA sample) gathered during an investigation (usually referred to in the professional literature as 'material', a term taken from CPIA), and to make decisions based on that information. ACPO described five principles underpinning the investigative mindset (ACPO Centrex, 2005, p 63). These are summarized in the table, and can be memorized using the mnemonic UPERE.

Principle	Explanation
Understanding the source of material	Understanding how a deleted SMS has been recovered from a mobile phone
Planning and preparation	This is in terms of the gathering of material, eg planning a witness interview
Examination	This comprises: • account (eg given by a victim); • clarification (eg investigate any apparent contradictions); and • challenge (both the meaning and reliability of material)
Recording and collation	Making adequate records, storing material correctly, establishing access arrangements
Evaluation	Identify further action that may be needed (eg fast-track actions to find other materials). 'Gap analysis' (see 24.4.4)

(Based on ACPO Centrex, 2005, pp 60–3 but authors' own interpretation)

An investigative mindset helps maximize the amount of information gathered, and that its reliability is effectively tested, appropriate actions are initiated, proper records are kept, and that material is appropriately stored. The same principles should be applied for every piece of information uncovered in the course of an investigation. As an example, take a piece of evidence discovered such as a CCTV image. Investigators should:

- understand the source of the CCTV;
- plan and prepare how best to examine the material (ie what is the most appropriate format for the examination);
- examine the material for what it can add to the investigation;
- record the outcome of the examination (eg as suitable notes) and ensure integrity of its storage; and
- evaluate it in terms of what is already known within the investigation, how it interacts with other evidence and what it means in terms of the future focus of enquiries.

This approach encourages officers to be thorough and thoughtful in relation to the material they obtain. Rather than accept it at face value, or make assumptions relating to its importance, they are required to examine it with a critical eye. However, the more serious and complex a case, the more onerous this task becomes.

Investigators need to keep an open mind in relation to alternative explanations of the material they uncover. APP suggests it is sometimes useful to generate hypotheses based upon available facts. They posit that hypotheses should not be generated unless and until all material evidence has been gathered, and they caution investigators not to try to find material that fits the hypotheses, but instead to alter hypotheses to fit the material. Whether this advice is sufficient is open to debate, but it is important that investigators understand that a valid intention would be to prove or disprove any given hypotheses, fitting nicely with the notion of an open minded and transparent investigation. Investigators are also encouraged to use the National Decision Model (NDM) when making decisions within a criminal investigation (see 6.5.2).

24.2.2 Managing and recording investigations

Effective communication is a key component in case management, as the investigator will interact with other officers, members of the police family and members of the public. It provides clarity between all of the 'players' within a particular investigation. How else would it be possible to gain information and evidence from others, and to brief other professionals on the status of the investigation and of the needs of the case?

Risk-management is also important, and must be borne in mind throughout an investigation in relation to colleagues, as well as to victims, witnesses, and members of the public. There are several examples in IPCC related cases where police failed to appreciate the real risks posed to victims of crime (for instance, the investigation into the death of Tania Moore, 2006). The police have been criticized for their failure to recognize risk, particularly in relation to their poor response to domestic abuse cases (HMIC, 2014). This is important, especially where the police become aware of a threat to life. They have a duty to protect life where there is a real and immediate risk. This derives from a duty to protect life emanating from Art 2 of the European Convention on Human Rights and outlined in an ECHR ruling (*Osman v UK* (2000) 29 EHRR 245).

Records of the investigation must be kept so that investigations are auditable and transparent. As such, depending upon the level of investigation, decisions, actions, and strategies will be recorded in a variety of media by investigating officers. For example, in a volume crime investigation and for routine priority crimes, the investigation is likely to be recorded within the electronic crime report. However, the investigation of a serious or major crime will be recorded on a decision log or policy file, which will set out the key strategic decisions (for further information see ACPO Crime Committee (1999) *Revised Guidelines For the use of Policy Files*). The policy file could become very important where ownership of an investigation is transferred to another officer—not uncommon in the uncertain world of policing—so it is crucial to have an accurate record of what has been done.

24.2.3 Allocation of resources for investigation

Each police force is required to make strategic decisions concerning the investigation of crime, and these often depend on whether the crime is a volume, priority, or major crime. The distinction between volume, priority, and major crime is determined largely at the BCU level by the Tactical Tasking and Coordinating Group (TCG). They will also decide how to tackle volume crime in their particular area (see 23.6.2).

Volume crime as defined by the NPIA (on behalf of ACPO) is 'any type of crime which, through its sheer volume, has a significant impact on the community and the workload of the local police ...' (NPIA/ACPO, 2009, p 8). It usually includes: street robbery; burglary, of dwelling-house and other ('non-dwelling'); theft (including shoplifting); theft of vehicles and from vehicles; criminal damage; common assault; and illegal possession of controlled drugs (often linked with acquisitive crime). Priority crimes for many BCUs in recent years have included street robbery, burglary, and car crime. Hence a priority crime might also be a volume crime, and vice versa, but the terms are not synonymous. In order to ensure that volume crime is accorded sufficient attention the *Practice Advice on the Management of Priority and Volume Crime (The Volume Crime Management Model)* (2009) (often referred to as VCMM) sets out the minimum standards of response for volume crimes identified by the TCG process (see 23.6.2).

Major crime generally includes any crime that includes serious violence (eg murder, manslaughter, and stranger rape) or the potential for serious violence, and that requires resources beyond those of a single BCU. Any crime of grave public concern (eg the abduction of a child), terrorism, or the threat of terrorism is also likely to come under the umbrella of major crime. Major crimes are classified as shown in the table.

Category	Definition
A+	Public concern and the associated response to media intervention are such that 'normal' staffing levels are not adequate to keep pace with the investigation
A	An incident of grave concern or where vulnerable members of the public are at risk; where the identity of the offender/s is not apparent, or the investigation and the securing of evidence requires significant resource allocation
B	The identity of the offender/s is not apparent, the continued risk to the public is low, and the investigation or securing of evidence can be achieved within normal resourcing arrangements
C	The identity of the offender/s is apparent from the outset and the investigation and/or securing of evidence can easily be achieved

For each force a senior detective officer (eg a superintendent) will head a Major Crime Unit. He/she can designate any crime as a major crime, in order that the appropriate resources can be made available for its subsequent investigation.

24.2.4 Witnesses in Investigations

The evidence of a witness (including victim(s)) may be vital in obtaining a conviction. The term 'victim' is normally associated with a person who has been disadvantaged, suffered injury, or been damaged as a result of an event, but the victim is usually also a witness (but see the important discussion relating to use of the term 'victim' or 'complainant' in 17.6.1). Many, if not all, witnesses will co-operate if officers provide reassurance and information about what to expect: see, for example, <http://www.cps.gov.uk/victims_witnesses/resources/index.html>.

There are various categories of witness, and these are important for determining the form of the dialogue between the witness and the police officer and the means by which evidence is obtained.

A defence witness is a person who the accused is going to call to give evidence at the trial in relation to an alibi or to other matters. The name, address, and date of birth of any such witness must be disclosed in advance to the prosecution (s 6 of the Criminal Procedure and Investigations Act 1996) as the police may wish to interview him/her. Some defence witnesses may be intimidated or reluctant to assist, fearing, for example, police coercion to change his/her account. In these circumstances consultation with the CPS is advised. Any interview with a defence witness has to comply with the relevant Code of Practice (under s 21A of the Criminal Procedure and Investigations Act 1996).

A significant or key witness is someone who can provide evidence that is particularly important to a case. They are designated as such by the SIO, usually in a serious or major crime enquiry involving an indictable offence such as murder, manslaughter, rape, kidnap. The witness may have witnessed the offence (or part of it) or may stand in a particular relationship to the victim, or have evidence or intelligence to offer. An interview with a significant witness may be visually recorded if it seems that this will contribute significantly to the investigation (see 25.6.1).

Investigation and Prosecution

'Vulnerable' and 'intimated' witnesses may require 'special measures' during investigations. The definitions for these categories of witness are provided in Part II of the Youth Justice and Criminal Evidence Act 1999. We provide a summary here:

A vulnerable witness (s 16) is any person:

- under the age of 17;
- with a 'mental disorder' (this is the phrase used in the Act);
- with significant impairment of intelligence and social functioning (eg a learning disability); or
- with a physical disability or a physical disorder.

An intimidated witness (s 17) is:

- any elderly and frail person;
- a witness suffering from fear or distress in relation to testifying in the case;
- any witness who self-neglects or self-harms;
- any complainant in a sexual assault case;
- a victim of domestic violence, racially motivated crime, or repeat victimization; or
- a relative of the victim in a homicide case.

Witnesses under 17 years of age and complainants in sexual cases always require special measures. Other vulnerable or intimidated witnesses may require special measures, but further assessment will be required through the use of an MG2 form. More information on special measures can be found on the CPS website.

A 'reluctant witness' is a witness who declines to co-operate, or who makes a statement but then refuses to attend court. He/she may fear repercussions or reprisal, or might simply not want to assist the police. If the police can establish that he/she has important evidence to offer, a witness summons can be issued to compel attendance in court (see Home Office Circular 35/2005).

Some witnesses are granted anonymity in the interests of justice. However, a key principle of criminal justice is that the defendant must receive a fair trial, so the police must obtain as much corroborative evidence as possible in any case where witness anonymity might be involved. Certain conditions must be met for a 'witness anonymity order' (under the Coroners and Justice Act 2009) to be issued by a court. For example the order must be necessary to protect the safety of the witness or another person, or to prevent any serious damage to property, or to prevent real harm to the public interest—and the court must take the witness's feelings into account on these matters. The order must also be needed for the defendant to receive a fair trial (and without the order either the witness would not testify or the public interest would be harmed if the witness were to testify without anonymity). The main case on this issue is *R v Mayers (Jordan)* [2008] EWCA Crim 2989. This case dealt with several separate investigations into murder and drug-dealing, where anonymous witnesses were allowed to provide evidence at the different trials of several defendants. Each appealed on the grounds that the witness anonymity orders should not have been allowed in their trials. The Court of Appeal upheld the decision to allow the orders, provided that the criteria outlined above were satisfied.

24.2.4.1   Offenders as witnesses for the prosecution

The Serious Organised Crime and Police Act 2005 (SOCPA) established a number of important new powers to help the police tackle serious organized crime. For example, agreements can be made with offenders who offer to assist with the investigation or prosecution of offences committed by others. The agreement must be in writing and could state, for example, that the person will not be prosecuted (an immunity notice under s 71), or that certain pieces of evidence will not be used (a 'restricted use undertaking' under s 72).

In order to benefit from the agreement the person must fully admit his/her own criminality, agree to cooperate in full, provide all the information he/she has regarding the matters under investigation, and give evidence in court if required. For example, a witness against the accused may also be a co-accused, as in the Rhys Jones murder in 2007. In that case the CPS was originally going to charge a co-accused with firearms offences but instead offered him immunity from prosecution provided he met certain conditions, including attending court and giving a truthful account. He accepted these terms and the CPS was able to use the new evidence to charge a suspect with murder.

24.2.5   Evidence in investigations

Evidence usually falls into one of four categories: oral, real, documentary, or hearsay. We also consider bad character evidence. The nature and types of evidence are covered during initial police training, for example in LPG 1.7 'Investigation and Interviews'.

Real evidence exists as an object, for example as microscopic bloodstains or particles of explosive, or a hammer. An item of real evidence is known as 'an exhibit'. The reporting or the arresting police officer is responsible for ensuring the secure retention of exhibits. There must be an auditable trail for real evidence, from the moment it was discovered or recovered until it is produced in court. This is referred to as 'continuity of evidence' or the 'chain of evidence'. In complex cases, an exhibits officer will be appointed, and in some police forces a designated specialist is responsible for safeguarding certain materials, such as forensic items or CCTV footage. Further details on the procedures for ensuring the continuity of evidence are provided in 11.2.6 and Chapter 26.

A document is of course also 'real evidence', but is separately classed because of its referential nature, and because authorship can often be proven. The medium through which it is written can vary from a 'Last Will and Testament' on parchment with spidery copperplate writing, to an electronic file recording the use of a credit card over the internet. A handwriting expert may be needed to testify that, within limitations, the author of one particular document is likely to be the author of another particular document. This becomes even more complex when it comes to electronic text, and specialists differ over degrees of certainty about the authorship of, for example, web documents, particularly if they are not signed or copyrighted. The requirements for 'continuity of evidence' also apply to documents (see also 26.5.5 on forensics).

24.2.5.1   Hearsay evidence

Hearsay evidence is when one person reports in court what another person has said or written outside court. For example, the witness might give evidence that she heard a man say that he saw his friend stab someone in an argument. This would be hearsay, because she did not see the stabbing, she is only reporting that she heard the man talking about it. . This kind of evidence has generally been treated with an element of suspicion, and was usually rendered inadmissible in court because of the potential for ambiguity or malice. Part of the reasoning for caution with hearsay evidence is that the defendant cannot cross examine the person who made the relevant statement (ie the man who saw the stabbing in the example above) because he is not there giving the evidence himself. It was considered that hearsay evidence should only be allowed as evidence in court in specific circumstances. The Criminal Justice Act 2003 changed the law relating to the admissibility of hearsay evidence in criminal proceedings, and can be seen as a major shift in attitude towards this type of evidence (see 27.5.2.3 for more details). The new law was predicated upon the assertion that juries in particular could be trusted with more evidence than before, even if that evidence was either hearsay or bad character evidence. Properly directed, the reasoning went, they could make decisions without assuming guilt. Whether this is true or not is open to debate, but the net effect of the 2003 changes was to increase the amount of evidence potentially admissible at trial. The old law was criticized (Spencer, 2016) for being too complicated, difficult to find (because it was in different Acts of Parliament or case law, some of which extended back into previous centuries), and too inflexible. In an infamous trial for indecent assault (*R v Sparks* (1964)) the court would not allow a defendant to use certain hearsay evidence and he was convicted, even though that evidence might have exonerated him if the jury had heard it. (He subsequently appealed and was successful, but only on other grounds.) In the 2003 Act there is a specific clause allowing for flexibility and admissibility of evidence that would be in the interests of justice for a court to hear. If *Sparks* were to happen today, it is likely that he would be able to use the hearsay evidence in his defence.

A trainee officer does not have to learn all the details of all the provisions for hearsay, but he/she must remember to make a PNB record of exactly what was said.

24.2.5.2   Bad Character Evidence

Bad Character Evidence (BCE) can sometimes be used in criminal cases, and officers should always consider whether relevant BCE exists. Bad character is defined by s 98 of the Criminal Justice Act 2003 as evidence of:

- misconduct (including previous convictions, cautions, and offences for which a person has been charged, but the charge has not been heard or the person was acquitted (s 112)); or
- a disposition towards misconduct, for example 'other reprehensible behaviour' (s 112), which, for example, could include anti-social behaviour, persistent lying, and racist behaviour.

Thus the law makes it clear that reprehensible behaviour falling short of a conviction counts as bad character, as well as obvious instances, such as previous convictions. For instance, a person may have a propensity to be violent if he/she gets drunk, and this may become relevant in a case of assault against a family member, irrespective of whether the accused has been previously convicted in relation to similar behaviour. The evidence for BCE cannot come from the offence currently under investigation, nor can it be related to the process of the current proceeding (eg the defendant not attending court when required). Therefore police officers should record matters that might relate to bad character evidence contemporaneously, and provide such intelligence to the relevant department. This information could be crucial to a subsequent criminal investigation.

BCE is likely to be covered during initial police training as it features in IPLDP Operational Module 9 'Prepare and present case information, present evidence, and finalise investigations' and under LPG 1.4 'Bad character evidence'. It will also be covered in CKP in Knowledge of interviewing suspects in relation to priority and volume investigations within a policing context Here we have provided a simple overview of BCE to the extent which is relevant to the trainee officer. The CPS website provides information on bad character evidence and the College of Policing Authorised Professional Practice website also contains further information (under the heading *Prosecution and case management*).

24.3 The Criminal Procedure and Investigations Act 1996

The Criminal Procedure and Investigations Act 1996 (CPIA) requires investigators to provide a list of unused material to the prosecutor, who will then consider what material might need to be disclosed to the defence out of fairness. As already indicated above, the CPIA is seen by some as something that only comes into play *after* an investigation is complete. Seen from this perspective, it does not seem to require any attention until the very end of an investigation. But in fact, the CPIA and its associated codes require exactly the opposite.

The definition of a criminal investigation in s 22 (and honed by the Code of Practice), makes it clear that responsibilities and duties apply right from the very start of a criminal investigation. Relevant material (any evidence that might be pertinent, see 24.3.1) must be recorded and retained, and lines of enquiry that might exonerate a suspect must also be pursued. Subtly, the Act and Codes ensure a shift towards a truth-seeking investigation, rather than one that is merely trying to prove the guilt of a suspect. The CPIA should be seen as a set of legal responsibilities that run through an investigation from the moment it begins. If an investigation was a stick of rock, you should be able to cut it open, and see CPIA at its heart, running all the way through it. In major crime investigations particularly, a disclosure officer and other staff are appointed at the earliest stage to ensure that all relevant material is dealt with in the correct fashion.

Some of this relevant material will be used as evidence for the prosecution case. Any unused material is then revealed to the CPS who then decide which parts of the revealed information should be disclosed to the defence. You should note that 'revealing to the CPS' and 'disclosing to the defence' are both often (confusingly) referred to as 'disclosure'. These matters are covered during initial police training as part of the IPLDP module LPG 1.7, and in a number of Diploma in Policing assessed units, notably the unit 'Handle information and intelligence that can support law enforcement' and the Certificate in Knowledge of Policing unit 'Knowledge of handling information and intelligence'. The information presented here is drawn from the CPIA and its associated Code of Practice, and the Disclosure Manual (CPS, 2006).

Some officers regard revelation to the prosecutor and disclosure to the defence as a process that both confuses the courts and facilitates the work of the defence. However, investigations need to be conducted as a search for the truth, and police investigators are obliged to search for evidence which will not only point to guilt, but also to innocence. It could be said that disclosure helps create a 'level playing field' because the prosecution has access to significant professional services and capabilities for producing evidence for the prosecution, while the defence case is sometimes constructed by only one person, the defence solicitor.

To illustrate the importance of this topic, imagine a case in a local magistrates' court. The prosecution counsel opens the case by outlining the circumstances of a major public disturbance in a town centre, witnessed by a number of people. Officers from the nearby police station and surrounding areas had attended and a woman was arrested. The arresting officer consequently provided a statement regarding the arrest, and further witnesses provided statements which provided good evidence of an assault by the defendant. In court, one of the witnesses gives evidence for the prosecution, and is then cross-examined by the defence counsel. Next, the arresting officer (AO) takes the witness stand and the prosecution asks him to outline the evidence of the arrest. After this has been done, the defence counsel rises, and says:

> **Defence**: Officer, I have only two questions for you…we will hear shortly from my client that there were several other police officers at the scene of the alleged assault. Who were these other officers and why are they not giving evidence today?
>
> **AO**: There were approximately ten officers at the scene; I do not know their names as they came from a neighbouring police area.
>
> **Defence**: Officer, the last witness has told this court that, when you arrived at the location, you had a conversation with him about what actually happened. Where are your notes of that conversation?
>
> **AO**: I have no record of the conversation; I remembered the name and address and then a statement was taken later.

The defendant now takes the stand and tells the court the reason for the assault was self-defence and that the arresting officer was completely wrong about how drunk she was. The defence counsel asks his client if there is anyone who can corroborate this, and she replies that, if the other police officers and witnesses had been at court, they would be able to confirm her account. The focus of the defence lawyer has now switched from what his client actually did at the scene (which is what you are probably thinking is the most important issue), to examining whether the police officer had kept proper records of the events, including whether the identity of the other police officers present had been noted. The defence applies to stay the proceedings on the basis that his client is being deprived of the right to a fair trial under Sch 1, Art 6 to the Human Rights Act 1998 (see 5.4), stating that the prosecution have effectively prevented their access to a number of witnesses who are crucial to their client's defence. Alternatively they might apply for a stay of proceedings on the grounds of an abuse of process. The magistrates retire to deliberate.

Whether the application would have been successful or not in this imaginary case is irrelevant here. The point is that a lot of time and effort can be wasted if important information is not recorded, and that cases can be lost as a consequence.

TASK 1 What sort of information could the arresting officer have recorded in relation to this case?

24.3.1 Relevant material

Material is said to be relevant when it has a bearing on any offence under investigation or any person being investigated, or on the surrounding circumstances of the case. 'Material' is any information and objects obtained in the course of a criminal investigation, and includes written materials, videotapes, and information given orally.

In general terms, all relevant material obtained or generated during the course of an investigation must be recorded and retained, even if it is not subsequently used by the prosecution. If it is not recorded (or is recorded incorrectly), or is not retained then it is 'lost' to the defence, and hence has not been properly shared with them through the CPS. This could be a serious loophole that can be exploited by the defence as illustrated at the start of 24.3. The responsibility to record and retain relevant material does not relate just to prosecution material, but also to material which might assist the defence. As an example, imagine that CCTV recordings of an incident involving assault at a nightclub in the centre of a town have been collected. If the recording showed the suspect talking to a bouncer outside the club, this could be an alibi for the suspect and the material would be relevant. It may be difficult though to decide whether materials are in fact relevant, because the defence strategy cannot be predicted in advance.

It is sometimes necessary to liaise with other organizations or individuals when building a case file. Communication for this purpose should be done taking into account the circumstances under which the information is shared. There are instances where there is a statutory obligation to share information (for example, under a freedom of information request). In other situations there may be a statutory power to share information, but not an obligation. Any statutory purpose for sharing the information must be identified, and if there is none, the risk of sharing the information must be assessed. This will take into account the source of the information and the possibility of its further dissemination, the common law duty of confidentiality, and possible breaches of the Human Rights Act 1998 and the Data Protection Act 1998. Police forces often have Information Sharing Agreements (ISAs) that help to streamline the exchange of information.

Any sharing of personal information (eg medical information, or religious or political beliefs) must be deemed necessary for the purpose for which is being shared (that is, it must not be shared out of mere curiosity or interest). The information must be accurate, judged on its own merits, and decided on a case-by-case basis, and its relevance should be clearly explained. The College of Policing document *Information management: Sharing police information* (available online) provides further details and explanations.

24.3.2 Record, Retain, and Reveal

The officer in charge of the investigation is responsible for ensuring that relevant material is recorded in a durable or retrievable form. This could be in writing, on tape, or on a computer drive. The record should be made when received or as soon as possible afterwards. The contents of any material (eg a recording) deemed not relevant should be summarized before discarding the material.

The following is a list of material which is routinely recorded and retained, as described in para 5.4 of the CPIA Code of Practice:

- **Crime reports** (including crime report forms, relevant parts of incident report books, and officers' PNBs).
- **Custody records.**
- Records derived from **tapes of telephone messages** (eg 999 and 112 calls) containing descriptions of an alleged offence or offender.
- Final versions of **witness statements** (and draft versions, where their content differs from the final version), including any exhibits mentioned (unless they have been returned to their owner, on the understanding that they will be produced in court if required).
- **Interview records** (written, audio or video records, of interviews with actual or potential witnesses or suspects).
- **Communications between the police and experts** such as forensic scientists, reports of work carried out by experts, and schedules of scientific material prepared by the expert for the investigator, for the purposes of criminal proceedings.
- Records of the **first description of a suspect** by each potential witness who purports to identify or describe the suspect, whether or not the description differs from subsequent descriptions by that or other witnesses.
- Any material casting **doubt** on the reliability of a witness.

There is a particularly important point concerning potential witnesses who the police know about but have not interviewed. In the case of *R v Heggart and Heggart* (November 2000 (CA)), it was determined that the courts should assume that any evidence from uninterviewed witnesses would either undermine the prosecution case or assist the defence case. Therefore, a record should be made of any witness details and what they observed in relation to the incident at the scene. There is, however, a notion of proportionality here: there would be no expectation to record the details of all 25,000 spectators at a large football match.

Material relevant to an investigation must be retained for a certain period of time. The length of time varies, depending for example on whether the case continues to court, the outcome, and the length of sentence following conviction (see para 5.8 of the CPIA Code for more detail). Some of the relevant material will be exhibited as part of the prosecution case, but some will not. This 'unused material' will be 'revealed' to the CPS who will then make decisions regarding disclosure to the defence (see 24.3.3).

24.3.3 Disclosure

Disclosure is providing the defence with copies of, or access to, any material which might reasonably be considered capable of undermining the case for the prosecution against the accused, or of assisting the case for the accused, and which has not previously been disclosed. The CPS decide on what should be disclosed and usually the police disclose it when the decision has been made. In routine and minor cases, the arresting officer or the case officer will also be the disclosure officer. In more serious cases the disclosure officer is a specific and dedicated specialist role, and will not necessarily be a police officer.

The forms used for disclosure are MG6 B, C, D, and E (see 27.4.2 on MG forms). The disclosure officer ensures that copies of these forms are provided to the CPS which reviews them and decides what else should be disclosed and when. Some of the more sensitive information revealed to the CPS will not be disclosed, such as personal details of a CHIS (see 23.3). The police will then disclose the selected items to the defence.

TASK 2

1. Reference is made earlier to material that is relevant but will not be used as evidence. In relation to the disclosure process, what is the term for this material?
2. Who is responsible for examining the records created during the investigation with a view to revealing the material to the prosecutor?
3. Who makes the decision regarding what unused material is actually disclosed to the defence?

The failure to disclose certain information led to the convictions of 20 appellants being quashed in the high-profile case of *R v Barkshire and others* ([2011] EWCA Crim 1885). The appellants had been convicted of conspiracy to commit aggravated trespass in preparation for protests against climate change at a power station at Ratcliffe-on-Soar. The prosecution failed, amongst other things, to disclose the action of an undercover police officer who had infiltrated the group and could have been seen to be inciting the events himself. The convictions of a further 29 appellants in the case of *R v Bard (Theo)* ([2014] EWCA Crim 463) involving the same police officer were also quashed.

24.4 The Investigation Stage by Stage

The response to priority and volume crimes involves many different police staff, from call handlers to trained investigators. The majority of incidents attended by members of the police family are usually dealt with by the first attending officer (FAO). In many circumstances he/she may, in the end, be the only investigator.

The quality of an investigation and the chances of a successful prosecution are enhanced by actions taken early on in the investigation. These actions include locating, gathering, and retaining material, and making an initial report. Call handlers, public-facing support staff, and police officers are all obliged to record, retain, and reveal information to the investigating officer or disclosure officer, and must follow the specified procedures described for Management of Police Information (see 6.8.2) and in the CPIA and its associated Code of Practice (see 24.3). If other investigators are subsequently involved they should not underestimate the potential benefits of questioning and gathering evidence from the person reporting the crime and from the person who received and wrote the initial report.

Some of what follows is an interpretation of the NPIA/ACPO 2009 document *Practice Advice on the Management of Priority and Volume Crime (The Volume Crime Management Model)*, 2nd edn (NPIA/ACPO, 2009), see this document for further detail and APP relating to investigations. We have attempted to describe the procedures adopted in a 'typical' police force, and present the investigation of priority and volume crime as a series of separate activities (for simplicity) but in practice they are more likely to overlap and merge into a single process. The various activities described here will not all necessarily feature in any particular investigation, or in the precise order implied.

Investigation and Prosecution

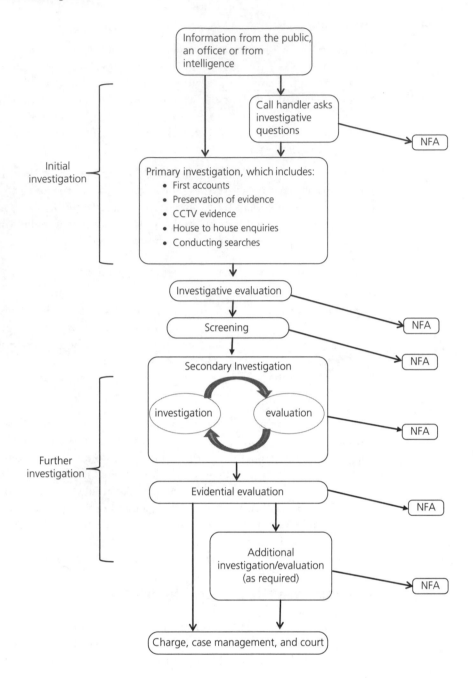

At any stage of the investigation it might become clear that it is necessary to arrest the suspect. Suspect management is an important part of any investigation (see 24.4.3.1). It could also become clear that the case will have to be filed as undetected, or that no further action is required (NFA).

Trainee police officers will be involved in both the primary and secondary investigations into priority and volume crimes during their second year of initial training (or earlier in some forces). The actions outlined here could provide evidence of competence at PIP Level 1 (see 7.5).

24.4.1 Initial investigation

Initial investigation covers a wide range of activities involving police officers and other policing staff. Investigating begins at the very moment a police officer arrives at an incident or a call handler answers a call from a member of the public. An investigation can be instigated proactively as a consequence, for example of research and development of intelligence gathering, or reactively when new information becomes available from sources such as:

* the general public;
* partnership agency reports;
* intelligence derived from other crimes or new information received about an old crime leading to a subsequent re-investigation;
* self-generated police actions, for example discovering a cannabis factory through the use of a thermal imaging camera.

24.4.1.1 Call handling as initial investigation

Many investigations start when a member of the public calls the police or emergency services. Call handlers play a key role in the initial investigation and screening, for example their guidance to a caller may help preserve forensic material at a scene. Their questions are part of an initial investigation and the appropriate response can then be determined. Call handlers collect a large amount of information and may use scripts or computer dropdown menus to help ensure all relevant information is gathered.

Depending on the BCU deployment policy, officers may be dispatched to a location (there may be a dedicated team of officers for attending volume crime scenes). If immediate attendance is not required the caller will probably be transferred to a 'crime bureau' where details of the incident will be considered and recorded. This may be the end of the investigation for that incident, unless any further information comes to light to necessitate further investigation.

24.4.1.2 Primary investigation

Police officers may be deployed to a location based upon the decisions of the call handlers, or may encounter an incident whilst on patrol. An officer's initial appraisal of the situation and a few preliminary questions will often be sufficient to determine whether any persons present could reasonably be suspected to have been involved in a criminal offence. The answers to these questions comprise the 'first account', sometimes referred to as an initial account, and would aim to establish:

- the type of alleged offence;
- the approximate time of the alleged offence;
- the scene of the alleged offence—only sufficient general knowledge to understand what might be said in an interview; and
- how the alleged offence came to the notice of the police.

A police officer who is trying to discover whether, or by whom, an offence has been committed can question any person from whom useful information might be obtained (PACE Code A, Note 1). If there are reasonable grounds for suspecting that the person has been involved in a criminal offence then a caution must be given before asking any further questions (see 10.3 on cautions). Any conversation that takes place with a suspect before a caution is given should be summarized in a PNB entry, as it could be used in court. Remember that once a suspect has been arrested he/she cannot be interviewed about the offence except at a police station (Code C, para 11.1) unless the delay would irretrievably hinder the investigation (see 10.8.6).

In the majority of cases, the most beneficial way of using witness evidence is to ask the witness in the presence and hearing of the suspect(s) to explain what he/she saw or heard. Care must be taken in cases of domestic abuse or sexual offences where the victim might be reluctant to speak in front of the suspected abuser (see 13.6 and 17.1). This will be a judgement call by the officer, based upon the circumstances of the case. The answers given by a witness should be recorded word for word in a PNB entry or equivalent. The record could later be used as evidence in court as part of an officer's duty statement (see 10.12 on duty statements, and 27.5.3.2 on using a PNB in court).

First accounts from witnesses can also provide the information required for planning an interview with the suspect, or for constructing a 'handover pack' for other officers to conduct the interviews (see Chapter 25 on interviews and 10.14 on handover procedures). A first account can also be compared with an account given under oath verbally at court, and any inconsistencies between the two accounts would require an explanation from the witness.

Information about all the witnesses, and any actions, statements, comments, or other relevant material (see 24.3) must be recorded, ensuring compliance with the CPIA. A case could be undermined in court if the defence asked a police officer about something a witness had said and the officer had no record of it (see 27.5.3). If for some reason a PNB record cannot be made, the record can be made separately, on a clip board for example. The use of the PNB and making PNB entries is covered in 10.2.

Written police records of victim and witness early accounts may be admissible as evidence (s 116 of the Criminal Justice Act 2003). This may be necessary if a witness or a victim cannot appear in court in person for example if he/she is seriously ill, or cannot be found, or is unwilling to give evidence. The police records of such accounts must be recorded verbatim. In addition a victim might tell a third party about the events in relation to the offence, and this 'hearsay' is potentially admissible as evidence in court (see 27.5.2.3). A record must be made of the names and addresses of any other people the victim has told about the incident so these can be followed up. Concerning the account from the third party, it is vital that a verbatim PNB record is made if the police record is to be admissible in court.

In addition to obtaining first accounts, other actions are required as shown in the table. These actions would generally be taken during the 'golden hour' or as 'fast track actions' (see 11.2.4). A trainee police officer could be involved in any of the actions listed here. The National Decision Model (see 6.5.2) would be used to help decide what actions to take. There will probably be a need to prioritize those early actions that can be realistically pursued at the time.

Taking a report of a crime	All actions taken to trace witnesses and suspects should be recorded. A list should be made of any other enquiries that have been made, or could be made
The crime scene	The scene should be preserved for the CSI, to avoid contamination. This might require a cordon (see 11.2) for a large or serious crime scene
CCTV evidence	The location of cameras that could have recorded the incident should be recorded (for CPIA purposes and evidence recovery). The CCTV hard copy should be preserved, recovered, and exhibited where possible (see 24.4.1.3)
Managing witnesses	First accounts must be recorded, including full names and addresses. These accounts might suggest further potential witnesses, and these should be recorded in full
House-to-house enquiries	These are likely to concern witnesses or potential witnesses. A record should be made of all persons spoken to, and of any absent potential witnesses (for a future visit). The content of the discussions should be carefully noted, including any refusal to reply
Other evidence	Photographs, plans, and maps might suggest opportunities for obtaining forensic evidence. All documents, captured texts, images, or sequences from electronic devices should be retained
Taking statements	Statements should be obtained as a matter of urgency where violence has occurred (or been threatened), where a suspect has been detained, or if witness contamination must be avoided (eg where a description of a person is relevant)
Recording actions taken	Before going off duty, full details of all actions taken must be recorded, as handwritten PNB entries or electronic entries (depending on the circumstances)

(Adapted from *Practice Advice on The Management of Priority and Volume Crime (The Volume Crime Management Model*, 2nd edn (NPIA/ACPO, 2009))

With regard to possible witnesses, any people in the vicinity who were not involved or who did not see what happened should be eliminated from the enquiry. Careful judgement is needed to establish who was a material witness to the event (who actually saw it) and who was not. This is not as easy as it sounds because people can become over excited when they think they have witnessed a crime and will be keen to provide their (possibly derivative) account. Note, however, that an effective response to supporting survivors, victims, and witnesses will improve the quality of investigation, by maximizing the availability of evidence (and it will also help increase public confidence in the police).

The aim would be to complete all the actions listed in the table so that the information can be pieced together. It is important to realize that a primary investigation is an integral part of the whole investigation (eg as a precursor to an evidential evaluation and possible secondary investigation) which may lead to prosecution; the primary investigation is not simply a collection of information concerning an alleged crime. The primary investigator produces a crime report which is sent to the principal screener or in some forces links directly with the crime bureau to provide information for the crime report. It is important that the FAO is thorough in considering all of these initial actions, so that a professional product is either handed to an investigator who may take the investigation further, or it is filed with no further investigation necessary.

24.4.1.3 Obtaining CCTV evidence

CCTV evidence can also form part of a primary investigation. It can be used to establish the sequence of events and to provide evidence, including supporting the defence case. Relevant material would include footage that showed the suspects were near to the relevant vicinity around the time the crime was committed. ACPO has produced Practice Advice on the use of CCTV in Criminal Investigations, available online; we summarize the key points here.

Ideally CCTV footage should be obtained early on during the 'golden hour' to avoid it being lost, but it is sometimes difficult to obtain straight away. In theory, any officer could seize and exhibit CCTV evidence but when and who depends on the circumstances. A trainee officer could ensure that the recording system is safe and secure before referring the matter to his/her supervisor; specialist services might be required.

The storage format and technical requirements for recovering recordings should be established before accessing the equipment. If the footage contains relevant material, it should be seized in accordance with the rules about the preservation of evidence (see 11.2.6 on exhibits and 24.3.1 on relevant material). For any further viewings, working copies must be made.

Often the images are stored on a disc, and taking away the machine (or its hard drive) is not always possible. For copying digital storage media footage, ACPO's four principles must be followed (see 21.4). The ACPO Good Practice Guide for Digital Evidence, Version 5 (available online) makes it clear that seized hard drives should be placed in anti-static bags, tough paper bags, tamper evident cardboard packaging, or wrapped in paper and placed in aerated plastic bags.

In 2014, the Information Commissioner's Office (ICO) produced an updated Code of Practice for the use of surveillance cameras and personal information, and this is complementary to the surveillance camera Code of Practice issued in 2013. Businesses need to comply with certain regulations to legitimately utilize any of these devices, and it is useful for trainee officers to know about these, and about the rights of individuals to find out about what information is held about them.

24.4.2 Investigative evaluation and screening

As part of a first formal investigative evaluation the crime will be screened to decide if it should be classed as mandatory, priority, or non-priority. This process will also assess the quality of the initial and primary investigation, and ensure that all evidence-gathering opportunities are exploited (for the current incident and for other related incidents). A principal screener will normally be an experienced police officer with investigative skills at PIP Level 2 or above. (The exact role title can vary from force to force, but it may also be undertaken by Crime Management Unit staff.)

Non-volume serious crimes such as homicide and rape will be classed as mandatory and will certainly be assigned for secondary investigation. The probable 'solvability' of priority and/or non-priority crimes will also be assessed, and a secondary investigation will be allocated for any crimes which are part of a series, involve a named suspect, or for which there is good evidence or credible intelligence linked to a named offender. To determine the future direction of the investigation, APP suggests that four important questions need to be asked: What is known? What is not known? What are the consistencies? What are the conflicts? These will help determine whether the investigation needs to be filed with no further action because no leads exist and little else can be done, or whether it needs to be handed on for further investigation because more lines of enquiry exist and/or suspects might be known.

In a complicated or lengthy investigation there will need to be a number of staged investigative evaluations to maintain focus. These will form part of an on-going secondary investigation, and will be conducted by the officer leading the investigation. You can see the cyclical nature of the process of investigative evaluation in the flow chart above. There will be further investigation, and then investigative evaluation and so on until the case is ready to be subjected to some form of evidential evaluation (assuming a suspect has been arrested at this stage). If the investigation does not uncover a suspect despite lengthy enquiries, it may be filed. Each evaluation should be recorded so that decisions can be reviewed throughout the investigation.

The VCMM makes it clear that, as a minimum, an investigation plan, sometimes part of a 'handover package' (see 10.14), should be prepared for any secondary investigation. If the decision is not to investigate any further then the crime report is filed ('finalized') as NFA (no further action) and the reasons for the decision are recorded. Much of this process has received criticism, as there are indications that a significant number of cases are screened out at an early stage, and receive little investigative attention. Sir Peter Fahey stated that Greater Manchester Police could only investigate four out of every ten cases reported due to lack of resources and strategic priorities (*The Daily Telegraph*, 4 September 2013). However, as we explain in 24.4.1, there is always some sort of investigation before any decision to file a case is made.

The principle screener can allocate secondary investigations to a variety of investigators performing different roles. These could be patrol officers, neighborhood officers, volume crime investigators working as part of a volume crime investigation team, or officers on specialist squads (eg a burglary squad). Depending upon individual force protocols, a trainee officer might be allocated particular volume crimes to investigate as lead investigator, such as domestic abuse, hate crime, and public order offences.

24.4.3 Further investigation

Once allocated a crime to investigate, officers will need to decide upon what other actions and strategies they will use to progress the investigation. Investigative actions are any activities that could lead to uncovering important facts, preserve relevant material, or lead to a resolution to the case (APP, 2015). The investigation plan from the principle screener will help direct any secondary investigation and will identify relevant lines of enquiry. These may be, for instance, to trace witnesses, identify a victim, or to protect scenes. The plan will set out the minimum enquiries expected, but for other investigative strategies the investigator has some discretion for a particular case. Any fast-track actions may have already been completed in the initial and primary investigation phase before being allocated to an investigator. The investigator should consider the possible strategies and actions that could be used and then select the appropriate way forward for the particular investigation. In serious cases the police might for example decide to employ a media strategy to ask the public for assistance with a challenging investigation. This would not be necessary in a shoplifting case where the offender has been caught in the act and arrested immediately in possession of the stolen goods. Sometimes in these less serious cases, where a person is 'caught on camera' committing minor crime but has not yet been caught by police, the police might publish a 'rogues gallery' to try to find out who the suspect is. This would depend upon the individual facts of a case.

Strategies that can be employed are numerous. They include activities such as house-to-house enquiries, the use of the media, searching, forensic retrieval, e-fit circulation, statements from witnesses with full descriptions, capturing text or other electronically generated data, and interviewing. Each strategy employed must be carefully planned and executed, and APP is a very good place to start when considering how to implement each one. In addition, whether a person to be interviewed by the police is a witness, a victim or a potential witness or victim, he/she is entitled to be treated fairly and with dignity. As a result, in any interaction, a person's individual needs must be considered. For instance, the person could be a vulnerable witness (see 24.2.4) who would require some assistance when providing evidence to the police, or a vulnerable suspect who would need an appropriate adult, family member and/or solicitor present when interviewed at a police station. The person may have other special requirements, for example he/she may speak a different language (and would therefore need the services of an interpreter), or have physical disabilities that would require assistance from a specialist adviser. Not only does this professional approach treat people in an appropriate manner, it also ensures that any evidence obtained is not tainted by poor practice.

The guidance in APP distinguishes between actions that are undertaken generally in order to trawl for information (for instance house-to-house enquiries) and those with a specific aim in mind (ie to trace a suspect). Each investigator has discretion as to which strategies to utilize in the current investigation. The choices made concerning actions and strategies should be recorded as the investigation progresses.

As more evidence is gathered the investigator will need to conduct further investigative evaluations (see 24.4.2). This might lead to further lines of enquiry, the employment of other investigative strategies, a decision to arrest, or a decision to proceed no further with the investigation. Once a potential suspect is identified, the investigation will move into the suspect management phase (see 24.4.3.1). Both the VCMM and APP consider this in detail as it is a key part of any investigation. Arrest strategies are discussed in detail, as well as search strategies and interview strategies. Trainee officers should seek advice from peers and supervisors if in any doubt about to how to progress the suspect management phase of an investigation.

24.4.3.1 Suspect management

Once a suspect has been identified, a range of options will need to be explored. If the suspect has not already been arrested, consideration would need to be given to arrest, search, and seizure of evidence, and the appropriate timings for each action. The lawfulness of and necessity for any arrest would need to be considered. It may not be as simple as going to arrest someone at his/her home. First, consideration needs to be given to what is known about the suspect and his/her criminal history, for example has he/she been violent to police officers in the past? Careful planning would then be required in relation to safely effecting an arrest. Additionally, what if he/she is not at home when officers attend? How do you deal with the issue of the suspect being potentially alerted to the fact that you have called to speak to him/her? What if he/she either decides to go into hiding, or to dispose of evidence? Consideration would need to be given to an application for a search warrant from local magistrates so that that you attend with a power to effect entry to property even if the suspect is not at home (see 9.7). That way any potential evidence could be secured despite his/her absence. Whether this is necessary, proportionate and legal is a key consideration for the investigator, and this requires careful thought and planning. Consideration will also need to be given to the police station(s) where the suspect(s) will be taken following arrest, particularly if a number of suspects are to be arrested at the same time.

Once a suspect is in custody, key considerations include the medical condition of the suspect, whether any 'bad character' exists, whether any identification procedures are applicable, further searches of premises, when to interview, who is to conduct the interviews, and the exact nature of the interview strategy (see 10.8 on detainees and Chapter 25 on interviewing). Whilst 'no further action' is a potential outcome of an investigation, there are many criminal justice methods of disposal, ranging from charge to formal caution, to fixed penalty notice (see 10.13). If a charge is advised (see 27.3), the investigation then moves into the case management phase (see 27.4).

24.4.3.2 Evidential evaluation

If the investigation has progressed through secondary investigation, then a further evaluation is necessary. Again this will be undertaken by the officer in charge of the investigation. This is called an evidential evaluation, and considers whether there is sufficient evidence to allow for a criminal justice disposal, or whether no further action can be taken because all leads have yielded no further evidence. The evaluation will consider the strengths and weaknesses of the case, and whether there is (in the opinion of the police) sufficient evidence to charge. The evidential evaluation stage never takes place in a vacuum—investigators will liaise with peers, supervisors, case review officers or even evidence review officers (EROs) to consider whether there is enough evidential material to place before the CPS for a charging decision, or whether the case should be filed pending further evidence coming to light. If the CPS are consulted, investigators will usually submit an advice file (MG3) for a decision on disposal. The CPS may provide advice about evidential gaps (see also 24.4.4) that would need filling before a suspect could be charged, so an investigator can seek that evidence before any final decisions are made. For more on CPS advice and charging, see 27.3.

24.4.4 Gap analysis

Allied to the concept of the investigative mindset, and particularly to the principle of investigative and evidential 'evaluation', is the notion of a 'gap analysis'. This is the periodic analysis of material gathered during an investigation in order to identify and then fill any gaps in investigative and evidential knowledge. It is often referred to as the '5WH' approach; the 'Who? What? When? Where? Why? and How?' of the alleged offence. Investigators are encouraged to utilize this when considering the progress of their enquiries, thereby conducting a more methodical and thorough investigation.

Gap in Knowledge	Explanation
Who?	The identities of witnesses, suspects, victims, etc
What?	The sequence of events leading up to, during, and after an alleged offence
When?	The time(s) of events linked with the alleged offence
Where?	The locations linked with the alleged offences
Why?	Motivation—why this place, this time, this alleged victim?
How?	The means of conducting the alleged offence

24.5 Trainee Officers and Investigations

Trainee police officers may be directly involved in undertaking criminal investigation, and this will provide many opportunities for collecting evidence for the Diploma in Policing assessed units. The evidence could include PNB entries and witness statements. Trainee officers will be expected to attain PIP level 1 status which will allow them to 'own' investigations into priority and volume crime offences. They would not take charge of investigations into more serious crimes, but could be present as a first attending officer (FAO). So all trainees need to understand all the principles discussed here, so they could deal competently with any crime incident until other support arrives, or even take ownership of less serious volume crime investigations.

The IPLDP 'Crime Investigation Model' may be used during Phases 3 and 4 of initial police training. It consists of seven stages: instigation, initial response, investigative assessment, suspect management, evidence assessment, charge and post-charge activity, and finally court (Home Office, 2004). These inevitably relate to the various stages of investigation covered in 24.4 (although the names of the stages employ slightly different wording). In other chapters we examine many aspects of the IPLDP's seven stages and we discuss most of the remaining ones here.

Students undertaking the Certificate in Knowledge of Policing (see 7.2.1 and 7.3) will study the underpinning knowledge required to 'conduct priority and volume investigations' and may also be assessed when undertaking an investigation scenario (eg a simulated burglary).

The links between investigative activities and NOS Units/QCF Diploma Units

Example of activity	Linked NOS units	Linked QCF Diploma unit(s)
Control room instruction, incident log, etc	BE2	Support victims, witnesses, and vulnerable people
Risk assessment, recording the incident, etc	BE2, CJ101, CK1, CK2, CD1	Support victims, witnesses, and vulnerable people. Interview victims and witnesses in relation to priority and volume investigations
Provide immediate support to victims, etc	CI101, 4G4	Support victims, witnesses, and vulnerable people
CPIA 1996, protecting the scene, minimizing contamination, etc	CD1	Provide an initial response to policing incidents
Identify and question witnesses, CCTV, etc	CI101	Conduct priority and volume investigations
Force intelligence reports, CHIS, etc	CI101	Conduct priority and volume investigations
Initial lines of enquiry, description, names, etc	CI101	Conduct priority and volume investigations
PNC, NDNAD	CI101	Conduct priority and volume investigations
Arrest strategy, PACE Act 1984/SOCPA 2005 powers of arrest, etc	CD5	Use police powers to deal with suspects
Legal authority, seizure of items, proportionality, etc	DA5, DA6	Conduct police searches
PEACE, interview strategy, etc	CJ101, CJ201	Interview victims and witnesses in relation to priority and volume investigation. Interview suspects in relation to priority and volume investigations
CPS charging standards, prepare case files, evaluate investigation, etc	DA5, DA6, 2G4	Handle information and intelligence that can support law enforcement

(Based on Home Office, 2005d and NPIA, 2010a)

24.6 Answers to Tasks

TASK 1 A police officer attending an incident is a potential witness for both the prosecution and the defence. If he/she talks to witnesses or potential witnesses, their details and what they observed in relation to the incident should be recorded. If there are groups of people milling around, the officer might decide to stay in the area in case of any further trouble; such observations and any decision taken should be recorded. In the case of an arrest, any assistance provided to an arresting officer should be recorded. On the other hand, if it is clear that his/her colleagues require no further assistance, this should also be recorded as a PNB entry.

TASK 2

1. Unused material.
2. A disclosure officer is responsible for examining the records created during the investigation (and any criminal proceedings arising from the investigation). He/she will also complete the appropriate forms (MG6 series) to reveal relevant material to the prosecutor.
3. The prosecutor.

25 | Investigative Interviewing

25.1 Introduction

As a crime investigator our fundamental task is to recreate a moment in time, without the aid of a time machine, to disprove or prove that a crime has been committed. Central to this process is the collection, collation, and evaluation of many differing categories of information. Stewart (1985, p 1) correctly observed that, 'Information is the lifeblood of criminal investigation and it is the ability of investigators to obtain useful and accurate information from witnesses and victims of crime that is crucial to effective law enforcement'.

Interviewing witnesses, victims, and suspects is a key part of the police investigation process, and a 'frontline' police officer will carry out an interview nearly every day. The modern approach to police interviewing in the UK is to see the interview as a means of seeking to establish the truth. This sounds obvious but it does in fact represent a marked change in emphasis from the past: it is no longer simply a case of working through a list of 'points to prove'. Instead, interviewing is now much more of an information gathering 'inquisitorial approach' (see 5.1) and the term *investigative* should be firmly in the mind of the officer, who should remember that 'the interview is a central part of my investigation and can significantly affect the outcomes'. In the past (particularly in the 1970s and 1980s) the police were sometimes accused of using oppressive techniques for obtaining a confession, and there were a number of notorious miscarriages of justice where innocent people were wrongly convicted or the guilty were incorrectly acquitted.

The advent of the PACE Act 1984 represented a major step forward, as for the first time the police were obliged to routinely audio-record interviews. There were many benefits to this (both legally and ethically), but the interviews also provided a rich source of data to be examined by researchers, particularly psychologists and criminologists. They found there were a number of areas of poor practice in interviewing. An influential report (Baldwin, 1992, p 34) notes that when interviewing suspects the main weaknesses were 'a lack of preparation, a general ineptitude, poor technique, an assumption of guilt, unduly repetitive, persistent or laboured questioning, a failure to establish the relevant facts and the exertion of too much pressure'. This and other reports led to the development of a standardized approach to interviewing, and more importantly, to the adoption of the PEACE model, and increased standardization of interview training across the whole of England and Wales.

The PEACE model (see 25.3 onwards) was a reaction to the perceived shortcomings in police interviewing. However, a remarkably high proportion of suspects still confess to crime during the interview process. For example, Gudjonnson *et al* observed in 2004 that about 60 per cent of suspects in England confessed to the police during interviewing, and that this proportion had remained relatively constant for the previous 25 years (Gudjonnson *et al*, 2004). The precise reasons for this are unclear.

In this chapter we will examine investigative interviewing processes and procedures in depth, and the recommended methods for conducting interviews. The IPLDP covers this in detail, and trainee officers will also practise interviewing procedures and techniques, including how to follow the relevant codes and legislation. The information provided here is also relevant to the 'Investigation and interview' heading in the Learning Diary (Phase 3). If you are on a pre-join course at a university, college, or with a private training provider (see 7.2.1) you might have the opportunity to explore some more of the underpinning theory and research involved in police interviewing—for example, in relation to memory enhancement, lying and deception, and false confessions. The Certificate in Knowledge of Policing has two assessed units that are relevant: 'Knowledge of interviewing suspects in relation to priority and volume investigations within a policing context' and 'Knowledge of interviewing victims and witnesses in relation to priority and volume investigations'. The College of Policing published Authorised Professional Practice covering 'investigative interviewing' in 2013 and further information and guidance from the CoP can be found on their website.

25.2   Key Principles for Interviewing

In order to establish an ethical framework to police interviewing some general principles have been adopted by the police service. These principles apply to all interviews, and assist with effective planning and implementation. Home Office Circular 2/1992 on investigative interviewing outlines the following seven principles:

1. The role of investigative interviewing is to **obtain accurate and reliable information** from suspects, witnesses, and victims in order to discover the truth about matters under police investigation.
2. Investigative interviewing should be approached with an **open mind**.
3. Information obtained from the person who is being interviewed should always be **tested** against what the interviewing officer already knows or what can reasonably be established. When questioning anyone, a police officer must act fairly in the circumstances of each individual case.
4. **The police officer is not bound to accept the first answer given**. Questioning is not unfair merely because it is persistent. Even when a suspect exercises the right of silence, the police still have a right to put questions.
5. When conducting an interview, **police officers are free to ask questions** in order to establish the truth: except for interviews with child victims of sexual or violent abuse which are to be used in criminal proceedings, they are not constrained by the rules applied to lawyers in court.
6. Vulnerable people, whether victims, witnesses, or suspects, must be **treated with particular consideration** at all times. The interviewing of victims, witnesses, and suspects is an everyday part of the police role.
7. The interview is the formal means by which vital information and evidence is obtained in relation to incidents. This requires specific skills to obtain this information and evidence in a way that **conforms to the laws of the land**.

(Further details concerning the seven principles may be found on the College of Policing website under the 'Investigative interviewing' Authorised Professional Practice heading.)

In essence an investigative interview should be lawful, in that the information should be obtained in accordance with statute so that it may be usefully admitted in evidence if required. The information should be obtained in an ethical manner, bearing in mind the individual's rights, such as freedom and dignity. The investigative interview should maximize the opportunity to establish detailed information, which can be used to establish the reliability and veracity of the interviewee's account. It should also meet and extend the aims and objectives of the overall investigation. The outcomes of the interview must stand up to judicial review and challenge by the criminal justice system.

The legislation around police interviewing is complex, and here we cover the basics, sufficient for the trainee officer. The following legislation is also important for interviewing:

- ss 76 and 78 of the PACE Act 1984, including provisions under Code C, Code E, and Code F;
- Part III and ss 34, 36, and 37 of the Criminal Justice and Public Order Act 1994 (CJPOA), including 'special warnings' (see 25.5.9);
- the criminal law relating to the offence(s) for which suspects are charged;
- the Human Rights Act 1998 (see 5.4);
- the CPIA 1996; and
- the Youth Justice and Criminal Evidence Act 1999 (especially on 'vulnerable', 'intimidated', and child witnesses).

Other legislation covers specific provisions which we will refer to later, but those noted here are the principal sources governing the legality of what a police officer can do and say during an interview. Legislation such as the PACE Act 1984 and its Codes of Practice have certainly helped to reassure the public, lawyers, academic commentators, and the police themselves that interviewing is now more tightly controlled, more ethical, and often more effective. Of course, simply knowing the law is not enough: applying the law is the key role for a police officer. If mistakes are made through incompetence, poor practice, or acting in 'bad faith' during the interview process, parts of the evidence may be rendered void or inadmissible. This could mean that a guilty person might avoid prosecution and be free to offend again, or an innocent person might be wrongly charged and convicted.

Copies of the PACE Act 1984 and the CJPOA 1994 (available on the www.legislation.gov.uk website) should be to hand while reading this chapter.

25.2.1 Strategic Oversight

Since the recognition of investigative interviewing as a crucial part of the criminal investigation process, and in line with a professionalization agenda, the National Strategic Steering Group on Investigative Interviewing (NSSGII) oversees the development of both witness and suspect interviewing. It aims to develop policies, practices, and procedures that are appropriate for modern investigative activity. Working in conjunction with the NSSGII, each police force now has a force lead on investigative interviewing, and coordinators at both regional and national levels provide advice and guidance to practitioners on current best professional practice. In addition, at the tactical level, trained and qualified interview advisers are available to support colleagues in formulating both suspect and witness strategies. All of this is a far cry from the pre-1990s, when officers conducted interviews with little or no guidance or support, mainly to obtain a confession. This was sometimes to the detriment of major investigations when poor and illegal tactics were exposed at court (see for instance the IRA cases in the 1970s and 1980s, the Maxwell Confait case in the early 1970s, and the George Heron case in the early 1990s).

25.3 What is an Investigative Interview?

Before looking at the PEACE model in more detail we should first attempt to identify what we are trying to achieve. There are a number of definitions of an interview, the one most often quoted by trainee officers is provided in PACE 1984, Code C, para 11.1A. This states that an interview is 'The questioning of a person regarding their involvement or suspected involvement in a criminal offence or offences which, under Code C paragraph 10.1, must be carried out under caution'. However, this definition does not include witnesses, nor does it provide us with any real focus to the process. To maximize the information gathered, we also need to recognize the importance of the key component of an interview, namely the dyadic conversational process. A more useful definition of an interview is that 'An interview is a conversation with a purpose and therefore needs to be appropriately managed' (Shepherd and Kite, 1988).

The common element in all investigative interviews, with a witness, victim, or suspect, is face-to-face communication between two persons. The interviewer must therefore be aware that the conversational process is central to the success of the encounter, and that social skill and appropriate conversational behaviour will affect the outcomes of the interview.

We have all assimilated the norms of conversation through our everyday lives, and have generally learnt to follows these 'rules' without even thinking about it. Consider a recent productive social conversation you have had, face to face with a friend. It is highly likely to have started with saying 'Hello' in some manner that is appropriate to your relationship and status (for example a handshake, high 5, kiss, or hug). After that you will have generally chatted, taking conversational turns, exchanging anecdotes, news, and possibly even gossip. When the conversation started to come to an end you will have used language to indicate this to the other person by saying something like 'Oh, it's been really nice talking...' to see if you are both ready to disengage and depart. If you are both ready to do this you will go through a process of saying 'Goodbye', and again, this will be in a manner appropriate to your relationship and status. Without giving it any thought you will have followed the sequence:

- Greeting;
- Mutual Activity;
- Closure.

An investigative interview is a 'conversation with a purpose' so we cannot approach it in exactly the same manner as a social conversation, but we can model our behaviour on this familiar social model. We can also manage the 'conversation' in accordance with our predefined investigative objectives and overall aims, which are the 'purpose' of the conversation.

Shepherd (2007, p 21) defines the model of conversation management as, Greet, Explain, Mutual Activity and Closure (GEMAC). This is an extremely useful, practical and transferable model that can be used for any investigative interview process, and it could be said that the PEACE model echoes this approach. The GEMAC model provides an investigative interviewer with a framework for decoding the underlying conversational process, and will help establish and develop detail to an extremely high level. The SE3R approach (Shepherd, 2008) is also widely used ('Survey, Extract, Read, Review, Respond'), and this also helps the interviewer to gain a fuller and more detailed understanding of the relevant events.

Police forces in England and Wales use the 'PEACE' approach to interviewing: Planning and Preparation: Engage and Explain; Account, Clarification, and Challenge; Closure; and Evaluation (CoP, 2013q). Each of these elements will be considered in turn, but the detail will depend on whether the interview is with a suspect or a witness. The key points to consider are as follows:

- **the objectives** (what is to be achieved and how: remember, the emphasis is on establishing the truth (see Chapter 24 on investigation));
- **the relevant law** (eg recent stated cases, and intention, effect of drink/drugs on intention, recklessness, etc);
- possible **defences** (eg, statutory defences, reasonableness, mistake, coercion, duress, self-defence);
- possible mitigating and aggravating factors; and
- **pre-interview briefing** (to solicitors or legal representatives: see 25.5.4).

We devote considerable time to looking at the preliminaries, because establishing an appropriate tone, mood, and format for an interview from the very start is beneficial to the overall process. Most interviewees will not know what is happening and may need reassurance; he/she may have never even been in a police station before.

For an evaluation of the use of PEACE by police forces in England and Wales, see Clarke and Milne (2001) and Walsh and Milne (2008). In the latter case the two researchers found particular concerns within the PEACE stages of rapport building, and the lack of summarizing during the interview. Clarke, Milne, and Bull looked at PEACE interviewing again in 2011 and found that further improvement in training was required, particularly in terms of the communication skills of interviewers (Clarke *et al*, 2011). It might be worth thinking about this as you read through the rest of this chapter.

Further information on the history of PEACE together with a detailed explanation is provided in *Investigative Interviewing: the conversation management approach* (Shepherd and Griffiths, 2013).

25.3.1 PEACE—planning and preparation

Many aspects of an interview appear to be merely practical issues, but on closer inspection several of these factors could also influence the whole outcome of the interview, so careful planning is essential. For example, if other officers are to be present this is likely to affect the approach. There is no substitute for careful and detailed planning; every interview is different and every witness, victim, or suspect will behave differently, so interviewers must be prepared for these differences and plan accordingly. The plan should be in writing.

Practical aspects to be covered in the plan include:

- the order of interview if more than one person is to be interviewed;
- who will be present, and the seating plan (how will this affect communication?);
- the time and location;
- the timing of breaks; and
- the recording medium and how the product will be later presented.

For interviews with suspects (see 25.5), there are other practical considerations, such as recording the interview and the PACE requirements for rest and review times. Reference should be made to the PACE Codes of Practice C, E, and F.

As well as covering the practical aspects, the plan should take into account all the topics that need to be covered; these will be the interview objectives, one of which will be selected as the key objective (see 25.3.1.1). The College of Policing APP suggests that a properly conducted 'wants analysis' will help an investigator in formulating objectives. There is a truism in interviewing which is often overlooked: *'If I know what I want to know, I will know when I have been told it'*. At face value this appears obvious but it can be challenging to actually define what you need to 'know' in order to be able to accept or reject an investigative hypothesis. This always requires careful thought, and must be completed prior to the encounter.

An interview plan helps an interviewer keep track of what has been covered and what remains to be explored. SE3R can be used as an *aide memoire* during the interview. It will also help if the accounts from different interviewees contradict each other, or vary significantly from what seem to be the facts. The plan may contain a series of prompts, thereby enhancing topic selection and thoroughness, but these should be used with care to ensure the interviewer appears professional and in control of the interview. Remember that whatever sort of plan is used, the interview plan is relevant material (as set out in the CPIA 1996) and must therefore be retained as a document to be revealed (see 24.3).

Certain information is required about the interviewee in advance, as part of the preparation process, for example:

- Has his/her identity been confirmed? A Livescan and IDENT1 check could be used (see 26.5.4).
- How old is he/she? (Establishing the age of a person is not necessarily a simple process. Some adults will claim to be younger in an attempt to avoid prosecution.)
- Is he/she on the force's intelligence database? Is he/she suspected of other crimes elsewhere or flagged as active or of interest to other police forces or agencies (for instance on the PNC or PND)?
- Is he/she already on bail? Is he/she in breach of bail, an ASBO, or a court order, or wanted for a crime elsewhere?
- Does the interviewee have any medical or mental health conditions to take into consideration?

Normally the same interview team would conduct all the interviews relating to one incident. However, once the arrest and detention procedures are complete, the responsibility for an interview is sometimes handed over to another officer (perhaps from a dedicated unit for prisoner handling). In such circumstances, the interviewing officer will need to be fully briefed so he/she can prepare properly for the interview (see 10.14 on handover procedures). In these situations, SE3R is an invaluable tool to assess, analyse, assimilate and become fully conversant with every detail of a case.

25.3.1.1 Establishing the Aims and Objectives of the Interview

The aim of the investigative interview is to establish a detailed explanation (an account), and to compare it to the material facts that have been established from witness(es) or other evidential sources (for example from CCTV or forensics). For this we will need interview objectives (see 25.3.1.2 for some examples), and one of these should be identified as the key objective.

When we formulate objectives we are defining the parameters of the account to be obtained from an interviewee, and we are seeking to obtain detailed information that can be used to test the reliability and veracity of the account given and of other accounts and evidence. For example, we may have physical evidence from the scene of a road traffic collision in the form of a skid mark left by a motorcycle; this indicates the motorcycle was moving at a high speed. If we obtain witness testimony from the driver of a vehicle overtaken by the motorcycle (indicating a similarly high speed and reckless behaviour), this would put the physical evidence into context and would also help corroborate it. All this information in turn could be used to deconstruct the motorcyclist's account; he states that he was adhering to the rules of the Highway Code. This illustrates how one (or more) interview(s), in this case with a witness, can inform interview(s) with another person (in this case with the suspect).

25.3.1.2 Using questions

Open questions (which normally cannot be answered with a simple yes or no) are preferable, as this invites a fuller, richer response. The interviewer should ensure that the interviewee provides as much detail as possible in his/her own words, as this makes any potential evidence more powerful. The use of leading questions which might cause a person to overstate or understate the truth should be avoided. In a suspect interview, in order to prove the *mens rea* (see 5.3.2) the interviewer might ask an open question, for instance starting with 'explain how you were you feeling when you…?' or 'tell me what you were thinking when you were…?'.

The opening questions of the interview are very important as these tend to set the 'agenda' and tone for the rest of the interview and also, to a certain extent, dictate interviewing tactics. The first questions should reflect the key objective (s) for the interview. For example, imagine that the interview concerns a case where a man is accused of stealing a chocolate bar from a shop. He was observed to enter the shop, walk to the confectionery display, look furtively over each shoulder, select a chocolate bar and place it into his pocket. He then walked calmly from the store and was challenged and detained by a member of staff outside, where a chocolate bar was recovered from his pocket.

From this we can identify a number of key material facts:

- he was inside the shop;
- he carried out various actions inside the shop;
- he walked from the shop;
- he had a chocolate bar in his possession when stopped.

The aim of the interview will be to establish his account in detail, so our interview objectives here could be:

- Explain (in detail) his reason for going to the shop.
- Explain (in detail) his actions inside the shop prior to the confectionery display.
- Explain (in detail) his actions at the confectionery display.
- Explain (in detail) his route after leaving the confectionary display.
- Explain (in detail) his possession of the chocolate bar.
- Explain (in detail) what he was thinking at each of the above points in the chronology.

Note that these are not specific questions but are instead 'questioning areas' that can be developed conversationally by the interviewer who now '...*knows what she wants to know...*'.

The key objective here would probably be 'Explain (in detail) the man's possession of the chocolate bar'. This provides a starting point for the conversation and can be used to formulate an opening question such as 'Tell me in detail how the chocolate bar came to be in your pocket?' or 'Explain in detail how the chocolate came to be in your pocket when you were stopped outside the shop?' Both these questions are open-ended and both address the key objective. By starting with the correctly selected key objective, the interviewee is drawn towards focusing on the salient issues, and this can be used to develop the other objectives in turn. Once all the objectives have been met (in detail), the interviewer has established an account that can be tested against other evidence to determine the reliability and veracity of the interviewee's account, which was the overall aim of the interview.

25.3.1.3 Using bad-character evidence

Interviewers must carefully assess at the planning stage whether any relevant bad character evidence (BCE, see 24.2.5) will be raised. The previous behaviour would have to be relevant to issues in the current investigation. For example, many theft convictions would add very little to an assault case where the key issue was whether the suspect intended to commit GBH. BCE can be used by interviewing officers to rebut an innocent explanation, to suggest untruthfulness, or even to demonstrate that the suspect committed the crime on the basis of 'unlikelihood of coincidence'. (For example, a person's offending history might make it seem more likely that he/she is the offender for the current offence (*R v McAllister* [2009] 1 Cr App R 129)). This type of bad character evidence was used in the conviction of Levi Bellfield for the murder of Amanda ('Milly') Dowler (*R v Bellfield*, 2011).

There are no hard and fast rules as to when to raise such issues in interview, but it does make sense to include it in the plan as a separate objective to explore, once other objectives have been fully covered. Then each previous conviction or incidence of behaviour can be explored in fine grain detail until all relevant areas have been discussed. Any similarities or other reasons for raising the material should be discussed within the interview.

25.3.2 PEACE—engage and explain

The aim of this phase of the interview is to create an environment that encourages the interviewee to cooperate with the interview process. It builds upon the 'greeting' phase and seeks to establish a productive social and conversational dynamic for the encounter. This is known as 'set induction' and has two important aspects:

1. Orientation of the interviewee regarding the context of the encounter, and orientation towards the task in hand and the expected outcomes.
2. Behaviours required by both parties to undertake the agreed mutual activity.

The interviewer should explain what is going to happen and how things will proceed, as this will help to reassure and relax the interviewee and provide the correct conversational dynamic for the encounter. If the interviewee understands exactly what the interviewer is trying to achieve, and what is expected from him/her in terms of content and detail (and why), then it is more likely that this will be achieved. It will also help to reduce anxiety in the interviewee, and he/she will probably perform better and be more likely to provide the information the interviewer requires. Adopting a consultative and non-threatening manner will improve the chances of the interviewee cooperating; this is vital as encouraging the person to talk is a primary aim of the interview process. The interviewer should definitely not simply read from a plan, as this does not help build a rapport, and is likely to convey a general lack of competence and professionalism (see 6.11 on communication).

In this stage of a PEACE interview, the interviewer should:

- **establish a rapport** by including introductions, concerns, considerations, and by using appropriate humour. This will help establish common ground and hopefully create a cooperative atmosphere;
- **explain the reasons for the interview** (for a suspect, this should include an explanation of the alleged offence, the grounds for arrest, and that the interview provides an opportunity for the suspect to put his/her account of what happened, and for the police to seek the truth);
- **set out the route map**—what happens during and after the interview process, and the general (not the specific) line of questioning;
- **describe the routines**—depending on the nature of the interview this might include explaining why certain persons are present, the recording procedures, the need for interviewers to refer to their notes and make further notes, the production of exhibits, etc;
- **state the expectations**—ground rules such as no over-talking or interruptions, politeness, time to think, and the need to seek clarification of questions and answers; and
- **explain the interviewee's legal rights** and the role of the solicitor and legal advisers.

For suspect interviews, any significant statements or silences must be put to him/her at the start of the interview in compliance with the PACE 1984 codes of practice (Code 10.4). Suspect interviews are covered in more detail in 25.5.

Setting the right tone is very important: not all interviewees and suspects are guilty. The rule of thumb would be treat people as you would wish to be treated yourself. For each interviewee any cultural or behavioural factors should be noted and taken into account. For example, asking directly how he/she wishes to be addressed might provide an easy ice-breaker at the beginning of the interview. An interviewer could also offer the interviewee a cup of tea or other refreshment (if available—there is a certain loss of face otherwise!).

25.3.3 PEACE—account, clarifications, and challenge

This is the main part of the interview. The interviewer should first seek a 'free' account, without any interruption if possible, focusing on the key objective(s). The account should then be developed by conversational probing of what has been said , moving systematically from one objective to another, clarifying or seeking greater detail. Turnbull and the ADVOKATE checklist could be used here, if appropriate (see 10.5.3). Each objective should be explored in 'fine grain detail', thus exhausting relevant questions on that objective before moving on to another.

A good strategy to develop is using the interview objective as a conversational 'opener', and to let a free narrative develop. The on going narrative can then be used to formulate the next question. This will create a continuous sequence where each question will seem to flow from what the person has already said. The interview will feel more like a natural conversation, where the interviewer is really listening to what the interviewee says. This is almost always more productive than a disjointed series of questions and answers. It requires great concentration on the part of the interviewer and needs practice. Appropriate training from a skilled practitioner is also essential.

The account should then be summarised before selecting the topics that are relevant, in dispute, and checkable. These will then be examined in greater detail. To clarify the account the interviewer may need to seek new/additional information, before summarizing again, with commitment and agreement if possible. The account should make chronological sense. The account and topic phase of the interview should establish the interviewee's full and detailed account.

25.3.3.1 Challenging

Once the complete account is established it can be compared with the evidence, and any inconsistencies can be challenged. Challenging should be restricted to inconsistencies and facts (that can be checked and proved, and are also admissible). The interviewer should take care not to criticize or accuse—but should instead ask for explanation where discrepancies emerge. The challenge phase should not be a confrontation; hard-to-answer questions can be asked in a socially skilled and conversational manner. The interviewer must also consider whether a special warning is needed, see 25.5.9.

One effective conversational method of challenging is to:

1. Confirm the detail given by the interviewee in the account.
2. Reveal the detail that contradicts this or is inconsistent with it.
3. Ask an open-ended question.

This approach can be illustrated in a suspect interview as follows, (where I is the interviewer, S is the suspect and detail X is contradicted by information Y):

I: In your earlier account you said X (detail), do you agree? [Point 1 above]

S: Yes

I: The evidence shows Y. How do you explain that? [Points 2 and 3 above]

The suspect then needs to account for the inconsistency in what she has said, and this can then be further probed. The interviewer should listen carefully, because the suspect may now start changing her account (which should have been fully developed, summarised and agreed in the topic phase of the interview). An interviewer can be robust and persistent in line with the seven principles (see 25.2) without being confrontational and oppressive.

> **TASK 1** What special interview techniques may be used to help the interviewee's recall, particularly for witness interviews?

25.3.3.2 The importance of breaks

Breaks are useful for making arrangements and gathering thoughts, particularly if the interview has taken an unexpected turn; the plan may need to be revised. It may be useful to structure this part of the interview as follows:

- Account Phase – use the key objective and develop a detailed account.
- Break – analyse information, review plan, undertake relevant fast track actions.
- Topic Phase – develop topics that are relevant, checkable, and in dispute.
- Break - analyse information, review plan, undertake relevant fast track actions, plan challenges.
- Challenge Phase.

After a break it is good practice to summarise what has been said and to invite the interviewee to comment on the accuracy of the summary. This demonstrates that the interviewer has been listening carefully and has realised the significance of what has been said, and that the interviewee is being taken seriously.

25.3.4 PEACE—closure

The interviewer should aim to maintain the good rapport built up during an interview as it might be necessary to interview the same person again, especially if any new evidence emerges or the CPS provides guidance. Before finishing the interview the interviewer should:

- review the interviewee's account in full;
- allow the interviewee the chance to correct, confirm, deny, alter, or add to his/her account;
- ensure that all the planned objectives and topics have been covered;
- check whether the interviewee (or the solicitor, if present) wants to ask any questions; and
- explain what will happen in the future.

The interview can then be formally closed. This is likely to include recording the time when the interview finishes. For interviews with suspects, there are additional requirements relating to recording the interview (see 25.5.7).

25.3.5 PEACE—evaluation

The evaluation stage includes not only an evaluation of what has been achieved but also how well the aims and objectives set by the interviewer were met. The interviewer should refer to his/her plan and reflect on what went well, what might have gone better, and (for next time) which areas he/she would try to develop or improve. The following questions might be relevant:

- Have other reasonable lines of enquiry (such as an alibi) been discovered?
- Have other forensic opportunities been discovered?
- Have all the points to prove from the offence under investigation been covered?
- Have the statutory defences, mitigation, or explanation, perhaps pointing to innocence been considered?
- Have the objectives been achieved?
- Does the interview add to the investigation as a whole?
- Have the requirements of the CPIA 1996 been satisfied?
- How have I performed, and what can I learn from this interview to develop my skills?

Trainee police officers could assess their personal level of skills and knowledge about interviewing, and use this as a basis for Learning Diary entries. All other officers conducting interviews should regularly evaluate their performance to ensure continuing professional development.

25.4 The Needs of the Interviewee

Many suspects will be anxious and want to know what is going to happen next and in the longer term. The common questions are 'will I be released?', 'will I get bail?', and 'how long will I be here?'. Remember that there is a presumption in law that a suspect will be bailed, and that bail periods will be generally limited to 28 days (The Police and Crime Act 2017, effective from 3rd April 2017). If the suspect asks, then the interviewer should answer fairly and honestly but should also explain that he/she cannot determine the decisions of the custody officer or the CPS reviewing lawyer. Obviously, there should be no attempt to gain a confession through promise of favours such as early release or bail, as this could render any subsequent confession inadmissible at court. (Further information on admissibility is provided in 25.5.1.2.)

25.4.1 Meeting the needs of all interviewees

The interviewer and the custody officer should be alert to the special circumstances involved in interviewing a person with a physical or mental impairment. They should always try to ascertain the nature and extent of the impairment, although the individual may or may not be willing to divulge it and the PACE Act 1984 'allows police officers to proceed on an assumption'. This obviously needs careful and sensitive handling, for example by asking 'do you have a physical impairment we should be aware of?' (You may need to explain what 'physical impairment' means to the interviewee by giving examples or explaining in everyday language.)

For a profoundly deaf individual a 'signer' may be required. A partially deaf person will find it easier if he/she can see the interviewer's face in order to lip-read, and people should speak one at a time. A deaf person's attention could be attracted by lightly touching his/her sleeve. The force diversity team may be able to provide Braille texts which explain, for example, a suspect's rights, the caution, and the management of tapes after interview (although not all blind people can read Braille).

Other impairments such as speech impediments may be more difficult to deal with, but interviewers should always be sensitive to the individual's needs and requirements, and should try to satisfy these needs. The simple question is: 'Have I done all I can to ensure that this person is not disadvantaged in any way because of a disability or impairment?' If this is the case, then all reasonable steps have been taken. No one should be placed at a disadvantage in a police interview because of physical or mental impairment; the criminal justice system is not well served unless this principle is upheld.

25.5 Interviews with Suspects

A suspect interview is defined as 'the questioning of a person regarding his/her involvement or suspected involvement in a criminal offence or offences which must be carried out under caution' (PACE Code C, para 11.1A). This applies to any conversation (no matter how short and wherever it takes place) once a caution has been given and it is irrelevant whether or not the suspect has been arrested. Not all suspects are arrested, for example a suspect on the street being reported for a road traffic offence (see 10.13.1.1), or a suspect who volunteers to be interviewed to assist with the investigation of an offence.

Interviews with suspects will often take place at a police station. Suspects who have been arrested must be interviewed at a police station (PACE Code C, para 11.1). Suspects who have not been arrested and who volunteer to be interviewed to assist with an investigation would normally be interviewed at a police station, but could be interviewed at another location such as his/her home. Suspects being reported for a road traffic offence would usually be 'interviewed' in the street.

25.5.1 General rights of the suspect

The suspect has the normal rights of being treated with dignity, fairness, and objectivity, and the right to free independent legal advice (FILA) during interview, and for a vulnerable person, an 'appropriate adult' should also be present (see 25.5.1.1). A number of laws and associated Codes regulate the process of police interviews, in order to protect the interviewee. The suspect should be assessed as 'fit for interview'. Normally a doctor or custody nurse will make this decision considering whether the suspect is ill, hurt, or suffering from a psychological condition, but it can be decided on the person's own say so, supported by the custody officer's independent observations.

Unquestionably, there have been many instances in the past of the police abusing their powers to question suspects (some of which may have been motivated in part by the so-called 'noble cause corruption' discussed in 6.5.3). This could range from oppressive behaviour used to obtain confessions under duress, to a lack of safety provisions when interviewing a vulnerable person (eg due to a disability or learning difficulty). A recent example of where the suspect's rights were denied prior to arrival at the police station was the Halliwell case (see 25.5.1.2). The custody officer and the suspect's legal adviser both have a responsibility to monitor the suspect's rights and the process of interviewing, and this has greatly reduced the opportunities for foul play. The suspect should have his/her rights explained, and this should be reinforced with a written explanation.

The EU directive 2012/13/EU enhances the rights of suspects at police stations, and covers the right to information in criminal proceedings. It enshrines the right of a suspect to information concerning procedural rights (such as right to free legal advice and to silence), information relating to the reason for arrest and the suspected offence, and access to case file material that relates to the legality of the arrest (Cape, 2015). So as soon as the custody officer becomes aware of the existence of material relevant to the legality or otherwise of the arrest, he/she must communicate this information to the suspect. This will allow the defence to make submissions to the custody officer (and beyond) regarding the suspect's continued detention. Cape (2015) suggests that the problematic issue will be how much information is provided to a suspect and/or his solicitor prior to interview. The amended PACE Code C 11.1A states: '... they and, if they are represented, their solicitor must be given sufficient information to enable them to understand the nature of [the suspected] offence and why they are suspected of committing it, in order to allow for the effective exercise of the rights of the defence'. *R v Roble* [1997] Crim LR 449 states that a legal advisor must be in a position to 'usefully advise his client'. Police officers have discretion when deciding which material will be disclosed, and will need to consider the matter carefully at the planning stage. This area has produced some interesting case law (see *R v Howell* [2003 EWCA Crim 01] and *R v Knight* [2003 EWCA Crim 1977]).

25.5.1.1 The presence of an 'appropriate adult'

The PACE Act 1984, Code C, para 1.4 states that an 'appropriate adult' must be provided for any person detainee suspected or known to be:

- 'mentally disordered or otherwise mentally vulnerable' (see 13.2 and 13.7.3);
- under the age of 18 (since October 2013, PACE Code C, para 1.5A); or

- likely to find an interview problematic due to an impairment such as a serious visual handicap, deafness, illiteracy, or who has difficulty in articulation because of a speech impediment.

The appropriate adult is there to act on behalf of the suspect and advise when necessary. He/she will also facilitate communication between the interviewer and the interviewee, and observe whether the interview is being conducted properly and fairly. It is usually the custody officer who considers whether an appropriate adult is required.

PACE Code C, para 1.7 sets out the categories of person who can be an appropriate adult, and his/her duties are also described. The appropriate adult for a juvenile is, first, a parent or guardian, or, if the juvenile is in care, a suitable representative from the care authority or voluntary organization. If neither of these is available a social worker may stand *in loco parentis* (in the place of a parent). As a last resort, any responsible person aged 18 or over who is not a police officer or employed by the police may act as the appropriate adult. PACE Code of Practice C Note 1B states: 'A person, including a parent or guardian, should not be an appropriate adult if they are: suspected of involvement in the offence; the victim; a witness; involved in the investigation, or have received admissions prior to attending to act as the appropriate adult.' For a person who is 'mentally disordered' or has a reduced mental capacity (see 13.2.4), an appropriate adult is a relative, guardian, or other person responsible for his/her care and custody. Alternatively, it could be someone who has experience of dealing with mentally vulnerable people, such as an approved mental health professional (AMHP) or a specialist social worker. Failing this, any responsible person aged 18 or over can act as the appropriate adult, but as stated earlier, anyone connected with the police is not eligible.

The appropriate adult will be invited to sign the custody record to show that he/she understands the responsibilities involved. The interviewer should check that this has been done before the interview begins. An interview involving an appropriate adult may take longer, especially if it involves interpretation, for example by a signer. Translation from one language to another takes at least twice as long as normal, so allowances should be made for this. There are advantages: the interviewee has more time to consider his/her replies, and the interviewer will have more time to observe and consider the suspect's non-verbal communication (NVC) and demeanour (although of course any interpretations must always allow for cultural and linguistic diversity, see 6.11.2).

25.5.1.2   Confessions, oppression, and unfairness

Any statement that is in any way adverse to a person (eg admitting to a crime or even to being present at the scene of a crime) can amount to a confession under s 82 PACE. The statement can be made to any person, not just a police officer, and can include written or spoken words, actions, or even silence. Even though a person may have confessed in one of these recognized ways, the evidence might not be admissible in court. The defence can argue that a confession should be rendered inadmissible because:

- it was, or may have been obtained by oppression (s 76 PACE);
- something was said or done likely to render the confession unreliable (s 76 PACE) (eg inducements were offered, threats were made, or the caution was not properly given);
- the manner in which the evidence was obtained would mean that it would be unfair to admit it (s 78 PACE); or
- it is too prejudicial to admit it (eg that the offender has previously confessed to a similar but more serious offence, and the bench or the jury might concentrate on the seriousness of that offence rather than fully consider the evidence in the current case) (s 82 PACE).

Many of the unfair practices that were adopted in the past by the police to secure a 'confession' from a suspect in custody have been identified and made less likely, if not impossible, by legislation and practice guidelines.

Oppression usually means behaviour akin to breaching a person's human rights under Article 3 of the ECHR (this refers to torture, inhumane or degrading treatment, or the use or threat of violence). Case law has widened the definition of oppression to include 'exercise of authority in a burdensome, harsh or wrongful manner' (*R v Fulling* [1987] 2 All ER 65), as well as 'questioning which by its very nature, duration or other circumstances (including the fact of custody) excites hope (such as the hope of release) or fears, or so affects the mind of the subject that his will crumbles and he speaks when otherwise he would have stayed silent' (*R v Prager* [1972] 1 WLR 260, 266, adopted by the House of Lords in *R v Mushtaq* [2005] UKHL 23). This definition can encompass many situations, and it is unsurprising that defence solicitors often argue that a confession has been obtained by oppression. If the court or the defence raise the issue of oppression, the burden of proof is on the prosecution to prove beyond reasonable doubt that it was not obtained in that manner.

Inducements to confess could include offers to grant bail, or for the police to refrain from arresting family members. Threats could be suggesting that bail would not be granted or that family members might be arrested.

Section 78 of PACE underpins many strategies used by defence solicitors, as it allows for any potential prosecution evidence to be rendered inadmissible (not just confessions, see *R v Mason* [1987] 3 All ER 481). To use s 78, the defence has to show that the manner in which the evidence was obtained means it should not be admitted as it would be unfair to the proceedings. The defence might argue, for instance, that DNA evidence should not be admissible because the prosecution have not proven continuity of the evidence from the moment it was found to the moment it was examined at the laboratory (implying that it might have been contaminated). Note, therefore, that if a s 76 argument does not succeed the defence could argue that a confession should be rendered inadmissible under s 78 instead.

The Halliwell case is a recent example of where the suspect's rights were denied. A superintendent was judged to have breached PACE by interviewing the suspect in circumstances that were oppressive and that deliberately denied him his rights (both ss 76 and 78 PACE arguments were employed by the defence). Halliwell was arrested for abduction of Sian O'Callaghan who had been missing for several days, but some of the interviews were conducted prior to arrival at a police station, under the guise of an urgent interview, without caution, and without a solicitor (without Halliwell's express agreement). He confessed to the murder of O'Callaghan and another woman, and was subsequently charged with both murders. After lengthy legal arguments at the start of the trial, all of Halliwell's confessions were ruled inadmissible and the second murder case failed. The O'Callaghan case continued based upon other evidence, and Halliwell was convicted. There was extensive media coverage and an IPCC investigation ensued. The superintendent was found guilty of gross misconduct for the breaches and was given a final written warning.

25.5.2 Planning suspect interviews

As well as the general PEACE considerations for planning interviews covered in 25.3.1, there are other factors that apply only to suspect interviews to consider, such as:

- the legal framework for interviews with suspects;
- the suspect's right to a free independent legal adviser and for the adviser to be present throughout the interview; and
- the arrangements for recording the interview.

These requirements need to be covered in the interview plan. The interviewer also needs to consider what defences the suspect might employ and how these might be countered.

One of the first things to consider for a suspect interview is what potential offence or offences are being investigated. Remember that, if an offence has actually occurred, the following must be proved:

1. **Criminal intent** (*mens rea*): What was in the suspect's mind at the time? Why did he/she commit the offence?
2. **Criminal action** (*actus reus*): What did he/she actually do? How did he/she do it?

For each offence the following will be required: the points to prove, the evidence that the suspect committed the offence, case law and the specific parts of the criminal law under which the suspect may be charged. The relevant legislation should be consulted and the key points established. Information such as witness accounts or statements should be considered, and this will help clarify the contribution the interview will make to the investigation.

25.5.3 Defence solicitors

The defence solicitor is the defendant's legal adviser, and is obliged to prevent his/her client from further assisting the police by way of self-incrimination, if that is not in the client's interest (PACE Code C, note 6D). The solicitor's only role in the police station is to protect and advance the legal rights of his/her client (PACE 1984 Code C Note 6D).

A 'duty solicitor' is drawn from a retained panel of solicitors available to advise an arrested person who does not have a solicitor of his/her own available for the interview. They provide 'free and independent legal advice' (FILA) and are there to advise their clients at any time. They are of course independent of the police and the CPS. The custody officer will make the initial contact with the solicitor, following a request from the detained suspect (see 10.10), and the interviewer will then become the point of contact for the defence solicitor. (Note that confidential handover documents or witness statements should not be attached to the custody record.)

25.5.3.1 Active defence

A solicitor might adopt an 'active defence' role (Ede and Shepherd, 2000). If the evidence looks weak or merely circumstantial, the solicitor will probably advise the suspect to remain silent or to submit a jointly prepared statement. It is sometimes difficult for a trainee officer to accept that a solicitor can advise a suspect against providing details about a crime or admitting guilt, and more experienced police officers may also argue that there is no 'level playing field'. It is important to recognise these are emotional reactions, and that it is essential to remain objective and focused on the real evidence. There may be sound reasons for a legal adviser to advise the suspect to remain silent or reply 'no comment', for example there may have been very little pre-interview disclosure. The decision to make 'no comment' and the possible reasons could be examined by the court (see for example *R v Howell* [2003] EWCA Crim 01). A jury may adversely interpret a suspect's silence at interview (see 25.5.9.2 on adverse inference).

Sometimes an admission of guilt is better for the client, especially if there is strong or irrefutable evidence, or strong mitigation (an excuse or reason for what has been done).The solicitor might try to dominate an interview (an accepted tactic), particularly if the interviewing officer seems to lack experience or is unprofessional. If a solicitor is disruptive there is a risk of 'losing the interview', so the interviewer may need to speak out and take control (a good command of the relevant areas of PACE 1984 Code C Note 6D and 6E will be needed). However, it is very rare for a solicitor to behave so inappropriately that the police interviewer has to exclude him/her from the interview under PACE CODE C 6.9 and in any case the whole interview is recorded; the court will take a negative view of a disruptive solicitor, and this might even prejudice the suspect's defence.

25.5.4 Briefing a solicitor before an interview

Before the interview begins the solicitor must be briefed (provided with the relevant information) so that his/her client may be usefully advised (see *R v Roble* [1997] Crim LR 449). The interviewer must plan what to disclose, considering:

- what is the evidence?
- what evidence should be disclosed immediately or withheld (at least for the time being)?
- at what stage of the interview will particular evidence be disclosed?
- can the withholding of all/some/any evidence be justified? (see *R v Imran & Hussain* 1997).

Any evidence derived solely from intelligence should not be disclosed at this stage as the protection of sources is an important consideration. Forensic evidence, or details of a particular MO can be disclosed at the discretion of the interviewer, being mindful of the amount of detail and how this could be used by the suspect to construct a false alibi or defence. If there is any doubt over whether it is appropriate to disclose particular evidence prior to interview, the interviewer should seek advice and guidance from a supervisory officer or qualified interview advisor. In some situations a fuller disclosure might facilitate a frank and productive interaction between the suspect and the police—the skill is to recognize the situations where fuller disclosure would be beneficial. Where the disclosure is limited, the solicitor is more likely to ask difficult questions and to advise the suspect to remain silent at interview. If further material is disclosed during an interview, the solicitor is likely to immediately ask for a private consultation with his/her client. These consequences should be considered and planned for.

There are two major warnings which must be heeded when briefing the solicitor: never overstate or understate the evidence, and never express a view on the likely outcome for the client. The case of *R v Mason* [1987] 3 All ER 481 is a good example of where a solicitor was misled (as well as the suspect). Police told them both that the suspect's fingerprints had been found on a broken bottle from the scene of an arson attack, but this was not true. The court took a dim view of investigators having deliberately lied to an officer of the court (the solicitor), and rendered Mason's subsequent admissions as inadmissible under s 78 of PACE.

Ideally, the police officer and the defence solicitor will meet in a quiet room, and there will be no interruptions. However, sometimes they will end up discussing the matters in a busy corridor, or by phone which makes it more difficult. At the start of the meeting the interviewer should explain that he/she will answer the solicitor's questions when the disclosure of evidence is complete. Sufficient time should be allowed for the solicitor to take notes, although an audio-recording will be made in serious cases. The case against the suspect should be outlined, including the evidence upon which the interview will be based, and up-to-date information about the welfare of the client should also be provided. Then the solicitor can be invited to ask questions; this needs careful handling, as being over-defensive and disclosing only in response to the solicitor's questions may increase the likelihood of a 'no comment' interview. The interviewer must however also guard against saying too much. A solicitor may try different tactics, such as switching abruptly from questions about evidence to questions about other aspects of the case. The interviewer needs to remain calm and self-possessed, and will of course be able to deal more confidently with such situations if he/she knows all the details of the case, and has a thorough understanding of the relevant law.

A record should be kept of the details that have been disclosed. The disclosure process can also be audio-recorded, and a copy given to the solicitor. This is common in serious offences and is also advocated by the Law Society to ensure transparency and ethical practice by all parties. Such a recording may be crucial evidence in arguing there has been recent fabrication, particularly when a solicitor has advised 'no comment' on the basis of there having been little or no disclosure of information.

25.5.5 The start of a suspect interview

The time spent on engaging and building rapport with the suspect, explaining what is going to happen and following the procedures properly, may all prove productive later on. In addition, no irregularities will have been provided for the solicitor to use in the defence of his/her client.

At the start of the interview (or after a break) and before asking any questions about the offence, the interviewer must caution the suspect (see PACE Code C, paras 10.8 and 11.4) and check his/her understanding of the caution. A detailed account of the various cautions and their use is given in 10.3. The interviewer might say to the suspect, for example:

> 'You have an absolute right to remain silent if you wish, you do not have to speak to me or answer any of my questions. However, if this matter goes to court at a later date and at court you rely on a fact in your defence that the court think you could have reasonably given me here today, then the court are entitled to ask themselves "why did you not reveal this fact at the time of the interview?" They might think that the facts you give in defence in court are untrue or have been fabricated since the interview, and they may be less likely to believe you. And remember, everything being said here today is being recorded and could be played in court.'

The solicitor should not be asked to explain the caution, or to acknowledge that his/her client understands it—this is the responsibility of the interviewing officer.

Certain additional information must be provided to the suspect depending on the circumstances and location of the interview. A suspect who has been arrested and who is being interviewed at a police station must also be reminded that he/she is entitled to free legal advice in person or on the phone, and that the interview can be delayed until it is obtained. Such reminders and the suspect's response should be recorded in the interview record (Code C, para 11.2). Other information that must be provided to the suspect is given in the table.

Circumstances and location of interview with a suspect who has not been arrested	Additional information to be provided to the suspect
Suspect is on the street being reported for an offence	That a failure to cooperate (eg by not providing a name and address when being reported for an offence) could amount to committing a further offence or lead to arrest (Code C, para 10.9)
Suspect has volunteered to assist with the investigation of an offence and is being interviewed (Code C, para 3.22)	That he/she can leave at any time, and can also obtain free and independent legal advice if he/she agrees to remain (Code C, para 3.21)

Any significant statement (see 10.4) should also be discussed. The suspect must be given the opportunity to clarify, confirm, deny, or add to an earlier statement. Sometimes it may be difficult to distinguish between a significant statement and a 'relevant comment' (again see 10.4), but if there is any doubt, the statement or comment should be put to the suspect at the beginning of the interview, after caution and before questioning.

25.5.6 Tactics during interviews

The interviewing officer should be polite, rational, and professional, and proceed with the interview as planned. However, interviewees may be hostile and refuse to cooperate. A common temptation for an interviewing officer in such circumstances is to confront the solicitor or to start rushing the questions, but this must be avoided. The interviewing officer must not be drawn into asking closed questions (requiring a yes or no reply), or into speeding up, allowing little time for answers (as if a 'no' answer is expected). Nor should the suspect be asked to justify why he/she is not answering the questions. The simple advice in this situation is to adhere to the PEACE model of interviewing, and not to be thrown. Skilful and persistent questioning may slip under a hostile suspect's defences, and by following a new line of questioning the suspect may forget to continue to 'brazen it out' with a repeated 'no comment' and suddenly provide vital evidence or information.

Most defence solicitors, particularly duty solicitors, will have a good understanding and plenty of experience of the PEACE interview model and the approaches which an interviewing officer is likely to adopt. For example, the solicitor will know that the interviewer will try to build a rapport with the interviewee but it is very unlikely that he/she will assist with the process. If the interviewing officer starts with a few informal words about a non-contentious topic (such as whether the suspect would like a drink) to encourage the suspect to open up, the solicitor is likely to challenge its relevance unless it relates directly to the suspect's welfare. Therefore, all opportunities to build a rapport before the interview should be recognized and utilized to the full.

The PACE Codes of Practice provide some guidance on what is acceptable behaviour by the solicitor in an interview. A legal adviser is permitted to seek clarification, offer the client their advice (including not to answer a question), and can also challenge an improper question or the manner in which it is put. A legal adviser may not, however, answer questions on the client's behalf or provide him/her with written responses to quote. (See PACE Code C, Notes 6D and 6 E.)

The solicitor will also closely monitor the interview process itself. This is because, however overwhelming the evidence, any flaw in police procedure can lead to charges against the suspect being dismissed, or an application at trial to have the evidence ruled inadmissible. A solicitor has no obligation to immediately point out any police failing or non-adherence to the appropriate Codes, and may only mention it later when it is of particular advantage to the client, for instance in court. This is one of the reasons why the interviewing officer needs to know the law and the associated police procedures very well indeed. Asking leading questions, adopting a threatening or bullying manner, or seeking to offer the suspect a lighter sentence in exchange for giving more evidence will all prompt the solicitor to intervene (and rightly so). If, however, the interviewing officer is acting fairly, proportionately, and properly, then the solicitor's grounds for intervention are much reduced.

25.5.6.1 Prepared Statements

The solicitor may present the interviewer with a written 'prepared statement'. This is often written by the solicitor and the suspect, and signed by the suspect. The suspect might then not want to say anything more about the matter, and may make this clear at the start of the interview (after the caution). The most appropriate response in such a situation is to temporarily suspend the interview and consider the contents of the statement. It can then be included in a revised interview plan, and the interview re-started. The receipt of a prepared statement does not mean the interview process is over. As an interviewer, you still have the right to ask relevant questions relating to the investigation.

The case of *R v Knight* [2003 EWCA Crim 1977] should be studied by all interviewing officers as this provides useful guidance on what to do when presented with a prepared statement. If the factual defence is stated in the prepared statement in writing, and the suspect gives oral evidence at court which is wholly in line with statement, then no adverse inference can be drawn. The case makes it clear that the purpose of s 34 of the Criminal Justice & Public Order Act 1994 is to encourage the early disclosure of a suspect's account and not the scrutiny and testing of it by police in interview. Had the latter been intended, parliament would have used significantly different language, as questioning the contents of a statement would be a significantly greater intrusion into a suspect's general right to silence than the requirement to disclose his factual defence. However, *R v Knight* recognises that a prepared statement does not give automatic immunity to adverse inference as the prepared statement might be lacking in detail or deficient in another manner.

All prepared statements should be carefully analysed (using SE3R for example), and any omissions noted. The case of *R v Lewis* [2003] EWCA Crim 223 is particularly relevant in this context. If the prepared statement lacks detail, including explanatory detail, this gives the interviewer the opportunity to ask question about what is **not** contained in the statement. In the case *R v Lewis* it was observed that 'a fact supporting a fact, is also a fact that can reasonably be expected to be mentioned'. The careful analysis of the content then gives rise to new interview objectives, based on information that is not included in the prepared statement. These objectives can then be developed during a further interview, being mindful that it is highly likely this will be a 'no comment' interview.

25.5.7 Recording suspect interviews

The tenet of PACE Code E (para 3.1) is that an audio-recording should be made of all interviews under caution with suspects in indictable or triable either way offences. Investigators are not precluded from recording interviewing in other circumstances, providing they comply with the relevant codes (note 3A). Many interviews are now visually recorded, so Code F will apply.

25.5.7.1 Recording interviews with suspects who have not been arrested

If a suspect is not under arrest but is interviewed voluntarily at a police station, then the interview should be recorded whenever possible. However, Codes E and F (in force since October 2013) state that a sergeant (or higher rank officer) can authorize an interview to continue without audio-recording in prescribed circumstances, for instance where:

- the custody officer believes there will be no prosecution from the outset;
- equipment has failed or no room is available and the custody officer believes it would cause unnecessary delay (Code E, para 3.3A);
- the suspect objects to an audio-recorded interview (Code E, para 4.8).

If the suspect refuses to be audio-recorded, a written record of the interview should be made. The decision to continue recording the interview against the wishes of the suspect may be commented upon in court, as this could be seen as being oppressive (PACE Code F, Note 4G). The evidence could then be rendered inadmissible under s 76 or 78 (see 25.5.1.2).

If the interview takes place other than at a police station, for example at the roadside in relation to a motoring offence, or at a juvenile's home (with an appropriate adult), the PNB is the most appropriate place to record such an interview in writing, complying with PACE Code C, para 11.7. This can be enhanced by the use of Body Worn Video (BWV) cameras (of evidential quality) now being used by a number of police forces. However BWV should not be relied on; using the PNB as the primary evidential record remains best practice (the contemporaneous note interview process being recorded by the BWV for transparency).

25.5.7.2 Procedures for recording interviews

Audio- recordings of interviews are made using tapes, CDs or secure digital networks, depending on the facilities available. PACE Code E (2013) makes various provisions for the use of all of these different types of media.

For tape and disc recordings, the sealed recording media must be shown to the suspect at the start of the interview to show they are new, sealed and have not been tampered with. The following information must be recorded as a PNB entry, or on the paper seals to be wrapped around the media at the end of the interview (see PACE Code C, para 11.7, PACE Act 1984):

- the time, day, date, location of the interview;
- the name, rank, role of the interviewer;
- the name, address, date of birth of the interviewee; and
- the persons present and a description of the layout of the room and the equipment.

If a tape recorder is being used, when it is first switched on there will be a continuous sound while it is winding on to the recording part of the tape. This must be explained to the suspect.

Two recordings are made simultaneously (sometimes three are made, depending on the equipment). At the end of the interview one of them will be sealed as the 'master recording'. The other(s) will remain with the case file; these are known as the 'working' copy/ copies. A further copy will also be provided for the solicitor on request. The master recording is filed by the designated responsible person, and will not be opened unless it is needed in exceptional circumstances, or is to be examined on the direction of a judge or a senior member of the CPS.

> **TASK 2** Find out what happens to the working copy of the recording.

At the end of the interview and before switching off the machine, the interviewing officer must record the time when the interview finishes. For discs or tapes, the labels must be signed by the suspect, the interviewing officer, and the solicitor, and the master recording must be sealed in the presence of the suspect. If a suspect or the solicitor refuses to sign the labels, this has to be recorded. (Note that no signing is required for a recording made on a secure digital network.) The suspect should be told what will happen to the recordings, and this is reinforced by providing a written explanation on a pre-printed card.

Where the interview is recorded onto a secure digital network, Code E makes separate provisions for the start of the interview. In brief, the recording medium would need to be switched on immediately the interviewer enters the room with the suspect, and the interviewer must log directly into the secure digital network and commence the recording. The interviewee must be told that the interview is being recorded onto a secure network, that the recording has begun, and of his/her rights of access to it should a prosecution ensue. At the end of the interview (as with all interviews), he/she will be provided with a notice about the rights of access to the recording. The interviewer should also make a PNB note of the date and time, together with the identification number of the recording.

Interviews are sometimes visually recorded. PACE Code F states that there is no statutory requirement to do this, but provides examples of circumstances where an investigating officer might consider it useful to do so. These examples include where the suspect has requested it, where there is a need for an appropriate adult, and where the officer wants to question after charge (Code F, 3.1). At the start of a video-recording, the interviewing officer must explain that a visual recording is going to be made, and then unwrap the recording media in the presence of the interviewee, load the equipment and start recording. Similar legal necessities apply to video interviews as for audio interviews (ie caution, significant statements or silences, etc). The suspect has the right to object to the visual recording at this point; the interviewer will explain that the visual recording cannot be completed and then stop the recording (see Code F). The interview will then be recorded using audio equipment. Once a video-interview is complete, any recording media used must be sealed in the presence of the interviewee, and he/she must be informed about the uses to be made of the recording and his/her rights of access to it. The suspect will be supplied with a copy of the recording as soon as possible after being charged or notified of an impending prosecution (Code F, 4.19).

Further details concerning recorded interviews may be found in the 'investigation' area of APP on the College of Policing website. Note that under the PACE Act 1984 there is no requirement to record the suspect's NVC , apart from the interviewing officer making references to actions.

25.5.8 Taking offences into consideration

Admissions of other offences can sometimes be treated as TICs ('taken into consideration'). These assist police to solve crimes, they promote a victim's 'closure', they allow victims to claim compensation, and they allow the police to gather essential intelligence relating to criminal activity. A suspect may wish to tell the police about other offending behaviour in order to 'get it all over and done with', fearing for instance that further evidence of his/her offending behaviour could emerge over time, leading to repeated arrests.

TICs should be discussed with suspects, of that there is no doubt. However, no admissions to crimes should be obtained by inducements or favour (see 25.5.1.2). Safeguards have been put in place to prevent abuse of the TIC system; in the past, some criminals undoubtedly 'assisted' the police by admitting to offences they had not committed, hoping for more lenient treatment. But in fact the opposite applies—the Sentencing Council (2012) make it clear that where a defendant has admitted TICs, the sentence should reflect the totality of the offending.

It is legitimate for an officer to ask a suspect if he/she wishes any further offences to be taken into consideration, as long as the officer adheres to the warnings above. Where a suspect discusses another crime he/she has committed, the officer should obtain sufficient detail of the crime to be able to satisfy the points to prove, as if the case was going to court as a charge. This includes seeking out any evidential material that may already exist, for example forensic evidence. Each subsequent admission should be dealt with in the same manner, providing a thorough and professional response to the investigation of the other crimes. Officers will also need to check whether the admitted crimes have already been reported, or whether they are new crimes that should be recorded as such. The MG18 form must be completed so that the prosecutor and the court are made aware of any relevant factors, and also the MG19 form which relates to possible compensation for victims. If the suspect then refuses to accept the TICs in court at a later stage, he/she will already have been warned that the offences concerned could be investigated separately.

Sentencing guidelines (issued in 2012) made it clear that TICs are unlikely to be accepted for sexual or violent offences, or for offences more serious than the main charge. If there is any doubt about the appropriateness of certain charges or TICs, advice is available from the CPS (see 27.3), custody officers, and PIP Level 2 investigators. Further information is provided on the CPS website.

25.5.9 Special warnings and adverse inference

Special warnings are used when the suspect fails to, or refuses to answer questions satisfactorily after due warning. If he/she presents a 'no comment' interview when asked questions, or fails to respond to questions based on special warnings, then at trial a judge may advise the jury that they are entitled to draw an 'adverse inference'.

25.5.9.1 Special warnings

The use of a special warning (ss 36 and 37 of the CJPOA 1994) is, in a sense, a further caution to the suspect and his/her legal adviser. A special warning may be needed for a suspect who has been caught directly in the commission of a crime (*in flagrante* or 'red-handed').

Section 36 warnings relate to a suspect's refusal to account for objects, marks, or substances, or marks on such objects. Further details are shown in the flowchart.

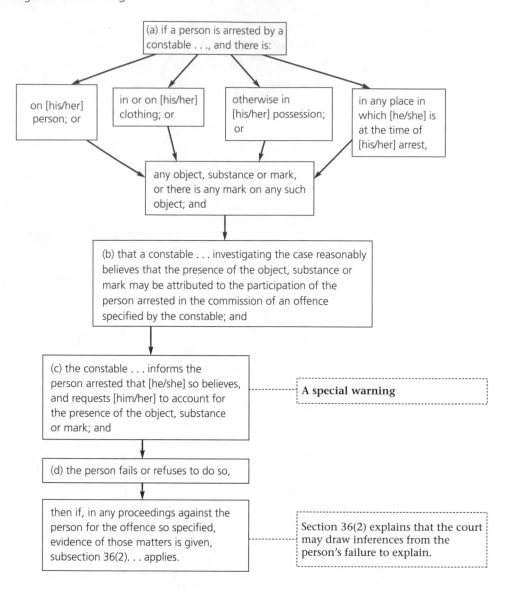

(a) if a person is arrested by a constable . . ., and there is:

on [his/her] person; or

in or on [his/her] clothing; or

otherwise in [his/her] possession; or

in any place in which [he/she] is at the time of [his/her] arrest,

any object, substance or mark, or there is any mark on any such object; and

(b) that a constable . . . investigating the case reasonably believes that the presence of the object, substance or mark may be attributed to the participation of the person arrested in the commission of an offence specified by the constable; and

(c) the constable . . . informs the person arrested that [he/she] so believes, and requests [him/her] to account for the presence of the object, substance or mark; and

A special warning

(d) the person fails or refuses to do so,

then if, in any proceedings against the person for the offence so specified, evidence of those matters is given, subsection 36(2). . . applies.

Section 36(2) explains that the court may draw inferences from the person's failure to explain.

Section 37 warnings relate to the failure of a person to account for his/her presence at a place at or about the time of an alleged offence. If a police officer believes that the suspect's presence is attributable to his/her participation in the offence, then the suspect must be warned that 'adverse inference' could be drawn if no explanation is provided. If a suspect has given a reasonable account of the fact in question, a special warning should not be used as it could be interpreted as oppressive behaviour and the suspect's legal adviser would almost certainly intervene.

The special warning should include the following five points, put in ordinary language which the suspect will understand:

1. the nature of the offence being investigated;
2. the particular fact the suspect needs to account for;
3. that the interviewing officer believes that the fact arose because the suspect was involved in the offence;
4. that inference may be properly drawn if the suspect fails to account for that specific fact; and
5. that a record of the interview is being made.

Once any particular special warning topic has been probed in fine grain detail, it is important that interviewees are made aware of when the special warning no longer applies. Special warnings indicate that the suspect needs to explain something, so if he/she does not, an adverse inference can later be drawn at court. If a special warning no longer applies, an interviewee should be made aware so that they no longer feel compelled to answer and their normal right to silence now applies. Suggested wording and more guidance on special warnings may be found in the 'investigation' area of APP on the College of Policing website. It may be necessary to give several special warnings, if a number of separate material facts have been identified under s 36 or 37.

25.5.9.2 Adverse inference

'Adverse inferences' under ss 34–37 of the CJPOA 1994 can be drawn if the defendant presents new significant information in court. It must be information concerning a fact in his/her defence, such that the court would expect it to have been reasonably divulged earlier (at interview or before the time of charging or reporting (either in the interview in general, following a caution (s 34), or after a special warning (ss 36 and 37)). The jury would be entitled to ask themselves 'why didn't he/she mention this earlier?' and may conclude that the defendant has recently fabricated the fact, or that the new information is untrue. Therefore, during a police interview the suspect **must** be asked all the relevant questions to cover possible defences. After all, if the crucial grounds for defence were not covered during the interview, then the defence might be able to argue in court that the defendant would have provided the information at interview 'if only he/she had been given the opportunity'. Where an investigator feels that adverse inferences could be drawn as a result of silence or failure to answer questions, APP suggests that an adverse inference package is compiled for the CPS, to highlight where this might be the case. Always seek advice from peers, supervisors, and consult APP guidance before undertaking this work.

> **TASK 3** When should the special warning be used—before caution, during the 'engagement' phase, or at the end of the interview, as things are being brought to a close?

25.6 Interviews with Witnesses

The PEACE process applies to all interviews (see 25.3) but interviews with witnesses are **not** governed by the PACE Codes of Practice, so there is more flexibility. Different approaches and techniques for gathering witness testimony can be adopted (eg video- or audio-recording), depending on the category of the witness and the nature of the interview in prospect.

Ideally, interviewers should only know a little about the alleged offence(s) before the interview. This is because too much knowledge might result in the interviewer contaminating the interview by inadvertently introducing information not already mentioned by the witness. Another pitfall can be the interviewer failing to ask all the questions which would be needed to fill any 'gaps' in a witness's account. This can happen when the interviewer subconsciously supplements the account with his/her own knowledge of the offence.

APP suggests that a witness interview strategy should be developed in the early stages of an investigation. This is particularly important in complex investigations where there may be a number of victims and witnesses, but may still be important in volume crime cases. Any strategy should consider such issues as: appropriate level of interviewer required, how the evidence is to be captured (ie audio, video, statement), location of interview (ie police station, home address, sexual assault referral centre), and any vulnerabilities or particular needs of the witness or victim (see 25.6.2).

25.6.1 Recording witness interviews

The account from a witness is usually written up on an MG11 as a witness statement (see 10.11). Some categories of witnesses and victims (eg vulnerable or intimidated witnesses, see 24.2.4) are interviewed away from a police station at designated facilities with suitable recording facilities (see 25.6.2).

In a serious crime the interview with a significant witness is often video-recorded to capture his/her initial oral account of events. This has numerous advantages for the investigator; for example, it is less obtrusive and more fluent than the stop/start approach required for a written statement, so the witness may be more forthcoming. In addition, the witness's own words and intonation are recorded, thus reducing the risk of the statement-taker unintentionally influencing the content. A video-recording can also help assess the witness's ability to provide convincing oral evidence from the witness box ('come up to proof')—some witnesses may not be able to perform reliably in court due to nervousness, forgetfulness, or confusion. After the interview a ROVI (record of a video-interview) document may be prepared by the police to help inform decisions on criminal charges, or a full witness statement (MG11) can be prepared. The existence of the video-recording must be revealed (see 24.3) to the CPS. The subsequent use in court of evidence derived from video-recordings is covered in 27.5.2.5. Vulnerable witnesses can be supported by the use of intermediaries. This may eleviate communication problems and allow better evidence to be obtained. For further information, see *Making the most of working with an intermediary* (Lexicon Ltd, 2014).

25.6.2 Achieving Best Evidence

Interviews conducted in compliance with Achieving Best Evidence (ABE) guidelines are used for a witness who has been assessed as having a particular vulnerability, or characteristics that will require a particular approach or special measures. The definitions of vulnerable and intimidated witnesses are provided in 24.2.4. Each witness must be assessed prior to formal interview in order to identify whether this is required. Interviewing officers should use the special measures available so they can offer reassurance in the face of questions from a witness such as 'Will I have to face him in court?' or 'Will everyone be able to hear all this?'.

Interviews that are likely to be more difficult or protracted will be conducted by specialist officers qualified to at least PIP Level 2 (see 7.6.1.1) and will follow ABE guidelines. APP makes clear the similarities between the PEACE model of interviewing and ABE, demonstrating that the phases are essentially the same. The phases identified in an ABE interview are: establishing rapport, initiating and supporting a free narrative account, questioning, closure (Ministry of Justice, 2011). Guidance is also available regarding the structure of visually recorded interviews with witnesses (NPCC, 2015a), and this should be read in conjunction with the ABE guidance. Trainee officers may engage with such witnesses in obtaining vital first accounts, or might attend a full interview to brief and assist the interviewing officers. Where a first account is being obtained, it cannot be stressed enough that it is imperative to ask open, non-leading questions, and to record what the person says verbatim in contemporaneous notes (usually in your PNB).

25.7 Interviews and Criminal Intelligence

An often overlooked by-product of a formal police interview is the 'intelligence interview'. An intelligence interview is the process through which the police attempt to gather criminal intelligence on the activities and lifestyle of the interviewee and others. It is a separate process from an investigative interview, and must be undertaken by specialist intelligence officers. A trainee officer is unlikely to be involved in the detail of any of this, but it helps to know that it happens.

All police officers should be alert to the potential for an intelligence interview and carefully note those people (known as 'subjects' in this context) who would have access to information about targets whose criminality comes within the force's strategic intelligence requirement. The access which the subject has should be reported to the BCU Intelligence Unit, who will arrange for an interview. This is often carried out by a fully trained intelligence analyst or researcher who does not work 'in the field' (so that other criminals who may be in the vicinity will not recognize him/her). Any interview conducted whilst the subject is in custody (and this is often the only opportunity for a secure approach) must be recorded on the custody record, but there must be no specific reference to the interview's purpose. The record will simply show the transfer of custody from one police officer to another. In order to enhance confidentiality intelligence interviews should not be recorded on tape and no other people should be present. Any information obtained will be recorded on a 3 × 5 × 2 (see 23.5.2).

An Investigation Anonymity Order (IAO) can be used when a person (other than a witness) can assist the police with relevant information or intelligence, but he/she wants to remain anonymous. This is only possible in certain circumstances and for certain offences, as set out in the Coroners and Justice Act 2009. The legislation is primarily intended to tackle 'gang culture' crime, but may in time be extended to cover a wider range of criminal acts. An IAO prohibits the disclosure of information that identifies the person or might lead to his/her identification. The case must involve murder or manslaughter with a firearm or knife, and the suspect must be between 11 and 30 years of age and belong to a group of people of a similar age. This group ('gang') should also be identifiable by the types of criminal activity undertaken by its members, and also be likely to use intimidation against a member who provides the police with relevant information about the offence.

25.8   **Answers to Tasks**

TASK 1 For interviews with cooperative witnesses the 'cognitive interview' (CI) technique could be used. This uses memory-enhancing techniques such as context reinstatement, which involves recreating the other events that were also encoded at the same time (or before or after) the event of interest. You are probably familiar already with this idea—for example, what techniques do you use to locate misplaced keys? If you want to know more about the cognitive interview and other interview techniques then *Investigative Interviewing—Psychology and Practice* by Rebecca Milne and Ray Bull is a good start (Milne and Bull, 1999). Although CI may be part of PEACE training, it is not often used by police officers investigating volume crimes.

TASK 2 A shortened version of the interview will be prepared as a transcript for the reviewing lawyer (a Short Descriptive Note (SDN)). It is not usual practice for a full transcript (Record of Taped Interview or ROTI) to be made, as this is very time-consuming and therefore costly.

TASK 3 Many police practitioners argue that the best place to use a special warning is after the suspect has had a full opportunity to account for what happened, but has not done so. This would probably be during the 'challenge' phase of the PEACE interview (see 25.3.3.1).

Investigation and
Prosecution

26 | Forensic Investigation

26.1 Introduction

This chapter is concerned with the use of forensic investigation and the role it plays in policing. We will concentrate on the aspects of forensic investigation that are most relevant to initial training, exploring not only the subject of forensic investigation itself (and its relationship with forensic science) but also the role of police officers in assisting the Crime Scene Investigator (CSI), such as 'bagging and tagging' evidence, and collecting evidence from suspects. An understanding of forensic investigation and how a police officer supports that process is vitally important in terms of both convicting the guilty and exonerating the innocent. This importance is reflected in the IPLDP: there are a large number of learning outcomes that relate to forensic investigation in the modules OP 3, LP 1, and LPG 2.

This chapter will help a police officer in training to develop the underpinning knowledge required for a number of Certificate in Knowledge of Policing units, the Diploma in Policing assessed units, several of the PAC headings, and entries for the Learning Diary Phase 3 and SOLAP. It will also be of interest and value to students on pre-join programmes (see 7.3.1) at a university, college, or with a private training company leading to the Certificate in Knowledge of Policing (see 7.4): many such courses will include modules that cover basic forensic science and investigation.

The apparent obsession with detail in packaging and exhibiting can seem odd to the uninitiated but there are serious consequences in making errors or from failing to follow accepted procedure. As an example, this is an extract from the judgment in *R v Hoey*, by Weir J (2007):

> It is not my function to criticise the seemingly thoughtless and slapdash approach of police and SOCO* officers to the collection, storage and transmission of what must obviously have been potential exhibits in a possible future criminal trial but it is difficult to avoid some expression of surprise that in an era in which the potential for fibre, if not DNA, contamination was well known to the police such items were so widely and routinely handled with cavalier disregard for their integrity.

> (*R v Hoey* [2007] NICC 49 (20 December 2007))

* Scenes of Crime Officer, a role now more usually performed by CSIs

The material covered here is particularly relevant to two of the Diploma in Policing assessed units: 'Use police powers to deal with suspects' and 'Conduct police searches'. In particular, the following learning outcomes and assessment criteria are relevant:

Name of Diploma unit	Learning outcome	Assessment criteria
Use police powers to deal with suspects	Be able to arrest and detain suspects in line with legal and organisational requirements and timescales	Preserve evidence during the arrest in line with approved practice
Conduct police searches	Understand legal and organisational requirements in relation to searches	Explain how to secure potential evidence from search scenes
Conduct police searches	Be able to conduct police searches of premises, vehicles, and outside spaces in line with legal and organisational requirements	Conduct police searches (preventing loss or contamination of potential evidence)

Name of Diploma unit	Learning outcome	Assessment criteria
Conduct police searches	Be able to conduct police searches of premises, vehicles, and outside spaces in line with legal and organisational requirements	Maintain the integrity of seized items, including through the use of appropriate packaging and storage
Conduct police searches	Be able to conduct police searches of individuals in line with legal and organisational requirements	Control individuals (preventing loss or contamination of evidence)

It is also relevant to parts of the Certificate in Knowledge of Policing units 'Knowledge of using police powers to deal with suspects' and 'Knowledge of conducting police searches'.

26.2 Principles of Forensic Investigation

Some key principles underpin the application of forensic science to criminal investigation. For example that:

- all things are unique;
- when two objects come into contact they exchange material; and
- forensic science is context-sensitive, which means that forensic evidence is given meaning when its place or role within the investigation is understood.

Forensic investigation is a tripartite arrangement which involves forensic science, the investigator, and the CJS. It has potential to support both criminal (and civil) investigations.

26.2.1 Locard's Principle

We take a knife from a drawer and replace it. In so doing, material (eg sweaty deposits from our fingertips) is transferred from the hand to the knife and may remain there, for a little time at least. Material is also transferred from the knife to our hand—for example, particles of dust or even tiny fragments of the wooden handle. Edmond Locard (1877–1966) is credited with the development of this Principle of Exchange. His assertion was that material from the crime scene would be found on the suspect and vice versa and is commonly expressed as 'every contact leaves a trace'. As a simple example, an offender could leave fingerprints, blood, and shoe marks at the crime scene and might take away fibres or glass fragments on his/her clothing; the contacts have left a trace.

Locard's Principle has been a mainstay of forensic investigation principally because all matter is divisible if enough force is applied (Inman and Rudin, 2002), that is; objects break down during contact and, potentially, most things ultimately erode to become smaller and smaller. Some of these contacts cannot actually be proven because the quantities of the physical material transferred are too small to be located by current technology. Kirk (1953) wrote that failures by investigators to find or understand physical evidence were the only real problems with forensic evidence, rather than the veracity of the evidence itself. Fortunately the principle can also be extended to include the impressions left at crime scenes by tools, weapons, and other materials. Locard's Principle is really inductive reasoning by another name and hence cannot be considered a scientific law in the usual sense, but until relatively recently this did not much concern the courts. (Inductive reasoning involves generalizing from a number of previous examples to establish a rule or theory. The fingerprint, for example, is still assumed to be unique and this is based on the assertion by fingerprint experts that no two fingerprints have yet been found to be the same. Perhaps the most famous example of inductive reasoning is that 'all swans are white', which is based upon repeated observations of white swans. It would be entirely natural, therefore, to have every confidence in the statement until the day that a black swan is observed.) In practice, Locard's Principle manifests itself in reverse in forensic investigation—evidence of transfer is used as a demonstration of contact.

Trust in the principle requires a leap of faith but, even after assuming we can find the transferred material or an impression, we then need to show that it came from the particular source in question. This brings us to the concepts of individualization and uniqueness.

26.2.2 Individualization

According to Kirk (1963, p236) 'all objects in the universe are unique' so no two things can actually be identical, apart from at an atomic or molecular level. Thus, everything we are concerned with in forensic investigation should be considered as unique, or a one-off. This represents another leap of faith on the part of the investigator and forensic scientist because, again, this concept is not strictly a scientific law. (It cannot be considered to be a scientific law because there is no way it could ever be falsified.) However, as with Locard's Principle, the criminal justice system (CJS) does not consider this a particular problem and it is doubtful whether the idea that all things are unique has ever featured in deliberations in the courts.

Many objects which appear to be identical are markedly different, and those that are very similar (perhaps too similar to measure any differences) become visibly or measurably unique during use. This unique quality is brought about by the development of individual characteristics. The majority of industrial processes impart very similar characteristics to the same products, so they appear identical to the naked eye. A standard 'slot' screwdriver for example will be made on a production line, and every screwdriver will appear identical. The tip will be hammered flat and the blade ground to pre-set dimensions, creating an edge which is generally very similar in every screwdriver of that type. During subsequent use (and misuse) each screwdriver will, however, develop unique characteristics, which provide the means for the forensic scientist to tell them apart, or individualize them.

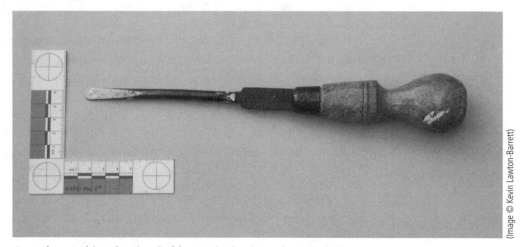

(Image © Kevin Lawton-Barrett)

A used screwdriver has inevitably acquired unique characteristics

Anything which can be associated with its source is said to have individual characteristics: for instance, a fingerprint to a finger, a tool-mark to a tool, and so on. There are different types of characteristic in the classification of evidence to help us understand this. Consider, for example, a number of unused, apparently identical screwdrivers of the same brand. These will have:

- class characteristics which are qualities produced by a controlled process, typically a manufacturing process: for instance, a brand of screwdrivers, where each one is similar to the naked eye. An example could be a 10mm slot screwdriver;
- sub-class characteristics which are the features on a batch of screwdrivers, particularly those which distinguish them from other batches—these features may be imparted by poor quality control or minute changes in settings, grinders, and so on. A batch of screwdrivers may be almost imperceptibly different to other batches;
- the individual, unique screwdriver. It shares the same characteristics in the class and sub-class but Kirk's statement tells us that it is unique—as are all other screwdrivers.

Individualization follows from the premise that two items (such as a screwdriver and a scratch it made) are derived from a common source, so any marks the screwdriver makes can potentially be matched with it. This process is easier if the screwdriver has been damaged or modified by use because the unique qualities of the screwdriver will be more noticeable.

26.2.3 Applications to criminal investigation

An investigator will use evidence of transfer in an attempt to prove that contact has occurred. Although any police officer may be involved in searching a crime scene—whether a place, person, or thing—the majority of scenes are examined by specially trained CSIs. Transfer can be demonstrated by the so-called traces that comprise debris—glass, paint flakes, hairs, DNA, and fibres for example (see 26.5.1 for more detail). Second, there are 'impressions' (see 26.5.2) which include 'prints' made by fingers, shoes, tools, typewriters, and printers. Note also that Locard's Principle is not restricted to these traditional and tangible examples: it can also be extended to intangible digital data held by electronic media, such as computers, discs, and mobile phones.

Locard's Principle is primarily used to create physical links between the differing parts of an investigation. This is set out in its simplest form in the following diagram for an offence against a person.

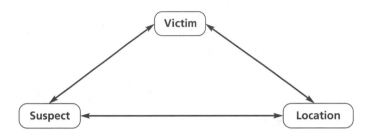

The links are normally created by forensic scientists comparing a 'questioned sample' with a 'control'. It is the examination of articles for individualizing features and subsequent comparison to another object which creates evidence that can be used by the CJS.

Clearly, the link may be between two or more people, a suspect and the scene only, or any permutation of these. A chief aim of forensic investigation is to locate and recover the physical material or impressions which will allow the links to be made. The best links are two-way between every facet, because this reinforces the strength of the evidence.

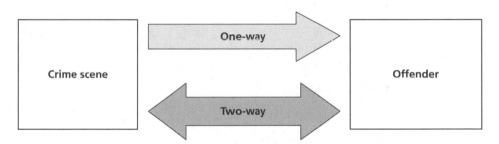

A mechanical fit (sometimes called a physical fit or jigsaw fit) between two or more fragments is an extended application of the theory that all things are unique and can be individualized. In its simplest form, imagine that an object breaks into several parts, and that those parts are later found separately. If the parts can be reconstructed as 'a fit', then it is a reasonable assumption that they must all originate from the same source. This would provide exceptionally powerful evidence in a police investigation. For example, small fragments of a blade were found in the chin of a deceased male and a suspect was found in possession of a damaged craft knife. The blade of the craft knife and the metal fragments were reconstructed successfully to rebuild the blade in its original form. (However, whilst this is acceptable to the court as proof that the craft knife was involved in the murder, it does not prove who committed the offence.)

In a more common scenario, imagine that a window has been forced using a screwdriver. The CSI will recover control samples from the crime scene (see 26.6.2.1), perhaps a sample of paint and a cast of a tool-mark, and will aim to have these compared with the 'questioned samples'—a sweater and a screwdriver taken from a suspect. This may provide strong evidence of association. However, if a corner of the screwdriver blade had broken off and become lodged in the window frame it should fit exactly with the damaged screwdriver blade, and this would provide even stronger evidence of association. (The actual fit would depend on a number of factors, including whether the screwdriver had been used after the break occurred and how effectively it was preserved by the police officer who took control of it.) However, the question now arises: Who was holding the screwdriver when it forced the window? The investigator needs to be able to 'put the suspect at the scene', so evidence of transfer between the suspect and the window (or other parts of the crime scene) would be important here. Any paint flakes on the suspect's sweater or other clothing could be compared to the control of paint removed from the crime scene. Thus: two forms of evidence would have been employed—the mechanical fit *proves* the involvement of the screwdriver and the paint flakes are *strongly supportive* of the notion that the suspect was present during the commission of the offence. A variety of physical evidence types supporting other forms of evidence (eg eye witnesses, CCTV, stolen property) can support the contention that the suspect committed the offence in question.

If Locard's Principle is accepted as really meaning all things erode or break down, then it continues to apply after the commission of the offence, so evidence will inevitably continue to change: fibres on the guilty party are lost, shoes continue to wear out, screwdrivers are modified, and DNA decays. One key objective for the police therefore, is to intervene as quickly after the crime as possible to recover the potential evidence and prevent any further change.

26.3 Forensic Science and Investigations

Forensic science is commonly described as the application of scientific disciplines to the legal system. The fields of science so employed are many and varied: from archaeology through every conceivable speciality to zoology, and any of these may potentially have a role in the investigation of an offence. Experts in these fields may work independently or be employed by a Forensic Science Provider (FSP, but normally just called the 'lab'). They will produce evidence for the investigator by analysing and interpreting the material provided to determine facts or form opinions about the case. The scientist can later make statements of fact (what she did during the examination) and opinion (what she believes her analysis means).

The evidence may point to the guilt or innocence of a suspect, neither of which should be a consideration for the scientist. There are a number of important ethical principles which the scientist is bound by, the key one being to discover the truth and to be unbiased. This is also the essence of a police investigation and the primary focus of the criminal court.

Forensic investigation is often concerned with two main forms of (largely physical) evidence: corroborative evidence (material that will confirm or refute a hypothesis about the crime, for instance that a powder is, or is not, heroin) and inceptive evidence, which identifies an unknown, for example a person.

The investigator may employ forensic investigation and forensic science in a variety of ways when considering these two main forms of evidence. These include:

- Describing the *modus operandi* (MO): the attending CSI or scientist can help form a hypothesis about the method used by the offender to commit the crime. This would be at an early stage in a forensic investigation. The data can be analysed for patterns to link offences. For example, a CSI may link a number of burglaries based upon MO, fingerprints, or a shoe mark left at several crime scenes, or a scientist may be able to interpret the patterns of blood splashes at the scene of a violent crime to describe the mechanics of an assault.
- Answering questions posed by an investigator in order to progress an enquiry: for instance, whose DNA is on this knife? Is there a connection between the weapon used in this crime and this suspect?
- Establishing that an offence has occurred: by examining exhibits it may be shown that an offence has been committed, for instance: following the analysis of a white powder; the classification of a firearm; the calculation of alcohol in urine or blood.
- To corroborate or refute witness statements: this is particularly useful when applied to very specific issues raised during interview.
- To establish physical links between different people, crime scenes and exhibits such as drugs or stolen property and weapons.
- To identify an individual: fingerprints and DNA (and some other techniques) can be employed to identify people, including suspects, arrested persons, or the body of a deceased person.
- To further inform an enquiry: often by clarifying issues or providing some form of descriptive information or intelligence. An example would be a specialist helping to identify the make and model of a vehicle involved in a 'hit-and-run' road traffic incident.

26.3.1   Working with forensic scientists

Efficient communication with forensic scientists is vital to the investigative process. In volume crime this is normally carried out by the CSI, but in major crime it will be a senior CSI, and sometimes one or more investigators assist at a case conference held by a Forensic Management Team (FMT). In order to provide an efficient and effective service to the police, the forensic scientist expects:

- unbroken continuity (or 'chain of custody') of evidence (see 11.2.6);
- correct packaging with intact integrity seals;
- utmost care in preventing contamination (see 11.2.5.1);
- a clear communication which explains the investigative need and describes the perceived relevance and place of the evidence (context);
- guidance regarding 'points to prove';
- up-to-date information whenever the investigation changes tack; and
- clear guidance on any deadlines, such as bail dates or court appearances.

It is important to remember that forensic evidence is context-sensitive. This can be difficult to understand, the misunderstanding being based upon the notion that a particular type of evidence is 'good' or 'poor'. Fingerprints and DNA evidence are often regarded as good because each can easily provide clear differentiations, but their significance depends on their location or 'context'. For example, a fingerprint found near the point of entry in the female toilets of a burgled pub was found to belong to the barman. The context of this apparently innocent mark changed when, during interview, he categorically denied ever having been in the toilet. In another case, blood found on an assault suspect's clothing was initially explained by the fact he had helped an injured stranger in the street. However, on closer analysis it was apparent that the blood must have spattered onto his clothing, which indicated he may have been involved in an offence.

In order to provide the correct information and to explain its importance to the case, a form (MG21) is used to guide the investigator through the submissions process. Police officers must follow force procedures regarding the submission of exhibits to laboratories to avoid problems in any subsequent prosecution. Laboratory submission forms, fingerprint documentation (even for negative results) and CSI worksheets are disclosable under the CPIA (1996) and all the physical or digital materials recovered as evidence can be examined by defence experts upon request.

26.3.2   The role of the Crime Scene Investigator

The CSI is typically the first port of call for all enquiries regarding forensic science, such as taking samples from suspects and victims and the examination of crime scenes. Chief amongst the CSI's crime-based activities are:

- photographing crime scenes, articles, or people associated with crime, such as weapons, injuries, victims, and suspects (but not so-called 'mug shots');
- the location, assessment, and recovery of exhibits and physical or biological evidence (including fingerprints) from crime scenes;
- the packaging, storage, and documentation of recovered material;
- attending post-mortem examinations for sudden and suspicious deaths;
- providing advice to police officers and investigators on matters related to physical evidence, photography, and laboratory submissions; and
- gathering intelligence (from utterances, personal observations, or physical material) to support the NIM (see 23.6), and for use in databases.

CSIs are also involved with non-crime incidents such as sudden deaths, suicides, and fatal industrial accidents (on behalf of HM Coroners and in support of Health and Safety Executive investigations). They may also be involved in the recording of loss through fire prior to arson being ruled out, especially at high-value scenes and those of significant public interest.

The majority of CSIs in the UK police are police support staff attached to a force's scientific support department (sometimes shared with other forces). This includes other complementary services such as a photography unit and a fingerprint bureau with experts who identify suspects from crime scene fingerprints and manage IDENT1 (the national fingerprint database), and a laboratory for enhancing fingerprint evidence. Computer forensic investigators and technical services (responsible for covert intelligence and evidence-gathering technology) may work in the same department.

Qualifications and Training

26.4   **Establishing the Time and Date of an Event**

This is about establishing the precise time that an event occurred (eg when an image on a computer hard drive was accessed) and is sometimes known as 'time-and-date-stamping'. Some evidence may occur in a physical form which shows it was created during the commission of the offence, and this is potentially of great value. For example:

- in the investigation of an assault, the distribution of blood on the suspect could indicate that she had been present during the assault, and even establish her distance and position in relation to the victim. DNA analysis of the blood on the suspect's clothing could establish it was from the victim, so proving the suspect's clothing (and probably the suspect) was present when *that person* was assaulted;
- when investigating a case of criminal damage to a church window the presence of unusual stained glass from the window on the suspect's head hair and upper clothing may indicate that he was in close proximity when *that* window was smashed;
- for an offence where a firearm had been used, finding firearm discharge residue (FDR) on a suspect may show that he was present when **a** firearm was discharged. However, it does not necessarily prove that he fired *that* particular gun.

Challenging suspects in interviews, however, can be used to reinforce many forms of evidence. CSIs and forensic managers prefer absolute statements from suspects because this can make the context of the evidence stronger. If a suspect or other person makes an early statement, this information should be carefully considered: it may be of value to the scientist and must, at least, describe any admissions made. In addition, when a laboratory result is received officers might consider their interview strategy; that is, how best to employ the information received to drive the investigation forward.

For example where a man is suspected of a shooting, the forensic manager and scientist will consider the value of any potential FDR evidence after interview thus:

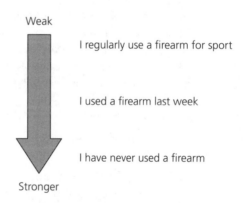

Weak

I regularly use a firearm for sport

I used a firearm last week

I have never used a firearm

Stronger

Clearly, if the man denies the use of firearms on any occasion then any FDR located on his body or his clothes would provide the basis for challenging the veracity of any statement he makes in his defence. The evidence against him would be strong. If this were the case, consideration must be given to his activity in recent days:

- Has he been in the vicinity of a firearm which has been used?
- Was he arrested by an officer who recently used a firearm, say, for sport?
- Was he conveyed in a vehicle which had contained people who were contaminated with firearms residues?
- Was he arrested by an officer who was environmentally contaminated through using firearms at work?

The forensic scientist would need to know this sort of information so that an informed assessment of the significance of the contamination could be made. To explore this further you may wish to look at how FDR evidence was used in the wrongful conviction of Barry George in 2001; the defence raised the possibility that his coat had been contaminated by armed police officers when they searched his home address. He was subsequently acquitted in 2008.

> **TASK 1**
> 1. What does FSP stand for?
> 2. Who is credited with the development of the Principle of Exchange?
> 3. List three things for which an investigator might employ forensic science.

26.5   Types of Forensic Evidence

Forensic evidence can be classified in a number of different ways, but in this section we have chosen a relatively simple method:

- trace evidence; very small quantities of material (DNA is considered separately);
- impressions or marks (fingerprints are considered separately);
- DNA evidence (a type of trace evidence, but with special features);
- fingerprints (impressions, which also leave a trace of sweat, and can be printed in blood or other materials); and
- documents, firearms, and CCTV.

A great deal of intelligence can be recovered from crime scenes and this can be stored in a variety of databases, such as IDENT1, the National DNA Database and footwear collections which will be discussed later. The information taken even from a crime scene with limited evidence can be valuable when it is compared to other crime scenes, including the MO, the size of tool marks and even the behaviour of the suspect. This information can be stored in crime systems (like Genesis) or forensic management databases such as Locard and Flints, and may be capable of linking offences through their analysis.

For digital devices, finger prints, DNA, and fibres (from users, their clothes, and the environment in which the items have been stored or used) can be present. There is however a potential conflict of priorities when considering the seizure of physical and intangible evidence from a digital device, so advice should be sought from a CSI and Computer Forensic Investigator. Evidence from digital devices such as computers and tablets is covered in 21.5.

26.5.1   Trace materials as forensic evidence

Trace material can be any material transferred from the suspect to the crime scene (or a victim) and vice versa. It ranges from common materials such as fibres, glass fragments, and paint flakes transferred during property crimes to the more exotic, such as pollens, soils, and even insects or their fragments. Imagination is important here and consideration should not be limited to any specific groups: creativity is a vital element in forensic investigation. DNA trace evidence is covered separately in 26.5.3.

26.5.1.1   Glass

The manufacturing processes vary depending on the type of glass required and this provides varying degrees of discriminatory power (ie the ability to distinguish one object made of glass from another). The addition of colourants and physical processes can make this outwardly common material very useful in the right criminal circumstances.

Glass is a mix of silica, sodium carbonate, and calcium compounds which are smelted to form the base material to which physical processes or chemical additives are applied, imparting a number of properties. All glass can be chemically analysed and its refractive index measured (how much it slows down light that passes through it). The following types of glass are often encountered in an investigation:

- Plain window glass (or float glass): the most common window glass manufactured today. It breaks relatively easily.
- Georgian wired glass: reinforced with wire mesh of varying sizes, used for security (because it is difficult to penetrate), and fire resistance (it remains in situ longer than float glass).
- Toughened glass: inherently strong and normally difficult to break—used in telephone kiosks and the side windows of vehicles. It breaks easily if struck with force near the edge, forming thousands of cube-shaped granules.

- Laminated glass: two sheets of glass which sandwich a plastic filling which prevents the pane shattering and retains it in the frame. Windscreens and many low-level windows are constructed in this way.
- Container glass: eg bottles, drinking vessels, older TV and computer screens.
- Optical glass: found in lenses.
- Mirrors.

Shards of glass may be exceptionally sharp and small, and can be very dangerous. Personnel should always wear goggles and gloves when dealing with broken glass and avoid large, unsupported broken windows which may collapse without warning.

Glass found on the suspect or other articles can be compared to samples recovered from the broken window frame by a variety of analytical techniques. Where the glass is unusual (perhaps very old or specially coloured) the scientist may provide a forensically important statement. Glass can be broken in a variety of ways and different authors have different views on classification but, in a criminal context, glass is typically broken by moving objects (varying speeds), by some form of stress, by heat, or by an explosion. Frequently, the cause is deduced at the scene, but windows and glass objects can be reconstructed in order to demonstrate the cause, point, and (using some fractures) even the direction of the breakage. One of the most valuable attributes of breaking glass is a process called backward fragmentation, where breaking glass throws out fine particles which may land on the offender in a characteristic way, and which can demonstrate that he/she was in the vicinity of the window when it broke.

26.5.1.2 Fibres and paint

Fibres can be natural, man-made, or mixed. They are frequently transferred from clothing, seats, and carpets on to receptive surfaces, especially when the contact has been violent or has occurred over a long period. They are often ignored because they are (wrongly) thought by many to be very similar and common. However, manufacturers use different fibre mixes and dyes and so a garment or other fabric may have an unusual or characteristic mix. Man-made fibres, in particular, can survive conditions which cause decay in natural materials such as wool or cotton. A process called fibre mapping can be carried out in significant crime scenes, where every fibre is lifted onto hundreds of adhesive tapes. This can demonstrate the position of, for instance, the suspect at a crime scene. Note, however, that poor crime scene management can compromise the success of such procedures.

Paint is applied to window and door frames, manufactured objects, and cars as a protective or cosmetic coating. Its chemical components are designed to give the paint specific properties, such as rust-proofing, weather-proofing, fungal resistance, and even as an identification measure. These elements and the enormous variety of colour and finish types ensure that any surface which has been chipped or scraped may be usefully examined and compared with paint fragments found on a suspect's clothing, tools, vehicle, or other objects in his/her possession. The more layers of paint, the more likely the profile can be demonstrated as unique. Some paints are unique or very unusual such as military (infrared absorbing) coatings and paint used on colour-coded scaffold poles. Other dye and marker traps are normally categorized separately to paints. They are made up of unique combinations of animal and plant material or chemical markers and are often used to trap thieves by proving ownership of stolen property.

26.5.1.3 Soil, plants, and insects

Soils are found nearly everywhere, but they can vary significantly over short distances because of a number of important geological and geomorphological ('rock shape') factors, such as the source rock contributing to the soil. In a simplified description, the scientist examines the minerals, organic material, and grain size of the sample. In some situations the soil has been modified by the inclusion of chemicals and waste material from industrial and other processes, and this can be useful in identifying locations. Soil is almost always sampled during exhumations to demonstrate that any toxins found in the body of the deceased have not leached into it from the environment. The main general limitation for soil evidence is demonstrating that it came from a *very specific* location related to the offence (perhaps a few square metres of a field) but it should be noted that—while difficult—it is not necessarily impossible.

Vegetative material can often be used by forensic botanists to identify the species of a plant from small fragments of leaf, stem, seed, flower, or wood. Palynologists can identify the species of plant from the pollen transferred onto clothing, vehicles, and illegal substances such as cannabis resin. The precise mix of plant types at, say, the crime scene, can often provide particularly powerful forensic evidence.

Insects are generally sensitive to their food source and climate (apart from the common pest species) and, as a result, many species are found in limited ranges. When insects are identified during a forensic investigation they may be helpful in determining the geographic origin of materials. Forensic entomologists can also use known data on insect life cycles—especially that of blowflies—to identify when a body became available for them to feed upon. This may be of value when attempting to determine the time or date of death.

By using all these naturally occurring types of evidence, the source of materials such as cannabis resin, or the previous locations of vehicles and people can often be established.

26.5.1.4   Toxicology

This is a specialist field engaged in the analysis of poisons and drugs and may be crucial to an investigation, for example:

- to calculate whether a person is over the drink-drive limit;
- to establish that alcohol or drugs may explain behaviour such as violence or drowsiness (particularly relevant to 'date-rape' offences); or
- to establish cause of illness and death.

Roadside breath tests are the most common forms of toxicological measurement carried out by the police, but these are normally used as screening tests (see 19.9.4) prior to more stringent evidential tests (see 19.9.5). A variety of field-test kits and covert-sampling devices can be employed to screen for drugs, but the opinion of an expert toxicologist should be sought to provide evidence suitable for a prosecution unless force policy allows the suspect to make a guilty plea prior to caution, or if there is an intervention model in place at the time (see 12.5.3.1). Elaborate and expensive analysis would therefore not normally be required (or at best, not even embarked upon), since the case will not go to court in these circumstances.

In driving cases, where the driver claims to have drunk alcohol only after an incident, specialist laboratory submission forms should be used to request a 'back calculation' (see 19.9.5.3). Police officers should always seek the advice of a CSI based at the Basic Command Unit (or a Scientific Support Unit adviser), since the forms required for such a calculation can be quite complex and require other factors to be considered, such as medication, food consumed and any ill health. Regardless of this, original bottles and glasses should be seized where possible, and marked up to show what the suspect claims to have drunk—remembering that a 'gulp' or 'swig' is not a scientifically accepted measurement of alcohol consumption!

Commonly, blood or urine is sent for analysis for toxins, but other samples from the body tissue of deceased victims (including from the eyes) may also be used, depending upon the circumstances. Toxicology samples must always be treated as a potential health hazard.

26.5.2   Impressions as forensic evidence

These are the marks left by fingers, shoes, tools, tyres, stamping machines, printers, and typewriters, etc. Whilst these can be a direct 'stamped' effect, many are made up of irregular scrapes and smudges and even cutting or drilling marks. Fingerprints are covered separately in 26.5.4. All forms of impression can be easily destroyed: be cautious about what is touched and where people walk.

26.5.2.1   Footwear marks

Shoe or other footwear marks are a useful but potentially short-lived form of evidence. Footwear is readily modified by use when people walk over surfaces which scratch and tear the soles or add particles such as glass and stones. The resultant damage occurs at random and is therefore unique to every sole. When a shoe leaves an impression at a crime scene the mark can be compared with the shoe in question. However, the shoe must be located and recovered before the relevant damage to the sole is further eroded, as this could reduce the value of any comparison.

The marks can be on a flat, apparently two-dimensional surface, or they can be impressed into a soft substrate to form a three-dimensional pattern. Importantly, the surface must be fine enough to receive the mark: soft clay is clearly better than coarse sand.

Trainers in particular are readily identifiable (either from databases or by an expert) and this data can be used for intelligence purposes in order tentatively to link crime scenes. Forensic Management Systems used in force, or external databases like The National Footwear Database provide a valuable intelligence tool (see also 26.6.1.5). The addition of MO, times of offence, and target properties can make such databases invaluable. Under the PACE Act, 1984, (as amended) police forces can make good use of shoe marks and their intelligence databases by taking shoes from prisoners in custody and scanning the sole patterns for future use (see 26.6.1). It should be noted that this would of course only provide intelligence data on the shoes worn at the time of arrest. The database can also provide information on offences where a *similar* sole pattern has occurred and, therefore, assist in linking crimes.

In theory, marks should be present at almost every crime scene, since almost all offenders will walk within the venue so all personnel in attendance should use the Common Approach Path (CAP) to a crime scene (see 11.2.2). A variety of techniques can be used to recover the marks: photography, casting, lifting, or removal of the surface upon which the mark rests.

26.5.2.2   Tyre marks

Like footwear, vehicle tyres leave impressions which are commonly found in soft soils, on roads, smooth concrete floors, glass, and paper—particularly at 'ram raids'. They are also modified by the surfaces over which they pass, and may pick up 'inclusions' such as glass and gravel. On a suitable surface these individual details will be impressed as a two or three-dimensional pattern. The impression may be of a rotating tyre or a skidding tyre. The full circumference of a car tyre is approximately 3.14 times the diameter, so a full rotation print of a 50 cm diameter car tyre is over 150 cm long. (Finally, that school geometry has proved useful!) Never assume that only part of a print needs to be preserved: as much as possible should be retained for the CSI. The laboratory can assist in identifying the make and type of tyre from a recovered print, which may include or exclude vehicles from the enquiry.

26.5.2.3   Other types of marks

Tool or **instrument marks** are marks imparted to receptive surfaces by the application of force. These marks can also be left by objects such as rocks, baseball bats, and any suitably hard object which meets a softer surface, but typical examples are those made by forcing a window or cashbox. The marks can be made by:

- levering, to force open a window, door, or cashbox—one edge of the target surface acts as a fulcrum or pivot and both this and the opening part will be marked;
- striking an object, or person, with a weapon or similar;
- cutting—the action caused by scissors, wire cutters, and bolt croppers; and
- drilling—the waste material and hole from drilling can bear the impression of the cutting edge of the drill bit.

The actions used will be cut into or impressed onto the surface with the shape of the tip or edge of the device. This will have been individualized through its manufacture and previous use, as can be clearly seen on the milled edges of scissors and pliers for example (see 26.2.2).

Stamps, dyes, and manufacturing marks are impressions deliberately pressed into a surface, similar to tool or instrument marks. For instance Vehicle Identification Numbers (VINs, see 16.8.1) are often faked or amended: a particular stamp can be compared to VINs on suspect vehicles. Where metal factory waste has been stolen it may be beneficial to take some of the remaining material to scrap dealers to compare it with scrap they have recently accepted because it is reasonable to presume the waste has identifying features and unique cut edges that can be usefully compared to the factory cutting machines.

Any material which is set in a mould or extruded also takes on an impression of the mould or extrusion head, particularly where debris has built up. Examples include apparently identical copper pipes, plastic bags, and plastic components. These can be compared because many objects from a single batch will have similar characteristics. If for instance half a batch of copper pipes has been stolen and is recovered by the police then extrusion marks can show they originate from the same batch. Extrusion marks were especially useful in the 1970s and 1980s when terrorist bombings were investigated: the offenders often used several bin bags from the same roll, and they were found at different locations, allowing the police to link several offences.

Printers, copiers, and typewriters can also provide useful evidence. Modern copiers (and all printers) are digital, which means that the pages which have been printed are digitally stored within the device's limited memory for some time after printing. Paper feeders and rollers may also impart marks. When the metal letters, golf ball, or daisy wheel are damaged or aged they take on individual characteristics which are easily compared with characters contained in seized documents. Photocopiers superimpose an image of the glass screen (the platen) on the copies they produce. The more damage (or dried correction fluid) on the platen, the better the scientist's chances of demonstrating an association between a particular copier and paper evidence. Most colour printers are also capable of 'printer steganography' where the serial number of the machine and date are printed onto the document; this can be used for tracking forged documents and money. The fonts chosen by typewriter manufacturers can be identified when found on letters or other material. Plastic ribbons, correction ribbons (which physically lift letters from paper) and other components can be very valuable where an offender has used such a machine.

Bite marks are another form of impression, and are valuable sources of evidence. The position, number, layout, orientation, and cutting surfaces of teeth make our dentition highly individual. It is the role of the *forensic odontologist* to compare marks found on victims and in foodstuffs with the teeth of the suspect. This is carried out by taking a three-dimensional dental impression of the suspect's teeth and comparing it with photographs or with impressions of the injury or damage. Older bite marks on skin may be visible under ultraviolet (UV) lighting and can be photographed some time after the incident. The apparent lack of a bite mark on skin is not, therefore, a 'lost cause'. (Whenever bite marks are found, DNA may be present and consideration must be given to preserving this evidence.)

26.5.3 DNA evidence

Every cell in the human body—with a few exceptions—has a nucleus which contains chromosomes. Chromosomes are made up of genes which provide instructions to the body cells to manufacture proteins, and therefore govern the biological and physical processes in the body. The genes are made of DNA and every nucleus contains a copy of the DNA for the entire organism, so a cell from a person's cheek contains exactly the same material as a white cell from his/her blood. A large proportion of DNA is the same for all humans, but small differences occur between individuals and these account for variations such as hair and eye colour, other physical characteristics, and genetically related illness. However, the chromosomes also contain sections of DNA called Short Tandem Repeats (sometimes called 'junk DNA') which have no apparent function. The coding in STRs varies significantly between individuals so it is therefore very useful for forensic analysis. Many texts refer to DNA as the 'blueprint' for humans and other living things, but the term 'DNA fingerprinting' is not to be taken literally—fingerprint patterns cannot be established through DNA analysis.

DNA is typically found on articles or at scenes yielding blood, semen, saliva, hair with roots, some bodily secretions, and pieces of body tissue (all of which are a health hazard). This biological material also needs protecting from us if it is to be used as evidence because our own DNA can easily contaminate it. At the laboratory the material containing DNA is often clearly visible (such as blood or a cigarette end). It is extracted and copied many times using a process called Polymerase Chain Reaction (PCR) to ensure enough is available for analysis. Put simply, the different STRs are measured and compared to the suspect's sample or data stored in the National DNA Database. On some articles (like tools or weapons) the amount of material containing DNA can be so small it is invisible, so the PCR process is continued several more times. CSIs and scientists refer to this as Low Copy Number DNA, DNA LCN or 'touch DNA'. This has yielded sufficient DNA for analysis from a number of unexpected sources such as tools, clothing grabbed by the suspect, and weapons, particularly where fingerprints could not be found.

26.5.3.1 DNA variability and forensics

Clearly, there would be limited mileage in comparing common genetic material (such as eye colour) to identify suspects. The analysis of DNA samples highlights the differences between the DNA of different individuals. One limitation with DNA is that identical twins and triplets are almost certain to share the same DNA profiles, because they came from the same fertilized egg which divided to produce more than one foetus. (There is a very small possibility that their

DNA has mutated, but this is not likely to be discovered in routine forensic tests.) Twins or triplets from different eggs are called fraternal (or non-identical) twins or triplets and their DNA differs considerably. Note that identical twins and triplets have different fingerprints (all fingerprints are unique, see 26.5.4) so this can be used to distinguish one from another.

A DNA 'hit' is a calculation concerning a selection of a person's STRs and is supplied by the scientist as a 'match probability'. If the match probability is one in a billion, it means that there is one chance in a billion that another person selected at random has the same profile. It does not mean that there is a one in a billion chance that the suspect is innocent, nor does it mean that there is a one in a billion chance that someone else left the DNA at the scene (the prosecutor's fallacy). If the DNA recovered for analysis is degraded through age or lack of proper handling, the match probability applied to the comparison may be reduced, which can cause some concern, but remember that other evidence should be used to support the prosecution case. A new DNA system called DNA 17 has now been brought online in the UK. It uses more STRs than previously and has even greater match probabilities than the SGM+ system which was routinely used up till 2015. The DNA 17 system contains all of the STRs used across many countries, so a DNA sample from a crime scene in the UK can easily be compared with records on a database in another country (and vice versa).

Mitochondrial DNA (Mt DNA) is a different form of DNA which can be extracted from bone, hair, faeces, and teeth. It is found in the cytoplasm of all cells inside tiny structures called 'mitochondria' (rather than in the cell's nucleus), and forms a loop; this makes it more resilient to external influences so it may last for many years. It does, however, have limitations in that it cannot uniquely identify a person: it can only identify the maternal line. This means, for example, that a person has the same Mt DNA as his/her siblings and mother (and her siblings), all the way up the female line. Fathers do not share their Mt DNA with their children because at fertilization only the sperm head enters the egg (and the tail containing the mitochondria is left outside the egg). Mt DNA analysis can be beneficial when applied to the study of old and degraded samples where normal (nuclear) DNA is unavailable. It was famously used by the Forensic Science Service (FSS) to identify the bodies of Tsar Nicholas II, Tsarina Alexandra and their three children, whose bodies were found near Yekaterinburg in Russia, in 1991 following their murders by the Bolsheviks in 1919.

Y STRs are a variable genetic feature found on the Y chromosome, so they can only be used for the identification of men (as women do not have a Y chromosome). It can be used to determine paternal ancestry by studying a specific set of STRs. In Western culture (though not in Iceland, where surnames are passed on in a different way), this is traditionally paralleled by the transfer of the surname; hence Y chromosome analysis has gained commercial popularity as a genealogical tool and may assist in some investigations. The value of Y STRs is, of course, diminished in males with uncertain paternity.

26.5.3.2 The National DNA Database

The National DNA Database (NDNAD) is a database containing records of the DNA of persons who are arrested, cautioned, convicted, and charged for recordable offences, and also some volunteers, missing and vulnerable people. It is the property of the police and is managed by the Home Office. The database stores records on DNA recovered from crime scenes (where applicable) and from all people who have been sampled under legal and operational criteria. On 30 September 2016 the database contained the DNA data of some 5.2 million individuals and 537,000 crime scene samples (see <http://www.gov.uk>). Approximately 80 percent of the retained samples are from males.

The elegance of the system is that although many offenders who commit minor crimes will move away from criminal activities, others will continue as volume-crime offenders or will step up their activity to more serious offences. By taking the DNA sample of new volume-crime offenders, the police effectively 'bank' this intelligence for future investigations, as they do with fingerprints. There may also be a deterrent effect. The NDNAD's true strength however lies in making 'cold hits' which is when a sample from a crime scene or victim identifies a suspect. In many of these offences there was no other way that this might have occurred.

Each time a new crime-scene or suspect sample is received it is entered in the database and cross-checking occurs. The NDNAD can also identify links between crimes. This may not seem hugely significant, but consider the case of John Wood who normally assaulted two young girls in 1988 in Canterbury in Kent, and was not apprehended at the time. He was arrested in 2001 in Derbyshire for shoplifting £10 worth of groceries, and the arresting PC took his DNA sample. It was matched to DNA found at the crime scene in Canterbury, and Wood admitted the offences and was sentenced to 15 years in prison. Your local force will have similar success stories where the NDNAD has solved old and new crimes.

26.5.4 Fingerprints

About 5 per cent of the human body is covered in skin that bears ridge detail. This is found on the fingers, palms, soles, and toes. Every finger, toe, palm and sole pattern on every person is considered by the criminal justice system to be unique, including those of so-called identical siblings. The tiny ridges consist of small features such as forks and spurs, which are normally referred to as '*minutiae*'. It is the combinations and positions of these features which make the fingerprints unique. The ridges develop in the womb and remain identical (apart from size and scarring) until death—and beyond if the body is sufficiently preserved.

Finger marks can potentially be found on all the finely textured surfaces we touch. They can either be a physical impression or a print consisting of sweat and contaminants. The receiving surface must be sufficiently smooth to accept the mark. (There is an analogy here with the pattern of a shoe impressed into soft clay compared to one impressed into shingle.) For a non-porous surface, the easiest way to determine whether it might yield fingerprints is to scratch it gently with a fingernail (clearly, this practice should be carried out with caution, and never at serious or major crime scenes). If the scratching action makes virtually no noise then the surface could be a good source of fingerprints. If it makes a noise (due to it being rough) then the surface might be unsuitable. Porous surfaces, such as paper and wood, can bear fingerprints but only if the surface is fine enough.

26.5.4.1 Locating fingerprints

Latent marks are invisible. CSIs usually make them visible using a fine brush to gently dust a surface with powders, and searching with a torch. This is the most common procedure; the fabric of the building can be examined, and bulky items left in place, rather than being recovered as evidence. The mark may then be photographed and, where appropriate, lifted with an adhesive material and placed onto an acetate sheet. Positive (or patent) marks are visible, often printed in dirt or blood, and can be photographed. Plastic marks are three-dimensional patterns impressed into putty, clay, or chocolate for example. They can also be photographed and even cast using a silica gel if the surface is firm enough.

On some items, such as paper, there may be no visible marks, but it is *presumed* that marks are very likely to be present. Such an item can be seized and packaged for later chemical or physical enhancement by employing specialist light sources, physical treatments and chemical dyes to enhance the non-aqueous components of sweat (salts, fats, oils, and amino acids make up about 1.5 per cent of the content of sweat). It is worth bearing in mind that, even if items from a crime scene have been handed back to the owners, paper exhibits can still produce meaningful fingerprint evidence years later. Consider fingerprints on documents from the DVLA to show ownership of vehicles in the distant past, and old passport applications, cheques, letters, and diaries.

Occasionally, laboratory personnel visit complex scenes and search the fabric of the building using chemicals and light sources. Whilst CSIs routinely 'dust' smooth non-porous surfaces, marks may be found on many other surfaces such as textured plastics, polythene bags, paper, smooth wood, and even wall coatings. The majority of marks at scenes or on exhibits are invisible, which means they are easily damaged by thoughtless actions.

Note that it is always better to preserve a whole crime scene rather than just the point of entry because as an initially nervous and sweaty-palmed offender moves through a building, his/her hands dry out sufficiently to leave marks of good quality further inside the scene.

26.5.4.2 IDENT1

The IDENT1 database contains the fingerprints (so-called 'tenprints') and palm prints of arrested persons, and crime-scene marks recovered by CSIs and other personnel. This national system contains in excess of 8 million sets of fingerprints and palm prints. IDENT1 compares: crime-scene marks to crime-scene marks to search for links between offences; tenprints and palm prints against crime-scene marks (and vice versa); and new tenprints to those already on file to confirm identity or to establish that an arrested person is not using a pseudonym. Once the system identifies a suspect print, a chain of at least three experts then verify the result before providing a statement of evidence.

IDENT1 is linked to the Livescan tenprint scanners in police stations. These capture suspects' fingerprints by scanning electronically, and have improved the quality of tenprints since forces stopped routinely using ink and paper. As the finger and palm prints are already on the system, the identity of a suspect with an existing criminal record can be verified in about ten minutes through IDENT1, a so-called Live Identification. Portable 'Lantern units' are also linked to the system for making identifications while on patrol.

26.5.5 Evidence from documents and CCTV

Here we examine the evidence available from handwritten and printed documents, and public safety or security CCTV systems.

26.5.5.1 Evidence from documents

Under the term 'documents', forensic investigators normally include all letters, paperwork, invoices, cheques, transfers, application forms, handwriting, and any other written material, whether handwritten or printed by typewriter, computer printer, photocopier, or other device.

The writing on a document (eg a hate-mail letter) can be compared with material obtained during the investigation with samples provided by a suspect. Handwriting samples are used most effectively when a variety of material is submitted for comparison, and not just samples produced in front of a police officer. For example 'course of business' handwriting samples (such as diaries, letters, general paperwork) can be sourced from his/her home address, work, or other places. Some samples may be *known* to have been written by the suspect, but for others this might not be so certain. A document can also be analysed for 'impressed' handwriting. Typically this is found when a pad of paper is used and an impression of writing on one page is transferred to the pages below. It is enhanced using Electrostatic Detection Apparatus (referred to as ESDA).

Printers and typewriters can also be analysed and compared with a specimen document. The presence of printer-head faults, 'banding', or damage to paper caused by rollers may be reproduced under laboratory conditions and compared with the suspect document (see also 26.5.2.3).

The physical features of paper can also be compared, such as tear marks, staple holes and batch faults in envelopes (such as poor cuts). Other features such as watermarks, obliterations, paper type, security inks, concealed marks, and 'reactive fibres' can be analysed in a number of ways, for example by microscopy and by using a Video Spectral Comparator (VSC). A VSC employs different wavelengths of light and is particularly useful in identifying handwritten additions to cheques and payment forms, and for revealing obliterated text. When a suspect is identified, the investigator should also exploit any fingerprints on paper, and take samples for potential DNA on envelope flaps and stamps.

26.5.5.2 CCTV footage

At some crime scenes, CCTV footage might provide vital information. Most CCTV cameras are automatic and many are actually unmonitored, with tapes being renewed on average about every seven days. Digital storage systems almost certainly last longer than this but are likely to be overwritten at some stage. Copies of CCTV recordings can be obtained with appropriate authorization so that a forensic analyst can enhance the images and conduct a more thorough analysis (see 24.3.1.3). CCTV footage should not be ignored or simply deleted if the activity which concerns the investigator is not seen on the tape or disc. Such actions may be challenged at appeal: in *R (Ebrahim) v Feltham Magistrates Court* (2001) the investigating officer did not seize a CCTV tape because he saw nothing of significance on it, but this was challenged on the ground that a fair trial would not be received as a result. CCTV tapes and discs are disclosable material under the CPIA (see 24.3).

26.5.6 Firearms and forensics

Firearms and spent bullets or cartridges are a rich source of evidence. In a typical offence a firearm is used to threaten, injure or kill a victim, and the offender leaves with the weapon, leaving only a bullet (or lead shot), a spent cartridge and perhaps some damage to a building where a bullet has passed through. Later, a suspect might be arrested and his home searched, revealing a suspicious firearm which must be linked to the shooting in question (or indeed any shooting), and to the person who fired the weapon. The categories of firearms, their component parts, and the associated legislation are covered more fully in Chapter 18.

For intelligence purposes the National Ballistics Intelligence Service (nabis.police.uk) hub laboratories can examine spent (used) bullets and cartridge cases found at crime scenes. When a weapon is fired, the barrel and the firing mechanisms leave marks on the bullets and cartridge cases. The examiners will look for these marks, and they can be used to establish links between crime scenes from where other bullets and cartridges have been recovered. Clearly, one firearm can be used at a number of crime scenes so the intelligence provided by NABIS can be very useful. In this respect the functionality of their database is similar to that of IDENT1 and the NDNAD in that links can be generated and crime series can potentially be identified and detected. Recovered firearms can also be test fired at the hub laboratory to generate spent bullets and cartridges for the same purpose.

Bulleted cartridge component	Available evidence
Cartridge case	The actions of loading, firing, and ejecting the cartridge will scratch the polished brass casing and leave comparable marks upon it. These marks are caused by the magazine (if used), the ejector, extractor, breech face, and firing pin. Since bullets, cartridge design, and extractors vary, it may be possible to identify the type of weapon from which the cartridge was ejected. Manufacturer's details, calibre, and type of round are normally engraved on the head stamp (the base) of cartridges. Despite the high temperature generated during firing fingerprints can potentially be recovered from the brass case
Bullet	This will normally identify the calibre of the weapon used, and since there is huge variation in bullet design, specialist rounds and sometimes the type of weapon can be identified. Most important, though, is the scratched impression on the bullet of the rifling grooves within the gun barrel. Variations in the twist (left or right) and the number of grooves may assist in the identification of the make and model of the gun used, and can be compared to a suspect weapon. Even badly deformed bullets are useful to the scientist as a means of eliminating weapons
Powder	During burning, the powder gives off smoke and particulates which are emitted from the muzzle and frequently around the mechanism of the firearm itself. Minute particles of the bullet, unburnt powder, and other debris are ejected in several directions. This may include small particles of lead, barium, and antimony, which form small granules. These 'firearm discharge residues' (FDRs) can be found on the clothing, face, and hands of the offender and other people and items in the vicinity. Swabbing kits are available to retrieve this material. Suspects should be swabbed as soon as possible because the residues fall off easily. It should be noted that the presence of FDRs does not necessarily prove involvement in the offence

Shotgun cartridges vary both in their overall design and the number and size of lead shot they contain (see 18.5). CSIs and forensic scientists can use these features to derive evidence.

Shot cartridge component	Available evidence
Cartridge case	This is normally retained in the weapon until reloading; however, it may be ejected by automatic or self-loading weapons. It can be used to establish the bore of the weapon and the manufacturer and type of cartridge. Scratches on the brass base and the impression of the firing pin and breech face can be compared to suspect weapons. In automatic weapons marks from the extractor, ejector, and magazine may be found
The shot	The size of the shot may eliminate some types of cartridge from an enquiry. The spread of the shot is useful in establishing the range of the weapon (when the possible use of a 'choke' is taken into consideration)
Powder	FDRs are available, but in most sporting shotguns the FDRs are ejected through the muzzle, since the breech is sealed
Wadding	The presence of wadding indicates that a shotgun has been discharged. It can frequently give an early indication as to the bore of weapon used, and a hint as to the cartridge manufacturer. Wadding is normally badly deformed during discharge, so irregular lumps of plastic, felt, or cork at the scene should be collected and preserved. Plastic wadding fired from a sawn-off weapon can sometimes be compared to the finish at the sawn-off muzzle end: if the finish is poor, the wadding may bear scratches which can be reproduced during controlled tests

Firearms may also require classification to establish the holder has committed an offence relating to a particular category of firearm. Test firing may also be required to check that they function, and to support or refute statements about trigger sensitivity or any issues with the mechanism (for instance when they fire 'accidentally'). The most frequently asked questions at the laboratory are:

- Is this weapon a firearm as defined by the legislation (see 18.3.1)?
- Is this weapon an imitation firearm (see 18.8)?
- What type of weapon fired this bullet (or recovered cartridge case)?
- Did this weapon fire this bullet (or recovered cartridge case)?
- How far was the weapon from the victim?
- Can this weapon fire accidentally?
- Do these swabs/items of clothing bear FDR?
- Which is the entry wound/exit wound on this victim?

(Adapted from a number of unpublished Forensic Science Service publications.)

TASK 2

1. List three types of trace evidence or material which might be found at a burglary.
2. List three types of impression.
3. List three sources of DNA.
4. Which does mitochondrial DNA establish: male or female lines?
5. Which parent provides a boy's Y-STR?

26.6 Taking Samples in Investigations

The objective of taking samples from suspects, victims, and crime scenes is to demonstrate a link between them, preferably during the offence in question (see 26.2.3). Forensic evidence has the potential to produce powerful forms of evidence which might 'include' or 'exclude' people and other things from an enquiry, and can also produce investigative leads. Procedures must be strictly followed in order that samples have a clear provenance and do not become contaminated with other material. Typically, if a sample is taken from one person or place then a corresponding sample should be recovered from elsewhere for comparison. A sample taken from a known source, such as DNA from a person or a scrape of paint from a window frame is known as a 'control' (see 26.6.2.1).

Whilst the crime scene is normally examined by CSIs, any people who are suspected of having been involved in the offence will also need to have samples taken. This can be carried out by custody staff, a medical practitioner or police officer in the custody area, a hospital, or at a person's home or place of work (depending on the person and the circumstances).

26.6.1 Taking samples from people

We have already discussed the requirement to link suspects, victims, and venues as part of an investigation but samples are also occasionally used to establish identity.

The samples taken from people can include a variety of trace evidence and DNA-rich material in or on any part of the body, including foreign blood, saliva, and semen (all sources of DNA); firearm and explosive residues; trace material such as glass, paint flakes, fibres, grease, plant debris, or soil; bite marks, weapon marks, and bruises; chemicals, such as alcohol, toxins, and drugs within the blood and urine, or chemical traces upon the skin; fingerprints; and handwriting characteristics.

It is important to distinguish between people in custody and others who are voluntarily providing evidence or material which can eliminate them from the offence. When taking forensic samples from suspects (whether arrested or not) the procedures set out in PACE Code D must be followed (see 26.6.1.1). However, there is no equivalent PACE Act requirement for people such as victims and witnesses who provide samples to assist police investigations. This means it might not *always* be necessary for a police surgeon or other medical practitioner to take certain types of sample. Police officers must, however, treat victims, witnesses, and volunteers in accordance with the Human Rights Act 1998 (see 5.4). This is an important consideration when arriving at a scene or dealing with a victim who attends the police station where no CSI or medical assistance is immediately available.

As noted earlier, people are crime scenes and are sources both of evidence (potentially to be used in court) and intelligence (eg to provide leads in an investigation). Hence samples from a person can be used to:

- prove or disprove his/her involvement in the offence;
- corroborate or refute statements;
- show a link between him/her and another person, the scene, or an exhibit;
- establish drug, toxin, or alcohol levels in the body; and
- provide a reference sample (DNA, fingerprints, or footwear impressions) for direct comparison, for elimination, or for a database.

Normally DNA and fingerprint samples provided by suspects are retained in databases for 'speculative' (untargeted) searches, but most other samples are destroyed after the case is complete. Ensure you follow local protocols on retention and disposal.

26.6.1.1 PACE Code D

When taking forensic samples from suspects, parts 4–6 of PACE Code D must be followed (see the table).

Part in Code D	Procedure covered
4	Identification by fingerprints and footwear impressions
5	Examinations to establish identity and the taking of photographs
6	Identification by body samples and impressions

This includes suspects who have not been detained but are instead attending a police station 'voluntarily' (see para 5.19). Note that when PACE refers to a suspect attending a police station 'voluntarily' this is not referring to a member of the public who 'volunteers' to submit to some form of sampling.

Some of the key points from this part of Code D are that:

- samples should be relevant and should be proportional to the offence (unless they are for speculative searching and are covered by blanket policies, such as taking fingerprints, DNA samples, and photographs);
- appropriate adults are required in many circumstances, including taking samples from juveniles, the mentally disordered, or the visually impaired; and
- a full record must be kept about consent, authority, and warnings to the detained person.

The PACE Act 1984 defines two types of sample: non-intimate and intimate. An easy way of remembering the distinction is that: a sample is non-intimate if it is outside the underwear and not an orifice, but if the area to be sampled is an orifice or within the underwear (including a bra), then it is intimate.

A non-intimate sample includes:

- a sample of hair (other than pubic hair) and includes hair plucked with the root;
- a sample taken from a nail or from under a nail;
- a swab taken from a non-intimate part of a person's body (not from inside a nostril or ear);
- an impression of the skin from a non-intimate part of the body (such as the ears, lips, knees, feet or elbows); or
- saliva.

An intimate sample is:

- a dental impression;
- a sample of blood, semen, or any other tissue fluid;
- urine;
- pubic hair; or
- a swab taken from any part of the genitals or from any orifice other than the mouth.

A non-intimate sample may be taken by a police officer, detention officer, or CSI, and reasonable force may be used. Intimate samples must be taken by a registered medical practitioner (a doctor, dentist, nurse, or paramedic) and force may not be used.

Intimate samples are essential when attempting to establish the existence, or otherwise, of a 'two-way transfer' between the parties (see 26.2.3) to prove a sexual assault, rape or other serious offences against the person. Note that in cases of sexual assault and murder the intimate *and* non-intimate sampling of prisoners and victims will ideally be conducted by a specially trained Forensic Medical Examiner (FME) or other registered medical practitioner. Police officers and CSIs might assist however, especially with note taking and packaging.

26.6.1.2 What samples should be taken?

The types of sample taken from victims and suspects will depend on the nature of the offence. The following table describes the *minimum* samples for consideration (represented by a tick in the table). Note that PACE Code D and the Human Rights Act 1998 must be complied with, and the reasons for taking a particular sample must be noted in each case.

Minimum samples

	Cheque or other fraud. Hate mail	Burglary or other property crime	Sexual assault or rape	Theft from motor vehicle with damage caused	ABH and other assaults	Homicide victims and suspects
Blood and/or urine for toxicology			✓		✓	✓
Clothing (inner)			✓		✓	✓
Clothing (outer)		✓	✓	✓	✓	✓
DNA	✓	✓	✓	✓	✓	✓
Fingerprints	✓	✓	✓	✓	✓	✓
Hair (combing)		✓	✓	✓	✓	✓
Hair (pulled/cut)		✓	✓	✓	✓	✓
Handwriting sample	✓					
Photographs of injuries		When relevant	When relevant	When relevant	When relevant	Effectively mandatory
Sexual offence kit			Mandatory			Normally used
Shoes		✓	✓	✓	✓	✓

26.6.1.3 The sampling procedure for taking evidence from people

Upon delivery to a custody area all arrested persons are subject to mandatory sampling where their fingerprints, DNA, and a photograph are taken. Force policies may also require the scanning of shoe patterns. In the case of DNA this will not be required if a successful profile has been created previously. Sampling of suspects for evidence to link them to recent crimes should be carried out as soon after arrest as possible to recover the maximum available material. Do remember that, in major crimes and sexual offences, you should contact a CSI for advice if you wish to carry out Livescan fingerprinting or DNA swabbing prior to the arrival of the medical practitioner, because evidence can be lost during these processes. If there is a long delay between offence and arrest (even years), the CSI should be consulted because non-intimate samples, and material recovered from the crime scene, may still be useful.

Brand-new, unused packaging equipment must be used, since old equipment is a source of contamination. Specific kits are available, for example for the sampling of hair or urine, and these should be used where accessible. Personnel should wear gloves as a minimum form of protection and, for serious offences, or where health warnings exist, officers should wear protective clothing to protect themselves and the evidence from contamination. The CSI should be informed when samples have been taken, so that correct transport, storage, and subsequent preservation can be arranged. Blood, semen, and saliva contain DNA and should normally be frozen immediately, but if the target material is similar to a paint or oil, it is best practice to air-dry the samples securely, or to freeze them if this is not possible.

Samples from the exposed skin, hands, head, and mouth should be taken first (before clothing samples) in order to prevent material from those areas contaminating the clothing or vice versa.

26.6.1.4   Head hair samples

Head hair (including beard hair) may contain glass, plant material, foreign hairs, and other particulates and should be dealt with before clothing is removed. This will limit contamination by or from other samples (especially important in offences where windows have been smashed). Head hair samples can be used for the following purposes:

- recovery of fibres, hair, and particulate material and traces, wet or dry blood;
- comparison (as a control) with the subject's hair (structure, length, colour, and treatments) when found at scenes or on other people;
- chemical analysis to demonstrate long-term drug use or metals poisoning; and
- DNA analysis from the cells forming part of a hair root.

Any hat should be removed and exhibited first. Where religious head coverings are worn, such as turbans, it is good practice to ask permission from the person first and, time permitting, make arrangements for alternative head coverings prior to removal.

The samples must be taken over a sheet of pre-folded paper (at least A4 size) which catches debris. The hair should be combed from front to back all over the head so that debris falls onto the paper, continuing until no more debris is found. Clearly, this is not easy when the person is not compliant. The paper and comb should both be exhibited. For a person with matted hair or dreadlocks, a glove can be worn and the hair gently 'brushed' with the hands, or a new small hairbrush can be used with care. The paper containing the debris, the glove, and the comb or brush should be exhibited. Any blood or other matted material in the hair should be cut out over a sheet of pre-folded paper, and the scissors should be exhibited along with the cut section and the paper.

A 'control' of head hair is also required and ideally this is pulled out (so it contains the root material and can be identified as belonging to that person through DNA) but follow local advice because some forces may prefer the hair to be cut. At least 25 control hairs should be taken, including all colours and length variations.

26.6.1.5   Clothing and footwear samples

Given that footwear can leave marks, and that clothing can leave impressions or fibres at crime scenes, these forms of evidence can be very powerful. In the laboratory the scientist may wish to take test impressions or use control samples of fibres to establish whether the footwear or clothing was worn by a person involved in an offence. Fibres, hair, wet or dry blood, etc can transfer between different parties during offences against the person and during property crimes, so they are potentially very useful as evidence. Damage to clothing can provide information about weapons used on a victim, and damage to fibres can indicate proximity to fire or an explosion.

When taking clothing from suspects and victims, the person must stand on a clean paper sheet to catch any debris which may fall because material recovered from the floor has no known provenance. The clothing should be removed in a logical manner, normally starting with jackets and sweaters, followed by shoes, trousers and socks. Each piece should be separately exhibited and packaged in front of the subject. Notes should be made about the condition of clothing: its size, the presence of blood, colour, logos, and any damage. (This avoids the need to open the packaging later, to screen or describe the contents.) A final search of pockets may be carried out within the bag to prevent the unnecessary loss of material.

When all the clothing has been taken the officer should ask the subject to brush off his/her bare feet onto the paper sheet before stepping off, because material on the sheet will otherwise adhere to sweaty feet. The paper sheet on the floor is now an exhibit, and must be treated with care before being folded and dispatched for analysis.

Footwear impressions can provide important intelligence information since they can be compared against patterns stored in the National Footwear Database. This can be searched for footwear matches, which is particularly relevant for premises-related crimes such as burglary. Shoes which may be needed for the analysis of trace materials and DNA should not be scanned or copied as this can contaminate the shoes or cause the loss of material.

Qualifications and Training

26.6.1.6 Skin swabs and nail scrapings

Swabs from the skin may show the presence of blood, saliva, or chemical residues such as explosives traces. Generally, this is best left to a CSI (particularly explosive and firearm traces and the photography of blood) or a medical practitioner, but do not permit unnecessary delays to occur. CSI training officers or a CSI 'on area' will be able to provide information on the latest protocols for recovering blood and other fluids from non-intimate areas on suspects' skin. Note that bite marks on people may contain DNA from another person that will need to be preserved; a CSI should be contacted immediately.

Nails may have skin or other debris beneath them. They are cut or scraped by using a 'nail module' which typically contains cocktail sticks, A4 paper, bags, and clippers. Hold the hand firmly and carefully clip or scrape the debris from all the nails of one hand onto the pre-folded paper. Place the cocktail stick (or clippers) inside the paper before folding it, then put everything in the bag and seal it in the presence of the suspect. The samples from each hand form separate exhibits.

26.6.1.7 Buccal swabs and other samples for DNA analysis

DNA can be extracted from buccal (mouth) swabs and pulled hair for inclusion in the NDNAD, and for direct comparison to crime scenes and victims. The subject should not eat, drink, or smoke for at least 20 minutes before the test as this allows the mouth to regenerate dead or damaged cells. The DNA sampling pack contains a buccal swab kit and a hair sampling kit. The gloves must be worn and every effort must be made to avoid contamination—biological material can be very easily contaminated by people talking, coughing, or sneezing over it, or otherwise mishandling it. The sampling process should be carried out *before* completing the associated paperwork, because if the swab is accidentally dropped, the entire kit must be disposed of and a new form would have to be completed for the replacement swab kit. After taking the sample it should all be sealed in the 'tamper-evident' bag, arranged so the forms can be read through the bag. Force protocols must be followed regarding subsequent handling and storage.

Under the PACE Act 1984, a suspect may refuse to provide a buccal swab, in which case he/she may elect to provide a hair sample (pulled, to include the root). The hair sampling site can be chosen by the suspect on condition that it is not in an intimate area. Note that although Code D, para 6.7 refers to the use of 'reasonable' force to take non-intimate samples, buccal swabs should not be taken by force because the swab tip can be dislodged inside the mouth and presents a risk of choking. Swabs of blood or other DNA-rich material on the skin should ideally be taken by a CSI or trained custody personnel.

26.6.1.8 Prints and impressions from people

Fingerprints are a useful and non-invasive form of evidence. The regulations governing their use by the police are provided in Code D, paras 4.1–4.15. Police officers receive training on how to fingerprint suspects using Livescan (in all main police stations), Lantern—a portable device for use on patrol—and ink systems. Livescan and Lantern have the advantage of being digital devices that are linked to IDENT1, so they are quick and accurate. Ink systems include using traditional copper plate and printers' ink, and peel-apart pre-inked strips. The latter have the advantage of being portable, and they are mainly used to take elimination fingerprints from, for example, victims of crime.

Fingerprints can be used to identify a person as part of immigration enquiries, such as for a person detained under the Immigration Act 1971, Sch 2, para 18(2). They are also used for identification in relation to s 141(7) of the Immigration and Asylum Act 1999 when a person:

(a) fails to produce identity and nationality upon arrival to the UK;

(b) is refused entry but temporarily admitted;

(c) is to be removed as an illegal entrant or deported;

(d) is arrested under the Immigration Act 1971;

(e) has made a claim for asylum;

(f) is a dependant of any person listed in (b) to (e).

All police officers are qualified to take fingerprints, but other impressions can be problematic. For instance Code D para 6 covers the more unusual body impressions (eg ears and feet), which can be problematic, so the advice of a CSI should be sought. A registered dentist is required under PACE to take impressions of a suspect's teeth (an intimate sample under Code D).

26.6.1.9 Handwriting samples

A person providing a handwriting sample should sit at a table without being able to view any of the existing handwriting evidence. A ballpoint pen is used—not a pencil or a felt tip because they do not always show the construction of each letter, which is important. The officer then dictates what is to be written. Under no circumstances should the subject simply be asked to write 'the quick brown fox jumps over the lazy dog'. This sentence would be of little use since a person's writing style is partly determined by the letters before and after every other letter, so it might not provide the combinations required for the investigation. The sample material must be written in the same format as the document for comparison: if the original is in capitals, then the sample piece must be in capitals, and so on. If the writing was on a specific form, the supplier should be asked to supply blank samples; dummy cheques are available from CSI or Fraud Units if necessary. The person should be asked to write out the contents of the document a *minimum* of five times (unless this would be unreasonable), and for cheques, at least 15 samples are needed. He/she should sign and date every page, and each completed sample should be removed so the writing style used previously cannot be seen and copied. The subject may, obviously, attempt to conceal his/her true handwriting style but may start to revert to type after several samples. (This is why 'course of business' handwriting, perhaps taken from the home or workplace, is useful.) Even though the final results may be 'obvious', the samples should still be submitted to a suitable facility for expert opinion. Note that your forensic supplier may accept scanned copies by email for an initial assessment.

26.6.1.10 Photographs

Taking photographs and searching for identifying marks is covered in Code D (paras 5.1–5.18 for a detained person and paras 5.19–5.24 for a person who is at a police station but not detained). The Code is not explicit regarding injuries, but it is common, especially in major crimes, for suspects to be examined by a doctor (or nurse) and to be photographed by a suitable person to provide evidence of injury. Photographs of a recent injury may indicate a suspect's involvement in an offence, for example burns from arson attacks, and bruises or lacerations caused by one or more parties defending themselves in an assault case, especially when a victim of strangulation has fought back. Valuable identification evidence can also be provided by taking photographs of certain features, such as tattoos and scars.

> **TASK 3** Imagine you are a police officer. Consider what you might do if:
>
> - A woman attends the police station and claims to have been 'date-raped'. GHB and Rohypnol (examples of so-called 'date-rape' drugs) are rapidly excreted from the human body. Would you find a 'urine module' and request an immediate urine sample? How might this affect potential DNA evidence?
> - You attend a robbery and a man says he bit the offender. He can still taste blood in his mouth. Would you ask him to spit into a sterile bottle?
> - A victim claims a man sexually assaulted her and ejaculated over her hand. Would you glove or bag her hand, or even take a swab from it (if trained)?

26.6.2 Sampling from crime scenes

This is a complex area so CSI trainers provide training for new officers and those on refresher or detective training courses. This Handbook can be used as a guide, but CSIs are able to provide the most up-to-date information on local force protocols.

A force is likely to employ specialist CSI staff whose chief role is the recovery of physical material from crime scenes. However, a police officer may seize exhibits in the course of duty at crime scenes, for example when part of a search team (see 9.8), or if it seems there are only one or two items to seize and they can be safely recovered without a CSI (eg documents, cheques, or a single moveable shoe mark)—note that local policies on CSI deployment and evidence seizure must be followed. There may also be situations where the CSI is unable to attend, or where evidence could be lost if not recovered immediately (eg a shotgun cartridge on a windy day).

Evidence at crime scenes can include a wide range of potentially valuable material, but it will be mixed up with lots of other 'everyday' items. The best way to identify sources of potential evidence at volume crime scenes is to speak to the victim. The CSI will question the victim at a common domestic burglary regarding probable entry and exit routes, what has been disturbed, and what was stolen. This informs the search for evidence which, typically, follows a common pattern. The CSI then assesses the risks and hazards and examines external areas for evidence first, particularly the point of entry and especially if the weather might destroy it. This is followed by a search of the internal areas and focal points such as searched drawers and other disturbed articles. The victim assists but does not control the process. Contemporaneous notes are taken, and packaging is completed at the scene.

Typically (though not always at volume crimes), photographs are taken first, because the process is non-destructive. Then DNA and other trace evidence are taken, with fingerprinting carried out last, because the powders are contaminants. Each piece of evidence is packaged, marked, and labelled according to force protocols, and its position and description recorded on a worksheet. In a standard volume crime scene, common forms of evidence include:

- tool-marks and shoe marks outside the premises, particularly near to the point of entry (these are photographed and then cast using a silicon gel and plaster of Paris);
- broken glass (broken during entry?) for use as a control to match to any suspect's hair and clothing;
- shoe marks on windowsills (can be photographed and lifted onto gel or tape). Shoes can also leave prints some distance into a crime scene, especially on recently waxed floors and gloss doors (see 26.5.2.1 for details);
- fingerprints left by a suspect climbing into the premises, pulling out a glass pane, leaving ornaments outside, or while searching (see 26.5.4.1 for details);
- DNA, if the suspect has sustained injuries, left strands of pulled hair, consumed food or drinks, or discarded a cigarette;
- glove and fabric patterns, prints left by the ears, nose, elbows, and even lips, which have all been found at crime scenes, and can be used by the scientist with varying degrees of success; and
- control samples of fabrics to compare with fibres on the suspect's clothing.

26.6.2.1 Recovering 'controls'

A control is for comparing with other samples, for instance comparing a fibre from a sofa in a crime scene with fibres found on a suspect. A control (in crime scene investigation terms) comes from a known source, so in this example it would be material cut from the sofa. This would then be compared to fibres found on the suspect's clothing (and vice versa, with his clothing acting as a control). Where only a simple control of material is needed without a full scene examination, then a suitably trained police officer may gather the samples, but for anything more complex the CSI should be tasked. Police officers can, however, take glass and paint controls in order to save time and inconvenience.

Glass controls should always be taken from the supporting frame because glass on the ground has 'no provenance' (its origins are unknown). Where no glass remains in the frame a police officer must be certain (and be able to satisfy the forensic scientist and a potential jury) that the glass originally came from the frame. Thick gloves and goggles should be worn to prevent injury. At least six pieces should be taken and marked on one side with an indelible felt pen or 'chinagraph' pencil, to indicate the inside or outside surface. Samples from all around the break should be included. For a hole in toughened glass, the cube-shaped debris should be removed from around the hole (see 26.5.1.1 on different types of glass). If a large laminate window has been broken, the slabs can be extremely dangerous, but the complete thickness must be sampled and not just the dusty ground glass on the surface. Shoe marks may also be present on window glass.

All glass fragments should be placed into a suitable sturdy box with every edge sealed with tape. No fragments should puncture or be able to escape through the box, and an outer polythene bag is essential. The window void and its exact position above the ground should be measured, and the information recorded on a plan drawing.

Paint controls from window and door frames should be sliced with a new sharp knife from several areas around the damage. (However, if a tool mark is present, it may be advisable to call a CSI instead.) The sections of the paint should be at least 20 mm long, and some base material should be included if possible. Sampling vehicle paint is complex: call for the assistance of a CSI. Note that adhesive tapes should never be used to recover paint samples. The fragments of paint should be placed into a paper fold (see 26.7.1) and then put into a polythene bag. Paint is brittle so it may lend itself to a mechanical fit—if this seems likely the entire object and all the chipped paint are needed, so a CSI is almost certainly required.

26.7 Seizure and Packaging Techniques

Using the correct seizure procedures and methods for packaging prevents damage and contamination and is, effectively, a demonstration of the care and skill that accompanied the seizure of the exhibits. Local force protocols will be based on those laid down by forensic science laboratories and these must be followed. Guidance can be found in the FSS publication *The Scenes of Crime Handbook* (probably available to police officers through their local force, and available as a PDF online, or from Scenesafe). For the seizure and packaging of objects related to cyber-enabled or cyber-dependent crime, see 21.5.

26.7.1 Types of packaging and how to use them

Paper bags should have the top folded over twice (approximately 25 mm (one inch) per fold). The joint should be sealed over with a signature seal (an adhesive label with the officer's signature, name, and number). The entire join between folds and bag should then be completely sealed. An exhibit label can also be attached if required. Note that some forces require the factory-sealed base of the bag to be folded and sealed in the same way as the folded top.

For **polythene bags** a tamper-evident bag should be used if available. If the bag is plain however, a signature seal and a complete seal of tape should be tented over the open top, with the ends of the tape pinched off and cut about 10 mm from the bag. An exhibit label can also be attached if required.

Nylon bags should be sealed by twisting into a 'swan neck' as shown in the photograph, and then secured with tape or a cable tie (without 'teeth' as these could puncture the bag). The sealed nylon bag is then placed in a polythene bag, swan necked, and sealed.

(Image © Kevin Lawton-Barrett)

A Nylon bag 'swan necked' prior to securing with a cable tie

The entire package should then be placed in a rigid container, signature sealed, and labelled. Nylon bags containing hydrocarbons should not be stored close to other samples (see 26.7.2).

Boxes can also be used, but the items must be immobilized inside the box with string or cable ties. All the open edges of the box must be sealed with tape and signature-sealed as shown in the photograph.

(Image © Kevin Lawton-Barrett)

Police evidence box

Paper folds are required for the safe collection and storage of dry materials such as powders, paint fragments, and hair combings, (but not glass: use a small box). The diagram shows a common technique used to construct a 'paper-fold' container. The paper should be pre-folded before use, and the debris worked down into the greyed section before refolding and sealing into a suitable polythene bag.

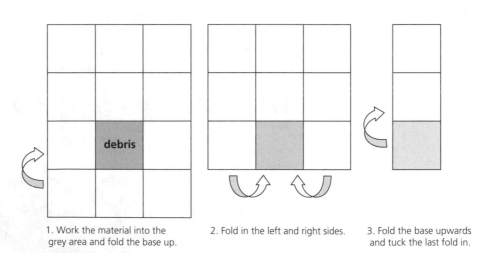

1. Work the material into the grey area and fold the base up.

2. Fold in the left and right sides.

3. Fold the base upwards and tuck the last fold in.

26.7.2   Packaging procedures for some common items

In these examples it is assumed that the officer has access to packaging materials with pre-printed exhibit labels attached. If labels are not printed on the package then paper versions are available but personnel should also write onto the package in case the label becomes detached.

Bedding, fabrics, clothes, and shoes must be sealed into paper bags which allow them to breathe. Sealing articles which are even slightly damp into plastic encourages the growth of mould and bacteria. A health hazard warning label should be used if any biological material might be present or where it is known or believed that articles have come from a potentially contaminated source (eg a known drug addict).

Articles that are **slightly wet or soaked** with non-flammable liquids (including blood) need to be dried. A CSI should be contacted urgently for advice and assistance with drying. Fabric items bearing wet blood must not be folded as this causes the blood to transfer to other parts of the article. In an emergency the wet items could be placed in a polythene sack for transport but urgent CSI advice is required, and it should all be sealed into a robust paper sack for protection.

Articles which may bear **flammable substances** should not be stored in paper bags because flammable chemicals (ignitable liquids or accelerants) will evaporate through paper sacks and be lost, as well as contaminating other material in storage and transit. A nylon bag should be used for hydrocarbons (eg petrol, diesel, or paraffin) and for non-hydrocarbons such as methylated spirits, alcohol, and acetone. The nylon bag should then be sealed *within* a polythene bag. Where biological material such as blood or semen is also believed present, the CSI should be consulted, since DNA may be destroyed by flammable substances. It is likely that the CSI will recommend immediate transport to a laboratory.

Sharps, bladed weapons, screwdrivers, and other pointed objects represent a very serious health hazard. Needles from syringes should be disposed of in a sharps bin prior to packaging the syringe if specialist syringe and needle storage boxes are not available, but this does not apply in major-crime cases: advice will be required. For knives and blades a knife tube should be used where possible, but a clean, unused, sturdy box could also be used. Care should be taken with screw-thread knife tubes as the screwing action can easily force the point of a knife blade through the lid into the hand. The two halves of knife tubes and sharps packs should be sealed together with tape and signature-sealed prior to packaging in a polythene bag. Blood soaked or wet weapons may need air-drying to prevent rusting or DNA decay.

Firearms represent a serious and immediate high-risk hazard. It is best practice to call for the assistance of a Firearms Officer and CSI to properly record the making-safe process. Any firearms of forensic interest can then be sealed in boxes with a safety certificate but those surrendered to the police (perhaps after the death of the owner) may simply require a label.

Bottles and glasses must be immobilized in a sturdy box to protect fingerprints or DNA, and prevent damage from any sharp edges. Bottles and glasses for back-calculation alcohol analysis (see 19.9.5.3) must be marked to show the levels the suspect claims to have drunk.

Urine samples may be required in a crime investigation or be taken from drivers under the Road Traffic Act 1988 (see 19.9.5.2). Custody officers have access to 'RTA-type' urine kits which contain a special preservative, but the urine can also be collected in a plastic pot, which is then decanted into a suitable bottle containing a preservative. The bottle must be properly secured and placed in a rigid outer container.

Documents should be packed in stout card folders or boxes to prevent people leaning on the documents or writing over them.

TASK 4 If you are a trainee police officer discuss the following questions with a BCU, CSI, or your trainers. If you are a student you could raise them in a seminar:

1. At a major crime scene, what are the usual problems with the CAP and cordons?
2. What is the better form of evidence: a fingerprint or DNA? (People are very likely to have different views, based almost entirely upon the perceived context of the evidence.)
3. What is worse, genuine contamination of an exhibit, or the suspicion of contamination?

TASK 5

1. A police officer is taking a DNA sample from an arrested person. He accidentally drops the swab on the floor. What should he do now?
2. Which PACE Act 1984 Code applies to fingerprinting suspects?
3. Imagine you have a quantity of fine debris you wish to store. Taking a sheet of A4 paper, make a paper fold to retain it.
4. Clothing thought to be contaminated with hydrocarbons (eg petrol) is packed into what sort of bag?
5. In an emergency, can a police officer lawfully ask a victim to provide a urine sample if he/she says he/she was the victim of a drug-induced rape?
6. A police officer attends a crime scene and takes a control sample of glass. How many pieces should she take? From where? How should she mark them (if at all)?

26.8 Answers to Tasks

TASK 1

1. Forensic Science Provider. Most forensic services were previously carried out by the Forensic Science Service (FSS) but this was closed by the Government for financial reasons and the work has been taken over by a range of private sector companies. The FSS archive still exists for research and cold case investigations.
2. Edmond Locard.
3. A possible list:

   - describing the *modus operandi* (MO);
   - answering investigative questions;
   - to establish that an offence has occurred;
   - to identify an offender or suspect;
   - to corroborate or refute witness statements;
   - to establish a physical link between suspect, crime scene, and victim;
   - to identify an individual; and
   - to further inform an enquiry.

TASK 2

1. Fibres, glass, paint, soil, pollen, etc. You could also include DNA-rich material.
2. Tool marks, shoe marks, impressions from stamps and dyes, extrusion marks, finger marks, clothing, gloves, etc.
3. Blood, semen, ear wax, mucus, saliva, etc.
4. Mitochondrial DNA comes from the female line, that is, from the mother, and is found in all her children.
5. The Y-STR comes from the father and is passed only to his sons.

TASK 3 In all these instances you could lawfully have taken the evidence. If you elected not to do so the evidence could quite possibly be lost.

It is acceptable, in an emergency and when a CSI or medical assistance is not available, for anyone to take a sample from a victim in a case such as this. Clearly, the dignity and psychological well-being of the victim must be uppermost in your mind, but there are occasions when decisive action will benefit the investigation. Crucially, you would have to have access to appropriate sterile equipment for the task and you would preferably have received previous training.

Many police forces have evidence kits at the front counter for just these unlikely situations. Out on Supervised or Independent Patrol these kits might not be available, so personnel may have to 'make do', but immediate actions like these can be required at any time.

TASK 4

1. Common Approach Paths sound simple but raise many problems, not least of which is selecting a good route and location. Essentially, they should be on a hard surface and should not be the offender's or victim's likely route to or from the crime scene. The next issue is how to mark a CAP on a windy day without anything to secure the tape. This cannot really be done until assistance arrives. CSIs will probably be able to explain that, with hindsight, the FAO could have employed better tactics.
2. Fingerprints are assumed to be unique, but there is disagreement over this issue since it is difficult to actually prove this point in a scientific sense. Our DNA is unique, too, but many people feel more comfortable with DNA because it has been the subject of much recent research. The best evidence, ultimately, only occurs where the context for it is right: thus on one occasion DNA can be of no use, whilst the next day it is very powerful.

In terms of speed, the turnaround for a fingerprint in an emergency can be a few hours from any point in the UK by using Livescan or Lantern, digital photography and secure email, or by driving the fingerprints direct to a fingerprint bureau. For DNA, forensic scientists are now deploying fully automated 'Rapid DNA' technology in some areas, which can reduce the analysis time to about 2 hours, but if this is not available, the best that DNA can manage is around 12 hours.

3. If the CSI knows contamination has occurred he/she can warn the scientist, and occasionally there may be a way to overcome the problem. If there is a suspicion or accusation that it has occurred then there may be no resolution, particularly if the Crown is 'ambushed' in court. By ensuring rigorous standards at the scene (or elsewhere), and by admitting mistakes the prosecution might be able to rebut these accusations. The most important point is: never allow contamination to occur. But if it does then honesty is the best policy.

TASK 5

1. Destroy the entire kit and start again with a new kit.
2. Code D.
3. Compare the result to the diagram in 26.7.1.
4. Nylon. Nylon bags are crinkly and rustle like a crisp packet: remember 'Nylon is Noisy'.
5. Yes. There is nothing to prevent an officer asking for a sample in an emergency (and assisting, to an extent, in its collection). However, the human rights of the individual must be respected and officers should act with common decency.
6. Six pieces from the frame (around the hole), and mark the inside or outside of each piece.

27 | Prosecution and Court Procedures

27.1 Introduction

Prosecution, as all experienced police officers know, is often a lengthy and complex affair, and many aspects are not solely in the control of the police. There are two forms of prosecution: written and criminal charge. Written charge is a relatively straightforward process (see 10.13.1.1). Here we cover the more complex process of criminal charge.

The police decide on charging in the case of most 'volume crimes' that are either summary only or (in the case of an envisaged guilty plea) either-way offences normally dealt with at magistrates' courts. The offences that can be prosecuted by the police are known as 'specified proceedings' and are listed in the Prosecution of Offences Act 1985 (Specified Proceedings) Order 1999. These include: careless or inconsiderate driving; failing to comply with a traffic direction; failing to stop, report an accident or give information or documents; being drunk in a highway, other public place or licensed premises; and throwing fireworks in a thoroughfare.

The Crown Prosecution Service (CPS) make the decisions on charging for indictable offences and/or more complex or sensitive cases. Once a decision to charge has been made, the CPS will run the case to conclusion, working closely with the police officer in the case (OIC).

In this chapter we look at the role of the CPS and examine the aspects of the charging, prosecution and court procedures which are most relevant to trainee officers and students on pre-join programmes.

27.2 The Role of the Crown Prosecution Service

The CPS was set up in 1986 under the Prosecution of Offences Act 1985 as an independent prosecuting authority for England and Wales. It is independent of the police, and is therefore an important mechanism for maintaining fairness in the criminal justice system. CPS lawyers (Crown prosecutors) are solicitors and barristers who are responsible for prosecuting criminal cases on behalf of the Crown.

Where a case is serious or complex, Crown prosecutors advise the police in the early stages of the investigation, sometimes about possible lines of investigation, and always in terms of decisions about charging. These types of cases should not be charged by the police without the authority of a Crown prosecutor. Crown prosecutors prepare and then present cases in court. The CPS also provides information and guidance to victims and witnesses, and will help support them through the prosecution process.

The CPS is divided into 13 areas across England and Wales. Each area is headed up by a Chief Crown Prosecutor, who in turn is answerable to the Director of Public Prosecutions. The Director of Public Prosecutions is the head of the CPS and works under the superintendence of the Attorney General. The Attorney General oversees the work of the CPS and is accountable to the Government in terms of its performance and conduct.

Crown prosecutors are governed by the Code for Crown Prosecutors. This is a public document and is available on the CPS website (CPS, 2013a). In short, it sets out that before pursuing a case, the Crown prosecutor should be sure that there is sufficient evidence to provide a realistic prospect of conviction, and that it is also in the public interest to pursue a prosecution. Only when both of these elements are met should a case be charged. The same standard applies in cases where the charging decision has been made by the police. There is one exception to this and that is where a case is charged on the threshold test (see 27.3.2).

27.3 The Charging Process

As mentioned in the introduction to this chapter, the police are responsible for charging decisions in most cases involving straightforward summary offences, and in lower level either-way offences that are likely to be dealt with in a magistrates' court. The charging decision should be referred to the CPS for indictable-only cases, and for more serious or sensitive either-way offences likely to be heard at the Crown Court. Charging advice is normally provided to the police in one of three ways: CPS Direct; the direct submission of a case file; or through a face-to-face meeting.

CPS Direct provides most of the charging advice given to the police. It consists of teams of Crown prosecutors across England and Wales who are available 24 hours a day, seven days a week, 365 days of the year. The police telephone CPS Direct and transmit the evidence electronically, so the advice may be provided straight away. At this point a suspect could still be in custody and the police may be requesting charging advice on the threshold test (see 27.3.2), or the suspect may have been bailed pending a charging decision—in which case the charging advice is likely to be given in line with the full code test (see 27.3.1). Charging advice is requested on police MG3 forms (see 27.4.2), and the Crown prosecutor sends the advice to the officer electronically, on a CPS MG3 form.

For cases that are more complex and/or sensitive, a file can be submitted directly to the CPS. A Crown prosecutor will then review the file and provide charging advice to the police. Again, charging advice will be sought and given on MG3 forms.

Face-to-face meetings or sometimes video-conference style meetings are held for more large scale, complex, sensitive, and serious cases. By their very nature these cases will require more time and may involve the examination of large quantities of evidence.

27.3.1 The full code test

The majority of cases will be charged using the 'full code test'. This is set out in the Code for Crown Prosecutors, but it also applies for cases where the charging decision is made by the police. There are two stages to the full code test. First, the prosecutor must be sure that there is sufficient evidence to provide a realistic prospect of conviction. This is different to the test set down for a jury deciding on guilt. A prosecutor does not need to be convinced of guilt beyond any reasonable doubt, but must be sure that a properly directed and impartial jury, acting in accordance with the law, is more likely than not to find the defendant guilty. When the prosecutor is trying to decide whether the evidence is sufficient, he/she needs to be sure that the available evidence is reliable, credible, and capable of being used in court. If there is not sufficient evidence to provide a realistic prospect of conviction then the case fails at this stage and the suspect should not be charged, no matter how serious the offence is. If the prosecutor decides there is sufficient evidence to provide a realistic prospect of conviction the second stage of the test is applied.

The second stage of the full code test considers the public interest. If there is sufficient evidence then a case will normally proceed unless there are significant public interest factors which suggest that the case should not go ahead. Public interest factors can include:

- the age of the suspect;
- the circumstances of and the level of harm caused to the victim;
- the impact on the community;
- whether there may be a source of information that requires protection; and
- whether a prosecution is a proportionate response or whether the suspect could be better dealt with by a method which diverts them from the court process, such as a caution.

There is no exhaustive list of public interest factors, and there may well be factors unique to individual cases. If a case meets the full code test then the appropriate charge(s) should be selected and the suspect charged as soon as practicable (CPS, 2013a).

27.3.2 The threshold test

The threshold test is used when there is a time limit and a decision has to be made on whether to charge or grant bail. It applies in cases where further evidence still needs to be gathered but the suspect would pose a significant risk if granted bail. There are two factors that must be considered when applying the threshold test. First, is there a reasonable suspicion that the suspect committed the offence? This must be decided using the evidence available at the time. Once reasonable suspicion is established, the Crown prosecutor must then decide whether there is further identifiable evidence to be gathered, evidence that could ultimately provide the prosecution with a realistic prospect of conviction (in line with the full code test). If both factors are met then the threshold test may be properly applied and the Crown prosecutor is likely to authorize a charge (CPS, 2013a).

Once the suspect has been charged he/she must be placed in front of the next available court for the magistrates to decide whether to remand the defendant in custody or grant bail. The CPS, working together with the police, may apply for the suspect to be remanded in custody, and the court makes the actual decision.

When a case has been charged under the threshold test it must be kept under constant review to ensure that it is progressing as anticipated. The evidence must be reviewed on a regular basis to make sure that the decision to keep the defendant on remand is still appropriate. As soon as practicable the full code test must be applied and met in order for the case to continue.

27.3.3 Investigative advice

In the case of very large scale, complex, or sensitive cases the police may decide to seek advice from the CPS at a very early stage in the investigation to ensure that the correct evidence is identified and gathered from the outset. This may involve a number of consultations, and the CPS may also provide written advice setting out further actions for the police to complete ('action plans'), before charges are actually authorized. However, it ultimately saves the police from pursuing unnecessary lines of enquiry and ensures that the appropriate and required evidence is gathered as soon as practicable.

27.3.4 Selecting the correct charge

A CPS 'charging standard' can be used to determine the precise charge (or charges) made against an individual. For example, a suspected shoplifter might be charged with 'Theft contrary to sections 1(1) and 7 of the Theft Act 1968', in which case the charging standard would involve a consideration of the five elements of the offence (dishonesty, appropriation, property, belonging to another, permanent intention to deprive, see 16.2).

When selecting the charge the Crown prosecutor or police officer should make sure that the charge fairly reflects the seriousness and the full extent of the offending. The charge selected should also give the court adequate sentencing power. Once charged, the 'suspect' becomes a 'defendant'.

27.4 Preparing and Submitting Case Files

Successful investigations normally require good quality and accurate case files. It is important that case files are completed accurately, logically and with integrity for a prosecution to succeed. The case file will include the interview record (see 25.5.7) and the MG6 forms (see 27.4.2), charge sheets, lists of exhibits (often forensic evidence), and so on. The National Audit Office revealed in 2011 that 79 per cent of police prosecution files reviewed did not contain the necessary paperwork for the cases under the Streamlined Process guidance (National Audit Office, 2011, p 5). More detailed information on the case-building process is provided in s 1 of the 2011 edition of the *Prosecution Team Manual of Guidance* (ACPO, 2011d) and the *Director's Guidance On Charging 2013*, 5th edn, May 2013 (available online).

This topic is usually covered during the second year of initial police training. The 'Finalize Investigation' PAC heading lists the following as targets to be achieved before Independent Patrol; 'Complete pre-charge files', 'Complete post-charge files', and 'Complete summons files'.

27.4.1 The National File Standard

The National File Standard (NFS) is described by the CPS and the College of Policing as providing a 'staged and proportionate approach to the preparation of case files' (CPS, 2013b; College of Policing, 2014h). The purpose is to provide the prosecutor, the defence, and the court with proportionate and relevant information throughout the case. The files submitted to the prosecution from the first hearing must contain the core information which the prosecutor will need to complete a Case Management Form. The content required for a case file depends on whether a guilty or not guilty plea is expected (ACPO, 2011d).

27.4.2 MG forms

The forms for case files are often referred to as 'MG forms' (the MG stands for Manual of Guidance). Each MG form will show the suspect's details and the case file reference number. It is likely that such information will be accessed through an interface with the NSPIS (National Strategy for Police Information Systems) Custody and Case Preparation Programme which will have been uploaded when the suspect was first presented to the custody officer upon arrest (see 10.10.2). (Note that some forces are phasing out their current NSPIS contracts in favour of alternatives.) Here we cover only the MG forms that a trainee police officer is likely to require. These are for:

- straightforward cases where a guilty plea is entered (and there are no complications such as certain sensitive disclosure issues); and
- contested ('not guilty' pleas), and Crown Court cases.

Charging decisions are usually based on the information received by the CPS in a pre-charge expedited case file. This will include forms MG3 and MG3A and any key evidence (ACPO, 2011d). Once the charge has been made, a post-charge expedited file is required for the court. If a 'not guilty' plea is entered, or if the case is to be heard in Crown Court, upgrading to a Full File is required. If the case is disposed of at the first court appearance, then of course no upgrading is needed.

The forms required for each eventuality are shown in the table. A tick indicates that a particular form will almost certainly be needed, and a question mark indicates that it might be needed. The *Prosecution Team Manual of Guidance* provides detailed guidance on the completion of MG forms (ACPO, 2011d).

Form	description	straightforward pre-	straightforward post-	contested pre-	contested post-	full file
MG2	Special Measures Assessment				?	
MG3	Report to Crown Prosecutor	✓	✓	✓	✓	✓
MG3A	Further report to Crown Prosecutor	?	?	?	?	
MG4	Charge sheet		✓		✓	
MG4A	Conditional bail form		?		?	
MG4B	Request to vary police conditional bail		?		?	
MG4C	Surety/Security		?		?	
MG5	Police Report		✓		✓	✓
MG6	Case file evidence and information	?	?	?	?	
MG6B	Police officer/staff's disciplinary record					?
MG6C	Schedule of non-sensitive unused material					✓
MG6D	Schedule of sensitive material					✓
MG6E	Disclosure officer's report					✓
MG7	Remand in custody application		?		?	?
MG8	Breach of bail conditions		?		?	
MG9	Witness list		✓		✓	✓
MG10	Witness non-availability		✓		✓	✓
MG11	Witness statements	?	?	?	?	?
MG12	Exhibits list					✓
MG15	Interview record: this could be a SDN, a ROTI, or a ROVI*		?		?	✓
MG16	Bad character/dangerous offenders				?	?
MG18	Offences taken into consideration		?		?	?
MG19	Compensation form (plus supporting documents)					✓
MG21/21A	Forensic submissions				?	✓
MGDD A/B	Driving under the influence of alcohol/drugs forms	?	?	?	?	?
SDN	Short Descriptive Note; may be written on MG15, MG5, or officer's MG11		✓			✓
Phoenix print	Computer print-out of the suspect's previous convictions, cautions, etc	✓	✓	✓	✓	✓

Form	description	straightforward		contested		full file
		pre-	post-	pre-	post-	
PNC	Print of suspect and key prosecution witnesses' pre-convictions, including simple cautions, conditional cautions, reprimands, final warnings, PND etc	✓	✓	✓	✓	✓
Copy of documentary exhibits/photos			✓	✓	✓	✓
Police racist incident form/crime report			?		?	?
Crime report and incident log				✓	✓	✓
Any unused material which might undermine the case		✓	✓	✓	✓	✓
Custody record						✓

* ROTI: Record Of a Taped Interview; ROVI: Record Of a Video-recorded Interview; both are written documents summarizing the content of the recordings

27.5 In Court

The role of magistrates' courts and the Crown Court is explained in 5.5. Here, we will concentrate on what happens at court, with particular emphasis on the likely role of a trainee officer.

The course of events in both the magistrates' courts and the Crown Courts follow certain routines and patterns depending on the type of hearing. Below you will find a description of the people who are most likely to be present in the magistrates' and the Crown Court.

Participants in the court room	Description of the role
The Magistrate(s)	Unpaid, specially trained volunteers who hear cases in the magistrates' court. They are **not** legal professionals. Also known as 'lay magistrates'
District Judge	A legal professional drawn from the rank of solicitor or barrister—hears cases in the magistrates' courts only
Court legal adviser	A legally trained professional who advises the lay magistrates on matters relating to the law
The defendant	The person who is charged with the offence with which the court is concerned
Representative for the prosecution	In the magistrates' court this may be a solicitor, a barrister, or an associate prosecutor. (Associate prosecutors undergo a legal training programme before they are able to undertake advocacy work in court. They are able to review and present straightforward cases, and with further training may present trials involving summary only non-imprisonable offences.) In the Crown Court it must be a barrister, or a solicitor who has undertaken further training and obtained 'higher rights of audience'. He/she may be employed by the CPS, or be a barrister from the independent bar who has been instructed by the CPS
Defence	A legal professional acting on behalf of the defendant. Again, this can be a solicitor or a barrister in the magistrates' court. In the Crown Court it must be a barrister or a solicitor who has undertaken further training and obtained 'higher rights of audience'
The Public	Courtrooms are open to the public and anyone may attend a hearing. There are certain exceptions to this where the court may be closed to the public, for example where the defendant is a youth
The Judge	A legally qualified professional, normally drawn from the rank of solicitor and barrister, who has held their qualification for a period of at least five years
The Jury	The jury in the Crown Court consists of 12 members of the public who have been selected from a panel of people who have been 'summonsed' for jury service
Witnesses	People who have witnessed elements of the offence that need to be proved in court. The defence may wish to test a witness's evidence by cross-examination. Professional witnesses may also be called to give evidence in relation to particular evidence, for example a doctor may be asked to give evidence in relation to injuries he/she has examined
The Media	Usually present at major trials, court reporters are sometimes also present at the magistrates' courts and are likely to report on cases of local interest

Some court rooms are still the more traditional, grand, imposing wood panelled rooms, but many court rooms are located in modern buildings and are far removed from the scenes you may see in television dramas. Wigs and gowns are not worn in the magistrates' courts where proceedings are generally a little less formal. To learn about the processes, there is of course no substitute for visiting courts and observing the procedures live.

For a trainee police officer, giving evidence features as one of the PAC headings, a key aspect of qualifying to undertake Independent Patrol. However, after qualifying, a police officer might not attend court again for some time; indeed, to some extent the opportunities to experience court during training are specially arranged. A police officer is more likely to give evidence in court if he/she is a detective working on volume crime or is involved in a major police operation. Court appearances for police officers are less common now partly due to the increased proportion of early 'guilty' pleas. This increase is likely to be in some part attributable to advances in DNA evidence, the increased availability of discounted sentences in return for a guilty plea at an early stage, and also the increased use of statutory fines and penalties (see 10.13.2). However, as court appearances by police officers now tend to relate to more serious offences and involve a substantial criminal trial, it is all the more important to get it right.

27.5.1 The adversarial justice system in court

In court, contested hearings are undertaken by two 'adversaries' or opponents, these being the representatives for the defence and the prosecution. Occasionally a defendant elects to conduct his/her own defence, but he/she will not always be permitted to cross-examine all witnesses (see 27.6.2.3 for details).

The defence and the prosecution must comply with certain rules concerning the evidence. The prosecution has a duty to ensure that all relevant evidence (and unused material) is disclosed under CPIA (see 24.3). The Criminal Procedure Rules govern the process, and these are updated every year. Part 1 sets out the overriding objective that the court should be able to deal with cases justly:

> 1.1.—(1) The overriding objective of this procedural code is that criminal cases be dealt with justly.
> (2) Dealing with a criminal case justly includes—
>   (a) acquitting the innocent and convicting the guilty;
>   (b) dealing with the prosecution and the defence fairly;
>   (c) recognising the rights of a defendant, particularly those under Article 6 of the European Convention on Human Rights;
>   (d) respecting the interests of witnesses, victims and jurors and keeping them informed of the progress of the case;
>   (e) dealing with the case efficiently and expeditiously;
>   (f) ensuring that appropriate information is available to the court when bail and sentence are considered; and
>   (g) dealing with the case in ways that take into account—
>   (i)   the gravity of the offence alleged,
>   (ii) the complexity of what is in issue,
>   (iii) the severity of the consequences for the defendant and others affected, and
>   (iv) the needs of other cases.

In accordance with the overriding objective of fairness, the defence are unlikely to succeed if they seek to ambush the prosecution with a piece of evidence or a point of law at a late stage in the proceedings (for example, see *Gleeson* [2003] EWCA Crim 3357).

The defence occasionally challenges the prosecution's case and asks for the prosecution to cease. For example, the judge can be asked to dismiss the case at a Plea and Case Management Hearing (PCMH) before the trial begins. The admissibility of critical evidence might be challenged, and if successful the case for the prosecution inevitably fails. Alternatively, in certain circumstances, the challenge might come later on in the trial by way of a 'half time submission' by the defence, once the prosecution have closed their case. A challenge is very likely to occur if a key witness fails to confirm (orally) the evidence in his/her written statements. The judge can also halt a trial for similar reasons and direct a jury to acquit, but this is rare.

By way of example, the defence could challenge the following issues (this is not an exhaustive list):

* whether the alleged offence actually took place (eg in a rape case, when a point to prove has not been established in the evidence);

- whether the defendant carried out the relevant acts (perhaps he/she has an alibi);
- whether the defendant had the requisite intention (the act was unintentional or there were justifiable reasons for the act, such as self-defence); and/or
- whether the process which brought the defendant to court was at fault.

This last point can be used even if it seems very likely the defendant clearly did commit the crime (eg if there is very strong DNA prosecution evidence) and there is little to be said in mitigation. The defence could claim for example that the relevant PACE 1984 and CPIA 1996 Codes of Practice had not been followed, and suggest that the trial is flawed and unfair, and the judge will be asked to dismiss the evidence and any related charges. Indeed, it is the role of the defence counsel to expose flaws in the prosecution case if that helps the defendant. Some people feel uncomfortable with these aspects of the defence counsel's role, believing such approaches to be morally ambiguous. This misses the point: the role of the defence is to do anything (within legal and ethical bounds) to act in the defendant's best interest, including exploiting loopholes in the law.

So, in this sense, the police have to get it absolutely right, every time. That is why we place so much emphasis here on getting the procedure right.

27.5.1.1 A court as a public arena

Both the Crown Court and magistrates' courts have a public gallery, and anyone can watch any trial or hearing in progress (although in exceptional circumstances a case is held in private and the public are excluded).

When friends or relatives of the defendant and the victim are present, public order problems may occasionally occur. If this seems likely the ushers and security staff should be alerted to this possibility. The judge or chairman of the bench may warn the public gallery about the possible consequences of disruptive behaviour, such as removal or arrest for contempt of court. Whilst efforts have been made to alter courtroom layouts to avoid such a possibility, a member of a jury may still be intimidated by glares and gestures from the defendant's circle of associates. In such circumstances the public gallery may be cleared, leaving the press bench to represent the public's interest. It is not just in the courtroom that these problems arise, however: in communal corridors, cafes, and smoking areas, the defendant's associates and the witnesses for the prosecution have opportunities to meet. If necessary, separate rooms are available in most courts for witnesses to sit away from other people. Intimidation of juries and witnesses is covered in 14.6.

Police officers are not immune from threats or intimidation, and should identify and bring to the court's attention any person who challenges, or seeks to threaten or intimidate an officer. Common times for this are when a police officer is leaving court at the close of the day, or is away from the court during a lunch break.

27.5.2 Court procedures

Evidence is usually presented in court in the form of the testimony of a witness. Witnesses give evidence of what they heard, saw, smelled, tasted, or felt. Sometimes, an expert witness may be asked to give an opinion, such as a pathologist giving an opinion on the cause of death in a murder case, but ordinary witnesses (including police officers) will seldom be asked for an opinion. Witnesses who attend courts frequently (eg police officers) are known as professional witnesses, as distinct from expert witnesses.

On the basis of the given evidence, the bench or district judge (in a magistrates' court) or the jury (in the Crown court) will decide whether the accused is guilty or not. In the case of the Crown Court, if the accused pleads guilty, there will be no need for a jury, and the hearing will be much shorter.

27.5.2.1 The notification to attend court

At the outset witnesses are 'warned for court'. For a magistrates' court the notification to attend will be a simple letter or notice stating the date and time. For the Crown Court, there are two forms of witness warning—a 'conditional' and a 'full' warning. A conditional warning is used when the witness's evidence is not likely to be contested and so the witness may not be required to attend court. If nothing more is announced or communicated then he/she can 'stand by' and is unlikely to give evidence (until either side move to have the witness called—perhaps if the trial takes an unexpected turn). Note, however, that he/she still should not discuss the evidence with any third party. A witness receiving a full warning will certainly be called to attend, but still might not be called to give evidence.

Waiting for a case to get to court can be a frustratingly long and drawn-out process for a number of reasons; for example the volume of cases any given court has to deal with, or difficulty finding a date when all witnesses and legal representative can attend court. Once in court, a case may still not be heard quickly: it may be put back, postponed, rescheduled, or otherwise not heard on that day for any number of technical or procedural reasons.

27.5.2.2   The oath

Evidence must be given on oath by any witness or defendant at a statutory legal process, including a magistrates' court or the Crown Court. The Perjury Act 1911 and the Oaths Act 1978 require that a person must be sworn in the particular form or manner which is binding on his/her conscience. Those adhering to a religious belief touch or hold (covered or uncovered) their respective holy books when giving the oath, but there may be other observances involved such as a ritual washing.

Perjury is when a person lies under oath. This is a serious criminal offence under the Perjury Act 1911. A person commits perjury when he/she wilfully makes a 'statement material in that proceeding, which he knows to be false or does not believe to be true' (s 1(1) and (2)), having been lawfully sworn as a witness or as an interpreter in a court or tribunal, or before any person legally empowered to hear and assess evidence. A court determines whether the statement was 'material' or not for the proceedings (s 1(6)). The false statement must have been made deliberately and not merely by mistake, and the testimony of only one witness (alleging that the statement was false) is not sufficient for a conviction (s 13).

Perjury is an offence in criminal and civil proceedings, punishable on indictment with a maximum of seven years' imprisonment or a fine (CPS, 2012a), and the punishment must reflect the seriousness of the original offence (*R v Dunlop* [2001] 2 Cr App R (S) 27). Although perjury will in most cases amount to perverting the course of justice, the two offences (perjury and perverting the course of justice) should not be confused. Perverting the course of justice could be arranging a false alibi, but lying about it in court would be perjury. A prosecution for perjury is appropriate when making a false statement in court is the principal act, but not if the false statement is part of a series of acts aimed at perverting the course of justice (SFO, 2010). Aiding, abetting, counselling, procuring, or suborning another person to commit perjury carries the same penalty as perjury itself (s 7(1)).

27.5.2.3   Giving evidence

Oral evidence is the most common form of evidence presented to a court. It is verbal, spoken evidence. A witness will say 'I saw him push the block over the parapet of the bridge', or 'I heard her scream and then felt a hand on my bottom', or 'The drink tasted really bitter after I came back from the toilet'. It is what has been directly experienced by someone on the spot at the time that the alleged offence was committed. A witness to an act must have perceived (seen, heard, felt, tasted, or smelled) that act directly, through his/her senses. Under s 9 of the Criminal Justice Act 1967, if both sides agree, a witness statement can be read out in court in the place of oral evidence from the witness (and hence is often referred to as a 'section 9 statement').

Real evidence is any article or thing which can be produced for the court, supported by testimony to link to the accused, such as 'This is the iron bar I saw him holding'.

> **TASK 1** Can you think of potential problems associated with the use of, and production in court, of 'real evidence'?

The evidential link to the accused generally has to made through supporting testimony, such as 'These bloodstains were recovered from the clothing worn by the accused at the time of his arrest, and which match the blood type of the man found lying in the stairwell'. The significance of a piece of real evidence often has to be explained in court, especially if the relevant item is not within everyone's common experience, such as an explosive detonator for triggering a bomb. Large items, for example a lorry, a crash site, or piece of machinery, may be visited by a court if the evidence is vital for a case.

There must be an auditable trail for the article produced as real evidence, from the moment it was discovered or recovered until it is produced in court. This is referred to as 'continuity of evidence' or the 'chain of evidence'.

Documentary evidence is a separate class of real evidence. The rules about the legal status of documents are complex but the general point is that the document should be produced in court by the person who created it and who can testify to its contents. This is not always possible (eg for a will) but a court can ask for a handwriting expert to testify that, within limitations, the author of one particular document is likely to be the author of another particular document.

Hearsay evidence is 'any statement not made in oral evidence in the proceedings' (s 114 of the Criminal Justice Act 2003); it is one person's account of what another person said. There have been concerns that hearsay evidence might breach Article 6 of the ECHR (which establishes the right to a fair and public hearing) by not allowing the defence the opportunity, for example, to cross-examine an absent witness. The ECHR found that this was unfounded, and stated that the circumstances of each trial need to be taken into account (*Al-Khawaja & Tahery v UK* [2012] 2 Costs LO 139).

TASK 2 There are a number of exceptions which allow for hearsay evidence to be used. Can you think of any possible exceptions that might apply?

The four 'gateways' to admissibility of hearsay evidence are:

1. The CJA or any other Act indicates it may be used. (This will include, for instance, when a witness cannot attend court due to illness, and statements from a person (eg a victim's friend) about what the victim had said about the incident (s 120 of the CJA).)
2. Any of the common law exceptions preserved by the CJA (including confession evidence).
3. All parties to the proceedings agree to the evidence being given.
4. The court concludes that in the interests of justice the hearsay evidence should be admitted.

Gateway 4 is particularly useful for hearsay evidence that does not fit any of the recognized exceptions (it is sometimes referred to as the 'safety valve'). It was used when the Court of Appeal (Criminal Division) accepted hearsay evidence consisting of a police officer's record of a conversation with a 14-year-old witness. This contained details of the witness's relationship with the offender, and was accepted on the grounds that it was useful to confirm evidence given by the witness earlier, despite it having been later denied (*Burton v R* [2011] EWCA Crim 1990).

Bad Character Evidence (BCE, see 24.2.5) can be used in court but the defence or the prosecution must first apply to the judge under s 100 of the Criminal Justice Act 2003. The main principle is to protect a witness or victim from having irrelevant aspects of his/her previous history brought up (see s 101(1) of the Criminal Justice Act 2003 for the full list). Where the defendant wishes to raise the previous sexual history of a complainant, this is likely to be excluded by virtue of s 41 of the Youth Justice and Criminal Evidence Act 1999 (YJCEA 1999), unless it is relevant and admissible. Case law shows that judges are unlikely to allow BCE evidence to be introduced unless it is really significant and relevant (see *R v Bovell* [2005] 2 Cr App R 401).

TASK 3 Find out which MG form is used to record BCE in a defendant's case file.

Witness evidence is given from the witness box (often surprisingly small and modest in reality, unlike those you may have seen on TV or film). The witness should face towards the judge or the bench when giving evidence. Evidence can take a number of forms such as oral, real, documentary, or hearsay, and these are covered in detail in 24.2.5. Evidence-in-chief is the evidence given by the witness in response to the party that called him/her as a witness.

In most straightforward cases oral evidence is given 'directly', which means providing a detailed and accurate chronology of events without any prompting. Under s 9 of the Criminal Justice Act 1967, a witness statement can be read out in court in the place of oral evidence from the witness (and hence is often referred to as a 'section 9 statement'). In more complex cases, and always at the Crown Court, evidence is given in response to questions that seek to draw out detail from the witness, usually following the chronology of the events.

A police visual recording of an interview with a significant witness (see 25.6.1) may be shown to the court, particularly if there are inconsistencies between the oral evidence and the recorded evidence. A recording is not usually permitted as the sole source of evidence-in-chief, apart from when 'special measures' apply (see 27.5.2.5). This commonly happens in cases involving rape or sexual abuse, and especially where the witness is a child. The court can exclude a recording if there is insufficient information about where it was made, or if the recording contains serious violations of the rules of evidence.

27.5.2.4 Cross-examination

Cross-examination takes place once the evidence has been given (either directly or in response to the counsel's questions). The opposing counsel is likely to ask questions. This may be quite stressful for the witness, but there are a variety of 'special measures' available for vulnerable and intimidated witnesses (see 27.5.2.5), and aggressive questioning is not normally tolerated by magistrates or judges. If the defendant is conducting his/her own defence it will sometimes be inappropriate for him/her to cross-examine a particular witness, particularly in cases involving domestic violence for example. In such circumstances an application can be made by the prosecution for a legal representative to be appointed to act on the defendant's behalf, for cross-examination purposes only (s 36 of the Youth Justice and Criminal Evidence Act 1999).

After the cross-examination, the counsel that called the witness has the right to ask further questions (re-examination), but this questioning is restricted solely to matters that arose in the cross-examination, and is usually seeking clarification and removing ambiguity. And finally, the magistrates or judge may need to ask questions of a witness, though they will be very careful not to take over the role of either counsel.

After a witness has finished giving evidence the magistrate or judge gives permission for him/her to leave the witness box. There are two forms of 'permission to leave' and these are:

- to be stood down, which usually requires a witness to be available for recall; and
- to be discharged, which means the court does not expect him/her to be recalled so he/she may leave the court.

The witness can sit in the public gallery once he/she has been discharged.

27.5.2.5 Special measures in court

Special measures are available to assist some vulnerable and/or intimidated witnesses (as defined in 24.2.4). Special measures are important in terms of witness well-being, which in turn impacts on the quality of the evidence he/she is able to give. All children under the age of 18 are eligible for special measures. Vulnerable witnesses are eligible if the quality of their evidence is likely to be adversely affected due to their personal difficulties, as are intimidated witnesses whose quality of evidence is likely to be diminished by reason of fear or distress. An application is made to the court explaining what type(s) of special measure is being applied for, and how and why this will assist the witness and improve the quality of their evidence. The application is made by the CPS, based on information provided by the police.

The various types of special measure are set out in ss 23–30 of the Youth Justice and Criminal Evidence Act 1999 (YJCA 1999):

- screens are positioned around the witness (s 23). This is helpful in that the witness will not be able to see the defendant and vice versa. However, it does mean going into the same room as the defendant which may be too difficult for some witnesses;
- a TV live link is used so the witness gives evidence from another room within the court building or, sometimes, a different building altogether (s 24). Evidence is relayed live to the court room on large TV screens. This means that the witness doesn't have to go in to the same room as the defendant. It does mean that the defendant will be able to see the witness on the TV screens, although it is possible to apply for the TV screens to be screened off in court so that the witness can't be seen;

- evidence is given in private—members of the public are excluded from the court room and only one nominated member of the press is permitted to stay for the proceedings (s 25). In practice this is not used very often but can be employed in very sensitive cases, or where intimidation is an issue;
- wigs and gowns (judges' and lawyers') are removed to create a less intimidating environment (s 26). This is particularly relevant to cases involving children;
- video recorded interviews can be used as 'evidence-in-chief' (s 27)—this allows the witness to give his/her account in a more relaxed environment, closer to the time of reporting the offence, hopefully resulting in a fuller more detailed account. The witness will however still be cross-examined by the defence;
- a pre-recorded cross-examination is used (s 28). At the time of writing this is not yet fully operation in England and Wales, but recent pilots have provided encouraging results;
- intermediaries (such as a speech and language therapist) are used to help with communication and understanding (s 29); and
- communication aids (such as a computer) are used by the witness when giving evidence (s 30).

Each special measure may be used individually or in combination with others in order to ensure that the witness has the best possible opportunity to provide high quality evidence. It should be noted that special measures are not guaranteed until the court has ruled on the application. Therefore, while it is a good idea to explain the available options to eligible witnesses at an early stage, premature promises should not be made.

27.5.2.6 Hostile witnesses

A barrister can ask for a witness to be deemed 'hostile' by the judge. This is when a witness has made a statement previously but declines to confirm certain details in court, and is assumed to be deliberately not telling the truth. (He/she may have been asked to change the details or fall silent rather than incriminate the accused.) The judge will announce his/her decision to the court, often giving reasons. The witness can then be cross-examined and challenged about the change of evidence, and the inconsistencies with previous statements and accounts will be explored.

27.5.3 Giving evidence as a police officer

Early on in his/her career a police officer is most likely to give evidence in court as the 'officer in the case', the 'OIC'. If this applies to you, your BCU Administrative Unit will help arrange a suitable date for the hearing.

This is the final phase of the investigation in a sense, because it is the calling to account of the case against the accused and a consideration of the evidence. A police officer's role is to explain what he/she has done, heard, seen, or recorded, as clearly and as concisely as possible. Any witness, including you as a police officer, should avoid discussing the case in detail with colleagues or associates before, and certainly during, the trial, because recollections can be contaminated by verbally revisiting the circumstances.

27.5.3.1 Preparing for giving evidence as a police officer

After the case file has been prepared, further planning and preparation is needed for the actual process of giving evidence. As the officer in the case you would have to:

- review the case, reread the case papers, and reread your PNB;
- ensure you have a copy of your duty statement to use as a reminder, if required, while giving evidence (permitted under s 139 of the Criminal Justice Act 2003);
- familiarize yourself with the rules of evidence (particularly on hearsay evidence and opinion);
- speak to the CPS lawyer who will be prosecuting;
- prepare for dealing with predictable but difficult questions from the defence, for example on certain points of evidence;
- check that everything in the case is administratively in order, including labelling the exhibits; and
- check the arrangements for witnesses, payment of witnesses, and holding areas, particularly if they feel vulnerable to intimidation—often a room is set aside for witnesses.

You could also visit the court premises and sit through part of another case, before checking the exact location of the courtroom for 'your' case.

27.5.3.2 In the witness box as a police officer

It is becoming increasingly common, particularly in magistrates' court cases for police officers to give their evidence via video link from their police station in order to save time and resources. However, there will be times when you will have to attend court in person, and in any event this guidance applies equally (where practicable) to both scenarios. After taking the oath or affirming you introduce yourself by rank, police number, name, and the police station where you are based. When you are responding to questions try to address your answers to the judge and jury, or the magistrates.

If you want to refer to your PNB in court, you should ask for permission. The defence may ask you to explain the manner and time of making your notes, and whether your notes represent a 'contemporaneous account' (written at the time) or whether you wrote up your PNB afterwards. Any notes made reasonably soon after the event should be acceptable, but if there is a significant time lag (two days or longer) the defence is likely to question you very closely and probably in a hostile manner. The court, prosecution, or defence may want to examine the entry itself, so make sure that your grammar and spelling are always up to scratch and that your handwriting is at least legible! They might also examine it to look for any evidence of collusion with other officers (see 10.2.3).

When giving evidence you could be tempted to try to learn your evidence by heart and then recite from memory, but this is most inadvisable. For a start it will sound rehearsed and artificial. Secondly, the defence may try to put you off with questions so that you lose your thread and flounder, and finally it suggests that maybe you do not have the confidence to rely on your recall of events. There is nothing wrong with referring to your PNB entries—after all, the lawyers and the judge constantly refer to their notes. However, you should not rely on your PNB exclusively as that will not create a good impression. It is much better to speak clearly and confidently, referring only now and then to your PNB to refresh your memory, or to quote a particular detail. Always avoid hearsay or bad character evidence unless it has been confirmed to you that it has been admitted. We discuss how to create a good impression in more detail in 27.5.3.4.

27.5.3.3 Cross-examination

As a witness you can ask the defence or anyone else to repeat a question which you did not hear, did not understand, or which you want clarified. (It also gives you an extra moment to think.) You should remain polite and courteous at all times, and be prepared for the unexpected, for example:

'PC Winn, what formal training have you had in interview techniques and did that training, if indeed you had it, cover the use of oppressive interrogation?'

Here the defence is using a common tactic of double questioning, as well as launching straight into querying the officer's qualifications. She might choose to reply as follows:

> [to the judge] I was accredited Tier 2 Investigative Interviewing, which means I am qualified by the police in investigative interviewing, which incorporates questioning styles. I did the training at the Police training centre in August last year. I routinely undertake interviews at this level and believe I have an understanding of the term 'oppressive' as it applies in the Police and Criminal Evidence Act 1984, section 76.
> [turning back to the defence] Would you repeat the second part of your question, sir?

Note her politeness and refusal to be flustered or stampeded by the defence's approach. In fact, the completeness of her first reply establishes her as a professional and credible witness, and the defence may seem merely querulous (questioning for its own sake). If the defence persisted in making an innuendo in such a deliberately challenging tone the judge might intervene to ask where it is leading and how is it relevant, and whether the defence is raising an issue for consideration for exclusion of the evidence. You might also have noticed how PC Winn 'collects' the question from the lawyer and delivers her answer directly to the judge, before politely asking the defence lawyer for the second part of his question. This emphasizes that she has been attentive and is not to be hurried into giving confused (or confusing) answers to compound or complex questions.

The use of body language can certainly help control pace and speed. It would be best to turn back to a person asking a question only when you think you have given a complete answer and you are ready for the next question. Some eye contact with the jury is always helpful as they are the people you would need to convince on issues of fact. You should avoid a one-to-one 'conversation' with either the defence or the prosecution counsel as this is likely to be irritating to the jury (they may feel distanced from the proceedings).

The defence may use a variety of approaches such as trailer questions, multiple questions, hypothetical questions, topic hopping, or out-of-sequence chronology. These should be dealt with one at a time. It is important to portray yourself to the jury as a competent professional.

The defence counsel will sometimes attempt to persuade juries that collusion has occurred between officers and that adjustments have been made to match their accounts. It is important that you limit yourself to recollections about matters that you have personal knowledge of, and can convey directly to the court, and do not adjust your evidence to correspond with another's. Imagine if you truthfully recalled in your evidence to the jury that your recollection is that the car you saw was green, and your colleague following you into the witness box had said it was red? Both of you are telling the truth, one possibly mistaken, but this would be far better than you 'changing your recall' to having seen a red car—when the car was in fact later proved to be green! (See 10.2.3 on 'conferring with others' and your PNB.)

There will be occasions when your evidence as a police officer is favourable to the defendant, and naturally enough the defence will want to make use of this. You should expect to be questioned about how you conducted the investigation, about the evidence you have already given, and asked for any additional facts which you have not already given. It is often not what you say that is fertile territory for the cross-examination—but rather what you did not say.

27.5.3.4 Creating the right impression

The impression a police officer creates in court, as we have noted earlier, will influence his/her credibility, particularly as some members of the jury might be subjective and 'go by feel', rather than by objective fact.

When giving evidence as a police officer you should always watch your general attitude and remain calm, polite, and courteous at all times, even in the face of inflammatory questioning or an apparent attack on your integrity. Rising to the bait will only serve to assist the defence. If in court you appear intolerant or impatient, or reply in kind, then your credibility as a police officer on oath or affirmation in court would be at risk. Police officers are subject to personal scrutiny (as any other witness can be); your record, your training, your job performance, and even your personal life may be closely investigated by the defence. Anything which can undermine your credibility or make the jury dubious about the reliability of your testimony may be exploited by a defence lawyer, who will not hesitate to confront you with it during cross-examination. In the same way, any obvious bias demonstrated by a police officer against a defendant will be deeply unhelpful to the prosecution case and may in fact help the defence.

When giving evidence you should speak clearly, keep your voice at an audible volume and try not to talk too quickly. Clear concise language should be used. No one would advise you to talk like a legal textbook but you should avoid using colloquial speech or slang terms unless you are repeating something you have heard as part of your evidence, in which case you should say exactly what you heard, no matter how obscene or objectionable the language. Another temptation is to say too much and to keep on talking, but you should keep your answers short and to the point.

For example:

> **Prosecutor:** Constable Winn, did you see the injuries?
>
> **PC Winn:** Yes, I did. This was at first during the initial interview, when Ms Bent showed me an extensive bruise to her left eye and cheekbone. She was then examined by the custody nurse for other injuries.
>
> **Prosecutor:** What did you do next?
>
> **PC Winn:** I arranged for the custody nurse to examine Ms Bent and prepare a body map of injuries, and arranged for them to be photographed

> **Prosecutor:** With what result?
>
> **PC Winn:** We have the injuries photographed and listed. She was advised to attend A and E immediately after the interview, and I have obtained a doctor's report and statement.
>
> **Prosecutor:** Your Honour, I refer to the statement taken from Dr Salim Khan, A and E House Officer at Albright Hospital, in bundle 6, document 44A.

Notice that PC Winn gives clear answers, but does not elaborate (she knows that the prosecution—or the defence—will follow up with another question if there is more to be said). Note too that she does not try to give a medical opinion, nor to paraphrase Dr Khan's evidence or statement. This would be inappropriate because PC Winn has no medical qualifications and knows that she cannot speak with any authority. However, the court may allow PC Winn to comment on whether the apparent injuries were consistent with assault, based on her knowledge and experience as a police officer. The temptation to use someone else's evidence in your answers can be strong, especially if you know the case well and have carefully read all the statements and written evidence, but you must resist.

The use of acronyms (eg BCU, TIC, ETA, SIO) and overly technical words (eg 'haematoma' (a bruise) or 'lacerations' (cuts)) should also be avoided as they may confuse and irritate the jury. You might appear to be trying too hard to impress if you say something like this (especially if your grasp of the meaning of words is a little shaky).

> I proceeded in a southerly direction towards the connurbative encompassment of commercial premises which is characterized by the soubriquet of 'shopping mall'. The chronological observation which was then essayed by myself was recorded contemporaneously as 13.45 hours, British Summer Time. It was at that juncture that I espied the trio of adult males engaging in what I deemed to be behaviour which warranted a sufficiency of explanation as to make my legitimated suspicions subside...

Perhaps all you needed to say was:

> I was on patrol in the shopping centre at 13.45 when I saw three men behaving suspiciously, so I challenged them.

Even this is fairly formal, but it has the great merit of being brief. Remember the impression you are creating as a concise, well-prepared professional.

You certainly need to be organized and to appear to be organized: 'Um...I will just check...' or 'Um, I seem to have mislaid it...' are not likely to impress the jury and risks losing their attention. The statement 'May I please refer to document 24 in the bundle, M'Lord?' is far more professional and courteous. Using the correct terminology to address the court will certainly help create a good impression:

- 'Ma'am' or 'Sir' for the lawyers on either side;
- 'Your Honour', 'My Lady', or 'My Lord' for the Judge in the Crown Court (depending on the status of the Crown Court);
- 'Your Worships' for the magistrates' court and 'Ma'am' or 'Sir' if addressing them individually; and
- 'Ma'am' or 'Sir' for a district judge in the magistrates' court.

It would be easy for us to ignore your appearance through some sense of 'politeness' and respect for individual personal style, but non-verbal communication (see 6.11.2) is a powerful influence—you need to look as smart as you sound. A smart uniform, polished shoes, and neat hair can seem petty restrictions, but they help you assert your authority (see 3.5) and will boost your confidence in the witness box. Actions also convey attitudes; hands in pockets, fiddling with buttons or your glasses, and constantly shifting through documents create a poor impression.

27.5.3.5 **After giving evidence**

You should wait in the witness box until the magistrate or judge gives you permission to leave. If you are in doubt about whether you are being 'stood down' or 'discharged' (see 27.5.2.4) you must speak to the CPS lawyer prosecuting the case at a convenient moment, and remain available within the court building.

If you wish to remain in court you are entitled to do so, and can sit in the public gallery. However, witnesses and family for the accused could also be there, so you might not feel particularly comfortable. You should also avoid making eye contact or nodding in agreement; this sort of action on your part might encourage the defence to question any influence you may be having on the jury or the magistrates, and could easily lead to criticism of your conduct in open court.

You would also need to take care in relation to other witnesses who have not yet given evidence. Imagine you travelled to court with a colleague and that you have given evidence and been discharged, but she is going to give evidence the following morning. You travelled together by car and intend to return home the same way; however, you would need to take care not to talk about the case. The following morning she may be asked about how she travelled, who with, and whether the case was discussed. The defence may look for forms of collusion, or inconsistency between her written statement and the evidence she gives orally, and suggest that any differences are an indication that she changed her account to suit others. You will need to ensure this type of situation does not arise.

27.6 Answers to Tasks

TASK 1 You might have referred to the 'continuity of evidence'. You will remember from many examples in this Handbook that this is a mundane but vital part of case preparation.

TASK 2 The exceptions usually agreed to be taken as evidence are declarations on the point of death; and statements made as confessions (if the witness heard the confession him/herself).

TASK 3 Form MG16 is used.

Bibliography and References

ACPO (2006a), *Murder Investigation Manual*, 3rd edn (Wyboston: National Centre for Policing Excellence).

——(2006b), *Practice Advice on Search Management and Procedures 2006* available at <http://www.kent.police.uk/about_us/policies/n/documents/n37search%2Bmanagement.pdf> (accessed 23 January 2014).

——(2006c), *Practice Advice on Stop and Search 2006* available at <http://content.met.police.uk/cs/Satellite?blobcol=urldata&blobheadername1=Content-Type&blobheadername2=Content-Disposition&blobheadervalue1=application%2Fpdf&blobheadervalue2=inline%3B+filename%3D%22436%2F865%2FPractice_Advice_on_Stop_and_Search.pdf%22&blobkey=id&blobtable=MungoBlobs&blobwhere=1283565271771&ssbinary=true> (accessed 19 March 2014).

——(2008), *Practice Advice on Analysis* available at <http://www.acpo.police.uk/documents/crime/2008/200804CRIPAA01.pdf> (accessed 17 April 2011).

——(2009), *ACPO Guidance on Investigating Child Abuse and Safeguarding Children*, 2nd edn, available at <http://ceop.police.uk/Documents/ACPOGuidance2009.pdf> (accessed 11 March 2014).

——(2010a), *Guidance on Investigating and Prosecuting Rape* (abridged edn) available at <http://www.acpo.police.uk/documents/crime/2011/20110303%20CBA.%20Guidance%20for%20Investigating%20and%20Prosecuting%20Rape_Public%20Facing_2010.pdf> (accessed 20 December 2013).

——(2010b), *Guidance on the Investigation, Cautioning and Charging of Knife Crime Offences 2009* available at <http://www.acpo.police.uk/documents/crime/2009/200907CRIKCO01.pdf> (accessed 8 April 2010).

——(2010c), *Guidance on the Management, Recording and Investigation of Missing Persons* available at <http://www.acpo.police.uk/documents/crime/2011/201103CRIIMP02.pdf> (accessed 14 April 2011).

——(2010d), *Manual of Guidance on Data Protection*, Version 3.0 (London: ACPO) available at <http://www.acpo.police.uk/documents/information/2010/201002-im-data-protection-mog.pdf> (accessed 11 March 2014).

——(2010e), *Manual of Guidance on Keeping the Peace* available at <http://www.acpo.police.uk/documents/uniformed/2010/201010UNKTP01.pdf> (accessed 5 February 2012).

——(2011a), *ACPO Uniformed Operations Policing the Roads—5 Year Strategy 2011–2015* available at <http://library.college.police.uk/docs/ACPO/ACPO-policing-the-roads-2011.pdf> (accessed 3 March 2013).

——(2011b), *Annex A ACPO's Statement of Risk Principles* available at <http://knowsleychildcare.proceduresonline.com/pdfs/acpo_statement_risk.pdf> (accessed 27 February 2014).

——(2011c), *Guidance on the Management of Police Information* available at <http://www.acpo.police.uk/documents/information/2010/201004INFMOPI01.pdf> (accessed 11 March 2014).

——(2011d), *Prosecution Team Manual of Guidance* available at <http://library.college.police.uk/docs/appref/MoG-final-2011-july.pdf> (accessed 21 December 2013).

——(2011e), *Strategy & Supporting Operational Guidance for Policing Prostitution and Sexual Exploitation* available at <http://www.acpo.police.uk/documents/crime/2011/20111102%20CBA%20Policing%20Prostitution%20and%20%20Sexual%20Exploitation%20Strategy_Website_October%202011.pdf> (accessed 8 January 2015).

——(2012a), *ACPO Good Practice Guide for Digital Evidence March 2012* available at <https://www.cps.gov.uk/legal/assets/uploads/files/ACPO_guidelines_computer_evidence[1].pdf> (accessed 3 May 2016).

——(2012b), *Guidance on Safeguarding and Investigating the Abuse of Vulnerable Adults* available at <http://library.college.police.uk/docs/acpo/vulnerable-adults-2012.pdf> (accessed 31 January 2015).

——(2013), *Interim Guidance on the Management, Recording and Investigation of Missing Persons 2013* available at <http://www.acpo.police.uk/documents/crime/2013/201303-cba-int-guid-missing-persons.pdf> (accessed 11 March 2014).

——(2014a), *A Guide to Investigating Child Deaths* available at <http://www.app.college.police.uk/app-content/major-investigation-and-public-protection/child-abuse/police-response/risk-and-associated-investigations/> (accessed 31 January 2015).

——(2014b), *Preventing and prosecuting female genital mutilation* available at <http://www.college.police.uk/en/22021.htm> (accessed 9 January 2014).

ACPO Centrex (2005), *Practice Advice on Core Investigative Doctrine* (Camborne: National Centre for Policing Excellence).

Aitken, C, Connolly, T, Gammerman, A, Zhang, G, and Oldfield, R (1995), *Predicting an Offender's Characteristics: An evaluation of statistical modelling*, Police Research Group Special Interest Series 4 (London: Home Office).

Akers, S (2009), *ACPO Gangs Network* Letter to the LGA, 21 January 2009. Was available at <http://www.lga.gov.uk/lga/aio/874167> (accessed 14 April 2011) but is no longer available: please try other library resources.

Alderson, J (1998), *Principled Policing: Protecting the public with integrity* (Winchester: Waterside Press).

Allcock, E, Bond, JW, and Smith, LL (2011), 'An investigation into the crime scene characteristics that differentiate a car key burglary from a regular domestic burglary', International Journal of Police Science and Management 13(4), 1–11.

Angiolini , E (2015), *Report of the independent review into the investigation and prosecution of rape in London* available at <https://www.cps.gov.uk/Publications/equality/vaw/dame_elish_angiolini_rape_review_2015.pdf> (accessed 15 March 2016).

APCCS (2013), *Police and Crime Commissioners* available at <http://www.apccs.police.uk/page/pcc-candidates> (accessed 13 February 2013).

Audit Commission (1993), *Helping with Enquiries: Tackling crime effectively* (London: Audit Commission).

Baldwin, J (1992), *Video Taping of Police Interviews with Suspects—An Evaluation. Police Research Series Paper 1* (London: Home Office).

Banton, M (1964), *The Policeman in the Community* (London: Tavistock).

BBC (2016), *Hundreds of police accused of sexual exploitation* available at <http://www.bbc.co.uk/news/uk-38240524> (accessed 1 March 2017).

——(2017), *Police pay out at least £22m to informants in five years* available at <http://www.bbc.co.uk/news/uk-38902480> (accessed 1 March 2017).

Belviso, M, De Donno, A, Vitale, L, and Introna, F (2003), 'Positional asphyxia: reflection on 2 cases', American Journal of Forensic Medicine and Pathology 24(3), 292–7.

Berne, E (1968), *Games People Play: The psychology of human relationships* (Harmondsworth: Penguin).

Bichard, Sir M (2004), *Return to an Address of the Honourable the House of Commons dated 22nd June 2004 for the Bichard Inquiry*, Report HC 653 (London: The Stationery Office).

Blackburn, R (1995), *The Psychology of Criminal Conduct: Theory, research and practice* (Chichester: Wiley & Sons).

Blair, Sir I (2005), *The Richard Dimbleby Lecture 2005: Sir Ian Blair* available at <http://www.bbc.co.uk/pressoffice/pressreleases/stories/2005/11_november/16/dimbleby.shtml> (accessed 13 April 2011).

Bloom, B, Engelhart, M, Furst, E, Hill, W, and Krathwohl, D (1956), *Taxonomy of Educational Objectives: The classification of educational goals; Handbook I: Cognitive Domain* (New York: Longmans).

Bottoms, A and Tankebe, J (2012), 'Beyond procedural justice: A dialogic approach to legitimacy in criminal justice', Journal of Criminal Law and Criminology 102(1), 119–70.

Bowers, KJ, Johnson, SD, and Pease, K (2004), 'Prospective hot-spotting: The future of crime mapping?', British Journal of Criminology 44(5), 641–58.

——Hirschfield, A, and Johnson, S (1998), 'Victimisation revisited: A case study of non-residential repeat burglary in Merseyside', British Journal of Criminology 38(3), 429–52.

Bowling, B, Parmar, P, and Philips, C (2008), 'Policing ethnic minority communities' in T Newburn (ed), *Handbook of Policing*, 2nd edn (Cullompton: Willan), pp 611–41.

Bradford, B, Jackson, J, and Stanko, E (2009), 'Public encounters with the police: On the use of public opinion surveys to improve contact and confidence', Policing and Society 19(1), 20–46.

Bradley, The Rt Hon Lord (2009), *Lord Bradley's Review of People with Mental Health Problems and Learning Disabilities in the Criminal Justice System* (London: Department of Health).

Bryant, R (2008), *Investigating Digital Crime* (Chichester: John Wiley & Sons).

——and Bryant, S (2014), *Policing Digital Crime* (Farnham: Ashgate Publishing).

Bullock, K and Tilley, N (2003), *Crime Reduction and Problem-oriented Policing* (Cullompton: Willan).

Button, N (2009), *National Fraud Authority Fraud Typologies and Victims of Fraud: Literature Review* available at <https://www.gov.uk/government/uploads/system/uploads/attachment_data/file/118469/fraud-typologies.pdf> (accessed 23 January 2015).

Caless, B (2008a), 'Corruption in the police: The reality of the "dark side"', The Police Journal 80(1), 3–84.

——(2008b), 'Persistent dark matter: Police corruption in the last ten years', Ethics in Policing 1(2), 16–28.

——and Owens, J (2016), *Police and Crime Commissioners: The Transformation of Police Accountability* (Bristol: Policy Press).

Campbell, A and Muncer, S (1989), 'Them and Us: A comparison of the cultural context of American gangs and British subcultures', Deviant Behaviour 10, 271–88.

Canter, D and Alison, L (2000), *Precursors to Investigative Psychology: Criminal detection and the psychology of crime* (Aldershot: Ashgate).

——, ——, and Fritzon, K (1998), 'Differentiating arsonists: A model of firesetting actions and characteristics', Legal and Criminological Psychology 3, 73–96.

Cape, E (2015), 'Transposing the EU Directive on the right to information: a firecracker or a damp squib?', Criminal Law Review, 1, 48–67.

Center for Problem-Oriented Policing (2009), *Community Safety, Crime & Drugs Audit, 2004*. Was available at <http://www.popcenter.org/problems/residential_car_theft/PDFs/BrightonHove.pdf> (accessed 23 July 2009) but is no longer available: please try other library resources.

Centrex (2005), *Level 1 Investigator Professional Development Portfolio*.

CEOP (2013), *Welcome to CEOP's thinkuknow website* available at <http://www.thinkuknow.co.uk/> (accessed 12 March 2013).

Chan, JBL (2003), *Fair Cop: Learning the art of policing* (Toronto: University of Toronto Press).

Chapman, R, Smith, LL, and Bond, JW (2012), 'An investigation into the differentiating characteristics between car key burglars and regular burglars', Journal of Forensic Science 57(4), 939–45.

Chartered Institute of Arbitrators (2009), *Mediation* available at <http://www.ciarb.org/information-and-resources/jargon-buster/> (accessed 13 April 2011).

Chenery, S, Henshaw C, and Pease, K (1999), *Illegal Parking in Disabled Bays: A means of offender targeting*, Police and Reducing Crime Briefing Note 1/99 (London: Home Office).

Clarke, C and Milne, R (2001), *A National Evaluation of the PEACE Investigative Interviewing Course*, Home Office Report PRAS/149 (London: Home Office).

——, ——, and Bull, R (2011), 'Interviewing suspects of crime: The impact of PEACE training, supervision and the presence of a legal advisor', Journal of Investigative Psychology and Offender Profiling 8(2), 149–62.

Clarke, RV (1999), *Hot Products: Understanding, anticipating and reducing demand for stolen goods*, Police Research Series Paper 112 (London: Home Office).

College of Policing (2013a), *FAQs* available at <http://www.college.police.uk/en/18060.htm> (accessed 11 February 2013).

——(2013b), *Intelligence collection, development and dissemination* available at <https://www.app.college.police.uk/app-content/intelligence-management/intelligence-cycle/#prison-intelligence> (accessed 1 March 2017).

——(2013c), *Investigation Investigative Interviewing* available at <https://www.app.college.police.uk/app-content/investigations/investigative-interviewing/> (accessed 1 March 2017).

——(2013d), *Operational Review* available at <http://www.app.college.police.uk/app-content/operations/operational-review/#officers-conferring> (accessed 1 March 2017).

——(2013e), *Pre-Join to Policing Programmes* available at <http://www.college.police.uk/What-we-do/Learning/pre-join-to-policing/Pages/Pre-join-in-policing.aspx> (accessed 11 March 2016).

——(2013f), *Professional Entry to Policing: Pre-Join Strategy & Guidance* available at <http://www.college.police.uk/What-we-do/Learning/pre-join-to-policing/Documents/Professional_Entry_to_Policing_Strategy.pdf> (accessed 28 December 2015).

——(2013g), *Risk* available at <https://www.app.college.police.uk/app-content/risk-2/risk/> (accessed 23 March 2015).

——(2014a), *Code of Ethics: A Code of Practice for the Principles and Standards of Professional Behaviour for the Policing Profession of England and Wales* available at <http://www.college.police.uk/What-we-do/Ethics/Documents/Code_of_Ethics.pdf> (accessed 13 January 2017).

——(2014b), *Domestic abuse (consultation)* available at <http://www.app.college.police.uk/consultation/domestic-abuse-consultation/consultation-questions-consultation/> (accessed 6 January 2015).

——(2014c), *High Potential Development Scheme* available at <http://www.college.police.uk/en/8563.htm> (accessed 11 March 2014).

——(2014d), *High Potential Development Scheme (HPDS) Manual of Guidance* available at <http://www.college.police.uk/en/docs/HPDS_MoG_2013_final.pdf> (accessed 11 March 2014).

——(2014e), *Job related Fitness Test for the Police Service of England & Wales, Sept 2014 Winsor Recommendation 33* (Ryton-on-Dunsmore: College of Policing).

——(2014f), *Major investigation and public protection Responding to child sexual exploitation, Risk Factors* available at <http://www.app.college.police.uk/app-content/major-investigation-and-public-protection/child-sexual-exploitation/#warning-signs> (accessed 20 January 2015).

——(2014g), *Professional Entry to Policing* available at <http://www.college.police.uk/en/docs/Professional_Entry_to_Policing_Strategy.pdf> (accessed 11 March 2014).

——(2014h), *Prosecution and Case Management* available at <http://www.app.college.police.uk/app-content/prosecution-and-case-management/charging-and-case-preparation/#summonsing> (accessed 9 January 2015).

——(2015a), *Arrest and other positive approaches* available at <https://www.app.college.police.uk/app-content/major-investigation-and-public-protection/domestic-abuse/arrest-and-other-positive-approaches/> (accessed 26 December 2015).

——(2015b), *Call handler and front counter staff response to a domestic abuse incident* available at <https://www.app.college.police.uk/app-content/major-investigation-and-public-protection/domestic-abuse/call-handler-and-front-counter-staff-response/> (accessed 26 December 2015).

——(2015c), *Current and Former Approved Providers* available at <http://www.college.police.uk/What-we-do/Learning/Policing-Education-Qualifications-Framework/Pages/Policing-Education-Qualifications-Framework.aspx> (accessed 24 April 2017).

——(2015d), *Female genital mutilation* available at <https://www.app.college.police.uk/app-content/major-investigation-and-public-protection/female-genital-mutilation/> (accessed 28 December 2015).

——(2015e), *Figures on Disapproved Register published* available at <http://www.college.police.uk/News/College-news/Pages/disapproved-register.aspx> (accessed 1 March 2017).

——(2015f), *First response* available at <https://www.app.college.police.uk/app-content/major-investigation-and-public-protection/domestic-abuse/first-response/> (accessed 26 December 2015).

——(2015g), *Investigative development* available at <https://www.app.college.police.uk/app-content/major-investigation-and-public-protection/domestic-abuse/investigative-development/> (accessed 26 December 2015).

——(2015h), *National Policing Police Community Support Officer: Operational Handbook* available at <http://recruit.college.police.uk/pcso/Documents/National_Policing_PCSO_Operational_Handbook.pdf> (accessed 1 March 2017).

——(2015i), *National Policing Curriculum* available at <http://www.college.police.uk/What-we-do/Learning/Curriculum/Pages/default.aspx= (accessed 26 March 2015).

——(2015j), *Possible justice outcomes following investigation* available at <http://www.app.college.police.uk/app-content/prosecution-and-case-management/justice-outcomes/> (accessed 27 January 2016).

——(2015k), *Review of the Implementation of Pre-entry Programmes for Policing Version 1.00 College of Policing Limited* (unpublished).

——(2015m), *Stop and Search* available at <https://www.app.college.police.uk/app-content/stop-and-search/> (accessed 15 March 2016).

——(2016a), *Developing and delivering an education qualification framework for policing The College of Policing response to the consultation* available at <http://www.college.police.uk/What-we-do/Learning/Policing-Education-Qualifications-Framework/Documents/PEQF_2016.pdf> (accessed 1 March 2017).

——(2016b), *Home Page* available at <http://www.college.police.uk/Pages/Home.aspx> (accessed 29 December 2015).

——(2016c), *Major investigation and public protection Missing persons* available at <http://www.app.college.police.uk/app-content/major-investigation-and-public-protection/missing-persons/?s=missing+persons> (accessed 25 November 2016).

——(2016d), *Major investigation and public protection: Missing Persons, Quick reference guides* available at <http://www.app.college.police.uk/app-content/major-investigation-and-public-protection/missing-persons/quick-reference-guides/> (accessed 25 November 2016).

——(2016e), *Major investigation and public protection: Missing person investigations* available at <http://www.app.college.police.uk/app-content/major-investigation-and-public-protection/missing-persons/missing-person-investigations/> (accessed 25 November 2016).

——(2016f), *Major investigation and public protection: Specific investigations, Missing Children* available at <http://www.app.college.police.uk/app-content/major-investigation-and-public-protection/missing-persons/missing-person-investigations/specific-investigations/> (accessed 25 November 2016).

——(2016g), *Mental Health* available at <http://www.app.college.police.uk/app-content/mental-health/?s> (accessed 25 November 2016).

——(2016h), *National Investigators' Examination* available at <http://www.college.police.uk/What-we-do/Development/Specialist-roles/Pages/NI-Examination.aspx> (accessed 1 March 2017).

——(2016i), *National Police Promotion Framework (NPPF) Step Two Legal Examination Rules & Syllabus 2017 – Final Version 1.1* available at <http://www.college.police.uk/What-we-do/Development/Promotion/Documents/NPPF_Rules_Syllabus_%282017%29_Final_Version_1_1.pdf> (accessed 1 March 2017).

——(2016j), *National Policing Curriculum* available at <http://www.college.police.uk/What-we-do/Learning/Curriculum/Pages/default.aspx> (accessed 1 March 2017).

Cope, N, Fielding, N, and Innes, M (2005), 'The appliance of science? The theory and practice of crime intelligence analysis', British Journal of Criminology 45(1), 39–55.

Cottrell, S (2013), *The Study Skills Handbook (Palgrave Study Skills)*, 4th edn (Basingstoke: Palgrave Macmillan).

Coventry University (2015), *Certificate of Knowledge in Policing (CKP)* available at <http://www.coventry.ac.uk/course-structure/2013/cuc/professionally-accredited-programmes/certificate-in-knowledge-of-policing-ckp/> (accessed 26 March 2015).

CPS (2006), *Disclosure Manual* available at <http://www.cps.gov.uk/legal/d_to_g/disclosure_manual/> (accessed 23 July 2009).

——(2007), *Acquisition and Disclosure of Communications Data Code of Practice* available at <https://www.gov.uk/government/uploads/system/uploads/attachment_data/file/97961/code-of-practice-acquisition.pdf> (accessed 11 March 2014).

——(2009a), *Guidance on Prosecuting Cases of Domestic Violence* available at <http://www.cps.gov.uk/publications/prosecution/domestic/domv_guidance.html> (accessed 22 May 2010).

——(2009b), *Offences Against the Person, Incorporating Charging Standard* available at <http://www.cps.gov.uk/legal/l_to_o/offences_against_the_person/index.html> (accessed 10 July 2010).

——(2012a), *Perjury* available at <http://www.cps.gov.uk/legal/s_to_u/sentencing_manual/perjury/> (accessed 21 December 2013).

——(2012b), *S 67 Voyeurism* available at <http://www.cps.gov.uk/legal/s_to_u/sentencing_manual/s67__voyeurism/> (accessed 21 December 2013).

——(2013a), *The Code for Crown Prosecutors* available at <http://www.cps.gov.uk/publications/docs/code_2013_accessible_english.pdf> (accessed 2 February 2016).

——(2013b), *The Director's Guidance On Charging 2013—fifth edition, May 2013 (revised arrangements)* available at <http://www.cps.gov.uk/publications/directors_guidance/dpp_guidance_5.html#a16> (accessed 26 December 2015).

——(2014), *Honour Based Violence and Forced Marriage: Guidance on Identifying and Flagging cases* available at <http://www.cps.gov.uk/legal/h_to_k/forced_marriage_and_honour_based_violence_cases_guidance_on_flagging_and_identifying_cases/index.html> (accessed 29 January 2015).

——(2015), *Domestic Abuse Charge Sheet* available at <http://www.cps.gov.uk/publications/equality/ﬁﬂﬁﬂﬁﬁﬂﬁﬁ_abuse_charging_advice_sheet_2013.pdf> (accessed 26 December 2015).

—— (2016), *Former police officer sentenced for preying on domestic abuse victims for sexual gratification* available at <http://www.cps.gov.uk/news/latest_news/former_police_officer_sentenced_for_preying_on_domestic_abuse_victims_for_sexual_gratification/> (accessed 1 March 2017).

CPS and MPS (2015a), *Joint CPS and Police Action Plan on Rape* available at <http://www.cps.gov.uk/publications/equality/vaw/rape_action_plan.pdf> (accessed 29 January 2015).

—— (2015b), *What is Consent?* available at <http://www.cps.gov.uk/publications/equality/vaw/what_is_consent.pdf> (accessed 29 January 2015).

Crawshaw, R, Devlin, B, and Williamson, T (1998), *Human Rights and Policing: Standards for good behaviour and a strategy for change* (The Hague: Kluwer Law International).

Croall, H (2011), *Crime and Society in Britain*, 2nd edn (Harlow: Pearson Education).

Cumbria Police (2014), *Making Cumbria an even safer place: A Police and Crime Plan for Cumbria 2013–2017* available at <http://www.cumbria-pcc.gov.uk/media/9811/Police%20and%20Crime%20Plan%202013-17.pdf> (accessed 12 February 2014).

Daly, M (2003), *My life as a secret policeman* available at <http://news.bbc.co.uk/1/hi/magazine/3210614.stm> (accessed 23 July 2009).

Davis, M (1996), 'Police, discretion, and the professions' in J Kleinig, *Handled with Discretion: Ethical issues in police decision making* (Lanham, MD: Rowman & Littlefield).

Delattre, EJ (2002), *Character and Cops: Ethics in Policing*, 4th edn (Washington: AEI Press).

Department for Children, Schools and Families (2009), *Safeguarding Children and Young People from Sexual Exploitation* available at <https://www.gov.uk/government/uploads/system/uploads/attachment_data/file/278849/Safeguarding_Children_and_Young_People_from_Sexual_Exploitation.pdf> (accessed 8 January 2015).

Department for Transport (2013), *Driving under the influence of drugs: Report from the Expert Panel on Drug Driving* available at <https://www.gov.uk/government/uploads/system/uploads/attachment_data/file/167971/drug-driving-expert-panel-report.pdf> (accessed 11 February 2016).

——2016, *Reported road casualties Great Britain: 2015 annual report* available at <https://www.gov.uk/government/uploads/system/uploads/attachment_data/file/556396/rrcgb2015-01.pdf> (accessed 1 March 2017).

Department of Health (2000), *No Secrets: Guidance on Developing and Implementing Multi-Agency Policies and Procedures to Protect Vulnerable Adults from Abuse* available at <https://www.gov.uk/government/uploads/system/uploads/attachment_data/file/194272/No_secrets__guidance_on_developing_and_implementing_multi-agency_policies_and_procedures_to_protect_vulnerable_adults_from_abuse.pdf> (accessed 31 January 2015).

—— (2015), *Mental Health Act 1983 Code of Practice* available at <http://www.crisiscareconcordat.org.uk/wp-content/uploads/2015/01/Code_of_Practice.pdf> (accessed 28 December 2015).

Devon and Cornwall Police (2014), *Substance Misuse Referral Schemes* available at <http://devon-cornwall.police.uk/FOI/Doc/fa8da6bd-cbf3-43b6-bdbd-91da5ba67cbb/p?D280.pdf> (accessed 31 March 2015).

Directgov (2011), *Uninsured Driving* available at <http://www.direct.gov.uk/en/Motoring/OwningAVehicle/Motorinsurance/DG_067639> (accessed 31 March 2011).

—— (2013), *Police officer recruitment update—February 2013* available at <http://www.dorset.police.uk/default.aspx?page=301> (accessed 3 March 2013).

Dunnighan, C and Norris, C (1996), 'A risky business: Exchange, bargaining and risk in the recruitment and running of informers by English police officers', Journal of Police Studies 19(2), 1–25.

——and —— (1999), 'The detective, the snout, and the Audit Commission: The real costs in using informants', The Howard Journal 38(1), 67–86.

Eddlestone, J (2012), *Blind Justice: Miscarriages of Justice in 20th Century Britain*, e-book, Bibliofile publishers.

Ede, R and Shepherd, E (2000), *Active Defence: Lawyer's guide to police and defence investigation and prosecution and defence disclosure in criminal cases* (London: Law Society Publishing).

EHRC (2015), *Newsletter* available at <http://www.equalityhumanrights.com/college-policing-and-commission-announce-new-police-training-stop-and-search> (accessed 25 January 2016).

Ekblom, P (2001), *The Conjunction of Criminal Opportunity: A framework for crime reduction toolkits* at <http://webarchive.nationalarchives.gov.uk/20100413151441/crimereduction.homeoffice.gov.uk/learningzone/cco.htm> (accessed 11 March 2014).

Elliott, J, Kusher, S, Alexandrou, A, Dwyfor Davies, J, Wilkinson, S, and Zamorski, B (2003), *Review of the Learning Requirement for Police Probationer Training in England & Wales* (University of East Anglia and University of the West of England).

Ellison, M (2014), *The Stephen Lawrence Independent Review: Possible corruption and the role of undercover policing in the Stephen Lawrence case* available at <https://www.gov.uk/government/uploads/system/uploads/attachment_data/file/287030/stephen_lawrence_review_summary.pdf> (accessed 4 March 2015).

Emsley, C (1996), *The English Police: A Political and Social History*, 2nd edn (Harlow: Pearson Education).

Environmental Audit Committee (2012), *Wildlife Crime* available at <http://www.publications.parliament.uk/pa/cm201213/cmselect/cmenvaud/140/140.pdf> (accessed 30 January 2013).

Everson, S and Pease, K (2001), 'Crime against the same person and place: Detection opportunity and offender targeting' in G Farrell and K Pease (eds), *Crime Prevention Studies*, vol 12 (Monsey, NY: CRC Press).

Experian (2016), *Fraud costing the UK economy £193bn a year* available at <https://www.experianplc. com/media/news/2016/fraud-costing-the-uk-economy-193bn-a-year/> (accessed 1 March 2017).

Farrall, S and Gadd, D (2004), 'Evaluating crime fears: A research note on a pilot study to improve the measurement of the "Fear of Crime" as a performance indicator', Evaluation 10(4), 493–502.

Fielding, NG (2005), *The Police & Social Conflict: Rhetoric and reality*, 2nd edn (London: Routledge-Cavendish).

Fineman, K (1995), 'A model for the qualitative analysis of child and adult fire deviant behaviour', American Journal of Forensic Psychology 13, 31–60.

Flanagan, Sir R (2004), *A Report on the Investigation by Cambridgeshire Constabulary into the Murders of Jessica Chapman and Holly Wells at Soham on 4 August 2002* (London: HMIC).

Flatley, J, Kershaw, C, Smith, K, Chaplin, R, and Moon, D (2010), *Crime in England and Wales 2009/10* Home Office Statistical Bulletin 12/10 (London: Home Office).

Flynn, C (2011), 'Examining the Links between Animal Abuse and Human Violence', Crime, Law and Social Change 55(5), 453–68.

Forced Marriage Unit (2014), *Statistics January to December 2013* available at <https://www.gov.uk/ government/uploads/system/uploads/attachment_data/file/291855/FMU_2013_statistics.pdf> (accessed 9 January 2015).

Francis, B, Barry, J, Bowater, R, Miller, N, Soothill, K, and Ackerley, E (2004), 'Using homicide data to assist murder investigation', Home Office Online Report 26/04 (London: Home Office).

Fuller, E (ed) (2008), *Drug Use, Smoking and Drinking among Young People in England in 2007* (National Centre for Social Research, National Foundation for Educational Research).

GMC (2008), *Licensing and Revalidation* available at <http://www.gmc-uk.org/7a_Licensing_and_ Revalidation.pdf_25399016.pdf> (accessed 11 March 2014).

Goldstein, H (1990), *Problem-orientated Policing* (New York: McGraw Hill).

Gudjonsson, G, Sigurdsson, J, and Einarsson, E (2004), 'The role of personality in relation to confessions and denials', Psychology, Crime & Law 10(2), 125–35.

Haigh, J (2006), 'Forensic science and the legal process' available at <http://www.maths.sussex.ac.uk/ Staff/JH/Fslp/FSLPnotes.pdf> (accessed 23 July 2009).

Harfield, C and Harfield, K (2005), *Covert Investigation* (Oxford: Oxford University Press).

——and —— (2008), *Intelligence: Investigation, Community, and Partnership* (Oxford: Oxford University Press).

Harris, D, Turner, R, Garrett, I, and Atkinson, S (2011), *Understanding the Psychology of Gang Violence: Implications for designing effective violence interventions*, Ministry of Justice Research Series 2/11, March.

Heaton, R (2000), 'The prospects for intelligence-led policing: Some historical and quantitative considerations', Policing & Society 9, 337–55.

——(2008), 'Measuring crime reduction: Geographical effects', The Police Journal 81(2), 95.

Henriques, R, Sir (2016), *An Independent review of the Metropolitan Police Service's handling of non-recent sexual offence investigations alleged against persons of public prominence* available at <http://news.met. police.uk/documents/report-independent-review-of-metropolitan-police-services-handling-of-non-recent-sexual-offence-investigations-61510> (accessed 1 March 2017).

Herbert, N The Rt Hon (2011), 'Restorative justice, policing and the Big Society', Restorative Justice Council, Manchester, 22 February.

Herring, J (2007), *Family Law*, 3rd edn (Cambridge: Pearson).

Highway Code (2004) available at <http://www.direct.gov.uk/en/TravelAndTransport/Highwaycode/ DG_070190> (accessed 11 March 2014).

HM Government (2014a), *Modern Slavery Strategy* available at <https://www.gov.uk/government/ uploads/system/uploads/attachment_data/file/383764/Modern_Slavery_Strategy_FINAL_DEC2015. pdf> (accessed 23 January 2016).

——(2014b), *Multi-agency practice guidelines: Handling cases of Forced Marriage* available at <https:// www.gov.uk/government/uploads/system/uploads/attachment_data/file/322307/HMG_MULTI_ AGENCY_PRACTICE_GUIDELINES_v1_180614_FINAL.pdf> (accessed 9 January 2015).

HM Government and College of Policing (2014), 'Out of Court Disposals Consultation Response' available at: <https://www.gov.uk/government/uploads/system/uploads/attachment_data/file/370053/ out-of-court-disposals-response-to-consultation.pdf> (accessed 23 January 2016).

HMIC (2002), *Training Matters* (London: HMSO).

——(2003), *Diversity Matters* (London: HMSO).

——(2005a), *Inspection of Kingston upon Hull BCU Humberside Police July 2005* available at <http://www. humberside.police.uk/about-us/inspection-reports/basic-command-unit-bcu-inspection-reports> (accessed 11 March 2014).

——(2005b), *Police National Computer Data Quality and Timeliness Second Report on the Inspection by HM Inspectorate of Constabulary* (London: HMSO).

——(2006), *PNC Compliance Report: City of London (Aug 2005)* (London: HMSO).

——(2009), *Adapting to Protest* available at <https://www.justiceinspectorates.gov.uk/hmic/media/ adapting-to-protest-20090705.pdf> (accessed 4 March 2017).

——(2010), *Anti-social Behaviour: Stop the rot* available at <http://www.hmic.gov.uk/media/stop-the-rot-20100923.pdf> (accessed 2 March 2011).

——(2011), *Policing Public Order* available at <https://www.justiceinspectorates.gov.uk/hmic/media/a review-of-the-august-2011-disorders-20111220.pdf> (accessed 4 March 2017).

——(2012a), *A Review of National Police Units which Provide Intelligence on Criminality Associated with Protest* available at <http://www.hmic.gov.uk/publication/review-of-national-police-units-which-provide-intelligence-on-criminality-associated-with-protest-20120202/> (accessed 6 March 2012).

——(2012b), *A Step in the Right Direction: Policing anti-social behaviour* available at <http://www.justiceinspectorates.gov.uk/hmic/media/a-step-in-the-right-direction-the-policing-of-anti-social-behaviour.pdf> (accessed 2 January 2015).

——(2013a), *Crime Recording in Kent: A report commissioned by the Police and Crime Commissioner for Kent* available at <http://www.hmic.gov.uk/media/crime-recording-in-kent-130617.pdf> (accessed 11 March 2014).

——(2013b), *Stop and Search Powers: Are the police using them effectively and fairly?* available at <https://www.justiceinspectorates.gov.uk/hmic/media/stop-and-search-powers-20130709.pdf> (accessed 11 March 2016).

——(2014), *Everyone's business: Improving the police response to domestic abuse* available at: <http://www.justiceinspectorates.gov.uk/hmic/wp-content/uploads/2014/04/improving-the-police-response-to-domestic-abuse.pdf> (accessed 6 January 2015).

——(2016a), *Best Use of Stop and Search revisits* available at <https://www.justiceinspectorates.gov.uk/hmic/publications/best-use-of-stop-and-search-revisits/> (accessed 1 March 2017).

——(2015b), *Integrity matters An inspection of arrangements to ensure integrity and to provide the capability to tackle corruption in policing* available at <https://www.justiceinspectorates.gov.uk/hmic/wp-content/uploads/police-integrity-and-corruption-2015.pdf> (accessed 1 March 2017).

——(2015c), *Stop and search powers 2* available at <https://www.justiceinspectorates.gov.uk/hmic/wp-content/uploads/stop-and-search-powers-2.pdf> (accessed 11 March 2016).

——(2015d), 'The depths of dishonour: Hidden voices and shameful crimes, An inspection of the police response to honour-based violence, forced marriage and female genital mutilation' available at: <https://www.justiceinspectorates.gov.uk/hmic/wp-content/uploads/the-depths-of-dishonour.pdf> (accessed 4 December 2016).

Home Affairs Select Committee (2015), *The College of Policing in the first two years* available at: <http://www.publications.parliament.uk/pa/cm201415/cmselect/cmhaff/800/80005.htm> (accessed 31 March 2015).

Home Office (1989), *Criminal and Custodial Careers of those Born in 1953, 1958 and 1963*, Home Office Statistical Bulletin 32/89 (London: Home Office).

——(1997), *Police Health and Safety, Volume 2: A guide for police managers*, Police Policy Directorate (London: Home Office).

——(2001), *Policing a New Century: A blueprint for reform*, Cm 5326 (London: Home Office).

——(2005a), *Code of Practice for Victims of Crime* available at <http://webarchive.nationalarchives.gov.uk/20100418065544/http://homeoffice.gov.uk/documents/victims-code-of-practice2835.pdf?view=Binary> (accessed 3 April 2012).

——(2005b), *Initial Police Learning and Development Programme (IPLDP), Letter to Chief Police Officers 7 November 2005* (London: Home Office).

——(2005c), *IPLDP Central Author Practitioner Guidance*, Community Engagement & Professional Development Units (London: Home Office).

——(2005d), *Rationale for Changing the Overall Module Structure of the IPLDP*, IPLDP Central Authority Executive Services (London: Home Office).

——(2007), *Safer Communities: Towards Effective Arson Control* available at <http://webarchive.nationalarchives.gov.uk/20120919132719/http://www.communities.gov.uk/publications/fire/safercommunitiestowards> (accessed 13 April 2011).

——(2009a), *Explanatory Memorandum to the Criminal Justice and Immigration Act 2008 (Violent Offender Orders) (Notification Requirements) Regulations 2009 No. 2019* available at <http://www.legislation.gov.uk/uksi/2009/2019/pdfs/uksiem_20092019_en.pdf> (accessed 20 December 2013).

——(2009b), *Guidance on Designated Public Place Orders (DPPOs): for Local Authorities in England and Wales* available at <http://tna.europarchive.org/20100413151441/http://www.crimereduction.homeoffice.gov.uk/alcoholorders/alcoholorders016.htm> (accessed 7 July 2010).

——(2009c), *National Domestic Violence Delivery Plan Annual Progress Report 2008/2009* available at <http://webarchive.nationalarchives.gov.uk/20100418065544/http://www.homeoffice.gov.uk/documents/dom-violence-delivery-plan-08-09.html> (accessed 10 July 2010).

——(2009d), *Together We Can End Violence against Women and Girls: A strategy* available at <http://webarchive.nationalarchives.gov.uk/20100413151441/http://homeoffice.gov.uk/documents/vawg-strategy-2009/end-violence-against-women2835.pdf?view=Binary> (accessed 10 July 2010).

——(2010a), *Call to end violence against women and girls: strategic vision* available at <https://www.gov.uk/government/publications/call-to-end-violence-against-women-and-girls-strategic-vision> (accessed 9 February 2014).

——(2010b), *Drinking Banning Orders (DBOs) on Conviction*. Was available at <http://webarchive.nationalarchives.gov.uk/+/http://www.homeoffice.gov.uk/about-us/home-office-circulars/circulars-2010/003-2010/> (accessed 4 April 2011) but is no longer available: please try other library resources.

——(2010c), *Policing in the 21st Century: Reconnecting police and the people* (London: Home Office), available at <http://www.homeoffice.gov.uk/publications/consultations/policing-21st-century/> (accessed 19 May 2011).

——(2010d), *Statutory Guidance: Injunctions to prevent gang-related violence* available at <http://www.official-documents.gov.uk/document/other/9780108509599/9780108509599.pdf> (accessed 5 February 2011).

——(2011), *Missing Children and Adults* available at <https://www.gov.uk/government/uploads/system/uploads/attachment_data/file/117793/missing-persons-strategy.pdf> (accessed 11 March 2014).

——(2012a), *Crime in England and Wales: Quarterly Update to September 2011–19* available at <http://www.homeoffice.gov.uk/publications/science-research-statistics/research-statistics/crime-research/hosb0112/hosb0112?view=Binary> (accessed 10 January 2013).

——(2012b), *Domestic violence disclosure scheme pilot: guidance* available at <http://www.homeoffice.gov.uk/publications/crime/dvds-interim-guidance?view=Binary> (accessed 21 December 2012).

——(2012c), *Ending Gang and Youth Violence: one year on* available at <http://www.official-documents.gov.uk/document/cm84/8493/8493.pdf> (accessed 10 January 2013).

——(2012d), *The Police Act 1996 (Equipment) Regulations 2011 and the Police Act 1996 (Services) Regulations 2011 Impact Assessment* available at <http://www.homeoffice.gov.uk/publications/consultations/cons-2010-police-procurement/police-act-ia?view=Binary> (accessed 7 March 2012).

——(2013a), *Domestic violence and abuse: new definition* available at <https://www.gov.uk/domestic-violence-and-abuse> (accessed 20 December 2013).

——(2013b), *Penalty Notices for Disorder (PNDs)* available at <http://www.justice.gov.uk/downloads/oocd/pnd-guidance-oocd.pdf> (accessed 11 March 2014).

——(2013c), *Surveillance Camera Code of Practice* available at <https://www.gov.uk/government/uploads/system/uploads/attachment_data/file/204775/Surveillance_Camera_Code_of_Practice_WEB.pdf> (accessed 11 March 2014).

——(2014a), *Anti-social Behaviour, Crime and Policing Act 2014: Reform of anti-social behaviour powers: Statutory guidance for frontline professionals: July 2014* available at <https://www.gov.uk/government/publications/anti-social-behaviour-crime-and-policing-bill-anti-social-behaviour> (accessed 1 March 2017).

——(2014b), *Best Use of Stop and Search Scheme* available at <https://www.gov.uk/government/uploads/system/uploads/attachment_data/file/346922/Best_Use_of_Stop_and_Search_Scheme_v3.0_v2.pdf> (accessed 26 March 2015).

——(2014c), *Home Office Counting Rules for Recorded Crime* (London: Home Office).

——(2014d), *Home Secretary outlines reforms to the Police Federation* available at <https://www.gov.uk/government/news/home-secretary-outlines-reforms-to-the-police-federation> (accessed 26 March 2015).

——(2014e), *Strengthening the Law on Domestic Abuse—A Consultation* available at <https://www.gov.uk/government/uploads/system/uploads/attachment_data/file/344674/Strengthening_the_law_on_Domestic_Abuse_-_A_Consultation_WEB.PDF> (accessed 6 January 2015).

——(2015a), *Crime Recording General Rules* available at <https://www.gov.uk/government/uploads/system/uploads/attachment_data/file/489732/count-general-january-2016.pdf> (accessed 22 February 2016).

——(2015b), *Hate Crime, England and Wales, 2014/15* available at: <https://www.gov.uk/government/uploads/system/uploads/attachment_data/file/467366/hosb0515.pdf> (accessed 22 February 2016).

——(2015c), *Operation of police powers under the Terrorism Act 2000 and subsequent legislation: Arrests, outcomes, and stop and search, Great Britain, financial year ending 31 March 2015* available at: <https://www.gov.uk/government/statistics/operation-of-police-powers-under-the-terrorism-act-2000-financial-year-ending-march-2015> (accessed: 25 January 2016).

——(2015d), *Statutory Guidance Injunctions to Prevent Gang-Related Violence and Gang-Related Drug Dealing* available at <https://www.gov.uk/government/uploads/system/uploads/attachment_data/file/432805/Injunctions_to_Prevent_Gang-Related_Violence_web.pdf> (accessed 11 March 2016).

——(2015e), *Working together to safeguard children. A guide to inter-agency working to safeguard and promote the welfare of children* available at <https://www.gov.uk/government/uploads/system/uploads/attachment_data/file/419595/Working_Together_to_Safeguard_Children.pdf> (accessed 23 December 2015).

——(2016a), *Ending Violence Against Women and Girls Strategy 2016-2020* available at <https://www.gov.uk/government/uploads/system/uploads/attachment_data/file/522166/VAWG_Strategy_FINAL_PUBLICATION_MASTER_vRB.PDF> (accessed 23 October 2016).

——(2016b), *Forced Marriage Unit Statistics 2016* available at <https://www.gov.uk/government/uploads/system/uploads/attachment_data/file/505827/Forced_Marriage_Unit_statistics_2015.pdf> (accessed 1 March 2017).

——(2016c), *Hate crime, England and Wales, 2015 to 2016* available at <https://www.gov.uk/government/statistics/hate-crime-england-and-wales-2015-to-2016> (accessed 1 March 2017).

——(2016d), *Home Office counting rules for recording crime; Section A: Whether and when to record*, available at<https://www.gov.uk/government/uploads/system/uploads/attachment_data/file/566188/count-general-nov-2016.pdf> (on 26 November 2016).

——(2016e), *Home Secretary announces reforms to IPCC* available at <https://www.gov.uk/government/news/home-secretary-announces-reforms-to-ipcc> (accessed 24 March 2016).

——(2016f), *Police powers and procedures England and Wales, year ending 31 March 2016 Statistical Bulletin 15/16* available at <https://www.gov.uk/government/uploads/system/uploads/attachment_data/file/562977/police-powers-procedures-hosb1516.pdf> (accessed 1 March 2017).

——(2016g), *Police Workforce, England and Wales 31st March 2016* available at <https://www.gov.uk/government/uploads/system/uploads/attachment_data/file/544849/hosb0516-police-workforce.pdf> (accessed 17 January 2017).

——(2106h), *Seizures of drugs in England and Wales, year ending 31 March 2016* available at <https://www.gov.uk/government/uploads/system/uploads/attachment_data/file/564412/seizures-drugs-hosb1316.pdf> (accessed 19 April 2017).

——(2017), *Best Use of Stop & Search Scheme* available at <https://www.gov.uk/government/uploads/system/uploads/attachment_data/file/346922/Best_Use_of_Stop_and_Search_Scheme_v3.0_v2.pdf> (accessed 1 March 2017).

Home Office Select Committee (2015), *Evaluating the new architecture of policing: the College of Policing and the National Crime Agency—Home Affairs, Certificate in Knowledge in Policing* available at <http://www.publications.parliament.uk/pa/cm201415/cmselect/cmhaff/800/80008.htm#a13> (accessed 31 March 2015).

Home Secretary (2012), *Conference Speech to The Police Superintendents' Association 11 Sep 2012. Home Office* available at <https://www.gov.uk/government/speeches/police-superintendents-association-conference-home-secretarys-speech> (accessed 26 February 2016).

Hughes, K, Hardcastle, K and Perkins, C (2015), *The Mental Health Needs of Gang-Affiliated Young People* available at <https://www.gov.uk/government/uploads/system/uploads/attachment_data/file/398674/The_mental_health_needs_of_gang-affiliated_young_people_v3_23_01_1.pdf> (accessed 12 January 2016).

Humberside Police (2015), *Wanted Person* available at <http://www.humberside.police.uk/sites/default/files/Wanted_Persons.pdf> (accessed 27 January 2016).

IDMG (2015), *2015 Report of the Inter-Departmental Ministerial Group on Modern Slavery* available at <https://www.gov.uk/government/uploads/system/uploads/attachment_data/file/469968/IDMG_Report_Final.pdf> (accessed 24 December 2015).

Ingleton, R (2002), *Policing Kent 1800–2000* (Chichester: Phillimore).

Inman, K and Rudin, R (2002), 'The origin of evidence', Forensic Science International 126, 11–16.

Innes, M (2014), *Signal Crimes: Social Reactions to Crime, Disorder and Control*, (Oxford: Oxford University Press).

——(2005), 'What's your problem? Signal crimes and citizen-focused problem solving', Criminology & Public Policy 4(2), 187–200.

Institute of Alcohol Studies (2015), *Alcohols impact on emergency services full report* available at <http://www.ias.org.uk/uploads/Alcohols_impact_on_emergency_services_full_report.pdf> (accessed 1 March 2017).

——(2016), *Youthful Abandon* available at <http://www.ias.org.uk/uploads/pdf/IAS%20reports/rp22072016.pdf> (accessed 1 March 2017).

IPCC (2014), *Police Officers Subject of a Complaint* available at <http://www.ipcc.gov.uk/page/police-officers-being-subject-complaint> (accessed 24 March 2014).

——(2015), *Statutory Guidance to the police service on the handling of complaints* available at <https://www.ipcc.gov.uk/sites/default/files/Documents/statutoryguidance/2015_statutory_guidance_english.pdf> (accessed 28 December 2015).

——(2016a,) *IPCC independent Investigations – information for police officers, staff and their representatives* available at <https://www.ipcc.gov.uk/sites/default/files/Documents/complaints/Key%20messages%20for%20officers%20document%20-%20FINAL.pdf> (accessed 1 March 2017).

——(2016b), *IPCC investigation after death of Staffordshire Police detainee* available at <http://ipcc.gov.uk/news/ipcc-investigation-after-death-staffordshire-police-detainee> (accessed 1 March 2017).

Iranian and Kurdish Women's Rights Organisation (2014), *Postcode lottery: police recording of reported 'honour' based violence* available at <http://ikwro.org.uk/wp-content/uploads/2014/02/HBV-FOI-report-Post-code-lottery-04.02.2014-Final.pdf> (accessed 10 January 2015).

Jackson, J, Bradford, B, Stanko, B, and Hohl, K (2013), *Just Authority? Trust in the police in England and Wales* (London: Routledge).

Johnston, D and Hutton, G (2005), *Blackstone's Police Manual, Volume 2: Evidence and Procedure* (Oxford: Oxford University Press).

Jones, T and Newburn, T (1998), *Private Security and Public Policing* (Oxford: Clarendon Press).

Joyce, P (2011), *Policing: Development & Contemporary Practice* (London: Sage Publications).

Junger, M, West, R, and Timman, R (2001), 'Crime and risk behaviour in traffic', Journal of Research in Crime & Delinquency 38(4), 439–59.

Justice (2011), *Mediation and alternatives to court* available at <http://www.justice.gov.uk/courts/mediation> (accessed 21 December 2012).

Kent Online (2013), *Kent Police officer Eileen Arthurs tells misconduct trial of friendship with convicted criminal and ex-Page 3 model* available at <http://www.kentonline.co.uk/gravesend/news/kent-police-officer-eileen-arthu-a54538/> (accessed 1 March 2017).

Kent Police (2010), *Neighbourhood Watch* available at <http://www.kent.police.uk/advice/community_safety/initiatives/nwatch.html> (accessed 13 April 2011).

Kershaw, C, Nicholas, S, and Walker, A (eds) (2008), *Crime in England and Wales 2007/08: Findings from the British Crime Survey and police recorded crime*, Home Office Statistical Bulletin 07/08 (London: Home Office).

Kirk, P (1953), *Crime Investigation: Physical Evidence and the Police Laboratory* (New York: Interscience Publishers Inc).

——(1963), 'The Ontogeny of Criminalistics', Journal of Criminal Law, Criminology and Police Science 54(2), 235–238.

Kolb, D (1984), *Experiential Learning: Experience as the source of learning and development* (Upper Saddle River, NJ: Prentice Hall).

Law Commission (2014), *Reform of Offences against the Person A Scoping Consultation Paper Consultation Paper No 217* available at: <http://lawcommission.justice.gov.uk/docs/cp217_offences_against_the_person.pdf> (accessed on 6 January 2015).

Lee, M and South, N (2003), 'Drugs policing' in T Newburn (ed), *Handbook of Policing* (Cullompton: Willan).

Leishman, F and Mason, P (2003), *Policing and the Media: Facts, fictions and factions* (Cullompton: Willan).

Leukfeldt, E and Var, M (2016), 'Applying Routine Activity Theory to Cybercrime: A Theoretical and Empirical Analysis', Deviant Behaviour, 37:3, 263–280.

Lexicon Ltd (2014), *Making the most of working with an intermediary* available at <http://lexiconlimited.co.uk/wp-content/uploads/2014/11/intermediary-toolkit-update-251114.pdf> (accessed 1 March 2016).

Lincolnshire Police (2011), *Drugs and Alcohol* available at <http://www.lincs.police.uk/Youth-Lincs/Teen-Lincs/Drugs-and-Alcohol.html> (accessed 7 April 2011).

London Evening Standard (2012), *Notting Hill Carnival: 'Body armour' gang held on way to festival* available at <http://www.standard.co.uk/news/crime/notting-hill-carnival-body-armour-gang-held-on-way-to-festival-one-man-remains-critical-8083875.html> (accessed 20 February 2013).

Luft, J (1970), *Group Processes: An introduction to group dynamics* (Palo Alto, CA: National Press Books).

Mackie, L (1978), 'Race causes an initial confusion', *The Guardian*, 14 June.

Macpherson, Sir W (1999), *The Stephen Lawrence Inquiry* available at <https://www.gov.uk/government/publications/the-stephen-lawrence-inquiry> (accessed 4 April 2014).

Madden, V (2015), *Understanding the Mental Health Needs of Young People involved in Gangs* available at <http://www.mac-uk.org/wped/wp-content/uploads/2013/03/Mental-Health-and-Gangs-Report-2013.pdf> (accessed 19 January 2016).

Marshall, B, Webb, B, and Tilley, N (2005), *Rationalisation of current research on guns, gangs and other weapons: Phase 1* (London: University College London/Jill Dando Institute of Crime Science).

Mason, F and Lodrick, Z (2013), 'Psychological consequences of sexual assault', Best Practice and Research Clinical Obstetrics and Gynaecology 27, 27–37.

Matassa, M and Newburn, T (2003), 'Policing and terrorism' in T Newburn (ed), *The Handbook of Policing* (Cullompton: Willan).

Mawby, RC (2008), 'Community policing' in T Newburn and P Neyroud (eds), *Dictionary of Policing* (Cullompton: Willan), pp 40–1.

McKee, C (2014), *Home Office Statistical Bulletin Crime Outcomes in England and Wales 2013/14* (London: Home Office).

MIB (2013), *Annual report and accounts 2013* available at <http://view.digipage.net/00000817/00017508/00089004/> (accessed 31 March 2015).

Miller, J (2003), *Police Corruption in England and Wales: An assessment of current evidence*, Home Office Online Report 11/03 available at <http://webarchive.nationalarchives.gov.uk/20110218135832/http://rds.homeoffice.gov.uk/rds/pdfs2/rdsolr1103.pdf> (accessed 23 July 2009).

Milne, R and Bull, R (1999), *Investigative Interviewing: Psychology and practice* (Chichester: John Wiley & Sons).

MIND (2010), *Achieving Justice for Victims and Witnesses with Mental Distress* available at <https://www.cps.gov.uk/publications/docs/mind_toolkit_for_prosecutors_and_advocates.pdf> (accessed 27 February 2014).

——(2013), *Police and Mental Health: How to get it right locally* available at <http://www.mind.org.uk/media/618027/2013-12-03-Mind_police_final_web.pdf> (accessed 27 February 2014).

Ministry of Justice (2010), *Offences Of Stirring Up Hatred On The Grounds Of Sexual Orientation* available at <http://www.banksr.co.uk/images/Other%20Documents/Judicial%20material/circular-2010-05-sexual-orientation-hatred.pdf> (accessed 11 March 2014).

——(2011), *Achieving Best Evidence in Criminal Proceedings* available at <http://webarchive.nationalarchives.gov.uk/20130128112038/http://www.justice.gov.uk/downloads/victims-and-witnesses/vulnerable-witnesses/achieving-best-evidence-criminal-proceedings.pdf> (accessed 23 December, 2015).

——(2013), *Out of Court Disposals* available at <http://www.justice.gov.uk/out-of-court-disposals> (accessed 17 January 2015).

——(2015), *Code of Practice for Victims of Crime* available at <https://www.gov.uk/government/uploads/system/uploads/attachment_data/file/470212/code-of-practice-for-victims-of-crime.PDF> (accessed 27 December 2016).

——(2016), *Multi-Agency Public Protection Arrangements Annual Report 2015/16 Ministry of Justice Statistics Bulletin* available at <https://mappa.justice.gov.uk/connect.ti/MAPPA/view?objectId=7674832> (accessed 1 March 2017).

——, Home Office, and Office for National Statistics (2013), *An Overview of Sexual Offending in England and Wales* available at <https://www.gov.uk/government/uploads/system/uploads/attachment_data/file/214970/sexual-offending-overview-jan-2013.pdf> (accessed 20 December 2013).

——and the Youth Justice Board, (2015), *Youth Out-of-Court Disposals Guide for Police and Youth Offending Service* available at <https://www.gov.uk/government/uploads/system/uploads/attachment_data/file/438139/out-court-disposal-guide.pdf> (accessed 27 January 2016).

Morris, W, Burden, A, and Weekes, A (2004), *The Case for Change: People in the Metropolitan Police Service* (Morris Inquiry) available at <http://www.policeauthority.org/Metropolitan/downloads/scrutinites/morris/morris-report.pdf> (accessed 19 July 2010).

MPS (2014), *Met Briefing Note; Body Worn Video (BWV)* available at <http://www.met.police.uk/docs/body-worn-video.pdf> (accessed 31 March 2015).

Myhill, A and Bradford, B (2011), 'Can police enhance public confidence by improving quality of service? Results from two surveys in England and Wales', Policing and Society First 1–29.

National Audit Office (2011), *The Crown Prosecution Service, The introduction of the Streamlined Process* available at <http://www.nao.org.uk/wp-content/uploads/2011/11/10121584.pdf> (accessed 17 January 2015).

——(2012), *Home Office and National Policing Improvement Agency Mobile Technology in Policing Report by the Comptroller and Auditor General*, HC 1765, Session 2010–2012, 27 January (London: The Stationery Office).

——(2016), *Upgrading emergency service communications: the Emergency Services Network* available at <https://www.nao.org.uk/report/upgrading-emergency-service-communications-the-emergency-services-network/> (accessed 1 March 2017).

National Sexual Assault Hotline (2012), *How Long Does it Take to Recover?* available at <https://ohl.rainn.org/online/resources/how-long-to-recover.cfm> (accessed 8 January 2015).

NCA (2015), *National Referral Mechanism Statistics – End of Year Summary 2015* available at <http://www.nationalcrimeagency.gov.uk/publications/676-national-referral-mechanism-statistics-end-of-year-summary-2015/file> (accessed 4 December 2016).

——(2016), *NCA Strategic Cyber Industry Group Cyber Crime Assessment 2016* ver. 1.2 available at <http://www.nationalcrimeagency.gov.uk/publications/709-cyber-crime-assessment-2016/file> (accessed 1 March 2017).

NCDV (2015a), *ASSIST* available at <https://www.assist.uk.net> (accessed 26 December 2015).

——(2015b), *Third Party Injunction Referral* available at <http://www.ncdv.org.uk/information-for-police-agencies/third-party-injunction-referral/> (accessed 26 December 2015).

Neighbourhood Watch (2014), *Our mission* available at <http://www.ourwatch.org.uk/about_us/our_mission/> (accessed 11 March 2014).

Newburn, T (1999), *Understanding and Preventing Police Corruption: Lessons from the literature*, Police Research Series Paper 110 (London: Home Office).

——(2007), *Criminology* (Cullompton: Willan).

——(ed) (2011), *Handbook of Policing*, 2nd edn (Abingdon: Routledge).

——(2015), *Literature review—Police integrity and corruption* available at <https://www.justiceinspectorates.gov.uk/hmic/wp-content/uploads/pic-literature-review.pdf> (accessed 27 Dec 2016).

——and Neyroud, P (2008), *Dictionary of Policing* (Cullompton: Willan).

Neyroud, P (2011), *Review of Police Leadership and Training: Volume One* (London: Home Office), available at <http://www.homeoffice.gov.uk/publications/consultations/rev-police-leadership-training/report?view=Binary> (accessed 11 April 2011).

——and Beckley, A (2001), *Policing, Ethics and Human Rights* (Cullompton: Willan).

NFA (2014), *National Fraud Authority Annual Report and Accounts 2013–14* available at <https://www.gov.uk/government/uploads/system/uploads/attachment_data/file/324138/40817_HC_371_NFA_ARA_Web_Accessible.pdf> (accessed 23 January 2015).

NHS (2013), *How to Spot Child Sexual Exploitation* available at <http://www.nhs.uk/livewell/abuse/pages/child-sexual-exploitation-signs.aspx> (accessed 8 January 2015).

Nozick, R (1974), *Anarchy, State and Utopia* (Oxford: Blackwell (2003 print)).

NPCC (2015a), *Advice on the structure of visually recorded witness interviews* (3rd Edition) available at <http://library.college.police.uk/docs/appref/NPCC-(2015)-Guidance-Visually-Recorded-Interviews%203rd%20Edition.pdf> (accessed 10 March 2016).

——(2015b), *Questions and Answers* available at <http://www.npcc.police.uk/About/QuestionsandAnswers.aspx> (accessed 29 December 2015).

NPIA (2007), *Practice Advice on Critical Incident Management* available at <http://www.acpo.police.uk/documents/crime/2007/200708-cba-critical-incident-management.pdf> (accessed 16 March 2011).

——(2008a), *Guidance on Investigating Domestic Abuse* available at <http://www.acpo.police.uk/documents/crime/2008/2008-cba-inv-dom-abuse.pdf> (accessed 20 May 2010).

——(2008b), *National Policing Improvement Agency Circular NPIA(WSU)(RAP)(08)1*. Was available at <http://policerecruitment.homeoffice.gov.uk/documents/npia-08-012835.pdf?view=Binary> (accessed 17 March 2011) but is no longer available: please try other library resources.

——(2008c), *Subject Area Breakdown—OSPRE® Part I Inspectors' Examination 2008 OSPRE® Part I*. Was available at <http://www.npia.police.uk/en/11795.htm> (23 July 2009) but is no longer available: please try other library resources.

——(2010a), *Initial Police Learning and Development Programme, Programme Handbook*, March, Final Draft Version, National Police Improvement Agency.

——(2010b), *Missing Persons: Data and Analysis 2009/10*. Was available at <http://www.npia.police.uk/en/docs/Missing_Persons_Data_and_Analysis_2009-10.pdf> (accessed 14 April 2011) but is no longer available: please try other library resources.

——(2011a), *Initial Police Learning and Development, Review and Guidance on Pre Join Programmes in England and Wales 2011*. Was available at <http://www.npia.police.uk/en/docs/Pre_Join_Guidance_0111_CA_HA_Ful_doc__6_.pdf> (accessed 13 April 2011) but is no longer available: please try other library resources.

——(2011b), *Neighbourhood Partnerships*. Was available at <http://cfnp.npia.police.uk/1521.aspx> (accessed 13 April 2011) but is no longer available: please try other library resources.

——/ACPO (2009), *Practice Advice on the Management of Priority and Volume Crime (The Volume Crime Management Model)*, 2nd edn, available at <http://www.acpo.police.uk/documents/crime/2010/201002CRIPVC01.pdf> (accessed 13 July 2010).

NPT (1995), *Police Probationer Training Foundation Course Notes* (Police Central Planning & Training Unit, a division of National Police Training), p 4.

NSPCC (2005), *Understanding the links, child abuse, animal abuse and domestic violence* available at <https://www.nspcc.org.uk/globalassets/documents/research-reports/understanding-links-child-abuse-animal-abuse-domestic-violence.pdf> (accessed 4 December 2016).

Nunn, J (2016), *Drug Driving over the Prescribed Limit in London - Placing the offending in a theoretical context* Canterbury Christ Church University Master of Art dissertation, unpublished.

ONS (2014), *Crime in England and Wales, Year Ending June 2014* available at <http://www.ons.gov.uk/ons/dcp171778_380538.pdf> (accessed 6 January 2015).

——(2015), *Public Perceptions of Crime* available at <http://webarchive.nationalarchives.gov.uk/20160105160709/http://www.ons.gov.uk/ons/rel/crime-stats/crime-statistics/focus-on-public-perceptions-of-crime-and-the-police--and-the-personal-well-being-of-victims--2013-to-2014/chapter-2--focus-on-public-perceptions-of-crime.html> (accessed 28 February 2016).

——(2016a), *Crime in England and Wales Bulletin tables* available at <https://www.ons.gov.uk/peoplepopulationandcommunity/crimeandjustice/datasets/crimeinenglandandwalesbulletintables> (accessed 1 March 2017).

——(2016b), *Intimate personal violence and partner abuse* available at <http://www.ons.gov.uk/peoplepopulationandcommunity/crimeandjustice/compendium/focusonviolentcrimeandsexualoffences/yearendingmarch2015/chapter4intimatepersonalviolenceandpartnerabuse> (accessed 4 December 2016).

——(2016c), *Population Estimates for UK, England and Wales, Scotland and Northern Ireland* available at <https://www.ons.gov.uk/peoplepopulationandcommunity/populationandmigration/populationestimates/datasets/populationestimatesforukenglandandwalesscotlandandnorthernireland> (accessed 1 March 2017).

——(2017), *Crime in England and Wales: year ending Sept 2016* available at: <https://www.ons.gov.uk/peoplepopulationandcommunity/crimeandjustice/bulletins/crimeinenglandandwales/yearendingjune2016> (accessed 1 March 2017).

Office of the Children's Commissioner (2012), *'I thought I was the only one. The only one in the world' The Office of the Children's Commissioner's Inquiry into Child Sexual Exploitation in Gangs and Groups*. Interim Report, Office of the Children's Commissioner, available at <http://www.childrenscommissioner.gov.uk/content/publications/content_636> (accessed 5 March 2015).

Ofqual (2016), *The Register* available at <http://register.ofqual.gov.uk/> (accessed 16 March 2016).

Owens, C, Mann, D, and Mckenna, R (2014), *The Essex Body Worn Video Trial* available at <http://college.pressofficeadmin.com/repository/files/BWV_Report.pdf> (accessed 31 March 2015).

PCeU (2014), *What we do* available at <http://content.met.police.uk/Article/What-we-do/1400015320495/1400015320495> (accessed 11 March 2014).

Pease, K (1997), 'Crime prevention' in M Maguire, R Morgan, and R Reiner (eds), *The Oxford Handbook of Criminology*, 2nd edn (Oxford: Oxford University Press).

——(2002), 'Crime reduction' in M Maguire, R Morgan, and R Reiner (eds), *The Oxford Handbook of Criminology*, 3rd edn (Oxford: Oxford University Press), pp 947–79.

Peters, R (1973), *Authority, Responsibility and Education* (London: Allen & Unwin).

Police Federation (2011), *Policing the Riots* available at <http://www.polfed.org/documents/PR_Policing_the_riots_submission_to_HMIC_011211.pdf> (accessed 11 March 2014).

PredPol (2014), *Policing Meets big data* available at <http://www.predpol.com/about/> (accessed 11 March 2014).

Public Health England (2016), *Local Alcohol Profiles for England* available at <http://www.lape.org.uk/> (accessed 1 March 2017).

Rawlings, PJ (2002), *Policing: A short history* (Cullompton: Willan).

Reiner, R (2000), *The Politics of the Police*, 3rd edn (Oxford: Oxford University Press).

——(2010), *The Politics of the Police*, 4th edn (Oxford: Oxford University Press).

Re-Solv (2013), *Working to prevent VSA* available at <http://www.re-solv.org/> (accessed 11 March 2014).

Rogers, A (1996), *Teaching Adults*, 2nd edn (Buckingham: Open University Press).

Rose, G (2000), 'The criminal histories of serious traffic offenders', HORS 206 (London: Home Office).

Rowe, M (2002), 'Policing diversity: Themes and concerns from the recent British experience', Police

——(2014) *Introduction to Policing*, 2nd edn (London: Sage).

Scarman, Lord (1981), *Report into the Brixton Disorders*, Cmnd, 8427 (London: HMSO).

Sentencing Council (2012), *Assault Definitive Guidance* available at <http://sentencingcouncil.judiciary.gov.uk/docs/Assault_definitive_guideline_-_Crown_Court.pdf> (accessed 6 February 2012).

Sentencing Guidelines Council (2007), *Sexual Offences Act 2003, Definitive Guidance* available at <http://webarchive.nationalarchives.gov.uk/+/http://www.sentencingcouncil.org.uk/docs/web_0000_SexualOffencesAct1.pdf> (accessed 23 December 2012).

——(2012), *Offences taken into consideration and totality-definitive guideline* available at <http://sentencingcouncil.judiciary.gov.uk/docs/Definitive_guideline_TICs__totality_Final_web.pdf> (accessed 11 March 2014).

SFO (2010), *Perjury* available at <http://www.sfo.gov.uk/media/103061/perjury%20web%201.pdf> (accessed 21 December 2013).

Shepherd, E (2007), *Investigative Interviewing: A Conversation Management Approach* (Oxford: Oxford University Press).

——(2008), *SE3R: A resource book*, 4th edn (East Hendred: Forensic Solutions).

——and Griffiths, A (2013), *Investigative Interviewing: The conversation management approach*, 2nd edn (Oxford: Oxford University Press).

——and Kite, F (1988), 'Training to Interview', Policing 4, 264–280.

Sherman, L (2013), 'The Rise of Evidence Based Policing: Targeting, Testing and Tracking', Crime and Justice 42:1, 377–451.

Shorter Oxford English Dictionary (2002), 5th edn (Oxford: Oxford University Press).

Simmons, AJ (2001), *Justification and Legitimacy: Essays on rights and obligations* (Cambridge: Cambridge University Press).

Skills for Justice (2011), *Policing Professional Framework* available at <http://www.skillsforjustice-ppf.com/?r_id=1> (accessed 3 April 2012).

Smith, MJ and Tilley, N (2005), *Crime Science: New approaches to preventing and detecting crime* (Cullompton: Willan).

South Wales Police (2015), *YES – I do have the Certificate of Knowledge in Policing* available at <http://www.south-wales.police.uk/apply-for-a-job/police-officer/questions-answered/<> (accessed 31 March 2015).

Spencer, J (2016), *Evidence of Bad Character*, 3rd edn (Oxford: Hart Publishing).

Stelfox, P (1998), 'Policing lower levels of organised crime in England and Wales', The Howard Journal 37(4), 393–406.

Stewart, JK (1985), 'Interviewing Witnesses and Victims of Crime' *US Department of Justice, National Institute of Justice, Research in Brief, December1* in: Milne, R and Bull, R (1999), *Investigative Interviewing: Psychology And Practice* (Chichester: Wiley).

Stone, V and Pettigrew, N (2000), *The Views of the Public on Stops and Searches* (London: Home Office).

Taylor, M (1986), 'Learning for self-direction in the classroom: The pattern of a transition process', Studies in Higher Education 11(1), 55–72.

Taylor, P and Bond, S (eds) (2012), *Crime Detection in England & Wales* (London: ONS).

Thornton, S (2007), 'Introduction' in *ACPO Practice Advice: Introduction to Intelligence-led policing*, ACPO Centrex.

Tilley, N (2008a), 'Modern Approaches to Policing: Community, problem-orientated and intelligence-led' in T Newburn (ed), *Handbook of Policing* (Cullompton: Willan), pp 373–403.

——(2008b), 'Problem-orientated Policing' in T Newburn and P Neyroud (eds), *Dictionary of Policing* (Cullompton: Willan), pp 225–7.

Tong, S (2008), 'Interagency Approaches to Policing' in T Newburn and P Neyroud (eds), *Dictionary of Policing* (Cullompton: Willan), pp 148–9.

Tor (2016), *Tor* available at <https://www.torproject.org/> (accessed 15 March 2016).

Tyler, TR (2003), 'Procedural justice, legitimacy, and the effective rule of law' in M Tonry (ed), *Crime and Justice: A Review of Research*, volume 30 (Chicago, IL: Chicago University Press), 431–505.

UK Parliament (2013), *Clare's law: The Domestic Violence Disclosure Scheme—Commons Library Standard Note* available at <http://www.parliament.uk/business/publications/research/briefing-papers/SN06250/clares-law-the-domestic-violence-disclosure-scheme> (accessed 20 December 2013).

Vodafone (2015), *Tackling crime with technology* available at <http://www.vodafone.co.uk/cs/groups/configfiles/documents/contentdocuments/pdf_met_police_case_study.pdf> (accessed 26 January 2016).

Vrij, A (2008), *Detecting Lies and Deceit: Pitfalls and opportunities*, 2nd edn (Chichester: Wiley-Blackwell).

Waddington, PAJ (1999), *Policing Citizens* (London: UCL Press).

——Stenson, K and David, D (2004), 'In proportion: Race, and police stop and search', British Journal of Criminology 44, 889–914.

Wadham, J (2004), 'Conference on data protection and information sharing', 15 July (London).

Walby, S and Allen, J (2004), *Domestic violence, sexual assault and stalking: Findings from the British Crime Survey*, Home Office Research Study 276.

Walby, S, Towers, J and Francis, F (2014), 'Mainstreaming domestic and gender-based violence into sociology and the criminology of violence', The Sociological Review 62:S2, 187–214.

Walsh, D and Milne, R (2008), 'Keeping the PEACE? A study of investigative interviewing practices in the public sector', Legal and Criminological Psychology 13(1) February 2008, 395–7 (19).

West Yorkshire Police (2009), *IPLDP Programme* available at <http://www.bishopgarth.com/programme.html> (accessed 23 July 2009).

WHO (2008), *Classification of Female Genital Mutilation* available at <http://www.who.int/reproductive-health/topics/fgm/overview/en/> (accessed 28 December 2015).

Wilson, J and Kelling, G (1982), 'Broken windows', Atlantic Monthly, March, pp 29–38.

Wilson, JQ (1996), 'On deterrence' in J Muncie, E McLaughlin, and M Langan (eds), *Criminological Perspectives: A reader* (London: Sage).

Wiltshire Police (no date), *What is a major incident?* available at <http://www.wiltshire.police.uk/index.php?option=com_content&view=article&id=173&Itemid=393> (accessed 30 January 2014).

Wolfenden Report (1957), *Report of the Committee on Homosexual Offences and Prostitution*, Cmnd 247 (London: HMSO).

Woodhouse, J (2013), *Extreme Pornography Commons Library Standard Note SN/HA/5078* available at <http://www.parliament.uk/business/publications/research/briefing-papers/SN05078/extreme-pornography> (accessed 27 February 2014).

Wright, A (2002), *Policing: An introduction to concepts and practice* (Cullompton: Willan).

Index